Where Do We Go From Here?

Charleston Conference Proceedings 2015

Edited by Beth R. Bernhardt, Leah H. Hinds, and Katina P. Strauch

Cataloging-in-Publication Data on file at the Library of Congress.

An electronic version of the proceedings is available at http://docs.lib.purdue.edu/charleston/

Contents

Preface and Acknowledgments

"Where Do We Go From Here?" was the theme of the 2015 Charleston Conference, which took place in Charleston, South Carolina, on Wednesday, November 4 through Saturday, November 7, 2015, with over 1,700 participants. The far-ranging and diverse program, which focuses on the purchase and lease of information of all types and in all available formats, is curated by an able team of Charleston Conference directors headed by Beth Bernhardt and Leah Hinds, who have worked long and hard to compile this volume. Thanks are due to Leah and Beth and to all the Charleston Conference directors who helped in assuring timely and professionally peer-reviewed submissions. Thanks are also due to the Purdue University Press team: Dianna Gilroy, Production Editor; Liza Hagerman, Assistant Production Editor; Katherine Purple, Managing Editor; Bryan Shaffer, Sales and Marketing Manager; and many others behind the scenes. Last but not least, many thanks to all the authors and presenters of this amazing group of papers in this volume!

In 2015, the Charleston Conference included fourteen preconference sessions, covering the following: introduction to library research data, an acquisitions bootcamp, understanding the library market, legal issues in libraries, citation analysis, assessment of academic library value, defining discovery for your library, developing a collection development allocation formula, e-resource management, streaming video in the academy, KBART, an Ithaka S+R workshop, visualizing usage data, and negotiating with vendors. Fourteen plenary and Neapolitan sessions; several hundred concurrent sessions; and lively lunch discussions, PechaKucha-like shotgun "shorts," and poster sessions spiced up the offerings. The popular Neapolitan format was continued from 2014, allowing three plenary-level speakers to speak in large rooms during the same time slot. The conference directors also continued Charleston Premiers during Saturday morning breakfast which were refereed and allowed companies to make five-minute presentations about new and emerging products.

The Charleston Conference has a plethora of additional offerings including juried product development forums for publishers or vendors who want to get feedback from librarians about new or emerging products, dine around dinners on Friday night at some of Charleston's well-known restaurants, a gala reception on Thursday evening at the Charleston Aquarium, and the Vicky Speck ABC-CLIO Leadership Award for someone connected with the Conference.

In 2015, the Conference was able to use the newly renovated Gaillard Center that had just opened. The Gaillard is able to accommodate larger groups than our other venues, which gave a more formal feel to the Conference than in the past. There were several "newness" glitches, but they have hopefully been rectified for 2016. The 2015 lead keynote presentation ("Star Wars in the Library") by Jim O'Donnell of Arizona State University energized the attendees. Courtney Young of Pennsylvania State University spoke about the "Value of Libraries." The Friday keynote was Katherine Skinner (Educopia Institute), who talked about making an impact through collaboration. Neapolitans included the following topics: think like a start up; the secret life of articles; and real-life examples of industry consolidation, innovation in open access monographs, text and data mining contracts, and shared print in Orbis Cascade, the library-publishing landscape, and change management with metrics.

There were breaks in the plenary and Neapolitan talks when a lively Oxford-style debate ensued between Maria Bonn (University of Illinois) and Derek Law (University of Strathclyde) on the proposition that "Altmetrics are Overrated."

The Saturday sessions were equally stimulating. Beginning with Premier five-minute refereed presentations by new companies and products, the next plenary and Neapolitan talks dealt with studying satisfaction with book collections, comparing search engines and discovery services, and much more.

The concurrent sessions, lively lunches, poster sessions, shotgun sessions, and the like that were submitted and refereed by the editors are grouped into six categories in this volume: Collection Development, End Users, Management and Administration, Patron-Driven Acquisitions and Interlibrary Loan, Scholarly Communication, and Techie Issues.

Many new ideas and innovations are implemented and shared at the Charleston Conferences!

Reports of numerous of the plenary sessions and concurrent sessions are included in this volume, many transcribed ably by Caroline Goldsmith. Archives of many of the papers are also loaded online at the Conference website: docs.lib.purdue.edu/charleston/

And, of course, the city of Charleston was as beautiful and vibrant as ever!

The next Charleston Conference will be held November 2–5, 2016, with the theme "Roll With the Times or the Times Roll Over You!" There will be several new offerings; several preconference sessions; and Charleston seminars as librarians, publishers, vendors, aggregators, and consultants from all over the world explore important changes within the industry that impact the way in which information is leased, acquired, and made available. Charleston Conference information will be updated regularly. For archives and further information, visit: http://www.charlestonlibraryconference.com/

See you in Charleston in November!

Katina Strauch, Founder and Convener, Charleston Conference

Bruce Strauch, Owner, Charleston Conference

Introduction

The Charleston Conference continues to be a major event for information exchange among librarians, vendors, and publishers. Now in its thirty-sixth year, the Conference continues to be one of the most popular library-related conferences in the United States and globally. With record numbers for 2015, Conference attendees continue to remark on the informative and thought-provoking sessions. The Conference provides a casual, collegial atmosphere where librarians, publishers, and vendors talk freely and directly about issues facing their libraries and information providers. All of this interaction occurs in the beautiful city of Charleston, South Carolina. This is the twelfth year that Beth R. Bernhardt has put together the proceedings from the Conference and the eighth year for Leah Hinds. We are pleased to share some of the learning experiences that we, and other attendees, had at the conference.

The theme of the 2015 Charleston Conference was "Where Do We Go From Here?" While not all presenters prepared written versions of their remarks, enough did so that we are able to include an overview of such subjects as collection development, management, end users, scholarly communication, and technology issues. The unique nature of the Charleston Conference gives librarians, publishers, and library vendors the opportunity to holistically examine these and other points of interest.

Katina Strauch, founder of the conference, continues to be an inspiration to us. Her enthusiasm for the conference and the proceedings is motivating. We hope you, the reader, find the papers as informative as we do and that they encourage the continuation of the ongoing dialogue among librarians, vendors, and publishers that can only enhance the learning and research experience for the ultimate user.

Signed,

Co-Editors of the 34th Charleston Conference Proceedings

Beth R. Bernhardt, Assistant Dean for Collection Management and Scholarly Communications, University of North Carolina at Greensboro; Main Conference Director

Leah Hinds, Assistant Conference Director

Plenary Sessions

The Value of Libraries: An Association Leadership View

Courtney Young, Head Librarian and Professor of Women's Studies, Penn State Greater Allegheny

The following is a transcript of a live presentation at the 2015 Charleston Library Conference.

Courtney Young: Good morning. Thank you so much for inviting me to be here. I see that the front seats are nice and available, just like when I do course-related instruction. That's good. So, good morning. It's really great to be here with you and at the Charleston Conference. As you can see from the title of my presentation, I will be talking about "The Value of Libraries: An Association Leadership View," and this, of course, is going to be filtered very much through my academic librarian lens, but I will be talking a little bit about other types of libraries as well.

So, as ALA president, I worked with members from all different types of libraries and from all types of library-related roles to highlight areas of interest and emphasis with the Association's mission and vision, and for me that is diversity, career development, engagement, and outreach. I believe that these are the things that really bring value to being a member of the Association and, in turn, the work that we do in and for libraries. They also help us to have a positive impact on the communities that we serve, and in my case those are campus communities. I've come to realize that these three areas from ALA's mission—diversity, career development, and engagement and outreach—are what have helped me, someone who is a frontline librarian in an academic library who is working with traditional- and nontraditional-age undergraduate students from around the world, to do my job better and to be a change agent for those whom I teach. This opportunity to see how libraries of all types are serving their communities has really allowed me to bring back some new ideas and to take different approaches to the way that I do my work. It's also raised my profile among the campus faculty and staff whom I work with so they really get a better sense of the type of impact that librarians and libraries can have on the national level. They are really surprised that, "Wow, libraries are doing an awful lot. This is kind of an important role." I would say, "Hmm, just a little bit."

The chance to serve as the Association's chief spokesperson meant, among things, speaking with the media about libraries. Often this was around that question of, "Do we still need libraries?" Yeah, exactly. I'm glad there was at least one chuckle. What do today's libraries have for 21st-century users? In many cases they were talking about the country's over 16,400 public libraries, but often when I talk about libraries that is what they are thinking about. They're thinking about the public library. And that's okay on a certain level, but academic libraries, which in some communities function as the public library, are just as dynamic and exciting, but also as at risk and challenged as their public counterparts. Which brings us to questions about the value of libraries.

If I look back on my presidential year, I do have a few thoughts on this. First, the value of academic libraries. Now, the Association of College and Research Libraries, ACRL, produced *The Value of Academic Libraries: A Comprehensive Research Review and Report* in 2010. This report provides "1) a clear view of the current state of the literature on the value of libraries within an institutional context, 2) suggestions for immediate 'Next Steps' in the demonstration of academic library value, and 3) a 'Research Agenda' for articulating academic library value" (ACRL, 2010, p. 11). Many of the next steps in that report reflect a national dialogue on public and school libraries. These include linking libraries to improve student retention and graduation rates, enhancing library contribution to student job success, and demonstrating and developing library impact on student learning. This is likely because the executive summary states in the report's scope, "this report includes significant research from other library types: school, public, and special libraries as they offer," and I quote again,

http://dx.doi.org/10.5703/1288284316226

"examples of numerous library value approaches and lessons learned from each" (p. 11). I'd also like to note that the report purports the need to promote and participate in professional development and leverage library professional associations. ALA went on in this by adding professional and leadership development to its new strategic directions that were approved by the Association's council in June of this year. This for me is a real recognition of the fact that professional and leadership development of librarians and library workers is essential to ensuring high-quality professional practice and the future of libraries and information services, increasing the diversity of library professionals and sustaining their professional growth through multiple strategies, and aligning leadership development and continuing education with the best thinking about the changing information environment. And I think that there are a few people in this room who know a little bit about that changing information environment.

I had the opportunity to attend the 2014 South Korea Library Association conference. And in her presentation, "Skills for the Librarian of the Future," the US information resource officer, Alka Bhatnagar, noted the service philosophy for 21st-century librarians as being "user-centric, high-quality resources and services to meet the exponentially growing recreational and knowledge needs of the globally networked current, potential, and future diverse community users in a conducive environment" (Bhatnagar, n.d., p. 31). So, if you think about those pieces that she calls out, it's user-centric, they're high quality resources and services, it's growing recreational and educational needs, it's globally networked, it's current, it's future, it's also potential, it's diversity as well—all taking place in an environment that is conducive to all of these things. Now, even though I know that she was talking about public community-focused libraries, this sounded a lot to me like the experiences that we're shaping in today's academic libraries. It's that intersection of resources and services to support our students' academic and social personal needs that connects them with the world. It recognizes and celebrates diversity all in the right locations that are outfitted appropriately. So, for this morning I'm going to share a few thoughts about libraries' value through advocacy, through partnerships, and through diversity.

First, I'm going to start with advocacy. Now see, advocacy is the foundation of that value piece. It is defined as a public support for, or recommendation of, a particular cause or policy. It is one of ALA's new strategic directions. So, when it comes to advocacy, the American Library Association aims to advocate for the public value of librarians, libraries, and information services and seeks to focus on its mission and priorities working with three key constituents: ALA members, libraries, and the public. Now, the key components of this area are to bring support for libraries and librarianship through public awareness—providing a vision of innovation, enabling the future of libraries and promoting libraries as centers of community engagement and participatory librarianship—and also by promoting ALA's core values and emphasizing the impact of libraries to form a basis for advocacy and community conversations. If we start with that educational piece—when you first tell someone that you are a librarian, so that they won't say, "Do we still need librarians? Do we still need libraries? You must really like to read"—an effective advocacy campaign on behalf of libraries of all types will remind their communities of the vital roles that libraries play. It will raise that community's profile and ultimately will build support. We need to build support with our faculty, both those who are full-time as well as part-time, our students, who are often based in their department or discipline, or their student groups that they are associated with, as well as our campus staff. They often work directly with our students via academic affairs and student affairs, as coaches, and as part of the writing center staff. Another advocacy piece that is related is library spaces. The themes I highlight when I speak to the media regarding public library centers and library projects, either new or renovated, include new technologies, including computer centers and wireless access. It is more community and performance spaces, like the one we're in this morning. It's about auditoriums and meeting rooms, as well as vibrant and comfortable spaces. So, our advocacy for transformed library spaces are also key in terms of the advocacy work that we do on campus.

Once our libraries were constructed to be warehouses of printed volumes that would not even leave the confines of the building. Our academic libraries are now dynamic, multipurpose, multifunctional spaces. Who has the best hours on campus? Likely, it's the library that has the best hours on campus. At some colleges and universities we are the first to open and we are the last to close; and then, of course, in some places we are open 24/7 and perpetual access to the library is just a given. Academic libraries are being reconceptualized to allow students to work directly with each other as well as to effectively engage in virtual collaboration. There are quiet study areas which we still do need. Group study areas which our students are demanding more and more; computer and other digital media labs. Our print collections still have a real role to play in the student's life on campus, and so access to those materials is also part of that design. The beauty of the way 21st-century libraries are being built or renovated is that they are not only setting students up for academic success while they are in college or at the university, but also for life after college. These blended spaces for group work and quiet study with access to various technologies and experts, often referred to as *knowledge commons* or *information commons,* look a lot like those modern-day office spaces where students go to work once they graduate. We need to create and seize opportunities to advocate for the library and articulate its value. This means that all members of our library staff must become advocates and they should be empowered to speak to the library's strengths and contributions to the campus community. It's not just the job of the dean or the director or the associate university librarians, it's everyone's job to have that advocacy role. So, just as I have been prepped to talk about why libraries are still important in the age of Google, and the types of services and resources that are available, everyone on staff needs to be educated and encouraged to articulate the value to our constituents.

Next: partnerships. This might not seem earth shattering, but sometimes a reminder is a good thing. During my presidential year, I observed how important advocacy and partnerships are for libraries, and the unique role that partnership plays in the US versus in other countries that I had the opportunity to visit. So, for example, through a lot of hard work and advocacy, public libraries were included in the Workforce Innovation and Opportunity Act, ensuring that public libraries are recognized as places where jobseekers can go for job search assistance and employment training. My international travel demonstrated to me that this notion of partnering with other agencies—other social agencies, government agencies, other folks in the community—was not necessarily the norm. In our academic libraries, we are also partnering with other groups on campus and across the campus—sometimes with departments, sometimes with specific faculty. We are partnering with those units so that we can help in providing tutoring to our students through our tutoring centers and our writing centers, as well as our international programs for those students who often come to our campuses ahead of when other students arrive on campus. My year as president demonstrated to me that it is important to continue to be aggressive in building those partnerships and even expanding on the partnerships that we currently have in place. I also think we need to recognize partnerships that we have with publishers and vendors who are also a part of our library community, many of whom possess library school education and started off in our library schools as students alongside us. As publishers, in addition to developing products and functionality, often with librarian input, we are also working with many members of faculty to help them publish their research and facilitate access to their work. Some of our biggest supporters in the library advocacy arena have been our publishers, and for that work I am incredibly grateful.

Diversity, inclusion, and equity. Now diversity, which is also beginning to include inclusion and equity, is becoming more inclusive when we say it these days—a little ironic. It is a programmatic priority in the American Library Association, and it focuses not only on fostering the diversity of the profession but also on working to ensure that we are serving all members of our communities, all segments of our populations. The 1990 Diversity and Collection Development Interpretation of the Library Bill of Rights states, and I will quote, "Librarians have an obligation to select and support the access to materials on all subjects that meet as closely as possible the needs and interests of all persons in the community which the library serves. This includes materials that reflect the political, the economic, religious, social, minority, and sexual issues" (Office for Intellectual Freedom of the American Library Association, 2006, pp. 117–118). Libraries and librarians are critical to literacy and multicultural awareness. Library programming is an opportunity to foster intellectual and cultural enrichment. Again, our libraries are an opportunity to foster intellectual and cultural enrichment. So through speaker series, One Campus, One Book projects, even art installations—these are all examples of library programming that is taking place that not only brings the academic community together, but also provides opportunities for diversity and inclusion, particularly when you consider that libraries are designed as destinations for our undergraduates, our graduate students, faculty, staff, and community members. Now diversity and librarianship really go hand in hand, and I believe this is essential for everyone who is working in a library, or pursuing a degree in library information science or a related field. Those librarians or libraries whose librarians and staff or volunteers have a significant impact on their communities, they not only understand this but they embrace it as well. And they are showcasing that their libraries are not only a rich source of diversity but are places where difference is truly welcome. Now ethnic and racial diversity are usually what come to mind first when people mention the term *diversity,* but it means a whole lot more. There is, of course, gender, gender identity, gender expression, national origin, religion, social class, age, sexual orientation, physical and learning abilities. And of course in our university setting, we're talking about our students who are coming to us as traditional-age students, because they're undergraduates, adult learner undergraduates, our graduate students, our international students, our first-generation students, and then of course our faculty, our staff, our administrators, our alumni, our community users. These reflect all the ways in which our communities exist and all the ways in which our communities are changing.

Over the course of my career, I've come to realize that libraries are probably the richest source of diversity in our communities, and in some cases I would even go as far as to say that they are the richest, most untapped source of diversity in our communities. The richest untapped source of diversity. A place where the potential for successful understanding, inclusion, and equity can exist. I have to take a moment to recognize the fact that we are in Charleston and that we are a very short walk away from the Emanuel African Methodist Episcopal Church. Cynthia Graham Hurd was a public librarian who, along with eight members of her congregation, lost their lives on June 17 as a result of a senseless, racially motivated hate crime. We have a long way to go as a society, but when it comes to getting to that place where equity and inclusion are a valued way of life, I strongly believe that libraries and librarians can lead the way and play an active role in healing our communities and creating those much-needed safe environments for all.

The changing demographics in the United States have, and will continue to have, a huge impact on our communities. In 2012 the US Census Bureau numbers showed that the population aged five and under was at 49.9% minority. The nonwhite population increased by 1.9% to 116 million, which is 37% of the US. The fastest percentage growth is among multiracial Americans, followed by Asians and Hispanics. Non-Hispanic whites make up 63% of the US, Hispanics 17%, Blacks 12.3%, Asians 5%, and multiracial Americans 2.4%. Now trends indicate that the United States will become a majority minority country in a rapidly approaching future and communities nationwide are seeing demographic shifts that impact programming, collections, outreach, and staffing. Of course these figures do not provide us with snapshots of other dimensions of diversity. For example, physical and mental disabilities are increasingly visible. In a 2012 disability status report from Cornell University, 12.1% of the US population was indicated to have a disability.

Now, going back to another thing that Alka Bhatnagar noted in her presentation in South Korea, she said, and I'll quote, "The relationship between libraries and their communities is at a critical intersection. There has never been a more rapid period of change affecting libraries and their communities. As a result, there has never been a better opportunity for library employees to act as leaders for positive change" (Bhatnagar, n.d., p. 10) So, as academic librarians, staff, and supporters, we are uniquely positioned to build a community of advocates to collaborate and build partnerships and foster diversity, equity, and inclusion. Our collections, our programming, the services that we provide, the resources that we provide, these all lend to that opportunity within our academic libraries.

One final thought, particularly since this session is being streamed: When I became president, I knew one of my unique contributions could be in the area of social media. I personally was participating in this space in a way that other presidents had not, which isn't to say anything about previous presidents, but just to say that that's just part of who I am, particularly as a "Gen Xer." I know that social media is related to library services, marketing, and the like and can be hit and miss, but I'm also so proud of this profession's willingness to experiment and model the aspirational behavior that is so important in our communities today. I also discovered social media's power as an advocacy tool. It is a strong partnership tool and it is also a way to engage diverse populations in groups in real conversations, not just a one-way output for information. I'm excited that by using social media we can make connections, we can build relationships, and we can improve our professional skills by tapping into an amazing personal learning network. And on that note I look forward to the work ahead and continued improvement of my skills as an advocate, a partner, and a champion for diversity, equity, and inclusion. I look forward to spending time with each of you during this conference and, of course, on social media. Thank you.

References

Association of College & Research Libraries. (2010). *The value of academic libraries: A comprehensive research review and report.* Retrieved from http://www.ala.org/acrl/sites/ala.org.acrl/files/content/issues/value/val_report.pdf

Bhatnagar, A. (n.d.). *Skills for the librarian of the future.* Retrieved from http://photos.state.gov/libraries/korea/49271/october_2014/Skills%20For%20Librarian%20of%20the%20Future.pdf

Office for Intellectual Freedom of the American Library Association. (2006). Diversity in collection development: An interpretation of the Library Bill of Rights." In *Intellectual Freedom Manual* (7th ed., pp. 117–118). Chicago: ALA Press.

Star Wars in the Library

Jim O'Donnell, University Librarian, Arizona State University

The following is a transcript of a live presentation at the 2015 Charleston Library Conference.

Jim O'Donnell: Good morning. The saga continues. About 15 years ago I delivered myself of some opinions about the future of libraries and librarianship in a book called *Avatars of the Word.* The guilty words are here on-screen before you now. You will recognize that academics are given extra points anytime we can use the words "Henry James" in a sentence. That explains some part of this, but I did venture myself to compare the future of librarianship to the mythic heroes Natty Bumppo and the Jedi Knights of Star Wars. I did not ask permission of Natty Bumppo, of librarians, or of the Jedi Knights before I undertook to say these things, and I thought I had escaped safe and sound. Until last February the Jedi came back for me and informed me that I was being appointed University Librarian at Arizona State University. I took a deep breath. It is one of the most exciting institutions of higher learning in North America. I think and say whatever I get the chance that I think we have the best and most venturesome president in higher education. He has charged us to think big and to do bigger in the libraries, and that is what will be trying to do. At the same time, there are plenty of times when I wake up in the morning and ask myself just what I've gotten myself into and whether this isn't the Jedi's way of coming back to exercise their revenge.

So I enter the saga of Star Wars in "Episode Six: The Revenge of the Jedi." I realize I need to do a small footnote right there because many of you will be remembering right now that you saw a movie called *Return of the Jedi* and you are not quite sure about this one. The true Star Wars fans among you will know, however, that the first version of that film was to be called "The Revenge of the Jedi," and it went very far forward in that direction until George Lucas or someone decided that the integrity and good character of the Jedi meant that they didn't engage in revenge. Well, be that as it may, there are opportunities for librarians everywhere, and one that my colleagues took at Arizona State University Library was to score a copy of a promotional poster for the original title of the movie to go along with our collection of documents and, yes indeed, Star Wars toys that we have in the special collections at ASU. Collections are often driven by opportunity. "Episode Six: The Revenge of the Jedi" then is the space in which I find myself living and working. I'm mostly going to fast-forward through this part, however. It has many skirmishes and excitements of one kind or another that I'm living. Some of the most inspiriting episodes, well, they come from meeting and working with smart and hard-working and open-to-change colleagues in the library and beyond at ASU. The more nail-biting episodes have come from other, somewhat predictable, directions. The one to which I will point as perhaps my biggest single learning at the ground level, operational level, skirmish level of librarianship in 2015 is that whatever we think may happen in the future, right now when it comes to electronic books in our libraries, things aren't working. We're getting products whose functionality is limited and crippled in a variety of ways. On one of the aggregator sites that we use we are told that you can copy 38 pages or print 76 pages of a given book. Eh, what's that about? When was the last time with a print book you said, "I think I'll copy 38 pages?" It hasn't happened to me. We also are finding ourselves limited by things like simultaneous user numbers and checkout periods. You can check out one of our e-books for 14 days. You have no incentive to give it back early so you've used it for 10 minutes and it is kept out of sight for 14 days until someone else is able to use it. This simply doesn't work. The prices aren't sustainable. We have hard work to do in that area and many others. But, I want to concentrate for today on thinking forward to the next exciting episode of Star Wars. You're getting now, here, the special advanced preview of what you will be able to see in the theaters starting in mid-December, and you can reveal as many of the plot details as I give away to all of your friends. I'm not sure how popular that will make you, but I hope it helps.

http://dx.doi.org/10.5703/1288284316227

And so I'm going to talk about what seemed to me to be three very high priorities for librarianship, and then at the end of those three priorities I will ask a question that points further forward into galaxies yet undiscovered. I talk about three because of an old friend who likes to say that if you have more than three priorities, you really don't have priorities. The discipline of three is a way of thinking about what is genuinely strategic and what is genuinely important. In a new job, you are often being torn by all of this week's crises and this week's needs, while you think forward to a future seen only intermittently and only in glimpses. Today I want to look flatly at that future and describe for you how it seems to me as a newcomer to this profession where the central issues for our success for the decades to come may lie. I am by training and practice a professor of ancient classics. This gives me the habit of thinking about the long-term. I am not necessarily always thinking forward 2,500 years, but it is useful, I believe, to look forward 20 or 50 or 100 years and ask yourself where you want to be, where you need to be in that time, and then work backward to what would be the most important things to work on for now.

So, I have three simple principles to enunciate and about which to say a few words. The first is a discovery that perhaps is easier to make at Arizona State University than at some others. Arizona State University has over 80,000 students in what we now call our full immersion programs. We also have over 20,000 online degree candidates, and those numbers are going up rapidly. When you hear the promotions on NPR that count how many current online degree programs ASU has, whatever number you hear is incorrect because we just rolled out another one this week. So, we have to think about those online students, but my discovery is that we are already there in the universe of online students for all 100,000 of our education seekers. Yes, we have gate counts in our main building of 1 million and half a year; on a busy Tuesday or Thursday in term time, more than 10,000 people come into our largest building; about another six or seven come into another building about three blocks away. But if you track those students through our buildings, the use they are making of our material collections while they are there verges on the trivial. I have been joking that the average number of customers, faculty or students, whom you can find in our stacks of our libraries looking for a book at any given moment is consistently through the day exactly one. Why is that the case? Well, I'm not even in the stacks. I'm still active in my scholarship; my office is on the same floor with history, philosophy, and religion. When I want one of the books from those stacks, yes, I go online. I click a couple of times and I pick it up at the front circulation desk on my way out of the building that evening because it is just plain easier to do. I'm an online student in that regard. But, if all of our students are online students and need to be served in that way, we have important changes to make in the way we imagine our services. With luck, very soon we will have an opportunity to renovate completely the main building in which we work on the ASU campus, and if that comes to pass soon it will be an opportunity to use that as a forcing function to change the way we think of our services. What happens when we don't have a core collection and core users and then supplementation online, but rather we have a library accessed mainly online and physical service points on our campuses that deliver the appropriate services to those who come in the building looking for them, and support the delivery of services for those people and all the others when they are not in the building? It means we need to think about how we can deliver every service we have to every one of our users, wherever they may happen to be. It means we need to build, of course, our discovery tools; that's a "this year" kind of task. I would point very quickly in passing at the work of David Weinberger at Harvard, who's been talking about the library-sized hole in the Internet. There is a library-sized hole in the Internet: We're too hard to find. Our content requires you to think of yourself first, most of the time, as a library user before you begin to get access to it. We need to change that. We need to have tools that are so powerful and so effective that people say to each other, "I'm not doing one of those stupid Google searches again. I'm using the library search because that's where I find the good stuff." And I do deeply believe that we have the "good stuff" in our libraries.

But, I'm particularly concerned in this context about what happens to our traditional, physical collections. I strongly believe that we need to make the content of those collections available to all of those online users. I'm proud to say that right now, if you are an online student at ASU and you want to have access to one of our books that is only available in print, we will in fact mail it to you. It is a little sobering to realize that our demand for that service is running around 150 volumes a semester, but at least at that level we can afford to provide that service. But, we need to get past that. We need to get past that by addressing what I call the "crisis of the boomer books." The books that are themselves baby boomers of the library. The efflorescence of publications that appeared in the 1950s, 1960s, 1970s, justified the building of our great stack towers, and now have filled our shelves for in many cases more than 50 years. As long ago as 10 years ago, it was discovered by an Ithaca study that 83% of the books in our research libraries are presumably in copyright post-1923. That was using data of 10 years ago. That percentage has to have gone higher. We are now the custodians of huge collections of the cultural heritage of the 20th century, which can be accessed mainly, almost exclusively, only in print, only with the physical artifacts, at a time when information users' behaviors are increasingly focusing on what is available here, now, in my hands. I say that it is a vital strategic task for us as a culture to imagine how our libraries can be genuinely online libraries, not merely by digitizing that content, but by making it available to users. I think, hope, and believe that we are coming to a point where even the most restrictive views of rights holding, and the prerogatives that come with rights holding, will be competed with the recognition that if you are not making your content digitally available, your content will be increasingly invisible and unused. I'm talking to senior scholars of my acquaintance about the challenge they will face as they retire and leave their great books behind on the library shelves if those books are not readily available in some form for a wider audience.

Those books themselves also provide a serious conservation issue, as many of them are reaching that stage of advanced middle-age where they need to see the doctor just a little more often than they used to once upon a time. I have in mind, for example, a typical best-selling novelist of the 1950s, Allen Drury *(Advise and Consent).* What's become of Allen Drury lately? How many of you have read an Allen Drury novel? Not as many as used to. Of his 25 books, we have 23 of them in the ASU library, I'm happy to say, but only 9 of them are available on Kindle, and Kindle is a lousy format if you want your book to survive. Sixteen are in the collections of HathiTrust, but HathiTrust of course is only able to provide limited search access to them. My example is to say that if anyone wants Allen Drury's books to be known or remembered 5 or 15 or 20 years from now, they will have to cross a bar into the world of digital information. And the challenges of doing that case by case right now are prohibitive. We may indeed soon, fingers crossed, have a new librarian of Congress, and therefore new leadership for the copyright office. I see that as a moment we should all seize upon to bring stakeholders of various kinds together for conversation about what it will take to get us to the end state at which the default for the books that have made up the culture of the last hundred years and before, the default situation is that they be available digitally, accessible digitally, for some price. Of course my favorite price is zero, but for some reasonable price. I think I'm willing to pay the fair market price for a 1950s best-seller novel because I think that fair market price is probably $.05 or $.10 and maybe we can negotiate it down in a "big deal." I say the pricing doesn't matter so much as long as the pricing is sustainable. The access is what we need. If all of our students are online students, then we need to deliver information in forms in which they will use it, and in which it is sustainable for us for the longest term.

Second principle: Knowledge is a verbal noun. Now, I need to do a show of hands, and this stage, for those of you who haven't been up here, it is a little challenging for this. So I have a question and I'm going to squint into the lights. How many of you since you got up this morning have engaged in sophisticated text and data mining against very large datasets? May I have a show of hands? Okay. Bad answer. You're wrong. You're all wrong.

I'm going to ask exactly the same question again and I want to see the show of hands. How many of you since you got up this morning have done a Google search? Show of hands? Much better answer. Correct. My point is those two questions are functionally identical. The knowledge use practices we engage in depends, in ways that we've barely come to realize, on access to huge collections of information structured in a wide and divergent variety of ways, accessed with incredibly powerful tools. Google does now against what's arguably the largest dataset in the history of this galaxy that kind of searching all day, every day, and we take it for granted. But think of your practice with a Google search as well. What happened to that Google search you got this morning when that page of results showed up with your first page of hits? Did you get out a spiral notebook and write down and take notes on everything you were finding in your Google search? I doubt it. Do you download all of your Google searches to your own machines and back them up and preserve them for all time? I doubt it. No, you clicked on a link and that Google search and its results disappeared. Or you "X'd" out of that window, satisfied with the information you'd had and those results disappeared. But, at the moment you had those results, at the moment you did that search, that question you were asking and the results that you got was the most important thing in the universe for you. It was knowledge of extraordinary sophistication and now it is gone. Because you were making that knowledge on the fly; you were using it and you were going on to make additional knowledge. If we are talking about flipping models in our libraries, this is the fundamental ontological flip of all flips. We no longer should think of libraries, no longer should think of knowledge, as stable collections of information which can be consulted and used and recorded and preserved; rather, we need to think of our libraries as places in which new knowledge is being made all the time. Many of us are experimenting with so-called maker spaces in our libraries. My argument here is simply that we have always been a maker space, but now we need to conceive ourselves in those terms, conceive the support of our users as people who are making knowledge all the time, and making new knowledge, using our tools. And we need to know how to compete and keep up with the best tools and the best ways of using. As we talk about renovating our main building, I have been saying I would be satisfied if we just blew out all the walls to the outer shell and left a completely blank, empty space, facilitating modular adaptation over time. We are just on the point of building a more sophisticated geospatial data center, and that is an important thing to be doing now—to connect to a big data analytics center—of course, but I am only too well aware that in probably only 5 or 10 or 15 years from now we'll be looking at each other and saying, "Remember back when geospatial was big? Boy, those were the old days!" We don't need hard carved into our buildings a geospatial research center endowed by the geospatial family to be carrying us forward 15 years from now. We will need to keep up. We will need to adapt. We will need to have the new skills for our librarians in order to support new skills for our users.

Third principle: The printed book has a long and glorious future in front of it. I believe that strongly. Nothing I said before about the need to digitize the printed book should speak against that. We will be preserving, and conserving, and caring well for the printed books in our collections. But when I think forward 20 years, and I think forward to the next provost in 20 years, I can predict this with absolute certainty: There will be provosts in our institutions in 20 years who say, "Excuse me, you have how many square feet of off campus high-density shelving space, air conditioned in a way that seems contradictory to our commitment to support a sustainable global environment? And just exactly how many of those objects are being pulled out of those buildings on a day-to-day basis?" I know well, as well, that when the provost says that 20 years from now, some librarian is going to answer, "Well, um, let me get back to you on that. It's probably not very many." That's not a sustainable future. We need to be thinking now and making an object of our study among academics and librarians what we expect for the print collection of the future. I'm looking to design a position to post in a few weeks which will be something like curator of the print collections of Arizona State University—separate from managing our larger collections issues, but thinking about how we handle the books we put in our off-campus shelving facilities. But at the same time thinking about which books we have in which buildings on our campus for what purpose. I think that means we need to kind of do a zero-based budgeting exercise about the books that we have in our buildings. Right now, the books we have in our buildings are the ones that we have just bought and the ones that have survived various culls and purges to off-campus shelving based on frequency of use. But frequency of use is a very slippery category. Among other things, it becomes a self-fulfilling prophecy. If you say something hasn't been used much and you take it out of your main buildings, it will be used less. And if you carry the question of frequency of use to its logical extreme, you wind up with a very simple and jejune and small collection back on your main campus in your main buildings which would not represent well the riches of our collections and the possibilities for our students and our faculty to make use of those collections. Should we be rotating books up to the front of the line? I know of one library where it is said that new Italian fiction always goes straight to off-campus shelving because there isn't much audience for new Italian fiction. This says to me, should we have a 3-month period in which all of the new Italian fiction is put on the front shelves to remind people of the riches of Italian culture and to introduce them to things that they would otherwise fail to see? I'm just groping forward and thinking about this, but it does seem to be an underlying principle that we will need to be intentional, and deliberate, and focused in what we do with our print books as we build the collections of the future. Another thing that is obvious, and others have said it, is that as we move forward the print books that we cherish and sustain, particularly in our main buildings, will increasingly be those that we regard as genuinely special collections. And what will differentiate us one library from another 20 and 50 years from now is not which databases we subscribe to, but what unique materials we have in our libraries, including our bootleg Star Wars posters.

So, those are my three principles. All of our students are online students, *knowledge* is a verbal noun, and the printed book has a glorious future in front of it. Those each represent huge challenges and tasks for us in librarianship, as all of you well know and recognize. Those are the areas in which I think we should be putting focus for the next 5 and 10 years because those are the areas that will make the most difference for our success in years to come. When we get distracted by the skirmishes of the moment—by, let's say, arguments with vendors about e-book interlibrary loan practices—I think we need to be referring those skirmishes to these major principles as we think about the future we want to build. But let me then point one question further beyond that and ask you what a universal library would be like, the universal library of that distant future. I have one very clear picture of what it won't be like. This is the library of the Jedi from those movies. We live in the 21st century; therefore when this image appeared in the movies, there was a small skirmish of intellectual property in discussion with the library of Trinity College, Dublin. This space resembled, it was said, a little too much The Great Hall of Trinity College. I am proud of the academic profession to say that Trinity College decided to take no legal action on the basis of this. But this is the Jedi library. It embodies two things that I think are absolutely untrue about the universal library of the future. First, it is the collection of stuff all in one place. No, that is not the future. But, more important than that, it was the collection for the Jedi themselves. It was a collection for a defined body of users in a particular place with their Jedi Knight Net ID cards authenticating themselves for access to the building, and the online databases. And you see a little Jedi action going on down on the main floor there. At Arizona State University, one of our leading principles in the last decade has been that we will define our success not by who we exclude, but by whom we include; and it is one of the things that makes me proud of the institution that we have been creative and successful in finding ways to incorporate students and faculty into our university who would not have had those opportunities before. We have tripled, for example, in the state of Arizona the number of Native American students who attend ASU and get degrees. We are now producing more Native American PhDs per year than any other university in history. That comes with effort, but it is an embodiment of the recognition at our institution that we succeed when we make success possible for all who come from whatever backgrounds and from everywhere.

That means that we need to think forward to what it will take to build that library collection of the future, and I use the singular there. It really is a single library collection without duplication of activities, without duplication of efforts, no longer negotiating 1,000 different licenses for 1,000 different communities, but finding a business model whereby we can sustain publication and access, and make the most universal access possible. And, one more time, flip the model away from imagining that we have many libraries and some collaborative activities, to making the collaborative activity on the fundamentally core collection of library materials and resources the main business, and allow all of our individual libraries to be points of access, points of service provision, points of collection of special collections, no question, in that larger global kind of service.

There are asterisks on the possibility of doing this. One asterisk is the inertial asterisk of wishing to keep control for ourselves of our own material. But even what we collect in our special collections should be made intellectually accessible and, where possible through digital representations more than just intellectually accessible, to the widest possible range of users. Not just those in our university communities, but those well beyond. I joke about Jedi Knight ID cards, but library cards have been the feature of our institutional and social practice for many, many years. We are all in favor of the widest possible access to our materials, and think of your day job. We all keep checking ID cards. We all keep talking about who is authenticated into our system. We all keep talking about the limitations on use, not the ultimate expansion of that use. But I would suggest the principle there are no good reasons—and I am emphasizing good—there are no good reasons why all of the riches of the best of our university and academic research libraries in the world should not be available to students in community colleges, to students in secondary schools, to people who don't live in privileged first world countries, to people who don't have their Net ID card in any form or another, but still have a fundamental human right to inquire, to explore the results of human inquiry, to learn, to benefit from that, and to make new knowledge. The biggest asterisk on that future will be, of course, that there will be opposition from cultures in places at which the possibility of globalized access to information is unwelcome. I think that if 100 years from now we have come to a point at which there really is a universal access to library information throughout the world, then many other things in the world will have gone well. And I would turn that around and say that if you do not succeed in achieving that kind of collection, that not so many things will have gone so well. Some other things will have gone badly.

If the first three principles I outlined suggest very large, very expensive, strategic tasks for all of us in the immediate and near future, asking this question poses what seems to be the mother of all strategic questions about the future of libraries. And to suggest that, as we go forward as librarians, we need to think that we live indeed not simply on a small speck of dust floating around a particular sun in a particular corner of the universe, but that even in libraries we live in a very large galaxy, among many other galaxies that we know of in the world in which we live.

And so, I come to the end of these remarks by wishing you the very best that I possibly can. When you saw the title of my remarks you probably should've been able to predict what my last words to you would be, and I will indeed utter them now: May the Force be with you!

Needle-Moving Collaboration: From Act to Impact

Katherine Skinner, Executive Director, Educopia Institute

The following is a transcript of a live presentation at the 2015 Charleston Library Conference.

Katherine Skinner: Thank you so much, Anthony, and thank you to all of you for being here so bright and early in the morning. I'm going to move fast so if you didn't get coffee, you're probably going to regret it in a couple of minutes, but you're going to be awake. So, today what I'm going to be doing is I'm going to be challenging all of us in this room to think about the roles that we need to play, all of us, to move the needle in scholarly publishing. Nobody here is exempt, and I will say that again: Nobody here is exempt. Every single one of us has a role to play. Every single one of us is needed as we are moving into the next generation of scholarly communications, all of us.

In order to kind of illustrate action and the need for action, I'm going to start with my favorite tigress. This is Mohini. So, this tigress and her story appeared first in *The New Scientist* back in 1984. It was a story told by David Challinor, who was a long-beloved representative of the Smithsonian National Zoo. And so Mohini was a gift to President Eisenhower. She was the first white tigress to arrive in the United States. Beautiful, fantastic, totally exotic for the 1950s America and she was placed in a 12 × 12 cage in the lions' area, which is what you did with animals back then. So, in that lion's den on concrete she paced back and forth, back and forth in her 12 × 12 pen for years. But the Smithsonian Zoo was one of the first zoos in the United States to really pursue natural habitats, and so in the early 1970s they started to build Mohini a new area to live in. Acres and acres of grass, and they were really, really excited to let their tiger out and see what she was going to do. So, when they released Mohini, she was a little set in her ways. And so everybody's watching—there's great anticipation—and what does she do? She claims a 12 × 12 area and starts pacing it, and she wore out the grass underneath her feet. She paced back and forth, back and forth, back and forth for months. And the story illustrates what happens if we don't act and if we don't recognize the kinds of opportunities that are in front of us. In the academic publishing landscape, I think it is a story that we need to hear and that we need to think about because we've had an established way of doing our business that has worked really well for centuries. Maybe not quite so well in more recent years, but it has worked pretty well for centuries, and now we have got this opportunity to do so much more and I'm not sure that we're there yet.

Sociologists and naturalists would call Mohini's plight *isomorphism,* which is a fancy word for habit. She was hindered from experiencing what she could have, and in taking advantage of what she could have, because she was stuck in her habits, and we can see this all around us. So all of our partners on this journey—and you see kind of an illustration here, a lot of the ones that come to mind when we think about scholarly publishing—we have arguably been wearing pretty serious tracks in our own 12 × 12 confines. Most of publishing today is still adhering to rules that were established a generation ago. And I'm going to argue today that all of that is changing, whether we want it to or not, whether we participate or not, actively; that we are in a critical moment now; and this critical moment is every bit as dramatic as Mohini's shift from the concrete cage to the grassy acres. We've all got a choice to make in this moment.

And this is a critical moment. So what do I mean by critical moment? This starts to illustrate it. And I will let this sink in for just a second. So, what I want you to note in this image is all of the loss. Right? There's the loss of the pipe, the loss of the glasses, the loss of the hat and the toupee, which is my personal favorite part, and the loss of the oar, the loss of control. I mean, he has completely lost control, and so have the two very helpless women who are not doing a whole lot to assist the man. But I do want to take issue, and the name of this painting is *A Critical Moment,* and I

http://dx.doi.org/10.5703/1288284316228

do want to take issue with that name because I'm not sure that this is the critical moment. When I think about the critical moment, I think about that moment that preceded this. What happened that allowed this moment to take place?

The moment of opportunity is what I like to focus on when I'm thinking about critical moments, not the moment of loss. Hopefully we don't get the moment of loss, because we take advantage of the moment of opportunity. And not every era gives us the opportunity to experience critical moments, especially not like this day and age. Every generation thinks it is living in unique times, but we really do live in pretty intensively changing times. Not every era brings that, so we're creatures of habit, by and large, as humans; change of the field-wide or system-wide level is usually restrained by the boundaries that are around the field. So, if you think about the way that gears reinforce each other and encourage stasis, they don't like to let go. That's what the systems that we embed ourselves in—including the business systems like academic publishing—that's what they do. And for the most part that is a good thing. We need predictability; that's why we function this way. But those things can get in the way when we're ready to change. And in particular, when we're thinking about change, one of the things that is hard to realize when you're in the middle of something is that one organization, or one institution, or one small cluster, or one stakeholder group has a really hard time bending these gears enough to actually get them to go out of alignment so they go somewhere new. One of the things that I think we expect to happen, and that we fund to happen, and that we try to invest in is innovation in small spaces. That doesn't work unless it incentivizes all the players in the system. You can't incentivize one stakeholder group and expect everything to change, and I'm going to illustrate that in just a couple of minutes.

When we think about this critical moment, and some of the markers of it, and some of the ways that we know that we really do have a lot of things aligning that open up a moment of opportunity—a moment where we can make great changes that aren't necessarily permissible in the human system under regular circumstances—some of those changes are here. Technological change: I don't even have to tell y'all how fast it's going because all of us are experiencing it on a daily basis. New competitors: We've got a lot of them in this field. Some of them are driven by commercial interest; others are driven by more academic interests. There are clashes of values that are happening on a regular basis, and it's something that has increased dramatically over the last generation of scholarship. We also have huge political shifts, and this is going on in the broader environment. So, looking at the way that the kind of shifting priority has happened from the public good, which used to be more or less an accepted part of the American life, to more privatized interest and the concentration of wealth in very, very few hands, so the political shifts kind of merge in with this economic concentration, though they are distinct, and when you put all of those factors together and then add to it the information deluge, we've got huge opportunities. It's not comfortable times we're living in. We really do have huge opportunities for change, and change is coming. If we're in a critical moment, if by this definition we're in a critical moment, then what do we do? We've got two main choices: We can continue to walk in our 12 x 12 confine and do what we're used to, or we can try to game the system for good and create some transformation ourselves. I like that latter option for opportunity, and sociology gives us some really great tools towards that end.

How do we game the system? We start with research. Research from disciplines like sociology and economics and business can tell us a whole lot about field transformations, which is what we are really experiencing right now. Lots of fields are changing; it's not just the academic publishing field, but we feel it here, and those disciplines—sociology, etc.—have demonstrated repeatedly that fields do tend toward stasis. So, think about the gears again. But, major change does become possible occasionally, and when those moments come up we can change or we can be changed. You can witness the Catholic Church in the age of Gutenberg just as an example. I won't go into a deep illustration of that, but the printing press transformed one of the most powerful institutional forces on the planet at the time, and certainly in the Western world. When fields become unsettled, the process of change usually unfolds from innovations, but not innovations that take place at the center. They usually take place on the fringes of the field, which is not where we expect to see them. This is due to the habituated behaviors, so the Mohini kind of mindset, and the way that we treat our vested interest. If we are at the center, there is really nothing incentivizing us to have the kind of breakthroughs that tend to happen more on the fringes. So we really have to watch the fringes in order to anticipate where change can really come from.

And then, third, and I think most overlooked within our respective fields, researchers have also shown that it is not lone geniuses that produce change. Innovation is not something that happens because a lightbulb goes off over somebody's head and they come up with this brilliant idea and that idea is what changes everything. That is what we tell ourselves, and I think the American mythos in particular—with the focus on frontier mentality and those kinds of things—I think the US is extremely prone to this kind of lone genius fallacy. But it is a fallacy, and it has been pretty well debunked in sociological circles. Instead, those innovators are always a key part; if they are successful they are always a key part of a larger cultural system that includes the production, the distribution, and especially the reception. And that system always depends upon networks of people. You cannot do this—you cannot have change happen without networks of people driving it. To say that a different way, change doesn't arise because one amazing individual somehow displays his or her extraordinary genius, devising some magical new innovation that completely changes the world. Instead, it happens through the activities of networks of people. I can think of no better illustration for this than the Castellers in Barcelona, who literally build human castles, and do so by strengthening the base with arms that stretch to shoulders and basically make a proportional infrastructure to support the people that they are elevating.

Now what do we do with that information? So, if you buy what I've said so far, then we can play a little game of "if-then." If a field is a somewhat stable enterprise, and if innovation tends to happen on the fringes, and if networks are what's needed to move those innovations from the fringes to the center, then we all need to work deliberately field-wide, which is not something that we would comfortably do, in order to manage our efforts using networks to ensure that we align and not compete. We need to work toward a common goal that's at the field level. We need to stop thinking only about the here and now and start thinking about where we want to go and how to get there.

What might that look like? Let's shift gears for just a minute, and in order to really position where we are right now I want to make sure that we are all on the same page. I'll recognize and own that my perspective on this is my own perspective on this. It is as grounded as it can be from history and sociology, but I will recognize that there may be some things in the following slides that others would paint a little differently. I want to put us in the historical context that we are operating in today. This image is of the first research journal. This is *The Philosophical Transactions of the Royal Society,* and this was published 350 years ago. I had the great pleasure of seeing this, which is actually Christopher Wren's personal copy, when I was in Oxford, England, for FORCE 2015 earlier this year. This was an incredibly important innovation and it exemplifies impact. Three hundred fifty years ago, basically what happened is this got published and it laid the groundwork for everything that's come since. But there are some reasons that that happened. The innovation itself was good, and one reason is that this encapsulated research. It gave an easy way for scholars and researchers to get information back and forth to each other. It was a good mechanism for registering, for disseminating, and for recording and archiving one's research, so I don't want to take away from that. But that in and of itself did not make this successful. What made this successful is it had a ready society that adopted it and adapted it and quickly started using it. The Royal Society played an incredibly strong role here, and it was something that had already been there. This was not a new society: It was a ready network of influential players and, as we'll discuss a little bit more in a few minutes, that is the kind of linchpin in these environments.

Then the third factor that played into its favor is that this came into being right at a moment when scientific discoveries were on the rise and when a lot of people actually had the means to both do research and to appreciate this kind of recording of it. Building on this first journal publication from roughly the late 1600s, all the way up until the 1970s, 1960s, we had a pretty well established way of doing things. It relied on our publication of journals and of monographs, and publishers served as the gatekeepers, the editors, the producers, and disseminators of scholarship. The academic libraries purchased them and cataloged them and preserved them. Everybody had a role and the system functioned really, really well for a long time. And then things happened. The unsettling of this relatively healthy system and the resulting articulation of crisis can be traced back all the way to at least the 1970s, and I suspect the 1960s, though I haven't found that proof yet. And notably this was a really volatile moment for Western markets, and we can't take this out of that context. Now conventional wisdom today, and the wisdom that I was taught, is that this all happened for two reasons—that the scholarly communications crisis happened for two reasons—(1) the shift from print to digital, and (2) the consolidation, the now infamous bundling practices. Right? But that explanation is not right. It is way too simple and reality is way more complicated than that. So, where did the destabilization come from? One of the causes was the Xerox machine. The Xerox machine, as it says, makes copies of anything on ordinary paper, including books. In the late 1960s this became a technology that was being used by scholars, and it cut into journal subscriptions. Very quickly, scholars were able to take a piece of what they wanted and actually take it back to their offices. This really changed some of the subscription behaviors of individual scholars. Now, that alone didn't do it. We also had the diversification, very quick diversification, of fields. Disciplinary specialization started to be on the rise in the 1960s, 1970s. For example, you had anthropology splinter off into subdisciplines, and those subdisciplines splintered off into subdisciplines, and each of them had to have their own society and their own journal. Suddenly there was a lot more competition for society memberships, and so again, subscriptions dropped. Also, libraries couldn't keep up with the sheer volume of content that was coming out, so that too led to a drop in subscriptions from the library side.

Now that matched up with another phenomenon, which was the emergence and attention that was given to publishing and higher education rankings. For both disciplinary departments and across the university, the value of publishing included what it was doing for the ranking system. Again, there was an increase in the supply of journals and journal articles, so libraries' acquisitions budgets continued to suffer and subscriptions continued to drop. And the net effect of all of this—and I will give a shout out to Sarah Glassmeyer, who produced this graphic, and there are some more updated versions of this out there as well—but the drop in revenues from subscriptions weakened the societies. There was an open door for consolidation, and again this was all taking place in Western markets, where consolidation was already happening across other industries like music; you name the industry, it was consolidating. As I say, commercial publishers bought out a lot of the weakened societies, and you can see here how that played out in one particular area. But the commercial publishers were feeling the burden too. It's not like they were these protected creatures that were hugely successful. Instead, they knew that they were in a subscriptions spiral, the same as everyone else. The libraries would drop subscriptions, or people started dropping subscriptions, and then the prices had to rise to accommodate that, and then they'd drop more subscriptions, and so the spiral went forward and it spiraled really out of control, and it was hurting the commercial publishers as well as the noncommercial publishers. But, the commercial publishers were the ones that decided that they had to do something, and they found an opportunity to move strategically towards an electronic future at the same time as they were addressing this problem.

Now it is really important to recognize that the innovation which was the Big Deal, the bundled subscriptions, was really an accident coupled with serendipity, right? This was not a deliberate scripted takeover of the scholarly journal space. It was a really, really good guess in the right direction that just happened to snowball. But why did it snowball? It was a good innovation in some ways, but why did it snowball? It's because all of the players in the system embraced it. Not a single player, not a single sector, stepped back from this and said, "We're not going to play this way." And that is what enabled its success. So, Academic Press was the one that initiated the idea over in the UK. They spotted a source of funding and saw that the UK's higher education funding council had a grant program that was available, and they pitched a project at it, and that project led to the funding of a multiple journal, or multi-journal, and multi-year license that provided all of the UK's higher ed establishments with free use access to all of AP's titles. This seemed like a win for everybody, right? Academic Press had a dependable revenue stream, which was nice, and the way to actually start exploring the digital without it being quite as much of an investment as it might've been. UK's higher education funding council was really happy because they had a strong project that filled an established and notable gap, and libraries and researchers were happy because they had huge vastly increased access to content, especially through some of the early consortial relationships. Everybody got something out of this, and it was a bold move in a critical moment, much like the critical moment that we're living through today, and it was well played, more by luck than by aim, and that is really, really important to recognize.

The sense of crisis that permeated the scholarly communications landscape left the Big Deal largely under analyzed, even by AP itself, which later admitted that they were going on gut and really had not analyzed thoroughly the model that became the new base model for academic publishing. There were a few people in the field, mostly librarians, who did point out from the beginning, and I do want to say that the Big Deal was a short-term win for individual institutions and potentially a long-term loss for the whole field. But because it appealed to so many local interests, most institutions bought in. We are really bad about doing this, folks. We think local, we do not think at the field level, and that gets us into a lot of trouble. I think where we are today we can tie directly to that, and where we go tomorrow, we need to be thinking about that so that we avoid hitting the same calamity. Once they bought in, their campuses had huge access to content and they don't want to give that up. So, the deal with the devil. I don't think any of the players here are devils, and I also think that the biggest problem here is that the problems that the Big Deal sought to address weren't actually addressed by the Big Deal. It just postponed the inevitable. The subscription crises continued to go where it was going; the shrinking budgets of libraries, that hasn't changed. If anything it has gotten dramatically worse. Library budgets have continued to decrease, journal prices have continued to increase, and now libraries have been trapped for long enough and have kind of occluded what was happening—not intentionally, but by design—because they were trying to protect their campuses. What we have at this point is a weakened system. It's not just a troubled system, which is where we were in the 1970s—now it's a really weakened system. Part of what weakened over this was the relationships between the different sectors. Because it became the libraries against the presses, especially the commercial presses. Or it became the libraries and the university presses not working together, but actually working at odds with one another and having a lot of resentment because, of course, monograph purchases dropped radically and so the university presses were doubly impacted. Groups that should've been great supporters of each other, and great supporters of the academic promise, and supporters of knowledge dissemination have gotten focused on these other things. These other things have really split us apart and are very divisive; most of the outfits that have tried to resist the Big Deal just continued that same sensation of divisive action instead of trying to find some grounds on which we can all unite. This is a systemic problem, and I do mean a systemic problem. Note that there are no new purchasers arising in this space so themarket share, the amount of money that is there to spend, has decreased at the same time as the content has dramatically increased, both in price and amount.

Scholarly communications is not the sole burden of libraries. It is not the sole burden of publishers. There are a lot of stakeholders and a lot of interests in the landscape, including the authors who we often don't have in, for example, this room. But until this moment, the crisis was absorbed a lot by the libraries, and now the libraries can't absorb it anymore. The range of approaches that have been attempted to resolve the crisis or to change it, again, most of those have actually inadvertently reinforced the main problem, which is that the different sectors aren't talking to each other, and certainly aren't talking to each other straight. I'm going to say that one of the things that is a problem right now is that we haven't found a way to incentivize a sufficient percentage of the stakeholder groups that have interest in the landscape. In order for any entity to have an impact on the system that lasts, we've got to have the players from across the system actually unite around something. Whether that is done purposefully or accidentally, it doesn't matter. But we've got to be in that crucial sociological phenomenon where a network really takes the innovation back into the system.

How do we align? We're in a new critical moment—one where change is imminent. We know change is coming and we know that we've got a lot of factors aligning again, much as we did in the 1970s, and we've been talking around the big thing that's changing for decades. More recently we've gotten closer and closer and closer to what the crux point is, and the word that resonates here is a big one, and it's one that means a lot of different things: *data.* This is what's coming and we know it. It's already here. But today I am not wanting to talk about the typical data conversations that we've had over the last five years: how to publish it, or how to cite it, or how to preserve it. Those are all important things, but there is something much bigger looming. What's important about data in academic publishing today is how it's starting to be collected and how it's being used in predictive analytics, and the implications of what that could mean, not just for academic publishing but for the whole academic system.

How many people here remember *Money Ball*? *Money Ball*, both the book and the movie, do a really good job of exemplifying what happened with the Oakland Athletics back in the late 1990s/early 2000s with super metrics. They were one of the first really popularized ideas of what data can do. In essence what they did at the Oakland Athletics, where they didn't have much money, is they constructed their team one year not by the collective wisdom of the players, and the coaches, or the scouts, and the front desk, and all the people who usually got involved in that kind of baseball selection, but instead from analytical gauges of player performance. What Oakland did was it demonstrated, as it started winning games, that the effective use of data could move a team from the bottom of the heap close to the top. The value in this case was placed on things that lead to wins in baseball games. So, on-base percentage and slugging percentage, which, as it turned out, once they did the math, those things mattered a lot more than the things that were driving the decisions of most coaches and scouts and others, like batting average. Again, let me emphasize the value here was placed on wins. So, as we move from the field of dreams to the field of publishing we need to ask the question, "Where will the value be placed?"

It's a really, really, really important question because digital technology is making it possible for publishers and libraries to gather data on the dissemination and use of digital scholarly publications in absolutely unprecedented detail and on an unprecedented scale. Data arising from the digital distribution of content provides us with all sorts of new opportunities. There are lots of good things here to help us understand what is going on in the scholarly communications ecosystem, but it also raises a huge range of questions—ethical questions and ones that we really haven't begun to grapple with. The high cost of providing data and providing data-related services, those are reinforcing the inequities that are already there within the academic publishing landscape so that those who have enough money

to actually understand what's going on also have increased ability to act. Those practical challenges associated with gathering and assessing and disseminating or interpreting usage data are really, really important to who is going to be able to play in the next generation. Even those libraries and publishers who do have sophisticated data management systems lack the crucial contextual data to basically mark their own performance by. They may be able to analyze their own, but can they tell what's going on in the aggregate? If you're not able to measure your impact then, again, you've got some problems here. Data about the published works you're using is playing a growing role in the assessment of research performance. For scholars this is huge, and it's going to be informing how decisions about scarce resources are allocated—what gets published and what we do with those publications—and it's going to be a determining factor in things like permission and tenure. It's something that has those scholars who are paying attention, which is a tiny minority, but has them very, very concerned right now, and we need to be listening to those concerns and amplifying them with concerns of our own. The increasing availability and value that is placed on data—usage data—creates important ethical challenges for organizations that are gathering this information. So, in particular, where is the transparency around the data algorithms and about data accuracy? What are they measuring? We don't know right now for most of the things that are happening within the system, and we are sufficiently not asking and we are sufficiently not controlling it, and that is a problem. And the "we" here is all of the different players in this system, not any one player. Even if data is accurate and we understand the algorithms that are used to analyze it, the data still raises really urgent questions. How will personally identifiable information be tied to a scholar? How will measures of the attention given to a scholar's work impact that research career, the trajectory, and what we value? What is it that we're going to value—what sells? Or is it going to be that we value what transforms? And what transforms doesn't tend to transform in the moment that you put it out there. We all know this. We are in academic publishing, and some of the most important texts that have been published were underappreciated in their own time. As we're using usage data to shape the new forms of scholarly inquiry, we've got to recognize that's actually what we are doing. It's not just that usage data is going to help us to somehow better market, better understand, better anticipate. It's that it fundamentally could change what we are publishing in ways that could privilege the commercial interest over the actual intellectual interest. I think this is already happening, and I think it is terrible, and I think it is dangerous.

What do we do about this? We have a system that's changing. The implications are just very, very severe. I can't make that point strongly enough in this talk. We can choose to sit by and let a few dictate what that aggregated data look like, who holds them, how they control them, how they dole them out, etc., or we can work together to determine that as a community. I'm going to encourage us to choose the latter, and I want us to think about what that might look like and what could make it possible for us to align.

Basically the question here is, how do we move from act to impact? In the social sector, initiatives that are geared towards system-level transformation have been increasingly turning to methodologies that cultivate multi-stakeholder licenses in order to create and sustain transformative change: environmental improvement, or reduction in homelessness, or reduction in teen pregnancy rates—all of these types of things. We've got some really, really well-proven methods that do a lot to make those changes happen. And in these approaches the system-wide changes encouraged through the work of cross-stakeholder networks—that comes right back to the sociological principles that we were talking about. And what they share in common is a number of very specific pieces. So, they share a common agenda where cross-stakeholder groups come together and say, "You know what? We may disagree on a lot of things, we may be competitors, but we agree on this one central thing." It can't be a platitude. It's got to be something that is measurable. You've got to have shared measurement systems that allow each one of those stakeholder groups to map back progress, both of the whole group towards the whole and then of side projects and initiatives towards the whole. This is about alignment. Mutually reinforcing activities have to be there, and have to be constantly recalibrated, to make sure that all of the players in the system continue to get enough out of the pathway that is moving forward to stay involved and to keep moving those gears in a new way. Continuous communication—absolutely mandatory, and it's got to take place from a neutral space, and that neutral space has got to be funded well enough to actually do that work. It is one of the most underfunded things that we do, and we need glue to hold a group together. We rarely provide it in the academic publishing community, and it is one of the reasons why multi-sector stakeholder initiatives often splinter. I know that that works because I put it into practice in a lot of different ways through Educopia projects, and also because I've studied this extensively so when I ask you guys to trust me on it, I'm also going to say that if anybody wants to talk to me about how this has worked and how lightweight this can be, I'd be happy to.

But I'm going to turn in the last 2 minutes—and Anthony I promise it will be 2 minutes—towards a project that we are lovingly calling "Project Meerkat" that grew out of the Scholarly Communications Institute a month ago. This is a proposal that we are just starting to vet. A few of you in this room have probably already seen it, and hopefully many of you will see it in the coming weeks. What we did at the Mellon Fund Scholarly Communications Institute under the leadership of Kevin Hawkins, who was the head of my group from the University of North Texas, is we looked at usage data in one very specific area: monographs. And what we became quickly obsessed with are the challenges in the ethical implications of that data, and who holds that data, and how that data is used. What we've done now is we've put together a proposal. We got pretty juiced up about this, and we've put together a proposal that would do a seed-funded project that would have the following aims. In essence the important parts are the three bullets:

- *Usage data modeling:* How do we collect and share information about monograph usage? How do we share it? With each other and with others that are not necessarily part of gathering it?
- *Usage data ethics:* What are the principles that we all need to adhere to in order to protect the academic integrity of what we're publishing?

And then, finally:

- *Cooperative infrastructure:* How do we incentivize all of the groups to be there because they all own and govern it?

We've got a number of deliverables that we have outlined again with this now very drafty proposal that we are just vetting. This is not an active initiative yet, but it would have three sets of deliverables, and I think that the crux piece here is that data ethics piece. It would map with and include, it would have to include a lot of other relevant efforts. There are a lot of other things going on in the area of data analytics. What we're talking about here is not doing something different from that. It is approaching it in a different way. So the outcomes here would be knitting together a different type of scholarly communications infrastructure. Not one that is utopian, where all of us suddenly love each other, and it is all equal and somehow that works for everybody. No. There are going to be more successful and less successful players commercially. There are going to be more successful and less successful players in terms of what their ratings are, etc. But ultimately all of us will be moving in a more unified direction, and one that protects the thing that I think all of us are most motivated by, which is academic integrity and which is, I think, under fire right now if we are not very, very careful with what usage analytics does for us in the future.

So on that very positive end note, I'm going to go ahead and transition and say that these are the people that have been working on this proposal with me, and again I'm going to say that it is still in the vetting stages right now. Don't be afraid—if you'd like to see it—to reach out to any one of us and ask. Over the course of the next couple of weeks we will be rolling it out further and really testing this to see if it is something that we can make fly. So, I am truly grateful for your attention. I had to rush through so many things. This is so painful. I would have loved to talk to you guys for an hour, but I don't think that that was what the conference organizers meant. So, I will stop talking now and hear from you.

The Long Arm of the Law: Privacy Explored

Gary Price, Cofounder and Editor, infoDOCKET

William Hannay, Partner, Schiff Hardin

Lisa Macklin, Director, Scholarly Communications Office, Emory University Library

Moderated by Ann Okerson, Senior Advisor on Electronic Strategies, Center for Research Libraries (CRL)

The following is a transcript of a live presentation at the 2015 Charleston Library Conference.

Ann Okerson: Well, good morning and welcome to the sixth session of the "Long Arm of the Law." Thanks to Katina for thinking these topics are so important that she makes sure that we get a certain amount of airtime for them each year. Every year we pick a topic or a court case or something that we're going to follow in this session that will be of value to many, many in the audience: librarians, publishers, and others. This year we decided to focus on privacy, which is a topic that is touching us all in every layer of our lives. Privacy is the ability to control into whose hands information falls. It is important because it protects the rights and freedoms of all of us to live as we please. Our speakers today are bringing to us important perspectives about privacy in the library, in publishing, and other settings. I'm going to be very brief with these introductions. We're going to just run through them all very quickly. The speakers will each take about 15 minutes, and then with good luck we'll have some time left over for audience discussion.

Our first speaker is Gary Price, who is known to you in many ways for his work with *Library Journal,* keeping us all informed and up to date with infoDOCKET. He is going to speak about technologies that libraries and publishers use—deploy, often inadvertently—and how they might compromise our privacy. The other day Gary told me that my most frequently used airline, United, doesn't encrypt their itinerary information enough and it might be possible for people who care to do this to find out where I'm going, and that freaked me out. So, Gary is going to talk about things like that. His mission here is to put the fear of God into our minds as we go forward. Bill Hannay, who is a repeat, regular offender here and one of our most popular speakers, is going to talk about the larger legal context, continuing a topic that he started last year, which was the right to be forgotten. And then Lisa Macklin is going to bring the discussion directly into the academic setting and discuss things that will be of issue in our library context. So, that is our lineup for this morning, and we thank you for being here. We hope there is something in here of value to everyone. So, Gary . . .

Gary Price: All right. Thank you, Ann. Good morning, everyone. To continue with the Kenny Rogers theme, hopefully by the end of this you won't call me "Coward of the County." Okay. I'm here to put the fear of God in you, and hopefully in the next 12 minutes we'll do some of that and also impart some useful knowledge to you as well. So, library and Internet privacy. Bottom lines at the top: awareness by all parties, discussion, and education is a must and needed now. The privacy that people expect from the library, and have come to expect from the library over many, many decades, is not where it should be in the digital age and we need to do more. The first place to begin is with discussion, education, and knowledge of first ourselves and then our users. Some of the good news is that there is work being done by many organizations. Now in the last couple of years we've seen interest from NISO. They have a privacy initiative. The American Library Association just released e-book privacy guidelines (http://www.ala.org/advocacy/library-privacy-guidelines-e-book-lending-and-digital-content-vendors), for example, and there is another funded project from the Knight Foundation called the Library Freedom Project. We are also seeing more publishers getting involved. Some examples, and database

http://dx.doi.org/10.5703/1288284316229

providers—BiblioCommons, Project Muse, OverDrive, BilblioBoard—are all now encrypting the entire process, which includes the personally identifiable data (your name, if you have to register), but what I'm talking about is also the transmission of data over the Internet, and we'll talk more about that in a moment.

Privacy is more than encryption. It is the local data: How is it stored? The transaction laws: Is the data being scrubbed? How often? Does your library—and I've seen this in some of my research, privacy policies from some libraries haven't been updated in years: Is your library doing that? Are you disclosing what's going on in a clear manner, not on page 43 of some statement? What are we doing with sharing with vendors? We can share with vendors some of the things that Katherine [Skinner] was talking about—we can use some of this data—but we need to let our users know what's going on. We ask transparency of others, but we're not doing the job that we're asking of others. We need to do a better job. The same thing is going with data storage. There are third parties involved. The library is just not a single building now. The data is flying all over the place. What is your relationship with the vendors? What are their privacy policies? How will they contact you? Will they contact you? How long after might there be a data breach? Is the technology configured correctly? Opt-in services the vendors provide: What are they doing with that data? If you're e-mailing results to a group of people, is that data being saved? If it is, is it being scrubbed after x amount of days? Is it just immediately disappearing? We need to understand these things and work with our vendors on these types of issues. Is there a response plan in place locally that, if there is a data breach, what will happen? So, it's awareness, training, staying current, and being vigilant because all of this changes on a very regular basis.

I also have seen over the last few years that perhaps we're a bit scared of what might happen, but in my view that's kind of burying your head in the sand. And in this day and age we can lose a lot of respect from the general public and our users for something that they respect us for—being a pillar of privacy in our communities—with just one simple data breach, and the fact that somebody can easily say, "Well, you never told us." I believe in this day and age we need to be out front on these issues and, again, the transparency that we ask of others, we need to become better at in this particular topic. We need to be preemptive versus reactive. If just about every European website can have a cookie disclaimer on it, something that simple, why aren't we doing the same thing? For example, when somebody borrows a book from an e-book provider and puts it on their Kindle, that data is being shared with a third party. Are we simply even disclosing this to our users? And one thing that I've also learned over the last few years is everybody has a different level of comfort with privacy. So, if somebody doesn't want their data stored indefinitely with Amazon, are we showing them how to remove the data off of the Amazon server? Are we providing them that information? From what I've seen we need to do a better job.

Now, we can talk about all the ethical reasons and "this is what we have always done" reasons, but put all of those aside for a moment. In the last few years, privacy, data surveillance, and the like have become a major topic both in the US and around the world. My belief is that privacy, library privacy and privacy in general, can be a wonderful marketing opportunity for us as a community to show our relevancy—something we are always looking to do—with an issue that a lot of people are talking about and interested in. For example, the community campus can be a privacy clearinghouse and leverage respect for our past efforts, and public respect.

I'm going to skip through these [slides] and I'm going to show you a little bit of a live demo, so let me scroll through this here, and we'll go over here. So here it is, ladies and gentlemen. Your term for this part of the presentation is *sniffing*, and this is an open-source-type piece of technology that I am, on a level from 1 to 10, on a scale from 1 to 10, I am probably a 2 or 3 at. You can take intensive classes on this. This tool called Wireshark has conferences that keep people updated. In a nutshell, this is all of the Wi-Fi traffic flowing through this room right now. You can break it down and actually see sometimes, if it is unencrypted, what somebody is doing. So I will now, with the next tool I'll show you, it makes it a little bit easier to see what I'm talking about. This is a piece of software—again, open-sourced—developed by a student at Iowa State University. Instead of writing a master's thesis paper he developed this software. This takes all of the data coming off of the unencrypted cookies coming through Wireshark and makes them much more easy to view without having to have a master's degree in that particular product. And this is how—one of the tools—that I learned that Ann's airline and another European airline is sending data unencrypted—including the passenger's last name and their passenger record number over the Internet unencrypted—which I found to be rather shocking.

Here are all of the people on Wi-Fi on the network right now. There's probably more, but this is what we're seeing right now. Now, you're going to say, "Well, Gary, so what if I'm learning that you're searching x library and it says that you're looking up whatever?" Well, another thing that's going on right now, especially when you're thinking of government surveillance and surveillance by others, is that whatever you're doing—somebody is searching books.Google.com—this tool also is identified with the exact what is called the MAC address, which is the unique ID of that person's computer or electronic device, so there's two pieces of data. There is no one holy grail of data. In this day and age, having enough distinct data points makes it relatively simple to figure out who that specific person is. So, you can see now what people are looking at—somebody's looking at the CBC—that kind of thing. So those are the two particular tools.

Now, let me go back to my slides for a moment and give you a couple of actual examples. Am I scaring the heck out of you? This is one slide, if we can do this here. Can you see this right here? I'm not going to make this one too big. Here is a practical tip for you—especially for those of you who own Apple devices, very often your device is named after you. So, one of the things floating through is not just that MAC address but it's your specific name. You can see that here. (Play from current slide.) You can see that somebody named Jeff W., I blanked out his full name, was on the Wi-Fi yesterday at one of the conference hotels. Do you see where I'm going with this? It's these distinct, a number of these distinct data points merged together, which can be easily done now, makes it very simple to figure out who someone is and where they are.

Another thing that we're dealing with now all over the Internet are things called tracking scripts and beacons. These are pieces of code embedded in the webpage that can provide all sorts of data. Again, these are the types of analytics we were talking about earlier—whether or not it is a good thing or bad thing, that is up to the organization—but my point is, gaining that knowledge and sharing what's going on with our users. Also now we are seeing beacons used in a mobile setting, allowing people to be tracked throughout the store or throughout the library. If your library is doing that, what are you doing with that data after the person walks out of the library? And are you informing them in the first place that that's going on?

Your IP address can share a lot of information with you. Now in this, case at my hotel, you're able to see specifically where I am. This IP address is tied to Charleston, South Carolina, but I've also been in locations where it not only says that you're in this city but where in this city you're at. You're in the lobby, for example, of the Mayflower Hotel in Washington, DC. This is again more of a specific example of the Cookie Cadger tool I just showed you. Here I am, 9cf3, and here I am searching the library of Congress OPAC, and you can see all of the search suggestions as I'm typing in. All of that is being sent over the Internet unencrypted. Here is another view of that data. You can see the referrer says I was looking at loc.gov, and then my search term. This is another example, and in this case the Google Analytics we're sharing show that this person was coming from library.caltech.edu. This by itself isn't a bad thing, but again my point, my takeaway from this, is we need to understand what's going on first and then share that data with our users.

Here is an example of a PubMed search. You probably can't see it from here, but you can see all of my search terms and the specific data fields I was searching. So, become privacy literate, first step. It needs to be a major part, in my view, of any digital literacy campaign that you're doing. Awareness of tools and concepts to minimize exposure: So I've shared some of those with you. I know Lisa [Macklin] is going to—hopefully we will have time to talk about some of the things that you can do if this is an issue for you at the library level. But also for an individual, remember everybody has a different threshold of comfort. There are tools that you can use, but while you can't—I would never get up here and say that you can be completely private online and I can guarantee it—but there are tools to, let's say, put "roadblocks" up to make it a little bit more challenging to get to some of this data. It's not rocket science to use them.

Stay current: Things change quickly, we all know that. And discuss issues with colleagues and our users. There are a lot of ethical issues, which we will get into moving forward and then teach our colleagues and users. I've also on the slide deck that you'll get included some other examples. This for example: the article *Exposing the Hidden Web: An Analysis of Third-Party HTTP Requests on 1 Million Websites*(http://arxiv.org/abs/1511.00619v1) was just published in the past month. So, again, I promised I would go a little bit short to stay on schedule. I want to make Ann a happy lady. One final comment: These types of tools, Wireshark and Cookie Cadger, don't just work on Wi-Fi. You could plug an Ethernet cable on here and get the same type of data as well. So, we will have questions later. Thank you very much for your time and attention. I hope I've scared you just a little bit. Thank you.

Bill Hannay: The title of my program is "Please Remember to Forget." Catchy, right? I'm sure you will remember because this program is all about forgetting. And the larger topic, where's all this privacy stuff going? Is it going to turn into a flood, or is it just a ripple? We'll talk a little bit about this.

As I mentioned last year, Europe, the European Union, is very big into privacy issues. In particular, unlike the United States, they have a very broad-reaching data privacy statute. It's called a "directive," but it's effectively a statute. And its idea is to protect individuals in the processing of data about them. What they focus on is personal data. Now, personal data actually has a very broad definition in Europe: Any information relating to any individual. Any individual! Any information! Whether it relates to personal, private, or professional life. It can be a name; it can be a photo; it can be an e-mail address. They don't have Social Security numbers over there, but if they did, Social Security numbers, medical history, really anything about them, particularly if it happens to be of a deleterious nature. And why are they concerned about this? A great quotation from the memo written in the European Union government, "With social networking sites, cloud computing, location-based services and smart cards, we leave digital traces with every move we make." Gary just showed you some of your traces: all you in the audience just buzzing around the Internet when you're supposed to be listening to us. "We need a robust set of rules to make sure people's right to personal data protection . . . is made effective" (EU Memo/12/41, Brussels, 2012, http://europa.eu/rapid/press-release_MEMO-12-41_en.htm?locale=en, para. 1).

I kind of admire the European Union government because they have apparently a sense of humor. This is actually an official government cartoon that's on their data privacy website. It looks like a student going into the free Internet café and coming out embarrassed and totally naked because of the information that this person has logged onto the Internet doing an Internet search. I am reminded of going into a library one time a couple of years ago and waiting in line to speak to a human being who was a reference librarian. And there was a young person, who looked like a high school student, standing, talking, kind of whispering to the reference librarian. Whisper, whisper. And the librarian leans back and says, "Mildred! Where do we keep the books on sex change operations?!?" So, information about oneself can be disclosed in a number of ways.

You may remember last year we talked about a man named Mario Costeja Gonzáles. And he asked Google to take down some information about him—that is, remove it, as in take down, because this deleterious information, this negative information about him had long since ceased to be accurate and it was embarrassing. If you did a search on his name, it would come up with a couple of articles about the fact that he had, well actually I won't mention it because I don't want to publicize what his problem was. He wanted this taken down, and they said, "Oh no, we couldn't do that." So he goes to the government agency in Spain and asks them to make Google take this down. They enter an order, Google appeals, it goes all the way to the European Court of Justice, which is, on a regional basis, like our United States Supreme Court; it's the highest court in Europe. The Court affirms the order of this Spanish privacy agency and makes Google take this down. But more than that, not just fix the problem for Sr. Costeja Gonzáles, but to actually order Google to set up a whole system to do this for anyone who is subject to the data privacy laws, or the protections of it. What they ordered was that Google remove from the list of search results any webpage links relating to an individual if such information is "irrelevant" in relation to the purposes for which data is collected. You have to balance individual rights against the collective rights of the public to know things.

Google has set up this system, and there's a request form here that you can go on the website and say, "I'd like you to remove the following information." And they have been, this process has been used an enormous amount in the past year. As of this week, 338,000 requests have been filed with Google in Europe to remove information from 1.2 million URLs. Of those, 42% have actually been removed, these search results. Now understand, what that means is, it's not whatever the URL is has been removed from the Internet, it's that Google's results will not produce that URL. You can maybe still find it some other way if you happen to know it, but you can't search for it. So, almost 10,000 URLs, the listing of them was removed from Facebook.

For example here, here's one that in the UK someone said that I'd like you to remove a minor crime that I was involved with. Google did remove it, and then the newspaper that had reported it originally then filed a news report about the removal of the report, and Google took that one down too. So the long arm of the law extends on a continuing basis.

The EU is actually thinking of strengthening this whole process and reaffirming the right to be forgotten. They prepared an elaborative directive in 2012, just a few months ago the Council of Justice Ministers approved it, and it will now go to the EU Parliament and the broader Council for further action, and I expect that it will be enacted. It addresses a number of things, not just right to be forgotten, but they have reinforced the notion that if an individual no longer wants their personal data processed, and there's no legitimate reason to keep it, then it should be removed. But, this proposal recognizes something that was somewhat unclear under the prior codification, which is that this is all subject to a careful balancing of the right of freedom of expression, for newspapers to print articles. Even though a newspaper may be required to take it down, or Google's search will not find it, that has to be taken into account.

Here's a statement recently from the EU Justice Commission, sort of the equivalent of our attorney general:

> The right to be forgotten is . . . not an absolute right. There are cases where there is a legitimate reason to keep data in a database. The archives of a newspaper are a good example. It is clear that the right to be forgotten cannot amount to a right to re-write or erase history. (European Commission, 2015)

Again, a balancing of the public's rights and private rights.

To update you on this thing: Not only are there the hundreds and thousands of requests that are going in Europe, it now is beginning to impact in the United States because a French agency has ordered Google to take down information—to remove, to "delist" information—from its US-based website, from Google.com; not just Google.es or Google.fr in Europe, because they've been doing that. But now this French court says in order for this to be fully effective, this whole right to be forgotten thing, you have to take it down everywhere that you, Google, have a website. And so if you've got Google.com in the US, it's got to come out of that, too, because someone in Europe could link to Google.com and do the search, which would otherwise be prohibited in Europe. The logic of this is, it's an evasion otherwise. Well, Google is not taking this lying down. They're going to appeal to the European Court of Justice again. They've said, "We're not going to do this. We're going to take the heat and we're going to go and appeal because you don't have any jurisdiction." And what the French agency says is that it isn't a question of jurisdiction over the United States—what we're saying is if you've got a website somewhere else and someone in Europe can link to it, then you've got to carry the right to be forgotten all the way through those websites.

So, what is the significance of that to us in the United States? Well, if they're compelled to take out information, to take down, to remove, to delist information that you would otherwise be able to find in the United States, it will no longer be available to you. And this is in order to protect the rights of someone in Europe. In the US, we don't have the right. We can't ask Google to take down negative information about us. If there was a copyright violation, we can ask them to do that, but not privacy. But, if you're going to do a search on Google.com, there will not be as much information there as there once was. And so it does impact us in the United States.

Just to close here, I just want to explain if you have something to hide, you can now take steps and then safely say [singing]:

> The light is green, the web is clear,
> So if you want to go surfing, dear,
> I'm delighted, I'm delisted, I'm de-Googled!
>
> I understand the reason why
> You're curious, and just want to pry:
> You're de-nosey, you're de-snooping, you're de-peeping
>
> You can tell at a glance
> That the EU has taken a stance.
> You can hear their Court of Justice
> Murmering low:
> "You'll never know."
>
> So, please be sweet, my chickadee,
> And when you ask me, I'll say to thee,
> It's delightful, it's delisting,
> It's debatable, it's deletable,
> It's defensive, it's delib'rate, it's deleted,
> It's de-Googled.

Lisa Macklin: So, that's a hard act to follow. I do have to tell you that I once sent a friend of mine a birthday card that said, "In honor of your birthday, I will not sing." And so I will not sing and you should be very grateful for that. So, I'm going to talk to you about privacy in libraries and really try and take what Gary and Bill have said and kind of bring them back into our everyday lives, if you will.

So, in the US we have several sources of privacy. As Bill mentioned, in the US we don't have this sense of privacy and privacy laws that they have in Europe, and so we find that we do have a patchwork, if you will, of federal laws—FERPA being an example within higher ed—and state laws. There is a common law right of privacy and there are some state statutes for privacy, and then we also have some state statutes specifically for libraries that really do vary by state, and they do dictate the confidentiality of library records. However, those state laws often don't include library records that might be hosted by a third party, for example. And there's a list of various state laws on the ALA website, so if you're not familiar with your state law I would suggest that you take a look there and really begin to understand what your state law says regarding privacy.

We also have institutional policies on privacy if you're in an academic institution; however, much of our own library policies really are not stemming as much from a law as they are stemming from the ALA code of ethics. And essentially that code of ethics has been the grounding of library policy for a number of years, and it's essentially protecting the library user's right to privacy and to confidentiality. This goes to that core library mission of providing open and equal access to our collections, and we do this in order to enable education and free inquiry, those kinds of cornerstones of a democracy. However, privacy is not absolute, and we have to balance user privacy with our other constraints around efficiencies, requirements of law enforcement, and then just plain old Internet security. Much of our privacy practices are really rooted in our history of deleting circulation records when somebody has returned a book. They're really grounded in the days of almost complete print collections. However, technology has expanded both our collections and our services, and Gary has demonstrated how easy it is to track a user on the Internet. So, let's talk about doing a privacy audit for library services and what you might want to think about.

Three questions that I think are worth asking . . . First of all, do you have a library privacy policy? Have you reviewed it lately? Does it pertain only to your print collections? Does it apply to online collections and take into account the changes that we've seen recently? Does it align with federal and state law in your institutional policies? I came up with, well, let me backtrack a tad bit. I do want to say that policies are really important because they provide transparency, and they do provide assurances to our users, but it's in implementing practices that I really think we can make the most difference. And I do think that we all have a role to play in that, so I came up with kind of these three questions. Use them if they're useful to you, but I don't think that we always ask these questions when we should.

The first is, what data is being collected? And Gary gave us examples that I don't think some of us are always aware of. Who has access to that data? And then do users have the option to opt out? So, putting that another way, can users search, access, and read anonymously? Or, if they're using a particular service, are they actually automatically getting tracked in ways that they don't realize? For systems librarians and technologists—really looking at ILS systems, search and discovery systems, mobile apps, library webpages—we need to consider what data is really being collected. How securely is it stored? How securely is it transmitted? Is personally identifiable information encrypted? For our vendor colleagues, have you tested your systems for vulnerabilities? If you provide hosting services, how securely are patron and user data stored? For those who do usability testing—of which, quite frankly, I'm a big fan—I think we need to be aware for collecting personally identifiable information as part of usability testing, realize that we probably need to be anonymizing that information. We need to make certain that the participants understand the parameters of the data collection, and the use that we're going to make of that data. For scholarly communications librarians, most of our institutional repositories do have basic hit and download information, which is pretty generic and anonymized, but we do have some repositories that have sensitive data and other kinds of things where you have to register as a user to actually download the files. So how are we tracking that information, storing it? Do we delete it on a regular basis?

For collections librarians, do you know what data the vendor of those collections and online materials is collecting? Is there digital rights management software attached to those files? How is that data collected used? With whom is it shared? Now, data collection is not, in and of itself, a bad thing. We in libraries need to know how our collections are used. We make collection decisions on a regular basis based on use statistics that are provided from vendors. But do we need that information for each individual user, or is that information in the aggregate really what it is that we need to make those decisions? So, for electronic resources librarians, are you negotiating for terms in your license agreements that protect user confidentiality and privacy? We can do, by contract law, what we don't necessarily in this country have laws to protect privacy for. For publishers and content providers, we need your help. We understand that you have a desire to track your content and how it's used, but we ask that you also understand that tracking and storing who is reading what is in direct conflict with our values and our ethics. Katherine touched on this in her presentation as well.

Liaisons and subject librarians, I will echo what Gary has already said—that we really need to be teaching our users, including our faculty as well their students, about privacy as part of information and digital literacy. So you have a very big role to play in educating users. We need to support our users' ability to make informed choices. I've used Facebook here as an example, in part because they have improved their user privacy over the last several years, often as a way of reacting to user feedback. And when I logged into Facebook a couple of days ago it asked me if I wanted to review my privacy settings, so they've gotten more proactive in how they really approach privacy. But I think we in libraries really need to be proactive. We shouldn't be waiting for an incident or user demand to really be addressing user privacy.

For all of us, whether you are a librarian, a technologist, a publisher, or some combination of the three, you need to understand the contours of privacy law, and our legal and ethical obligations. And most importantly, as Gary showed, we really need to understand how technology works, both to invade our privacy and to protect our privacy. We need to regularly question privacy implications of new tools and services. And we need to keep current, which I realize is a huge challenge since technology is going to continue to change. So Gary's infoDOCKET is one great example of that. The ALA's Washington office is also another example where they regularly will have information about privacy.

Finally, and most importantly, be an advocate. We all have a role to play, and I've given you this laundry list not expecting you to go back to your institutions and do everything all at once. But my hope is that each of you can have a takeaway from this panel discussion to do, that you will go back to your institutions and think about and consider. As our collections are becoming increasingly digital, and our services are often hosted on platforms and servers even outside of our own institutions, our sensitivity to patron privacy really does need to increase. Fulfilling our library mission of providing equal and open access to our collections to enable education and to enable free inquiry relies on libraries remaining a trusted institution. When users recognize or fear that their privacy or confidentiality is compromised, then the freedom of inquiry no longer really exists. And that, I think, is the thing we need to guard against. Thank you.

Reference

European Commission. (2015, June 15). *Stronger data protection rules for Europe* [Press Release Database; European Commission—Fact Sheet]. Retrieved from http://europa.eu/rapid/press-release_MEMO-15-5170_en.htm

Hyde Park Debate, Resolved: Altmetrics Are Overrated

In Favor: Derek Law, Professor Emeritus, University of Strathclyde

Opposed: Maria Bonn, Senior Lecturer, Graduate School of Library and Information Science, University of Illinois

Moderator: Rick Anderson, University of Utah

The following is a transcript of a live presentation at the 2015 Charleston Library Conference.

Voting took place prior to the debate on the resolution "Altmetrics are Overrated." The vote was 44 in favor of the resolution, and 43 against the resolution.

Rick Anderson: All right. Welcome, everybody, to our annual Hyde Park Debate. My name is Rick Anderson. I am at the University of Utah, and I am serving as moderator today. I'd like to welcome our combatants. First, we will hear from, as befitting his position in favor of the proposition before us, we will first hear from Derek Law, who is Emeritus Professor of Informatics at the University of Strathclyde. We will then hear in opposition to the proposition Maria Bonn, who is senior lecturer at the Graduate School of Library and Information Science at Illinois University. For those of you who aren't familiar with how we do this, each of our contestants will open with a 10 minute prepared statement. Each of them will then respond to the other with a three-minute prepared statement. We will then have the balance of our time given over to a Q&A and discussion with the audience, and then we have 5 minutes left in our allocated time where we will close the discussion and have an exit poll, and whichever of our debaters has moved the larger number of people toward his or her position will be declared the winner.

Derek Law: (Written statement provided to moderator prior to debate)

Chairman, colleagues, distinguished visitors—and supporters of Altmetrics, it is my privilege to propose the motion that this house believes that Altmetrics are overrated. Now, when considering your vote, please note that it is not required to believe that they are wrong, ridiculous, and a pernicious delusion—as I do—but simply that they are overrated. You should answer the proposition as put. I should make clear from the start that it is my view that the fundamental problem with such metrics is that they focus on what is measurable at the expense of what is important. They make quantitative, not qualitative, judgements in order to aid administrators rather than to advance research. The most meretricious of all of these metrics is Altmetrics, a term first coined five years ago.

I want briefly to explore four key points as to why I hold this view.

Firstly, we don't really know what they are, nor do their supporters. Secondly, they mechanistically measure meaningless data rather than using knowledge and skill to evaluate and judge. Thirdly, they rely on populist social media, highlighting what is deemed newsworthy, not what is important. Fourthly, they are very susceptible to gamification, a horrid neologism which has superseded the good old-fashioned word "cheating."

Now let's start by a quick look at the Altmetrics manifesto website. The first thing we note is the uncertainty over what the term actually means. Is it alternative metrics? (Yes, according to the site.) Is it an acronym? (No, because it could only stand for "A Load of Trash.") Or does it stand for article level metrics? (No, but that's a common usage.) Actually, none of this matters since, judging by the website, the most contentious issue to be decided is whether Altmetrics is a single word or whether there should be a dash between alt and metrics. The manifesto asserts that no one has the time to read everything. Perhaps if less time was spent on this introverted, narcissistic drivel of whether or not there's a dash, a little more time could be spent reading real research literature.

http://dx.doi.org/10.5703/1288284316230

Having discovered that the proponents of Altmetrics differ on what it means and how it is spelled, let me next turn to the issue that it eliminates judgment in favor of someone else's number crunching. And very crude and unsubtle number crunching at that. There are huge differences between disciplines and how they communicate. What is appropriate for theoretical physics will not be appropriate for, say, Italian renaissance philosophy. And there must be huge unease once commercial companies step in and block usage through subscriptions. Equally, we are all aware of how, say, Google search results are manipulated and doctored by the algorithm used and how product placement becomes an issue.

Altmetrics is to metrics what alternative medicine is to medicine. It is the last refuge of the over-indulged self-absorbed first world middle classes who refuse to believe the evidence-based judgements of real science. There is an implicit assumption that nobody in the non-English speaking world and in developing countries who cannot or may not use Twitter and Facebook has anything useful to say. Just in passing we may note that 80% of the world's medical literature relates to diseases which kill only 20% of the world's population. Yet South literature relating to malaria or AIDS or dengue fever will largely be ignored by Altmetrics. At the moment, they rely on a very small dataset of around 3.5 million articles—compared with the fifty million in existence, growing by two million a year—and that excludes books, book chapters, conference papers, book reviews, and so on. Of course that number can and will be increased, but it will never capture all output in all disciplines. More importantly, Altmetrics relies on crowdsourcing rather than expert opinion and is almost entirely populist. It's like politicians arguing about the number of lines on each others' faces rather than addressing the real issue of economic growth.

And who would you trust? Speaking on October 7 at a conference held in Amsterdam, Juan Pablo Alperin, an online publications scholar at Simon Fraser University in Canada, said: "After five years, we still don't have much of an idea of what we're measuring." All that Altmetrics enthusiasts have discovered is that their new metrics gave different results to traditional scholarly citations. Alperin's Twitter-based survey of discussions about Brazilian science also revealed that more than a third of those tweeting papers were not academics.

The general public is being asked to judge or influence the impact of scientific work, and any metric that relies even a little bit on public input will prove invalid. Altmetrics may be expected to grant high scores to works on climate change skepticism and on intelligent design, groundlessly raising pseudoscience to the level of science, at least in terms of measured impact. There are already numerous questionable publishers willing to publish articles on such topics. Popularizing Altmetrics means articles about Bigfoot and about astrology will register a greater impact than articles about curing cancer and discovering the nature of dark matter, for there are many more people interested in popular topics than there are interested in scientific ones.

Consider whether you would put your trust in Twitter or in the Nobel Prize Awards panels. Look at this year's crop of awards as an example. I shall mention only four.

Firstly, Angus Deaton, Nobel Laureate for Economics. Except Twitter assumed that it was an English comedian of the same name. There was a huge Twitter traffic about the comedian's improbable success.

Or what about the guy who won the Peace Prize for work in the Middle East and knowing the difference between Hamas and ISIL? With Twitter, step forward Donald Trump, who is much better known than the Tunisian National Dialogue Quartet. I believe he's also an American comedian.

Then the Nobel Prize for Literature. Some woman from Belarusia or somewhere in central Asia. Kim Kardashian was it? Certainly she's a bigger name on Twitter then Svetlana Alexievich.

And finally the winner of the Nobel Prize for Medicine, the Chinese researcher Tu Youyou. She only ever published in Chinese, so doesn't feature at all on Twitter or Facebook. But hey, who needs Tu youyou when we have U2 too. That Bono is much more interesting on the role of traditional medicine in healing his injuries.

This leads naturally to the topic of gamification and how metrics can be manipulated. Now this is not uniquely a difficulty for Altmetrics. The most infamous case—although not the most discussed on social media—is probably that of the Netherlands. When the Dutch government began to use citation counts as a way of measuring how research funds should be distributed to universities, behavior changed within six months. Where Dutch academics had previously cited non-Dutch articles in great quantities, almost overnight they began to cite each other, pushing up their scores and therefore research income. And if we look at Altmetrics, much the same is true. The web is awash with tales of gamification and also helpful tips on how to push your ranking up, including paying companies to promote your research on social media. We have seen a good example of this within the last few weeks, where Amazon has begun to take action against some 1,400 people accused of writing high scoring reviews for a fee.

I have to say I am familiar with this skewing of statistics from personal experience and the principle that it's not what you know but who you know. My most cited publication is a small one and a long way from being my best. There were several co-authors, including Tim-Berners Lee, inventor of the World Wide Web. I'm not self-delusional enough to believe that my name is of any interest in this context. But social metrics push it up the rankings thanks to his involvement. So one trick for those of you who want to play with Altmetrics is just to make sure you have important co-authors. Another interesting fact is that there is a very limited correlation between Altmetrics and citation. However, there is a strong correlation between a high Altmetrics score and the appearance of a paper in Retraction Watch. In other words, bad papers get high scores.

And so to conclude:

- It is unclear exactly what Altmetrics are
- They measure what can be measured, not what is important; using populism, not quality, as the arbiter of value
- They can be manipulated to influence outcomes and personal standing
- They are aimed at informing the decisions of bureaucrats, funding agencies and government so that they can abdicate responsibility for making qualitative judgements and so pass the buck

The first metrics were invented a thousand years ago. Altmetrics has all the value, relevance, and accuracy of the eleventh century debate over how many angels could dance on the head of a pin.

And so I beg to move the motion that Altmetrics are overrated. Thank you.

Maria Bonn: (Written statement provided to moderator prior to the debate.)

Friends, Charlestonians, those who are not my countrymen, oh, I mean my esteemed opponent, and honorable moderator. Welcome. It is my privilege today to stand in opposition to the proposed resolution that Altmetrics are overrated. I will begin by demonstrating my contrarian impulses and posit that the problem with the resolution is not its patent absurdity (she says, looking meaningfully at her opponent) but its phrasing. Perhaps there was a typo? Altmetrics aren't overrated; ALL metrics are overrated. Altmetrics arise in response to over simplified citation counting and impact factors, but are a symptom of the same cultural disease—er, condition—which they seek to cure. (Here I am put in mind of my greens-averse daughter who, when presented with her first plate of kale, muttered, "Great what do you call this? Alt-spinach?" In our attachment to and desire for numbers by which we can measure the value and contribution of scholarship, we see manifest our pernicious (information) science envy; we believe that truth only emerges from numbers, and quantification becomes almost a form of religious expression. We place our faith in counting, but numbers without interpretation offer limited value to understanding.

But wait. Let me contradict myself: all metrics are overrated? Yes. And all metrics are valuable. Do I contradict myself? Well then I contradict myself. We are large. We contain multitudes. Here, I no doubt reveal my earliest disciplinary principles and practices, wherein, as an instructor of rhetoric and composition, my constant exhortation to my students, often in the form of red ink marginalia, was "supply supporting evidence." If you want to make a good argument, if you want to tell a good story, you need to be able to substantiate your claims, to provide illustrative details. You know, the difference between "I had breakfast" or even "I had a good breakfast," and "I had some cheesy grits with two poached eggs and some collards sautéed in bacon fat, with a good sized mug of a rich dark roast coffee to go with." And now, I come clean as not an information scientist, but an information humanist, one who values interpretation, critique, and critical approaches to data over the data itself. Like any other good knowledge worker, I want to understand the fields in which I toil, and I want to share that understanding with others. I want to hear and to tell good stories about the value and the reach of scholarship. And to tell those stories, I need material. And metrics, of all kinds, are good material.

It is because of these propensities on my part that I was so delighted when I first happened upon the work of ImpactStory. ImpactStory, its website tells us, is "an open-source, web-based tool that helps scientists explore and share the diverse impacts of all their research products—from traditional ones like journal articles, to emerging products like blog posts, datasets, and software. By helping scientists tell data-driven stories about their impacts, we're helping to build a new scholarly reward system that values and encourages web-native scholarship." I read this and say to myself, "finally, we are getting at the narratives needed to substantiate the claims of scholarly impact. Well, I wait patiently, but, for the most part, I have yet to hear these stories. I look at altmetric profiles, and the narrative material is rich, but I'm still listening for the voices telling those stories. What, exactly, are our scholars having for breakfast?

In the summer of 2014, the journal that I edit, the Journal of Electronic Publishing (a journal which proudly uses altmetrics, by the way), published a special issue on "Metrics for Evaluating Publishing Value: Alternative and Otherwise." In response to my call for submissions, and in the pages of the issue, I see attention to a variety of ways of measuring value, from the Altmetrics of blog link backs and tweet counts, to the attention of book reviewers, to computational analysis for measuring impact of documentaries intending to promote social justice. These reports, dare I say, stories, lend specificity to my point that there are many ways we can tell stories about the attention garnered by publication and about the use to which scholarship is put. For instance, we can conduct network analysis and produce visualizations; we can illustrate international impact by mapping metrical data with GIS; we can count sales of books, celebrate awards, collect curricular evidence of course adoption. All are ways of making an impact case, and all require interpretation and articulation to be meaningful.

I should avoid the pitfall into which, ahem, others tumble, of being too broad brush in my generalizations. My old shop, as well as my current publisher, Michigan Publishing, making me proud, seems to be starting to spin some yarns. In a case study published by Digital Science this year, Charles Watkinson, the director, begins laying out some of the uses of Altmetrics:

(And here I quote at length from the case study) In the first example, he—that is, Charles—highlights an open access article on female photographers in Bengal, India:

> The publishing strategy employed by the editor and authors in this case was to use an open access model to disseminate this article widely to get more recognition of the work of these pioneers in India. The strategy succeeded judging by the spread of social media coverage the article received. The

second example has a legal context that is steeped in American history. The Altmetric attention to an article on Habeas Corpus and past suspensions of civil liberties by US presidents, in this case Abraham Lincoln, could have an impact on modern policy making in this area via coverage in media such as Salon, The Huffington Post and The Nation. The third example highlights the attention that open access monographs have the potential to get. A book on the principles of web writing for teachers and students at liberal arts colleges is attracting a lot of scholarly and social buzz and this can be measured and explored using Altmetrics. (Altmetric, n.d.)

So here, I pump my fist in celebration of narrative, but I also take a turn slightly in my argument, because now I ask, "Where are the numbers?" The scenarios here are seductive. Now substantiate them and allow those of us who are listening to judge whether this is the story the numbers are telling. Give me confidence these aren't tall tales.

Yes, I want it all. I want the words and I want the numbers, lots of numbers of lots of kinds. But overall, at our moment in time, I mostly find myself like my children often were at bedtime, wanting more stories, more stories. Tell me about the research article that informed a senator who proposed a new policy. Tell me about the book that was assigned in a freshman course and changed the shape of an undergraduate's major and led to a career that was entirely different than planned. Tell me about my witty remark at a Charleston Conference session that was retweeted across the globe, picked up by a journalist, and ended up in translation in a Japanese language newspaper being read by a market trader on her way to work in the morning.

I stand by my position on this resolution. Altmetrics aren't overrated. But they are under used. By all means, establish and record Altmetrics. And then use them, and help our scholars to use them. Analyze, interpret, articulate, and argue, with supporting evidence. Let's apply our considerable professional intelligence, as librarians, as publishers, as hybrids of the two and information workers of all types, to making good evaluative use of the tools we have at hand and becoming good storytellers. With such a vast metrical harvest, what kind of meal can we bring to the research table? If it's rich in both kale and spinach, perhaps we'll see improved scholarly health. At this point you may be playing exasperated Watson to my meticulously observant Holmes (and yes, it would really please me if you were thinking that I have a bit of an air of a female Benedict Cumberbatch), and you are muttering, "Enough with the tediously obsessive accumulation and analysis of evidence." But this is what is needed to find a solution (and a greater than 7% one at that). It is, you see, elementary my dear Mr. Law. Altmetrics are NOT overrated.

Rick Anderson: Derek, your response.

Derek Law: Thank you for that eloquent discourse. My loquacious opponent does indeed have the air of a female Benedict Cumberbatch, although the last time I saw him he was wearing a bit more makeup, who, of course, specializes in the smooth delivery of works of fiction, telling tall tales. It is perfectly fitting that she is speaking in an opera house where she might be seen to be playing the character of Poobah in the Mikado. Poobah, the Lord high everything else, whose specialty is a tale full of corroborative detail intended to give artistic very similar to an otherwise bold and unconvincing narrative. This year's altmetric conference in Amsterdam took place just after I had to submit my written statement; sadly it confirmed everything I had been arguing. There was a debate about Altmetrics itself and what the term meant. There was a debate, but no clarity on what the word impact means and indeed exactly what we're trying to measure, and we still haven't had the answer to this because the impact cannot possibly be the same for researchers as for institutions and for readers and for funding agencys. There was also lots of discussion on the lack of standards or principles in the field, again a topic not addressed so far. The fact that there is not a pool of common data between Altmetrics providers makes it difficult to compare anything. A recent study that was presented at the conference compared Altmetrics data from different providers for a similar sample of DOIs and found completely different results. To me, the case is so obvious that I thought I'd actually spend my minute and a half rather better by reading you a small chapter from one of the greatest works of American literature of the 20th century from one of my all-time favorite authors, James Thurber. In *Fables for Our Time* he tells the tale of the fairly intelligent fly. "A large spider in an old house built a beautiful web," note from 1939 that sly, prescient dig about the Web of science. A large spider in an old house built a beautiful web to catch flies. Every time a fly landed on the web the spider quickly devoured him so that when another fly came along he would think the web was a safe and quiet place. One day, a fairly intelligent fly buzzed around for so long without alighting that the spider appeared and said, "Come on down." But, the fly was too clever and said, "I never alight where I don't see other flies, and I don't see any other flies in your house." So he flew away until he came to a place where there were a great many flies. He was about to land there when a bee buzzed up to him and said "Hold it, stupid, that's flypaper. All of those flies are trapped." "Don't be silly," said the fly "they're dancing." And so he landed, and became stuck with all of the other flies, and the moral of this fable is there is no safety in Altmetrics—sorry there is no safety in numbers, or in anything else. They are overrated, and I urge you so to vote. Thank you very much.

Maria Bonn: First they throw an opera house at me, and then this Scotsman with a razor-sharp wit and tongue to go with it. But, we're not scared. So, my esteemed opponent levels several related criticisms at Altmetrics. One cluster of these decries the sort of information with which Altmetrics equips us; he tells us that Altmetrics focuses on what is measurable at the expense of what is important, that they mechanistically measure meaningless data rather than using knowledge to evaluate, that they eliminate judgment in favor of what's important, in favor of someone else's number crunching. Excuse me, I couldn't agree more. But the fault, Mr. Law, is not in our metrics but in ourselves. If we make poor judgments in our use of those metrics, take ourselves to task, don't blame the bricks for the shoddily constructed house. My opponent also likens Altmetrics to alt-medicine, the last refuge of the overindulged, self-absorbed first world middle classes, oh and of millions of rural Chinese. At least in the last century, when we're sick, you see, we reach for what heals us. Emergency surgery rocks; so does a couple of acupuncture sessions for the right ills at the right time. When my 86-year-old mother's arthritis acts up, she reaches for the needles. She is also impressed by high numbers of Twitter followers, but my opponent would see that as a problem because my mom, a two-year college dropout and once a professional typist, you see, is definitely one of the general public, and Mr. Law has no truck with that hoi polloi. I would not be so bold as to speculate on how he voted on the recent ballot on Scotland's independence, but I detect in his remarks at least a lingering fondness for some kind of scholarly aristocracy. He tells us with dismay that Altmetrics are almost entirely populist. True, maybe, but if it is, isn't that great? If I, as a researcher, learned from this Brazilian study that Mr. Law cites that more than a third of those tweeting my paper were not academics I'd say, "Wow, cool!" and if this knuckleheaded public is giving bad science high scores in social media, it might be because it's being called—it's calling out those bad papers for public shaming.

Let me highlight one of my opponents other claims. He tells us the first metrics were invented 1,000 years ago and then some stuff about angels and pins, but funny I remember some stuff in the Iliad about numbers of spears and swords and that were being used by the Trojans to tell them a story about their chances in battle. What's lying in wait inside the Trojan horse of my opponent's claims?

Following a Q&A session, a final vote was taken on the resolution "Altmetrics are Overrated." 77 were in favor of the resolution, and 51 were opposed to the resolution. Derek Law was declared the winner of the debate.

Reference

Altmetric—Case study: Michigan Publishing. (n.d.) *Altmetric.com*. Retrieved from https://www.altmetric.com/case-studies/michigan-publishing/

The Secret Life of Articles: From Download Metrics to Downstream Impact

Carol Tenopir, Professor, University of Tennessee

Lorraine Estelle, Director, Project COUNTER

Wouter Haak, Vice President Research Data Management Solutions, Elsevier

Meg White: Welcome. This is part of our Neapolitan sessions here at the Charleston Conference. You are in ballroom number two for *The Secret Life of Articles*, so if that is not where you're meant to be, now is the time. My name is Meg White, I will be your moderator for the session, and I'm going to quickly turn it over to our wonderful panel of speakers. Just to remind you, if you have questions we are going to do our best to reserve some time at the end of the talks for those questions. Don't be shy, we will invite you to approach the mic and let's really get as much out of these three wonderful folks who are here to share with us today by giving them our questions at the end of the session. So, with that, we are going to get started. It's exactly 10:30, and I will turn it over to Carol for *The Secret Life of Articles*.

Carol Tenopir: Okay. Thank you, and I know that in the earlier session, the acoustics were a little problematic. I think this room is a little better, but if you have trouble hearing me or if I am swallowing words or wander away from the microphone as I sometimes do, raise your hand at me or make a sign and I will remember to come back. For those of you who are regular Charleston attendees, and I know there are quite a few, some of you may remember that last year we introduced this "Beyond Downloads Project" at a session and we were in the middle of collecting data. The project is complete now, at least the research aspect of it is complete, so I'm going to present some of the research, at least some of the key takeaways from the project on article sharing. We are really looking at the idea of the impact, but more at the instances of sharing, so I am kind of digging deep into article sharing. I'll give you the results of the research project, and then Lorraine and Wouter are going to tell you about some of the practical implications from each of their perspectives, and some of the next steps that both COUNTER and Elsevier are doing. So, I am doing the research part and they are doing the "what happens next" or "what are the implications."

I do need to start by acknowledging that this was a wonderful team across kinds of organizations and an international team, and I want to thank all of the team members. There are some others that are here: Hazel Woodward is in the front, and I think Anthony Watkinson is walking over here, and those of you that I don't see right now, apologies, but we had a really quite wonderful team working together. So, at the "Beyond Downloads Project," our real motivation is we wanted to know what are Project COUNTER reports missing? What are those downloads reports missing in terms of use? And we really wanted to look at this issue of how much do scholars share articles once they've downloaded something? How do they share? What do they share and how much does that measure—is there a way to measure total use of an article, not just downloads, which we've gotten down really well thanks to COUNTER and lots of the extensions and things that libraries and publishers have done. But the assumption is that only tells part of this story now that we know that there's a lot of sharing going on. Are there ways to calculate and measure that sharing and what is—is it possible to look at a more complete measure of value because a lot of our applied measures of value of library collections, applied measures of journals or articles, are based on amount of use, and with sharing if we're not measuring that complete use, how do we measure value in a more complete way? So those were kind of the motivations.

Another motivation was to initiate discussion of these issues, and I think that has certainly succeeded judging from the size of the crowd last year and this year as well, and the discussion will

http://dx.doi.org/10.5703/1288284316231

continue, I'm sure. We did use several methods in the research portion of the project, and I'm going to talk about where we started, which was the focus groups and interviews. We did focus groups and interviews in both the US and the UK. We had a total of 29 participants, academics but ranging from senior academics to PhD students so we had a good mix of ages. We had less of a mix of subject disciplines. We are really science- and social science-heavy, so I'm not going to give you a lot of conclusions about humanities scholars. We are really focusing on sciences and social sciences among our populations. The focus groups helped inform an international survey, which we had responses from 69 different countries; about a quarter of them were from the US, but the other three quarters were spread out everywhere, and yes, we really did have 1,000 responses. So two days before it was supposed to close we had 996 or something, and I said "let's keep it open until least we have 1,000." As soon as they got to 1,000 we closed it because the math is really easy when it's 1,000. So, it looks a little odd. We don't have 1,000 to every question, but we do have 1,000 responses. Again, there is a good range, excluding humanities—we had just a few humanities, but it is a good range. About a third are from sciences and the rest are engineering, social sciences, so that is our group that we're looking at.

Good age range; they range in age from 18 to 83. The average age was 48 and about a quarter are 39 and under, so they do skew a little on the older side in terms of 40 and over. As you can imagine, we recorded in the interviews and the focus groups, and the survey had an incredibly wide range of opinions and behaviors when it comes to article sharing. Different motivations, different behaviors, different opinions, etc. I'm going to give you a feel of some of that range but also a feel of the things that I think are the main messages when you look at—or the main takeaways when you look at all of these results and what do kind of the average or indicative sorts of behaviors and opinions tell us.

So, five key takeaways from my part. The first is that sharing of scholarship is a means to an end, and the end is not the sharing. The end is the scholarship or the science or getting the work done. A little bit about function or purpose or motivation of the sharing drives the form or format of what is shared. The third is that e-mail seems to still be the most popular or is the most popular number one choice, but version matters, and I will show you that in a second. The library is still key when it comes to initiating the sharing, but we'll look and see how the library fits in there.

Okay. So first, means to an end. This is a word cloud from the question how do you feel about your work being shared with others? And you'll notice there are some very interesting words in here like happy, good, free, fine. We had 690 opened comments in the survey, and I must share that researchers and teachers and scholars like to share. It makes them feel good. They like to have their material shared and they like to share the works of others. The vast majority of the comments are positive; only a few expressed reservations and most of the reservations came with, "It is my work being shared. I want to make sure that the proper citation is included so that I can credit for it." So, it isn't negatives about the act of sharing. Very few comments in terms of worrying about whether it is legal or not legal, or whether it is appropriate or not—"it makes me feel good to have my work shared and it makes sense." Again, we have a lot from both the focus groups and the open-ended comments. We have a lot of really rich quotations and things that show what people are feeling, and, again, scholars on why they share: they find it useful to further their scientific and academic discovery, to facilitate collaboration when it's their work, to further their own work. Sharing is often initiated by others who are interested in an author's work and ask for something, and an author will share it or they ask for something of somebody else and they'll share it and again; this message is that sharing is a natural part of scholarship. They share materials for good reason. It is part of what they have always done; it is just easier now and they look for the ways that make it easy.

The second most common reason is if somebody asks for a copy of an article, either of their own article or of somebody else's article, the person who is asking has a reason to believe that the person they're asking of may have a copy, and the idea is they're trying to get around a pay wall or if they don't have access. So this idea of helping a colleague fulfill an information need was mentioned by many. I share because one of my colleagues doesn't have a good collection or does not have access or the cost per article is too high, so I'll share whether or not it is strictly legal. ANd it was interesting in the focus groups to have people say, "Oh, I just thought it may not be legal but, what the heck, I'm going to do it anyway." There are a couple messages here: convenience, fitting in with their work, and helping others are all more important than the letter of the law. We also asked about embargoes, about what are reasonable embargoes, and the longer the embargo the less reasonable people thought, although there wasn't much—there weren't many fans of any length of embargo, if I put it bluntly; but with the longer embargoes we got a lot less people saying that they agree.

Scholars who work in a research group are more likely to share their articles or the works of others than those who work alone. So, many of the scholars say that their sharing will increase, or they expect it to increase, or it has increased over the last few years. If you put that together, they think it will increase, plus the tendency of work to be done more often in research groups, the tendency of more co-authors on papers—this idea that sharing is going to increase anyway but research groups are going to increase, collaborations increase; you put those two together and I think you can pretty safely say that the instances and the amount of sharing will increase into the future. And add that to sharing becomes easier; I think that is a pretty safe assessment that people are going to share and find the need to share and find ways to share.

That leads me to the next point that is function drives form. We assume that sharing meant sharing the full text, but it doesn't always mean that. It became clear fairly early on that there are two main methods of sharing. One is to share just the citation and most people do that; they say when that researchers who work in their group or who they're sharing with have easy access to the articles, so then they would likely share a link or a citation. Sharing the full document in PDF is still the favored form of sharing; sharing of full text is most common when access may be an issue or when it's easy to do. And so we found both. What's interesting about this when we are talking about calculating amount of sharing is when you share a citation, your downloads may go up. When you share the full text your downloads may go down, so there's a little bit of balancing going on here. The instances of sharing full text as reported were still higher than the instances of sharing citations, so it doesn't quite balance out but there is a bit of bouncing. One thing drives usage statistics up; one thing drives usage statistics down. When we ask more details about their most recent shared link or reference, we found that when they're sharing by e-mail they said they shared an average of about 11 times, 10 to 11 times, per download, so for every download it's about 10 more times the link or reference so that might make it go up. For teaching, learning management software is the preferred method of sharing and that's slightly higher, about 14 times per download. We asked also about full text, what's the average time of share, or how many times did you share the last full text you downloaded, and it's about the same. They share via e-mail most commonly again about 11 times, and then full text is more likely to be shared on research social networks for example about 11 times.

So, not surprising now after what I just said, that e-mail is number one but what surprised us is how much it is number one. You know, academics are not always the first to change. They do change if things are easier, and right now for most of them e-mail is the fastest and easiest. Remember sharing is not the main purpose. Sharing is to get to the main purpose of learning or helping their research, so if it is easier to share for research, for e-mail, they'll do it. About 74% said that e-mail is their preferred method of sharing, followed by cloud services like dropbox and then internal networks. Notice that things that you would expect, systems designed specifically for sharing, don't make those top three; those come afterward. Both general social networks and research social networks—doesn't mean that they're going away but a lot of the comments expressed the idea that there are so many choices right now I'm not sure it's just easier to send somebody something when the choices settle down in the research and social networks, and that becomes easier then we expect these to get more popular. It doesn't mean that they aren't using them, because clearly they are—it's just that we asked, "What's your preferred method?"

For teaching, e-mail again by far number one but in here number two is learning management systems sharing with students and then internal networks number three. Again the research sharing networks, both general and specific, come after those. However, if you look at the number of times you share and your preferred method versus the number of people you think are reached, you can't just do a calculator so the number of people who were reached becomes in the hundreds or thousands people estimate depending on the method, so if they want to reach hundreds or thousands, research social networks are going to reach a lot more people than e-mail will, for example, which is a more one-to-one sharing—general social networks in the hundreds as well as internal networks for more people. So, if you think of, instead, one download equals 10 shares, 10 times I share, then I might share 10 times if it reaches hundreds, and I have to say times hundreds if I'm going to look at reading, so 1 x 10 x 100 is potential readership or potential people that this particular article is reaching, so the numbers get bigger depending on the method quite quickly.

Version matters. There are some people in this audience that might not like to see this but when sharing articles, either your own work or the work of others, which version do you prepare to share? Guess what? It is the final published version. We had a lot of people who commented that it gets too confusing to have various kinds of preprints, accepted manuscripts, and all of these other versions. I want to share the one that will be cited and the one that we know people will find again, so the final published version is what people prefer and want to share overwhelmingly of both their own and others' work. And again lots of comments about this—this first comment—a main point is that I want to share the version that has the publisher and journal stamp on it. I want to show that it is the final version, and I particularly like the second quote, "I'm a little fish let them come for me." There was a fair amount of this kind of like, "I'm just doing my job. It's not having that much of an impact and I'm going to do it, just come if you will." There's another quote I wanted to read that's on here. But, content providers in general have to realize that the relationship between seller and buyer has fundamentally changed in the last 20 years. In order to get someone to pay you for something they can get without your permission, you need to (1) make the process of obtaining your product legally at least as effortless as the process of obtaining it illegally, and (2) make it so cheap that it's not worth pirating. Some very opinionated but perhaps wise scholars here and perhaps since this project was done, some of you are aware of the hashtag "#Icanhaspdf," which is this kind of copyright freely, share copyright papers, and the article it describes. The first one that I saw, academics have found a way to access insanely expensive research papers for free, so there is this whole pirate bootleg kind of community.

So the last is the library—is key, sort of. We asked about the average number of downloads for your last research project and for your last teaching term. Put these together, assume two terms per year, and you put one project you have, maybe 115 or 120 downloads. Where those downloads come for research the library and publisher is still the number one, teaching is still number one but less so, so this is where the downloads are coming. All of these others are coming from other places and just because the library downloads is a source of download doesn't mean that is the complete source of count of use, because we asked when you share it, when you return to that article, when you reread an article, most of them do not download again. Only 10 to 12% say they download again. What they do is they go to a saved copy. People are saving and so those download counts don't get to rereading, and they don't get to sharing, except for those few that links are shared.

Okay, so, let me wrap up my part and then turn it over to the others. Again, sharing is a natural kind of behavior of science—that download counts underestimate the true amount of use of articles but sharing is done because it helps disseminate results, support research, and helps people share in ways that are convenient, and they share because it is convenient. They don't want to stop and think, "Should I be doing this? How do I do this? I just want to do it." And any policies or measures from publishers I think must fit those preferences and the likely behavior, because you don't want to have punitive kinds of policies. You want to be part of that research conversation and not seen as an enemy but seen as a partner, and, again, I think downloads are really just the tip of the use iceberg. Let me turn it over now to Lorraine Estelle who is the new director of Project COUNTER.

Lorraine Estelle: Good morning, everybody. Before I start I would just say that I've been with COUNTER since June and I'm speaking to slides which are not my work; they are the work of my predecessor, Peter Shepherd, who was the last director of COUNTER, so I just want to make clear that I'm not plagiarizing his work. I'm giving him credit for it. So, in terms of COUNTER, what we have been looking at is calculating sharing metrics. Is it possible and what are the approaches that can be taken? And clearly we could see from the project that there was a very wide range of sharing mechanisms and all of them different, not comparable, and clearly we're in an area where there are no standards yet. And we also found from the project that the data collected is likely to go out of date very quickly. Two approaches can be considered when we're thinking about calculating sharing metrics. The databased approach—employing usage data from publishers and citation data where such data is comprehensive and reliable. So there are limits there because that data has to exist. The other approach, survey-based approach, is using an online community as a basis for monitoring sharing behavior over time. Again, we have to think about how frequently that would have to happen and therefore how feasible that would be. So, really just looking at those problems in a bit more detail, data on article sharing by formal and informal methods will be difficult to collect reliably owing to the large number of channels used and as I say the lack of standards at the moment. The mix of sharing methods used varies from discipline to discipline and from year to year. And if we were to use a databased approach, really it would seem to make sense to supplement that with the surveys from time to time.

So we then really come to the question is a sharing calculator possible? I think we can say that it is difficult, it's early days, and there are problems to address and in the project we can see that there are outliers that really skew the results, and demographics matter a lot and make a big difference. So, an approach that we have considered here is a range of sharing with a lower—using the lower range and upper range, and here in the table you can see this approach and I think it is very useful looking at the range across those different categories that Carol was telling us that she found that the researchers have been using and again. We can see there right at the top e-mail is the winner for sharing with the highest range. So that may be one approach that we could build on.

Carol, again, pointed out demographics do matter and it will be no surprise to hear that the younger the researcher, the less formal their methods for sharing. And, again, I think what Carol said the researchers of the slightly more mature years—more formal sharing—they post class but when they do they have greater reach. And of course disciplinary differences, social scientists share more via social media so they have really embraced it, the social scientists. So when we think of the original question of thinking about a calculator, can it be done? Well any estimate on a number of times an article is shared per download depends on many things. There are lots of things going on there. An alternative to the exact calculator might be as we said that range of sharing for those different categories, and this range could in turn be combined with download numbers to estimate a level of factual posts downloaded usage.

I am, when we're talking about sharing, also going to use this presentation as an opportunity to highlight two of the projects that are going on in this sort of area of COUNTER working with CrossRef. So, we have the DET and the DUL, and if you get them confused, well you're joining me there. I get them quite confused. So the DOI event tracking (DET) initiative really looks at creating an open common infrastructure to track activities around DOI's, recording user content interactions, so articles but also other items at the DOI level. The distributed usage logging (DUL) initiative—again really very similar—similar infrastructure but a peer to peer system for the exchange of usage data on user content interactions. So, for example, you might have the exchange of data from a publisher's platform at an institutional repository, and there you would see the use of an article in those two places. So, I think those initiatives are something we're working on and which will also give us that wider picture. So, thank you very much, and now I'm going to hand it over to Wouter, who is going to tell you about his project.

Wouter Haak: Thank you. I guess hopefully everybody can hear me and you probably immediately note my accent. I'm not American. I'm Dutch, so I'm sorry for that already. I'm also a product person, so that means that my job is to actually translate insights into products that lead to results. That's my life, that's what I like doing, and I particularly like doing that online. So, I'm not going to talk about policy implications. There's actually another discussion later today that will discuss how sharing affects changing publisher policies. I highly advise you to attend that session as well if you're interested in that. I'm going to talk about products and researcher behavior and what this may mean for you as a librarian from my perspective being a publisher. So, let me start with Mendeley because as you may know Mendeley was acquired by Elsevier a couple years back, and Mendeley is a collaborative sharing platform. Let me just give you some metrics of what sharing on Mendeley is doing. So, sharing is growing. As you can see from the start of Mendeley sharing has grown tremendously, double-digits every year. So, obviously Mendeley is a popular tool, and it is growing in popularity, but aside from that it is really the group, and this is just one picture—this is groups. They're growing tremendously, and a Mendeley group is a group where you invite others to privately share references and full-text documents with others. It is very popular as you can see. And then the articles they're sharing—that is growing even faster. So as you can see the number of articles shared on Mendeley with other researchers is growing tremendously. Now, to Carol's research, this actually is the tip of the iceberg because most researchers share by mail. Now, our challenge is we actually wanted to make it so easy to share with others on platforms like Mendeley, and actually I'm broadening the scope here because it could be Mendeley, it could be Papers, it could be ReadCube, but of course our focus is on Mendeley. We want to make it so easy that researchers will prefer to share on collaborative platforms that we can then use to improve their research and to help you as a librarian.

So, what I would like to talk about is three actions we've done. So, first of all, we've created a "My Research Dashboard" where we now feed back to the researcher what's happening with their article. Secondly, we're now testing in institutional dashboards, where we're giving back to you as a librarian metrics about what's happening with the articles including sharing and collaboration, and thirdly we've joined forces with other publishers to create a movement to kind of outline principles, what constitutes simple, seamless, and good sharing, and all three I want to highlight quickly.

So, first of all, let me just show you some screenshots of the "My Research Dashboard." So, and I guess maybe in the back you can't completely read this, resolution is always an issue, but basically this tells the researcher how many views, how many citations of the articles that he has published with Elsevier and non-Elsevier. This is the full world of your research, and why is this important? Particularly, early-career researchers have a hard time kind of establishing how they're doing because they need to wait for the first citation or they need to judge by the impact factor of the journal how well they're doing, as you know the first citation could take as long as two or three year, and the impact factor of the journal is a gross kind of collection of an aggregate result. It doesn't say anything about your success as a researcher on that particular research. So, that is why we're starting to feed back these signals immediately after you publish your article to get earlier signals about how you're doing, who's reading you, and what they are doing with your article—and that's also why sharing is so important.

So, this is feedback from Mendeley. For example, this article has not just been downloaded and viewed many times but it's also been added to a Mendeley library 548 times, and by the way, out of those times that people added to their library, 16 people decided to share it in their group. Now, that is a very strong signal and very strong, let's say, following of what happens with articles. First you glance at it, then you read it, then you deep read it, and then you decide to share with your fellow collaborators. This is what we're doing with the sharing. We know that sharing is important, so therefore we thought we need to feed this back to the research community. When we presented this to a group of librarians last year, the first question we got is, "Hey, can we get this?" We were like, "Yeah, why not?" So, that leads me to the institutional dashboard. We believe that you as librarians should get better controls of what's happening with your authors, your readership, and what's happening around your institution, so we're creating a—this is actually a markup of a prototype that is now live at a couple of universities we are working with. We are creating a prototype where we again give you feedback about usage and statistics and stories about what's happening at your institution. But sharing and collaboration is important, so, for example, this a picture of the collaborations that happened at your institution internationally in the last three years, so we're trying to zoom out from the article and researcher level to an institutional level and help you understand what's happening with your authors.

Having said that, this is explaining why we believe it's really important to feed back sharing to researchers, to institutions, because it's happening and it's increasing as the research showed. Now it's an incomplete picture, so, for example, we can't track e-mail usage and we can't, we as Elsevier, can't for example track what's happening with our documents on, for example, ResearchGate or Academia. But we're talking to those platforms and we're talking to other publishers, and what we said is actually, "Sharing isn't bad. Sharing is actually a good thing," usually, and that is actually also what your research showed. Usually, researchers share amongst fellow researchers that are actually—we like them to read those articles, so we don't care that much about entitlements in research collaboration groups. We actually want to enable that as seamless as possible, so what we did is we got together with a group of publishers—and actually I happily see a couple of them sitting in this room—driven by the STM to create principles for sharing for social collaborative networks (SCNs), and this is difficult, right, because what is an SCN? We said well, probably, let's use a broad definition. We want to apply principles for sharing of articles on social collaborative networks, and what we did is with that group and together with the STM we came up with a set of initial principles and we started a consultation, and that was back in March, and we asked the whole community including you for feedback, and actually a lot of feedback came so what happened is 50—actually I think it was more than that—52 people gave feedback from librarians, institutional repositories, SCN's, other publishers, and actually also we got a lot of response privately. All of those responses were analyzed and we actually said, "Okay, that is actually really valid feedback." So, we changed the principles based on that consultation. And based on that, we have now come up with a new set of what we call "voluntary principles" because anybody can sign up to it where we say first of all publishers actually facilitate the dissemination and discovery of their authors' scholarly articles. That may sound very basic but is actually really important. It means that we actually want to help authors share their work and researchers share their insights with their collaborators.

Secondly, we say sharing should be allowed within a research collaboration group. It is really important. Sharing should be allowed. There should be no doubt about that. Any publisher that signs up for these principles allows sharing in private collaboration groups. Those groups can be of subscribers and nonsubscribers, so we're actually okay with researchers that are entitled to share with other researchers that are not entitled.

It's very important. That may sound very trivial; it is actually—a lot of the feedback that we got was, "That's happening all the time already," but I did talk to some librarians and they're worried to endorse some sharing tools because they're like, "Well, we know that sometimes illicit sharing is happening, and actually through these policy changes that we're going through we are actually allowing this." So, we're allowing you to endorse sharing and collaborative tools and to help your researchers do this. We even say, look, it can be researchers sharing with other researchers and it can be researchers sharing with the wider public. That's okay as well. What we do say is that commercial research is different. Commercial researchers from highly paid organizations—there's different tools, different mechanisms to facilitate that. There are already several platforms facilitating that. We do want to kind of follow those mechanisms. The only thing we're asking back in return is that those platforms that endorse this as well, we'd like to follow and track the usage. We would like to work with COUNTER and CrossRef to track the usage and sharing going on. Why? Because we want to feed that back in those dashboards that you've seen and in the reports to institutions. We want to use their signals to improve our recommendations engines.

I was really impressed with the speech this morning by James O'Donnell with the Jedi sword who said your task as a librarian should be to help researchers with discovery. Well the same holds for us. We're actually in that boat together. Our engines, our discovery engines, are power-fed by the user signals. That is why this is so important that we track those user signals because our recommendations are worth nothing if we don't understand what's happening with the articles, and it's our responsibility to give good recommendations to make researchers read less because they need to read the proper stuff.

So, we are actually working together on standards with all of the standards organizations to make this more of a standard mechanism, and we're changing our policies to reflect these principles. So far only, I should say only, actually in publisher time frame it's actually amazing—publishing is not that fast. Three publishers have changed their policies, so Nature, Springer, Elsevier, and Wiley, but that's a large portion of articles out there. So, I talked to other publishers. I hear rumors that more publishers will follow so I think this is a good thing. So what I'm really asking you as a library community is do you feel comfortable with this? Do you think this is the right direction? Do you feel that you are supportive of this? If so, I would really encourage you to endorse this movement because we want to enable sharing. We want to help sharing. You can help me by endorsing this or leaving your feedback on the STM Association site. I'm sure this presentation will be shared at some point, but I think the simplest way to do it is if you Google for STM principles or STM consultation, you'll also land on this. The importance of this I can't underestimate because research sharing is increasing. COUNTER and CrossRef are actively making this happen. What I would like from you is the support so that we can clearly communicate to all of the platforms and publishers out there that this is important. So, please help me with that. Thank you.

Innovation in Open Access Monographs, Archives, and Journals

Brian Hole, Founder and CEO, Ubiquity Press

Alison Mudditt, Director, University of California Press

David Parker, Head of Editorial, Alexander Street Press

Moderated by Rick Anderson, University of Utah

The following is a transcript of a live presentation at the 2015 Charleston Library Conference.

Rick Anderson: So, first we're going to hear from Alison Muddit, who is the director of the University of California Press, and she's going to talk about the UC Press's new and very exciting monograph publishing program called Luminos. Then we will hear from Brian Hole, who is the founder and CEO of Ubiquity Press, and he's going to discuss the way in which Ubiquity Press provides a platform on which others can innovate with openness; and the third speaker will be David Parker, who is head of editorial at Alexander Street Press, and he's going to describe an interesting new initiative in open access for archival materials. Following him, I'll make a couple of very brief synthesizing remarks and then we'll open up the remainder of the time for a discussion. Alison.

Alison Mudditt: Thank you. Okay, so I'm so excited to be here to talk about one of my favorite topics, the open digital feature of the monograph, and I would like to acknowledge that there are a lot of interesting things really happening in this space. I'm going to focus on what we've been doing at UC Press with our Luminos program, and there are a lot of really interesting other programs out there that are happening at university presses here in the US. So, we started thinking really seriously about open access at UC Press a few years ago, as we started to think about the digital future beyond books and journals, and we really saw this and saw open access as integral to that future. It is in perfect alignment with our mission as a university press, both to democratize access to content and also to increase the impact of the scholarship that we publish. But, as we started to think about monographs, we kept on stepping back to a series of crises; depending on who you spoke to, it was either the crisis of the monograph itself or the crisis of the humanities or even the crisis of the university press. And so we really wanted to unpack that to better understand what we were dealing with, as we tried to think about models for dealing with monographs. That said, the one thing that was really clear to us was that the monograph remains a vitally important vehicle for scholarly communication in the humanities and the humanistic social sciences. And so, as we thought about the monograph, we wanted to make sure that we were not only preserving the monograph but also reinvigorating it with more open digital models.

As a starting point we sort of looked across the landscape at what was happening in open access and we thought about what this told us about what may or may not work for monographs; and the first conclusion—this is a pretty obvious one to many people but I think it is worth underlining—was that the hybrid models that were being developed were really developed for STM journals and for fields primarily in the life sciences where there are large research grants that pay the cost of publication. This brought us up against one of the first challenges for books, given (1) they were expensive, and (2) they are in fields that don't have those grants. There were no obvious funding sources—certainly no single funding sources in the underfunded humanities and social sciences that were really going to be able to cover the costs of publication in the way article processing charges (APCs) have begun to for gold OA journals.

The next challenge, and this is really more as we started talking to faculty, is a whole series of cultural concerns about moving to a digital open

http://dx.doi.org/10.5703/1288284316232

access model for monographs; and yes, there is an attachment to printed books, but I think there's a great discussion of this in Geoff Crossick's recent Higher Education Funding Council for England (HEFCE) report on the landscape for open access monographs, and he talks about an attachment to the materiality of the book, the visual grammar that is created through things like footnotes and indexes and all the other apparatuses of book publication, all things that haven't really been well-captured by the digital form at this point in time.

Next, a key concern, particularly among junior faculty, as you might imagine, is the question as to whether the digital open access book will have the same legitimacy, promotion, and tenure as the traditional print monograph. And then I think, finally, an added complexity of monographs is that we are looking to move to digital and open access at the same time, and if you think back to journals, by the time mandates became a big deal and open access became more of an issue for journals, digital had been the norm of publication for a decade or more. I would say with monographs we're really grappling with both of those two things simultaneously.

As we started to think about what we wanted to do in the monograph space, the first thing that we set out to do was to really think about a model that would address what we identified, now respected as the two primary concerns of monographs. The first concern is that the presses and libraries in the current model are under increasing financial strain, whether you want to call the model broken or not, but certainly under increasing financial strain. And the second is the issue of access. As a university press, we believe that we have a responsibility to disseminate the scholarship we publish as widely as possible, certainly to all who are interested, ideally to all would profit from it, but very definitely we want to be represented in the 300 or so research libraries in the West who can afford to buy monographs these days. At the same time we wanted to make sure that we preserved what really works so well about the monograph, and one of the things that we have been very careful to do in the Luminos model is to make it clear and to ensure that an open access monograph is exactly the same as any other UC Press monograph in the important areas of selection, peer review, approval by our editorial committee, and the editorial development of the book.

As we started to think then about business models, we really identified the fact that this is a problem that libraries and publishers are unable to solve on their own, and so we moved back to thinking about collaborative ways to address the problem. The business model that we developed is one that really shares the cost of publication among the people that we identify as the key stakeholders. You'll see that there is an author's contribution to that—you know, what in the journals' world has become known as an article processing charge (APC). We are assuming that comes from the author's institution but at the same time recognize that not all institutions are able to fund this. There's also a library subsidy that comes from a mention model that I'll talk about more in a moment. But there is continuing subsidy from UC Press; we always support all of the monographs we publish, and then there are print editions available and so we are hoping to generate revenue from printed titles.

Since we are at a library conference, why don't we dive a little deeper into the library venture model. It is kind of, you know, in many ways, an NPR-type model. We have four levels of membership. Membership is, of course, completely optional for all libraries and there are different levels of benefits for libraries at each of the four levels. So one benefit that is consistent across all of them is that faculty at the library and institutions will all receive a discount on that title publication fee to publish within Luminos. And so the library revenue that we generate is used in two ways: the first is to help support the publication costs of the books that are published in the Luminos program and anything that's left from that goes into a waiver fund which we are using to support authors at institutions that genuinely cannot afford the cost of the publication.

So, we're at a point now where we've published the first six books in the series, and that has all happened over the last couple of months, so there's not a lot of data to report at this time. It's very early days, but the data is of course all available on the websites and you can see exactly how many uses and downloads on this there have been. We've had a great reception from libraries. We've signed up a good number of library members and had a really positive response from authors and I think there are really two ways that the model has really resonated among our authors. The first is among authors who want to be read and not simply published; and the immediacy of being able to see the dialogue and those kinds of things has really been great for authors. And the second is among the increasing number of humanists and social scientists who are doing multiform work and being able to reflect this fact in their publications in a way that the traditional monograph doesn't allow them to. So that said, I'm really excited about what we've done with Luminos so far and I'm really ambitious about where we could take it. I do think that there are some pretty big issues for us to address if we really want to move open access forward, and these go beyond simply proclaiming the benefits of open access. I think the first and perhaps most difficult one is winning over faculty opinion. We all—libraries and publishers—spend a lot of time in rooms like this talking about open access. There is a really important group of stakeholders who are not here and involved in this discussion and we have very, very different points of view; but you know, the root of this is the entrenched value system, where the newer publication is most important in the career of any academic and they, like we are, human, and most of them will choose prestige over the ideals of OA, and so there are some really significant changes that must happen there, which I think we all have to accept, that will take a really long time.

The next challenge for monographs, I think, are issues to do with licensing and rights. We've adopted a pretty open approach, offering any of the Creative Commons licenses for monographs. The OA purists argue anything that is not CC-BY isn't real open access, but I think for us to really move forward with monographs we have to be a little more open-minded than that, and then there's the technology issue. I think the experience of reading a digital open access monograph has to become a lot closer to the experience of reading a physical book for it to become an acceptable alternative.

Finally, there are the issues around business models and funding. I think that we're doing a lot to really scaffold together what we can with Luminos and to start to address some of the real issues of moving to a digital open access model for monographs, ones that go well beyond how we pay for them. At the same time, I think, for us to see OA ventures scale in the way that many of us would like them to, there's going to have to be some pretty significant top-down change to the financing of these models. So, in conclusion, I hope and think that we are making a real contribution with Luminos, along with many other publishers in this space, to try and develop sustainable models, and I hope we're demonstrating that open access models can not only be just as good as but perhaps better than the traditional monograph. Thank you.

Brian Hole: Good afternoon, everybody. So, there's a background to this slide (see Figure 1).

Figure 1. Hole's first slide in his presentation.

I was asked originally to talk about what the state of open access was when I first came into it. So, this slide symbolizes that. I used to work at one of the large publishers and left there to go back to University College London (UCL) to get my PhD and discovered at that point that publishers weren't as loved as I thought they had been. I'm blabbering and so forth. I also found that open access was a big issue, and because of my publishing experience I was asked to help out with some of the smaller journals that operated on campus, and we looked at all the opportunities to get them published in open access and we couldn't find anything that cost us less than $20,000 a year for publishing print books. And that was the genesis for setting up Ubiquity Press. So I found out that open access was out there, but especially in humanities no one could quite yet reach it and at the same time I was doing my research. I'm an archaeologist so I was working up in India a lot of the time and very, very few people could access it, even if it was supposed to be open access through programs like Canary and so forth which are very where with all programs but in reality don't reach more than 10 or 20% of people. So that was a real driver for us to set up the company and get moving.

And so what we did was we set up and we aimed to be as low-cost or as cost efficient as possible. So we set up an APC of around 10% that would beat the other publishers and we did that by using open source software for our platform, by being just very, very cost-conscious from the beginning and that was really, really critical in the humanities so we eventually got to the point then where we had a lot of success with humanities journals because we worked more with them, and societies and libraries were willing to pay the charges that we were asking for because we were very transparent about it. We were saying, "We're not spending money on our expensive yacht." It's actually going into everything like running our office, building our platform, doing the typesetting, and so on. That was very critical.

And then what we did was we took the platform and we decided to open it up and let other presses use it as well, because we'd become a fairly successful, smaller, growing open access publisher in our own right, with books and monographs and things like that, so we opened up the platform and decided to let university presses take advantage of it and other societies; and what we do generally is they use the platform, the software, they run the front office of the press, and we offer everything else in terms of the infrastructure, editorial support, typesetting, copy, and all that kind of thing, and what we aim to do is to de-risk university publishing for them, make it sustainable, and provide a solution to university presses so they can take on big publishers. And we do things, we push things automatically to use our repository and build our user base up as well-shared between all of the universities, peer review, that kind of thing. And that has taken off very well also.

I'll just point out three quick case studies. Because our platform is extremely cost-efficient and allows others to take it with low risk and allows them to innovate on top of it so in a way we've done our bit, now we're trying to get other people to come up with new business models in open access, try out new things, because when open access is operated successfully it won't just be done in one particular way. It won't just be an APC model; there can be lots of different approaches depending on different disciplines and situations that will work.

So, the first of those—and Alison has already talked a little bit about University of California Press using the platform—UC Press uses it for *Collabro*, which is a large journal that they launched, where because the fees we charge are quite low they are able to charge a little bit more for staff and things like paying peer reviewers and really iterate around that model and try and come up with a solution that fits the academic community and some of the problems they've been having not being rewarded by larger publishers, and so on. And plus the Luminos platform that Alison's just mentioned, and then another one is the Open Library of Humanities, once again addressing the fact that this would not be extensive in the humanities, but if you offer things at a reasonable value, then libraries, for example, are probably going to be willing to contribute and back you. The Open Library of Humanities has a library membership model for journal publishing, which has taken off extremely well. I imagine most people here will have been involved in that at some point by now. Another one—I can mention about 10 or 20 different things—but the other one that I'm going to bring up that you might have seen recently is the initiative called LingOA which is from the linguistics community, and essentially what happens there is they built up a large fund to be able to pay the APCs for journals in the linguistics community that want to go fully open access. So, we have journals who negotiate with their publishers to see if they will be allowed to go open access. If they're not allowed, they leave those publishers and come across to the platform. And LingOA is an initiative that is backed by the Dutch government and universities and they put together a fund to pay these fees for five years. There've been a few recent high-profile moves on that same space.

So, the aim of all of that is, then, that we try to make a community of all these initiatives working together. The end of this slide (Figure 2) is to talk about the importance of teamwork.

Figure 2. Hole's second slide, representing teamwork.

The idea being birds that fly in formation are 80% more energy efficient, and that's kind of the idea of a platform, that all these different initiatives share the same infrastructure, same services, and they network together and they can actually be much more efficient working together. And I saw, believe it or not, a book on birds' migration, which talked about the way in which a bird falls behind and another bird will go back and help it fly to the front, and the model is "no bird left behind." But as a result of that we have really well-established presses like UCP but we also have a huge number of journals from countries like Sri Lanka, so we're trying to build a proper global community together therefore, working towards open access together.

And then I was also asked to say what I think the future is and to take a few steps further and I'm not sure I have video to play. This is actually John's Horn swallows doing crazy things. Okay so for some reason I can't play it. What that was really just showing is that we are actually very, very ambitious about the platform and we don't want to stop with just ten presses working together. We want to get up into the hundreds and we want those presses to be very successful so we want to see journals moving away from publishers who don't want to support them in an open access business model. They should come over and start working with the presses that do have the ability to support them and then together we can form an agreement about what infrastructure we should have. Thank you.

David Parker: This would be a really easy platform to take a dive off of. So, I'm David. I'm with Alexander Street. Our model at Alexander Street is making silent voices heard, and a big part of that for us is bringing new archived content to the scholarly community. We see these dusty boxes of archives and we see opportunity. Digitizing them has been in our DNA for long time. Open access, though, was a new initiative we wanted to engage in, and so we started looking at the landscape of current initiatives in archival open access publishing, and largely two models appeared. The first, government or institution funded, and we know that that is wonderful for OA but it is also constrained by limited dollars. And then we also saw the sales threshold model that Reveal Digital and others have popularized. We really like this model. We believe it's a great way to bring archives to open access but the challenge with the sales threshold mode is that it is delayed indefinitely. You establish a target of, say, $500,000 and you gotta get there. It could take two years, it could take five years, it could take ten years. So, we wanted to embrace a model or try a model that would do something a little different. We also, when talking to faculty and talking to the complex mix of rights holders we deal with, realized that we were running up a big challenge, which is that some of the rights holders we deal with are never going to go open access. Some of them are definitely going to go open access. Faculty, however, when they experience our content, regardless of whether it's open access or not, they want it on a unified single platform.

Which brings me to our new initiative launching early in 2016: Anthropology Fieldwork Online. So what I want you to imagine is the world's biggest database of field research notes all in one place. If you think about the twentieth century, it was seminal for anthropology in defining how the discipline was going to operate through the practice of ethnography. So, early in the century folks like Bronislaw Malinowski wrote these great ethnographies. Later on, people like Margaret Mead wrote ethnographies, which progressed the practice of the discipline, and for that 250-page monograph you have now that they've written, underneath it are boxes and boxes and boxes of fabulous field notes, and when you start diving into the—if you're geeky anthropologist like I am—you love it. You're thinking, "Wow, how can we bring this to life?" But, again, you deal with these complex rights. We have institutions, individuals, we've been in the basement of spouses of deceased anthropologists looking at their notes; it's a really interesting, complex web of content rights that we have to navigate, and again we have to get all of this material digital, discoverable, on a single platform, and when possible, open.

So, how are we going to do it? We're launching Anthropology Commons. Anthropology Commons—think of a coin, Anthropological Fieldwork Online is on one side of the coin; flip the coin over—that's Anthropology Commons; and both of them are discoverable, searchable, on one platform, on two sides of a coin. There are three ways we're making content open access via the Anthropology Commons. The first is, from every sale we make of Anthropological Fieldwork Online, we are contributing 10% to sponsoring open access content in the Commons. The second model is our delayed OA model, and these are from some of the archives that have said to us, "We have a mission to sustain. We need to generate some revenue, but after a certain period of time we are willing to go open access." So, that's five years in our model. Five years of sellables in Anthropological Fieldwork Online and then the content moves over into the Anthropology Commons. And finally is the third model, sponsored content, and that's where our 10% is going but also, many of the archives that we've spoken to say they would be willing to underwrite digitization and evince costs so that content can be immediately open access. Also, many of the archives participating in the delayed model have told us they would like to kick back a bit of the royalty to the sponsorship pool.

So how does this work in practice? How many of you know who these folks are (see Figure 3)?

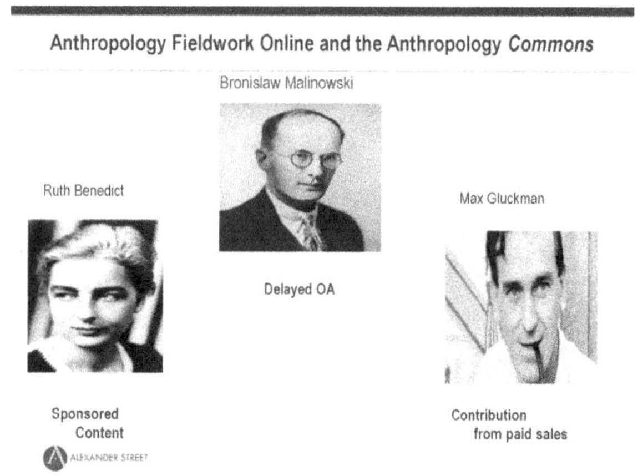

Figure 3. Hole's third slide: Anthropology fieldwork online and anthropology Commons.

Any of these folks? One or two hands. But, again, you're not geeky anthropologists like me. So these are examples of archives, or part of the anthropologists that we are targeting in looking at the archives to bring the content to life. So, for example, Ruth Benedict. If this works out for us, we believe it will, we're very close to an agreement, this would appear immediately in our sponsored content. We are underwriting the cost of bringing all of her archival content that is immediately available to open access, and it is fascinating stuff. Bronislaw Malinowski is the granddaddy. In my first anthro course I had to read *Argonauts of the Southern* [or *Western*] *Pacific*, I can't remember now. That will be delayed OA. And then Max Gluckman, he's the founder of the Manchester School of Anthropology, and his content is coming via the Royal Anthropological Institute, and they have to earn a royalty, so it would be always in that sellable part of the Anthropology Fieldwork Online, but again 10% is going over into sponsoring content. So that is our model. That is an example of how Anthropology Fieldwork Online and Anthropology Commons function together online like two sides of the coin.

So last, the future of open access archives. I should've written from my perspective not from our perspective, but you know the Library of Congress has said that less than 10% of their content is now digital let alone open access, and if the Library of Congress is less than 10% I think we can assume that the rest of the world's archives are about 2%. And part of this is that archives don't benefit from the need to publish behind open access journals and monographs.

Figure 4. Hole's fourth slide: Open access archive landscape . . . from our perspective.

You saw my comment earlier in the slide (Figure 4) that archives don't seek tenure so funding isn't always flowing towards getting archives open and digital, but on the other hand I think that makes it an opportunity for innovation because it's not constrained by the various publisher models that define how things are going with journals and monographs, notwithstanding the great new initiatives of my copanelists. So, I do think we're in a time of opportunity for new models in open access archives. I'm a big fan of Ray Kurzweil. A lot of people think he's nuts. He said that in less than 50 or so years the pace of technology innovation and biology innovation will make it so that none of us have to die. It's "the singularity," he calls it, and in a lot of ways he's crazy, that doesn't make any sense, but Ray says that the reason we think he's crazy is because we look at everything in a linear change model but really change is exponential, especially with technology, so he says that if you take a step back and you look at the pace of change in its exponential nature, you'll see that it's really moving way faster than you realize, and I believe that is the case with open access archives. I think we are just on the cutting edge of it and there's going to be a lot more great new innovation. My last note: Anthropology Commons is only the beginning for us. Stay tuned and see what we do in other areas at Alexander Street. Thank you.

Text and Data Mining Contracts: The Issues and Needs

Nancy Herther, Sociology Librarian, University of Minnesota

Daniel Dollar, Director of Collection Development, Yale University Library

Darby Orcutt, Assistant Head, Collection Management, North Carolina State University Libraries

Alicia Wise, Director, Elsevier

Moderator: Meg White, Executive Director of Technology Services, Rittenhouse Book Distributors

Meg White: Good afternoon, folks, and welcome. This is our second Neapolitan session of the day in ballroom number two, so if that is not what you were looking for now is your time to make your escape. We thank the audience for your stamina at the end of a very long day, but we're glad you're here for what promises to be a very interesting session. So I'm going to turn this over to Nancy and her panel for "Text and Data Mining: Licensing Issues."

Nancy Herther: And thank you, Meg, and welcome to all of you here today. I'm glad you've been able to find us and I certainly again agree. It's kind of been a long day. It's a great conference; I'm sure you agree as well, but we're getting so much information. We're hoping that we can organize the session a little bit differently. We're going to be having some presentations and then really we're going to turn it over to you. I had a chance to work on a couple of articles for Katina for the website on text and data mining, and one of the things that I found in doing that was that, at least here in the United States and Canada and North America, it's still so fresh, it's still so new, there are so many questions and a lot of the answers that one organization doesn't necessarily work at all for another. So it was very interesting, and quite an education for me, and because of that the lesson I took from that was we need to start talking a lot more about text and data mining, what's happening around us. Maybe if you don't have a lot going on, then understand and listen and share with the people around you who maybe have a little bit more experience. There is no one formula. We don't have any one way of doing it. Someday we might but we don't today. I want to introduce our three speakers who are going to speak for 5, 7, 10 minutes on their experiences with text and data mining. We have three wonderful perspectives here. They're going to present to you certainly not the only perspectives that we might have, but I think all of these are valuable. They have all agreed that they would be happy to take your questions, and answer whatever questions you might have and give you whatever sort of information or insight that they have to give you. I'm going to go ahead now and introduce our speakers; excuse me for the paper here. So, our first speaker is Daniel Dollar. He's the director of collection development at Yale University Libraries, and he has been involved and he's currently involved with their budget management, an important aspect when it comes to collections, the collection steering committee, and also the executive committee for the library as a whole. He has written on a variety of different issues, certainly e-books and a lot of transformations that we have seen here, and he's going to give us a perspective being from a large, very multidisciplinary institution and the issues that he sees that are important, and how it impacts his practice as well as the current structures that exist at Yale. Our next speaker is someone who has been an academic, understands academic research. She has a PhD in anthropology and research, and that is Alicia Wise. She has been at Elsevier since June of 2010. She is leading the universal access team. In this role she is responsible for access and related policies, building relationships with other stakeholders in scholarly communication, and she has also worked for the UK Joint Information Systems Committee first to manage national

http://dx.doi.org/10.5703/1288284316233

negotiations for access to a broad range of intellectual property issues; she has experience on different aspects of these sorts of issues that we're looking at today. In Great Britain text and data mining is developing very differently than it is here in North America, so I really appreciate her perspective on this as well.

Our last speaker here, our last specialist, is Darby Orcutt. He is the assistant head of collection Management and chair of the humanities and social sciences subject team at the North Carolina state University Libraries. He has negotiated content mining access with numerous vendors, including the first ever blanket mining agreement between an institution and a major commercial vendor of historical abstracts, and that was from Gale, and similar first institutional agreements with accessible archives, Unlimited Priorities, Adam Matthew, and others that are going to be announcing in the near future. So I want to turn this over to Daniel Dollar now, our first speaker, and again we will have lots of time for questions, insights, concerns, etc., from you as we go. Thank you.

Daniel Dollar: Thank you, Nancy. All right. So, let me start my timer here. Okay. "Text and Data Mining: Licensing Issues." You saw, some of you may have seen, the video that Elsevier created on text and data mining; it's a nice overview. I'm taking this from LIBER, the Association of European Research Libraries Text and Mining website, where it talks about text and data mining as basically its machine-read material; its copying of large quantities of material which can sort of concern people when you talk about copying, but it's in order to extract data and then recombine it to find patterns. I thought it was very interesting that this morning we had Jim O'Neil talking and saying how many of you have done text and data mining. And it was like okay, every time you do a Google search, so we're all text and data miners whether we knew it or not. But, it is certainly something that is critical if we're going to try to understand a large corpus of material. We are moving beyond I think, like the horse and buggy era where we call things "e-journals" and "e-books." I mean, as the content has moved into a digital age and we have to think in new ways in order to make sense of this huge corpus of material and text, and data mining is a tool to do that and really see this as becoming an everyday tool or part of a toolkit for the discovery of new knowledge, and even in the humanities it is going to become a mainstream part of scholarly inquiry. That is what we see coming, or envision.

What are the challenges? I see four challenges: legal, pricing, access, and library support. On the legal licensing side, our position is, wait for it, we really don't see a reason to have to have separate TDM licenses. The output is subject to the same terms and conditions undertaken with any research using licensed resources, and making lawful use of the content when employing TDM is still governed and subject to the license agreements that we've signed. We can't do text and data mining and just throw content out on the web or re-create the products that we've licensed for the whole world, but we can make research use of that content again within the context of our licenses. We do accept the premise that the right to read is the right to mine whether it's close, human reading or distant, machine reading of the material and if it—Susan Riley from LIBER who was supposed to be here on this panel, you got me instead, yay! But, if she was here from LIBER I think she would talk a little bit about how in Europe they feel that they are behind. The researchers there are behind us in terms of our ability to make use of text and data mining because of fair use and the way it is interpreted in the United States. And I would direct you to the LIBER website for more information about their rationale for that.

Dropping into pricing: as a research library, we are paying a premium for content and so if we are paying a premium for content, for digitized content, then it should come with text and data mining as a matter of course. You know, I sort of think of the analogy of when back in the 1990s we started getting content on discs but you couldn't print or you couldn't save it because you were worried about what would happen to the content. We sort of got past that—we got past the early days of e-journals when we were worried about electronic ILL, I sort of feel we're in the same sort of early stages with text and data mining. There's a lot of concern—what's going to happen? The content is going to get out on the web and bad things are going to happen, but from the library's standpoint and we're paying this premium for content, if you're going to have these kinds of restrictions that in a few years I'm going to have to go back and buy text and data mining rights, then didn't I pay full royalties the first time around? Actually I already paid it more than once because I bought it on microfilm but let's—you know, oh well. We'll get it right one day, but I'm quite concerned as a chief collection development officer at my institution, going in and making six-figure purchases, or high five-figure purchases, and I'm going to have my colleagues or the person who comes after me saying, "What in the heck was he doing?" By not including this and not making sure that this was clearly understood when we made this acquisition.

Access: so in terms of access, you know, getting the raw data either on a drive or putting it in a secure location in the cloud where we can actually do text and data mining. We've had some success with vendors where we have been able to do that, we were able to get research output from that text and data mining and then point back to the publisher's website for the human readable content, and that's a real win because we're making new discoveries, our researchers can make new discoveries; it points back to the platform where we have the human readable licensed content, and what do you know? It drives up usage so it's a good thing.

So, APIs come out and are a major issue when we talk about text and data mining, and there's good and bad. We look at what JSTOR is doing with the Data for Research Program as good. It's not mediated. We are also optimistic about what the HathiTrust Research Center is working on. They're trying to work on an API to mine all of the content within HathiTrust, and that includes the post-1923 content, which is quite problematic. So, we see those as advantages. We take a Dem view with API, where it's going to be mediated or potentially mediated by others sort of looking over the shoulder of the researcher, potentially. And that accessibility: this is something that I can only touch on briefly. I understand that UC Berkeley is making some use of text and data mining for accessibility issues, and so I don't know all the mechanics of how they're doing that but it is an interesting idea that maybe they can take that content and put it into forms that can be used with someone who has disability needs in very controlled ways.

And then the final challenge is library support. We think of the sciences, the labs, linguists, those folks generally have quantitative data science skills or expertise in their labs or their departments. The humanities not so much, and so we see digital humanities centers as helping bridge the gap and helping the humanists sort of tap into these rich resources and make use of them in new and exciting ways, but that has a financial cost. Even, wait for it, at Yale it has a cost. I mean every position we hire for has to go through our Executive Council, and we have long debates. I mean we have caught up to the rest of the world and so—but we have to make these investments. We've received a grant. We're hiring and building out a digital humanities lab, and again it is a significant financial impact for us. It's not free, and even if we can make use of the content using TDM we have to make an investment on our side.

So, thank you. These are three of my colleagues who are instrumental in helping me with this presentation but don't hold them responsible for what I said. Thank you.

Alicia Wise: Hey, everybody, it's terrific to be here today and I really enjoyed already learning from my fellow panel members. We've had some lively discussions in preparation for this, which got me thinking afresh and I hope the discussion today will continue that. So, let me offer a publishing perspective on the same space. TDM is interesting and it's challenging for all of us, and it's really important I think that libraries and publishers work together because we are all supporting researchers so that the more we are aligned the easier it is for them. We have a wide array of TDM programs. We're actually working in close partnership with specific universities. We have a policy but we also have service channels, so we're supporting TDM miners through a development portal and we provide quite a lot of technical support and services beyond just access to the content. Some of our corporate customers, for example, work with us quite closely to develop TDM software and tools. That isn't a call that's been made on us for the academic community, or at least not yet, but it's perhaps something that will come in the future.

We have been engaged in text and data mining support for almost 10 years now. It started off in a very small way with one group of researchers in California who wanted access to our publications for developing text and data mining tools back in 2006, and so that was interesting—those really early adopters. We stepped up I think and made a scale change in our support for TDM, and in about 2013 when we engaged in around 30 pilot projects to better understand the challenges of mining for researchers and libraries and publishers and we kind of thought it would explode at that point, but interestingly I think we along with other publishers are seeing a slow, steady growth in interest in text and data mining and it hasn't been that explosion yet. It still feels like we're very much in the early phases. We're still actually engaging with early adopters, which is interesting.

Okay, so some of the challenges from a researcher's perspective: they need access to computers and code and things that they may not easily have. A lot of the early adapters are actually writing their own code, and that's a barrier potentially to the wider use and uptake of mining. They have to deal with access to content in a variety of different formats across different platforms, and there's a lot of refinement and testing and learning and gurning through data and the outputs to kind of get meaningful results, and I think gaining access to those different platforms and permissions to mine across all the different platforms is of course a challenge for them and something that would be helpful for all of us to help resolve.

I hesitate to say to librarians what some of your challenges may be. I'm sure you know that better than I do, but we do hear from our library partners that actually it is pretty demanding for you all because you're supporting a wide array of research projects on your campuses and they may have really different mining requirements, so developing the expertise, hiring people with the right expertise to really be able to provide tailored support, is a new challenge. It's a hassle for you as well if there are different access requirements and permissions and things across different platforms, and something that Daniel and Darby really brought home to me is that your user privacy is really important to you. So what your users are doing across different platforms and how that is being monitored or tracked is a concern. Any additional cost at all is going to be a challenge, and we are also hearing from librarians that they're sometimes concerned about how TDM figures are being factored into the counter usage statistics, so they want to see publishers reporting separately on machine users and human users.

From a publisher's perspective, there are other publishers in the audience, for example, from Sage, so this is one perspective, but again we're having to support TDM projects across a wide range of subject areas—arts, sciences, and humanities; those have very different support requirements. We also are supporting users with a wide array of technical experience, so when they're mining they're actually often writing programs that are then being run on our platforms, and many miners are very sophisticated and they have terrific software—that's not always the case though. We do have examples where somebody lets their software loose and they haven't really tested it well and it kind of goes crazy, so this is one reason we do ask miners to tell us what their e-mail address is so that if their program kind of goes wild unintentionally we can get into quick contact with them and ask them to please stop running that code.

Legal challenges: we are a global publisher. Every law in every country and every state is different, and yet we need to have a simple easy-to-use service that is understandable that works across all of these different boundaries, national boundaries and institutional boundaries. So, in our case we have come up with one clause that we insert into all of our site license agreements that covers text and data mining from an institution's perspective. We agree that separate agreements aren't necessary, but we do need some kind of license in place because not every country has the same approach. And privacy for users is also important to us to maintain their respect and our credibility. We need to very much respect user privacy and we do.

Ok, and then, finally, we have to find ways of supporting miners, the machine users in a way that won't undermine the quality of service that we are providing to human users, and this is actually the reason we use an API service and let the miners go to town on that. It's a completely different platform actually than our human users are experiencing and interacting with. So, one doesn't affect the performance and speed of the other. We have a TDM policy. We don't make any additional charge for text and data mining. I know other publishers have other approaches, and I've got some sympathy for that. It is not inexpensive to develop the infrastructure and so forth for text and data mining, so if you have concerns about that from other publishers, you know, engage in dialogue with them. But I would urge you to be open-minded and sympathetic about the fact that they may be incurring new costs as well. And we also have made a firm commitment that if any researchers in academic institutions want to mine content that their institution doesn't actually subscribe to or have access to—that we'll respond and be really flexible there. So we have universalacess@elsevier.com, where you can make those sorts of inquiries if you need that support.

There is a registration portal and I've personally registered for an API key, and you guys are right—it is a pain in the ass! So, we have some work to do, I think, to get this streamlined a little bit more, and the idea is that we do want that user's e-mail address in case we need to get in contact with them about their code. We used to ask them questions about their subject area and their projects so that we could learn ourselves what they were requiring in different subject areas, but we want to step away from asking intrusive questions. They don't want to fill in forms for us, and we now have pilots so we've got that understanding. There's a simple click through license for our TDM service,s and I've shared it with Daniel so he can tell me afterward if it's simple enough or if we need to continue refining it, but one of the things I've discovered in preparing for this session is that the way it's been installed, there's actually another click-through license before you get to the TDM license, which is not intended. That's just an error in how it's been implemented, so again, on behalf of Elsevier and other publishers, if you or your users are interacting with our TDM services and you find stupid, awkward things like that, let us know. It's probably a mistake rather than a conspiracy or deep evil, honestly.

Okay, so we've rolled out the TDM access clauses into all of our site licenses, again at no additional cost. If anybody has been missed and wants them, just get in touch with your account manager or contact that universal access e-mail address. The big thing though is that we recognize that miners, that librarians don't only need access to Elsevier content. We honestly do get that, so we're partnering with other publishers through CrossRef on an industry-wide text and data mining service, and this essentially gives researchers a way to get API keys and permissions and to go to town across our platforms so they can access a wide variety of content. So, here are the publishers currently participating. We have about 13 1/2 million articles at this point in the service, and that can grow quite drastically. It is estimated that we are on a course for about 36 million by the middle of next year, and that service from CrossRef and the cross-platform mining is a completely free service as well. So, there's more to be done; there is more refinement; we want to work closely with librarians and we want to work closely with other publishers, and I'm looking forward to learning more about how we can do that more effectively. Thanks, everybody.

Darby Orcutt: Well, my thanks to Daniel and Alicia for really spelling out in a clear fashion the issues and the complexities of all this. I think what I'm going to do is simplify things. I'm a simple guy; I'm a "get it done" kind of guy, and my experience has been in the trenches of working with many, many vendors to try to cut to the heart and to make a deal to make this happen, and I think I have some solutions to some of these and at least one solution that we need to go ahead and move on with regard to this complex area.

A few years ago, or a couple of years ago, actually, this really came to my attention when I attended a campus colloquium at NC State on mining. This was sponsored by one of our social sciences units, and I was shocked to find hundreds, yes hundreds, of faculty and graduate students in attendance, and when one of the speakers asked, "How many of you are engaged in this activity?" almost every hand went up. I knew that there were a lot of folks working in these areas, but what I didn't know was just how many were already doing this and how many were not using necessarily library resources to do this. Now, certainly we have some library resources that particularly social scientists know they can get datasets from, and that's great but I also found in the course of this session that a lot of these folks were using whatever dataset they could find on the web—whatever was convenient, whatever seemed to be well structured data but not necessarily the best data to answer their particular research questions, and we in libraries particularly are worried about, well, if you're like me you're worried about the role of the library and research heading into the future. Here we are providing these wonderful resources, and are our users really actually taking advantage of them? We need to make it easier. We need to open up our collections for computer-assisted research. We need to open it up for these sorts of research informatics like mining.

I also, as I looked around the library community at the time, found a lot of folks who said, "Oh yeah, we've had that on our radar for a long time. Oh yeah, we have that as part of our license agreements, yeah, part of our checklists, we ask for mining rights or access rights." And I had one colleague from another institution who said, "Oh yeah, we've negotiated those rights with a couple of dozen vendors." I said, "Send me a list." And they sent me a list, and probably the most interesting was, I'm making this up, but the *Journal of Esoteric Studies* and the three titles they published, they had mining rights to that; there were no major publishers on the list. None of the content that our users would really be wanting to do was opened up for this. I think really as I found in rolling up my sleeves and working with vendors on this, I found a "push me/pull me" on both sides of this equation. On the vendor side there's this fear of letting the data out, and I think that it is sometimes a very well founded fear. There have been instances I've learned of, in confidence, where content has gotten out there and been posted on the web—usually it's in China but, hey, and so there's this fear of letting things out, and I think on the other hand a lot of vendors have a real fear of being last to the gate. They recognize that this is an area that they really need to respond to, but they're really not sure how to do that. They're afraid that their content will become devalued if they don't offer it, but they're really not sure how to do that. On the other hand, I think we have this "push me/pull me" of librarian confusion. For one, I think that I find on the library side a lot of misunderstanding of vendor capacities, and that's a big problem. This is something again I learned from talking with vendors. One of these issues, for example, is the issue of siloed content. A lot of vendors are a little reticent to release their data because they're a little embarrassed. What on the front end looks like a seamless product or a seamless set of products is actually all kinds of mishmash of different datasets, because these are the things that have been developed over time and they shouldn't feel embarrassed about that. Certainly we in libraries understand that issue, but I think that is one of the things that is going on, and there's this fear that maybe people won't know what to do with that. They won't how to grapple with this data that is not in a single structured format. But that's okay. That's what researchers do. I think also that librarians oftentimes expect an awful lot—and Alicia alluded to this—expect an awful lot for no additional cost, and that's something that I have found—that's actually confusion both on the library inside and oftentimes on the vendor side. Librarians think, "Hey, you can create an API or you can customize the dataset and that's no big deal." Well sometimes it is, and I know also that in talking with the vendors sometimes the vendors think that providing data is a very expensive proposition because their only experience with it has been with providing customized datasets that have required a lot of staff hours from very experienced, expert programmers and such.

I think also librarians grapple, and a colleague was mentioning this to me last night, addressing the present needs and addressing the future. One of the things that we should be doing, and libraries is thinking toward the future about, is thinking about what our users will need versus the sort of—now it's just the early adopters, as Alicia said. And so I think that really thinking about what are we doing when we put together agreements for mining, we're not building a bridge to nowhere. We're building the bridge that is across that great chasm where all of our researchers are headed toward, or a great many of them. And I think the biggest confusion all around on the part of both libraries and vendors is what do we do now? Where do we go? How do we take all this morass of confusing things and turn it into meaningful action? And I appreciate that when we talk about these things, talking about mining implies new services, it implies new support—it implies new roles; this is for libraries and for vendors, and I can't answer all of that and what that will look like, but I can tell you the first step.

I've been advocating, and this is what has allowed me to ink so many of these first of kind deals with a great many vendors, so I've been advocating for a very basic access model, and I realized just this morning I finally have my snappy name for it: the Basic Access Model, BAM. Let's move toward BAM, you know—hey, in the real world there's oftentimes a BAM that comes right before mining activities, right? Am I taking it too far? The Basic Access Model, well our idea of basic access will change over time but what does that mean right now? How do we get access to this particularly, and at this point it's our early adopters, it's our high-end researchers; first of all, we need to get all the data. We need to get all the files for those researchers. I've learned that speaking of raw data, that's not the terminology oftentimes to use in the vendor community. For some, actually creating raw data is an extra step for them so I say, "Well, what format do you have the data in? Send me those files." I want to include not just the text files but also the image files, and there are a couple of important reasons for that. First, depending on the researcher and what they want to do, those things can be extremely, extremely important. Secondly, as we look to the future, we talk now about text and data mining. I prefer to use the term "content mining" because there already are researchers who are or are thinking about mining images, mining video. Let's think about—let's have a generic term for talking about all of these formats that will become an important part of mining activities in the future.

Next, we need to have clear and appropriate cost recovery agreements. It's not fair to ask the vendors to do all this for free, but at the same time let's have a reasonable cost model for this. Now, when I worked out the agreement with Gale, the solution that we came to, a very inelegant one, but maybe the best one, was that the content we needed—they delivered all of the files to us on physical hard drives and they charged us the cost of those hard drives. That's fair. That was what we negotiated. Why? Because even with all the wonderful bandwidth that we have at NC State it would take a long, long time to download all of that data and, in fact, one of my colleagues from the library took the hard drives and walked them over to our laboratory for analytic sciences where one of our faculty, Paul Fife, got together a team and started to mine 19th century British newspapers—an inelegant solution. That's what is basic at this time. It will change. Bandwidth will increase; hey, we can make changes, but if he is right now, he and a team of researchers are working on this data. If we waited, and again, people ask me, "Why didn't Gale provide an API? Why didn't Gale do something better?" Gale should instead be applauded for going ahead and taking this step and becoming the first major commercial vendor of historical archives to offer this type of blanket access to a campus, and they've now turned around and opened that up to any of their customers. If we waited for them to get it all together it would've taken some time, and again that's not just Gale—that's any vendor right now. They're all working on these issues, but we need to make sure that we nail down that basic access for our researchers now.

I mentioned blanket access. That is another important key. We want to mirror the access that we have for close reading of this content, so we don't want to have an additional login. We don't want to have—as it's been a point of contention between me and one vendor, we came to agreement on everything except they want to know, they want every single person who's going to mine that content to register their name and their project with the vendor. Absolutely not! Would we sign a license for content for a database that had those terms? Absolutely not. There are a lot of good reasons why our researchers would need to keep their research private at least for a time. I had one researcher who was going up for an NSF grant, a very competitive grant, and he wasn't quite ready to reveal his great idea for what he was going to do. On the flip side, do probably 99% of our researchers want to report that to the vendor, want to be able to have these conversations about the data and what they're doing? Absolutely. But that needs to be their decision, not a requirement.

Lastly, we really need to have in this basic access model. We need to make sure that there are no special restrictions on mining activities or the outputs. And Daniel alluded to this; these things are already covered by our terms, they're covered by copyright, they're covered by the provisions of fair use. The irony is I've had a lot of vendors who say, "Oh, we want to limit the number of words that can be put out there, we want to limit the number of characters." No. We don't need to do that. We don't have to have a special agreement, and in fact the irony is that of folks who are mining, and this is particularly in text mining environments, their outputs generally cite less of the text than those people who were doing close readings because their outputs are quantitative, not to mention that many of these researchers are doing close reading and computer-assisted distant reading and putting their interpretations together. Well, where do you draw the line? Do they have to follow these restrictions because they had a mining element to their research, or can they follow these because they were also doing regular just using the database? Again, we don't need to complicate things. That's why I'm advocating for this: the Basic Access Model. BAM! Thank you.

Don't Get Married to the Results: Managing Library Change in the Age of Metrics

Corey Seeman, Director, Kresge Library Services, University of Michigan

The following is a transcript of a live presentation at the 2015 Charleston Library Conference.

Corey Seeman: Thank you. Thank you very much. I'm going to spend a lot of time talking about my library and myself so I'm not going to do any introductions. I'm Corey Seeman, director of Kresge Library Services at the Ross School of Business at the University of Michigan. My presentation, "Don't Get Married to the Results: Managing Library Change in the Age of Metrics," is all about the program changes that we've gone through, and when I posted it on Twitter it went to Facebook and my stepbrother Blaine freaked out because he saw that all that came through in his feed was a Tweet or a Facebook post from me saying, "don't get married," and I mentioned to him that that would be something that my wife would present on.

So, I've been at the University of Michigan for 10 years. It will be 10 years later this month and if we want to use an altmetric that's four football coaches, so it's kind of an interesting way to think about things. So, last week I was on campus and I saw this wonderful squirrel and he just captured what I want to do. He was sort of measuring the acorn that got away. So what I'm going to do today is talk about some opening thoughts on assessment, problems with numbers, library changes and you, about Kresge Library and what we're doing—and if at any point I move away from the mic, please let me know—and then telling your story, and this is really about what we're trying to do at Kresge.

So, I am a bit of an iconoclast when it comes to assessment. I think that we can rely on our gut to be a little more definitive about what we're doing. Oh, by the way the slides are available online. There's a tiny URL that will show up again at the end. I think that assessment needs to be periodic and continual, but it can't be the sort of "hear all and end all." One of the things that was really wonderful—so I saw a colleague from Grand Valley in the audience. Grand Valley State University in Allendale, Michigan has a library that anyone would be envious of, and they had a conference this August that was fantastic: "Re-Think It: Libraries for a New Age." This is a picture of the library. It helps when Steel Case is a partner, but they really did a great job, and it was all about design thinking, which is really about empathy, which is really about understanding the end users. This is a dynamic—this is a graphic that really focuses on what our world looks like in business, and I know there are a couple business librarians here. The resources, the faculty; maybe in history it's more similar, but at least in business the student needs are different than the faculty needs. So, faculty needs include scholarly journals, articles, books, datasets, etc. Students' needs are articles, company and industry information, and market reports. The community, we work with alumni—we have some alumni resources—they are more geared toward students, so assessing becomes very tricky when we're looking at different populations with different needs. And then, finally, I was talking to my colleague from Michigan State and said all of my pets will make an appearance somewhere. This is my cat, Cosmo, and the reason why I chose this picture is because he's in a Postal Service box, and in academic campuses, I feel very strongly about this, we are on-campus monopolies. We are sort of the way that people get information and so we have to work differently. If we think about some of the frustrations that we have with IT departments, who are also on-campus monopolies, we will sort of get the same thing.

I want to talk a little bit about some problems with numbers. Okay, so it's a political season. It will continue to be a political season for one more freakin' year. Stupidity with numbers—so for those of you who are keeping score: 271,000 jobs, 5% unemployment, that's good news, unless you're Ben Carson, Donald Trump, etc., etc. So, Kohl's pricing is something I've always talked

http://dx.doi.org/10.5703/1288284316234

about in so far that it's part of the ridiculous notion of numbers when you spend $55 and realize you've saved over $200. John Oliver has a great piece on school testing that I encourage everyone to look at. And then Halloween—so we had two trick-or-treaters. We live out in the middle of nowhere; we bought a big candy bag and so we were able to give that out. Yeah, bad return investment, but happy kids so it was worth it. In my picture, that's my dog and those are my nieces. That's my dog, Flapjack. So, big data, we were talking little earlier—so Gary (Price) freaked us all out; he freaked me out about "big data" and I think that people are really excited about the possibility and the potential, but I don't really see that this is just right around the corner for us. I think that it may actually be years before we can harness some of this information so I'm not that enamored with it.

So, back to Kohl's, retail pricing is really important. So, this is a business database and we're told that for our $5,000 quarterly investment our students have downloaded $3.7 million worth of content. Now no one at University of Michigan can turn $5,000 into $3.7 million, not even Coach Harbaugh. So, I'm going to think that these numbers maybe aren't as accurate or useful. And then another thing about retail pricing: I'm not hugely enamored with a cost per use. I think it's a good metric, it's good to know, but it doesn't really tell the whole story. I did notice George's Loan Company on King Street: "Money to loan on articles of value." So, if we just had pawn shops near our campuses we would know what books are valuable. And there's my cat, Wanda, proving once and for all that cats prefer print to "e." So, we are trying to connect a usage with value, but it's not always clear cut and I think that we're trying to find, we're trying to answer the question, we might be burning daylight. So, more problems with numbers: we are very good about making tiny cuts. If we go flatline we all know that we have to reduce resources so we make small incremental changes and then taken holistically or taken over the course of a matter of years we end up with some big problems, that we really changed our fundamental value and that we drop below the just noticeable thresholds. This is a can of Chase and Sanborn, which was a very popular coffee brand and now it's really kind of the worst coffee you can get, so the small changes over the years can lead to bigger issues.

This is something I found from *The Economist* very recently. Most of us flew here, and it's very sad, but treating flyers well apparently is bad for airlines' bottom line. This gentleman here is cramped in his seat. I flew on a 757 and I didn't have half that much room so I'm not sure how he did well, but when we sit there we have a service that we are providing to a campus and the more that we do, it does provide some benefit but it's not really adding sometimes to our bottom line and then change happens. So this is the Chase Furniture Company, which is one of three furniture stores north of here on King. I'm at the Hyatt Place so I've been walking back and forth and it's now the Charleston College of Law. One furniture store just closed and the other is still open, probably not for long. This is Reed Brothers, which is a fabric store that I went into. There is a sign that says "stereo department," and I think it's a trap, so I didn't go down that road—so I'm not sure exactly where that path, I'm not sure exactly what it is. But this is the dynamic of what we're dealing with. Very quickly through this, Katherine (Skinner) talked this morning about "Moneyball." I've done some stories about or some articles about baseball history as well back in the day, talking about how we spent more time talking about contests then context, and so that's really where I think the metrics do us poorly.

So, in summary here when we think of library statistics a lot of us think of items, access, usage, headcount. A lot of us have been talking about what are the outcomes not the outputs, and we're trying to make connections that are really hard to find. What is the library contribution toward retention, for example? What is the library contribution to faculty's success and to tenure promotion? And I think that there are a lot of issues here that are really very tricky. And then we also love to oversimplify our numbers. So, this was from two winters ago. It was −21°. I drove the car and it had a thermometer in it; well it was my wife's car, so everyone loves dashboard indicators and they do a really, really great job of sort of dumbing down what's going on, simplifying it. It does a really good job and I'll get back to this at the end—it does a great job of telling you how you're running, but it doesn't necessarily tell you about environments at your institution.

Library, change, and you. So, change of course is a very personal experience, and your mileage may vary and we all have change from a very distinct point of view. If you ask anyone in the library field 35 years ago when the conference started, they would tell you "Oh my gosh, things are changing so much with the OCLC. We used to do such curated cataloging records." I believe right now we're at the tip of real systemic change. I'm in a departmental library, a small 19 person library that's now even smaller. Medical libraries, science libraries, and business libraries have all been contracted. One of the things—this is the Skillman Branch, 1931 in Detroit. It is a beautiful building, and across the façade it says, "The fountain of wisdom flows through books." It is a really beautiful sentiment and certainly the case in 1931. But, the changing use of space is something that is really important. Steven Bell, who talked at—he gave a keynote a couple of years ago—did a great column not that long ago about an external forces. We always talk about internal change that we want to do and that's great, but the external forces are the bigger issues and he talked about Sweet Briar closing, or closing and then not closing, and LaSalle University dealing with dramatic decreases in tuition dollars—this is just my thought in summing it up: our virtue is not our salvation. That's what I said: it was me.

So about Kresge, I'm going to go through this quickly so I can move on. So we're an independent library. We were built in the 1980s, and when you have a library built in the 1980s you have lots of stacks and you have lots of items. We were open 108 hours a week. We had seating for 700 students, very visible, very citifying. We originally had a collection of 140,000; then it was reduced to 70, but we were in a constant state of library erosion. Here are some pictures, very crowded, and it wasn't like this was the one day a year it was crowded. This is pretty much Monday afternoon to Thursday at five. At U of M, Thursday is your drinking night so everyone—Thursday night the place clears out and then Friday as people sober up they come back in so it's usually around 10 or 11. We don't have that anymore and then in the bottom you can barely make it out but that's a giant mascot, Sprout, because General Foods was recruiting that day. I'm going to skip over this because they just created—I'm going to read this really quickly and I apologize. This just came from some Ross faculty who are writing about the Ross project, and I want to talk about it positively so I'm going to read this. This just came yesterday: "The second challenge involves the downsizing of Kresge library. As a result of the construction of the new building on the Ross School Campus and the demolition of the former library location, Kresge Library lost its entire physical space. The library was no longer a place with **stacks of books**," and I'll explain why it's bold, 'and journals nor a "go-to" place for students to study. The leader of the library relayed his unit's choice to avoid soaking, rebelling or resisting. Instead, the positive pillar was consciously employed as a reminder to look at this process in a particular way towards focusing on what we might have and what is working right rather than what we lost. The library director was able to create a positive vision for an ephemeral library,' and explained that, "including publishing academic journal articles, his vision on the library of the future. These articles and his leadership allowed Ross to become a pioneer in creating the library of the future." Okay, so two things. So first thing, I'm going to go to the second thing, I'm referring to this as the ethereal library, not ephemeral library, so I made that clear. I grew up in New Jersey so the fact that I can say anything is pretty awesome, and I asked them to change "stacks of books" because "stacks of books" sounds like we're an episode of "Hoarders" yet to come. But I think this captures what we're doing. It's not on the slides that are available because again I just got it but I guess it will be coming out in print at some point soon.

This is our library. Twenty-seven thousand feet, now we're around five and change. There are six group study rooms across the top. There are a few tables, a few terminals for Bloomberg and things like that, and then we have open office behind. There is very little room for stacks; almost nothing. We have room for about 200 books, which incidentally is the same number that the Mission San Juan Capistrano had in 1834, so I thought that was cool. I think they were trying to prove a different point. When we first started designing this we were really trying to bend over backwards to create a space that students could still use, and then it dawned on us: we can do it. There's not enough real estate. So we have to sort of realign. Failure, very importantly, is an option that we can deal with. In the discussion that we had with the leadership team we talked about the academic nature of the collection. We talked about the fact that 90%, our estimate, did not have a digital counterpart, and if we were to get rid of it, it's gone, and people asked the question "well, maybe it wasn't that important if it didn't have a digital counterpart." And of course in this crowd you're like "AHHH!" But, you know, for people trying to fit a lot of building in a small space it becomes a question that they ask. We did have some redundancy with the main library and our colleagues at the U of M have been great—they actually took on our unique content. We did have circulation of around 10,000 to 14,000 a year over the last couple of years. It wasn't insignificant; it was actually pretty decent. But, the big thing for us I explained is that if we go this route I can't collect print. I can't collect nonelectronic format. I won't have the space and in the end that was determined to be okay. So, in the end we lost our space. So, we're shifting from a library of space to a library service, and there are some very, very interesting things.

To follow what Katherine (Skinner) said this morning, it is not only our moment of loss, but it is also our moment of opportunity. So to talk about those things sort of at the same point, this is actually—people have heard about moving of the tree. That's the tree they moved to the front of the school. That's the last cart of books that rolled out of the building, and the library is to the right of the tree. Libraries are going through all sorts of shifting right now. A lot of librarians are taking on more teaching roles instead of being bibliographers, and it really is a whole lot of change going on. The library did not close, although I was asked last night "oh, you're here? I thought your library closed." It's totally legit. I can understand that and what I'm saying is that we didn't close—we lost our lease. So, what are we doing now? We are trying to be very entrepreneurial. We have a long history of doing that and we're doing that with all except the bottom one. Entrepreneurs will always talk about a new approach to a problem, new worlds, new market opportunity, creative thinking, empathetic focus, willingness to fail. The exit strategy, and that came up in the session yesterday; we don't have an exit strategy right now, so that's really how we're just a little different, but what we wanted to determine was how do we tell the story? So we only got the 200 books. Aerostats are a breeze. I've got that going for me, and we used our budget really to reframe how things are going. The change of library as a place to library as a service was huge. Gertrude Stein's quote about the Oakland of her youth, "There is no there there," is really about not being able to recognize the place that you worked and the place that you used. For us the big thing is the loss of established identity, and so, you know, you see a building that's open and it's great to and that's all wonderful.

So, a lot of the things that I want to talk about for the next 10 minutes or so really stem from my dad and here we are, here he is. My dad was a great innovator in the New Jersey retail space. He owned a clothing store, and it was one of the first true discounters in New Jersey and it really kind of started a movement with discount malls and so the retail focus really helps us, helps me at least, frame what we're trying to accomplish. Balancing is really important. Academic librarians try to balance from today and tomorrow, build the collection for now and down the road. There are opportunities to do that but we're not really in a great shape to do that, and I think it's kind of a big obligation for us right now and so we're really focused on the short-term, which really creates a very, very different kind of library. Thinking about the future is really a good thing. It's not something that we can easily do right now, and here's a squirrel burying nuts for later and squirrels; by the way, do remember where they have put those nuts as they cash them all over the grounds.

The big thing for us is that the school—our mission is the mission of the school. So the school went through and they were talking about positive pillar; there are four pillars: action, analytic, boundaryless, and positive. And everything that we do what Ross School of Business needs to funnel into one of those. So, we do not have our own specific mission at Kresge. We basically say "it's that," and so what we've done is we've created a document that says "for each of these four things, here is how we support it," and we control that but it really ties us to what the leadership team wants, which I think benefits us at the end.

Connecting with stakeholders is really important. We had conversations with faculty, staff, and students, ironically after the decision was made, for whatever reason. The communication was such that it would all happen very, very quickly. This is the Kresge staff, the great people I work with. Actually, we first found out that this might be happening during a shifting process, and we were integrating some books and we couldn't really stop in the middle of it so we had to go through it even though we knew it was possible—we did this in the summer of 2013. By going through this work we actually were able to create a clean slate and try to figure out what is needed by our community, and we used the mission sort of as a North Star reference and we moved in that direction.

One of the things that's really important, although we are hard to find and a lot of people think we are closed and there's a lot of confusion about Kresge, communication is, of course, a huge issue. We're still central to reference, and our reference numbers are pretty consistent and actually maybe even trending up. We have an expanded role. We have some capacity that we have been able to redirect to reference, and so we have actually more people doing reference than before and this is one of the academic deans and one of the faculty members—very important in MAP, which is our multidisciplinary action program where we have our embedded librarian program. So, you know, if our reference numbers imploded in addition to our space they would be making some dramatic changes, but the service again saved us. We've always strived for sort of the high-class problem. The high-class problem is one of trying to figure out capacity versus the low-class problem trying to figure out how to get people to use it. We have way too many low-class problems in publishing, librarianship, etc. This is our annex. We actually couldn't find space in the Visgo for this, so the great people over at Law set us up, which is actually symbolic. I'm looking over my friend, Breezy, from Michigan State, as their business library is also in the Law, so we have that in common. They're good friends at East Lansing. So we were doing what the school needed, so a lot of people are erring toward sort of creating—we want to teach classes, we want to be more educators, would want to do bigger and loftier things. What we determined was that there was an opportunity to go in and actually create, have the library manage a program that the school wanted, and it was an exam and assignment program so that they could hand back exams—the students could look at it but they had to be returned. This was a service that was run through our faculty support unit, and they couldn't handle it so was folded into the library, which actually was great for the circulation staff who didn't have anything to circulate. So, it actually did fantastic things because it was a service that the school wanted. Most importantly from my perspective, it saved jobs and it produced a real value in it was a real win—we needed one.

From our exit survey—we don't survey but the school surveys the students; we have some MBA student exit surveys—the good news is: "Kresge libraries are amazing"; "D" who is one of our employees: "D" was a great help for one of my projects"; "Shout out to Sally, who was beyond phenomenal during our MAP project"; Laura Burnish gets a lot of praise here as well. "Kresge team might be one of the best at the school." That's all good. On the downside: "Kresge being closed for the second year was a big loss"; "Will it get better in the new building?" Maybe, maybe not. One of my favorite ones was there were lot of people complaining about the library being closed and one person complained about the hours of the library, and so, well, if it's closed are there hours? But, the students were equating Kresge as space, not service, and this is actually something UNCG Greensboro's Tim Bucknell, at a presentation that I went to yesterday, was talking about: how people who are coming into the library are not using materials; they are not using a lot of the materials but they are using the flat surface. They're using it as a place to study and that is what our students wanted, and that was a great session with Rick (Anderson).

And so the time horizon of our work has really changed and this has been really tricky. I have realigned us for the short-term and so it's the short tail. Okay, it's all I got. Speaking of metrics that don't mean anything, I have over 17,000 pictures on Flickr of University of Michigan campus squirrels, so every so often you'll see a number that doesn't make any sense and that's two of them. So, what we're trying to do is we're trying to share our accomplishments as they resonate with our stakeholders. It's not aligned with the profession, it's not aligned with tradition, but it's going to, actually, I think put us in a better spot down the road. From the budget request we have shared the ways that we manage these spaces and these issues. We changed our names to Kresge Library Services because Kresge Library connotes a place. Services at the end connotes what people can expect to find there. We moved to electronic course materials thru study.net. Reference location after-hours help has moved a lot, but our reference interaction has actually increased, I think.

The last thing I want to talk about a little bit: here's a picture of me when I was four—I'm the little one. That's my older brother and my dad in 1968. When you're going through dramatic changes, there is a great tendency to go back and think about the way things were. We don't have the opportunity to do that, and I think a lot of people if they're in this position may not have this. I've given staff a lot of flexibility to choose their own path. Some people I know are looking and that's fine. It's a different kind of library, and it's not the library that everyone necessarily wants to work at. We want to consider services that are going to meet the needs of the school rather than ones that we need to sell with. The title comes from something my dad always told me: "Don't get married to the results." And it's really—I think very, very useful because it is that, and it was always something he would say whether something happened good or bad, and sure he got married four times in his life so maybe there's a different message here. But one of the things that we've especially found in big change—we've decided that we weren't going to start with any predetermined measures of success, so we didn't have—we needed reference to go up by "X" amount; it doesn't really matter. What we wanted to do was we wanted to look at what we were doing, tweak, and be nimble enough to change. We look at usage stats really as indicators, not validator's, and so we try to tell that story as best as we can. And having the appearance of success doesn't mean you actually have it, and so that's one of the things that I think we need to be really careful about: not to say that we need to live in a paranoid world, but we need to live in constant sort of reflection of what our schools need. And you know if too many metrics like school testing, getting back to that reference to John Oliver, could be at the expense of other elements. If we wanted people to use our resources we could thrust the discovery layer down their throat. It's not always what people need, and so it's really a matter of trying to be attuned to what our patrons need and don't let yourself be judged by what we didn't accomplish. I mean, I have a very patient boss right now. I have a different boss and I will have a different boss in January, but they are very, very good about understanding the role that we are going into. And then one closing thought: so one block from here, if you go down Calhoun and you go to Bay, this happened. This was my mother's car. My mother used to live here and she'll live here again, and so we were driving back from Fort Sumter. It was our first visit to town and we were rear-ended, and so when people love talking about dashboard indicators, I will share that dashboard indicators are wonderful to tell you how you're doing but it doesn't necessarily tell you about the idiot behind you. That is a very, very tricky situation on our campuses, on our universities, on our communities, etc., so being aware of all of that is something that is really important. The slides are right here, a tiny URL CHS 15 Cory, and with that we're at 11 o'clock so if you need to leave early to get your next session, that's great. If you have questions, we will do that. So, thank you very much for your attention.

GOBI, YBP, and Overdrive: Changes in the E-Book Distribution Landscape

Kari Paulson, VP Market Development, ProQuest

Steve Potash, President and CEO, Overdrive, Inc.

Dan Tonkery, President and CEO, Content Strategy

Moderator: Nancy Herther, Sociology Librarian, University of Minnesota

The Following is a Transcript of a Live Presentation at the 2015 Charleston Library Conference.

Nancy Herther: Thank you very much and I hope you will all find places to sit here. Hopefully this is going to be a wonderful session. We've designed this so that we have wonderful people up here with great experience, but at the same time we want to know your questions. First, a note on the title. We certainly are going to be looking at all of the major sorts of changes and issues that are coming up from all of the vendors. Obviously we couldn't fit all of the vendors up here, so in planning this program I tried to put together three people that I knew could do the job, and I'm hoping that those of you out in the audience who are working with other companies that are involved with this feel free to join the conversation and the discussion. As Charles was saying, we're planning on cutting this off so that we have a minimum of 10 minutes at the end because we really want this to be a conversation, a discussion with you.

So, the plot thickens when it comes to e-books. We're hearing more and more about them. The penetration is obviously there. In the *New York Times,* however, not that there isn't controversy, just in September there was a big discussion and articles concerning the e-book sales slippage, the fact that the data is still a little bit bumpy. We're not seeing that continuous movement and just a couple days ago *Simon & Schuster* reported that their e-book sales are down and the American Booksellers Association released their information, and in their information what they found is that for some of their publications the e-book versions are not doing well. On the other hand, the American Booksellers Association has now added a "Buy Now" button for their IndieBound series so that it's easier for people going into the database to locate books from one of the members of the Association to be able to get it right away in various versions. So, it's very difficult to be able to say anything dramatic, or I shouldn't say that—it's easy to say things that are dramatic, I guess, but conclusively about e-book sales because we really don't have good statistics on this yet. There is an awful lot of self-publishing and other things going on, and we just haven't really gotten the kind of statistical evidence that we need to feel confident about saying things. As far as other trends going on, we're not going to cover them here, they're but interesting, because there's always something going on with e-books. Both Poland and Germany are starting to advocate for the sale or resale of e-books, the development of a used e-book market, and in the EU and countries that might be a little bit easier—they have a different structure than we have here. Also, about a month ago Waterstones decided that they're not going to sell the Kindle because the sales of their print books are going up so high. The Kindle hasn't been as strong so they've decided to sort of pull that for the time being. Statistics that came out in terms of book sales for e-books find that the majority of e-books in the United States, approximately 75%, are still coming from Amazon so the end-user market is still extremely important in this area.

And lastly, I guess, I do want to mention some of the people that aren't up here. Amazon, obviously, is a major player. It would be wonderful if they would be willing to come to conferences like this but you can send them an e-mail and they don't respond. Same thing for Alibaba. They're a big, huge corporation, an important corporation moving into this area with very, very deep pockets. They're not here. I want to apologize as

http://dx.doi.org/10.5703/1288284316235

far as EBSCO not being here to directly talk about YBP and the acquisition of that, but I hope if there are representatives here that you will feel happy to kind of join in our conversation. I guess one last thing that I want to point out in terms of companies, again, talking about the amazing importance of companies that don't usually attend this conference, the front page today of the *USA Today* talks about the five companies and between Amazon and Alphabet—we always know it is Google—that's well over 50% of the online market these days in terms of online dollars so there are many parts of the e-book arena that we're not able to bring to the fore here. However, I'm hoping because again picking wonderful people here who have experience and who have been here for a long time I think is going to give us that depth of experience; context based on the past but as well as give you some insight into what we all see happening. Certainly I think we are going to be seeing a lot more internationalization. I think we already are and again you'll be hearing about that.

We're going to start with Steve Potash and he is another long timer in the CD-ROM and even other sorts of areas going back to the 1980s as I do. Overdrive is definitely the leading digital content provider and has certainly not only announced a lot of global expansion back at the Frankfurt Book Show—a lot of global expansion with some of their institutional buyers—but they're now in more than 50 countries, which is pretty amazing, and they're offering content in 50 languages. So they are doing very, very well. Steve has been head of Overdrive from the beginning. He still is, and recently the big news, of course, that bodes well for the future, especially for that internationalization, is the fact that they were purchased by Rakuten which is a major Japanese firm. He will be our first speaker today, talking about what he sees for the industry and for what's happening.

I'm going to give the other introductions as well kind of starting out here rather than walking back and forth. As you can see, we only had room for three people here. And the next person who is going to be speaking is Kari Paulson, and she is also a relative newcomer from the standpoint of some of us, but when it comes to e-books she has been around for a long time. She is a founding member of EBL and started working with e-books in 1998, back when it was in Australia, and she moved to San Francisco with the acquisition of the company by ProQuest, so she is now a vice president of market development for books with ProQuest. And ProQuest of course also has Ebrary, and they've been making some other interesting corporate announcements in the last few months that again point to a lot of not just stability but a lot of positive, optimistic options for the future, so I'm very happy that she's here to join us.

The last speaker is somebody else who's been involved in e-books going back to the floppy disk era and so on is Dan Tonkery. And Dan has been a librarian for 45 years. Most of his career involved the automation of technical services, and when he shifted to the commercial world working with the National Library of Medicine, UCLA Library, he was the AUL for technical services. He has run different companies as president or CEO, but for the last seven years he has been the president of Content Strategies and he works with a variety of different companies, individuals, firms, venture capital, and large libraries, and he is someone who has been graced with a lot of wisdom when it comes to what is happening with books and certainly with e-books and with the e-book industry. So I'm going to turn this over to Steve Potash and I hope that you remember that at the end we're going to be saving—and I'm going to be sitting in the front row to make sure that everybody stays pretty much on time here because we really want your input and your questions and your insights in terms of where the industry of e-books is going and taking us. So, thank you, and Steve, for coming.

Steve Potash: Thank you. Good morning. Thank you again, Nancy. I'm delighted to be here, and as most of you know Overdrive is best known for the success we've had listening to public librarians and delivering what they've asked for—for what your communities and what your readers want. Let me just—so I won't have to give too much background on Overdrive, who in our audience has either had experience through a public library or school with Overdrive's product? Thank you.

Okay, so we'll just go fast. What you may not know though is in addition to the 93% of the North American public libraries we serve, our fastest growth is in education. Now we tackled K–12 first because of the need and how public librarians are helping parents and teachers and their communities and, as a result of that over the last two or three years, our collection and our services and our tools and the access models are now giving us the wherewithal to start coming back into higher-ed and academic, a market which today we serve. We serve hundreds of universities and research and national libraries all over the globe and I'm excited to be here at the Charleston Conference to meet with the academic publishers and talk to some of the universities who are looking to supplement your online databases and journals with every other kind of book with one purpose in mind: go where the readers are, and mobile first. This is kind of what is driving us.

Without talking too much about what Overdrive is doing, when Nancy asked me to focus my comments on one or two areas, looking at the topic of the session, let's talk about two big trends and where the market is going. For e-books it has to be number one: a proliferation of new access models for content. Overdrive set up our B2B Marketplace for librarians and teachers and educators and corporate knowledge centers to acquire permission for copyrighted digital books, digital audiobooks, streaming video, magazines, and newspapers, and it primarily started by evangelizing to the publishers and the rights holders under our most popular model: "One Book One User." I will say we now have hundreds of publishers that permit simultaneous access. In the school model and for the school market we now have major trade educational academic publishers giving us what I call "classroom sets." So, bulk discount so every student for the quarter, for the semester, for the school year, has their own copy. We are now proliferating what we call the "book club model." So if everybody reads or a city or Mayors Book Club reads, we want low-cost simultaneous access. We also are live now with what we call CPC, cost per checkout, so it's pay as you go; we've done that with the Hollywood Studios because we have to pay on every few. We are now with patron-driven acquisition and in the public library we call it "recommend to library" and let the librarian mediate whether they want to add these titles are not. So this is one of the most exciting trends, and I can tell you now that we've had most of the trade market, and of course the educational and the academic markets know digital books in public, and academic and school libraries increase their brand, their value proposition, which helps reinforce print sales and other content. We are now evangelizing that you should make your content available under any model the buyer wants. So it's really exciting that I have some publishers that didn't even allow library lending 5 years ago, and now some of their bestselling in prints and titles can be bought under three or four different options. We're just saying to give the customers more ways to buy your products, and you will sell more, whether it's here or abroad.

Access model is great, and by the way, just to mention we are very proud that we're learning some of the academic and research and professional markets. Three years ago we signed an agreement with LexisNexis, and Overdrive is in almost every court system, law firm, law school. I was just at Harvard Law School Library, and Overdrive has a very simple way of going forward. We ask our customers, we asked our librarians: how do you want it to work? And this is something that has kind of driven our evangelizing the flexible content models and improving the user experience, and when Nancy talked about the landscape, the big three or four that are making the markets: Google, Amazon, Apple, and who else did you mention? Microsoft! Let's throw them in for good measure. I'm proud to say because this is where people work and live and play, if you go to Bing.com and search for a book, Sycamore Road Book—above the fold because Overdrive also believes in open industry standards. We helped invent and popularize that e-pub file format; we are very big fans of HM05 and at developer.overdrive.com, your library, your institution, or your vendors can get no-cost open API's, so Microsoft, Google, Amazon, and who is the fourth? Apple! We are either partnering with them for deep integration so their users can discover and utilize library and research materials on their native devices or partnering with them with apps and then Chromebooks as they go around the world into classrooms.

The second topic that Nancy suggested and especially as a result of the change of ownership we enjoyed earlier this year—and that wasn't the first time—five years ago Overdrive was fortunate enough to have a private equity fund invested in us, but with a private equity fund you have a kind of three or four year window, so we were in our fourth year. We were always profitable, growing great, but it was time for them to go. Don't repeat this. They're wonderful people. So when you get to a strategic partner like Rakuten, who is one of the global leaders in e-commerce, and they have a visionary founder and CEO, Mikitani Hiroshi—they have just provided us the long-term capability based on their pillars of digital content, and they own a variety of streaming video companies around the world and digital book assets—that has helped accelerate our ability to aggregate content and enter some new markets. But even before the recent transaction, we were very fortunate that we developed from day one a vision that we don't know what the business model will be. We don't know what container we will read the books from and so we will have to develop multilingual, multicurrency, open systems, and I'm proud to say that the fastest-growing areas of content for us are non-English materials in the US library. You go to the San Francisco Public Library, and they have 10,000 simultaneous release Chinese e-books for readers of all ages, and Overdrive is selling English-language material worldwide into institutions, international schools, and national libraries. It couldn't be a more exciting time to bring digital content, premium digital content, enhanced digital content with the new e-pub 3 standard now that we are doing with one click, without an app—synchronized children's book or language learning with the words highlighting and the pages turning, engaging readers who want to learn a language or for young children or supporting literacy campaigns. I can mention some of my favorites but many of them are very silly, but we do also have Superman, Avengers, and Frozen from Disney. We're excited about reading for all readers of all ages, and it's that instant access and gratification that we're excited to bring to higher-ed and academic markets. I will also just quickly mention that Overdrive has been extraordinarily proud to be partnering with the ALA in their campaign "Libraries Transform," under the leadership of the current ALA president, Sari Feldman. She has set forth a vision and a mission for all divisions of ALA to reimagine and challenge ourselves to deliver value to our communities, value to our readers, and I'm very proud to be working directly with ALA and many of their divisions and supporting a series of vision there. I am done. I'm going to keep under budget here on my time, Nancy, and I look forward to the questions or a chance to chat afterward. Thank you.

Kari Paulson: Thank you, Steve. Hello, everyone. So, one thing—when I found out I was going to be participating on a panel with Steve Potash I thought, "Great!" because Steve and I are fellow travelers in the e-book world, and we actually were previously partners, our companies, when I worked for e-books.com, which is where EBL developed out of Australia way back when we worked with Overdrive as a wholesaler. They supplied some of the e-books we sold in the retail space, so we've sort of known each other and continue to bump into each other along the way over many, many years, and it's really interesting to be standing here right now sort of where we are today. I don't know that either one of us could have anticipated that this is where we would be at this point in time. So, it is—I was thinking about it as I was sitting here how fun it's been to sort of be involved in e-books and their nascence, and to be here today seeing the things that are happening. At ProQuest, for example, who would have ever thought that the e-book companies would be buying the print companies. It was unthinkable in the days that we were starting, and you can forget how fun it is on a daily basis but it really is exciting to be a part of this evolution.

So, I'll talk a little bit about ProQuest and our acquisitions, and I know there are many acquisitions, or not many but some recent acquisitions, that don't have to do with books; I'm not going to focus on those. My focus is really going to be on what we're doing in the book space and some of what's driving that. But I can say as somebody who's come into ProQuest as a recently acquired business that I do understand the drivers for why ProQuest acquires the companies we do. We do have a primary mission to empower researchers and enable them to reach superior outcomes, and the primary way we do that is by focusing the institutions that serve these researchers. And we are continually scanning the landscape in our services and our products and in what libraries are asking for to identify the gaps. And that certainly has been a primary driver when it's come to books or e-books. So, in early 2011, for those of you who don't know the progression of the e-books and books acquisitions at ProQuest, ProQuest acquired Ebrary, and Ebrary at the time was one of our—as EBL—one of our primary competitors, and I remember at the time thinking, "Oh, my gosh; it's over. I'll just go home. Stop. Put our tools down. It's all going to be over." But, of course, that didn't happen. We continued to work in slightly different ways and we had different strengths. In early 2013 ProQuest then acquired EBL. One of the primary drivers for acquiring EBL—well ProQuest already had an e-book platform, Ebrary—was that we had different strengths and we had developed some different products, different access models, and different functionalities that were really complementary to each other, and by bringing them together, I think it was identified that we could have a much stronger offering for libraries. We also had some geographical differences, so as a company that had grown out of Australia, EBL certainly had strengths in North America, but we were particularly strong in Europe and the UK and Australia and the Austral-Asian market, so it really was a nice complementary fit for ProQuest to be able to expand its support and services in all the regions it was operating in. So, as a part of that acquisition we've been bringing these two products together. I can also say that the reason ProQuest bought these multiple book companies or e-book companies has not been just a market play. If it were, what you'd see is getting rid of the company that they bought and those people, just bringing those products in and then not necessarily bringing in the diversity of different functions. What we've seen instead or what we've done instead is—I as the president of EBL was actually brought in as the GM of the e-books group at ProQuest, and my role was to help bring Ebrary and EBL together and I'm still obviously involved in that process. But we also kept the development team, the sales team, the account managers, and created roles so there wasn't a single person who left or was let go as a part of that process, and that I can say is a consistent pattern I've seen with ProQuest and the acquisitions. It really is about expanding functionality and filling those gaps.

So, in early this year, 2015, ProQuest acquired Coutts. So with Coutts, that is the print business and MyiLibrary. So now three e-book businesses and a print business, and you know to some people it may be a head scratcher as we were watching this transition from print to "e," why would an e-business buy a print business? But I think, and we've obviously seen this with some of our peers in the marketplace with EBSCO and YBP, what was the driver for this? I can tell you that the primary driver was to fill the gaps, the gaps that we were hearing from our customers, the gaps that we were feeling in terms of the solutions that we needed to provide and I think the reason why, you know there was a point in time that we used to sort of back at EBL think "Oh, wouldn't it be awesome if we could go buy a print company, wouldn't that just turn the industry on its head and be so shocking?" Of course it was really out of reach at the time, but I think as we are progressing in this transition to "e" to "p" or "p" to "e" we are hitting more of an inflection point where these gaps in workflow, really what's happened, especially in the academic library space, is e-books have kind of been rammed into a print workflow as best as they could. And being able to see what's here or there, it's gotten quite complex and complicated, and we're at a point that when we look at journals, we don't talk about e-journals and print journals so much the way we did 5 or 10 years ago—we talk about journals. I think we are starting to get to that point with books, and there is need for more consolidated acquisition, selection, discovery management workflow. That was the primary driver for the acquisition. And we've also got to a point I think where you know the print companies were previously buying the e-companies, the e-companies are now buying the print companies because as we're, I mean at ProQuest we had on our strategic roadmap a plan to build out a number of workflow solutions that we knew were missing and needed to be filled. There was the option to do that organically and slowly over time. We did and continue to partner with other companies to build those solutions between our companies, but we found that it would be a much faster route to market to be able to acquire a company like Coutts and work together really under the covers to bring these solutions together. We also with Coutts saw it as an opportunity again to really invest in those geographical strengths that we had, especially in markets like the UK and Europe, where Coutts is a very strong print supplier.

So, back to that question of partnerships, although we have acquired multiple companies and as a part of our strategy to bring the right solutions, that isn't at the expense of our partnerships, so we are continuing and we believe that partnerships are still imperative in terms of bringing the right solutions to you as a community and as our customers. So we continue to partner with YBP, OCLC, all of the places that you are asking us to, all of the vendors and suppliers you are asking us to work with, to ensure that what you're doing in your library, you are able to still have a seamless and satisfactory workflow.

So, I think those are the primary things I wanted to cover. I know we want to have a lot of questions. One other point, and I know this has come up, is the question about, well, what about competition? There's a lot of consolidation and I know there's a lot of concern in the marketplace around the rapid nature of some of the acquisitions we've seen. We see it in publishing: publishing houses, the smaller publishers, and this was talked about by Taylor and Francis in our session yesterday. Some of the smaller publishing houses are not in a position to invest, and so they are at a point in time where they're willing to be acquired by some of the bigger publishing companies. When I look around and I see that while there is consolidation—I shouldn't even use the word consolidation, but there is some merging of companies and services—it opens the door and it creates a gap for other companies at the edges to step in and I think we've seen that a little bit with e-books where we have JSTOR and Project Muse and some of these other companies stepping up and becoming a larger part. We're hearing more and more of libraries talking about them as platforms and solutions. So, there is a bit of an organic process involved, and I hope that more small companies continue to come in, drive some innovation, and keep it a diverse marketplace.

One final comment: sorry I said the last comment was a final one, but also as I was thinking about these "e" and "p" acquisitions, as print sales are declining and e-sales are growing there is for all of us—it's beneficial that the upside of "e" is still being invested back into the "p" workflow and support for those formats because we had primarily had our workflows driven by the print suppliers and the print workflow solutions. As print declines, the ability to invest in building out increasing amount of workflow solutions for electronic becomes more difficult. So, with the combination of "e" and "p," under the same company we are able to continue to invest that upside back into a more holistic workflow across books in general. Thank you.

Dan Tonkery: Well, good morning. My presentation is perhaps a little different. I'm not going to tell you about the great features of the company that I have or anything like that. I'm going to talk a little more about numbers. So, if you don't like numbers you can go ahead and fall asleep right now and it will not disturb me. I've been in this business for 45 years, and for 15 of those years I was a librarian. I was a real card-carrying librarian. I worked 10 years in the National Library of Medicine. I worked at UCLA, and then I fell off the wagon and I went to the dark side, and the last 30 years of my career has gotten darker and darker and darker and there is a group of people I don't know—and none of you probably know any of these people who work in the shadows of our industry. They're the people who buy and sell the companies for the companies that we're talking to, and they don't get up at a meeting and I've seen probably 10 of them at this meeting. They're the people who are running around talking in the corners. They're the people who are having private meetings in rooms. You never see them. You don't know who they are, but that's the group that somehow I have fallen in with, you know. The thieves, horse traders—anything you want to call them is probably fine just as long as you don't ever mention their names. And so consolidation in the book industry or any serial publishing has gone on for many years. The historical trend was subscription agents bought other subscription agents. Book vendors bought books vendors and publishers bought publishers, and that's the way we've operated for the last 30 or 40 years, and then there's been a change in our community and I think that change is the one that many of you may not even recognize or what's going on. You may have heard their names and I think that the consolidation now that you see out there is not being driven by the market. It is being driven by a group, a very select group, of venture firms. This is venture plays. This is not, you know—I can tell you almost with certainty that EBSCO didn't wake up one morning and say, "Oh, we should buy Yankee today!" You know, it didn't happen that way, okay? You know what happened—Baker & Taylor in 2006 was bought by Castle Harlem partners, and they paid $455 million in 2006. They expected great things. Baker & Taylor had been owned by four other venture firms, so they keep—a hundred million dollars sells to one group for two hundred, and then the two hundred sells—anyhow, Castle Harlem and their great wisdom paid $455 million for something that didn't even have the lipstick on the pit bull, you know? They sort of looked at the tail and thought, "Oh, that's a nice ass." So, they paid $466 million for something that probably wasn't worth half that. So, what do you do? Okay. For 2 years they took this pony around and tried to sell it. I mean, they dressed it up, put new coloring; they colored in some of the dark spots hoping that they could find a buyer for this thing called Yankee, and there were multiple people bidding and sure enough EBSCO won the bid. Now why would EBSCO pay a shit-load of money, in my world, for something that probably wasn't quite worth all of that? They bought that because, believe it or not, Yankee holds, and I'm talking about the academic market not the school and public library—forget that market, that's not a market that I pay attention to—84% of the US market, academic market, is controlled by Yankee. Good deal. So, but in the end of the day, Yankee generates a significant amount of money and pays back half of the investment that Castle Harlem has paid. So, okay, they are feeling a whole lot better now because now they only have a couple hundred million invested in Baker & Taylor instead of half a billion, so that works well. Well, as soon as that happens, ProQuest is not dead, yet. They decide that, "Oh, Coutts would be a good fit for us. Oh man, that's really good." Well, it only has about 15% of the market. I'm not sure what you can do with that one way or another. I mean, and the people at Ingram in Nashville, when they put that on the loading dock and shut the door and held their breath hoping, "Someone take it off our hands!" it was exciting.

So anyhow, we get into the e-book world and we've been talking about the big players, the big players—nobody says 75% of the e-book revenue in the United States is controlled directly by the publishers. Not Ebrary, not Yankee, not anybody else. Just understand that 75%, in some cases it's higher than that, of the total e-book sales are controlled directly by the publisher, and that number seems to be increasing. Part of the reason I think is number one: better price, and number two: often DRM free. So, I thought, you know "Gee!" I surveyed 15 of the large STM publishers to get their numbers, and it actually went from 60% to 85% so 75%—sort of a ballpark number but, you know, you talk to a Springer sales rep. Or you talk to an Elsevier sales rep. And you say, "What are you selling today?" and they'll say, "Well, everybody has the journals. But we're selling a lot of e-books." And I said, "Well, how are you selling those?" "Well, direct." That is a direct sale, direct sale, direct sale. So, all of these other companies, and you worry about the big three or whatever it is, are dealing with less than 20% of the market, and then you'll find out that if you talk to some of the big science publishers, they don't even make their entire list available to aggregators and it's like you have to call the publisher and say, "Okay, I want these books." "Okay, you can have these books, but these three you have to buy through an aggregator." So it's a little crazy but everybody is fighting over this very tiny portion of the market, and I'm not sure that that's going to change. Except to have more stuff go to the publishers and so then what you also see is that Amazon is not asleep at the wheel and so Amazon is gradually ranking up their library sales and you'll see that if you talk to the university presses, 40% of the University presses' sales today are through Amazon, and their largest e-book format is Kindle. So, there's a tremendous amount of, you know, several of the large presses, and I'm not talking about Oxford or Cambridge because those are really not university presses and what we consider a university press. I'm talking about places like California or Michigan or Rutgers or whoever else—40% of the sales through Amazon with an increasing; I mean, it's almost to the point where academic libraries are no longer the principal sales channel for a University Press. Okay?

So, anyhow, as I said, I'm more about the numbers and I think that from my standpoint, I'll just end it by saying that I think that many of the recent acquisitions that the venture guys have sold, and it's the venture guys selling, you know, Baker & Taylor never saw a dime of the money for Yankee. It went right to the venture guys and it's the same thing with many of the others. The prices are just outlandish. I mean, they are really crazy prices and whether it's Ex Libris and the $500 million or whether it's the other companies, I think that the venture guys are driving up the numbers to the point that there's not going to be money for development, and the library community is the one that's going to suffer from that because if you've been bought by the venture firm there are certain expectations and they expect a certain delivery of numbers or they change people like people change underwear. I mean it's like you're gone if you don't hit your numbers. And so it's a very ruthless business and the money for development is what you're trying, it's what you need as the library community—that money gets strangle-holded, and so because you paid too much you can't put money into development and it ends up making your life worse.

The Young and the Restless: Young Eyes Scan the Scholarly Communications Landscape

Mara Blake, Data Librarian, University of Michigan

Hannah Scates Kettler, Digital Humanities Librarian, University of Iowa Libraries' Digital Scholarship & Publishing Studio

Jen Maurer, Library Sales Representatiive Midwest, Cambridge University Press

Dan Valen, Product Specialist, Figshare

Moderator: Mark Sandler, Director Center for Library Initiatives, Center for Library Initiatives

The following is a transcript of a live presentation at the 2015 Charleston Library Conference.

Mark Sandler: Okay, I'm jumping in. 45 minutes goes by pretty fast, so I'm just going to kick this off. I'll say good morning, everyone. I know there's stiff competition here among programs, not to mention the many delights of Charleston itself, so thanks for coming and we're going to try to put on a good show for you.

So, I'm Mark Sandler. I'm director of the CIC, Center for Library Initiatives, and I don't want to waste time trying to explain to you what that is, so someday you can look that up, but I'll say on a personal note I'm 69 years old. I'm the oldest person at the Fun Run on Thursday morning at 6:30 a.m., and I actually have a retirement date in sight now on Leap Day coming up in February, and once you get to that point in life, you start to think about how libraries could possibly survive without me going forward and how will Charleston Conference ever draw a crowd or manage to put on all these programs if I'm not there to babble on through them, so for all of you out there who have been sharing my angst about whether this is the end of time, I guess I really am delighted for the opportunity that Katina gave me to pull together this program and reassure everyone that we're in good hands and there are bright days ahead for our library and publishing space.

So, I'm very thankful for some of my younger professional friends here who have agreed to come and talk about how the present-day workplace feels for them as some of our younger colleagues and how their scope and their very long futures in this scholarly information space. So, I'll just call out names here, to my left, Mara Blake who is a spatial and numeric data librarian at the University of Michigan, Jen Maurer, who is a library sales rep at Cambridge University Press, Hannah Scates Kettler, who is a digital humanities librarian at University of Iowa, and Dan Valen who is a product specialist at Figshare. So, I asked these folks to avoid PowerPoint and just approach this as a conversation, but first I'm going to ask each of you folks to just take a few minutes to introduce yourselves and sort of tell us about your current positions and how it is that you sort of got to the—how it is that you came to this industry and space and kinds of work that you're doing now, and in what ways the roles that you've played to date have and haven't lived up to your expectations. So, with that, let me ask Mara to come up first and do a little intro. Thanks.

Mara Blake: Thanks, Mark. Good morning, everybody. As Mark said, I am Mara and I came to this scholarly information space through an interest and love for research. I always loved doing research in the library, and after completing my bachelor's degree I kind of didn't know what I wanted to do with my life, and I ended up in an office job in the public sector, and I found it mind numbingly boring, and so I really knew I needed something that was going to be more intellectually engaging and something that would have a lot of variety and excitement and change. So I ended up in library school and I expected this kind of profession in this area to be something

http://dx.doi.org/10.5703/1288284316236

that would have a lot of change and something that would really keep me engaged. As a researcher, I had already seen databases go from command online searching to graphical user interface searching, so I saw some of that already from the outside, and I've had kind of two main trajectories in my career so far. The first is a move to increasingly larger research institutions and the second is a move from social science librarianship to data librarianship. So, my first job out of library school was at a small liberal arts college as a social science librarian, and I would say that that job to a "T" met my expectations about what a library job would be in terms of instruction and research consultations and title by title selection for collection development. I liked that job, and there was a lot of embeddedness with the campus and one-on-one contact with students and faculty. But, after doing that for a while, I really wanted to move to an institution where they would be heavier duty research and media research. I also had some responsibilities for data in that role and really liked them and wanted to have more of that. I wanted to do more of that, so I made a move to a smaller ARL library to a role that had both liaison responsibilities to the social sciences as well as a defined data role as part of that job. I also was assigned to learn geographical information systems and support geospatial data from the library, and as part of that work it really expanded what I thought library work could and should be in this new area that was really exciting, and so it changed my assumptions a little bit.

And after doing that for a while I wanted, I liked everything I was doing, but, I wanted a more narrow focus where I could really develop a deeper expertise in some of the areas I was working in, which is how I ended up in my current role at the University of Michigan as a spatial and numeric data librarian. It feels like a pretty good fit in terms of I'm busy, just like I wanted to be, but I have a narrow enough focus but I have a chance to be good at what I'm doing. And I would say that I always wanted to work in a big research institution. I thought it would be the most exciting collections, the most interesting research on campus that you'd get to work with and the most resources to do projects through the library, and I would say that has definitely met my expectations in my role so far, but I did along the way find a lot of valuable things about working at smaller institutions that I didn't necessarily expect in terms of engagement that doesn't scale as well to a larger institution. It's harder to replicate there. But I am so fortunate where I am now, both in terms of financial resources, but also of resources in my colleagues and things that are available to me on campus, and I really value those things. Naïvely what I didn't expect would come with that would be the larger bureaucracy that goes with a larger library at a larger institution, and so I've had to adjust my skills in terms of navigating those types of structures as something that I just consider a part of my job, and that's something that I didn't expect but have learned along the way. So, that's kind of the rough outline of how I got here and I would say that I wanted was to not be bored and I'm definitely not bored and I do not expect to be bored going forward, so I really love that. Thank you.

Jennifer Maurer: My name is Jennifer Maurer. I am a library sales rep at Cambridge University Press. I wish that my entrance into the publishing world were quite as rich as Mara's, but I came in via Craigslist. I took a year off after I graduated, did some retail for a year, and thought, "It's probably time for a 9-to-5 job." I went to Craigslist and thought, "A Spanish and music degree, how about administrative assistant?" Editorial assistant sounded kind of interesting. I sent my résumé to Springer, and that is kind of how I started. I've done a few different things. I've worked at a few different places. I've been in this world about almost seven years now, but as I mentioned I started out at Springer in editorial and then moved to an account development role at Springer which was—I think it is—still evolving, but the best way I'll describe it is a little bit of marketing, a little bit of sales, some post-sales support, some training support, but after that I think how I've made my changes through the different roles that I've had has been somewhat influenced by life personal choices and not necessarily not feeling fulfilled in the roles that I've had. After Springer I moved to Columbus, Ohio, for a year and worked at OCLC, which was really interesting and then just simply missed home, which is New York, so I started at

Cambridge in sales. I think one of the things that I really appreciate about this industry is the ability to try new things and to move around pretty seamlessly. The fact that things are changing so rapidly really presents a lot of opportunity that to just try something and if you don't like it try something else, and I think that's been one of the most exciting things to be a part of this field. What keeps me here and still trying new things within publishing is simply the people. Everyone I meet is very interesting and pretty willing to talk and share their story and that's probably why I've sort of evolved into a sales role. I think it really affords the opportunity to listen and make some good connections, and I'd say I think that is sort of what's guided my path thus far. So, I'm really happy to be here today and I am excited and a little surprised to see how many people are in the room but it's great. Thanks so much for being here.

Hannah Scates Kettler: Hello, everyone. My name is Hannah Scates Kettler. I am the digital humanities research and instruction librarian at the University of Iowa Libraries, a DH librarian for much shorter. I'm a part of the digital studio or, excuse me, we just recently changed our name, the digital scholarship and publishing studio, which was recently formed in the libraries. Previously it was two different departments, one within the library called digital research and publishing for which I worked for, and another group called the—let me look it up—the digital studio for public arts and humanities, which was supported outside the library by the provost, and those two merged quite recently and I did work for that one as well so a little bit of outside/inside of the library. Previously to that actually I was an archaeologist for a few years so there's kind of a nontraditional background there.

So, my day-to-day actually includes consulting and research on various different methodologies and platforms, active development as a partner in digital projects that come from our students and faculty. We are building out resources for projects instigated by other librarians, so a little internal/external work there. Sometimes we publish those projects as part of our digital library in our institutional repository or as part of our digital editions, which are kind of standalone digital monographs, if you will. In addition to the resource development and publishing role, I kind of hold, I act as one of the touchpoints for the different departments on campus that work with digital scholarship such as ITS, informatics advanced technology and research groups, student organizations, and academic departments as well as a conduit for internal library resources, including our special collections, preservation conservation, and our subject librarians. So, there's a lot of talking, which I actually enjoy and a lot of meeting new people as they come in.

So, the reason I got into this work was I was quite interested in differentiated learning and teaching. I'm very much a visual learner and a lot of archaeology is text-based, and I didn't actually get a lot out of that so I started creating 3-D reconstructions so I could learn, and so one of the those—the idea was then how is this supported within my library resource as an archaeologist? How can I use the library to access these different types of information? And that's where I started my interest there and I submitted some 3-D reconstructions I did as an undergrad in my institutional repository, and at that time I actually didn't know anything about proprietary format so I submitted something that no one else could open or use, and the librarians at the time didn't know anything about 3-D and so they took it and thought it was fine. They did realize after I left that you couldn't open it and that was a problem. Thankfully after I got my master's degree from Kings College in digital humanities I did come back and started working for the same library, and I got a chance to redo that and now it's in a PDF format, which makes way more sense.

So, I've been working in the library now for about three years. In my position I'm actually allowed a fair amount of latitude. In the past three years I wrote the job description, so it's kind of nice; it lived up to my expectations, as you might imagine, but there were some things that did catch my attention, which was I felt that I wanted to be a part of this new cutting-edge proactive development for digital resources and there were structures in place like Mara mentioned, structures, conditions, bureaucracy that kind of retarded that development a little bit. At the same time, these structures did provide a comfort, a thoughtfulness in how we develop our resources so that we can reach the largest group possible. So, I guess there's a checking of my idealism in free technology and were going to move this in two weeks crumbs, if you know what that is, "at job" development, that kind of stuff, so there's a little bit of checking that at the same time it hasn't really been hampered too much. There is a lot of openness that I found within the library that has been uplifting, so that's kind of my background and how I got into this. I really like it, actually.

Dan Valen: Hello, my name is Dan Valen. I am the product specialist at Figshare, and product specialist is vague by design because I'm also the only full-time North American employee for Figshare. I actually got started in publishing about seven and a half years ago at Springer, and similar to Jen, I graduated with a degree in English and economics and didn't really know what I was going to do with that and Springer was actually the first place that called me back. I had an interview and a job offer out of college about a month after I graduated, so I moved up to New York City and I spent a few years in editorial and then moved into the trade side of things, which is working with print, and then finished out my time working in licensing, so licensing out electronic content to university librarians, which is how I really got exposed to this space. And Mark actually held a similar session when I was at Springer where he brought a bunch of early career professionals from the CIC and a bunch of folks from Springer and put them in a room and said, "Alright, let's talk things out." When I was actually working at Springer at that time I was in, I was working with what we call the "college market," which is kind of your nontraditional customers for a huge STEM publisher, and I was excited to be able to go and talk to all these Big 10 schools and see what do they have to say about all these huge publishers and see what their feedback was, and everyone was just talking about open access. I was like, "Whoa, there is a pretty big disconnect here," to what I was coming at this from and what the younger librarians are thinking about, and so I started looking at alternate business models and different ways to think about this. I actually was an advisor for a company called ReadCube and sat on their advisory board, and that's kind of how I found my way into the digital science world. One of the founders of ReadCube asked me to pull together a business plan and I was just like, "I've never been asked to do that. I have no idea how to do that." So about two years ago, November, I met with somebody from Digital Science at a coffee shop and it also was at the end of November, and it was full on "Movember" mode and I had a giant mustache and it was really embarrassing, but I was there to talk with him about ReadCube and this idea of like a new business model, and how do we fix things, and all he could do was talk about FigShare and I'm like, "What is a FigShare?" So, we actually spent about three and half hours chatting and I really wanted to get involved, and that's kind of where I landed now and it's great. I truly believe that in your professional life you should do business with people who believe what you believe, and now when I go and talk to universities and talk about open access and open science and how to facilitate that, there are a lot of nodding heads and ways to change this and take it forward, so it's super exciting. Yeah. That's pretty much it, so.

Mark Sandler: Okay, so you feeling optimistic now like I promised? So, some of the things these folks have in common is that they're young and smart and articulate, by my reckoning incredibly poised and dressed up, full-functioning information professionals. But I wanted to just as a first question to you all, drill down and look at some of the differences between you. So, Dan and Jen, for lack of a better word, are working on the quote/unquote "vendor side" of our space, and Hannah and Mara are working on the library side, and I wondered if you guys could talk a little bit about how you think your workplaces are doing at assimilating younger workers and bringing them along?

Dan Valen: I guess I'll start. It's pretty good from a FigShare perspective. It's interesting because no one at FigShare right now is over the age of 40, so it really does foster to a younger group of individuals and we also have pretty much a flat structure so everyone's input is really valued, which is something that I really, really appreciate coming from a much larger, entrenched industry. The fact that we all can share these ideas and they're all heard, I mean, we do have one ultimate decider if we hit a blocker but, for the most part, it's really accommodating to the younger crowd for sure.

Mark Sandler: Some of you at more venerable institutions, want to take a crack?

Hannah Scates Kettler: I guess I would say working with a large institution where there's a much more mixed demographic age-wise than FigShare, there's a tradition I think of fostering kind of young voices, if you will, early career, I guess, voices and trying to get their input especially I think they're energizing, say, and kind of a new influx to the gene pool and they do listen. Whether or not things get acted upon I think has less to do with a hindrance because of the age difference; I think it is more either your traditions, well mostly the bureaucracy, right? They get heard but they also need the top brass, the typically older generation to kind of root for those things as well, so it's not that their voices aren't heard, there just has to be a few more voices added to it I think to help kind of credidate that kind of input.

Mara Blake: I want to echo a little bit what Hannah said where in all of my roles I felt very empowered with my own time and things that only involved me, but that when it went beyond that and involved other people or other resources that was a different thing to navigate. It depends on the institution a lot, and a little bit that I alluded to before in bureaucracy it's really, "Can you figure that out? Can you make it work for what you're doing?" But I would say that that is in some ways equal opportunity for all ages, but it does require kind of a bigger buy-in from a bigger group of people.

Jen Maurer: To piggyback off of that just a little bit, I think that one of the challenges in, and I'm speaking across sort of all three organizations that I've been part of, which have all been pretty big, well-established across the age demographic, I think that one of the challenges is finding those opportunities for empowerment and making sure that when you are in your own space, when you do have the opportunity to grow, that you're really seizing upon the opportunity even if it might not appear that it's immediately an opportunity to do that. I think that also it's not—we're sort of talking around this like "young versus more seasoned" thing, and I truly believe that is something that young people, or at least myself, I feel like I have learned, and continue to learn, is there is something to learn from everybody that you meet, so whether it's your more seasoned colleague, who is a little bit harder to work with, there is a learning opportunity there. Your younger colleague who was really excited to hear your ideas and is willing to let you fly and do what they see you can, they're ready to give you the space to do that, but it's just making sure that we are kind of listening across the spectrum and not cutting ourselves off too soon too. I hope that makes sense.

Mark Sandler: Back to the more seasoned moderator. I will, just to drill down just one more layer on this theme, Dan and Jen, or actually all of you, do you have like start-up envy, Silicon Valley envy, Google envy, I mean, do you have a sense about the difference between sort of working in these younger, freer organizations, you know, where you just see people hanging around ping-pong tables and playing beach volleyball as compared to a much more established organization with some of the street cred that comes with a venerable imprint or, you know, a 200-year tradition and a football team at a university. Do you want to just comment on that about you know as you are sort of walking around Brooklyn or walking around Iowa City, do folks look and go, "Oh yeah, you should be out there working on the West Coast," or do you feel pretty good about how these, I guess, what these other, more established organizations offer younger folks?

Dan Valen: Well, even when I was at Springer people said that I looked like I should be working at a start-up and they had a nickname for me there. But, I saw a panel a couple of months ago where people are kind of talking about innovation, and why innovation isn't happening as much as it should in this space. In my time spent at Springer there was this idea that this is the way that we do things, we can be a little bit flexible in either way, but this is the way that it's kind of always been done. We can introduce new models but it still—this is where we're at and with the whole idea of the start-up it does allow you to be more nimble and to have a little bit more mobility and change directions on what you're focus is, build new tools faster. I think the analogy that was used that really stuck with me was there's not a lot of innovation in publishing because that's like asking Hilton to create Air B&B. If the business model is working, why would they change? So, from that standpoint, I think it really enables you to grow faster and make different changes to kind of disrupt what is happening, what is the status quo, so you have the big thing that works really well, a well-oiled machine, and then you have the "crazy kids" who have all of these ideas that are seen as radical, and you kind of have to wedge yourself in there and show through your hard work that you can actually change things.

Mark Sandler: Jen, I hope I'm not putting you on the spot here, but you worked with a 500-year-old Cambridge University Press. I think they say they accomplished the books that Adam and Eve were reading so, you know, say something nice about what it means to go into an office like that that has that kind of history?

Jen Maurer: I think that being around people who have been around is actually a really good learning experience. There are challenges. I think one of the hurdles that I think that I've had to go through in each place I've been, I won't just limit it Cambridge, but getting over the perception that as a young person I think that I know it all and I don't feel that way. I don't approach my job that way, but I know that there is a period of adjustment, and it's about building trust and helping your colleagues around you get to know who you are and helping them feel comfortable with the level of experience that you do have. You know, sometimes there are things that I might have just a better handle on because I've done it differently but it takes time. I don't think that I'm at a disadvantage by being where I am. I think it is actually a pretty interesting challenge trying to navigate the space I'm in, and you know if I were so miserable that I think you have to find the good in experiences that you're in regardless of whether it's the glamorous job that you think you should have or the one that you find yourself in, so I guess I'm sort of touching on the, "Am I jealous of cool start-up companies?" Not really. It would be cool. Maybe someday. I don't think that I'm at any disadvantage to be where I am right now. It's all a growth opportunity.

Mark Sandler: Do you want this one, Mara?

Mara Blake: Sure. I just had a quick thought. One is that I'm not jealous of the volleyball because I'm terrible at it, but the second is that in the library what I envy a little bit about those companies, especially some larger technology companies, is that they have a little bit of leeway to fail in projects that we don't necessarily feel like we have in the library where I feel like we feel like we're trying new things, but there is a lot of pressure for them all to succeed and that is kind of a lot to take on as a librarian, as an individual, in the library.

Mark Sandler: Interesting. So, here's an unhappy thought for you but you know probably 2045, 2050, or 35 years from now you're still going to be dragging your sorry selves to Charleston and this conference, so what do you think those programs are going to look like then? What is the space going to look like? Are librarians and publishers still going to be jabbing at each other about price and terms? Is Silicon Valley just going to be all over that exhibit space and a whole lot of these much more established conceptions of libraries and publishing houses will have pretty much receded into a past memory? What is your sense of Charleston 2050?

Hannah Scates Kettler: Okay. Well, I was just going to speak a little bit toward 2050. I will probably have a cane or something, but I think that the Charleston Conference itself will still be relevant and useful. In terms of like library spaces, I'm drawing off of my experience at the University of Iowa Libraries, where we're actually in the process of renovating quite a bit of the space to reflect what the students have been asking for, which is collaborative spaces, access to digital material, which may or may not link back to our physical collections, more openness with special collections, group study space, that kind of stuff. So I think libraries will kind of continue to evolve to reflect this kind of knowledge creation that I think is being called for as opposed to just a place to find the knowledge. It's actually going to be a place to generate and collaborate and come together, so I think it's happening now and I think it will continue to happen as we know it takes a little while not only because of what the expectations of what a library is and how that changes and how quickly that might change, but also you have to have the funds for it, the space for it, etc. I think it will kind of continue to evolve in those, kind of, what I see as a very positive kind of space where people can come together and talk about hard issues, can create projects or exposés, if you will, installations, that speak to these harder issues that bring different types of people together in the same space, because I think the library is seen as a meeting place of a lot of different diverse kinds of disciplines just naturally because we house books and things that are from different disciplines, but now it's becoming this place with those disciplines can actually meet and I think it will continue to evolve that way.

Dan Valen: Yeah, I think one thing that Hannah said that really resonated with me is the idea of the library to help foster creation of content. And so not necessarily the library as publisher, I'm not going to go down that road, but the idea that I had the benefit of being able to visit the Hunt Library at NCSU, and if you don't know what that is you should look it up. It's one of the most inspiring spaces that you can go to if you are super into libraries, but it's the whole idea of helping foster creation amongst the researchers and having librarians kind of move into a nontraditional role of capturing this content and moving it along. You still have those parts of the library, the archiving, the preservation, being the voice of record, but libraries have the benefit of, in almost every campus that I visit, of being located smack dab in the center of campus, so it's always the whole idea of the open-door policy, this is where knowledge should be generated, how you use technology to leverage that? How do you empower libraries and librarians to kind of shift their focus and really engage with theirfaculty, with their staff, with the researchers? So, I kind of see a future where I can throw out open access and go down that road as well, but it is this whole idea of open knowledge because the Internet has really democratized pretty much everything except for academia, and it's ironic because it came out of academia, so how do you use tools to create efficiencies, make content openly available, and collaborate across universities, across countries?

Mark Sandler: Interesting. So, I definitely want to leave a few minutes for you all, although there weren't too many minutes to divvy up. Let me toss out one last question and that is if your bosses were to toss you the keys on Monday morning and say, "Here, you drive," what do you think would make your respective institution stronger and more vital in the lives of students, researchers, authors, scholars—what is on your mind that you would like to take the reins and do sooner rather than later?

Hannah Scates Kettler: I guess I'll start. The thing that is really occupying my mind right now, well, it's still 3-D, we're still trying to figure that out but by extension, just how do we preserve, present, and publish different types of data that don't fall within the norm, non-textual, visual data, experiential data, that kind of stuff.

Mara Blake: So, I'm so excited to answer this question because I am working on that project currently, and it's happening and that is across the CIC a collaborative discovery portal for geospatial data and scanned maps, and we have nine institutions working on it right now. I just came from that meeting and when I started this job that I have, it was my hope that something like this would happen and it is happening and it's what I would've done if I could and I can so it's really amazing.

Jen Maurer: I think I would love to see some better mechanisms for feeding some of these great projects that are going on in our libraries back into an organization like Cambridge, and I will even say it's just Cambridge-specific, but I think the dangers at big established organizations is that we think we know and there's just one of the good things about coming to this conferenceis having conversations with folks like the people to my right and left and seeing that there are some really cool things happening out there. How can we figure out how to partner, partner differently, partner better, and I think that there is real opportunity for us to facilitate those conversations differently, facilitate them better, facilitate them at all, so I think that is something that I would be really interested in pursuing Monday morning at 9:30.

Dan Valen: And something that Mara said earlier, the whole idea of being willing to try things and fail, it's something that I've really had to get used to doing because our founders pretty much said I can run and do what I need to do, so that aren't really that many restrictions. It's this whole idea of figuring out how to pursue our mission and so the scariest thing for me is failing, I guess. But, yeah, I like that I'm able to kind of take this idea forward and run with it. It's pretty liberating and equally scary.

New Platforms and Discovery Tools: Toward 21st-Century University Presses and Libraries

Angela Careno, Head of Collection Development, New York University

Helen Cullyer, Program Officer, Mellon Foundation

Susan Doerr, Operations Manager, University of Minnesota Press

Ellen Faran, Director Emerita, MIT Press

Leila Salisbury, Director, University Press of Mississippi

Tyler Walters, Dean, Virginia Tech University Libraries

Moderated by Charles Watkinson, Associate University Librarian, University of Michigan

The following is a transcript of a live presentation at the 2015 Charleston Library Conference.

Leila Salisbury: Good morning. I am thrilled to see all of you here this morning. We're very fortunate to be joined by some very sharp thinkers from publishing on funding and librarianship who are going to talk with us about how scholarship can be curated and interpreted and used better by our patrons. First thing this morning we're going to hear about two Mellon-funded projects designed to break new ground discovered only in the linking of humanities texts and to create iterative editions of scholarly that will work alongside scholarship itself. Talking about these two programs will be Susan Doerr, who is the operations manager at the University of Minnesota Press and co-principal investigator for the Manifold Scholarship Project, and Ellen Faran, who is the director emerita of the MIT press and is the project manager for the UPScope project. Then we'll hear from Helen Cullyer, program officer in the scholarly communications division of the Mellon Foundation who is helping fund these two projects and many others, and she's going to talk with us a little bit more broadly about Mellon's work and interest in this area. Then we're going to hear from Angela Careno, head of collection development for the division of libraries at NYU, and Tyler Walters, who is dean of university libraries and professor at Virginia Tech. So we'll hear from all ends, and I'm just going to turn it over to the panel and listen and leave little time for questions this morning.

Susan Doerr: Good morning. I'm Susan Doerr with the University of Minnesota Press and I'm pleased to present to you Manifold, which is our new publication platform for a new type of scholarly publication, which we are calling the "Internet edition." Manifold is close to two parts in the project. The first is the development of the platform itself, where you will publish the work. The other is changing the workflow for authors and for publishers so that we can produce these works in a consistent and revocable way without re-creating them over and over each time.

So, Manifold has inspired some experiments that we've done at Minnesota. One of those is called Forerunners: Ideas First. And, so the idea with Forerunners is trying to create a new place where scholars can formally publish their work that they are doing that is in progress, so Forerunners are 25 to 30,000 words. They are what we have been calling "gray literature," that space where they are not yet meant to be a full monograph, but they are ideas and scholars want to publish them and start having dialogue on them. We've used some new tools to publish them quickly. These can be done in 12 weeks instead of 12 months and some of them are turning into full monographs, and so for example the green book *At the Anthrocene* by Jussi Parikka is now a book called *A Geology of Media.* In the Manifold platform that could've

http://dx.doi.org/10.5703/1288284316237

happened, and the Forerunner could exist with the monograph, and you could just move between them to see the changes and adaptations that Jussi made. Now you have a print object and a field project, and you have to go from one to the other.

So, this new monograph format, the integer edition, not a great word integer edition, but the idea here is that they are networked. They're of the web. They are published with enhanced resources like video. They can have audio; they can have additional maps, additional photos, whatever scholars can think of they can turn into a digital file as part of the project on Manifold. And it is really important for us—we're not thinking about Manifold publications as books per se. Instead we are calling them "projects," and those "projects" are basic resources and texts, and they will be monographs, and we will produce a released version in Manifold and in print so it's going to be a hybrid project where we will have both the container, a static addition, and the dynamic addition living on the web.

So, in creating Manifold we have a prototype called Debates in the Digital Humanities. This is an open access website. It is currently housed at CUNY, and you can read the full book, you can interact with the book, you can interact with other readers through the annotation features, but to date it wasn't scalable. It was designed for one book and you needed some programming knowledge in order to get the text on there. What we've done with Manifold or are in the process of doing is making this something that any university press or just generally publishing production staff will be able to upload and put text into Manifold. You don't need to be a programmer in order to use it as a tool. So this is Manifold on a skylight. And we want readers to be able to read on whatever device they have in their hand. If they're sitting at their computer, they can read on that screen. If they've got their phone, they can read it on that screen. For a tablet, they can read on that screen. We want them to be able to interact on any device that they're using, and so in doing our wide framing and considering our features we've got all the potential devices in mind so that we can make a good experience, a beautiful experience, no matter what they're reading.

So, the platform is built for authors and publishers. This is a publishing tool. It is not a production tool, and it is important to make that distinction. When you are loading a work into Manifold, the two platforms that we are taking and adjusting are either E-pub or Markdown. You still have to do all of the production work in the publication process to get to that E-pub. You still do your copy editing outside of Manifold. You still do your proofreading outside of Manifold and what you bring into Manifold, what we process, is the E-pub file and then all the resources.

The Manifold library is a collection of projects, and it's a collection of formally published books. And these are not books in Manifold. These are just some pretty covers we've done. But the idea is that it will be a mix of works in progress, the early editions and then the formally released version, and we are preparing Manifold in a way that it will be a toolset that you can use and install yourself if you want to publish books and we will be giving it away. This is open source and it will be free. And it should be—anybody with basic tactical knowledge should be able to install it and use it to publish. But, reading is really only the beginning for scholars, students, readers, anyone coming to a Manifold pub, we want them to be able to do more than read, and so annotate, contribute, discuss, all of these are the kinds of features, social media integration, we want it to be networked, and we want this to be a dynamic experience, not the flat replication with the static reading experience we have today. Reading is interactive, so why can't you interact? We want to be able to add that interactivity, and we want in some cases if the authors want to have dialogues with their readers, we would like to be able to have that on the platform.

Going back to our Debates in the Digital Humanities platform, we are currently doing an assessment analysis of how annotation has been used on that platform so that we can anticipate and solve some of the problems we have there in the Manifold platform. We are committed to open, so as we do the code, as we do the process, everything will be visible if you want to follow along. You can either follow along on your log and we'll be releasing development versions as we go, and we've in fact decided to adjust some of the previously published books so you can see how content renders and interact with it as we build it. It will be an open source code-based, so anybody can use it, adapt, it take it, and do your own thing if you don't like how we've built it. But, if you want to use it the way we've built that, you're welcome to do that too. And some of the books that we publish will be open access. So that doesn't mean that everyone has to publish in open access if they use Manifold to publish themselves. We feel like open is a really important priority, is part of this project. So follow us along, and if you have any questions you are welcome to e-mail me, or you're also welcome to tweet me and I will respond.

Ellen Faran: I'm Ellen Faran. I am the project manager for the planning grant for UPScope, which is the working title for an online resource for university press monographs. UPScope is a project of the Association of American University Presses, AAUP, and a planning grant is funded by the Mellon Foundation. We are hoping to have a full implementation proposal for the project next spring.

UPScope will provide a single place for peer-reviewed scholarship collected and curated by university presses. We are exploring a full range of access and delivery models for the platform, seeking to meet the current and evolving research needs of scholars. The improved discoverability of our content will support existing purchasing practices, and as a service to UPScope users, we plan to provide purchasing and paid access options on the platform. Beyond gathering university press content in one place, UPScope will feature an innovative search function. Our inspiration is AcademyScope, now online at the National Academies Press. AcademyScope uses a natural language search called Related Engine and uses the full text of books to go deeper than metadata in order to identify connections among titles. This search algorithm is what's known as an inference engine. It can extract key terms from full text to create indexes; they can map to existing taxonomies, thereby revealing relationships across fields and leading to novel discovery. And they have a way cool visualization, which I am not able to show you because I have a mere screenshot here, but this is all animated. If you select a major topic on the right-hand list, subtopics literally bubble up to show you what's happening and you get a spider web network of the book you're after and the books that are connected to it. This is so inaccurate that I'm sure you want to check it out. The way to find it again is AcademyScope or go to nap.edu.

Many of us have long envisioned the collaborative all university press catalog in the sky. Even better the timing of this planning effort for UPScope means that we can marshal tools for uses far beyond a catalog: desemantic search and options for process sharing and content delivery. So, please stay tuned for more news about UPScope.

Helen Cullyer: I don't have slides, so I'm just going to sit here I think and talk for a few minutes. So, I'm Helen Cullyer. I'm the program officer for scholarly communications at the Andrew Mellon Foundation and I worked very closely with Don Waters, who I'm sure many of you know. I just very briefly want to take you through some of our funding priorities and strategies. I'm not going to speak in depth about Manifold and UPScope, but rather place those initiatives in the broader context.

So, since sort of mid-to-late 2014, we've been engaged in a pretty major scholarly publishing granting initiative. Our goals are to assist not-for-profit publishers to disseminate and produce high-quality humanities publications on the web, to do that in a way that's financially sustainable, and to make those publications as broadly accessible as possible. We are focused on sort of a couple of broad areas. Firstly, the sort of financial and economic questions, more sustainable financial models, and we have quite an emphasis at the moment to try to determine the cost allocation, so some of you may have seen Nancy Mera's presentation yesterday. This is a study still in progress, Ithaca SNR, to really do a pretty broad survey of monograph publication costs across US university presses, so it will be a very large sample, and to figure out standardizing out what those costs really are, and I think having seen some of that preliminary data, the important thing to really realize that you can't really reduce the cost of the monograph to one number and there are questions about direct costs, indirect costs, and kind costs. And we've also been doing some work with institutions: Michigan, Indiana, and Emory to figure out institutions' appetite really at the senior level of the administration to pay fees for their faculty to publish open access monographs, assuming standard peer-reviewed editorial procedures, revocable processes, and it seems actually that for those three institutions there is some appetite to do that. Obviously there are some issues surrounding sort of equity, what about the institutions that couldn't pay? What about non-tenure-track faculty? So, this has been an interesting set of investigations to really figure out at the level of not discipline variants but deans and provosts sort of pushing a little bit on how institutions are going to think in going forward about funding publication in the humanities and social sciences.

The other area that we're really focusing on is the development infrastructure, both human and technical, for peer review, editing, production, marketing, dissemination, discovery of scholarly publications and humanities, and by scholarly publications we're really thinking about sort of three different areas: journals, books, and also non-book-like things, so things like the products of digital scholarship that could really only be disseminated on the web and can't be printed, and that really stretch the definition that we have sort of the monograph to its breaking point.

Just to give you a few examples of the UPScope and Manifold that we will be funding in the general space that will combine the humanities collaboration between Montgenevre, now at Burbank, and the Ubiquity Press. So this is a mega-journal in the humanities, so a journals funding model contributed by—funded by—contributions by libraries, and if you saw Brian Hall from Ubiquity Press' presentation yesterday or day before, the great thing about this is really the low cost of journal production on that level. In the book space, sort of the evolving e-book space, the monograph I think is an evolving genre as we've heard with Manifold. One project that is just in the planning phase right now and will be moving forward to the implementation phase next year is Muse Open. Project Muse has been planning—is planning right now—to develop the capacity to host already E-pub books on its platform alongside content behind a paid wall. So that seems really important. As the publication becomes more mainstream, to get those homemade publications on the platforms along with subscription content.

And then the third one, and this is relating to the space of the non-book-like, non-monographic forms, Stanford University Press has received funds from us to start publishing what's called an interactive scholarly works. So these are works that really can't be considered books—like in any sense—may be so rich in multimedia, data, also interactive, they may have interpretive text, but it may be nonlinear that they really can't be thought of like a monograph or like a book in any meaningful way. And so they are developing not only sort of production and dissemination workflows, mechanisms for those, but they're also just figuring out peer review. How these objects, complex projects peer review. There needs to be a level of sort of technical peer review as well as peer review of the content, so they will be developing hopefully some best practices or something that will move toward best practices for peer review of those new genres.

I want to address very briefly the role of libraries. UPScope and Manifold are actually two projects that don't really involve libraries in the development, but we do have a number of grants that do involve libraries and publishers working together, and I think those libraries increasingly supporting digital scholarship, some are becoming some publishers themselves, and some libraries are becoming integrated with the presses. There are multiple roles libraries can play. So just to focus on sort of one of those roles, actually publish those roles, we have a grant at University of Illinois at Urbana–Champaign, one of several grants, that is helping institutions and their libraries provide better support for humanities scholars who want to develop nontraditional humanities publications. So it's these interactive scholarly works and humanities projects. And helping them to think about the early stage of research and development what the publication outlets are going to be. What the formats are going to be. What the venues, channels for publication are going to be, and in the case of UYUC, it may be that some of the faculty are working with some of the people on digital scholarship and scholarly communications, and the library may end up publishing with university presses, and in other cases they may end up publishing through the library, but the idea is to get scholars thinking about publication as they are developing new research. That's all. Thank you.

Angela Carreno: I'm Angela Carreno, head of collection development at New York University, and I do not have slides either so I'll just stay here. Even before I heard about Manifold, I was definitely aware of the need for some outlet for linear, static text that makes allowances for what scholars are working on, and as a librarian, there was no easy way to think through it when those questions came in. And, on September 15, Rick Anderson posted something on *The Scholarly Kitchen* about an experiment taking place at the University of Utah in collaboration with Oxford University Press, and a library effort in collaboration with a scholar to add to the print version of the book primary source material and allowances for scholarly commentary and crowdsourcing options for gathering additional primary sources, etc., and I know that they used a blog platform. I said, "Okay, well . . ." And it was kind of exciting that a press was okay experimenting with a library and was going to be okay with the static print version combined with full-text coverage of the open version with all of this iterative functionality, so that sounded exciting to me, and I have a colleague in my library who was approached by a scholar in our Hebrew and Judaic Studies Center; she published a book with Yale University Press. And what she wanted was some sort of way to map their world using GIS technology. And the question was whether or not the librarian could help her, can we get this online, and is there some way to connect it with the book? And I know that she has been engaged in an effort in collaboration with this scholar to make it happen and is very excited about the work she's doing. So, and she's using Omeka. Okay? Then, I am involved in collection stewarding committee meetings where we worry about the dissertation and our archiving role and the excitement in monographic students about digital humanities and experimental ideas and how important it is for us to think of ways to archive whatever it is, any kind of book. So platforms are very important, and the fact that it's open source is very important, and finding a collaborative, central way to take advantage of the platform that scales and is sustainable is important, and I'm glad we have these projects going on because I sure need help. When it comes to UPScope, I do not see libraries using it for vendoring, distribution, workflow, and processing. That isn't the idea. I am super excited about search that's taking advantage of natural language queries, and I'm super excited about the metadata, and I think both need to be shared to the advantage of both.

Tyler Walters: Good morning, everyone. So, my challenge is to say a few things that everyone hasn't said yet. Right? Two good essay projects I need you to pick up on UPScope, in essence we can talk about that, I mean I would agree in terms of the library perspective. It has this potential to be this really great search discovery resource of course for our users, for students and faculty on our campuses, and frequently this is mediated by libraries who are looking at specialized resources for teaching; students and faculty have utilized such specialized resources to find things. I'm particularly struck by the nature of a lot of publishing. Academic publishing these days is highly interdisciplinary, and I think as a faculty member or student we are looking for resources. If you have an engine like this you've probably discovered things from authors and probably even subject areas that you may not have thought about on your own, have for the system. It is just that you are able to find things that are written in just the right way and perhaps learn of people in certain disciplines working together and drawing from one of those works that again you haven't previously thought of on your own. More specifically, I think the data that will come out of this search tool is going to be a lot of use not just to publishers, but to the library student who would really like a better understanding of user behavior, user searching, and being such a highly specialized database, I think these libraries would like to learn from this as well and to better understand what our users are doing, what they're seeking, work that has been produced in universities. I, too, I don't think that libraries are going to use it as a vendor tool, again that's not the purpose of this. Again, I think a lot is to be said for the data and interdisciplinary-ness of it all. Maybe also think about with all of this material online. Inevitably you can't print an online resource, and the thing you wonder about as AAUP and presses in general is the electronic path as libraries are self-serving, if there wasn't any off-duty potential of collaboration with another institution for preservation of these materials down the road.

Manifold—this is another very terrific project where I think many of us have thought about, "Yes, we need this dynamic, iterative, web-based resource that is based on library literature." I'm sure many of us probably had that thought 20 years ago and think about it. Hyperlink, on the web through a browser, obviously, all of us in this ecosystem have struggled with this in these last few years. How do we get to this point where it is very easy to build such resources and sustain them and use then them in an instructional way? So, Manifold has I think, I don't want to set too high a bar for it, but Manifold points in that direction of being an open source platform that would be very easy for people to use, for presses to use, for the builders of content especially to be using and pushing out there. It reminds me of a lot of the digital humanities resources that we see in this building oftentimes in conjunction with the libraries who help produce these matters and to manage and maintain them. So, again I think it applies to that future of, wow, this is actually being built really of the press at the University of Minnesota. There's a lot of interest, a lot of potential stakeholders and others involved, and I think to with any classically or digital humanities resources, once these things are built, how do we preserve and sustain them? They take on a scholarly life of their own clearly in conjunction with the monograph that published. They become a value-added scholarly resource on their own, these dynamic versions of these books, and I like to think that they're called projects. We know what books are in print, but we also know what e-books are, we always think of e-books right? It's a PDF or E-pub file—very, very flat. It's still kind of black letters on white paper, open screen. So this gets us far beyond that and helps us to think about using the dynamic web in a way that it was really intended from the beginning. That some of the questions going forward for Manifold is, it's great, it's going to be offered as an open source tool to be used in part for this to be built and sustained over time, will others contribute to sustaining Manifold and developing it, evolving in overtime. Because usually you see those really great open source platforms that really make it for the long haul arose from the main stakeholders at the same time, it usually is a visionary institution and/or a person who is putting this platform together, and they have that here at the University of Minnesota, and I'm in great support, and I think Manifold is tracking right where it needs to track. Also from the library perspective of libraries are certainly production units in a lot ways, and some of us run publishing programs, so this will be interesting to see the future of library publishers actually pick up the use of Manifold in their own operations. That's all of my comments right here.

Susan Doerr: So, Tyler, if I could just respond really quickly. So, I didn't name our partners and that was an oversight. We are partnered with the Digital Humanities Center at Manifold, and that is the digital scholarship opportunity and that goal specifically. So, as we are building this, digital humanities projects are very much top in mind because those are the folks that we are working with to build it as well as our technology partner called Cazgir Coding Technology and our dataset programmer is a humanities scholar himself, so everyone coming together around this project, our scholars and authors and interest in building the tools they wanted to see because of the tools they want, and in terms of the code development, we've committed 10 years of funding to continue support for the Manifold platform, and that is coming from both CUNY and the University of Minnesota because we want to see this succeed.

Summon, EBSCO Discovery Service, and Google Scholar: Comparing Search Performance Using User Queries

John Vickery, Analytics Coordinator, North Carolina State University Libraries

The following is a transcript of a live presentation at the 2015 Charleston Library Conference.

John Vickery: Definitely thanks for coming on a Saturday morning. You know, I want to congratulate us all for sticking around to talk about search performance, and then at the same time maybe get a little worried about us, but mainly I think we should feel excited that we have stuck around. I'm used to Charleston sort of in the small rooms at Francis Marion, you know where we're all kind of in a small little group, so I'm going to try to not wander away from the mic. I usually tend to wander around a little bit, so if you can't hear me, if I kind of step off to the side, start flapping around or something and I'll try to get back to a nice sort of podium stance up here, and I'll also try not to fall off the podium.

So, again, thanks for coming. I'm John Vickery from NC State Libraries and I need to back up. My colleague, Karen Ciccone, who I worked with closely on the project, was unable to make it to the conference. I wish she could but unfortunately she couldn't make it. We were originally scheduled to present this together, so what you see me presenting, we definitely worked together as a team and then that's also part of a larger team effort, so this definitely wasn't just me. I should be up here with several other folks who couldn't make it today.

Today I'm going to talk about a project that a team of us did at NCSU to compare the search performance of Summon, EBSCO's Discovery Service, and Google Scholar. Here's what we will be covering. I definitely plan to leave time for questions, so hopefully we can kind of have a little bit of a discussion afterward or don't feel shy to ask questions at the end or even grab me afterward if you want to just kind of take the discussion offline.

I'll start by giving a little background about the project and our objectives. We'll then get into the methods of how we coded and analyzed the data, and I'll talk about the idea behind randomization tests and why we used that method so if you pulled up the actual blurb to the talk you saw I mentioned randomization tests, so another thing that I think is kind of exciting for us to be talking about today, and then finally we'll take a peek at the results of our comparison.

So, a minute ago I mentioned that the project was a team effort. It was put together by our web scale discovery product team. Karen and I wrote about the project in an article for *Evidence Based Library and Information Practice*. The article was published I think in February or March of this past year. It's open access, so Google it, pull it up, you can read it now while I'm giving you the talk. And if you really want to kind of take a deep dive into some of the idea of randomization tests a little bit more and how we implemented them using SAS, you can take a look at an article I did for the SAS Global Forum this past spring if you follow that link, or maybe Google the conference proceedings and then if you want to maybe implement the code yourself or really start playing around with it, the code is in the conference proceedings paper as well but you can check out the GitHub space and download the code and play around with it. I should say I program in SAS, but I know you could implement the test we did in Aura or Python, or pretty much any analytics language of your choice, so what I'll be talking about is how I did it in SAS. I'm not going to get into the code and whatnot, but that is SAS code on GitHub and in the conference proceedings, but again you could implement this in several different ways. And again, if you decide to take a look at the code and you have questions, please get in touch with me. I'd be glad to talk about it more.

Okay, so a little bit about the project. Similar to many libraries, at NCSU we've invested quite a lot of time, effort, and money into implementing a web scale discovery service. So, we think it's

http://dx.doi.org/10.5703/1288284316238

important to periodically review the landscape, review competing products, and see if maybe it would be a better fit for us because of price or effectiveness or any other consideration so our web scale discovery product team is charged with testing and evaluating our existing service as well as other potential products. Our team is made up of about nine librarians. Some of them may be in the room now but not to worry, you can flag yourself down, and we covered several departments in the libraries. We tried to touch all of them. We range from public services, tech services, collections, and IT, and at NCSU we've been using Summon since 2009.

Something a little different about how we use our discovery service—we primarily use Summon to populate the articles section of our quick search application. So, if you could kind of see that. I've been in a couple presentations here and screenshots tend to get kind of washed out. But, if you are a user at NCSU's library website, we present folks with sort of the large single search box. If you were to enter a search in there, that search is spread out into both our website, article results, and book results, so what we're using our discovery service for is to populate this article section, these article results. So, we'll give you the top three and if you click "see all results" you'll be passed into the Summon interface. Most of our users don't actually even get to the Summon interface, and this has implications in how we designed the test as well, but back when we implemented Summon in 2009, it was actually I think the only discovery service that had an API that we could leverage for this purpose. So, 2009 was a long time ago, and since of course other services have the API functionality, in particular EBSCO's that we wanted to evaluate.

So, in April and May of 2014, we set up a trial of EDS, and it was during that time that we ran the tests. So we were testing in the spring of 2014 and did data analysis over the summer. Of course there has been other really good studies that compared discovery services. I would encourage you to take a look at these two from 2013. Asher, Duke, and Wilson compared the performance of Summon, EDS, and Google Scholar, and their study quality was judged on whether or not articles selected by test subjects were scholarly publications, so peer-reviewed articles. Rochkind, if I'm pronouncing that right, published a study that compared user performance for search results from several of the available discovery services. In that test subjects were presented with a side-by-side view of two discovery services, and they were asked to select which results set they preferred. Both of those studies had test subjects enter hypothetical searches, and so the main difference between these two and our study and where we think our study contributes to the literature and to the community is that we used actual search queries from our Summon logs. So, we actually found the actual text that was entered into a search and used that as the basis of our search as opposed to asking users to enter in, maybe pick some searches that you think you might want to do.

The primary objective of our study was to answer the question of which discovery service produced better results for the type of searches typically performed by our users. And we can get a sense of what "typical" is by examining a Summon search log. So what I was mentioning before as opposed to hypothetical kind of "try to come up with a question on your own," we were actually drawing the real researcher questions that our users, faculty, students, staff, we didn't know who they were, were entering into a search. So, the Summon logs contained the actual queries that the users entered, and from looking at the logs we know that about three-quarters of the searches are for topical-type sort of broad searches where you're looking for a general area, and about 25% are known-item type searches, so this would be where a user actually pastes in a citation to an article so they know exactly what they were looking for and they're going to go get it. Or maybe they typed in a title keyword or a piece of the title of the work. So, because of how these two searches differ, we wanted to separately evaluate how the discovery services handled them. So, here's a couple examples. This shouldn't look particularly surprising to anybody but you can see the difference. These are actual searches from our logs of known-item search queries on the left and topical search queries on the right. So, when we're looking at our search logs, this is the kind of how we're going to see the difference in those. We would've had again about 75% of the searches be topical and 25% be known-item, so you can see where someone has actually pasted in the citation to that internal medicine article there.

In the title of the presentation we talked about Google Scholar. So far we have kind of just touched on Summon and EDS, but we needed to consider our 800-pound Google gorilla. So, why did we throw that into the mix? So, first I should say that discovery services like Summon and EDS, they offer clear benefits to libraries that Google Scholar doesn't. In particular, Google Scholar's terms of service—they don't allow results to be presented outside of the Google Scholar context. So, at NCSU where we use the API functionality to populate that articles section of our quick search app, we couldn't do that even if we decided we wanted to sort of say, "okay, we want to use Google Scholar." We can't use it in the way that we have our environment set up now. So, we also know that the Google universe is sort of the "go to" place for many of our researchers, and we could maybe say most, I'm not sure. So we really wanted to see how that fared as well.

Okay, now we're going to start getting down into the weeds a little bit with the methods. This is kind of the part where I get the most interested and sort of my interest is usually inversely related to other folks' interest, so a little "nerd alert." So, hopefully this is the kind of stuff you might want to talk to me about later or just kind of hang on and we can get through it. Okay, so let's talk about how we coded and analyzed the data. The first and probably the most important thing that we did again was to use those actual user search queries from our Summon search logs. So we wanted to try to replicate the experience, really see what our users saw as closely as possible to really replicate what results they were getting. Now it's not uncommon for these searches to have punctuation errors because people probably type better than me, but you're going to get extraneous characters, sort of overly broad topics, but we kept those exactly as they appeared, so if someone had mistyped something, we just copied and pasted that query into our test to see how it worked. So, a few examples. You can see where there is a "G" in front of plants or some misspellings or "new class of drugs patent," maybe something that doesn't necessarily come off as a well-thought-out topic, but it could've just been mistakes in the typing or how the student or faculty framed the search.

Another really important aspect of the methods was that we generated a random sample from the search logs. I know we all know that this is basic standard practice, but it was really important for us to get a representative sample or a representative dataset to test. So, we started with about a year's—I think a complete year's—worth of Summon's search logs, and we generated a simple random sample so no stratification, just a random sample of 225 queries. The 225 number we felt like was large enough to be representative, but it also worked well with our team of nine members because we gave each team member 25 queries to test. A couple team members were not able to actually complete the test, so our final analysis dataset was down some from 225, but it still after sort of some post-talk power tests came out sufficient to detect an effect that we wanted to detect. So, team members, the nine of us, we used our judgment to classify each query as either topical or a known-item search, and going back to that slide I showed a minute ago, it was generally very easy. In our discussions amongst the team we didn't have a whole lot of talk at all about "I couldn't decide, was this topical or not?" It really was quite clear so that was our first decision point was "Is this query a topical search or a known-item search?" And we're going to split our analysis based on that. For topical searches we recorded the number of relevant results within the first 10 results, and we used our judgment again to consider a result relevant if it matched the presumed topic based on kind of title and abstract only. So, we didn't really dig deep into the result list. We tried to—I guess in a lot of ways we were trying to put ourselves in the frame of a user, a student maybe, and say if you are scanning this result list you're not going to necessarily read every article. You're going to make the decision at that time: "Is this relevant? Do I want to dive into it more or pass?" For known-item-type searches we asked two questions. One was, "Did you find the item and was it in the top three results?" We know from some of our testing that it's relatively uncommon for folks to actually get past those top three. We limited ourselves to the top 10. I think in a future test, if you wanted to really get even more strict, you could say limit that the entire test environment to just the top three results. Since we used a random sample, the distribution of the topical to known-item that mirrored the overall distribution, so again we within our sample dataset of 225 we had about 75% of those were topical questions and 25% were known-item. And at this point we've got the dataset up for two different types of analysis. For the topical searches we have count data, and for the known-item searches we have binary sort of "yes"/"no" categorical data.

After all the team members coded their data, we had a series of spreadsheets that looked like this. These are examples of the known-item searches with the "yes"/"no." Team members—this is sort of half the spreadsheet. The way we presented it to our team members was a spreadsheet with a list of their 25 queries to test, they needed to make that first judgment of topical or known-item, and then they would respond in the various columns depending on how they determined it whether it was known-item or not. And this would be how they recorded the topical or broad searches, what we also called it. So, for the topical searches, the way the test was designed we had the dataset up appropriately for a repeated measures ANOVA, so analysis of variance, and then what that test is designed to detect is any overall difference in the average number of relevant results for each of the three products. So in a repeated measures ANOVA, we test each subject multiple times, once under each condition. And let me show you how we were viewing this as that set up. So you can think of the query text as the subject and condition one will be testing under EDS, condition two under Summon, and condition three under Google Scholar. So, kind of in general you may see this kind of design in like a medical study or something where one individual was given three different drugs over different periods of time, but it was the same individual that was being tested, so in a sense the query text is the individual and the discovery service is the condition that we tested under.

So, we pulled the data into SAS, and again like I said you could use other analytic tools. SAS is the one I tend to use, and the first stop was to make some plots or some graphs of the data and get some basic stats. I'm going to kind of jump ahead a little bit and show you the plot of the known-item searches first, and when I saw it, it was kind of a little bit of a spoiler for the results section because it was a pretty boring graph. It was like a tie. So, in some sense, we didn't always need to run complicated analysis. After kind of viewing this we thought, "Well, that was kind of interesting. It's a tie." I'll make a comment though about the actual dataset of 44, that got a little too small after some of the folks had to drop out of the test, so sort of in a follow-up this would be an area that would really want to address as to kind of take a deeper dive into the known-item type queries. We had a large enough dataset for the topical searches, but this was kind of pushing the boundary on known-items of this would be a spot to, sort of the weakness of the study and where we would really want to evaluate it more in-depth. And then for the other question of was it in the top three results? All but one of the queries was in the top three for Summon, and all but two for EDS and Google Scholar. So, again, really close basically in some senses a tie for the known-item type searches.

So, let's go back to the topical searches. These are the average number of relevant results for each of the three discovery services. Summon and EDS are basically tied. You can see 4.76 and 4.83. That's really close, and then you can see that Google Scholar had about one additional relevant result per result set within the first 10. So, overall these are coming in really, really close. When we plotted it out you can see the distribution of the number of relevant results so you see EDS is blue, Google is red, and Summon is green. You can see where they had the frequency of 0 relevant results, 10 relevant results, and so we've got the distribution from 0 to 10, and you can see that there is enough variation to kind of warrant a closer look, so different from the known-item we're kind of seeing a little more variation where we'll want to kind of dive a little more deeper into it. But at the same time this is where I started to get nervous about using a regular repeated measures ANOVA, because like all statistical tests, there's assumptions that you have to meet and one of them you know you can breed, whether or not this is one you need to worry about all the time or not, but one of them is that the data should be normally distributed. Get you a nice bell curve and this is really, really, really not a nice bell curve. In my analysis work I typically don't get a nice bell curve. One day I feel like I'm going to find one but in library data I never do. Ever. But one day maybe I'll just get a nice normal distribution. So, in order to get around the possible violations of the assumptions that are regular repeated measures of ANOVA, we decided to use what's called a randomization test. Now the concept could be maybe a little complex, but I kind of find that randomization tests are in a way easier to conceptualize than the normal parametric equivalent. So, what in the world is a randomization test? The concept goes back to the 30s with R. A. Fischer. This is a picture of him and others and the basic outline of the randomization test—you might see it called randomization tests or permutation test—is that you randomly shuffle the data and repeatedly calculate your test statistic and the "P" value, that marker of statistical significance, where you want it to be under .05 or .001 is the fraction of how many times the test statistic for the shuffled data, that rearranged data, is equal to or more extreme than the observed test statistic. All right. If you're still awake, give yourself a cheer. You just made it!

Okay, now the practicality of the method, however, was limited by computing power until relatively recently because even with small datasets the number of possible permutation gets really, really big really fast, so our dataset had 139 observations, so 139 rows, and the way that we're permeating the data was within that row.

So we would take an answer from EDS and put it in the Summons slot. This is randomly generated so or the number recorded for Google Scholar and slot that into the EDS slot. So the formula gives you the possible number of permutations, but that is six to the 139th power. You know, I put that in and tried to like put all the zeroes out there. It's a really huge, huge number. So, that's why they weren't doing it in the 30s, because they couldn't write fast enough. But, you don't actually have to do it that many times. Typically you'll see randomization tests done in the low thousands or ten thousands, which for your computer is nothing. You can run a randomization test and do ten thousand iterations of it and it's really quick.

The basic steps: you calculate your test statistic. In our case we were doing ANOVA, so we chose the "F" statistic—that's the standard one for ANOVA. You rearrange the data like I was saying before. You're going to shuffle it up and then you're going to calculate the test statistic for this shuffled up data. Then you're going to do number two and three many times. I heard a presentation the other day where someone was referring to this as like, "wash, rinse, repeat," because this is kind of where you're reading the back of the shampoo bottle. You're doing number two and number three many times, but your computer is actually doing it, and then your "P" value is the fraction of how many times the statistic for the rearranged data, all of it put together, is equal to or more extreme than the observed test statistic.

Okay, so let's look at the results. You've kind of suffered through the methods. We saw that the known-item searches were basically a tie but the topical searches where we applied these randomization tests. Okay, histograms I love. Histograms I think they're fun to look at. Hopefully you do too. With the topical searches our randomization test showed that there was an overall difference. If you think back to that table where I showed you the average results, we had Summon and EDS as a tie, and Google just about won. But we are looking for is whether or not that slight difference was due to chance or whether or not there was an actual overall difference. So, here's what it looks like plotted out the results of our randomization test. And what you want to notice about this plot is the area of the graph to the right of the redline. It's that little bitty shrunk down spot. So, that's sort of the graphical representation of the "P" value. That's our "P" value of .002, which is a really, that's a small number, and so that's strong support for an overall difference. Basically what we're seeing is that it's really unlikely that we would've gotten our observed difference, our observed "F" value of 6.3, just by random chance alone. So, were saying to ourselves, "Wow, there really is a difference in these three products!" Now again the difference was slight, but there really is a difference. It wasn't just chance. Now, our ANOVA test or our randomization test shows that there is an overall difference, but it doesn't show us where. So, we don't know which discovery service is accounting for the difference. I mean, we can have an idea of that based on our table of looking at the average number, but in order to figure it out we had to do pair wise comparisons, so we did more randomization tests. This time comparing the possible pairs. So, Summon to EDS, EDS to Google Scholar, and Summon to Google Scholar. Here is what we got comparing Summon to EDS. What you want to take away from this graph as opposed to the previous one is the large "P" value and the shaded red areas. What this tells us is that there is essentially no difference in the way we measured relevant results in our test between Summon and EDS. So if we have Summon and EDS folks here you're basically tied according to the way we tested it. So, I don't know, you can take it out into the hall and see who's really winning. Now, I think of a lot of times when you read studies you get excited for a difference. We were excited to see a difference based on the "F" test that we did a minute ago, but this sort of no difference, this tie for us at NCSU had really important implications. It actually was really in a sense very helpful because it meant that we could basically take performance out of the evaluation equation. So when our team is looking at which product to choose and what factors to weigh we can say to ourselves "performance isn't one of those," and in our case and the way we tested it, performance isn't in the equation, so we can focus on backend functionality, the knowledge-based piece that comes with the discovery services. We can focus on user interface so our user research team might want to go out and do a test and just focus on which interface works best for our users or we can look at cost, so it's basically just simplifying our decision making, which is really important and really helpful for us at NCSU.

Okay, so what about Google Scholar? This is Summon compared to Google Scholar, and you'll notice a difference here as opposed to a lot of red if you can actually see what you want to focus on again is the area to the right of the red lines, and just a very little red shaded area, and that's the graphical representation of our really small "P" value. So again this is saying that Summon in fact according to our test did significantly, you know, in a statistical sense, outperform Summon. So Google really did have better results. I'm sorry; this is showing that Google Scholar did in fact, thank you, outperform Summon. Statistically. Okay, and so now we've got to compare EDS to Google, and no surprise we basically—another version of that previous histogram. Again we saw a slight difference with Google Scholar outperforming by almost one relevant result, and our randomization test showed that that was super, super, super unlikely to have been just based on random chance alone. So again Google Scholar did outperform it as the way we tested it, both Summon and EDS. And again this has important implications for us at NCSU. On the one hand we are not able to plug Google Scholar into our infrastructure the way we've designed it, the way we want to use it, but we can also say to ourselves and I guess that our users are actually getting good relevant results when they choose to go to Google Scholar, which we know they are. So, basically the same story between EDS and Summon—Google Scholar did actually outperform them, but do recall that it was a relatively slight difference.

So, a few takeaways. Summon and EDS basically tied, so they're going to have to duke it out in areas outside of performance, or maybe that will change if we redo the test at a future point or or if any of you guys decide to you might see a difference in their performance, but for us at

NCSU it took performance out of our evaluation equation. It's simplified our decision making. We were able to focus on cost, backend performance, and user interface. Google Scholar came out slightly ahead like we just saw. Again it's kind of important for our users because we know that is what they're using, and this is my little takeaway hopefully that you guys might want to consider a randomization test as something in your toolbox of hypothesis testing. It might be an option for your data because again in my experience I typically don't get nice, normal data, so it's been helpful to have a sort of a more robust, nonparametric test that we can turn to. Thank you very much. I'm definitely happy to answer questions if you have them.

End of Conference Poll-a-Palooza: Part II

Derek Law, Professor Emeritus, University of Strathclyde

Erin Gallagher, Electronic Resources Librarian, Rollins College

The following is a transcript of a live presentation at the 2015 Charleston Library Conference.

Erin Gallagher: All right, welcome. Good afternoon. And thanks for sticking around for this. It's been a busy three days, and I know that everyone has been talked at a lot for the last three days, so what we're going to do today is more interactive. You'll get a chance to be part of the discussion today, maybe more than you have in the last few days, and it's also going to be fun, it's going to be low stress, it's going to be dynamic, and it's going to be a palooza, ultimately. So, thanks for coming to the end of conference Poll-a-Palooza, Part II. I'm Erin Gallagher. I'm the e-resources and serials librarian at Rollins College, and I also write a weekly column for *Against the Grain* called "Hot Topics." I am joined by Derek Law, professor emeritus from the University of Strathclyde, who will be regaling us with something completely different a bit later.

In case you are wondering what a "palooza" is, which Derek was just asking me earlier, so here's what it is. According to the very reputable source, urbandictionary.com, a palooza is "an all-out crazy party; partying at one place with a ton of people like there's no tomorrow." All right. Thank you. So, in case you were wondering, that's exactly what's about to happen. Has anyone done any sort of live audience polling thus far? If you were at the Hyde Park Debate yesterday, which was just marvelous, it was really enjoyable, then you may have taken part in the poll "Are Altmetrics Rubbish or not?"

Derek Law: Yay!

Erin Gallagher: Victorious! So, we're going to be using the same software today, Poll Everywhere. There are a couple of ways that you can respond: you can go to the site at polleverywhere.com/chsconf or you can respond via text. These instructions are going to be up there when the polls come up every time anyway so you don't have to memorize them. This is the second time I've done this end-of-conference Poll-a-Palooza, and last year one of the questions I asked was, "What do you think will be the hottest topic of Charleston 2015?" These were some of the responses I got, that people responded the most often with, and some of them are pretty accurate. I'd say open access has been pretty hot this year, right? Who has attended a session involving something to do with open access? All right, okay. I think we all have. So somebody had a crystal ball last year and knew that that was going to happen. Some of the others, not so sure—e-books, DRM, big packages, that's definitely been pretty hot this year. Is it dead yet, print, you know, I'm not totally sure what the prevailing sentiment is, but I don't think it is. Streaming video, the Swets debacle, how quickly that did not become a hot topic. So, I'm going to ask this one again when we do our polls, and then it will be interesting to see next year if any of our predictions come true in 2016 for the hottest topics of Charleston. So, were going to get started right away with some polling. And you've already started answering so, good for you.

All right. I like to start out with a question that gets everybody familiar with responding to the polls. So, where you all from—city, state, company, planet, that sort of thing. Unfortunately, this isn't like a high school reunion where whoever traveled the farthest gets a prize. Though I do say, is that London, England, or Ontario? All right. If there was a prize I'd say so far—oh gosh, we've got Japan, Saudi Arabia, wow, we've got some people who have traveled really far to come to this conference, which I think it's definitely worth it. It's my favorite conference of the year. All right. Oh, Australia, okay, somebody won! All right, you can still continue to respond but I'm going to go ahead and move on. Also the tenor of the questions today, I want this to be fun but also informative, so we're starting out with some general questions about the conference and

http://dx.doi.org/10.5703/1288284316239

I'm going to move on to some questions that involve common themes that have risen throughout the sessions, things that I've pulled from my "Hot Topics" column, things that have, you know, that have come out of a lot of news involving library and information in bookselling throughout the year, and then ending with some other fun ones, but what I really hope is going to happen is that this leads to some lively conversation so don't feel like if you have a question you have to sit on it. Please speak out, raise your hand, stand up, you know, do the sort of things that would be expected at a palooza and feel free to add to the conversation. I do want to add, so Derek asked me earlier what exactly is a palooza and beyond the Urban Dictionary definition I was thinking what the heck is—where did I get the idea of tacking "palooza" onto the end of this, and I realized that it came from—has anyone ever been to the music fest Lollapalooza? Okay, Nicole, nice, we really have some people that went to Lollapalooza. So, I was explaining to Derek what that was, and I realized that's the only other context in which I've ever heard this used.

I'd like to know if you are a first-time attendee of the Charleston Conference. Also, if your answer is "C: What's the Charleston Conference?" then I guess you just showed up for the food and we're all a bunch of librarians. Oh, wow. We've got a pretty good mix of first-timers and veterans. Nice. That's really good to know that we've got a lot of people that it is your first time here. Who knew that it was going to be this hot? Okay, yeah. I live in Orlando, Florida, so this is nice to me but I realize it's probably pretty melty for everybody else.

This is one of my favorites to find out: What is your favorite session type? Oh, also Neapolitan isn't the ice cream, in case you were wondering. Derek, you're not responding.

Derek Law: No, I thought it was ice cream. You've not told me what it is.

Erin Gallagher: Oh good, we've got some "G's" going on, "happy hour."

Derek Law: How can you be in two places at once and attend a concurrent session?

Erin Gallagher: These are highly philosophical questions. I'm not sure I'm prepared to answer these. This is a palooza after all.

Derek Law: This is clearly altmetrics here. I do not believe only 4% of people go to happy hour at the bar.

Erin Gallagher: See, this is anonymous everybody, too. Nobody knows who's responding what. Actually, yes, you can vote as many times as you like so that's once again altmetrics at work, right?

Audience member: It will only let you vote once.

Erin Gallagher: Oh, really. Maybe with the multiple choice I think you can only vote once but with the open-ended questions you can respond as many times as you like.

Derek Law: What you need is Irish election software. Vote early, vote often.

Erin Gallagher: Hey, now. My name is Erin Gallagher, so.

Derek Law: She's quick. She is quick.

Erin Gallagher: Well, we've always had to be. I'm definitely interested to know what you think of the new Gaillard Center. Also, am I pronouncing it correctly? I just think it's absolutely stunning. It's gorgeous. Beautiful venue. I also think it could use a few more signs. I got very lost yesterday on my way to the Hyde Park Debate. Kind of a maze, yes, that's a good way to put it. Oh, I saw something that said "you aren't," so does that mean that I did not pronounce incorrectly? It's "Gay-ard?" Okay.

Derek Law: "Nookes and crannies."

Erin Gallagher: "Nookes and crannies," ooh. I want to know more about those. Oh, "weird sign for nonexistent ladies room on the second floor." Make a note. "Unpronounceable yet gorgeous." Oh, that should be their promo. All right.

All right, here's what I want to know—oh, this is the hottest buzzword of the 2015 Conference: "Hard to start day in room not allowing coffee" (shown on screen). Hey, it's a palooza, that's why, you know . . .

Audience Member: In the French language "Gaillard" in French means a vigorous, healthy old man.

Erin Gallagher: Well, then.

Derek Law: Thank you very much!

Erin Gallagher: This is why I'm really glad to be in a room of scholars. Thank you very much. "Gaillard."

Audience member: But you know that most of the people here say "Gill-Yard."

Erin Gallagher: See, that's why I was wondering. I thought, "Is that a Charleston thing or is that actually how it's pronounced"?

Audience member: It's "Gill-yard"!

Erin Gallagher: Maybe there's not a wrong answer here. You say "Guy-ard," I say "Gall-ard." "Amazing record attendance"—that's nice to see. "Open access," "sharing," "reading," "food," "Katina," "need coffee." Was that for the previous question or was that for this one? "Grits." Derek, are you a fan of grits?

Derek Law: What?

Erin Gallagher: Are you a fan of grits, the food grits?

Derek Law: Yeah, we put it on the road when ice is there to stop people sliding.

Erin Gallagher: Okay, then I guess you are a fan, okay.

Katina Strauch: Hominy. There's hominy grits.

Derek Law: Hominy grits, yes.

Erin Gallagher: All right, so I'm going to be taking these responses and compiling them for our Poll-a-Palooza for next year, and we'll see if our predictions of hottest buses come true. Yay! There's one that says "Yay!" All right we're moving onto the next question.

What do those stats mean? We're going to start with some serious questions now. How do you purchase e-books? DDA/PDA/EBA/choose your favorite acronym. Do you purchase through publisher/aggregator packages, title-by-title, we don't purchase e-books? Okay, those of you responding "other," if you're so inclined I would love to hear what else you are doing.

Audience Member: All of them!

Erin Gallagher: All of the above? Okay, maybe that's "other"?

Audience member: Well, A, B, C.

Erin Gallagher: If there is an "other" that I didn't catch here though, please feel free to share. I'd be interested to see how these responses would match up if I had done this same question even five years ago. Also, let me know if you need more time. Is everyone doing pretty well with the polling software? It's working for everybody? Okay, great, good. I like to ask my students—part of my liaison duties at Rollins involve working with the English department teaching library sessions for the English classes, and I always like to ask the students, "Who likes to read an e-book? Who likes to read a book entirely online?" So, that's why this whole buzz topic of "Is print dead yet?" it seems like such an obvious answer that it's "no," because when I asked the students who were between the ages of 18 and 21 mostly if they like to read books entirely online I might get one tentative little hand coming up so I think that answers the question.

Derek Law: Although, I would like to ask the second question: When did they last read a book in any format?

Erin Gallagher: Well, I like to be a bit more positive in my instruction. Have you ever taken a MOOC? And when I asked—my mom is here visiting with me. She is not in the audience today, but I was telling her about polling and I asked, "Do you know what is a MOOC?" And she said, "Is that like a hip, new, alternative milk?" Okay, so we got some "What the heck is a MOOC?" MOOC, Massive Online Open Course, it's freely available courses offered by a lot of institutions and organizations and colleges, and they have varying levels of sophistication and value, and I wanted to ask this question because one of our librarians was on a sabbatical all last year and part of what she did during that sabbatical was takes several MOOCs and try them out, and I think out of those there were maybe only one or two that proved to be really valuable, so does anybody have any that they've taken and found to be worth sharing? Yes?

Audience member: Copyright X.

Erin Gallagher: Copyright X?

Audience Member: Yes.

Erin Gallagher: And who offers that?

Audience member: Harvard does.

Erin Gallagher: Harvard. Okay, I think I've heard of that one. By the way, if anyone needs a microphone if you want to speak and you feel like you might need a little bit of amplification, then our dear friend might be able to bring you a microphone. Yes?

Audience member: Or as I said two years ago that the time would be that every one of you should take a MOOC. If you met a MOOC, you'll figure out what it's like and you'll have your own opinion. It's amazing that only 20% of you would take a MOOC. You're missing out on an important, important phenomenon in our world.

Erin Gallagher: That's good to hear. I admit I have not taken one, so, and now I'm inspired. Yes?

Audience member: I took a music one that was the "History of Jazz," and it was really good and one on Sonata.

Erin Gallagher: Okay. I like to hear that. You don't necessarily have to take ones that relate to your day-to-day; it could be kind of fun, too. Has anybody else taken any others that are kind of off the beaten path? Yes?

Audience member: Equine Nutrition.

Erin Gallagher: Equine Nutrition! Wow! All right. Horse health. Oh, okay. I lied about the microphone. You're just going to have to shout. All right, at this point DDA, or demand-driven acquisition, is and this is open-ended, friends, so you can respond as many times as you like and it's anonymous. Responses might be things like "old hat" or "not something I would touch with a 10-foot pole" or "fantastic." Oh, wow! The negativity. Oh, gosh, I'm so glad I just co-authored a book on use driven acquisition. "A malicious quagmire." "Where articles should be." I like that! I don't know who said that but I agree and I totally salute you. Oh, I see "gotta also ask if we ever completed a MOOC." Good point, whoever mentioned that. Maybe that will be for next year. "Worth exploring," "too expensive and we dropped it," oh, that's in all caps, someone is serious. All right. Well, I am very interested in these answers, and so if you want to come talk to me afterward about this in more detail I'd like to hear more about why this is getting such negative feedback. "An interesting idea." Would—do you think that DDA would be better received if we had more options for formats beyond just books, e-books? Yay/nay? That's a little on the fly question.

Derek Law: I love that one, "Where our expectations went to die."

Erin Gallagher: "Works well with video." I agree. We have found that to be working quite well for us. "More expensive than the good old days."

Oh, alright. Let's try the next one. Oh, here we go. Hot, hot topic. Do you use alternative metrics to measure the impact of your own research and publication activities? How about you, Derek?

Derek Law: I hadn't heard of them until the last few weeks.

Erin Gallagher: Oh, wow! You fooled us. So, we've got some "yeses," those of you are saying "yes," I'd love to hear more about what you're using, what sort of sources of measurement are you using—social media? Maybe nobody wants to admit that they said "yes?" I'm getting some "What the heck are altmetrics?" So Derek did a really lovely job of providing us with an analogy yesterday that it's a bit like alternative medicine, and I was also—the first thing I thought of was alternative rock music from the 90s, hence the palooza theme, but as far as, "What the heck are altmetrics," you know, Derek, you want to give us 10 seconds?

Derek Law: A snare and a delusion. They rely on the assumption that people who don't know anything know what's good. It's a bit the same as giving them—as using demand-driven acquisition. You leave it to the general public to decide what is good and what is bad. It bears no relation to what is important. It's just what can be measured, and the assumption is if you can measure it that's good enough, and the other thing that I liked is the highest correlation, I read when I was writing this up, the highest correlation that you get with altmetrics is with retraction watch. It shows that what it is measuring is bad science, which I find fascinating.

Erin Gallagher: All right, Derek. Next year, you and me, "Is DDA rubbish?" It's on! All right open-ended question: "How do you market open access resources to your user community?" And the answer to this might be "I don't," but in any case I'd love to hear about what you're doing. Okay, "B." That's—whoever is using "B's" to market open access resources, see me after. I want to know how you're doing this. You're including them in catalogs, digital commons, Facebook. Was Facebook with the altmetrics question? I learned a lot about what different libraries are doing with open access resources as far as marketing here.

Derek law: I like the idea of having a budget for open access.

Erin Gallagher: Well, you know. Actually, that is what we're doing right now, and it does involve the budget. What kind of throwing money at our faculty to get them interested in publishing in open access and then it's getting a foot in the door for us, hopefully. "I have no users." So, I'm assuming we have like some vendors or publishers in the audience. If this doesn't totally apply to you, you can make something up. I'm interested in—there are quite a few Facebook answers here. If anyone has answered Facebook and feels confident and if you want to share how are you marketing open access resources via Facebook? All right, well, you don't have to, but . . .

Audience Member: Well, we have particular programs online for open access publishing we can find and control (inaudible).

Erin Gallagher: Good to know. Yet we do similar things. We have the blog and pushing things to Facebook.

Audience member: Yeah, it's getting bigger.

Erin Gallagher: Right. Thank you. Instruction classes, definitely, I was very interested to know if you're promoting open access in instruction as well. That's something that we're thinking about doing more. "LinkedIn"—is that where things go to die? I don't think so, but I've heard that.

I'm very interested in this one: Do you consider Wikipedia to be a valid educational resource for college students? Maybe that's another one for next year's debate. This is great. I'm seeing lots of "yeses," "it depends." I think it does kind of depend in some ways. We have a faculty member in the English department at Rollins who teaches a class every couple of semesters called "Writing About Wikipedia," and it involves students working in groups or working independently to improve Wikipedia entries together. I learned a lot by partnering with this faculty member on exactly what goes into the vetting process at Wikipedia as far as what they allow to be posted, and I was really surprised to find out how quick they are at identifying erroneous information and pretty much shutting you down. In fact, just recently I became aware that the Rollins College IP addresses are being blocked—people are being blocked from editing Wikipedia from our IP ranges—and the reason being there seems to be one person who consistently goes in and adds erroneous Crayola crayon colors to the Crayola entry, some of which are downright racy, so we're working on correcting that.

Derek Law: I guess Donald Trump has to do something in his spare time. I really like the story of the Bodleian Library and its special collections, and there were a lot of erroneous entries about their special collections but the librarian, very cleverly I thought, rather than just moaning and writing and complaining and getting them to change it assigned members of her staff to writing up entries about the Bodleian special collections with hot links through to catalogs and things like that, so they used it as a positive attitude or attribute rather than just complaining about it. I thought it was really good.

Erin Gallagher: Very nice. I like that idea. All right, so I'm definitely interested to know if you will be implementing any new programs or adjusting existing programs at your library or organization based on what you've learned here? I know I will be for sure, especially regarding open access marketing, management, collecting. For those of you who are responding yes, anyone want to share what you might be implementing or changing at your place of business? We are all going to be getting rid of DDA, apparently, and buying open access materials.

Derek Law: And Altmetrics.

Erin Gallagher: And altmetrics. Doing altmetrics. So it looks like yes, we got a pretty good amount of people who are going to be shaking things up when you get home. Yes?

Audience member: Dan Tonkery said that 75% of e-book sales were coming through publishers, and we haven't been able to find these publishers, so I'm thinking that that I need do that.

Erin Gallagher: Hmm. That's very interesting to hear. So publishers as opposed to aggregators, I would imagine. Okay. All right. Well, I'm sure they're pretty compelling reasons behind that. Anyone else? Yes?

Audience member: I would reconciliate into finding out where this money goes for e-books.

Erin Gallagher: Okay. Very important. Maybe talk to me afterward. I need to know how to do that. Yes?

Audience member: (inaudible 27:06)

Erin Gallagher: Oh, ok. Definitely a worthy undertaking. Anybody else? All right. Well, we're all just going to go shake things up. Let's have a little bit more fun with our questions. What's the best book you've read this year? I want to know because I need some reading material. Derek, how about you?

Derek Law: It's the best book because I read it every year. It's *McCarthy's Bar.* It's all about getting drunk in bars in Ireland. It's a travel book. Can I have just 1 minute for the story? It's a journalist in Birmingham and England who is made redundant at the age of 50 and couldn't get another job. He had a big payout and he decided he'd write a book. It's the only book I've ever bought in paperback then gone out and bought the hardback, and he says when he starts the book that there's always one bit of advice you get from your grandmother that you remember, and the bit of advice he had from his grandmother was "never walk past a bar with your name on the door," and his name is McCarthy, so he went to Ireland and just goes around every bar finding out what the Irish think of themselves and having a great time. *McCarthy's Bar.* I don't need to tell you the author because it's in the title—*McCarthy's Bar.*

Erin Gallagher: Oh. Should I do the same thing in Ireland?

Derek Law: Oh, yes!

Erin Gallagher: Look for some pubs with "Gallagher" in the name? One of them I saw was "My own book" was the best book you've read this year. Anybody want to share what is your own book? Is Stephen King in the audience? I mean, I wouldn't know which one because he's published about eight books this year. I'm a huge fan, by the way, I'm not dissing him. Okay. I haven't read most of these, so this is great. I'm getting some really good ideas. I think the best book I read this year, I finally read Nathaniel Philbrick's *In the Heart of the Sea.* Has anyone read that one about the whale ship *Essex?* There's a movie coming out next month, so please read it before you see the movie. It's really fantastic. Derek and I share a love of maritime adventures, by the way.

Derek Law: Put the two of us in a rowing boat and there's no stopping us.

Erin Gallagher: All right, this is the most important question by far of all of the polling questions: What's your favorite restaurant in Charleston. Sorry, everyone, I moved on a little quickly. "Justine's" Yes! Last year I asked this question and I got a lot of responses that said "Not this." Has anyone eaten at Aww Shucks Oyster Shack? Yeah. Il Cortile Del Re was always my favorite. Am I correct that that that is not there anymore? I read online, because I was looking it up to take my mom there, and I read that it's not there anymore. I know, it was always my favorite. "Anything that sells barbecue," all right. Well, Derek, did you have an answer to this one?

Derek Law: Well, I had lots of nice places, but the one that I thought was really great is just across the street is Ladles, the soup kitchen. That was a brilliant place for lunch.

Erin Gallagher: I haven't been able to get in there. It was like a line out the door every time.

Derek Law: Yeah, it is really, really good.

Erin Gallagher: I like that this is anonymous because last year somebody said McDonald's. You got to branch out! "Subway." Yes! Eat fresh, even in Charleston! Alright, we're moving on.

Any suggestions for the 2016 Charleston Conference theme? Where do we go from here? Feel free to get real "pun-y" with this too. I like some good puns. Oh, "no theme." Wow, going to get crazy. "Like a publisher," aww, or a vendor! Full disclosure, I used to work for a vendor and so my first four Charlestons were here as a vendor and you do leave feeling a little battered.

Derek Law: "I love altmetrics."

Erin Gallagher: I love altmetrics. I like "Standards in the Sky." That's really good whoever came up with that one. That's the kind of thing I like to see. So, next year is going to be very interesting. Especially the timing of the conference is always so crucial with election years.

Derek Law: The idea of Trump budgeting makes you glad that words like "oxymoronic" do exist.

Erin Gallagher: These are some great ones. Katina, are you getting some ideas for next year? All right. "Been there, done that." Well, all right, moving on. If you come up with other really, really good ones feel free to just tell Katina. Oh, yes, yeah.

All right. All right, what do you think will be the hottest topic of Charleston 2016? I'm very interested in this so that we can look next year and see if any of our predictions came true. This one really might be Trump, I don't know. "Death of the ILS." "The Weather." I mean, if we're being really honest, yes. "Who isn't owned by ProQuest or EBSCO?" I think that might be the winner, that's good. These are going to be great to look at next year. I hope everybody comes back next year because we going to be looking at these. "Where libraries fit in." Oh, boy.

Audience member: The EBSCO ProQuest merger!

Erin Gallagher: Oh, boy. All right, well we'll see how many of these come true. This may have been my last one.

Derek Law: Trump buys ProQuest.

Erin Gallagher: Yes it is. All right. So, without further ado, my esteemed colleague and new friend and fellow maritime scholar, though I don't put myself in your same category, I'm just more of a reader, Derek Law is going to regale us with some end of conference comments. However, Derek, I would like to point out that if you would like to get a real sense of the kind of person who Derek is, is to check out his and I believe his now defunct blog called "Long Overdue" and as he describes it, it is a dated blog of library jokes and stories so I wanted to share just a couple of my favorites, one of which was, "What did the spider do inside the library computer? It made a webpage." Now, but this one's even better, really. "Why did the librarian slip and fall on the library floor? Because she was in the non-friction section." Did you make these up? These are so funny. All right. There are lots of changing light bulb jokes too, like "How many academic librarians does it take to change a lightbulb?" and, you know, I'll let you answer that one, but thanks so much for participating in the polls everyone and without further ado, Derek Law.

Derek Law: Actually, has everybody heard of David Beckham the footballer? Because my favorite joke is David Beckham goes into the library and he goes up to the desk and he says, "Can I have a Big Mac and fries, please?" And the counter assistant says, "You're in a library," and he says (whispering) "I'm sorry, can I have a Big Mac and fries please?" Okay. Where is the slideshow button? Slideshow. Okay. Well, I have been asked to do a summing up. Summing up is almost impossible as the conference has become so big. This is the 35th Charleston Conference, so happy birthday Charleston Conference. Almost 1,800 registered, almost 500 first-timers, 291 sessions, it's physically impossible to attend everything, and therefore I can only give you some of my prejudices, not really sum up everything that happened. But, one of the notable features for me is 549 speakers of the 1,800 registrants. One of the great things about Charleston is that it's about sharing. I know of no other conference where the ratio of speakers to attendees is so high; it's not as in so many conferences about 50 people standing up at the podia like this and handing down tablets of stone to the ignorant masses. It's about a third of the conference sharing their experiences, their plans, their projects, and their ambitions with each other. It's the most sharing conference I'm aware of. The other thing I love about Charleston is the quotes that we always get at the beginning, the conference theme, and I've heard lots of them over the years. This time it's from our guest Martin Luther King's speech "Where do we go from here?", one of the great speeches by this famous speaker, but it only tells half the story because this is the catalogers' way, as we all do, we know we learned we catalog from the title page not from the cover but we then, in this case, lose some meaning. "Where do we go from here: Chaos or community?" It's the sort of subtitle that doesn't appear on the title page. Is it chaos? Well, we're all working or have been working separately in little boxes, and again one of the great things about Charleston is the way in which it encourages people from different disciplines, from different areas, from different activities to come together with their diverse perspectives on a whole range of topics. And at a time of radical and fundamental change, this has been a theme coming through; it is more important than ever that all of those in the information stream, the information flow, are working together toward common ends.

In the UK, a survey was done recently, which showed that the public library, that the library is the second most used, still the second most used public service. It's hugely popular with the public. I should perhaps add that the most popular and most heavily used public service is crematoria. Now, can't you see we have a great advantage over crematoria because we can get repeat business! The other bit of advice I always love is of Bjorn Borg, the tennis player. When he gave up the professional circuit he took up coaching, and what he would do, I gather, is that he would play a couple of games with whoever he was giving some coaching to, and he always had a single bit of advice, which he gave to those he was coaching, and that was, "Always change a losing game." And I thought that was a great motto, a great bit of advice to give, a great thing to work with. If it's not working don't try and improve it and tinker with it, change it fundamentally. Because what we're going through, and this was again a theme of some of the planetary speeches, is that we are going through not an upgrade, but an upheaval, and always change the losing game. One of my favorite authors that I like to read is Clay Shirky. He tends to be talking about journalism, but the sort of things he talks about because it is part of the information seen as well to me apply just as much to libraries and publishing. "The hard truth about the future is that nobody knows for sure what will happen; the current system is so brittle and the alternatives are so speculative that there's no hope for a simple and orderly transition from state 'A' to state 'B'. Chaos is our lot; the best we can do is identify the various forces at work shaping various possible futures." Which to me sums up where we are in the state of chaos perfectly.

But what we have, and what Charleston produces, is that sense of community, which can take us forward. I like that phrase yesterday from Katherine Skinner about conditions aligning, things beginning to come together, working together, making things happen, and I've always liked alliteration. That's the trouble with being a librarian, I guess. I like the four "S's," and you get these all at Charleston: sandboxes, showcases, sharing platters, and survival kits. There are all kinds of different sessions. It's not just about people standing up here talking down. I've been in meetings this week of six people and meetings of 1,000 people, and all of them have values of different kinds and bring knowledge of different kinds. So I'm a great believer in community.

Something else I'm doing made me think of an analogy, which was something I know absolutely nothing about but I like the analogy, which is the way in which gardens changed in England between the 16th and the 18th centuries. The traditional English garden was a very small, very regimented, this is the one at Hampton Court, everything divided into tight little boxes, everything perfectly articulated, everything very neat and tidy, but the boxes very separate and very much a part. They were traditional, formal box gardens, which were first introduced in France and then moved to England in the style that somebody called "Le Notre." But, then along came the Industrial Revolution and along came Capability Brown. He worked at the time of the Industrial Revolution and he revolutionized gardens, great house gardens in England and the United Kingdom. Great sweeping vistas, using technology to dig big lakes and using technology to build bridges across those, have big sweeping views of what was going on, everything linked together, the water, the landscape, the views all linked together. He literally opened up new vistas. The other thing I love about him is that he invented the "HaHa," you know that little step in gardens that you fold down. "HaHa," the original LOL. So he took the time, he seized the moment, he saw the alignment of things coming together and he changed fundamentally the way that gardens looked in big posh houses of the sort that you now pay $20 to visit.

So, when are we going to create our pleasing vistas for the future? Well, Charleston is a great start. That's why you're here. I hope that all of you—half of you here will be back next year and instead of being first-timers you'll be second-timers. Charleston is also for me an experience of the senses. And all five senses starting with sight, the beauty of Charleston, it really is a gorgeous city, the Gaillard Center, I come from near France, so I'm going to call it "Guy-yard." The Gaillard Center performance hall is really wonderful. Last night I heard screaming outside. It was cheerleaders practicing out in the park. Wonderful. The aquarium, all sorts of views of sharks and things that work with publishers. Come on, it's a joke! And then other too, other characters. Tony, where's Tony? Anthony, our style icon up at the back there. These are pictures of players in the Rugby World Cup, which happened in the last month for those of you in America who went out the first round. These are pictures from the Rugby World Cup of people who have clearly seen Anthony and have used him as a style icon. The one at the top right is the one I love but here we go. So, Charleston is an experience of the senses. So, sight we have done. Taste, lots of food and wonderful canapés. You know canapés—it's the French hors d'oeuvres. Lots of food, and thank you to all of the sponsors and hosts who have given us so much of that wonderful food. I enjoyed lunch today, particularly. Smell: did you see the gas leak in King Street. Well, you can't see a gas leak, but the thing that I loved about that was how many emergency vehicles does Charleston actually own? That must've been about 20 of them out there when they thought that was a gas leak. All the sirens going, wish my grandson could've been there; he would've loved it. I could think of lots of other smells, but that's the most delicate one to mention. Hearing: one of the things about having so many speakers and so many sessions is I tried to do a rough calculation and reckon that you've all heard something like 4 million words over the last three days. That's quite a lot to take in. And lastly touch: the Francis Marion lifts are rather small, so can I apologize to all of those that I may inadvertently have touched over the last three days.

Anthony Watkinson: That's your story!

Derek Law: But at least it's a story. So, really, as well as trying to sum up very briefly, I'd like to do some thanks to the community who support and run and organize the Charleston Conference. The sponsors who have fed us wonderfully well during the week, and the exhibitors who informed us, but, perhaps most importantly for me, they give you all sorts of things to put in the Christmas stockings, the Santa stockings for my daughters and grandchildren, some wonderful toys in there that will be going into Christmas stockings. I'm Scottish, I get to be mean. And the conference team, it would be invidious to name any name in particular. There's been a huge conference team who you have seen all around you, information desks, back of house, front of house, they've all been absolutely charming, absolutely friendly, wonderfully helpful, and they've done a great job. And to you, the participants, a new record of almost 1,800 all learning, training, and for me most importantly sharing. That's been the community that has come together over these last few days. And of course Katina, the "Fons et Origo" of the conference. For those of who didn't benefit from a classical education, that's Fons as in "source and origin," and not as in Henry Winkler, although we have had happy days.

It would be traditional in my part of the world to finish with "Auld Lang Syne." Now hardly anybody knows the real story of "Auld Lang Syne." And these two verses are the two middle verses, which nobody ever sings but are some of the most important for me because "Auld Lang Syne" is about remembering childhood friendships. It's about remembering being together, and it tells the story of Burns and his friend. They'd run about the hills together and they wondered around together in the old days and they'd paddle the boats and they played together as children, and then the friend moved overseas to Jamaica to the plantations and they were separated for years, but they remember every year with a toast those friendships. So "Auld Lang Syne," which I'm not going to try and sing to you, is all about friendship. It's not about the end of the year. It's about friendship and that's the other great thing that one gets in Charleston. So, see you next year, November 2nd through the 5th. I like that effect. See you next year in Charleston and welcome returned then. Thank you. I'm sorry I forgot one joke I was going to tell about Katina, not a joke really, just a question. Did you all see Katina sitting in the box in the Gaillard Center in the opera house? I couldn't make up my mind. Did it look like Queen Elizabeth and Prince Philip sitting there in their majesty or did it look like Statler and Waldorf?

Collection Development

One Library's Successful Venture in Providing Comprehensive Streaming Media Services

Allyson Mower, Scholarly Communications & Copyright Librarian, J. Willard Marriott Library, University of Utah

Mary Ann James, Electronic Resources Manager, J. Willard Marriott Library, University of Utah

Catherine Soehner, Associate Dean, Research and Learning Services, J. Willard Marriott Library, University of Utah

Maria Hunt, Head, Scholarly Resources and Collections (retired) , J. Willard Marriott Library, University of Utah

Dave Heyborne, Scholarly Resources Analyst, J. Willard Marriott Library, University of Utah

Joni Clayton, Head, Media and Classroom Services, J. Willard Marriott Library, University of Utah

Abstract

Thoroughly understanding what professors and instructors needed to accomplish their teaching goals with streaming video was the first step enabling one academic library to successfully manage a rapid increase in demand for streaming media. The second element was incorporating an expert understanding of copyright law and the nature of the video marketplace.

This paper will strive to educate librarians and other professional library staff on how they can best integrate media streaming into mainstream library services for their campus faculty, as well as how to provide a full range of streaming services. The paper also will address workflow, communication with faculty, budget and license negotiations, copyright principles, fair use, and content delivery.

Introduction and Background

University libraries have always engaged in the business of providing their campus communities with resources for research and teaching. As technology has changed, the delivery method for providing these resources has also adjusted in order to make content more easily and quickly accessible. One excellent example of this is the provision of media, especially film.

Historians document that motion pictures made their debut in the late 1800s and by the 1970s 16mm films were regularly used in educational settings from grade school through higher education (Mintz and McNeil, 2013). Many university libraries developed extensive collections of 16mm film, including archival collections of university activities (Brancolini, 1993). As technology advanced, 16mm films were replaced by collections of videos in Beta and VHS formats, then DVD, and finally Blu-Ray as physical forms of film. Providing access to films in physical formats such as VHS, DVD, and Blu-Ray had obvious disadvantages for library users. There were only so many copies available to students who were required to view certain films for their coursework and only so many machines available to play these physical formats causing stress on both the library and the students.

As computer technology improved and the Internet matured, videos were increasingly created in digital form and films on VHS and DVD were capable of being digitized and streamed. Streaming allowed access to the films any time, anywhere the Internet was available. Many university libraries began to offer media

http://dx.doi.org/10.5703/1288284316240

streaming services to their campus communities such that a faculty member could request the streaming of a film for their course, the library would digitize and stream the film, and students could easily access the required film any time (Snyder et al., 2001). These services began appearing in the early to mid-2000's when film publishers and vendors were primarily offering the physical forms of film as the dominant method of purchasing and accessing a film.

However, the marketplace was shifting. Film publishers and vendors began to embrace the new technology and their offerings expanded to include streamed versions of their films for a price. As such, libraries have responded to the new marketplace by adapting and updating their media-related services. Getting clear about what library users needed in order to accomplish their teaching and learning tasks along with incorporating expert understanding of copyright and the marketplace allowed one university library to successfully manage these significant changes while still meeting user needs.

Literature Review

The most recent journal article on the topic of media streaming services offered by an academic library includes Rebecca Schroeder and Julie Williamson's 2011 article, "Streaming Video: The Collaborative Convergence of Technical Services, Collection Development, and Information Technology in an Academic Library" (2011). The article discusses the creation and implementation of Brigham Young University's streaming device, BYUGLE, and the adaptations in collection development that the new technology precipitated.

Library Trends published a special issue in 2010, edited by Clara Healy, titled "Current Trends in Academic Media Collections and Services." Two of the articles from the special issue focused on new models in video acquisition, delivery, and patron access (Bergman, 2010; Handman, 2010). Other articles discussed training in media librarianship, copyright scenarios, and a case study on using Netflix to augment the library's collection (Laskowski, 2010; Russell, 2010; and Healy 2010).

The Association of College & Research Libraries issued *Guidelines for Media Resources in Academic Libraries* in 2012 (ACRL, 2012) and the Association of Research Libraries released a related SPEC Kit in 2001 on instructional media services provided by libraries (ARL, 2001). As noted by Schroeder and Williamson, much of the literature focused on the technical aspects of video streaming and less on the collaborative and nuanced approaches to streaming as it pertains to instructional needs, library acquisitions, information technology, and the legal and film market landscape.

Knowing What Professors Want

As we investigated how best to offer streaming media services, the need for a workflow system immediately became apparent. The workflow involved discovering, researching, licensing, purchasing, and administering the content professors and instructors wanted. The solution we arrived at came in three-parts: a request form, a ticket tracking system, and a status page which faculty could use to check on existing requests. Each of these parts are described below.

The request form was originally designed to handle book and journal purchases and had to be expanded substantially to support the streaming media process. We needed specific information from professors and instructors about the courses or scholarly projects each film would be used for to ensure that we pursued the proper kind of licenses and licensing periods. Did they need the film for more than one semester? If streaming was not available, could we meet their need by placing it on reserve? Could they show it during face-to-face class time? Balancing the complexity of questions with the desire to create a streamlined form arose as one of the primary challenges.

To track and manage requests once submitted by faculty, we opted to have the system send completed request forms to a separate help ticket system. This allowed us to resolve the request through a workflow process with steps such as:

- Purchase investigation
- Contacting vendor
- Prepare for streaming
- Ready for CORAL

This was a natural way to integrate the process of tracking requests with our existing trouble ticket management system and maintain an efficient workflow.

As the new request and ticketing systems began to see greater use, faculty wanted an easy way to check the status of a request while it was being processed. As you will see later in the paper, streaming media can be time consuming to license, so unlike most purchase requests the library receives, it can often be difficult to complete a streaming request in under a week or so. To address this issue, the library's information technology group built a small web application that would read the information from the ticketing system and then display the information in a simplified format for professors and instructors. Professors and instructors use the web application to determine when their requested films expire and to decide whether or not to renew their request for a future class.

Expanding the Budget and Negotiating Licenses

In order to meet faculty demand for streaming media, we had to find additional funds. Initially, we had a small budget of $25,000 allocated for the audiovisual (AV) collection with an emphasis on keeping up with current DVD and Blu-Ray content. This allocation was split between two staff members who selected in those formats. Occasionally, librarian-led college and interdisciplinary teams augmented the AV budget and utilized firm order funds to purchase AV material in a subject area.

We also changed the scope of what we purchased by focusing more on immediate teaching needs. This meant we stopped buying new AV content and reallocated what remained of the existing AV budget towards streaming video. During the 2013-14 fiscal year, we allocated $30,000 for streaming licenses and added it to the original $25,000 we had for AV material. We also relied on our database budget to initiate subscriptions to streaming media collections such as Films On Demand or Medici TV. We also asked for additional funds solely for streaming media during the 2014-15 budget cycle.

Media Streaming Licenses

As we expanded the service, we discovered that licensing streaming media presented unique challenges. Each vendor had different terms, prices, and renewal dates for content, making it difficult to budget, especially when the number of films and their individual prices were not known until each title was researched and pricing finalized with the vendor. To the extent possible, we negotiated for perpetual rights in order to keep staff processing time to a minimum and to help professors plan for future courses. While most of the content came with a license agreement, some purchases did not and terms were simply noted on the invoice. Occasionally permission was given to stream the film without having to pay for streaming rights. In those cases written permission was given either by e-mail or a separate document.

Teaching Exemption, Lending, and Public Performance Rights

When it came to access, we carefully reviewed terms to avoid agreeing to any explicitly prohibited in-class viewing clauses or terms not allowing us to loan the physical item. This would negate the already-established face-to-face teaching exemption (Section 110(1)) and the first sale doctrine (Section 109) in the US Copyright Act. These cases were rare, but did happen. We also used the license negotiation process to clarify public performance rights, which typically cover screenings that occur on campus, but outside of class. For the most part, teaching faculty do not require public performance rights and we preferred to not pay additional fees for that type of permission. If the vendor still included the right in the renegotiated price, we recorded it in our electronic resource management system so that campus patrons wanting to hold a screening event in the future could do so with the licensed title.

Single Title Licensing Versus Databases

Licensing films individually by title rather than subscribing to collections or databases was costly and time consuming due to the processing required. On average, purchasing a single streaming title required approximately four hours of staff time from the time a request was made to the point of notifying the professor about the film's availability. Of the 1,920 streaming requests received between spring semester 2013 and summer semester 2014, we purchased approximately 500 single titles representing over 2,000 hours of staff time (see Table 1 for request statistics).

Single-title licensing was also duplicative. We discovered that many faculty requested the same titles, making streaming video databases an effective collection development strategy. Collections of streaming video opened up more content for more people affiliated with the university and MARC records could be loaded into the online catalog. Despite these conveniences, fewer rights holders offered their films through streaming video databases. Only 115 of the requested films were available in video databases that the library had access to making this a less dominant option in the video marketplace.

Keeping Track of Permissions, Licenses, and Expiration Dates

To help track the range of licenses required for streaming media, we created a separate, internal process using the open source electronic resource management software CORAL. We used the software to manage basic information about a streaming resource such as instructor, course, semesters needed, cost, how the film should be accessed, what type of license was used for the purchase, and vendor contact information. Expiration dates were entered and the system alerted staff when titles expired. Most importantly, the license, invoice, and any additional correspondence that provided permissions were attached to the CORAL record as a pdf. This helped clarify questions about public performance rights that would come up after an item had already been licensed.

Addressing Copyright

A basic understanding of copyright provided the necessary foundation to expand the library's streaming media services. This allowed us to intelligently negotiate licenses and have a fuller knowledge of what academic libraries could do when it came to audiovisual material. In the broadest sense, copyright represents an individual right and consists of five components that rights holders can transfer or license either in whole or in part. Essentially, copyright protects the creators of original literary, dramatic, musical, artistic, and other intellectual works and the protection extends to both published and unpublished material (Title 17, *US Code*). The following list includes the typical (and exclusive) rights that come with being a copyright holder:

- To reproduce the work
- To prepare derivative works
- To distribute copies of the work
- To perform the work publicly
- To display the work publicly

Streaming a movie involved at least two (and possibly four) of the five exclusive rights authors and creators had in a work—copying and distribution. Once streamed, the work could also be considered a display and a performance. In order to engage in these rights, we either needed to be a copyright holder, have permission from the rightsholder, or rely on exceptions provided for in the US Copyright Act. This required copyright market research: finding copyright owners, figuring out how rights holders published and distributed their works, and determining availability of permissions—either direct or through a vendor.

Copyright Market Research

We developed a market research workflow in order to accurately and fully respond to the professors' requests and move the tickets through the process. First we checked the US Copyright

Office online catalog of registration records to determine the rights holder. Next, we searched for each film title in a collection called Campus eMedia, administered through the statewide education network to see if rights had already been purchased for student and faculty use. Then we searched video streaming databases that the library had already licensed and the feature film company holdings where we had an existing contract.

After the on-campus resources had been exhausted, we moved to searching a film-specific website called canistream.it which helped us establish if the streaming version was available for individual purchase through vendors such as Amazon Prime, iTunes, Google Play, or others. We also searched the general web to see if an institutional streaming version of a film was for sale on other film websites or the production company's site. Using the information from the copyright registration record, we e-mailed rights holders or vendors to ask about availability or permission to stream. If no streaming resources were found and the production company did not license streaming, the title was considered in context of the fair use exception in the US Copyright Act.

Fair Use

The US Copyright Act accounts for and defines fair use as the ability to copy for purposes of criticism, commenting, news reporting, teaching, scholarship, and research. Measuring and applying what constitutes a fair use remains subjective, but guidance exists to help navigate its flexible nature within institutions whose mission centers on teaching, scholarship, and research. An institution's copying and reuse policy provides initial guidance and so do campus attorneys. In addition, the American Library Association has a fair use evaluator and the Association of Research Libraries produced fair use guidelines in 2012 (Brewer, 2008; ARL, 2012).

When it comes to fair use, it remains important to balance the purpose of the use with the nature of the work and the impact on the market for the work both in terms of purchasing and permissions. We considered all these factors in context of the University's policy on copying for academic use and in light of the copyright market research we conducted at the beginning of the workflow.

Delivering the Content

Once sufficient copyright market research, negotiations, purchases, or fair use evaluations occurred, we prepared the work for faculty and student access. If the rights holder or vendor did not supply a mechanism for streaming video, we delivered content through the library's streaming information technology system, which consisted of a storage server housing the digitized video and a web server that used an in-house database to provide titles through an authenticated interface. The server system restricted downloading, copying, and link capturing. Each film received a unique URL that we delivered to faculty via e-mail with specific instructions on limiting use to students enrolled in the course. Depending on the title, some links were added to the catalog.

Hosted Content

If the film requested by the faculty member existed as part of a licensed database, we shared the link, provided information about the database, and explained that it did not have to be restricted to the class, since databases were usually licensed for campus-wide access. We also explained that students would need to authenticate if they viewed the film while off campus.

While most licensed video databases remained accessible for the entire campus, some hosted content was restricted to only the students enrolled in the course. One example of restricted, vendor-hosted content included Swank Digital Campus. The company offered feature, studio films by semester or year. Access was temporary and only for students registered in the course; titles did not become part of the library's collection. We helped instructors facilitate access for students through course management software by securely embedding links to the film. Figures 1 and 2 illustrate this process. We

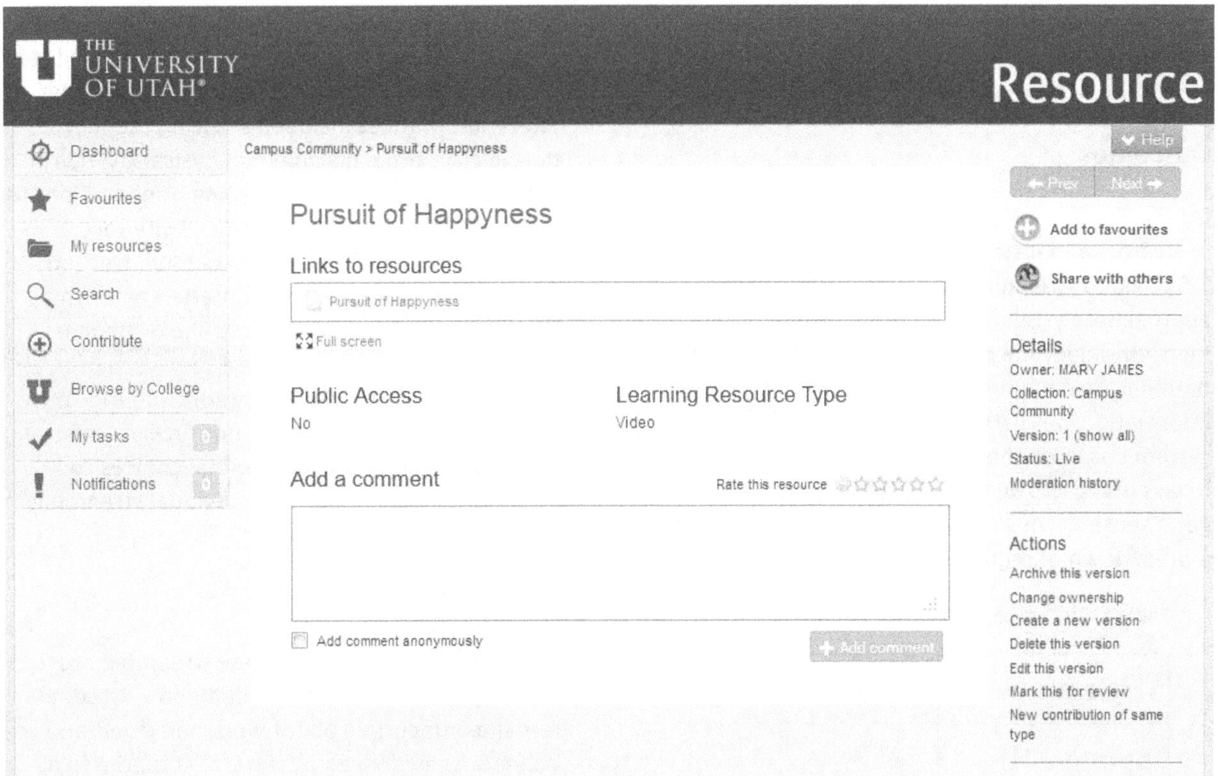

Figure 1. Link to hosted content embedded in course management software.

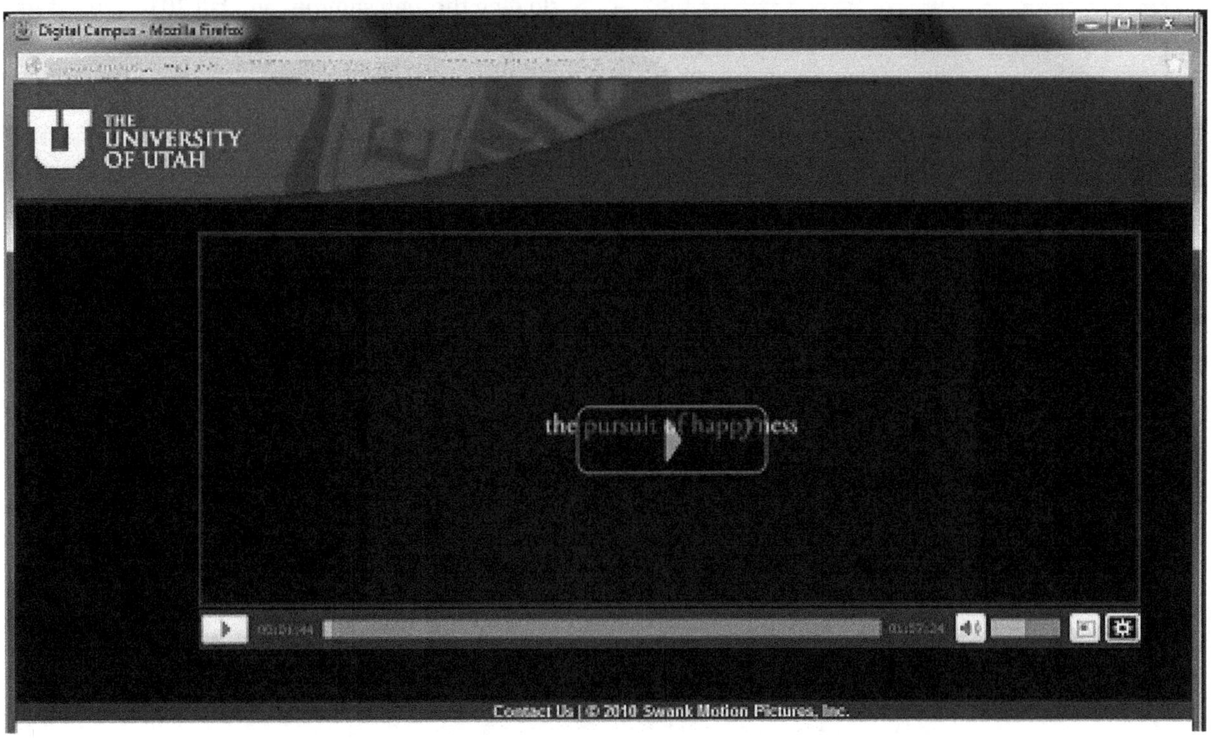

Figure 2. Film connecting to hosted content website via course management system.

communicated the delivery outcome to professors and instructors via e-mail and tracked completion within the ticket system.

Outcomes

During the first academic year of the service, professors and instructors submitted a total of 1,612 video streaming requests. We delivered approximately 1,200 of the requested films either through single-title purchase, licensed database, or in-library streaming. As noted above, this information was gathered through the ticket system based on the assigned workflow status (e.g., purchased, denied, streamed [fair use]). To get a sense of the flow of demand, Table 1 shows a breakdown of requests by semester.

Table 1. Streaming requests by semester.

Semester	# of Requests
Spring 2013	621
Summer 2013	164
Fall 2013	378
Spring 2014	449
Summer 2014	99
Fall 2014	81
Spring 2015	92
Summer 2015	36

We denied approximately 400 of the requests because the film's copyright holder or vendor did not offer an institutional streaming version for the library to purchase nor did the request favor fair use since the rightsholder offered individual on-demand streaming options for students to purchase. The professor or instructor received this information by e-mail, which also included a list of alternatives to meet his or her teaching needs. These alternatives included showing the film during class time, placing the physical DVD on short-term checkout, or selecting brief portions to digitize and post to the course website for asynchronous viewing. Professors followed-up with us by e-mail and many opted to place the DVD on reserve, some chose to show the film during class, and a few desired to have clips created. Since it fell somewhat outside the scope of the library service, we did not receive information regarding professors' choices to direct their students to the individual streaming purchase options.

Conclusion

The first six months of the new streaming process was critical. While we knew demand existed, we remained uncertain about workload levels and the budget. As evidenced by the statistics, the first semester (spring 2013) had the highest number of requests, followed by spring 2014 semester, then slowing through summer and fall 2014 semesters.

We discovered that our preference was to license films for multiple years, especially popular titles. While perpetual rights were more expensive at the outset, they enabled us to save in the long run both in terms of money and staff time. The money would be spent, but it would free up funds for more resources in the next fiscal year. In addition, we would not have to spend time renegotiating new terms the next time a professor requested the title.

Now that a full academic year has passed, we have sufficient data to predict demand, budget, and workload in order to continue the popular service. In the end, we feel confident in saying that providing comprehensive streaming media services and collections for professors and instructors represents an important and manageable role for academic libraries.

References

Association of College and Research Libraries. (2012). Guidelines for media resources in academic libraries. Retrieved August 20, 2014, from http://www.ala.org/acrl/standards/mediaresources

Association of Research Libraries. (2012, January). Code of best practices in fair use for academic and research libraries. Retrieved August 15, 2014, from http://www.arl.org/storage/documents/publications/code-of-best-practices-fair-use.pdf

Bergman, B. (2010, Winter). Making the most of your video collection: Trends in patron access and resource sharing. *Library Trends, 58*(3), 335–348.

Brancolini, K., & Provine, R. E. (1993, December). Video Collection and multimedia in ARL libraries. SPEC, Systems and Procedures Exchange Center Kit 199. Retrieved from http://eric.ed.gov/?id=ED368390

Brewer, M., & American Library Association. (2010). Fair use evaluator. Retrieved October 8, 2015, from http://www.librarycopyright.net/resources/fairuse/

Copyright Law of the United States of America. (1976). 17 U.S.C. Section 106.

Handman, G. (2010, Winter). License to look: Evolving models for library video acquistion and access. *Library Trends, 58*(3), 324–334.

Healy, C. (2010, Winter). Netflix in an academic library: A personal case study. *Library Trends*, *58*(3), 324–334.

Laskowski, M. M. (2010, Winter). A media librarian's education: An assessment of the availability and need for specific training in media librarianship issues and practices. *Library Trends*, *58*(3), 324–334.

Mintz, S., & McNeil, S. (2013). The emergence of motion pictures. Retrieved July 5, 2014, from *Digital History*: http://www.digitalhistory.uh.edu

Russell, C. (2010, Winter). The best of copyright and VideoLib. *Library Trends*, *58*(3), 324–334.

Schroeder, R., & Williamsen, J. (2011). Streaming video: The collaborative covergence of technical services, collection development, and information technology in the academic library. *Collection Management*, *36*, 89–106.

Snyder, C. A., Logue, S., Carter, H., & Soltys, M. (2001, October). Instructional support services. SPEC, Systems and Procedures Exchange Center Kit 265. Retrieved from http://www.arl.org/component/content/article/6/1769

Collaborative Collection Development: Engaging Liaisons and Sharing Information

Alana Verminski, Collection Development Librarian, University of Vermont Libraries

Abstract

Librarians at the Bailey/Howe Library of the University of Vermont found themselves in a challenging situation at the start of the 2016 fiscal year. Facing nearly unprecedented budget reductions, librarians were forced to assess current collections and expenditures, and look ahead to an uncertain future. With a critical eye on existing collection development practices, Bailey/Howe librarians embraced a spirit of collaboration and piloted a new evaluation project which engaged librarian liaisons and supported a more informed renewal decision-making process.

The collection development librarian worked closely with the liaison program director to design a project which asked liaisons to rank the library's electronic resources. The project required liaisons to provide feedback on existing resources in a holistic manner, which would be used by the collections team for renewal and cancellation decisions. This exercise provided the added opportunity for bridge-building between library departments and improved transparency. Liaisons were asked to rank electronic resources in their subject areas and evaluate multidisciplinary resources as a group. The collection development librarian supplied liaisons with resource lists which contained current and historic pricing and usage information. Additionally, the collection development librarian met with liaisons to discuss usage statistics and developed a quick reference sheet about usage data for liaisons to consult as needed. Although budget reductions are an unfortunate, yet common, reality in most academic libraries, the approach taken by Bailey/Howe librarians laid a foundation for collaborative collection development and liaison engagement.

Introduction

For two consecutive fiscal years, the UVM Libraries budget remained flat funded. In late FY 2015, forecasts indicated the Libraries could expect a reduction in funding starting with FY 2017. Already experiencing financial pressure, Bailey/Howe librarians were forced to evaluate current collection development procedures and ask difficult questions about future strategies and methods. Coinciding with these considerations were questions about the degree of liaison involvement in collection development.

The UVM Libraries revamped its earlier bibliographic instruction program in 2007 to reflect then emerging trends in information literacy. Librarians were give liaison assignments which most closely reflected their research and instruction experience. The focus of the new program, like its earlier iteration, was on instruction services and research support. Although liaisons did not have collection development decision-making power, they were often consulted as part of renewal decisions, but not in a systematic manner. Little effort was made to inform liaisons of current collection development trends and initiatives, and liaisons' experience with collections and perspectives on collection building varied widely.

The UVM Libraries already had experience making collections decisions cooperatively. The Bailey/Howe Library Collections Team reviews requests for new resources and evaluates renewals for continuing resources. The Collections Team includes representatives from Collection Management Services, Information and Instruction Services, Special Collections, and the Dean's Office. These representatives are responsible for sharing information with their departmental colleagues and seeking input on renewal decisions when needed. Historically, liaisons were contacted if a resource in their subject area was considered a possible candidate for cancellation and asked for input on how well the resource fit with existing curriculum and its relevance to the given discipline. Liaison feedback was highly valued by the collections team and often stood in the way of resource cancellations.

http://dx.doi.org/10.5703/1288284316241

The previous method of soliciting liaison feedback for renewal decisions worked during periods of fiscal ease, but budgetary pressures made it necessary to critically assess the Bailey/Howe Library's subscription resources systematically. Liaisons were contacted at time of renewal to provide input on a single resource. Often point of contact was made very close to the renewal deadline and via e-mail, so liaisons were not asked or did not feel as though they had a real opportunity to more thoughtful consider the resource in the context of the larger collection. A true in-depth evaluation did not always take place and therefore most resources were renewed for lack of an effective process to critically assess their value.

At the start of FY 2016, the collection development librarian and acting liaison program director partnered to develop a pilot project aimed at gathering all liaison feedback in a holistic manner. The goal of the project was to sensitize liaisons to the current budget situation, improve information sharing between technical and public services, and begin teaching liaisons about the inner workings of collection development and electronic resource usage statistics. The collection development librarian considered it an underuse of liaisons, who have the most interaction with faculty and students and awareness of the current curriculum, to not establish an open channel of communication and systematic means of gathering liaison feedback. The project was presented as a learning opportunity for not only the liaisons, but the Bailey/Howe Library's recently hired collection development librarian.

Literature Review

Bailey/Howe librarians are surely not the first to critically evaluate collections in response to budget pressures. In the past decade, countless academic libraries were forced to cancel subscription resources to align annual expenditures with reduced budgets, while identifying and preserving essential resources. Evaluation criteria, rubrics, and decision matrixes are useful tools in collection assessment projects, and can instill consistency in rankings and gain buy-in from project team members. As described by McManus and Foudy, members of the Electronic Resources Committee at University of Maryland Libraries developed a decision grid to prioritize resources and identify candidates for cancellation while engaging subject librarians. Four overarching criteria were used to rank resources: access, cost-effectiveness, breadth/audience and uniqueness (McManus & Foudy, 2005, p. 535). Blackburn, McFarland, and Reed at Vancouver Island University developed a 27-point rubric, which aided serial cancellation decisions and ensured decisions were made in a thorough, well-documented manner which could be defended if necessary (2013).

Furthermore, Emery and Stone presented broader considerations for electronic resource review in their 2013 Library Technology Report. In addition to analyzing usage statistics and gathering input from users, Emery and Stone remind readers of other contributing factors, including successful implementation, resource activation, and platform migration, which could impact recorded usage and users' perception of a resource (2013, p. 26–29).

Looking at assessment from an earlier stage in the electronic resource life cycle, Bhatt reinforced the need for liaison engagement and systematic procedures to solicit meaningful feedback that can be used in decision-making for electronic resource trials. As described in the 2015 article, Bhatt revamped existing practices to become more collaborative and consistent across resources, while relying on the participation of subject librarians (p. 124–125). Purposeful, consistent, and documented processes are essential as libraries make difficult decisions that impact collections and acquisition dollars.

Gathering Feedback From Liaisons, Holistically and Purposefully

Budget pressures triggered a need for holistic collection assessment and a systematic approach to gathering meaningful feedback from librarian liaisons at the Bailey/Howe Library. The collection development librarian and acting liaison program director expected liaisons to share more thoughtful feedback when given more time and information to evaluate resources. At the start of the project, both project leaders made a point of emphasizing how the feedback from liaisons would be factored into renewal decisions by the collections team.

Early in the 2016 fiscal year, the collection development and acquisitions/e-resources librarian met with liaisons to present updated information about the budget, explain how the collections team made renewal decisions, and describe the information and data which factored into those decisions. This meeting was intended to inform recently hired librarians and remind all liaisons of collection development procedures. In a later meeting, the collection development librarian engaged liaisons in a conversation about usage statistics, answered questions, and gave liaisons a document which could serve as an easy reference when presented with usage data in the future (see Appendix A).

Liaisons were given four weeks to rank electronic resources in their subject areas and assign a ranking to multidisciplinary resources. A meeting was scheduled after the four-week period in which liaisons could discuss multidisciplinary resource rankings as a group. The collection development librarian developed criteria to assist in the ranking of resources, which was given to liaisons along with resource lists which contained current and historic usage and pricing information (see Appendix B). Resources could be be placed in three categories:

Level 3: Resources in this category are essential to the discipline and canceling these resources would severely impact the research and teaching of our primary user community. Alternative sources do not exist for the information contained in these resources.

Level 2: Resources in this category are relevant to their discipline and valuable to the library's primary user community. Alternative sources for discovery and access of information may exist.

Level 1: Resources in this category are not essential to their discipline or relevant to current research and teaching endeavors on campus. Cancellation of these resources would pose minimal impact to faculty and students.

Liaisons were encouraged to add comments, ask questions, and consult with the collection development librarian for overlap analysis between resources. Liaisons were asked to consider the uniqueness of content, information access and discoverability, ease of use, and if the resource met the information needs of the library's primary user community: teaching and research faculty and students.

At the end of the four weeks, the collection development librarian met again with liaisons to answer questions and facilitate a discussion about multidisciplinary resources. As part of this meeting, liaisons had the opportunity to explain their rankings and hear the opinions of colleagues. The collection development librarian followed up with liaisons individually to discuss subject-specific resources. By the end of this meeting, all electronic resources were assigned a final ranking, which was shared with the collections team along with any comments from liaisons.

Lessons Learned

In addition to the rankings and comments received from liaisons, this project garnered fascinating—and as the case for some, unexpected—results. Perhaps the most significant benefit was the opportunity for open discussion about collections and collection development practices. Liaisons seemed to relish the chance to ask questions and voice concerns about how decisions were made. Liaisons were given the most up-to-date information about the budget's impact on collection development, which served to sensitize librarians to the overall situation and necessity to relinquish unneeded and lesser-needed resources. This level of engagement was a much needed step, especially as the library looks ahead to uncertain times. As a result of this project, the collection development librarian and a handful of liaisons are planning a smaller, targeted assessment project. The collection development librarian is optimistic about continued collaborative efforts with liaisons, which will only serve to benefit the collection.

The evaluation criteria also generated a discussion among project members. Many liaisons were inclined to evaluate a resource according to the resource's overall value to its discipline and rank resources highly, even if recorded usage was low. The collection development librarian encouraged liaisons to consider the current curriculum and research happening on campus and recognize some resources, though valuable, did not fit local information needs. Other liaisons questioned promotion efforts and the potential connection between promotion and usage, and wondered if faculty and students were even aware of particular resources.

Final rankings and additional comments from liaisons were particularly valuable. Liaisons used the project as an opportunity to express concerns about resources in their subject area and explain the rationale behind rankings. One liaison made note of recent cancellations made in her subject areas and the need for fair and equal consideration, while another liaison pointed to the absence of resource promotion in his liaison areas as possible cause for low usage. Some liaisons even made suggestions for further, future analysis and the potential for cancellations based on findings. Also of interest was the uneven treatment and evaluation of multidisciplinary resources. Liaisons were asked to assign a ranking to each of the multidisciplinary or reference resources. At the project's final meeting, liaisons were to discuss those rankings and determine a final ranking as a group. The majority of liaisons did not rank the entire list of multidisciplinary resources, citing a discomfort and feeling of unpreparedness with assigning a ranking to resources to which they were unfamiliar. Although a handful of liaisons did rank each multidisciplinary resource and provide comments along with rankings, the overall number of rankings for multidisciplinary and reference resources was surprisingly low. This acknowledged unfamiliarity with resources, especially reference resources, was particularly interesting to the collection development librarian.

As intended, the project impacted the collection team's renewal decision-making process. The rankings helped the collections team prioritize and establish a baseline of essential resources. Decisions can be made more efficiently, because liaison feedback is readily available. Liaisons are still contacted if further information is needed, or when a resource is recommended for cancellation. Thus far, liaisons seem to be more willing to discuss renewals, and more often those conversations are happening in advance of renewal deadlines and face to face. Within six weeks of finishing the project, the collections team was able to make an informed decision to cancel a poorly ranked online reference source. The liaisons were in full support of the cancellation, which the collection development librarian fully attributes to the evaluation project.

Future Projects

With the potential for budget reductions looming, the collection development librarian expects critical assessment of collections to continue. This initial project was very much a learning opportunity, and the collection development librarian intends to refine and repeat the project in the next fiscal year. In the next iteration, the project will be based on an evaluation rubric, rather than criteria and ranking which can be misinterpreted or interpreted differently across liaisons. Greater effort will be made to conduct overlap analyses and truly determine if content is unique or accessible elsewhere. Although liaisons were encouraged to request an overlap analysis from the collection development librarian in this project, none did. This absence of analysis weakened the overall evaluation for many resources as uniqueness of content was assumed, but not verified.

In a future evaluation project, the collection development librarian would like to explore grouping liaisons according to subject area. In such an arrangement, liaisons can exchange ideas and better address the many resources which span disciplines and local liaison assignments. The collection development librarian would like to see greater collaboration among liaisons, especially when evaluating online reference materials or broad multidisciplinary resources, which impact all liaisons areas. Perhaps asking the liaisons to work in groups or clusters would facilitate such cooperation.

References

Bhatt, A. (2015). E-Trials in academic libraries: 101 and beyond. *Journal of Electronic Resources Librarianship, 27*(2), 121–127. http://dx.doi.org/10.1080/1941126X.2015.1029424

Blackburn, J., McFarland, D., & Reed, K. (2013). *Culling the herd in hard times: Implementing an evidence-based "big deal" cancellation support tool at VIU Library*. Retrieved from http://libguides.viu.ca/c.php?g= 188987

Emery, J., & Stone, G. (2013). Ongoing evaluation and access. *Library Technology Reports, 49*(2), 26–29.

Foudy, G., & McManus, A. (2005). Using a decision grid process to build consensus in electronic resources cancellation decisions. *Journal of Academic Librarianship, 31*(6), 533–538. http://dx.doi.org/10.1016/j.acalib.2005.08.005

Appendix A

Electronic Resources Usage Statistics (Briefly) Explained

Usage statistics can be tricky business. The glossary below aims to clarify and define the common metrics used in tracking usage statistics so liaisons can be more informed and better oriented to provide feedback on renewals and engage faculty in discussion. Any questions about usage statistics should be directed to Alana Verminski in Collection Development.

Most database vendors follow the standards established by Project COUNTER. These standards were designed in 2002 so librarians could rely on consistent and reliable usage statistics for comparison across platforms. Release 4 of the standards was issued in April 2012 and vendors were given until December 2013 to become compliant with the new standards.

Summary of COUNTER Usage Reports and Metrics: Databases

Searches: A use is recorded each time a user enters terms into a search box.

Result clicks: A use is recorded each time a user clicks on an item found in a list of search results.

Record views: A use is recorded each time a user views a full database record (the "detailed" record). A user could arrive at this record from a list of search results, from browsing within the database, or from entering a full record from another record within the database.

Session: A use is recorded each time a user enters a database.

Summary of COUNTER Usage Reports and Metrics: E-Books

Successful title requests: A use is recorded each time a user accesses a complete electronic work (typically an e-book or reference work).

Successful section requests: A use is recorded each time a user accesses a piece (or section) of an electronic work (such as a chapter or specific entry of a larger work).

Searches: A use is recorded each time a user enters terms into a search box.

Summary of COUNTER Usage Reports and Metrics: Journals

Successful full-text article requests: Usage is recorded each time an article is downloaded as a PDF or the HTML full-text is accessed. We usually describe this metric as the number of full-text downloads.

Access denied to full-text articles: Usage is recorded each time a user from one of our registered IP addresses is denied access to a journal article on a particular platform because the library does not subscribe to the journal. This metric is described as the number of "turnaways" or "denials."

Summary of COUNTER Usage Reports and Metrics: Multimedia and Streaming Video

Successful full multimedia content unit requests: A use is recorded each time a user accesses an item which is not textual (such as an image, streaming video, or downloadable audio or visual files).

Points of Interest

In the transition from Release 3 to Release 4, COUNTER significantly changed the way usage is recorded for databases. When comparing usage between 2012 and 2013 or sometimes even 2013 and 2014, these changes will be visible in usage reports. Different metrics are used and for our local reports. Jimmy will note those changes.

Unfortunate for us, not all database vendors and publishers are COUNTER-compliant. Usage drawn from these content providers will not compare well with their COUNTER-compliant counterparts. In these cases, Jimmy will request more information about what type of usage is being tracked and recorded from our vendor reps. Non-COUNTER usage can be murky, and if anyone has questions about the usage, please get in touch with Alana or Jimmy and we'll try and clarify.

Cost-Per-Use

Cost-per-use (CPU) is a simple measure to gauge our return on investment for our subscriptions. CPU is calculated by dividing the annual cost by the annual usage. Ideally, we like the CPU to be below the cost to access the same item via ILL.

More Information About Project COUNTER

Project COUNTER: http://www.projectcounter.org/

Glossary of Terms used in Release 4: http://www.projectcounter.org/r4/APPA.pdf

List of COUNTER-compliant vendors: http://www.projectcounter.org/compliantvendors.html

Appendix B

FY 2016 Electronic Resources Review

Criteria and Questions to Consider

HOLISTIC Evaluation of Electronic Resources

The following criteria and corresponding evaluation process is designed to gather meaningful input from librarian liaisons, which members of the collections team can consider when making renewal decisions for existing electronic resources.

By reviewing resources according to subject area, liaisons can compare content and consider the uniqueness of each resource and its contributed value to the collection.

Questions to Consider

The questions listed below are designed to assist in critically evaluating each resource in the following areas:

1. Access & Uniqueness of Content
2. Ease of Use
3. User Community

Ranking Criteria

Each database will be ranked on a scale of 3 to 1.

Resources ranked at a Level 3 are essential to their discipline and cancelling these resources would severely impact the research and teaching of our primary user community. Alternative sources do not exist for the information contained these resources.

Level 2 resources are relevant to their discipline and useful to faculty and students. Alternative sources for discovery and access of information may exist.

Resources that are not essential to their discipline, contain information that can be accessed elsewhere, and pose a minimal impact to faculty are ranked at Level 1.

For More Information

For guidance in interpreting usage statistics, see the Electronic Resources Usage Statistics document uploaded to the Collections Team SharePoint Site.

For questions about overlap or gaps in content, consult with Alana. An overlap analysis may be possible depending on the availability of title lists.

CRITERIA AND RELATED QUESTIONS	YES	NO	N/A	COMMENTS
ACCESS & UNIQUENESS OF CONTENT				
Does this resource meet the research and teaching needs of one or more academic departments?				
Is the information contained in this resource available elsewhere (e.g., another library resource or freely online)?				
Can the information contained in this resource be discovered elsewhere (e.g., in an index, database, Primo Central Index, or research guide?)				

Vhat makes the content of this esource unique or essential to he discipline, if at all?				
EASE OF USE				
1 your opinion, can users of this esource quickly and effectively each relevant information?				
oes the database require a ser to create an account to earch and access information?				
o any impediments exist in the ıterface, e.g., unclear language, oorly located search boxes, or ifficult navigation?				
re search functions robust?				
USER COMMUNITY				
; this resource multidisciplinary nd of value to multiple cademic departments or isciplines?				
; this resource used by a articular department, class, or rogram?				
oes this resource have broad ser group, including faculty, ndergraduate and graduate tudents, and other esearchers?				

Giving Subject Specialists the Tools They Need to Succeed: The Collection Development Training Manual at the University of Maryland

Margaret Z. Saponaro, Interim Head of Collection Development and Librarian for Journalism, University of Maryland Libraries

Abstract

The University of Maryland Libraries (UMD) employs over 40 librarians with collection development responsibilities. These subject specialists represent a range of varying experience levels with collection development—from new librarians to seasoned veterans. Although many subject specialists are required to use the same tools for their collection development activities, materials to support these activities were not always easy to find, nor was there one place available to direct new subject specialists who needed resources to assist them with their responsibilities. This paper describes the process undertaken to develop of a toolkit for materials for subject specialists at the UMD Libraries, including the key issues identified by subject specialists and members of the Libraries's Acquisitions unit, the framework developed for the toolkit, and the implementation process for the toolkit.

Introduction

At the University of Maryland Libraries (UMD), over 40 librarians have responsibilities in collection development. Called subject specialists, these individuals represent a range of experience levels, from newly hired librarians to those with many years of experience at UMD or elsewhere. During 2014, the author, then the librarian for journalism and hearing and speech sciences, was approached by the associate dean for collection strategies and services to participate in a job enrichment program (job rotation) in the collection development department. The enrichment program is available to staff and librarians throughout the UMD libraries, and provides participants with an opportunity to explore an area of interest outside regular job responsibilities for a defined period of time. After exploring options for the job rotation, creating a training manual or toolkit for subject specialists to facilitate their collection development activities was selected as the job rotation project. This was done primarily because of the author's prior experience with and interest in collection development instruction (Evans and Saponaro, 2005; 2012), and the timeframe for the project (March-August, 2014).

Design Process

At the outset of the project, a three-pronged approach was developed in order to create a toolkit that adequately met the needs of subject specialists at UMD. This process consisted of conducting a literature review, holding in-person interviews with selected individuals in both public and technical services, and creating, distributing and analyzing the results of an online survey sent to individuals with selection responsibilities at UMD.

The literature review was intended in order to identify best practices in training for librarians with little background in collection development. However, a search of the literature accessible via *Library and Information Source Complete*, *ERIC*, *Education Research Complete* and *Google Scholar* revealed that very little current research existed with examples of training manuals for collection development librarians. Despite the lack of current research, two articles (Perkins, 1982; Carter, 2004), did provide useful background on the topic.

Despite the lack of current research, a review of websites on the subject did yield several examples and ideas for areas a training manual should

http://dx.doi.org/10.5703/1288284316242

include or address. Of note was the Collection Manager's Manual from the University of California, Santa Barbara Library (UCSB, http://collman.library.ucsb.edu/). Through the inclusion of a First Day Kit for Collection Managers (http://collman.library.ucsb.edu/firstday.html), the UCSB site acknowledged the needs of new selectors. This idea resonated with the author, as well as the manager of collections and the associate dean for collection strategies and services. Other online manuals of note included those from Cornell University (http://www.library.cornell.edu/colldev/cdmanualcontents.html) and Rutgers (http://www.libraries.rutgers.edu/rul/staff/access_serv/coll_mgt/coll_mgt.shtml).

The second step in the process was to conduct brief (20–30 minute) in-person interviews with individuals from public services, collection development, and acquisitions in an attempt to determine a list of elements to include in the manual. A total of eighteen interviews were held during a six-week timespan. The individuals selected for interview represented a variety of experience levels and job responsibilities at UMD, in order to try to capture as many viewpoints as possible. Interviews with acquisitions and collection development personnel gave the participants an opportunity to identify frequently asked questions or workflow issues encountered when working with selectors, as well as indicate training needs that would fall outside the scope of the *Manual*. The interviews also were useful in identifying existing resources that could be included within the *Manual*. Interviews with subject selectors gave the participants an opportunity to reflect upon areas or processes where they encountered challenges or had frequent questions, and identify areas where their selection work could be facilitated. In order to respect the privacy of all those interviewed, results of the in-person interviews were shared in aggregate with the associate dean for collection strategies and services and the manager of collections.

Since not all subject specialists could be interviewed individually, the third step in the process was to create and distribute an online survey to all librarians with collection responsibilities. The survey itself was designed using the *Qualtrics* survey platform, which is available via site-license at UMD. The survey contained six questions, and respondents were asked to provide input on the following:

- Areas of collection development where they have frequent questions
- What policies and procedures do they need to be able to refer to on a regular basis
- Their preferred method of learning
- Other questions or concerns that could be addressed in an in-person training session
- What tools and resources they use for selection
- What items would be considered "must haves" in a training manual

Respondents were also asked to indicate the number of years they had worked in collection management/selection at the University of Maryland Libraries for classification purposes. Respondents self-reported themselves into one of four groups, based on their length of service at the Libraries. The highest number of responses (39%) came from librarians with one to five years of experience at UMD. The second highest response rate came from librarians with over ten years of experience (26%). The online survey was open for a total of 13 workdays (18 calendar days). There were 31 responses to the survey for a total response rate of 65.9%. Survey responses were anonymous and results were shared with the associate dean for collection strategies and services and the manager of collections.

Key Issues Identified

A number of issues came to light as a result of both the in-person and online surveys. Areas that could be addressed through the *Collection Development Training Manual* included:

- Policies and procedures—including links to the UMD Collection Development Policy, a timeline for selectors, policies for gift books, information on realignment/weeding and the desiderata process, and an overview of the Research Data Services unit at UMD

- Tools for selectors—including information on or links to the online acquisitions system (such as resetting passwords, requesting reports, checking fund code balances), the online ordering systems (such as login information, creating folders and notifications, training opportunities), commonly used forms for ordering print and electronic resources, tools frequently used in selection (such as e-mail reflectors, websites, *CHOICE*, or other resources suggested in survey responses)
- Helpful resources/appendices—including a glossary of terms and a contact list for questions

Other notable requests included providing an overview of the UMD philosophy of collection development—including what are priorities for withdrawing materials, a list of acronyms used in collection development, and a list of talking points about the libraries's special collections unit that selectors could share when working with individuals in their subject disciplines.

Subject specialists also indicated an interest in a wide range of training opportunities, ranging from how to transfer money within fund codes to how to check fund code balances. Although providing training programming was outside the scope of the job rotation project, these themes were shared with the associate dean for collection strategies and services and the manager of collections for further action.

Toolkit Framework

Because the largest number of survey respondents fell in the category of new librarians, it was evident that a prominent section of the *Manual* be devoted to "Resources for New Selectors." This section would serve as a "quick start" by providing an overview of the collection development unit, as well as links to items/tools such as the acquisitions and ordering systems used at UMD, a timeline or calendar of selection activities, a list of selectors by subject, a list of selection tools, and a contact list for questions.

A guiding design principal for the *Manual* was that wherever possible, the *Manual* would link to existing content on the Libraries's public website, the Libraries's Intranet or elsewhere on the Internet, rather than duplicating content that already existed. It was hoped that by linking to existing content, that would help keep the *Manual* current.

Content included in the *Manual* was divided into five sections, including the aforementioned "Resources for New Selectors" section. Other sections of the *Manual* are:

- Overview of the collection development unit—including an unit overview and links to key committees and task forces
- Policies and procedures—including links to key policies such as gift items and the desiderata process
- Tools for selectors—providing links to overviews for the acquisitions and ordering programs used at UMD, listings of gift funds and selection tools, and an overview of research data services and special collections and university archives
- Helpful resources and appendices—including contact information for collection development, acquisitions and vendors, and a glossary of terms

Although much of the content in the *Manual* could be linked from existing pages from the Libraries's public website or Intranet, documents created by the author specifically for the *Manual* included:

- Sample completed forms for requesting print and electronic materials (materials request form and electronic request form), along with completion instructions for each
- A suggested list of reflectors, journals, and other resources used in the selection process, including those items identified by the selectors themselves

- A glossary of terms for acquisitions and the online ordering system

Other items in the *Manual* contributed by colleagues included a collection policy for Research Data Services and key talking points on special collections and university archives.

Throughout the development of the *Manual* framework and individual components, the author collaborated with colleagues from the acquisitions unit of the libraries as well as the UMD representative from YBP. The expertise of these individuals was invaluable in creating tools that would be useful for selectors.

Implementing the Toolkit

Because the *Manual* included proprietary information from one of the vendors for the UMD Libraries, the decision was made to house the *Manual* within the staff-only Library Intranet (Libraries Intranet or LIBI), based on the *Drupal* open source platform. In addition to linking to existing resources such as listings of departmental liaisons and the Libraries's gifts in kind manual, the author created a total of 19 new pages for LIBI in the span of four months. The graduate sssistant for collection development assisted the author in creating and linking many of the pages, as well as with proofreading and troubleshooting the *Manual*.

Once complete, the manual was reviewed by the associate dean for collection strategies and services and approved for distribution. At this point, a link to the *Manual* was prominently placed at the top of the "Resources for Selectors" section of the existing collection development page on LIBI.

Additionally, once the *Manual* was finalized and linked, an overview of the project was shared with subject specialists at the collection development assembly meeting held in January 2015. Since that time, components of the *Manual* continue to be updated as services, policies, processes, and resources change. New selectors are given an overview of the *Manual* during an orientation session with the Interim Head of Collection Development.

Conclusion

The Collection Development Training Manual project spanned 10 months and involved the time and energies of many individuals throughout the UMD Libraries. It provided the author with an opportunity to explore an area of interest and experience with specialized CMS and survey tools (Drupal and Qualtrics). One unexpected result of the project was the number of issues raised by selectors that may otherwise not have been realized or acted upon had this project not occurred. The Manual continues to be used by selectors and components within it are regularly updated as needed. It is hoped this tool will continue to benefit selectors at the UMD Libraries for many years to come.

References

Carter, N. F. (2004). Bibliographer's manual: A new life, a new process. *Collection Management, 29*(1), 31–41.

Dubicki, E. (2007). Basic marketing and promotion concepts. *Serials Librarian*, *53*(3), 5-15.

Edward Evans, G., & Saponaro, M. Z. (2012). *Collection management basics.* 6th ed. Library and information science text series. Santa Barbara, CA: Libraries Unlimited.

———. (2005). *Developing library and information center collections.* 5th ed. Library and information science text series. Westport, CT: Libraries Unlimited.

Perkins, D. L. (1982). Writing the collection development manual. *Collection Management* 4(3), 37–48.

Back to the Future: Re-Examining the Need for Shelf-Ready Processes in the E-Book Environment

Susan J. Martin, Acquisitions Librarian, Texas Woman's University

Pamela D. Ward, Director of Technical and Access Services, Texas Woman's University

Brittney L. Washington, Library Assistant III, Texas Woman's University

Abstract

Shelf-ready processing of print materials is a commonly available service from library book vendors, and many libraries outsource these services in order to help save staff time and costs, and to expedite the process. However, in the age where print monographs are increasingly replaced with e-books, do these services still make fiscal sense? In the spring of 2015, the Texas Woman's University Libraries were looking to expand shelf-ready services to a second vendor, but before doing so opted to do a feasibility study to see if shelf-ready services were still needed and economical. This paper presents the findings of a two-month study done at the Texas Woman's University Libraries on their outsourced and in-house cataloging workflows. The study examined the amount of time it took to receive the materials after ordering, the various costs involved, including shelf-ready fees and internal staff costs, as well as the number of print materials being purchased over the past three fiscal years.

Introduction

Texas Woman's University (TWU) is classified as a Doctoral/Research university. One of four independent public institutions of higher education in the State of Texas, it is the nation's largest university primarily for women. With campuses in Denton, Dallas, and Houston and a total student enrollment of over 10,000 FTE, TWU offers both traditional and online degrees from the Bachelor's through the Doctorate in the liberal arts, nursing, health sciences, sciences, business, and education. TWU Libraries hold 686,588 volumes, subscribe to over 2,000 journals and databases, and have a collections budget of $1.6 million.

Texas Woman's University Libraries went shelf-ready in March 2012 in order to save staff time and money processing firm order print books. The Libraries had just experienced a significant reduction in their budget which resulted in the elimination of several staff positions. We assumed that routine copy cataloging took up a large portion of staff time and was not cost effective. With these two assumptions in mind, weinvestigated using shelf-ready services, which are a common and popular book vendor service. We thought that by receiving the bulk of our firm order books "shelf-ready," cataloging staff would be free to do other tasks and projects.

Questions were raised as we prepared to expand to another vendor: Is the quality of cataloging and physical processing acceptable? How many and what sort of changes do staff need to do with these books? How many days from order placement until the items are available? What is the true per book cost? Do we purchase enough print books that outsourcing still makes sense? What other efficiencies or technologies can we capitalize on? In light of these questions, we wanted to compare the two workflows, in-house copy cataloging and shelf-ready, before making any additional outsourcing commitments. A two-month study tracked all print books received from order to shelf; and a complete cost analysis of the entire acquisitions and cataloging processes was done. For this paper we were asked by our administration to use pseudonyms for our vendor names, and we are honoring this request.

Structuring the Study

We were inspired by a study done by Rebecca Schroeder and Jared L. Howland of Brigham Young

http://dx.doi.org/10.5703/1288284316243

University. Their study focused specifically on looking to see if shelf-ready should be used for print approval items, which was different than our focus, but the overall goal was similar and we found that their methodology was sound.

We derived our study sample from the print titles we received during April and May 2015. We normally receive a significant portion of our print firm order materials during this time, and thought it would provide a good representative sample. We ended with 355 titles from a variety of vendors. The items were tracked using two forms which followed each workflow process, shelf-ready items and in-house (see Figures 1; 2, on next page). Using the unique Alma-assigned Purchase Order Line number, each item was tracked by date and time as it progressed through the workflow. Any corrections made to the shelf-ready materials for either the MARC record or physical book were noted. The tracking stopped with the date the item was sent to circulation to be shelved.

Copy Cataloging Shelf-Ready study	Shelf Ready Shelf-Ready Study
POL-	POL-
Acquisitions	**Acquisitions**
Date received:	Date received:
Time received:	Time received:
Cataloging	**Cataloging**
Received in:	Received in:
Date/time work began:	Date/time work began:
Date/Time finished:	Date/Time finished:
Physical Processing	**Modifications made**
Received in:	MARC (overlay? Edit?)
Date/time work began:	Barcode:
Date/Time finished:	Label:
Date to circ:	Date to circ:

Figure 1. Tracking work forms.

Findings and Analysis

As shown in Figure 3 (p. 122), shelf-ready materials took consistently longer from order to shelf, and cost significantly more per item than materials ordered for in-house processing. The shelf-ready books averaged 28 days from order to shelf compared to 10 days for all other materials. Cataloging staff spent 1.5 minutes per shelf-ready book performing quality control checks to ensure accuracy; a final physical processing check took an additional minute. In-house materials took longer, 10 minutes per book with an additional 2 minutes for physical processing. We noticed that cataloging times varied depending on the vendor, and after looking at some of the specific titles (specialty DVDs, kits, dissertations), we concluded that the variation in time corresponded with difficulty of cataloging the item, and that the more sophisticated items were not able to be ordered shelf-ready.

The order-to-shelf result from our SRV was not a surprise, as we had initially thought it took a long time compared with materials received from others. However, the per item cost of purchasing and processing was a surprise, as we uncovered costs which were not readily apparent. Our shelf-ready fee is $5.99 per book, which covers cataloging and physical processing. This cost appears on our invoices and is the only cost we commonly associate with the process. However, we incur an annual charge ($2,800) in order to use the SRV's ordering system. We divided out that cost, and it added an additional $4.77 per book for our sample, making our total shelf-ready cost to be $10.76 per book. We also have our own internal costs for acquiring, cataloging, and processing. Each shelf-ready item incurred an extra $0.48 OCLC charge and $8.68 worth of TWU staff time, bringing the final per item cost to $19.92.

In comparison, all other materials were ordered, received, and on the shelf within 10 days. Each of these items incurred $2.85 for physical processing (including OCLC) and $9.27 of TWU staff time with an average per book cost of $12.12. Vendor A's (V-A) order to shelf time was 11 days with a per

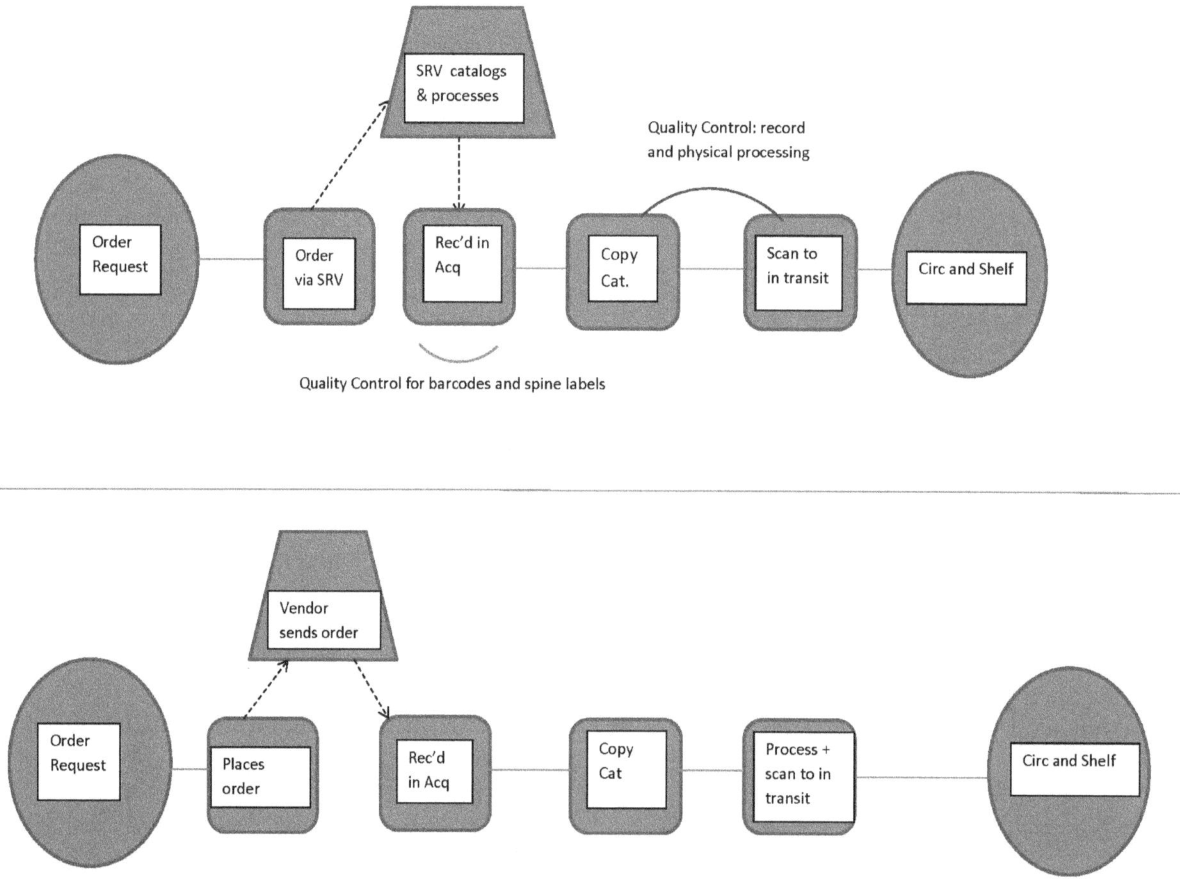

Figure 2. Workflows.

book cost of $13.05. Vendor B's (V-B) was the most expedient and cost effective, with just over 7 days from order to shelf, and a total per book cost of $11.05. At $19.92 the cost of a shelf-ready item was at least $6.87 more (and as high as $8.87) than any of the materials processed in-house.

The Libraries would benefit from having greater control over the cataloging quality and process, as well as see a significant savings by eliminating the costs incurred by a duplicate shelf-ready workflow. As shown in Figure 2, all shelf-ready items are quality control checked using a workflow that mirrors the in-house one. This workflow was implemented from the onset of the service, and was kept due to the amount of corrections—actual and perceived. Figure 4 (p. 123) outlines the cost per book for the 523 shelf-ready books received in FY15, along with the cost per book if the same 523 items were acquired through a different vendor. The costs in red are the savings. V-B would realize the greatest savings, due in part to its automated ordering system, which saves significant ordering time and is free to use. We also see significant savings when we apply the per book costs to the entire 1200 items received in FY15. The library could potentially save $5,244.00 on per book processing costs.

The shelf-ready quality control workflow is faster, but the amount of time saved is negligible. Divided evenly, we would need 8.34 hours of time per week, leaving almost 32 hours for e-book cataloging and other projects. Receipts do not come in evenly—April and May tend to be our busiest months, whereas almost nothing is purchased during the summer. Large projects will have to be saved for the slower period. However, the library will save significant staff costs by

	Shelf-Ready Vendor	Vendor A	Vendor B	Misc Vendors	All non SRV
Average Order to Receipt (days)	27.04	10.08	7.07	18.7	9.73
Average Order to Shelf (days)	28.54	11.15	7.88	20.23	10.73
Average cataloging time (min)	1:27	14:57	4:16	4:16	10:12
Average processing time (min)*	1:00	2:09	1:26	1:26	1:51
Average cost for Shelf-ready services**	$10.76				
Average processing cost (TWU)***	$0.48	$2.85	$2.85	$2.85	$2.85
Average staff cost (ACQ)	$7.25	$8.75	$7.25	$8.75	$8.25
Average staff cost (CAT)	$0.42	$0.89	$0.72	$0.87	$0.82
Average staff cost (PROCESS)	$0.12	$0.22	$0.18	$0.27	$0.21
Average staff cost (TOTAL TWU)	$8.68	$10.20	$8.20	$9.88	$9.27
TOTAL COST from order to shelf (not including item cost)	$19.92	$13.05	$11.05	$12.73	$12.12
TOTAL COST w/KAPCO (student applied)	---	$14.25	$12.25	$13.93	$13.32
TOTAL COST w/KAPCO (staff applied)	---	$15.55	$13.55	$15.23	$14.62

*In house processing did not put on Kapco covers during this time, but in the future, they will be.

That will add an additional 10 minutes of time or $1.20 of student time or $2.50 of staff time.

** SRV includes $5.99 shelf ready fees and a $4.77 Ordering System cost

*** TWU processing costs are estimated at $2.57 (barcodes, labels, covers, etc. plus $0.48 for OCLC. Shelf-ready items also incurr this OCLC charge

Figure 3. Times and costs.

eliminating the duplicate workflow. Additional savings could be accomplished by retooling the physical processing workflow to use student workers and to move some of the processing into acquisitions.

We also wanted to see if our assumption on errors was correct. For our shelf-ready sample, we tracked 98 items, and due to our cataloging standards, 46 of those MARC records needed some sort of editing (removal of extra 856 fields, addition of a subject heading) or a complete overlay of the MARC record. This yielded us a 47% correction rate. We did not have any physical processing errors for the sample; however, this may be a false result due to a discovery of how the items are quality controlled. We assumed physical processing quality control took place only in cataloging and processing, and expected any errors to be discovered there. However, when we mapped out the workflow and spoke with the staff involved, we discovered that the majority of physicsal processing mistakes are switched barcodes and spine labels, which are spotted and corrected upon receipt in acquisitions.

Twenty-eight days and a 47% error rate still seemed high. So, we opted to verify our study data to see if it was an anomaly. We checked receipt times by downloading all print receipts from the past three fiscal years from Alma. We discovered that shelf-ready titles averaged 42 days from order to receipt, and in-house materials came in around 34 days. V-A was the quickest with 9 days, but some specialty vendors took as long as 36 days for the item to arrive. We did not order with V-B prior to FY15, and could not do a comparison. We learned that our shelf-ready receipt rate for our study was better than the past three years.

To verify the error rate, we selected 98 random titles received between September 2013 and March 2015. Each MARC record was checked by using Alma's View Versions in the metadata editor which shows the MARC record history for that particular title (order record, original vendor supplied record, and any edited version) along with who edited it and the date. The new sample yielded a 38% correction rate with 37 MARC

	Shelf-Ready Vendor	Vendor A	Vendor B	Misc Vendors	All non SRV
FY15 estimated costs 1200 firm order items	$23,904.00	$15,660.00	$13,260.00	$15,276.00	$14,544.00
Cost savings		$8,244.00	$10,644.00	$8,628.00	$9,360.00
Cost for 1200 items with Kapco (student)	---	$17,100.00	$14,700.00	$16,716.00	$15,984.00
Cost savings		$6,804.00	$9,204.00	$7,188.00	$7,920.00
Cost for 1200 items with Kapco (Staff)	--	$18,660.00	$16,260.00	$18,276.00	$17,544.00
Cost savings		$5,244.00	$7,644.00	$5,628.00	$6,360.00

Figure 4. Cost estimates and savings

records having been edited or overlaid immediately after receipt of the vendor supplied record. Our new sample had a better rate of success, but we find that 38% is still too high to be acceptable.

Our findings were mirrored by several local peer libraries, four of which use shelf-ready services and four of which do not. The four libraries that used a shelf-ready service reported order to receipt times ranging from 10 to 26 days. For error rates, 3 of the libraries reported that they were low, but could not provide quantifiable numbers. One library had tracked their shelf-ready error rates and reported that they were close to 50%. Two of the libraries that do not use shelf-ready services fully catalog and process all their materials in-house. Both libraries receive significantly more print materials than we do (14,000–18,000 print items). They handle this load, along with e-books and other materials with 5 FTE (3 professionals and 2 library assistants) and 6 FTE, respectively, which is comparable to our 4 FTE in cataloging (1 professional and 3 library assistants).

Two additional institutions, St. Edward's University (SEU) and Columbia Gorge Community College (CGCC), have completely forgone the traditional book vendor in favor of using Amazon with a Prime membership that includes two-day shipping to supply their firm order print and media material. Copy cataloging and processing for all print and media materials is done in-house. CGCC has only 2 FTE for all library operations, and they treated 664 items with a 2-day turn-around time this past fiscal year, and SEU processed 1,100 items with 2 FTE (1 professional and 1 library assistant). Librarians at SEU and CGCC have written extensively about their experiences with library vendors and their decision to use a nontraditional acquisition method in light of receipt times, questionable cataloging records, and declining print numbers in favor of e-books.

We examined the possibility of using Amazon as our primary vendor. We searched Amazon to see how many of our SRV and V-B sample titles were available. Out of 203 titles, 201 were available with Prime shipping, and only 2 were not Prime eligible, but were still available for purchase. The discounts offered by Amazon are comparable to our traditional book vendors, and the large inventory and fast shipping make Amazon an attractive option. The drawback is the amount of staff time needed to manually key in orders and invoices. If Amazon develops API ordering and invoicing with Alma, we will seriously consider Amazon as a primary vendor.

Shelf-ready processing made sense in the print environment. However, as information access has moved from print to electronic, we have seen a decrease in print monograph purchases. Over the past three years, our print receipts have averaged out to be 1239 per year. At the same time, e-book selection has increased (see Figure 5 on next page). This change is more than just a swap of form, print to digital, but it is reflective of how libraries are selecting and managing the content of their collections.

Static library budgets do not afford as much collection building as they did in the past. Collection development now focuses on what is actually needed at a particular time rather than what might be needed. Focusing more on their own unique archival materials, libraries are leasing access to a focused set of resources within the larger body of knowledge to support their

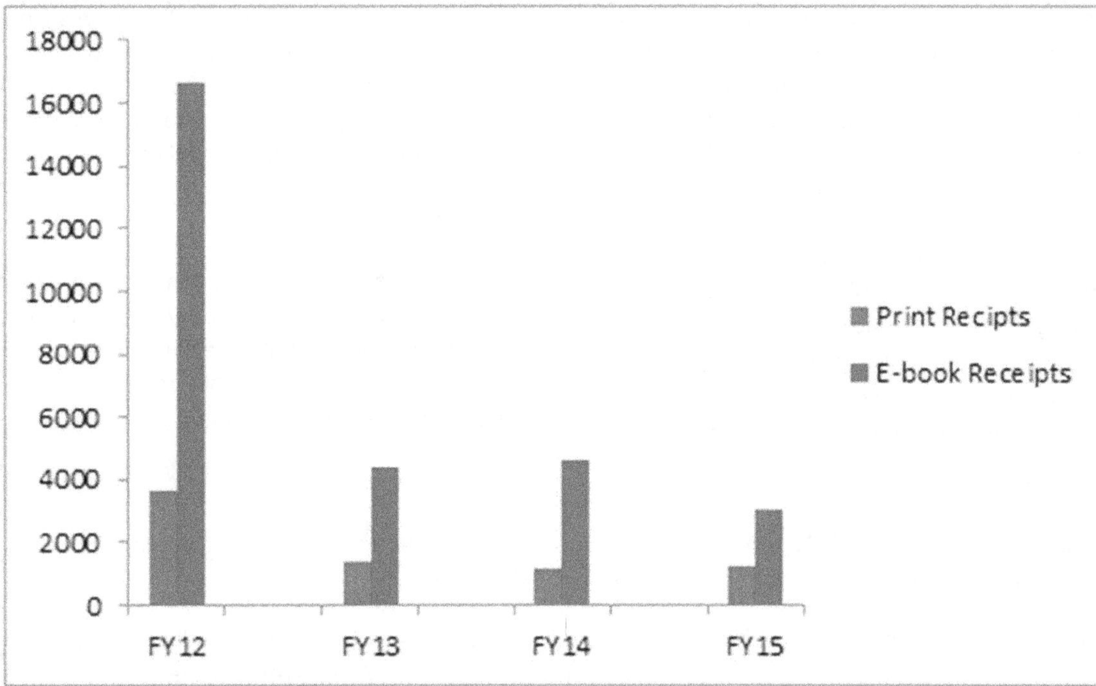

Figure 5. Cost estimates and savings

university's curriculum, new teaching methodologies such as the "flipped classroom," and online degree programs.

Changes in the industry inspire a fresh response. Today libraries have moved toward a just-in-time (JIT) purchasing model; waiting weeks to obtain materials is not an option—firm order e-books are available within a day or two and pay-per-view article services provide instant access. Moreover, libraries have embraced demand-driven acquisitions (DDA) services as a means of providing access to a large body of information in an instant and economical way.

We can also apply this JIT model to print materials. With smaller amounts of print items, the Libraries should be able to quickly obtain and make them available by seeking out vendors with the fastest shipping times. Additionally, ILS and content vendors are closely collaborating and creating sophisticated acquisitions APIs which interface seamlessly. These acquisition APIs reduce the time (and therefore cost) acquisitions staff spend keying in orders and invoices.

This evolution of vendor cooperation and integration has a positive effect on cataloging as well. Staff is able to locate and process vast numbers of records in-house due to the advanced searching capabilities in OCLC and import/export improvements in our ILS and third party products, such as MARCedit. The techniques used by book vendors to locate and process MARC records are easily duplicated by our own staff.

Recommendations

We recommend the following:

- Discontinue our shelf-ready service.
- Return all firm order cataloging and processing to utilize our in-house expertise.
- Focus on quickly obtaining print materials which will build in a cushion of time for cataloging and processing.
- Use Vendor B as our primary vendor for our print materials.
- Purchase an Amazon Prime membership to utilize their 2-day free shipping for rush orders.
- Reassess in fiscal year 2017.

This return to the traditional workflow will benefit both library and patron. The library will realize substantial savings over time in staff and processing costs, as well as a cleaner catalog. Patrons will have new materials on the shelves in an expedient timeframe. We will be poised to fulfill any requests for the material even after it has been ordered. Once the item is in-house, it's simply a matter of pulling off of the cart and processing immediately. However, if the item requested is waiting to be processed off-site, there's little we can do to expedite the process. In terms of our catalog quality, we will have better control and quality of our MARC records from thebeginning. Finally, all print items would be funneled through one workflow eliminating the need to having a separate cataloging workflow for a small portion of print materials.

Outcomes

We presented our study findings to our Libraries' administration team, and they agreed with our recommendations with the caveat to carefully examine workflows and rote activities that could be handled by other staff and students.

References

Ferris, K., & Buck, T. H. (2014). An ethos of access: How a small academic library transformed its collection-building processes. *Collection Management, 39*(2), 127–144.

Greene, B. (2014). Responsive acquisitions: A case study in improved workflow at a small academic library. Retrieved from http://www.inthelibrarywiththeleadpipe.org/2014/responsive-acquisitions-a-case-study-on-improved-workflow-at-a-small-academic-library/

Martin, S. J., Ward P. D., & Washington, B. L. (2015). [TWU_raw data Back to the Future.] Unpublished raw data set. Retrieved from http://hdl.handle.net/11274/7305

Schroeder, R., & Howland, J. L. (2011). Shelf-ready: A cost-benefit analysis. *Library Collections, Acquisitions & Technical Services, 35*(4), 129–134.

An Account and Analysis of the Implementation of Various E-Book Business Models at Queensland University of Technology, Australia

Martin Borchert, Associate Director, Library Services (Information Resources and Research Support), Queensland University of Technology

Colleen Cleary, Library Resource Services Manager, Queensland University of Technology

Abstract

Queensland University of Technology (QUT) is a leading university based in the city of Brisbane, Queensland, Australia and is a selectively research intensive university with 2,500 higher degree research students and an overall student population of 45,000 students.

The transition from print to online resources is largely completed and the library now provides access to 450,000 print books, 1,000 print journals, 600,000 e-books, 120,000 e-journals and 100,000 online videos. The e-book collection is now used three times as much as the print book collection.

This paper focuses on QUT Library's e-book strategy and the challenges of building and managing a rapidly growing collection of e-books using a range of publishers, platforms, and business and financial models. The paper provides an account of QUT Library's experiences in using patron-driven acquisition (PDA) using e-Book Library (EBL); the strategic procurement of publisher and subject collections by lease and outright purchase models, the more recent transition to evidence-based selection (EBS) options provided by some publishers, and its piloting of e-textbook models. The paper provides an in-depth analysis of each of these business models at QUT, focusing on access verses collection development, usage, cost per use, and value for money.

Introduction

QUT (Queensland University of Technology) is a leading Australian university located in the city of Brisbane. QUT Library supports the university through the provision of its learning support services, research support services, and collections of online and print resources. Its monograph collection consists of 600,000 e-books and a much reduced print collection of 450,000 books. The 2015 Library resources budget is about $14 million, of which 93% will be spent on online resources, $1.5 million on e-books, and $500,000 on print books.

QUT Library buys resources intending them to be used. QUT Library users now make one million e-book uses and 400,000 print loans, holds and renewals a year, and nine million full-text journal article uses per annum.

The Library is e-preferred and prefers access over ownership models. Approval plans with book suppliers are used. Patron-driven acquisition (PDA) has been the major means of providing access to a large number of e-books via e-Book Library (EBL, a ProQuest business) since 2005, with over 300,000 EBL titles now available. The JSTOR demand-driven acquisition (DDA) collection was introduced at QUT in early 2015.

From early 2015, the Library sought to diversify its e-books procurement options by trialing a range of evidence-based selection (EBS) offerings from Elsevier, Taylor & Francis, and Wiley. This paper provides a detailed account of QUT Library's experiences with both PDA/DDA and EBS and e-textbook e-book business models and makes some observations and suggestions on collection development, usage, and affordability.

Literature Review

A number of papers were found to specifically assess the PDA or DDA models. Goedeken (2015) provides a history of the PDA model and an account of three examples of e-book collecting in libraries using ebrary PDA, ebrary Academic

http://dx.doi.org/10.5703/1288284316244

Complete lease model, and selection via YBP-approval plans at Iowa State University. An understanding of user behavior and the availability of large leased content collections was thought to empower libraries to provide better collection services to clients. Miller (2015) and Downey (2013) found that DDA e-books were more used than print books. Cramer (2013) explains the business model and speculates on some of the effects of DDA on the collection development activities of libraries (how it interplays with other selection, procurement, and access models) and on scholarly publishing. Proctor (2012) advises libraries to procure e-books and especially older titles using PDA and to firm order where there is evidence of demand, rather than signing up to large collections of back titles for which there may be limited demand. e-Book packages are beginning to resemble e-journal big deals and are mixing content libraries want with content they don't. Herrera (2012) provides an account of collection development with respect to e-books at the University of Mississippi and how a limited PDA trial was undertaken with two subject collections. It was found that PDA access could support the development of interdisciplinary collections, but would require a broad profile supported by additional funds, and balanced with other collection development approaches could provide the best of both access and collection development goals. Harloe (2015) describes the application of DDA to a consortia library model and how costs can be shared across member libraries. Only one paper (Proctor, 2015) was found to review the EBS model (where it was called the sunk cost model) and in this instance the Elsevier EBS product at the University of Wyoming. The author recommends libraries carefully consider their initial level of investment as many academic monographs have low demand and circulation.

QUT Library's E-Book Collection Development History

QUT Library's e-book collections have grown to over 600,000 in ten years. The *Library Collection Development Manual* includes section CDM 3.2.1 Electronic Books and CDM 5.1 High Use Materials, which are most relevant to this paper. About 70% of the Library resources budget is spent in foreign currencies (not Australian dollars) and purchasing power has been greatly affected by the Australian dollar moving from US$1.10 in 2011 to below US$0.70 by late 2015.

QUT Library's EBL profile has generally included all titles from 2006 onwards. Short-term loans (STL) are made available for the first three usages of a book and auto-purchases are made on the fourth use. The combined effects of increased usage, rising costs imposed by publishers, and a weakening local currency exchange rate against the US$, has had the effect of greatly increasing QUT Library's EBL costs from A$352,000 in 2009 to $853,000 in 2013 and up to $1.6 million in 2014. Usage during this time has increased from 11,401 STLs and 1,712 auto-purchases in 2009 to 33,411 STLs and 4,647 auto-purchases in 2014. The 78% increase in EBL costs between 2013 and 2014 (USD) was very largely a result of increased demand, which from June 2014 has been exacerbated by publishers increasing STL costs from 10% to 15%, and to as high as 60% of the purchase price of the book. As a result, the average STL cost has increased from US$12.90 in 2013 to US$20.63 (60%) in 2014, while the average auto-purchase cost increased from $116.44 to $161.45 (39%).

In 2015, the Library allocated A$1 million for EBL and opted to implement mediation on all patron requests in mid-2015. To reduce demand, access to mediated rental titles was removed from ProQuest Summon and provided via the classic catalogue and the EBL native interface only. For 2015, the Library also wanted to diversify its e-book purchasing by implementing EBS with Elsevier, Taylor & Francis, and Wiley.

In the twelve months prior to the EBS, QUT's use of Elsevier titles via EBL was high, with 2,017 STLs and 230 autopurchases, costing US$72,612 and $58,901, respectively. The library could afford to license a limited EBS to update its previously acquired subject collections and include one new discipline, and the corpus comprised 1,155 titles with publications years 2009–2015 at a precommitment cost of US$79,615 (A$101,149). QUT Library would own 377 titles at the end of the EBS 12-month period based on US$211 per title average. 969 duplicating titles were removed from QUT's EBL profile.

QUT's use of Taylor & Francis and associated imprints was high and QUT spent US$271k on 9,706 STLs and US$340k on 1,527 autopurchases on EBL in the twelve months prior to the EBS. Taylor & Francis would license only five times the value of titles compared to the up-front commitment, and a limited budget restricted QUT's EBS corpus to titles in EBL with copyright dates from 2012 to 2015. An EBS collection of 7,765 Taylor & Francis titles costing GBP136,557 (A$269,822) was implemented in March 2015 and duplicating titles were removed from QUT's EBL profile. At the end of the EBS period QUT Library would own 1,411 titles based on GBP96.73 per title average list price. The EBS model allows the library to own more of the content.

QUT's use of Wiley titles via EBL was also high, with 4,035 STLs costing US$90,795 and 654 autopurchases costing US$164,469 in the twelve months prior to the EBS. 16,665 Wiley online books including 2015 publication dates costing US$105,000 (A$140,788) were implemented on the usage-based collection model (UCBM), and 10,061 duplicating titles (or 60% of the UBCM content) were removed from QUT's EBL profile. There were 1,583 owned EBL titles that were duplicates of the UBCM and these were left in the UBCM to be eliminated from the final selection of perpetual content. At the end of the EBS period QUT Library would own 621 titles based on average cost approximately US$169.

One hundred and forty JSTOR DDA titles were implemented in March 2015 with a US$5,000 (A$6,159) deposit, and in September 2015 this collection was broadened to 4,532 titles. Using this model, four PDF downloads or six chapter views triggers a purchase. 3,445 duplicating titles were removed from QUT's EBL profile.

A Cengage e-textbook pilot program was implemented via the Council of Australian University Librarians (CAUL) consortium using the EBL platform to make seven broadly used Australian texts available in e-book format for the first time in 2014 and 8 of 20 titles available in 2015. A trial of 21 Oxford University Press titles was also implemented in 2015.

In 2015 the Library implemented an e-textbook trial with Pearson and licensed 49 titles in semester 1 at a subscription cost of A$18,100 and 46 titles in semester 2 at $15,607.

Results

Elsevier EBS Compared to Collection Purchases (Figure 1)

The EBS model shows a high level of usage compared with the Elsevier collections, which have been owned since 2012 and especially compared with 1.72 uses per title across the entire QUT e-book collection in 2014. The EBS cost per use is higher than the collection purchase cost; however, the latter were available for a much longer time. It is to be expected that per title usage on older content would be lower than the more recent EBS titles.

Elsevier EBS Impact on EBL Costs (Figure 2)

As QUT implemented mediated PDA from June 11, the post-EBL expenditure is extrapolated based on the previous three months and estimated to have reduced by only US$3,076. The extra cost of the EBS is therefore US$76,539. Note that the EBL spend on the content the EBS replaced was only 11% of total EBL spend on Elsevier content and it was never expected that the EBS could eliminate all EBL expenditure. There are a number of variables affecting comparisons of EBL spend before and after the EBS, such as the increasing usage trend on EBL (for instance, there was a 13%

EBS March to August 2015 (1,155 titles)			Collection Purchases 2007–2012 Cumulative Use (1,142 titles)		
Total Use (Section/Chapter)	Cost Per Use	Use Per Title	Total Use (Section/Chapter)	Cost Per Use	Use Per Title
9,757	US$4.07 / A$5.42	8.29	45,508	A$2.53	9.60

Figure 1. Elsevier EBS compared to collection purchases.

EBL Costs	STL	%	US$	Auto-purchase	%	US$	Total	%
Pre-EBS								
All Elsevier EBL Titles	2,017		$72,612	230		$58,901	$131,513	
EBS EBL Titles	304	15	$8,635	38	16	$6,113	$14,479	11
Post EBS Annual Projection							$128,437	

Figure 2. Elsevier EBS impact on EBL costs.

increase in EBL transactions in 2014 over 2013 despite that for nine months of 2013, QUT exposed its full profile from 2006 for only three months of the year); higher STL and auto-purchase charges in 2015 compared to 2014; and that not all content on EBL was included in the EBS.

EBL Value of EBS Usage (Figure 3)

An alternative calculation estimates the EBL value of EBS usage as follows in Figure 3.

Based on just the first six months of usage, the effective value from the EBS would be: Total EBL usage value on suppressed titles US$87,547 plus value of usage on additional content US$22,208—cost of EBS US$79,615 = US$30,140.

EBL and EBS Cost Per Use and Titles Owned (Figure 4)

Again using the EBL value of EBS usage to calculate, the cost per use was lower for the EBS. Additionally, the cost per title owned was lower using EBS and more titles are owned for your money in EBS; however, more titles can be made available for access via EBL PDA without an upfront commitment.

EBS drove more usage via ScienceDirect than the equivalent content was previously used on EBL. EBS represents a cost-effective alternative to collection purchases. In terms of being an alternative to the EBL model, it is not a fair comparison. A more comprehensive EBS collection would be needed to fully evaluate the cost-effectiveness of the model and completely eliminate the EBL costs for Elsevier imprints.

Taylor & Francis EBS

During March to September 2015 the Taylor & Francis EBS selection resulted in 4,416 e-book section (chapter) uses, which extrapolated for 12 months at $269,822 equals $35.64 per usage, improving over time. Of the 7,765 titles, 27% were used during the six-month period.

Taylor & Francis EBS Impact on EBL Costs (Figure 5)

Projecting the three-month post EBL costs US$225,197 to a full year of usage (US$611,348 reduced to US$562,992) and including the cost of the EBS (GBP136,577/A$269,822), the extra cost is A$205,348.

EBL Titles	Usage	% of Titles	Times Used	STL Cost Average US$32.20	Auto-purchase Cost US$	Total Cost US$
379	6,554	23	4 or more	$21,638	$57,666	$87,547
155	256	16	1 to 3	$8,243		
590	0	61	STL Total	$29,881		
Non-EBL Titles						
59	2,980	43	4 or more	$5,700	$15,189	$22,209
25	41	18	1 to 3	$1,320		
54	0	39	STL Total	$7,020		

Figure 3. EBL value of EBS usage.

Elsevier	Cost/Title	No. Titles Owned	Cost Per Use
EBL PDA	US$257 / $343	340	US$13.36 / A$17.81
EBS	US$211 / $281	377	US$4.07 / A$5.40

Figure 4. EBL and EBS cost per use and titles owned.

EBL Costs	STL	US$	Auto-purchase	US$	Total US$
Pre-EBS	9,706	$270,945	1,527	$340,403	$611,348
Post-EBS	2,943	$110,530	519	$114,667	$225,197
Annual Projection					$562,992

Figure 5. Taylor & Francis EBS impact on EBL costs.

EBS did not sufficiently curtail the usage and cost of EBL; however, as stated above, there are a number of variables affecting comparisons of EBL spend before and after the EBS, including higher STL and auto-purchase charges in 2015 compared to 2014. To estimate the potential cost of EBL transactions had the EBS not been undertaken, the EBS usage is calculated in EBL terms.

EBL Value of EBS Usage (Figure 6)

Using just the EBL usage costs for the six month EBS evaluation period US$178,797/A$238,396 and subtracting the cost of the EBS, this is an extra cost of A$31k. There were several issues affecting the EBS success, including mismatching between EBL and T&F eISBNs, which beset the suppression of T&F EBS content on EBL resulting in some content not being suppressed; the late supply of MARC records for a proportion of content; and a small proportion of titles having older copyright dates. Although the uncalculated EBL value of the second half of the EBS usage period also needs to be considered, it appears that the EBS has not been as effective in curbing EBL expenditure as anticipated.

EBL and EBS Cost Per Use and Titles Owned (Figure 7)

Once again, the cost per use, cost per title owned, and number of titles owned favored the EBS. However, more titles can be made available for access via EBL PDA without an upfront commitment.

Wiley EBS

The 2015 Wiley EBS selection resulted in 23,385 e-book section (chapter) uses during the seven months from March to September 2015 (excludes 2,998 usages on titles already owned), which for

EBS Titles	Usage	% of Titles	Times Used	STL Cost Average US$38.00	Auto-purchase Cost US$	Total Cost US$
233	1,723	3	4 or more	$26,219	$51,563	$178,797
1,850	2,693	24	1 to 3	$101,014		
5,682	0	73	STL Total	$127,234		

Figure 6. EBL value of EBS usage.

Taylor & Francis	Cost / Title	No. Titles Owned	Cost Per Use
EBL PDA	US$767 / A$1,022	233	US$40.48 / A$53.98
EBS	GBP96.73 / A$191	1,411	GBP18.03 / A$35.64

Figure 7. EBL and EBS cost per use titles owned.

12 months extrapolated at US$105,000 equals US$2.61 per usage. Of the 16,665 titles, 71% were not used and of the 10,404 titles suppressed from EBL, and 84% were not used.

Wiley UBCM Impact on EBL Costs (Figure 8)

Projecting the three-month post UBCM EBL costs to a full year of usage (US$164,469 reduced to US$61,152) and including the cost of the EBS, the extra cost is US$1,683.

In March 2015 Wiley introduced an embargo on STLs for current-year content and hence a proportion of these STL costs would no longer have been incurred for the current year publication dates. This is estimated at about US$23k per annum in STL costs eliminated by the embargo. This is an advantage of the EBS in that the EBS provides access to the 2015 titles without embargo. However, factoring in the impact of the embargo, the cost difference is therefore higher than calculated above.

EBL Value of UBCM Usage (Figure 9)

Using just the first six months of usage, the effective value from the EBS would be: total EBL usage value on suppressed titles over six months US$122,657 plus value of usage on additional non-EBL content US$144,624—cost of EBS US$105,000 = US$162,281/A$216,374.

Wiley advised after EBS commencement that 1,278 titles available via EBL were excluded from the UBCM. Matching analysis confirmed that 20% of the previous 12 months' STL transactions were for titles not included in the UBCM. The exclusion of textbook and premium content is one reason the EBS did not curtail the usage and cost of EBL to the extent the library was hoping. However, considering the EBL value of the EBS usage the EBS appears to be a cost-effective alternative.

EBL and EBS Cost Per Use and Titles Owned (Figure 10)

Once again, the cost per use, cost per title owned, and number of titles owned favored the EBS. However, more titles can be made available for access via EBL PDA without an upfront commitment.

JSTOR DDA

From March, 2015 through October 20, 2015, there were 17 e-books purchased for a total of $782. There were a total of 538 chapter views and downloads for a cost-per-chapter view and download of $1.45. The 538 chapter views and downloads were across 155 titles and this was across 34 publishers. When the corpus was increased from 140 titles to 4,532 titles, the average number of e-books accessed each month increased from 10 to 63 and the average downloads and chapter views increased from 45

Wiley	Cost / Title	No. Titles Owned	Cost Per Use
EBL PDA	US$199 / A$265	616	US$12.61 / A$16.82
EBS	US$169 / A$225	621	US$2.61 / A$3.48

Figure 8. Wiley UBCM impact on EBL costs.

EBL Titles	Usage	% of Titles	Times Used	STL Cost Average US$20.80	Auto-Purchase Cost US$	Total Cost US$
616	8,188	6	4 or more	$38,438	$52,311	$122,657
988	1,534	10	1 to 3	$31,907		
8,457	0	84	STL Total	$70,346		
Non-EBL Titles						
775	12,199	15	4 or more	$48,360	$65,813	$144,624
912	1,464	18	1 to 3	$30,451		
3,334	0	67	STL Total	$78,811		

Figure 9. EBL value of UCBM usage.

EBL Costs	STL	US$	Auto-purchase	US$	Total USD
Pre-UBCM	4,035	$90,795	654	$73,674	$164,469
Post-UBCM	519	$9,093	216	$15,368	$24,461
Annual Projection					$61,152

Figure 10. EBL and EBS cost per use and titles owned.

to 133 per month. The purchases per month did not change. QUT was projected to spend $3,500 based on the titles selected, but to date has only spent $782. QUT needs more time to assess the usage of the JSTOR DDA collection, and to assess any effect on the usage and cost of use of JSTOR titles in EBL.

E-Texts

The QUT usage of the seven Cengage 2014 e-texts was 298 in 2014 (Aug/Dec) and 955 YTD Oct 2015. Cost per use extrapolated for 2014 is US$3.72/A$5.31 and cumulative cost per use is very good at US$1.43/A$2.04. The usage of the 30 titles purchased in 2015 was 255 YTD Oct 2015 and extrapolated cost per use is US$10.84/$15.48, which will of course improve over time. Not all titles are set texts at QUT, which will affect the comparative usage rate of titles.

The QUT usage of the 21 Oxford e-texts during the six-month period March 30 to October 8, 2015 was 798 views of 20 titles, at US$3,500, equating to US$2.19/A$3.12 per use, which is a comparatively good return on investment.

The QUT usage of the Pearson e-texts was 5,369 hits during the period of almost six months from April 22 to October 8, 2015, equating to A$1.68 per use extrapolated over 12 months. Fifty-eight of the titles received hits and 43 titles received 10 hits or more and only 12 titles received five hits or less. Although the Library licensed 49 titles in semester 1 at a cost of A$18,100 and 46 titles in semester 2 at $15,607, only nine of the semester 2 titles were made available, and as these were not invoiced they have been excluded from the cost per use the calculation.

QUT's EBL usage of e-textbook titles was not affected as the e-text pilots did not include titles previously available via EBL. Pearson has since provided a new pricing structure and service guarantee which will make the e-text model more attractive to libraries.

Conclusion

EBS can be effectively used by libraries to provide access to collections of e-books at a predetermined cost, resulting in the selection of best-used titles for perpetual access. For all EBS publisher collections used at QUT, the usage of e-books will be sufficient to create a selection list for perpetual access; however, for all publishers involved, a smaller pool of titles was available via EBS than from EBL PDA. EBS is not a replacement for EBL PDA when considering it provides only a subset of titles for procurement via the EBS model.

The EBS e-book business model has the advantages of providing budget certainty to libraries; libraries can select the up-front financial commitment they can afford; patrons can choose from a wide choice of titles; usage data is used for selection (DDA); only titles that are used are purchased; dollars are spent on procuring used titles in perpetuity; current-year embargoes can be avoided; there are no STL costs; and the library ends up owning a greater number of titles as a result of the up-front investment. The EBS cost per book is lower than the EBL PDA cost per book. This is an important factor for the libraries which value the collection development approach over the access approach. However, calculations of the EBS usage on suppressed EBL content indicates that the actual impact of the EBS was much more effective than indicated by before and after EBL expenditure comparisons in isolation. There are many other factors to consider, such as changes in content, pricing, and demand.

Disadvantages include: publishers may limit access to a ratio of titles per spend; fewer titles are made available to users; libraries may be required to preselect a pool of titles to be selected by patrons; it is complicated and high workload to manage and provide; EBS titles need to be deduped against other access packages in order to prevent double purchasing; not many publishers provide EBS; and finally, many titles in the EBS collections were not used at all during the access period. Where publishers had restricted the size of the EBS collection, EBS did not have as much effect as anticipated in reducing the demand for and cost of publisher titles via EBL. The QUT EBS pilots highlighted the importance of publishers providing comprehensive and accurate information, including correct details of EBS content and comprehensive supply of MARC records. It also highlighted that libraries need to take care with matching of eISBNs to facilitate deduplication. We don't yet know if the model will increase in prevalence or if it is a passing phase in publishing.

The Cengage and Oxford e-textbook pilots have successfully provided access to a range of e-texts at an affordable price. The Pearson e-text pilot was successfully implemented in semester 1, 2015 with good cost per use.

Looking to the future, QUT Library is planning to continue to use EBL PDA, JSTOR DDA, and some publisher EBS models. It would be helpful to QUT if publishers facilitated EBS hosting on EBL (ProQuest e-book Central) in 2016, as this would eliminate the very substantial workload associated with deduplication across multiple e-book platforms due to platforms using different eISBNs.

QUT will continue with the Cengage and Oxford e-Text pilots and will also continue with the Pearson e-Text pilot as they are providing good value.

References

Cramer, C. (2013). All about demand-driven acquisition. *The Serials Librarian: From Print to the Digital Age, 65*(1), 87–97.

Downey, K., et al. (2013). A comparative study of print book and DDA e-book acquisition and use. *Technical Services Quarterly, 31*(2), 139–160.

Goedeken, E., & Lawson, K. (2015). The past, present, and future of demand-driven acquisitions in academic libraries. *College and Research Libraries, 76*(2), 205–221.

Harrera, G. (2012). Deliver the e-books your patrons and selectors both want! PDA program at the University of Mississippi. *The Serials Librarian: From the Printed Page to the Digital Age, 63*(2), 178–186.

Harloe, B., et al. (2015). What's the use of use: Return on investment strategies for consortial DDA programs. *Journal of Library Administration, 55*(3), 249–259.

Miller, L. (2015). Demand driven acquisition e-books have equal cost per use as print, but DDA has a much more active use overall. *Evidence Based Library and Information Practice, 10*(1), 89–91.

Polanka, S. (2013, March–April). E-Book access: Business models for subscription services. *Online Searcher, 65*.

Proctor, J. (2015). Demand-driven acquisition and the sunk cost model. *Collection Building, 34*(1), 2–5.

Proctor, J. (2012). Avoiding e-book "big deals": Alternatives to e-book backlists. *New Library World, 114*(7/8), 301–307.

Implementing Collection Life Cycle Management

Annie Bélanger, Associate University Librarian, Information Resources & Academic Excellence, University of Waterloo Library

Abstract

In a time of increasing physical collection space pressures and rapidly evolving higher education institutions, a holistic understanding of the collection life cycle, a strategic approach to collection development and retention, and increased stakeholder engagement is needed. Some librarians struggle with what materials to withdraw, especially if there is faculty opposition, and how to move forward collaboratively. This article will explore leveraging the experience of leading the local culture shift in a large Association of Research Library, the principles, policies and methods required to shift mental models towards what must be retained, facilitating withdrawal decisions, and connecting collection development with ongoing collection management.

Why Collection Life Cycle Management?

The last decade has been a time of reduction in stack space, for a wide range of reasons. Increasing pressure to ensure that precious square footage is focused on user needs has precipitated a reduction of stacks in many libraries. Off-site storage facilities are notoriously full, with some seemingly on life support. Increasingly, libraries are having to weed print collections, whether in the campus libraries or offsite storage. There has been a range of success based on stakeholder management and selector engagement.

Many struggle with what materials to withdraw, especially if there is faculty opposition. The just-in-case approach of collection building is set in direct conflict when there is discussion of withdrawal—"How do we know this won't be valuable in 10, 20, 50, 100 years?" The very essence of the definition of research libraries since the end of WWII is challenged by the need to withdraw beyond basic housekeeping. Evidence-based practices are challenged when so much emotion and the definition of a profession is tied into the collections.

A holistic understanding of the collection life cycle, along with a strategic approach to collection retention, assists a library in moving the conversation from one of loss to one of empowerment and proactive engagement. Collection life cycle management (CLM) shifts mental models towards what must be retained, facilitating withdrawal decisions and connecting collection development with ongoing collection management. Further, CLM allows us to enhance stakeholder engagement at the level of overarching principles and areas of focus, and not at the title level, which has been found to be an impediment to good process management.

It allows us to create multiple paths for material to move through, with a clear understanding of these paths and their associated intentions. It gives us permission to buy materials that have at most a midterm use and flag these for early withdrawal. It provides a cohesive framework to manage collections from the start to the end of their life cycle.

Exploring a Shift to a CLM Approach

The road to implementing CLM will vary among institutions, in part due to the selector model in place and its history. Here, I will attempt to breakdown what is often an organic model with overlap into a set of concrete steps. Any one institution may be starting at any one step, depending on their collection culture.

The first step, if there is such a concrete thing, will be to create buy-in for the concept. I suggest breaking this process down into manageable pieces. To begin, acquire a solid understanding of where your institution is and the gaps that need to be filled before a culture shift can occur. At

http://dx.doi.org/10.5703/1288284316245

Waterloo, a palpable difference in the approach in thinking to collections occurred after five years.

The second step, and one your institution may have completed, is to create collection development policies and, if possible, an overarching collection development strategy. Collection development policies clearly articulate what is being purchased, and why and by whom, defining the incoming materials. Sometimes, they provide a way to refuse requests for materials that do not fit the goals of the collection. The acceptance of donations should align with these policies to ensure a cohesive collection.

The third step in moving to CLM is to get buy-in for collection evaluation. This is commonly perceived as a task that requires a great deal of time; however, the benefits are profound. Collection evaluation

- Strengthens decisions regarding the life cycle of a collection
- Ensures that individual collections encompass materials that effectively meet the changing research needs of its users; gives opportunity to identify and remedy a collection's weaknesses; exhibits proactive engagement with a collection
- Helps maintain librarians' accountability to users, academic departments, and stakeholders

In critically asking questions, librarians will determine the unique facets and focal points of a collection, aiding them in the selection of evaluation methods to target key materials for retention. I will not explore collection evaluation methods in this paper, but rather the high-level questions that frame the evaluation.[1]

Librarians need to consider the following questions in direct relation to their collection:

- What are the collection's focal points or areas of concentration?
    - What are the objectives of the collection?
    - What kinds of materials are vital? Conversely, what kinds of materials are no longer vital?
- Is the collection strong and relevant? Conversely, what are its weaknesses?
    - Are collection materials meeting the research needs of its users?
- Are materials being used regularly by students, faculty, etc.?
    - In what ways are materials being used by students, faculty, etc.?
- Is the collection supporting or impacting other collections?
- Are certain material formats more desired than others?

As well, collection evaluation should be done in the context of the library's specific goals regarding user needs and research outcomes. As such, knowledge of the local institution policies is key. Further, librarians should keep in mind academic departmental research and teaching needs in the short- and long-term. Librarians can refer to academic departmental documentation and correspondence, such as:

- Minutes from academic departmental meetings
- Undergraduate and graduate affairs reports presented to faculty councils

---

[1] Information on evaluation methods is in the CLM toolkit: http://subjectguides.uwaterloo.ca/collection life cyclemanagement.

- Recent changes made to program or course descriptions
- Recent consultations with department and faculty

The fourth step is to begin working on collection retention policies to support each of these recognized benefits and lead to effective and responsible decision making in the form of strategic withdrawal action. Strategic retention ensures that collections remain relevant by explicitly identifying necessary materials to be retained over the long-term.

Collection retention policies are a critical component of shifting the conversation from one of loss to an empowered discussion of material that is both valuable and of value to the institution's constituency. Retention policies will foremost institute an efficient, streamlined collection evaluation process that can be carried out on a regular basis, in a manageable manner, by all librarians. Focusing on retention will help to efficiently structure the withdrawal review process by promoting a proactive approach to collection retention and withdrawal that facilitates continuous review rather than a reactionary and defensive "crisis management" approach when required. The policies directly address the often unique long-term research needs particular of individual collections, saving librarians considerable time and effort in identifying fit and assuring that their collections are perpetually relevant to the students and faculty using them. Last, they improve communication with faculty members in regard to collection maintenance.

Each collection retention policy must include specific statements that speak to the collection areas that will generally be retained, such as specialized topics that support the specific department; primary sources (this might include print sources such as diaries and correspondence, as well as electronic sources such as raw datasets); works published by university students and faculty (books, conference proceedings, etc.); materials collected by other departments that are deemed no longer relevant but which have research value for a specific department; and classic retrospective works that contribute to the strength of the collection (seminal works, core titles, standards, patents, etc.). This list of collection retention areas is not exhaustive. Because each collection has a unique focus, librarians may need to create further retention statements. Similarly, they may feel the need to modify existing retention categories. Librarians should ensure that they remain at a high enough level that no one title is mentioned. If such detail is wanted, it should be a follow-on to the policy in term of LC class and title-level retention rules that can be used by the collection maintenance and cataloging teams.

Keep in mind that the collection retention policies are meant to reaffirm the principles and key areas in collection development policies. The retention policies should not contradict these policies; however, they may not include all areas of the policies since the retention policies are meant to identify materials that need to be kept over the long-term, whereas the development policies include short-, mid-, and long-term needs.

The last step is to create a collection philosophy.

Implementing CLM at Waterloo

In this section I explore Waterloo's experience of moving to a CLM approach starting with piloting a retention policy to living with proactive, ongoing collection stewardship.

In 2008, Waterloo desperately needed to withdraw material, yet mired in a sense of loss, it was essentially paralyzed. Both main libraries were over 90% capacity, with some floors close to 98%. The long-term storage facility had only several years of transfer left, at a limited pace. The collection maintenance unit was desperately aware of the situation, as each collection shift had created a growing workload due to the stack capacities, quadrupling of the cost of these shifts. During this time, over 30,000 monographs and many print serials titles were being received.

After moving into a crisis management mode to draw down a floor that had received a fire warden warning because aisles were encroached by book trucks filled with materials, I started exploring ways to think about the issue over the long-term. As a newer member of the library, my first step was to understand what had been done in the past, what a successful management of the collection might look like from a different vantage point, and what was different now that made something we tried in the past not possible.

In 2005-2006, the library had moved to a more standardized approach for collection development policies. These were created in consultation with the relevant academic departments and were to align with higher level collection policies, such as the statement on the purchase of textbooks. In the same timeframe, the local consortia, the Tri-University Group of Libraries (TUG) had created a Preservation of TUG Last Copy Agreement,[2] which had preceded a significant deduplication effort of the shared long-term storage facility.

In listening to the librarians and the collection maintenance unit,[3] a few concepts came into focus. The first was that the term "weeding" was used to represent (1) shifting to the long-term storage and (2) withdrawal outright, with the first meaning the most frequently applied. Second, for many, tonnage was still foremost in defining what it meant to be an ARL-level research library. Third, there was a concern that withdrawing a book meant we were not trusting earlier collection decisions and potentially short-changing future researchers.

Waterloo needed a way to both validate those concerns and mitigate the risks by a strategic approach to drawing down the size of its collections. Coming from a varied background, I started to think about the life cycle of print materials along with the policies, procedures, and practices that ruled their existence within the library. I developed two simple flowcharts, one with an overlay of these policies and procedures (Figure 1) and another with their role (Figure 2), to illuminate the situation.

Using a project management approach, a pilot was developed as a way to test out these ideas in a collaborative, engaged way. The pilot created collection retention policies so the collection could be evaluated in tangible ways on a consistent basis. Therefore, collection evaluation would become an ongoing task for librarians as

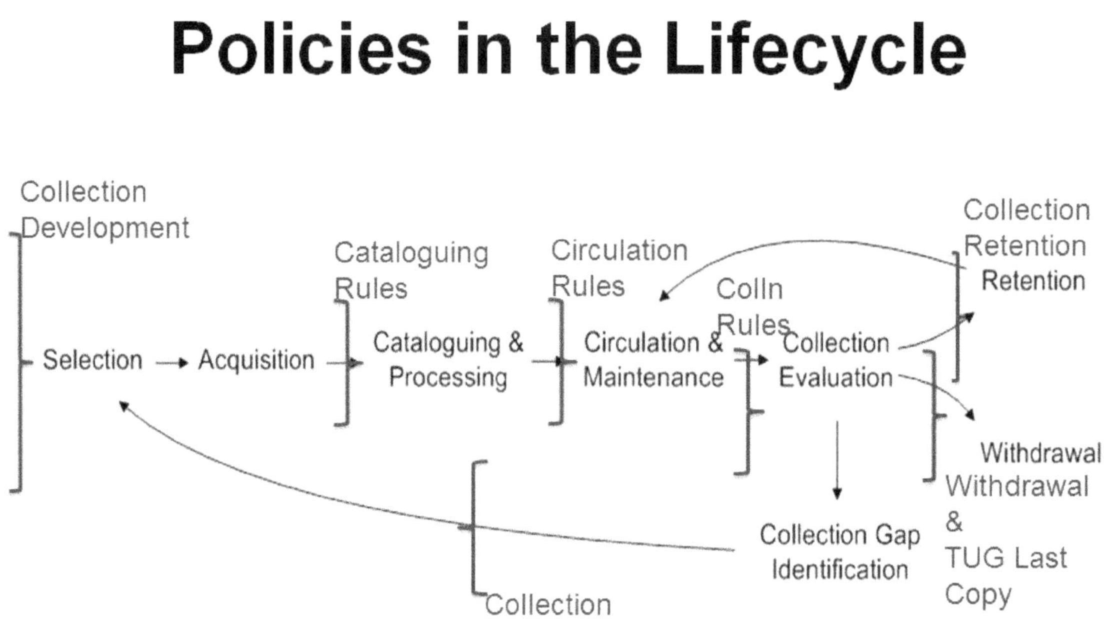

Figure 1. Policies in the life cycle.

[2] The Preservation of TUG Last Copy Agreement is at: http://www.lib.uwaterloo.ca/staff/irmc/last_copy_agreement_sept06.html.

[3] Liaison Librarians at Waterloo

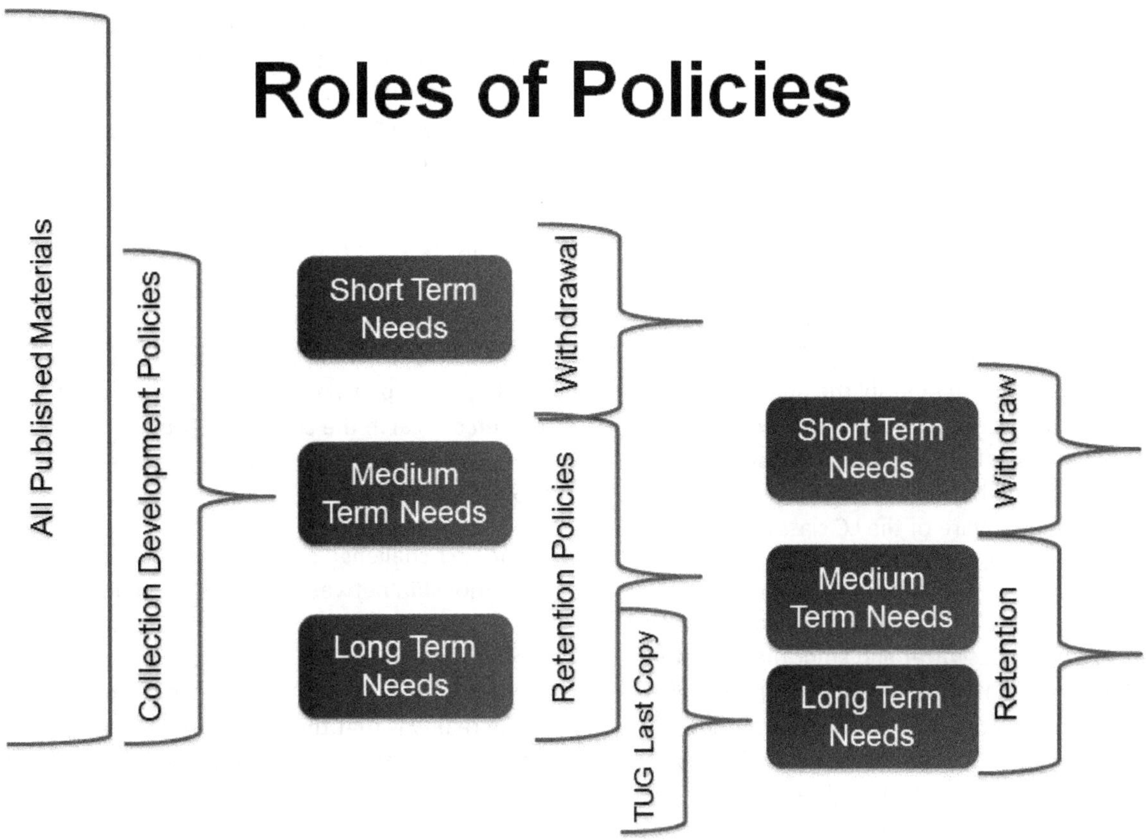

Figure 2. Roles of policies.

opposed to a task which is completed in crisis mode when print collections need to be withdrawn due to space issues. Continuous collection evaluation would allow librarians to examine the weaknesses and strengths of their collection and ensure that collections remain relevant to users.

The pilot began in 2010, with two librarians drafting retention policies and providing feedback on the toolkit as well as training needs. In early 2011, librarians received training, enabling them to evaluate their collections and draft retention policies. Over the following year and a half, librarians drafted their collection retention policies with support from an MLIS intern.

A large part of this project required the intern to provide support to the librarians when they were creating their collection retention policies. The answers to their questions were established by critical judgement and impressionistic analysis and thus used the knowledge they possess in their subject field. In addition, other evaluation tools and methods used usage data and user statistics. In many cases, an MLIS intern collected the necessary statistics by running various reports. The collected data, often displayed on excel file sheets, was then presented to the liaison librarian so that he or she could make appropriate retention decisions.

The arts and humanities librarians completed their policies first, while the science, technology, engineering, and math (STEM) librarians were to do so in the second phase. The collection retention policies for the STEM librarians posed a different challenge. The wording associated with the collection retention policies was much more congruent to the arts and humanities fields. The STEM library has a different concentration with regards to its collection, which focuses much more on recent publications and current development with little classic retrospective works being retained. This meant that the wording for the policies had to be reworked as well as the approach to the development of the collection retention policy.

To identify classic retrospective works for STEM subject areas, an MLIS intern identified core older titles by generating book citations in Scopus that are specifically related to the Waterloo faculty. Additionally, STEM librarians requested that the research areas pertinent to their subject fields be mapped to Library of Congress subject headings and Library of Congress classification numbers, allowing librarians to identify the appropriate subject headings that correspond directly to research areas in their subject field. I supposed that the arts and humanities librarians were generally more aware of the LC class since the monograph is still a dominant purchase.

Once the policies were drafted, the withdrawal exercises became swifter and smoother. In late 2012, the Arts & Humanities Library undertook its first visual inspection to identify duplicates and noncritical superseded editions. Every duplicate and previous edition was brought to the appropriate librarians for review and decision making: retain, shift to long-term storage, or withdraw. In approximately six months, the stacks were brought to 80% capacity from 96% capacity, with very few titles being lost. The plan was to repeat the exercise in the STEM Library immediately, but a consortia project overtook this, and the exercise is now planned for next year.

In 2012, the TUG libraries (University of Guelph, University of Waterloo, Wilfrid Laurier University) undertook a project to complete a large-scale print monograph deduplication of low-use items across our main libraries and shared storage facility. Though there was mild discomfort among the librarians about using a metrics-based approach, the assurance of retention LC classes and a review by special collections for valuable books allowed us to move forward. The retention classes were drawn directly from the retention policies.

Most recently, in 2014, the library undertook the subscription collection review (SCR), reviewing every ongoing subscription, which accounted for over CAD8.5M in yearly expenditures. The principle of strategic retention and curation underpinned the exercise, which is still ongoing and likely to become the way the library operates in terms of renewals.

Over these past five years, there have been many lessons learned from challenges in implementation. The following section will outline some of the key challenges and the accompanying glimmer of wisdom. Before proceeding though, it is key to emphasize that an active champion has been critical in the continued progress and dedication to an approach that requires more planning.

The first challenge concerned the expected relationship between the collection development and retention policies: were they to be different or to refer to each other. We worked on emphasizing the relationship between the two. The reality is that the first dictates what is added to the collection and the other is used to decide what should be retained, and therefore withdrawn. Thes two policies are then closed by the withdrawal policy and the TUG Preservation of Last Copy Agreement.

The second challenge was that a wide range of evaluation approaches could be used, including the order in which people undertook projects. For example, some librarians drafted their policies first and evaluated the collection to validate and revise. Others dug deeply into evaluation and stakeholder engagement to ensure the policy was in line with ongoing needs. Similar outcomes arrived with retention projects. The key was to let them use collection knowledge and ensure that while a framework was provided, you don't oversteer.

The third challenge was the power of faculty influence. Many librarians felt pressured to keep everything, thus finding it difficult to make retention decisions when they felt they needed to report back on each decision. We were in many cases able to engage them through the collection development and retention policies to give input at a higher level, allowing them the ability to act independently at the title level.

The fourth challenge was in many ways hesitance. Collection maintenance is often seen as a low priority, regularly put off since there is no time or because it can be an overwhelming, intimidating exercise. Getting rid of materials does not always sit well. The key lesson is that shifting a mental model not easy. We approached this by building trust, an unwavering champion who demonstrated its need at regular meetings.

Training a New Librarian in the What, How, Where, and Why of Health Sciences Collection Management

Susan K. Kendall, Health Sciences Coordinator, Michigan State University Libraries

Mari Monosoff-Richards, Health Sciences Librarian, Michigan State University Libraries

Abstract

Collection management for the health sciences, particularly clinical medicine, is an increasingly complex job which, anecdotally, is usually given to experienced librarians. Health sciences libraries tend to delegate collections responsibilities to one librarian who holds all of the institutional collections knowledge. Replacing these people as they retire or move on can be difficult unless new librarians become trained in collections work. At the Michigan State University Libraries, recent search committee experience revealed that an entry-level health sciences collections position attracted fewer applicants than entry-level health sciences positions for instruction, liaison, or educational technology. This may reflect the focus of library school curricula as even applicants for the collections position generally had very little relevant exposure to the subject in library school or internships. Health sciences librarianship in general can involve a lot of on-the-job training, but supervisors hiring new librarians for collections may find themselves starting from scratch. This poster will demonstrate a detailed training program developed to teach a newly graduated librarian how to develop and manage an extensive clinical medicine collection at a large university library serving medical schools. The step-wise approach focuses on learning by doing, moving from the specific to general principles rather than the other way around. Decision making for selection of materials is approached from multiple angles: institutional analysis, subject analysis, and publisher and vendor knowledge. The new librarian will provide insight into which parts of the training were most helpful.

Introduction

Recent trend pieces on health sciences librarianship have focused on new and emerging roles for librarians such as those described in a systematic review of job announcements and the literature (Cooper & Crum, 2013). The review notes that many of the new roles or new twists on old roles involve outward-facing, liaison, or instruction-related activities. Meanwhile, preservation of books and journals tend not to be a focus. Collection development (beyond the idea of preservation) was not addressed as a role specifically, so it is interesting to consider where health sciences collection development librarians fit into these trends. Certainly collecting and preserving physical materials is less and less a concern for health sciences librarians, particularly in light of the recent downsizing of many health sciences libraries (Freiburger, 2010). On the other hand, while "collection development" is a traditional role, it is also a dynamic and very relevant role for today's health sciences libraries. In her chapter, "Collection Development in Health Sciences Libraries," Holly Phillips describes collection development as the "art of understanding and meeting user information needs through careful assessment of the population served, evaluation and acquisition of resources in a variety of formats to serve those needs, and ongoing maintenance and care of the collection, including deselection" (Phillips, 2014). The chapter goes on to detail how complex collection development is in today's world, how it is encompassing ever newer skill sets, and how central collections remain in the mind of library users and health sciences library missions.

If collection development as a role for health sciences librarians is not represented heavily among new job descriptions or in discussions of the futures of health sciences libraries, yet the jobs of collection development librarians are complex and central to library missions, how are health sciences libraries filling these roles? One can perhaps assume that experienced librarians are assigned these roles, particularly where collection development is centralized in one

http://dx.doi.org/10.5703/1288284316246

librarian's position rather than shared among several subject specialists. It is also likely that more librarians are needed to teach classes, work directly with faculty and students, and do more of the outward-facing jobs than are needed in the collection development role. However, for the future of health sciences libraries, there will be a need to train new librarians in the skills of collection development and management. This training may be more and more the job of supervisors, as it appears that library school curricula are tending to de-emphasize collection development, at least in the health sciences. Perhaps this is in response to fewer job postings for collection development and the above-mentioned trend reports about new and emerging roles. The data is anecdotal, but recent search committees at the Michigan State University (MSU) Libraries found that an entry-level health sciences collections position attracted fewer applicants than entry-level health sciences positions for instruction, liaison, or educational technology. Furthermore, applicants for the collections position had very little relevant exposure to the subject in library school or internships. Health sciences librarians at Michigan State University who received their MLIS degrees within the last 10 years and who represent five different programs in the United States and Canada all report that collection development classes were minimal, optional, or sometimes nonexistent.

Despite these trends, the MSU Libraries decided to hire and train a newly graduated librarian with no professional experience to manage a medical collection which serves two medical schools. The librarian would manage the collection under supervision from a health sciences collections coordinator librarian, but the expectations were that the new librarian would eventually manage the large and complicated collection mostly independently. An extensive training program was needed. The Medical Library Association has published a number of recent books and book chapters covering collection development in health sciences libraries, including the aforementioned chapter by Phillips which covers philosophy, trends and more general issues, and more specific resource-oriented books like *Introduction to Reference Sources in the Health Sciences and The Medical Library Association's Master Guide to Authoritative Information Resources in the Health Sciences* (Huber & Swogger, 2014; Thompson, Higa, Carrigan, & Tobia, 2011). *These are all geared towards self-education and as references for collection development librarians. While informative for a new librarian, though, they are not enough to train a beginner.* A search for materials geared for supervisors training new librarians in collection development yielded only two books which address the training of new collection development librarians at length. These were the American Library Association's *Guide for Training Collection Development Librarians* and *Recruiting, Educating, and Training Librarians for Collection Development* (Fales, 1996; Johnson & Intner, 1994). While dating from the 1990s and not specific to health sciences, both books were relevant and useful as background for building a targeted in-house training program for the new librarian.

Developing the Training Program

The American Library Association's *Guide for Training Collection Development Librarians* begins with some important assumptions about collection development. First, that training new selectors is extremely important because of the cost and importance of collections for the library. Next, that selectors come to the job often with not much subject knowledge. This is especially true for health sciences where it would be extremely rare, for instance, that someone would have deep subject knowledge of clinical medicine. Third, that there are macro and micro aspects of the training needed. Selectors need to be aware of the philosophy of the institution, current trends, the publishing world, research process, and scholarly communication issues. Simultaneously they also need to learn local procedures for purchasing, local policies, the operations of other units in the institution (such as cataloging or acquisitions), and management skills. Training adult professionals also requires some assumptions. The training should be planned sequentially, involve evaluation by trainer and trainee, be flexible, involve short- and long-range plans, use different teaching methods for different types of information, and involve multiple people. Ideally, the adult trainee will help develop a personal learning program, understand the big picture, and see why they are doing various tasks.

This same guide proposes 14 different training modules that can be used as templates to develop an in-house training program: ethical, legal, and cultural considerations; planning; collection development policies; selection and review processes; approval profiles; budget processes; library department operations; marketing, outreach, and communication with constituents; the selector knowledge base; navigating the electronic environment; collection assessment; deselection; conservation and preservation; and fund-raising and donors. To develop a specific training program for the new librarian for health sciences, ideas were taken from some of these 14 modules. Other thoughts came from Soete (1994), who suggests a training program begin first with a needs assessment of the trainee and proceed to development of training objectives, identification of methods, activities to pursue, development of performance goals and expectations, and finally evaluation of the program.

Developing the in-house training program geared towards teaching a new librarian how to manage a clinical medicine collection began with a needs assessment at the librarian's interview and continued after she was hired. Supervisors can expect a range of possible experience that can be tangentially related to subject expertise. Full understanding of the knowledge gaps can take time as they may not be readily apparent in a new hire's cv. The supervisor spent considerable time talking with the new librarian informally, asking questions, being alert to questions and comments from the new librarian, and synthesizing these into a coherent list of gaps to be addressed in training. Soete warns against overwhelming the trainee with a long list of undifferentiated needs but suggests sorting by urgency.

Because the librarian was new to the profession, there were many knowledge gaps, and the list of areas for training could potentially have been overwhelming. On a macro level they included learning the subject area along with key textbooks and reference sources; knowing the publishers and platforms for clinical medical materials; knowing the MSU Libraries' current subscriptions and holdings; and understanding the budget. On a micro level, learning the procedures involved would be a lot more straightforward. Of all the knowledge gaps, the following were identified and sorted as most urgent for initial training:

1. Knowing relevant departments and people involved in acquisitions and collection development at the Libraries
2. Knowing which databases, e-book packages, and other resources the libraries already has
3. Understanding how to choose monographs to purchase to support the institution's user groups
4. Understanding how to monitor the monograph fund
5. Understanding procedures for selecting new monographs in electronic or physical format

Monograph selection was chosen as a first step in the training process, because ordering for those needed to begin right away, stakes are lower with one-time purchases, and individual small purchases can help build confidence for larger decisions. Serials renewal often happens more automatically and decisions about new serials could wait. The training program was designed to begin with institutional and subject specifics rather than with general collection development principles. This goes against some of the suggestions from the books on training collection development librarians. General principles, including trends and issues in collection development and the field of clinical medicine, are important to include in a training program and would eventually be addressed with articles and discussions, but, while the librarian was given several articles on collection development to read and found them interesting, they did not help her get started with her day-to-day job. Instead, identifying the University's residency specialties to help learn local needs and medical specialties, core textbooks to purchase using review services, and learning publishers and platforms for e-books would help the new librarian begin to make decisions.

Module 1 (monographs) of the training process is included in the appendix. A philosophy of the training was that the librarian learn through doing and that very little of the training was hypothetical or merely "for educational purposes." On the other hand, the steps were deliberate, specific, and prescriptive because the librarian was starting at a basic level. The program began with the librarian learning *what* to purchase (step A) and then later *how* to purchase. Learning what to purchase required the librarian to learn about the subject area and user groups, and that was accomplished first by learning about the residency programs offered at the institution. Residents require more advanced and research materials than are needed by medical students, and the kinds and sizes of residency programs give an indicator of the strengths and focus of the institution. The librarian was next given the collection development policy to help her learn call numbers and existing collection strengths and priorities in order to match against what she had learned about the residency programs. Although all the training books consulted recommend using the collection development policy as a training tool, the new librarian was not able to use the policy as initially envisioned. At a large university with medical school, so many subject areas were collected as the "research" level that nothing stood out as unique. The majority of time spent in the first part of the training was in learning how to use *Doody's Review Service*, an online service which rates medical books and provides helpful information on core titles, publishers, and online availability for collection development librarians. The librarian was asked to develop title lists for each residency program identified, learn key titles in each field, and begin generating a list of books to purchase if key titles were not already owned. This task accomplished the goals of learning how to use a selection tool, developing more familiarity with important books in various fields, and getting started with choosing materials to purchase.

Step B of module 1 was to help the librarian prepare to purchase monographs by focusing on publishers. Current collecting of monographs in the health sciences, with a focus on electronic materials, can no longer be based solely on whether a book is on an important subject or by a known author. Purchasing e-books involves knowing platforms, packages, and licensing terms, all of which are dependent more on the publisher than on the author or subject. The new librarian was asked to sort potential purchases by publisher and begin dealing with purchases one publisher at a time. As she went through her potential purchases by publisher with the supervisor, she began to learn when she could choose books title by title and when that wasn't possible. She was able to develop a plan for how to purchase the books she had already identified in step A.

The last step of module 1 was training on the local specifics of purchasing such as how to use vendor platforms, how to work with the acquisitions department, and how to use the budget. While these can be complicated, they were made simpler by all the organizational and planning steps that had already occurred. Budgets can be a complicated area, and the new librarian found that notions of budgets based on personal finances did not always apply.

Module 2 of the training program focused on databases (see appendix). The new librarian was asked to go through each database on the library website that was tagged for the health sciences. She was to determine for each database the kind of content included, the subject areas covered, and the audience for the database. "Databases" included literature indexes as well as full-text e-book and journal packages, so it comprised a significant part of the medical collection. The new librarian was asked to create user-centered summaries of each database that could be used on the library website. While this task doesn't necessarily appear to be collections-specific, it is important to get a new librarian to learn about the existing collection. Older books on collection development training tell the supervisor to have the new librarian walk the stacks to familiarize herself with the collection. Today's digital libraries make that impossible or, at least, less helpful as a training exercise.

Assessing the Training Program and Future Directions

From the beginning, the new collection development librarian was given performance goals and was involved in helping to evaluate her training program. For each aspect of the training program, the new librarian wrote down her thoughts about what she had learned. She found that several of the steps fulfilled the goals of helping her to learn about the University's user groups, about the collection, about the types of materials available for purchase, and about vendors and platforms. While it is tempting to learn the procedures of ordering and get started more quickly, she saw the value in all the preparation work. Sometimes she indicated that training goals could be made clearer. For instance, she found the collection development policy not to be helpful in learning subject areas of focus or call numbers. The collection policy may be useful, but may be easier to understand once the librarian has started to do more purchasing based on other aspects of the training. In other cases, the new librarian was unaware of all the reasons behind a certain task and the competencies that it was meant to develop. This underscores that supervisors will be more successful the more transparent they are about learning objectives and about why tasks are assigned.

References

Cooper, I. D., & Crum, J. A. (2013). New activities and changing roles of health sciences librarians: A systematic review, 1990–2012. *Journal of the Medical Library Association, 101*(4), 268–277. http://dx.doi.org/10.3163/1536-5050.101.4.008

Fales, S. L. (Ed.). (1996). *Guide for training collection development librarians*. Chicago: American Library Association.

Freiburger, G. (2010). Introduction: Be prepared. Loss of space for medical libraries. *Journal of the Medical Library Association, 98*(1), 24. http://dx.doi.org/10.3163/1536-5050.98.1.009

Huber, J. T., & Swogger, S. (2014). *Introduction to reference sources in the health sciences* (6th ed.). Chicago: ALA Neil-Schuman.

Johnson, P., & Intner, S. S. (Eds.). (1994). *Recruiting, educating, and training librarians for collection development*. Westport, CT: Greenwood Press.

Phillips, H. E. (2014). Collection development in health sciences libraries. In S. Wood (Ed.), *Health sciences librarianship* (pp. 90–96). Lanham: Rowman & Littlefield.

Soete, G. J. (1994). Training for success: Integrating the new bibliographer into the library. In S. Johnson & S. S. Intner (Eds.), *Recruiting, educating, and training librarians for collection development* (pp. 159–169). Westport, CT: Greenwood Press.

Thompson, L. L., Higa, M. L., Carrigan, E., & Tobia, R. (2011). *The Medical Library Association's master guide to authoritative information resources in the health sciences*. New York: Neal-Schuman Publishers.

Appendix: Training Program

Module 1: Clinical Medicine Collections—Monographs

A. Subject Areas

1. Learn and list residency areas for the medical colleges and read about colleges on their web sites.
    a. Look at medicine collection development policy.
    b. Note any questions/potential areas of collecting depth that do not match what you've learned about the colleges
2. Look up *Doody's Core Titles* for residency subject areas, list a few top titles by star rating for each.
    a. Compare your list of *Doody's Core Titles* for specialties against the *Library Medical E-Books LibGuide*. Any discrepancies?
    b. For any titles not on the *LibGuide*, do we have these in the catalog? Electronic or print? Any titles we should buy? Start a "to buy" list.
3. Examine e-book usage stats for McGraw-Hill Access products, Ovid, and ClinicalKey. How do the most highly used books compare in subject area with what you've learned above?
4. Goals:
    a. Be able to list from memory one or two "name" books for different subject specialties.
    b. Update collection development policy if needed.
    c. Have a "to buy" list begun for next fiscal year.

B. Prepare for Purchasing Monographs

1. Arrange "to buy" list from part 1 into publishers. Check for e-book availability in *Doody's*, and make note of availability online. Check spreadsheet on publisher platforms.
    a. Elsevier: Clinical Key or Elsevier Science Direct.
    b. McGraw-Hill: Access products, McGraw-Hill eBook Libraries.
    c. Lippincott Williams & Wilkins: Books@Ovid or Lippincott Health Libraries.
    d. Cambridge: Cambridge online.
    e. Wiley: Wiley Online Library.
    f. Aggregator platforms: ebrary, EBSCO online, R2.
    g. Societies: American Academy of Pediatrics online, Psychiatry Online (American Psychiatric Association).
    h. Not available online—buy print.
2. Arrange Rittenhouse slips by publisher. Note which ones are available in online packages:
    a. Elsevier.
    b. McGraw-Hill.
    c. Lippincott Williams & Wilkins.
    d. Thieme.
    e. Taylor and Francis.
    f. Wiley.
    g. Oxford.
    h. Cambridge.
    i. Society publishers (American Academy of Pediatrics, American Psychiatric Association, American Academy of Orthopaedics . . .)

j. Special: history of medicine, consumer health, medical humanities, sociology, ethics, undergraduate topics, etc.
k. Drug guides.
l. Board review preparation.

3. Select titles from "special" areas to be purchased as print books (will need input from supervisor for this).

C. Procedures for Purchasing Monographs

1. Review budget online. How much money is available for monograph purchases for the year?
2. Review approval plan for medical books.
3. Review how-to procedures for purchasing printed books:
    a. Selecting approval books.
    b. Purchasing a book using Rittenhouse slips.
    c. Purchasing a book using WorldCat.
    d. Purchasing books using Rittenhouse carts online.
5. Learn to purchase electronic books
    a. Purchase books on R2 platform.
    b. Begin creating spreadsheet of Books@Ovid titles to purchase.

Module 2: Clinical Medicine Collections—Databases

A. Medical Database Collection

1. Go into each database tagged "medicine" and look for answers to the following:
    a. What kind of content is it: abstracts of scholarly articles, textbooks, videos, images, or some combination of these?
    b. Is the content inside the database full text (textbooks or journal articles) or is it only abstracts (like PubMed) with links out to full text that resides elsewhere?
    c. What subject areas are covered by the database (for example: psychiatry only, internal medicine, all areas of medicine, or biomedical research?)
    d. Based on the answers to #1, who is the audience for this database: researchers, all physicians, medical students, residents, pediatrics residents, premedical students, or the public?

BAM: The Basic Access Model for Content Mining Agreements

Darby Orcutt, Assistant Head of Collection Management, North Carolina State University Libraries

Abstract

The Basic Access Model (BAM) provides a reasonable and practical framework of business terms for libraries and vendors to agree on how to facilitate user access to digital content for content mining purposes, as well as a principled and agreed upon industry foundation for future cooperation. BAM has already opened up significant content for mining access. The sooner we can open up our collections—both as libraries and as vendors—to the new and emerging tools and methods of content mining researchers, the more relevant we and our collections will be.

Background

The need for much deeper library support for text and data mining (TDM) research came especially clear to me a couple of years ago at a campus colloquium on mining. Hundreds of faculty and graduate student researchers showed up—a far larger crowd than I had expected, and a crowd that was not simply interested in mining activities, but already engaged in them. Yet, I was simultaneously dismayed at the quality of the datasets that many of these researchers were using. Certainly many were using datasets from the ICPSR (Inter-university Consortium for Political and Social Research), federal government, and other standard sources, yet it seemed at least as many were simply downloading whatever datasets they could conveniently find via Google.

As a librarian, I knew we had better content available through the Libraries that could much better answer many of their research questions. But I also knew that we had thus far done little to expose to our users what data we had, and that most of it was not available in ways that would easily allow for computational research. Furthermore, this was not an institution-specific situation. Surely, I thought, research libraries could do better than we were. If we are serious about being relevant sources of information for researchers now and in the future—indeed, if we value the continued existence of the institution of the research library—then I realized we needed to be opening up our collections for computational research immediately.

Push Me/Pull Me

Librarians have been talking about establishing text and data mining agreements with vendors for quite a few years now, but little progress has been made. The current scene seems dominated by vendor fear and librarian confusion, but each of these conditions operating within a push me/pull me relationship to itself. Vendors, especially commercial vendors, simultaneously fear letting their data out into the world and not adapting well to the changing context of scholarly activity; in other words, they want to hold and protect the value of their content on the one hand, while also not missing the opportunity to increase the value of their content (or not allowing its value to diminish) by withholding it from the new and emerging ways in which academics now and increasingly will need to use it.

Librarians themselves largely seem to feel torn in different directions too, confused mainly by pragmatic versus idealistic desires. At the institutional level, they generally privilege present needs of access over what they perceive as future needs of supporting mining activities (resulting, for one, in not pushing too hard for TDM agreements). At the larger professional level, however, librarians as a whole seem rather more idealistically than pragmatically focused. They misunderstand the current or near capacities of vendors, including how silo-ized is much content that may appear homogenous via a front-end interface, how historicized and uneven is much metadata, and especially how costly it might be to

http://dx.doi.org/10.5703/1288284316247

provide the "perfect" interface or even APIs, as well as quibbling amongst themselves as to exactly what researchers will need. The result is near-deadlock, with continued non-access for computational researchers.

Breaking Through the Logjam

The big confusion all around centers on what to do and where to go from here. For both vendors and libraries, the move toward computational research implies new services, new means of support, and new roles. I recently began exploring the possibilities for these on the library side in an article in *Online Searcher* (Orcutt, 2015). While I can't answer all of these questions—and moreover, I believe that there are multiple acceptable and contextually appropriate decisions around this support that will need to be made at the local—I am certain that our first step needs to be nailing down agreement on a basic level of access for research.

This is what I've been doing for the North Carolina State University (NCSU) Libraries, but also with a hand toward getting commercial vendors to offer like terms to their other library customers. Beginning with Gale in June 2014, we have inked several first-ever blanket mining agreements with commercial providers of especially primary source historical content. And, as Gale did just a few months later in November 2014, many of these vendors have (or will soon) be offering these same terms to other institutions. Several press releases (with more to come) detail some of these successes:

Gale:

http://www.infodocket.com/wp-content/uploads/2014/11/final-Gale-data-mining-press-release-1103142.pdf

Unlimited Priorities/Accessible Archives:

http://www.unlimitedpriorities.com/2015/03/unlimited-priorities-and-ncsu-libraries-partner-to-create-model-data-mining-agreement/

Adam Matthew:

http://news.lib.ncsu.edu/blog/2015/08/14/ncsu-libraries-adam-matthew-digital-strike-groundbreaking-content-mining-agreement/

The Basic Access Model (BAM)

The key to opening up these rich datasets to computational research is to focus on a core level of access for mining purposes, with both library and vendor meeting at a reasonable, practical, and sustainable agreement regarding how to make this content available to researchers now, without the need to define and articulate the complete future landscape of what vendor and library roles, services, and support for mining activities may become. My Basic Access Model (BAM) is not a model license, but rather a model framework of business terms to ensure researchers can access these often superior (although never perfect) datasets. And while our shared understanding of what constitutes "basic" may change a bit over time, this is what it includes now:

1. Library customers can access *all* data—This includes all associated metadata and image files. In fact, I much prefer to speak of "content mining" than TDM, as the former is more inclusive of the sorts of formats that only the most advanced researchers are currently mining but will eventually become much more commonly mined.
2. Clear and appropriate cost recovery agreements—These should spell out in advance actual and reasonable costs of such recovery. Too many institutions have found that they and vendors differ over what constitute the bases of "cost recovery," so agreement in principle alone is not sufficient. Vendors would do well to publish clear and reasonable cost schedules for particular datasets. Providing basic access for content mining should not be a profit center for vendors,

although I do see opportunity for vendors to develop at scale and monetize add-on services (particularly teaching resources for mining activities) (Orcutt, 2015). Although it may sound archaic, the easiest and least expensive delivery option for very large datasets at present is actually physical delivery of hard drives (something that will certainly change over time!).

3. Access for researchers must be blanket access—In other words, access to data for mining (or distant reading) purposes should mirror usual individual (or close reading) access, allowing for anonymous access so long as institutional affiliation is confirmed, and without need to indicate what, how, or why research is being conducted (as some vendors desire). Libraries have vested interests in protecting their users' privacy, as well as ensuring against potential overt or *de facto* censorship of a line of research. And while the overwhelming majority of content mining researchers welcome conversation and transparency with vendors about their research questions, there are legitimate reasons why a researcher may wish to delay or forgo divulging their ideas (for example, a pending grant application).
4. Lastly, there should be no special restrictions on mining activities or their products—These uses by scholars are already covered by existing contract terms, copyright, and fair use. Access to data for content mining does not give a researcher any special rights to share or publish, but neither should it remove any usual abilities to do so. Motivated by fear, some vendors attempt to more strictly limit, for example, textual citations by mining researchers (to a certain number of words or characters); ironically, the products of text mining research are often more quantitative or algorithmic in nature, and are likely to cite less (and less of the essence) of texts than more traditional scholarship.

Next Steps

Libraries and vendors alike should look to the BAM model as both a present means for content mining access to data, and as a principled and agreed upon foundation for future cooperation between content providers and libraries. Certainly tools, support, instruction, services, staffing, infrastructure, and needs related to content mining will give us plenty to discuss, develop, and figure out over the conceivable future. Yet, the sooner we can open up our collections—both as libraries and as vendors—to the new and emerging tools and methods of computational researchers, the more relevant we and our collections will be to academic research, scholarship, and the discovery and production of new knowledge.

References

Orcutt, D. (2015). Library support for text and data mining. *Online Searcher, 39*(3), 27–30.

Changing the Conversation: Using Agile Approaches to Develop and Assess Collections Holistically

Genya O'Gara, Associate Director, Virtual Library of Virginia (VIVA)

Cheryl Duncan, Director of Cataloging and Acquisitions, James Madison University

Abstract

In 2013–2014, James Madison University (JMU) Libraries embarked on an endeavor to create a flexible, holistic model for developing, managing, and assessing collections. The effort began by surveying what qualitative and quantitative data was being collected that could inform big-picture questions about whether library collections were meeting evolving campus research needs. The investigation included an in-depth literature review, the launch, evaluation, and adoption of several pilot projects, and ultimately the construction of an evaluation rubric and disciplinary subject snapshots that articulate both the impact of collections and potential gaps within them at institutional and departmental levels.

In order to remain agile as the pieces were built, JMU took an iterative pilot approach that included collapsing siloed funds, revising allocations, and implementing a structured multi-year campus-wide continuing-resources review. The process also included the adoption and evaluation of contemporary content development methods, including a consortial DDA program, curation of local digital collections, and hosting of campus research and open access publications.

These proceedings detail the results of this two-year venture and the mechanisms developed for expressing a holistic value of collections to stakeholders.

Introduction

It is no surprise to hear that the content scholars are producing and relying on has been rapidly changing, as have scholarly communication norms throughout disciplines. Although there is still a strong reliance on traditional materials in many disciplines, including monographs and journal articles, today's researchers also rely on datasets, digital libraries, open access publications, streaming video, visualizations, and the ability to use, reshape, and re-share the products of their scholarship in new ways.

Academic libraries and librarians are striving to meet both emerging and traditional needs. To do this they are being asked to wear many hats, from bibliographer to data visualization specialist, from intellectual property expert to grant reviewer. Rarely in this environment is there time to pause and reflect on whether or not current approaches are meeting campus needs holistically. Without this time and space, more often than not librarians are applying traditional collection development and assessment strategies to a changed environment, and are unable to clearly link the efforts put into the development of collections to the current goals and aspirations of their institutions. The professional literature of the past few years, with one notable exception, bears this out, focusing primarily on the assessment or development of a specific tool or format, rather than attempting to examine collections as a whole (Duncan & O'Gara, 2015).[1]

At James Madison University (JMU) the Libraries are committed to flexible collection development to meet emerging needs, but struggle, like many institutions, with deciding what to discontinue in order to meet those needs, how to measure success, and how to articulate the value and impact of collections to stakeholders. In

[1] A notable exception was the article "Challenges and Possibilities for Collection Management in a Digital Age" (Horava, 2010), and the literature was only reviewed through July 2014.

http://dx.doi.org/10.5703/1288284316248

preliminary efforts toward more flexible and holistic collection development JMU had begun the process of retraining and reallocating staff, streamlining processes, and developing workflows for ingesting content that supported new research needs. In the spring of 2013 the Libraries were ready for the next level of this endeavor and embarked on the development of a tool to better assess as a whole where collection development efforts were succeeding or falling short.

Background

JMU is a comprehensive, four-year public university with an emphasis on undergraduate research and engagement. Collection development is accomplished through several channels. Local and rare collections are developed by the digital and special collections units and consist of JMU-authored publications, ETDs, manuscripts, and archival collections. Circulating collections are developed by subject liaisons, primarily through one-time purchases and approval plans. Continuing resources, including journals and database subscriptions, are reviewed by four groups of affiliated subject librarians (referred to as clusters) and then recommended to the Collection Development Committee (CDC), which approves new resources. An elected representative from each of the four subject clusters (social sciences, arts and humanities, sciences, and applied health sciences) sits on the CDC, as well as the Director of Collections. This group is also responsible for reviewing general resources and recommending and implementing new collection development practices.

Like many libraries, JMU has struggled with expanding resource costs and flat materials budgets. A scholarly communications task force[2] had documented changing disciplines on campus, and yet there had been little room, either in the budget or in the current workload and workflows of librarians, to meet emerging needs while continuing to develop more traditional collections (Brantmeier et al., 2013).

The Pilots

With the goal of freeing some of the materials budget to meet new campus demands, and to experiment with new methods of content development, the CDC began examining allocation models. Conversations about alternate approaches led to some immediate pilots, including identifying a subject cluster to pilot a collapse of siloed firm funds in interdisciplinary fields, the development of collection snapshots, a review of all continuing resources, and streamlining the development and assessment activities leveraged on JMU collections. These pilot projects, approached iteratively, helped to shift the organization's overall approach toward collection development.

With these projects underway, the development of a collections evaluation rubric also began. Beginning the work on the rubric simultaneously ensured a mechanism to gauge the impact of new approaches, while deliberately evaluating for a holistic value of collections in meeting the needs of stakeholders.

Collections Snapshots

Collections snapshots were developed to support subject librarians in conversations with faculty about what collections supported specific disciplinary work and how these collections were being used. These one-page documents were created upon request—a significant change from the previous practice of compiling massive spreadsheets with usage and title information for monographs, journals, and databases within each subject area. Although the statistical and financial information found in this previous document was valuable, it was a large amount of work for a fairly underutilized internal tool. It also didn't include information about more specialized content that might be important only within a particular discipline.

The primary purpose of the snapshot is to represent collections in specific disciplinary areas

[2] "Scholarly Communication Taskforce: Final Report and Recommendations" (Brantmeier et al., 2013) details the findings of the group.

more fully and visually, by both use and format, and to not isolate particular resources. For example, a one-page document might include information on print, e-book, and journal holdings distributed across identified Library of Congress classifications and aligned with specific programs. Corresponding use percentages are included in the form of overlaid graphs and other data visualizations (Figure 1). Snapshots are customized by discipline, so a science snapshot may include the impact factors of journals, and the media snapshot might include streaming statistics. These one-page documents are outward facing, and attempt to reflect what is valued and used by a particular discipline.

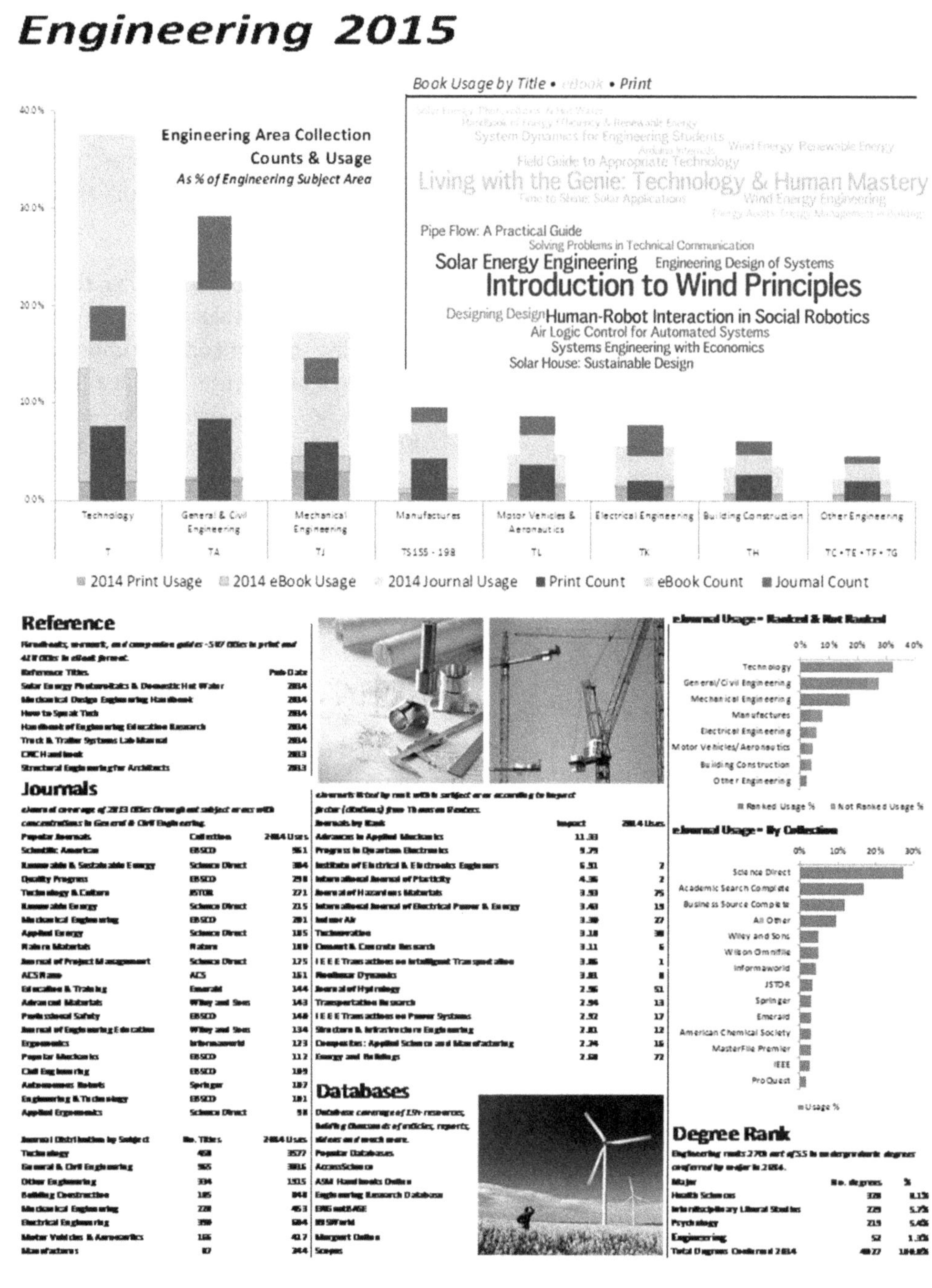

Figure 1. Example of 2015 engineering collections snapshot.

Continuing Resources Review

In order to create greater flexibility for new types of continuing resource needs, meet the inflationary costs of current subscriptions, and prepare for a projected state budget reversion, a review of all continuing resources was implemented. Structured in two parts, the libraries began with a database review designed to leverage qualitative and quantitative data in the decision-making process. Information about resources was presented to subject librarians for review through an internal SharePoint form that included costs; past, current, and projected subscription charges; and use information represented graphically and numerically (Figure 2). Subject librarians were asked to contribute to the form information on the ease of use, the audience resource, the availability of consortial products, and faculty feedback.

Clusters of affiliated subject librarians reviewed the resources and identified approximately 10% in cancellations from combined subject areas for the CDC's review. This approach took the burden off of individuals and allowed for multidisciplinary decision-making.

The second part of the process was a journal review that included many of the same data points as the database review, but additionally contained aggregated rankings and comments from faculty. In order to obtain this information, the Journal Review Tool (Figure 3) was built. This web tool allowed faculty to record and submit responses to a proposed cancellation list that represented the top 25 percent of highest cost per use subscription titles, distributed across the clusters' broad subject areas. The methodology for processing the feedback was approached in two ways. First, the rankings of the users who provided feedback were weighted based on how closely research and teaching subject areas matched the journal subject areas. For example, a weight of 1 was given for direct associations between users and journal subject areas, a weight of 0.5 was given for partial associations, and a weight of 0.1 for tangential associations.

Rankings of must keep, keep if possible, and can cancel assigned points (10, 5, and 1), and these points were multiplied by association weight factors, and summed and averaged over the total number of rankings for each title. This surfaced titles that closely associated users had ranked as vital to the collections. Other data points, such as impact factors, cost-per-use, and JMU authors within a publication, were also considered. The formula to combine these data points is detailed more fully in the 2015 article "Building holistic and agile collection development and assessment" (Duncan & O'Gara, 2015).

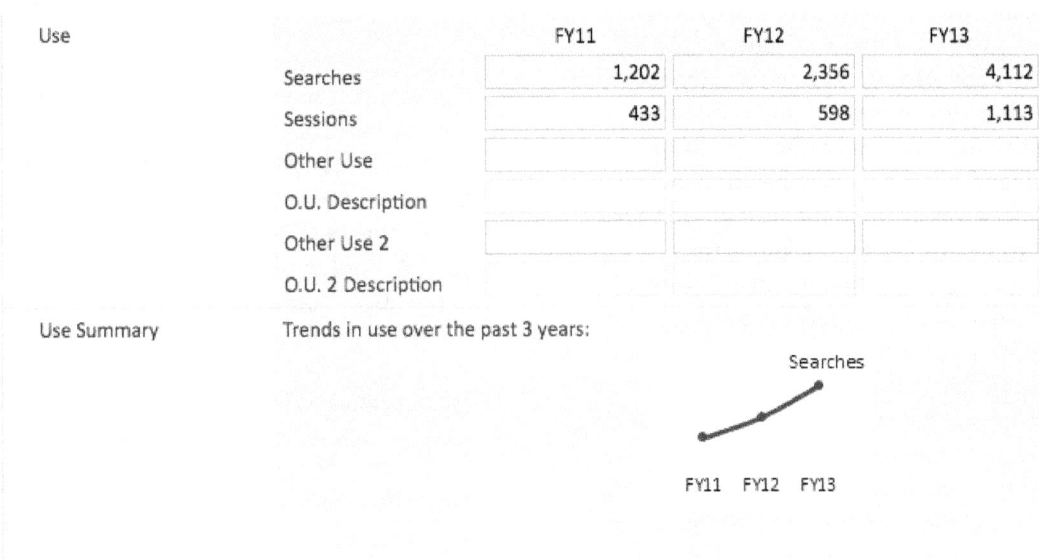

Use		FY11	FY12	FY13
	Searches	1,202	2,356	4,112
	Sessions	433	598	1,113
	Other Use			
	O.U. Description			
	Other Use 2			
	O.U. 2 Description			
Use Summary	Trends in use over the past 3 years:			

Figure 2. Example of use represented over time in the JMU database review.

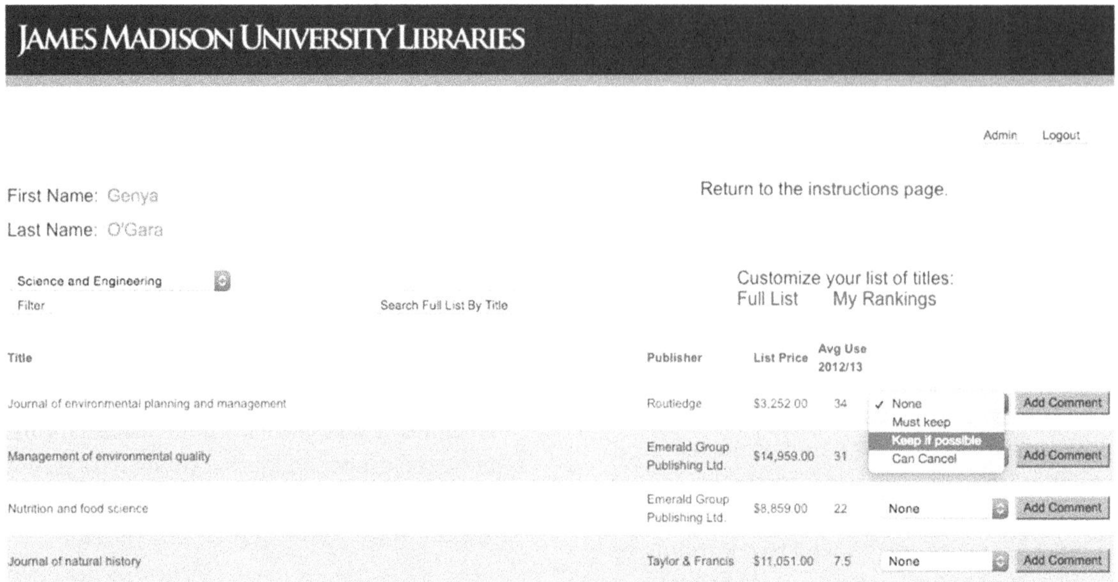

Figure 3. Example of user ranking view taken from the JMU Journal Review Tool.

As with the database review, clusters of affiliated subject librarians reviewed the results and made recommendations for cancellation to the CDC. This multi-pronged review allowed for the incorporation of individual feedback and quantitative data, provided information in a manageable way to selectors, and gave campus stakeholders an active voice in the process.

Collapsed Funds

The Collapsed Fund pilot was identified early on as a way to break down collecting silos, encourage interdisciplinary selection, give liaisons more flexibility, and align subject selection with the University's college structure. JMU's subject liaisons were already divided into four subject clusters to support collaborative collection development, but the applied health sciences (AHS) cluster was deemed the best group to pilot this due to several factors, including the increasing college enrollment and an interest in new curricular tools to support emerging career opportunities within health sciences fields. Therefore, finding creative solutions to meet the program's expanding needs was a priority for this cluster. In this model the slips previously reviewed individually would now be available for the group to review, and the fund lines for individual slips collapsed into one. This allowed librarians to spend more widely in new areas that needed additional support or to decide collectively to put the funds towards one-time purchases that would support all areas.

Results of the first year of the pilot were compared to the previous year's patterns and initial evaluation pointed to success. Spending patterns during the collapsed model year stabilized and fiscal year deadlines were consistently met. This had the added benefit of reducing some of the end-of-year spending blitz for acquisitions, and helped to alleviate some of the pressure librarians sometimes felt to "spend it or lose it," which was detrimental to thoughtful collecting decisions. In visualizing expenditures across departments in comparison to full-time equivalent students (FTE), spending appears to now be more aligned with departmental FTEs. The pilot was successful enough that two additional clusters adopted the approach, and it is expected to become business as usual for all clusters next year. A more in-depth examination can be found in the 2014 Charleston Proceedings: "Moving Librarian Collecting from Good to Great: Results from the First Year of a Librarian Liaison Collaborative Monographic Purchasing Project" (O'Gara, Schubert, Sapp, & Mungin, 2014).

Evaluation Rubric

While the new approaches initiated by these pilots and projects enabled JMU to more easily select, manage, and promote collections as one

Collections . . .	Baseline	Developing	Excelling	Data Source
are **responsive**	2 of 4 clusters agree that spending shifts by department are in response to changing demographics/new programs	3 of 4 clusters agree that spending shifts by department are in response to changing demographics/new programs	4 of 4 clusters agree that spending shifts by department are in response to changing demographics/new programs	5 of 4 clusters agree spending shifts are in direct response to changing demographics/new programs
meet evolving campus needs	Report detailing departmental needs has been completed	Subject librarians have reviewed the report and advocated for new resources/collections services	Where appropriate, L&ET collections/services have been developed in response to these articulated needs	*Biannual Scholarly Communication Task Force reports:* Use as a framework to examine campus needs
are **user focused**	Review and develop ratios based on current make up of departments and profiles	Modify the profiles that are the most "skewed" in terms of their ratio of readership to disciplinary demographics	Biannual review to ensure that readership to disciplinary demographics are aligned across fund codes	*OIR demographics:* Evaluate disciplinary approval profiles alongside FTE at graduate and undergraduate level for readership levels
are accessible in users' **physical and virtual spaces**	Perceived mean of 6.50/libqual lite	Perceived mean of 7.00/libqual lite	Perceived mean of 7.50/libqual lite	*LibQual Lite:* Results from Question 8, "Print and/or electronic journal collections I require for my work"
align with **campus research and curricular foci**	> 30% of departments have current subject snapshots	> 50% of departments have current subject snapshots	> 90% of departments have subject snapshots and/or representation in multidisciplinary snapshots	*Collections snapshots by discipline:* used to solicit feedback from departments
are **resourced**	50% of liaisons report do not note additional resources needed	> 25% of liaisons report note additional resources needed	0 liaisons report no additional resources needed.	*Liaison reports:* Noted additional fiscal resources needed
include **local collections and campus research outputs**	> 30% of departments are represented	> 50% of departments are represented	> 90% of departments are represented	*Institutional repository adoption*: Adoption by college (e.g., every college has a

Figure 4. Partial view of the JMU rubric.

entity, the question of how to evaluate disparate content holistically remained. How do libraries determine that all of the collections, taken as a whole, support the mission of the libraries and educational technologies (LET), and in supporting this mission, promote JMU's aspirations? How do we make decisions grounded in data? Is there a way to see at a high level where future efforts should focus? Can we do this without adding additional data collection efforts to already overburdened library staff? These questions led the Libraries to consider how "the temperature" of collections might be taken, without starting on a massive new data collection effort, and while still ensuring that the collections were directly supporting the big picture goals of the campus community. To do this the Libraries began testing potential "temperature taking methods," which ultimately led to the development of a rubric to frame this work.

Although every academic library is different, there are some common elements to be considered when creating a rubric, including: the larger institution's values and strengths, community demographics, college and department foci, research outputs, budgets, resource diversity and depth, campus scholarly communication practices, and any consortial or collaborative collecting.

JMU's rubric (Figure 4) is based on these elements, as well as on concepts drawn directly from the mission and purpose statement.[3] Evaluation is based on factors (temperature takers) that measure some aspect of the priority concepts (e.g., Collections are . . .) statements. This approach relies on data and activities that are already being collected, focuses efforts at a high level that aligns with the mission, and facilitates timely reactions to evolving collection needs.

As noted, these particular elements are based on local priorities, as are the measures and the data sources. The rubric is meant to be a living document, and other objectives, measures, and data sources may be selected for future inclusion. For example, LET has been working with JMU's Office of Access and Inclusion on ensuring that collections are inclusive and support a diverse community of learners; therefore, the Libraries may choose to include this as an objective within future rubrics. Mission and focus of the university and libraries may also change over time and the rubric would be adjusted to reflect changing priorities. As a living tool, the rubric must be malleable if it is to serve as a mechanism for evaluating the Libraries collections holistically. Targets and results, both quantitative and qualitative, should be visualized to better understand gaps, and focus organizational efforts when discussing campus's resource needs.

The intention of the rubric is not to be prescriptive, but rather to serve as a framework for a community conversation about the purpose of the collections as a whole at a given institution. Many different evaluation points, data sources, and measures exist, and these will necessarily differ from institution to institution, subject area to subject area, and as new data sources become available. As institutional aspirations evolve, objectives too may be expected to change. The hope is the rubric is flexible enough to accommodate this change and stable enough to show areas of strength and gaps in resources.

Next Steps

JMU continues to move forward in broadening the initial pilots, reducing content and format silos, and more fully applying and testing the rubric. Currently, collection snapshots for over two-thirds of JMU's academic departments have been made available to liaisons, and an externally facing collections-wide snapshot has been created for a holistic overview. Future versions of this document will include visualizations from the rubric to highlight LET's progress.

In context of the more traditional collecting methods, the Libraries's approval profiles are being further collapsed and revisited, PDA and POD opportunities are being reviewed, reference resource development has been distributed among the clusters, and remaining single funds are being merged into shared cluster funds.

---

[3] The following bolded concepts drawn from the JMU LET mission and collections department purpose statement are what the rubric aims to measure: "By building responsive collections across disciplines to meet the evolving needs of scholars and faculty at JMU. By developing, maintaining, and enhancing user focused collections in all formats and spaces, both virtual and physical, in support of the Libraries' mission *to build learning and information environments where people connect with ideas and each other to discover, create, and share knowledge."*

Simultaneously, in light of the changing approaches to collecting and ongoing efforts to revamp JMU's liaison program, the subject clusters are being reexamined with the goal of structuring these groups to focus on broader academic support needs and to include services such as instructional technology support, data curation, and digital publishing.

These, and other assessment efforts within the libraries, have jump started the development of a statistical hub that will facilitate the submission, storage, querying, and reporting of all the Libraries's raw statistical data. This will increase the consistency and efficiency of statistical reporting across the organization and provide a greater number of data sources for the rubric.

Those pieces of the rubric itself which have not been fully applied will be employed in their entirety over the next year. JMU plans to use the rubric to track the progress of its collections to ensure focused support of the University's mission and aspirations.

Conclusion

JMU will continue to implement what works, and equally as important, be willing to walk away from practices and measures that fall short, are no longer applicable, or don't directly support mission and vision. The Libraries now have a framework for making these decisions that allows big-picture user needs to be addressed more promptly, and ensures good stewardship of the University's resources. Managed change for collections and content that garners the buy-in and active participation of library staff and campus entities has fostered a more collaborative, flexible, and holistic approach to collection development at JMU.

References

Brantmeier, E., Cockburn, B., Liu, C., O'Gara, G., Schubert, C., & Shorish, Y. (2013). *Scholarly communication task force: Final report and recommendations*. James Madison University's Libraries and Educational Technologies.

Duncan, C., & O'Gara, G. (2015). Building holistic and agile collection development and assessment. *Performance Measurement and Metrics, 16*(1), 62–85.

Horava, T. (2010). Challenges and possibilities for collection management in a digital age. *Library Resources & Technical Services, 54*(3), 142–152.

O'Gara, G., Schubert, C., Sapp, L., & Mungin, M. (2015). Moving librarian collecting from good to great: Results from the first year of a librarian liaison collaborative monographic purchasing project. *Proceedings from the Charleston Conference, 2014: The Importance of Being Earnest*. Retrieved from http://docs.lib.purdue.edu/charleston/2014/Collection/9/

Purchasing E-Books from Life and Physical Science Society Publishers: Trends and Considerations

Kelli J. Trei, Biosciences Librarian & Assistant Professor, University of Illinois at Urbana-Champaign University Library

Erin E. Kerby, Veterinary Medicine Library & Assistant Professor, University of Illinois at Urbana-Champaign University Library

Abstract

This study evaluates e-book publishing by professional life and physical science societies. In order to be good stewards of their resources, collection managers should always be aware of digital rights management (DRM) restrictions and access issues when contemplating an e-book purchase. This can be difficult due to the wide variety of publishing models employed by society e-book publishers. In this study the authors examine various life and physical science societies that publish e-books, including factors such as DRM and access conditions, and purchasing options. The results provide information for collection managers to consider when purchasing e-books from society publishers, as well as allows them to advise patrons when access to e-books may be limited to society members.

Introduction

Professional societies in the sciences provide important opportunities for members and major contributors in the field to share information. These societies provide valuable opportunities for professional development, collaboration, and the creation or influence of scientific legislation and policy. The information is frequently produced in the form of conference presentations and so-called "grey literature," peer-reviewed journals, and sometimes books, which have historically been offered in print. Some societies publish books themselves in-house, and others do so through commercial publishers. While some of these organizations have begun offering e-books, their output varies significantly from a substantial collection to a single title. The variation creates many differences in the functionality of the books, for example a book with printing restrictions that may be read on a society's website or a book that can be downloaded and printed. For this reason, collection managers should always carefully investigate digital rights management restrictions and access issues when contemplating an e-book purchase. In this study we examine various life and physical science societies that publish e-books, revealing factors such as DRM and access conditions, and options for purchasing.

Literature Review

As primarily non-profit organizations, professional societies traditionally have spread the costs of publishing to members via dues and merchandise, and in some cases via institutional subscriptions. However, the peer review process and editing that are so important to scholarly research require a robust and sustainable publishing system, which some societies find easier to achieve by partnering with commercial publishers (Yess, 2004). Much of the scholarly literature concerning society publishing looks specifically at journals. In 2005, a study of the journal publishing practices of members of the Council of Academic Societies found that almost half of the journals were published in conjunction with a commercial publisher (Byrd, Bader, & Mazzaschi, 2005). This suggests that the cost of publishing is one that some societies are not able to fully absorb and sustain on their own.

The 2015 STM Report (Science, Technology, and Medicine) relayed information from Outsell, Inc. that the STM e-book market is growing much faster than the print book market and STM market as a whole (Ware & Mabe, 2015). It is not clear that all society publishers are able to mirror this trend. Although results from studies determining

http://dx.doi.org/10.5703/1288284316249

actual usage of e-books vary quite a bit, they have shown that the more e-books a library acquires, the more they are used (Lamothe, 2013). There is also some indication that STEM fields show more preference for e-books than other fields (Frame, 2014; Marshall, 2014). This can make it a challenge for librarians as they try to plan for future collections.

A Taylor and Francis survey conducted last year in conjunction with the Association of Learned and Professional Society Publishers (ALPSP) found that the most revenue that society respondents gained from publishing was 5–25% (Frass, Gardner, & McCulloch, 2014). The study also indicated that 28–47% of respondents were considering publishing new journals or open access journals for revenue. Thirty percent of respondents felt that society publications are very important in attracting new members. Furthermore, the majority of respondents found that high quality online publishing and "partnering" to improve the journals were most important in terms of journal publishing. The largest percentage of respondents indicated that a journal publisher brought greater discoverability and better financial return to their society publications. Only 10% were concerned with combined book and journal publishing options. This concentration on journal output may be related to the fact that journals remain the primary way scientists convey significant research.

The STM report points to a number of similarities between the journal and e-book markets. For example, journals are often packaged into bundles for libraries and library consortia, and the e-book market is trending toward this model as well (Ware & Mabe, 2015). There is one notable difference between the journal and e-book markets, however—namely that end users are more likely to purchase e-books than journals, effectively cutting out the library as middleman. This may have implications for society publishers concerned with costs and revenue.

In addition to the murky nature of e-book publishing by societies, the usability of resources is an ever present concern. DRM and usage restrictions create a significant barrier for users, especially in institutional settings. Previous studies have shown that publishers are responding to these usage concerns, and purchasing from a publisher rather than an aggregator reduces DRM restrictions and access issues (Kerby & Trei, 2015). Discoverability, usability, and dissemination of member-contributed content, as well as facilitating collaboration, are important roles filled by societies. Transitioning publishing models for online journals to books produced by a society would face many of the same financial constraints and technical challenges. This research begins to uncover some of the issues faced by society publishers and what that means for usage and access of the resources.

Methods

To compile the list of society publishers, the authors consulted the Association of Learned and Professional Society Publishers (ALPSP, http://www.alpsp.org/Ebusiness/AboutAlpsp/ListofMembers.aspx) and the Society for Scholarly Publishing (SSP, http://www.sspnet.org/about-us/organizational-members/) member lists. They also referred to the list of societies in the University of Illinois online journals and databases list at http://sfx.carli.illinois.edu/sfxuiu/az, and searched in the following subject areas for the terms "society" or "association":

- Agriculture sciences
- Chemistry
- Environmental sciences
- Health sciences
- Life sciences
- Physics

Further entries were added based on the authors' professional experience and recommendations from other subject specialist librarians. The list was compiled in alphabetical order and then each society's website was searched to determine whether the society published e-books. If so, then findings were recorded for each of the following categories:

- Published by society or external publisher
- Purchase options
- DRM restrictions

- Usage allowance
- MARC record availability

When the information was not readily available on the website, the authors contacted the society to inquire about the missing information. Eighteen societies were contacted, and responses were received from 11.

Results

There were 149 life and physical science societies identified via the methods described above. Of these, only 34 produce any kind of e-book content. One society, the American Society of Limnology and Oceanography, produces one e-book in PDF format for free download from the site, whereas all other societies offer e-books for purchase to either individuals or institutions. The authors were unable to obtain information about institutional purchasing from four of the publishers: the American Heart Association, the American Medical Association, the American Phytopathological Society, and the Australian Entomological Society. Of the remaining 29

Society Publisher	Individual Purchase/Subscription Available	Institutional Purchase/Subscription Available	Marc Records Available
American Society of Agricultural and Biological Engineers	Yes	Yes	No
Acoustical Society of America	Yes	No	No
America Academy of Pain Medication	Yes	Yes	Yes
American Ceramic Society	Yes	Yes	Yes
American Chemical Society	Yes	Yes	Yes
American Geophysical Union	Yes	Yes	Yes
American Geriatrics Society	Yes	Yes	No
American Heart Association	Yes	Unknown	Unknown
American Medical Association	Yes	Unknown	Unknown
American Meteorological Society	Yes	Yes	Yes
American Oil Chemists' Society	Yes	Yes	Yes
American Physiological Society	Yes	Yes	Yes
American Phytopathological Society	Yes	Unknown	Unknown
American Society for Microbiology	Yes	Yes	Yes
American Society of Agronomy	Yes	Yes	Yes
American Society of Health-System Pharmacists	Yes	Yes	Yes
American Society of Limnology and Oceanography	Free	Free	No
Australian Entomological Society	Yes	Unknown	Unknown
Biochemical Society	No	Yes	Unknown
Crop Science Society of America	Yes	Yes	Yes
Endocrine Society	No	Some Titles	Yes
Entomological Society of America	Yes	No	No
European Respiratory Society	Yes	Yes	Unknown
Faraday Society	Yes	Yes	Yes
Geological Society of America	Yes	Yes	No
Institute of Physics	Yes	Yes	Yes
Nutrition Society	Yes	Yes	Yes
Royal Astronomical Society	Yes	Yes	Yes
Royal Astronomical Society of Canada	Yes	No	No
Royal Society of Chemistry	Yes	Yes	Yes
Society of Dairy Technology	Yes	Yes	Yes
Soil Science Societ of America	Yes	Yes	Yes
Water Environment Federation	Yes	No	No
World Wildlife Federation	Yes	Some Titles	Some Titles

Table 1. Purchasing options and MARC record availability.

Society Publisher	DRM Restrictions	Additional Terms
America Academy of Pain Medication	None	
American Ceramic Society	None	
American Chemical Society	None	"DRM is governed by existing ACS License"
American Geophysical Union	None	
American Geriatrics Society	None	
American Meteorological Society	Restricted	
American Oil Chemists' Society	Restricted	
American Physiological Society	None	
American Society for Microbiology	None	
American Society of Agricultural and Biological Engineers	None	
American Society of Agronomy	None	
American Society of Health-System Pharmacists	Restricted	May only print page in use.
Biochemical Society	Restricted	Cannot download entire book.
Crop Science Society of America	None	
Endocrine Society	Varied	Aggregators have DRM restrictions. Books published by Wiley have no restrictions.
European Respiratory Society	Unknown	
Faraday Society	None	
Geological Society of America	None	
Institute of Physics	None	
Nutrition Society	Restricted	
Royal Astronomical Society	None	
Royal Society of Chemistry	None	
Society of Dairy Technology	Restricted	
Soil Science Societ of America	None	
World Wildlife Federation	Varied	Springer published volumes have no DRM, others do.

Table 2. DRM terms and conditions for institutional purchases.

publishers, 25 offer purchasing options for institutions for at least some of their titles (Table 1). These titles are offered in various ways: published by a for-profit publisher such as Springer or Wiley, published on a platform native to the society itself, or offered through aggregators such as EBSCO or ebrary.

The availability of these e-books from any society varied widely from a single PDF title hosted on the society's website to an entire collection and robust member interface. Most publishers posted DRM and usage allowance on their website or have provided information to the authors.

Although the European Respiratory Society has not responded, of the other 24 societies, 71% provide unlimited concurrent usage of the titles and 67% have no DRM restrictions (Tables 2 and 3). Usage and DRM restrictions are frequently different for individual users—most of the time more restricted. Although the Biochemical Society and European Respiratory Society have not responded regarding the availability of MARC records, of the other 23 societies with institutionally available titles, 87% did provide records, either themselves or through the company providing their content (Table 1).

Society Publisher	Usage Options	Additional Terms
American Society of Agricultural and Biological Engineers	Unlimited Concurrent	
America Academy of Pain Medication	Unlimited Concurrent	
American Ceramic Society	Unlimited Concurrent	
American Chemical Society	Unlimited Concurrent	Monitor for excessive downloads
American Geophysical Union	Unlimited Concurrent	
American Geriatrics Society	Unlimited Use, Limited Concurrence	5-25 concurrent users based on package.
American Meteorological Society	Varied	Purchased through aggregator.
American Oil Chemists' Society	Varied	Purchased through aggregator.
American Physiological Society	Unlimited Concurrent	
American Society for Microbiology	Unlimited Concurrent	
American Society of Agronomy	Unlimited Concurrent	
American Society of Health-System Pharmacists	Varied	Subscriptions available based on concurrent user or unlimited concurrent.
Biochemical Society	Unlimited Concurrent	
Crop Science Society of America	Unlimited Concurrent	
Endocrine Society	Varied	Purchased through aggregator.
European Respiratory Society	Unknown	
Faraday Society	Unlimited Concurrent	Limit is course pack downloads.
Geological Society of America	Unlimited Concurrent	
Institute of Physics	Unlimited Concurrent	
Nutrition Society	Varied	Purchased through aggregator.
Royal Astronomical Society	Unlimited Concurrent	
Royal Society of Chemistry	Unlimited Concurrent	Limit is course pack downloads.
Society of Dairy Technology	Unlimited Concurrent	
Soil Science Societ of America	Unlimited Concurrent	
World Wildlife Federation	Varied	Purchased through various providers.

Table 3. Usage allowance for institutional purchases.

Implications

The results of this study suggest that no single e-book publishing model is working for the majority of society publishers. Some have chosen to use a more traditional model for book publishing by offering e-book titles individually. Others are treating their e-book content similar to their journals, even to the point of bundling all e-content together into packages available by subscription or purchase for institutions.

The vast majority of societies provide e-book content to individuals. Occasionally, this is a benefit of membership in the society, but many times membership only provides a discount on e-book pricing. For example, in this study only the American Physiological Society and European Respiratory Society offer free e-books or access to full-text for members. Others provide a discount of some sort, such as the American Society of Agricultural and Biological Engineers and the Royal Society of Chemistry, both of which give download credits with membership. Four societies in this analysis restrict e-book content to individuals. One, the Royal Astronomical Society of Canada, provides its one e-book to members only when contacted directly. Rarely do societies exclusively offer content to institutions, but it does happen. The Biochemical Society formerly offered its *Biochemical Society Symposia* in e-book format to institutions subscribing to its e-content platform; now this content appears to have been wrapped into an e-journal produced by the society. Additionally, the American Chemical Society only sells the print versions of monographs to individuals. As over 80% of societies studied offer e-books in some way to institutions, most recognize the likelihood of their use by researchers in academia. Unfortunately, the manner in which these e-books are available varies widely, creating inconsistencies for users accessing the content and for those making purchasing decisions.

As with e-books purchased from any vendor, libraries are primarily concerned with patron needs. Consequently, DRM and access restrictions severely hamper the value of an e-resource. Across the board it was clear that DRM and usage restrictions were more stringent for individual members than for institutions. The majority of the societies make their e-book content available to institutions with little DRM or usage restrictions. As is true with the e-book market as a whole, society e-book content is much more likely to be free of restrictions if purchased from the publisher itself, rather than through an aggregator. Thirteen of the societies publish their content on a native platform. In these cases, the platform may have customizable features. For example, individuals may create a personal login with the American Society of Microbiology and the American Chemical Society, through an institutional subscription, and "favorite" titles and chapters, or save searches for easy content access. Since the majority of publishers provide MARC records for institutions, it allows easy addition to library catalogs, increasing findability for the user and requiring fewer resources from the subscribing institutions.

It can be challenging for a collection manager to predict if and where an e-book from a society publisher might be available, particularly with titles from societies with less publishing output. The findings of this study will assist collection managers in locating this content and making purchase decisions. The platform structure, number of titles, usage restrictions, and cost must be balanced with needs and priorities of the institution. In particular, e-books with DRM and access restrictions that limit usage and download of content create barriers for end users that a print volume might alleviate. To make their e-books more attractive to libraries, society publishers need to offer their content without DRM restrictions and with unfettered usage options to increase the value for institutions and use of their materials.

Conclusion

Though relatively few life and physical science professional societies publish e-books, the majority of those do make their e-book content available to institutions. They also generally provide unfettered access to this content. Society publishers do produce less e-book content than journals, but many still choose to share research and conference proceedings in this way. The preference for electronic journal content by scientific societies is unsurprising, as the process of peer review is stronger and more prevalent in these publications. However, whether they see e-books as a way to increase revenue for the society, or as an important contribution to scholarly communication from a trusted source, some scientific societies are clearly following the trend of increased e-book publishing. Future research could include evaluating usage of society publications and investigation into member perception of e-book content produced by these societies.

References

Byrd, G. D., Bader, S. A., & Mazzaschi, A. J. (2005). The status of open access publishing by academic societies. *Journal of the Medical Library Association, 93*(4), 423–424.

Frame, R. M. (2014). A comparison of use between e-books acquired in bulk packages, individual titles, and user requested titles at a health sciences library. *UNC Chapel Hill Theses, 1*(1).

Frass, W., Gardner, V., & McCulloch, A. (2014). Open access and society: Impact and engagement. *Taylor & Francis Editor Resources*. Retrieved September 27, 2015 from http://editorresources.taylorandfrancisgroup.com/open-access-what-do-researchers-really-think/

Lamothe, A. R. (2013). Factors influencing the usage of an electronic book collection: Size of the e-book collection, the student population, and the faculty population. *College and Research Libraries, 74*(1), 39–59.

Marshall, D. H. (2014). Digital collection development for unique users: A veterinary medicine library's approach. *Interlending & Document Supply, 42*(4), 171–175. http://dx.doi.org/10.1108/ILDS-09-2014-0041

Ware, M., & Mabe, M. (2015). *The STM report: An overview of scientific and scholarly journal publishing* (4th ed.). Lincoln: Libraries at University of Nebraska–Lincoln.

Yess, M. E. (2004). Publishing ECS content. *Electrochemical Society Interface, 13*(1), 15–16, 52.

Acquisitions Everywhere: Modeling an Acquisitions Data Standard to Connect a Distributed Environment

Eric M. Hanson, Electronic Resources Librarian, North Carolina State University Libraries

Paul W. Lightcap, Collection Strategist and Head of Acquisitions, Florida State University Libraries

Matthew R. Miguez, Metadata Librarian, Florida State University Libraries

Abstract

Acquisitions functions remain operationally crucial in providing access to paid information resources, but data formats and workflows utilized within library acquisitions remain primarily within the traditional integrated library system (ILS). As libraries have evolved to use distributed systems to manage information resources, so too must acquisitions functions adapt to an environment that may include the ILS, e-resource management systems (ERMS), institutional repositories (IR), and other digital asset management systems (DAMS).

This presentation is intended to articulate a vision for applying standards-based practice—as already employed for resource description—to acquisitions functions in a variety of metadata schema and systems. Utilization of standards will be demonstrated in the proposal of a core acquisitions element set that can exist in any system, with proofs of concept including demonstration of the element set within MODS, JSON, and how it may be reflected within the ILS and ERMS.

Building on these proofs of concept in recording interoperable acquisitions data will be an explanation of possible applications, including an exploration of more robust support for semantic web technologies. In particular, this presentation will explore how this element set could utilize published linked datasets, such as the North Carolina State University Organization Name Linked Data and Global Open Knowledgebase (GOKb) linked data service, to provide more accurate and efficient identity management.

Introduction

While substantial work has been done over the past decade to develop and implement standards for resource description, electronic resource management, and discovery within libraries, the realm of acquisitions data and functions—that core set of financial information and accounting practices crucial to growing and maintaining the bulk of what any library counts as its collections—has yet to be comprehensively addressed. Acquisitions functions remain complex for practitioners, demanding adherence to local procurement rules and standard accounting practice, with a continually increasing demand for, on one hand, instantaneity and flexibility, and on the other, transparency and consistency. Perhaps exactly this combination of complexity of practice and the hope for a single, comprehensive solution, has until now composed a seemingly insurmountable obstacle to standards application within the acquisitive world.

Instead of a total solution that fully accounts for competing demands and exception-ridden workflows, this proposal defines and extends the use of a common core set of elements already part of daily acquisitions work through application across the many systems currently used to manage all forms of paid content. The inspirational models for this work can be found in overlapping communities of practice as have developed the Program for Cooperative Cataloging's BIBCO Standard Record metadata application profile and the Dublin Core Metadata Element Set. This core set of acquisitions elements intersects with work already done as part of the NISO Cost of Resource Exchange (CORE) recommended practice, (http://www.niso.org/publications/rp/RP-2010-10.pdf); this work both

http://dx.doi.org/10.5703/1288284316250

supports and extends the CORE efforts, though, in that it proposes a somewhat shifted element set, makes explicit—through proofs of concept—applications for this element set across different systems beyond the ILS/ERMS/vendor triad, and demonstrates initial steps forward in utilizing semantic web technologies. The use of this proposed element set is intended as the first step in an iterative approach, acknowledging that any initial application must cross a low threshold in order to move toward normalizing certain crucial acquisitions data, expanding the use of this data in various library and resource management systems, and laying the groundwork for an evolving conception of distributed acquisitions data and workflows.

The Legacy Challenge, Compounded

As the next-gen library services platform (LSP) market has matured and concerns about age and functionality of the legacy ILS have increased, many libraries have already begun to move ahead with the next round of systems migrations, (Breeding, 2015a; Breeding, 2015b), or at least to prepare for such a move. Considering an ILS migration resurfaces worry about challenges faced in past migrations, topmost of which is concern about data loss. This is particularly noted as impacting acquisitions data such as resource cost, fund, and vendor (Farrell & Truitt, 2003; Butler & Larmore, 2006). While there is some indication that progress has been made in maintaining such legacy data during recent migrations to library services platforms (Fu & Carmen, 2015), it should be noted that the underlying connection between description and acquisitions metadata remains somewhat tenuous.

Many libraries have attempted to address these weak connections between descriptive and acquisitions data by utilizing not only an ILS, but also an ERMS. Through combined reporting from both systems—and, indeed, duplicating data stored within these systems—libraries have developed a point-of-need solution for recorded data that is otherwise missing or difficult to extract. Beyond this, though, libraries have needed to capture and report on data that cannot be adequately mapped within and reported from either the ILS or ERMS, and so have further duplicated data with the introduction of additional helpmates, such as separate spreadsheets or external databases. In sum, even with the development of new technologies to manage the largest volume and highest portion of expenditures—traditional print and electronic resources—but no accompanying efforts to standardize and deeply link an acquisition element set, libraries have built up an environment of additional systems and substantially duplicated data, without any capability for mutual understanding and interoperability.

Compounding technical worries of data loss and data structure are substantial environmental shifts: the emergence of data-driven culture, a growing emphasis on evidence-based practice, and an ever-increasing scrutiny on expenditures, especially within public institutions. Put succinctly, the demands to immediately and consistently report on expenditures for licensed and purchased resources, correlated to discipline and use, continue to grow. Such an expectation goes far beyond accountability to the citizenry for public expenditures; as experience over the past decade within college and university libraries amply shows, libraries are more regularly expected to report on total expenditures in support of departments or majors, including historical reporting to show trends or past years' oversights. Years of strained funding and implementation of different budget models within parent organizations such as activity-based, performance-based, or responsibility center budgeting, have amplified the demand for robust expenditure analysis mapped to use and areas served. Libraries have been called on to advocate for their funding based on credible data—or, in the case of budget reductions, to produce meaningful analyses that support strategic cuts.

All of these competing concerns and demands alone still would not necessarily prompt rethinking our practices. If resources remained in traditional formats and were acquired through traditional means, perhaps the most effective solution would be to redouble focus on library

```xml
<?xml version="1.0" encoding="UTF-8"?>
<mods xmlns:xlink="http://www.w3.org/1999/xlink"
      xmlns:dcterms="http://purl.org/dc/terms/"
      xmlns="http://www.loc.gov/mods/v3"
      xmlns:xsi="http://www.w3.org/2001/XMLSchema-instance"
      xmlns:mods="http://www.loc.gov/mods/v3"
      xmlns:flvc="info:flvc/manifest/v1"
      xmlns:acq='http://someURI.host'
      xsi:schemaLocation="http://www.loc.gov/mods/v3 http://www.loc.gov/standards/mods/v3/mods-3-4.xsd">
      <extension>
         <flvc:flvc>
            <flvc:owningInstitution>FSU</flvc:owningInstitution>
            <flvc:submittingInstitution>FSU</flvc:submittingInstitution>
         </flvc:flvc>
         <acq:acq>
            <acq:invoice>
               <acq:customerID>http://viaf.org/viaf/125490841</acq:customerID>
               <acq:vendorID>https://www.lib.ncsu.edu/ld/onld/00000728</acq:vendorID>
               <acq:invoiceID>001A</acq:invoiceID>
               <acq:invoiceDate>2015-08-15</acq:invoiceDate>
               <acq:orderID>8675309-1</acq:orderID>
               <acq:orderFiscalCycle>2016</acq:orderFiscalCycle>
               <acq:orderType>One-time</acq:orderType>
               <acq:totalPaid currency="USD">127.50</acq:totalPaid>
               <acq:listPrice currecy="USD">150</acq:listPrice>
               <acq:invoiceLine id="001">
                  <acq:fundID>FAKABTL</acq:fundID>
                  <acq:accountNumber>123456</acq:accountNumber>
                  <acq:materialType>application/pdf</acq:materialType>
               </acq:invoiceLine>
            </acq:invoice>
         </acq:acq>
      </extension>
      <titleInfo lang="ita">
         <nonSort>Il</nonSort>
         <title>secolo</title>
         <subTitle>Gazzetta di Milano</subTitle>
```

Figure 1. Example of element set as an acquisitions extension in a MODS record.

Summary | Full Description

Title:	Il secolo: Gazzetta di Milano.
Type of Resource:	text
Genre:	newspaper
Issuance:	serial
Frequency:	Daily
Date Issued:	1885-04-10
Publisher:	Sonzogno
Place of Publication:	Milano
Extent:	4 p. : ill. ; 59 cm.
Language(s):	Italian
Summary:	This issue contains Le colonie; Attraverso i secoli: Arti vecchie sempre nuove: Corrispondenza Telegrafica del secolo: Sul segreto e sulla liberta' del servizio telegrafico; Il comunicato degli eredi Garibaldi; Il Giudizio del "Fascio" ; La politica di Mancini; L'abbandono di Caprera; La battaglia nell'Afganistan; I membri del Ministero francese; Quello che i governi fanno del denaro pubblico; Il Crematoio di Firenze; La questione agraria nel Mantovano.
Identifier:	FSU_ilsecolonewspaper_04101885 (IID)
Subject(s):	FSU_ilsecolonewspaper_04271885 Ohnet, Georges, 1848-1918 La signorina di compagnia 54 La grande marniera 6
Use and Reproduction:	Use of this item is provided for non-commercial, personal, educational, and research use only. Florida State University Libraries is providing access to these materials for educational and research purposes and makes no warranty with regard to their use for other purposes. The written permission of the copyright owners and/or other rights holders such as holders of publicity and/or privacy rights is required for distribution, reproduction, or other use of protected items beyond that allowed by fair use or other statutory exemptions see Title 17, U.S.C.. For information about the copyright and reproduction rights for this item, please contact Special Collections & Archives, Florida State University Libraries, Tallahassee, Florida: https://www.lib.fsu.edu/department/special-collections-archives.
Owner Institution:	FSU

Figure 2. Same record displayed within the FSU Digital Library, demonstrating public masking of acquisitions data.

services platform functionality, emphasizing integration and centralization. The scholarly record has changed, though, as has the way that libraries support the research and educational efforts of their constituencies. Libraries have expanded the types of information resources that may compose collections, and added systems to support management and access to this varied content. Libraries have moved well beyond purchase of print and electronic books and journals. Collections now include purchased and licensed digitized manuscripts, satellite images, videos, datasets, and many other digital artifacts (whether born digital or digitized), that libraries must describe and host. Neither the integrated library system nor the ERMS is the appropriate repository for such digital objects or their metadata; instead, libraries have developed institutional repositories and other digital asset management systems to serve this purpose.

A Lightweight Standard

Standards, as acknowledged within the semantic web and metadata communities, are crucial in facilitating interoperability, enhancing reliable retrieval, controlling duplication, and making maintenance and data migration simpler. We propose a lightweight standard, not a deviance from predominant current practice, in the form of a set of core acquisitions elements.

This element set was conceived as lightweight in application, with no substantial technological impediments to implementation. It was modeled from significant data elements extant within the systems already in use to manage content: the ILS, ERMS, IR, and digital library (DAMS), with examples ranging across content types. The intention was to demonstrate how such an element set, if standardized, could not only allow for robust meta-analysis but also lay the foundation for moving forward acquisitions practice to use linked data, support all content types and systems, and start to transition from ILS-centric practice.

Acquisitions metadata is managed in both formal and ad-hoc systems. This leads to duplication of information as data is replicated within different systems to answer different questions. This differs from resource description practice where efforts are directed at creating interoperable standards to minimize the duplication of effort. Beyond an increase in effort, maintaining multiple data siloes can lead to "data drift" as information in one silo is updated but not refreshed in others. This problem is being addressed in the resource description community through the use of semantic web technologies. A strategy specific to acquisitions would be to bundle acquisitions metadata into the resource description. This way, wherever the record moves, its acquisition information moves with it.

How can acquisitions data be bundled to resource description? The information serialization technologies XML and JSON can be of service. Both technologies are system independent, and widely understood by the information and technology communities. Their widespread use has been supplemented with a variety of solution packages for every common programming language and standardized schema to solve wide-ranging problems from warehouse and inventory management to bibliographic description. These advantages have spurred the resource description community to develop a kaleidoscope of description standards built in XML.

The system agnosticism of XML and JSON means they can be ingested and exported from any system that can access and understand the rules of the format.

This is a fixed set of data mostly useful for reporting, but by standardizing and fixing the information to the resource, the need for ad-hoc data tracking practices could be eliminated. The data needed for financial reporting and analysis will move with the resource description when systems change. A publicly maintained and documented serialization standard ensures long-term access to the encoded data, and efficient analysis of data across distributed systems.

A few use cases can demonstrate the immediate utility of adopting a standardized acquisitions metadata element set. Current practices preclude acquisitions analysis at the level of consortia, even if expenditure data were able to be shared, as data recording practices are too different, and the systems for storing the data have no common language. Performing high-level analysis requires too much data clean-up and reconciliation to be feasible. If a standard element set were adopted, this process would be greatly simplified, even among members storing data in different systems.

Another use case would be performing meta-analysis against collections held in distributed systems. The ERMS, ILS, and DAM have different strengths for content management and access. As a result, paid content is hosted in an increasing number of systems, which leads to additional systems being used to track acquisitions data. For instance, supporting a STEM program might require purchasing datasets, digital images, and interactive licensed content along with more traditional library acquisitions. Common external systems such as spreadsheets are used to track all of this spending, and correlate it to resources. With acquisitions data bundled into the resources, collecting this data for aggregate analysis would require only a few queries against the different hosting platforms.

As the conversation around acquisitions metadata develops, a core element set may be extended to answer more complex questions such as cost-per-use or other dynamic data. The community can also look to resource description for other insights. Open Archives Initiative (OAI-PMH) is a simple web-service for standardizing the remote harvesting of descriptive metadata. In a distributed information environment, a similar service can be developed to standardize acquisitions information collection across different systems, communities, and consortia. When all of the different systems speak the same language, they can all report on the same questions.

Linked Data for Acquisitions

Given that this metadata schema is designed to be interoperable with multiple systems, identity management for customers and vendors becomes an important consideration. Different systems frequently use different labels for the same organization (e.g., "Royal Society of Chemistry," "Royal Society of Chemistry Publishing," "Royal Society of Chemistry Pub"), which complicates any attempt to consolidate information from multiple data sources. To solve this problem, organizations can be identified by Uniform

Figure 3. Acquisitions data harvested from feed.

Resource Identifiers (URIs) that can exist independently from the labels used by each system. There are many potential sources of URIs for organizations, including the Virtual International Authority File (VIAF), Library of Congress Name Authority File (LCNAF), International Standard Name Identifier (ISNI), DBpedia, and the North Carolina State University (NCSU) Organization Name Linked Data (ONLD).

The NCSU ONLD set is based on the NCSU Organization Name Authority, a tool used to manage the variant forms of names for serial and e-resource publishers, providers, and vendors in E-Matrix, a locally developed electronic resource management system. This dataset was enhanced with links to related descriptions in VIAF, LCNAF, ISNI, DBpedia, and Freebase. The NCSU ONLD served as the seed data for organizations in the Global Open Knowledgebase (GOKb), which is an open data repository that contains key publication information about electronic resources as represented within the supply chain from publishers to suppliers to libraries. It is also used by the AgriProfiles project (formerly AgriVIVO) to help manage organization names.

The NCSU ONLD can be used to transition a set of organization labels into a set of URIs for those organizations. In the NCSU ONLD, each organization is assigned a URI and a preferred label, as well as storing a list of alternate labels. With this information, the NCSU ONLD can be used to crosswalk different labels coming in from different data sources to a single URI that identifies the organization. By checking a list of organization names against the NCSU ONLD, a list of ONLD URIs could be generated for any organization labels that matched against either the preferred or alternate labels. Additionally, any VIAF, LCNAF, ISNI or DBpedia URIs that are provided through the ONLD could be used as identifiers for any of the matching organizations.

By describing customers and vendors using URIs rather than labels, it is much easier to build organization-oriented reports based on elements from multiple data sources. Integrated library system (ILS) payment data can be compared to the list price on vendor title lists for calculating the cost savings associated with different vendors. The amount for content covered by a particular vendor license could be generated using licensing data from an ERMS and payment data from the ILS. Usage data from an ERMS could be analyzed by subject area based on call number data from the ILS and proprietary subject classifications from a vendor title list. With a thoughtful and consistent approach to identity management that utilizes URIs across multiple data sources, more complex scenarios could be devised that would have been unthinkable in previously siloed systems.

The Next Step Forward

The proposed core element set, applied within different schema and utilizing URIs where possible, is but a first, tentative step toward standardizing acquisitions data. The authors understand that development and application of standards within the large community of practice of resource acquisitions necessarily requires a broad base of participation to further develop the proposal. It is the hope that this initial suggestion may prompt participation from acquisitions and metadata practitioners to further develop use cases, continue to refine the proposed core element set, and build additional proofs of concept across myriad systems to fully explore the utility of standards development for acquisitions. A solicitation for participation to achieve these goals will be shared widely in the coming weeks across acquisitions and metadata communities, but directly contacting the authors to indicate interest in moving this project forward is also encouraged.

References

Breeding, M. (2015a). Library systems report 2015. *American Libraries Magazine.* Retrieved from http://americanlibrariesmagazine.org/2015/05/01/library-systems-report/

Breeding, M. (2015b). Library services platforms: A maturing genre of products. *Library Technology Reports, 51*(4). http://dx.doi.org/10.5860/ltr.51n4

Butler, T. L., & Larmore, D. P. (2006). Biz of acq—The conversion problem: One state's migration of acquisitions data. *Against the Grain, 18*(3). Retrieved from http://docs.lib.purdue.edu/atg/vol18/iss3/29

Farrell, K. T., & Truitt, M. (2003). The case for acquisitions standards in the integrated library system. *Library Collections, Acquisitions, & Technical Services, 27*(pp. 483–492). http://dx.doi.org/10.1016/j.lcats.2003.09.012

Fu, P., & Carmen, J. (2015). Migration to Alma/Primo: A case study of Central Washington University. *Chinese Librarianship, 40*, 1–14. Retrieved from http://www.iclc.us/cliej/cl40FC.pdf

A Crossroads for Collection Development and Assessment, Its Fallout, and Unknowns: Where Do We Go From Here?

Thomas Reich, Collection Development Coordinator/Head of Acquisitions, University of Wisconsin–Stevens Point

Abstract

Where do we go from here? Achieving goals of sustainable resource collections through a thorough collection assessment is evermore challenged by fallout and unknowns lurking ubiquitously. There is an ever-increasing competition for both physical space and economic space. We're at an important crossroads for collection development, collection assessment, and libraries themselves. Change and assessment must be sustainable. To be effective, change must create its own momentum. Three years into our collection assessment project, momentum has been steady and efforts continue. However, we've encountered fallout and unknowns which we hadn't planned on, and these are of an institutional and political nature.

At the 2013 Charleston Conference I presented my paper: "Less Is More: The University of Wisconsin–Stevens Point Collection Assessment Program." For the first time in decades, the UWSP Albertson Library had started a weeding and collection assessment of our entire stacks print holdings. In 2012–2013, our seven-floor learning resource center faced a pending renovation project slated for 2017. Dutifully, we vetted and adopted a thorough collection assessment plan though our collection development committee. Weeding of the collection was initiated so collections occupied "less" space, while at the same time we set out to enhance the collection so that it provided "more" up-to-date core densities, addressing academic core resources and campus-wide curricula changes.

Collection assessment was to result in better use of physical space and "more!" Areas within the University Library once devoted to stacks were aggressively cleared of library resources, as a result of plans not totally associated with "weeding" or collection assessment, instead by plans for a reconfiguration of an institutional nature. Entering into our collection assessment project we knew to expect a variety of unknowns and even "fallout." In some ways we planned for the human and technical elements of collection assessment, and but not for unknown institutional elements. We had heard stories from other academic libraries that purposely did not make weeding lists public. Thereby, we expected fallout would occur from faculty resisting weeding. Yet, we felt by initiating a project that paired assessment (weeding) with enhancement (adding core titles) would effectively counter such concerns. In the large part, we were right: open communication with all academic departments did insure continued momentum. We made sure our assessment project included focus groups and an "open door" policy. We invited all campus faculty to review potential discard lists, posted by LC ranges. We developed a LibGuide that is vital for campus input and momentum in our project: http://libraryguides.uwsp.edu/ca.

Unfortunately, the past 3 years have been soured by state politics and an outright budgetary attack by the Wisconsin legislature, and governor, on publically funded higher education. Political and legislative mandates initiated huge budget cuts to the University of Wisconsin system, and even removed tenure protections from the state statutes, promising increased "flexibilities" as rewards for compliance. Political powers even worked to erase the "Wisconsin Idea" from state statutes—that measure ultimately failed when faced with a huge public outcry.

Twice in the last 3 years, the UW system budget faced 20% reductions in state funding, complicated by tuition freezes. All in all, each campus has looked to its units for budget paybacks and program prioritization. Most campuses have reduced the number of employees, through early retirement measures, selected incentive buyouts, not filling vacancies,

http://dx.doi.org/10.5703/1288284316251

and layoffs. Campuses across the University of Wisconsin system continue to slash programs as they cope with a second round of fiscal cuts—a $250 million state budget cut. Although methods have varied, each of the system's 13 comprehensive campuses, 11 two-year UW colleges, and the University Extension, have eliminated positions and programs. Our campus entered an era of program prioritization and pleas for differential tuition. In 2015–2016, 76.5 full-time equivalent (FTE) positions were or will be eliminated at UW–Stevens Point as a result of reductions in state support. Work on Fiscal Year 2017 continues. It's too soon to know if any additional FTE reductions will be required.

UW Libraries have taken more than their share of cuts in positions, programs, and base budgets. In March of 2015, the UW–Stevens Point University Library FY 2015 acquisitions budget took a huge hit, with 60% of its purchasing funds being "swept" by our division director for payback to campus Academic Affairs. In August, 2015, a move was made by the chancellor and provost to reinvest in strategically significant areas—instruction and student services and the library—restoring $120,000 to provide materials (books, journals, electronic databases) to support the instructional program. However, by mid-semester, it was announced that the library acquisitions budget would be frozen again on March 31, 2016, and likely swept clean by June, as any end of the fiscal year monies would be needed elsewhere. Where do we go from here?

Like all academic libraries, the Albertson Learning Resource Center continues to undergo changes in collections, services, and an ever-increasing emphasis on reorganization of services, both complicated and facilitated by new discovery tools, changes to our integrated library system, and changing workflows. The initial charge for our collection assessment project was one of collection enhancement and retooling of spaces for more user friendly areas, including individual study areas, group presentation rooms, hands-on teaching labs, additional emerging technologies, possibly a learning commons, and more. Instead, reconfigured space is needed for academic service units that are part of a rushed proposal to form a "University College." The image of any construction zones, alone, strikes a vein of contrasting hypocrisy amidst a climate shouldered with budget shortfalls.

When initiating our collection assessment project we knew that surprises are to be expected. Yet, unknown to us at the time, administrative space studies and institutional redesign plans were operating behind the scenes, unknowns that would have a direct impact on library holdings and resources. In 2013, administratively, without any departmental or faculty discussion, the University Library had merged with other academic service units (career services, academic advising, tutoring, disability services, and assistive technology) to form a newly bequeathed Division of Academic Success. Shortly thereafter, the UW–Stevens Point chancellor and provost charged a task force, led by the new division head (our library director), to explore the creation of a University College "designed to aid students in transitioning to university study and support and retain them throughout their academic careers." The goal was to create a unit that would have student success (retention) as their primary function. Questions became numerous, and continue to this day, about developing a new college, which will be headquartered in the Albertson Learning Resource Center.

Initially, local budget reductions delayed the effort to move forward with the creation of a University College. However, this fall semester the proposal suddenly moved forward, with little discussion. The renewed call outlined the University College as the central home for all major academic support services and retention programs, including the University's general education program and first year seminar. Also, a new center for inclusive teaching and learning would be created so that the University's professional development related to teaching, learning, advising, undergraduate research, and diversity would be appropriately aligned with student retention efforts. Eventually, the University College is to become the home for the university's diversity-related activities for students, faculty, and staff to ensure that diversity is integrated into all academic support services and retention programs. These moves are touted to ensure that the learning outcomes of the core curriculum can be effectively integrated across both curricular and co-curricular activities.

The provost announced that in recognition of budget reductions, the structure will involve no new positions or funding. A dean's position will be retitled from the existing director of academic success. A .5 FTE assistant dean/director of the library will be created from an existing library faculty position, similar to a chair's release in the colleges; noting that this would have to be done with or without the University College effort, due to a pending retirement in summer of 2016. However, not noted was the fact that in addition to the switch of the library director faculty position to division head, the Library has lost three FTE positions, with two faculty resigning (taking jobs outside the UW System) and one staff retirement (that was not replaced.) Campus administrators determined that none of those FTE would be filled, resulting in increased workloads and stresses for others. Also, it was revealed that funding for a teaching center director will be redirected "from existing professional development uses in order to serve a broader audience." To that effect, a moratorium was placed on tuition reimbursement for faculty/staff, which is a significant downside to professional development.

The updated proposal went to shared governance, Common Council, as an information item. Library faculty and staff, while not necessarily opposed to the idea of the forming of a new college, felt they had not been part of the discussions or the task force efforts as this model was generated. At Common Council concerns were raised on a number of fronts, including: costs, resources, positions, mission, and structure. The Provost apologized to those who felt left out of the process, explaining that the task force was created to explore the idea and to look at redundancies in certain areas; further explaining that there is no new money associated with the proposed University College, but current budget lines and some vacant positions will be repurposed. The one new hire is anticipated to be the director of the teaching center. A question was raised: where are the resources coming from for remodeling that is being done? Others asked regarding the creation of a new college on campus: who or what is the authority for this? Why the push to have this University College put in place by January 2016 when it has not been vetted or discussed through faculty governance channels? The provost noted, according to state statuette, only the creation of a new college that holds and offers academic programs needs to go through a different vetting process. Since this college will not offer academic programs, the vetting process is different.

Where do we go from here?" Work continues; some unknowns may soon become known, even as I post this paper. The University of Wisconsin system regents are scheduled in the second week of December to rule on the creation of the University College, and differential tuition for UW–Stevens Point.

A side note of importance on global literacy: Withdrawals, transfers, replacements, and gifts are all key factors in collection maintenance and development. At the University of Wisconsin–Stevens Point Albertson Library we have found that weeded collections and unneeded gifts can open new horizons, which impact global literacy and contribute to the quality of life for people of lesser developed regions. Literacy partnerships are two-way relationships involving mutual planning and conduct of programs and projects. We believe that education and access to books are basic human rights. Working together, with our literacy partners, we cycle many of our withdrawn titles to help fund high-impact literacy projects. By finding old books new homes, we have created a sustainable solution for diverting books from landfills. The Better World Books (BWB) donations and discards program helps us manage and ease our workflows related to withdrawn books and unneeded gifts. We've partnered with BWB (http://www.betterworldbooks.com/) and our nonprofit foundation, the Wisconsin/Nicaragua Partners of the Americas, Inc. (http://www.wisnic.org/). In addition, we have a yearlong library book sale that includes selected gift books and older withdrawn titles of higher value. A percentage of proceeds from BWB and the library book sale are shared with the Wisconsin/Nicaragua Partners of the Americas (W/NP). The Library's share of BWB proceeds is used to support the purchase of CORE (resources for the college library) items for our library collections, thus enhancing key needs of our collections. Proceeds from the book sale are used to support the purchase of current paperbacks and audiobooks for the leisure reading collection, to encourage reading for the fun of it!

The mission of W/NP is simple and effective: helping people improve their quality of life in practical, sustainable ways through a network of citizen and institutional involvement throughout the state of Wisconsin and the republic of Nicaragua. People-to-people programs promote cultural awareness and community development. Over the past 50 years, the W/NP "Sewing Centers" transitioned into "Learning Centers" as more skills became increasingly necessary and useful. Each of the Learning Centers maintains the common goal of providing opportunities for skill enrichment and development, yet each self-governed Learning Center is unique and special in its own way. By working together identifying needs and desired goals, the support from Wisconsin has been tremendous through the gathering of supplies for the Learning Center (LC) classes. Each LC is autonomous with organization and management by the women of their communities. Class subjects are in response to requests from community members. All classes are designed to include skill-building, personal dignity, and self-sufficiency, with a focus on employment for (rural) women. The program is focused on the care of families and communities and the encouragement of members to assume leadership responsibilities, and strives for international understanding and friendship. The Opening Doors project is intended to give business training plus a small amount of funds to enable men and women to start business enterprises, thus learning while actually running their businesses. Many of the participants in the Learning Centers learn skills that they would like to use to start a business, but do not have the necessary funds or business knowledge. In 2013 and 2014 eighteen learning centers from different parts of Nicaragua participated, benefiting about 100 people and their families. Promoting education at all levels continues to be a primary goal for individual book donations, Better World Book funds assist to build collections at the Learning Center libraries, which help make significant improvements for a student's educational experience.

Weeding Out in the Open: What Will the Neighbors Think?

Michael DeMars, Systems Librarian, California State University, Fullerton

Ann Roll, Collection Development Librarian, California State University, Fullerton

Abstract

Weeding is often an emotionally charged topic for both librarians and faculty. A healthy print collection needs weeding, but the campus community is often nervous and concerned about this practice. In preparing for a large scale monograph deselection project at California State University, Fullerton's (CSUF) Pollak Library, library faculty and administration grappled with how to productively and efficiently involve the large CSUF teaching faculty in the weeding process. Library systems staff developed an innovative web-based tool that enables faculty to easily provide feedback on deselection candidates on a title by title basis. This paper explains the thoughts behind the project, the creation of the deselection database and user interface, how the weeding project was received by teaching faculty, and the results of an initial pilot.

Introduction

Like many libraries, California State University, Fullerton's Pollak Library has been actively engaged in transforming its collections and physical space. Pollak Library proactively collects in electronic formats when possible and aims to provide spaces for student collaboration, study, and teaching. This transition has naturally led to a desire to deselect print materials that are unlikely to be needed in the future. While deselection projects for print journals and audio-visual materials on older formats have progressed smoothly, the campus expressed significant concerns about weeding the monograph collection. Library administration sought a method for campus teaching faculty to be engaged in the weeding process, while still moving forward with necessary deselection. In order to provide a streamlined approach to accepting feedback, library systems faculty and staff developed a custom online interface, in which teaching faculty could review titles slated for weeding on a title by title basis if desired. This paper describes the reasons behind the creation of the interface, the results of an initial pilot, and plans for ongoing weeding at Pollak Library.

Deselection Preparation

With over 38,000 students, California State University, Fullerton (CSUF) is one of the largest campuses in the 23-campus California State University (CSU) system. CSUF is a predominantly undergraduate and master's level institution, and Pollak Library's collecting focus is curriculum-driven. As a whole, the CSU system has been analyzing the future of print collections and library spaces as a part of the Library of the Future (LOF) initiative. LOF, along with an upcoming renovation of the library building, prompted Pollak Library to actively approach deselection. Historically, Pollak Library had not proactively weeded, and as a result, numerous editions of the same titles, outdated content, and unnecessary duplication existed in the monograph collection.

To embark on a large-scale weeding of the monograph collection, CSUF worked with Sustainable Collections Services (SCS) to enable more robust data-driven decisions. In summer 2014, Pollak Library loaded its monograph data into SCS's GreenGlass online tool, which allowed librarians to analyze the collection using our circulation data alongside WorldCat holdings, availability in HathiTrust, and multiple other data points. Subject librarians were each assigned appropriate sections of the collection to weed. The majority of librarians were philosophically ready for the task but had workload concerns, while a few were opposed to large-scale weeding. The collection development librarian held multiple meetings to discuss weeding strategies and practices as well as training sessions on the use of GreenGlass.

http://dx.doi.org/10.5703/1288284316252

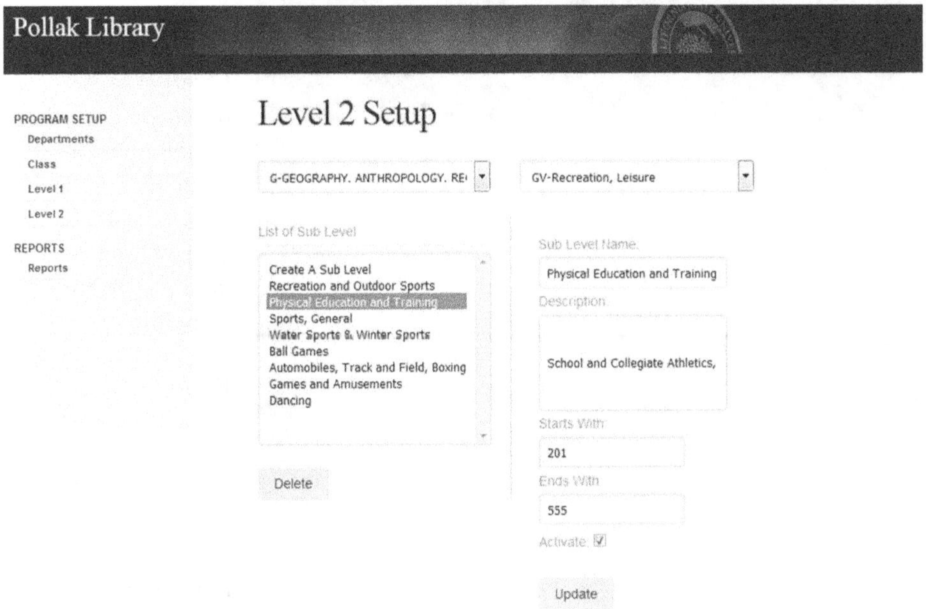

Figure 1. Administrative interface for librarians to separate lists by call number.

Change in Leadership and Approach

Shortly after the data load to GreenGlass occurred and initial weeding assignments were made, a new interim university librarian was appointed. As a member of the teaching faculty and a former chair of the academic senate, the new interim university librarian was especially interested in involving the teaching faculty in the weeding process. In addition, at an academic senate meeting, the Provost had assured faculty that they would have some involvement.

Prior to the start of the weeding process, faculty were surveyed on their opinions and perceptions of a number of library services and initiatives. On the topic of the upcoming weeding project, free text responses ranged from "I'm extremely supportive" to "I think this is a disaster!!!!!!!!" While there had always been a plan to make the list of deselection candidates available for comment in some form, such as via an Excel file posted on a LibGuide or moving the books to a specific area of the library for perusal, the new leadership wanted the process to be as transparent as possible, and very easy for faculty to provide feedback. Library systems faculty and staff were charged with creating an online system in which faculty could browse or search the list of deselection candidates, review necessary data points from GreenGlass (such as total checkouts and WorldCat holdings), and request that titles be retained or sent to their departments if weeded. Each department would have a single login and password, and only one "vote" per department.

In order to make the navigation as simple as possible for faculty, Library Administration requested that large lists of weeding candidates be broken down into smaller lists of approximately 200 books. Librarians created descriptive headings for each list, and library systems staff developed an administrative interface for librarians to create the headings and descriptions based on the call number ranges, as shown in figure 1.

Theoretically, this allowed departments to divide the list among colleagues by their areas of expertise. While each department had only one login name, faculty also entered their e-mail addresses as they logged in. The addition of e-mail addresses at login enabled the library to identify if individual faculty members were making numerous retention selections. Figure 2 shows this breakdown and description as viewed by a faculty member, and figure 3 shows a sample of

Initial Pilot

After the interface was fully developed and librarians were trained to break down their lists into smaller portions, an initial pilot was conducted in the spring 2015 semester. Systems staff loaded a list of 1,744 low-use items in the GV (recreation and leisure) classification range to the weeding interface. Librarians expected that the kinesiology faculty would be most interested in

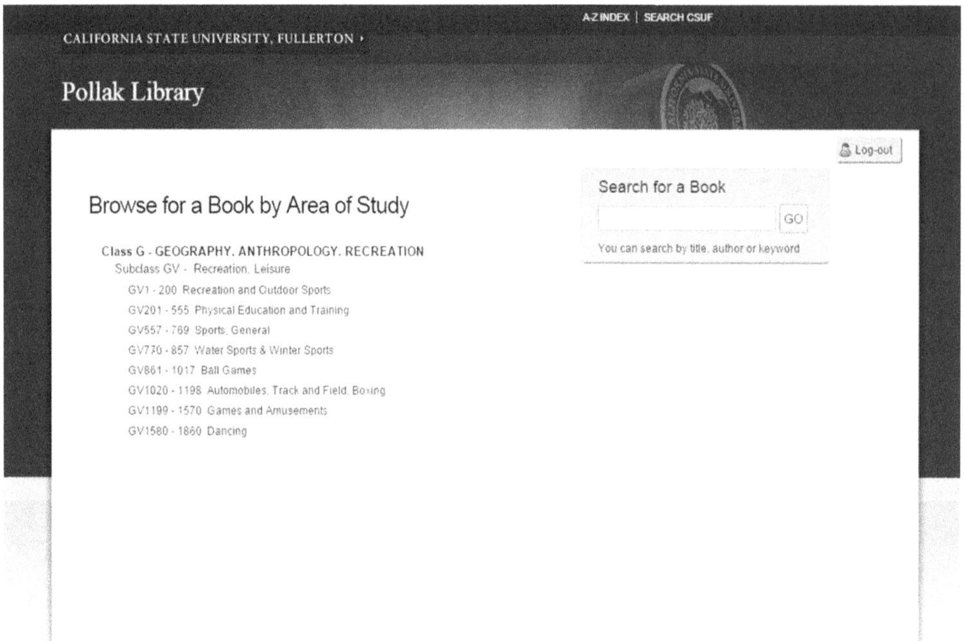

Figure 2. Browsing by classification in the weeding interface for faculty feedback.

this subject area, and so the liaison librarian attended a department meeting to describe the process, show examples of items on the weeding list, and answer questions. The department faculty members were receptive and agreed to participate in the process. Faculty in other departments were informed via e-mail messages, online announcements, and a presentation at the academic senate by the interim university librarian. While it was expected that kinesiology faculty would be most interested in the titles on the pilot list, all departments were given the opportunity to use the interface and provide feedback. The associate university librarian sentall department chairs e-mails including login information, details on the project, and instructions for using the interface.

Results of the Pilot

CSUF has over 2,100 faculty across 67 departments. Since most departments would not have a strong need for the books in the GV section, the library expected a small number of departments to participate in the pilot. Nine departments made retention requests, as entered by 20 faculty members. Four of the departments did not comply with the "one vote per department" rule, as multiple faculty made entries on the same title in some cases. One faculty member requested that 1,716 of the 1,744 books be retained in the collection, and so if all requests were honored, then only 23 books would be withdrawn, representing only 1% of the list presented. If this single faculty member's requests are ignored, then 1,095 books (63% of the list)

TITLE & AUTHOR	CALL NUMBER	TITLE CIRCULATION	Retain in Collection	Send to Department
The environmentalist's bookshelf : a guide to the ... By- Merideth, Robert W Published- 1993	GF 41z M45 1993 US Holding=200	***Recorded Checkouts= 0*** Last Checked Out= Never	☐	☐
Human development and the environment : challenges ... By- *Not Available* Published- 2002	GF3 H75 2002 US Holding=200	***Recorded Checkouts= 0*** Last Checked Out= Never	☐	☐
Interactions of the major biogeochemical cycles : ... By- *Not Available* Published- 2003	GF3 I28 2003 US Holding=200	***Recorded Checkouts= 0*** Last Checked Out= Never	☐	☐
The environmental future; proceedings. Edited by N ... By- International Conference on Environmental Future (1st : 1971 : Jyväskylä, Finland) mn Published- 1972	GF3 I37 1971b US Holding=200	***Recorded Checkouts= 0*** Last Checked Out= Never	☐	☐
The human habitat; contemporary readings [compiled ... By- Wheeler, David L Published- 1971	GF8 W45 US Holding=179	***Recorded Checkouts= 0*** Last Checked Out= Never	☐	☐

Figure 3. Titles listed in the weeding interface for faculty feedback.

Figure 4. Required comment box for retention requests.

would be weeded, and 649 books (37% of the list) would be retained based on the feedback from the other faculty. Of the 649 titles to retain, 306 of them had never circulated, and 221 of them had not circulated in twenty years. The interim university librarian requested a meeting with the faculty member who requested that nearly all the books be retained and her department chair. Both declined the meeting. Currently, none of the books from the pilot have been withdrawn. It is unlikely that they will all be retained permanently, but a long-term plan has not yet been established.

Future Directions

Ultimately, the pilot was a failure. The development and use of the interface enabled faculty participation, but also seriously hindered the weeding project. A significant amount of library staff time was invested in development, testing, and training for the interface. Subject librarians also spent considerable time separating their lists of weeding candidates into smaller lists. Some librarians also mentioned that after they put a lot of work into creating an appropriate list of weeding candidates, they disliked that any faculty member, regardless of discipline, could veto the decision.

However, the library administration sought to continue using the method with some adaptation. In consultation with the academic senate executive committee, the online interface was adjusted to require that any faculty member who requests the retention of a title provide a reason. Previously, the intention had been to make retention as easy as possible, and it was quickly recognized that additional justification was necessary.

Currently, in the fall 2015 semester, a list of over 30,000 books across a wide range of disciplines has been input into the interface for faculty feedback. A reason for retention is now required. Users must provide written justification for their retention requests before they can continue reviewing titles, as figure 4 illustrates. Due to the increased number of titles and the additional labor on the faculty's part, the library does not expect the same result as the pilot.

Going Local: Creating Unique and Special Collections in an Academic Library

Arielle Lomness, Collections Librarian, University of British Columbia, Okanagan Campus Library

Abstract

Over the past two years, the University of British Columbia–Okanagan Library has undertaken a review to update their special collections and focus on the local geographical areas and targeted populations. From this, a localized, accessible, and unique collection has emerged that can better serve the students and faculty on campus, as well as community user groups in the area. This project helped to grow the community engagement focused strategic direction of the university and increase the visibility of the library in the surrounding community through building new relationships.

This paper will focus on examining the roles libraries can play in developing targeted and focused special collections, drawing from recent experience in reimagining and expanding an existing special collections section within a newer academic campus library. It is hoped that this paper can spark considerations of the impact special collections can have on the strategic goals of a library or university or college, and on the roles and responsibilities academic libraries have in preserving local history.

Preface: A version of the history, project overview, and results section has been published by the Okanagan Historical Society. Berringer, H., Gattrell, J., & Lomness, A. (2015). Special collections at the University of British Columbia's Okanagan Campus Library: Expanding our community's access to local history. In D. Gregory (Ed.), *Okanagan history: The seventy-ninth report of the Okanagan Historical Society* (pp. 106–113). Kelowna, BC: Okanagan Historical Society.

Introduction

Special collections remain common among academic institutions, ensuring that rare and unique materials are preserved for long-term availability. Over the course of the past two years, we, the University of British Columbia (UBC) Okanagan Library, have been reimagining how special collections are defined on our own campus and specifically how they are tied to the local community engagement endeavours of our library. The following is an overview of the history of the campus, the project and its results, and relevant literature consulted while creating goals for the project and following its completion.

History

In 2005, UBC expanded to include a second campus in Kelowna, British Columbia, taking over one of the existing campuses of the Okanagan University College (OUC) (Mortenson, 2005). Over the past ten years, the Okanagan campus has become increasingly integrated into the local community and has settled into its Okanagan Valley surroundings. While a form of special collections has been a part of the UBC Okanagan Library since our inception, it was not until 2012 that there was a strong desire for change; a call to reimagine and refocus our special collections to match the campus's emerging role in the community.

With the creation of a new campus came much of the research collection materials previously held on the same site by OUC. During the transition, both circulating and special collections were reviewed and divided based on content type, relation to teaching and learning, and space. The result for special collections was a variety of print monographs that did not carry a strong focus, nor a foundation for future growth. Limited acquisitions criteria allowed for almost anything to be deemed worthy of being placed in the newly minted campus collections.

Over the first several years, the monograph-focused special collections was moved around the library building, residing in many different spaces. First, the collection was held in a room designed with purpose-built cabinets to house the materials. Doubling as a silent study space for

http://dx.doi.org/10.5703/1288284316253

students, this room offered access to the collection at any given time. As we moved through a period of renovation in 2012, the room that once held this collection was removed, and the materials were displaced into a storage closet in a locked hallway. Day-to-day access was no longer an easy task, and often required patrons to schedule access to use the materials. The visibility, accessibility, and usefulness of the collection, which we had long been offering to our patrons, had decreased. It was time to push forward, change, and reimagine the collection, not just in terms of its past, but what it could be for the campus, for the institution, and for the local community.

Project Overview

The project itself, to revitalize the special collections, began in the fall of 2013, with the hope of designing a collection that would serve to match the goals and priorities of our library, the strategic directions of the university, and the needs of the community members looking to access research materials. The landscape of the region was also taken into account when analyzing and brainstorming what the UBC Okanagan Special Collections (OSC) would look like.

One of UBC's main strategic directions/pillars for the institution was to commit to promoting high impact and locally focused community engagement practices. More specifically for the library, our patron groups were driving this intention. Not only did we serve our campus community—students, faculty, staff, etc.—but also our community patrons, who relied on accessing materials in our library that otherwise could not be found locally. Making available resources that were coming through document delivery from the main campus reinforced the need for an initiative to better serve the research needs of the area—focusing on providing the locally produced and focused materials to those living in or visiting the area. With limited preservation-driven post-secondary institutions in the area of the province, it was important to ensure that the historical values of the local region were being retained and maintained.

We began first by mapping out the local collections focus at institutions throughout the province. Most of the major regional areas were being covered in existing special collections. Regarding the areas that were remaining, we had conversations with other academic institutions to better understand their situation and goals and to ensure that there was comprehensive coverage without overlap. Following the preliminary mapping of the province, we considered what we as a library wanted to include in our goals for the project. We wanted to ensure that all monographic titles, serials, maps, and other materials published in or about the Okanagan-Similkameen area were being covered in our plan for the reimagined collections. In addition, we wanted to bring in pieces from our campus community, highlighting unique publications and projects from students and faculty. Through the analysis of the existing holdings and extensive collections development endeavours with the main campus's rare books and special collections (RBSC), we were able to create a robust collection of materials to make available locally to those patrons seeking to research the community.

Next steps included opening a new accessible space where anyone could visit and use the collections, tearing down the boundaries that had been created only a few years prior. In addition, we strove to create an atmosphere that was inviting to patrons and worthy of showcasing our holdings. Open-facing glass cabinets, hung photographs, and displayed artifacts make for a vibrant space worthy of highlighting the locally focused materials. We received additional funding to put toward having two dual master's of library and archival studies co-op students. During their time with us, they were able to work on identifying and acquiring monographs to address gaps in our collections and arrange and describe our first two community donated archival collections, respectively.

While our initial intention was to focus only on locally published materials, by the end of the project, we had expanded to encompass unpublished items, archival holdings, and artifacts. As we move forward, there is an ongoing commitment to preserving the local community's history, moving now into the realm of digitizing photographic collections that document the multitude of industries and families from the region's history.

Results

The beneficial outcomes of this project on our library have highlighted the importance of local collections in academic libraries. The level of engagement that has ensued and positive feedback received has created a space that is welcoming to visitors and is worthy of long-term impact in the local and campus communities.

In creating our special collections, partnerships were a foundation and should be a driving force behind any locally focused collection. The work that we have been able to do with other academic institutions in the province has laid the groundwork for future relationships and preservation activities that might arise. For example, through conversations with colleagues at one of the province's colleges, it was determined that due to space concerns they were no longer able to preserve all of the history from the Kootenay-Boundary region of the province. It was agreed that the OSC would preserve any donated material documenting or published in this nearby region. Internal partnerships with units on the Vancouver campus have also furthered the goals of the project; from collections development conversations with RBSC, to digitization initiatives with the UBC Digitization Centre, we have been able to promote ourselves as a fixture in the Okanagan-Similkameen region.

Another valuable outcome of building the OSC has been our outreach endeavours. Speaking to community members, societies, and local historical committees have all offered the opportunity to interact with a patron group that we do not always regularly encounter in academic libraries. In addition, being able to host special collections focused events in our spaces has given them the opportunity to come in and see the collections firsthand. The reciprocal trust that has been developed ensures that the ongoing growth of the collections is supported both on campus and in the community.

Throughout the process of developing the locally focused collections, we had the added advantage of receiving gift-in-kind donations. As mentioned above, the overall collections became more robust over the course of the project; much of that had to do with the community's increased investment in donating materials to the OSC. Countless members of the community generously donated rare and out-of-print monograph titles, along with much more—including photographic collections, unpublished pamphlets, and other unique and original items.

The added advantages to the on-campus community have included the addition of study space and the integration of the special collections into teaching and learning. Study space has always been a precious commodity on our campus, and with the creation of a larger space for the OSC in the library we wanted to ensure that students had access to the silent area. Since the opening of the space, students have used the area on a daily basis. Additionally, the space and the materials have begun to be incorporated into teaching and learning on the campus, another strategic direction for the Okanagan Library. Students are using the historical materials to document how historical research moves from primary to secondary source material in the local area and to see firsthand how history is being preserved. Overall, it has been reassuring to see the collections reaching broad patron groups and supporting the strategic initiatives set out by our university.

The results of the project have far surpassed the original intent we had when looking to revitalize our existing collections. They have demonstrated the overarching importance of documenting the local history and supporting other community-focused initiatives, both locally and more broadly, which cover similar topics. This process highlighted the importance of using the partnerships and goals driven from an institution's strategic direction to facilitate unique and special collections in academic libraries.

Literature Review

The literature surrounding special collections and archives in academic libraries has spanned many decades. For the purposes of this project, both before and after, we were most interested in discovering instances where academic libraries had also looked to reimagine or refocus their special collections, or had created collections, over the past few years, targeted at documenting the history of the local community around their institution. We found a shortage of literature directly relating to these topics, presumably since many special collections have been founded earlier in an institution's history. Much of the literature is related to incorporating special collections into teaching and learning and also about reinforcing partnerships and supporting strategic goals.

Most closely related to our situation was an article around the acquisition of three special collections at the Waterford Institute of Technology (WIT), based in Ireland (Darbey & Hayden, 2008). The case study documents the steps the library took in acquiring these collections, the reasoning behind their importance, and the factors involved in preserving and storing them long term (Darbey & Hayden, 2008). The fact that institutions frequently acquire collections without a strong intention of making them available quickly or possibly ever was observed (Darbey & Hayden, 2008). This is still a factor for donations that we receive. Our processing of monograph acquisitions is quick and straightforward, usually taking up to a couple of weeks to complete, while our archival holdings require more attention to detail, supplies, and long-term project time. Fortunately, we have been able to apply student work hours to helping make these collections available. If this additional support had not arisen, the scale of our donations acceptance could have decreased. The estimated time that it would take to process a collection should be considered before accepting any donation in order to avoid a situation where the items would remain unprocessed and unused in a backlog.

Aligning with the strategic directions of both the library and the academic institution should be considered overwhelmingly important whenever beginning a new project, whether that be building a special collections or another venture. Germano and Stretch-Stephenson (2012) discuss goal setting and the benefits this exercise can have on aligning a project with the strategic directions of the institution or library, as well as the possibility of failure if goals are very clearly unattainable. In relation to the WIT example above and similarly tied to our creation of a more defined special collections, goal setting can truly make or break a project. Without direction, whether that is the goals of the academic institution, those of the library, or simply those of a team within the library, a project could miss the mark. Other literature also discusses the broader impact of a library's structure on its projects in relation to how closely it has updated and reimagined itself alongside the academic institution (Nutefall & Chadwell, 2012; Franklin, 2009). Libraries must be willing to adjust and change in order to respond to the needs of the patrons. Finally, Harris and Weller (2012) state that special collections can be prominent outreach opportunities, a goal that is consistently included in strategic directions of many academic institutions. Seeing these collections as opportunities only broadens their purpose and helps to ensure their future.

Teaching and learning was also represented throughout the literature in various forms. In particular, it was argued that library instruction for special collections is distinct from regular library instruction and should be treated as such, focusing on celebrating the differences (Samuelson & Coker, 2014). Our own endeavours to educate students on campus using the materials in our special collections have mimicked this approach. The assignments vary in form from regular information literacy (i.e., our Library Introduction session to first-year English classes), instead working to create an environment of hands-on and practical knowledge learning. Carter and Whittaker (2015) comparatively explain that special collections are making a move beyond preservation to be represented throughout the research process, and they certainly hold educational value on an academic campus. In addition, they touch on elements around locally focused collections, emphasizing the need for "destination collections," or collections that will draw visiting researchers to use them (p. 361). Not only are these collections valuable in educating the campus community about the region right outside its doors, but also the larger community outside the institution.

While literature was challenging to find in relation to our exact situation, elements of previous case studies and research provided valuable justification for our approach to the project, both from the onset and after completion. Overall, we see that special collections are an evolving piece of academic libraries, and one that can certainly be used to our advantage.

Future Considerations

The following are future considerations that we were unable to cover in the scope of the original project and literature review. These considerations fall into two categories: how can we more thoroughly investigate the role academic library special collections can play within their local and campus communities, and more specifically, how do special collections evolve in relation to the similar collections of other local preservation bodies.

- What do we need to be doing to ensure we are effectively meeting the needs of the regional community (i.e., ongoing consultation, surveys, focus groups, etc.)?
- To what extent should we be collecting everything versus creating more specialized and focused collections in academic libraries?
- How best can we be promoting the use of these collections in the classroom?
- How can we break down barriers and misconceptions around special collections to better promote access for students?
- Is there a broader place for academic libraries to be taking on local collections that otherwise might live in a community archives or museum?
- In "academic towns" where community archives or museums may not exist, is there a greater need to facilitate creating special collections?

Conclusion

As mentioned previously, the overall project came to include much more than expected. Advantageous goals, partnerships, and donations helped to shape the locally focused special collections into what it is today. Understanding the ongoing nature of our commitments within the library has helped to spark new goals and has reinforced the alignment with the institution's strategic directions. As the literature reinforces, strategically based goals can help to increase outreach, teaching and learning, and partnerships both on and off a campus. We hope that our special collections will continue to grow and positively impact both the campus and the local community.

References

Carter, L. R., & Whittaker, B. M. (2015). Area studies and special collections: Shared challenges, shared strength. *portal: Libraries and the Academy, 15*, 353–373. http://dx.doi.org/10.1353/pla.2015.0017

Darbey, N., & Hayden, H. (2008). Special collections for beginners: A case study of special collections at Waterford Institute of Technology Library Service. *New Library World, 109*, 258–272. http://dx.doi.org/10.1108/03074800810873605

Franklin, B. (2009). Aligning library strategy and structure with the campus academic plan: A case study. *Journal of Library Administration, 49*, 495–505. http://dx.doi.org/10.1080/01930820903090862

Germano, M. A., & Stretch-Stephenson, S. M. (2012). Strategic value planning for libraries. *The Bottom Line: Managing Library Finances, 25*, 71–88. http://dx.doi.org/10.1108/08880451211256405

Harris, V. A., & Weller, A. C. (2012). Use of special collections as an opportunity for outreach in the academic library. *Journal of Library Administration, 52*, 294–303. http://dx.doi.org/10.1080/01930826.2012.684508

Mortenson, B. (2005, July 5). OUC keys passed to new institutions [media release post]. Retrieved from https://news.ok.ubc.ca/2005/07/04/ouc-keys-passed-to-new-institutions/

Nutefull, J. E., & Chadwell, F. A. (2012). Preparing for the 21st century: Academic library realignment. *New Library World, 113*, 162–173. http://dx.doi.org/10.1108/0307481211218543

Samuelson, T., & Coker, C. (2014). Mind the gap: Integrating special collections teaching. *portal: Libraries and the Academy, 14*, 51–66. http://dx.doi.org/10.1353/pla.2013.0041

Changing Operations of Academic Libraries

Jim Dooley, Head, Collection Services, University of California, Merced

Abstract

The University of California, Merced (UC Merced) opened in 2005. Both the campus and the library are celebrating their first decade of operation. This paper will examine decisions made at the founding of the library and which of these decisions remain valid today. The focus will be on collections, technical services, reference services, instruction, digital assets, and space.

The University of California, Merced Library: "Not What Other Research Libraries Are, What They Will Be"

This motto, created by Donald Barclay, one of the founding librarians at UC Merced, is still on the home page of the library's website. It reflects the approach taken to the creation of a new research university library on a new research university campus. For the most part, members of the initial cohort of librarians had many years of experience in large, traditional research libraries. All had opinions as to what was working or not working in those libraries. They also realized that the founding of UC Merced gave them the opportunity to reexamine established ways of building collections, providing services and using space. Even though the results of this reexamination would need to be implemented within the structures of the University of California, the founding librarians would have the opportunity to develop a research library model that reflected 21st century thinking in librarianship and that also worked in the UC Merced context.

Both the library and the campus have now completed ten years of operation. This is an appropriate time to examine initial decisions in collections, technical services, reference services, instruction, digital assets, and space and see how these initial decisions have played out during the past decade.

The University of California, Merced, the tenth campus in the University of California (UC) system and the first new American research university in the 21st century, welcomed its first class in 2005. The initial class comprised 875 students, mostly undergraduates. At the end of its first decade of operation UC Merced has 6,700 students including almost 400 graduate students. There is a proposal currently under review (the 2020 Plan) to construct sufficient academic buildings and student housing to allow the campus to grow to 10,000 students including 1,000 graduate students by 2020. If approved by the University of California Board of Regents, the 2020 Plan envisions the University of California partnering with a commercial developer to build almost one million assignable square feet of new construction (effectively doubling the size of the existing campus) with occupancy of some of the buildings in 2019.

Collections and Technical Services

In 2005 the library opened with the following collection development parameters:

- *Support the emphasis on interdisciplinary work.* Rather than have traditional academic departments, faculty were to be organized into research groups with members from various disciplines. To support the vision, collections needed to be built primarily to support this interdisciplinary work, rather than the individual research interests of particular faculty.
- *Utilize system-wide structures as much as possible.* For collections this meant participating to the greatest extent possible in UC-wide licenses for journals, e-books, and databases negotiated by the California Digital Library (CDL), an office of the University of California Office of the President. It also meant utilizing the

http://dx.doi.org/10.5703/1288284316254

internal UC ILL system to access the 39 million volumes in the UC collection.

- *Favor access over ownership.* The primary goal was to provide access to information resources, not to build an owned collection of a particular size.
- *Prefer resources in electronic format while at the same time providing information resources in the most appropriate format.*
- *Collect only electronic federal government information.* The UC Merced Library became an all-electronic Federal Depository Library in 2004 by relying on Marcive's Documents Without Shelves service.
- *Do not collect microforms.* At the same time the library did purchase equipment to enable reading, printing, and scanning of microforms received through ILL.
- *Use ILL to meet the needs for retrospective print.* Focus print book acquisition on prospective titles.
- *Do not have subject selectors.* There was not a sufficient number of librarians to assign as selectors.

In 2015 all of these parameters are still in effect, with one partial exception. The library has begun to develop some retrospective print collections in support of teaching and research in the humanities. The goal is to develop core collections of titles that need to be physically at UC Merced because the need for these titles cannot be adequately met by ILL. While there still are no librarian selectors, the library is exploring ways to improve communications between the library and the faculty.

Currently the UC Merced collection is 91% electronic by format and 85% electronic by expenditures. CDL licensed resources comprise 65% of the collections budget. There has been widespread acceptance of electronic journals and an increasing acceptance of e-books. At the same time, there remains a continuing demand for print books—both retrospective and prospective—in the humanities.

In 2015 the library has 116,300 current serial subscriptions, the vast majority in CDL-licensed packages, and 21 print serial subscriptions. An approval plan supplemented by firm orders at faculty request is used to acquire print books in the humanities and social sciences (the science approval plan was cancelled several years ago). These titles are in turn supplemented by strategic gifts. Currently the print book collection comprises 123,000 volumes. Available e-books total 1.2 million volumes, with 800,000 acquired through UC consortial licenses negotiated by the CDL. The remaining 400,000 e-books are available through local licenses: 128,000 volumes through a subscription to ebrary Academic Complete; 216,000 volumes through an EBL demand-driven acquisitions (DDA) plan with three short-term loans (STLs) and purchase on the fourth access; and 55,000 volumes through a DDA plan with MyiLibrary with purchase on the second access without STLs. The large number of titles available through DDA plans is contrary to standard collection development practice. This approach was taken at UC Merced in response to the rapid, uncoordinated increases in faculty hiring and creation of academic programs at a start-up campus as well as the lack of librarians to do title-by-title selection. Given these circumstances, the librarians believed that it made sense to have a large number of titles available through DDA. This approach worked well until the summer of 2014 when many publishers significantly raised STL rates. This action forced the library to reduce the number of titles available in the EBL pool by 50% in order to remain within budget.

From the beginning, technical services has been a very lean (but not mean) operation. Currently collection services comprises one librarian who primarily manages collections and provides general supervision of technical services, and two staff who manage electronic and print collections and who supervise two student employees (1 FTE). This staff has been able to assemble a current collection of 1.47 million titles primarily through the extensive utilization of vendor services. Examples are the receipt of files of MARC records from vendors and the use of shelf-ready services for approval and firm order books. Technical services staff are also greatly assisted by the work of the University of California Shared Cataloging Program that provides MARC records for CDL-licensed electronic resources.

Reference

The library has employed a triage reference system from 2005 to the present. No librarians have ever sat at a reference desk at UC Merced. There is one services desk that is primarily staffed by student employees supervised by access services staff. Since 2014 this desk has also been staffed by campus Information Technology (IT) staff and is the primary public contact point for campus IT services. Reference questions that cannot be handled by student employees are referred to a librarian. Students can also schedule an in-person meeting directly with a librarian. The student employees at the services desk are supplemented by additional "roving reference" student employees who receive additional training. These students wear a special t-shirt for identification and circulate through the library to provide assistance if asked. The library is part of the UC-wide 24/7 digital reference service using OCLC's QuestionPoint technology. Both librarians and select library staff cover UC Merced Library's assigned hours. A number of questions received each day during normal business hours are from UC Merced students who apparently would rather ask a question online than in person.

Instruction

From the time of initial planning even before the library opened, it was clear that there would not be sufficient librarians to meet demands for in-person library instruction as the campus grew. Therefore, the librarians developed various online, asynchronous tools that could at least supplement in-person instruction. The first such tool was the library tour originally on the iPod Touch, now on the iPad Mini. The tour is updated annually to reflect new shelving locations after stack shifts, new services, such as campus IT staff now at the services desk, etc. The reach of the instruction librarians is also increased by the development of online tutorials, both locally and in cooperation with other UC libraries. The library instruction program has forged close working relationships with the campus writing program. Even so, the library still had to cancel in-person support for Writing 1, the most basic level writing course, in order to concentrate on supporting Writing 10, the next level course. While all sections of Writing 10 are visited by a librarian, several sections have an "embedded" librarian who works with the students on the research process throughout the course. In 2014 a drop-in writing center was established in a library instruction room. Librarians continue to provide instruction to individual classes upon faculty request.

Digital Assets

Digital Assets in the UC Merced Library is active in four areas: Supplemental Course Resources (SCRs), digitization projects, electronic theses and dissertations (ETDs), and data curation. The first service developed by Digital Assets was Supplemental Course Resources. This is the library's implementation of electronic reserves in which links to journal articles, e-books, or digitized chapters of print books are placed in the course management system. Until very recently, the library did not have a print reserve operation but used SCR to meet the need for course support in a manner consistent with copyright law. In the fall of 2015 the library began a small-scale pilot with a few faculty of a print reserve system. Books are placed on reserve if the amount of text requested to be scanned exceeds fair use or if the library doesn't have an e-version of the title.

Beyond SCR, Digital Assets has pursued a variety of digitization projects. The first was a project funded by a grant from the Institute for Museum and Library Services (IMLS) to digitize art from the Clark Center for Japanese Art and Culture in Hanford, California. Another was the digitization of a collection of Japanese medical woodblock prints from the University of California, San Francisco. Currently, Digital Assets is working on several projects related to the themes of food, water, energy, and health. An example is a collaborative project with the University of California, Riverside to digitize records of irrigation districts as well as other records related to water in California. Another example is a project in collaboration with the UC Division of Agriculture and Natural Resources to digitize the records of the county extension offices in California. Recently Digital Assets completed the digitization of over 2,000 costume renderings by Dunya Ramicova, a UC Merced faculty member who has had a distinguished career designing for opera and theatre. This collection, along with the Clark Center collection, is now available on Calisphere, a portal to digital collections from the UC Libraries as well as other libraries, archives, and museums in California.

The UC Merced Graduate Division adopted a policy at the opening of the campus that all graduate theses and dissertations would only be accepted in electronic form. Instead of shelving print copies of theses and dissertations, the library uploads digital copies to the UC open access institutional repository and digital publishing platform, eScholarship, maintained by the CDL. If authors have executed release forms, ETDs are accessible to the public through eScholarship. Those lacking release forms or under embargo are preserved in a dark archive at the CDL. It has taken some time to develop workflows between the library and the CDL and between ProQuest and the CDL, but these workflows are now in place. OAISTER records are generated from the files in eScholarship and uploaded into WorldCat. These records are edited by UC Merced in accordance with the system-wide policies for cataloging UC theses and dissertations.

Data curation has become an important focus within research libraries. Within the University of California the CDL has developed several important services in support of the UC Libraries role in data curation. The UC Merced Library seeks to utilize these services, not duplicate them. The first is the UC institutional repository, eScholarship, and the associated digital preservation repository, Merritt. Originally developed as a means of displaying and archiving text, these complimentary services now accept datasets as well. The CDL has also developed a persistent identifier service for datasets, EZID, and a tool for developing data management plans required by funding agencies, DMP Tool. At UC Merced Digital Assets functions primarily as a broker linking faculty with CDL services or the services of other repositories, such as the San Diego Supercomputer Center. In July 2013 the University of California Academic Senate adopted an open access policy covering tenure-track and tenured faculty. Recently the University established a parallel policy to cover all UC employees including lecturers and librarians. The CDL has worked to implement technologies to facilitate the deposit of articles into eScholarship. The campus libraries, including the UC Merced Library, provide outreach to faculty and now to other employees in support of the policies.

Space

The UC Merced Library building was designed to maximize the amount of user space, not the number of books housed. The current library space is approximately 80,000 sq. ft. on three floors. Design priorities were to maximize the use of natural light and to make the building as open as possible by utilizing large staircases between floors. This space will support approximately 850 users at one time using a combination of wooden tables, extra-wide carrels, and soft seating. All of the study tables and carrels have power and data. During the afternoon and evening, current occupancy averages 70% with occupancy as high as 90% during midterm and finals periods. The building was designed with thirteen-, four-, and six-person collaborative workrooms equipped with screens and white boards. These rooms are so popular that an online reservation system had to be implemented. The theoretical capacity of the book stacks is 200,000 volumes, although the practical capacity is closer to 185,000 volumes.

The library building was designed with a café serving hot and cold food in a multistory glass atrium. Several of the glass walls can be raised in appropriate weather. With a café in the building, the librarians decided that it didn't make sense to attempt to limit food and drink within the building, even though this was contrary to accepted library practice. For the past decade, there have been no restrictions on food and drink anywhere in the building, except in special collections. The results continue to be positive:

students do not need to sneak food and drink into the library, library staff do not have to spend time being food police, and spills are reported and cleaned up promptly.

Conclusion

With very few exceptions, the approaches developed by the founding librarians remain valid after a decade of operation. The transition from print to electronic journals is nearly complete. The transition from print to electronic books has proceeded at a much slower rate than expected in the humanities and social sciences. Even though the library maintains its policy of preferring information resources in electronic formats, considerable time and expense continue to be devoted to maintaining a print approval plan, purchasing print copies at faculty request and now beginning retrospective purchasing of print to build core collections. While expenditures on print in the sciences are negligible, expenditures on print in the humanities and social sciences are likely to remain significant for the foreseeable future.

As a result of anticipating a faster transition from print books to e-books, the founding librarians did not see the need to establish a print reserve system. In fall 2015 the library yielded to the requests of various humanities faculty and began a pilot print reserves program. It is unclear if this program will need to be continued at some level in the future.

The foundational principles are still in effect. The library continues to build primarily electronic collections through CDL-negotiated UC-wide licenses. Reference services continues to employ the triage model; the only significant change is the addition of the 24/7 chat service. Instruction librarians continue to leverage technology to meet increasing demand. The development of digital library content and services continues to grow in importance. The library building remains a heavily used campus hub. At the end of its first decade of operation the UC Merced Library is poised to join UC Merced in the next decade of growth.

Moving a Library Can Be Easy, but Planning and Project Management Is Key

Katie Gohn, Head of Collections, University of Tennessee at Chattanooga

Abstract

In the summer of 2007, the University of Tennessee at Chattanooga (UTC) received 48 million dollars to plan and build a new library. Planning for the moving of the collection began shortly thereafter. This paper details specific collections projects completed by UTC Library faculty and staff that resulted in a flawless move that took only 11 days to complete. The luxury of time to complete a collection inventory and accurate measurement was key, but so was selecting the right people for the project.

Moving an entire library collection to a new facility doesn't happen very often, and I would dare say that many librarians will never experience the utter stress and joy involved in such a huge endeavor. That said, whether you are moving your collection within your existing facility or to a completely new space—there are two ingredients that will help make the move much smoother: planning and a sense of humor! Without proper planning and coordination, a library move can be a disaster leaving you with collections in a mess and items not being available to your patrons. Proper planning and coordination allow for a smooth and "easy" move with little downtime and an orderly and available collection quickly. This paper will discuss how the UTC library staff successfully moved the Library's collection from one building to a brand new facility with little mistakes. Focus will be placed on important points to consider to ensure success in your library move. Oh, and a sense of humor—that will get you through all the rough patches because there will be rough patches!

In the summer of 2007, the University of Tennessee at Chattanooga (UTC) received 48 million dollars to plan and build a new library. The library and the entire UTC campus was thrilled, and a bit scared. This was a huge undertaking. At the time of funding, no building design or programming plans had been discussed. One thing was certain: the move was going to be a monumental undertaking, and as all good academic institutions do, committees were immediately put in place to begin planning the new building and the move in earnest.

The library put together a committee named the Internal Library Building Committee. This committee was focused on all aspects of planning associated with the move to the new library. This included not only the physical move of the collection, but the programming and design of the building. As specific projects came up, and as the library moved closer to the actual move, a separate team led by staff members from the materials processing department with members from library IT, special collections, and library administration was formed to plan and work through the minute details associated with moving the physical collections. This team was small and agile, which allowed the group to communicate effectively and switch gears mid-project based on data and findings as work was completed. The team met weekly or more if needed and worked off of project plans and action items assigned to individual members. One project manager made sure that all projects running in parallel were being completed and any issues needing follow-up or discussion were tracked. Most importantly, having a member of library administration on the team allowed for finite decisions to be made. This allowed projects to move more quickly because decisions did not have to be funneled up the chain of command.

Because the new facility was not designed and the physical move was years in the future, the library had the luxury of time to plan and coordinate efforts surrounding the move of the physical collection. That said, without floor plans, shelving selections, and building programming, planning for the exact move of the collection was going to

http://dx.doi.org/10.5703/1288284316255

be an ever-changing and fluid process. The one thing that could be accomplished without knowledge of building specifications was one of the major pillars of any successful move and can be summarized in one phrase: "get to know your collection."

With a move looming in the future, it became imperative to begin accounting for the collections currently housed within the Lupton Library. It quickly became clear that the library's collection had not been reviewed since it was moved into the current facility 35 years earlier, and it is possible that it had never been adequately reviewed and weeded. With this in mind, the first project related to the move was a review and inventory of the entire collection. A collection review and weeding project is not something to undertake without caution, especially at an academic institution where such a review has never occurred. Faculty needs and concerns were of the utmost importance and the collection review was open and transparent, and involved faculty at every step. The review involved library liaisons reviewing the collection by call number in four phases. Each phase focused on a different subject area, and all recommendations for discard were posted for faculty review and comment at the end of each review cycle. The overarching goal of the review was "a balanced collection that provides appropriate coverage on a topic, while preserving Intellectual Freedom in a constantly changing society" (Wikipedia). The review began in the fall of 2010 and was completed in spring 2012.

An inventory of items was pulled from the library's ILS, and each item was given a measurement of 1.25 inches. A size estimate was given so that the committee could determine current collection size and estimate size following discarding. In order for the review to be accurate and complete, another large project needed to be completed—barcoding bound serials. Bound serials were non-circulating at the time of the review, but in order to properly inventory and estimate size of the collection, all bound serials had to be barcoded. The materials processing department, along with a select group of volunteer librarians, worked tirelessly to barcode all bound serials prior to the collection review beginning.

During the review, it was estimated that up to 25% of the collection would be effectively weeded. This was based on an initial review of the collection based on circulation statistics, age of content, and first review by subject liaisons. This number was used in initial design and programming of the new building, which was happening in parallel with the collection review process. The first plans had collections filling both the ground floor and the third floor with discrete collections like reference and popular materials living in small footprints on other floors of the now five-story building. Because it was estimated that up to ¼ of the current collection could be weeded, the internal library building committee began looking at ways to compress the collection into one floor.

A decision to utilize compact shelving on the ground floor to house monographs, serials, documentary film, microfilm, microfiche, and oversized collections was made. This freed up space on the third floor for more group study rooms and shared university space, but created a more complicated move of the collection due to the interfiling that would need to occur in order to house various collections on one floor. Soon after the decision to use compact shelving was made, specific shelving units and shelf sizes and configurations were also selected. This forced those planning the collection move to make some mapping decisions related to the collection before the collection review and inventory process completed. It would have been better to complete the inventory and weeding process before making these decisions to ensure that the collection, after weeding, would actually fit appropriately within the selected configuration. But, as with any building/construction project, this is not always possible and those on the move committee had to become flexible and creative in approaches to solving problems that these early decisions created later in the process.

It should be noted here that one decision in particular had a larger impact later in the project than the main decision to use compact shelving.

This was the decision to house call numbers M and N on oversized shelving carriages. These call number ranges house a large collection of musical scores and art books that are often oversized. When this decision was made, it meant that the collection had to be considered in two distinct sections: A–L and P–Z, because everything pivoted around the larger carriages in M and N. Since the majority of our expected future growth and the majority of our bound journal collections live in P–Z, it meant that if weeding predictions from the review project did not meet projections as expected, then that section of the collection was not going to fit.

After the first initial review was completed and lists of suggested discards were provided to faculty, it became clear that faculty were not comfortable with the amount of discarding that was suggested by librarians. Thus, far less than the 25% of items ended up being removed from the collection. This meant that there would be significant issues with overcrowding in section P–Z. Although it was a fact that weeding projections did not match with weeding reality, it often was forgotten when architects, planners, and others began making change suggestions on the ground floor. It also became problematic as the compact and fixed shelving was actually being installed because some shelving that was originally intended to be double-sided ended up being fixed one-sided shelving at the end of a section or against a wall. Support COLUMN placement also ended up consuming whole columns of shelving. All of these design decisions and construction obstacles ate away at precious square footage. Take this as a cautionary tale—always underestimate weeding and overestimate space needs, because changes in design, construction issues out of your control and underestimations of collection size can have huge impacts on your moving plans and leave you scrambling in the last few months.

At this point, the collection projects paused so that the library could do two things to transition from Innovative's VTLS to OCLC's WorldShare Management Service (WMS) and crunch numbers related to the collection review and weeding process. This is important to note because it took quite a bit of time to transition the catalog, and during this time we did not want to move too many things around in the building because we wanted to keep our data stable for the bulk load of data to the new system. It also took a bit of time to get accurate numbers from the collection review and weeding. Once we were back up and running in the fall of 2012, we began our final planning for the move of the collection that was slated to occur in the spring of 2014.

It became clear after completing the collection review and rerunning the numbers that more precise measurements of the collection were necessary to make an accurate plan for consolidating and moving the collection to one floor. At this point, all small discreet collections were physically measured. This included, CD's, LP's, Microfiche, Microfilm, Microcards, textbooks, and children's books. The reference collection and general collection (monographs and bound serials) were measured and inventoried in a more systematic way. Student workers—armed with wireless barcode scanners, laptop computers, tape measures, and spreadsheets—stored and shared via dropbox and scanned the barcode of the first and last book on each shelf. They also took the total measurement of books on the shelf (not each individual book, but the total amount of space taken up by the books on the shelf). As the students completed inventorying and measuring sections of the collection, librarians were able to review the data and compare it against the inventory of the collection from our WMS system. Not only did this process provide us with a much more accurate measurement of our actual collection, but mistakes in shelving, shifting, and barcoding were uncovered and corrected. If you have time to perform an inventory and accurate measurement of your collection in a systematic way, it is well worth it. It allows you to accurately pinpoint problems to specific call number areas. This is really important if you are planning on interfiling any collections.

Occurring in parallel with the inventory process, student workers were also looking for and pulling all items that would be considered oversized by the new shelving standards. Students used cardboard templates cut to the size of the largest "regularly-sized" book. When they came across items that were possibly oversized, they compared those items to the template and pulled any items that were bigger than the template. This pull was important because with compact shelving, oversized items could not be placed on their sides and still allow the compact shelving to close completely. All oversized items were checked a second time by members of the materials processing department and shelved in two locations in the current library building. These two locations would then be consolidated into a single oversized section on the ground floor of the new library. The only problem that we ran into with oversize was not having an actual floor sample of the shelving provided until late in the process. Once we had the shelving unit, we could mock up our planned shelf sizes to make sure that items fit as expected and that our shelving plans would work appropriately. I would suggest getting a sample shelving unit as early in the project as possible to avoid any issues with shelf size or configuration.

Reports generated from the inventory and measuring project that ended in fall 2013 provided much more accurate data related to the size of the collection. Armed with this data, we crunched numbers and combined total measurements and item counts from disparate collections in order to get accurate mapping of the collection within the new shelving schema. Once all collections had been combined into a single shelving location on the ground floor, as predicted, the collection was extremely full in section P–Z, and in particular in P and Q. To be a bit more specific, we were looking at shelving fill rate numbers higher than 90% in some sections. To put that in perspective, it meant that we would only be leaving about 3 inches per shelf. One new book, the need to shift, or a mistake in measurement and the collection had nowhere to go. This meant that more targeted weeding in P–Z had to occur.

Because bound serials are typically larger than your average monograph, the team decided to focus on weeding serials. Armed with a targeted area to pull from, the team ran overlap reports that compared physical serial holdings against e-journals holdings. Because the library had gained faculty approval during the collection review project to weed physical copies of journals that were available online, the library did not have to seek permission for this weeding project. Student workers began pulling journals where the online holdings completely overlapped physical holdings with no gaps. Over 10,000 volumes with an average measurement of 2.5 inches each were weeded. This gave us a bit of wiggle room in P–Z, but the collection was still tighter than we wanted it to be on move in. But, we were happy because we knew everything would fit!

Running simultaneous with all the collection move projects, a subcommittee of the Internal Library Building Committee was charged with producing the request for proposal (RFP) for the move of the collection. Because this was a move of over 400,000 items, which included our special collections, we knew this was not something we could undertake ourselves. Drafting began in the fall of 2013 and a bid was awarded in spring 2014. When drafting the RFP, it is important to meet with your campus or agency procurement department to make sure that you are drafting your RFP appropriately and including all legal requirements of the institution, and in our case the state of Tennessee. We also took the opportunity to ask for opinions on a few questions that had come up. Namely, should we host a pre-proposal conference, should it be mandatory, should we require a presentation, and how should the committee evaluate the proposals (point system, rubric, etc.)? We gained valuable information in this meeting and were able to write up an RFP document that met all our needs.

In the midst of finalizing the RFP, the library received news from the architect and construction manager that the project was not on schedule for an early summer 2014 occupancy. A date later in summer 2014 was given, but it became clear quickly that this date was also in jeopardy because it was running too close to the beginning of the fall semester. This forced the library move committee to redraft the RFP to allow companies to provide two bids: one for the move of the circulating and reference collection and another for the move of special collections. Companies could submit one proposal for both, two separate proposals, and one proposal for either move. We did this in order to provide ourselves flexibility in moving if the date continued to be pushed back and we were forced to move in two cycles. This would ensure that the main circulating collection was moved and ready for students when the building opened, without forcing a hurried move of our expensive, fragile, and rare special collections.

Within our RFP, we were very specific. Vendors actually praised us for creating an RFP that was very detailed, because it allowed them to properly and adequately bid on the project. We not only described in detail what needed to be moved, but we provided detail about logistics and floor plans of the current building so that bidders would understand how they would have to work logistically. For example, one line in the RFP says, "both buildings have a single delivery elevator located at the rear and public access elevators that reach all floors" (RFP). Our objective is specific and to the point:

> The contractor must move approximately 450,000 print volumes, 10,000 rolls of microfilm, 18 cabinets of microfiche, 10,000 AV items (video and audio), approximately 1,435 linear feet of boxed archival materials and 8,500 books from the library's Special Collections in multiple locations, and possibly other small groups of items from the old building to the new structure. (RFP)

The scope of work in the RFP included specific details about discrete collections, their size, current location, where they will be moved to, and any special treatment or note specific to the collection. Furthermore, specifics about how the move was to proceed, our requirements for the protection of the collection, communication expectations, expectations of responsibility (who packs and unpacks, etc.), broad fill rate expectations, and a description of the interfiling that would need to occur and what the responsibility would be for marking interfiles prior to the move was included. The RFP went on to include sections on handling and moving conditions specifying how the mover would prevent damage, protect collections, and prevent accidents, and a requirements section specifying what information the bidder/mover would need to provide in their bid—the agreement to attend an on-site visit and a pre-proposal conference, and the possibility of a presentation, a thorough explanation of their move methodology with answers to specific questions like:

- Who will manage the project?
- Will the vendor use local moving staff or bring their own?

The requirements section also included the need for both professional and institutional references, move methodology, cost proposal, and a general list of our other requirements that were not included in other sections. Other requirements included details like:

- The vehicles used to transport books, collections, and items shall be closed and locked when loaded and not attended.

Being explicit in your expectations is of utmost importance. You do not want to award the contract only to find out that you and your mover don't see eye-to-eye on some details. Remember, it is your collection and you create the expectations. Library movers with experience expect you to be mandating specific protocols.

The RFP was awarded in late spring 2014 to Hallett Movers. Hallett specializes in commercial and library moving, and has been in business since 1926. This company was chosen based on their professional and thorough response to the RFP, but more importantly, their references. I cannot state enough how important references were in the decision-making process. References provided detailed information about the professional nature of the companies, how conflicts and problems were resolved, how materials were handled, and how communication was coordinated. They provided detailed information about their particular move and why the company they chose either helped or hurt the outcome. Choosing the right company for your particular move is one of the most important things you can do. Following up with references and asking specific questions of them can make your choice much easier.

As I mentioned above, the RFP touched on the number of interfiles that needed to occur with the consolidation of the collection onto one floor. At the writing of the RFP, there were right at 1,300 call number integrations that needed to occur. These were mostly consolidation of serial runs that were housed between two floors in the current building. Within the RFP, we stated that the moving company would be responsible for 900 of those 1,300 integrations. This meant that the library was responsible for completing 400 integrations before the movers arrived. It was to our utmost advantage to complete as many integrations as possible so that the move time would be shorter and less complicated. Also, with fewer integrations there would be less room for errors. To tackle the integrations, data from the item inventory and measurement project was pulled that provided information on each integration. We analyzed the data and separated integrations out by the number of volumes and space needed for each integration. Because we knew how much space was available on each shelf of the library, we were able to pinpoint integrations that could be accomplished with little to no shifting. We created google sheets for student workers to work off of and set them about pulling items and completing the "easy" integrations. At the same time, our stacks maintenance supervisor was leading another group of student workers on shifting projects that would accommodate integrations that were more complicated and required more shelf space. Our goal was to continue integrations up until the moving company arrived on site.

We had begun the integrations project by focusing on serial runs. At the time, serials were housed on two floors. Everything pre-1950 was housed on the 3rd floor along with the library's monograph collection. Everything post-1950 was housed on the library's 2nd floor. No monographs were housed on the 2nd floor. We focused on moving serial runs from the 3rd floor down to the 2nd floor. However, after analyzing our data more closely, we shifted gears and stopped focusing on format type and started looking at how we could create fewer integrations by creating longer contiguous runs of call numbers. This meant that we began moving monographs and serials up and down between floors in order to fill in gaps in call number sequences. This ended up being a winning strategy, and when we finished integrations in October 2014, we were left with only 286 integrations.

During this same time period, staff and student workers from special collections performed a final inventory and measurement of all collections (manuscripts, rare books, university archives, and art and artifacts.) Special collections were housed in three different locations within the current building, but would need to be relocated to one space within the new building; a closed stacks location utilizing compact shelving. The final inventory ensured that all boxes, art pieces, and various items were properly tagged and labeled so that movers would be able to relocate them appropriately in the new space and so that the special collections staff would be able to account for all objects once they had been moved. Student workers along with two staff members completed the inventory in approximately 3 weeks.

With so many things moving around in the building during the fall of 2014, and because the move was scheduled at that point for early December 2014, it did not make sense to spend valuable staff time changing catalog locations for items we were interfiling. If our building were more complicated (more floors, more unique collections) it would have been imperative to keep the OPAC up-to-date with shelving location changes. However, since items were either on the 2nd floor or the 3rd floor, we decided to focus on the physical moving of items and provide signage to patrons that said, "Can't find your item, check on the 2nd floor/3rd floor." We also provided lists of completed integrations and moves to all service desks so that they could assist patrons with locating items. Since we would be bulk changing all locations in our OPAC in one fell swoop with the move to the new building at the end of the semester, providing good signage and information to our public services staff made more sense than wasting staff time to make catalog changes. After the integrations were completed, student workers tagged each of the remaining 286 integrations. These tags read like end-cap signs. They included the call numbers of the items that needed to be pulled from another floor to fill the gap. These tags also served as important indicators to patrons for where items were currently living within the collection. If a patron came across one of the bright pink tags, they could read it and know to go to the other floor if their item fell between those call numbers.

Hallett's pre-move team arrived on site in mid-November 2014. This team worked closely with the library move point person on finalizing details. They worked quickly to measure the entire collection, got a handle on the number and size of interfiles, began analyzing their measurement numbers, and mapped the collection into the new space accordingly. We worked with them to provide optimal fill rates per particular call number ranges based on our prior analysis of the collection. With their data, we were able to accurately map out the collection and spread fill rates and empty shelves across the entirety of the main collection. In P–Z, which was very crowded, we worked to gain as much growth room as possible in particular areas; squeezing more of the collection into specific call numbers that were not growing. Once we settled on fill rates, Hallett tagged the entire collection. Using the fill rates by call number range, a team of taggers armed with numbered and color-coded tape and measuring string worked through the collection, tagging books and shelves. These tags were then replicated on the empty shelving within the new building. When the movers arrived, they simply matched up tags from the old building to the corresponding tags in the new building. What this meant was that the movers did not have to work sequentially through the move; starting at A and ending at Z. Movers worked in multiple areas of the stacks simultaneously. This same system was used within the various locations housing special collections in the current building as well. It allowed for items in disparate locations to be effectively mapped and combined into single shelving locations within the new special collections stacks in the new building. This method proved very advantageous in our move in particular because we were moving into compact shelving, combining items from disparate locations, and working on a short time frame for completion.

The moving crew arrived on campus on December 8, 2014. They were given 3 weeks to complete the move. This would have them completing the move of both the general and special collections by December 29th. Because the library had completed so many collection clean-up projects, completed the majority of the integrations, and worked closely on mapping and measuring the collection with the movers accurately, the move ended up finishing on December 19, a mere 11 days after beginning. The library movers were able to work throughout the collection and move between the buildings efficiently. No technical problems were encountered, and open lines of communications between mover and library point personnel worked flawlessly. The collection remained open to patrons via a paging service throughout the entire process. Special collections, including art and artifacts, was moved after the general collection on the final day of the move. Special packaging and care were used in the transition of materials. Library staff chose to move the most rare and expensive items ourselves.

In the end, the library collection was only closed to the public for browsing during those 11 days. The collection opened officially in the new building on December 29, 2015 and has not been closed since. We have had no major problems with the collection since the move. Things were shelved properly and we have not had to perform any major shifts. The physical move of the collection ended up being the one project that occurred with zero problems. This was due to the time taken to clean up the collection through inventorying, measuring, weeding, and interfiling that was completed before movers arrived.

In the end, the key to our success lay in two areas: the luxury of time to plan and prepare and the people chosen for the move committee. UTC, in the end, had 7 years to plan for the move. This is both a luxury and a curse. With so much time to plan, there was so much time for things to change. On the other hand, we were afforded the opportunity to complete an entire collection review and inventory process that many libraries would not be able to complete. That said, without this data, it would have been almost impossible to have accurately mapped our collection to the new building without running into major space problems. In terms of people, the UTC Library put together a smart, agile, and knowledgeable team to take on the move. A project manager was able to coordinate the larger projects and handle any small issues that came up throughout. Other team members focused their talents on data mining and projections, stacks maintenance and student worker management, RFP drafting, and campus communications. Weekly and sometimes twice weekly meetings kept everyone informed of project timelines and objectives. I will point out that having a staff member on the committee who was astute at Excel, Access, and math in general was also helpful when it came to mapping collections, figuring fill rates, weeding, and figuring out creative ways to solve space problems. Finally, I can't say enough for having a dedicated group of student workers who completed a whole lot of work in a short amount of time. Any library planning a move should consider asking their campus for a larger student allocation to help with projects surrounding their move. Students can perform a plethora of tasks that just cannot be completed by library staff alone. Finally, attention to detail both in project planning and choosing the right library mover for our project proved exponentially beneficial.

In a library move, the details matter. Underestimating the intricacy of your move, the size of your collection, and the time it takes to complete a necessary project, or not utilizing the right people can mire your project and leave you with having to make drastic decisions in the end. Worse, you could be left with a project that is over budget and not completed to your satisfaction. Knowing your collection is important, but planning what you want your collection to be in your new space takes time, people, and good planning.

Creating a Standard of Practice for License Alternatives

Christina M. Geuther, Electronic Resources Librarian, Kansas State University Libraries

Mira E. Greene, Head, Content Development & Acquisitions, Kansas State University Libraries

Abstract

A gap exists in library literature for license alternative practices. Although licensing processes are a new concept, there is enough knowledge of best practices that will apply to alternatives. Much of the life cycle of electronic resources with and without licenses remains the same; therefore, a workflow can be framed for alternatives. Kansas State University created a standard workflow for managing license alternatives in its management systems Verde and Alma. We based this standard on the differences between licenses and their conventional alternatives, the NISO Shared Electronic Resource Understanding, and terms of use without registered or signed agreement. Aspects of this presentation will also apply to institutions without electronic resource management (ERM) systems. After considering the acquisition and review practices of license alternatives, a discussion of interlibrary loan as well as enforcing terms in the patron community will be offered. Interlibrary loan staff will easily interpret their procedures of fair use based on documentation in the ERM.

Why Document Alternatives?

License alternatives are handled differently in the workflow process. Unlike the conventional negotiation process when the licensor provides a standard license amendment appropriate for the electronic resource, the licensee reviews the terms and requests modifications or supplies possible addendums, which are reviewed by the licensor for new language and provided feedback with a modified document if the requests are accepted, and the licensee reviews the modified license to decide to accept and sign; the license alternatives are not negotiable. While libraries have a standard of best practices for licensing with policies and checklists, license alternatives are not as easy to determine and document. However, interlibrary loan department and fair use needs anticipate direction on electronic resources obtained by libraries. Therefore, it is imperative to document and copy the alternative license at the time of purchase.

SERU: A Shared Electronic Resource Understanding

A Shared Electronic Resource Understanding (SERU) was adopted as a NISO Best Practice in 2008. At that time the focus was on electronic journals; however, it has expanded into e-books. SERU offers an alternative for publishers and libraries to license agreements. The SERU statement expresses commonly shared understandings of the publisher, the subscribing institution, and authorized users on the nature of the content, user of material, online performance, and archiving and perpetual use. Use of SERU gives benefits to both publishers and libraries by removing the overhead of license negotiation. By registering for SERU, the publisher and institution have a cooperative and collaborative relationship with a mutual understanding between both parties.

Terms of Use With or Without a License

Terms of use may appear outside of a license or the SERU agreement. Some vendors list authorized users, interlibrary loan, and other terms of use on their website in a section for librarians; or it may be even more hidden in a Frequently Asked Questions section. Nevertheless, these terms of use should be treated with the same weight as a license agreement. They should be documented in the electronic resource system or modules to give collection development librarians and interlibrary loan staff direction.

http://dx.doi.org/10.5703/1288284316256

K-State Libraries's Process for License Alternatives

Kansas State University has two standardized workflows for processing licenses and license alternatives in the electronic resource management system. They are similar in structure and outcome. For licensing, there are five major steps: acquire first draft of license from vendor and the business terms requested by content development librarians; negotiation of license terms and addenda; submit to local signatories and vendor, and await countersignature; documentation of license terms and file management; and interpret license upon staff request. For the license alternative workflow, there are again five major steps: contact vendor for most recent terms of use and to ensure there is not a license that can be negotiated; consider terms of use and whether the needs of the library will be met; register for SERU when applicable; documentation of terms of use and file management; and interpret SERU or terms of use upon staff request. The difference between the two workflows is that negotiation is not taking place for the license alternatives, although our workflow establishes the same procedures for checking against policy and a checklist with the same concerns for all documents considered.

First, the electronic resources librarian contacts the vendor for most recent terms of use and to ensure there is not a license that can be negotiated. The vendor's website may or may not have all of the information you need to make a collection development decision. Terms of use may be listed, but it is possible that there could be further documentation from contacting a vendor. If the vendor does not have terms currently in place, try suggesting the SERU and proceed with Step 2. If there is a license that can be negotiated, use a licensing workflow. Finally, if there are terms of use only, make sure they are the most recent and check how regularly they may be updated. There may be other issues present if your state has requirements of purchases and contractual obligations. For example, in Kansas we have a required state form for purchases over a certain amount, and that must be incorporated in a license.

Second, the librarian must consider terms of use and whether the needs of the library will be met. Review the terms of agreement as carefully as when negotiating a license. Terms of agreement outside of a license cannot be negotiated, so contact the vendor and document areas needing clarification. Apply the same checklist and red flags as licenses. Checklists are quick visual guides for navigating sometimes complicated terms. A checklist may be used in the creation of a licensing and license alternative policy as well as part of the process of reviewing the terms. Policy enforces consistency in reviewing terms and agreements, and facilitates understanding among library staff assessing collection development once a resource is approved. One of the red flags Kansas State University considers is indemnification. Indemnification can go two ways: by the library or the vendor. Watch for language calling for the library to indemnify the vendor, because it carries the obligation to legally defend or pay legal fees to defend the other party from a third party's claims that may result from the agreement. Also look for the specified venue where legal action to resolve a dispute should take place, especially if your institution is restricted by law to its own state. What are the user restrictions? At Kansas State University, we have to consider our collections' purpose as a land grant university. We have to ensure walk-ins, who are unaffiliated persons using an electronic resource on-site.

Third, the library will register for SERU when applicable. Confirm the use of SERU with the vendor. This may be the first time a vendor has used SERU or they may have little experience, so check the NISO registry for SERU participants. Your university should be listed with up-to-date contact information. Then link the SERU license record to the appropriate electronic resource in the electronic resource management system or unified resource management system. At Kansas State University, we keep one SERU license record to update. We do not modify the terms of SERU to call for separate records for each electronic resource. This procedure was changed when we migrated from Ex Libris Verde to Alma resource management.

Recording in the Electronic Resource Management System

Documentation of terms of use and file management must be completed in a timely manner. When working with the license interface of an electronic resource management system, the text input fields for terms are laid out in a particular order that may not be reflected in the terms of use needing to be documented. Answering each field requires working back and forth between the sections of a document. Accordingly, it is easier to first make a template of the ERM license interface in Microsoft Word. Reread the Word document against the SERU or terms of use. Then copy the information over to the license form of the ERM/URM. Attach a copy of the terms of agreement to the form. Make a screen capture of the terms posted on the vendor website at the time of agreement. E-mail communication can be used in legal exchange, so at Kansas State University we maintain any vendor e-mails with clarification of terms in a backed up hard drive. We have a practice of maintaining those licensing and license alternative exchanges for at least five years, although we have used even older recorded e-mails for negotiations.

Outcomes: Enforcing Terms, ILL, and Fair Use

At Kansas State University, the three most common reasons to interpret license alternatives for staff are: public services refers a patron who wants to use an electronic resource in a manner that may be reflected in the terms of use; fair use implications are unclear; and the management system license interface does not have enough information to answer a question. In our case, the electronic resources librarian does not have much contact with patrons and works behind the scenes in technical services. First, library staff contacts the electronic resources librarian to interpret the terms of agreement. Then the electronic resources librarian looks through documented e-mails in the backed up licensing hard drive and the most current agreement in the management system to identify whether the staff's terms of use question has an established answer. If the documentation shows an unclear answer, the Electronic Resources Librarian becomes the main contact for communication over the matter with the vendor licensing representative. The issue is treated in the best interest of the university, whether reading the gray area at an advantage or deciding to be conservative based on most practices (such as avoiding systematic downloading). If, on the other hand, when the electronic resources librarian looked through the documentation in the licensing folder and management system, there is a clear answer, she cites the terms of agreement by e-mail exchange with the staff and appropriate patron.

Interlibrary loan uses the license information documented in the ERM/URM to determine permissions. The license module in Alma was configured to have the ILL information in the uppermost portion of the interface. The process of documenting the terms of use and SERU gives ILL and consistent workflow and the ability to make these determinations without intervention of the electronic resources librarian. They can quickly decide whether the permissions allow sharing of the material.

Conclusion

Kansas State University has found that developing a standard of documenting license alternatives has cut staff time answering questions on terms, interlibrary loan, and fair use. By developing a workflow for documentation, records are streamlined and consistent. The record only has to be updated at the time of purchase unless a question on enforcing terms is requested. Whether a library uses an electronic resource management or not, there is a standard and checklist that will make license alternatives manageable for library staff.

Resources

Albitz, B. (2008). *Licensing and managing electronic resources*. Oxford: Chandos.

Bosch, S. (2005). *Guide to licensing and acquiring electronic information*. Lanham, MD: Scarecrow Press.

Collins, M. (2007). SERU: An alternative to licensing—An interview with Selden Durgom Lamoureux. *Serials Review, 33*(2), 122–128.

Eschenfelder, K. R., Tsai, T. I., Zhu, X., & Stewart, B. (2013). How institutionalized are model license use terms? An analysis of e-journal license use rights clauses from 2000 to 2009. *College & Research Libraries, 74*(4), 326–355.

Lipinski, T. A. (2013). *The librarian's legal companion for licensing information resources and services*. Chicago: Neal-Schuman.

NISO. (n.d.). *SERU: A Shared Electronic Resource Understanding*. Retrieved from http://www.niso.org/publications/rp/RP-7-2012_SERU.pdf

Rupp-Serrano, K. (2005). *Licensing in libraries: practical and ethical aspects*. Binghamton, NY: Haworth Information Press.

Outsourced and Overwhelmed: Gaining a Grasp on Managing Electronic Resources

Matthew D. Harrington, Data Projects and Partnerships, North Carolina State University

Abstract

Outsourcing the management of electronic journals has significantly reduced the autonomy academic libraries have over their collections' metadata, as well as the ways in which that data is collected, organized, and made available to the library. However, the ephemerality of this metadata makes quality control burdensome and costly on the corporate end and necessitates ongoing title tracking and maintenance for the library. As a result, the quality of data in outsourced knowledge bases is often inversely proportional to the library's tolerance of "bad data," as well as its inability to tell the difference. This session demonstrates how an MS Access database was constructed that integrates data from various sources in order to reconcile e-journal and e-book title lists, process yearly subscription changes, and manage the distribution of work to departmental staff. As such, it both serves as a reconciliation tool with administrative functions for linking and displaying summary data about subscribed packages, and it provides a workflow tool with a user interface designed for staff to easily manage ongoing subscription maintenance. Electronic resources are dynamic by nature, and a management system should have the ability to track and respond to these changes. This easily maintained tool offers a model for managing change across the interrelated applications that manage electronic resources.

Introduction

Managing title lists has become an increasingly difficult task in the context of big publisher deals and the various packaging models used to describe these bundled sets of titles. Not only are these title sets too large to manually sift through for inconsistencies, but they change too frequently to justify such labor-intensive title-matching. Contributing to the problem is the outsourcing of data management to commercial products that may or may not communicate with each other. Subscription agents, knowledge bases and publishers may all communicate title lists to a library, but it is often the library's responsibility to ensure those title lists are accurate and uniform.

Therefore, to manage electronic resources, libraries must regularly perform title list reconciliation. What gets paid to the publisher must match what is both discoverable and accessible by the patron. However, electronic resources are not static, and this is where resource management becomes critical. Libraries cannot let go of their management responsibilities simply because commercial management services have been contracted. Though these services can automate many of the daily, monthly, and annual maintenance tasks associated with electronic resources, these are not enough. The library must have a tool that can monitor change and respond to inconsistencies among these systems to ensure title lists reconcile between those services.

Electronic resource management systems, or ERMS, often fail on this level. Though they may maintain records of licenses and perhaps even include some assessment metrics, they rarely flag problems that require staff attention. Therefore, the reports produced by these ERMS rely on the assumption that data are correct but lack the ability look for data discrepancies. IMPART (Integrated Multi-Package Reconciliation Tool), the electronic resource management database described in this paper, attempts to tackle some of the recurring issues that have arisen from the overwhelming amount of electronic resource data that must be managed and the loss of autonomy over that data once the management has been outsourced to commercial services.

Data and Data Integrity

Data are messy, and though everyone involved with data management may want clean and consistent data, there is rarely such thing as a

http://dx.doi.org/10.5703/1288284316257

perfect match or one-size-fits-all approach. Libraries can, however, focus their efforts on the few percentiles that have discrepancies. These data issues range from slight inconsistencies that can be ignored to large-scale issues that lead to misinformation in the reports relied upon to make key collection decisions. Therefore, libraries, and especially technical services departments, must be able to identify which problems can be found, which ones require a solution, and which ones can be solved. These are overlapping but not congruent categories, and the ultimate goal is to continually increase the overlapping area through new tools and new ways of looking at data.

To manage so much data, libraries often rely on commercial services to maintain that data and help organize it, and while these can ease the burden for certain tasks, they can also lead to data integrity problems if there is no communication of data among these different services. Electronic resources pose a particularly messy problem because the library has the least amount of autonomy over both the content and the metadata. There may be multiple systems managing details related to an item, none of which communicate directly with each other. The result is redundant data stored in varied systems, each managed by a different organization or service, and when a change occurs, such as a title transfer or title change, the data must be updated in every system separately, which never happens simultaneously. Furthermore, the ILS often depends upon data integrity, so this places the library in a middle-man position in which it must receive information from one source and communicate that information to another source in order to maintain the integrity of the data that

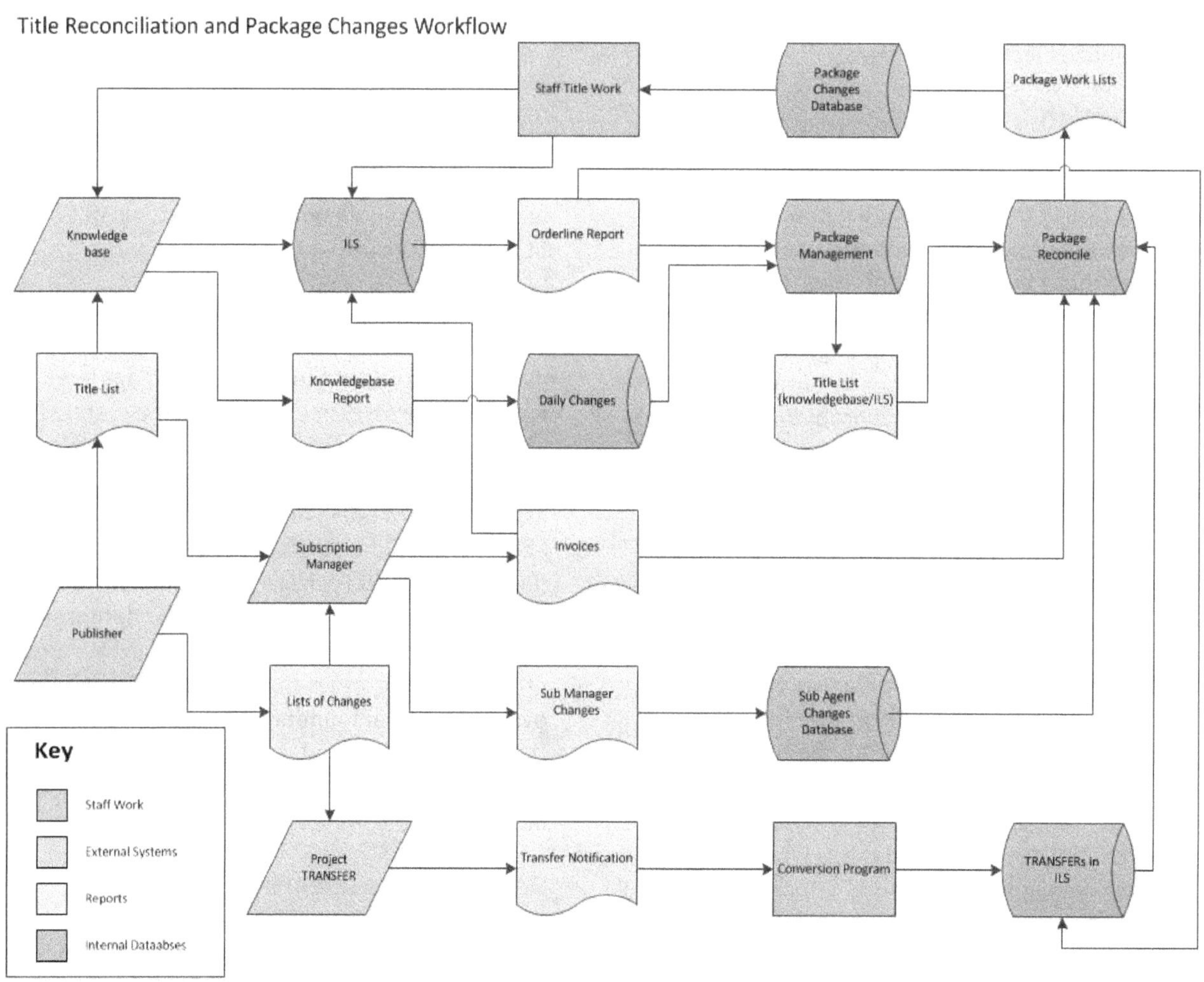

Figure 1. Data flow for title list management.

is stored by each. As an example of this, figure 1 illustrates the flow of data from different commercial systems, through reconciliation databases, to staff for processing, and finally back to the commercial knowledge base.

One of the problems encountered in this middleman position is linking data together. Outsourcing the management of electronic resources to multiple services leads to multiple identifiers, which may present problems when forming links between that data. In addition to the identifier used to locate materials on shelves, there are international identifiers for books and serials, OCLC numbers, subscription identifiers, knowledge base title IDs, proprietary identifiers supplied by publishers, and even locally created identifiers in the ILS. These may not all refer to the same type of object, but they all relate to each other, and creating links between them allows the library to manage resources more efficiently.

Some of these links may already be in place to automate matching invoices to orders or linking data in an ERM. However, unless all services are supplied through the same company, it may be more difficult to see a link that connects the title ID assigned to your order by a subscription agent to the database code your knowledge base may have assigned to denote the package containing that title. Finding links between these sets of data often falls upon the library. Therefore, understanding the nature and context of these identifiers is key to managing the links between data sources, and consequently, the integrity of the library's data.

Data Reconciliation

Reconciliation is all about maintaining data integrity. Whether payments are to be matched to invoices or orders to holdings, reconciliation involves ensuring two sets of data link correctly and match as expected. Problems occur when a portion of one dataset does not link to a portion of the other dataset or vice versa, and these often stem from changes in the data that affect the relationships between them. Therefore, reconciliation is also a continual process of relationship maintenance, and those relationships are often created from the data supplied by the various vendors managing one element of the maintenance process. The key to adapting a model to a specific group of vendors, commercial products, and ILS reports is to analyze the common elements that link together the varied sets of data from these systems. Sometimes this requires changing the way data is maintained in the catalog, and sometimes new procedures are needed to periodically collect data.

The database at NC State University was constructed incrementally as needs developed. Its original purpose was to reconcile serial title lists from large electronic journal packages, which ultimately meant ensuring the publisher lists matched orders in the catalog. This naturally grew to encompass title lists from our knowledge base and subscription agents, as well. With four possible lists to compare, it was evident that an important piece of the process would be to continually maintain matching title lists between the catalog and knowledge base while reconciling those as a whole against title lists received annually from various publishers and the subscription agent managing those subscriptions. Therefore, the first priority was to automate the reconciliation between the orders in the ILS, which meant relying on daily order reports provided through the ILS's reporting module, and the daily holdings report from our knowledge base, which was provided for download each day.

Although the ISSN was an early candidate for linking these datasets, using the proprietary identifier from the knowledge base proved most useful because the majority of the title records in the catalog for large e-journal packages were delivered through the MARC record service provided by the same company, and that meant nearly all of the titles in need of reconciliation contained the knowledge base identifier in their 001 field. This identifier was also available in the daily report of all serials holdings. After quickly cleaning up the 001 fields, which resulted in a shared identifier between titles in the ILS and titles in the knowledge base, all that was left was matching specific subscriptions to their appropriate holdings. Database names from the knowledge base had already been added to a specific field of the order record, so logically this field was normalized and linked to the holdings in the knowledge base through their database details report, which included a database code. This created a shared composite key identifier for both the knowledge base holdings and ILS orders.

The initial database ran simple queries that compared the two lists and combined attributes from each source of data. Not only could a single line of data include costs from the ILS and coverage dates from the knowledge base, but it was possible to find all records that appeared in one list but not the other, which is ultimately the premise for reconciliation. And because the process of linking records from each source had been automated, updated reconciliation lists could be run as quickly as the source reports were made available by the ILS and knowledge base. This allowed regular reconciliation reports to be generated and distributed to staff, who could then review the unmatched titles to determine the cause.

Matching to publisher lists meant using a different key, though. The only identifier provided by most e-journal publishers is the ISSN, and because there is so much inconsistent use between the print ISSN and electronic ISSN, conversion to an ISSN-L almost always yields fewer broken links. By adding the ISSN-L to the existing reconciled list of titles from the catalog and knowledge base, it becomes possible to link these to publisher-supplied title lists. All inconsistencies can then be sent to staff for review. For regular reconciliation reports, this worked very well. However, the management cycle for electronic resources involves more than quick, reactive reconciliation.

Managing electronic serials means processing annual changes, and this entails not only processing those changes, but also discovering those changes and distributing them to staff. This had previously been managed through spreadsheets and Google Docs, but for the 2015 subscription year, a new workflow tool was designed to manage this process. Title transfers and subscription changes were collected from sources such as Project TRANSFER and publisher sites, and these were then compiled into a list of changes, which could be formatted into a database table capable of tracking the renewal process. One column in the table held a staff person's initials so that tasks could be distributed. Each staff member had a queue, which was simply a filtered version of the table by the initials column, and throughout the process of making modifications to orders and knowledge base holdings, they checked off boxes in the database to keep a record of what had been done and what tasks remained. Staff had previously used databases for regular title maintenance and cancellation projects, so they were already accustomed to working in a database environment. The success of this database prompted a proposal to consider the possibility of integrating it and the reconciliation tool into a single database capable of collecting and reconciling title lists while also providing a dashboard for staff to manage the individual title work assigned to them within the database.

Integrating Databases and IMPART

By the beginning of 2015, there were four databases involved in the serials reconciliation process at NC State University. The two primary tools were the reconciliation database and title work database already described. In addition to these, a separate database was created that simply looked for daily changes occurring in the library's knowledge base holdings, and that involved comparing holdings lists from different days. Updated title lists from publishers appear in the knowledge base without warning, and with no means for proactively searching for these updated holdings, those changes may not be known to the library until a problem is discovered by a patron. Even large-scale changes may be missed if no process for finding these updates is in place. Maintaining a database that compared each day's holdings avoided this issue. When updates were made to the knowledge base, this database highlighted them so that corresponding updates could be made to the holdings displayed in other systems. Mistakes also happen, and when updated title lists contain bad data, those errors were easily identified using this database, and immediate corrections could be made.

Project TRANSFER e-mails also alerted the department to publisher changes, and these e-mails were collected, formatted into a spreadsheet, and periodically matched against orders in the catalog using a fourth database. The resulting list of transfers was then directly added to the package changes database for staff to review during the renewal process. Eventually this process was simplified by downloading data directly from the Project TRANSFER ETAS system.

These four databases provided the foundation for IMPART's design. The original premise was to use a single database tool to perform all of the reconciliation functions in the department. It needed the ability to access updated data reports to remain current, it needed to compile archival title lists for reconciled title collections, and it needed to route all reconciliation problems to the staff member assigned to manage that collection of titles. To ensure IMPART met the first of these requirements, its source data was collected into a single space and linked to the database through the use of linked tables. Queries within the database could then format the data directly from the source file, update any necessary identifiers, and create formatted, local tables from which to run additional reconciliation queries. These formatting queries can be captured using macros so that updates can be made easily using a button from a database form. Once the data is updated, simple queries that search for matches based on key identifiers were run to produce lists of all matched records, as well as lists of all unmatched records. The former were exported and archived once the problem titles from the latter query were resolved.

This model is not limited to e-journals, though. In addition to the reconciliation functions for online serials, an additional set of queries was designed to reconcile e-book packages. These operate from source files exported from the ILS, the commercial knowledge base, and the publisher, and like all other source data for the database, the files can be overwritten with updated title lists in order to rerun update queries within IMPART. Therefore, producing a new reconciliation list is almost fully automated.

Figure 2. IMPART main menu.

As figure 2 illustrates, IMPART is divided into two portals, one for staff to access title work that has been routed to their queues and one for the administrator to perform all of the necessary reconciliation functions that discover that title work. Therefore, once reconciliation queries have been run, additional functions allow these to be assigned to staff according to the name of the package by linking to a table containing all of the staff managing packages. Assigning title work creates a record in a separate table, which staff access when they open their assigned queue, and these are then filtered by staff initials. Figure 3 shows the staff view within those queues. Work tasks have three statuses; they can be marked as in process, completed, or if newly assigned, neither. Instructions for specific workflows can be automatically added based on the type of task, and linked documentation explains how to process each update. These queues can also be filtered by staff in different ways, such as limiting the display to tasks marked "in process."

Beyond IMPART

Once IMPART had the ability to fulfill each of its original three goals, additional functions were added. Using files exported from Project TRANSFER's ETAS database, functions that match these against order records in the ILS to create a list of all publisher transfers matching a

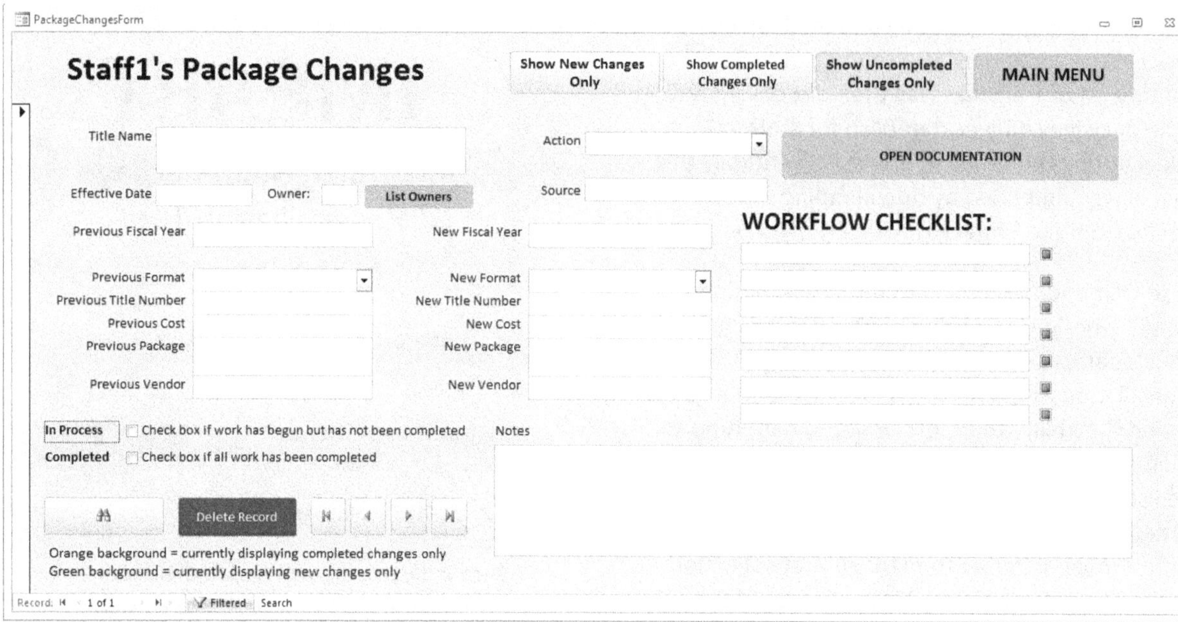

Figure 3. IMPART staff queue.

subscription were added to IMPART, and it could then assign the transfers to staff for processing. This simplified and automated a potentially time-consuming process. Invoices from the subscription agent could also be matched against orders in the ILS to find items that do not match correctly or to compare encumbered money in the ILS orders to the invoice amount provided by the subscription agent. The daily knowledge base changes previously monitored were incorporated through an additional function, and like other reconciliation processes, problems can be routed to the appropriate person. Additionally, if links were made to COUNTER usage reports, usage data could be imported and linked to the costs included in the ILS orders to produce cost per use reports. With so much data to organize and interpret, especially in technical services departments, there are many potential uses for tools such as IMPART. The key is finding where data intersects and how those intersections can be exploited.

Managing electronic resources is becoming more complicated as the multitude of those resources increases and their stability decreases. Management tools such as IMPART are now necessary to keep track of what has been purchased and what should be accessible. However, it is just one of many local databases created to address maintenance issues at NC State University. There is no one-and-done solution; this maintenance is a perpetual process, and libraries will have to continue to discover how electronic resources can be managed more effectively in this environment.

"But That's the Way We've Always Done It": Shifting From a Liaison to a Centralized Model of Collection Development

Amanda R. Scull, Collection Development Librarian, Keene State College

Abstract

This session discussed the shift away from a subject liaison model of collection development to a centralized model in a small academic library from the perspective of a newly centralized Collection Development Librarian. The session addressed the limitations of the subject liaison model, the challenges faced during transition, and the functional realities of centralized collection development. I discussed outreach, selection, and assessment as the three major areas where the change to centralization has required new policies and approaches to communication.

Background

Keene State College is a public liberal arts college in Keene, New Hampshire with approximately 4,800 students. One way in which Keene State differs from many libraries is that the librarians have faculty status. This means that Mason Library's eight tenure-track librarians are required to demonstrate teaching, scholarship, and service to the College in addition to their roles within the library. All of the librarians teach instruction sessions as well as full courses within the information studies minor.

Until July of 2014, the librarians utilized a subject liaison model wherein each librarian served as liaison to four or five departments and was responsible for outreach, instruction, and collections work in those areas. There were several issues with this model; namely, the fact that being assigned as a liaison to a department did not necessarily mean that a librarian had any expertise in that subject area. Librarians were not hired with particular liaison areas as part of their qualifications, and most of the librarians had similar backgrounds in the humanities.

Additionally, as job titles, because more specialized the available time and level of interest in collections work, varied among the librarians. No longer were "reference and instruction" librarians being hired, but instead one position became the academic technology librarian, another became the undergraduate experience librarian, and so on. The result from a collections standpoint is that the amount of time devoted to selection, deselection, and assessment manifested in an unbalanced collection.

Shifting the Model

Under the subject liaison model coordination of collections work fell under the access services librarian, as just one of her many and varied responsibilities. The librarians decided that an open position would become a collection development librarian in order to facilitate a shift away from both the subject liaison model and the jack-of-all-trades access services librarian position. The model adopted was a functional liaison team model, which created a collections team and an instruction team. The collections team consists of the collection development librarian, the head of technical services, and the archivist as the three positions that deal most directly with collections. Under the new model, the members of each team are responsible for outreach and for coordinating work in that area.

However, in practice this shift centralized collection development (outside of the archives) under the collection development librarian position. All assessment, acquisitions, deselection, collections outreach, and projects are managed by the collection development librarian position. While all of the librarians are consulted and their input and assistance with collections work is solicited and appreciated, there is no requirement for them to participate. This meant that I needed to streamline processes and prioritize collections work when I arrived on July 1, 2014.

http://dx.doi.org/10.5703/1288284316258

Selection

Prior to my arrival, selection decisions were passed directly from each librarian to the acquisitions manager. This often consisted of a catalog left in her mailbox full of sticky notes or circled entries, or e-mails containing links to resources. This meant that there was very little organization, guidance, or, most importantly, record keeping, and the librarians interested in selection work continued to do so in this manner after the shift. Since part of my responsibilities involve tracking, assessing, and directing acquisitions, as well as managing the budget, I sought a system that would provide a better, more complete view of selection. The head of systems created an internal purchasing database to facilitate this. The front end is a form that librarians complete to suggest an item for the collection, with required fields such as Title and ISBN. On the backend, the suggestions are arranged in table format, contain all of the information necessary to locate the item, and can be exported to Excel.

The database was not immediately well received, mainly because it asked more work of the librarians than their previous way of selecting materials. However, streamlining this process has been extremely beneficial both with regard to time spent on acquisitions and on data management.

Assessment

I was told upon my arrival that a comprehensive assessment of the full print collection had not been conducted, so I embarked upon that project almost immediately in order to approach further changes with a complete understanding of the collection's condition and our needs. I used several different measures: circulation statistics, syllabus analysis, program size analysis, peer library and list comparisons, and the age of the collection. The collection analysis and reporting of the data took approximately eight months to complete, work that I mostly completed myself with the assistance of a support staff person. Under the subject liaison model this workload would have been shared, so this was certainly a challenge under the new model wherein it was mainly my project.

However, the results of the assessment have been invaluable in demonstrating how old the collection is, how drastically circulation is dropping, and how program needs are changing. I used the assessment results to identify four priority areas to focus on each semester over the next three years, beginning with those fields wherein up-to-date information is most important (such as health science).

Outreach

These priority areas are being addressed through outreach to those departments. Under the functional liaison team model, outreach work is meant to be shared among the team members; but in practice it does not make sense for the archivist to meet with the health science department, for example. Thus when one person is managing outreach to 36 departments, it is important that outreach efforts be manageable and purposeful. During the fall of 2015, I met with four departments to share the results of the assessment with them, learn more about their curricula, and solicit their input on acquisitions work. Additional outreach efforts, such as targeted outreach for new resources, has been sidelined in favor of this outreach initiative because there simply is not enough time to do everything.

Deselection

Prior to the collections shift, deselection was handled in what was determined to be the best way possible to promote transparency and avoid political headaches. Approximately 2,000 books would be identified for deselection at a time, and an Excel sheet of titles would be sent to all of the faculty on campus asking for their input. It is no surprise that some people would copy and paste entire sections of the list, if not the whole list itself, and send it back with a message saying that the library must keep those volumes.

Part of targeted outreach to priority areas was shifting this process to a method of targeted deselection as well. I explained the need to conduct deselection to the departments I met with in the context of the assessment data (namely age and circulation). After identifying items for deselection, I invited the faculty members in only those departments to come to the library and review the physical volumes. They could then speak with me about volumes they identified as necessary to keep in the collection. Only a few faculty members did come to review the books, but those who did often had no objections after seeing the condition and obvious age of the print books on the shelf.

Reflections and Future Directions

I have completed a number of projects this year, including a reference weed and shift, video streaming workshops, weeding the bound periodicals and initiating their shift into the main collection, hiring and training a new subscriptions supervisor, and improving budget and spending documentation. This is all in addition to the faculty responsibilities of teaching courses, writing and presenting, and serving in professional organizations and on campus committees.

Centralized collections work is clearly a full-time job, and that can be problematic at Keene State where the librarians are 50% faculty and 50% librarian. It is not possible to be half a collection development librarian, and it therefore can be difficult to juggle administrative and faculty responsibilities. Centralized collection development may be a preferable model for institutions of the same size where the librarians do not have faculty status. When librarians do have those extra responsibilities, having a small centralized collections department or two collections librarians might be preferable.

There are many benefits to the system of centralized collection development, however, particularly at a liberal arts institution where the collection should be considered as a whole instead of in pieces. When one person is overseeing all of this work, the right hand always knows what the left is doing. Additionally, having in-depth knowledge of the resources available is an advantage when providing instruction to students.

Priority areas have been identified for each semester for the next three years so that the print collection can be systematically improved. During this time I also plan to conduct more thorough assessment of electronic resources and further develop some other initiatives that are currently in the early stages of conception.

Acquisitions in a Nutshell

Linda Creibaum, Acquisitions and Serials Librarian, Dean B. Ellis Library, Arkansas State University

Jeff Bailey, Library Director, Dean B. Ellis Library, Arkansas State University

Star Holloway, Serials Access Librarian, Arkansas State University

Abstract

Designed specifically for librarians new to the field of acquisitions, this session featured an informal introduction to the basics of acquisitions librarianship from three standpoints: a veteran acquisitions and serials librarian, a library director with a background in acquisitions, and a librarian who began her first professional appointment in 2013.

The session covered a variety of issues related to the acquisition of both monographs and serials in various formats, plus database and backfile purchases. Discussions included definitions, ordering considerations, avoiding purchase of duplicate resources, negotiating prices and access options, licensing, selecting vendors and jobbers, and various services that vendors' representatives can provide to assist librarians. The presenters discussed various aspects of access versus ownership of e-books and periodicals and the impact of each on space and budgets both current and future, and suggested the best times in the annual budget cycle for different types of spending decisions.

Introduction

The session opened with the introduction of presenters Linda Creibaum, Jeff Bailey, and Star Holloway; a brief description of their professional backgrounds; and a statement that the session was not specific to the procedures, resources, or services of Arkansas State University. Instead, the presentation would be an open presentation of a variety of issues related to library acquisitions, and the fact that every library does things differently due to a variety of factors.

Holloway began with a brief review of terms such as firm order, standing order, license, embargo, and backfiles that led into a conversation about some similarities and differences between acquisitions, collection development, and collection management. The discussion pointed out that there are many varieties of organizational structures for academic libraries and that the makeup of the unit(s) that perform these functions is likely different in almost every library.

Discussion Topics

Creibaum introduced the topic of general ordering considerations for each library. This included the value of obtaining trials before making final database purchasing decisions, and the difference between canceling and not renewing a subscription. Also discussed were issues associated with the purchase or subscription of resources with license agreements and the need for each institution to have an authorized person designated to read and approve each license.

The presenters covered various steps to take when a subscription ends. These include giving the vendor sufficient notice of non-renewal and getting the word to the campus community. Remember to notify library personnel so they can remove the resource from a discovery service, disable and remove links on website(s) and in course management systems, delete records in the library catalog and journal A to Z lists, and update other materials, including user guides.

Creibaum and Bailey discussed their experiences with selecting vendors and ordering resources. Different ordering considerations and/or purchasing or access arrangements can exist for different types of materials. Acquiring e-books includes the decision as to whether to subscribe, purchase, or lease titles via demand-driven acquisition. Print book and media purchasing

http://dx.doi.org/10.5703/1288284316259

involves considerations beyond price and availability such as approval plans, shipping charges, return policies, and the usability of the vendor's website. All these factors, plus any others which may be unique to the individual library, should be considered when choosing a vendor or jobber. Bailey addressed the importance of including customer service and response time as criteria in any bid process that may be required when selecting vendors or a subscription agent.

Holloway then addressed services vendor representatives may be able to provide to assist acquisitions librarians in their jobs. These services may include overlap analyses and title comparisons between resources, combined invoicing, and possibly information on packages of titles for libraries with limited funds or a very specific content need.

Vendors who supply a wide range of products for libraries are often able to list multiple subscriptions on a single invoice, or may be able to modify the start/end dates for database subscriptions to be payable at a more convenient time in the library's budget cycle.

Bailey mentioned the importance of tracking annual expenditures for budget planning purposes, and also that there is a great need for both long and short range budget planning. Long range planning considerations may include platforms that provide legacy access for online journals no longer available from any other source and digital preservation considerations.

As the session drew to a close, Creibaum discussed the role acquisitions can play in weeding and freeing up shelf space, including options to keep, store remotely, or weed print volumes as digital copies are acquired. Librarians were also reminded to carefully check all invoices for errors, including errors in prices, subscription dates, and even the name of the subscriber.

Attendees were advised to consider using end-of-year funds for one-time purchases of either firm order items or static online content such as datasets or journal backfiles, though library personnel should be aware that there are sometimes annual hosting fees for datasets and backfiles.

The Library's Role in the Changing World of Textbooks: Where Do We Go From Here?

Emily Ray, Metadata and Discovery Services Librarian, University of Arkansas at Little Rock

Abstract

This presentation examines the library's role as options proliferate regarding textbooks in higher education—due to the high cost of textbooks. It considers the prioritization of textbooks outside the university and the library, and it covers both the Ottenheimer Library's (at the University of Arkansas at Little Rock—UALR) pilot project to purchase textbooks and the experience of two other libraries with purchasing textbooks, print and electronic. It looks at the growth of open educational resource (OER) textbooks and how they are presented to potential users. The author also discusses the results of three libraries with pilot projects to incentivize faculty to switch to OER textbooks and how these projects impacted the libraries.

The Library's Role in the Changing World of Textbooks: Where Do We Go From Here?

So why is this a topic? Briefly, the cost of textbooks is increasing rapidly. There are many gory statistics, but to quote only one, recently NBC news used Bureau of Labor statistics data to state that from 1977– 2015 textbook costs have increased 1000% (Popken, 2015).

The skyrocketing cost of textbooks is seen as a financial burden on students and negatively impacting students' learning. The increasing cost of textbooks has made it outside universities as a problem. State legislatures, public interest research groups (PIRGs), and main stream media are paying attention to the rise of textbook costs while prices increase for academic journals and the "crisis" for academic presses has not received such attention. Cost of textbooks is a cause célèbre, at least partially, because dealing with the cost of textbooks is easier than addressing the cost of tuition or higher education as a whole.

This topic was the title of a talk at Charleston in 2009, so what has changed since then? Since 2009, there has been the growth of open education resources (OER). In addition to the popularity of OER, more libraries are experimenting with textbooks, and more outside actors are involved. Libraries are increasingly involved formally with teaching and learning and are looking to demonstrate their roles in student retention and student success.

The University of Arkansas at Little Rock's Experience

This is a brief description of the University of Arkansas at Little Rock (UALR). It is a state institution, part of the University of Arkansas system, but not the flagship university. There has been a declining enrollment and many nontraditional students attend UALR. Fall 2015 brought an enrollment of 8,902 students, including undergraduates, graduate students, and PhD candidates in engineering and computer science.

In summer 2014, UALR's provost asked the then library director if the library could provide some free access to textbooks for the fall semester, as cost is identified as the leading factor in students dropping out of UALR. The library was given no additional funds for this endeavor. Prior to this the Ottenheimer Library at UALR had a policy of not purchasing textbooks, but faculty copies of textbooks were placed on reserve.

The Collections team in the library took on this project. They conducted a brief literature review, including reading a 2013 report on Wichita State's 2012 pilot project with e-textbooks revealing high levels of student discontent with e-textbooks. In addition, they surveyed UALR's peers—mainly metropolitan, mid-sized public universities. None of the peer libraries were buying textbooks, but some were thinking about it (Grajek, 2013).

http://dx.doi.org/10.5703/1288284316260

UALR decided to purchase print textbooks and place them on reserve as we were expected to provide access at the start of the semester, with the added benefit that this would bring students into the library where they could see our other services as well. We focused on core curriculum courses—a subset of these are mandatory for first-year students—and looked for classes with large number of sections and high enrollment.

We roughly budgeted $2,000 for this pilot; we spent $1,600 total. For that fiscal year, our total materials budget was $1.4 million (this year it's $1.2 million). Last fiscal year we spent $16,900 on monographic purchases, including this budgeted $2,000. So for UALR, while $2,000 is small, it is not an insignificant amount of money; what we spent purchasing textbooks was almost 10% of our monographic funds for FY15.

For the fall semester we purchased three copies each for two history courses, one theater course, one communications course, one psychology course, one biology course, and one algebra course, totalling $875 for the fall semester. For spring semester, we spent another $758 on predominately science courses from the core curriculum, since these courses have expensive textbooks and were covered less by the first half of the pilot. Specifically, we purchased one anatomy and physiology textbook and two chemistry textbooks.

We did heavily promote in the library. We also e-mailed all faculty about the pilot and brought it up at the Dean's council meeting.

For the pilot, what we bought was heavily used. No textbooks disappeared. The core curriculum history textbook, for which we purchased three copies, in one year had 106, 96, and 97 uses for the three copies respectively. For a core curriculum Theater class, the three items had 34, 30, and 26 uses. The biology textbook items had uses in the 30s and 20s. The college algebra book was our one misstep as it was not used much. For the spring semester textbooks, the anatomy and physiology textbook and one of the two chemistry textbooks were heavily used.

On the flip side, as of fall 2015 UALR has new online-only programs for some degrees, and these textbooks are only available to students on campus. Only a year after our pilot three titles are on new editions; for these the library made the decision to keep the older editions on reserve. UALR expanded the core curriculum in fall 2015. All of the classes for which textbooks were purchased are still part of the core curriculum, but there are an additional ten classes.

Other Libraries Purchasing Textbooks

Interested in the experiences of those doing this on a large scale and with a larger budget than us, I spoke with Eric Elmore Electronic Resources Coordinator at University of Texas at San Antonio (UTSA). UTSA has a student population of 29,000. The library had been receiving requests for textbooks and purchasing them, but not systematically. Beginning in fall 2014, they began identifying requests for textbooks, purchasing and routing them to the reserves desk. They are e-preferred, only purchasing print when requested or when an e-textbook is unavailable. UTSA acquires unlimited multi-user textbooks when possible, or e-books with two or three users. If they see many turnaways, they purchase additional copies or access. Regarding print, fewer of the large introductory class textbooks are available as e-textbooks, and they have been purchasing new print editions for these textbooks, which has proven to be expensive.

There has been very little faculty pushback regarding spending on a textbooks, as the cost of a degree is an issue, and this project is seen as working to support retention. The UTSA library did put this program in their annual report (E. Elmore personal communications, August 25 and 27, 2015).

The Collections team in the UALR library also spoke with the collection development librarian at the University of Central Arkansas, when we were considering options at the start of our pilot. I followed up with Renee LeBeau-Ford, the collection development librarian.

University of Central Arkansas is a state school, not part of the UA system. UCA has predominantly traditional college age students, who live on campus. Their library is open 24 hours a day.

They budget $10,000 a year for purchasing textbooks and have been purchasing textbooks for 5 years. They run a list of textbooks for the upcoming semester against their holdings, and EBSCO e-book availability, to identify what they already have access to. They are e-book preferred, but do take into consideration when a preference for print is expressed. Many of the traditional textbook publishers are not producing e-books for their classes, so they are buying print in those instances.

The library sends a list of the textbooks the library has before the start of each semester to department chairs, or if the chair is known not to send stuff on, they e-mail the faculty directly. Frequently, faculty members ask the library to purchase their textbooks, or one will offer to bring a copy over as a personal copy. They are purchasing new editions, and sending older editions to the main stacks, where they do circulate.

At the start of a semester, students arrive on campus on Sunday and classes start on Thursday. On the first Monday students are in the library to check on their textbooks, and the library posts spreadsheets by department so students can see if their textbooks are available.

LeBeau-Ford stated the project was "hugely popular." After 5 years, there's word of mouth and students know about the textbook program and look for it. Financial aid also has the spreadsheet and if a student's financial aid is late coming in, they can know if their textbooks are available.

LeBeau-Ford described this project as gratifying to work with the faculty (R. LeBeau Ford, personal communications, October 15, 2015).

So far in 2015 I've been talking about buying print books, which is not very innovative and this is an innovation session, but there are other options, most prominently open education resources, or OER. OER have similar goals to open access, but OER are usually licensed, frequently using Creative Commons licensing (n.d.).

Using Creative Commons CC BY licensing, you do not pay to access the content, but you can't make profits off it for yourself, either. You can edit and adapt original content created using this type of licensing as long as you attribute it to the original creator and identify what you've changed.

This would seem to work well for textbooks, which would need to be updated as knowledge continually changes or grows, or at least changes.

Many libraries and other organizations are creating or compiling lists of portals for OER textbooks and resources. I will provide a couple of examples; first: MERLOT (Multimedia educational resource for learning and online teaching, n.d.), created due to the California SB-1053 California Digital Open Source Library legislation (2012) (https://www.merlot.org/merlot/index.htm).

Some of the content listed are collections of academic material or archival material, such as "Documents of the American South" and "Sage American History."

This is Fresno State's portal (n.d.): http://coolfored.org/facultyshowcase.html.

It looks more like traditional textbooks, with descriptions by faculty of how they used these texts in classes. Southern Connecticut State University has a lib guide about OER teaching materials (2015): http://libguides.southernct.edu/c.php?g=7150&p=34680.

I found the Southern Connecticut State portal among the most helpful. It has a list of OER portals, description of OER, and OER policy guidelines from Educause (n.d.). It lists steps for turning classroom materials into OER content and contains a great video testimonial from a physics professor. He describes the following: how he saw an OER textbook in a National Science Foundation (NSF) workshop and tested it by using one module in his course, and then the whole textbook; the adaptions he made under the Creative Commons licensing; students reactions as wholly positive;

and that students could purchase a $13 print textbook instead of a previously $175 textbook.

I only show a couple of portals because there are a lot of these portals, and they seem to have many of the same links to Open Stax, Merlot, Educause's seven steps to OER, etc. But also because it appears that there are 3,000 textbooks, but once you start looking for a specific topic, the process becomes complicated.

SUNY open textbooks (n.d., http://textbooks.opensuny.org/) is an open access textbook publishing initiative established by the State University of New York libraries and is supported by SUNY Innovative Instruction Technology Grants. It looks like there are about 10 textbook titles currently available, and more in progress.

So OER content exists in these resources, but does one use it, or get to faculty to use it?

Encouraging Faculty to Use OER Textbooks

I talked to three libraries involved in pilot processes of incentivizing faculty to work with OER textbooks: those at the University of California, Los Angeles (UCLA), North Carolina State University (NCSU), and University of Minnesota (UMN).

To learn about UCLA's experience, I spoke to Dawn Setzer, director of library communication. Starting in the 2013–2014 school year, UCLA used a fund originally created to cover open access journal publishing fees for faculty and grad students to now offer grants to faculty to switch from proprietary textbooks to alternatives. Grants for an enrollment under 100 students of $1,500 or $2,500 for enrollment above 200 students (n.d.).

Early in their pilot project a mechanical engineering professor wrote up his course notes toward making a textbook, wanted to supplement it with some material from an open textbook, and wanted charts and graphs in a proprietary textbook. The professor contacted the publisher (strategic decision to have the faculty member, not a librarian, contact them) with his request for access to the charts and graphs. The publisher agreed, if the textbook was listed as an optional text for the class at the bookstore.

For a theater class with an expensive collection of plays, the library subscribed to a database that contained the plays. So the cost of the textbook was removed from the student, but really taken on by the library, while the plays were also made available to more students on campus.

To support a Child development class that didn't use a traditional textbook, but course readings and videos of observing children, this content was acquired by the library.

Finally, there was the example of an English professor with a course on Victorian novels. For the professor's course the library digitized some Victorian novels from UCLA's special collections, and then sent them on to HathiTrust (n.d.). However, when a different professor teaches the course on Victorian novels, he or she might not use these novels, as they might want to cover other topics or authors in the field (D. Setzer, personal communication, October 2, 2015).

At North Carolina State University (NCSU), there is the Alt Textbook Project, about which I spoke to Will Cross, director of copyright and digital scholarship (n.d.). They have a similar grant program to that of UCLA. They have a workshop for interested faculty where they go through the process, the goals, and OER issues faculty might encounter. Faculty from undergraduate and some graduate courses participated. The courses that participated were STEM heavy, which makes sense considering NCSU's academic focus. From the first year of the grant program 9 of 11 recipients were creating their own content.

According to Mr. Cross, NCSU is comfortable having the faculty rely on resources that are open for their students, but not to the world. They are working to encourage faculty receiving grants to create truly open content.

However, for their program, they are willing to use fewer open resources, where costs savings will be high for the institution. NCSU describes their program as so far saving $200,000 for students. In NCSU's program, the library has not purchased any additional content, aside from what the grant covered. They are using the grants to purchase, not as a carrot for the faculty to take on extra work of reconsidering their textbooks or creating OER content (W. Cross, personal communication, October 2, and 15, 2015).

For the University of Minnesota Partnership for Affordable Content, I spoke to Shane Nackerud, Technology lead, Library Initiatives.

Similarly, UMN offered grants of $1,000 to $1,500 offered to faculty to consider switching from proprietary textbooks to OER or licensed content (2015). Like UCLA, a mixture of faculty from humanities, sciences, more undergrad than graduate classes participated.

He provided an example of a statistics professor who wanted the grant to create an open web page of content, but not require that content be used in his course. Once informed that wasn't sufficient for the grant, the professor did explore the OER resources available and found some good content, though still not exactly what he wanted. However, the library could license his textbook as a multi-user e-book so 58 students in his class will now no longer have to spend $254. That is a savings of $14,732 for one class in one semester.

So far the library spent $20,000 licensing content for this initiative. Again, students in these instances aren't paying for the expensive textbook, but someone else is. It is worth nothing that the three institutions I spoke to are all state universities, but they are all large ones with substantial budgets.

Mr. Nackerud did share a few examples of resistance. Two faculty members participated in the grant process but did not seem to want to give up their proprietary textbook, and he had to encourage them to look and consider OER materials, but described this as part of the process.

He also relayed the example of a Dean who expressed concern about the project, referencing academic freedom, and the idea that authors make money off of copyright, which are arguments not commonly mentioned in literature regarding OER (S. Nackerud, personal communication, October 5 and 7, 2015).

More Examples on OER and Textbooks

I have another experience to share from my home institution regarding OER textbooks.

UALR is part of the UA system led by the UA Board of Governors, which has created a brand new UA system-wide online-only education program, e-Versity, with lower cost per credit hour than any of the UA branches (n.d.). This is different from UALR's online-only programs and UA Fayetteville's online-only programs.

In one of the four slides advertising e-Versity states "no charge for textbooks" as part of the advertisement. Here, free OER textbooks are for the students' benefit. But not just for the students' benefit, it is also for lower overhead for the institution.

State Legislatures' Interest in OER

I mentioned in the beginning that even state legislatures were interested in the cost of textbooks. And this is just a selection, not all state laws or initiatives regarding textbooks.

The Ohio state legislature is considering a law to eliminate sales tax on textbooks (Siegel & Berliner, 2015) South Carolina is considering a minimum adoption of textbooks for upper level divisions of 2 years and lower level divisions of 3 years to create good buy-back value for students (2015).

This process can be described as nibbling at the edges.

In 2015 Connecticut passed an act concerning the use of digital open source textbooks in higher education. This act creates a consortium that shall "assess the use of high quality and affordable digital open-source textbooks . . . promote the use and access to open-source textbooks . . . and collaborate for the purposes of developing and acquiring open-source textbooks. "

So no real specifics, but this legislature is promoting open source textbooks.

I left the first and most important legislation for last, which was in California, the state that first looked at the issue of textbooks. In 2012 California passed two state laws on this issue (Senate Bill 1052 and Senate Bill 1053), with the aim to "provide for the creation of free, openly licensed digital textbooks for the 50 most popular lower-division college courses offered by California colleges."

However, I had a hard time finding those OER textbooks for the 50 most popular courses in 2015.

The California Open Education Resources Council lists 18 courses with recommended OER textbooks. As the website describes it, "the COOL4Ed Course Showcase will be continually updated during the duration of the project (2014–2016), and it will eventually reflect approximately 50 courses and a number of peer reviewed open textbooks for each course."

I think this illustrates that with a lot of interest and support from different stakeholders, including faculty and university administration, and where state government put in $5 million of state funds, as well as other private grants, it remains difficult to create OER textbooks and be in a position to use them on the scale matching the interest.

In a situation ripped from the headlines, at Cal State Fullerton, in the week of October 20, 2015, one week before this conference, a faculty member was reprimanded for selecting a nondepartmental textbook, instead of the textbook chosen by the department. The reprimanded professor chose a cheaper proprietary textbook combined with OER content. Seventy faculty members have signed a letter supporting him in challenging the reprimand (Reprimanded for Assigning Affordable Textbooks?, 2015).

As the *Inside Higher Ed* column put it, academic freedom of the department to pick a standardized textbook versus the academic freedom of the professor to pick a less expensive textbook? (Jaschik, 2015).

In review, UALR and two other libraries with larger budgets have been purchasing textbooks in print and e-book format, with varying degrees of coverage for courses. The cost is saved from the students, but switched directly to the libraries. The textbooks are still proprietary, but available immediately.

More conceptually, with more innovation, other schools are incentivizing and guiding faculty to switch to OER texts. It has been an involved but beneficial process with a range of products. The cost is saved from the student, and in some of this the cost has been switched to the library, in some instances covered by grants, and in some others OER content has been created and is available to others.

So to respond to the question "where do we go from here?" finding content, guiding others to find content, making that content discoverable, understanding the licensing, determining when it is worthwhile to purchase content, and providing access are all work that is part of librarians' expertise. Librarians can provide valuable and realistic guidance in this endeavor, but it's best to be aware of the immediate financial implications for these projects.

References

California State Senate. (2012, September 27). SB-1052 Public postsecondary education: California Open Education Resources Council. Retreived from http://leginfo.legislature.ca.gov/faces/billNavClient.xhtml?bill_id=201120120SB1052

California State Senate. (2012, September 27). SB-1053 Public postsecondary education: California Open Digital Source Library. Retrieved from http://leginfo.legislature.ca.gov/faces/billNavClient.xhtml?bill_id=201120120SB1053

Creative Commons Attribution—ShareAlike 4.0 International. (n.d.). Retrieved from http://creativecommons.org/licenses/by-sa/4.0/

e-Versity University of Arkansas System. (n.d.). Retrieved from http://eversity.uasys.edu/

Fresno State Affordable Learning Solutions. (n.d.). OER-Textbooks. Retrieved from http://fresnostate.edu/academics/als/textbooks.html

Grajek, S. (2013). Understanding what higher education needs from e-textbooks: An EDUCAUSE/Internet2 Pilot. Retrieved from http://net.educause.edu/ir/library/pdf/ERS1307/ERS1307.pdf

Hilton C. Buley Library at Southern Connecticut State University. (n.d.). Open access resources: Teaching materials. Retrieved from. http://libguides.southernct.edu/c.php?g=7150&p=34680

Jaschik, Scott. (2015, October 21). Can a professor be forced to assign a $180 textbook? *Inside Higher Ed.* Retrieved from https://www.insidehighered.com/quicktakes/2015/10/21/reprimanded-assigning-affordable-textbooks

MERLOT. (n.d.). Retrieved from. https://www.merlot.org/

Minnesota Libraries. (2015, spring). Partnership for affordable content. Retrieved from https://www.lib.umn.edu/elearning/partnership/awards and https://www.lib.umn.edu/elearning/partnership

NCSU Libraries. (n.d.). Alt textbook project. Retrieved from http://www.lib.ncsu.edu/alttextbook

Open Textbooks SUNY. (n.d.). Retrieved from http://textbooks.opensuny.org/

Popken, B. (2015, August 15). College textbook prices have risen 1,041 percent since 1977. *NBC News.* Retrieved from http://www.nbcnews.com/feature/freshman-year/college-textbook-prices-have-risen-812-percent-1978-n399926

Reprimanded for assigning affordable textbooks? (2015, October 21) *Inside Higher Ed.* Retrieved from https://www.insidehighered.com/quicktakes/2015/10/21/reprimanded-assigning-affordable-textbooks

Siegel, J., & Berliner, D. (2015, August 25). Bill would exempt textbooks from Ohio sales tax. *Columbus Dispatch.* Retrieved from http://www.dispatch.com/content/stories/local/2015/08/25/bill-would-exempt-textbooks.html

South Carolina General Assembly. (2015, March 10). S. 528 – Textbooks. Retrieved from http://www.scstatehouse.gov/sess121_2015-2016/bills/528.htm

State of Connecticut General Assembly. (2015, January). An Act concerning the use of digital open source textbooks in higher education, HB-6117. Retrieved from https://www.cga.ct.gov/2015/fc/2015HB-06117-R000224-FC.htm

UALR Core Curriculum. Retrieved from http://ualr.edu/catalogs/undergraduate-catalog/academicpol/competencies-core/

UCLA Library. (n.d.). Affordable course materials initiative. Retrieved from http://www.library.ucla.edu/about/collections/collection-development-initiatives/affordable-course-materials-initiative

Do-It-Yourself Title Overlap Comparisons

Melissa Belvadi, Collections Librarian, University of Prince Edward Island

Abstract

Discovery service indexing content can be highly customizable, which makes traditional title overlap analysis published by third parties less meaningful for a library making new subscription or cancellation decisions. This article presents a method for conducting basic title overlap analyses in-house at minimal cost, tailored to the specific configuration of the library.

Why DIY Comparison?

Whether it be for new programs, new competing products, or cancellations, librarians make decisions about which abstracting and indexing (A&I) and full-text products to subscribe to. Often, we turn to our scholarly literature, where colleagues have performed painstaking comparisons between specific products. Readers could be confident that if they licensed the same product, they would have access to the content that was tested in the article.

However, we now have a new kind of finding tool: the discovery service (DS). DSs are used by many library patrons for research as they would previously have used a single A&I database. They are substantial investments, so librarians making budget-driven subscription decisions need to take their DS into account.

But DS content is highly customizable. This article uses EBSCO Discovery Service (EDS) as the exemplar, but other DSs may be similar.

A library EDS license starts with a basic index, which includes over 250 million citations.

The library then adds whatever databases, A&I or full-text, are licensed with EBSCO. That includes both EBSCO-produced and third-party products, like EBSCO's Business Source, CINAHL, and SocIndex, as well as Medline, ERIC, PsycINFO, and MLA.

Then the library can choose to add any from hundreds of other sources available from third parties. Some, like the Harvard Bibliographic Dataset, are free. Others, such as MathSciNet and Web of Science, are only an option if the library is a mutual customer.

Finally, the library can provide its own metadata to include, known in EDS as a "custom catalog." The Library's literal catalog is the usual first choice. But they can provide other sets such as the metadata from their institutional repository.

EBSCO reports that there are about 850 sources that can be added to the basic index, with up to about 2.5 billion records as of October 2015. It is likely, then, that no two EDS libraries have the same search content available, even aside from the custom catalogs.

So the traditional methods of comparing two products, by either searching sample topics or title overlap, do not provide useful data for other libraries if one of those products is a DS. Each library needs to conduct its own analysis against its DS configuration.

Why Title Overlap Analysis?

There are two common ways to compare A&I products: sample topic search results analysis (STSRA) and title overlap analysis (TOA). STSRA involves searching the products side-by-side with the same set of search topics and then comparing the results, usually by some combination of recall (looking for known good articles that should be in the results) and precision (quality of the relevance of the results). STSRA is the ideal, but to do it effectively requires both significant subject expertise and a substantial number of discipline-specific sample topics that are appropriate for the research demands of the institution. Perhaps a grant can be obtained on rare occasions, but that

http://dx.doi.org/ 10.5703/1288284316261

would not be a method for everyday use. So TOA is the next best option.

TOA involves comparing the indexing coverage of specific journal titles, taking into account depth of indexing (cover-to-cover or selective) and years of coverage.

What TOA does not do is compare the quality of the metadata available in each product. Thus it has serious limitations for collection decision-making. The quality of metadata, particularly controlled-vocabulary subject terms, is very important to a researcher's success. The power of a professionally maintained and carefully applied subject thesaurus should not be taken lightly in such decisions. Some databases, like CINAHL, PsycINFO, and Historical Abstracts, have specialty metadata (e.g., the age and gender of research subjects, the time period of the historical research, etc.) that is valuable to researchers in those specialties in producing high quality results. Because a DS is designed to search literally hundreds of millions or even billions of records, there has never been a time that surfacing to the top of the relevancy ranking the best possible results has been more important.

So TOA should be considered just one tool. In particular it can be helpful in the negative result case, when there is such insufficient overlap that the product under consideration would definitely provide unique indexing content. In that situation, the more difficult STSRA is unnecessary because in the absence of adequate content, significantly poorer results in terms of "recall" is a certainty.

What About Google Scholar?

The one DS that is available for free to all library patrons is Google Scholar (GS). Increasingly, faculty and student researchers are turning to GS before library-licensed databases, with one study suggesting that close to 20% of researchers are using GS first (Hightower & Caldwell, 2010). It is possible that such choices are far more widespread than many librarians realize. So librarians testing A&I product content may want to include GS in their list of "competitors" along with their DS.

Workflow

UPEI's Robertson Library staff have developed a TOA workflow to compare products using Google Sheets, which is very similar to Microsoft Excel, and undergraduate student assistants who are hired primarily to provide technical support to patrons on a scheduled-shift basis. This workflow has been used to evaluate several existing products as well as products under consideration for new subscriptions. This fills up the downtime that students at a service point have when not helping patrons and thus does not require any new funds. Depending on the time of semester and length of the title list, the 10-hour-per-week IT student assistants can complete a TOA in just a few weeks. The task is ideal for that work environment, because the task is done cell by cell, so there is no loss of accuracy when they pause and resume around patron interactions.

Selecting Titles to Compare

TOA does not always mean evaluating every title covered in an index. Every institution has its own research areas of interest, and in some cases, an index may include many journals that are not within that scope.

Further, if the analysis involves an existing subscription, the library may have fairly precise title-level usage data about citations or abstracts viewed by its users. The librarians may thus restrict the analysis to those titles with demonstrated interest by their own patrons.

Some index publishers divide their lists into "core" titles that are fully covered versus "selective" titles which only include specific articles relating to the theme of the index. It is reasonable then to consider only conducting the overlap analysis on the "core" titles, with perhaps a small random sampling of the selective titles.

Finally, when considering products to support an entirely new program area, the primary concern may be to make sure the index covers the "most important" journals, whether that be judged by the faculty or by various external metrics such as impact factor or H index.

This last method is especially useful because unlike the usual methods, which tend to be one-sided in starting with a specific product's content and comparing the DS and GS to that (a process that is inherently biased in favor of the product), this one allows one to discover weaknesses in the product as well as the comparison targets.

However the title list is compiled, they need to be "cleaned up" as much as possible with regard to abbreviations, subtitles, punctuation, and the like, especially if GS will be included as a comparison target, because GS does not provide ISSN searching.

Spreadsheet Use

The recommendation is to have one spreadsheet file with one "master" worksheet, which contains the list of titles of interest and where the analysis will take place. Other worksheets will contain whatever other lists may be used to compare data, such as the coverage data for the product, or title lists of other competing products if the analysis will involve more than just the DS and GS.

A general principle for working with spreadsheets is that when an entire column contains formula-generated values, and the data it is drawn from is not going to change, use "autofill" to populate the entire column, open up a new empty column next to it, copy the entire formula-generated column, then use "Paste Special – values only" to copy all of the data into the new column, finally deleting the original formula-generated column. The reason for this is that maintaining large numbers of formulas (each cell down the column is a separate formula) significantly impairs the response time of the spreadsheet. Tip: autofill only works if it is immediately to the right of a column that has data in every row (otherwise it stops at the first blank).

Handling ISSNs

After establishing the desired title list, the second step is to reconcile ISSNs among the products. Generally the best way to get accurate results is by ISSN searches. However, title lists and data sources can vary as to whether they use the print ISSN, electronic ISSN, or both. Also, the absence of the hyphen in the list can easily cause spreadsheets to treat the ISSNs as whole numbers and drop leading zeros. Here are some tips for getting ISSN columns useful for testing:

1. When importing csv/tsv data into Excel, do not open it directly with Excel. Instead, start with a blank spreadsheet and use Data – Import from file to insert the data into the worksheet. That allows you to specify that the ISSN column(s) be treated as "text."
2. In Google Sheets, if the ISSNs were converted to numbers upon upload, create a corrected column using a formula like this: =text(A2, "0000-0000") (then autofill the column down) where column A has the ISSNs listed as numbers that have lost their leading zeros.
3. If your ISSNs lack hyphens, open a new empty column and use the following formula to add them. This assumes your list starts in row 2 and the ISSN is in column A: =left(A2,4)&"-"&right(A2,4) . Normalizing all of the ISSNs to include the hyphen is recommended because it guarantees that the cell contains text, and not a numeric value.
4. If you have two columns of ISSNs, for print and electronic, normalize both.

Formulas for Data Entry

The third step is to set up the columns to be filled in. Here is an example of a set of columns to use when comparing a list of titles for a potential new index, to GS and to EDS:

- The start/end date coverage of the index being tested:
  - If the vendor provides a list to pull this data from, upload it as another worksheet:
    - Normalize the ISSN data as above.
    - Create a single column combining the start and end indexing dates. For instance, if the start date is in column F and the

end column is in column G, use: =F2&" - "&G2.

- Use either index/match or vlookup to insert this data into the column in the main sheet:
    - Vlookup is easiest if the ISSN column comes before the coverage range. For instance, if your vendor coverage worksheet is called "db" and the ISSN column you will match on is in column C in "db" and column B in the main worksheet, and the combined coverage range is column H, use this formula in the new column on the main worksheet: =vlookup(B2, db!C:H,6, 0) (then autofill). The "6" refers to the fact that column H is the sixth column in the range from C to H, and the "0" tells Excel or Google to only report back an exact match.
    - Index/match can be used instead of vlookup if the coverage column comes before the ISSN column. The equivalent index/match formula for the vlookup situation above is: =index(db!H:H,match(B2,db!C:C,0)). Note that since columns C and H are specified without counting relative position, this method would work if they were switched, whereas vlookup requires the ISSN column to be before the coverage column.

- The number of hits for the title in the index (if available, e.g., a current or trial subscription).
    - If it is possible to create a column of direct persistent links, by either ISSN (ideal) or journal title, into the index, do so as in the examples for GS and EDS below.
    - Otherwise try to give the student as complete a search text as possible to save time and error. For instance, with Proquest's interface, which as of the time this was written did not allow the generation of persistent links by formula, we created this column, and had the student just copy and paste each into the Proquest search box (this example illustrates how to combine both the print and e-ISSN if you have both for maximal accuracy): ="ISSN("&B2&") OR ISSN("&C2&")".
    - The student can retrieve both the total hits and range of coverage years as separate data columns if coverage years were not available as per above.
- Link to search GS by journal name
    - Assuming the title is in column A, and the assistant gets the word "Search" to click on: =hyperlink("http://scholar.google.ca/scholar?as_vis=1&hl=en&as_publication="&A2&"&as_sdt=1,5","Search").

- GS does not offer an ISSN search, so consider results of very short titles that may be substrings of longer journal titles carefully.
- Hit count in GS (result of using the "Search" links): GS allows for a quick filter of results by 2011+, 2014+, or 2015+, or a custom range or just the count of all of the results.
- Link to search EDS by ISSN (in the B column):
  - =hyperlink("http://search.ebscohost.com/login.aspx?direct=true&bquery=IS+("&B2&")&clv0=Y&type=1&site=eds-live&scope=site","Search").
  - If you have both print and e-ISSN, use the print column for EDS searches.
- Hit count in EDS—total results as it appears at the top, which is already deduped.
- Range of dates covered in EDS—the student can see at a glance the starting and ending dates of coverage. This could be important because sometimes the specialty indexes cover earlier years than the dataset that EDS is using does.
- If the index you are testing is actually a part of your DS, like Historical Abstracts is for UPEI's EDS, create a test profile within the DS, which includes everything that your live one does except the one index you are testing. In EDS this is very easy to do as the administrative account service makes it easy to copy an entire profile's settings and then just turn off that one database. In this situation, modify your EDS search link to refer to that profile instead of your default live one, by adding: "&profileid=" and the code you named it in the administrative service.
- If the product being tested is a full-text product, you may also want to include a column with your current full-text holdings. If you can provide a "Search" link column into your holdings (e.g., your A to Z service), provide that column and the separate column for the holdings summary itself.
- You may also have a column indicating if the indexing is "core" in the product being tested, or if it is important to your program, or peer-reviewed.

Once the spreadsheet is set up, complete the first few rows to provide examples to your student assistants. It is also a good way to troubleshoot any problems with linking formulas. Then give it to the assistants to work on.

Analyzing the Collected Data

The fourth step is to analyze the data. How to do this will depend on which columns you have used.

- The easiest first step is to use Data – Filters to see which rows have 0 hits in your DS or GS. If there are many, and if high importance titles are among them (which you also use Filter to see), this might just decide the matter without further analysis.
- You may also want to consider a very small number of hits to be effectively 0. There are a couple of ways to do this depending on if you are using Excel or Google Sheets. But the one that gives the most control is to create calculated columns with criteria for then filtering on.
  - For instance, if you want to see all rows where both GS and EDS have fewer than 100 hits, you could use this formula, where the GS hit count is in column G and the EDS hit count is in column I: =if(and(G2<100,I2<100),0,1). In this example, the column will show 0s when both GS and EDS are below 100, which you can then use Filter on to show matching rows.
  - You could also use COUNTIF at the bottom of that column to get a gross count of the zeros, e.g.

=countif(J2:J250,"0") if the above is in column J from row 2 to 250.

- If you have importance designations (e.g., if you labeled some titles "core"), you may want to compare the index's hits to GS and EDS and count up only for the core titles; if column C has the 'core' label and column D has the index's hits, and G and I as above: =if(and(C2="core",G2<D2,I2<D2),0,1).
- If you prefer more readable labels instead of using 0,1 to indicate criteria matches, you can use words like "good" and "bad" in place of the "0,1" at the end of the IF (use the quotation marks around them); countif will accept strings, e.g., =countif(J2:J250,"good").

Endnote: All spreadsheet formulas with more detailed instructions are available at: https://goo.gl/hgJoJi

References

Hightower, C., & Caldwell, C. (2010). Shifting sands: Science researchers on Google Scholar, Web of Science, and PubMed, with implications for library collections budgets. *Issues In Science & Technology Librarianship, 63*. http://dx.doi.org/10.5062/F4V40S4J

The New Collection Development: Planning and Assessment to Promote Innovation

Daniel C. Mack, Associate Dean, Collection Strategies & Services, University of Maryland

Abstract

Library collections are in the midst of a radical transformation. Rapidly evolving technology, innovations in distributing and accessing content, new models of pricing, repurposing of library spaces, and shrinking collections budgets create a new environment for collection development. This new environment requires that librarians participate in a variety of new collection development activities beyond just selecting content.

In the emerging library collection development landscape librarians must engage with the disciplinary content of collections as well as a range of other areas. New areas of responsibility might include: information technology, including issues of personal data curation; copyright, open access, and scholarly communication; new modes for delivery of content; budgeting, development, fundraising, and stewardship of resources; collections issues regarding space, preservation, curation, and storage of collections in all formats; and integrating collections issues into instruction, reference, readers' advisory, programming and other engagement with the library's users, and funders and other stakeholders.

These and other activities continue to take an increasing amount of time and effort on the part of collection development librarians. In many cases, however, librarians and library administrators are not adequately prepared to incorporate these activities into their portfolios. The audience will engage in a dialog about incorporating new and emerging collection development activities into training programs, strategic plans, work plans, and assessment activities. Attendees will leave with tools for incorporating innovation into their institutions' operations.

We all know that library collections are in the midst of a radical transformation. Rapidly evolving technology, innovations in distributing and accessing content, new models of pricing, repurposing of library spaces, and shrinking collections budgets create a new environment for collection development. This new environment requires that librarians participate in a variety of new collection development activities beyond just selecting content. This paper focuses on academic libraries, and the issues are broadly applicable to libraries of all types and sizes.

In the emerging library collection development landscape librarians must engage with the disciplinary content of collections as well as a range of other areas. Some of the traditional areas of concern for collection development include:

- Subject coverage
- Scope and depth
- Geographic coverage
- Chronological coverage
- Languages
- Formats

With changes in technology, user needs, funding, and library services, collection development personnel have adopted new duties. New areas of responsibility might include:

- Diversity, equity, and inclusion
- Information technology, including issues of personal data curation and bibliographic citation management
- Copyright, open access, digital rights management, and scholarly communication
- New modes for delivery of content, including demand-driven acquisition and other types of evidence-based collection development

http://dx.doi.org/10.5703/1288284316262

- Budgeting, development, fundraising, and stewardship of resources
- Collections issues regarding space, preservation, curation, storage, and access to collections in all formats
- Integrating collections issues into instruction, reference, readers' advisory, programming and other engagement with the library's users, and funders and other stakeholders

These and other activities continue to take an increasing amount of time and effort on the part of collection development librarians. In many cases, however, librarians and library administrators are not adequately prepared to incorporate these activities into their portfolios. This paper addresses the process of incorporating these new collection development issues into the library's planning and assessment programs. It does not focus on the specifics of planning and assessment. A selected bibliography provides recent sources for information about planning and assessment for collection development.

Most libraries address at least some of these emerging issues. However, many libraries do not view these issues through the perspective of collection development activities.

A holistic approach to planning and assessment should not only involve collections issues, but also include collection development personnel. They can bring their unique perspectives to the conversation, as well as ensure that library-wide efforts address collection development priorities and policies. Unfortunately, many libraries focus on collections as objects while excluding the programmatic endeavors that are part of the art and science of collection development. For example, in your library, how is collection development involved in planning and assessment for decisions about matters such as planning for library spaces, acquisition of and training for new technologies, and issues of diversity, equity, and inclusion? All of these concerns affect not just library collections, but also the art and science of collection development. How can planning and assessment holistically incorporate collection development to encourage innovative ideas and new projects?

In the 21st century we have incorporated new roles for collection development librarians. The transformation from bibliographer to subject specialist has already happened in most academic libraries. As part of this metamorphosis, librarians with collection development responsibilities may now also serve as liaisons to specific user communities; act as teachers for information literacy, media use, and lifelong learning; mentor users as research consultants and interpreters of content; and serve as coordinators of spaces and technologies that promote use of collections. These new roles are necessary to promote innovation and foster success among our users. Holistic collection development planning and assessment require:

- A library-wide commitment to a holistic view of not just collections, but also of collection development
- Engagement and outreach beyond the library and the academy
- Accountability at every level, including frontline personnel, supervisors, department heads, and senior administrators
- Ongoing planning and assessment to direct resources to strategic priorities
- Support for innovation, which by definition means doing new things, or doing old things differently

Individual personnel should incorporate innovation, assessment, and planning into their own work plans, which should likewise inform departmental tactical plans. The library's organization-wide strategic planning should both reflect and inform departmental and individual planning activities.

Administrators can incorporate innovation throughout every level of planning in several ways:

- Asking each subject specialist, curator, archivist, or other collection development librarian to identify how their collection development activities can support innovation

- Incorporating at least one collection development goal that supports an innovative initiative into each librarian's work plan
- Always focusing on developing *user-focused* collections
- Being an advocate for both collections and users

For example, individual work plans could include activities such as:

- Supporting development of a library maker space by de-duplicating print serials runs for which the library has perpetual access to reliable digital surrogates
- Supporting diversity, equity, and inclusion by working with acquisitions to ensure that licenses for digital resources permit reformatting of content for users with special needs
- Supporting faculty grant applications by collaborating with technology personnel to advise on data curation requirements

One important issue to address is how to identify relevant data to collect and analyze, and how to employ this data in the creation of meaningful assessment measures relating to new collection development activities. Some specific examples from individual work plans might include the following questions:

- How many volumes can I withdraw? Translate this into how many square feet of library space can be repurposed to support the new innovative maker space.
- How many licenses will I review? How many users requested assistance with content reformatting?
- How many faculty did I assist with grants? What is the total dollar value of the grants?

There are two important considerations to keep in mind. First, who will coordinate data collection? Establishing specific personnel responsible for gathering, analyzing, and reporting data is vital. And second, everyone in the organization must recognize that not everything is quantifiable. When appropriate, any assessment plan including collection development should identify qualitative measures as well.

Of course, planning and assessment to support innovation requires not only action on the part of frontline personnel, but also commitment and effort from supervisors and administrators. Management can begin by taking some initial steps:

- Requiring innovation in individual work plans
- Rewarding success and permit failure. Note: success in this case means trying something new that supports strategic priorities. Exploration sometimes must permit failure.
- Engaging collection development librarians in decisions about spaces, programs, and technology in all aspects of library planning
- Providing tools, technology, and resources necessary for new initiatives
- Being an advocate for your collection development librarians within the library, throughout the institution, to the central administration, and to external partners
- Making middle managers central to successful planning and assessment in a large organization
- *Not calling something a priority if you are unwilling to allocate resources to it*

Assessing collection development should be an ongoing activity. Unfortunately, many libraries confuse analysis of *collections* with assessment of *collection development activities*. Assessment can include issues such as evaluation of *collection content* to redirect resources in support of changing mission and goals of the institution, including curricular changes, redirection of the research enterprise, especially if the institution supports advanced research, and the needs of other stakeholders such as citizens for land-grant institutions. Assessment of *collection formats* can enable the library to make creative and informed decisions about leveraging budgets, supporting the needs of specific disciplines, and empowering users with special needs. Assessment of *collection spaces and facilities* can help in the development of technology-rich, collaborative spaces that promote innovation and creativity, as well as provide for excellent, state of the art support for print and other legacy formats (this is also a good opportunity to educate stakeholders that user spaces *are* collections spaces). Assessment of *collection-related technology* can facilitate discovery, access, and use of collections in all media and formats, and can also offer users new tools to explore the content of collections and to create new information.

Many libraries already do many of these activities, but may not be coordinating, budgeting, or evaluating these activities holistically. A holistic approach requires that the library be programmatic in it its planning and assessment endeavors. A move from *random activities* to *demonstrable results* is as much a change of mind-set as it is a change of action. To make this happen, a library must:

- Incorporate support for innovation into collection development activities
- Include activities in individual work plans, departmental tactical plans, and library-wide strategic priorities
- Hold frontline personnel, managers, and administrators accountable
- Work with your institutional culture
- Keep it simple and start small

Many librarians and managers have found that checklists are one easy and effective way to keep track of new activities. A variety of widely available formats makes the creation of useful checklists easy. Libraries can use Word, PDFs, web forms, or whatever other format works best for their institution. Some content for a planning and assessment checklist for collection development librarians includes:

- Reviewing collection development policies: do they address spaces, technology, diversity, and other issues?
- Polling faculty and students for new initiatives in teaching and research and other innovation endeavors
- Asking the following questions: what priorities drive the rest of the library, and what are their synergies with your collection development activities?

As in every collection development activity, communication and collaboration are the keys to success.

Managers and senior administrators can also benefit from a checklist covering such issues as:

- Providing staff with the training, technology, tools, and other resources necessary for innovation
- Involving collection development librarians with planning and assessment at every level
- Viewing collection development librarians as experts and resources for user needs in all library programs and operations

It is worth repeating that, as in every new initiative, communication, and collaboration are the key to success.

References

Agee, J. (2005). Collection evaluation: A foundation for collection development. *Collection Building*, *24*(3), 92–95. http://dx.doi.org/10.1108/01604950510608267

Asogwa, B. E. (2014). Libraries in the information age: A measure of performance, competencies and constraints in academic libraries in Nigerian universities. *Electronic Library*, *32*(5), 603–621. http://dx.doi.org/10.1108/EL-07-2012-0097

Association for Library Collections & Technical Services (ALCTS). (n.d.). Collection assessment resources. Retrieved November 12, 2015, from http://www.ala.org/alcts/resources/collect/collmgt/collasmt

Austenfeld, A. M. (2009). Building the college library collection to support curriculum growth. *Collection Management*, *34*(3), 209–227. http://dx.doi.org/10.1080/01462670902975027

Blake, J. C., & Schleper, S. P. (2004). From data to decisions: Using surveys and statistics to make collection management decisions. *Library Collections Acquisitions & Technical Services*, *28*(4), 460–464. http://dx.doi.org/10.1016/j.lcats.2004.09.002

Bobal, A. M., Mellinger, M., & Avery, B. E. (2008). Collection assessment and new academic programs. *Collection Management*, *33*(4), 288–301. http://dx.doi.org/10.1080/01462670802369875

Borin, J., & Yi, H. (2011). Assessing an academic library collection through capacity and usage indicators: Testing a multi-dimensional model. *Collection Building*, *30*(3), 120–125. http://dx.doi.org/10.1108/01604951111146956

Brennan, D. (2015). Collection assessment and the library liaison program. *Pennsylvania Libraries: Research & Practice*, *3*(1), 41–52. http://dx.doi.org/10.5195/palrap.2015.88

Brown, J. M., & Stowers, E. D. (2013). Use of data in collections work: An exploratory survey. *Collection Management*, *38*(2), 143–162. http://dx.doi.org/10.1080/01462679.2013.763742

Carroll, D., & Cummings, J. (2010). Data driven collection assessment using a serial decision database. *Serials Review*, *36*(4), 227–239. http://dx.doi.org/10.1016/j.serrev.2010.09.001

Chadwell, F. A. (2009). What's next for collection management and managers? Successful collaboration. *Collection Management*, *34*(3), 151–156. http://dx.doi.org/10.1080/01462670902974921

Chan, G. R. Y. C. (2008b). Aligning collections budget with program priorities: A modified zero-based approach. *Library Collections Acquisitions & Technical Services*, *32*(1), 46–52. http://dx.doi.org/10.1016/j.lcats.2008.06.001

Ciszek, M., & Young, C. L. (2010). Diversity collection assessment in large academic libraries. *Collection Building*, *29*(4), 154–161.

DeVoe, K. (2006).Collection assessment in the digital age. *Against the Grain*, *18*(5), 1–18.

Corrigan, A. (2005). The collection policy reborn: A practical application of web-based documentation. *Collection Building*, *24*(2), 65–69. http://dx.doi.org/10.1108/01604950510592689

Costello, L. (2015). Assessment of undergraduate-driven acquisitions at a small college library shows both costs and benefits. *Evidence Based Library & Information Practice*, *10*(1), 92–94.

Craig, C. (2010). Collections assessment: A dubious investment. *Against the Grain*, *22*(2), 42–44.

Crosetto, A., Kinner, L., & Duhon, L. (2008). Assessment in a tight time frame: Using readily available data to evaluate your collection. *Collection Management*, *33*(1/2), 29–50. http://dx.doi.org/10.1080/01462670802157908

Danielson, R. (2012). A dual approach to assessing collection development and acquisitions for academic libraries. *Library Collections, Acquisitions, & Technical Services*, *36*(3/4), 84–96. http://dx.doi.org/10.1016/j.lcats.2012.09.002

Franklin, B. (2012). Surviving to thriving: Advancing the institutional mission. *Journal of Library Administration*, *52*(1), 94–107. http://dx.doi.org/10.1080/01930826.2012.630244

Hoeth, K. (2005). Meeting the accountability challenge. *Library Issues*, *26*(1), 1–4.

Kelly, M. (2014). Applying the tiers of assessment: A holistic and systematic approach to assessing library collections. *Journal of Academic Librarianship*, *40*(6), 585–591. http://dx.doi.org/10.1016/j.acalib.2014.10.002

Knowlton, S. A., Sales, A. C., & Merriman, K. W. (2014). A comparison of faculty and bibliometric valuation of serials subscriptions at an academic research library. *Serials Review*, *40*(1), 28–39. http://dx.doi.org/10.1080/00987913.2014.897174

Leonard, M. F., Haas, S. C., & Kisling, V. N. (2010). Metrics and science monograph collections at the Marston Science Library, University of Florida. *Issues in Science & Technology Librarianship, 62*(62).

Leyham, A. (2008). Exploring interlibrary loan usage patterns and liaison activities: The experience at a US university. *Interlending & Document Supply*, *36*(4), 218–224. http://dx.doi.org/10.1108/02641610810919570

Mack, D. C. (2014a). Beyond the bibliographer: Assessing collection development activities in the new digital library, in D. C. Mack and G. W. White (eds.), *Assessing liaison librarians: Documenting impact for positive change* (pp. 71–80). Chicago: ACRL.

Mack, D. C. (2014b). Designing and implementing a liaison assessment program, in D. C. Mack and G. W. White (eds.), *Assessing liaison librarians: Documenting impact for positive change* (pp. 139–144). Chicago: ACRL.

Mack, D. C. (2007). Library liaisons and the organization: An open system view of collection development in the academic library. *Against the Grain*, *19*(5), 32–38.

Martin, H., Robles-Smith, K., Garrison, J., & Way, D. (2009). Methods and strategies for creating a culture of collections assessment at comprehensive universities. *Journal of Electronic Resources Librarianship*, *21*(3/4), 213–236. http://dx.doi.org/10.1080/19411260903466269

Masuchika, G. (2012). Building by benchmarking: A method of creating and evaluating an Asian American studies collection. *Library Collections Acquisitions & Technical Services*, *36*(1–2), 1–7. http://dx.doi.org/10.1016/j.lcats.2012.03.001

McClure, J. Z. (2009). Collection assessment through WorldCat. *Collection Management*, *34*(2), 79–93. http://dx.doi.org/10.1080/01462670902722213

Mcclurg, C., Stieda, V., & Talsma, N. (2015). Comparing subscription-based anatomy e-resources for collections development. *Medical Reference Services Quarterly*, *34*(3), 282–295. http://dx.doi.org/10.1080/02763869.2015.1052690

Meier, J. J. (2010). Solutions for the new subject specialist librarian. *Endnotes, 1*(1), F1–F10.

Nagra, K. A. (2009). The evaluation of use of electronic resources and services in academic libraries: A study of e-metrics and related methods for measurement and assessment. *Journal of the Library Administration & Management Section, 5*(3), 28–41.

Newton Miller, L., Sharp, D., & Jones, W. (2014). 70% and climbing: E-Resources, books, and library restructuring. *Collection Management, 39*(2/3), 110–126. http://dx.doi.org/10.1080/01462679.2014.901200

Obrig, K., Lee, Y., Yohannes, S., Brown, S., & Williams, L. (2011). Conducting a journal assessment using an enhanced ms access database. *Journal of Electronic Resources in Medical Libraries, 8*(1), 35–49. http://dx.doi.org/10.1080/15424065.2011.551489

Oluwakemi, T. K., & Adeyemi, J. A. (2010). Acquisition and use of library resources in a university of technology: A statistical record assessment. *Library Philosophy & Practice*, 1–5.

Phillips, L. L., & Williams, S. R. (2004). Collection development embraces the digital age—A review of the literature, 1997–2003. *Library Resources & Technical Services, 48*(4), 273–299.

Poole, J. (2009). Academic branch libraries: Assessment and collection development. *Journal of Library & Information Services in Distance Learning, 3*(3/4), 192–205. http://dx.doi.org/10.1080/15332900903182655

Prottsman, M. F. (2011). Communication and collaboration: Collection development in challenging economic times. *Journal of Electronic Resources in Medical Libraries, 8*(2), 107–116. http://dx.doi.org/10.1080/15424065.2011.576585

Saunders, L. (2015). Academic libraries' strategic plans: Top trends and under-recognized areas. *Journal of Academic Librarianship, 41*(3), 285–291. http://dx.doi.org/10.1016/j.acalib.2015.03.011

Singh, H., & Mahajan, P. (2015). Library collection assessment: A case study of two universities in the region of Punjab, India. *Chinese Librarianship, 39*, 52–69.

Sinha, R., & Tucker, C. (2005). New program growth and its impact on collection assessment at the UNLV Libraries. *Library Hi Tech, 23*(3), 362–371. http://dx.doi.org/10.1108/07378830510621775

Stoller, M. (2005). Building library collections: It's still about the user. *Collection Building, 24*(1), 4–8. http://dx.doi.org/10.1108/01604950510576065

Streby, P. (2005). The conspectus: Time for a comeback? *Against the Grain, 17*(3), 54–58.

Taylor, M., & Heath, F. (2012). Assessment and continuous planning: The key to transformation at the University of Texas Libraries. *Journal of Library Administration, 52*(5), 424–435. http://dx.doi.org/10.1080/01930826.2012.700798

Teel, L. M. (2008). Applying the basics to improve the collection. *Collection Building, 27*(3), 96–103. http://dx.doi.org/10.1108/01604950810885997

Trail, M. A., Chang-FitzGibbon, K., & Wishnetsky, S. (2012). Using assessment to make difficult choices in cutting periodicals. *Serials Librarian, 62*(1–4), 159–163. http://dx.doi.org/10.1080/0361526X.2012.652931

Tucker, C. (2007). Collection development: Current options and future concerns. *Against the Grain, 19*(5), 44–50.

Tucker, J. C. (2009). Collection assessment of monograph purchases at the University of Nevada, Las Vegas Libraries. *Collection Management, 34*(3), 157–181. http://dx.doi.org/10.1080/01462670902962959

Urquhart, C. (2005). Assessing impact: Let us count the ways? *Library & Information Update, 4*(12), 26–28.

Waller, J. H. (2013). Undergrads as selectors: Assessing patron-driven acquisition at a liberal arts college. *Journal of Interlibrary Loan, Document Delivery & Electronic Reserves, 23*(3), 127–148. http://dx.doi.org/10.1080/1072303X.2013.851052

Way, D. (2009). The assessment of patron-initiated collection development via interlibrary loan at a comprehensive university. *Journal of Interlibrary Loan, Document Delivery & Electronic Reserves, 19*(4), 299–308. http://dx.doi.org/10.1080/10723030903278374

Wexelbaum, R., & Kille, M. A. (2012). The relationship between collection strength and student achievement. *Advances in Librarianship, 35*, 113–132. http://dx.doi.org/10.1108/S0065-2830(2012)0000035009

White, G. W. (2004). Collaborative collection building of electronic resources: A business faculty/librarian partnership. *Collection Building, 23*(4), 177–181. http://dx.doi.org/10.1108/01604950410564500

Wiersma, G. (2010). Collection assessment in response to changing curricula: An analysis of the biotechnology resources at the University of Colorado at Boulder. *Issues in Science & Technology Librarianship, 61*.

Wisneski, R. (2008). Collection development assessment for new collection development librarians. *Collection Management, 33*(1/2), 143–159. http://dx.doi.org/10.1080/01462670802158088

Does Format Matter? Reader Preferences in an Academic Library Context

Jennifer L. Robertson, EResource & Mathematics Web and Scholarly Communications Librarian, University of Toronto Libraries

Weijing Yuan, Head, Licensing & eResource Acquisitions, University of Toronto Libraries

Marlene van Ballegooie, Metadata Librarian, University of Toronto Libraries

Abstract

Although many academic libraries have dramatically increased their e-book acquisitions in recent years, questions linger about format preference. When a scholarly monograph is made available in both print and electronic formats, which format will users prefer? Does format even matter? At the University of Toronto Libraries, we analyzed usage data for scholarly monographs from three key university presses, covering thousands of titles over several years of publication. By comparing print and e-book usage patterns of identical titles, our goal was to examine format preferences and determine if there are differences in usage across subject disciplines or publishers. Through this analysis, our aim is to question whether continued acquisition of the same content in multiple formats is necessary and desirable, especially in an era of rapid technological change, increased pressure on library acquisitions budgets, and diminishing physical storage space.

Introduction

Integrating e-books into a library's collection development strategy requires understanding of how they are used relative to their print counterparts. When a scholarly monograph is made available in both print and electronic formats, which format will users prefer? Does format even matter? Are the same titles used in both formats? Are e-books used more as they are more accessible? Do usage patterns vary by subject or publisher? This study tried to answer these questions by analyzing usage data for e-books from three key university presses, covering thousands of titles over several years of publication, which were available in the University of Toronto Libraries collections.

The University of Toronto Libraries is comprised of forty-four libraries on three campuses and has rich and diverse collections that serve the teaching and research needs of the University's 67,000 students and over 7,000 faculty members. The collection development department in the central library system usually licenses electronic resources for the entire University. Other libraries have acquisitions budgets independent of the central library to meet local needs.

Over the last decade and a half, the library's e-book collections have grown tremendously and there are now close to 1.7 million e-books. The library has focused on licensing e-books for perpetual access, with unlimited concurrent users and without restrictive DRM whenever possible, and purchasing frontlist packages directly from publishers. For content in humanities and social sciences, even where frontlist e-book collections were licensed, print copies were still provided through the central library's approval plans as long as they fit the profiles. As a result, the library has built a large pool of titles with print and electronic equivalents.

Scope and Methodology

This book study focused on analyzing the usage of 6,555 print and online equivalents for three university presses: Oxford University Press, Cambridge University Press, and Duke University Press. For Oxford University Press, the study was limited to 3,624 Oxford Scholarship Online (OSO) titles with imprint years between 2010 and 2014. In the Cambridge Books Online collection, we analyzed 2,121 frontlist titles with imprint years between 2012 and 2014. Finally, for Duke University Press, 810 titles from the e-Duke Book

http://dx.doi.org/10.5703/1288284316263

Scholarly Collections with imprint years between 2008 and 2014 were considered for analysis. In all three collections, the backlist titles were excluded from the study due to the fact that the print and electronic versions were not available to users simultaneously.

Print data collection centered upon batch searching ISBNs against our Sirsi ILS system using a Z39.50 client. Once the resulting MARC records were de-duplicated and verified for correctness, the basic bibliographic elements were extracted from the MARC records. To obtain data pertaining to the individual copies of the print titles, custom API queries were used to retrieve the call numbers, number of physical copies, the circulation counts, and the date of last circulation. In cases where the library had multiple copies of a particular title, the data was aggregated to represent the total usage for the title. For the electronic data collection, we downloaded the COUNTER BR2 reports for all available years and merged them into a master spreadsheet for each vendor. This allowed for the calculation of monthly and yearly totals. Once all of the electronic usage data was collected, the ISBN was used as the match point to combine the print and electronic usage data into one master list.

Limitations

In the data collection process we encountered some limitations worth noting. The first limitation was that our print and electronic use data was not fully compatible. With the print data, we were only able to obtain the total charges for a title and the last date that the book was charged. Therefore, while we had a record of electronic usage by month and year, we could not get comparable statistics for the print equivalent. Inconsistencies in the COUNTER reports were also noted in the data collection process. For example, through the course of the study both Duke and Oxford switched from COUNTER 3 to COUNTER 4, and Duke migrated platforms from ebrary to Highwire, which likely affected how different vendor sites counted a "use." For this study, we consider Oxford, Cambridge, and Duke on the new Highwire platform to be counting chapters or equivalent, and Duke on ebrary to be counting all uses as a section. Another limitation of the COUNTER BR2 reports is that only used titles were included in the report. Without a full list of titles available on each platform, we had to make the assumption that the electronic version was available at same time as the print version and that if a title was missing from the BR2 reports this indicated that there was zero usage. In the electronic data collection process we also observed that COUNTER data was not available for the full date range of each press. For example, although we had print and online equivalents for Oxford since 2010, we could not get COUNTER data until March 2011. A final limitation worth mentioning is that the content we have locally loaded is unaccounted for in the study. For each of the university presses considered, we have an equivalent set of e-books loaded on local servers. However, due to the fact that we could not obtain compatible statistics for this content, we were required to exclude the locally loaded versions of the e-books from the study.

Results

Title Use by Format

Overall, close to 80% of books were used at least once, and patrons at the University of Toronto showed a slight preference for print. Print books were used 1.16 times more frequently than online books, where 66% of print books and 57% of online books were used at least once. Looking at the presses individually, Oxford print books were used 1.45 times more frequently than online books, showing a much stronger tendency to choose print. Use of Cambridge books was more balanced with a slight preference for online books, which were used 1.16 times more frequently than print, and Duke's print books were chosen only slightly more often than online. Oxford had the highest percentage of unused books at 24%, closely followed by Cambridge at 22%, while Duke's collection was very highly used with almost 90% of Duke's titles used at least once. Furthermore, Duke had the highest percentage of books used in both formats at close to 70%, with Oxford and Cambridge trailing behind at between 40–45%.

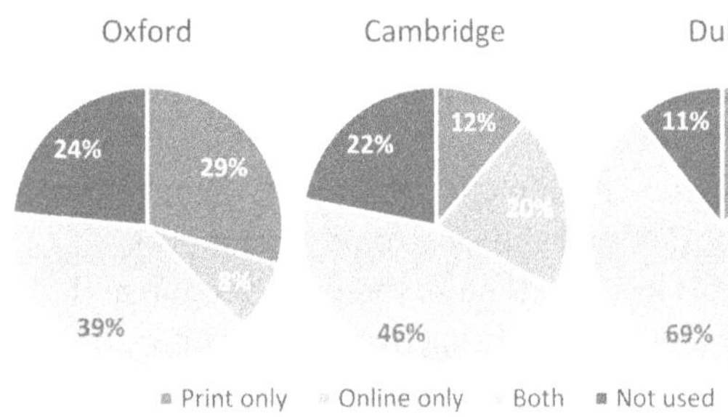

Figure 1. Title use by format.

Number of Titles by Publication Year

These column charts display the number of titles used by format and publication year. Looking at each press, the number of used print and online books progressively decreased in the last three publication years, most likely because newer books have had less time to be discovered and used. For Oxford, the gap between used print and online titles widened unexpectedly for the 2013 and 2014 imprint years, and Duke showed a larger than expected decrease in used online titles for 2013.

Percentage of Titles by Year Last Charged

For print books that circulated at least once, 77% were checked out in the last year, and the last two years accounted for over 90% of all title circulations, ranging from 89% for Oxford to 97% for Cambridge. So print books are still circulating, online has not replaced print, and most books that haven't been used at all continue to be used.

Total Use by Publication Year

Between the three presses, there were 30,805 print circulations and 351,752 online section views or downloads during the study period. Oxford had the highest number of circulations, but also the largest collection of books. Duke had the highest online use despite its smaller collection size, but this is likely due to the earlier start date and the difference in how the ebrary platform counts use. Use for Duke was also significantly smaller for the 2013 and 2014 imprint years and, while we expect newer books to have generated less use, this very large decrease is also a likely side effect of the platform migration.

Percentage of Print and Online Use by Range

Print and online use was also grouped into predefined ranges. For print books, the majority of use fell between 2 to 5 circulations with a very small proportion of use at 21 and over. For online books, the majority of use fell between 1 to 10 uses with a very small proportion of use generated at 51 and up. In both formats, Duke had a much larger proportion of books in the highest ranges.

Format Preference by Subject

After examining each university press collection as a whole, we analyzed them by subject.

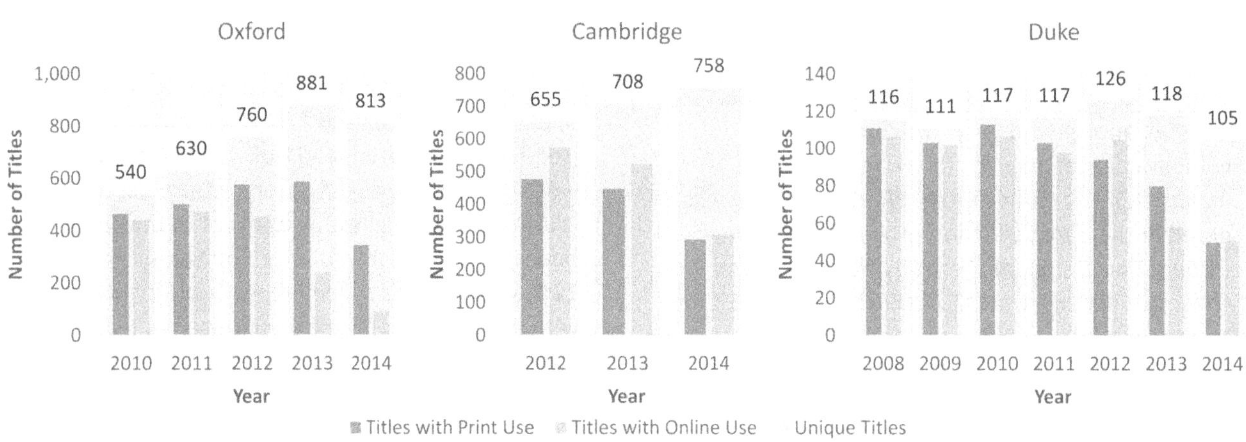

Figure 2. Number of titles by publication year.

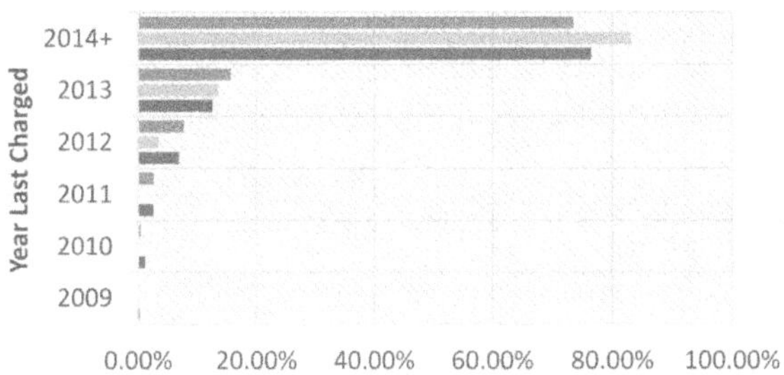

	2009	2010	2011	2012	2013	2014+
All	0.05%	0.46%	1.89%	6.38%	14.56%	76.67%
OUP	0.00%	0.49%	2.63%	7.72%	15.61%	73.55%
CUP	0.00%	0.00%	0.00%	3.38%	13.51%	83.11%
Duke	0.31%	1.22%	2.60%	6.87%	12.52%	76.49%

Percent of Used Collection

Figure 3. Percentage of titles by year last charged.

Categorizing titles by LC class produced 20 collection subsets for Oxford and Cambridge and 19 collection subsets for Duke. For all collections, subjects with less than 11 titles per subject were excluded.

To analyze the amount of use for both formats by subject, we focused on relative use. Previously we compared counts of used and not used books in both formats. With relative use, we compared the proportion of use for a subject relative to its size. A relative usage factor was calculated separately for each subject and format by dividing the proportion of use by the proportion of the subject within the collection.

Next we compared each relative usage factor to its expected use to determine whether a format generated use above or below the expected value. For example, if a subject's size takes up 25% of the total collection, it is expected to generate 25% of the collection's total use, and when this happens the relative usage factor equals 1. Where factors were greater than 1, the subject was well used in that format and generated more use than expected. For factors less than 1, the subject was underused. The amount a relative usage factor diverges from 1 indicates the percentage at which the subject is over- or underperforming. For example, for a subject with a relative usage factor of 1.20, use was 20% higher than expected, or 120% of its expected use, and for a subject with a relative usage factor of 0.70, use was 30% lower than expected, or 70% of its expected use.

After calculating the relative usage factors for each subject and format, we plotted the factors for online use against the factors for print use by subject on a scatterplot to view the overall pattern. Horizontal and vertical lines were inserted at 1 to indicate the expected use for each format. Comparing relative usage factors across all three presses, we found that for most subjects the use of one format was tied to the use of the other. Many subjects clustered around the expected use; if a subject was popular, use tended to be high for both formats and if unpopular, low for both formats. There were, however, subjects for each press that had relatively high or low use in one format only. For example, Oxford Technology and Cambridge Medicine had much

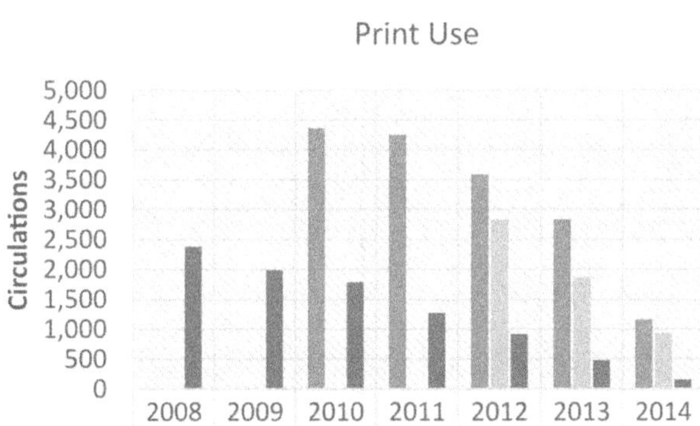

	2008	2009	2010	2011	2012	2013	2014
OUP	0	0	4,363	4,253	3,588	2,834	1,159
CUP	0	0	0	0	2,830	1,867	927
Duke	2,382	1,991	1,786	1,274	915	479	157

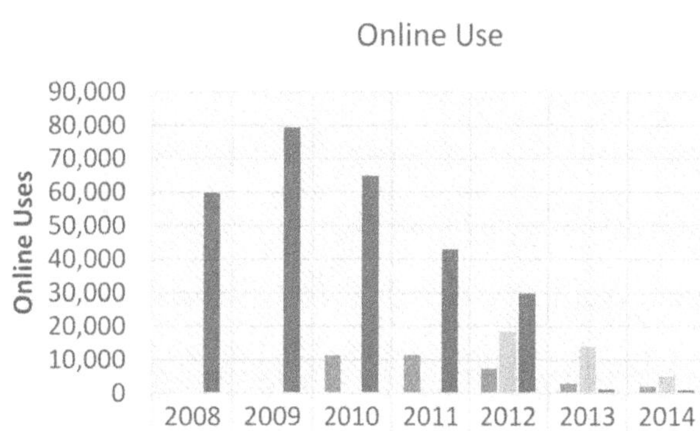

	2008	2009	2010	2011	2012	2013	2014
OUP	0	0	11,31	11,40	7,363	2,969	2,072
CUP	0	0	0	0	18,50	13,86	5,126
Duke	59,83	79,43	64,87	42,99	29,75	1,227	1,020

Figure 4. Total use by publication year.

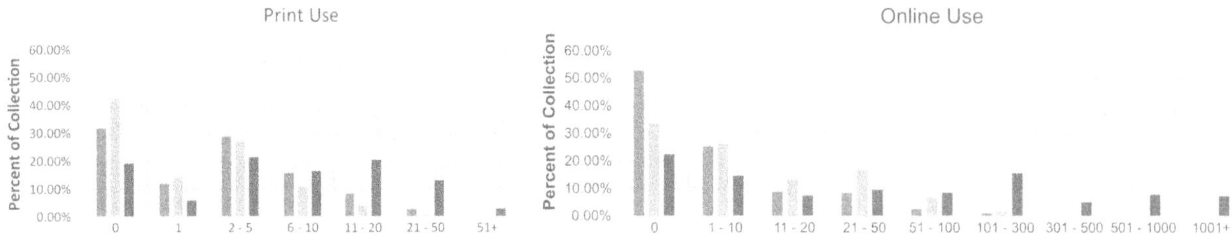

Print Use	0	1	2 - 5	6 - 10	11 - 20	21 - 50	51+
All	33.76%	12.02%	27.44%	14.42%	8.59%	3.30%	0.47%
OUP	31.82%	12.03%	28.89%	15.89%	8.50%	2.68%	0.19%
CUP	42.62%	14.29%	27.25%	11.08%	4.20%	0.57%	0.00%
Duke	19.26%	6.05%	21.48%	16.54%	20.49%	13.21%	2.96%

Online Use	0	1 - 10	11 - 20	21 - 50	51 - 100	101 - 300	301 - 500	501 - 1000	1001+
All	42.97%	24.45%	10.27%	11.58%	4.84%	3.16%	0.73%	1.05%	0.95%
OUP	52.98%	25.47%	9.02%	8.64%	2.65%	1.10%	0.08%	0.03%	0.03%
CUP	33.66%	26.40%	13.39%	17.30%	7.12%	1.84%	0.14%	0.14%	0.00%
Duke	22.59%	14.81%	7.65%	9.75%	8.64%	15.80%	5.19%	8.02%	7.53%

Figure 5. Percentage of print and online use by range.

higher use than expected for online and less than expected use for print.

Difference Between Print and Online Usage Factors

To explore format preference in more detail and help identify subjects where user preference for one format over the other was strong, we analyzed the gap between print and online relative usage factors by plotting the difference on a bar chart. Each bar represents a subject and the bar color indicates the preferred format. The endpoints of each bar are equal to the factors themselves, so the right edge of each bar is the factor for the preferred format and vice versa. The length of each bar is equal to the gap between the subject's print and online relative usage factors. Therefore, the longer the bar the more preference was shown for one format over the other.

Several subjects stood out either because of the substantial gap between print and online relative usage factors or the large distance from the line defining expected use. Some subjects seemed popular with the entire bar well to the right of the line of expected use, while others had bars well to the left and were underused in both formats. For Oxford, print exceeded online in 11 of 17 subjects, while the split was more even for Cambridge and Duke with just over half of subjects with a print preference. Where there were moderate to large gaps in relative format use, it was not the same subjects across all three presses, and a format preference exhibited by one press could be the opposite for another press. And while Oxford and Cambridge had several subjects with large gaps in format preference, Duke's relative usage factors for print and online tended to correspond more closely with gaps not nearly as large, which is consistent with Duke's more even format use.

Discussion and Conclusions

Does Format Matter?

When a book is available in both print and electronic formats, which format will users

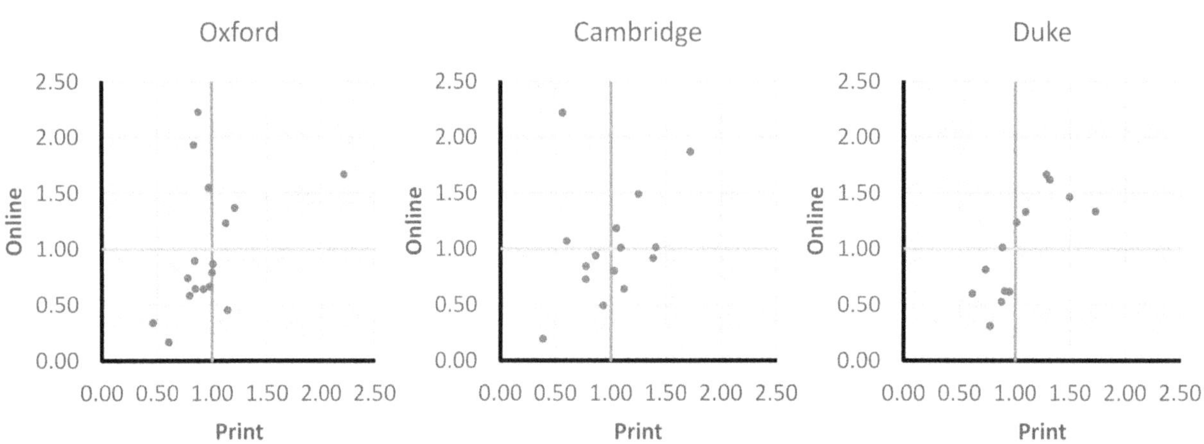

Figure 6. Format preference by subject: print versus online usage factors.

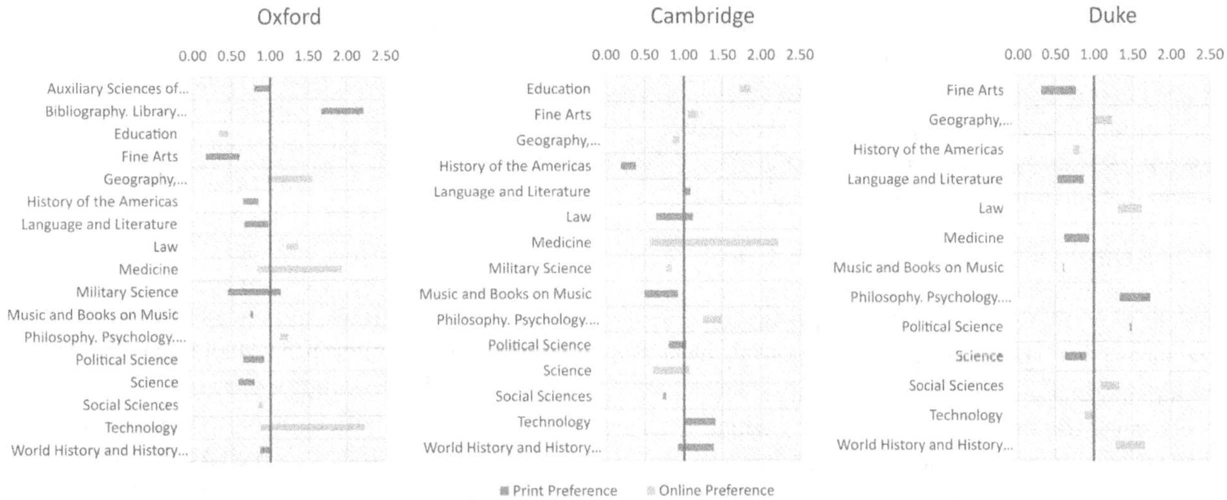

Figure 7. Format preference by subject: difference between print and online usage factors.

prefer? Although we came into the study with the assumption that our users would prefer electronic, by the end of it we were not entirely convinced. Our study shows that both formats were used quite extensively. For all of the presses considered, most titles had use in one format or another. Within the used portion of the collections, between 39% and 69% of titles were used in both formats. The circulation data confirms that print titles continue to be used several years after being released. In fact, the majority of print books circulated within the past 2 years. These statistics indicate that sthe presence of an electronic version of a book does not automatically displace the print title on the shelf.

Publisher Data, Knowledge Bases, and E-Book Use

In the data analysis, we observed that a substantial number of titles were used in one format only. For example, Oxford had an abnormally high degree of "print only" usage, and electronic usage in the last two years was comparatively lower than the other presses. A probable explanation for the low online usage of OSO content is that a large number of titles from 2013 and 2014 were missing from the Oxford Scholarship Online Frontfile package that we had activated within our electronic resource management system. In the University of Toronto's e-resource management context, the majority of catalog records for e-resources emanate from a MARC record service that is connected to titles activated within the knowledge base. As a result of the data omission within the knowledge base, we see a chain reaction that ultimately leads to no records in our library catalog and contributes to low use of the resources. Uncovering an anomaly such as this highlights the importance of a well-functioning supply chain for e-resource metadata and illustrates how critical it is in promoting the use of electronic resources.

Measuring Use

Throughout both the data collection and analysis processes we were continually faced with the question: Can the statistics truly gauge user preferences? When analyzing print and electronic usage, the statistics are not totally comparable. With print we are focusing on circulations of entire books which generally cover a long range of time. In contrast, electronic resource accesses tend to cover shorter periods of time and focus on chapters or sections of books, not books in their entirety. Statistics also cannot measure the intensity of use. Whether an item is used extensively or whether it is clicked on once and never consulted again, we really cannot gain any insight into this from the statistics. Similarly, by focusing print use on circulations, we only capture use that happens outside of the library walls when the patron physically signs out the book; we do not account at all for the in-house use of print items. The uniqueness of a user is also unaccounted for in use studies. Due to privacy restrictions, we cannot tell from the statistics whether many users are accessing an electronic book or one user repeatedly. Concerns like these are not new; they are well documented by previous studies measuring print and online use.

Although the statistics serve as an indication of use, we should not read into the statistics too deeply. The value of a study such as the one we conducted is not necessarily in the absolute numbers. What is of greater significance is the overarching trends that are represented within the statistics. In our analysis, we found that determining the "relative use" was more useful than focusing on the actual numbers, as it told us more about how resources were performing relative to other subjects within the collection, as well as which format tended to prevail in particular subjects.

Future Research

This study is one of the early steps in evaluating e-books at the University of Toronto Libraries. Through time, we hope to refine our process and use this study as a benchmark for future investigations. Due to the limitations of a purely statistical approach to use analysis, for future iterations of this study we are considering the inclusion of qualitative data to paint a better picture of user preferences. We hope that through surveys and focus groups we can gain more insight into how both print and online formats are used by patrons. Data in this study clearly showed that our patrons used both formats and in many cases preferred one format over another. It is therefore reasonable to conclude that format does matter. However, understanding why print books were still heavily used while e-books were also an option is a more complex question that warrants further investigation.

Evaluated, Removed, and Recycled—The Tale of Two Deaccession Projects Across the Disciplines

Martha Higgins, Research Librarian, College of William and Mary

Lauren Goode, Science Librarian, College of William and Mary

Mary Jordan, Collection Management Technician, Appalachian State University

John Abbott, Coordinator, Collection Management, Appalachian State University

Abstract

How have two midsized public university libraries approached large-scale weeding projects in their monograph and bound periodical collections? Space is at a premium in academic libraries as new roles combine and compete with traditional ones. How can the collection be refreshed to promote more use? Where will more collaboration and creative spaces be housed? How does a midsized library refine the collection to bring better campus alignment? How should the project begin? Who should be involved in planning? How can campus faculty be included in the deaccessioning process? How is the campus perception of the project handled? What should be kept, what sent off-site, and what discarded? What do you do with all of those discarded books and journals? How can the libraries work with campus sustainability goals? Do e-books play a part in what you keep and discard? How are different discipline areas handled when the book is valued differently? Are there useful guidelines like CREW (Continuous Review Evaluation and Weeding) that are applicable?

College of William and Mary

How does a medium-sized Carnegie-level institution with 8 PhD and 15 master's programs weed their collections? Very differently across the disciplines. Should the library do a massive weed all at once, or try a more piecemeal approach? Is there one right answer for all libraries? As space in the main library and the branch libraries, and even the off-site storage facility, is at a premium, similar to many libraries around the country, librarians were tasked with weeding our collections.

Two years ago, the reference department was tasked with weeding our reference area to create more space for students, and another possible open teaching area. I asked for help from all of the liaisons to pare down their subject areas within the reference collection. After several months of very slow progress, we were suddenly given a deadline, and a much bigger number to weed—now it was 50% to be removed from the areas. This was not received well by many of the librarians, as we also have a large genealogy collection within the reference area. Most new reference titles are being purchased electronically, but there are still many "standards" that are only in print. With a deadline looming, we needed to get serious about the weeding—what to send to the stacks, what to send to our off-site storage, and what to get rid of completely. After much negotiating and deliberating (and some arm twisting), the reference area was whittled down to 50% of the previous area, with new study spaces and a new teaching area now available.

The problem was what to do with those books we were weeding from reference? Weeding a reference area can be more complicated than you would first imagine: the enormous set of 1972 Italian encyclopedias—we *should* keep them because they are the definitive set and are not available in electronic form, but they have not been used in years. Okay, you think, send them up to the stacks . . . but wait, wait, there is no room in the stacks. Will anyone seriously ever ask that we bring over an encyclopedia from off-site? In total, more than 4,000 titles with almost 7,000 volumes were removed from the reference area.

http://dx.doi.org/10.5703/1288284316264

Of these, 25 guides were moved to the microfilm area, 25 large sets were moved off-site, 770 were "final exchanged"—our nice words for weeded—and the rest were sent to the stacks. In total, 444 Shelves were removed at 35" each equaling 1,295 linear feet. A major renovation of our microfilm area was also undertaken at this time, with more than 30,000 film, fiche, and cards being removed and the cabinets that held them, to make room for recording studios.

VIVA, the Virginia higher education library consortium also was conducting a shared collections project during this time, with VIVA members working on collaborative weeding, setting retention and purchasing thresholds, and distributing monographic subject collections across the Commonwealth. Liaisons were given "unique title" lists in each of our areas—these were titles that were held by only one library in the state, and by fewer than 10 in the country. One interesting statistic that was given to Swem Library during this project was that overall, out of more than 762,000 print items that this project looked at, 89% of our collections have been used or circulated at least once—this is a very high percentage for an academic library. During this project, many titles were sent to our rare books, or "medium rare" at our off-site stacks, or were discarded. But wait, why would we discard a rare book? Once we started actually looking at the materials, some were gold, and some were pyrite. Some examples of this were older articles from various journals that had been bound separately and cataloged, as well as dissertations (not done by William and Mary students) that had been purchased, but were now electronically available through ProQuest. There were also a lot of local history booklets, pamphlets, and items that were kept and put into medium rare.

Swem Library still does collect print books; in the 2014–2015 fiscal year we added 9,777 print titles. This was down from 2012–2013, in which 10,917 print titles were added. Swem subscribes to several DDA programs, as well as the EBSCO academic e-book package. Many of our faculty, especially in the humanities and social sciences still strongly prefer print books. Between the weeding of reference, and the continued purchasing of print titles with years of accumulation, many areas of the stacks were *full*, so full that the student shelvers would just shove the additional books on top and report that the shelf was full.

What is the easiest and fastest way to remove thousands of volumes from your shelves? Perform a JSTOR project. With JSTOR being a stable platform that nothing can be removed from, Swem thought this would be a safe option, and would not rile the faculty. Appalachian State did an enormous weeding of journals project last year, and it was very well received. We chose not to remove other vendors as our big packages are constantly changing. The discussions with faculty concerning this varied: some liaisons did mention it at faculty department meetings, while others trusted their judgment but assured faculty of the safety of their journals being accessible, and a LibGuide was created explaining the rationale of the weeding project with a link to appeal for retention of specific journals. There were several journals that were requested to keep in print because of the images and maps. Librarians checked, and double checked the JSTOR holdings with our print holdings, and all volumes not covered by JSTOR were retained. From the call number ranges C, D, E, and F, more than 6,700 bound journals were removed, and more than 13,000 from the entire collection. Students from the circulation department pulled the volumes, and a room was set aside to dissect the bindings and recycle the paper. The JSTOR project freed up more than 1,700 linear feet of shelf space, with large shifting projects that will be ongoing.

For several summers, various liaisons have conducted little weeding projects here and there when the stacks manager would point out the fact that no more books could fit into certain call number ranges, but something needed to be done on a larger scale. At a previous institution, with a colleague, we had done an extensive collection analysis weeding project that was based more strictly on circulation statistics and age. Looking back, some mistakes were definitely made on this project, and I did not want to repeat them. William and Mary offers a PhD in History, and is the home of the Institute for Early American

History and Culture, so having a strong history collection is extremely important. From previous weeding adventures, some necessary tidbits had been gleaned, first and foremost being to not rely strictly on reports produced from your ILS—actually going into the stacks shelf by shelf is a necessity. Yes, it is extremely time-consuming, but very worthwhile. There are so many cataloging questions and problems that arise, e.g., books that are not in the catalog but are on the shelves; over 100 books were found this way, and this was just by random chance, missing volumes, books with wrong call numbers, outdated formats, and other oddities including finding 14 copies of a 2-volume set on the shelves that were not all in the catalog. Don't let the judgments be left to working students just reading from lists—spend the time up in the stacks. There are so many things that you can learn: getting to know your collection so much better, what is up there, and what areas you really need to do some more intensive collection development in.

In History, you can't always judge the worth of a book by the newness or the number of checkouts—a lot of valuable material is *old*. Our circulation students are supposed to be recording in-house usage, but we know this is not always the case. Do we discard books because they are written by racists or during a time period that was not politically correct? We cannot erase history—these books are still part of the historiography, and should be kept. This is not the same in other disciplines, and each discipline needs to be treated differently when conducting library-wide weeding projects. Using a source such as the Resources for College Libraries, and following general guidelines like MUSTIE (Misleading, Ugly, Superseded, Trivial, Irrelevant, E for may be obtained elsewhere) are always good places to start. For the most part, what was weeded were copy 2's, (3's, 4's, and 5's) previous editions (keeping first editions of "classics"), alternate printings, and books in poor condition. Yes, people might want older travel books—several historical fiction writers ask for them regularly, so don't be so quick to throw those guides away. Balancing this out with the fact that we are not a Research One library, and do have limited space, is where the rock and hard place come in. This weeding project is continuing, and in total, over 3,000 items have been deselected in the D, E, and F call numbers.

The English liaison had different criteria, in comparison to disciplines where knowledge is more cumulative, the older materials retain their value better. Using "Selected Bibliographies" from the Norton Anthologies of English and American Literature, when working in the stacks, he checks to see if we have the standard edition, whether there is a newer scholarly edition in progress, and which are the highlighted critical works, the best biography, and so forth. These lists also tip him off to sets which may not have been purchased back in the 1980s or 1990s when less private money was available, or the state was pulling back library funds from the college, and he tries to fill in major titles.

The English liaison also shelf read at the same time and pulled out items out of place, took them to circulation to see if they were on a lost or missing list, and took items to cataloging that may have been miscataloged. And he pulled copy 2's of lightly circulated titles, damaged copies, and older materials which have been superseded by later revised editions where the editors have corrected errors, added to bibliographies, or just added new material. All of this takes far more time, but it is worth it for a better collection. Of course in literature, copy 2's are much desired for certain authors—especially the critical editions, so you must know what courses are being taught currently, and might be in the near future, so working with and knowing your faculty is a key component.

In Philosophy and Religion, the liaison was very careful to keep classic editions of certain works, so knowing your subjects is key. There are always preferred translations of classic works such as Plato or Aristotle or Nietzsche, as well as standard and new editions of the Bhagavad Gita, the Quran, and other religious works. Philosophy and Religion do not always have huge changes, and very few titles go "out of date." Sometimes, it usually comes down to experience: knowing which editions are often mentioned, or have been requested by faculty members and are used in classes is very helpful.

Weeding the Q's can be a much easier process than other call ranges. Science is quickly outdated and new materials on a given topic often supersede previous works. While it is important to retain foundational works as well as a small number of representative titles to maintain the historical perspectives, often older materials can be moved out or replaced. To determine if a work should be kept, it is searched in Worldcat, to ensure a rare piece is not discarded and confirm that the item is owned by one or more research institutions. If there is still a question, searching for information on the author can help make decisions easier.

The Chemistry Reading Room is one of two science branch libraries on W&M's main campus. The space is small, consisting of 450 linear feet and 4,932 volumes. Circulation in the collection is low, only 49 circulations (0.99% of the collection) for FY 2015, and faculty have referred to it as a "cute archive." The space is consistently used for students taking tests and studying; with academic space at a premium, the consolidation of materials into the main branch should be anticipated. In the summer 2015, the science librarian began an inventory of the collection. As a part of the inventory, duplicate copies, previous editions, damaged items, and outdated items not cataloged were removed from the collection.

A total of 92 items were deselected from the chemistry library, leaving a large portion of the collection remaining. A comprehensive weed will be required if and when the collection is moved into the main library. The inventory of the collection revealed that 757 items are "missing," defined as identified in the catalog as available in the chemistry stacks but not scanned during the inventory process. The number of missing items is 15.4% of the entire chemistry collection; judging from the lack of requests to locate missing materials, many items are simply no longer in demand. Collection usage will be a factor to consider in future weeding activities.

The Physics Library is the second science branch library. It is a much larger collection, containing 21,507 volumes over 2,000 linear feet. The collection is well loved by the faculty and students in physics and applied sciences. New book displays are popular, and a healthy monograph budget ensures that at least 6 linear feet of new materials are cataloged annually. Some areas of the collection were very tight in the shelves despite a weed during a 2011 renovation of the space. When shelving items the stacks would sway and sometimes books would have to be placed on top of other books.

Fearing for public safety, tired of breaking finger nails, observing students love of the space, and fantasizing over awesome programing opportunities, the science librarian proposed another weeding of materials at a faculty meeting. Physics is a scientific discipline which still values books and apparently weeding is a bad word, even if the weeds were dusty old duplicate copies of 1970s imprints. The idea for a comprehensive weed was rejected. The librarian made the executive decision to remove previous editions and duplicate copies of materials, with the exception of materials which were in high demand. To determine high demand, each item was checked for date last circulated and the total number of circulations. Generously, if each copy of an item had circulated in the last five years, both were allowed to stay. More than once, a previous edition had circulated recently, but the new edition had not, in those cases the previous edition was pulled to steer users toward the updated material. In all, 192 items were removed.

The branch libraries provide a unique opportunity for ongoing collection maintenance. The science librarian and a student assistant for the physics branch are the only library employees who check in and shelve materials. This is helpful because when shelving items, the surrounding items can be quickly evaluated and items which are duplicates or appear damaged can be pulled for evaluation. Tight areas can be cleared out before books start piling up.

Three years ago, our Geology department needed to reclaim the space occupied by their branch library to create needed lab space. Swem had to absorb the contents. This required a large amount of space, so there was serious weeding in the Q's and G's before the books and copious amounts of maps could be transferred. Over 1,900 volumes were removed from Swem in a 3-month time period, to make room for the books and clean up the collection. While the geology books should be in good order, there are still other areas in the main collection of Q's awaiting an evaluation. During the end of the spring 2015 semester, while participating in a shelving help project, 43 copy 2's and previous editions were pulled, just from a quick evaluation in areas where items were returned to shelves.

There are many opportunities for weeding in the future for the science collections. Future weeding projects will possibly require input from faculty members, and new backfile purchases will allow for the removal of additional journal runs which will free large shelving areas in the branch libraries as well as the main library.

With any weeding project, librarians run the risk of discarding material from the collections that may become useful in the future for historical reasons. This needs to be balanced against the current needs for space, and keeping current materials readily available. Checking the items' rarity in Worldcat when in doubt can help questions of what would be a tragedy to discard. Weeding can vary widely by discipline, type of library, and the reasons it is being done, but for each discipline, it should be conducted carefully and thoughtfully, and not rushed and done strictly by the numbers: it is about the journey as well as the destination.

Appalachian State University

Appalachian State University is a Carnegie-classified Master's/L institution located in the Blue Ridge Mountains of western North Carolina, and is one of 17 schools within the University of North Carolina System. Appalachian enrolls 18,000 students in 150+ degree programs at the undergraduate and graduate level, including one doctorate in education (EdD). A new campus library, The Belk Library and Information Commons, opened in 2005 with space for nine years of physical collections growth. Currently, the library's main book stacks house approximately 530,000 circulating items.

The library began an extensive review of collections and services in 2013. Under the guidance of the new dean, the library benchmarked against current and emerging visions of academic library collections and services. Though seemingly new, the now 10-year old building was designed with late 20th century conceptions because that was all we could understand at the time. It was clear the future of information resources would be different, but how, when, and with what price would these changes occur? Now it is clear that in those ten years much had changed for collections offerings, in technology related to patron use of information resources, and in patron's habits and needs.

The library retained an architectural firm in 2014 to assist in planning a renewal of the library. It was clear early on that transitions were underway in the use of collections and in the demand for new services. With those trends in mind, the library began thinking about an extensive review of collections to understand where space might be opened to grow into these changes. Several projects were outlined. Reference, A/V, bound journals, and main stacks were the first collections identified for evaluation.

Before the reviews were begun, the library reached out to the groups on campus to communicate the developing plans for the library renewal project; what the project's impetus was; and how the plan would be accomplished in space, time, and expense. Constituencies consulted included the provost, Faculty Library Committee, Deans Council, Council of Chairs, and campus physical plant. These presentations were met with interest and few questions. It would later become clear that back and forth communication between these groups and the general faculty could not always be relied upon.

Recent History of Collection Reduction at Appalachian

In 2012 and 2013, the library reduced the size of the reference collection by 80%; discarding 40% and transferring 40% to the circulating main stacks. The paper reference collection was little used by patrons or librarians. Twenty percent of the collection was retained. Similar projects were undertaken in the 16mm, VHS, and microfilm collections. There was no noticeable negative feedback following these projects, many of which freed space to move and expand the library's Digital Media Studio, a heavily used service.

In 2013 and 2014, the library examined the bound journal collection in comparison to our owned backfiles from major journal publishers, e.g., Elsevier, Springer, Wiley/Blackwell, etc., and from JSTOR. Bound volumes were shelved together in alphabetical order away from the main book stacks. The process was open and publicized to campus. A LibGuide was created explaining the plans to remove these journal volumes that were also included in the library's owned journal backfiles. An online form was available for campus patrons to recommend titles to be exempted from removal. Fewer than 30 titles were appealed and the reasons were most often related to format or illustrations. Almost 100,000 bound volumes were removed and routed into the recycling stream. Thousands of linear feet of compact shelving were freed to eventually be relocated to provide more shelving in the main stacks. One thing we did anticipate was the need for compact shelving in the main stacks, and areas of the stack floors were built to anticipate the relocation of compact shelves and the increased load associated with its shelving. The space opened by removing these bound journals will be used for more archives closed storage and for additional digital classrooms and services. There was little negative feedback during and following the project. We even received a few comments that it was about time the library performed this review and discarded these titles.

The Ongoing Main Stacks Review Project

Creation of the review list. In 2015, criteria were developed to evaluate low-use items in the main stacks. Using Innovative Interfaces' Create Lists function, straightforward criteria were applied against the main stacks holdings location: (1) The item was added to the collection prior to 1995, and (2) the item has no recorded use after 1995. The library had adopted the Innovative ILS in 1994, and the generated report reached back to the beginning of our collection use data. Recorded use included both checkouts and reshelvings. All in-house reshelved items were scanned before shelving and that internal copy use was recorded. If a patron consulted a volume and reshelved it themselves, that use would not be captured, but across 20 years the likelihood of a consulted volume always being reshelved by a patron was slim. We believed that there would be at least one captured use if an item was even marginally popular.

The criteria yielded a first list of approximately 90,000 items added more than 20 years ago and having seen no apparent use in the last 20 years. From date-due slips examined, some items on the list appeared to have had no use from the 1970s or earlier. The list became known as the zero list and was approximately 2,500 pages if printed out with 40 items per page in Excel. This first pass report represented 17% of the main stacks collection. Identification of these items was a first step to allow further review of these holdings' potential for retention or discard. We decided upon a three-part review process.

Three Levels of the Review

Level 1. Subject librarian review. The first review was a line-by-line examination by subject librarians searching for items that appeared somewhat foundational or canonical. Collection management at Appalachian is handled by a group of a dozen subject librarians with CM responsibilities divided in broad discipline categories: humanities, social sciences, business, education, and some narrower areas where a librarian has a particular disciplinary understanding. Before this line-by-line review began, the zero list's many imperfections were minimized via a thorough inspection overseen by the collection management technician, Mary Jordan. Mary identified and removed items that relate to unique areas of collection strength, e.g., Contract Bridge collection and books that had previously been identified by librarians for retention.

With the clean-up step accomplished, the resulting zero list was divided by appropriate two-letter LC classes, printed, and distributed to the appropriate subject librarians for the title-by-title review. Using a pink highlighter, subject librarians identified items that merited retention even if unused in 20 years. Each librarian applied their knowledge of the campus's curriculum and research to make these retention selections. Frequent trips to the stacks were essential. This process lasted six weeks. Approximately 10,000 items were removed from the zero list by these librarian reviews.

The resulting list of 80,000 was examined for patterns, and Table 1 summarizes those:

We wondered about the presence of rarer items on the zero list. To estimate the number of nominally rare books, which we defined as being held by fewer than five libraries in WorldCat, we hired two mathematics students to generate 2000 random numbers between 1 and 80,000, identify those selections on the zero list, and search those items in WorldCat. No more than 2% of the zero list was held by fewer than 5 WorldCat libraries. This 2% will receive additional attention in the Level 3 review process.

Table 1. Patterns in main stacks holdings versus the zero list items.

Broad Subject	Total in Main Stacks	% of Main Stacks	Total on Zero List	% of Subject on Zero List	% of Total Zero List
Humanities	296,082	56%	44,684	15%	56%
Social Sciences	90,929	17%	12,735	14%	16%
Hard Sciences	79,845	15%	12,591	16%	16%
Education	20,070	4%	1,479	7%	2%
Business	41,364	8%	7,969	19%	10%
Total	528,290	100%	79,458	15%	100%

We were surprised that the percentages on the zero list very closely matched those of the main stacks, i.e., social sciences LC classes accounted 16% of the zero list count and for 17% of the main stacks count. Interesting too was the apparent lack of use was spread somewhat evenly across the LC classes. That business had the largest percentage on the zero list was not surprising because of the fast-moving trends in that area make books obsolete more quickly. Education's small percentage on the zero list was likely the result of a very thorough weeding review of the "L" class in 2012. Overall, the lack of use was near 15% across the collection.

What stood out was the overall number of items in the broad humanities classes: 56% in the main stacks and on the zero list. Half of the library main stacks holds collections in literature, language, history, philosophy, religion, and fine and applied arts. The music collection is entirely held in the separate music library, was examined separately, and was not included in these main library review projects. Similarly, the Dewey-classed Instructional Media Center collection was not included in this review.

Level 2. Campus review of the list (ongoing in fall 2015). A LibGuide was created to inform about and include the campus in the main stacks review. The guide format was similar to that used successfully in the bound periodicals review project. The project background was covered; anticipated questions were answered; the review list was divided into narrow LC categories to facilitate faculty review of items in their areas of interest; and a comment form was created in SurveyMonkey for the input of titles suggested for retention. An e-mail was sent to campus about the project and included a link to the LibGuide. Three weeks were provided in early midsemester to examine the list and provide input.

Level 3. Item-by-item physical review by subject librarians (in 2016). After the appealed items are removed from the zero list, the lists will be divided between the two main stacks floors. The early library renewal construction is planned for the 2nd floor containing LC classes A through J. The 3rd floor contains K through Z. This lends an alphabetical approach; a comfortable fit for librarians. The recycling operation can handle the equivalent of 22 book trucks per week or roughly 2,000 books per week. The 2nd floor is anticipated to have 30,000 items to be removed, taking 15 weeks or one semester. To accomplish this, student workers pull items from the main stacks using the final zero list and deliver these on book trucks to the subject librarians. The subject librarians will examine each item for a third retain or recycle decision looking at the items in the university and library context.

Items not retained must then move through the library deaccessioning process to remove them from the catalog. There are considerable downstream effects on technical services and processing units receiving trucks of additional books each week to withdraw. This effect is repeated when the deaccessioned items arrive at the loading dock and campus physical plant's reception of tons of additional paper for recycling.

Interesting Aspects

Communication. We were strongly reminded that books possess a singular cultural meaning, particularly to those in academe. While the reference and the bound periodical reviews proceeded with ease, the main stacks review precipitated a much different and prolonged campus response. We learned that it is essential when beginning a stacks review project to understand how for many the book has iconic value that bound journals and other formats do not possess. This iconic value transcends perceived utility. 100,000 bound volumes were routed into recycling with little comment. The proposal that a smaller number of books join those journals in the recycling stream was unacceptable to a number of vocal faculty, most commonly from the core humanities departments. The STEM and social sciences departments offered few comments. Library representatives were called to faculty senate and to departmental meetings to explain and defend the library renewal. Clearly, the communication we expected to happen between the campus academic management groups and the faculty had not always happened. The early news of the renewal project may not have been communicated or it may not have been heard when it was communicated.

Faculty concerns centered on the loss of the books they might need in the future or on concerns that the removed books should find a home somewhere else after being withdrawn from our library. The iconic value lends itself to an attachment to books that is very strong and not to be underestimated.

For some concerned faculty, our reassurances were not convincing when provided an evidence that the books proposed for withdrawal were not rare and could be readily interlibrary loaned from nearby R-1 libraries committed to huge off-site storage facilities for low-use items. Giving up something (the books) the campus already owns and they might need someday was often not compensated for by the proposed opportunities for more creative and collaborative space or alternate delivery or substitution (e-book) options.

For those concerned that the withdrawn books still must have value and they should be sent somewhere to someone rather than be recycled, the options available are guided by the rules and regulations regarding disposal of state/institutional property. In our case, a few departments have requested the ability to review discards and move selected items to their departments. In a process handling tens of thousands of books through multiple steps for each item, having custom arrangements for some constituencies about some items may disrupt or fragment library workflows. Not accommodating some of those requests for custom arrangements can also have consequences.

One response to these concerns was that the review period for faculty was extended from three weeks to 2.5 months. At this writing we are halfway through that review period, and a few thousand books have been appealed through the LibGuide form. The overall lessons learned in a book stacks review center on the need for very broad communication from the beginning; the significant disciplinary differences in the perception of books; and the very special place the physical book holds in academe.

Keep Those Booktrucks Rolling: Strategies for a Major Move of the Library Collection

Edward F. Lener, Associate Director for Collection Management, Virginia Tech University

Leslie O'Brien, Director, Collections & Technical Services, Virginia Tech University

Ladd Brown, Head of Acquisitions, Virginia Tech University

Abstract

The University Libraries at Virginia Tech recently completed an extensive move of the physical collection and reduction of the stacks footprint in our main facility. This session relates key elements of what we learned during this multi-year process and share tips and strategies for an effective and efficient large-scale move. We cover ways to address such issues as project management, communications, staffing, identifying materials for storage or deselection, and processing of materials as well as how the process we used may be applied elsewhere.

Background

Between 2012 and 2015 the University Libraries at Virginia Tech moved its entire circulating collection in its main on-campus library facility. In the process significant numbers of volumes were moved to off-site storage or withdrawn from the collection entirely. The resulting reduction in the physical footprint of the stacks enabled targeted repurposing of spaces throughout the building for other needs.

We still have more moves ahead but would like to share some tips and strategies that we learned so far from our experiences.

The text and tables below are adapted from a poster session presentation given at the Charleston Library Conference in November 2015.

Some Major Milestones in the University Libraries (with approximate completion dates)

Construction of SCALE-UP classroom—February 2013

Expansion of 4th floor commons—summer 2014

Leased new warehouse space for 10 years—December 2013

Construction of library multipurpose room—January 2014

Downsizing and renovation of veterinary medicine branch—summer 2014

Completed upgrades to warehouse infrastructure—fall 2014

Table 1. The incredible shrinking collection—Newman Library, Virginia Tech.

Volumes by Floor	FY12	F13	FY14	FY15	Difference
2nd	172,907	73,808	72,935	0	
3rd	550,237	594,441	490,268	562,211	
4th	362,130	280,700	339,289	336,294	
5th	148,409	122,360	120,556	119,794	
TOTAL	1,233,683	1,071,309	1,023,048	1,018,299	–215,299

http://dx.doi.org/10.5703/1288284316265

Construction of ICAT studios—January 2015

Construction of R&I offices on 4th floor—summer 2015

Expansion of 2nd floor commons—summer 2015

Construction of digital humanities workspace—summer 2016

Construction of reserved faculty space on 3rd floor—summer 2016

Expansion of 4th floor commons phase 2—summer 2017

Tips and Strategies

The tips and strategies below are based on our experiences at Virginia Tech and are divided into four main categories. Each situation is unique, but these recommendations should help you better prepare for a move at your own library.

Project Management and Workflow

- Make a plan, but be willing to change it—Most helpful to us were detailed floor maps showing every range and the call numbers it held
- Seek to minimize the number of times any item is handled—Sometimes items must be moved more than once but doing so hurts efficiency
- Get started early and keep at it—Time moves quickly when the clock is ticking
- Identify what needs to happen next and try to keep at least one step ahead—Focus your time and energy wisely
- Expect the unexpected—In our case the only freight elevator was out of service for weeks

Staffing

- Have the staff on hand you need to do the job—Adding back two recent retirees made a world of difference for us, and no extra training was needed!
- Hire extra students—Moving is hard physical labor and turnover will be high
- Utilize staff from other areas during slow periods—Circulation staff provided valuable assistance during summer and breaks

Identifying Materials

- Find low-hanging fruit—We started with remaining print indexes and then moved to journal archives; both freed up large runs of shelf space fast
- Use overlap analysis to good effect—Tools such as Serials Solutions 360 can help identify what packages to buy
- Maximize archive/backfile purchases with a single vendor—Significant discounts can often be negotiated this way
- Rely on your partners to carry some of the load—We are part of a shared print repository system through ASERL
- Walk the stacks—All that dust is there for a reason!

Making It All Work

- Be strategic—Finding "push-back" from many humanities and social sciences faculty about moving their books on-site, we instead focused on journal runs, especially in the sciences
- Be strategic part II—We tried to add back extra study space along outer walls, which had both natural light and electric power
- Capitalize on opportunities—We were able to integrate much of our remaining reference collection back into the stacks
- Communicate fully—Misconceptions can crop up and the sooner you address concerns the better!

Rapid Collections Surveying With Book Traces @ UVa

Kristin H. Jensen, Project Manager, University of Virginia Library

Carla H. Lee, Senior Director, Collections Access and Discovery, University of Virginia Library

Abstract

Many donated books in circulating collections have value as historical artifacts due to unique interventions by their former owners, such as marginalia, inscriptions, and insertions. These interventions can potentially offer a trove of evidence of how books have been consumed across time and what they meant to past cultures, but are generally undocumented and therefore undiscoverable through library catalogs. Moreover, as circulating copies, these books may be vulnerable to damage, loss, and withdrawal. Book Traces @ UVa is a two-year effort to survey pre-1923 books in the University of Virginia Library circulating collection for uniquely modified volumes and enhance our catalog to make them more readily discoverable. Because our target population is large—more than 92,000 volumes—we are developing techniques for rapidly sampling the collection through a randomized, statistically representative selection from each call number subclass. We believe our statistical samples will point the way for deeper exploration of subject areas where the books are especially rich in evidence of historical readership, and in this paper we present some of our preliminary findings as well as an overview of our survey and sampling techniques. We also suggest how the Book Traces experiment in considering non-rare books as historical artifacts can reshape libraries' approach to retention and off-site storage decisions.

Introduction

Book Traces @ UVa is a two-year research project in the University of Virginia Library, funded by a CLIR Hidden Collections grant. This project got started when an English professor named Andrew Stauffer noticed that many of the older books in our circulating collection contain traces left behind by readers of the past: marginal notes, gift inscriptions, sentimental objects tucked between the pages, and so forth. Professor Stauffer started a crowd-sourcing website called Book Traces to collect examples, informally, of uniquely modified volumes in academic libraries, focusing on circulating collections.[1] This website has gotten a lot of press and you may have heard about it.[2] Book Traces @ UVa is the next, more formalized step beyond the initial Book Traces crowdsourcing effort. Professor Stauffer teamed up with the UVA Library's director of preservation services, Kara McClurken, to launch a more rigorous and methodical survey of the UVA collection.[3] Later in my paper I am going to talk more about the methods that we are using for this survey, but I

[1] http://www.booktraces.org/

[2] Jennifer Howard, (2014, May 5), "Book lovers record traces of 19th-century readers," *The Chronicle of Higher Education*, Retrieved December 1, 2015, from http://chronicle.com/blogs/wiredcampus/book-lovers-record-traces-of-19th-century-readers/52415; Alexis C. Madrigal, (2014, May 7), "What Is a Book? Not Just a Bag of Words, but a Thing Held by Human Hands," *The Atlantic*, retrieved December 1, 2015, from http://www.theatlantic.com/technology/archive/2014/05/what-is-a-book/361876/; Allison Meier, (2014, May 8), "The Call to Action to Save Digitized Books from Oblivion," *Hyperallergic*, retrieved December 1, 2015, from http://hyperallergic.com/125215/the-call-to-action -to-save-digitized-books-from-oblivion/; Eve M. Kahn, (2014, December 18), "Of Magic Lanterns and Screen Gems," *New York Times*, Art & Design sec, Retrieved December 1, 2015, from http://www.nytimes.com/2014/12/19/arts/design/of-magic-lanterns-and-screen-gems.html. Additional press citations at http://www.booktraces.org/press-for-book-traces/

[3] Project website: http://booktraces.library.virginia.edu/

http://dx.doi.org/10.5703/1288284316266

want to start with an example of the kind of book we are finding. I hope this will give you a hint of the motivations behind the survey.

We recently found a mechanical engineering manual published in 1876.[4] There are two inscriptions on the title page. One is by the original owner, one R. B. S. Nicolson, who was an engineering student at UVA in the late 1870s. The second inscription shows us that the book was later donated to the UVa Library by his brother, John. The real story, however, is inside. Bound into the back of the manual are several pages of lined paper for taking notes, and written on one of them we found this message:

> New York City April 13th 1912.
>
> It seems a desecration almost for me to write in this book so exclusively associated with my brother—but I am led to look into it for the first time in many, many years this Saturday night, the anniversary of his birth. He was born that memorable day, fifty one years ago, on which the Civil War between the North and the South began—fifty one years ago!! How life is slipping by!
>
> This book is a relic of my brother's first ambitions—viz, to be a civil engineer—and of his course at the University of Virginia to this end. Instead of continuing to this goal, he went into our father's business in Savannah in 1880, coming however to an early end. He was drowned at Tybee Island Ga. July 10th 1881.
>
> John Nicolson

This book is more than just a container for intellectual content. It is a double memorial to the young man who was born the day the Civil War started and died tragically young, just twenty years later. John Nicolson made tribute to his brother's memory first when he wrote this personal reflection in the blank notepaper leaves of the book and again when he donated it to the University of Virginia. Moreover, this book is a record, not just of the Nicolson brothers' kinship, but also of their affective relationship with the University of Virginia. As an artifact, this engineering manual gives us a little piece of family history, Southern history, and University history all rolled into one.

With Book Traces @ UVa, the basic question we are asking is, what *else* is "hidden in plain sight" in the circulating collection? We want to identify unique volumes with preservation needs and see that they get appropriate treatment to preserve their artefactual value. We also want to identify uniquely modified volumes as such in the catalog, facilitating research on them as historic artifacts. We are doing all of this with an awareness that there are space pressures on libraries across the country, and that there is some concern among scholars of nineteenth-century studies that circulating materials from this era may be vulnerable to withdrawal due to low circulation or shared repository status. Part of what we are doing is considering what kind of historical evidence might be lost in the case of withdrawals, and we want to offer a rationale for retaining uniquely modified volumes as well as a model for surveying collections.

Survey Procedure: The Why and How of Statistical Sampling

Our project started in April of this year and runs through March of 2017. We are working primarily in Alderman Library, the main circulating library for humanities and social science research at the University of Virginia. We are also drawing some books from off-site storage, but our project does not go into special collections because we assume those books are already well preserved and

[4] John C. Trautwine, (1876), *The Civil Engineer's Pocket-book (*10th ed.), Philadelphia: Claxton. Catalog entry for the UVA Library copy in question: http://search.lib.virginia.edu/catalog/u916173. For more on the book and the Nicolson brothers' history, see Kristin Jensen and Maggie Whalen, (2015, October 23), "Book Find: A Brother's Memorial," *Book Traces @ UVa*, retrieved December 3, 2015, from http://booktraces.library.virginia.edu /book-find-a-brothers-memorial/

protected against loss and damage. We are surveying only books published before 1923, for a few reasons. First, titles in this population are out of copyright and likely to be available in Google Books or HathiTrust; we want to make a case that uniquely modified volumes in local holdings may be overlooked if users turn first to digital surrogates. Secondly, pre-1923 volumes are also generally low in circulation, making their unique features less likely to be discovered serendipitously, and also potentially making them candidates for withdrawal when libraries develop shared repositories. At the same time, the low circulation of these volumes makes it more likely that loose insertions may be found intact. Thirdly, setting a 1923 cutoff means that most of the books in our survey were printed during the industrial period from about 1820 through the early twentieth century when print culture exploded and the relatively low cost of books meant that people could afford to own more books, personalizing them and often treating them as sentimental possessions. Finally, the history of collection development at the University of Virginia gives us another reason to focus on books from the long nineteenth century. Books from this time period in our circulating collection are likely to have been acquired as donations following the decimation of the UVA Library collection by a fire in 1895. Thus, they are likely to show evidence of personal reading practices rather than institutional use.

Narrowing our shelf list to pre-1923 monographs still left us with over 92,000 books to examine in the Alderman Library alone. Surveying such a large collection presents some challenges. At the outset, we did not know for sure how many books we would be able to survey in 3,000 hours of student worker time, which is the amount budgeted in the grant. We also did not want to wait until the end of the two-year grant period to get a sense of what we had on hand.

The solution that we came up with in the early weeks of the project was to start with a statistical sample. We did a few pilot surveys to iron out workflow issues, and then we brought in a fourth year statistics major named Jackie Morrogh to help us create a statistical sampling scheme. (Unfortunately, Jackie could not come to Charleston with me as a co-presenter, but I will try to do justice to her work.) We divided the shelf lists by Library of Congress subclassification, and Jackie calculated how big a sample we would need to take from each range in order to determine the "hit rate" with 95% confidence and a 5% margin of error. When I say the "hit rate," I mean how many books we would find with unique modifications that meet a certain threshold of notability. Taking a sample from each Library of Congress subclassification reduced the total population initially being surveyed from a little over 92,000 to a little under 19,000. In other words, during the preliminary sample period we are only looking at one-fifth of the population of interest.

The statistical sampling approach gives us some choices. We could look at a smaller subset faster and draw our conclusions with less confidence, or we could look at a larger subset for better confidence but spend more time doing it. We chose a sample size that we felt would be feasible to complete and a confidence level that we believed would allow us to draw some reasonably reliable conclusions about the collection.

Once we had decided on a statistical approach, the technique for generating shelf lists was fairly straightforward. Our statistician determined the number of books we needed to sample from each subclass. She assigned a random number to each line of the shelf list, then sorted each subclass of the shelf list by those random numbers. From the top of the randomized list, she selected the number of books needed for our sample.

For subclassification ranges with very few holdings, we have to look at every book or nearly every book in order to survey them with a confidence level of 95% and a 5% margin of error, but for larger subclasses, a much smaller proportion gives us an adequate sample. For example, we have over 15,000 pre-1923 monographs in the Library of Congress PR subclass, English literature, but we only have to look at 375 books to determine the "hit rate," the percent of PR books with unique modifications.

For another example, in the HQ range (covering the family, marriage, and women), we own 385 pre-1923 monographs and we are sampling 193 of them, about half. In call number subclasses with fewer than 140 books, the necessary sample size is so close to the population size, and so small, that we are actually surveying the entire population because it seems efficient to do so. By starting with the largest samples and working our way down the list to the smallest, we have been able to learn a lot about the largest subpopulations within our collection very quickly.

If we stratified the collection differently, such as by looking at all the A call numbers as one population, all the B call numbers as another population, and so forth, we would be able to take proportionally smaller samples and thus finish our entire survey even faster. The trade-off would be that what we learn about comparative hit rates would be accordingly large-grained. For example, if we had sampled all of the H call numbers as one population, we would not have learned that there is only a 5% rate of unique modifications among the HJ call numbers, representing books on finance, as compared with a 15% hit rate in the HB call numbers, representing books on economic theory and demography. We would still learn, however, that the hit rate is quite low in the A call numbers, representing general works, as compared with the H call numbers, representing the social sciences. And we would probably find a similar overall hit rate for the pre-1923 collection, around 12.5%.[5]

There are many benefits to starting Book Traces @ UVa with a statistical sample. Finishing the statistical sample has taken us only four months out of the two-year grant period, using about 500 student worker hours. While working on the statistical sample, we have also gathered data about our student workers' efficiency; knowing that they can survey about 38 books per hour allows us to plan our future work based on their efficiency as well as the hit rate data analyzed by our statistician. Even before finishing the sample, we had enough efficiency data to determine that we could finish surveying the entire Alderman Library population of pre-1923 imprints within the grant period, with time to spare. This was something we were not sure of at the outset. Now, knowing that we have time to survey other libraries within the UVA system, we can plan samples guided by our hit rate data from Alderman Library: we can choose to concentrate on subject areas that had the highest hit rates in the Alderman population in the hope that this will lead us straight to the richest seams of artefactual evidence.

Other Lessons Learned

I think doing the statistical sample has been the single most important choice we have made for learning a lot about our collection in a fairly small amount of time. That said, however, we have also benefited from putting some thought into designing an efficient process for carrying out the survey. Before hiring our student project assistants, I experimented with the surveying process, with an eye toward usability. Our process is designed to optimize a balance of speed and accuracy in recording data about the books in our open stacks. Our project assistants spend about 80% of their work time in the stacks, using a book truck as a mobile work station with a laptop, barcode scanner, and handheld "pen" scanner for text. Working from a list of pre-1923 monographs, the assistants pull each book from the shelf and give it a preliminary examination. If there is a bookplate, they use the pen scanner to record just the name on the bookplate; the bookplate census is a side project that will allow us to connect books donated by the same family. Books that have unique modifications meeting our criteria are set aside on the book trucks for further analysis; others are returned to the shelf. Near the end of each shift, the assistants do a second inspection of the books they pulled and record the

[5] At the time this paper was presented at the Charleston Library Conference, the survey had not yet been completed. It has since been completed and the results have been statistically analyzed. Our final overall hit rate for all pre-1923 monographs in the Alderman Library collection is 12.7%.

specific modifications, such as marginalia or insertions, using a Google form.

This two-step process promotes accuracy of description by allowing project assistants to concentrate on description separately from the task of finding and pulling books. It also accommodates one of the technical needs of the project: wifi is not fully reliable in the stacks area, so the assistants work offline using Excel spreadsheets for shelf lists in the stacks, then return to a central area to review the books they have selected and fill out the online descriptive form. Iterative design of the survey process has raised other technological considerations, too. For example, barcode scanners in raised cradles are more usable for this application than handheld scanners. For another example, laptop battery life is critical when students work in five-hour shifts and must roll their work stations through the stacks without plugging in.

I mentioned earlier that the statistical sample has helped us learn a lot about our collection in a short amount of time. Our findings are still preliminary: in fact, our project assistants will be wrapping up the last subclassification surveys in the next week or so, and the statistical analysis of our project data always lags two to three weeks behind the gathering of the data. However, we already have a lot of information about the relative hit rates in different subject areas. We expected to find a high hit rate in the P call numbers, covering languages and literature, and in fact we did.[6] We found a high hit rate in the B call numbers—representing philosophy, psychology, and religion—partly because we have a lot of books from two nineteenth-century philosophy professors who wrote in the margins a lot. It is also partly because we did some pilot work in the B call number ranges before starting the sampling scheme, and at that time our selection criteria were a little more inclusive.[7] We found a low hit rate in the A call numbers, which is not surprising: those represent "general works," which do not seem to call for a lot of personal engagement.[8]

To describe the types of unique modifications, or reader interventions, that we have been finding, we are using a modified set of terms from the RBMS Provenance Evidence Thesaurus[9] for research purposes, with the intention of eventually collapsing all the metadata into PET vocabulary for catalog description. The five most frequently found types of interventions are, in order: inscription, usually meaning the owner's inscription; verbal marginalia, which we are distinguishing from nonverbal marks; underscoring; nonverbal marginalia; verbal annotations, which we consider to be any sort of written marking that is not an inscription and does not interact as closely with the text as marginalia does; and finally gift inscriptions. Further down the list are things like insertions, authors' inscriptions, and doodles or artwork.

Another lesson we have learned is that it is considerably easier to survey books in bulk while they sit on open shelves in our main library. We have recently done a small pilot sample of books drawn from UVA's off-site storage facility, and the process was very labor intensive. When our project assistants are working in the open stacks, they spend roughly a minute and a half per book on our shelf list. By contrast, when we pulled books from off-site storage, the off-site staff spent roughly four to five minutes per book to retrieve each volume, route it to us, receive it back when we were done with it, and return it to the high-density shelving. Having discovered the labor requirements of surveying books in off-site storage, we are now making a point of surveying

[6] In the final statistical analysis (completed since this paper was presented at the Charleston Library Conference), 11 out of 16 sections in the P call numbers had hit rates above the library-wide average of 12.7%.

[7] In the final statistical analysis, 11 out of 15 sections in the B call numbers had hit rates above the library-wide average of 12.7%.

[8] In the final statistical analysis, 6 out of 9 sections in the A call numbers had hit rates lower than the library-wide average of 12.7%.

[9] http://rbms.info/vocabularies/provenance/alphabtical_list.htm

batches of books *before* they are scheduled to be moved to off-site storage.

The most important conclusion we have drawn is to confirm what Andrew Stauffer first discovered serendipitously. Many of the copies in our circulating collection have unique features that are not represented in digital surrogates created elsewhere. By considering each volume as a unique physical object, we can identify which ones have special interest as artifacts and as pieces of a distributed archive of the history of reading.

Reconciling E-Book Packages at NCSU Libraries

Christee Pascale, Associate Head, Acquisition and Discovery Department, NCSU Libraries

Xiaoyan Song, E-Resource Librarian, Acquisition and Discovery Department, NCSU Libraries

Abstract

As e-books become an increasingly large part of our collection, the NCSU Libraries acquisition and discovery department created an e-book reconciliation database to ensure that all of our purchased e-book package content is available in the ILS and throughout the Libraries discovery layers and to create definitive title lists that associate and articulate e-book titles with package purchases. This tool compares vendor title lists against ILS metadata in order to identify missing titles and generate reports. The paper will discuss what prompted the development of the database; present the e-book data flow in NCSU Libraries and e-book reconciliation workflows designed based on the data flow; report on our approach on how to collect e-book title lists, normalize metadata and identify matching point for the reconciliation; present our findings by analyzing the data; and discuss the most common e-books issues found in the reconciliation process, the causes and solutions for these issues.

Introduction

The NCSU Libraries acquisitions and discovery (A&D) department is currently staffed by twenty-four full-time employees divided into three units. The monographs and serials units each have nine staff members, and our data projects and partnerships unit (DPP) contains five staff members. We are a highly centralized, merged acquisitions and cataloging department. All unit staff perform acquisitions and cataloging tasks related to their functional areas. For example, staff in the monographs unit order, purchase, catalog, and troubleshoot non-continuing resources in all formats. Acquisitions and discovery handles purchasing, licensing, and access across all NCSU libraries and branches.

In 2014–2015, the Libraries acquired and managed approximately 34,000 combined monographic and serial e-resources. From an e-book perspective, this number includes e-book packages, firm e-book orders, e-book DDA/PDA titles, and e-book approval materials. We are a Serials Solutions customer and we typically manage a combined 555,000 unique serial and monographic titles in our Serials Solutions knowledge base.

NCSU Libraries purchased seventy-seven e-book packages in 2014–2015. This statistic represents the total number of packages acquired, as opposed to the total number of providers, as we purchased multiple packages from some vendors. From those seventy-seven e-book packages, we managed approximately 16,000 e-book titles in this fiscal year.

Last year the monographs unit team tackled a project to create an e-resource hub for our e-book packages. The e-resource hub is a Wiki-based tool that captures administrative metadata about our e-book packages. This includes data like: licensing, acquisitions information, access, and cataloging information. The e-resource hub was our first step toward capturing all known information about all our e-book packages in one space and helped inform a needs assessment for a possible e-book package electronic resource management (ERM) solution. Since an e-book ERM solution is still somewhere in our future, we realized we needed a tool to help us address more immediate concerns. We created the eBook Reconciliation Database, a Microsoft Access database, as this interim solution.

Currently our eBook Reconciliation Database includes title list data sourced from vendors and MARC record data about our e-book packages sourced from our ILS. As part of the design, we intentionally focused on e-book packages and left firm, DDA/PDA, and approval eb-ook orders out of

http://dx.doi.org/10.5703/1288284316267

the equation. We have a solid workflow for these e-book resources and, as a result, feel more confident in our management of these materials. The scope and volume of our e-book packages, however, demanded that we consider a tool that would help automate some identified problem areas.

Project Overview

We designed the eBook Reconciliation Database to initially address three specific concerns: access verification, title list certification, and a package/provider lookup tool. We needed a tool that would help us definitive describe what e-books we owned, their vendor and package association, and allow us to ensure we were providing access to those titles throughout all our discovery layers.

In our existing landscape, we had three elements:

1. Publisher title lists that represented purchased e-book content
2. Corresponding e-book packages activated in the NCSU Libraries Serials Solutions knowledge base
3. MARC records for each individual e-book title through Serials Solutions 360 MARC Record Service

Due to the sheer volume and scale of e-book titles purchased, we found we were unable to perform basic quality control for our e-book packages. We were unable to manually check that every e-book title in a publisher title list was activated in Serials Solutions. Instead we spot-checked titles when activating an e-book package in the Serials Solutions knowledge base. We were unable to follow up e-book front file content the year following to codify a final title list and ensure each title was properly activated in Serials Solutions. Finally, we were not able to check that Serials Solutions provided a MARC record for each title activated in the Libraries knowledge base.

We were relying on publishers to provide Serials Solutions with the correct information for each e-book package and for Serials Solutions to manage our e-book collections for us. We knew, however, that just because we did not have the staffing to manage the volume of e-books purchased did not mean we could rely on publishers and Serials Solutions to do this work for us.

For these reasons, we created a tool that would help automate e-book package processes, allowing staff to focus on problems by weeding out the titles that were correct. The volume of e-book packages purchased and titles included in each individual e-book packages is simply too great for us to manually ensure:

1. Every title included in an e-book title list is correctly activated in the Serials Solutions knowledge base
2. A MARC record is present in our library catalog for each title
3. We have access to every title on the title list at the publisher's site

The access verification functions of the eBook Reconciliation Database are designed to address these concerns. We load publisher-provided title list data and we load data from our ILS into the eBook Reconciliation Database; then write queries to compare the two sets of data. Through this reconciliation process, we ensure that every title included in an e-book package publisher title list is correctly activated in Serials Solutions and that we have a MARC record in our library catalog. The scale of e-book titles means we are not able to check access at the publisher's site for every single e-book title in every package, but staff do check access for problem titles and we have discovered and corrected patterns of access issues by this method.

We have learned that perpetual access as a licensing concept and perpetual access as an acquisitions concept do not necessarily agree. As companies are bought and sold, content changes platforms, or publisher's perform backend metadata cleanup, access to e-book titles we own "in perpetuity" is sometimes lost. Discovering titles that fall through the cracks and reestablishing access to those owned titles requires the Libraries be able to:

1. Demonstrate we own the title or titles in question through a license, a title list, or some other means
2. Provide proof of purchase

The eBook Reconciliation Database allows us to certify a title list, stamping it with a date and time giving us a title list of record. This title list shows we owned a title on a specific date and negotiate restored access. Acquisitions and dwiscovery staff troubleshoot e-book access issues reported by public services and the first questions we ask are: do we own this title and should we have access to this e-book title?

Performing access verification, title reconciliation, and creating title lists of record are critical to answering this question quickly and efficiently. We are halfway to our answer when we can say with certainty that, yes,

1. The title is included on a title list of record
2. We had access to it on a known date and time

Knowing this information allows us to use our e-resource hub to track down the last pieces of information we need to contact a vendor.

Workflows and Tools

We started the e-book reconciliation project with the pilot phase in December 2014. Through the pilot phase we built up the database with some sample data, identified different roles and tasks for staff with various levels of knowledge and skills, and established a set of workflow and documentation.

In May 2015, we rolled out Phase 1. During Phase 1, we applied the one-way reconciliation strategy, which identified titles shown in the publisher list but not in our ILS. Staff were trained with adequate e-book knowledge and skills to complete the assigned tasks. We completed 21 e-book provider/packages reconciliation.

Phase 1 was an incredibly valuable learning experience for us. It allowed us to ensure titles in the publisher provided list were activated correctly in our system and to identify common errors existed in our e-book data and to find solutions to correct those errors. We also discovered there was a significant delay for new e-book titles to appear in our knowledge base and realized it would be beneficial to create a reconciliation calendar for timely and efficient reconciliation. Moreover, to capture titles showing in our ILS but not in the publisher provided list, a two-way reconciliation strategy needs to be in place.

With the lessons learned and findings discovered during phase 1 we were very well prepared to move into Phase 2 in October, 2015. We modified the database to perform a two-way reconciliation, created the reconciliation schedule, streamlined the workflows, and provided more training to staff with new knowledge and skills. For the time being, we are working on reconciling 2014 e-book packages. And the report function to produce a certified title list is being implemented in the database. We will continue develop the lookup function in the database as our next phase.

There are a wealth of library systems including knowledge base, ILS, and discovery systems for libraries to choose from. These systems form a unique e-book data chain for different libraries. To design the reconciliation project, it's highly recommended to have a good understand of the data chain in your library system. At NC State Libraries, e-book titles are activated in the desired databases in Serials Solutions; MARC record service is activated in Serials Solutions and then loaded into our ILS, Sirsi. Finally the e-book data are pulled into our discovery system, Endeca, for patrons to discover. The data chain suggests that errors can be introduced while data are traveling from one platform/system to another one. The e-book reconciliation database has been designed to source data from the systems and capture errors presented in the chain.

The project is a collaborated effort between two units, Monograph unit and DPP unit, in our A&D department. E-resource librarians (ERLs) and staff are assigned with different roles and assignments. To manage and streamline the process, a seamless workflow with role assignments is indispensable. It starts with monograph ERL identifying the e-book packages that need to be reconciled. Staff then collect title lists from the publishers and Sirsi. The two title lists for a specific publisher are then compared and the mismatches are identified. Staff then identify and mark the issue with each title and take corresponding actions to resolve the issue. The reconciled final lists are then generated and sent to publishers for confirmation. This completes the whole reconciliation process.

An intuitive project management (PM) tool has proved to be critical to the success of the project. We've been using Trello as our PM tool. Trello is a free cloud-based PM tool. It contains three essential elements: board, list, and card. We built an e-book reconciliation board, and it included several lists as tasks/steps, and created a card for each provider package to be reconciled. The package cards were moved around between the lists as team members moved through the tasks. With Trello, we have kept all the communication in one place, eliminating the use of multiple excel files and e-mails, and the process has been transparent to all team members.

Staff were assigned to identify and mark status in the database. This can be challenging for inexperienced staff due to the complex nature of e-books issues with various scenarios involved. The decision tree workflow maps shown in Figure 1 proved to be helpful to staff. A decision tree is a decision support tool, which uses a tree-like graph to display decision points and chances. It turns complicated if-then scenarios into a straightforward tree-like graph. Following the decision tree workflow map, staff were instructed to mark the status for each title and to take corresponding actions.

The Database and the Reconciliation Approach

The database is built with Microsoft Access. There are two reasons why we chose Microsoft Access. First of all, as part of the Microsoft Office suite, we have access to the Access in our library. Secondly, our DPP unit has an ERL and staff who have experience and skills of developing databases in Access. They have built and maintained several databases for the department. The database has gone through evolution as we move along with the project.

The database has a dashboard shown in Figure 2, which includes a list of publishers that have e-book packages to be reconciled. Each staff member is assigned to one publisher. Clicking on each publisher brings up a table with a list of mismatched titles. The table includes several important elements including Type, ISBN, URL, Package, Status, and Publication Year. Type indicates the mismatch categories: No Sirsi Match or No Vendor Match. No Sirsi Match means the titles not showing in Sirsi, and No Vendor Match means they are not showing in the publisher lists. The Completed column is checked when all work is completed for the title. Package specifies the

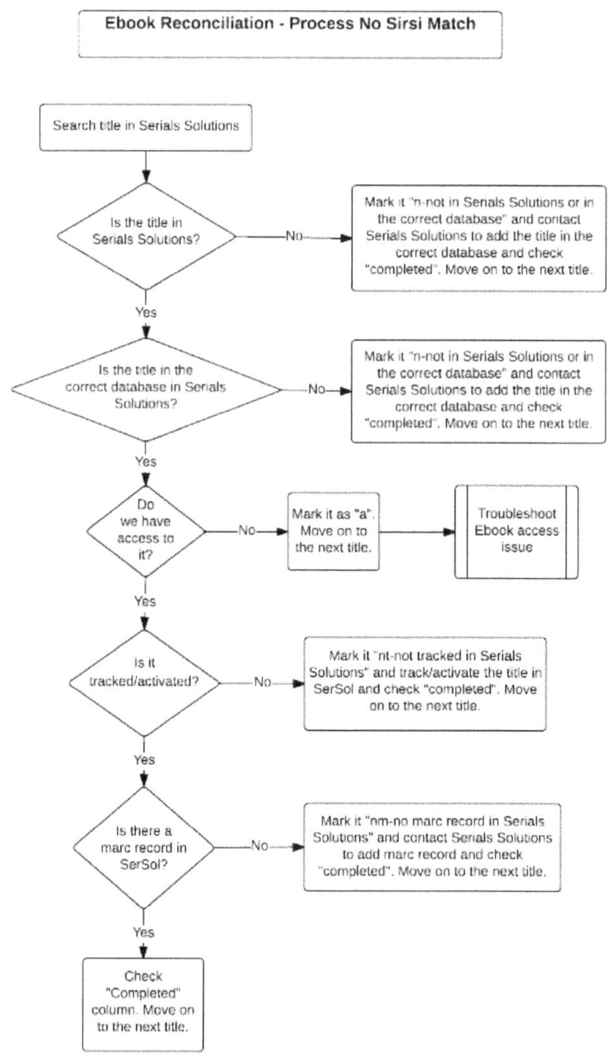

Figure 1. Decision tree map.

Figure 2. E-Book reconciliation dashboard.

Serials Solutions database that the title is or should be in, and it's manually ingested into the publisher title list by staff before the title list is pulled into the database. Staff rely on the package data to determine in which database the title should be activated. Status is used to categorize discrepancies between the two title lists. Several statuses have been identified during the reconciliation process and will be elaborated in the "Findings" section in this paper.

The reconciliation approach entails comparing two title lists for each publisher and identifying mismatches between the two lists.

Publishers were e-mailed to request the title lists for desired packages. Several metadata elements were required including: title, URL, ISBN, publication year, and package/collection. A staff member was designated to prepare the title list ensuring these essential data elements were included in the publisher list. The column names were standardized so that queries could be reused for all publishers/packages.

A custom bibliographic report was built in Sirsi to extract records from specific providers. The report was based on the provider name contained in the 856 field subfield z, which we requested as part of our MARC record service. See example below:

|zSpringer-Verlag SpringerLink ebooks—Behavioral Science (2009)

The URL or a portion of the URL was used as the identifier for matching titles on both lists. These are two examples of the URLs from the publisher list and the ILS list with the matching points underlined:

Publisher:
http://dx.doi.org/10.1061/9780784478851

ILS:
http://ascelibrary.org/doi/book/10.1061/9780784413654

This matching approach has been successful for many reconciled title lists. However, there are some publisher provided lists containing URLs with redirected DOIs. For example:

Publisher: http://dx.doi.org/10.1117/3.547461

ILS:
http://ebooks.spiedigitallibrary.org/book.aspx?bookid=149

OpenRefine Jython script was used to find the ending location of redirecting URLs. ISBNs did not prove to be useful because it's complicated to extract from Sirsi, and multiple URLs are often stored in MARC records and publisher lists.

Findings

Several most commonly seen issues have been identified and solutions have been provided to

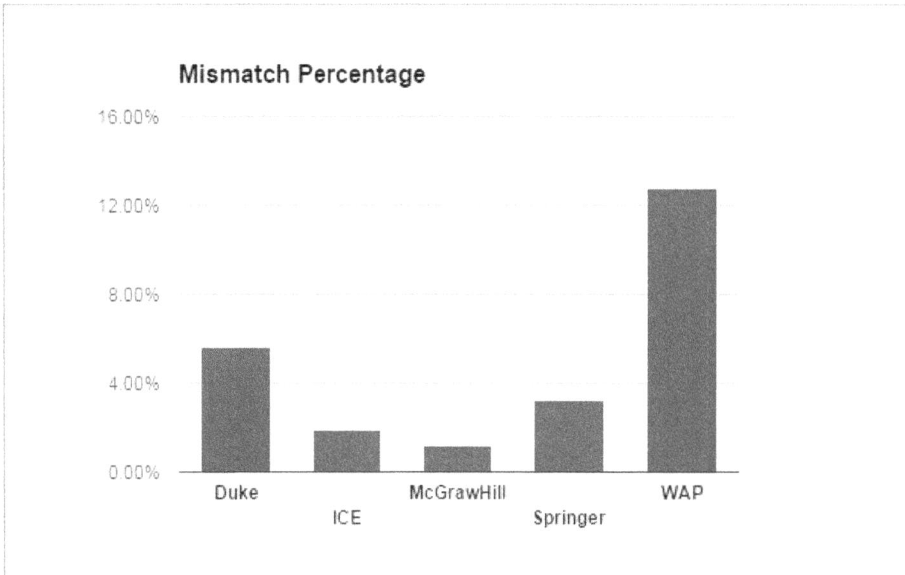

Figure 3. Mismatch percentage.

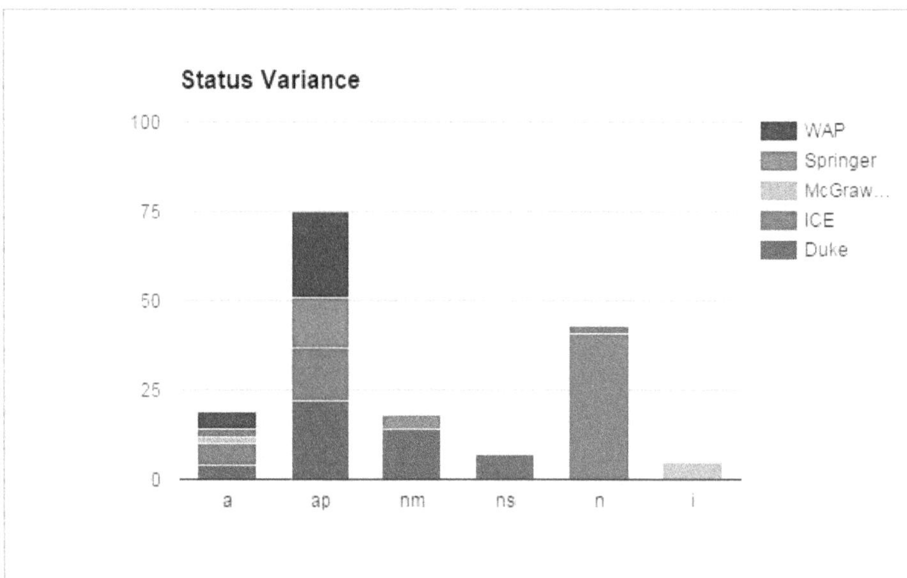

Figure 4. Issues/status variance.

resolve these issues. There were titles found not tracked in the correct database in Serials Solutions or not shown in Serials Solutions. Staff would activate these titles in the correct database in Serials Solutions or contact Serials Solutions to add them to the desired database. For titles without a MARC record in Serials Solutions, resulting in no Sirsi match, staff would request Serials Solutions to add a MARC record to the title. For no vendor match titles with access issues, we would delete the record in Sirsi. For other no vendor match titles with proper access, publishers would be contacted to confirm our rights, and if rights confirmed, these titles would be added to the publisher list. The reconciliation process allowed us to identify titles with access issues. The solutions to these titles were variant depending on the causes. For issues caused by incorrect URL, the URLs were corrected either in Serials Solutions, Sirsi, or in the publisher list. For vendor platform issues, publishers were contacted to resolve them.

To justify the value of the project, let's take a look at the percentage of mismatched titles for some publishers, shown in Figure 3. It's interesting to see that the number varies among the publishers with ranges from 1% to 13% for these publishers.

Furthermore, we are very much intrigued by the difference among all the found issues. The chart below brings our attention to the discrepancies for the mismatches. It shows the number of titles for each of the issues for these five publishers. The top one is "ap," which means add to the publisher list. These are the titles not included in the publisher list, but we have rights and access to them. This is caused by the fact that publishers keep adding titles to the packages after we collect titles from them. We feel fortunate to capture these constant changes, and meanwhile, it suggests we should perform the reconciliation soon after we collect the title list and the reconciliation process should be regularly conducted. The second large number of issues are titles either not in Serials Solutions or not in the correct database in Serials Solutions. This demonstrates that publisher and Serials Solutions are not consistent regarding what is included in a collection.

These discrepancies/issues reveal errors, legitimate or not. It also suggests the inconsistency among different segments in the e-book data supply chain. The reconciliation process allows us to correct these errors and maintain data integrity in the data supply chain.

Conclusion

NCSU Libraries eBook Reconciliation Database is an example of a homegrown tool that successfully facilitates management of e-book packages. The scale and volume of e-book package purchases necessitated that we create a tool to help address specific quality control concerns: access verification to ensure title-level representation throughout the Libraries's discovery layers; and, title list certification to definitively describe e-book package entitlements. By sourcing and comparing publisher title list data and ILS e-book MARC record data, we are able to take management of our e-book packages into our own hands for the first time. The local efforts we put forward may initiate a larger conversation with stakeholders in the e-book data supply chain on how to maintain data integrity in the system.

Eeny, Meeny, Miny, Moe: E-Books Changed Our Workflow

Denise D. Novak, Acquisitions Librarian, Carnegie Mellon University

Terry Hurlbert, Cataloging Senior Librarian, Carnegie Mellon University

Abstract

As the popularity and sheer number of e-books increased, it became evident that our existing process or workflow for acquiring and cataloging them would need some modification. This presentation will explain how the Carnegie Mellon University Libraries Technical Services implemented changes in workflow for ordering and cataloging e-books. Including the topics of technology, user expectations, and getting reference librarians on board, we'll cover the why of e-books, what has gone well, and where we go from here.

Carnegie Mellon University is a global research university of approximately 13,200 students, representing 114 countries. Over 5,000 faculty and staff representing 48 countries work and teach at the main Pittsburgh campus, Silicon Valley campus, and Qatar campus. The University Libraries in Pittsburgh are made up of three separate libraries. The Hunt library houses fine arts, humanities, and social sciences collections. It has recently become the home of the Integrative Design, Arts, and Technology Network (IDeATe). The Sorrells library holds the engineering, materials science, computer science, and robotics collections. The Mellon Institute contains biology, chemistry, and other life sciences collections. Users of these libraries need access to e-Books, and we're here to tell you how we do that.

Let's hop into Mr. Peabody's Way Back Machine for a moment. In 1999, Carnegie Mellon University Libraries purchased its first e-book collection through PALINET (now Lyrasis). It consisted of a collection of computer science titles which immediately became very popular. I thought, "Wow, this is the future and we should buy more e-books." Unfortunately, it wasn't that simple. It took some persuasion to get the publishers and librarians on board with the idea of offering users e-books, and we're still working with publishers and librarians on this front. I've found our STEM librarians to be very amenable to the e-book format. Most of their journals and proceedings are electronic, and they realized electronic access for users made more sense. I need to add that one of the big drivers for purchasing e-books is space. Both the Hunt Library and the Sorrells Engineering and Science Library have space issues. We needed more space for student study areas.

At this time, e-books were, for the most part, only available through the publishers who required license agreements for their titles.

License agreements with publishers are included in my routine. Our workflow for license agreements runs through the University Contracts Office. I do not sign license agreements, and the lawyers I work with understand the language much better than I do. When the publishers send me a contract, I read it over for items that are problematic. Ownership, usage rights, interlibrary loans, and library access (are all campuses included?). Then I send it over to University Contracts, who lets me know if there are issues they have questions about and then sign off on the license. I then forward an electronic copy of the signed license agreement to the publisher and in turn the publisher sends me a fully executed copy of the license. This is a pretty streamlined process.

In 2006, we signed licenses with ebrary and e-book Library (EBL), two aggregators of e-books. In addition we were still gathering licenses from publishers who weren't part of an aggregator's list.

When acquisitions staff began ordering e-books, the lines between acquisitions and cataloging began to blur. Acquisitions staff download the MARC records either from OCLC or the vendor/publisher website, and use MARC Edit to

http://dx.doi.org/10.5703/1288284316268

Title: INTEGRATIVE ALEXANDER TECHNIQUE PRACTICE FOR PERFORMING ARTISTS: ONSTAGE SYNERGY.
Author: MADDEN, CATHY
Publisher: INTELLECT LTD
Place of Publication: BRISTOL
Pub Year: 2014
ISBN: 9781783202201
Country Of Origin: UK
Binding: eBook
Pagination: 389 P.
Content Level: PROF
YBP Select: Supplementary
LC Class: PN2075.M34 2014
Subject Headings: ACTING--STUDY & TEACH.
YBP Interdisciplinary Topics: Psychological; Theatre/Drama
Approval Note: AUTH: UNIVERSITY OF WASHINGTON. GUIDEBOOK TO PSYCHOPHYSICAL MASTERY OF ACTING.
Aspects: Practical
Faculty Affiliation: U Washington
Language: English
OCLC: OCN892245928
NON-RETURN/NON-CANCEL YBP

alt-ed slip sent (12/17 /2014)
GobiTween (2 Slips)
alternate editions (1P/1E)
library activity (54 sold)

Supplier	Purchase Option	Library DDA	List Price	Status	Library Availability	Preview
+ EBL	1 User		20.00 USD	Available	Contract on file	Preview
+ EBL	3 User		25.00 USD	Available	Contract on file	Preview
+ EBL	Non-Linear Lending™	Yes	20.00 USD	Available	Contract on file	Preview
+ EBL	Unlimited		30.00 USD	Available	Contract on file	Preview
+ ebrary	3 User		25.00 USD	Available	Contract on file	Preview
+ ebrary	Multiple User Option (MUPO)		30.00 USD	Available	Contract on file	Preview
+ ebrary	Single User Option (SUPO)	Yes	20.00 USD	Available	Contract on file	Preview
+ ProQuest Ebook Central	1 User		20.00 USD	Available	No contract on file	
+ ProQuest Ebook Central	3 User		25.00 USD	Available	No contract on file	
+ ProQuest Ebook Central	Non-Linear		20.00 USD	Available	No contract on file	
+ ProQuest Ebook Central	Unlimited Access		30.00 USD	Available	No contract on file	

Library Note: *Add...*

Figure 1. User options.

add local information and load the records into our ILS.

Once YBP began offering e-books in the GOBI database we started ordering from them. This made sense to us because YBP is our primary book supplier. This change also meant we needed to sign a new license agreement with most publishers, reflecting the use of GOBI to order e-books. A portion of our approval plan with YBP, the Sciences, has become e-preferred.

Then something new was added to the confusion of e-books: different platforms. The decision to select the platform is made by the librarians requesting the title. It's not just the platform, but the number of users is also important. They know their users' needs.

E-book reader technology continues to change, and we do our best to stay on top of the latest technology so our users can download and read texts on a variety of devices. Our users' expectations are to be able to access e-books on any device they may be using, from smart phones to tablets to whatever comes next.

Finally, usage statistics no longer come from reports from our ILS but from aggregators/publishers websites. These statistics become more important as annual circulation figures drop from our print collection, which is a story for another day. And now, I'd like to introduce Terry Hurlbert, the cataloging senior librarian who will tell you her side of the story.

I'd like to make it clear from the outset that I'll be talking about "purchased" collections, not titles acquired via DDA. And my main focus is the workflow for loading e-book MARC records into our catalog (Sirsi/Dynix).

From the cataloging side of things, here's a little history: E-books were first on our cataloging "radar" in 2004 as we began to acquire a substantial number of individual e-book titles. Initial titles were requests from selectors that came via the acquisitions process or free titles for

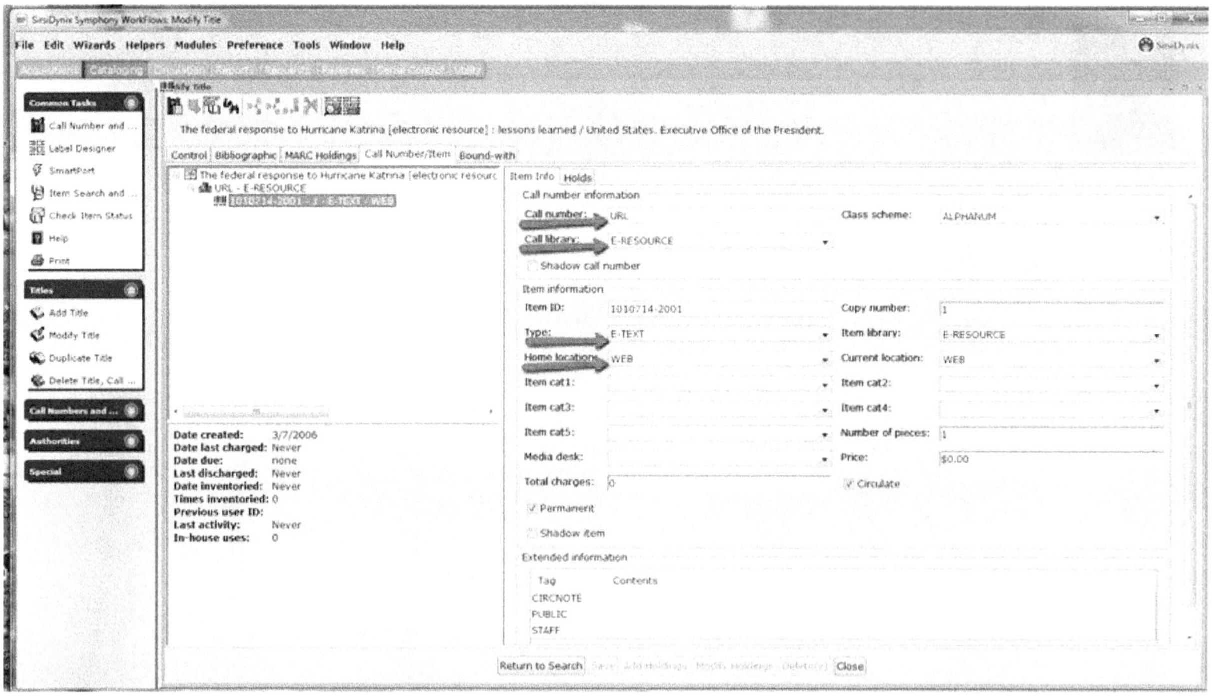
Figure 2. Workflows (cataloging interface) item.

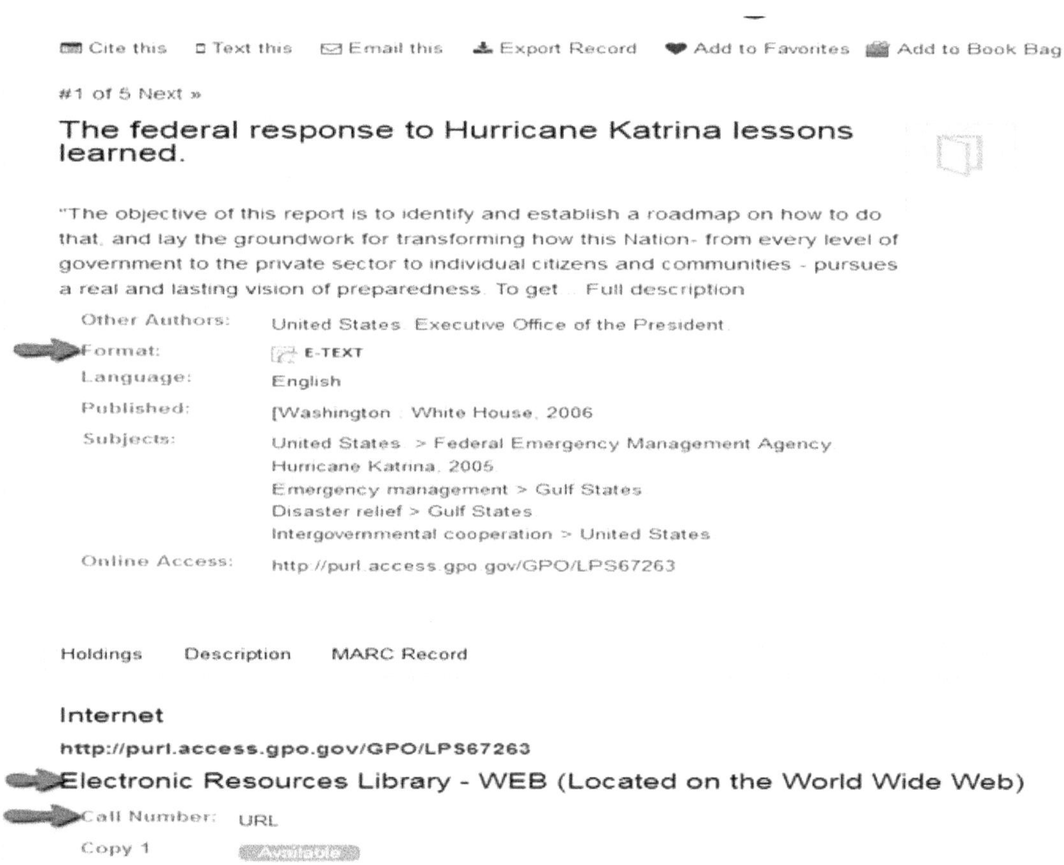

Figure 3. Public catalog.

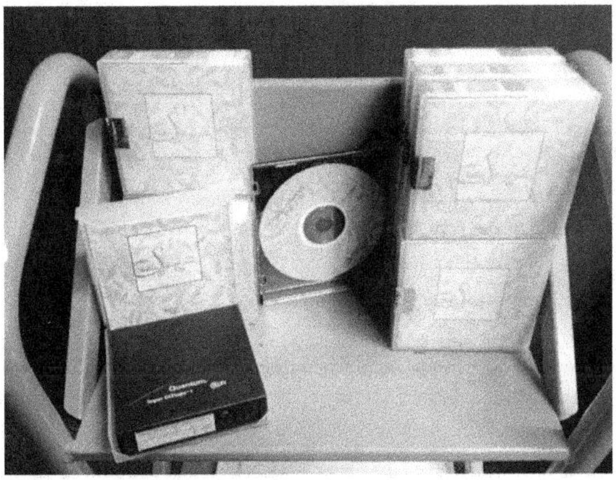

Figure 4. E-Book collections.

catalog. At this point, in addition to the bibliographic record, we needed to create an "item record" in our local system to make it clear(er) to users that the results they were retrieving included electronic books. Some standard vocabulary was needed, and we (acquisitions and cataloging staff) made some quick decisions about that terminology.

We chose the following terminology for the item record:

Library: E-RESOURCE

Call Number: URL

Item Type: E-Text

Location: WEB

This vocabulary has served us pretty well, and we haven't changed it over the years.

Here is how the display of this terminology looks in our public catalog (VuFind).

During these early years I used the order record provided by acquisitions to complete the cataloging in WorkFlows, or if it was necessary, located a record in OCLC or did original cataloging. This required communication with the acquisitions department—there were cases when the order records didn't exactly reflect what we eventually acquired. I had to be alert to such

Retrieving and Loading Files of MARC Records for E-Books

A. Retrieve MARC files for e-books from Vendor Web-Sites – Instructions
VENDOR XXX
Go to http://www.xxxxxxxxxxxxxxxxx.xxx
username: XXXXXX
password: XXXXXX

For recently purchased titles:

1. Login to XXXXX and go to the Reports tab and click on the Invoice Report link.
2. Create and save a list name, using "start list."
3. If applicable, use the browse function in the upper right-hand corner to search for orders using "invoice by date." Enter the dates for those orders for which you wish to download MARC.
4. Use the tick boxes in the right-hand column, "Select," to choose the titles of the MARC you would like (be sure to click on "Save Changes" in the light blue toolbar above). Or you may want to use the "Actions" drop-down menu to select MARC for all titles on the page (be sure to then click on the "Save" button next to the Actions menu).
5. When your list is complete, click on the "view this list" hyperlink to review the list you've made.
6. Then select "XXX MARC Records" in the drop-down export menu, and click on the "Go" button.
7. Your download of free XXX MARC will begin immediately; Save the file (MRC format is the default).
8. Use "MarcEdit" to add holdings information to the records in the file. **SEE MarcEdit INSTRUCTIONS**
9. Use "MARC Import" utility to import the file to the server. **SEE IMPORT INSTRUCTIONS**
10. Use report "Bibload ebooks with holdings" to load the records into WorkFlows. **SEE BIBLOAD INSTRUCTIONS**
11. Once the records are in WorkFlows spot-check a title or two to make sure that the links work and the items are correct

EACH WEBSITE HAS UNIQUE INSTRUCTIONS FOR ACCESSING AND RETRIEVING FILES

Figure 5. Detailed instructions for retrieving files.

B. Edit MARC files with MarcEdit - Instructions

.mrc files are purple .mrk files are blue

1. Open the MARC file that you have retrieved from the vendor. Because it is a MARC file it should automatically open in the MarcEdit program.
2. The "Input File" box will contain the file that you opened. It has the .mrc suffix. The "Output File" box will automatically contain a new file name for the MARC records in their "broken" form. This file will have the .mrk suffix and the records in it are the ones to which you will add holdings information.
3. Check the "MarcBreaker" circle, then click "Execute"
4. In the "Results" box you will see the number of records that were processed and how long it took. (If it is a negative number something has gone wrong)
5. Click the "Edit Records" box. The file of MARC records ready for editing will appear.
6. Under the "Tools" pull-down select "Add/Delete Field"
7. In the "Field" box type in "945"
8. In the "Field Data" box type in "$aURL$wALPHANUM$hWEB-TEXT"
9. Check the box for "Insert last"
10. Click the "Add Field" box
11. Close the "Edit Records" box
12. Close the file containing the MARC records. A window will pop-up asking if you want to save the changes. Click "Yes." The saved file will now appear as an .mrk file (blue)
13. Open the MarcEdit program. Select "MARC Tools."
14. In the "Input File" insert the .mrk file that you just created.
15. In the "Output File" name the file that you will use to import into WorkFlows. I usually put the word "READY" somewhere in the file name so that I know it is the version of the file that is ready to import. You must put ".mrc" at the end of this file name.
16. Check the "MarcMaker" circle, then click "Execute"
17. In the "Results" box you will see the number of records that were processed and how long it took. (If it is a negative number something has gone wrong)
18. You now have a file that is ready to import into WorkFlows and the records contain holdings information that will create items in Workflows.

ADD 945 HOLDINGS FIELD TO MARC RECORD

Figure 6. MarcEdit instructions.

discrepancies and to the fact that there might be many similar records for titles in OCLC for the same title. Since this was a new process we were aware that through experience and cooperation the process for ordering and then making titles available in the catalog needed to evolve.

As with many things in the cataloging world, you learn about a process, a standard, or an accepted practice by observing what others are doing and by exploring the topic on your own.

Between 2004 and 2011, I cataloged about 500 individual titles using this "system." Most were ordered through acquisitions, a few were requests sent directly to me, and a few required support from library information technology in order to store the purchased title on a library server and establish a URL/link.

Late in 2011, acquisitions staff began to do the "cataloging" of e-books, mostly individual titles, and smallish collections of titles including demand-driven acquisitions programs. As Denise has noted, they selected the appropriate record and after payment verified that the link was working.

Statistics for e-books that were added were reported to me (as compiler of all cataloging stats) by acquisitions staff.

Concurrently beginning around 2005, we began to acquire e-books via a variety of providers who delivered larger and larger numbers of titles as a package. Knovel, Credo, and Alexander Street Press were among them, and access to MARC records varied—some we ordered via OCLC, some we got directly from the vendor. I loaded these files of multiple records. One of my first memories associated with loading large numbers of records into the catalog was a huge file of records (thousands) delivered on tape/CD. I had to enlist the library information technology department to help load records that were provided in that format.

It didn't take long for files of MARC records to commonly be delivered via FTP or simple download. Individual instructions for retrieval of files for each vendor were a must. Keeping track of varying logins and differently designed websites became commonplace and time consuming. My activities focused on loading the MARC records,

C. Import and Bibload MARC files of e-books into WorkFlows - Instructions

IMPORT

1. In the "Utility" module select "MARC Import"
2. On the "Property" screen click "OK."
3. Under the "Import" tag fill in the "Source" box with the "READY" file that you created in MarcEdit.
4. Name the "Destination" file. (Usually I use the vendor name and date I created the file.)
5. Click "Import" at the bottom of the screen. This file will now appear in the list when you run the Bibload report.

BIBLOAD

1. In the "Reports" module select "Schedule New Reports."
2. On the "Set Session Settings" screen click "OK."
3. Under the "Templates" tab select the report, "Bibload ebooks with holdings."
4. Click "Set Up & Schedule."
5. Provide a "Report Name" in the box.
6. Click on the "Load" tab.
7. In the "File to Load" box insert the READY file that you already imported.
8. Click "Run Now."

Th10/10/2011

Rev.12/19/2011

BIBLIOGRAPHIC RECORD AND ITEM IN LOCAL SYSTEM

Figure 7. Instructions for importing records into ILS.

keeping up to date instructions for the sites, and compiling stats for records loaded.

The point here is not the content of the instructions, but that we needed unique instructions for each unique supplier of MARC records.

After file retrieval it was necessary to have instructions for editing the records in the files and loading the files into WorkFlows.

Steps 8–10 of the file retrieval instructions required additional levels of detail. For instance, step 8 involved using MarcEdit—a process that entailed additional steps.

I used MarcEdit to add a holdings field to each record and in some circumstances to add a local field to identify specific collections of e-books or subsets of a collection.

Another for instance, steps 9 and 10 of the retrieval instructions involved using the MARC Import utility and the Bibload Report in WorkFlows to load files of MARC records into our catalog—two other processes that entailed additional steps.

If all of this seems heavy on the "instructions" aspect, that's because it is. Attention to detail has always been important in cataloging, and MARC records for e-books has not changed that. I made these instructions available for use by cataloging and acquisitions staff.

More recently (the beginning of 2015), OCLC WorldShare has come to the fore as a way to manage MARC record delivery for selected vendor sets that were once delivered via WorldCat Collection Sets (a service that was discontinued at the end of March 2015).

WorldShare allows us to:

- Set up a library profile in WorldShare Collection Manager
- Enable MARC record delivery
- Define record editing and delivery options
- Opt in to desired collections

It is very helpful as a centralized location for retrieving files. WorldShare does not provide access to everything that we purchase, but is still a good, time-saving tool.

Here are some other details to mention about the process:

1. I usually test the links to a few records from a file before loading the MARC file. Generally everything is fine, but I have discovered instances when links were not working—a problem that requires follow-up with the vendor.
2. I eventually devised a report in WorkFlows to load files of records that contained new as well as updated records. It is important to be aware that everything is not necessarily a new record and plan for this possibility. It can be tricky in cases where I have added local information to records in a file, and then I have to overlay some of the records in that file. I don't want to lose the local information in the original file, so I have to plan accordingly.
3. The process of loading most large files is centralized with me. I trained another person on the cataloging team to retrieve files and load the records for our Qatar campus. This is a discrete task—not exactly simple but less prone to problems cropping up.

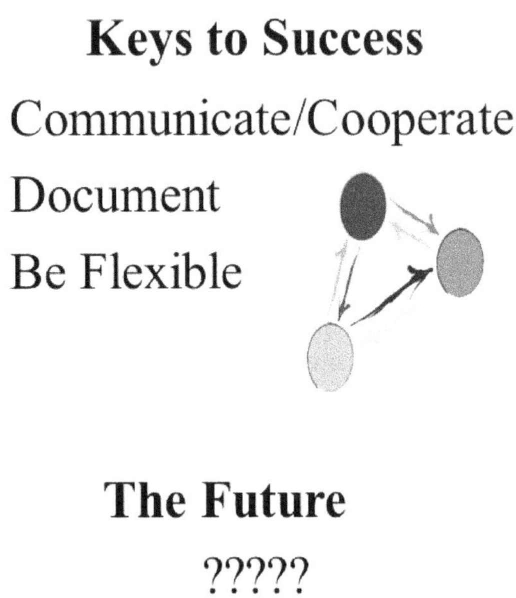

Figure 8. Keys to success.

Keys to success:

- Communication between teams/departments—cataloging and acquisitions have not been territorial throughout this experience; we have shared information and know-how
- Document procedures—for the sake of consistency and time efficiency
- Be flexible—whatever comes next, in weeks, months, or years, we will embrace

The Future

We're not sure what it will bring, but the same qualities and keys that have gotten us through this chapter with e-books will get us through the next.

Dollars and Sense: Examining the RFP Process

J. Michael Thompson, Head of Acquisitions, University of Houston

Arta Kabashi, Trainer, ProQuest

Carol Seiler, EBSCO Infromation Services

Eileen M. Johnson, Senior Associate Dean, Webster University Libraries

Abstract

While the Request for Proposal (RFP) is not an activity that all librarians encounter continually, it is an endeavor that all library service groups and companies undertake as an essential part of their ongoing operations. This article summarizes the 2015 Charleston session entitled "Dollars and Sense: Examining the RFP Process" which delved into the RFP process from multiple viewpoints, serving both as a review of the process itself and as an investigation of how the process can generate positive results for all parties involved. The panel consisted of a librarian from a large academic library, a librarian from a medium-sized academic library, a vendor representative, and an individual with considerable consortia experience. The academic librarians reviewed the generic and the institution-specific items that contribute to a successful RFP. The vendor representative discussed how the vendor reviews and crafts a response that fulfills the requirements of the RFP while providing contractual guarantees for themselves. The consortia representative looked at both how they respond to an RFP as well as what they require in an RFP; having a unique perspective of both sending out and receiving RFPs.

Introduction

There are cases in which the awarding of a contract at the conclusion of the request for proposal (RFP) process hinges solely upon bid price. However, when viewed as a whole, the RFP process can provide many opportunities for advantages that extend beyond mere price points. For example, the process can provide a platform for the review of current practices and planning for future needs. By its very nature, the process opens lines of communication which can foster greater understanding and agreement between libraries and their vendors. Of course, the resulting contract for goods and services provides financial and service assurances for both sides.

In order to realize the full benefits of an RFP, institutions and vendors need to work in concert with each other throughout the process. One useful approach to examine how the parties can best work together is to review the roles and responsibilities over the various stages of the process, which can be divided into five broad component parts:

1. Conception and conceiving
2. Responding
3. Evaluating
4. Awarding and contracting
5. Performance of the contract

Through a review of each stage of the cycle, the panelists explored approaches that would address the challenges and realize opportunities that exist throughout the process.

Conception and Conceiving

As with many aspects of life, proper preparation is the key to a successful RFP. It is advisable for libraries to begin planning for an RFP well in advance, especially if it has been a few years since a formal process has been completed. This involves both internal and external tasks.

An important first step will be to decide if an RFP is needed at all. The library's or institution's purchasing department may be able to indicate if

http://dx.doi.org/10.5703/1288284316269

there are circumstances in which the institution requires an RFP. If input from a purchasing department is not an option or does not seem to apply, a library may consider criteria including size, scope, and cost, as well as the time since the project was last formally bid. The library should also investigate the existence of pre-negotiated contracts at the local or state level that they can "piggyback" on, instead of starting with a brand-new RFP. Additionally, there are certain instances when the goods and services needed are only available through a single provider. In cases where no alternatives exist, the library should strongly consider bypassing the RFP process entirely in favor of formulating a sole source contract with that particular supplier.

Once the library has decided to pursue an RFP, another primary step is to review institutional and, if applicable, state requirements that will apply to the RFP and contracting process. For example, some states require an open bidding process with specific guidelines for posting the RFP. At institutions with less formalized RFP requirements, the librarian may need to develop an appropriate process for the project from the ground up.

The investigation of internal processes and procedures also opens communication with those within the institution who will be working with the library to complete the RFP, such as purchasing departments found at many larger institutions. It is a good practice to make these individuals aware of the library's upcoming RFP so that they get it onto their schedules. Additionally, this is a good time to review responsibilities and clarify who will be completing tasks such as submitting paperwork, drafting an award letter, and finalizing a contract. Finally, it is important to understand how evaluations are made, and what types of approvals will be needed to proceed with awarding and contracting.

The next step will be to develop a timeline. It is important to manage the project schedule by determining non-negotiable deadlines, establishing the ideal end date, and working backwards from there to determine how long each phase of the project might take. As the RFP progresses, the timeline should be consulted regularly to ensure that appropriate progress is being made.

Another key task is assembling the right team to work on the RFP. The team will need a charge that indicates whether it will be making the decision, or if it's just collecting information and making a recommendation for a higher-level administrator. If the team is making the decision, a person with decision-making authority should be included. Others to consider include those close to the work who understand the service being considered, and someone from library or institutional purchasing with strong vendor relation skills. Ultimately, the make-up of the team will depend on the dynamics of the organization and the people involved.

As the team is being formed, the group should solicit input from library staff members closely associated with the products and services. These conversations should include a review of current processes and questions regarding anticipated future needs. If the project is a large, public one, patrons or constituents may need to be queried as well, perhaps via surveys or focus groups. This is also a good time to conduct a thorough scan of the marketplace and to review sample RFPs. Potential vendors may be willing to provide well-written sample RFPs that correspond closely to the service being considered.

During this phase, the library may begin preliminary discussions with potential vendors. Giving vendors prior notice that the library will be issuing an RFP allows them to begin their own internal conversations and scheduling that will improve their ability to issue a timely response. The librarian must remain neutral during these preparatory discussions and structure them as simply notices regarding the expected timing and nature of the upcoming RFPs.

Some institutions proscribe RFP-related communication between potential vendors and individuals tasked with evaluating responses once the RFP has been issued. Regardless of formal institutional policy, librarians need to ensure that any communication between parties during the formal process does not provide advantages to one bidder over another. Additionally, it is recommended that all parties avoid engaging in activities which might appear to impact neutrality during the RFP process. For example, a librarian might consider turning down an invitation to have coffee with a vendor at a conference if there is not a specific topic to discuss that does not involve the outstanding RFP.

With the preliminary preparation completed, the writing of the RFP can begin. A successful RFP does not need to follow a set format, but most will include many of the following elements:

- Brief summary of the purpose of the RFP and scope of the project
- Approximate dollar value of the contract
- Note about the term of the contract
- Statement about the library or parent organization highlighting unique factors
- Request for proof of financial solvency/strength of the applicant

When writing the RFP, simple, precise language should be used. Language from sample RFPs can be used, particularly for generic sections such as those on when and how to return an RFP. For substantial requirements, though, the library should construct specific questions that will draw out targeted responses about how vendors will meet the library's unique needs. In other cases, an institution might have standard language that must be included. Also, take care to consider the information being requested. In certain cases, it may be better to ask for a summary of certain types of information instead of the information itself. If a library is not sure how it plans to use information it is requesting, it is wise to reconsider requesting it, or to reword the request significantly.

The requirements section is the core of the RFP, where a library describes its needs in detail, and asks vendors to explain how they will meet these needs. Libraries will want to give this section close attention, as responses to it will be used extensively during the evaluation phase. It is recommended that the RFP not be written too broadly or too narrowly. If it is too broad, it is likely that the library will receive responses from vendors that do not have a chance of getting the contract. If the RFP is written too narrowly, potential acceptable responses might be eliminated.

Many library services have a baseline set of functions that qualified vendors will provide in a fairly uniform way. The RFP might use a checklist or a series of brief yes/no questions to cover these basic questions without overemphasizing them. The library can then focus on asking questions about how vendors can meet its unique needs, and vendors can spend their time and energy detailing how they will meet the library's needs.

Specialty or less common requirements should be detailed in the RFP. Similar to writing a job posting, the library should include "required" as well as "preferred" detail here. Allowing for value-added services, longer terms, or flexible pricing will provide the vendor options to ensure all potential benefits of business with that vendor are listed.

The RFP may conclude with the criteria which will be used to evaluate responses as well as a request for information about costs. The evaluation criteria should be well-constructed and accurate; this will make the appraisal of the responses and eventual awarding of the contract more straightforward.

The RFP package will include a cover letter that might contain a contact for the vendors, statements protecting both parties' confidentiality, a request for references, and submission requirements including a due date and format. The cover letter should also indicate how long proposals should remain valid. If the parent institution permits, it might also include a statement delineating the library's rights regarding selection of a vendor.

Before sending out the RFP, it is helpful to reread the entire package, or have someone with fresh eyes check for mistakes or unclear instructions. The library will need to learn from its home institution whether it may just send the RFP directly to the vendors it has identified, or whether it is required to post public notices. For larger institutions, distributing the RFP will be handled through the purchasing department.

Responding

For nonprofit organizations, responding to the RFP is handled by the training team or team leads. Once the RFP has been posted, the team lead gathers all relevant documents and prepares a written response. It is useful to create a central document either on an internal network or a web-based file sharing system where team members can locate key due dates and relevant documents needed in preparing the final response.

In the event that a nonprofit is the issuing agency for the RFP, some time is taken to respond to questions submitted by responders. Use the open question period to clarify all outstanding issues and review the methodology for evaluation if not made previously clear in the RFP process.

The vendor process is similar to the nonprofit organization. The vendor will receive the RFP (or download it from the posted site) and begin to analyze it. The first read will allow the vendor to determine whether it can meet the base needs and if it should proceed with a response. The vendor may have a specific team devoted to responding to RFPs, or it might be assigned to various groups based on the content of the RFP. Preferred or value-added areas may need expertise within the company to ensure response is correct and thorough. Often a specific coordinator will be assigned to monitor the response process.

The response coordinator will pull out important dates, conditions, and any specialty requirements. A calendar will be set up and monitored. The coordinator ensures all areas of the RFP are appropriately answered and the response is sent within the time frame denoted in the RFP. The coordinator also assumes responsibility for ensuring any questions are sent to the library contact specified in the RFP. Required references are reviewed and contacted to ensure availability before inclusion in an RFP. Additionally, the response coordinator will do a final review to ensure consistency, clarity, and completeness of response.

Providing the vendors (via the RFP) a timeline of when the RFP will be awarded and when the contract would take effect also helps in crafting the response. Some RFPs will require specific formats in the return (PDF, MS Word, Excel for specific sections, etc.) or may require a certain number of bound print copies. The vendor appreciates acknowledgement of the returned RFP; this assures the vendor the RFP response was received in a timely manner.

Evaluating

The evaluation process may differ slightly depending on the type of library. A library with a less formal process may find itself solely responsible for making the final vendor selection. This offers more control and efficiency, but also means that the library is accountable for the final decision and communicating results to the respondents. In larger institutions with more formal processes, the purchasing department may gather the evaluations from the team members and communicate results themselves. The library under a more formal process may be insulated a bit from responsibility for the final decision, but that typically comes at the price of a more complex and sluggish process.

Regardless of whether an institution has a structured or unstructured RFP process, it is essential to provide a careful review of each application. One approach that has proven successful is first to perform a cursory review of each response and record initial impressions. Then, each response should be reviewed again, basing the evaluation strictly upon formal criteria as presented in the RFP. Any disparity between the two reviews should be explored to determine if any material evaluation issues have been found. The initial review can reveal if some responses should be eliminated immediately because they have failed to meet the basic RFP requirements. Also, if the cursory review reveals that some expected vendors are missing from the pool, the library or purchasing department may want to send a follow-up notice to them, especially if they have previously expressed interest.

If during the evaluation phase additional information is needed, requests can be sent to applicants either directly or through the purchasing department if required. Additionally, if no clear winner emerges from the evaluation process, follow-up meetings can be scheduled with the remaining respondents. Frequently these meetings will provide the vendors a chance to present the factors they feel differentiate their products and services from those of their competitors. The meeting can also provide a forum for the vendor to present their best and final offer (BAFO). To maintain equity, all remaining vendors should receive the same notice regarding what will be discussed and the expected outcomes of the meeting.

Awarding and Contracting

Once a decision has been made, the successful vendor should be contacted, referencing the submitted RFP response, their BAFO, and any other details agreed to in person. The notification of unsuccessful bidders can vary from situation to situation. At times notifications are sent once the successful respondent accepts the award. In other instances, notifications are held until a contract has been signed or once negotiations are well underway. In some cases, local policies and procedures dictate when notices are delivered. Regardless, both the successful and unsuccessful bidders should be notified.

Contracts are also handled differently across different organizations. Some institutions request the vendor to draft a contract that will be reviewed by an institution's general counsel. Other institutions have standard contracting forms which are completed internally with information specific to the current agreement. These "form contracts" are then sent to the vendor for their approval. In either case, the contracts are signed after both parties agree to the terms. Depending on the contract, this process can vary from simple to laborious. Once a contract has been signed, the library should obtain copies of all documents, to be used for ready-reference of specific contract details, in-house training, and as background material for the next RFP. At this point, library staff should be notified and preparations made to accommodate the new agreement (if necessary). This is also a convenient time to remind library staff of any binding confidentiality agreements.

The award process can be exciting for vendors who are awarded the contract or contemplative for those who are not. Once the contract has been awarded, it is important to communicate objectives, and set clear measurable milestones between the contracting parties. The vendor that has been awarded the contract will ensure that personnel are assigned to manage the new (or renewed) account. An unsuccessful bid is an opportunity to learn and grow. The vendor will contact the library or non-profit RFP agent to review the successful bid and evaluation criteria and learn what was undesirable or incomplete. This helps the vendor grow into a more competitive contender for the next RFP. Libraries should make sure that in all conversations institutional and state requirements are followed.

As a final note, once the process is over, it is useful for both libraries and vendors to evaluate the internal processes used in preparing, responding to, and evaluating an RFP. This will allow these organizations to identify any pitfalls encountered and be better prepared for the next RFP.

Performance of the Contract

Once the RFP is awarded and the vendor begins to service the account, performance should be monitored. If the vendor is not fulfilling the contract, the library will need to consult internal processes to review how to address the situation. Regular communication is critical. Minor issues should be discussed with the vendor promptly. If these or larger issues remain unresolved, it may be time to discuss with the institution's purchasing department the next steps for enforcing, or if necessary, voiding the contract.

The vendor also monitors performance. If an RFP is awarded based on a certain dollar figure, and that number drops significantly over the course of the contract, this may negatively affect the vendor's ability to service the account. Vendors may include a clause in the contract to that effect.

Conclusion

Going through an RFP can be a great deal of work, but in the end the results can be worth it. A carefully conducted RFP process can result in improved vendor services and pricing, enhanced communication channels, reexamined library processes and plans, and shared agreement regarding financial and service obligations.

Review in Motion: Multi-Year Electronic Resources Review at UTA Libraries

Peter Zhang, Department Head of Access and Discovery, University of Texas at Arlington Libraries

Ashley Zmau, E-resources Librarian, University of Texas at Arlington Libraries

Abstract

With a flat budget and ever increasing inflation for serials, UTA Libraries chose to embark on a multi-year electronic resources review process. Targeting low hanging fruits, the first step was to review subscription journals included in aggregator databases. This initial review process was also a relatively straightforward step to help new liaisons in a newly created Outreach & Scholarship department to get their "feet wet" with collection development. As liaisons became more acclimated, the second step in the following year was to review all single e-journal subscriptions, distributed amongst all liaisons. Guidelines and metrics were created to facilitate the review in addition to liaisons' empirical knowledge through their engagement with users. The third step was to review all databases and sustain a regular database review interval going forward. In the presentation, we will share with you our findings, guidelines, and metrics of the process.

Background

University of Texas at Arlington Libraries has operated under a flat materials budget for the past five years. During these years, however, serial prices steadily increased and, in some cases, increased dramatically (Bosh & Henderson, 2012). With inflation added to the baseline each year, it created a snowball effect, making it more and more challenging to sustain existing serials, let alone acquire new resources. Four years ago, 80% of our material budget was for serials. The number keeps going up, and is now at 97%. We have shrunk the monographic budget to shore up serials each year and implemented multiple DDA programs to meet users' needs for books in time. More needs to be done, especially on the serials' side. Although we were not preparing for a "Budget-ocalypse" (Enoch & Harper, 2015), we had reached a point of unsuitability of our resources. We chose to embark on a multi-year electronic resources review process where we first reviewed subscription journals also included in aggregator databases. The following year we reviewed all subscription journals. The third step will be to review all databases and sustain a regular database review interval going forward. We are very attentive to any impact on our users. The multi-year review plan is designed to minimize impact and create gradual buy-in from campus especially faculty.

University of Texas at Arlington Libraries went through a library-wide reorganization in 2013 to realign the Libraries with the University's vision. We placed a strong emphasis on engaging with faculty and students. The outreach and scholarships department was created to facilitate library liaisons' efforts with faculty. However, many liaisons were new to their role and did not have any collection management experience. Collection management in many ways is a science as much as an art. Close knowledge of how faculty and students use our resources gives meaning to the usage and cost data. Building relationships with faculty and gaining such knowledge takes time. However our budget situation demanded immediate action.

Opportunities

We decided to start with low hanging fruit: the de-duplication project. Over the years, as titles were changed or transferred, and as companies changed ownership, many our subscription journals also appeared in aggregator databases. There are some cases where such duplication makes sense; for example, embargoes on extended content. But in many cases, they do not. We pay for access twice to aggregators and publishers in addition to processing fees to subscription agents. With the instability of aggregator title lists in mind, we may potentially resubscribe when requested by users to meet

http://dx.doi.org/10.5703/1288284316270

their need "just in time." Another reason for this initial approach was to use it as a training opportunity to help new liaisons get their "feet wet" with collection management. They learned more about databases in their subject areas and how durable titles were in these databases. For the review, they evaluated coverage and embargo information and made a decision on whether or not to keep the subscription. The serials team identified subscription journals, which also appear in aggregator databases, by comparing subscription titles against our full-text titles in our link resolver's knowledge base. The following fields are set up in an Access database: title information, cost data, fund codes, subscription agents, decision checkboxes, and notes. Liaisons queried the database and identified titles based on fund codes in certain subject areas. They then recorded their decision, as well as notes. Using an Access database offered the advantage of allowing multiple staff to work on it concurrently; and progress and decisions could be easily queried and tracked. Project guidelines (Appendix A) and training sessions were offered to help liaisons understand the project's objectives and familiarize them with Access tables and queries.

The review went smoothly; there were only a few titles which needed additional deliberation. Results were given back to the serials team before the subscription renewal deadline. Seventy-five thousand dollars in savings was generated from cancelling duplicate subscriptions as a result of the review. Also, liaisons were exposed to additional evaluation factors, such as COUNTER usage data, cost-per-use, interlibrary loan requests, and so on. They now have a stake in the collection management process.

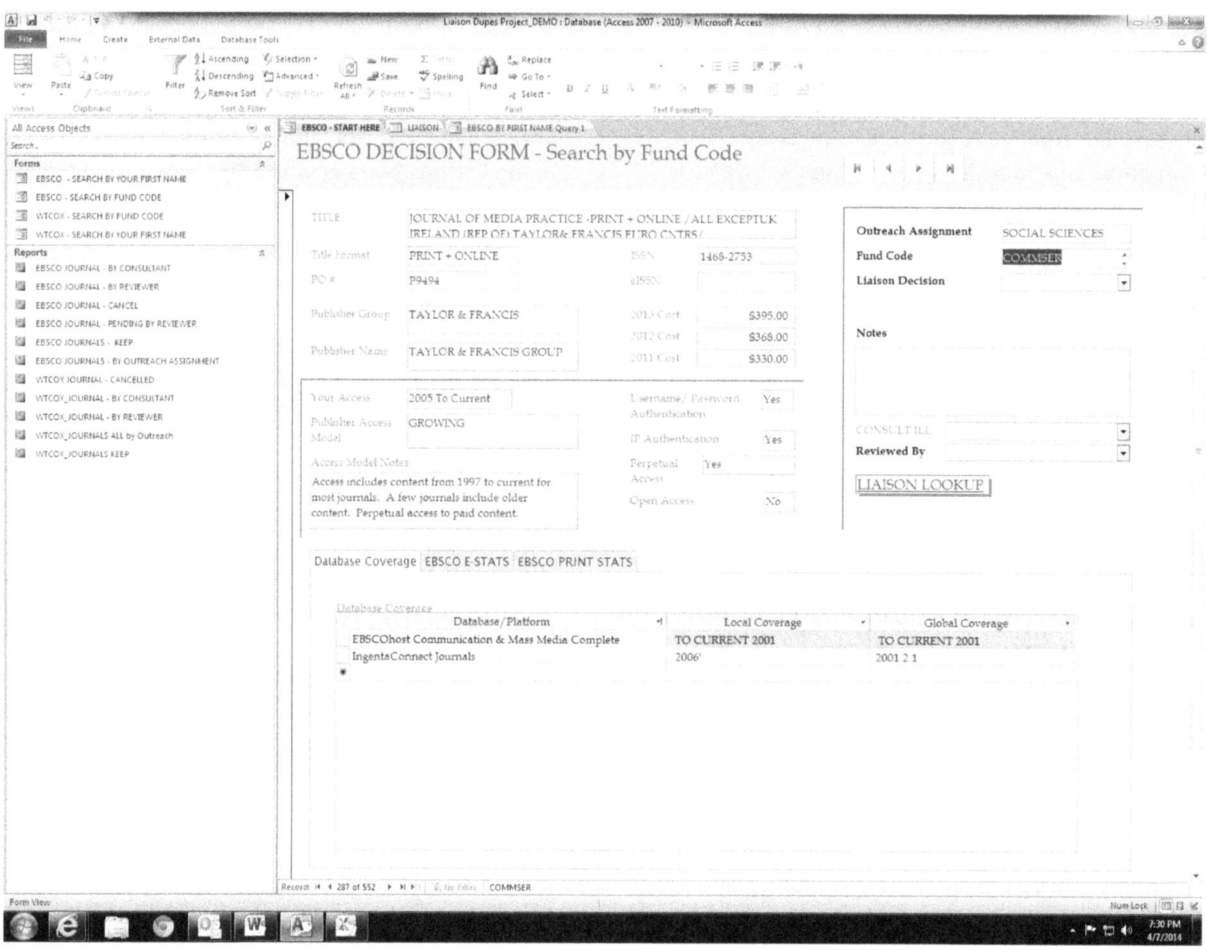

Figure 1. Access database fields.

For the Serials Review we initially wanted to consider all online subscriptions, outside of our largest "Big Deal" packages. We definitely wanted to get the biggest "bang for our buck" regarding the number of subscriptions evaluated versus potential savings. The serials team pulled our subscription lists from our two subscription agents and realized that the process would go much more quickly if we skipped membership or combination titles for now and returned to them at a later review. We also realized how many smaller packages we carried with our subscription agents, such as the University of Chicago and the Royal Society of Chemistry, and removed those as well. We were then left with a list of about 530 individual subscriptions which cost about $600,000.

The outreach and scholarship department brainstormed six thresholds of criteria (Appendix B) to evaluate for the serials review. With the idea that if a subscription met one threshold it would move on to the next, but if the subscription did not meet a threshold the evaluation ended there. Liaisons were encouraged to consider any duplicated access at the first threshold level, in case the de-duplication project from the previous year missed any stragglers. If there was complete overlap in access, such as within an aggregated database, they were told to cancel the individual subscription. However, if the access overlap was partial, such as with an embargo period, the liaison was encouraged to consider if the potentially missing content was vital to its related discipline. More often than not, liaisons decided partial overlap with another source did not justify cancelling the standalone subscription. Other thresholds included the number of UTA faculty publishing in the journal as well as JCR/SJR rankings. For the JCR/SJR rankings, journals ranked within the top 10% of their discipline were initially promoted to the next threshold within the review process. However, after 2–3 test examinations, it was decided to change the percentage to 5%. The change prompted about 10 more title cancellations and about $10,000 more in savings. In the end, from this first run of the serials review, we cancelled 100 titles and saved about $120,000. In the future we will evaluate online memberships, "Big Deals," and print serials.

For the database review we want to consider all databases or database-like (in function or cost) resources. Large e-journal packages will likely be considered in this review. Although the metrics for a database review may seem endless, we will focus on audience, impact, and relevance. Due to our organization's reorganization and change in leadership within the past five years, our databases in particular have not been holistically reviewed in several years. In the interim we gained a new University president and our largest academic programs, engineering and nursing, have substantially grown. With the database review, liaisons will be able to connect on a deeper level with their faculty and departments based on their prior review experience. This will also be a new opportunity to discuss how to best steward our financial resources to meet growing or new programs and initiatives on campus.

Conclusion

With a flat budget and ever increasing serials inflation, UTA Libraries has successfully embarked on multi-year savings projects. Online access redundancies were addressed with the de-duplication project and serials review, while the upcoming database review will be the spring cleaning action that the majority of our collections' budget has not had in years. These review projects have been instrumental in teaching newly minted liaisons within the recently formed outreach and scholarship department the basic tenets of collection management. These cost-saving measures have also provided them fodder to forge new relationships with their departments, and opportunities for fostering innovative partnerships. Designing the multi-year review process has instigated new workflows, such as an ongoing/annual database review and a complete overhaul of the workflow for resource suggestion. Technical services staff members within access and discovery have benefitted from the increased data population within their recently implemented electronic resource management system and have learned how to offer better internal customer service. Having proactively experienced varying collection review cycles, liaisons can now handle incoming requests from faculty with ease and are more familiar with their subject areas' strengths, weaknesses, and pressing needs. Due to the small bit of cushion present in this fiscal year's budget, a new knowledge management review committee has been formed to evaluate how the savings can be best spent.

References

Bosch, S., & Henderson, K. (2012). Coping with the terrible twins. *Library Journal, 137*(8), 28–32.

Enoch, T., & Harper, K. (2015). Planning for the budget-ocalypse: The evolution of a serials/ER cancellation methodology. *The Serials librarian, 68*(1–4), 282–289.

Appendix A

Criteria for de-duplication project

- Review the various information parts of the Access form related to each title, especially the following:
    - Title format (print, online, or print and online)
    - Access date coverage
    - Publisher access model and access model notes
    - IP authentication
    - Open access
    - Perpetual access
    - Review three tabs (Database Coverage, EBSCO E-STATS, and EBSCO PRINT STATS)
    - Need to check current database links in the Summon E-Journals tab, as titles may have left one database for another since the SFX harvesting was done last October
    - Liaison decision
        - Liaison decision options are: keep, cancel, or pending
        - If choosing to "keep" or "cancel," put into the "Notes" box a brief reason why, so in the future if we need to justify a decision, we will know
        - If working independently and the "pending" option is chosen, put into the "Notes" box reason that a consultation is needed and select the librarian you want to "consult" with using the drop-down arrow in the "Consult" box. Then send an e-mail regarding why you need to consult with them.

Appendix B

Outreach and scholarship threshold criteria for serials review

- Threshold 1: Cost per use in the previous year
    - Cost per use is less than $50
- Threshold 2: JCR ranking
    - JCR ranking is less than 20

- Threshold 3: # of total uses in the previous year
    - # of overall uses is greater than 40
- Threshold 4: # of UT Arlington faculty publishing in the journal
    - # of UT Arlington faculty publishing in the journal is 3 or more
- Threshold 5: Liaison knowledge of research in their discipline
    - Liaison justifies keeping the journal despite the metrics by providing discipline specific evidence. These will be reviewed by O&S department heads.

Leveraging Use-by-Publication-Age Data in Serials Collection Decisions

Matthew J. Jabaily, Information Services Librarian, Rhodes College

James R. Rodgers, Acquisitions Librarian, University of Memphis

Steven A. Knowlton, Collection Development Librarian, University of Memphis

Abstract

Traditionally, usage figures for electronic serials have lumped all years of publication together. New tools give librarians information about usage according to the year of publication. They allow us to analyze the usage of current material separately from usage of content published in prior years. The relative value of current subscriptions and backfiles has important collection development implications. For example, many libraries subscribe directly to titles that are offered in aggregated databases, but with embargoes. The relative value of current content distinguished from prior years may be useful in reevaluating such subscription decisions.

This paper discusses tools and techniques for analyzing usage by year of publication according to several measures—including COUNTER's JR5 report, Google Analytics, ILL reports, and token reports, and discusses how librarians can use these tools to aid in decision-making about serials collection development decisions.

The "serials crisis"—of periodical subscriptions eating up the budget for other materials—that libraries have endured since the late 1980s has spurred many laudable efforts to develop methods of identifying the serials of the most value to a library's patrons. Dozens of models for such evaluation have been published, involving any number of metrics as well as qualitative judgments. Amid the welter of bibliometrics ranging from Impact Factor to altmetrics, one measurement seems to always be included in serials evaluation models: usage (along with its derivative metric, cost-per-use—CPU).

Although a valuable metric, CPU is problematic for a number of reasons; in this paper, we will focus on complications that arise related to the publication date of materials. Traditionally, usage figures have counted all uses from a periodical title that occur in a given time period—regardless of the date of the article's publication. As Blecic, Wiberly, Fiscella, Bahnmaier-Blaszczak, and Lowery (2013) note, "the cost is for one given year while the retrievals reported in a year can derive from multiple volumes and years of the journal" (p. 180). So a reader who downloads in 2014 an article published in 2004 still triggers a count of one use. And a librarian calculating usage and CPU may accept that usage figure as indicative of the value of the current subscription to her community of users. In most cases, however, the situation is not that simple. Very often, the prior years of a serial title will be available to a library's patrons—because the library has perpetual access to previously subscribed content, because the journal's content becomes open access after a set period of time, or because embargoed access is available in an aggregated database. The current year's subscription really only purchases the current year's content.

We are not the first to discover this, of course. Earlier research identified this problem but required number-crunching that was beyond the capacity of most librarians to calculate improved estimates of the true cost of access to periodical content. And many libraries have dispensed with, or always lacked, efficient mechanisms for measuring print journal use. However, recent advances in data gathering and reporting have put estimates of use by publication year within the reach of many librarians. In this paper, we will discuss our observations of general trends in usage of periodical content according to the year of publication, using four tools: the JR5 COUNTER report, information from a publisher's "token" program, interlibrary loan reports, and Google Analytics applied to link resolver web pages. Further, we will explicate methods of calculating adjusted CPU figures. We will discuss how these

http://dx.doi.org/10.5703/1288284316271

new data and calculations apply to four different scenarios facing librarians charged with collection development decisions: whether to adopt a token program or a similar Get-It-Now program facilitated through interlibrary loan software; whether and how to abandon a Big Deal; and whether to purchase serial backfiles.

A Case Study in the Importance of Usage Figures by Year of Publication

COUNTER reports for usage figures have traditionally prioritized the JR1 report, which counts all usage of a given title, regardless of the date of publication. Until 2012, there were few alternatives except manual tallying. Until the ready availability of JR5 COUNTER reports, access to data by publication year has required either massive web server log data analysis projects (e.g., Huntington, Nicholas, & Jamali, 2006; Bollen & van de Sompel, 2008) for insights into local use, or reliance on proprietary usage data provided by publishers or e-journal service providers (e.g., Nicholas, Huntington, & Dobrowolski, 2005; Gorraiz, Gumpenberger, & Schlögl, 2014) for generalizations about user behavior from a global perspective. The COUNTER 4 Code of Practice, drafted in 2012, described the JR5 report and required COUNTER compliant providers to provide it by 2014. JR5 reports the use of periodicals by year of publication, and includes the use of archival packages in the report.

Inattention to the implications of publication data like those now available in the JR5 reports, and making decisions solely based on JR1 report data, can lead to poor collection decisions. In 2013, Rhodes College decided to abandon one of its Big Deals and instead adopt a token program. In a token program, the library prepays for a bundle of article access instances. Users coming through the library portal can find articles from the publisher via databases or a discovery layer, and when they download an article, one token is subtracted from the total number of tokens remaining available. Bulk discounts are offered for buying large quantities of tokens, but unused tokens expire after one year, making it important for the library to correctly estimate the number of articles that its patrons will read and purchase.

Librarians at Rhodes looked at their JR1 reports for the publisher from whom they were planning to buy tokens. Based upon that report they purchased 3,200 tokens, which represented between one-half and one-third of the previous year's use. Although some at the library initially feared they would run out of tokens, it became apparent as the year progressed that their patrons would use far fewer tokens than anticipated. Scrutiny of the usage log revealed that the tokens were only required for articles published during the current year. The previous subscription to a Big Deal had entitled Rhodes College to perpetual access to content published in the years covered by the subscription. As a result, only a fraction of the purchased tokens were redeemed before expiration. Although the college still saved money by dropping their Big Deal, much greater savings would have been realized if a more accurate calculation had been made.

Methods of Observing Patron Interest in Content According to Year of Publication

This observation led us to consider ways to explore the extent to which older content constitutes a portion of all the content used by our patrons. Four different methods are available. The first two are direct measures of use. The latter two indicate patron interest in content, but not necessarily successful access of it.

Token Information

Token reports are especially valuable because they give a clear picture of what content requires paid access. For example, open access articles will not be counted and downloads of different formats will not cause a single article to be double-counted. Comparing token reports to JR1 and JR5 reports may provide a method for measuring overall inflation due to double-counting in usage reports. Although we have preliminary token reports, they are not comprehensive enough to compare directly to our other data sources, and their data are not included in this paper.

JR5 Reports

Almost all major publishers have JR5 reports for use of serials during 2014 and afterward. JR5 reports are valuable because they can give title-by-title looks at the publication dates of articles viewed by the readers. Reports from large vendors allow us to identify trends across a diverse set of titles, while still being able to identify exceptions to the broad trends. A shortcoming of these reports, however, is that they only show data for titles to which a library already has access. Users' desire for articles that fall outside of the dates for which the journal are held are not measured. JR5 reports are prone to the same flaws as JR1 reports, including incidences of double-counting when a patron opens both html and PDF versions of the same article. As Bucknell (2011) notes, the design of a publisher's platform can influence usage counts, as publishers who don't provide abstract landing pages will often drive users to open an HTML version of an article to scan for its usefulness, then download the PDF version for deeper reading. In addition, as will be explored further, COUNTER reports record all usage within a single platform, whether it comes from the library's direct subscription or open access content; this may distort calculations of CPU.

Interlibrary Loan Reports

Libraries that use ILLiad software for interlibrary loan can generate reports indicating the year of publication for requested articles. The University of Memphis Libraries uses ILLiad to facilitate interlibrary loan requests. We generated a custom report in the ILLiad client of all of the filled article requests made in 2014, discerned the year of publication of each request, and calculated the relative number of occurrences of each year of publication. Interlibrary loan reports, of course, cannot give us an indication about how current collections are being used, but they are useful for a number of reasons. First, they are not limited by a vendor or disciplinary area, giving us a wider view of users' interests. Second, they can complement the JR5 reports, showing us which articles users want but to which they don't have access. This may also indicate weaknesses in a library's collection or the relative desirability of purchasing backfiles. Third, the additional effort required to place an interlibrary loan request indicate to us that these are high value items for users.

Google Analytics Applied To Link Resolver Web Pages

The University of Memphis Libraries uses SerialsSolutions 360 Link as its link resolver and has configured Google Analytics to track every time the resolver is used. Google Analytics records the Open URLs generated by each link resolution and the date of publication is included in the OpenURL. A fuller description of this method can be found in Knowlton, Kristanciuk, and Jabaily (2015). This allows us to calculate user interest in articles by year of publication. Link resolver tracking gives a very broad view of users' interest in articles, as it is not limited by vendor, discipline, or library holdings. Unlike the token reports and JR5 reports described above, this method measures interest instead of use; the full-text of the article may not have ever been successfully accessed. One limitation of link resolver data, however, is that they miss some full-text access. Any full-text access within the database that the user initially searched goes uncounted using this method. It also misses any use that did not come through a link resolver. If a user browses current issues of a journal online, this use is not measured.

Patterns of Patron Interest in Content by Year of Publication

University of Memphis Libraries has made use of three types of use statistics that allow us to look at article downloads and requests by publication year. Our data reflect usage recorded between January 1 and December 31, 2014. Here follows a brief summary of each set of data we obtained using these three methods. The first set of use statistics consists of 64,708 link resolver landing page URLs, collected using Google Analytics, and covers a range of publication dates from 1900 to 2014. The second set is 10,649 ILL requests, 2,202 of which were cancelled, and 8,446 of which were filled. It also records requests for articles published between 1900 and 2014. The third set consists of combined statistics from JR5 Counter reports for 140,151 full-text downloads for three large "Big Deal" e-journal subscription packages: Elsevier Science Direct Freedom Collection, Sage Premier, and Wiley Online Library. They comprise 3,745 titles published between circa 1986 and

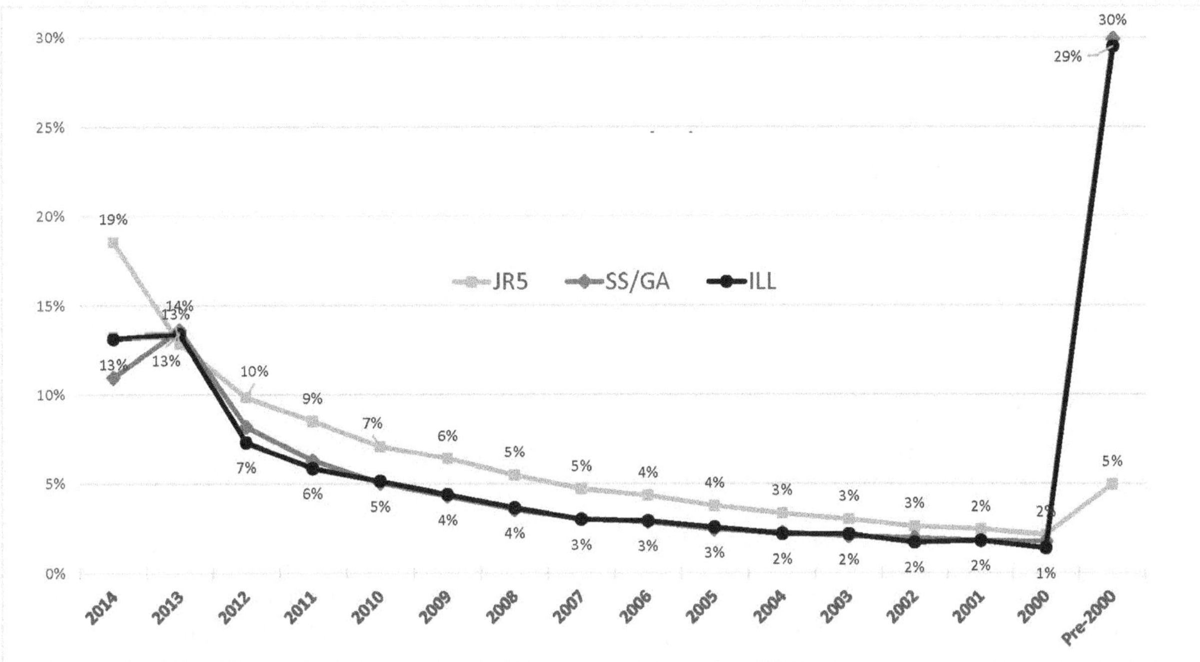

Figure 1. Percentage of use in 2014 by date of publication, according to three different measures.

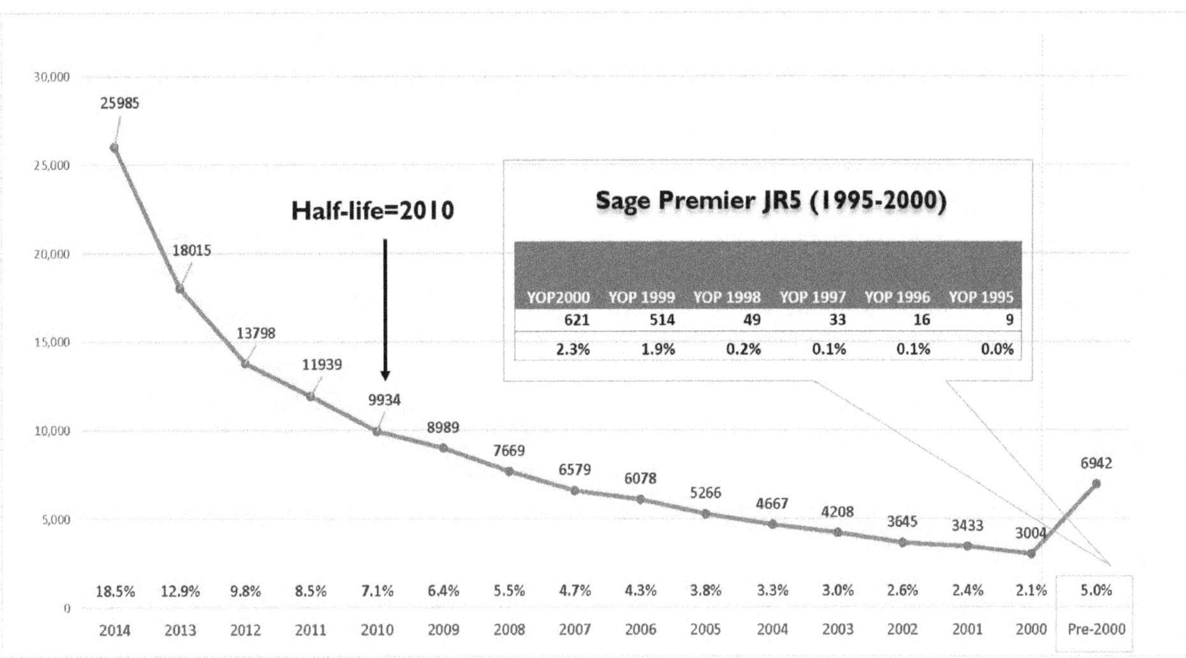

Figure 2. E-journal usage per JR5 reports with usage half-life.

2014. Between these three types of data we get a fairly complete picture of our users' interest and use. And perhaps most importantly for the purposes of this paper, they reinforce the fact that there is a clear predominance of use of the current year and an initially sharp decline and then a gradually flattening decline in use by publication age (see Figure 1).

When we speak of current year usage, we have to consider the cumulative nature of available articles, and since the rate of interest shouldn't be expected to keep pace with the rate of availability,

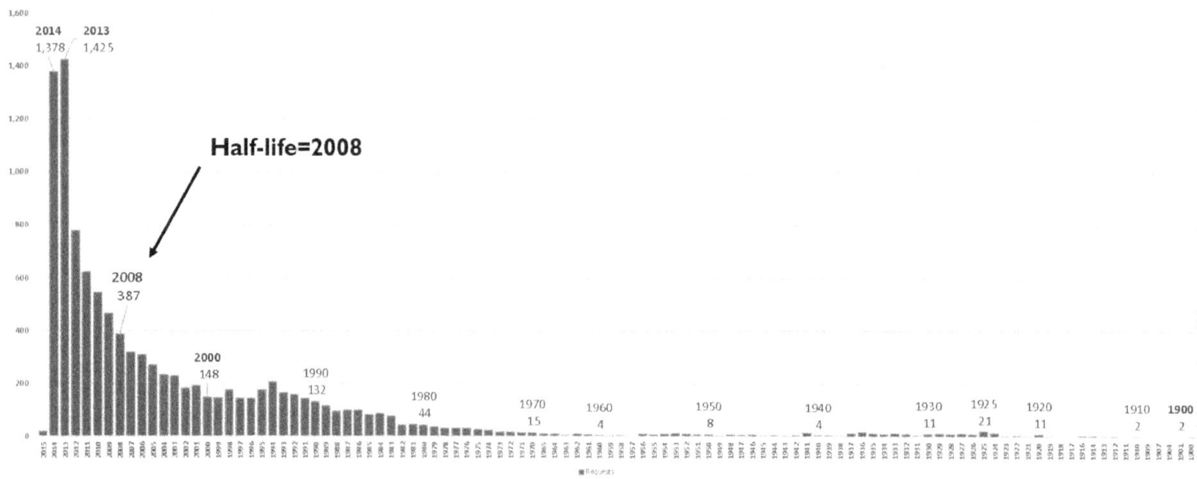

Figure 3. ILL requests by publication year with usage half-life.

one would expect there generally to be a lag before the full impact of currency is measured. That seems to be the case with ILL requests and our Google Analytics reports. Each shows that use of articles published in the most recent two years represents 13% of all use (about 25% for both years combined). However, the full-text downloads recorded in our JR5 reports seem to defy that pattern. In each of the three Big Deal packages, 2014 use exceeds that of any other year, and when adding in 2015 pre-publications and articles in press (ostensibly not available before 2014) it is as high as 20% of all uses. The flip at the end of the long tail in Figure 1 is a graphic conceit forced by one of the idiosyncrasies of the JR5 reports. Two of the three vendors reported pre-2000 use in combined groups of publication years 1995–1999, 1990–1995, and pre-1990, all shown here as pre-2000. The use by publication year before 2000 presumably follows closely to what is seen in the third Sage Premier package (see "Sage Premier JR5 1995–2000" call-out in Figure 2 below).

Our data follow patterns of usage by age of publication found in the literature. As Huntington, Nicholas, and Jamali (2006) describe patterns of use in seven months of OhioLINK weblog server data: "The general shape of the curve suggests there were, in fact, two stages to the decline. First there is a sharp decline phase. This period spans the first 8 to 9 years from publication date. Decline is most evident in the first 2 to 3 years, with usage falling by about a third over the first year and by about 60% by the third year. After the sharp decline period there follows a relatively stable or flat period of usage" (p. 1843).

Usage half-life, as introduced by Rowlands and Nicholas (2007) is another way to see the weight of currency in the distribution of uses by publication age. Both the concept and the behavior of charted data follow that of cited half-life, which, as the authors explain, is expressed as the median age of the articles [the author community] cite in their own publications. Typically, the citation time curve shows a sharp initial increase (authors'attention tends to focus on more recent papers) then a long tail off. Calculation of the 2007 usage half-life: the median age of all articles in journal J downloaded during 2007, regardless of their age (p. 226). To put it another way, usage half-life is the publication date before and after which there is the same number of uses.

Usage half-life for immediately available articles published between 1986 and 2014 (see Figure 2) is four years (that is, publication date of 2010). Strikingly, the usage half-life of all articles requested by our users, published between 1900 and 2014, and regardless of immediate access, as recorded by our Google Analytics data and ILL Requests (see Figure 3) is only six years (publication date of 2008).

When total uses for all 3,745 titles are aggregated the sharp decline and long tail chart very clearly. As you might expect, there is much greater variation when we look at titles grouped by subject, and of course even more so at the title level. By aggregating our JR5 data into subject categories, we get a sense of the different patterns of use by publication age in different disciplines or subject areas. The combined list of 3,745 titles was aggregated into 14 subject groups, based on a collation of subject assignments provided by each vendor, summarized in Table 1.

Subject	No. of Titles	Usage Half-Life
Agriculture, Aquaculture & Food Science	215	2011, 3 Years
Business, Economics, Finance & Accounting	349	2010, 4 Years
Chemistry	115	2011, 3 Years
Computer Science & Information Technology	156	2011, 3 Years
Earth, Space & Environmental Sciences	162	2011, 3 Years
Humanities	152	2012, 2 Years
Law & Criminology	51	2010, 4 Years
Life Sciences	449	2010, 4 Years
Mathematics & Statistics	72	2011, 3 Years
Medicine	846	2010, 4 Years
Nursing, Dentistry & Healthcare	179	2011, 3 Years
Physical Sciences & Engineering	362	2011, 3 Years
Psychology	182	2010, 4 Years
Social & Behavioral Sciences	454	2011, 3 Years

Table 1. Subject groupings of journals reported in three aggregated publisher package JR5 reports.

How total uses, use per title, and CPU correlate within subject areas warrants further exploration. Nonetheless, we can see in Figure 2 that use of material published in the current year ranges from 15% to 35% and does not necessarily correlate to the number of titles in that discipline. (Note that both the maximum and minimum current year use values are represented by the two subjects—law and criminology, and mathematics—with the smallest title representation in the combined packages.)

One can see significant differences in the shapes our charts take when comparing use by publication year for four different subject groupings (see Figure 5).

It is unclear to what extent preference for currency or other patterns in use by publication year can be observed on a global level when it comes to subject areas or disciplines. Certainly, some disciplines value currency to a greater degree than others, and there will be greater interest in older, seminal articles in some disciplines while that is not the case in others. And the makeup of a local population of users—with their particular habits and research interests—surely has a strong influence on the patterns of use by publication year in different disciplines.

According to our JR5 data, a good rule of thumb is that the most current year accounts for about 18–20% of use. This means that if a library cancels a title but retains perpetual access, it can expect to retain access to about four-fifths of its previous usage in the next year and would need to provide another means of access to meet about one-fifth of the demand. It is useful to note that the number of published current year articles grows over the course of the year. So, if a library cancels a title and is planning to rely on full-text from a source with a one-year embargo, the percentage of usage for which it will lose access is higher than it would be for an accumulating year. To approximate the number of articles accessed or desired "in the past year" requires adding a portion of the 2013 results to the 2014/2015/In Press numbers. So a library would retain access to between two-thirds and three-quarters of its use and need alternate access for the rest. Another consideration is that the JR5 reports we have from our publishers may overemphasize the demand for current articles because access to backfiles is limited in our collections. For collections with larger full-text backfiles, the percentages of use from the current year of publication may be smaller. The measurements of patron demand (ILL and link resolver analytics) show the same high demand for articles published in the current year and a steady decline in demand for articles published in each previous year, but the

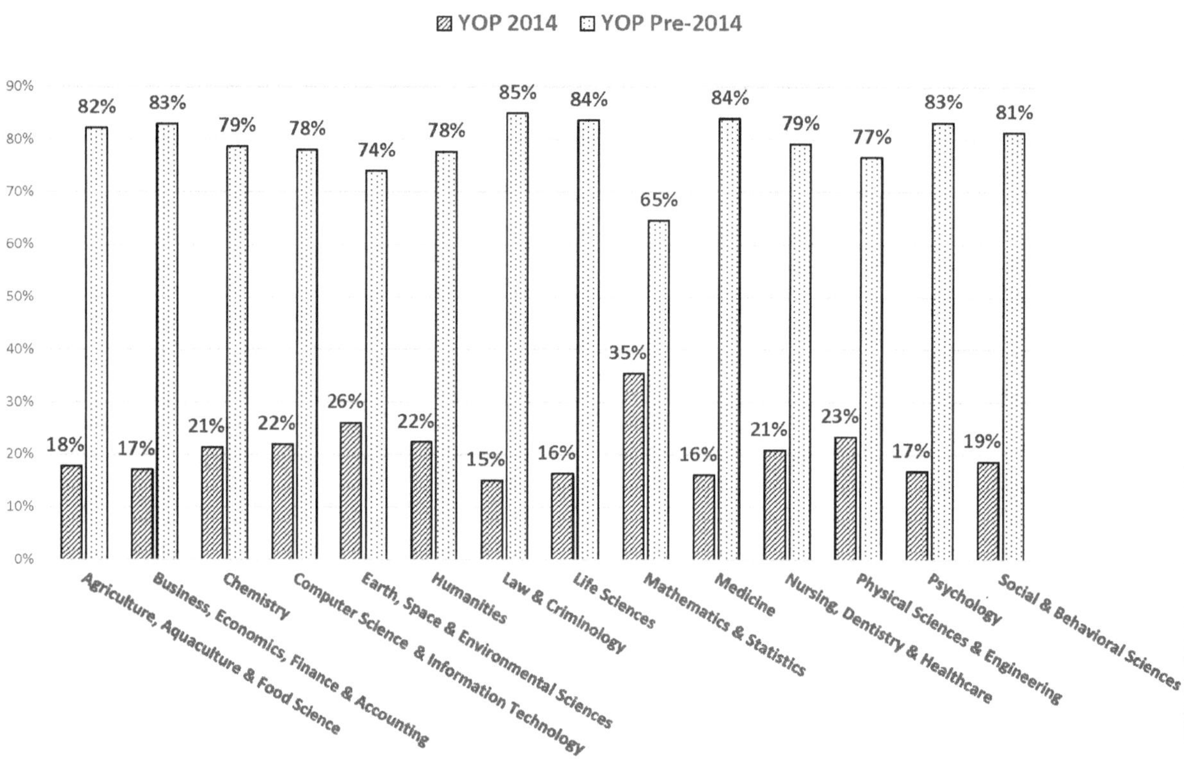

Figure 4. Current versus pre-2014 article downloads by subject.

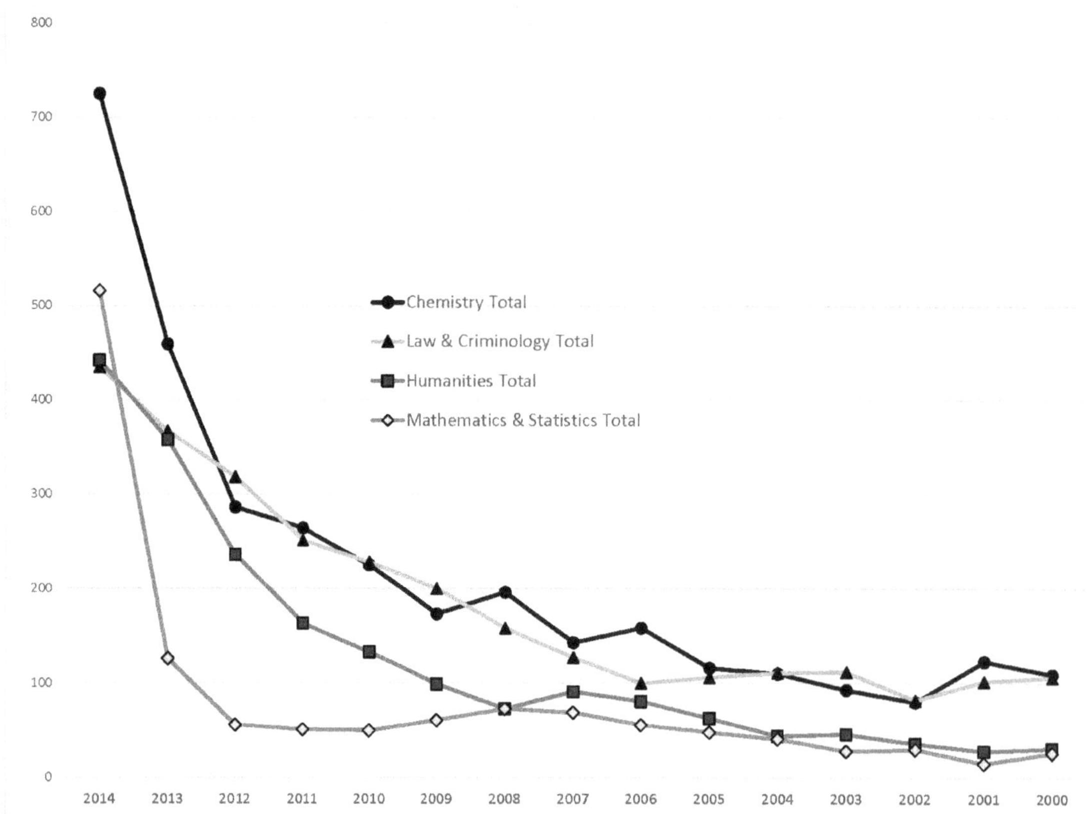

Figure 5. Comparing use by publication year for four subjects.

distribution is somewhat more even as the "tail" of the data is longer. Starr and Williams (2008) report that a similar pattern is seen in use of print journals.

Applications for Use-by-Year-of-Publication Data

The implications of this analysis are clear: the traditional way of measuring CPU fails to capture the real costs of each download. Except in those cases where a current subscription is required to access backfiles, the current year's subscription only obtains for a library the current year's content. Prior years' content has already been paid for. Therefore, a more precise measurement should be made. We propose measuring the cost-per-use-paid-for-this-year, or to be less awkward, an "adjusted cost per use" (ACPU). As mentioned earlier, another problem of traditional CPU is that it disregards duplication of content in aggregated databases. While many titles are embargoed for a year or more in aggregators, we have seen that current content makes up only a small part of total use.

Table 2 shows the difference between traditional CPU and ACPU for selected titles. We examined 32 of the most expensive titles in our portfolio and calculated the CPU. Then, by excluding the uses of content that was already paid for in prior years, we arrived at a much different ACPU.

These ACPU figures can reshape the decisions librarians make about serials expenditures. An obvious example is the token purchases discussed earlier. If the publisher offered perpetual access to their backfiles with the original subscriptions, then the library needs only to budget for the number of articles expected to be read from the years not covered by the backfiles. According to our results, this will likely be around 20% of total use. In the first year after cancelling direct subscriptions, this will often be a significant savings over the cost of the subscriptions—particularly if a Big Deal were subscribed. But in future years, more and more of the content that will be read will require tokens, as the owned backfile content moves farther backward from the current year. Strategic planning must take such changes into account.

Evaluating the Cost of Token Programs

To elaborate on the difference that is made by isolating journal usage by year of publication, let us offer an example from the University of Memphis. We looked into using a token program

TITLE	Paid in 2014	All Uses	Uses Unavailable Elsewhere	CPU	ACPU
Plant and soil	$10,390.83	3	0	$3,463.61	$10,390.83
Planta	$7,917.61	7	1	$1,131.09	$7,917.61
Addiction	$3,436.44	227	0	$15.14	$3,436.44
Journal of Optimization Theory and Applications	$3,343.23	13	1	$257.17	$3,343.23
Psychology & Marketing	$2,288.96	70	19	$32.70	$2,288.96
Machine Learning	$2,376.28	17	1	$139.78	$2,376.28
Journal of Financial Services Research	$1,669.06	12	2	$139.09	$834.53
Climatic Change	$5,252.93	49	11	$107.20	$477.54
Medical & Biological Engineering & Computing	$2,188.75	47	6	$46.57	$364.79
Journal of Applied Ecology	$1,772.64	22	5	$80.57	$354.53
Mean of 32 Journals	$3,460.22	69.2	32.2	$764.74	$1,628.44
Median of 32 Journals	$2,974.89	17	7	$139.09	$500.16

Table 2. Traditional cost-per-use compared to adjusted cost-per-use for selected titles.

from Wiley. Based on our JR1 usage data, we concluded that the cost of the tokens would be approximately four times greater than our subscription price. But by using JR5 data, we see that tokens needed for current year content would cost less than about two-thirds as much as we are paying in subscriptions. We will look into that as soon as our Wiley contract is due for renewal. (There may be some additional savings due to the fact that the JR1 and JR5 reports may be double-counting articles retrieved in both HTML and PDF format.)

Along with tokens from a publisher, libraries may also opt to participate in the Get It Now program from Copyright Clearance Center. With Get It Now, patrons who encounter an indexed article without full-text are given the option to click on a button in the link resolver that triggers an immediate purchase of the article. Prices vary by publisher, but librarians armed with the knowledge of their backfile and aggregator coverage can make much better estimates of the token or Get It Now purchases expected to occur. See Suhr (2013) for a more thorough discussion of Get It Now.

Assessing the Value of a Big Deal

JR5 data can also be helpful in evaluating the effectiveness of spending on a Big Deal. This year, the University of Memphis determined it could no longer sustain its ScienceDirect package. Although we were forced to opt out of the Big Deal by budget constraints, we found a way to use JR5 reports to maximize the access to Elsevier titles through judicious selection of direct subscriptions and reliance upon backfiles.

From 2005 to 2015, University of Memphis participated in the "Freedom Collection" Big Deal from Elsevier. In exchange for our retaining all our Elsevier subscriptions, we were entitled to full access to most other Elsevier titles. While we experience high usage and a low CPU for the package as a whole, its cost has grown to more than one-third of our entire materials budget. When we decided to get out of the Big Deal, we initially were looking simply at the JR1 usage data to determine which titles to retain. But when we looked at the JR5 data, we realized that a very different mix of titles could be subscribed to and still retain a lot of access.

There are two types of journals in our Freedom Collection package. Titles to which we had direct subscriptions, and additional titles included as part of the Big Deal. The direct subscriptions included perpetual access back to 1997. Additional titles do not have perpetual access. When we break the Big Deal, we will retain perpetual access to our direct subscriptions. With this in mind, we can calculate an ACPU that takes into account perpetual access rights. For titles with perpetual access, the ACPU is the cost of the current subscription divided by the number of uses for just the current year—because the previous years are already available whether we pay for the current subscription or not. For those titles that do not have perpetual access, the ACPU takes into account usage of all years back to 1997 because the current subscription will give us access to those older years of publication.

An example of calculating ACPU is shown in Table 3. Because Journal A does not have perpetual access, we can calculate that the year's subscription cost will cover all of the anticipated usage. Journal B does have perpetual access, so only that portion of usage that is anticipated to come from the current year will be underwritten by the subscription cost. As the table demonstrates, Journal A is more expensive and

TITLE	Perpetual Access?	Average Yearly Usage	Subscription Price for 2016	Traditional CPU	Expected Percentage of Uses to Pay for in 2016	Estimated Paid Uses in 2016	Adjusted CPU
Journal A	NO	154	$899.40	$5.84	100%	154	$5.84
Journal B	YES	208	$587.69	$2.82	19%	38.48	$15.27

Table 3. Example of ACPU calculation for titles with and without perpetual access.

receives fewer total uses but still has a lower ACPU because of Journal B's retained perpetual access.

By performing this calculation for all titles in our Freedom Collection package, we identified those titles with the lowest ACPU. We realized that we can cancel direct subscriptions to 255 titles while keeping 29, and take up 136 new direct subscriptions. We anticipate that we will continue to experience about 88% of the usage we saw this year, while cutting our expenditure by more than 50%. Next year, of course, will be very different, as those titles with perpetual access that we cancelled will lose another year's worth of content—and our ACPU will have to take that into account.

Experiences will vary with different packages. In some cases, the additional content provided by a Big Deal may make the ACPU calculations favor retaining a package. But the math is easily done and can provide clarity into the true value of a Big Deal.

Complicating matters is the fact that a subscription, if it includes perpetual access, "has also secured access to the current year's content for all *future* years" (Bucknell, 2012, p. 198). A subscription that has 100 uses of current content this year will have 67 uses of the same content next year, 51 uses the year after, and so on. Forgoing a subscription this year means losing all the future usage that would be included with perpetual access.

Purchasing Backfiles

One other use librarians may make of the data about use of older content is to assess the value of backfile packages. Many publishers offer one-time purchases of older journal content, typically with perpetual access. Torbert (2009) outlines several models of such offerings. Assigning a CPU to such titles has been difficult in the past. But with the estimates of usage by year of publication now available, it is much easier to make such calculations. If the library subscribes to the current year of a title, a librarian can extrapolate the usage of the older years according to the known progression. That extrapolation can be extended for a number of years to estimate the ACPU for a given title or for the whole package.

Conclusion

Librarians have been at a disadvantage compared to publishers for many years, as our tools to analyze the value of journal content were quite crude. With the advent of new tools including JR5 reports, interlibrary loan request reports, token usage reports, and Google Analytics applied to link resolvers, librarians can now see the usage patterns of journal content with much more granularity. While such tools do not answer all the questions a librarian may have—they certainly underreport the value of unique titles to specialized researchers—they do provide greater power in making the most cost-effective decisions regarding various options offered by publishers, whether they be tokens, Big Deals, individual subscriptions, or backfile packages.

References

Blecic, D. D., Wiberly, S. E., Fiscella, J. B., Bahnmaier-Blaszczak, S., & Lowery, R. (2013). Deal or no deal? Evaluating Big Deals and their journals. *College and Research Libraries, 74*(2), 178–193.

Bollen, J., & van de Sompel, H. (2008). Usage impact factor: The effects of sample characteristics on usage-based impact metrics. *Journal of the American Society for Information Science & Technology*, *59*(1), 136–149.

Bucknell, T. (2011). Usage statistics for decision making. *Serials, 24*(1), 17–20.

Bucknell, T. (2012). Garbage in, gospel out: Twelve reasons why librarians should not accept cost-per-download figures at face value. *Serials Librarian, 63*, 192–212.

Gorraiz, J., Gumpenberger, C., & Schlögl, C. (2014). Usage versus citation behaviours in four subject areas. *Scientometrics, 101*(2), 1077–1095.

Huntington, P., Nicholas, D., & Jamali, H. R. (2006). Article decay in the digital environment: An analysis of usage of OhioLINK by date of publication, employing deep log methods. *Journal of the American Society for Information Science & Technology*, *57*(13), 1840–1851.

Knowlton, S. A., Kristanciuk, I., & Jabaily, M. J. (2015). Spilling out of the funnel: How reliance upon interlibrary loan affects access to information. *Library Resources and Technical Services, 59*(1), 4–12.

Nicholas, D., Huntington, P., & Dobrowolski, T. (2005). Revisiting 'obsolescence' and journal article 'decay' through usage data: An analysis of digital journal use by year of publication. *Information Processing & Management*, *41*(6), 1441–1461.

Rowlands, I., & Nicholas, D. (2007). Understanding information behaviour: How do students and faculty find books? *Journal of Academic Librarianship, 34*(1), 3–15.

Starr, S., & Williams, J. (2008). The long tail: A usage analysis of pre-1993 print biomedical journal literature. *Journal of the Medical Library Association, 96*(1), 20–28.

Suhr, K. F. (2013). Get It Now: One library's experience with implementing and using the unmediated version of the Copyright Clearance Center's document delivery service. *Journal of Electronic Resources Librarianship, 25*(4), 321–325.

Torbert, C. (2009). Purchasing of electronic backfiles: Results of a survey. *Serials Librarian, 57,* 410–422.

When You Come to a Fork in the Road, Take It (15th Annual Health Sciences Lively Lunch)

Cunera M. Buys, E-Science Librarian, Northwestern University Library

Jean Gudenas (speaker & moderator), Head of Collections Management, Loyola University Chicago Health Sciences Library

Ramune K. Kubilius, Collection Development/Special Projects Librarian & interim Special Collections Librarian, Northwestern University, Galter Health Sciences Library

Elizabeth R. Lorbeer, Library Director and Chair of the Department of the Medical Library, Western Michigan University, Homer Stryker School of Medicine

Abstract

In this year's sponsored but no holds barred lunch, participants had the opportunity to contemplate examples of proactive approaches answering the question posed by the 2015 conference theme, "Where Do We Go From Here?" This year's lunch theme was inspired by a saying of Lawrence Peter "Yogi" Berra (May 12, 1925–September 22, 2015): "When You Come to a Fork in the Road, Take It." Researchers increasingly must meet various data management requirements and mandates, while educators are challenged by changing trends in providing curricular content. What choices do these challenges provide to libraries and librarians? In the best case scenarios, they utilize approaches espoused in Yogi Berra's advice—they follow paths (opportunities) that present themselves, and become partners.

In this year's sponsored but no holds barred lunch, participants had the opportunity to contemplate examples of proactive approaches answering the question posed by the 2015 conference theme, "Where Do We Go From Here?" This year's lunch theme was inspired by a saying of Lawrence Peter "Yogi" Berra (May 12, 1925–September 22, 2015): "When You Come to a Fork in the Road, Take It." Researchers increasingly must meet various data management requirements and mandates, while educators are challenged by changing trends in providing curricular content. What choices do these challenges provide to libraries and librarians? In the best case scenarios, they utilize approaches espoused in Yogi Berra's advice—they follow paths (opportunities) that present themselves, and become partners.

After greetings from Wendy Bahnsen on behalf of the lunch host, Rittenhouse, Ramune Kubilius presented the traditional brief "year in review" recap, highlighting news and trends that occurred or were noted since the Charleston Conference of 2014 that she listed on a handout entitled "Developments." The past year included anniversaries of independent publishers Karger (125 years) and Sage (50 years); retirements of the director of the US National Library of Medicine and of longtime key health sciences association personnel; industry mergers and acquisitions; a preponderance of news about datasets; open access developments; and critiques and initiatives in the realm of the peer review system.

Three panelists shared insights and opened the floor for lively discussion.

Are alternate open textbooks a solution for educators seeking health sciences curricular reading materials? In her presentation, entitled "Textbooks: Trends, Alternatives & Experimentation," Elizabeth Lorbeer discussed the current environment, experiments, and roles ("reinvented" expertise) librarians can share in order to help faculty and students. Her institution's library staff at a relatively new medical school has been able to become very

http://dx.doi.org/10.5703/1288284316272

involved in the selection and acquisition process for course materials, and was tasked with running of the medical school's bookstore. Experiments and initiatives have included the use of Inkling and Apple iBooks, institution as publisher (creation of open textbooks with accompanying peer review of content questions), and the use of Wikis for course materials. She ended with points that are food for thought. There is often the challenge of print versus electronic selection that can sometimes be driven by student preference. Not all online (e-books) offer annotation features. How should class notes and lectures be addressed? As for "must have textbooks," if the instructor wants students to have a particular book, the library can purchase it on their behalf and charge as cost of attendance. Other challenges and concerns include the need to restrict access to course materials only on the Intranet to be in copyright and licensing compliance, and a demand on libraries to spend finite collection dollars on examination review materials and resources, often driven by students who focus on them as a way to help them pass tests.

Cunera Buys described work she and Pamela Shaw (Biosciences & Bioinformatics Librarian, Northwestern University's Galter Health Sciences Library) have done in the data management planning arena, as part of a university working group. She provided background and shared results of a survey conducted by Northwestern University's E-Science Working Group that were first presented at a Medical Library Association 2015 annual meeting in a poster presentation entitled "Disciplinary Perceptions of Data and Data Management Practices." Libraries have a role in helping researchers understand funders' data sharing requirements, developing LibGuides, and knowing their constituents' disciplinary repository options when there are no institutional repositories that can accommodate datasets. Knowledge of our institutions' data management policies is key. Additional assistance includes help with and consultation on metadata, best practices (storing data on lab or personal computer desktops is not sharing or preservation), and the need to spell out specifics in data management plans. She shared some resources for librarians to become more familiar with data management issues and emphasized that datasets can and are part of libraries' collections. Librarians should consider what kinds of datasets they will store, what are their sizes, and how long will they be kept.

Moderator Jean Gudenas rounded out the panel by sharing highlights of a poster prepared for the 2015 Charleston Conference Friday evening poster session entitled "Expanding Limits with Get It Now." The question posed was whether access to material could be sufficient and provide cost-savings over ownership to a title. This is especially relevant considering that yearly journal subscription increases are not necessarily matched by yearly library budget increases and additional collection challenges such as expensive niche information needs that cater to a small population. As a supplement to document delivery solutions, Jean shared the steps her library took to identify a group of 100 high-demand, non-subscription journals to make available through Get it Now (Copyright Clearance Center), opting to make it an unmediated service. This solution was not set up lightly and incorporated an analysis of requests, exploration of cost per use in various alternative supplier (including publisher) options, a survey of users, and careful scrutiny concerning the expenditure of the amount in the deposit account.

Session participants took advantage of the opportunity to pose questions to presenters and share their own experiences and thoughts about best practices.

Libraries in a Bind: Practical Solutions and Human Responses to a Weeding Mandate

Alex McAllister, Humanities Librarian, Appalachian State University

Allan Scherlen, Social Sciences Librarian, Appalachian State University

Christina Mayberry, Collection Development Coordinator, Oviatt Library, California State University Northridge

Kathy Marks, Strategic Sales Director, Better World Books

Carla Caforio, Library Relocation Specialist, William B. Meyer

Abstract

Many university libraries are currently engaged in major weeding projects as they reduce their print book collections to make room for new space configurations to accommodate emerging library trends such as makerspaces and transitioning toward a predominately e-book collection.To address such a deselection project effectively requires both practical solutions and tact in dealing with faculty who seriously value their collections of print books. Librarians from two universities will share practical approaches to managing a large weeding project and for dealing diplomatically with book users affected. Representatives for deselection project services will also offer insights into their logistic support for handling weeding projects. Ample time will be provided for discussion where collection librarians can candidly discuss both the practical problems and user concerns faced when sandwiched between the demands of a major weeding project and the needs of faculty and students in book-reliant disciplines.

Introduction

The panel was introduced to the audience by Kathy Marks, the strategic sales director at Better World Books. Approximately 25 attendees participated in the session. Many participants had questions about communication and marketing of large weeding projects. The presenters created a weeding checklist that was distributed during the session. The checklist included information on preliminary planning for seeking feedback involved with a weeding project. The checklist also offered guidance with outlining workflow processes (see Appendix 1).

The Humanities and Social Sciences Academic Library Perspective

Alex McAllister, humanities librarian, and Allan Scherlen, social sciences librarian, both from Appalachian State University, presented an alternative perspective to some conventional notions of weeding presented in the library literature. Liaison humanities and social sciences librarians work closely with faculty and students: teaching classes, conducting research consultations, and ordering materials for these areas, which affords them a perspective different from library administrators and others in the library who may be viewing a large weeding project with a different, albeit, broader perspective.

McAllister and Scherlen noted a lack of discussion at other Charleston Conference sessions on diplomacy in weeding academic library book collections, especially in regard to working with faculty members who differ in their needs for and use of books in their research, such as differences in book use by scholars in the humanities versus in the sciences. Consensus among librarians, as revealed in conference discussions and library literature on weeding, shows that many academic librarians are comfortable relying upon egalitarian, use-based rubrics for weeding across the entire library collection without concern for

http://dx.doi.org/10.5703/1288284316273

treating the more monographic-reliant disciplines differently. For example, another session at the same 2015 Charleston Conference argued for weeding based on quantitative evaluation measures to determine the "life cycle" of books. The presenter at that 2015 session argued that, ideally, every book should have an end date attached to the book's record when it is acquired to let future librarians know when to weed that book from the collection.

The presenters suggested that weeding in academic libraries is fraught with challenges different from other kinds of libraries. Weeding humanities and social sciences areas of an academic library must be approached differently from other subject areas of the library. They discussed how some disciplines, especially in the humanities, may use more books than other disciplines, and may need older, unused books to mine as part of their research method.

One article that was discussed by ASU librarians sparked a lively discussion about working with humanities faculty members during a major deselection project. David Woolwine's *Collection Development in the Humanities and Social Sciences in a Transitional Age: Deaccession of Print Items* (2014) offers a contrasting opinion to today's trend toward adopting one-size-fits-all, use-based criteria for removing print books. More complex, discipline-specific criteria is needed for some disciplines, Woolwine would argue, that allows some lesser-used books to be retained. Woolwine constructs a thesis based on works by Andrew Abbott and others, which argues that humanities researchers use monograph materials more and in different ways than researchers in other disciplines, such as in the sciences. Because humanities scholars look at a library book collection as "a laboratory," they use books in ways that can be described as a kind of research method made possible in part by the exploration of the stacks. This includes the discovery of unknowns in the collection to reveal "holes" in prior research, which "can be determined only by reading." Humanities scholars, the article argues, use contemporary methods of online searching, but also approach research through methods such as "grazing" and following passages and citations among books in a collection. Thus, print books in the humanities and humanities-like areas of the social sciences are arguably less susceptible to obsolescence. Interestingly, a review of news about resistance to big weeding projects in academic libraries reveals that protest generally comes from faculty and students in the humanities. (For links to Woolwine, news articles, and other materials related to weeding, see OCLC's "Weeding and De-selection Bibliography" at https://www.oclc.org/sustainable-collections/bibliography.en.html).

The subject-specific approach to weeding was a major stimulant for discussion during the session. One questioner asked why materials that have not circulated in more than 10 or more years should be retained. A 2002 study by Jennifer Thompson was referenced (again from Woolwine) that found the median citation age for book citations in 19th century American and British literature to be 14 years, with most books showing a peak age range for citations between 6 to 10 years, followed by a lesser peak between 11 to 15 years. One audience member concluded that part of the discussion by noting the importance of regarding lists of books that have not circulated over a number of years only as a "review list" and not as the final discard list. In addition to reasons already discussed, some audience members expressed concern that interlibrary loan may be adversely affected by the large number of libraries removing much of their paper holdings.

The panel members asked the audience members if their library was planning, or currently going through, a major weeding project. Of the approximately 30 people in the room, almost all raised their hands. When the audience was asked if they were weeding to make space for more books or room for new services, many responded that their projects were driven by new and expanding services rather than growth. Many of the librarians appeared to be affiliated with institutions that have the option of sending weeded print books to an off-site storage facility.

A Solution?

McAllister and Scherlen were asked if there were some general conclusions they discovered from the process. The panelists summarized their findings into three principles:

1. A realization that consultation and communication are vital to the process.
2. Learning to adjust during the process even if that means changing course or modifying plans.
3. Having mutual respect among librarians and the user community, and to not take any of the reactions personally.

*****

Christina Mayberry, the collection development coordinator at California State University Northridge, presented information on a major weeding project that took place at CSU. She fielded a number of questions on the logistics and approach to determining criteria for materials that are to be deselected. Because CSU Northridge uses Better World Books, she was able to provide information about the benefits of working with a sustainable company that provides support to libraries conducting deselection projects.

*****

Kathy Marks, the strategic sales director at Better World Books, informed attendees about the benefits of working with Better World Books.

*****

CarlaCaforio, the library relocation specialist for William B. Meyer highlighted the benefits of using William B. Meyer services to lessen expenses required for weeding projects.

Appendix 1: Weeding Checklist

Stage 1: Preliminary Planning and Feedback

1. **Purpose**
   Outline purpose for the weeding project (e.g., book areas taken by new services, shelves at capacity, etc.)
2. **Scope & Criteria**
   Outline which areas of collections to weed and criteria to be used as well as track weeded volume
3. **Sustainability**
   Research sustainable disposal options for items to be removed
4. **Budget**
   Determine and outline all areas where costs could be incurred
5. **Timeline**
   Set preliminary timeline for the project
6. **Preliminary Outreach**
   Notify key constituents/stakeholders of general purpose and plans for project and invite feedback (especially from faculty)
7. **Preliminary Feedback**
   Incorporate feedback from stakeholders and modify basic plans accordingly (adjusting general plans for scope and focus as well as workflow and disposal accordingly)

Stage 2: Research and Outline Workflow Process

1. **Timeline**
   Revised timeline
2. **Personnel**
   Personnel involved in listing, evaluating, physically removing, deaccessioning, and disposing
3. **Vetting Process**
   Vetting items for removal (lists for bibliographers, lists for faculty, cart flow, etc.)

4. **Deaccessioning Process**
   Taking items out of the library system
5. **Disposal Plan**
   Book sale, vendor sale, recycling, or landfill
6. **Temporary Staging**
   Consider location, length of time, volume, etc. of removed items
7. **Execute & Monitor**
   Address record clean up, shift collections, track reporting, and incorporate key learnings into your library's collection development policy

A New Kind of Social Media Strategy: Collecting Zines at the Vassar College Library

Heidy Berthoud, Head of Acquisitions and Cataloging Services, Interim Head of Technical Services, Vassar College Library

Abstract

"Where do we go from here?" One way that the Vassar College Library is answering this question is by making concerted efforts to promote unique or rarely held materials—that is, nurturing collections that will make us stand out from the crowd. With that goal in mind, the Vassar College Library has spent the past year working to create a collection of zines.

This article will discuss the importance of social media in the acquisition of zines, using the Vassar College Library's experience as an example. Zines are DIY, self-published materials that are a vibrant and creative way to represent diverse points of view in your collection; however, with DIY publications come a host of new collection development and acquisition hurdles to consider. Since zines are produced outside of the purview of for-profit publishers, librarians cannot rely on our comfortable and well-established mechanisms to explore and acquire these materials. Using social media to inform collection development can be daunting, but if zines are a medium your library wants to pursue, doing a little bit of networking can go a long way.

Readers will learn about the Vassar zine collection development plan, and different ways that we use social media (particularly Twitter) to fulfill our mission. Different online zine distributors (or distros) will also be discussed, as well as the wealth of materials to be found from individual zinesters via avenues typically not utilized by libraries, such as Etsy. The topic of ethical zine acquisitions will also be explored.

Introduction

Zines are remarkably slippery to define; they almost seem to exist to defy categorization. They can come in many shapes and sizes. They can be typed, handwritten, collaged. They can be about any topic, created by any individual. At their core, zines are a do-it-yourself, creative form of publication. As Duncombe (2001) writes "zinesters privilege the ethic of DIY, do-it-yourself: make your own culture and stop consuming that which is made for you" (p. 7). For academic libraries, zines can add a new and welcome viewpoint; lacking the barriers to access present in more formalized publishing processes, the zine is a medium where anyone can make their voice heard. These small, self-made publications can add huge amounts of vibrancy to a collection.

The same qualities that make zines such diverse resources also serve to make them unruly for your collection development and technical services processes. Zines can and do present interesting challenges when it comes to researching, locating, and purchasing.[1] This paper will attempt to shed some light on how the Vassar College Zine Library is learning to take these challenges in stride.

Vassar College Zine Library

Vassar College is a private liberal arts college located in Poughkeepsie, New York. As of fall semester 2015, the full-time enrollment is 2,425. Creating a zines collection at Vassar College was something that Heidy Berthoud was interested in since starting her position in December 2012; she had previously worked with the zine collection at

[1] Zines can also present interesting challenges to citation methods when they are used in scholarly papers; this author referred to Giari (2009) for assistance in formatting.

http://dx.doi.org/10.5703/1288284316274

the University of Chicago Library and thought that zines would hold a certain appeal to the Vassar campus population.[2] However, it was not until the fall semester 2014 that the idea gained traction. To date, Vassar has purchased nearly 400 zines, and with the 2016 fiscal year, zines have been given an official slot in the acquisitions budget.

The focus of this project is to speak more in-depth on how the Vassar College Library goes about both researching and acquiring its zines, with a particular focus on its use of social media in these processes. Much of the collection development and acquisitions work is handled by Berthoud, the unofficial zine librarian and originator of the zine collection, though she is assisted in all things zine related by senior college student Matthew Higgins, the zine library's "zintern."[3]

Using Social Media in Collection Development

Finding zine content to purchase can be a time consuming process depending on your collection development goals. At Vassar, we have made the decision to center our zine collection on several key areas: namely, feminist zines, zines concerning gender and sexuality, and zines created by people of color. In order to fulfill this mission, we research zine content being created across the country, and even content being created abroad.

Since zines exist outside of corporate publishing models, zine librarians are forced to use unconventional methods to locate this content. There is no handy publisher's database listing thousands of available zine titles, no zine reviews being regularly pushed out to subject librarians for their consumption. There are resources available to zine librarians online via the ZineLibraries.info WordPress site,[4] but as every zine library is different, it is necessary, to a certain extent, to cultivate your own network of zine resources.

The primary way that Vassar is approaching this problem is through social media. Simultaneous with the public launch of our zine collection, we introduced the Twitter account @vassarzines and began following zine libraries, zine distros, and zinesters. We also utilize TweetDeck to track hashtags such as #zines and #poczines. These very simple steps have introduced us to a world of zine content that we might have otherwise overlooked. It was Twitter that led us to purchase such titles as *Black women & self care: Thoughts on mental health, oppression, and healing* by Naomi Moyer, and the edited series *Sonorus: Feminist perspectives on Harry Potter.*

Another quasi-social media site where one can locate zines is Etsy. A number of zinesters sell their creations in Etsy shops, and it is worthwhile for zine libraries to create an Etsy account. This functionality will allow you to "favorite" the zine shops you use. Etsy will provide automatic notifications whenever there is new content available in your favorite shops; they will also provide a list of recommendations based on your favorites, allowing you to potentially discover new content. While not a vendor database in the more traditional sense, Etsy can certainly be made to serve this purpose for zine acquisitions.

In order to continually expand our network of zine contacts, it has become part of our zine intake process to make note of a zinester's social media accounts and follow (or favorite) them, if possible. Additionally, we make a conscious effort to tweet about new acquisitions, including mentions of the zinester. In our view, these types of small interactions are simply part of being a good zine citizen. We like to publicly acknowledge our appreciation of the work zinesters create, and tweeting about our library content allows us to simultaneously spread the word about zines and build our own network of contacts.

[2] Her job talk was about acquiring and cataloging zines at the University of Chicago Library.

[3] Higgins also read and provided comments on this article.

[4] Or zine librarians to meet and exchange insights and expertise on a range of topics.

Methods of Acquiring Zines

As noted by Berthoud and colleagues (2015), "not all methods of acquisition are equal" (p. 4). The best—and most ethical—method of acquiring zines is to purchase content directly from the creator. The vast majority of zinesters are not making huge profits from their zines; many have other careers and pursuits, and are creating zines in their leisure time. Indeed, Wrekk (2009) notes that zines are "independently made for the love of creating and rarely make a profit" (p. 6). This kind of direct purchase ensures that one hundred percent of the cost of the zine goes directly to the zinester, which enables them to sustain their creative process. Moreover, when a library purchases content direct from the zinester, it shows that the institution respects the value of the zinester's work (Berthoud et al., 2015).

Libraries should also make it clear at point of purchase that the zines will be housed in a public space, not in an individual's private collection. Zines can be very personal items, and it is important to give the zinester the right of refusal; some zinesters may not feel comfortable with their work being available to so large an audience (Berthoud et al., 2015). When ordering for Vassar College, we also include a brief note, typically in the comments section of the online store form or the PayPal submission,[5] noting that the zines are being purchased for a library collection. To date, we have not received any notes from zinesters rescinding our purchase. On the contrary, a number of zinesters are extremely excited for the opportunity to have content they have created in our library, and many of them have mentioned us in kind tweets, or have sent along handwritten notes of thanks with our orders.[6]

While it is always preferable to purchase content directly from the creator, it is occasionally neither possible nor practical. When this is the case, the next best option is to use a zine distributor. Much like zines themselves, zine distros come in a variety of shapes and sizes. Some zine suppliers have both an online presence and a brick and mortar storefront, as is the case with Bluestockings in New York City, Quimby's Bookstore in Chicago, or the Portland Button Works and Zine Distro in Portland, Oregon. Other zine distros exist as an online presence only. For example, the Brown Recluse Zine Distro (BRZD) in Seattle is run out of founder Nyky Gomez's home (Gomez, n.d.). Other zine distros, like Stranger Danger Zine Distro, have existed in multiple locations with management being passed from zinester to zinester. Some distros will only sell zines by certain creators, while some build their zine catalogs around particular themes. If zinesters lack their own online store presence, you may be able to find their work in a distro. Because distros carry a range of content from different creators, it can sometimes be more convenient for libraries, both from a time and budget perspective, to purchase a single large order with a distro rather than a number of smaller orders with individual zinesters. Zine libraries will have to find a balance that works for their situation.

At Vassar, we try to purchase direct from the zinester whenever possible. This is especially true when we purchase zine content from abroad; we have a number of titles purchased direct from zinesters in the United Kingdom. However, we do have distros that we return to repeatedly in part for convenience, but mostly because we value the content they aggregate. BRZD is an excellent example; on the distro's website, Gomez (n.d.) writes that BRZD ". . . was created to support and center zines written predominantly by POC folks of all identities . . . [and] was born out of passion for zines and frustration at the lack of representation and meaningful zine material for People of Color" ("About Brown Recluse"). Our zine library appreciates the work that Gomez is

[5] Having a PayPal account is an absolute necessity for any library interested in starting a zine collection.

[6] In fact, we have received such a quantity of notes that we had to develop a workflow to process them. For each note, we know the zinester who created it and the package it was sent with, and we are seriously considering creating a separate archive to hold the various accoutrements received as part of our zine packages. In addition to notes, some zinesters have also sent us free stickers and buttons, and some highly decorate and ornament the packages themselves.

doing in promoting zinesters of color, and we show our support by being frequent customers of the distro.

Conclusion

No two zine libraries are exactly alike, so the strategies currently employed by Vassar College may not be the perfect solution for your home institution. Because there is only one librarian and one student zintern handling all aspects of zine development and acquisitions, it was relatively easy to create a social media strategy, and did not require buy-in across multiple staffers in multiple departments.

That being said, we would still highly recommend that any library considering a zine collection should explore ways in which they can make social media a regular part of their workflow. Turning to social media for assistance in both the collection development and acquisitions process has been hugely beneficial. This kind of networking has proven to be an integral piece in how we discover and purchase new content. Moreover, it has given us the opportunity to connect more fully with the community of zinesters, and play a role in helping to share their creativity with others.

References

Berthoud H., Barton J., Brett J., Darms L., Fox V., Freedman J., . . . Wooten K. (2015). *Zine librarian code of ethics zine*. Retrieved from http://zinelibraries.info/code-of-ethics/

Duncombe, S. (2001). *Notes from underground: Zines and the politics of alternative culture*. Bloomington: Microcosm.

Giari, K. (2009). *Cite this zine* (2nd ed.). Retrieved from https://zines.barnard.edu/sites/default/files/inline/citethis2010.pdf

Gomez, N. (n.d.). *About Brown Recluse Zine Distro*. Retrieved from http://www.brownreclusezinedistro.com/about-faq

Wrekk, A. (2009). *Stolen sharpie revolution 2: A DIY resource for zines and zine culture*. Portland: Lunchroom Publishing.

Teetering Between Two Systems for Managing E-Book Records

Stephen Francoeur, User Experience Librarian, Newman Library, Baruch College

Michael Waldman, Head, Collection Management, Newman Library, Baruch College

Abstract

Drawing on our experience with the Primo discovery service at Baruch College, we will discuss the extent to which libraries can expect that they can treat e-book packages in discovery services in the same manner that they treat journal packages. Given that many libraries are still trying to bridge parallel systems for the discovery of e-books—the catalog and the discovery service—this presentation will help organize the problem so that we can develop a deeper understanding of the challenges and outline a map for charting the way ahead.

Introduction

Like many libraries that have set up web-scale discovery services in recent years, we are still trying to maintain our legacy catalog at the same time and ensure that both are equally useful to our community. This balancing act has created a new set of tensions that we would like to explore in some depth today. Before examining these issues, we would like to first introduce Baruch College so you can get the necessary context to understand how the situation is playing out at our institution.

Baruch College is one of eleven senior colleges within the City University of New York system (CUNY), which has in total 21 campuses across the five boroughs of New York City. We are a commuter school in the heart of New York City with over 18,000 students, 35 undergraduate majors, 25 graduate-level specializations, and one doctoral program in business. Our library has 67 full time staff, 21 of whom are librarians. Our annual materials budget is currently $1.7 million, and we have over 650,000 electronic resources. Baruch's collection of e-books consists of roughly 280,000 titles.

For our presentation, it is important to keep in mind the consortia in which Baruch's library operates. We work within a very mediated environment where systems are centrally managed by a central CUNY Office of Library Services (CUNY OLS) for 21 CUNY schools. Since 2002, CUNY has used Ex Libris Aleph as its union catalog. Like other individual schools in the CUNY system, we at Baruch are not able to directly download or manipulate large sets of data. When uploading sets of records, files must be sent to the CUNY OLS, who vet them and add them to Aleph.

In 2005, the CUNY library system began using SFX as its link resolver. In fall 2014, the CUNY libraries launched a shared web-scale discovery service powered by Ex Libris Primo and locally branded as OneSearch. For both SFX and Primo, direct administrator access is limited to staff at CUNY OLS; we at Baruch must e-mail the central office to request changes, fixes, updates, and the like.

E-Books at Baruch

Some of our e-book collections are bought centrally by CUNY OLS for all CUNY libraries, such as ebrary, while other collections, such as Books24x7, are ones we got on our own. We acquire e-books in a number of different ways. Some are purchases, some are subscriptions. Some are bought on a title-by-title basis, while others are part of a package. Most are selected by library staff, but a growing number are selected through our demand-driven acquisitions (DDA) service from MyiLibrary.

Prior to our getting a discovery system, we only had to worry about one workflow to handle batch loading of e-book records. If we had at least fifty records, we had a time-consuming process that required a specialist who was, ideally, a librarian with cataloging experience. First, the purchase

http://dx.doi.org/10.5703/1288284316275

needed to be confirmed. Then the head of collection management would send the information to the metadata librarian and the user experience (UX) librarian (whose responsibilities also include assisting with the management of electronic resources). The information passed on would be about the resource itself (was it a one-time upload, was it a file that should be checked for newer titles, was this a DDA plan or a real purchase, do we want the records to go to OCLC). The information about the batch upload also had to include instructions about where to find the MARC record file and about any message we needed to add to the records.

The next step for the traditional workflow involved the metadata librarian, who would grab the file and use MarcEdit to edit the file. Next, the metadata librarian would send the file to the CUNY Office of Library Services so it could be loaded into an Aleph testing server. The metadata librarian would then review the records in the testing server and, if all was okay, authorize the files to be moved into the live instance of the catalog.

While the metadata librarian was getting the records into the catalog, the UX librarian, who also happens to assist with electronic resource management, would configure the resource in EZproxy if it were on a new platform and add links to it on the library's database pages.

Once the records were loaded into the live catalog, the metadata librarian would then record the number range for the records and the date of the load into a wiki page. If appropriate, the UX librarian of the head of collection management might make an announcement on the library's internal mailing list or staff blog to share the news about the new records in the catalog.

E-Books at Baruch Now That We Have a Discovery Service

Since we launched our discovery service from Primo last year, we have been presented with a new choice for e-books. We can either display the MARC records that we added to our catalog or, depending on the e-book platform, use records from the platform vendor that are available within the Primo Central Index (PCI). Just as we can activate in the PCI a database of articles so that it is discoverable in our instance of Primo, so too can we activate e-book packages.

This has changed our workflow with e-books. Now, when we get a new e-book platform, we check Ex Libris documentation to see if it is available as a package to be activated in the PCI. If it is, then we do so. But since we still want to make sure our catalog has the same set of e-books, we also have to continue the traditional e-book workflow of getting MARC records for those e-books into the catalog. This new workflow, though, has one new step: the central Office of Library Services (OLS) at CUNY adds an element to the MARC record so that they are not automatically ingested into the Primo Central Index as well. If we didn't take this step, we would find duplicates of e-book records in Primo: one from the vendor whose records we activated in the PCI and one from us—the MARC records that came over from the catalog.

Where E-Book Management Gets Problematic

This new option of using vendor records in the PCI should mean less work for Baruch and for the CUNY Office of Library Services. One time saver is something that happens rarely but can involve a lot of work in MARC records: vendors changing base URLs for books in their collection. We are dealing with this issue now, thanks to the merger of Springer and Palgrave Macmillan. All the URLs for our Palgrave e- books will soon change as they move over to the Springer platform, which means that we will need to update the URLs in the 856 field of our MARC records for those titles. But in the case of the records for those same titles that came from the vendor as a package to be activated in the PCI, the work of updating URLs is no longer our responsibility but rather that of Ex Libris and the vendor from whom they are getting the records. This kind of updating of URLs by vendors is something we are already used to in the case of serials, where libraries have been relying on knowledge bases from products like Ex Libris's SFX or Serials Solution's 360 Core to do that work for periodicals collections and aggregator databases.

It is not so simple for e-books, though. The problem is twofold. First, at Baruch we do not yet have the technology we know we need—a library services platform like Ex Libris's Alma or ProQuest's Intota. Such a system would integrate the cataloging, acquisitions, and serials management systems we currently have. Instead, we are trying to make sure that both our discovery service and our traditional catalog are both regarded by our users as places to find every single print and e-book that we have. And so we awkwardly remain straddling two systems—the catalog and the discovery system—and two workflows for handling e-books.

The other part of the problem, and this is not unique to Baruch, is that we are finding that there are some e-books we cannot easily get into our discovery service unless we rely on MARC records. This problem comes in two variations. First, there are some e-book packages we have at Baruch that are not available yet in the Primo Central Index. We would love to activate them in the PCI, but Ex Libris has not gotten the records yet or has not finished indexing them. The other variation on this problem is how to "activate" in the PCI those e-books that we have bought not as a package but instead on a title-by-title basis. Consider the reality that when we buy e-books individually, we have lots of choices about who to order from (such as EBSCO, Coutts, the publisher) and choices about what platform we want to access them on (such as MyiLibrary or the publisher's own platform). It is hard to conceive of how this variety of purchase and access options can be easily handled in the PCI. On a related note, there does not seem to be a way in the PCI to handle records for DDA titles.

There is also an issue relating to the speed with which Ex Libris gets updates to the e-book packages in the PCI. In theory, our traditional workflow for getting the latest e-book records for a platform we have had for a while means we can check as often as we like for new records. We could check monthly or even weekly. In the PCI, though, it is unlikely the e-book packages that we can activate will be updated more often than four times a year. So it is possible that our e-book records in the catalog will be more up to date than what we have in Primo.

In most cases, the indexing of e-books in the PCI does not make their full-text searchable. Only the metadata for the e-books can be searched. In the case of reference books, it is usually not the case that the indexing is at the entry level, which is a missed opportunity to open up these works to readers who might otherwise pass them by.

We recognize that some of the awkwardness of this situation is due to our need to maintain a legacy catalog and a discovery system at the same time. Some day when we decommission the catalog and move to a library services platform, the workflows for e-books will in theory be simpler. We also expect that in time Ex Libris will have added even more e-book packages that we can activate, maybe even all the ones we would ever have.

Until that day, though, we're having to work on our balancing act.

Preserving the Past for the Future: Moving Toward Best Practices and Tools for Thoughtful Monographic Withdrawal

Mary Miller, Director of Collection Management & Preservation, University of Minnesota Libraries

Jennifer Teper, Head, Preservation Services, University of Illinois at Urbana-Champaign

Abstract

This paper presents significant findings from a 2015 survey of the Association of Research Libraries (ARL) and Oberlin Group Libraries to learn how institutions make decisions to withdraw or retain print monographs. The survey was part of a two-pronged national study led by preservation and conservation experts to better understand which kinds of data, policies, data sharing mechanisms, and other communication strategies libraries use and need to make informed decisions about monograph withdrawals in their collections. This study reviews how policies are (or aren't) developed, what kinds of data are (or aren't) used, and which stakeholders are (or aren't) consulted. Trends in institutions by type and size (public versus private, state institution versus college) are also investigated.

Introduction

Libraries are withdrawing journals, and increasingly, monographs, from their print collections to recover space for programmatic use and other reasons. At the same time, relatively little is known about the long-term impact of current withdrawal practices on the future quality of legacy print collections, particularly for monographs. In the library preservation community, practices for print retention and withdrawal have been a persistent topic of discussion in recent years.

To date, there are few publications that examine or recommend practices for evaluating monographs for retention or withdrawal. Jake Nadal and Annie Peterson's 2011 white paper "Scarce and Endangered Works: Using Network-level Holdings Data in Preservation Decision Making and Stewardship of the Printed Record" provides a general outline for monographic withdrawal practices based on number of copies held nationally.[1] However, Nadal and Peterson's work makes recommendations based only on number of copies, not on condition of those copies remaining. Other recent projects have sought to derive data on the condition of commonly shared monographic titles, such as the UK-based 2006–2008 Identical Book Project (http://www.bl.uk/aboutus/stratpolprog/collectioncare/publications/articles/2007/identicalbooksp.pdf), or the University of Virginia's current Book Traces Project (http://www.booktraces.org/).

Based on the available research, and the preservation community's continuing interest in the impact of withdrawal practices on print monograph preservation, a 2014 forum was hosted by the University of Pennsylvania's Van Pelt Library. As a result of the forum discussions, two research groups were formed. The first group was charged with assessing analytical approaches to determine paper quality in bound volumes. The second group was charged with assessing current withdrawal policies and practices for monographs, and the likely long-term impact on preservation.

This second group, which included preservation administrators from University of Illinois, University of Minnesota, University of Pennsylvania, Northwestern University, and Yale

[1] Nadal, J. & Peterson, A. (2011). Scarce and endangered works: Using network-level holdings data in preservation decision making and stewardship of the printed record. *Jacobnadal.com*. Retrieved from http://www.jacobnadal.com/wp-content/uploads/2011/05/ScarceAndEndangeredWorksv7.pdf

http://dx.doi.org/10.5703/1288284316276

University, proposed a survey as a starting point. This resulting paper, presented at the 2015 Charleston Conference, summarizes preliminary findings of the survey. While further analysis of survey data and sample policy documents is needed, the authors draw some initial conclusions about current withdrawal policies and practices, and identify possible future directions.

Survey Methodology

An online survey was designed to gather information about policies and practices academic institutions currently use to make decisions about withdrawing print monographs from their collections. For the purposes of the survey, *policy* was defined as "any formal or informal written guidelines or other documentation, as well as unwritten practices, and may be inclusive of serials as well as monographs." The survey addressed:

- The existence and extent of current policies for withdrawing print monographs, on both an item-level and project-level basis
- How policies are developed
- Who makes decisions about selecting print monographs for withdrawal
- Information currently used in selecting print monographs for withdrawal or retention
- Information that would be desirable for future decision-making

During the summer of 2015, the survey was distributed to the Association of Research Libraries (ARL) and Oberlin Library director listservs, as well as the SCELEC (Statewide California Electronic Library Consortium) and ALA new director listservs. After the initial data collection period had passed, any libraries with known preservation programs (largely ARL member institutions) who had not responded were encouraged to respond through direct contact with their preservation administrators. (This may have caused a slightly higher response from preservation practitioners in the overall response rate, at 18% of the total responses.) Overall, the group received ninety-nine valid responses after removing multiple responses from a single institution.[2]

Data Analysis

The first section of the survey asked respondents to provide basic demographic information about their institution and their position, or role, within the institution. Overall, 60% of respondents were from ARL member libraries, 21% from Oberlin Group Institutions, and 18% were from "other" libraries.[3] Libraries ranged in size from 31.6% with print collections of less than 500,000, to libraries holding over 8 million print volumes (see Figure 1) and showed a fairly even distribution of size over the range of the respondents. In terms of position, 39.4% of respondents identified as senior library administrators, 18.2% as preservation/conservation staff, 32.3% as collection management/development staff; 1% identified as subject specialists, and 9.1% responded "other." (These respondents were largely technical services staff.)

Respondents were then asked if the institution had an institutional policy governing monographic withdrawal practices. Of the 99 responses, 80.6% responded that they did, and were asked to continue on for further data collection; the remaining 19.4% responded that they did not, and exited the survey. There was no observed correlation between the presence of an institutional withdrawal policy and the size of the institution; small libraries were as likely to have a policy as large ones. Of those institutions that have a policy, only 60% of respondents replied that their policy is written.

[2] It is worth noting that for most instances where multiple responses were submitted from the same institution, responses to our survey questions did not agree even across different units of the same library.

[3] "Other" responses were most often small liberal arts colleges.

Print Collection Size	
Less than 500,000 volumes	31.6%
500,000 - 1 million volumes	9.2%
1 - 3 million volumes	16.3%
3 - 5 million volumes	15.3%
5 - 8 million volumes	14.3%
8 or more million volumes	13.3%

Figure 1. Size of print collections.

Respondents were then asked how policies were developed and who helped to develop them. Over 85% of respondents replied that they developed their policy based on "discussions within the institution about local priorities and needs, comfort with risk, etc." (see Figure 2). The overwhelming selection of this response over other options (such as adapting language from other institutional policies, discussing policies with other institutions about cooperative or consortial priorities, or basing decisions on a study) suggests that policy development is still largely an internally focused process. Of those involved in the development of a withdrawal policy, the most common responses were "senior library administration" (79.2%), "collections management" (83.1%), and subject specialists (80.5%). Preservation staff were consulted in 51.9% of the overall responses, but when filtered by the 68.7% of institutions who *have* a preservation program, 71.4% of those respondents included preservation in policy development. This high correlation may be biased, however, by the high percentage of preservation administrators who were solicited in the final stages of data collection. Faculty involvement in the development of these practices was found to be quite low (only 29.9% of respondents saying that they were consulted in policy development, with smaller institutions markedly more likely to involve faculty than larger institutions.

How did you develop the policy? *(multiple selections possible)*	
We adapted language from the documentation of one or more institutions	16.9%
It developed from diszcussions within the institution about local priorities and needs, comfort with risk, etc	85.7%
It developed from discussions with other institutions about state/regional/consortial priorities and needs, comfort with risk, etc	23.4%
It is somewhat arbitrary	19.5%
It was developed from a study. If selected, please cite study or other relevant information here:	6.5%

Figure 2. How was the policy developed?

Policies were known and shared in a variety of ways, both formal and informal. While posted written guidelines were quite popular (51.9% of respondents noted that they had their policy posted either internally or publically), many relied on other means to communicate withdrawal practices, including training sessions (14.3%), verbal communications (59.7%), and simple historical practice (51.9%).

The next section of the survey delved into what the respondent's existing policies cover. When asked what their local policies encompass, policies most frequently covered duplicate print copies in the library (90.0% of all respondents) and withdrawal during preservation review (78.6%).

Withdrawal of duplicate holding across consortia was lower than expected in both ARL and Oberlin Group libraries (deemed most likely to be members of consortia) at 31.0% of ARL and 26.7% of Oberlin Group libraries. Similarly, policies encompassing guidelines for mass withdrawal (defined for these purposes as a programmatic approach to non-duplication within an institution, consortium, or other collaborative environment) was also lower than anticipated (only 15.7% of the total responses (see Figure 3).

Since several of these policy scenarios were dependent upon the presence of electronic copies, the survey asked respondents which repositories or content providers are included in their considerations. Responses showed that ARL and Oberlin Groups libraries rely most frequently on electronic copies in the HathiTrust (68.8% and 87.5% respectively), though the smaller "other" libraries were most likely to rely on locally digitized content, or digital content owned by

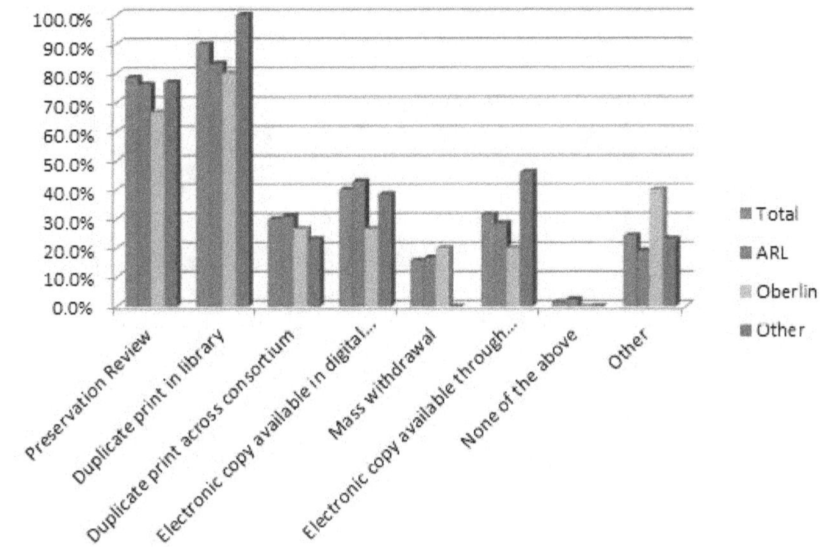

Figure 3. Institutional withdrawal policy coverage.

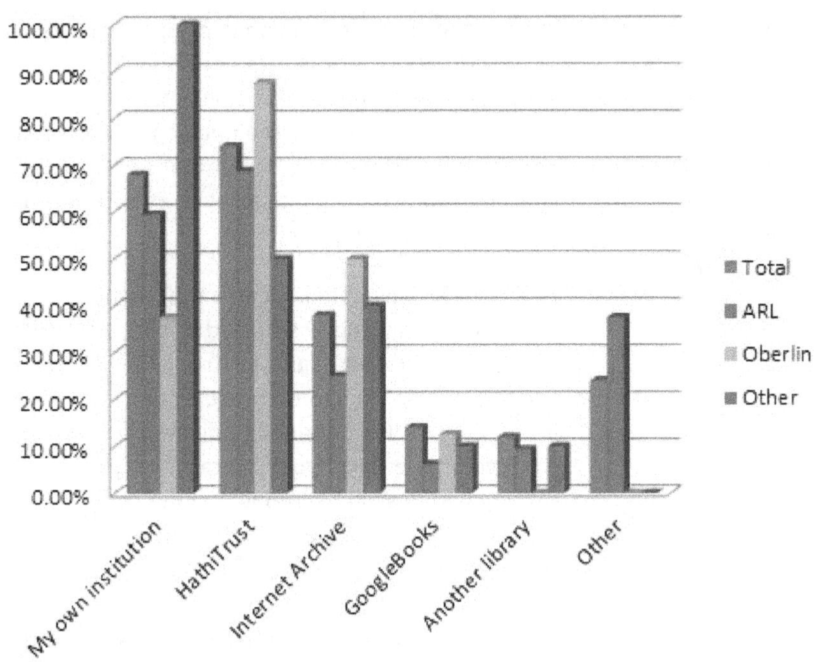

Figure 4. If the policy includes withdrawal of print monograph copies when an electronic copy is available, which repositories/content providers are included?

their own institution (100%). In aggregate, 74% of respondents rely on the HathiTrust and 68% rely on local digital copies (see Figure 4).

In the last question regarding withdrawal policy coverage, respondents were asked to identify which factor(s) they considered when deciding whether to retain or withdraw a monographic title. Unfortunately, the survey structure did not allow respondents to choose factors for different scenarios for withdrawing monographs (for example, individual item withdrawal versus large withdrawal projects). However, the responses still showed that libraries use a wide variety of factors, and in some instances almost any factor may be of value. The most commonly utilized factor for consideration appears to be physical damage, then embrittlement, provenance or other factors that render a copy unique, and input from collection development guidelines or staff (see Figure 5).

Finally, the survey asked respondents to consider what research or guideline development might be useful in the future as they withdraw print monographs from their collections. Overwhelmingly, when asked what element *is not currently* in their policies or procedures, but would be incorporated if easily accessible, almost 90% of respondents replied that "commitment to preserve at another institution" is the most desired element not currently available to them that would influence decisions. "Condition at another institution" fell significantly shorter in preference (just under 40% of overall responses responding that it would be helpful), and the development of a test to easily inform expected usable lifespan of a book (perhaps replacing the ubiquitous double-fold test

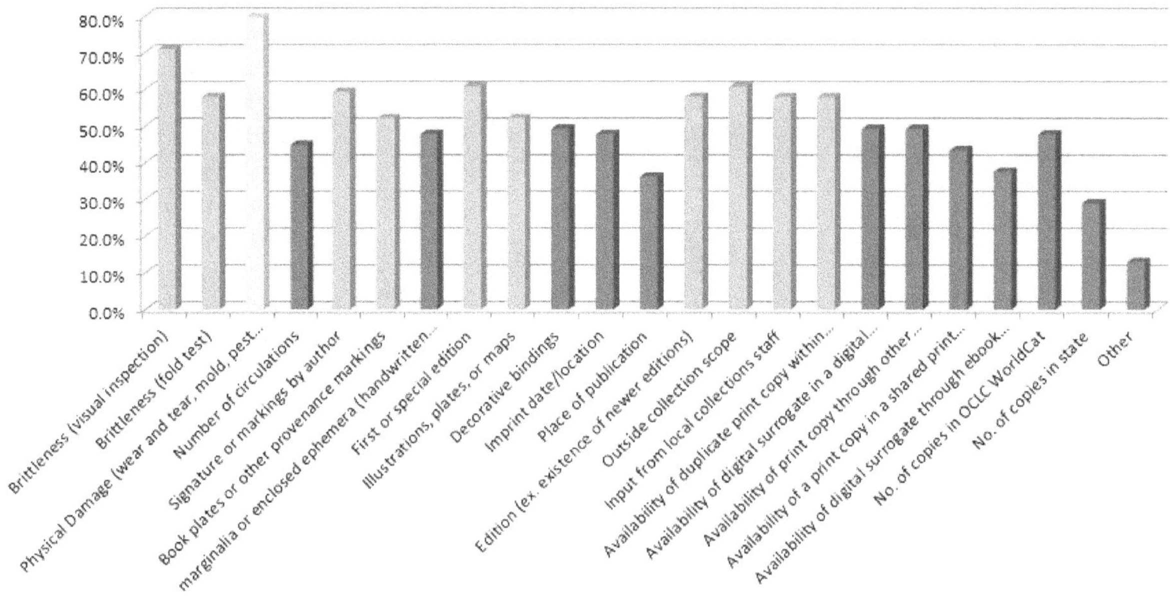

Figure 5. Current considerations for retention or withdrawal of individual items.

used to indicate current levels of embrittlement) was selected by only 25.8%. While "other" responses varied, "holdings at other libraries" was considered by some to be useful but not easily accessible at present (just under 5% of responses).

Survey respondents were also asked to provide relevant policy documents, which are currently being analyzed by the survey group.

Summary of Findings

While further analysis of the collected data is necessary, several trends and needs are already evident. Many libraries are operating without a guiding document that outlines when and how they withdraw monographs, and even those who have a policy frequently note that it is now out of date and in need of revision. In most cases, the development of such policies is an internal process that does not take into account external factors that may influence a decision to withdraw or retain a title, or the need for communication within and outside the institution. Policies often do not address consortial preservation considerations; the number of copies of a title available at the state, regional, or national level; or the condition of duplicate copies within the institution. And, more practically, many institutions have neither the necessary resources nor the infrastructure to implement such considerations on a practical level, even if they are included in a policy.

While the survey data indicates that many policies do not currently address shared or consortial print preservation, it also suggests strong interest in leveraging existing shared preservation infrastructure. Respondents indicated significant reliance on the HathiTrust Digital Library in making withdrawal decisions. In June 2015, the HathiTrust Board of Governors endorsed the final report of the Print Monograph Archive Planning Task Force, signifying a commitment to establishing a dispersed print repository.[4] Current recommendations include multiple overlapping retention commitments and building a dispersed collection that will "grow based on informed criteria such as optimal numbers of copies, geographical distribution, protection of scarce and unique titles, ongoing digitization, validation for existence and condition, and the movement into

[4] Hathitrust Board of Governors Steering Committee. (2015). *Summary and response to HathiTrust print monograph archives planning task force final report.* Retrieved from https://www.hathitrust.org/files /sharedprintreport.pdf

the repository of items not in the collections of Archive Holders or not yet digitized" (HathiTrust, p. 11). The survey indicates that some institutions are already committing to retain monographs on behalf of the academic library community, albeit on a much smaller scale; 19.1% overall, and 27.5% of responding ARL libraries replied that they currently serve as recipients for materials withdrawn from other libraries.

The survey results also indicated a broad desire for infrastructure to share information about institutional commitments to retain or preserve monographic holdings. While guidelines for indicating condition information and preservation commitments exist in the *Preservation & Digitization Actions: Terminology for MARC 21 Field 583,* few institutions currently utilize these guidelines. The potential for broader use of the *MARC 21* 583 field, or alternative mechanisms for sharing condition information and institutional retention commitments for monographs, is a possible topic of future study for the group.

The Future of Textbooks and Course Reserves in Academic Libraries: An Evolving Role and Emerging Opportunity

Osman Celik, International Acquisitions Coordinator, Gifts & Exchange Section Head, University of California Los Angeles

Roxanne M. Peck, Librarian for Digital Collection Management, University of California Los Angeles

Abstract

With the rising costs of textbooks, their affordability and accessibility in college and university campuses has emerged as a major financial obstacle for students. This challenge presents an opportunity for academic and research libraries in providing textbook affordability and accessibility for their students. Textbooks have been frequently excluded from the majority of academic and research libraries' collection development policies. Textbooks are often on the list of materials rarely purchased by libraries. Encouraging libraries to re-evaluate and re-strategize their traditional approach to textbook purchasing and course reserves is critical. Embracing more textbooks and expanding the course reserves has the potential to significantly improve user services in learning and teaching across campuses. Ultimately this evolving role for academic libraries provides another opportunity to demonstrate their value to campus administration and communities.

Room to Expand: Analysis of Collection Development, Textbook, and Course Reserves Policies

Many library collection development policies hold steadfast to a policy of either no textbook purchasing or making rare exceptions to purchase them. A random sampling of collection development policies for 30 ARL and ACRL institutions reveals that most ARL libraries have collection development policies that mention textbooks. Almost half of the ARL libraries that have collection policies posted also have a detailed textbook purchasing policy. Having reserves is an important aspect for ARL libraries, as evidenced by the fact that almost 80% have a dedicated reserves website or instructions for submitting reserves requests. ACRL libraries sampled had far fewer instances of collection development policies posted or reserves websites, and none of the libraries had a detailed textbook policy. See Figure 1 in the Appendix.

Closing the Gap in Service

The number of undergraduate courses offered in fall quarter far exceeds the number of classes served by the library course reserve system. This gap between classes offered and classes served provides the library with a chance to engage with faculty and students to demonstrate value and provide access to material used in the teaching classroom. See Figure 2 in the Appendix.

How Many Copies Are Enough?

It's not feasible to purchase a single textbook copy for all students in each course reserves class. However, the UCLA Powell (undergraduate) Library employs a general set of guidelines for purchasing titles not already owned by the library. See Table 1 in the Appendix.

Circulation Statistics

Over a period of 5 fiscal years, on average, 22% of all circulation statistics came from an item on course reserves. See Figure 3 in the Appendix.

Textbook Affordability

Analysis of titles available for students to purchase in the campus bookstore. See Table 2 in the Appendix.

Purchase Options

The campus bookstore offers students a variety of purchase or rental options for students. In spring

http://dx.doi.org/10.5703/1288284316277

2015, the top ten most expensive new books to purchase had multiple options to purchase either new, used, or rental copies of the book. Multiple choices afford students the opportunity to potentially save some money. However, students still need to look carefully at all options, since some rentals are more than the cost of the new text, and in other cases rentals are not much cheaper than purchasing a used copy. See Table 3 in the Appendix.

Potential Cost Savings

Usage of course reserve materials by students is hard to predict. Last minute research and studying means students may likely opt to purchase the item to ensure constant access and avoid regularly checking out an item on 2-hour reserve. Even if as few as 10% of students in a class relied solely on course reserves, they could potentially realize significant savings toward the cost of their education. See Table 4 in the Appendix.

Envisioning the Future

As demonstrated by the circulation statistics, course reserve materials are highly used year after year. Providing access to course reserves requires libraries to balance the needs of the students with the fiscal realities of limited library budgets. Libraries may not be able to afford purchasing all course reserve requests they received from faculty and students. However, an explicit local collection development policy acknowledging any limitations for textbook purchasing can help libraries to set realistic expectations regarding student needs without compromising the library budget.

Appendix: Tables

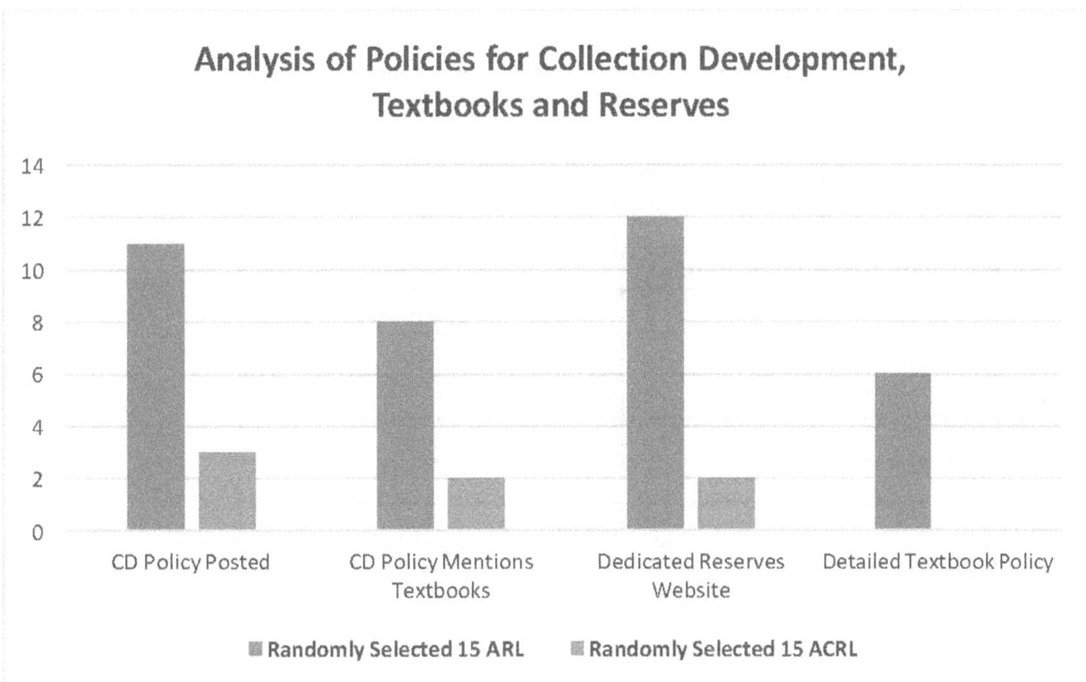

Figure 1. Analysis of collection development policies of 30 randomly selected ACRL and ARL Libraries.

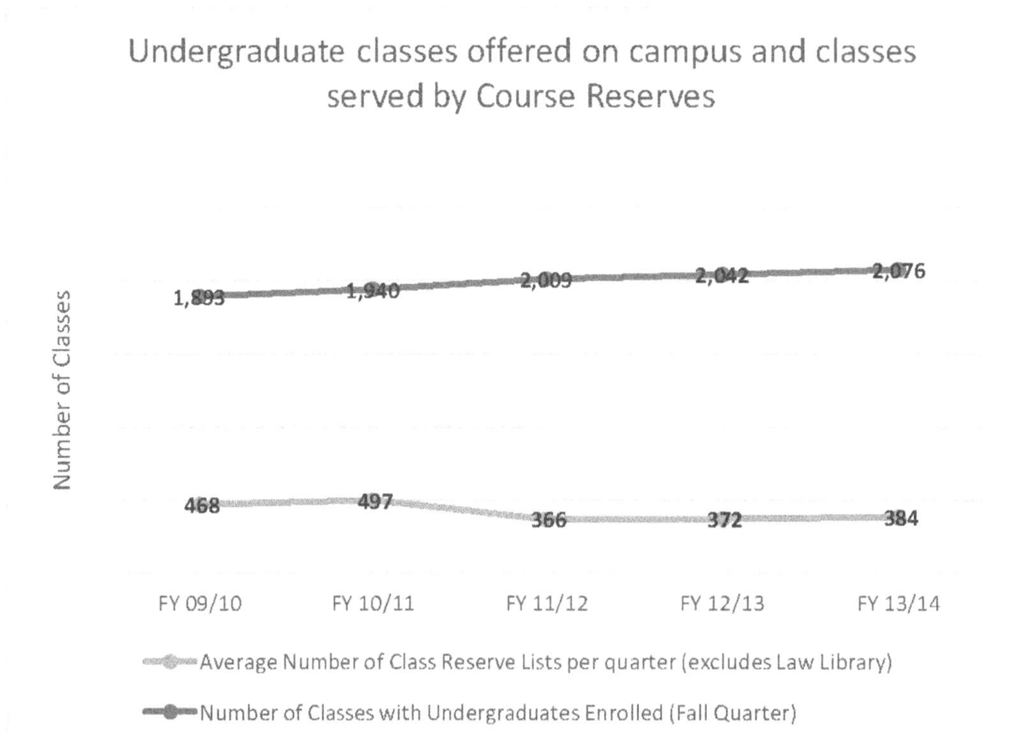

Figure 2. Undergraduate classes offered on campus and classes served by course reserves.

Table 1. Number of reserve copies purchased per class.

Guidelines for Reserves Textbook Purchases	
Class Size	Number of copies purchased
Less than 50 students	1 copy
50 – 120 students	2 copies
121 – 200 students	3 copies
201 – 299 students	4 copies
300 + students	5 copies

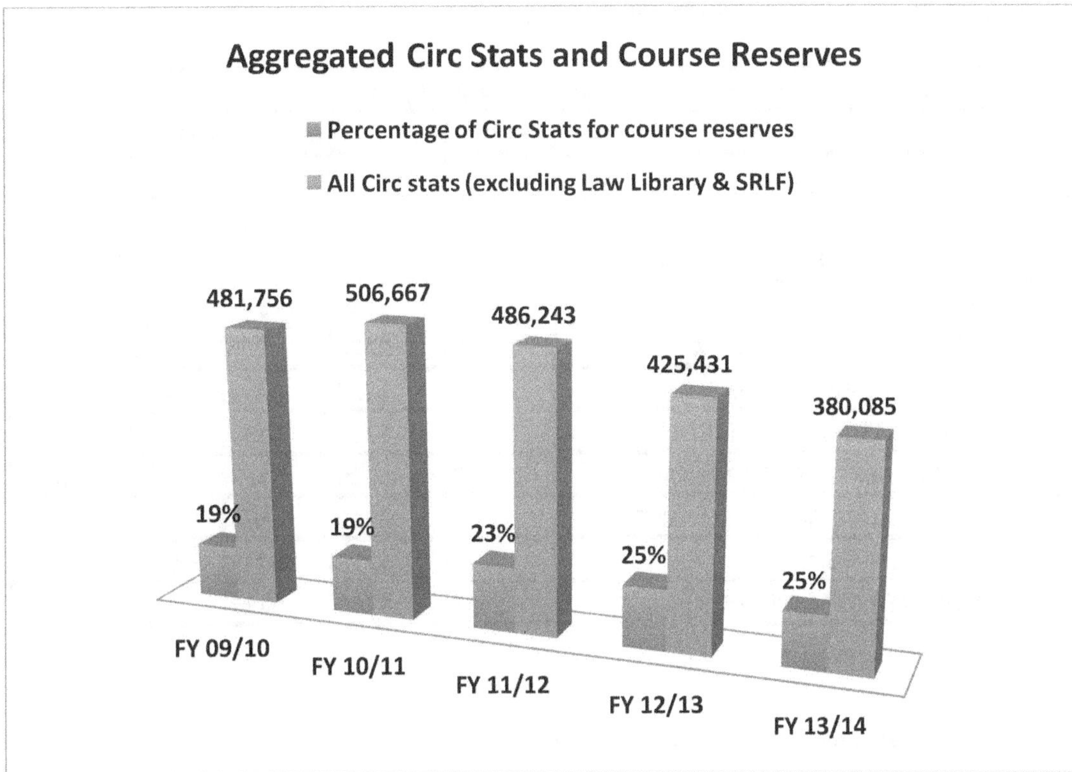

Figure 3. Library course reserve circulation statistics in comparison to overall library circulation statistics.

Table 2. Breakdown of textbook prices, spring 2015.

ASUCLA Bookstore Textbook Prices, Spring 2015		
New Book Price (List)	Number of titles	Percentage of All Costs
$100-$399	451	51%
$1-$99	2,528	49%

Table 3. Purchase options for the top ten most expensive books, spring 2015.

	Textbook Options for 10 Most Expensive Books, Spring 2015, UCLA						
			NEW	USED	DIGITAL	NEW	USED
	AUTHOR	TITLE	PRICE	PRICE	E-TEXT	RENTAL	RENTAL
1	BROWN	ORGANIC CHEMISTRY	$350	$263	$106	$190	$37
2	WINSTON	PRACTICAL MANAGEMENT SCIENCE	$331	$249	$186	$200	$87
3	CLARKSON	BUSINESS LAW	$326	$244	$98	$162	$29
4	WOOLDRIDG	INTRODUCTORY ECONOMETRICS	$317	$238	$96	$149	$55
5	REVSINE	FINANCIAL REPORTING & ANALYSIS	$302	$227	$203	$152	$64
6	BERK	CORPORATE FINANCE (3RD)	$297	$223	$131	$168	$127
7	ANDERSON	FUNDAMENTALS AERODYNAMICS	$293	$220	$183	$137	$123
8	ABRAHAM	INTRO REGRESSION MODELING (W/CD	$292	$219	n/a	$199	$174
9	YARBRO	CANCER NURSING	$291	$218	$245	$306	$306
10	MCDONALD	DERIVATIVES MARKETS	$283	$200	$117	$128	$82

Table 4. Purchase options for the top ten most expensive books, spring 2015.

Random Sample Class Textbook Costs by Course, Fall 2015	Number of enrolled students	Cost of new books per student	Cost for all students	Potential Savings if Students Used Course Reserves 10 %	20 %	30 %
Psychology 10	317	$213	$67,442	$6,752	$13,504	$20,256
Chem 14A	347	$199	$68,966	$6,905	$13,811	$20,715
History 114A	96	$175	$16,843	$1,680	$3,360	$5,040
Life Sciences 1	353	$146	$51,538	$5,154	$10,308	$15,462
Anthropology M151	73	$107	$7,811	$781	$1,562	$2,343
Scandinavian Studies 50	330	$55	$17,985	$1,815	$3,630	$5,445

The Unknown Path—Evaluating Electronic Resources for Access-Based Collection Development

Laurel Crawford, Coordinator of Collection Development, University of North Texas Libraries

Erin Miller, Electronic Resources Librarian, University of North Texas Libraries

Mark Henley, former Contracts Assessment Librarian at University of North Texas Libraries

Abstract

In 2015, the University of North Texas Libraries implemented an access-based collection development policy. This new policy, coupled with the increase of interdisciplinary studies at the University, dictated the necessity for a more exhaustive evaluation of continuing resources such as databases, journals, and standing orders before they are purchased. The collection development department created a rubric of criteria to address all aspects of the evaluation. This article will provide a brief description of access-based collection development and a detailed discussion of the rubric's criteria and how it will be implemented.

History

Formerly, University of North Texas (UNT) Libraries's collection development department operated on a traditional acquisitions structure. Selectors—usually public services reference librarians, who serve as subject librarians to assigned departments—selected monographs title-by-title to spend a small fund, which was allocated by department by a formula. These librarians usually have little exposure to or experience with financial or technical concerns. Collection development personnel did the actual purchasing after selectors communicated their choices.

The UNT Libraries have also experienced flat funding for the past several years. We have had to make very difficult decisions about what to discontinue and what to purchase. We began to ask ourselves: are we making the best use of the funds available to us?

We realized that the subject-expert librarians are not always in a good position to evaluate the added criteria that accompany Electronic Resource (ER) selection. There is much more to selecting ER's than simply content; there are also financial, usability, and contracting concerns. The traditional selection and acquisition model was not adapting well to the way we acquire ER's.

We believe, based on the literature and our own assessments, that the subject-expert's natural focus on narrow, traditional disciplinary subjects was neglecting the increasing importance of new, interdisciplinary areas of study. Some broad oversight of the collection was needed to address these collecting gaps.

A New Philosophy

To address these and other concerns, we adopted a new access-based collection development philosophy. We decided to choose access over ownership wherever appropriate, and take advantage of new acquisitions models such as demand-driven acquisitions (DDA) and pay-per-view. In sum, we are collecting for today's user rather than a someday user; and we think about collections as a *service* rather than an *object*.

However, the access-based approach wouldn't work if we continued allowing piecemeal selecting. We wanted to sculpt access on a macro level, then allow users to make the micro-level decisions within that framework. We decided to change the decision-making process. Under the old model, we more or less rubber-stamped selectors' decisions. We now take a team approach, with several acquisitions experts *and* the subject librarian guiding collection development decisions together. We see our

http://dx.doi.org/10.5703/1288284316278

objective as holistic collection-sculpting rather than piecemeal selecting. This vision requires a new attitude about assessment: we're now practicing rigorous evaluation of ER's *before* the decision to purchase.

Increased evaluation led us to a new set of principles by which we make these decisions:

- **Evaluation** of many more features of electronic resources than mere content
- Aggressive **negotiation** with vendors, on price, licensing concerns, and more
- **Transparency**, or the ability to justify our decisions to stakeholders
- **Documentation** of the decision-making process

In order to manifest this new philosophy, we had to put in place some infrastructure. We developed an evaluation rubric that helps us meet all of these goals *and* adhere to our principles. Although we're focusing on holistic collection development, we still have to evaluate each product on its own and make those one-by-one decisions. We evaluate each product on content, financial concerns, usability issues, and contract criteria. We also want to incorporate feedback from others when making the decision. The rubric functions as a place to collect and record input of various types and from various stakeholders.

Rubric Overview

The current version of our rubric is formatted as a spreadsheet with ten rows of criteria that are based on key components of library electronic resources. These are:

- Trial results
- MARC record availability
- Accessibility
- Subject area liaisons' review
- Curricular support
- Subject coverage
- Vendor support
- The availability of an access-based model
- License/contract concerns and usability

As the evaluation of a resource is undertaken, each of these criterion will be assigned a rating of either excellent, medium, or poor.

Two of the criteria ratings—*License/contract and usability*—are based on separate in-depth evaluations. For the other eight specific components listed, the ratings are clearly but briefly defined so as to provide consistency from one resource evaluation to the next. For example, the ratings for *MARC Records* are:

- Excellent: Available, no cost
- Medium: Available, at a cost
- Poor: Not available

The rating for *Trials Results* is differentiated not only by how positive the trial feedback was but also how plentiful it was, as well as by trial usage. The Electronic Resources Librarian promotes trials widely and collects information by e-mail as well as through online surveys that are provided for each trial. Low usage or limited feedback implies lack of interest rather than lack of awareness. The ratings for *Subject Area Liaison Reviews* are rated similarly on the amount of as well as content of requests and feedback from subject librarians.

Both the ratings for *Curricular Support* and *Subject Coverage* are supported with data and input from our Assessment Librarian. *Curricular Support* is determined by mapping the collection or resource being evaluated to disciplines taught at UNT. This allows us to evaluate whether the resource supports multiple departments by being highly interdisciplinary or not. An overlap analysis provides the data needed to determine *Subject Coverage*: whether or not electronic resource contains content that is duplicated within the collection or if it fills a collection gap.

Accessibility is an important concern in collection policy that we are currently looking at closely in order to improve and strengthen how our resources meet the needs of all of our diverse users. At this time, accessibility is evaluated based on the availability of Voluntary Product

Accessibility Templates (VPATs). These are forms completed by vendors that demonstrate how well a resource fulfills the guidelines put forth in Section 508 of the Rehabilitation Act of 1973. VPATs are available online at http://uniaccessig.org/lua/vpat-repository/. If a resource or vendor does not have a VPAT on file it may be possible to obtain one by contacting them.

Two criteria focus on concerns that are specifically important to the collection management team at UNT Libraries because of our specific interests and collection policies, but may not be applicable or valuable to all libraries. These are *Vendor Support* issues and whether or not *Access Based Models* are available. Finally, *Licensing Concerns and Usability* are important enough to each warrant separate evaluations, which we discuss in greater detail below.

Licensing Concerns

One way the rubric helps us to collect data and input from others is by helping us address contracting concerns. There is one criterion (or row) on the rubric that represents the entirety of contracting concerns. The Electronic Resources Librarian (ERL) guides and manages the entire evaluation process, but does not have time to review contracts herself without assistance—it is quite time-consuming. But it's also complex and high-stakes, so it needs librarian oversight. We outsource this responsibility to a staff person under the ERL's supervision. We created a checklist, explained in more detail below, to guide the staff member through the contract review.

Another element the rubric helps us to address is the timing. Formerly, the UNT Libraries negotiated license agreements *after* deciding to proceed with electronic resources purchases. There are many state, University, and library contracting requirements that require thorough review of all licenses. But we found that after committing to purchase, we had little leverage with which to negotiate license terms, and the lengthy review process delayed acquisition. Using the rubric to evaluate the license terms at the *early* stages of the acquisition process allows us to incorporate licensing concerns into the decision to proceed with ER acquisitions, and also expedites the process.

State Requirements Versus Library Concerns

It's important to note that we are evaluating resources on many more criteria than what is required by the state. The state of Texas seeks to create a business-friendly environment, but still places protections on state-funded entities. The University also has requirements for our contracts. However, the state and University leave many things up to us, so we also evaluate contracts and licenses based on criteria of importance to us.

In each state, the contracting laws, oversight, and procedures for public institutions are a bit different. Your institution should provide you with guidance on how to review your own contracts, but you should *definitely* add your own library-centered criteria to your decision-making process.

Some examples of state law requirements in Texas include *governing law*, *term* (time limit), and *confidentiality*. The *governing law* policy addresses the geographic location of the law(s) that will govern the agreement. In terms of the rubric, "Excellent" language would list the governing law as Texas. No mention of governing law would fall in the "Medium" category—this would be acceptable, but not ideal. "Poor" language in an agreement would specify any governing law other than Texas. This is a deal-breaker and must be changed to Texas before our institution will sign a contract. The state of Texas wants to ensure its contracts will not be subject to the laws of another country or state.

The *term* criterion addresses the time period covered by the contract. It has to be exact, which makes sense for clarity's sake, but also it also affects our promise to pay for the resource in question. If the contract specifies an exact time period, and covers only one fiscal year, the contracts earns a rubric score of "Excellent." If the contract extends beyond the current fiscal cycle, we must rewrite the language and be allowed to break the contract if funds are not appropriated to the University (or are greatly reduced) by the state legislature.

Finally, *confidentiality* clauses create problems for the UNT Office of the General Counsel due to the Texas Information Act regarding Freedom of Information Requests. But as librarians, we actually care about this section a great deal as well. If we are not allowed to share details in professional contexts, it hinders our ability to negotiate, and to collaborate with other institutions. For this criterion, nothing is actually better than something, so an absence of a confidentiality clause would indicate "Excellent" in the rubric. Language conditioned by the extent permitted by the Texas Information Act would indicate "Medium" on the rubric. The rubric considers any confidentiality language with no conditioning statements as "Poor."

Library Contracting Concerns

In addition to state requirements, the UNT Libraries also want to make acquisition decisions based on several library-specific and library usage concerns. Some examples of these concerns are *usage statistics* and *data mining*. The Libraries desire information on the *usage* of acquired materials. The rubric defines "Excellent" in this area as a license that promises the provision of COUNTER-compliant usage data. The rubric considers language "Medium" in this area when the promise of usage statistics by the vendor does not specify the type of data provided in the reports. If the rights holder provides no usage data, the product would earn a "Poor" score on the rubric.

Likewise, *data mining*, the analysis of large datasets, has emerged as new area of concern in libraries. The rubric defines "Excellent" language as that which explicitly permits data mining, "Medium" language as that which makes no mention of it, and "Poor" as that which prohibits mining.

Recording the Contract Evaluation

Historically, we had as many as 2–3 people working on reviewing contracts. As time went by, and contracts and licenses became more standardized, the contracts review became more routine. We also went from a paper-based filing system to an electronic one. Reducing the number of people and amount of time spent on contracts made sense. However, we still have a need for documentation of the review and negotiations and communication between the staff person and the librarian who now work on contracts. We created a checklist to serve the dual purposes of documentation and communication.

❑ Interlibrary loan	❑ Rights permitted and method of electronic provision is not restricted ❑ Rights permitted but method of electronic provision is restricted ❑ Prohibited by license (flag) ❑ Other: ______
❑ Course packs	❑ Electronic permitted, no record-keeping requirements, and no deletion at end of semester ❑ Electronic not permitted; record keeping requirements; deletion at end of semester (flag) ❑ Not permitted (flag) ❑ Other: ______
❑ Perpetual access, if applicable	❑ Contains perpetual rights language and fees are specific ❑ Add perpetual rights language and specify fees (flag) ❑ Other: ______

Figure 1. Contracts checklist.

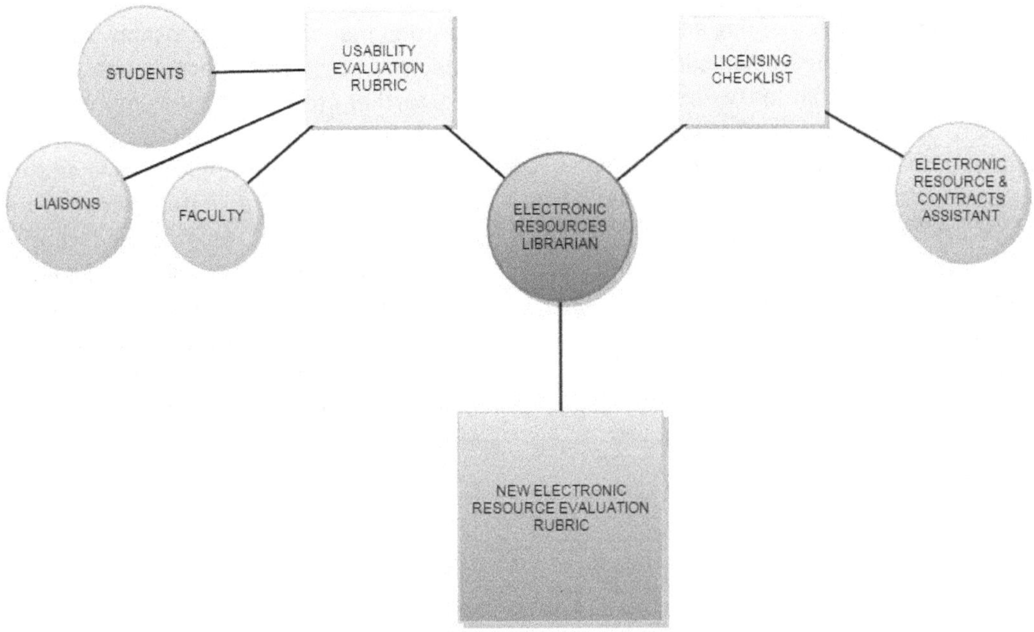

Figure 2. Evaluation workflow.

Here you can see a snippet of the contracts checklist (see Figure 1, "Contracts checklist"). It guides the staff member through the review, and through the rather complex process of various signatures and approvals. The checklist is then saved for documentation and submitted to the ERL for review. Benefits of the checklist include: it allows for outsourcing, provides two sets of eyes on a contract, and causes a natural pause for negotiation.

At the pause point, the ERL reviews the staff person's evaluation, represented by the checklist, and determines what actions should be taken. Options include:

- **Evaluate** all criteria to get a holistic picture of the value of the resource
- **Negotiate** with the vendor on negotiable criteria
- **Dictate** changes in the language to adhere to state law
- **Decide** not to purchase
- **Communicate** desired changes in language, features, etc.

This last point brings us to another "outsourced" criterion—usability. Similar to contracts, we ask others for their input, which is then incorporated into the rubric.

Usability and Workflows

In focusing on the interface of electronic resources, we decided that it is important to include not only an evaluation of usability by the ERL, but also on evaluations from actual users. For this reason we developed a separate rubric for usability designed to be completed by students as well as by subject librarians.

Our usability rubric is designed to assess the perceptions of users, either students or librarians, of task success and efficiency as well as overall ease-of-use and the availability of features designed to improve user experience such as help pages.

This rubric also uses a scale of excellent, medium, or poor for each criterion. It includes assessment of content, functionality, and appearance.

One of the challenges of implementing an evaluation process like this one is managing the information and workflows that make it possible. The ERL functions as the manager of this process and coordinates with the multiple people involved in the process. It is also the ERL who initiates the evaluation process, saves and organizes all the files and paperwork associated with or generated by the process, and who uses the general evaluation rubric to collate the licensing and usability rubrics. A workflow (see Figure 2, "Evaluation workflow") to define the ways in which information is shared and managed is key to making this possible.

Conclusion

The importance of carefully evaluating electronic resources before purchase is clear. When our collection management philosophy began to emphasize access-based acquisitions models we were further prompted to look more closely at our electronic resources and to communicate our needs more clearly to vendors. Furthermore, budget cuts have necessitated more careful acquisitions decisions. An organized, carefully planned evaluation process allows the library to evaluate the features of resources, provides information useful in vendor negotiations, and increases transparency and documentation of collection development decision-making processes.

Multiplying by Division: Mapping the Collection at University of North Texas Libraries

Karen Harker, Collection Assessment Librarian, University of North Texas Libraries

Janette Klein, Graduate Library Assistant, University of North Texas Libraries

Laurel Crawford, Coordinator of Collection Development, University of North Texas Libraries

Abstract

The University of North Texas (UNT) Libraries has developed a unique collection assessment tool, the Collection Map, to provide support for a new access-based collection development philosophy. UNT Librarians realized the limitations of traditional assessment methods to gauge the impact of emerging acquisitions models such as demand-driven acquisitions (DDA) and large interdisciplinary e-book collections. What was needed was a flexible, nimble assessment system to track access, holdings, and interlibrary loan (ILL) activity for each academic discipline. The Collection Map is a database that links items, and their associated data, to any one of several dozen overlapping subcollections via Library of Congress call numbers (LCCNs). The Collection Map's unique many-to-many relationship of subcollections to items and data enables librarians to demonstrate support for subject areas and to make more informed collecting decisions. This article describes the components and creation of the Collection Map, including manipulation of existing systems to extract data.

Introduction

The University of North Texas (UNT) Libraries Collection Development Department has developed a unique collection assessment tool, the Collection Map, to harness the power of available data and to provide increased purchasing flexibility. The Collection Map database links items, and their associated data, to any one of several dozen overlapping subcollections via Library of Congress call numbers. The Collection Map's unique many-to-many relationship of subcollections to items and data enables the library to demonstrate support for a wide array of subject areas, to make more informed collecting decisions, and to increase flexibility in purchasing. The Collection Map facilitates the compilation and analysis of data on multiple subject areas regardless of the original fund used to purchase the item, and regardless of the acquisitions model.

A Traditional Past

Traditionally, UNT libraries collections purchases were organized into over 60 disciplinary "funds" allocated by a formula. These funds were used for the tracking of funding availability and as a measurement of success. Funds utilized within this process were very narrow in scope due to the constraints of the organization and allocation process. Simultaneously, the monograph and journal collections within the UNT Libraries have undergone significant budget cuts for the past several years due to a variety of internal and external environmental factors. Collection selectors perceived that each available budget dollar was increasingly precious, and engaged in purchasing practices that included utilization of available funds to purchase items which were directly related to the discipline scope. Cooperative purchasing between funds was rare. Over time, maximization of resources or provision of support to major interdisciplinary purchases was reduced because funds were so segmented. Eventually we realized that allocation of money to these segmented funds could no longer ensure support for all areas in the collection adequately.

When creating reports and making decisions, key players relied heavily on data about materials based on what had been purchased from the individual funds. Every item was assigned to a single discipline by having been purchased using

http://dx.doi.org/10.5703/1288284316279

that fund. This method of assessment did not provide a clear depiction of the resources relevant to each subject or discipline as collection assessments were being conducted based upon viewing the purchasing and patterns through a single, rigid lens. The allocated funds were being used in three approaches that were both simultaneous and conflicting. The three purposes of the traditional fund allocation process included: control of the funding spent on subject areas; evaluation of success in meeting our collection development goals; and demonstration of support for subject-based programs.

Recognizing the deficiencies with the existing process, we decided to develop a flexible, nimble assessment system to track access, use, holdings, and ILL activity for each subject area. We, as an institution, needed to gather, and use, better information about collections than could be obtained through the use of the traditional fund allocation approach alone. And, we needed more flexibility and decision-making support for funding larger, non-traditional, interdisciplinary purchases.

An Assessment-Based Future

We stopped thinking in terms of funds, and started thinking in terms of call numbers. The classification of an item tells us much more about its relevance to multiple subject areas than the original fund used to purchase it.

Simultaneously, we created customized local collections that made sense to us, based on our needs. Usually these collections correspond to administrative or accredited units, like the Department of Philosophy & Religious Studies. We also made interdisciplinary collections of interest to research centers, minors, and special areas of emphasis, like LGBT and International Studies. We now measure access, purchasing, and use for dozens of these overlapping collections.

We now measure access, purchasing, and use for dozens of these overlapping collections (see Figure 1).

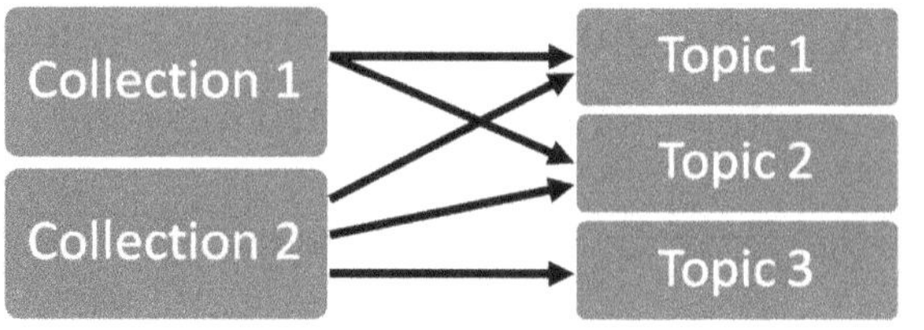

Figure 1. A many-to-many relationship.

In this way, we're able to do away with using budgeting as the primary (or only) method to design our collection—in other words, designating pots of funding to purchase discrete items in a certain subject area or format. The concept of "balancing" has become irrelevant; because the subcollections overlap to a high degree, the development for the whole collection is not zero-sum. Therefore, there is no need to allocate funds to each discipline. The test of success is no longer what we paid for, or even what we own. We changed the question: rather than asking "did we spend all of X fund," we began asking "do we support the research and teaching in X area?" Success is no longer based on balancing, formulas, or expenditures. This only worked because we were able to decouple the funding availability from the assessment data. We achieved greater funding flexibility and purchasing power by desegmenting funds and creating one big purchasing pool.

In order to make these ideas work, we needed a way to represent *all* of the granular topics relevant to each discipline or program. We also needed a way to map *many* overlapping call numbers to *many* collections. We decided to create a database in which one call number can be assigned to multiple collections. This database can be constantly updated to reflect new needs, and can connect our needs for information (usually based on administrative or accredited units within the university) to data about holdings, use, ILL, and access.

Overview of the Collection Map

Development of the Collection Map rested upon four key objectives and goals. The first was that the creation of the Collection Map will allow for proactive assessment of the collections while also facilitating the ongoing monitoring of collections by format and subject. The second objective was to implement and complete the mapping of the WorldShare Conspectus subjects to the UNT Libraries's collections. The third objective was to initiate comparison of the WorldShare® holdings with the existing UNT collections, and the final objective during the development of the Collection Map was the creation of a sustainable method to map different items to the UNT collections based upon Library of Congress Call Numbers (LCCNs). The overarching focus of the creation of the Collection Map was an emphasis on sustainability, as the Collection Map is intended to be utilized by key players within the UNT library structure by mapping/matching different items, regardless of format such as books, videos, musical scores—anything with a Library of Congress Call Number to the UNT collections.

The WorldShare Collection Evaluation System (CES) was utilized in this process as it uses WorldCat® data, thus allowing for ongoing comparisons between and against peer-institutions, a set of peers, and authoritative lists (e.g., *Outstanding Academic Titles*). Additionally, the subject categorizations within CES are based upon the Western Library Network, which became the Research Library Group network conspectus with which many of the collaborators within the Collection Map development project were already familiar. Authorization to use the conspectus list from WorldShare was obtained by the UNT Collection Assessment Librarian, Karen Harker, *prior* to starting development of the Collection Map.

Background

Historically, the YBP approval plan provided the foundation for the development of the UNT Libraries's collections. Within this process, LCCNs of interest to UNT Libraries were mapped to a single operating fund within the given fiscal year budget. This resulted in LCCNs being allocated to a single fund in a one-to-one relationship. As a result of connection between the YBP approval plan and the existing UNT Libraries's collections, UNT Libraries at the initiation of this process had a total of 59 subject-based collections. This led to the mapping of the 59 UNT Libraries's subject-based collections to the 11,251 WorldShare Collection Evaluation System (CES) Conspectus subjects. Please see Figure 2. UNT collection map pathway. During the development of the UNT Libraries's collections the realization was reached that certain LCCN ranges could belong to one or more collections and indeed that they should be placed within more than one collection to truly reflect the interdisciplinary nature of the items within the collections.

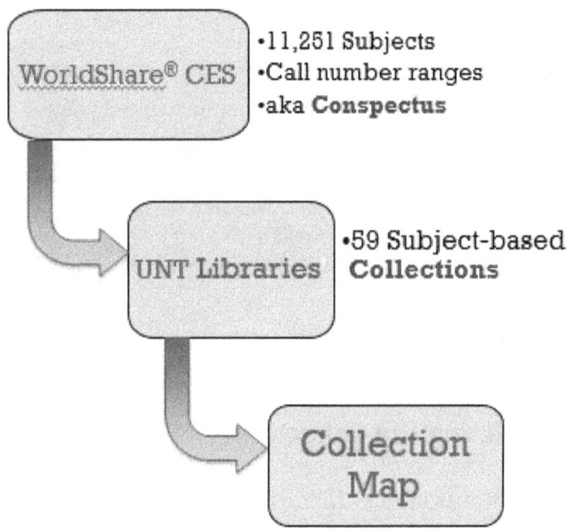

Figure 2. UNT collection map pathway.

Methods Overview

At the onset of the development of the Collection Map, the collection ranges were defined based upon LCCNs within Excel. The second step undertaken was the transference of the Excel data into an Access database created by the Collection Assessment Librarian. Access was selected as the principal database for this process as Access is more efficient for showing the multiple relationships amongst the individual components. Additionally, Access also allows for greater maneuverability and manipulation of the created collections. The third step included mapping as closely as possible, the UNT Libraries's collection ranges to the WorldShare CES Conspectus subject ranges. The fourth step was the process of selecting what items, such as book with LCCNs, can be assigned to the conspectus subjects. With a result that the selected items are indirectly mapped to the collection via the assigned conspectus subject. This process culminates with the selected items that can then be auto-matched to one range, which can reside in one or more collections as shown in Figure 3, "Overview of the methods used in developing the collection map." Each of these steps are presented in more detail in subsequent sections.

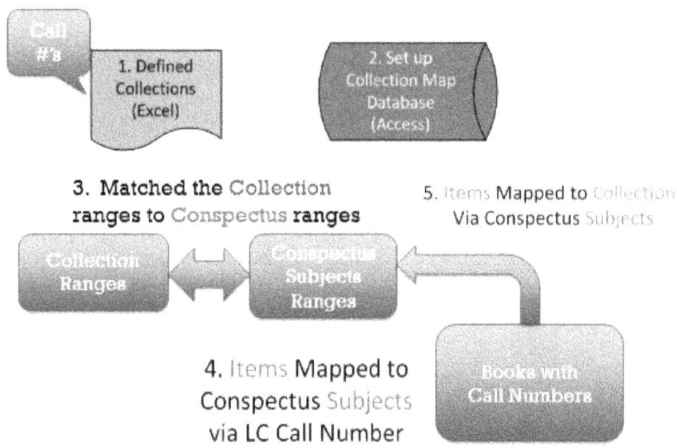

Figure 3. Overview of the methods used in developing the collection map.

Defining the Collections

As mentioned earlier, the initial set of ranges for each of the UNT Libraries's collections was derived from the YBP approval plan, which was used as part of the initial UNT Libraries's DDA profile. Historically, UNT had mapped funds to the approval plan. As such, the set of ranges to choose from was set by the YBP jobber, which did not necessarily match the Conspectus subject ranges as set by WorldShare CES. In that the WorldShare CES Conspectus ranges were specific in nature, while the UNT collection ranges were very broad. As mentioned earlier, the initial set of ranges for each of the UNT Libraries's collections (see Figure 4) was derived from the

Collection	LC Class	LC Range
Accounting	HF	5601-5690
Accounting	HF	5691-5716
Aerospace Studies	TL	500-779
Aerospace Studies	TL	780-786
Aerospace Studies	TL	787-4050
Anthropology	BF	1404-2049
Anthropology	BL	660-2699
Anthropology	CC	1-960

Figure 4. Original UNT collection ranges.

YBP approval plan, which was used as part of the initial UNT Libraries's DDA profile.

Establishment of the Conspectus Hierarchy

A hierarchy was developed for the Conspectus subjects that consists of three levels: division, category, and subject. Within this hierarchy structure there is no overlap in the Conspectus subjects as shown below with a division category of Philosophy & Religion being very broad and subdivided into two categories consisting of Ethics and Logic. The categories of Ethics and Logic each contain their own subjects such as Deductive Logic and Fallacies under the category of Logic. Please see Figure 5, "UNT collection map conspectus hierarchy."

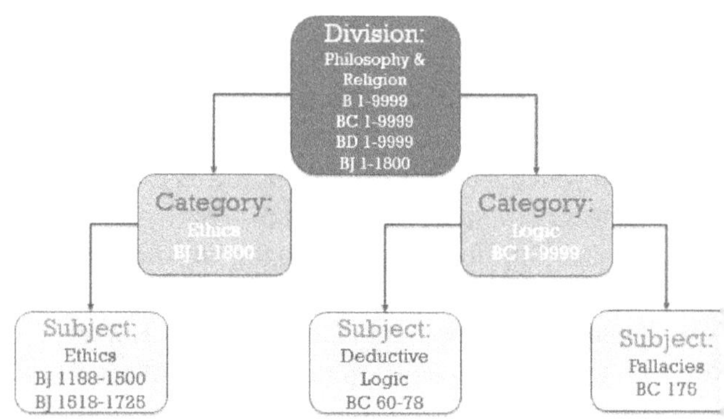

Figure 5. UNT collection map conspectus hierarchy.

Development of the Access Database

Due to the level of granularity within the WorldShare CES Conspectus, an Access Database was created to facilitate the establishment of relational tables connecting the divisions, categories, and subjects. Within this process each square as shown below in Figure 6, "UNT Collection Map Access database relationship tables," represents a table, and the lines between each table represent the links between the tables. Each of these tables contains the listings of Divisions, Categories, and Subjects as established by the Conspectus hierarchy. For example, the Conspectus Divisions are linked to the Conspectus Categories via the Conspectus Categories by Division table. As shown in the Conspectus Categories by Division table, there is a column for Division, which is the DivID from Conspectus Divisions table, and Category, which is the CatID from the Conspectus Categories table. Similarly, the Subjects are linked to the Categories by the Conspectus Subjects by Categories table. Thus, all of the Subjects are related to all of the Categories, which are related to all of the Divisions.

Mapping the WorldShare CES Conspectus to UNT Libraries's Collections

The next step in the process was to map the conspectus data to the UNT Libraries's collections as shown below in Figure 7, "Mapping of the WorldShare CES Conspectus to UNT collections." This phase used the call number mappings for the subjects that were developed based upon the approval plans with YBP. However, these ranges although similar were not identical to those defined in the Conspectus. Thus the decision was made to select the Conspectus subject that most closely approximated the YBP ranges. This phase of the development of the Collection Map

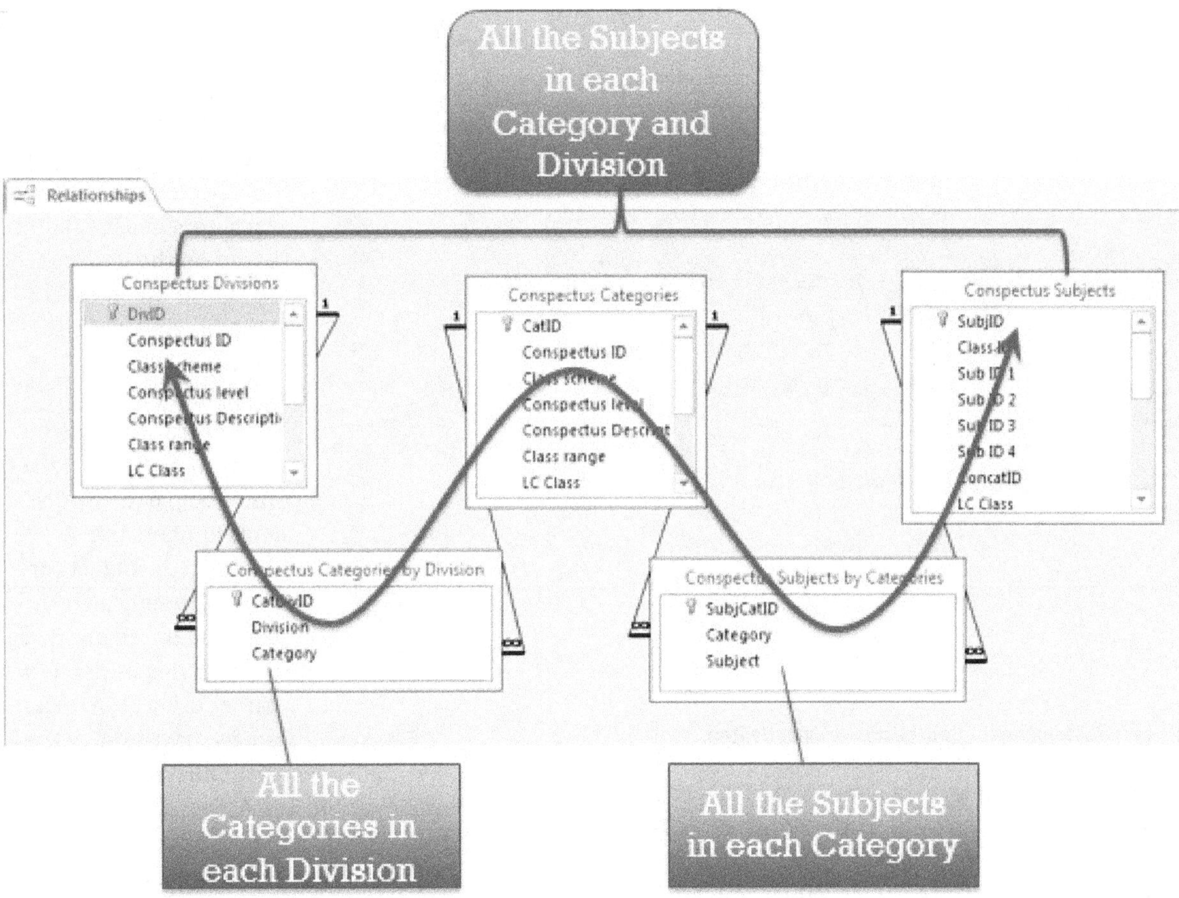

Figure 6. UNT collection map Access database relationship tables.

Figure 7. Mapping of the WorldShare CES Conspectus to UNT collections.

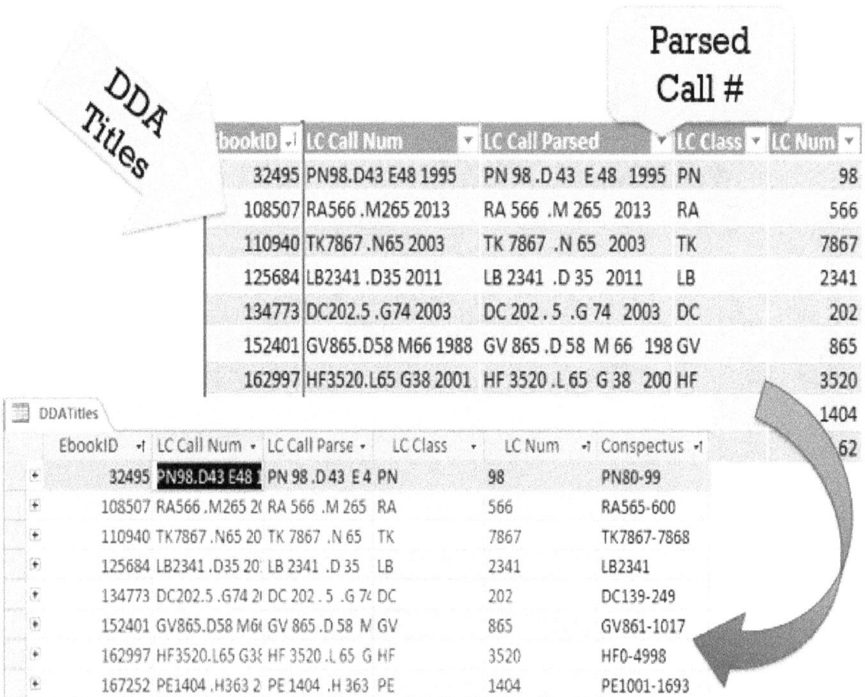

Figure 8. Assignment of Conspectus subject by item.

incurred the highest level of personnel cost in the form of both labor and time, as the entire process was manually performed with a review and decision being made for each individual line item, thus effectively "mapping" the YBP ranges to the closest-matching Conspectus ranges.

A significant advantage of the new Collection Map system over that of the historic YBP approval plan is that an association could be made for the same LCCN range to more than one collection. This is illustrated within Figure 7, "Mapping of the WorldShare CES Conspectus to UNT collections," as the range of HQ1101-2030 is associated with Women's and Gender Studies, Sociology, Educational Psychology, and Anthropology.

Mapping Items to the Conspectus

The fourth step in the process of the developing the Collection Map results in the assignment of the Conspectus subject for each item in a list that is based on the item's LC classification. In the example of DDA titles shown in Figure 8, "Assignment of Conspectus subjects by item," the LCCN is parsed into two parts—LC Class and Number. The Conspectus subjects are then automatically assigned based on the call number ranges defined earlier using an Access program written by the UNT Collection Assessment Librarian. The Access program initially looks up the LC class in the list of Conspectus subjects, and then finds the subject that includes

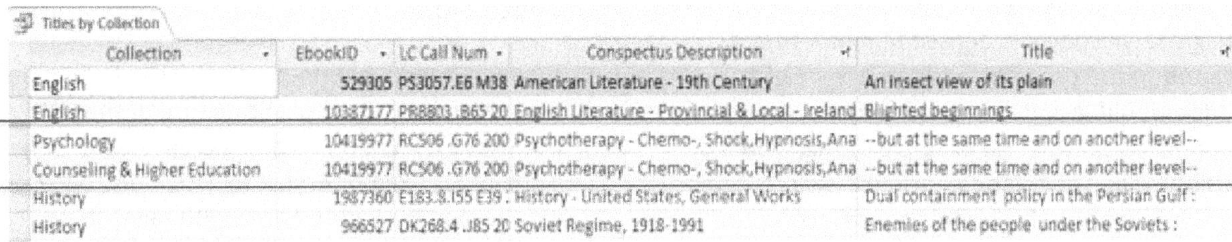

Titles by Collection

Collection	EbookID	LC Call Num	Conspectus Description	Title
English	529305	PS3057.E6 M38	American Literature - 19th Century	An insect view of its plain
English	10387177	PR8803 .B65 20	English Literature - Provincial & Local - Ireland	Blighted beginnings
Psychology	10419977	RC506 .G76 200	Psychotherapy - Chemo-, Shock,Hypnosis,Ana	--but at the same time and on another level--
Counseling & Higher Education	10419977	RC506 .G76 200	Psychotherapy - Chemo-, Shock,Hypnosis,Ana	--but at the same time and on another level--
History	1987360	E183.8.I55 E39 :	History - United States, General Works	Dual containment policy in the Persian Gulf :
History	966527	DK268.4 .J85 20	Soviet Regime, 1918-1991	Enemies of the people under the Soviets :

Figure 9. Assignment of WorldShare CES Conspectus subject by item through Access tables.

the LC number within its range. By default, the outcome of this process is that items are automatically mapped to the Collection Map as shown in Figure 9, "Assignment of WorldShare CES Conspectus subject by item through Access tables."

This results in any one item being assigned to one or more collections. Further, this facilitates a truly interdisciplinary collection map with one to many relationships existing within the collections through the mapping of item-level data with LC call numbers as shown in Figure 10, "Assignment of WorldShare CES Conspectus subject by item." Within this process zero-sum thinking has been eliminated. Due to the nature of the Collection Map, the sum of titles by collection is greater than the actual number of titles.

Improvements

Although this is a revolutionary process for UNT with significant areas of application, there are improvements yet to be realized within the process. A key area of improvement includes integrating resources currently without LC classification, such as interlibrary loan requests, media, and electronic resources into the Collection Map. Currently these items are being held in an "Excluded" category within the Collection Map. A second area of improvement is to review the UNT Libraries's collections to be more inclusive of related subjects. As part of the focus upon inclusivity, a proposal is to assign weights to the subjects by relevance based upon academic programs such as primary, which consist

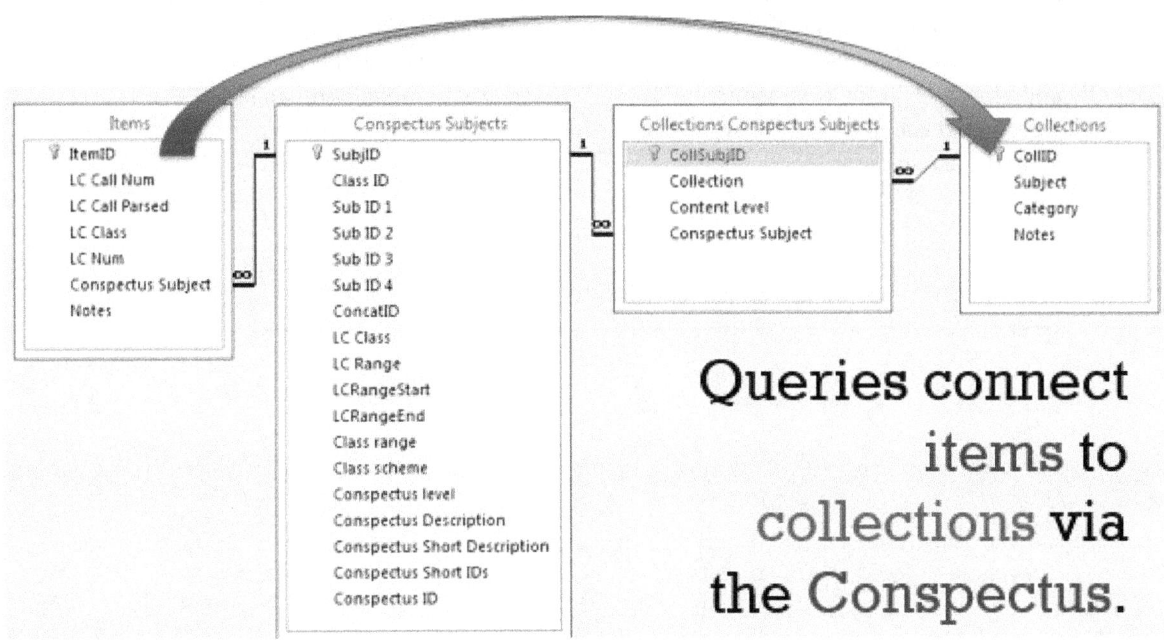

Figure 10. Assignment of WorldShare CES Conspectus subject by item.

of major topics related to the program, secondary weights, which would consist of minor topics related to the program, and tertiary weights, which would include required courses or supportive content. An example of this would be a program such as computer science, where items with a primary weight would contain computer-science-specific topics. Items with secondary weighting may include items and topics related to information technology, while the tertiary level would contain items and topics that support but are not specific to the program, yet that are still related in some way to computer science, such as mathematics. Within the proposal for a weighting structure it is clear that not all subjects are created equal, thus objective decision would need to be reached concerning both the weights to be applied and the placement of items within the weighted structure.

Utilization

The UNT Collection Map has tremendous potential to be utilized in a myriad of areas, such as for accreditation reviews, within ongoing and future in-depth college and departmental assessments, as a tool facilitating institutional peer comparisons, and for the evaluation of expenditures at the department, college, and institutional levels. The UNT Collection Map can be rapidly updated at any time in response to external and environmental changes, thus more efficiently and effectively using the resources available to best meet the needs of the students, faculty, staff, and stakeholders.

Conclusion

Through the development of the UNT Collection Map, a realistic and holistic picture of the UNT Libraries's collections is being created. No longer is the focus fixed on trying to assign one book or item to one designated area with many items' interdisciplinary nature going unrecognized. The creation of an interdisciplinary collection map facilitates a more realistic depiction of the UNT Library collections as a whole via its flexible, versatile, and sustainable framework. This is especially critical as we progressively continue to move toward an assessment- and evidence-based future.

The Collection Map structures collections data (usage, ILL borrowing, holdings, and more) in a way that makes sense to our local decision-making process. We have found this tool to be useful in answering the everyday questions that arise in the course of our collection development activities, such as how well we have supported a certain area of study, or whether a certain type of material has gotten historically high use. Challenges to using the Collection Map, ironically, center on its power and scope. We have so much data that it has been difficult to enfold it all into our selecting activities in a digestible, actionable way. We continue to work toward automation of the data and using our human resources efficiently to apply critical thinking to the numbers to create meaningful analysis.

Managing, Marketing, and Measuring Open Resources

Trey Shelton, Electronic Resources Librarian, The George A. Smathers Libraries at the University of Florida

Steven Carrico, Acquisitions Librarian, The George A. Smathers Libraries at the University of Florida

Ann Lindell, Head, Architecture and Fine Arts Library, The George A. Smathers Libraries at the University of Florida

Tara T. Cataldo, Collections Coordinator, Marston Science Library, The George A. Smathers Libraries at the University of Florida

Abstract

Academic libraries face many opportunities and challenges in managing, marketing, and measuring open resources (OR). Many questions arise when incorporating OR into an academic library collection. How do libraries select quality OR for inclusion in the collection? What tools and practices are used to manage electronic access? How can libraries better market OR to faculty? How can libraries measure the use and usefulness of OR? This paper outlines a project launched to improve the management of OR at the University of Florida's George A. Smathers Libraries; as well as incorporating feedback garnered at the Charleston Conference discussion forum on the topic, particularly on how academic and special libraries are handling OR offered to users.

Introduction

The University of Florida (UF) Libraries have been offering open resources to users for many years. Our definition of open resources (OR) includes both open access (OA) journals and books, as well as media and curricular materials often referred to as Open Educational Resources (OER). OR provided by the UF Libraries are collected from numerous channels. The largest segment of OR offered are catalog records downloaded using the vendor tool Serials Solutions for thousands of journals, e-books, and other resources from the Directory of Open Access Journals, PubMed Central, Highwire Press, etc. Additionally, OR are gathered from large repositories like HathiTrust and digital libraries such as Internet Archive. Digital content from the library's curatorial collections and the UF's Institutional Repository is also an important homegrown segment of these resources. The amount of resources being offered to users at the Smathers Libraries is substantial; as of 2015, approximately 70,000 e-journals and 220,000 e-books identified as OR were made available to users of the UF Libraries.

Despite all these open resources being made available, the UF Libraries have not developed systematic methodologies for review, selection, or deselection of these resources. Because machine-readable cataloging (MARC) records for OR are batch-loaded into the library's catalog and discover tools at frequent intervals, many librarians, subject specialists, and staff at the libraries are often unaware of OR content, particularly in their subject disciplines or areas of expertise. Unsurprisingly, marketing and assessment activities for OR are also not being performed in any sustained or systematic way. Thus, a team of four librarians launched a project to gather information and better organize the management of OR. Goals of the project were simple:

- Review the literature and lead a discussion at the Charleston Conference to determine current practices for managing OR at other academic and special libraries
- Develop new procedures and criteria for reviewing, selecting/deselecting,

http://dx.doi.org/10.5703/1288284316280

marketing, and assessing OR at the UF Libraries

- Incorporate knowledge gained into collection policies

Review and Selection

The review and selection process for open resources is very similar to the processes used for purchased online resources. Devising basic selection criteria is a recommended practice and can be adapted for OR (Johnson, 2013). Setting parameters for what is selected can include content or subject matter; language; scope; reputation of the author or publication; quality of scholarship; relation to curriculum and research; user levels; format; access; and whether a journal is peer-reviewed. An exhaustive review and set of important criteria for selection of OA journals were offered by Schmidt and Newsome (2007). Another important aspect of review and selection for libraries to consider regards hybrid OA journals and predatory publishers. Hybrid journals are publications that offer some or partial free access while other content must be purchased. Bulock, Hosburgh, and Mann (2015) highlight one problem associated with hybrids; many hybrid journals are listed as OA journals by knowledge bases and OPACs, which can only distinguish at the title, not article, level, leading to confusion and frustration for librarians and users alike. Predatory publishers are an even bigger nuisance. Predatory publishers can be defined by a set of characteristics that include lack of peer-review despite claims; dubious quality; or even in some cases charging author fees to make a profit. Berger and Cirasella (2015) provide an excellent review of the landscape of predatory journals and note that librarians must be careful in labeling a journal predatory; for example, not all OA journals that charge author fees are predatory.

One measure of a journal's quality has always been its inclusion in a reputable index. The Web of Science database has added some features that are particularly helpful with OA, including an OA filter in both Web of Science and Journal Citation Reports (the database for looking up Impact Factors and other metrics).

Managing Access and Discoverability

After selection decisions have been made, open resources, primarily OA journals and books, must be incorporated into a library's discovery and access points. There are many challenges associated with adding and maintaining OR in library systems, some of which are similar to licensed content and some unique to OR. Most of these challenges are related to the knowledge bases used to activate resources and the metadata, or lack thereof, on these resources contained in these knowledge bases. As Bulock, Hosburgh, and Mann (2015) point out, "A knowledge base's greatest strength—centrally managed collections—becomes a weakness when titles or holdings fall out of date and library staff have to initiate troubleshooting."

Metadata on open access titles, as listed in most commercial library knowledge bases, is very often lacking. Basic bibliographic information and date ranges of freely accessible content can be incorrectly listed or missing altogether, and predatory titles may be listed in broad subject-based collections next to legitimate gold open access (GOA) titles. Depending on the functionality of the knowledge base, selecting one title from a collection, often at the request of a subject librarian, requires selection of the entire collection. As proactive access checking is problematic even for licensed content, much less open content due to the sheer scale, it is not uncommon for libraries to provide notes on OA titles to users in link resolvers and other discovery points warning that the dates of accessibility may be incorrect.

As Lagace and Tananbaum (2013) state, "Thus in the case of hybrid journals—which consist of both open access and subscription articles—OA availability through a link resolver is often a 'hit or miss' situation when displayed on a library's service menu because the articles themselves are not tracked in these knowledge bases." This leaves librarians two choices, either include hybrid OA journals and know patrons will hit pay walls for subscription articles or exclude hybrid OA journals and know users will not be able to discover select OA resources through library systems. Some libraries have taken the route of excluding hybrid titles altogether.

Profera, Walker, and Cook (2014) called for publishers to ". . . provide stable link resolver data, adequate metadata, and standardized use statistics for their unpaid content." The National Information Standards Organization's (NISO) Open Discovery Initiative (ODI) (http://www.niso.org/workrooms/odi/) addresses many of the issues librarians have with discovery service indexes and knowledge base listing. Though ODI does not specifically focus on OR, it has the potential to have an impact if OA content providers are willing to participate. One attendee at the session pointed out that while it is important to maintain a certain level of service to our users, it is much more proactive and effective for librarians to work with standards organizations, like NISO, to develop national standards to deal with the issues we face; to focus on the macro, not the local. Finally, services such as the Open Access Button (https://openaccessbutton.org/) and 1Science (http://www.1science.com/) may provide local options that alleviate some of the technical pitfalls associated with OR.

Marketing Open Resources

Marketing of open resources can be as simple as making them discoverable alongside all other resources in the catalog, subject guides, and websites, as searchers are usually seeking resources on a topic rather than type of information container. Even those searching a known item are not necessarily concerned with their open or proprietary status. Marketing efforts can also be expanded to focus solely on OR. For example, one attendee mentioned how their library has created guides exclusively showcasing OR. Additionally, highlighting specific resources in instruction sessions, newsletters, correspondence, and conversations can increase use. Taking the time to specify the "openness" of OR should be encouraged. Attendees of the discussion forum pointed to the Association of Research Libraries (ARL) Scholarly Publishing and Academic Resources Coalition (SPARC, see http://www.sparc.arl.org/) as a resource for advocating and marketing open initiatives on campus.

Librarians point to liaise activities with faculty as a means to promote and advocate for open resources. This is logical since these are the users assigning resources to students and seeking publishing outlets; however, several attendees rallied around the idea of marketing OR to other user groups. Students could benefit an awareness of OR particular to their major, as they will likely lose access to licensed resources upon graduation and will need to know how to locate and use reliable, alternative sources. Additionally, instructional designers on campus who work with faculty to build online courses could benefit from learning about OR as they may influence faculty members' decisions regarding course assigned readings. Finally, one attendee referenced a mini-grant program their library offered to faculty to develop open textbooks for their courses.

Assessing Open Resources

Every library collection and incoming electronic resource, whether purchased or freely accessible, should undergo periodic evaluation and assessment to determine value to the research and instructional missions of the institution. Not surprisingly, the process of assessing open resources made available to users is similar to assessing purchased resources. The first phase of assessment is defining and categorizing the resources. There are several key questions that can help guide this process:

(1) How many resources and what formats are being provided?

(2) What subject areas/disciplines are being supported?

The first two questions necessitate creating several reports, most often generated from an integrated library system (ILS) or electronic resources management tool (ERM). There are various formats of OR. E-journals, e-books, and digitized texts and other objects are the most common. ILS and ERM reports can provide

Table 1. University of Florida title & usage report for open source journals.

Database/Provider	Subject Areas Supported	No. of Journal Titles	Uses	Avg. Use per Title
BioMedCentral Open Access	STEM; Med	332	19,696	59.33
Directory of Open Access Journals	STEM; Med; Hum & Soc Sci	6,155	65,071	10.57
Free Medical Journals	Med	1,673	25,181	15.05
Freely Accessible Journals	STEM; Med; Hum & Soc Sci	6,196	107,761	17.39
HighWire Press (Free Journals)	STEM; Med	474	40,407	85.25
Hindawi Pub. Open Access	STEM; Med	234	1,451	6.20
IngentaConnect Free/OA	STEM; Med	217	3,605	16.61
J-Stage (Japanese Sci & Tech)	STEM	536	5,405	10.08
Open Access Digital Library	STEM; Med; Hum & Soc Sci	4,427	36,798	8.31
Open Hum., OJS, Open Source, PLOS	STEM; Med; Hum & Soc Sci	454	12,079	26.61
PubMed Central	STEM	1,857	108,532	58.44
REDALyC & SCIelo	Latin America (all subjects)	1,258	8,229	6.54
Total		**23,813**	**434,215**	**18.23**

librarians a better sense of what and how many OR are made available across broad subject areas. Unfortunately, most of the MARC records for OR do not offer call number or subject headings, but often OA collections in knowledge bases are labeled with subject designations (e.g., "Freely Accessible Medical Journals") that can provide broad categories.

(3) What type of usage statistics are available and *what* is the impact of this data?

Inevitably, usage statistics play a crucial role in assessing electronic resources. Relying on usage should not be the sole measuring stick to determine collection and user value, but usage is certainly a cornerstone metric for librarians reviewing and deselecting OR. One problem with usage is that the definitions of the data collected often vary across publishers and platforms (for example, what constitutes a "download"). If applying a consistent statistical measurement, the reports can be quite useful. Table 1 shows a report generated by the ERM tool at the UF Libraries using a "click-through" metric (click-through is defined as the user accessed the provider's platform through the libraries link resolver). This report is a seven-year compilation of statistics for journal titles received and tagged as OR. It provides the name of the resource provider or collection, the subject areas supported, the number of titles made accessible, uses, and average use per title. Not only is the number of uses quite high (no. = 434,215) but the average use per title is very strong (avg = 18.23). This table shows only a summary of the usage in each collection, but the usage data is available for librarians to sort by subject areas, the individual journal titles, and usage for detailed review. Additionally, the COUNTER compliant Journal Report 1 Gold Open Access (GOA) can be used to assess usage of OA articles and journals from a particular publisher or provider.

(4) What qualitative assessments can be utilized?

Conducting qualitative assessment of e-resources is fraught with challenges. Librarians know how difficult it can be to get users to respond. Equally problematic is gauging user satisfaction and relevance across subject areas for hundreds or even thousands of open resources. It would be fair to assume that most of the OR made available to users go undiscovered; but, given the usage statistics and number of quality peer-review journals and respected OR available, users are placing value on at least a significant portion of these resources. Determining that portion is the key. Survey tools, focus groups, and one-on-one discussions with faculty and researchers are recommended methods of exploring user feedback. Usually the best approach to evaluating electronic resources, including OR, is to conduct a combination of qualitative and quantitative methods of assessment.

Impact on Collection Management

It is not just the abundant amount of open resources many libraries are offering users that is having an impact on collection development activities in academic and special libraries. It is the significant number of respected and important resources that are now available. Attendees overwhelmingly agreed that open access materials made available to users were considered part of library collections, which supports Bulock, Hosburgh, and Mann's (2015) findings that 71% of librarians considered OA materials as part of their library collection. As of December 2015 the *Directory of Open Access Journals* (DOAJ) listed almost eleven thousand peer-reviewed journals from over a hundred countries constituting more than two million articles (2015). While this metric seemingly validates libraries incorporating these and other high quality OR into collection building, a Google search of academic library collection policies shows little mention of OR. At the Charleston Conference discussion session on this topic, librarians in attendance reported OR were not systematically incorporated into formal collection policies; although many librarians indicated it would be very useful to have updated policies on OR to share with users and faculty at their institutions. Finally, incorporating OR into instructional activities was identified by librarians attending the discussion as an important future focus, which also ties into marketing efforts.

Conclusion

This project was immensely interesting and informative, and is still ongoing. Clearly there is a need for libraries to develop guidelines for reviewing and selecting open resources. Improving the discoverability and consistency of the resources is an important issue, as is finding better methods of marketing and sharing the wealth of OR that are available to users. A key step is using both quantitative and qualitative measures for assessing the OR being offered, to ensure the value of the resources and as an evidence-based means to deselect. Finally, creating or adapting collection policies for OR would be beneficial for libraries as a more formal reference for communication with stakeholders.

The project review and the informative discussion at the Charleston Conference will assist the Smathers Libraries in the management of OA resources going forward. Here are the key takeaways from the project and discussion forum:

- Developing a more organized and systematic process for review and selection of OA resources.
- Developing a systematic way to implement and track selector decisions and review metadata/links
- Developing improved ways to communicate with faculty and users about OA resource availability
- Developing routine OA resource evaluation processes
- Incorporating OA resources into collection policies

References

Berger, M., & Cirasella, J. (2015). Beyond Beall's list: Better understanding predatory publishers. *College & Research Libraries News, 76*(3).

Bulock, C., Hosburgh, N., & Mann. S. (2015). OA in the library collection: The challenges of identifying and maintaining open access resources. *The Serials Librarian, 68,* 79–86. http://dx.doi.org/10.1080/0361526X.2015.1023690.

Directory of Open Access Journals (DOAJ). (2015). *Directory of Open Access Journals*. Retrieved from https://doaj.org/

Johnson, P. (2013). *Developing and managing electronic resources.* Chicago: ALA.

Lagace, N., & Tananbaum, G. (2013). NISO Open Access metadata and indicators working group: Creating a cross-audience solution. *The Serials Librarian, 65*(2), 123–127. http://dx.doi.org/10.1080/0361526X.2013.813892

Profera, E., Walker, M., & Cook, E. (2014). Realizing the value of non-purchased content. *The Serials Librarian, 66,* 88–91. http://dx.doi.org/10.1080/0361526X.2014.879637

Schmidt, K., & Newsome, N. (2007). The changing landscape of serials. *The Serials Librarian, 52*(1–2), 119–133. http://dx.doi.org/10.1300/J123v52n01_11

What ARE We Thinking? Collections Decisions in an Academic Library

Tasha Cooper, Collection Development and Analysis Librarian, Syracuse University Libraries

Linda Galloway, Collection Development and Analysis Librarian, Syracuse University Libraries

Shannon Pritting, Director of Library and Learning Resources, SUNY Polytechnic Institute

Abstract

When faced with multiple competing priorities for investment in library resources, there are many important aspects to consider. From student enrollment to prominence of programs, there are both data-driven and intangible factors to weigh. In addition, most library collections now focus on the immediate needs of students and researchers instead of collecting for posterity. This just-in-time versus just-in-case collection development mindset prioritizes different resource attributes and requires an often unfamiliar level of acquisitions flexibility.

Collection development in academic libraries is challenging and complex. Some of the complexity is the result of numerous choices including, but not limited to:

Collection building philosophy: comprehensive or lean format options (print, electronic, streaming, etc.)

Selection options: firm orders and approval plans utilized by library staff or patron-driven acquisition

Additional factors: access models (IP-based or passworded); availability of COUNTER compliant usage statistics; accessibility; licensing terms; preservation and long-term access; pricing models; usability, etc.

Further complexity arises from institutional demands, such as curricular and research support.

The purpose of this paper is to provide an overview of collections preferences from several viewpoints. The authors will share factors to consider, pitfalls to avoid, and communication strategies to employ. A collaboratively-created checklist for adding scholarly resources is included, and a reading list for more in-depth treatment of this topic is provided.

Large, Interdisciplinary Institution

Syracuse University is a large and diverse private institution. With more than 20,000 FTE, 1,200 faculty, and 3,500 staff, meeting the research needs of this community requires a broad view of scholarship at the University. Faculty and students at Syracuse University have high expectations that library resources and services will fully meet their needs. The University's programs range from performing arts to biomedical engineering and everything in between. Some of the more highly ranked schools and colleges include the School of Information Studies (iSchool), the SI Newhouse School of Public Communications, the Maxwell School of Citizenship and Public Affairs, and the Martin J. Whitman School of Management. There is an increasing emphasis on serving veterans' needs with the development of the Institute for Veterans and Military Families that provides programs related to education, entrepreneurship, and transitioning to civilian life (IVMF, n.d.). In addition, a medical school to train doctors to care for military veterans at VA hospitals is also under consideration (Boll, 2015).

Collection development is accomplished at Syracuse University Libraries by a small team of collection development and analysis librarians with significant input from subject liaison librarians. The subject liaison librarians have close working relationships with the departments and colleges they serve and are well suited to contribute to collection development decisions.

http://dx.doi.org/10.5703/1288284316281

The collections budget has been healthy with realistic inflationary increases. The Libraries are fortunate that the central administration recognizes the need for highly regarded resources to support scholarship at the University.

While the Libraries are fiscally sound, staffing levels have declined after an unusual amount of staff turnover. This has led to collection development challenges as key staff are tackling multiple jobs with many competing priorities. As a result, there are electronic resource acquisition, management, and maintenance workflows that need attention and streamlining. These challenges affect the selection of resources because items under consideration need to be easy to acquire, maintain, and access.

One of the first considerations made when deciding whether to acquire a new resource is determining how well it fits in with the current collection. An overlap analysis (using Serial Solutions' product) can be conducted for journal or e-book packages. The Libraries also need to consider duplicative "types" of products owned. For example, do we currently have access to databases containing datasets, or do we need an additional product? The number of students and faculty who will benefit from a new resource is also a consideration, but many of the resources acquired are used by a narrow slice of the University community. While we rely on data-driven information when making cancellation decisions, much of the information used when making acquisition decisions is subjective. The number of students and faculty that could use a given resource is acknowledged, but so is the relative significance of the resource under consideration. New and underserved curricular needs may be of greater importance than many other factors, including prominence of programs. Syracuse University seeks to build collections to meet current and future campus demands.

Product access and usability issues are a major concern to the Libraries. We strive to acquire resources that are available to the campus community via IP authentication. The Libraries ask all vendors to fill out a Voluntary Product Accessibility Template (VPAT) that documents conformance with accessibility standards (ITI, 2015). Other product usability aspects include responsive web design (so that content can be easily read on most devices), unlimited simultaneous users, and the possibility of patron-driven acquisition for a resource.

The ease with which users can discover content is of significant importance to the Libraries. Resources, such as an e-book or journal package, that can be easily "turned on" in the discovery layer (e.g., Summon, EBSCO, Discovery Service, or WorldCat Discovery) are favored, as are those e-book packages that freely provide MARC records. Of increasing importance is the ability for users to discover library content via Google Scholar. In order for this to be accomplished, Google Scholar users must see at least the complete author-written abstract or the first full page without being required to log in or click through (Google Scholar, n.d.).

Of course, data are used to help make and support collection development decisions. When considering individual journal titles and journal packages, interlibrary loan (ILL) requests are used to assess needs. The Libraries often consider vendor-provided turnaway data (unsuccessful full-text e-book or article requests) as well. A demonstrated desire by patrons for unavailable materials is a compelling reason to acquire content. As alluded to previously, an overlap analysis, to determine uniqueness of content may also help inform decisions. The ability to assess materials after purchase or lease via COUNTER compliant usage data is also an important consideration.

There are many ways content can be purchased or leased by an institution, and these methods are very dependent on budgetary constraints and institutional preferences. Furthermore, content can be acquired via aggregators, publishers, or by individual selection. When conducting transactions with vendors, be certain that both parties are clear about the products and types of content access under consideration. Attributes desirable in one product (no DRM for e-books) may be irrelevant for other products (print books). In sum, there are many elements that influence collection development decisions at institutions. Librarians use a combination of institutional and subject knowledge, user input, data, and intuition to make informed and sound choices.

Small, Specialized Institution

SUNY Polytechnic Institute (SUNY Poly) is a new institution within the State University of New York. Formed in 2013, SUNY Poly is comprised of merging a small institute of technology, SUNY IT, with a division of the University of Albany, the College of Nanoscale Sciences and Engineering (CNSE). SUNY IT offered mostly undergraduate degrees in technology and professional studies, while CNSE offered mostly graduate degrees, with a small but growing undergraduate population. With the merger, SUNY Poly will become a PhD-granting institution, and will move toward becoming a research center within the SUNY system. The merged SUNY Poly includes two main sites, one in Utica, NY, and the other in Albany, NY, about 90 miles apart. The new SUNY Poly Institute focuses on both educational excellence and economic innovation through public-private partnerships. During its first year in 2013, SUNY Poly became number one in the nation in research funding from business (NSF, 2014). In addition to corporate funding, SUNY Poly has worked closely with New York state officials to attract high-tech companies to New York, with SUNY Poly serving as the research and development partner facilitating innovation hubs across the state.

While SUNY Poly's merger creates an exciting new institution to build new educational and research partnerships across New York State, providing library services to such an institution is challenging. Finding the best fit for library resources is the most difficult part of determining what collections services are needed. SUNY Poly's institutional makeup is one that allows it to serve many different niches, but often leads to difficulty in finding a cost-effective and user-friendly manner of providing access to research resources. SUNY Poly has several qualities that create issues with obtaining library resources: a relatively small student FTE (currently approximately 2,500), with small PhD programs, approximately 250 teaching faculty, with over 750 research staff, many of whom are engineers or scientists and actively engaged in research. Also, many of SUNY Poly's programs are in engineering and related Sciences, which many vendors use to create a subscription formula. Thus, although SUNY Poly is small, for subscription formula purposes, the large science FTE and large number of research scientists can make a full subscription to journal packages extremely expensive.

Since the merger brought together a party without any library staff (as it was a division of a larger University) and an institution that served a small campus that focused on teaching, the library staff is very small, with only 2.5 FTE librarians and 2 FTE staff. With a small staff, the amount of time that it takes to establish, maintain, and assess resources is paramount. Additionally, determining how easily it will be to either cancel subscriptions or move to a different access model is also important, as there are no staff who focus only on collection analysis. But with large amounts of funds dedicated to library resources, being able to quickly and easily interpret the cost per use for different models is necessary. Adding library resources is necessary for the research needs of the faculty and research scientists, and the library's budget has doubled each year since the merger. However, with the increasing amount of institutional investment in library resources comes increased scrutiny over funds allocated. It is essential for the library to be able to clearly demonstrate how it is serving in order to best negotiate the best option for the institution.

As a new institution focusing on high-level scientific research in very specific areas, one of the major issues has been deciding whether to "bundle" or not. Many libraries are "unbundling" or considering how best to move away from "Big Deal" packages (Bosch and Henderson, 2015). The process of unbundling is, indeed, a long and complex process; as such, the best strategy for SUNY Poly has been to avoid adding any new "Big Deals" whenever possible. To do so, SUNY Poly has taken an approach that prefers using pay per use models, or when relevant, a hybrid approach. However, when the cost is low, Big Deal packages still remain the best option, especially when the focus of the package connects to SUNY Poly's research interest. To get the best institutional fit involves a fair amount of risk, especially due to the low staffing and difficulty in getting access to faculty and research scientists to determine what specific journals and resources they actually need. Pay per use requires adopting a model that, for at least a year (due to journal subscription calendar timing) assumes that itemized article purchasing is the most cost-effective model. In a few cases, article download tokens have been quickly used up due to unforeseen demand for a specific title. Overall, the hybrid approach has proven to be the most successful, in which a portion of the journal package is a subscription, while the rest is available via pay per use models. And, as librarians are able to better communicate with research staff and faculty, and usage data becomes available, fine-tuning for the "right fit" will be easier.

SUNY Poly has negotiated many new subscriptions as it becomes a fully merged institution with a new focus on research, and an in-depth analysis of whether subscribing to the Big Deal or full access package is the best method was not always possible. But, some assumptions about Big Deals can be made, and were used to guide decisions. First, publishers who provide a tiered pricing model are more likely to provide cost-effective pricing for large journal packages. This has proven to be true for SUNY Poly for multiple publishers such as the American Institute of Physics. Second, if the publisher is a commercial, or for-profit publisher, it is less likely that the Big Deal bundle will be a resource that is affordable long-term, and a subscription will include price increases that other libraries have found to be unsustainable in the future (Bergstrom, Courant, McAfee, & Williams, 2014). Having the following criteria in mind when contemplating subscriptions has been useful in driving the dialog with research faculty and administration in discussing how SUNY Poly will build library services typical of a research university: is the publisher for-profit and do they offer tiered pricing. The trend of resisting or moving away from the Big Deal bundles is becoming a major trend in research libraries where subscription to such packages is prevalent (Strieb & Blixrud, 2014). As many of the researchers and faculty at SUNY Poly have experience with driving economic change, these discussions of market analysis and trends have proven helpful in allowing SUNY Poly to forego subscribing to large journal bundles and to initially look for different access options. With almost 25 years of history of large journal package trends to rely on, SUNY Poly has been able to broaden the discussion with faculty regarding how to meet research needs, while also helping to prevent adding services that will almost certainly not be sustainable in the long term.

SUNY Poly receives great benefits from its status as a member of the State University of New York system, and does receive some subscriptions such as access to Elsevier titles, as part of consortial negotiations. Other research institutions are able to negotiate large and increasing "substantial portions" of journal packages as a consortium (Strieb & Blixrud, 2014). However, SUNY Poly's status as a doctoral institution, and the absence of wide-scale cooperation of negotiating journal subscriptions as a consortia either within SUNY or other consortia, leave SUNY Poly to attempt to negotiate most subscriptions on its own. In the negotiation with vendors, not having a readily available consortium with which to bargain has been both problematic in bargaining power, but also leaves SUNY Poly to best consider its options in coordination with the vendor.

A perfect example of the hybrid approach of subscriptions has been SUNY Poly's strategy for American Chemical Society (ACS) journals. Although SUNY Poly's focus on nanotechnology and nanoscience is, essentially, interdisciplinary, there are many focused journals on "Nano" or "Nanotechnology" within many different disciplines. The ACS publication *ACS Nano* is one such journal that SUNY Poly must subscribe to, as usage is extremely high for this specific journal, but other ACS publications, although essential, do not get as much usage as others. SUNY Poly's ACS subscription in which some subscriptions are "all you can use" while others are "metered" has proven to provide a Big Deal-like experience for faculty, while providing the best cost per use scenarios. The four major areas that are most connected to Nanotechnology (Chemistry, Physics, Engineering, and Biology) are also the areas in the sciences with the highest price per title and highest amount of inflation and increases per year (Bosch & Henderson, 2015). With the highest cost for subscriptions, models are where pay per use will be of continued interest going forward.

As SUNY Poly is a new and evolving institution, the relationship with the vendor regarding journal subscriptions is one that is important at the outset. As one of SUNY Poly's goals in its strategic plan is to "upgrade" its Carnegie Classification, and slowly grow to add 30% more FTE, and grow new small, but highly desired, PhD and other graduate programs, having vendors who are willing to negotiate different models is essential. If SUNY Poly isn't able to establish models that work for our evolving nature, then pay per use models or supplementary programs for access, such as Copyright Clearance Center's Get it Now and reliance on Interlibrary Loan, become necessary. Although the approach of using ILL and other methods of providing access to pay per use material does not allow for unfettered access to content, the extra steps of clicking through link resolver pages to submit ILLs has been shown by Knowlton and colleagues to lead to almost one-third of users to determining they do not want to request the article (Knowlton, Kristanciuk, & Jabaily, 2015). Indeed, reliance on ILL and link-resolver-based access does lead to less usage, but with downloads and requests costing money, the filtering of downloads can lead to longer-term lower costs. With many endeavors of a merging institution competing for budget dollars, more funding for subscriptions not tied to specific initiatives will remain difficult. One advantage of ILL or purchase on demand is the ability to tie costs and purchasing back to specific departments and areas. With subscriptions, making the direct connection between the patron and the cost is less possible. Thus, when SUNY Poly isn't able to establish a relationship with the vendor that creates seamless access to the content, communication to faculty is key to let them know that ILL and purchase on demand of articles via ILL other methods is essential for access where data can then be used to request more funds to support specific programs.

SUNY Poly has merged at a time when most libraries are reviewing library resource acquisition, leading to different subscription models. As SUNY Poly matures and the academic journal market changes more quickly due to continued budget pressures in libraries, SUNY Poly will only understand its needs more, with more subscription options from which to choose.

Conclusion

The authors hope that their perspectives on collection development decisions in academic libraries will help colleagues choose resources wisely. A collaboratively created checklist of factors to consider when making these decisions is provided as a supplemental material. The bibliography also contains links to excellent resources that will help expand knowledge in collections acquisition.

References

Bergstrom, T. C., Courant, P. N., McAfee, R. P., & Williams, M. A. (2014). Evaluating big deal journal bundles. *Proceedings of the National Academy of Sciences, 111*(26), 9425–9430. http://dx.doi.org/10.1073/pnas.1403006111

Boll, C. (2015, August 6). University explores idea of veteran-focused college of medicine. *Syracuse University News*. Retrieved from http://news.syr.edu/university-explores-idea-of-veteran-focused-college-of-medicine-28979/

Bosch, S., & Henderson, K. (2015, April 23). Whole lotta shakin' goin' on | Periodicals price survey 2015. *Library Journal*. Retrieved from http://lj.libraryjournal.com/2015/04/publishing/whole-lotta-shakin-goin-on-periodicals-price-survey -2015/

Google Scholar. (n.d.). Inclusion guidelines for webmasters. Retrieved from https://scholar.google.com/intl/us/scholar/inclusion.html#overview

Higher education R&D expenditures funded by businesses: Fiscal year 2013—US National Science Foundation (NSF). (2014). Retrieved from http://ncsesdata.nsf.gov/herd/2013/html/HERD2013_DST_25.html

Information Technology Industry Council (ITI). (2015). Accessibility. Retrieved from https://www.itic.org/policy/accessibility/

Institute for Veterans and Military Families (IVMF). (n.d.). Retrieved from http://vets.syr.edu/

Knowlton, S. A., Kristanciuk, I., & Jabaily, M. J. (2015). Spilling out of the funnel: How reliance upon interlibrary loan affects access to information. *Library Resources & Technical Services*, *59*(1), 4. http://dx.doi.org/10.5860/lrts.59n1.4

Strieb, K. L., & Blixrud, J. C. (2014). Unwrapping the bundle: An examination of research libraries and the "big deal." *Portal: Libraries and the Academy*, *14*(4), 587–615. http://dx.doi.org/10.1353/pla.2014.0027

The authors wish to acknowledge prior work on this topic, and point readers to the following resources:

Anderson, E. (2014). *Electronic resource management systems: A workflow approach*. ALA TechSource: Chicago.

Dames, K. M., Gwilt, R. B., Warren, S. A., & Carrier, T. C. (2015). Collections and space: An update on Syracuse University Libraries' journals migration project. *Syracuse University Libraries*. Retrieved from http://library.syr.edu/about/PDF/20150406-journalswhite.pdf

Goedeken, E. A., & Lawson, K. (2015). The past, present, and future of demand-driven acquisitions in academic libraries. *College & Research Libraries, 76*(2), 205–221. http://dx.doi.org/10.5860/crl.76.2.205

Hosburgh, N. (2014). Managing the electronic resources lifecycle: Creating a comprehensive checklist using techniques for electronic resource management (TERMS). *The Serials Librarian, 66*(1–4), 212–219. http://dx.doi.org/10.1080/0361526X.2014.880028

Strader, R., Roth, A., Boissy, B., & Robertson, W. (2006). A collaborative checklist for e-journal access. *The Serials Librarian, 50*(3–4), 235–242. http://dx.doi.org/10.1300/J123v50n03_05

Sutton, S. (2013). A model for electronic resources value assessment. *The Serials Librarian, 64*(1–4), 245–253. http://dx.doi.org/10.1080/0361526X.2013.760417

TERMS: Techniques for electronic resource management. (n.d.). Retrieved November 2, 2015, from https://library3.hud.ac.uk/blogs/terms/

Checklist for Adding Resources

Evaluation and Selection

- o Resource fit with collection development criteria:
    - o Requested by faculty
    - o New curricular need
    - o Existing curricular need

- Access models:
    - Good usability and responsive content design (easily read on multiple types of devices)
    - IP based campus-wide access, or password protected access?
    - Unlimited simultaneous users or access "seats"
    - Demand-driven acquisition
    - "Get it Now" or other article purchase service
    - Interlibrary loan
- Content discovery:
    - Simple to add to discovery tools (Summon, WorldCat Discovery, EDS, etc.)
    - MARC catalog records available – plans for RDA?
    - Content discoverable in Google Scholar
    - Simple to remove from all discovery tools if no longer subscribed
- Accessibility for users with disabilities, as demonstrated through a Voluntary Product Accessibility Template (VPAT) (from the Information Technology Industry Council) and captioning for video
- Enhanced content access (or monetary credits) for resources with previously acquired print counterparts
- Perpetual access through participation in initiatives such as CLOCKSS, LOCKSS, or PORTICO
- Resource trial availability
    - Not needed – adding content to an existing platform or database
    - Yes, IP based so entire campus can use OR password protected trial for individuals
- Usage statistics that are easily accessible and meet Project COUNTER standards
- Decision Support Data:
    - Check consortial pricing and offers
    - Consider initial price AND cost of resource over long-term
    - ILL Data
    - Overlap analysis to determine unique contributions of resource
    - Citation data to determine field-weighted impact (e.g., SNIP)
    - Publication data to determine where faculty are publishing/editing
    - Turnaway data to document constituent need
    - Feedback from trials or other user experience analysis
    - Projected return on investment (ROI) for resource
- Add resource under consideration to the library's ERM to document decision-making process and track progress through resource life cycle

Acquisition

- Determine official FTE requirements of vendors (for example "science" students, all students, research associates included, other discrete populations)
- Licensing and renewal documentation that is clearly written and understandable. Request license modifications to meet institutional requirements and needs.
    - Does the license permit interlibrary loan of purchased e-content?
    - Does the license permit non-affiliated users to access in the library?
- Smooth and minimal set up for implementation, with minimal ongoing monitoring

Additional considerations

- Availability of in-depth, specialized research options, such as text mining
- Alumni access
- Open access (OA) credits for institutional authors who wish to pay article processing charges (APC) to make content OA. Can be a subscription credit or APC credit for authors.

End Users

Creating the Sandbox: The Juxtaposition of Collections and Student Development

Helen Salmon, Information Resources Librarian, University of Guelph Library

Linda Graburn, Information Resources Librarian, University of Guelph Library

Abstract

While academic library collections are typically built and assessed in relation to pedagogical or curricular needs and accreditation processes, they can also be intentionally developed, accessed, and promoted with more conscious attention to the developmental needs and context of the students who will use them. This paper will explore the roles that academic library collections play in relation to the psychosocial development of young adults. Drawing upon contemporary learning and young adult development theory, we will situate the role of academic library collections in relation to the various developmental stages, tasks, and learning challenges that young adults experience during a typical university experience. We will also explore how traditional ways of selecting, promoting, and providing access to library collections can be modified to create more direct and meaningful engagement for our students as they struggle to define themselves and to consider "where do we go from here?" for their generation.

Traditional Library Roles

Since their beginnings, universities have served as centers for the transmission and exchange of existing knowledge and for exploring and codifying new forms of knowledge. Libraries have traditionally supported this role by preserving the thoughts and writings of scholars (and society in general) and by providing a means for knowledge across many disciplines to be shared, preserved, and re-accessed across the centuries. As storehouses of knowledge, libraries and their collections help to preserve and reinforce the prevailing norms, thoughts, and social beliefs of a specific time and place. They thus serve an important social acculturation role in helping to educate and support the intellectual, emotional, and even moral growth of young adults as they prepare to enter the working world and to define themselves as individuals and as contributing members of society.

Modern academic libraries typically develop their collections very consciously and programmatically—to meet accreditation requirements, to support the university's formal teaching curriculum and research programs, and to enable program or course learning objectives. Allocation formulas, approval plans, and liaisons with academic departments all ensure that library collection budgets are aligned with the formal curriculum of the university and that purchasing of resources is largely confined to discipline-specific academic content. Reaching further into the past, however, university libraries served a more general societal role in supporting the development of the "whole" student, building collections which would promote literacy and engender the ability to think, debate, and develop moral reasoning and life skills beyond the formal curriculum. While universities no longer aim to inculcate specific cultural and moral values in their students, they do still serve an important and unique role in providing young adults with a place and a range of experiences which will support their transition into full adulthood. Contemporary academic libraries help to support this role and collaborate in the students' development by providing "spaces" (physical, virtual, collections) and services which allow students to be engaged, inspired, and challenged across multiple developmental domains.

Young Adult Development (Emerging Adulthood)

What are the developmental tasks and challenges of the average college-aged student? The pathway from adolescence to adulthood involves growing maturity and mastery across a number of

http://dx.doi.org/10.5703/1288284316282

psychosocial dimensions, including cognitive/intellectual, emotional, social, sexual, and applied life skills. Profound and sometimes rapid changes in all of these domains occur during the young adult years, and a variety of student development models and theories have been put forward to describe and categorize this stage of life development, and to try and explain the ways that students grow, develop, and mature during the university years, and in response to the university environment. These theories generally fall into several broad categories, which as a group paint a picture of the profound transitions that take place during young adulthood:

- *Psychosocial* theories of student development seek to define the developmental tasks, issues, and events that occur during young adulthood. Development is seen as a sequence of tasks or events that unfold as chronological age progresses and that is shaped by the individual's environment and significant life experiences. Erik Erikson defined development as occurring through and in response to a series of crises or decision points which provide the stimulus for developmental progression (Erikson, 1959). Arthur Chickering (1969; 1993) drew upon his extensive research with college students in the US to describe seven developmental "vectors" or deepening areas of competence which typify psychosocial developmental throughout the young adult years: these include intellectual competence, managing emotions, growing independence, maturing of interpersonal relationships, a strengthening sense of self-identity and integrity, and developing a sense of vocation in life.
- More recently, Jeffrey Jensen Arnett considered the global nature of the workforce in postindustrial countries and the need for advanced education and training to enter competitive job markets and its impact on the development of young adults. Demographically, there is a related delay in the average age of taking on the adult roles of marriage, career, and parenthood. Without these social norms and expectations, the early twenties are spent in self-focused exploration of diverse life roles, preparatory to transitioning to these adult roles. He coined the concept of "emerging adulthood" as a new developmental stage between adolescence and young adulthood (Arnett, 2001).
- *Cognitive-structural* theories explore the ways that individuals reason, think, and make sense of their environment and experiences. Development is hierarchical, with one stage each stage scaffolding upon and incorporating the previous stage. Jean Piaget (1958) theorized that the fourth and final stage of cognitive development, or the formal operational stage (from age 12 through to adulthood), sees the emergence of abstract thought and hypothetical reasoning abilities, and the ability to engage in systematic planning. In 1970, William G. Perry, Jr. outlined a sequence of approaches to learning and thinking which students move through as they progress from dualism to multiplicity to contextual relativism (1970). By the end of the university years, students come to understand that diverse opinions or answers need to be considered and weighed relative to their background context—they are not all equally valid. By this stage, decisions are based on an integration and weighing of various perspectives, and all solutions must be supported by reasons.
- In their 1986 book, *Women's ways of knowing: The development of voice, self, and mind,* Belensky, Clinchy, Goldberger, and Tarule refined upon Perry's model of intellectual development to recognize more specifically female pathways of cognitive development. "Women's ways of knowing" proposes a developmental pathway progressing from silence (disconnection from knowledge), to

subjective knowledge (recognizing the self and one's own inner feelings and experiences as authority), to procedural knowledge (recognizing that multiple sources of knowledge exist and can be explored and evaluated), to constructed knowledge (recognizing that knowledge is constructed, mutable and contextual).

- *Moral development* theories describe the gradual development of moral reasoning ability, that is, standards of what is right and wrong. Beginning in 1958, and building on Piaget's earlier work, Lawrence Kohlberg (1984) posits a moral ladder of progression in reasoning abilities during the college years through three stages: preconventional (right or wrong is dependent on authority and by the consequences for disobedience or compliance); conventional (morality is defined in conformity with social norms and societal laws); and postconventional (morality is defined in accordance with universal ethical principles and an individual's own principles). In 1982, Carol Gilligan (1982) both built upon and critiqued Kohlberg's work by proposing a theory of women's moral development which contrasted male views of morality, based on individual rights and rules, with female views of morality, based upon the caring aspects of human relationships. For women, Gilligan argued, Kohlberg's stages of moral reasoning should be recast as "stages of the ethic of care," whereby young women progress from a selfish viewpoint which valorizes personal survival (the preconventional stage) to a recognition that one has a socially assigned responsibility for others (the conventional stage), to an internalization of the principles of care for oneself and others (the postconventional stage).
- *Person-environment* theories explore the interaction between the person and their environment working together, and assert that positive outcomes for college students are associated with campus environments which encourage student engagement (Kuh, Kinzie, Schuh, & Whitt, 2005), which challenge and support them on multiple levels (Sanford & Adelson, 1962), and which provide a rich integration of academic and social systems (Tinto, 1994). These theories particularly focus on student success in transitioning to the world of work and careers.
- *Experiential learning* theory emphasizes the process by which individual students learn through experience. David Kolb (1984) presents an iterative four-stage experiential learning model which begins with a concrete experience, followed by reflective observation of that experience, followed by abstract conceptualization of that experience, followed by active experimentation based on learning acquired through the experience/reflection phases of the cycle. Kolb further argues that, to be effective, experiential learning must actively involve students, and that they must have the necessary skills (ability to reflect, analyze, and problem-solve) to benefit from the experience. In other words, stages of student development interact with experiences (curricular and noncurricular) in complex and reciprocal ways.

Finally, it is important to recognize that, while the wide range of student development theories provide useful frameworks for understanding the general experiences and processes of emerging adulthood, they also recognize that individual students will be affected by such factors as diversity (culture, ethnicity, gender), individuality (personality, temperament, learning styles, preferences, past experience), and the environment around them (campus climate, involvement in curricular and extracurricular activities). As well, for some students, emerging adulthood is even more complex and offers different and more difficult challenges—specific subgroups of college-aged students have unique needs and challenges. Students with physical disabilities, learning disabilities, or mental health issues will require more extensive and more targeted support as they seek to master the usual developmental tasks of young adulthood. International students entering North American universities face a variety of challenges beyond the normal adult developmental tasks, as they strive to acquire English language and writing skills, understand the academic approaches and expectations of Western universities, navigate the cultural practices and norms of a foreign culture, and establish the new social networks that are such a crucial aspect of the young adult life-stage.

It can be argued that, for all students, the line of demarcation between adolescence and adulthood is perhaps not as sharply defined as it once was, and the current cohort of college students tend to drive their own development more independently and with higher regard to their own developmental and utilitarian needs than that of previous student cohorts. Their style of learning is an iterative one, involving self-reflection and the development and maturation of their own personality constructs, rather than responding solely and passively to a curricular narrative owned and controlled by faculty experts.

Library collections can play a unique and important supporting role in this process of individualized exploration by providing the intellectual raw materials for students to interact with and explore, and to learn about how scholarship is produced and communicated. We need to question the assumption that universities or their libraries can control the ways that users' access and use information, and turn the lens around to view young adulthood from the perspective of our students, recognizing the full spectrum of their development as young adults. Recognizing their usual information-seeking practices, and within the context of their ongoing and unique developmental needs, we can create collections which supplement and complement the generic sources of information available on the Web with scholarly forms of communication, and with information customized to the developmental needs of emerging adults. These collections can be selectively inserted into student learning spaces (point-of-need access through learning management systems). They can also serve in a more general, noncurricular way as an intellectual sandbox for students to explore and use as they follow their own self-initiated intellectual and developmental pathways.

Campus Partners

If academic libraries seek to integrate their services and collections more deliberately into the overall university mandate to support student development needs, who might our natural campus partners be? Institutions of higher education of course recognize that their students have developmental needs beyond the cognitive and intellectual skills which are developed in the classroom, and student life services play a well-established and important role in identifying and supporting the full range of developmental needs of young adults. The "wellness wheel" model, originally developed by Bill Hettler (1976), is used as a standard model at many North American universities to promote balance for students across the intellectual, social, physical, spiritual, occupational, emotional, and environmental dimensions of life. Academic support skills, life management skills, mental and physical health supports, and social networks all fall within the domain of student life service centers in the modern university, and are seen as a crucial support for recruiting and retaining students through their university career. Other, more specialized units typically address specific types of student development needs—curricular committees deal with the integration of cognitive and learning development into the university's formal course design; and the needs of specialized subgroups of students (international students, student athletes, students with mental or physical challenges, first year students, etc.). All of these units think about student development needs from different perspectives, and all of them have the potential to be partners with their campus library in promoting the awareness, integration, and use of library collections in support of those needs.

Often, however, student life support units are somewhat cut off from the academic life of their university and from each other. They are frequently funded and managed differently than academic departments, and the academic skills promoted in the classroom are seen as separate and outside of the psychosocial development occurring in other aspects of a student's life. Our students are "whole" persons, but universities do not always do a good job at integrating support and providing student development opportunities in a holistic way across the full university experience. This bifurcation between the "academic" and the "student development" roles of a university can also extend to other academic support units (including libraries) across the university. The obvious role that library collections play in providing resources to support the formal curriculum is well-recognized. Less often recognized and acted upon, though, is the crucial role that academic libraries and their collections can play in providing "beyond the curriculum" support for students as they learn and explore the world around them—trying on and experimenting with new roles and viewpoints, learning how to recognize and integrate the world's complexity and to make choices, learning how to attain information on their own in order to question received wisdom. Even within libraries, front-facing library student support services such as information literacy or reference services tend to be separated from collections services, both in terms of budget alignment and organizational reporting structures. Collections practices and funding are "student focused" only insofar as they support the formal teaching goals of the university; rarely do they consider the needs of students as they make the transition to adulthood through multiple developmental pathways. Very recently, the ACRL framework for information literacy has evolved from a set of generic formal standards (levels of cognitive development) to a model which assesses each student's individual skill levels and personal context for information seeking and usage, recognizing that the student's particular developmental stage and needs should drive the learning process (ACRL, 2015). However, the potential for library collections to play an active and deliberate part in that developmental learning process remains largely underexplored—some possible approaches for using collections in this way will be explored in the remainder of this paper.

Library Roles in Supporting Student Development

Academic library collections can contribute to the "wellness wheel" of student development in many ways. Our collections, and the ways in which we can integrate and supplement them with the full spectrum of information available to society, can help to engender and deepen a number of cognitive skills in the students who work with them. By their very diverse nature, academic library collections expose users to multiple viewpoints on the world. The evaluation and integration of information is not a passive process—collections provide the ability to master information literacy skills in an applied context. By learning how to recognize different points of view, how to judge and evaluate various types and sources of information, and how to evaluate and critically assess the quality of scholarly communication, students develop more sophisticated and pervasive cognitive skills and frameworks for dealing with the world. Through contact with library collections and the development of the practical and cognitive skills needed to find and use information, students gain a deeper understanding of the scholarly communication cycle in general, and ultimately develop threshold concepts for their own academic discipline which can be integrated into their own developing intellectual constructs and sense of self. By providing wide-ranging and generic content that stretches beyond the formal curriculum to address the needs of young adults, libraries can aid the overall mission of the university by helping students to become more comfortable with diversity, ambiguity, and uncertainty, and with charting their own paths of inquiry independently from the requirements of their professors. This is an important developmental step for young adults, and its impact is felt across all of the major psychosocial domains. The ability to debate and to integrate varying perspectives, to support an argument with evidence, to understand the cultural and societal constructs which frame their society, and the basic ability to find and use information which meets both academic and personal needs—all of this can be supported by interaction with the raw materials represented by an academic library collection.

We can further promote intellectual growth and self-mastery of learning goals in a more applied way by inviting students and staff in other campus support units (student life, counseling services, wellness units) to become active partners in building those collections, through the use of patron-driven acquisitions purchasing models or active solicitation of student requests for leisure reading collections. We can enable access to library collections in ways which will deliberately enhance student engagement across multiple psychosocial domains and which will recognize and accommodate many different styles of learning. Something as simple as the harmony between the visual and physical elements of an academic resource and its intellectual content (whether it is a book, an e-journal, an e-book, or a streaming media object) can be a powerful shaper of a student's experience with it. The placement of physical collections and their integration with well-designed study and learning spaces, the promotion and visibility of leisure collections, and the provision of e-book platforms which engage students on functional and emotional levels as well as providing academic content—all of these approaches to acquiring and managing collections can have a direct (albeit not always obvious) impact on the learning and social environment of the university and the ability of students to successfully navigate the transition into adulthood.

The role of academic libraries as social learning spaces has been well-recognized over the past few decades, as they have been gradually evolving from a warehousing role (for print collections) to a role which prioritizes the creation of active student study and learning spaces. In addition to their traditional role of providing intellectual fodder for students' cognitive and moral development, university libraries now actively provide a range of physical and intellectual spaces where students can meet, encounter and test new ideas, engage in group learning activities, and form social networks which help to support them as they master the developmental tasks of young adulthood. The transformation of library collections space to support this type of active learning has been made possible by the careful and conscious management of print legacy collections. Most North America academic libraries have reduced their print collections footprint by adopting such strategies as offsite storage, resource sharing with other institutions, weeding of low-use materials, and replacing print collections with digital surrogates. The resulting savings in physical space are then repurposed for learning commons services and study spaces which more actively support and engage student development needs beyond the academic/cognitive domain to include social, emotional, and applied life skills as well. By providing spaces (virtual and physical) for students to interact with one another, there is the potential for them to engage more actively and collaboratively in using the library's collections, and to be inspired and shaped by that experience.

The transition of collections from print to digital has profoundly affected the ability of libraries to integrate their role and their resources more closely into the campus curriculum, and to target access to those resources in ways that are timely and therefore more effective in supporting student learning. In addition to increasing the library's ability to integrate resources into virtual learning spaces, the print-to-digital revolution has also allowed libraries to free up physical space for the creation of new partnerships between libraries and other units on campus who provide support for student development. Such partnerships might include a wide range of academic or administrative service units supporting generic and specialized student development needs—computing and technology skills, data and GIS services, media creation labs, digital humanities partnerships, and a range of specialized student support services which address generic skill development in writing, learning, or numeracy. Because of their central positioning on most campuses, and their long opening hours, libraries often also house services for first year students, international students, or students with disabilities. These services and partnerships exploit the space once used by print collections, but can also actively recognize and draw upon the contemporary ways that libraries acquire and serve up information. Deliberate outreach to student wellness and counseling units to select and provide resources (print and digital) which they can refer students to at the point of need will have a much greater impact than if we passively expect students to discover those resources on their own. The success of all of these partnerships and services depend upon access to good quality scholarly information and data, and the library's collections in turn can be selected and made accessible in ways which promote and support their use across the campus, in ways which recognize the full spectrum of student development.

Special and unique local collections in particular provide unique opportunities for students to work with and understand scholarly collections. Primary sources inspire and provide students with historical context for modern ideas and issues, and can be drawn into student learning spaces (virtual or in-person) to catalyze discussion, learning, and intellectual growth. In addition to supporting experiential learning objectives, engaging students in the creation and use of locally digitized content creates learning synergy by combining the practical work of digitization with the intellectual and conceptual aspects of working with collections. By integrating student-created digitized content into the curriculum, students create the learning objects that they and others will use in their studies. Digitization of special collections (whether carried out by students or not) enables the textual and historical analysis of primary sources and the creation of enduring instructional media. Partnerships with faculty and students can be undertaken to set priorities for digitization, and to incorporate digitization projects and the use of digitized or primary artifact collections as part of course design. These and similar projects which involve students as paid employees or volunteers in selecting or managing the library's collections can engender the development of a number of cognitive, academic and life/workplace skills, including:

- Generic employment skills (technical and interpersonal)
- Knowledge of digitization and curation practices
- Bibliographic and research skills
- Intellectual curiosity and an appreciation of the world's complexity and the variety and range of intellectual viewpoints in it
- Increased understanding of libraries, readership, and scholarly communication

Providing students with the opportunity to work with library collections can also have the side benefit of expanding student's understanding of the cultural roles and skills unique to libraries and librarianship, and how these contribute to the creation and preservation of scholarly knowledge. Through such work, students can move beyond an intellectual exploration of scholarly knowledge to consider such aspects of scholarly communication as:

- Collecting and organizing information as it is created
- Preserving knowledge (even as formats change)
- Making resources discoverable and accessible
- Being aware of emerging information technologies, and how to implement them
- Training others in information (and other) literacies
- Assessing, responding to and advocating for diverse user needs, communities, and preferences

Finally, we can use the public spaces in our libraries (meeting rooms, casual spaces, online and physical exhibition space) to promote and use our collections in ways that will challenge and nurture the intellectual, emotional, social, and moral development of our students. We can "open up" our collections by promoting them through special exhibits, sponsoring events which debate and explore current social issues or "library" values or issues such as censorship or literacy. We can provide spaces for students to curate, display, and celebrate their own intellectual work, so that libraries are seen to be a part of the intellectual life around them. In short, we can reinvent and revalorize the original role of library collections in the life of a university—a place where human thought in all of its richness is gathered together to be preserved, to be shared, and to serve as a catalyst for the discovery of new knowledge for the next generation.

References

ACRL. (2015, February 2). *Framework for information literacy for higher education*. Retrieved from http://www.ala.org/acrl/standards/ilframework

Arnett, J. J. (2001). *Adolescence and emerging adulthood: A cultural approach*. Upper Saddle River, NJ: Prentice-Hall.

Arnett, J. J. (2000). Emerging adulthood: A theory of development from the late teens through the twenties. *American Psychologist, 55*(5), 469–480.

Belensky, M. F., Clinchy, B., Goldberger, N. R., & Tarule, J. M. (1986). *Women's ways of knowing: The development of voice, self, and mind*. New York: Basic Books.

Chickering, A. W. (1969). *Education and identity*. San Francisco: Jossey-Bass.

Chickering, A. W., & Reisser, L. (1993). *Education and identity* (2nd ed.). San Francisco: Jossey-Bass.

Erikson, E. H. (1959). *Identity and the life cycle: Selected papers*. New York: International Universities Press.

Gfellner, B. M., & Bartoszuk, K. (2015). Emerging adulthood in North America: Identity status and perceptions of adulthood among college students in Canada and the United States. *Emerging Adulthood, 3*(5), 368–372.

Gilligan, C. (1982). *In a different voice: Psychological theory and women's development*. Cambridge, MA: Harvard University Press.

Hettler, B. (1976). The six dimensions of wellness model. Retrieved from http://c.ymcdn.com/sites/www.nationalwellness.org/resource/resmgr/docs/sixdimensionsfactsheet.pdf

Hettler, B. (1980). Wellness promotion on a university campus: Family and community health. *Journal of Health Promotion and Maintenance, 3*, 77–95.

Hinchcliffe, L. J., & Wong, M. A. (2010). From services-centered to student-centered: A "wellness wheel" approach to developing the library as an integrative learning commons. *College & Undergraduate Libraries, 17*, 213–224.

Kohlberg, L. (1984). *Essays on moral development volume II: The psychology of moral development: The nature and validity of moral stages*. San Francisco, CA: Harper & Row.

Kolb, D. A. (1984). *Experiential learning: Experience as the source of learning and development*. Englewood Cliffs, NJ: Prentice-Hall.

Kuh, G. D., Kinzie, J., Schuh, J. H., & Whitt, E. J. (2005, July-August). Never let it rest: Lessons about student success from high-performing colleges and universities. *Change,* 44–51. http://dx.doi.org/10.3200/CHNG.37.4.44-51

Long, D. (2012). Theories and models of student development. In L. J. Hinchcliffe & M. A. Wong (Eds.), *Environments for student growth and development: Librarians and student affairs in collaboration* (pp. 41–55). Chicago: Association of College & Research Libraries.

Piaget, J., & Inhelder, B. (1958). *The growth of logical thinking: From childhood to adolescence: An essay on the construction of formal operational structures* (Ann Parsons and Stanley Milgram, Trans.). New York: Basic Books.

Perry, W. G., Jr. (1970). *Forms of intellectual and ethical development in the college years: A scheme*. New York: Holt, Rinehart, and Winston.

Sanford, N., & Adelson, J. (1962). *The American college: A psychological and social interpretation of the higher learning.* New York: Wiley.

Tinto, V. (1994). *Building learning communities for new college students: A summary of research findings of the collaborative learning project.* Philadelphia: Pennsylvania State University, National Center on Postsecondary Teaching, Learning, and Assessment.

Tough Love: Guiding Student Researchers Toward a Better Future for E-Books

Emily O'Connor, Assistant Vice President of Academic Support, Rasmussen College

Kara Kroes Li, Director of Product Management, EBSCO Information Services

Melissa Fulkerson, Director, E-Book Sales, Elsevier

Abstract

EPUB has emerged as the standard format for e-books due to its numerous advantages over PDF, including superior accessibility, enhanced navigation, lighter file sizes, optimization for mobile devices, and support for non-English languages, to name a few. However, there is little understanding of EPUB's advantages among end users and little appreciation for EPUB's potential in academic libraries. This paper provides a literature review and perspectives from a publisher, an aggregator, and end users (higher education library) about solutions that drive increased knowledge and use of the EPUB format for e-books in the academic library. It will summarize the reasons for EPUB's ascendance among academic publishers, explain how PDF e-books present barriers to innovation and real problems for accessibility, and argue that the scarcity of EPUB in the academic library is mostly due to a lack of awareness of its benefits. It will give librarians some ideas on how to begin integrating EPUB into research instruction, and ultimately, it will suggest that both librarians and vendors take an active role in shaping the habits and thus demands of their users.

Introduction

EPUB has emerged as the standard format for e-books due to its numerous advantages over PDF, including superior accessibility, enhanced navigation, lighter file sizes, optimization for mobile devices, and support for non-English languages, to name a few. However, there is little understanding of EPUB's advantages among end users and little appreciation for EPUB's potential in academic libraries. Research has shown that most users don't recognize the EPUB format and prefer PDF due to its familiarity. This puts publishers and vendors in a difficult situation: continue to deliver PDF content at an increasing cost, both financial and in terms of usability, or risk turning users away by forcing them into an unfamiliar format?

Nomenclature and Background

While other e-book formats exist, this paper focuses on PDF and EPUB formats, because those two formats are most relevant to the academic research workflow involving e-books.

PDF

Portable Document Format, or *PDF*, was invented by Adobe Systems in 1992 and (as of 2008) is maintained as an open standard file format by the International Organization for Standardization (ISO) (Adobe Systems, 2015). PDF editing software is, however, proprietary and maintained by Adobe. Most PDF files are designed to be "flat documents," which means that you see the layout of the document exactly as its author intended, including print-corollary pagination. Variations of the flat PDF include options to make a document accessible, embed multimedia content, and create fillable forms (all options requiring the use of Adobe's proprietary software). PDF is a common file format due in some part to the ease of formatting from common document editing software, such as Microsoft Word, and the polished appearance of the final document.

EPUB

According to the International Digital Publishing Forum (IDPF), the organization responsible for standards related to electronic publishing and

http://dx.doi.org/10.5703/1288284316283

content consumption, EPUB "is the distribution and interchange format standard for digital publications and documents based on Web Standards" (2015, par. 2). Initially released in 2007, the IDPF released EPUB version 3 (EPUB3) in 2011. EPUB provides a user with a number of features that are focused on the accessibility of a web-based electronic document through the integration of Web standards such as dynamic linking; adjustable font size, background color, and text; integration of accessibility standards; searchable images, formulas, and tables; support for non-Roman languages; and integration of audio, video, and quizzes (version 3). EPUB's most visible (and differentiating) feature is its reflowable text, or optimized display, which resizes the document to fit screens for a variety of devices.

The Case for Accessibility

Accessibility is a key issue in the publishing world and, specifically, publishing in higher education. Section 104 of the *Code of Federal Regulations* (2000) stipulates that academic materials required for courses must be made accessible for all students. Accessibility is not limited to readers of Braille, but also readers with other visual impairments as well as motor impairment or cognitive challenges (Bide, 2014). Technological advances provide the means for publishers and aggregators to provide enhanced or alternate versions of materials more quickly and efficiently than print variations, in large part due to the advent and use of PDF and EPUB for material delivery to end users. However, while accessibility tools are available in the development of both PDF and EPUB files, the integration of accessibility features is not automatic; rather, the creator of a file must specifically leverage accessibility markup and specifications in a file. Only a PDF generated with accessibility checks through Adobe Acrobat Pro provides a user with options to include alternate text for figures, specified languages for text, character encodings, and a structure tree that references all document content (Adobe Systems, 2004). EPUB, on the other hand (specifically EPUB 3), provides the file creator with options to integrate enhanced navigation, add textual descriptions of illustrations, adopting MathML for typesetting equations, global language support, and rich media and hyperactivity. EPUB 3 also integrates the accessible DAISY format—the audio format standard for "talking books." As a result of these accessibility integrations in EPUB and the ability to implement integrations without the use of proprietary software, the Association of American Publishers (2013), the DAISY Consortium (2015), EDitEUR (2014) and others support the use of EPUB for e-book publication over PDF.

EPUB Perspectives

Despite the many superior qualities of the EPUB format, and the fact that virtually all academic publishers are producing it, EPUB runs a distant second to PDF in terms of usage in academic libraries and delivery from academic e-book vendors. The authors provide perspectives on the challenges and opportunities for integrating EPUB in the academic research workflow from the publisher, aggregator, and end user (higher education library), and offer potential solutions from these three critical perspectives.

The Publisher

The publisher perspective outlined here is that of Elsevier's Science and Technology Books portfolio, which publishes academic reference content in print and digital formats to support advancement of research science. Elsevier began creating EPUB files for books in 2010, mainly in an effort to meet the needs of several retail channel partners with proprietary e-readers. Elsevier saw an uptick in retail sales to consumers when content was made available, which gave evidence to a growing need for content optimized for mobile devices in the research community. Elsevier then began converting backlist titles to EPUB that were previously only available in PDF, so the available catalog could be as broad as possible and allow a consistent experience for users. The benefits to EPUB in the research community were clear—text that is reflowable and can be resized based on screen size allows a researcher to easily access the same book on their PC, tablet or mobile device through the reader of their choice, and offers a more streamlined workflow which no longer confines them to their desk when using book content, or requires them to struggle with a PDF that is not easily viewed on a mobile device in the field.

In 2013 when EBSCO and other library aggregators began accepting EPUB as a supported file type, it further advanced the possibilities for the use of this content in research and helped drive the return on investment that Elsevier and other publishers have put into making this content available in the academic market.

In addition to the simple—but impactful—improvements that EPUB allows publishers to bring to the traditional reading experience, it is also important that publishers look into how best to support additional accessibility features. Some of most forward-looking features of EPUB, and particularly the most recent EPUB3 standard, include things like adding textual descriptions to images and nontext elements. Similarly, adding interactive elements like charts and graphs that allow for data input, question-and-answer quizzes inline with text, and multimedia video are all part of the future landscape for scientific book content. One of the challenges however, is the limited rollout on the vendor side with regard to functionality with EPUB 3. Publishers would be in a better position to leverage these tools if all vendors, whether serving library or consumer markets, would rally behind support for EPUB3 functionality. There is the ability to gracefully downgrade an EPUB3 file so any reader only renders what it's capable of without creating a rift in the user experience. But in order for our industry to fully embrace the technologies available to us, more support is needed from the broader reseller marketplace that is hosting and delivering this content.

The Aggregator

The e-book aggregator perspective outlined here is that of EBSCO Information Services, which began integrating EPUB format e-books in the spring of 2013. At that time, EBSCO anticipated an inevitable transition away from the PDF format because of its many limitations. For trade content, the case for EPUB is simple, since the primary use case is offline, on a mobile device and the reflowable content is a near necessity. But for e-books in the academic library, where the primary use case is the online research workflow, the benefits of the EPUB format are lesser known. Academic monographs in EPUB format are full of rich, intratextual linking between sections and to/from end-of-chapter references, and they contain hyperlinked indexes and links to the open Web. They operate like and integrate with Web content, which makes online research using e-books much more efficient. They are also, for the most part, made highly accessible. So in light of the benefits to end users and the near-universal adoption of EPUB by publishers, EBSCO released an online EPUB viewer within the EBSCOhost platform, which is comaintained with the existing PDF viewer. Thus, the EBSCO engineering team is maintaining two platforms for e-books, so every feature has to be built (defined, planned, coded, tested, and released) twice. Sometimes this means equal time and resources for each format, other times there is substantially more effort involved with the PDF feature because the technology is so outdated. Initially, EBSCO accepted the dual format/dual platform situation with the hope that the EPUB viewer would soon displace the PDF viewer as the premier research platform, while the PDF viewer could be maintained at a basic level for backlist e-books or anything for which an EPUB version was unavailable.

But despite the initial optimism, EBSCO has been unable to retire support for the PDF viewer, and due to typical resource constraints within a software platform, it has been unable to fully develop the potential available for EPUB content. With each software release, EBSCO must allocate available resources across two platforms, which necessarily limits the rate at which it can develop for EPUB features. (Additionally, which such heavy use of the PDF content, EBSCO is unwilling to let the user experiences diverge beyond a reasonable amount). Other academic vendors have chosen to forgo an online EPUB experience all together. In short, because of the academic community's attachment to PDF e-books, EBSCO and others have been limited in the number of advanced EPUB features it has been able to introduce.

Why has EBSCO not forced the choice on its users, as consumer sites have done? First, as an aggregator, EBSCO has to support a range of market segments and user populations: technology-savvy users on one end of the spectrum and on the other, users still adjusting to e-books in general. Second, aggregators generally follow trends in scholarly research and introduce features based on demand—if enough researchers require integration with a certain citation management tool, aggregators will comply. But rare is the case where the aggregator is dictating the research trend—e-book aggregators generally don't have enough prominence in the scholarly research universe. And most importantly, EBSCO's users haven't yet gravitated towards EPUB in any statistically significant numbers. As recently as October 2015, EPUB use among EBSCO's academic customers accounted for just 6.28% of overall EBSCO e-book usage, and just 7.42% of total downloads.

To understand the reasons for the low usage of the EPUB versions, the researchers looked to data gathered by EBSCO's user research team on full-text linking and student research habits. In a study called "Library-ese," a survey of 208 US undergraduates designed by EBSCO's user research group to probe what library and research terminology students do and don't understand, the researchers found a remarkably high level of recognition with the PDF icon and acronym. This survey, along with several usability tests, have shown that students are not always sure which links take them directly to the full text in their information products, but that PDF represents a reliable and familiar choice. Seventy-two percent of students surveyed believed that clicking "PDF" provides them immediate access to full text, while HTML, e-book, and EPUB were selected at a much lower rate for providing immediate access to a full-text e-book (Lawrence 2015). In a related usability study, only 13% of students correctly guessed what EPUB is in a multiple choice question (Gambrell 2015). What Khalilah Gambrell, EBSCO Technical Product Manager for e-books, found anecdotally is that students think of "e-book" as the format and do not necessarily know or care about the difference between types of e-book formats. This presents a challenge for EBSCO as an aggregator. It would be easy to consolidate the e-book link to the EPUB version, where available, but until librarians understand and support that decision, EBSCO is hesitant to force that transition on them.

Another challenge for EBSCO as an aggregator is that publishers support different versions of EPUB (2.0 and 3.0), and those that produce EPUB leverage the navigation with varying degrees of elegance. Most publishers anchor links to chapters, so that if there is a reference to, say, "Chapter 9," the user can select that reference and be taken to that chapter. Many publishers also support links to end of chapter references, but comparatively few publishers link back from the end of chapter reference to the point in the book where the user left off. This two-way linking is where the biggest research efficiency is gained—so that users can check a reference and then "flip" back to their place in the book and not lose the integrity—or the flow—of what they were reading. EBSCO is undertaking efforts with publishers to encourage them to fully exploit EPUB advantages and partner to deliver best-in-class research experience.

Soon, aggregators must decide when and whether to establish the EPUB version as the primary e-book and begin to deprecate PDF support in favor of robust EPUB support. Continued research with end users and the promotional activities outlined in this paper should help make that decision more clear in the coming months.

The End User

The end user studied in this publication is a private college with program offerings in six schools (business, design, early childhood education, health sciences, nursing, and technology), operating residentially in five states and online. The three-part study focused on EPUB perceptions of college students as well as the faculty and staff who support college students through either curriculum and design or direct instruction. The study administrator (assistant vice president of academic support at the college) poses that in a higher education setting, many of the benefits of EPUB outweigh its PDF counterpart, including:

- Students and faculty more frequently connect to library resources on mobile devices; optimized display makes it easier for students to move from tablet to phone to desktop without compromising readability
- EPUB's features support accessibility needs in higher education classroom settings, especially virtual classrooms or courses in which electronic materials are required
- Dynamic text and multimedia integration make a once-static text interactive and engaging, providing the reader (student) intrinsic incentive to complete the material

Despite this improved functionality, users are reticent to select an EPUB file over a PDF file when provided with the option, because PDF is more recognizable. In partnership with EBSCO (its primary e-book provider), the college measured its e-book use by format selection and discovered that in peak usage periods, PDF full-text views numbered nearly 8,000 while EPUB views in the same period numbered less than 1,000. Through its library administration, the college sought to change EPUB perception through three channels: curriculum integration, faculty development, and student marketing and training.

Curriculum Integration

The college curriculum is supported by curriculum and instruction (C&I) team and course design teams that are tasked with partnering with school and programmatic leadership as well as subject matter experts and academic support personal (including librarians) to develop outcomes and curricula for courses and programs. At the course level, librarians are tasked with liaising with the C&I team to integrate library resources in courses as required or supplemental reading material, and then working with the course design team to ensure that library resources are appropriately linked within courses. Prior to this study, librarians as well as the C&I and course design teams placed no prioritization on EPUB resources: since as much as 75% of e-book usage at the college stems from course integration, the potential to improve EPUB usage as a result of changes in prioritization is significant. The library administrator provided training to both the C&I and course design teams on the value of EPUB (usability, accessibility) and instructions on identifying resources within the college's databases that are available in EPUB format. Beginning with new and revised course designs in fall semester 2015, the teams will prioritize resources with EPUB format if they fit other criteria for materials selection, and the library administrator will remeasure format selection to identify shifts in use.

Faculty Development

Resource selection for college courses is typically directed or at least guided by the faculty teaching those courses. As such, faculty play a critical role in the integration of library resources in course curriculum as well as the use of resources by students for assignments. In September, 2015, the study administrator hosted a faculty development session presented by EBSCO, its primary e-book aggregator. The session focused on the differences between EPUB and PDF, the value of EPUB, and opportunities for faculty to connect students to resources in EPUB format using the searching and linking tools in the college's library databases. A few weeks after the presentation, faculty ($n = 58$) were asked to complete a survey about EPUB; 7 faculty responded. The faculty who had an opportunity to try EPUB prior to or after the survey were positive about EPUB features but also identified a need to receive additional training on the availability and features of EPUB. The number of faculty who participated in the session and subsequently completed the survey is a small sample; the author plans to repeat the session during future faculty development and offer focus sessions to gather additional data.

Student Training and Marketing

Students are the primary users of library resources and typically require significant exposure to and training on library resources to become adept at use for research. The study administrators provided a free webinar on EPUB format to student tutors at the college. The tutors were not required to complete the training but were offered compensation (tutors at the college are paid for completion of any duties-related training). Following the training, participating tutors were asked to complete a survey about EPUB features. Of the 10 students who completed the training and the survey, 6 tried EPUB resources after the training was complete, which suggests that the mere exposure to format training increases the likelihood of use of EPUB use. Additionally, 80% of students surveyed somewhat agreed or strongly agreed that they are "more likely to select EPUB as my first choice of format for future online research" and that "EPUB makes my online research more efficient." Ninetey percent of students who completed the survey either somewhat agreed or strongly agreed that they would "definitely select EPUB books" for pleasure reading and for research. While the sample is small, results correlate to a positive impact on training to improve EPUB use by students.

Conclusions

The e-book publishing and aggregation market continues to change as use cases in public and academic markets change. In some instances, even the concept of a "book" is changing: where a course may have once required readers to purchase and read an entire text, students are now provided with or required to purchase a bundle that includes pages and chapters of a variety of articles and books as well as videos and other multimedia content. This evolving landscape, combined with the introduction of and improvements to increasingly inexpensive mobile devices, makes the EPUB format a particularly attractive resource. The literature and our studies suggest that while some use-case scenarios may require PDF availability, a more proactive approach to format selection includes extensive training on the features of EPUB for end users and extensive integration in courses where e-books are utilized as required or supplemental materials. The researchers hope that with the increase in demand, better availability and support across academic platforms will follow.

References

Adobe Systems. (2015). About Adobe PDF. Retrieved from https://acrobat.adobe.com/us/en/products/about-adobe-pdf.html

Adobe Systems. (2004). Creating accessible Adobe PDF files: A guide for document authors. Retrieved from https://www.adobe.com/enterprise/accessibility/pdfs/acro6_pg_ue.pdf

American Pscyhological Association. (2011). How do you cite an e-book (e.g., Kindle book)? Retrieved from http://blog.apastyle.org/apastyle/2011/06/how-do-you-cite-an-e-book.html

Association of American Publishers. (2013). AAP EPUB3 implementation project. Retrieved from http://02c494f.netsolhost.com/epub3implementationproject/

Bide, M. (2014). The case for adopting accessibility using EPUB 3. Retrieved from http://epubzone.org/news/the-case-for-adopting-accessibility-using-epub-3

Gambrell, K. (2015). [Full-text link display best practices]. Unpublished Raw Data.

International Digital Publishing Forum. (2015). EPUB. Retrieved from http://idpf.org/epub

Lawrence, K. (2015). Library-ese study. [Student perceptions of library terminology]. Unpublished raw data.

Modern Language Association. (n.d.). How do I cite an e-book? Retrieved from https://www.mla.org/style/handbook_faq/cite_an_ebook

US Department of Education. Nondiscrimination on the basis of handicap in programs or activities receiving federal financial assistance, 34 C.F.R. § 104 (2000).

Verma, P. R. (2015). Making publications accessible for all. *DAISYpedia*. Retrieved from http://www.daisy.org/daisypedia/making-publications-accessible-all

Effect of Library Advocacy on Mendeley User Adoption and Productivity

Yath Ithayakumar, Mendeley Market Development Manager, Elsevier

Helen Josephine, Head Librarian, Terman Engineering Library, Stanford University

Abstract

Millions of researchers and students currently use Mendeley.com, a free reference manager and one of the largest academic collaboration networks, to support them in reading, writing, collaboration, and publishing processes. Mendeley is an easy-to-use reference management tool with only self-help online tools available for researchers. However, in the last two years, with its integration with Elsevier, it has made available more varied support resources for new users. It is widely believed to be more effective to provide structured support for early career researchers versus just-in-time support for seasoned researchers; and structured support for STEM disciplines versus just-in-time for non-STEM disciplines.

This study first defines the baseline differences in user adoption and productivity rates between different disciplines (STEM versus non-STEM users) and academic statuses (undergraduates, graduates, post-docs, professors). Then, by applying different library resources (in-person training sessions, help aid, tutorial video, and on demand support) in selected US institutions, this project attempts to understand the effects of different support resources to eventual user adoption and productivity.

Objective

The objective of the study is to understand the user adoption and productivity rate of a reference management tool such as Mendeley between different discipline and academic statuses and how they are affected by different structured and just-in-time learning and support resources.

Academic Institution Participants

- Michigan State University: Tina Qin, qinna@mail.lib.msu.edu
- York University: Rajiv Nariani, rajivn@yorku.ca
- Montana State University: Hannah McKelvey, hannah.mckelvey@montana.edu
- Stanford University: Helen Josephine, helenj@stanford.edu
- Touro College: Carrie Levinson, carrie.levinson2@touro.edu
- Carnegie Mellon University: Lynn Berardm lberard@andrew.cmu.edu

Requirements to Participate for Academic Institutions

- Assign a librarian project lead
- Give permission to analyze new users' behavioral data between January 1, 2015 and May 8, 2015
- Give permission to send a user survey to all "new registered users" between the weeks of May 11 and May 20
- Librarian project lead to track and diary all known activities to promote Mendeley on campus
- Total commitment hours: eight hours per month, April and May

Benefits to Participate for Academic Institutions

- Librarian is listed on the poster session as co-author and can reuse findings
- Mendeley to provide data analyzed specific to the institution; no individual user info can be released

http://dx.doi.org/10.5703/1288284316284

Methods

Baseline/Current Context Analysis

Aggregated analysis on user adoption and productivity rate across worldwide users will first be conducted to establish the current as-is baseline. This will tell us the differences in behavior and activities of STEM versus non-STEM discipline areas as well as differences between academic statuses (undergraduates, graduates, post-docs, professors).

Selected, Longitudinal Study

With the cooperation and collaboration of 3-5 US and Canadian academic institutions, we will be following new users from January through May 2015 and examine their user behavior and usage of different learning and support resources. Both quantitative (data analysis) as well as qualitative (user survey) will be deployed to get detailed analytics as well as user feedback. In addition, reviews with librarians will also be conducted to get a thorough cross-section review.

Last, with the information from the baseline analysis as well as the selected longitudinal analysis, this will help both the software provider (Mendeley) as well as the librarian/information resources professionals to best charter the right designs and best practices to better enable students and researchers.

Analysis

- Mendeley user adoption is highly seasonal because of the influences of academic institutional terms
- Highest new user adoption months are September and January, matching to the start of new school terms

See Figure 1 in the Appendix.

- Mendeley active user numbers are also seasonal because of the influences of academic institutional terms
- A positive correlation ($R^2 > 0.5$) can be noticed in the active user numbers as new users continue to join Mendeley

See Figure 2 in the Appendix.

- "New user" adoption of the 6 partner universities seem to remain relatively consistent to the CONTROL line
- However, activities specifically at Stanford.edu, Yorku.ca, and MSU.edu have resulted in different patterns

See Figure 3 in the Appendix.

- "Active users" from the 6 partner universities seem to remain stable across all groups
- They appear relatively consistent from 2014 to 2015

See Figure 4 in the Appendix.

Library Activity Analysis

Definition

- Structured on-line (librarian initiated): library websites, LibGuide, tutorial videos
- Structured in-person (librarian initiated): classroom training, department updates, research group meetings, research day events, graduate/undergraduate services
- Ad hoc on-line (user initiated): online library chat, e-mail, phone call
- Ad hoc in-person (user initiated): in-library inquiry
- Social, promotions: blog, Twitter, Facebook, posters, eNewsletter

See Figure 5 in the Appendix.

- The 6 partner universities documented a total of 99 hours of libraries supporting Mendeley users during March through May 2015
- It is difficult to draw correlations based on limited data as well as not optimal user activity periods
- But it is interesting to see, again, the positive "new user" and "active user" activities during April in almost all the institutions

See Figure 6 in the Appendix.

See Figure 7 in the Appendix.

User Feedback: Learning Resources With Most Impact on Discipline

1. "Colleagues/collaborator" recommendation is the highest impact in all academic statuses
2. Professors are then most affected by "online video & tutorial" as well "newsletters and direct e-mails"
3. "Library website" has high impact on researchers
4. "Library training sessions" has high impact on PhDs

User Feedback: Learning Resources With Most Impact on Lengths of Usage

5. "Colleagues/collaborator" recommendation and "online video & tutorial" are almost equal in impact for all users
6. New users are most affected by various social media and direct communications (i.e., newsletter, department announcement)
7. "Library website" and "Library training sessions" are then secondarily effective for all users

Conclusion

Objective #1: To understand the user adoption pattern of a reference management tool such as Mendeley

- User adoption and user "activeness" is heavily influenced by seasonality
- Structured in-person training appears to have the most immediate impact on adoption numbers
- Other promotional activities (such as Research Day) seem to have a multiday effect

Objective #2: To understand differences between discipline and academic statuses and how they are affected by different learning and support resources

- "Colleagues/collaborator" recommendation is the highest influencer in all academic statuses as well as disciplines
- Professors are the most affected by "online video & tutorial" as well "newsletters and direct e-mails"
- Non-STEM disciplines (i.e., environmental sciences and humanities) are more favorable towards various library website and support services
- New users are most affected by various social media and direct communications (i.e., newsletter, department announcement)

Appendix

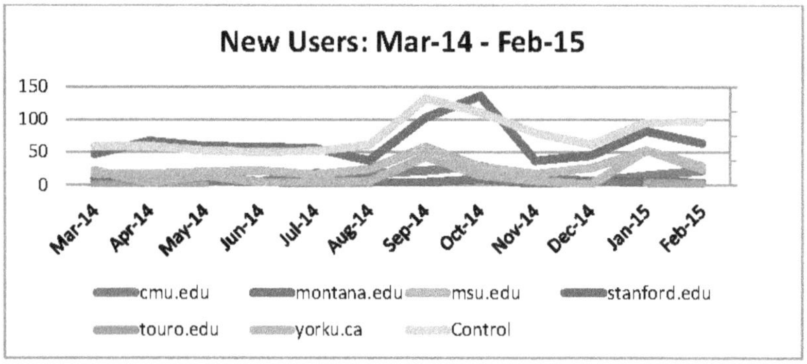

Figure 1. New users: Mar 14–Feb 2015.

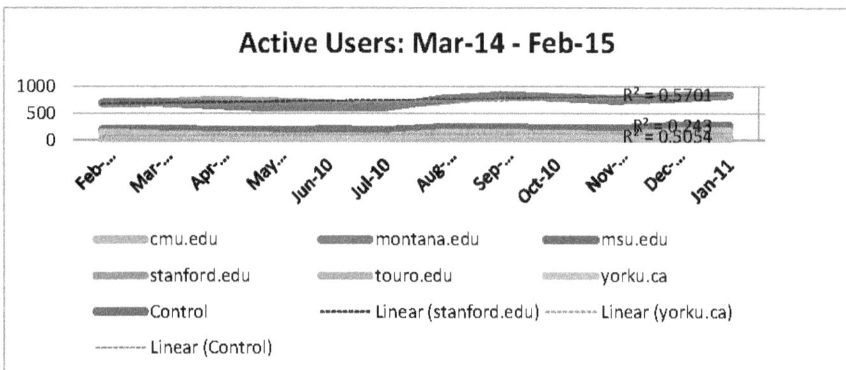

Figure 2. Active users: Mar 14–Feb 2015.

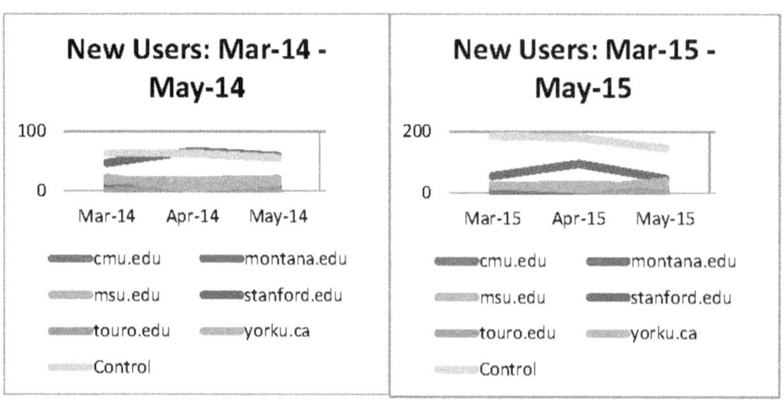

Figure 3. New users: Mar–May 2014; Mar–May 2015.

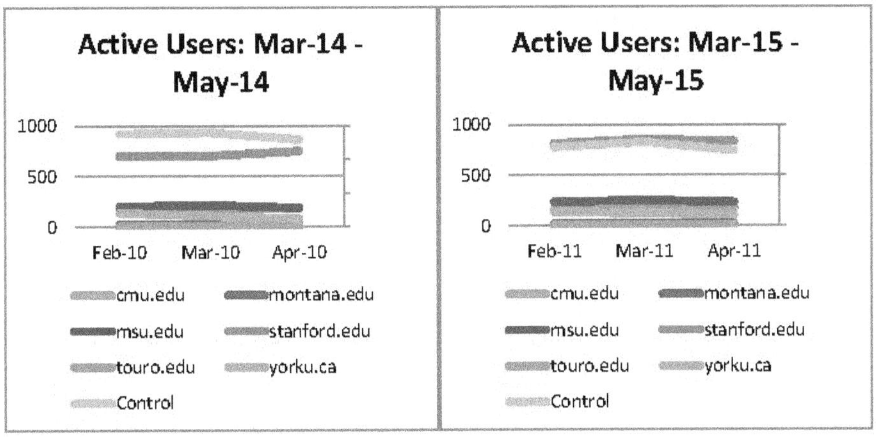

Figure 4. Active users: Mar–May 2014; Mar–May 2015.

MENDELEY

Analysis: Library Activity Analysis

Total amount of 'Mendeley' learning resources applied by each university through March – May 2015

	Carnegie Mellon University	Michigan State University	Montana State University	Stanford University	Touro College	York University
Structured on-line	64%	0%	20%	7%	25%	58%
Structured in-person	21%	80%	70%	21%	63%	12%
Ad-hoc on-line	0%	20%	5%	0%	0%	11%
Ad-hoc in-person	14%	0%	5%	71%	0%	10%
Social, promotion	0%	0%	0%	0%	13%	10%
TOTAL HOURS	14	10	10	7	4	54

*March – May 2015 Total library activities tracked by 6 partners

Figure 5. Analysis: Library activity analysis (Mendeley).

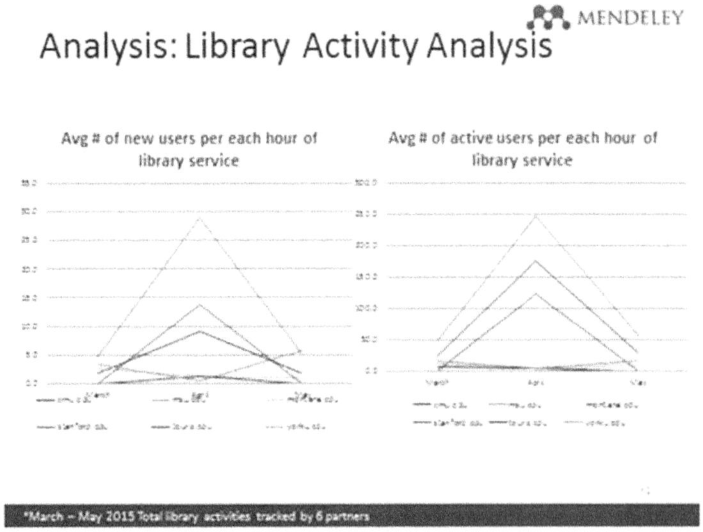

Figure 6. Analysis: Library activity analysis (Mendeley).

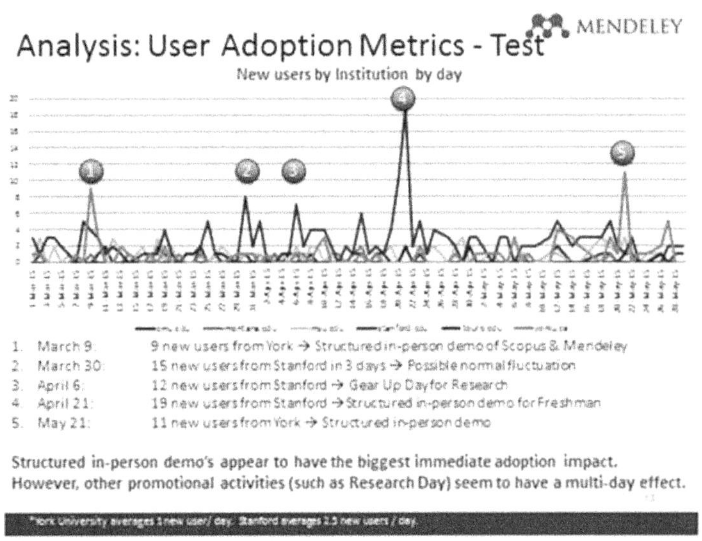

Figure 7. Analysis: User AdoptionMetrics – test (Mendeley).

Next Steps in Discovery Implementation: User-Centered Discovery System Redesign

Richard Guajardo, Head of Resource Discovery Systems, University of Houston

Kelsey Brett, Discovery Systems Librarian, University of Houston

Frederick Young, Systems Analyst, University of Houston

Abstract

This paper will discuss a discovery system redesign project at the University of Houston Libraries, and in particular the Discovery Redesign Team's collaborative, user-centered approach. Throughout the redesign process, the team collected information about the needs and expectations of internal and external users regarding the Library's discovery system. The team worked with two internal working groups to gather and evaluate the collected information. The results of this evaluation were used to make user-centered design decisions.

The Discovery Redesign Team worked with the Discovery Advisory Group, made up of library employees from various departments, to seek feedback and suggestions throughout the redesign process. Working collaboratively with this Group informed design decisions made by the team while also generating buy-in for the discovery redesign.

The team worked with the Discovery Usability Group to collect information from end-users to inform the Team's design decisions. The Committee held focus groups with the Library Information Desk staff to learn how the discovery system was serving users, and where it was falling short; they conducted usability tests with students to find out where users were experiencing breakdowns while completing common tasks. The methodologies and findings of the team's various activities will be discussed.

Changes to system interfaces affect both internal and external users. The University of Houston's discovery system redesign is an example of a successful, user-centered, collaborative design project.

Background

Over the past several years the University of Houston (UH) Libraries has made several attempts to implement a discovery solution that would provide an intuitive and seamless search and retrieval experience for users, and improve access to electronic resources. Initially, we offered our patrons federated search tools such as the Library Find developed by Oregon State University Libraries. Later we implemented the Encore platform from Innovative Interfaces, bundled with a federated search tool called Research Pro. At the time, both products required a heavy investment in staff time for implementation and maintenance. Encore was just completing its beta-test period and required installation of numerous updates; the number of resources available with these federated search tools was very limited. None of these products were well received by librarians and staff. In particular the Encore implementation left many here with a negative impression of discovery systems.

In 2010 we implemented SerialsSolution's Summon discovery system. Summon became the default search option on the library website, and was branded OneSearch. Electronic resources usage statistics in the following years indicated that Summon exponentially increased exposure to and use of electronic resources, an important consideration for the UH Libraries. Relevancy ranking and usability were also much improved from previous discovery implementations. These factors helped restore confidence in discovery among librarians and staff. However, Summon

http://dx.doi.org/10.5703/1288284316285

was not without its weaknesses. Summon had very few customization options, which was a point of frustration for the department responsible for managing it. Summon customers did not have a lot of control over what new features were implemented and when. For example, when SerialsSolutions developed Summon 2.0, customers were initially required to migrate to it by a certain date. Evaluations by the Summon community and our own internal evaluation revealed significant flaws in the 2.0 platform; we were not comfortable releasing it to our patrons, or being on the vendor's timetable for deploying new releases.

Two years after implementing our first discovery platform, we decided to take another look at the discovery systems available. Our reevaluation of discovery systems began in 2012. We used our previous experiences with discovery systems as a starting point for evaluating the options and in deciding on our next steps with discovery systems. In 2014 we implemented the Primo discovery system from Ex Libris; it was selected primarily for the customization capabilities available to us as customers.

We completed the Primo implementation during the spring of 2014, and launched the new system in a soft rollout on the first day of the 2014 summer session. We did not promote the new system to end users, and presented it as a OneSearch upgrade rather than a completely new system. Having fewer patrons on campus during the roll-out period allowed librarians and staff time to adjust to the new interface before the start of the fall academic session. Primo was implemented with few modifications. This allowed us time to become more familiar with the administrative functions, evaluate user feedback on the interface, and plan for additional features and customizations.

Conversations With Internal Users

At the UH Libraries the maintenance and development of the discovery platform is one of the responsibilities of the resource discovery systems (RDS) department. In order to foster buy-in from internal stakeholders, it is important that RDS work collaboratively with colleagues to make decisions about the system interface. This collaborative approach had been used before by RDS to facilitate the deployment of new OPAC releases and enhancements. The department worked closely with its OPAC Advisory Group. After implementing Summon, the OPAC group was asked to evaluate the interaction between Summon and the OPAC; the group eventually began evaluating the Summon interface as part of their charge.

As the discovery system became the prominent user-interface for search and access, the group shifted its focus to discovery and was renamed the Discovery Advisory Group (DAG). The members of the DAG represent various library departments and bring unique perspectives and experiences. During the initial implementation of Primo, the DAG provided support for including some OPAC elements into the discovery interface. For example, the material type icons used in the OPAC were carried forward into Primo as content types. The DAG also recommended that the advanced search and browse Search options be more prominent and allow users to conduct phrase searches for known items. Their perspectives were valuable and carefully considered as we made implementation decisions, and their involvement in the process helped strengthen buy-in and support for Primo from our colleagues.

We continued to collaborate with the DAG in the months following the Primo implementation to collect feedback and suggestions from various departments to improve Primo. One activity conducted by the DAG during that time was a competitive analysis of Primo instances at peer and aspirational institutions. This gave us several ideas about how we could improve our Primo interface, and we drew heavily from some of their examples while we developed it. One advantage of Primo was having access to a development sandbox where we could experiment with different ideas. RDS implemented several of the DAG's suggestions. We reviewed them together on the sandbox and decided which changes to implement on the live Primo instance. RDS made numerous changes to the look and feel of the Primo interface in the development sandbox, and

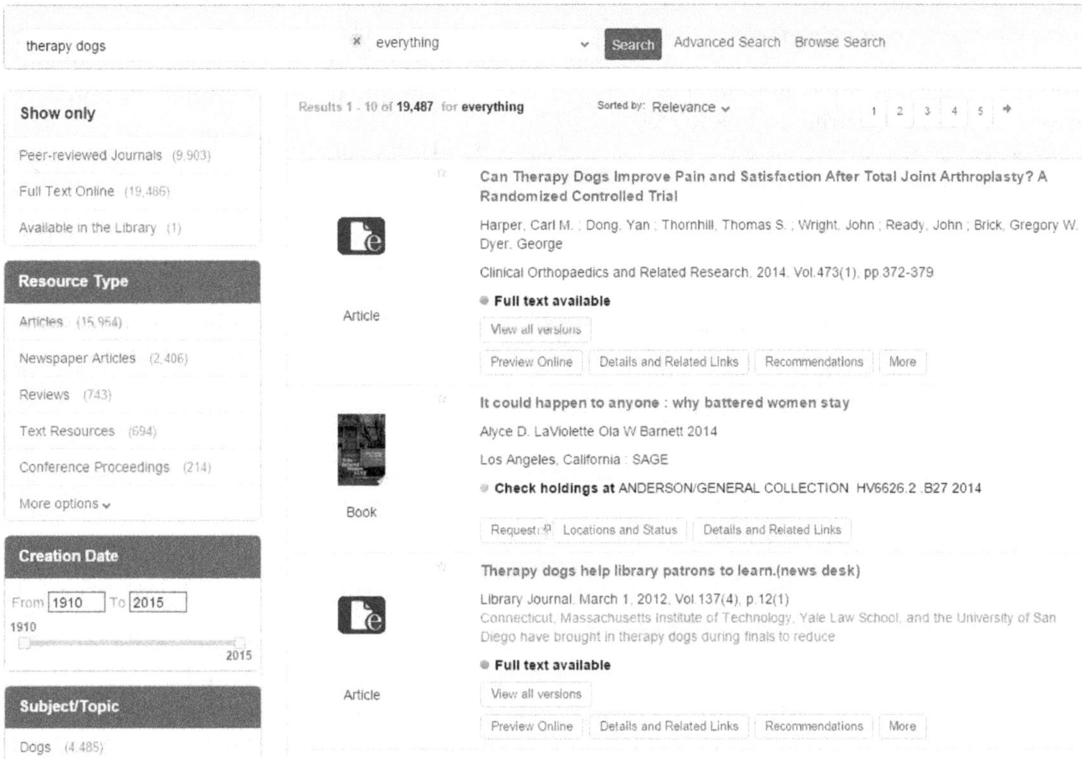

Figure 1. Primo: Soft rollout with minimal customizations.

planned to launch a redesigned interface in the summer of 2015—one year after the initial implementation.

Conversations With External Users

Just as it is important to work collaboratively with internal stakeholders, it is also important for RDS to collect feedback from end users to inform the development process. RDS works with an additional group, the Discovery Usability Group (DUG), which is made up of individuals from various departments and is charged with determining what our users need from a discovery system and testing the usability of the discovery system to help determine its effectiveness. Similar to the Discovery Advisory Group, the DUG started out with a focus on the OPAC and shifted toward discovery as it became the prominent search interface. The DUG uses a variety of methods to assess the discovery system, such as focus groups and usability testing. The results of these assessments are used to make recommendations for Primo customizations and developments. In the year following the Primo implementation, the Discovery Usability Group conducted a series of activities that helped RDS and the Discovery Advisory Committee determine needed improvements and make customizations to improve usability.

In the fall of 2014, the DUG conducted a focus group with student workers who staff the library's information desk, which provides both reference and circulation services. The focus group took place several months after the Primo implementation and the participants had experience with both Summon and Primo. The DUG was interested in their perspectives because they commonly assist users at the desk and see firsthand the strengths and weakness of the system. Several student workers attended the session and provided valuable feedback. Some of the primary takeaways from the focus group included the following:

- OneSearch is most useful for finding electronic resources—if a patron is looking for a physical item the library catalog is the preferred tool

- OneSearch is a good tool "if you do not know what you are looking for"
- The limit to full-text and limit to peer review features are extremely helpful when assisting patrons
- The "View Online" option is confusing because it opens in a small window within the search results page
- Finding an item in OneSearch that we do not have access to is not helpful for users
- The most used facets are resource type and date
- The current save functionality is not useful because it is not permanent
- Links that do not resolve properly are extremely frustrating but have noticeably improved
- Experiences with OneSearch are more positive than negative

Based on the feedback and suggestions collected from the focus group, RDS made several modifications to the discovery interface on the Primo sandbox. The facets were redesigned to look cleaner and less cluttered; enhancements to the date facet made it more functional; and the most useful facets were promoted to the top of the facet list. Additionally, the "View Online" tab was renamed "Preview Online" because it more accurately represents the function of the tab and search results that were limited to the Libraries's holdings as a default. RDS also began exploring the possibility of implementing accounts for users to permanently save search results.

In the spring of 2014, the Discovery Usability Group conducted a usability study to find out if users could complete common research tasks using Primo. The group developed a usability test which asked users to complete a set of common research tasks and verbalize their thought process as they completed each task. Because significant customizations had already been made to the development sandbox, the Group tested users on the sandbox rather than the live site.

Key findings from the usability study include:

- Users appreciate pre-search filtering options and expect more of them
- Users tend to change their search terms if they do not find what they are looking for
- Users typically do not make use of the facets
- Users click on the title to access resources rather than system-provided mechanisms such as the "Preview Online" tab
- Users do not understand the meaning of library and academic jargon such as peer-reviewed, Digital Library, and checkout
- Users do not readily distinguish between newspaper articles and scholarly articles

Several recommendations were made as a result of the usability study. RDS used the recommendations to make additional customizations in the Primo development sandbox. We renamed the "Peer-reviewed Journals" facet to "Peer-reviewed Articles" because the word "Journals" confused users trying to find an article. We removed the "UH Digital Library" as a limiting option in the drop-down menu next to the search box because participants misinterpreted it several times throughout the study. We added "Articles+" as an option in the drop-down menu in order to increase pre-search filtering options that participants expected. Finally, we ensured that a title click would take the user directly to the resource.

Some recommendations could not be implemented at the time due to limitations of the system or lack of consensus. Among these were call numbers that linked to their appropriate places on the stacks guide, and removing newspaper articles from the default search. It should be noted that many of the breakdowns identified during the usability study, such as misunderstanding academic jargon, cannot necessarily be addressed with technological solutions.

Redesign, Features, and Enhancements

An incremental approach to rolling out the discovery platform allowed RDS to make gradual improvements to its interface. These improvements were informed by the Discovery Usability Group's (DUG) analysis of external users and the Discovery Advisory Groups (DAG) input from internal users. To a great extent, we were able to keep the user's perspective in the forefront our our design decisions.

One of the reasons for selecting our current discovery platform, Primo, was that it provides users with the ability to customize their search experience. This functionality is made available in the "My Account" feature. Incorporating this feature into the discovery display was delayed because RDS wanted this feature to work in conjunction with a single sign-on solution for the library—which had not yet been developed but was under consideration. In the initial release, users only had access to the "e-Shelf." This allowed them to save search results, but only for the current session. Once the browser was closed, saved results were lost. Information provided by the DUG indicated that this was a point of frustration for users.

Wanting to fully implement the "My Account" feature, we began discussions with the library's web services and computer support and networking departments. After some investigation, it was determined that the implementation of a centralized authentication service (CAS) would allow us to roll out "My Account" features. A key factor in selecting the CAS was that it could be used with the library's off-campus authentication services, EZProxy. The CAS also has the potential to become a single sign-on portal for the library's online services. Once a user logs into one of the library's online platforms, they can use other library services without having to reauthenticate—thus providing a more seamless library experience.

With the implementation of the "My Account" feature, students have the ability to permanently save search results and have access to a customized relevancy ranking of search results based on a subject area they have associated with their user account. Off-campus users, once they log into their discovery platform accounts, are seamlessly authenticated for off-campus access to resources.

From internal users, there was a desire to have research guides display more prominently in the search results. To accomplish this, subject specialists added metadata—in the form of tags—to the research guides, using the guide's native interface. This additional data would be included in the XML export file. The normalization rules—used to ingest data into the discovery index—were modified to make use of the additional metadata. The result was a slight boost in visibility for the research guides in search results. The additional metadata also made it possible for patrons to find course-specific research guides by using variations of the course name or course number. In some instances, however, the guides were not displayed on the initial page of search results as desired. After some consideration, adjustments to the relevancy settings in the discovery platform were made; more weight was given to title and subject categories. This allowed us to achieve the desired result. It should be noted that adjustments to relevancy settings should be made sparingly and with care so as to avoid undesired changes in search results.

Another way that we improved visibility of the research guides was the inclusion of the subject area specialist's photo in the search results. These images were available in the research guide's native interface. The URL for the images was included in the XML export file. A local field was added to the normalization rules for research guides, and tweaked with HTML so that once processed, the subject specialist's image would appear in the search result. Custom CSS was applied to the images so that their appearance was consistent in the discovery interface.

One take-away from the focus group discussion with the Information Desk was that sometimes features need to be scaled back in order to be useful. The initial rollout of discovery interface was described as busy, cluttered, and difficult to read. A close examination of the information

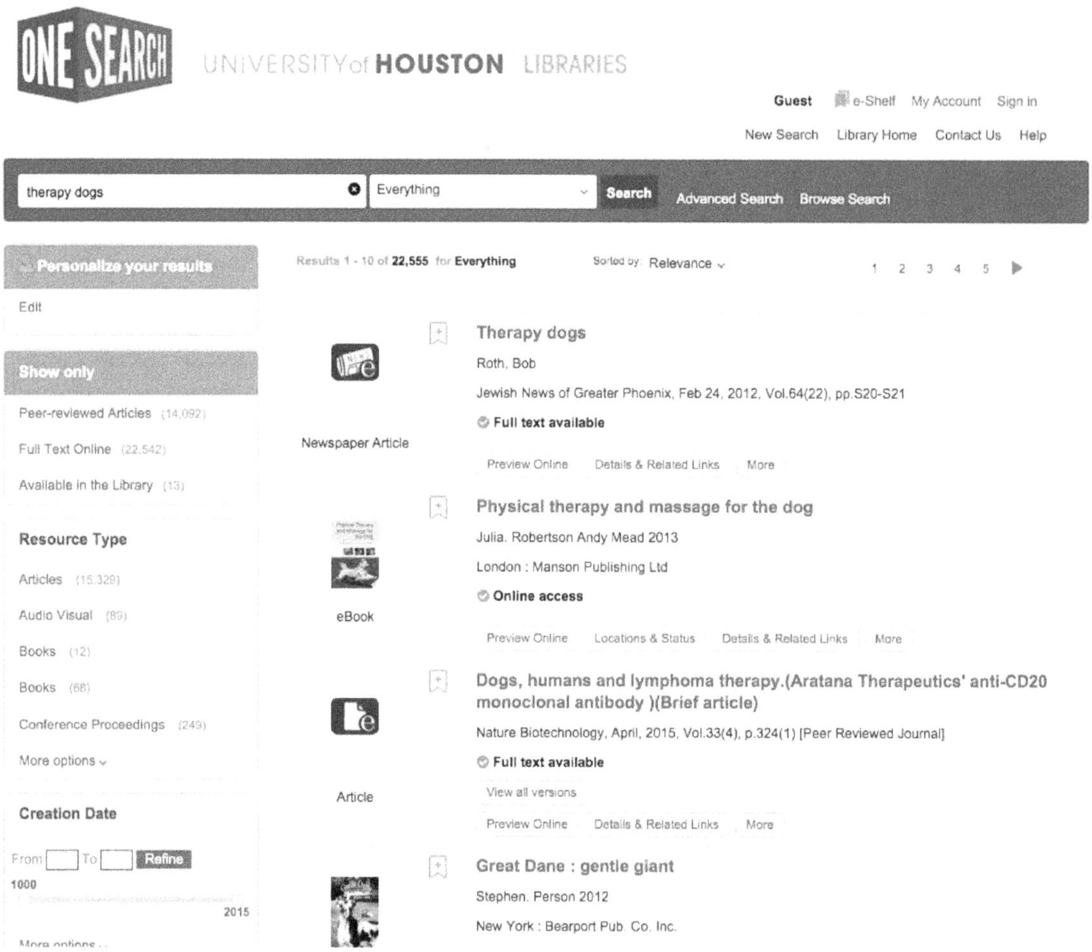

Figure 2. Primo: Results of redesign, summer 2015.

displayed coupled with feedback from the DAG's competitive analysis gave us some ideas about how to address this issue. We took the following actions:

- Redundant displays of information and features that were used infrequently were removed
- Features that were not easily understood, such as the Bx recommendations at the top of the search results display, were hidden
- Additional whitespace was incorporated into the display, especially within the facets groups and the details of individual search results
- Tabs in some areas were converted to buttons for a cleaner and more intuitive appearance
- Labels for facets and tabs, some of which contained library jargon, were modified in an effort to more clearly convey their purpose (e.g., "Queries" was changed to "Search History")
- Facets categories were prioritized—the most frequently used facets were moved to the top of the list, and the least used facets were removed
- The functions of some actions in the discovery display were modified to better meet user expectations (e.g., clicking the title now takes the user to full-text instead of taking the user to additional details about the item)

These adjustments to the discovery interface have remarkably changed its appearance and have received feedback from internal users indicating that the interface is easier to read and understand.

Conclusions

- Combining our previous discovery experience with a collaborative evaluation of the discovery landscape allowed us to select a system more suited to our user needs, as well as generate buy-in from internal users.
- Deploying the discovery platform during the summer session, when the user population is lower, allowed internal users the much needed time to become familiar with the new system, its features, and functions.
- Enlisting the experience and expertise of existing OPAC groups for discovery provided valuable user-centered input for the redesign. Information provided by the DAG and the DUG significantly informed decisions made for the redesign, inclusion of features, and deployment of enhancements.

Future Plans

- Continue conversations with internal and external users
- Work with branch libraries to develop scoped views
- Work with special collections to include finding aids in discovery
- Work with digitization services to improve access to digitized collections

The User-Driven Collection 4.0: The Next Phase in User-Driven Monographic Acquisition

Darby Orcutt, Assistant Head of Collection Management, North Carolina State University Libraries

Abstract

For more than a decade, the North Carolina State University (NCSU) Libraries has had some level of user-driven collecting. Periodically building upon the success of these programs, which has often entailed pushing vendor and library systems beyond their current capacities, the Libraries is now poised to move most of our monographic selection into user-driven pools.

Context

The "4.0" in my title refers to the fact that I realized I've now led or co-led at least four major stages of our user-driven book collecting—an approach to selection that was barely conceivable when I began my career.

In 2003 at the North Carolina State University Libraries, we modestly began our first user-driven acquisitions program, "Books on Demand." Frankly, it was not much of a stretch. When newer books that we did not own were requested via Interlibrary Loan (ILL)—and they fit certain cost and publisher criteria that mirrored those of our book approval plan—ILL staff purchased books for the collection rather than borrowing them. The overwhelming majority were titles selectors would have purchased anyhow if requested, so why not save the extra steps?

By 2009 or 2010, vendors finally offered somewhat robust "purchase on demand" models for e-book acquisition (what is known today as "demand-driven acquisition," or DDA). With increasing e-book availability, we soon also made the move with YBP, our primary monograph vendor, to "e-preferred" status, seeking to maximize our online holdings.

The size of our DDA program grew and grew, as did our proportion of e-book acquisition. A key factor in making these programs work was that we always *curated* the collection of potentially triggered titles—not on a title basis, but using various automated criteria available via YBP's profiling structure.

We were always a little ahead of the pack, however. Our first request to YBP to move to "e-preferred" came before they had a system for handling that. And our subsequent desires to push the envelope similarly were not—and in fact, *still* are not—directly available via YBP's current profiling capacities. This is not to say that YBP is behind their competitors, nor to say that they haven't been excellent partners in helping us figure out when and how to use their current system in ways that it was not intended to accomplish what we hope to do. And I know from my conversations with YBP that our approach to collection development is helping inform the next version of their GOBI database.

Books by Request (BBR)

In 2012, I conceived of and we implemented a new "Books By Request" (BBR) program, populating our catalog with titles not yet owned, indicating to users that these titles will be rush-ordered upon request (and there's a button right there with which they can do so). BBR is managed in-house, although requires the type of backend work that perhaps YBP could provide in the future. A user request results in an e-book purchase (if available), or a print purchase and patron hold if not.

A number of things had been bothering me about the ways in which our traditional book and slip approval plans didn't fully enable our preferences for e-books and DDA:

1. We were still acquiring a fair amount of print, despite rapid availability of many

http://dx.doi.org/10.5703/1288284316286

titles in e-book or even DDA versions shortly thereafter.

2. By purchasing print on a "just in case" basis, we were rewarding the very publishers who were not acting in the ways that we wanted (in other words, I wanted to encourage timely electronic and DDA availability, not fund their absence).

The benefits of this BBR program are many:

1. Every book purchased is a wanted (and likely used) book.
2. By waiting until time of need rather than time of publication, there is a greatly increased chance of e-book (or even DDA) availability.
3. Even if no e-book is available, there is a greatly increased chance of a more cost-effective paperbound edition having become available.

I will note that I do not necessarily regard BBR as a means of reducing costs. What it definitely does do is shift costs into the future (in other words, when the book is needed rather than when it is published). I first proposed implementing it in a particularly poor budget year, so that it would and did actually become part of our strategy for riding out a temporary drought—but time will tell if it reduces costs regularly or simply just better aligns collections expenditures with actual, expressed user needs. (If all it does is that, I'll be very happy!)

Prior to this approach, we were not taking advantage of changes in the marketplace. When I started at NC State in 2001, or even for many years after that, delaying purchase would not have made sense at all. In those times, academic books routinely went out of print and became unavailable. In today's world, delaying purchase generally lowers costs—and very little becomes unavailable (and almost nothing unpredictably so).

The Next Phase

Our current phase of BBR implementation essentially means a complete overhaul and replacement of our approval plan—and has required our working with YBP to engineer pools of potential titles using systems never intended for such complex criteria. What we are currently doing is thrusting virtually our entire approval plan (books and slips) into user-driven models, with DDA our preferred model, and automatically populating BBR records in our catalog. We have completed extensive analysis of the criteria by which we generate pools of possible monographic content from which users may select.

We found that publisher was the greatest predictor of future e-book availability—fortunately, because that is the highest-level filter that YBP offers for approval plans, and we had to essentially create extra, parallel approval plans to move from the excluded, book, slip outcomes of traditional approval plans to instead add an extra layer: excluded, book, auto-BBR slip, slip.

This may not (at least immediately) mean the end of title-by-title selection by our collection managers, although for many it will greatly reduce that burden, freeing their time for other significant activities. More importantly, this approach means that we are better aligning our actual approval expenditures with our goals: (1) addressing user needs, and (2) making sure our money flows most freely to those publishers who are offering not just the best content, but also our preferred format (electronic) and preferred model (DDA).

The 2014 Credo Survey

Adam McKiel, Dean of Library Services, Western Oregon University

Abstract

The Credo Survey addressed student research skills. Two parallel surveys over the same questions were addressed separately to students and faculty, which had respectively 2,606 and 472 respondents. Just less than 90% of the students were undergraduates split nearly evenly in progress to completion, with 87% of respondents attending full-time and a fairly representative spread of majors. Just less than 50% of the faculty had taught over 10 years with nearly even proportions spread across the first 10 years and with a representative sampling of disciplines. Seventy-seven percent were full-time. The majority of responses came from about a dozen institutions—half universities and half colleges or community colleges. This article reviews and compares the student and faculty responses. It also compares the student responses with similar questions from the 2012 Credo Reference Survey.

Survey Review

Finding Information

Faculty and Student Question 5: How often do you think your students [you], on average, use the library to do research or ask for help (not including studying, typing papers, printing, etc.)?

Answer Choices	Responses - Faculty	Responses - Students
At Least Once a Semester	53%	38%
At Least Once a Month	31%	29%
At Least Once a Week	15%	32%
Total Responses	424	2,477

Question 5 asked both faculty and students about how often students use the library to do research or ask for help (not including studying, typing papers, printing, etc.); once a semester, month, or week? Students viewed their use of the library for research as more extensive than faculty's perceptions. Students answered once a semester 39%, monthly 29%, and weekly 32%. Faculty answered 53%, 31%, and 15% respectively.

Faculty Question 12: Where do you think students start their research?

Answer Choices	Responses - Faculty	Responses - Students
Library - Encyclopedias	1%	1%
Library - Article Databases	7%	26%
Class Materials (textbook, notes, etc.)	9%	4%
Library - Catalog	1%	17%
Web - Google	72%	48%
Web - Wikipedia	10%	2%
Other (students only)		2%
Total Responses	392	2,315

In question 12, where faculty were asked where they think students start their research, 82% selected the web compared to 50% of the students. The faculty assumed students started in the library in 9% of the responses compared to 44% of the students' responses. Class material was selected by 9% of the faculty and 4% of students.

Faculty and Student Question 10: What do you think students are [What are you] most comfortable with regarding their [your] research skills? (open-ended responses)

Verbs	Students	Nouns	Students		Faculty	Nouns
Find/Search	1,114	Internet	170		Internet	25
Write	95	Online	167		Google	15
		Articles	158		Library	7
		Books	134		Database	7
		Databases	115		Online	3
		Google	49			
		Everything	30			
		EBSCO	9			
	Total Comments 2,092				Total Comments 339	

Question 10 was open-ended for students and asked, "What do you feel most comfortable with regarding research?" The most common verbs referred to the process of searching. Some variation of find or search was used in 1,114 of the 2,092 comments.

The most common nouns associated with what they liked were Internet (170 mentions), online (167), library (158), articles (134), books (126), and databases (115). All of these refer to online resources except libraries, articles, and books, which include both physical and online resources. Since library usage of print articles is a very small

http://dx.doi.org/10.5703/1288284316287

percentage of article usage and book versus e-book usage varies based on their percentage of availability, the term library refers mostly to online resources. There was a noticeable number of references to the wealth of resources available through the library and the ease of using them, more than recollections from other surveys indicate. There were only 95 appearances of the word write and 30 of the word everything. There were only 9 references to EBSCO and 49 to Google, which both figured less prominently than expected. Both changes may be associated to some degree with the increasing number of library systems that have discovery systems like Encore and Primo.

The faculty in question 10 were asked, "What do you think students are most comfortable with regarding their research skills?" The nouns the faculty used, in descending order, were Internet (25), Google (15), library (7), database (7), and online (3). There was no mention of books or articles in the 339 responses. Faculty commented on student use of the open web over library resources.

Faculty and Student Question 11: What do you think intimidates students [you] most about research assignments?

Students			Faculty	
Finding and Evaluating Appropriate Sources	320		Citations	61
Writing the Paper	249		Finding and Evaluating Appropriate Sources	26
Citing Sources	108			
Total Comments 2,136			Total Comments 354	

In question 11, students were asked, "What intimidates you most about research assignments?" "Finding" was the primary verb with 320 uses. Sources and information is what they were having difficulty finding. The most popular adjectives used to describe the difficulty were relevant, credible, and reliable. "Writing" was the second most used verb with 107 instances. The term "paper" was used 142 times in relation to comments like sorting it all out, putting it all together, and starting it. Citing sources was mentioned 108 times.

In question 11, faculty were asked, "What do you think intimidates students most about research assignments?" Faculty referred to the same problems the students reported. However, they mentioned them with different frequency. A greater percentage of faculty than students mentioned the problems students have with citations, which was mentioned 61 times in the 354 responses. Finding appropriate sources was reported 50 times with 11 of the responses referring to student difficulty evaluating information resources. Other prominent comments concerned students' difficulties with knowing how to begin, selecting the topic, organizing the research, and writing the paper.

Guidance and Instruction on Research Skills

Question 15 asked students, "Have you taken a course on information or research skills?" Twenty-six percent reported that they had.

Faculty Question 9: Do you give your students guidance on sources to use for research?

Answer Choices	Faculty	Students
Never	3%	5%
Sometimes	24%	46%
Frequently	32%	37%
Always	42%	12%
Total	425	2,513

Students and faculty appear to have different understandings of guidance and instruction concerning research skills, which show up in their responses to questions about who does instruction. The instructors reported providing instruction much more often than the students reported receiving it. Students and faculty have a reverse order set of responses to question 9, "How often do your instructors give you guidance on sources to use for research?" The students ranked options "sometimes" 46%, "frequently" 37%, and "always" 12%. Faculty ranked them 24%, 32%, and 42% percent respectively.

Student Question 13: Who do you ask for help when you have a research assignment?

Answer Choices	Student Responses	Faculty Responses
Your Professor	51%	34%
Classmate or Friend	27%	52%
Librarian	11%	14%
Family Member	6%	1%
Other (please specify)	5%	
Total Respondents	2,305	

Students reported asking instructors for help more often than faculty reported providing it compared to others to whom students might turn. Question 13 asked students, "Who do you ask for help when you have a research assignment?" Just over half (51%) of students selected their instructor. Classmates or a friend took second place at 27%, and librarians followed with 11% and family 6%. Faculty thought students asked a classmate or friend 52% of the time, their instructor 34% of the time, librarians 14% of the time, and family 1%.

Student Question 16: Have you received other types of instruction in research skills from a professor or librarian? Please select all that apply:

Answer Choices	Responses
English Class (professor)	73%
Other Class (professor)	35%
Library Presentation in Your Class (librarian)	35%
English Class (librarian)	27%
One-On-One Help From Professor	25%
Freshman Orientation	24%
Workshop in Library	13%
One-On-One Help From Librarian	13%
Other (please specify)	5%
Total Respondents:	2,223

Question 16 asked students, "Have you received other types of instruction in research skills [other than an information literacy course] from a professor or librarian? Please select all that apply." One hundred percent of the students (73% from a professor and 27% from a librarian) reported receiving library instruction in an English class. Students reported having other in-class presentations from both librarians (35%) and the class professor (35%). They also reported one-on-one help from both a professor (25%) and librarian (13%). The other categories of instruction selected were freshman orientation (24%) and workshops in the library (13%).

Faculty Question 17: Have you or a librarian given students instruction in research skills in your class?

Answer Choices	Responses
Yes - I Have	34%
Yes - Librarian	18%
Yes - Both	30%
No	18%
Total Respondents	374

Faculty in question 17 reported providing research instruction in their classes (34% by themselves, 18% by a librarian, and 30% by both). Only 18% of faculty reported not providing instruction in research skills in their classes.

Student Question 17: How useful was the research skills instruction you received?

Answer Choices	Responses
Not Useful At All	3%
Somewhat Useful	30%
Pretty Useful	47%
Very Useful	21%
Total Respondents	2,214

Nearly all of the students in question 17 reported that instruction in research skills was useful (97%). The breakdown was 30% useful, 47% pretty useful, and 21% very useful. So, regardless of what particular instruction the students are referring to, they overwhelmingly reported valuing it.

Student Question 18: How important is doing research to your field of study?

Answer Choices	Responses
Very Important	62%
Somewhat Important	33%
Not Important	5%
Total Respondents	2,256

Question 18 asked students how important doing research is in their field of study. Most, 62%, viewed it as very important, 33% somewhat important, and 5% not important.

Faculty Question 19: Do you use any of the following to deliver research skills instruction? Please select all that apply:

Answer Choices	Responses
Instructions on a Research Assignment	72%
Lecture	68%
In-class Practice	53%
Syllabus	49%
Homework Practice	45%
Supplemental Multimedia or Tutorials	41%
Learning Management System	34%
Total	348

In question 19, faculty reported using a variety of methods for providing instruction in research skills including instructions on a research assignment (72%), lecture (68%), in-class practice (53%), the syllabus (49%), homework practice (45%), supplemental multimedia or tutorials (41%), and a learning management system (34%).

Method of Teaching Research Skills

Faculty and Student Questions 19 and 22: What do you think is the best method for students [you] to learn these skills?

Answer Choices	Faculty	Student
Instructors Teach Research Skills in Disciplines	31%	32%
Take a Research Skills Course	25%	25%
Online Tutorials/Videos On-demand	9%	20%
Librarian Visits to All Classes With Research Assignment	17%	9%
Scheduled Research Consultations With a Librarian	10%	10%
Other (please explain)	9%	4%
Total Respondents	373	2,254

In questions 19 and 22, students and faculty respectively were asked "What would be the best way for you [students] to learn research skills?" Having faculty teach research skills in their classes was favored by the most students (32%) and faculty (31%). Taking a research skills course was second in order of preference for both students (25%) and faculty (25%). On-demand tutorials/videos were in third place for students (20%) and fifth place for faculty (9%). A scheduled research consultation with a librarian was in fourth place for students (10%) and for faculty (10%). Visits by librarians to the class were fifth for students (9%) and third for faculty (17%).

Importance of Teaching Research Skills

Faculty Question 21: If you provide research skills instruction—why do you teach it? Please select all that apply:

Answer Choices	Responses
Responding to a Lack of Student Skills	72%
Necessary in Your Discipline	47%
Responding to Student Requests	29%
I Do Not Provide This Instruction	11%
Mandated by Your Institution	9%
Total Respondents	362

When faculty were asked in question 21, "If you provide research skills instruction—why do you teach it? Please select all that apply," the top three selections were because students lack research skills (72%), it is necessary in their discipline (47%), and student requests (29%).

Faculty Question 20: How big of an impact did the research skills instruction have on the quality of your students' work?

Answer Choices	Responses
No Impact	5%
A Small Impact	27%
A Moderate Impact	50%
A Major Impact	19%
Total Respondents	354

In question 20, faculty were asked, "How big of an impact did the research skills instruction have on the quality of your students' work?" The responses were moderate (50%), small (27%), major (19%), and none (5%).

Faculty Question 15: How does a lack of student skills in this area impact your work as an instructor? (open-ended question)

Most Common Words	# of Times
Time	112
More	66
Research	67
Content	14
Total Responses	326

Question 15 asked faculty the open-ended question, "How does a lack of student skills in this area impact your work as an instructor?" "Time" (112) was the most common word used. The word "more" was used 66 times. Faculty reported using "more time" (26) covering basic "research" (67) skills. One faculty reported, "I have to spend a lot of time helping students and teaching them basic concepts about using research, even when I think they should know the information." The word "content" was used 14 times in sentences, e.g., "It takes away from the time that could be spent teaching other topics."

Faculty Question 23: What do you think is the most important thing students should know about doing research? (open-ended question)

Most Common Words	# of Times
Sources	45
Information	39
Find	28
Evaluate	13
Use	11
Citing	10
Time	9
Total Responses	301

Question 23 asked faculty the open-ended question, "What do you think is the most important thing students should know about doing research?" "Find" (28), "evaluate" (13), and "use" (11) were the most used verbs. "Sources" (45) and "information" (39) were the most common nouns. "Time" (9) was used mostly referring to the time it takes to do research. There were 10 references to citing sources properly.

Student Question 20: Since you have started college, what is the most useful thing you have learned about how to do research? (open-ended question)

Most Common Verbs	# of Times
Use	307
Find	268
Most Common Nouns	**# of Times**
Sources	495
Library	260
Database	254
Time	69
Wikipedia	43
Total Responses	1,966

Question 20 asked students the open-ended question, "Since you have started college, what is the most useful thing you have learned about how to do research?" The two most frequently used verbs were "find" (268) and "use" (307). The most frequently used nouns were "sources" (495), "library" (260), and "database" (254). "Research" was used 206 times as a noun and a verb. "Time" was used 69 times generally associated with managing it. "Wikipedia" was used 43 times. Of those 19 were about not using it and 24 about how to use it.

Research Skills

Faculty and Student Question 14: Faculty were asked their levels of confidence in students' information literacy skills as one of four levels: not very confident, somewhat confident, confident, and very confident; students were asked to rank their own confidence levels.

Summary Table Ranking of Percentages of Faculty and Student Confidence of Student Skills ("confident" + "very confident")

	Student Skills	Students	Faculty
1	Understanding the Ethics of Using Information	71	24
2	Choosing a Topic	70	41
3	Incorporating Sources Into Your Paper	67	24
4	Using Scholarly Information	67	18
5	Searching Library Databases	60	26
6	Narrowing a Broad Topic	59	20
7	Writing a Thesis Statement	57	17
8	Properly Citing Your Sources	57	22
9	Evaluating the Authority of a Source	53	16
	Total Responses	2,317	383

The responses for faculty and students across all of the skills followed skewed patterns in their average confidence levels. The students' confidence level overall was considerably higher on average than the faculty's. The students selected "very confident" on average across the skills 22% of the time, and the faculty 4%. Students selected "confident" 41%, and the faculty 19%. They selected "somewhat confident" on average 29% of the time, and the faculty 46%. Finally, students selected "not very confident" 8% of the time, and the faculty 31%.

Faculty had the most confidence ("confident" + "very confident") in students' ability to select a topic (41%) and the least confidence in their ability to evaluate the authority of a source (16%).

Students had the least confidence in "evaluating the authority of a source" (53%) and the most confidence in "understanding the ethics of using information" (71%). See the confidence rankings table below Question 14 for a comparison of the student and faculty rankings on all nine skills.

In the 2012 survey, students were asked, "When writing a typical research paper in a college or university class, do you generally feel prepared to conduct the required research?" Their responses roughly align with student responses in the 2014/2015 survey.

2014 Survey	Not Very Confident	Somewhat Confident	Confident	Very Confident
Faculty	31%	46%	19%	4%
Students	8%	29%	40%	22%
2012 Survey	Not Prepared	Somewhat Prepared	Adequately Prepared	Very Prepared
Students	3%	34%	46%	16%

The 2012 Credo Student Survey article can be found in *Against the Grain,* April 2013.

(McKiel, A. (2013). Information literacy and e-resources: The Credo student survey. *Against the Grain, 25*(2), 83.)

Summon, EBSCO Discovery Service, and Google Scholar: Comparing Search Performance Using User Queries

John Vickery, Analytics Coordinator & Collection Manager for Social Sciences, NCSU Libraries

Karen Ciccone, Director Natural Resources Library & Research Librarian, Science Informatics

Abstract

When the NCSU Libraries initially subscribed to the Summon Discovery Service in 2009, there were few other competitors on the market and none offered an API interface that could be used to populate the "Articles" portion of our QuickSearch application (http://search.lib.ncsu.edu/). Since then, EBSCO Discovery Service (EDS) has emerged as a viable competitor. Using a random sample of actual user searches and bootstrap randomization tests (also referred to as permutation tests), the NCSU Libraries's Web-Scale Discovery Product Team conducted a study to compare the search performance of Summon, EDS, and Google Scholar.

Introduction

This paper discusses a study done by the NCSU Libraries Web-Scale Discovery Product Team to compare the search performance of Summon, EBSCO Discovery Service, and Google Scholar. The paper provides background on the study and its objectives. We then discuss the study methods and results. This paper and the accompanying presentation at the 2015 Charleston Conference are drawn from a detailed article about the project published by Karen Ciccone and John Vickery in *Evidence Based Library and Information Practice, 10*(1) (2015). Readers are encouraged to consult that article for a more detailed discussion of the study. In addition, the SAS code written for the analysis is discussed in more detail in a paper by John Vickery in the 2015 SAS Global Forum Proceedings (2015). The code is also made available on GitHub at https://github.com/jnvickery/permutations.

Project Background

Similar to many libraries, the NCSU Libraries has invested substantial time, effort, and money into

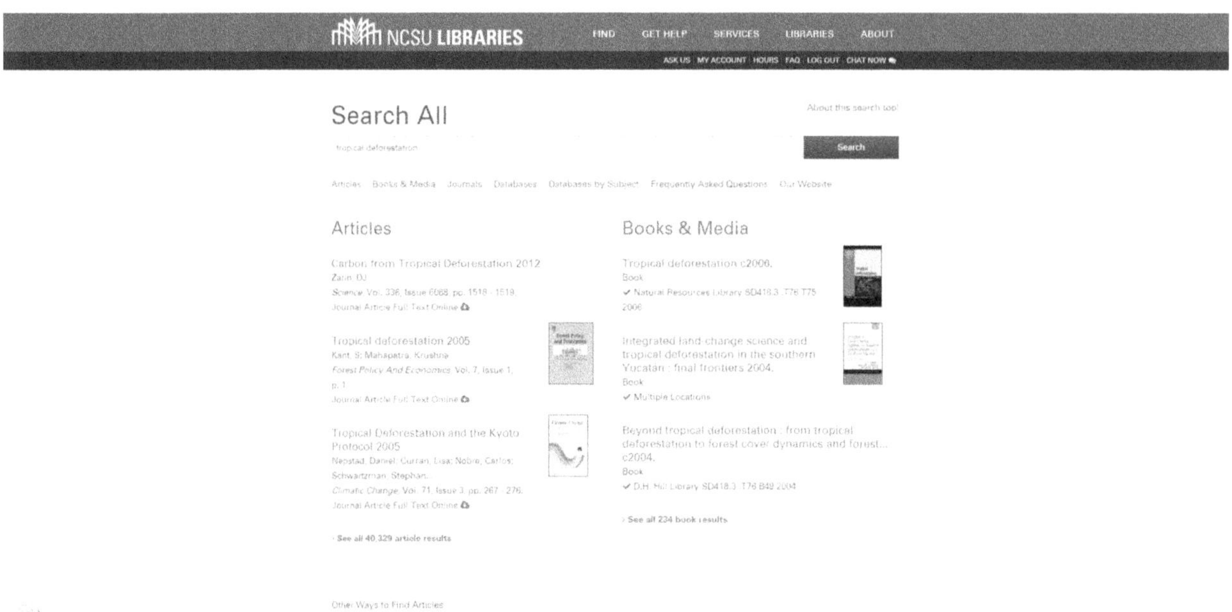

Figure 1. The NCSU Libraries's QuickSearch interface.

http://dx.doi.org/10.5703/1288284316288

implementing a web-scale discovery service. Given this investment, it is important to periodically review competing products to see if they would be a better fit for us either because of price or effectiveness. Our Web-Scale Discovery Product Team is charged with testing and evaluating our existing Summon service as well as other potential products. The team is made up of nine librarians representing public services, technical services, collections, and IT.

At NCSU, we primarily use the Summon API to populate the "Articles" section of our QuickSearch as shown in Figure 1. A search in the QuickSearch application presents separate results for Articles, Books & Media, Our Website, and other information.

In 2009, when the NCSU Libraries implemented Summon, it was the only product that had an API that could be leveraged to be used with our QuickSearch application. Since 2009, other products including EBSCO Discovery Service (EDS) have implemented API functionality. As such, the Web-Scale Discovery Product Team decided a comparison was warranted and a trial for EDS was set up in April and May of 2014 in order to conduct the study.

Other studies have, of course, been conducted to assess the performance of discovery services. In 2013, Asher, Duke, and Wilson compared Summon, EBSCO Discovery Service, and Google Scholar on the basis of search performance. Scores were based on librarian quality ratings of the resources selected by test subjects. Quality of resources was based on whether articles were from scholarly or non-peer-reviewed journals.

In 2013, Rochkind compared user preference for search results from the major discovery systems including EDS, Summon, EBSCOhost "Traditional" API, Ex Libris Primo, and Elsevier's Scopus. Users were presented with side-by-side views of results from two randomly chosen products. Users were then asked to indicate which set of results they preferred, with an option for "Can't Decide/About the Same."

Both of the above studies relied on test subjects entering hypothetical searches. The NCSU study differs in that actual user queries from the Summon log files were used. This provides a sample of actual research questions as well as a distribution of searches that accurately reflects the relative frequency of known-item to topical searches.

The primary objective of the study was to answer the question of whether Summon or EDS produced better results for the type of searches typically performed by our users. We can get a sense of what is "typical" by examining our Summon search logs. These logs contain the actual queries that users entered into the search box. From looking at these logs, we know that about three quarters of the searches are for "topical" type searches with the rest being "known-item" type searches where a user pastes in a citation or clearly enters title and author keywords. Because of how these two types of searches differ, the study was designed to separately evaluate how the discovery systems handled these types of

Table 1. Examples of known-item and topical search queries.

Known-item search queries:	Topical search queries:
Personal characteristics of the ideal African American marriage partner: A survey of adult black men and women	adderall edema
National cultures and work related values: The hofstede study	solar power coating nanoparticle
Adalimumab induces and maintains clinical remission in patients with moderate-to-severe ulcerative colitis	experimentation on animals
hill bond mulvey terenzio	conjugated ethylene uv vis
Sullivan A, Nord CE (2005) Probiotics and gastrointestinal diseases. J Intern Med 257: 78–92	religiosity among phd
Bryan; Griffin et al; Tierney and Jun	sleep deprivation emotional effects
Bone graft substitutes Expert Rev Med Devices 2006	Czech underground
Ann. Appl. Biol. 33: 14–59	toxicology capsaicin

searches. Table 1 lists examples of known-item and topical search queries from the Summon logs.

Discovery services such as Summon and EDS can offer several advantages over Google Scholar (e.g., API available, ability to save and e-mail results, ability to limit to peer-reviewed articles). However, we know that the Google universe is often the first choice of our users. Therefore, we were interested in how Google Scholar would perform as compared to Summon and EDS.

Methods

The study used actual user search queries from our Summon search logs. This differentiates the NCSU study from both the Asher and Rochkind studies (2013; 2013). The user queries occasionally contain typos, punctuation errors or extraneous characters. In addition, the queries could also be overly broad or otherwise problematic. Table 2 lists examples of problematic search queries from our sample.

The SAS software PROC SURVEYSELECT procedure was used to generate a simple random sample of 225 search queries. The sample was drawn from the approximately 664,000 Summon searches performed between January 1, 2013 and December 31, 2013. We determined the sample to be large enough to be representative of the population but also small enough to be manageable by the Web-Scale Discovery Product Team. Each of the nine members of the team was given twenty-five queries to analyze. Two team members were unable to complete testing, resulting in 183 queries tested.

Table 2. Examples of problematic search queries from our sample.

Problematic search queries:
Compendium of Transgenic Crop Gplants
suicide collegte
the over use of vaccinations
new class of drugs patent
technology behind online gaming
disney world facts
divorce effects on childreen
abortion is not morally permissible

Team members coded queries as topical search queries or known-item search queries. Team members entered each query into Summon, EDS, and Google Scholar. For topical searches, team members recorded the number of relevant results within the first ten results. A result was considered relevant if it matched the presumed topic of the user's search. Only the title and abstract were used to determine relevancy.

For known-item search queries, team members coded "yes" or "no" responses to the questions of "Did you find the item?" and "Was it in the top three results?"

The topical search queries were analyzed graphically as well as with a permutation test for repeated measures analysis of variance and pairwise permutation tests for comparing the means of the paired data. The permutation test code was written in SAS/IML software. The known-item search queries were analyzed using a graphical comparison of the number of found known items and a Mantel-Haenszel analysis to examine the relationship between discovery product and success of a known-item search.

About Permutation Tests

Permutation tests are defined in *A Dictionary of Statistics* (Upton & Cook, 2014) as follows:

> A simple type of hypothesis test. Denote the value of some test statistic by *T*. The observed data values are randomly redistributed amongst the experimental units. The test statistic is calculated for each such redistribution. Depending on the number of data values, either all possible permutations are made, or a random selection (of say 1,000 permutations) is made. For each permutation the value of the test statistic is considered. The significance of the value *T* is determined by the proportion of permutations that lead to values greater than, or equal to, *T*.

Table 3. Basic steps for a randomization/permutation test.

Randomization/permutation test steps:
1. Calculate test statistic for observed data
2. Randomly rearrange the original data
3. Calculate the test statistic for the rearranged data
4. Repeat #2 and #3 many times (typically several thousand)
5. Compute *P*-value as the fraction of how many times statistic for the rearranged data is equal to or more extreme than the observed test statistic

The concept of permutation tests was discussed as early as the 1930s by Fisher and others (Anderson, 2001; Good, 2005). However, the practicality of the method was limited by computing power. As the definition above states, the basic premise of a permutation test is that by randomly shuffling the data and recalculating a test statistic, a permutation test can calculate the probability of getting a value equal to or more extreme than an observed test statistic. Edgington and Onghena provide a detailed overview of using randomization tests to determine *P*-values in repeated measures designs (2007).

Results

For the comparison of known-item searches, the proportion of items found using Summon, EDS, and Google Scholar was nearly the same. Figure 2 shows the frequency of known items found between the three products.

For the question of whether or not a found item was in the top three results, the products performed nearly the same. All but two of the found known items were in the top three results for EDS and Google Scholar, and all but one was in the top three for Summon.

Adjusting or controlling for the sample query, no significant difference was found between Summon, EDS, and Google Scholar success rates, $\chi 2$ (2, N = 132) = 0.08, p = 0.96. The small sample size for known items (n = 44) was a limitation of our study. The test did not have the sufficient power to detect small differences (< 40%) in the performance of the products. We would suggest that subsequent studies use a larger starting sample in order to obtain sufficient known-item queries to detect small performance differences between products.

For the comparison of topical searches, the three products also performed similarly. Figure 3 shows the distribution of the number of relevant results for Summon, EDS, and Google Scholar.

Table 4 lists the mean number of relevant results for each product. The mean for Summon and EDS is nearly the same. Google Scholar appears to have on average approximately one additional relevant result.

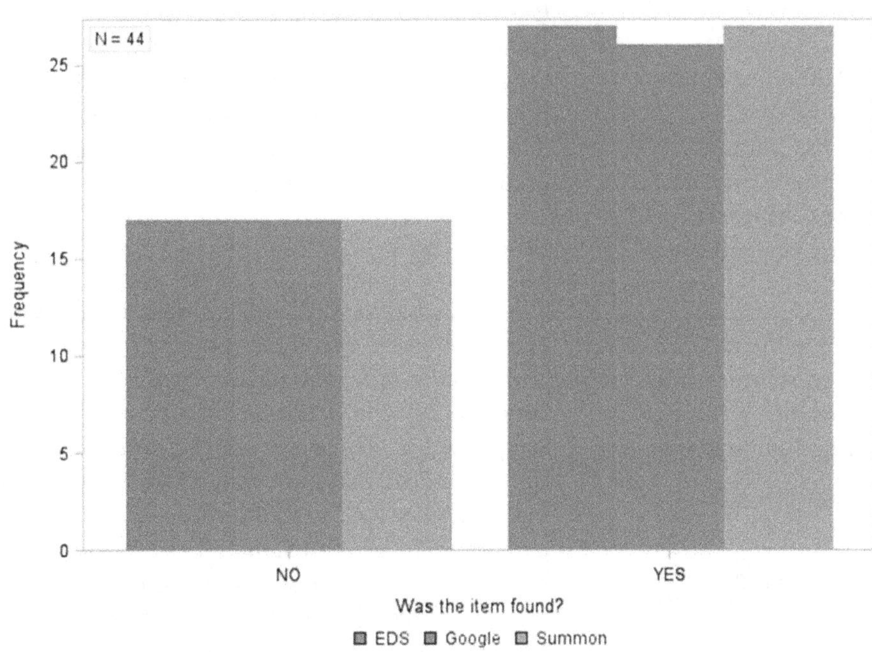

Figure 2. Frequency of known items found for EDS, Google Scholar, and Summon.

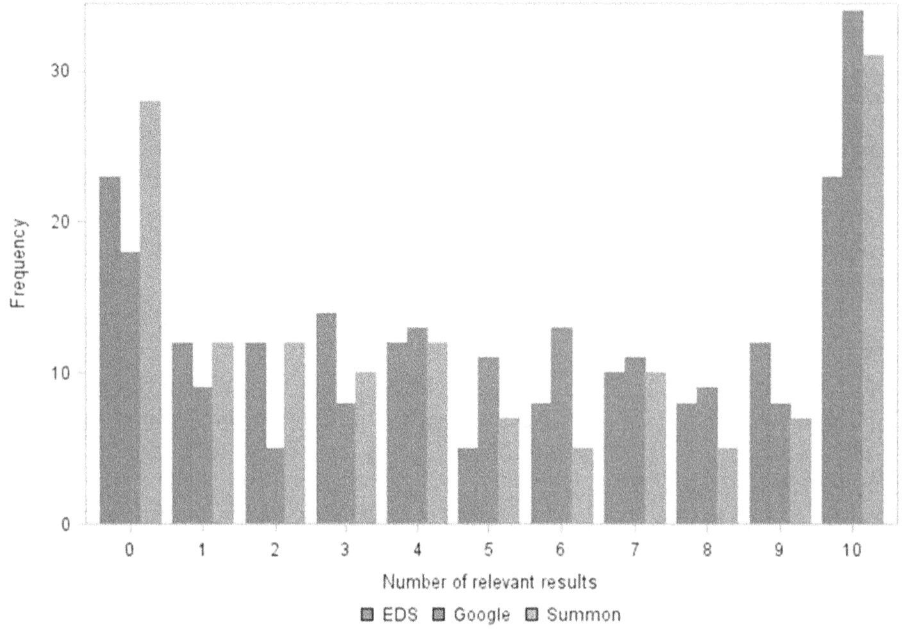

Figure 3. Frequency distribution of the number of relevant results from EDS, Google Scholar, and Summon.

EDS. The large P-value of 0.773 represented by the red shading of the histogram indicates no significant difference between the two products.

There was, however, a significant difference between the mean number of relevant results for Google Scholar and both EDS and Summon. In our observed data, Google Scholar outperformed EDS by an average of 0.85 relevant results. Figure 6 (see Appendix) shows a histogram of the results of the permutation test. As indicated by the small P-value of 0.004, the test indicates that it is highly unlikely that this difference was due to chance alone.

In order to detect any overall difference between the means, we performed a permutation test for repeated measures analysis (Good, 2005; Howell, 2006). Figure 4 (see Appendix) shows the results of ten thousand simulations of the F-statistic. The small P-value of 0.002 indicates that there is an overall difference in the means.

Given the indication of an overall difference in the mean number of results between the three products, we performed pairwise permutation tests to confirm where the difference occurred. The tests compared each of the possible pairs: Summon to EDS, EDS to Google Scholar, and Summon to Google Scholar.

There was no significant difference in the mean number of relevant results between Summon and EDS. Figure 5 (see Appendix) shows the permutation test results comparing Summon and

Table 4. Mean number of relevant results for each discovery product.

Discovery Product:	Mean number of relevant results
Summon	4.76
EDS	4.83
Google Scholar	5.68

Similarly, Google Scholar outperformed Summon by an average of 0.91 relevant results. Figure 7 (see Appendix) shows the results of the comparison between Summon and Google Scholar. Here again, the P-value associated with the test is 0.004 and indicates a significant difference in the mean number of relevant results between Summon and Google Scholar.

Conclusion

The NCSU Libraries's Web-Scale Discovery Product Team conducted a study to compare the search performance of Summon, EBSCO Discovery Service (EDS), and Google Scholar. A random sample of 183 actual user searches from the NCSU Libraries's 2013 Summon search logs was used for the study. No significant difference in performance between Summon and EDS for either known-item or topical searches was found. There was also no significant difference between the Summon, EDS, and Google Scholar for known-item searches. However, Google Scholar outperformed both Summon and EDS for topical searches. Given the lack of significant difference in performance between Summon and EDS, NCSU Libraries's decision to purchase one product or the other can be based upon other considerations such as technical issues, cost, customer service, or user interface.

References

Anderson, Marti J. (2001). "Permutation Tests for Linear Models." *Australian & New Zealand Journal of Statistics, 43*(1), 75–88.

Asher, A. D., Duke, L. M., & Wilson, S. (2013). Paths of discovery: Comparing the search effectiveness of Ebsco Discovery Service, Summon, Google Scholar, and conventional library resources. *College & Research Libraries, 75*(5), 464–488.

Ciccone, K., & Vickery, J. (2015). Summon, EBSCO Discovery Service, and Google Scholar: A comparison of search performance using user queries. *Evidence Based Library And Information Practice, 10*(1), 34–49. Retrieved from http://ejournals.library.ualberta.ca/index.php/EBLIP/article/view/23845

Edgington, E. S., & Onghena, P. (2007). *Randomization tests*. Boca Raton: Chapman & Hall/CRC.

Good, P. (2005). *Permutation, parametric and bootstrap tests of hypotheses* (3rd ed.). New York: Springer.

Howell, D. C. (2006). *Repeated measures analysis of variance via randomization*. Retrieved from https://www.uvm.edu/~dhowell/StatPages/Resampling/RandomRepeatMeas/RepeatedMeasuresAnova.html

Rochkind, J. (2013). A comparison of article search APIs via blinded experiment and developer review. *Code4Lib Journal, 19*. Retrieved from http://journal.code4lib.org/articles/7738

Upton, G., & Cook, I. (2014). Permutation test. In *A Dictionary of Statistics*. New York: Oxford University Press. Retrieved from http://www.oxfordreference.com/view/10.1093/acref/9780199679188.001.0001/acref-9780199679188-e-2108

Vickery, J. (2015). Permit me to permute: A basic introduction to permutation tests with SAS/IML. *SAS Global Forum 2015 Proceedings*. Retrieved from http://support.sas.com/resources/papers/proceedings15/2440-2015.pdf

Appendix

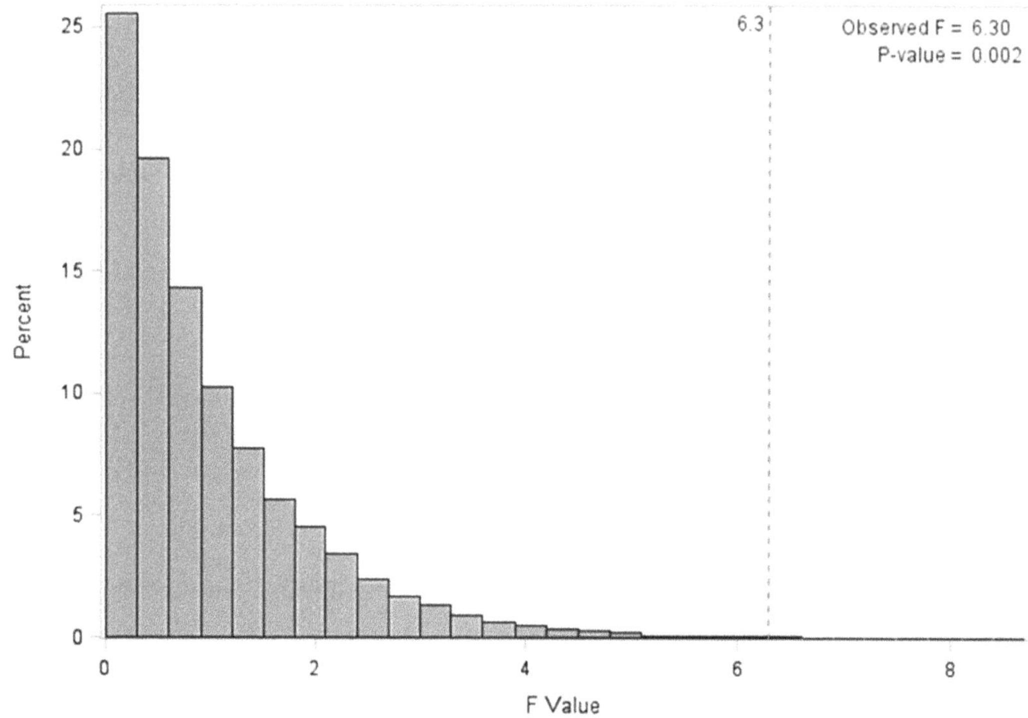

Figure 4. Bootstrap distribution of the *F*-statistic under the null hypothesis for 10,000 resamples indicates an overall difference between the mean numbers of relevant results for EDS, Google Scholar, and Summon.

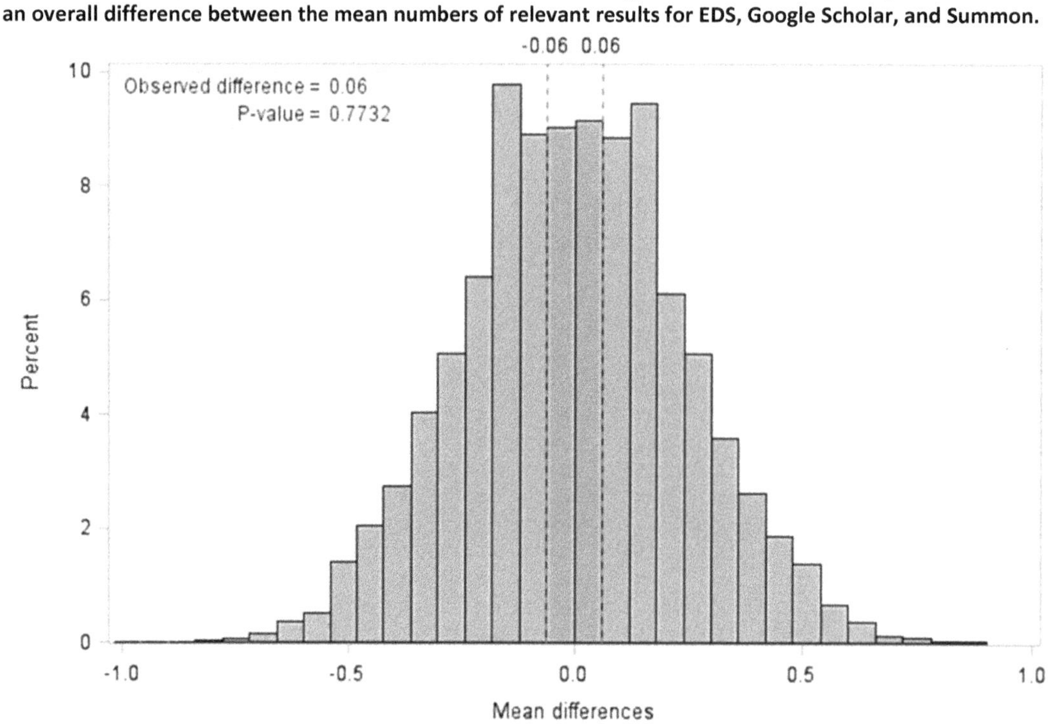

Figure 5. Bootstrap distribution under null hypothesis for 10,000 resamples shows that the observed difference in the mean number of relevant results between Summon and EDS was not significant.

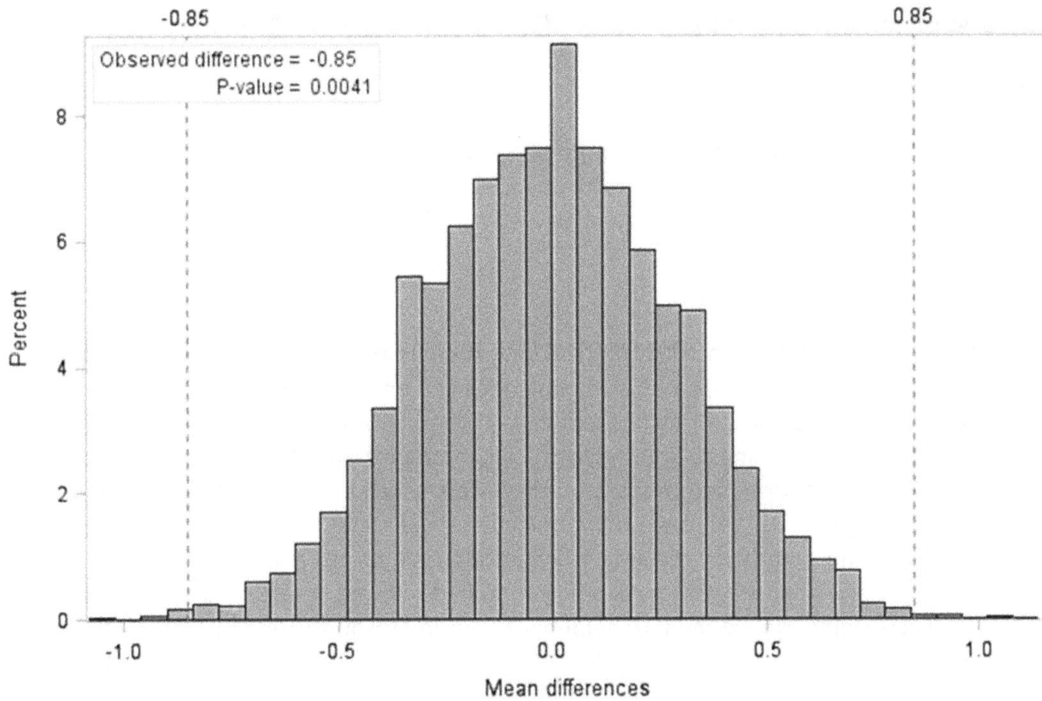

Figure 6. Bootstrap distribution under the null hypothesis for 10,000 resamples shows that the observed difference in the mean number of relevant results between Google Scholar and EDS was significant.

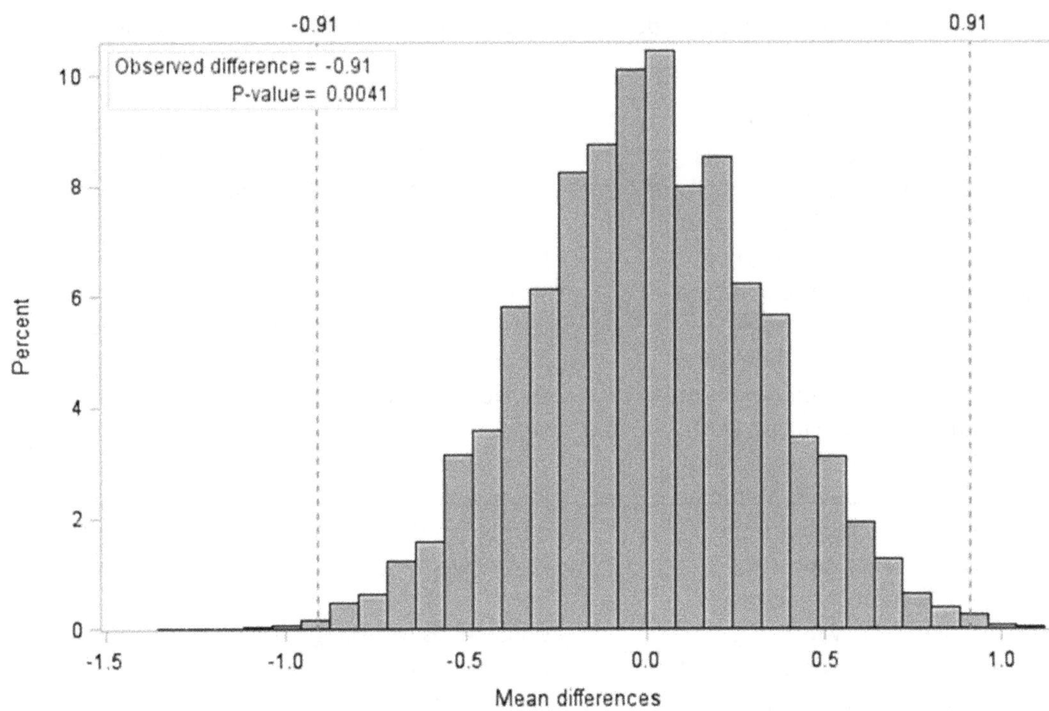

Figure 7. Bootstrap distribution under the null hypothesis for 10,000 resamples shows that the observed difference in the mean number of relevant results between Google Scholar and Summon was significant.

From Usability Studies to User Experience: Designing Library Services at the University of Kansas

Lea H. Currie, Head Of Content Development, University of Kansas Libraries

Julie Petr, Associate Librarian for Graduate Initiatives, University of Kansas Libraries

Abstract

The University of Kansas (KU) Libraries first made their discovery tool, Primo (Ex Libris), available to their users in the fall of 2013. Since that time, in spite of many upgrades and improvements, most librarians and library staff are still not using the tool for their own research. Last year, librarians from KU presented their findings at the Charleston Conference using a survey given to KU librarians that asked them to compare Primo to Google Scholar and their favorite databases. Librarians were asked to compare the three and make recommendations for improving Primo. This year, KU librarians designed a much briefer survey and asked all library staff to participate, including student assistants. Library staff were asked to use Primo to conduct research on a topic of their choice and use all aspects of Primo to find relevant results. They were then asked to describe what they used in Primo to lead them to helpful information resources and rank the first 10 results from their final search.

The purpose of this survey is to discern how our colleagues use Primo and how successful they are in retrieving the information they need when using this search tool. This study will help KU Libraries develop training for library staff in the use of this new mode of discovery and access. The search terms used in this study will also be useful in helping the discovery implementation team recreate the searches to test Primo in the future, after scheduled upgrades, in order to detect noticeable improvements or problems with the search results.

In 2014, University of Kansas (KU) librarians conducted a survey asking invited participants from the KU Libraries's staff to test the usability of the discovery tool, Primo. The participants were instructed to perform a known item search, a search for a designated topic, and a search for a topic of their choosing using Primo, Google Scholar, and their favorite database. They were then asked to compare and rank their results on a Likert scale of one to five, with one being very relevant and five being not relevant at all. Most of the participants had little success with Primo in finding relevant results, particularly with the known item search. Participants expressed frustration with the duplication of their results and little understanding of what was being searched. Furthermore, the survey took several hours to complete, which caused even greater frustration given the fruitless results. With only twelve participants, the results were not conclusive, but they did provide search terms to be used for testing Primo after upgrades throughout the last year.

In 2015, KU librarians redesigned the usability survey for Primo into a much shorter version. A call was sent out library-wide for participation in taking the survey, asking respondents to search Primo for a topic of their choice, something they would typically research. They were asked to describe the steps they took to get the best results and to rank the first ten results using a one to five Likert scale, similar to what was used last year. They were also asked to share three positive comments and three suggestions for improvement. They were instructed not to search more than thirty minutes. The returns from this survey were much more useful by addressing the positives of the Primo discovery tool and making suggestions for changes to Primo. To increase participation, there was a drawing of the participants for a fifty dollar gift certificate. Thirty five library staff members from across all library departments participated in the survey.

During the intervening year between the two surveys, Primo received two upgrades that

http://dx.doi.org/10.5703/1288284316289

improved its usability immensely. A "Browse e-shelf" was added, allowing users to browse thumbnails of the book jackets surrounding their Primo search results. Also added to Primo were advanced search options such as the ability to search by publisher, music publisher, resource type, and OCLC number. Users can now "Personalize their results" by choosing a preferred discipline and newer results to appear first. The "Did you mean?" option was also improved. Relevancy ranking and duplication were also refined. Due to these improvements, library staff members were much more successful this year in finding relevant results in Primo.

Some of the positives about Primo expressed by library staff were its user friendliness and ease of use. Survey participants found the relevancy of their results much improved overall and narrowing down results was made simple by using the facets on the left side of the results screen. Participants liked the mixture of formats that appeared in the results and were happy to see the format clearly labeled, taking the guess work out of deciding whether the item was a book, journal article, or another format. Other positive feedback included the ease of saving results to the e-shelf and ease of seeing the availability of an item. Participants found the option to "expand beyond library collections" extremely useful. They also found it easy to make adjustments to their original search, and overall they liked the seamless one-stop shop for scholarly resources.

Along with the many positives, library staff were able to give positive criticism and suggestions for improvement to Primo. Several of the participants would like to have the advanced search option as the default search box on the main library website. They would like to be able to sort their results from oldest to newest and wish there was a "mark all" option to save their search results. A few participants expressed their frustration with not understanding what Primo was searching and that known item searches, particularly for author and title combined, continued to be problematic. They also felt that the "print, e-mail, and export" options were too hidden in "Locations and Availability." In addition, participants found too much duplication in their results and reported that primary resources were displayed too far into the results. Several participants thought the login option was not obvious enough, and they were frustrated when they lost the filters chosen prior to logging in. One staff member suggested a rollover option so the user could see the abstract without clicking on the detailed record.

The survey designers shared a detailed report, which described the searches and feedback, with the discovery implementation team and provided a list of suggestions for improvement. The discovery implementation team worked through the list of suggestions, letting the survey participants know that their recommendations would be used to make further improvements to Primo when possible. They promised the survey participants that they would work with Ex Libris to improve duplication and relevancy rankings. They also began investigating methods making the advanced search more visible and labeling more understandable, particularly the e-shelf label. The discovery implementation team is also planning to make the "print, e-mail, and export" options more visible, as well investigate a way to sort results from oldest to newest. They also agreed that the option to mark all items to save on the e-shelf was a great suggestion. The suggestions also gave the team new topics for training library staff to use Primo successfully.

In summary, the Primo discovery tool continues to improve over time. Results from the surveys have been particularly instrumental in this process because they identified the concerns of the library staff, as well as the positive aspects of the tool. The discovery implementation team has successfully engaged the library professionals, assuring them that their input was essential and acting upon their concerns to improve the discovery tool. While the surveys continue to solicit a variety of suggestions for improvement, they also document greater overall support of the discovery tool.

How Do We Study Satisfaction With Academic E-Book Collections?

Beth Caruso, Library Research Assistant & Writing Program Lecturer, University of North Carolina at Charlotte

Alison D. Bradley, Head of Research & Information Services, University of North Carolina at Charlotte

Abstract

Much of the existing literature on patron satisfaction with e-books in academic settings does not differentiate between platforms, formats, and other conditions that drastically change the user's ability to read, annotate, and use e-book content. The Charlotte Initiative is a project funded by the Mellon Foundation to convene a working group that investigates principles for permanent acquisition of e-books for academic libraries. As part of this project, a user experience research team has been created to review the existing literature on patron satisfaction with multiple aspects of e-books. During summer 2015, this research team began a meta-study to determine areas of the user experience with e-books in academic libraries that have been studied comprehensively and to identify areas that have not received formal evaluation. In this paper, we not only convey the results of our research team's literature review but also provide criteria that librarians and institutions can use to guide assessments of user experience with e-books in academic library settings.

Introduction

Much of the existing literature on patron satisfaction with e-books in academic settings does not differentiate between platforms, formats, and other conditions that drastically change the user's ability to read, annotate, and use e-book content. This is a primary area of research being investigated by the Charlotte Initiative—a project funded by the Mellon Foundation to convene a working group of librarians, non-profit publishers, and consortial executives to study the permanent acquisition of e-books for academic libraries. Specifically, the project will consider ways that three core principles can affect the library market for the scholarly monograph in e-book format: unlimited simultaneous users, no digital rights management, and irrevocable perpetual access and archival rights.

As part of this project, a user experience research team was charged with reviewing the existing literature on patron satisfaction with e-books in order to conclude how academic libraries currently assess and evaluate patron satisfaction with their e-book collections. During the summer of 2015, the co-principal investigator and research assistant for the user experience research team designed and implemented a literature review and meta-study of the published literature on user satisfaction with e-books in academic libraries, in hopes of revealing how the current research climate might inform library best practices in e-book collecting.

A critical issue for the Charlotte Initiative is the impact of digital rights management (DRM) on the user, particularly in the ways the variations in DRM on e-book platforms can limit the use of academic e-book collections. From a user experience (UX) standpoint, we're considering DRM to be the technological restrictions on the use of content—the ways in which the product is designed that prevent people from doing the things they need or want to do through use of proprietary software formats that restrict access to or manipulation of the content of the e-book. DRM in this context is frequently raised as an issue in discussions of user opinions of e-books for academic use.

Methods

Since our charge was to review the published literature, we began by searching both the Library, Information Science, & Technology Abstracts with Full Text (LISTA) and the Library and Information Science Abstracts (LISA) databases, using the search terms "SU: electronic books AND academic

http://dx.doi.org/10.5703/1288284316290

libraries" (2,416 results) and "e-books AND academic libraries" (1,977 results). Other search terms were used, but yielded minimal results or many overlaps. Additionally, we reviewed several bibliographies to discover pieces that were not accounted for in the database searches and those regarding parallel subjects of potential use. Overall, we compiled 373 citations and abstracts into a shared spreadsheet, and once reviewed, coded 146 of them. We accounted for components such as the platforms or publishers studied in the articles (such as Springer, NetLibrary/EBSCOHost, Ebrary, Safari, and MyiLibrary); the DRM types addressed, if any (such as highlighting, note-taking, and file manipulation); the user group studied (which included any combination of students, faculty, librarians, libraries, researchers, and consortia); and the type of study conducted. Additionally, we noted the content of the study and how or if the study makes larger conclusions about UX, aside from simple like/don't like dichotomies, as well as those that warranted further consideration because of how they studied or discussed key issues in unique ways. We wanted to learn if an author concluded something about how users feel about e-books and whether or not they addressed differences in e-book platforms in reaching those conclusions. However, because these studies do not account for the same types of conclusions in the same ways, coding for conclusions and conclusion type was more difficult than expected. Within the set of 146 coded articles, we determined that 95 offer some conclusion about user satisfaction, meaning that the author makes a claim about their users' opinions, perceptions, or acceptance of e-books.

Variations in Precision of Study

The precision of the research reviewed varied a great deal. Some studies listed specific platforms available at their libraries, but often would not ask the subjects of the study to identify which platform they were most familiar with using. Many studies provided feedback specific to certain types of format and restriction that are not universal features of e-book collections. In other cases, this would lead to participants in the same study providing contradictory statements, with some respondents stating a dislike of e-books due to the inability to download or print while others in the same study cited ease of downloading and printing as a benefit of the collections. Many studies were not able to address how users felt about features and restrictions of individual collections, but some used focused techniques to gather feedback that was specific and defined. In "E-book Usage in Pure and Applied Sciences," Bierman, Ortega, and Rupp-Serrano (2010) conducted a two-stage study to address this confusion, following a widely distributed survey of faculty with individual interviews that included demonstrations of e-book features and restrictions, allowing the researchers to see exactly how each user reacted to the platform or features in question.

Many articles surveyed users and asked whether they commonly used personal e-books in addition to library collections or if they read e-books for pleasure or leisure as well as for research, but very few differentiated between those experiences and library collections in their assessments. Even with studies that attempted to determine which platforms a subject had used, they occasionally learned that the patrons could not differentiate between the various e-book platforms available. In Corlett-Rivera and Hackman's (2014) article "E-Book Use and Attitudes in the Humanities, Social Sciences, and Education," they asked directly which of seven popular e-book platforms in their library's collection the patron had used, and the most common response (at 23%) was "I don't know." In general, determining platform-specific feedback seems to require surveys that explicitly address only a single platform or personalized techniques such as focus groups, individual interviews, or usability studies.

What Do We Mean When We Talk About User Satisfaction?

Working definitions of "satisfaction" varied substantially, with common themes of satisfaction, preference, perception, or meeting expectations occurring throughout. Some studies simply extrapolated acceptance or satisfaction from usage data: if statistics show that a title has been used, or that usage of a collection increased over time, then the e-book format was at least accepted by their user community. In Timothy Bailey's (2006) article "Electronic Book Usage at a Master's Level I University: A Longitudinal Study," he reviews changing usage patterns in NetLibrary usage over a span of several years, and concludes, "The ever increasing amount of use demonstrated by the statistical reports available from NetLibrary indicates the acceptance of remotely accessible monographs by the AUM Library's patrons." Usage statistics are thereby used as a metric for acceptance: the researchers show that these people have used e-books or that collection usage has increased, and they extrapolate that to mean that they liked them.

Surveys were the most commonly used instrument, typically directly asking users if they liked, preferred, or accepted e-books. Corlett-Rivera and Timothy Hackman's (2014) research is an example of such a survey that asks detailed questions about their users' habits, preferences, and experiences with e-books broadly. Others conducted more detailed studies using techniques that directly evaluate the experience users have with a certain set of e-books. In a study at Miami University of Ohio, Q-methodology was used to study their users' attitudes and opinions toward e-books, and to develop a model that groups four types of user attitudes toward e-books: book lovers, technophiles, pragmatists, and printers (Shrimplin et al. 2011). The wide range of methodologies and techniques used to investigate user satisfaction makes it very challenging to draw conclusions about the current state of research in this area.

E-Books and Print Books

The expectations on the part of users, publishers, and librarians for e-books to function like print books recurred throughout the literature reviewed. A study conducted in 2005 examined comparisons in usage between a NetLibrary package and duplicate print titles in the circulating collection. They commented on the challenges of comparing print use with electronic use, and noted that while an e-book use could be "a thirty-second browse or a serious reading," it is equally unknown whether the patron actually read the book they borrowed when using circulation statistics to inform collection decisions (Christianson & Aucoin, 2005, p. 79). This concern is far more frequently noted in discussions of usage statistics of electronic materials than in circulations of print.

Many packages available to libraries limit usage of e-books to a specific number of users, intending to mimic the experience of a library purchasing a certain number of copies of a physical item to be made available to their users for a set period of time. Several studies noted patron frustration with this artificial restriction, particularly in light of electronic journal articles, which are commonly available to an unlimited number of users (See Owen, Riessen, Weir, DesRoches, and Noel, 2008; Staiger, 2012; and Slater, 2010, among others).

Aline Soules compares the assumption that an e-book must retain the general function of its print predecessor to the concept of the "skeuomorph," which she defines as follows: "Adapted from the world of architecture and ornamentation, a skeuomorph carries remnants of its previous existence as it evolves into its new self. It is similar to a molting snake. E-books have not yet cast off their print skins, and this colors many issues" (Soules, 2009).

Formats, Platforms, and Features

Although readers have expectations of how e-books should function, these expectations are not always met. In an attempt to reconcile expectations with provided features, most pieces that discuss DRM talk about specific features that platforms include or that agreements allow. Commonly addressed DRM features and restrictions, such as highlighting; annotating; changing font sizes; limiting page views; or the ability to print, save, copy, and paste appear throughout the literature reviewed. For example, page size is a frequently discussed feature, though on a tablet, the ability to enlarge a page may cause paragraphs or charts to separate, which can interfere with fluidity. On desktop computers, the user may select for the page to fill the screen, but then option buttons are not as readily available. If they downsize the page scale to reveal options, then the page is not as readable, because some platform readers take away space by cluttering the frame. Additionally, some features and restrictions overlap when a platform offers a feature that doesn't actually work. For example, on some platforms, readers can only retain their annotations by exporting them. However, if this function fails to successfully e-mail readers their notes, such as in a study conducted by Muir, Veale, and Nichol (2009), the feature that was meant to enhance a user's experience becomes a restriction.

Because features are presented in different ways on different platforms, users also can mistake those differences as rights restrictions. Inconsistency is a strong underlying negative factor of a user's experience, as they expect all e-books to operate the same way, regardless of platform (Soules, 2009, p. S3). In fact, while advocating for consistency, one of JISC's (2009) studies concludes "(DRM) systems should either be removed or developed in line with actual user behaviour" (p. 44), which many other studies also insinuate.

Although these issues cause frustration for users, those who require the use of assistive technology or text enhancements can find the use of e-books overwhelming to the point of non-use. We may generally think that a digital version of a text would be beneficial to those using technology such as screen readers or those requiring text enlargement, but the reality is that these features do not always work as they should, which can alienate users from the text and keep them from getting the information they need. As Diane Michaud (2013) states, "One common misconception is that 'available electronically' means 'accessible'" (p. 24). Michaud has found that in some cases, the e-book requested will not be in an accessible format, which requires librarians to contact the publisher for at least a tagged PDF version, if it's available. Some licenses also make full e-books impossible to download, and this obstacle could have implications for how users of assistive technology make use of full-text searching and other functions designed with general usability in mind.

Christopher Stephen (2009) goes a step further and claims that "if people cannot find and access the information, it has little [. . .] value" (p. 77), and calls for a change in the way an e-book's index is formed. He advocates for indexing "units of information" (p .78), generally at the paragraph level, so users can find information more easily than with traditional indexes. However, navigating a paragraph-level index could become cumbersome for readers requiring accessibility measures, so the implementation of alternate keywords for such an index is essential.

The need for more accessible navigation and search functions is in line with the earlier findings of Muir and colleagues (2009), who studied the accessibility of e-books by using multiple observation techniques to examine users' habits while taking on specific tasks. They noted that their "user-centered research [was] aimed to understand not only the characteristics of behavior but also why users behave in certain ways" (p. 93), since a then-recent JISC study called for "improved user experience or functionality [that is] explicitly linked to desired outcomes" (p. 105). Overall, the team recommended "a form of adaptive personalization. The concept is to make the service adapt to the user, rather than forcing the user to adapt to the system" (p. 105). Likewise, Cassidy, Martinez, and Shen (2012) "recommend that e-book publishers and platform designers attempt to provide as many options as possible for visually adjusting a text's display, as well as options for printing and converting text to speech, in order to provide the best possible experience to the maximum number of users, regardless of abilities" (p. 330). It is evident that both users and researchers see the need for at least some level of release of DRM restrictions, particularly to accommodate users with additional needs.

Although such endeavors will take time to implement, interested groups are already addressing similar issues. The Digital Accessible Information SYstem, or DAISY Consortium, is committed to bringing accessible e-books to everyone, no matter what their needs may be. Their standards, which they make available in what they call the "DAISY book," go beyond allowing the reader to simply read the text or access audio files of the text to including time-aligned navigation, "which enables the user to move smoothly between files while synchronization between text and audio is maintained" (2015, sec. 3). This assists in making information within an e-book findable, and therefore usable. Additionally, the World Wide Web Consortium (W3C) outlines four principles in developing accessible web-based resources. They stress that information should be:

- Perceivable—Information and user interface components must be presentable to users in ways they can perceive
- Operable—User interface components and navigation must be operable
- Understandable—Information and the operation of user interface must be understandable
- Robust—Content must be robust enough that it can be interpreted reliably by a wide variety of user agents, including assistive technologies (WCAG 2.0 Guidelines, 2008)

Although these principles are designed to relate to accessibility measures for web-based sources, they also echo the findings of many e-book usability studies. The principles can have major implications on how we envision e-book usability and are highlighted in recent studies as being of value to e-book design.

The concept of accessibility was not an original component of our charge, but throughout our research, it is clearly of serious importance when we consider e-book usability. If users are unable to perceive the information, operate the user interface, and understand and interpret the information they are given, e-books and their formats are less useful, no matter how many simultaneous users are allowed or what their preferences may be.

Next Steps

The original charge for the user experience research team was to examine the published literature on user satisfaction with e-books to establish how libraries currently assess and evaluate patron satisfaction with their e-book collections. Although the findings of this study were valuable, we realized that it is necessary to depart from the published literature to find out how satisfaction research is being put into practice in libraries.

How Recommendations From Studies Are Being Implemented in Practice

Throughout the published literature, researchers make determinations about user satisfaction with e-books and sometimes recommend action points that could help remedy issues that users are having. These action points can vary: some call for purchasing certain types of collections, or endorse e-books as a format to be added to an academic library's collecting profile. Others recommend additional promotion or discovery tools to promote their e-books more widely. Many suggest that more instruction or user guides would help users locate and use special features like annotation or highlighting. Reviewing and coding the content of the meta-study to analyze these various types of recommendation may reveal interesting patterns.

Even though recommendations for practice are posed in many articles written by librarians who work in a collection development unit, it is impossible to extrapolate whether those suggestions are being implemented in practice, or how they are being conveyed to the researcher's library team. We hope to investigate how published recommendations may or may not be reflected in institutions' practices by following up with the writers of these pieces via surveys, interviews, and other ways. Also, additional questions have arisen about researchers' affiliations and roles. Are there distinctions or differences between studies done by librarians with various roles in a library, or between practicing librarians and library science faculty members? Does research sponsored or conducted by a publisher's staff address these topics in the same way?

Finding and Starting Other Discussions

Even though a number of published articles convey usable statistics and conclusions, the bulk of the research/work that *directly informs practice* is not showing up in published journals. For this reason, we intend to move away from published pieces in two ways to investigate library practice that may not be recorded in the circulating literature.

First, many LIS professionals present their work on user satisfaction at local, state, and regional conferences, rather than publishing articles or reports. An immediate next step for our research team is to conduct a review of available conference proceedings for library conferences that focus on relevant areas, such as the Charleston Conference, ER&L, and ACRL, among others. We intend to investigate conference proceedings in the same ways in which we addressed the journal literature in order to determine which researchers we would like to contact for further discussion to find out the goals of their work and how they have designed their tasks.

Second, there are certainly even more initiatives that are not being put in front of the public eye, but instead remain as in-house, non-published, practical initiatives. They may not be labeled as *research*, but instead as *assessment*, designed to inform library practice. We hope to identify individuals and libraries that are investigating UX issues in their own institutions to have conversations about the necessity and goals of these initiatives, as well as their findings and next steps. A simple mention of this step at the Charlotte Initiative working group meeting uncovered at least three initiatives currently underway in members' institutions. Conversations with the people conducting these assessments will prove valuable, since they will be trying to implement or alter actual practice in their libraries.

Recommendations for Replicating or Designing Studies of E-Book UX and Satisfaction

In hopes of influencing the current direction of research on e-book user experience, we have defined criteria that you or your institution can use to guide assessments of user experience with e-books in academic library settings.

- Clearly identify the platforms in question. Discussing all platforms together leads to confusion as to how specific platforms handle certain functions. In these cases, participant responses aren't as helpful because readers cannot match the responses to the specific constraints the users are working within.
- Identify the current e-book format, as there can be multiple formats used on one platform
- Consider usage and accessibility separately. Different things work for different people. Features like page enlargement and variable fonts seem to aid in accessibility, but may conflict with adaptive software or assistive technologies that an individual prefers to use.
- Consider observing users' actual behaviors. When answering survey questions, many users may imagine other experiences they have had, and not the ones the survey intended to capture. For example, if the survey asks about library e-books, users may end up thinking of Kindle books or even very specific, one-time experiences. Observation can help researchers better understand how users experience e-books in very specific contexts.

While user experience remains complex and often frustrating to study, considering the perspectives of librarians, publishers, and users together is essential in this stage of development of the academic e-book market.

References

Bailey, T. P. (2006). Electronic book usage at a master's level I university: A longitudinal study. *Journal of Academic Librarianship, 32*(1), 52–29. http://dx.doi.org/10.1016/j.acalib.2005.10.004

Bierman, J., Ortega, L., & Rupp-Serrano, K. (2010). E-book usage in pure and applied sciences. *Science & Technology Libraries, 29*(1–2), 69–91. Retrieved from http://dx.doi.org/10.1080/01942620903579393

Cassidy, E. D., Martinez, M., & Shen, L. (2012). Not in the love or not in the know? Graduate student and faculty use (and non-use) of e-books. *Journal of Academic Librarianship, 38*(6), 326–332.

Christianson, M., & Aucoin, M. (2005). Electronic or print books: Which are used? *Library Collections, Acquisitions, & Technical Services, 29*(1), 71–81. http://dx.doi.org/10.1016/j.lcats.2005.01.002

Corlett-Rivera, K., & Hackman, T. (2014). E-book use and attitudes in the humanities, social sciences, and education. *portal: Libraries and the Academy, 14*(2), 255–286. http://dx.doi.org/10.1353/pla.2014.0008

DAISY Consortium. (2015). About us. Retrieved from http://www.daisy.org/about_us

JISC. (2009). JISC national ebooks observatory project: Key findings and recommendations. Retrieved from http://observatory.jiscebooks.org/reports/jisc-national-e-books-observatory-project-key findings-and-recommendations/

Michaud, D. (2013). Copyright and digital rights management: Dealing with artificial access barriers for students with print disabilities. *Feliciter, 59*(1), 24–30.

Muir, L., Veale, T., & Nichol, A. (2009). Like an open book? Accessibility of ebook content for academic study in a diverse student population. *Library and Information Research, 33*(105), 90–109. Retrieved from https://openair.rgu.ac.uk/handle/10059/795

Owen, V., Tiessen, R., Weir, L., DesRoches, D., & Noel, W. (2008). *E-Books in research libraries: Issues of access and use.* Ottawa, ON: Canadian Association of Research Libraries.

Shrimplin, A. K., Revelle, A., Hurst, S., & Messner, K. (2011, March). Contradictions and consensus—Clusters of opinions on e-books. *College & Research Libraries, 72*(2), 181–190.

Slater, R. (2010). Why aren't e-books gaining more ground in academic libraries? E-book use and perceptions: A review of published literature and research. *Journal of Web Librarianship, 4*(4), 305–331. http://dx.doi.org/10.1080/19322909.2010.525419

Soules, A. (2009). E-books and user assumptions. *Serials, 22*(3), S1–S29. http://dx.doi.org/10.1629/22S1

Staiger, J. (2012). How e-books are used. *Reference & User Services Quarterly, 51*(4), 355–365. http://dx.doi.org/10.5860/rusq.51n4.355

Stephen, C. (2009). From print to web: Indexing for accessibility. *Indexer, 27*(2), 14–32.

Web Content Accessibility Guidelines (WCAG) 2.0. (2008). *W3C.* Retrieved from http://www.w3.org/TR/WCAG20/

Cost Per User: Analyzing EZProxy Logs for Assessment

Tiffany M LeMaistre, Electronic Resources and Discovery Librarian, Nevada State College

Abstract

Cost per use has long been a staple of collection development decision-making for electronic resources, but what of the users behind those retrieval and search counts? Questions about the interdisciplinary usage of an e-resource, the depth of integration into a given program or course, and who will miss it if it is cancelled are generally relegated to the realm of anecdotal evidence. Researchers at Nevada State College have made efforts to remedy this gap in knowledge by analyzing EZProxy logs, which can be set up to capture unique user identifiers at the point of authentication into library electronic resources. When matched with institutional data about those users, this data can answer questions such as cost per user, percent of users within the institution as a whole or a specific department, and frequency and depth of use for the average user. Ultimately, librarians can even discover if library users have higher GPAs or make better grades on research assignments. This paper will provide a summary of the work of the research team at Nevada State College, currently in the midst of their first year of EZProxy log analysis.

About Nevada State College

Nevada State College (NSC) was founded in 2002 and quickly became the fastest growing institution of higher education in the state of Nevada, and one of the fastest growing in the country. The College has a diverse student population of about 3,400 students. Over fifty percent of the students are from culturally diverse backgrounds. More than sixty percent of the students are first-generation college students, and about seventy-five percent are women (Nevada State College 2015).

Serving a student population traditionally underserved by higher education is important to the mission and vision of Nevada State College. The College is constantly searching for solutions to help students succeed in their educational goals. One centerpiece of this effort is the use of data to drive decision-making. The Office of Institutional Research makes use of several online data dashboards and a behind-the-scenes predictive analytics framework to identify indicators that a student may be struggling, and proactively recommend services that positively correlate with student success outcomes such as advising and tutoring.

The Marydean Martin Library at Nevada State College initially became interested in EZProxy log analysis as a way of contributing to this predictive analytics framework by becoming a recommended service for student success. This paper will focus on the collection development aspects of the data. However, using the data to assess the library's contribution to student success and to identify and address equity gaps in library use are also important goals of the project.

Nevada State College's Marydean Martin Library is the first digital library in the state of Nevada. There are no open book stacks in the library building, and the vast majority of resource use comes from the online collection encompassing more than 1.4 million e-books and roughly 5 million scholarly articles.

How the Data Is Collected

EZProxy is OCLC's authentication system for managing access to online library resources such as e-books and electronic databases. Many academic librarians know it as the off-campus authentication system, but at Nevada State College EZProxy mediates on- and off-campus access. Librarians at Nevada State College made the choice to prompt for authentication on campus in order to capture all e-resource use in the log files. EZProxy logs are an optional feature of EZProxy, which can be setup to track and save user activity (OCLC 2015). Most libraries do choose to collect some form of a log file for troubleshooting or security purposes, but often the data collected is brief and automatically deleted after thirty to sixty days.

http://dx.doi.org/10.5703/1288284316291

At Nevada State College a comprehensive log file is collected, which includes, most notably, the unique user ID of the individual accessing library resources. The systems analyst in NSC's Office of Information Technology Services (ITS) protects the raw data with encryption. On a monthly basis, she uses a PowerShell script that parses the data into a CSV format and sends it to NSC's Office of Institutional Research (IR) using a scheduled job. In the IR office, the data is uploaded into a SQL database. SQL processes written by IR staff anonymize the data and match it with student data as well as usage data from other services on campus such as the writing center, advising, and tutoring. The library works with IR staff to create and maintain SQL update procedures that cleanup the log files, converting complex fields like the request URL into clear database and platform names whenever possible. Finally, the Director of Institutional Research visualizes the data in an online dashboard using Tableau.

With this workflow, all of the matched data is anonymous and raw library use data is encrypted and protected. So for example, the number of library users with a GPA above 3.5 that accessed the Discovery search is evident from the online dashboard. However, that a named user with a GPA of 2.8 accessed WorldCat Discovery on October 5th is not stored anywhere in the dataset.

For collection development purposes most of what librarians need to know about resource use is evident from the online dashboard. However, there is sometimes a need for deeper analysis such as the correlation between library use and GPA or the statistical significance of equity gaps in the usage of library resources by ethnicity or gender. When those needs arise, the quantitative Analyst from the Office of Institutional Research has been able to provide the library with statistical analyses based on the anonymous matched dataset.

This project involves a significant collaborative effort across the institution. Some librarians outside of Nevada State College have noted that the barriers to such a partnership on their own campuses may be too high to explore EZProxy log analysis. However, there are still valuable insights to glean from proxy log analysis that do not require any matching with student data. To illustrate this, the first portion of this paper will refer to a dashboard created within the library

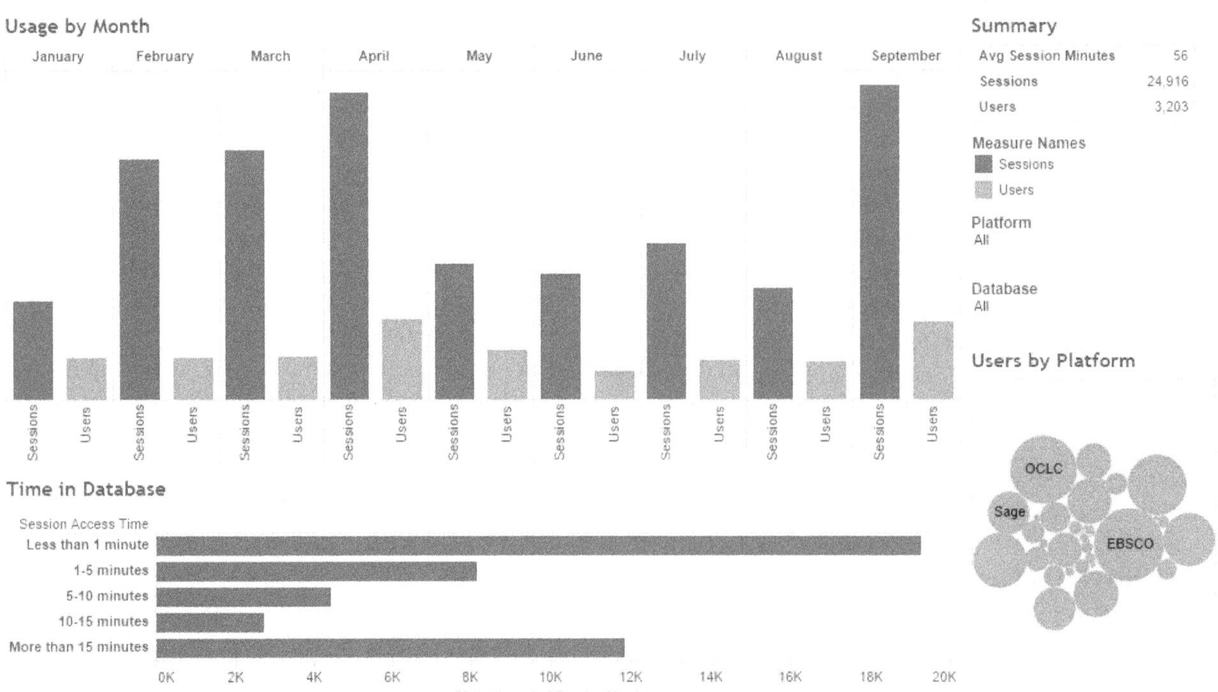

Figure 1. Screenshot from Tableau dashboard of Nevada State College's online resource use from January to September 2015.

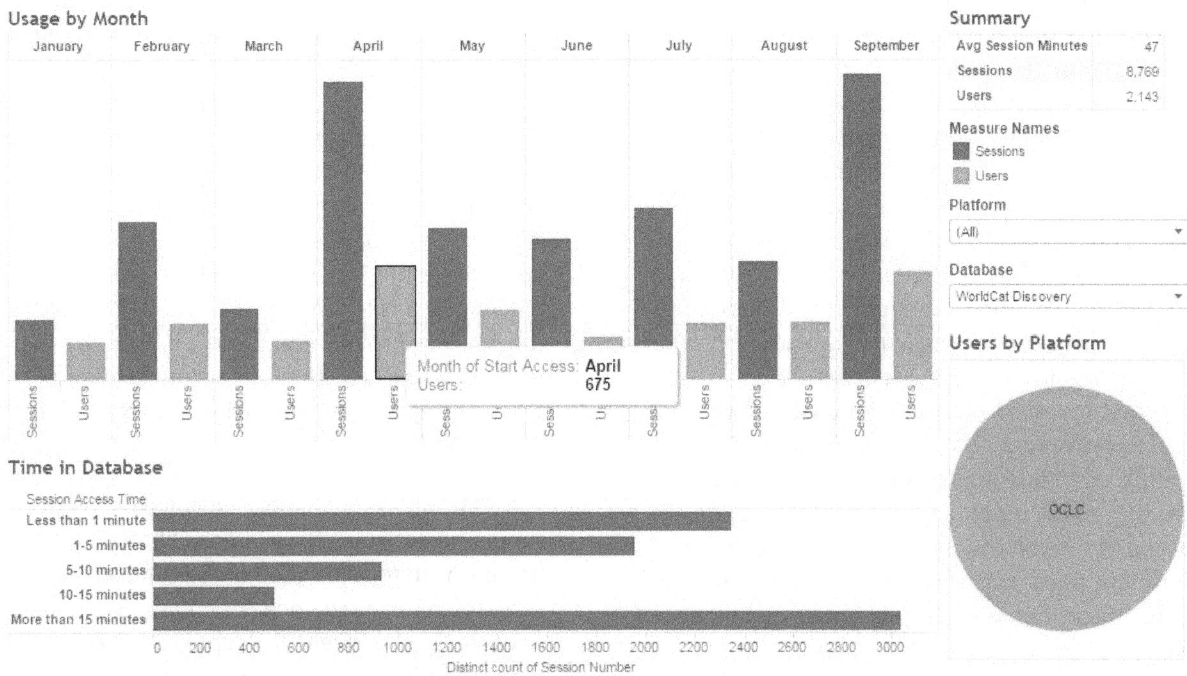

Figure 2. Screenshot of Tableau dashboard limited to WorldCat Discovery use with the cursor over April users bar revealing additional detail.

with anonymized EZProxy log data only. Then, the paper will explore the additional value from matching with student data through the dashboard created from the partnership with NSC's Office of Institutional Research and Instructional Technology Services.

Early Benefits of the Data

Without matching EZProxy log data with student data, a library can still use the proxy logs to determine the number of unique sessions and users for electronic resources. This can be useful in that it provides a true comparison across all electronic resources, offers an opportunity to calculate return on investment, and gives insight into frequency and patterns of use over time. Figure 1 shows an unfiltered view of an online dashboard created from anonymized EZProxy log data in Tableau. It shows the number of users and sessions by month and overall. A bubble chart displays the number of users by platform indicating high use of EBSCO, OCLC, and Sage.

All of the bars and bubbles in the online dashboard are interactive. Users can roll over them for more detail, or select them to filter the data presented. For example, Figure 2 shows a view of the dashboard limited to WorldCat Discovery use only using the dropdown menu under database. The cursor is over the users bar for April, showing the number of unique user IDs from the dataset for that month and resource.

Session length and average time are also included, but there are problems with these metrics. Since there is no logout feature of EZProxy, the difference between the start time of the first and last line in the log file for any given session or resource determines access time. The usefulness of this metric varies by platform as some databases create more lines in the log file than others based on similar user actions. User and session counts are the more reliable metrics available from proxy log analysis.

A True Comparison

The most consistent comparison of electronic resource use in the field today is COUNTER compliant usage statistics (COUNTER—counting online usage), but there are two problems with COUNTER. First, not all vendors are COUNTER compliant. Some of the major databases subscribed to by the Nevada State College Library still do not provide statistics in COUNTER format and a few do not provide usage statistics at all, making consistent comparisons with other resources impossible. Second, there are nuances within the COUNTER standard itself that can make comparing one resource to another challenging. For example, some of NSC's e-book providers only report COUNTER BR1 for title requests. Others only report COUNTER BR2 for section requests. It is clear that counting a use for every e-book title accessed versus counting a use for each section or chapter within a book that is accessed is a different measure, but there is no way of knowing exactly how much section requests are inflated compared to title requests unless the vendor produces both reports. Not all e-book vendors do. User and session counts from EZProxy logs allow librarians to use one standard metric to compare all resources regardless of platform or resource type.

Return on Investment

Another benefit of the EZProxy log data alone is that even without knowing anything about who the users are, having unique user identifiers tied to use can allow for a calculation of number of users and cost per *user*. This metric offers a different perspective than cost per use on whether the library is achieving economies of scale. It also allows for a calculation of return on investment for subscription resources that may be more palatable to administrators than efficiency measures like cost per use. Comparing cost per use to ILL fees or article purchase costs is an excellent measure of efficiency within the library, but it means little to outsiders. By contrast, cost per *user* is comparable to individual subscription fees to calculate how much the library is saving faculty and students by providing access to certain resources. It puts more emphasis on the value of the subscriptions provided by the library, and less on efficient spending of resources allocated to the library.

Usage Patterns

Without matching EZProxy log data with student data, librarians can also get a sense of usage patterns over time. They can calculate new versus repeat users of a resource and begin to understand how frequently users access certain resources. Currently, NSC's work with analyzing usage patterns from the proxy logs in the early stages. NSC researchers look at the number of users and number of sessions to get a sense of new versus repeat users. For example, for the Discovery search there were 2,143 total users and 8,769 sessions between January and September 2015. Since the Discovery tool was implemented in January, this means that at least 24% (2,143) of the sessions in WorldCat Discovery were from new users and 76% (the remaining 6,626 of the sessions) were from users who had accessed the service before.

Theoretically, a much more advanced analysis should be possible. For example, librarians should be able to determine the number of users who accessed a resource once, 2–5 times, 5–10, and 11 or more. Alternatively, they could analyze how many users accessed a resource once per semester, monthly, weekly, or multiple times per week. If it was of interest, a researcher could even determine what times of day or week experienced the highest traffic in certain resources.

Adding Student Data to the Analysis

The benefits of EZProxy log data alone are interesting, but the true power of EZProxy log analysis is evident from matching this data with data about users. This requires collaboration with campus stakeholders who have access to the data, as well as careful attention to issues such as anonymity and data security. As a result, the Library at Nevada State College chose to collaborate with experts on our campus in the Office of Institutional Research and Information Technology Services to achieve an analysis that goes beyond collection development and begins to address the library's role in student success.

Figure 3 shows a Tableau dashboard created by the NSC's director of institutional research. In this dashboard, the potential of EZProxy log analysis for understanding users is evident. The number of unique users by date from January through May 2015 appears at the top. In the online dashboard, users can adjust the slider below that chart to filter the display of all other dashboard elements to the date range desired. The percent of library

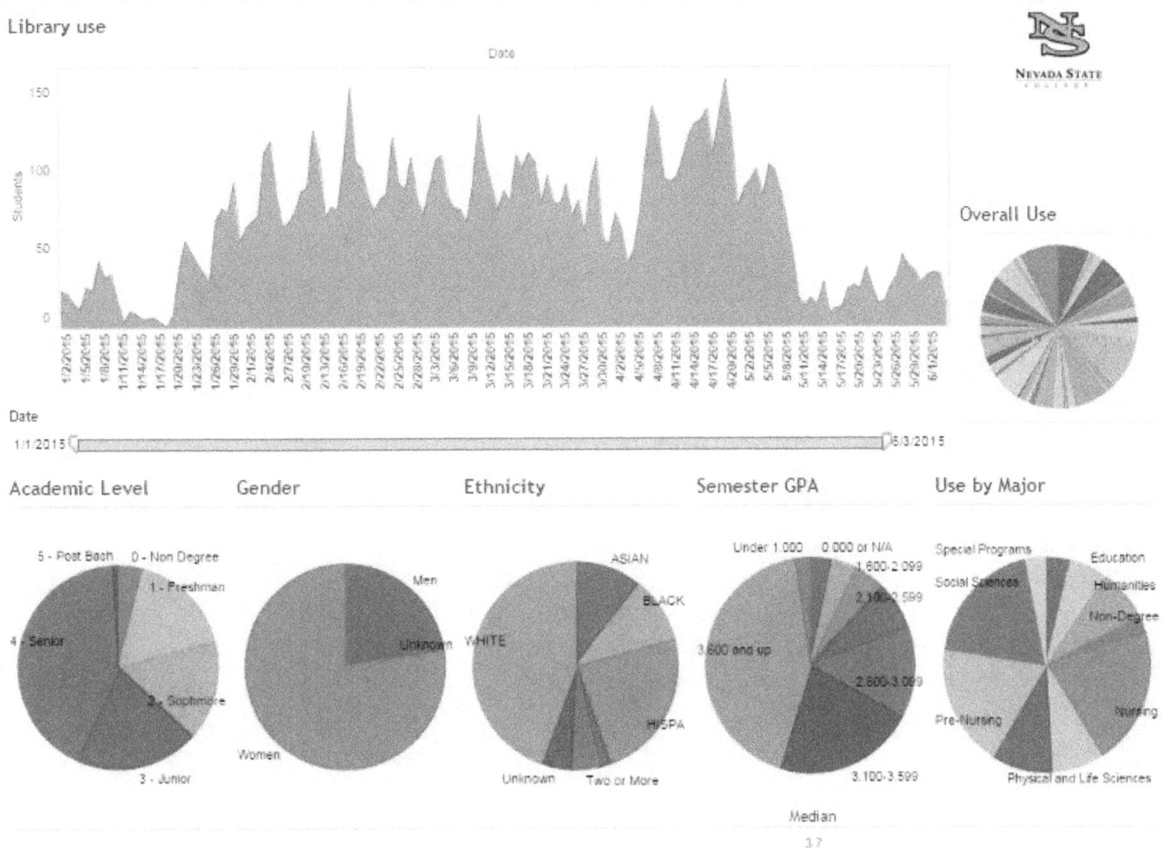

Figure 3. Screenshot from Tableau dashboard of Nevada State College Library's users.

users at each academic level and in broad disciplinary categories and GPA ranges appears at the bottom. The ethnicity and gender of library users is also included to determine if library users are a reflection of NSC's diverse student population.

On the right-hand side, there is a pie chart of Overall Use. In the online dashboard, rolling over the slices shows specific library resources such as JSTOR or Academic Search Complete. Clicking a slice will filter the dashboard to usage for that resource only. For example, Figure 4 shows the data limited to use of the WorldCat Discovery search tool.

This dashboard is useful for determining how representative library users are of the Nevada State College students as a whole. For example, underrepresentation from education majors is something librarians at Nevada State College have already begun to address with outreach to faculty in that program. Filtering to particular resources can offer further insights into the user group for that particular resource. For example, filtering to "historical New York Times" showed librarians at NSC that usage of the resource is broadly interdisciplinary and when considering a switch to the NYTimes.com platform there were several campus stakeholders that needed consultation.

From the dataset behind this dashboard, the quantitative analyst from NSC's Office of Institutional Research has already begun to communicate to the library about characteristics of library users. For example, her analysis of library users with spring semester data uncovered a statistically significant positive correlation between number of library sessions and GPA. When a full year of data is available for analysis in January 2016, the research team will pursue additional analyses.

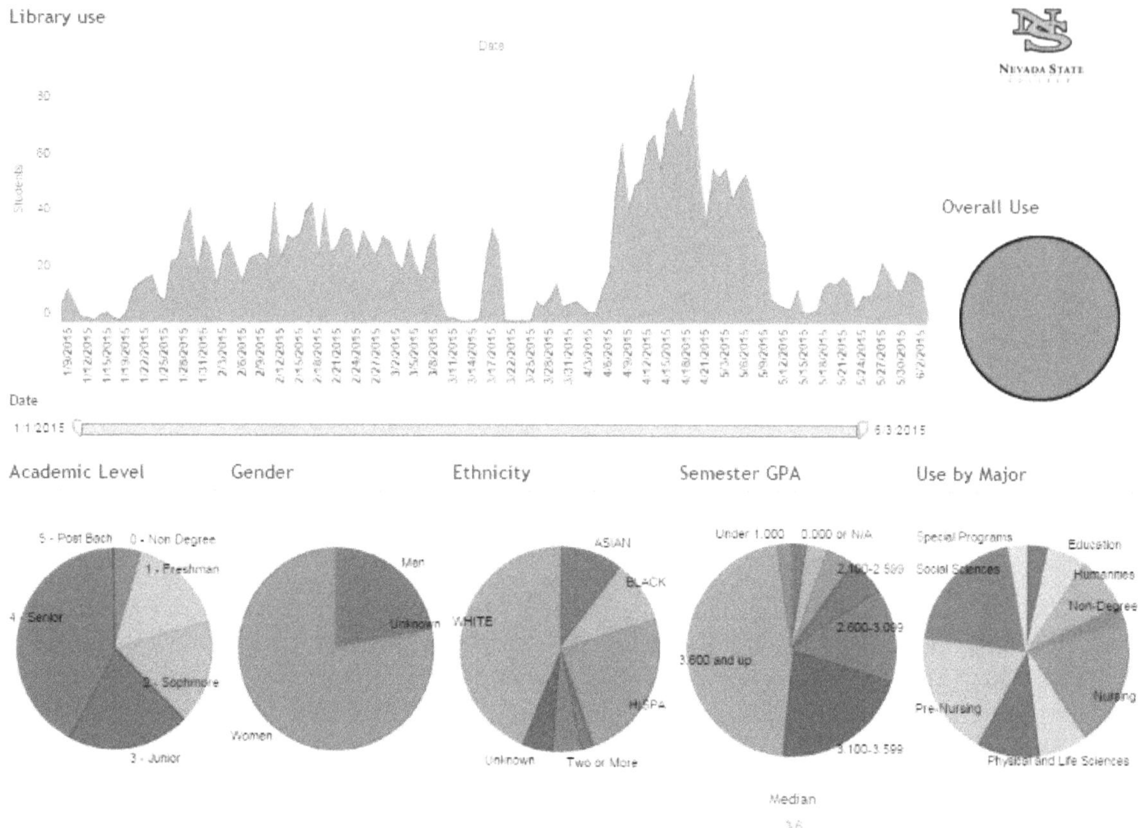

Figure 4. Screenshot of Tableau dashboard of library users limited to WorldCat Discovery use only.

Limitations and Future Directions

There are several limitations of this project, which we are currently attempting to address with further analysis. First, collection use is only one type of library use. Truly understanding the library's impact on student success requires other data points that correspond to services and spaces. Second, the current statistical analysis is in the exploratory stages. Researchers will need to conduct additional analyses before conclusions that are more meaningful are evident from the dataset. Finally, as with all correlational studies, we cannot infer causation even if we are able to demonstrate statistically significant results.

Incomplete Dataset

As a digital library with on- and off-campus authentication through the EZProxy server, NSC's EZProxy logs provide a relatively complete picture of collection use. However, there are still pieces missing. There is a small amount of print book circulation from interlibrary loan and other request services that it is our goal to include in future analyses.

Collection use is also only one small part of what the library has to offer. Librarians at NSC suspect that library services and spaces may be just as or potentially more important to student success than the resources we offer. Several other institutions who have pioneered work in matching student identifiers to student success metrics have combined other types of library use beyond the collection (Cox & Jantti, 2012; Evans, Bowe, Golian-Lui, & Luther 2015; Library Analytics and Metrics Project 2015; Regents of the University of Minnesota). Including additional data points like study room checkouts, library instruction attendance, and research consultations is one of the long-term goals of this project.

Statistical Analysis

So far, researchers at NSC have only run preliminary statistical analyses on the dataset that includes library users only and consists of correlations that do not attempt to control for potential confounding variables like high school GPA. At the end of one year of data collection, the research team is planning a more advanced analysis that includes success measures beyond GPA like retention and graduation rates, compares users to non-users of library resources, and controls for other variables that may influence college GPA like high school GPA.

Exploring Causation

As with all correlational studies, even if NSC researchers are able to demonstrate a statistically significant positive relationship between library use and student success outcomes, they cannot conclude that library use is the cause of student success. As a result, librarians at Nevada State College are in the early stages of exploring possible experimental designs that may be more suited to inferring a causal relationship. In one pilot project, librarians have worked with an English 101 instructor to add a research assignment to a course that did not have one previously and look for any relationships between library use and grades on that assignment in the fall 2015 semester. The study is a pilot because the sample size is small and there is no control group, but it has allowed researchers at NSC to explore possible methods for implementing an experiment that might encourage library use through changing course requirements and allow the researchers to look for any significant changes in student learning outcomes as a result.

Conclusion

Despite the limitations, this project has brought the library one step closer to understanding the impact of library resources. Instead of evaluating e-resources on retrievals or search counts, the library can understand the users impacted by those resources. Researchers at Nevada State College are now able to use the dataset to determine if library users are representative of the campus population. If discipline-specific or demographic groups are underrepresented the library can begin to investigate whether services and collections are actually meeting the needs of all students, and if not why not. Finally, the library can demonstrate and work to improve the connection between library use and student success outcomes like GPA. All of these are important steps in shifting assessment efforts from library outputs to library impact.

Acknowledgments

The author would like to thank Tina Buck and Nathaniel King for their comments and feedback.

From Chaos to Community: Two Libraries Finding a Unified Direction

Melissa E. Johnson, Electronic Resources and Serials Librarian, Augusta University

Rod Bustos, Assistant Director for Library Systems, Augusta University

Sandra Bandy, Chair, Content Management, Augusta University

Abstract

In January 2013, the University System of Georgia Board of Regents consolidated a health sciences university and a predominantly undergraduate liberal arts university. Each university had its own library, and the consolidation presented several challenges to the newly formed University Libraries. One major challenge was unifying the catalog as each library follows different classification standards. National Library of Medicine call numbers and Medical Subject Headings were utilized on the Health Sciences campus, and Library of Congress call numbers and subject headings were used on the liberal arts campus. After recognizing the differences in the catalog records, the Libraries asked "Where do we go from here?" A cataloging subcommittee was formed to identify ways to consolidate bibliographic records, streamline holdings, and turn chaos into community.

When an academic library and a medical library consolidate, there are two resulting options: chaos or community. In 2013 the University System of Georgia Board of Regents consolidated eight of their institutions into four. One of these consolidations was between Augusta State University, a primarily undergraduate liberal arts university, and Georgia Health Sciences University (formerly the Medical College of Georgia), the state's public medical school; the resulting university became Georgia Regents University (GRU), the state's fourth public research university (Board of Regents, n.d.). Effective December 1, 2015, Georgia Regents University will be called Augusta University.

Since each of the previous universities had their own library, the two libraries were consolidated under the umbrella of the University Libraries, which included the Reese Library on the Summerville campus, formerly the Augusta State University facility, and the Robert B. Greenblatt, MD Library on the Health Sciences campus. Each of the libraries had resources specific to the fields of study on their respective campuses.

Prior to consolidating the libraries, there was a lot of preliminary work done to merge some electronic resource subscriptions, clean up the backend of the ILS, and change the catalog interface. As with the other University System of Georgia institutions, the GRU Libraries used the Voyager ILS. Throughout the state it is referred to as GIL—GALILEO Integrated Libraries. Previously, the Greenblatt Library used the classic GIL catalog, which functions via WebVoyage software and provides patrons with a simple, easy-to-read list of items in the catalog. Classic GIL also updates immediately so that when a new record is added it can be viewed from the patron's perspective right away. Conversely, the Reese Library used the newer GIL-Find version that functions via VuFind software. It has an updated appearance with graphics for book covers providing visual appeal and links to Amazon reviews or Google Book previews. Records added into Voyager, however, appear in GIL-Find the next day after the update is run overnight. Upon consolidation, both libraries began using GIL-Find as their primary catalog interface.

After the initial consolidation of the libraries websites and catalogs was complete, some of the differences became noticeable. Where the Greenblatt Library utilizes the Medical Subject Headings (MeSH) and the National Library of Medicine (NLM) call numbers, the Reese Library uses the Library of Congress Subject Headings (LCSH) and Library of Congress (LC) call numbers. When cataloging, the second indicator in the 6 hundred fields signifies the vocabulary from

http://dx.doi.org/10.5703/1288284316292

where a heading comes; 0 in the field indicates LCSH and 2 indicates MeSH. There are some distinct differences between the two: MeSH uses the singular form of a subject and LCSH uses the plural; MeSH uses scientific terminology, LCSH uses common terminology; there is also the difference between generalized terms for MeSH and specific terms for LCSH (US Library of Congress, n.d.).

Both libraries had different physical locations for their resources. The Reese Library retained their print serials in the 2nd floor serials area whereas the Greenblatt Library kept them in the bound and unbound journals section on the second floor of their library. Both libraries had historical collections, but with different names. Reese's historic collection is called special collections, and Greenblatt's is called historical archives and collections. The book collections are maintained in various places, as well. Greenblatt's books are maintained in the book collection, core collection, reference, and historical reference. Reese's book collections, which number around 350,000, are held in various locations: browsing, reference, special collections, reserve, government info, and 3rd floor stacks. The Reese Library has been a Federal Depository Library for more than 50 years, and Government Information resources, including books, also appear in the catalog. The Government Information resources utilize Superintendent of Documents (SUDOC) call numbers.

If the same material was found at both libraries and used the same bibliographic record, the short display would show that it was available at the Greenblatt Library, as the display was showing the results in alphabetical order. If a different bib record was used for the same item, the resource would appear twice in the catalog, once for each library. The Reese library also used the same bib record for print journals and links to aggregated databases that contained the electronic version of the same journal. The Greenblatt Library had separate bib records for the print and electronic versions of the journals. The electronic journal links, however, for Greenblatt went directly to the publisher site.

As the catalog continued to be used, the discrepancies became more noticeable. A cataloging/link resolver committee was established to look at the differences between the two libraries; not only differences in the catalog for each library, but differences in the way each campus and library accessed their electronic resources. The Greenblatt Library utilized SFX™ for their electronic journals list and link resolver, and the Reese Library utilized EBSCO A-to-Z.

The cataloging/link resolver committee consisted of members of content management from Greenblatt Library and technical services at Reese Library, which are essentially the departments at each library performing the same functions such as managing serials, e-resources, and cataloging. The committee also included members from access services at both libraries and the systems librarian who is responsible for information technology at both libraries. The committee was given the charge to make usability easier for patrons.

Of this group, a cataloging subcommittee was created to identify disparities in the catalog and investigate ways to streamline the records. The group met monthly to identify the problems and made corrections. Other library catalogs from universities with both a medical campus and an academic campus were consulted to garner an understanding of how they handled similar situations. The University of Georgia Library's catalog was investigated as it has several libraries and locations.

One of the first decisions the committee made was to change some of the locations so there would be standardization. Previously the journal locations were the Reese serials area, 2nd floor, Greenblatt bound journals, and Greenblatt unbound journals (shelved with bound journals). The committee decided that there may be confusion for the patron when using the term "serial." Most professors require student to use academic "journals" for any research conducted. The term "serial" was replaced with "journal" in the location. The committee also opted that for each catalog entry's holding location, putting the library's name first; then the area designation, followed by the floor of the library, so that the patrons would not be looking for an item in one library that was actually held by the other library. The systems librarian was able to make global location changes so that the new journal locations were the Reese journals, 2nd foor, and Greenblatt journals, 2nd floor.

A similar designation was determined for books. Instead of Greenblatt books and Reese 3rd floor stacks, the new book locations were Greenblatt reference, 1st floor, Greenblatt core, 1st floor, Greenblatt books, 1st floor, Reese reference, 1st floor, and Reese books, 3rd floor. Again the systems librarian made the location changes. Although the cataloging module in Voyager still uses the original location codes, the public OPAC interface utilizes the new location display names to make it easier for patrons to find materials.

One of the problems that arose originally was in regard to materials available at both libraries. The short display of GIL-Find would sometimes have the call number for one library appearing with the location for the other library. For example, a patron searching for the *Publication Manual of the American Psychological Association* in the library catalog saw the short display, which indicated the book was available at the Reese Library, but showed the call number as WZ 345 A512p 2010, which is the NLM call number. The LC call number for the same book was BF76.7 .P83 2010. After the patron looked through the stacks at the Reese Library and could not locate any books with a call number of W, they requested assistance. Reviewing other library catalogs to see how similar circumstances were handled, the systems librarian changed the short display in the catalog interface to multiple locations and multiple call numbers. Once a patron clicks on the multiple locations link, the holdings information with the correct call number and library location are displayed.

The holdings information for print journals was also maintained in a different format. At the Reese Library, the holdings for print were listed as volume – volume on the first line; then date – date on the second line. Greenblatt listed their holdings as date – date, then volume – volume on one line. The committee elected to use the standard MARC 21 format for holdings – volume (date – date) format all on one line.

In relation to journals that were available online, Reese had "Full text electronic journal List" as the visible note in the holdings for any journals. This referred patrons to the main EBSCO A-Z™ menu where they could type in the name of the journal again. Greenblatt's holdings stated either "Available online" or "Full text available via link." Both libraries' holdings were changed to "Check online access" with the campus in parenthesis. Since many patrons are more familiar with the campus name when they are off-campus as opposed to the library name, the committee believed it would be easier for them to know which resource they could access. This was important as there are different subscriptions available on both campuses. Some resources are subscribed to for either one campus or the other, especially the medical resources. The systems librarian was able to establish an authentication process to enable patrons to access their campus-appropriate resources.

Another area which needed streamlining was the online resources available through the Reese Library. There were several locations for online materials including: e-books on EBSCOhost, e-books on EBSCOhost (GALILEO), Net Library, ebrary, GALILEO Films on Demand, and Reese Online. From the patron perspective there was an uncertainty about where all these locations could be found. By streamlining them all to say "Reese Online" and "Click here to access," it became easier for the patron to access the information they wanted.

The committee identified the changes that would be most effective and easiest to rectify. They will continue to examine ways to make the catalog function better for patrons. Where there was chaos, a library community which includes SUDOC, LC, NLM, and MeSH now exists. An upcoming challenge for the cataloging subcommittee is the implementation of ALMA, which is anticipated to begin mid-2016. The subcommittee will be conducting data clean-up for migrating to this new cloud-based ILS.

References

Board of Regents of the University System of Georgia (n.d.). Recommended consolidations. Retrieved from www.usg.edu/docs/consolidations.pdf

US Library of Congress (n.d.). 15.5 Differences between LCSH and MeSH. *Cataloger's Reference Shelf: CONSER Cataloging Manual.* Retrieved from http://www.itsmarc.com/crs/mergedprojects/conser/conser/module_15_5_ccm.htm

Leveraging Usage Data and User-Driven Development to Extend the Use of Collections

Kristen Garlock, Associate Director, Education & Outreach, ITHAKA

Abstract

In 2014, the JSTOR Labs team used an algorithm to identify more than 9,000 articles on JSTOR that exhibited patterns of use consistent with being used in the classroom or assigned as coursework. Using a low-cost rapid development approach called "flash builds," the team validated and built a prototype browser for this dataset with the direct involvement of teachers at the secondary and introductory college levels. This dataset is now available as "Classroom Readings," a free and open experimental resource. Classroom Readings (http://labs.jstor.org/readings) is designed to help educators find articles on JSTOR that are good candidates for teaching, adding value to the investments libraries have made in JSTOR collections.

Text

As larger proportions of library budgets are invested in electronic journals each year and we have more data about their use, we can leverage that data to help libraries get even more out of these investments. In 2014, JSTOR employed usage data analysis and rapid development techniques to build a new tool called "Classroom Readings." The tool enables educators to find articles that have been used in courses and filter the results by reading level and length.

When we began this project we did not initially set out to create this particular tool. Our original idea was to help support the use of content from JSTOR in teaching by creating expert-curated lists of articles and books that aligned with core first-

doi	discipline	article title
10.2307/450483	Language & Literature	Guilt and Death: The Predicament of The Ancient Mariner
10.2307/3175999	Language & Literature	Elephants in the Labyrinth of Empire: Modernism and the Menagerie in "The Old Wives' Tale"
10.2307/462329	Language & Literature	The Doll House Backlash: Criticism, Feminism, and Ibsen
10.2307/2933083	Language & Literature	Resistance, Rebellion, and Marriage: The Economics of Jane Eyre
10.2307/462130	Language & Literature	Frankenstein: Creation as Catastrophe
10.2307/2871293	Language & Literature	Is There a Performance in this Text?
10.2307/461329	Language & Literature	Alice's Invasion of Wonderland
10.2307/3844618	Language & Literature	"Jane Eyre", from Governess to Girl Bride
10.2307/3174801	Language & Literature	A Genealogy of Dependency: Tracing a Keyword of the U.S. Welfare State
10.2307/1343054	Language & Literature	The Marginal Gloss
10.2307/25115310	Language & Literature	"The Great Gatsby" and the Obscene Word
10.2307/461001	Language & Literature	Wuthering Heights and the Limits of Vision
10.2307/20027310	Language & Literature	What Is Security?
10.2307/3174406	Language & Literature	Transforming Franz Kafka's "Metamorphosis"
10.2307/2853637	Language & Literature	Mohammed and Charlemagne: A Revision
10.2307/25293689	Language & Literature	Faust's Damnation: The Morality of Knowledge
10.2307/2928384	Language & Literature	"Shaping Fantasies": Figurations of Gender and Power in Elizabethan Culture
10.2307/1343408	Language & Literature	A Few Canonic Variations
10.2307/2851941	Language & Literature	The Carolingian Age: Reflections on Its Place in the History of the Middle Ages
10.2307/3844619	Language & Literature	"Sympathy" in Jane Eyre
10.2307/20024056	Language & Literature	Deep Play: Notes on the Balinese Cockfight
10.2307/3174446	Language & Literature	Looking and Listening: The Construction of Clinical Knowledge in Charcot and Freud
10.2307/1261283	Language & Literature	Adam, Eve, and the Fall in "Paradise Lost"
10.2307/3844532	Language & Literature	Discovery and the Domestic Affections in Coleridge and Shelley
10.2307/30166165	Language & Literature	Kafka's "Metamorphosis": Rebellion and Punishment
10.2307/361359	Language & Literature	The American Civil War and the Problem of Inevitability
10.2307/1350027	Language & Literature	Moving Tropes: New Modernist Travels with Virginia Woolf / مجازات التنقل: ترحلات الحداثة الجديدة عند فرجينيا وولف
10.2307/3174621	Language & Literature	Feminist Critics and Literary Mothers: Daughters Reading Elizabeth Gaskell
10.2307/813939	Language & Literature	Gatsby: False Prophet of the American Dream
10.2307/372763	Language & Literature	Satiric Strategy in the Importance of Being Earnest

Figure 1. Thematic patterns in dataset.

http://dx.doi.org/10.5703/1288284316293

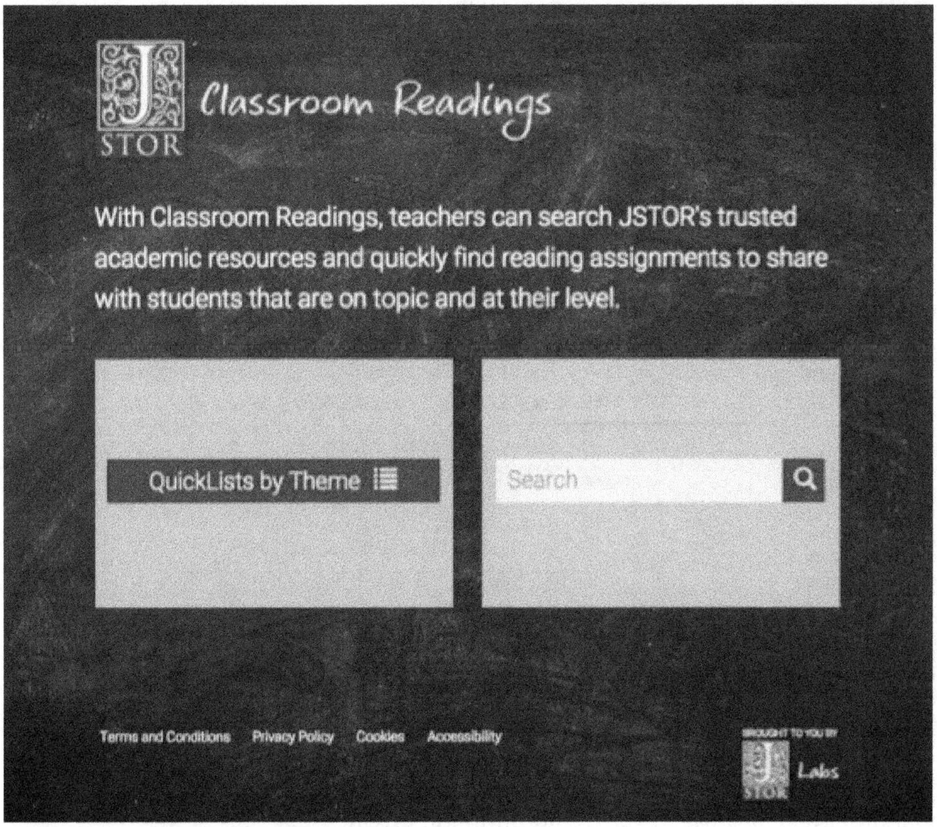

Figure 2. JSTOR Classroom Readings.

year courses. We quickly realized that such a manual, top-down approach would be time and resource intensive; engaging already busy subject matter experts to create these lists would be difficult. So, we took a step back and challenged ourselves to find another way to correlate content on JSTOR with course topics.

From years of anecdotal reports, we know that content on JSTOR is used in teaching in many ways, not just for research papers. But what content? How could we discover which articles were most useful in a teaching context? Would teaching use show up in the usage patterns?

We decided to experiment with looking for usage patterns that would distinguish use of an article assigned in a class versus use of an article accessed by an individual for a research paper.

Our data scientist created an algorithm to look for a "teaching use" pattern, which we defined as spikes in usage of an article at a single institution within a two-week period.

Using this technique, we identified about 9,000 articles that had this usage pattern in 2011–2013. In looking across this dataset, we saw some interesting trends: there was very little duplication of articles assigned across institutions, but there were strong thematic patterns. We thought that perhaps we could identify articles in a theme and use these as the basis for our course lists.

To help us explore the data in more detail, we created a rudimentary web browser that enabled us to much more quickly spot these thematic patterns, and we began to use it to build lists of content. This led to our a-ha! moment . . . perhaps this browser itself might have value to educators.

To test the concept of making the browser available to educators, we worked with our small JSTOR Labs team to build and test a prototype with high school and college teachers. Using a rapid development technique called a "flash build," we were able to quickly validate the concepts and features of most value.

The teachers were enthusiastic about the concept and particularly interested in the thematic lists, or QuickLists, as we named them. We refined the tool in July and August of last year, built a number of sample thematic lists, and rolled out the tool as Classroom Readings last fall. The tool is free and open for anyone to use, though links to the full-text content on JSTOR may require an institutional or individual account. Recently, we reran the algorithm against usage on JSTOR for January 2014–June 2015, and expanded the dataset to approximately 50,000 articles.

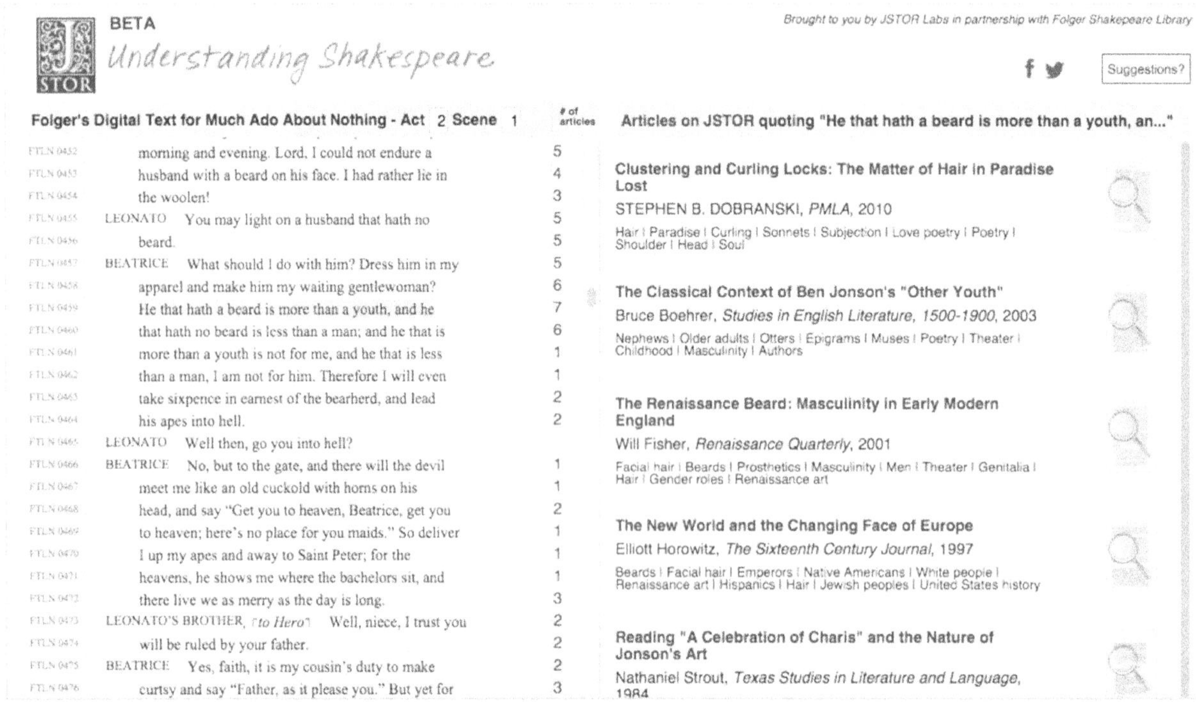

Figure 3. Understanding Shakespeare.

Of course, usage date can only tell us what's happening on-site, not about other teaching use via course tools and sharing of PDFs. In the future, it may be possible to enrich the dataset further by looking at other metrics and enabling educators to contribute to, review, or annotate the lists and content. Longer term, the features of Classroom Readings may be useful to incorporate directly into the main JSTOR interface; for right now, it's a beta tool providing a means to test the concept and features more broadly.

While not perfect or entirely comprehensive, the teaching use algorithm and digging into the data first helped us to develop hypotheses that could be tested through quick, low-cost methods. We've since used these techniques to build and test several other tools. One example is Understanding Shakespeare, a collaboration between JSTOR and the Folger Shakespeare Library. Using a matching algorithm developed by JSTOR Labs, we created links from the lines in the plays to the secondary literature on JSTOR.

We're also thinking about other usage analysis that might indicate opportunities to improve discoverability. Perhaps we could using an analysis of the frequency of search terms to identify topics that could be enhanced with on-site subject guides.

The teaching usage data might also be applied in other ways to help libraries. One librarian has suggested that being able to identify titles used in teaching might help with collection development. For example, would knowing that a title gets relatively smaller use overall but has strong teaching use impact a cancellation decision? These are some of the things we're thinking about to help students and educators, and to add value to the investments libraries have made in JSTOR.

Try, Try, Try Again: Better Faculty Outreach Through Trial and Error

Patti C. McCall, Physical & Life Sciences Librarian, University of Central Florida

Sarah D. Schulman, Account Development Specialist, Springer

Michael A. Arthur, Head of Resources & Acquisition Discovery, University of Alabama at Tuscaloosa

Abstract

Reaching out to faculty about library resources and services is an ongoing and sometimes mysterious process for vendors and librarians alike—one that, when effective, can contribute a higher ROI and improved collaboration between libraries and publishers. However, it can be a challenge to reach that sweet spot between "effective" and "annoying," especially in the face of seemingly nonresponsive faculty. A physical and life sciences librarian and former head of collection development and acquisitions from the University of Central Florida (UCF), and a Springer account development specialist, who works closely with academic librarians, weigh in on four different issues about improving outreach and identifying opportunities for outreach and collaboration.

Outreach Goals

The key goal for acquisitions librarians and subject librarians is to create awareness among faculty of library resources and increase the use of those resources. At the University of Central Florida (UCF), subject librarians actively work with their faculty to solicit feedback about the current collection and ways it can be improved, and, whenever possible, identify collaboration opportunities that often lead to successful grant proposals. Simple ways of measuring success include increases in constructive discussions with faculty, collaborations, instruction requests, research consultations, and use of library resources. While at UCF, Michael Arthur worked closely with subject librarians to facilitate successful relationships with teaching faculty. From the publisher perspective, Springer's outreach goals include helping customers attain a high return on investment, while also helping to market the library itself on campus.

Outreach Initiatives

There are a number of simple, but often overlooked, means of conducting outreach. In his new (and current) role at the University of Alabama, Arthur has participated in many new faculty events, introducing himself and learning about issues in their disciplines. Wasting no time, he is already in the early stages of working with faculty to evaluate the effectiveness of streaming video on classroom instruction. Patti McCall is also proactive and routinely takes steps to develop and enhance relationships with faculty, including:

- Attending on-campus events such as department seminars, dissertation defenses, and discipline-specific discussion groups
- Attending discipline-specific conferences (she is an active member of the Chemical Information Division of the American Chemical Society), and being present for faculty and student presentations and poster sessions at those conferences
- Making occasional presentations to student groups (such as the student chapter of the American Chemical Society)
- Personally welcoming all new faculty in her departments
- Regularly attending meetings with publisher representatives

She believes that being a presence in her departments and making personal connections helps build trust and establishes a reputation as being a go-to resource for her faculty and

http://dx.doi.org/10.5703/1288284316294

students. In her four years at UCF, she has slowly but steadily increased the number of instruction requests and research consultations but is careful to point out that building these relationships takes a great deal of time, effort, patience, and sometimes pure luck.

Examples of successful outreach include working with UCF's Faculty Center for Teaching and Learning (FCTL) to include a write up in FCTL's weekly e-mails, which are distributed to faculty campus wide and highlight a variety of library resources. Librarians are also frequent presenters at the FCTL's annual on campus conference.

Librarians and publishers also worked closely to hold a publisher forum at UCF, geared specifically to address the interests and needs of faculty. Key topics included how faculty can get published, open access opportunities and initiatives, and issues relating to digital rights management. The forum was well received and generated productive discussion with faculty in a variety of disciplines. There have also been collaborations with faculty that resulted in $2 million in grant funds for new collection-focused purchases between 2009 and 2014.

Of course, not all outreach efforts prove successful. Some departments have been simply unresponsive to repeated attempts by subject librarians to get input on collection development and in those cases; some of the collection development funds have been shifted to departments who show interest in working with their librarian. Other departments on campus have been unwilling to share in the costs of access to resources when they realize that those resources need to be available for all students and not just a select group in their department, a view that runs contrary to the library's collection development policy.

Outreach Challenges

Nevertheless, faculty outreach is not easy given the typical challenges: time (or complete lack thereof), limited budgets, and ever rising costs. There are other issues as well, such as departmental politics, heavy course loads, and a large number of adjunct faculty. These issues tend to make successful outreach difficult at best. In a school of 60,000-plus students, it is also difficult for a librarian to truly address each department equally. Unfortunately, faculty do not always understand the high costs and delivery models involved with the resources they desire, making collaboration difficult and sometimes even creating the misperception that the library is not responsive to their needs. They complain to the library but fail to make the administration, which is in charge of the purse strings, aware of their needs. Faculty may also be reluctant to collaborate because they view the work involved as part of their domain and not that of the librarian. Or, they may view the work involved as work to be addressed by the librarian and not their job. On the flip side, when these collaborations do work they almost always result in establishing solid long-term relationships.

Publishers: How Can They Help

With flat or soon to be cut budgets, librarians can be leery of publishers looking to yet again attempt to sell them (or bypassing them and going directly to faculty) something that the library simply cannot afford. Sarah Schulman noted that her role is not to sell more products, but to work with librarians to find ways to make the most of resources they currently own. Helping librarians discover who among their faculty have published in specific journals or identifying faculty who might be interested in resources the library currently owns can be very helpful in fostering relationships. McCall pointed out that publishers should not simply focus on dealing with acquisitions staff. They should work with subject librarians who know their faculty best and are responsible for promoting the use of resources and soliciting valuable feedback. Leaving the subject librarian out of the loop generally results in that librarian not having the latest and most useful information that would benefit the faculty. At UCF, publishers such as Springer, Sage, Gale, and Taylor & Francis have helped to facilitate outreach by participating in and providing funding for outreach events and providing promotional materials.

Conclusions

Outreach is often difficult yet necessary and frequently proves beneficial for faculty and students by creating an awareness of library resources, promoting their use, and even finding the funds to purchase new resources. There are no easy formulas and sometimes the best of efforts fail, but patience and communication are essential.

We're Not So Different, You and I: How Librarians and Publishers Use Statistics in Different Ways to Achieve Similar Goals

Sarah D. Schulman, Account Development Specialist, Springer

Alexis Linoski, System Libraries Resource Development Director, Texas A&M System Libraries

Abstract

Statistical gathering and analysis plays an important role for librarian and publisher alike as we strive to predict and decipher end user behavior and improve collection development. During this session, hear from a librarian who works with a large university library consortium, and a representative from a major publisher, on how statistics factor into our workflow—and the stories they can tell about how content is being discovered and used. Learn about specific projects and applications from each side, and hear how analyzing end user behaviors helps refine everything from services we provide to institutional decision making. There will also be time for audience members to ask questions and share their own experiences.

Springer

The Account Development (AD) team at Springer collaborates with academic and government library customers to help them attain the best possible value from purchased content. Statistical gathering and analysis is just one method they use to work toward this goal.

What type of statistics do we look at and why?

1. **COUNTER reports:** On a quarterly basis, each AD team member gathers and records in a central datasheet the

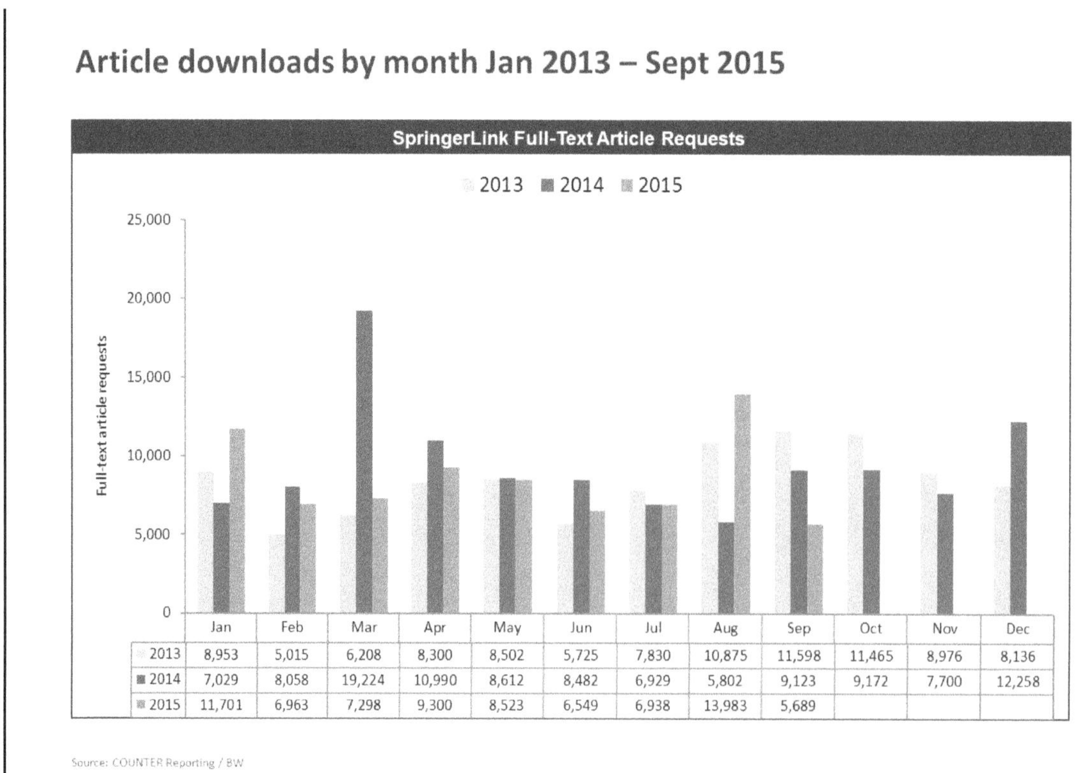

Figure 1. This chart compares three years of journal article COUNTER usage on a monthly basis.

http://dx.doi.org/10.5703/1288284316295

English-language packages: chapter denials by eBook package Jan – Sept 2015

eBook Package	Contemporary	SBA
Behavioral Sciences	146	192
Biomedicine & Life Sciences	653	693
Business & Economics	227	88
Chemistry & Materials Science	187	304
Computer Science	10	74
Earth & Environmental Sciences	56	183
Energy	9	
Engineering	406	86
Humanities, Social Sciences & Law	515	316
Mathematics & Statistics	236	633
Medicine	1,205	336
Physics & Astronomy	80	237
Professional & Applied Computing	20	
Total	**3,750**	**3,142**

Source: COUNTER Reporting / BW; Springer Book Archive = CY 2004 or older; excluding Protocols

Figure 2. This table shows e-book chapter denials, or turnaways, by subject collection and age (contemporary versus archival).

COUNTER statistics for every "key customer" in our dedicated regions. A "key customer" is defined as one who has purchased or renewed any Springer products that year (including journals, books, and databases). The AD team mostly works with academic institutions with a Carnegie Classification of Master's Large or higher, although there are some exceptions. In addition to COUNTER statistics, the central datasheet for each region shows how much customers spend per product, the previous year's usage, and a percentage showing how much COUNTER usage has increased or decreased from the previous year.

Gathering COUNTER statistics on a regular basis and recording them in a central document provides a one-stop method of monitoring usage, spending, and cost per download. Is usage increasing each year the way we want it to in relation to spending increases? Where is usage decreasing or remaining static? Keeping an eye on this information helps the AD and sales teams ensure that all customers are getting the best ROI and usage.

2. **Account reviews:** Throughout the year we visit most (if not all) key customers along with our regional sales counterparts to present account reviews. These detailed PowerPoint presentations show a visual, in-depth analysis of the most current usage and denial statistics per product. Please see Figures 1 and 2 for specific examples.

Performing these account reviews serves a number of purposes. Much like with the central document for quarterly COUNTER statistics, it provides an easy way to compare usage trends per customer on a monthly basis in addition to annually. By looking at the most and least used subject

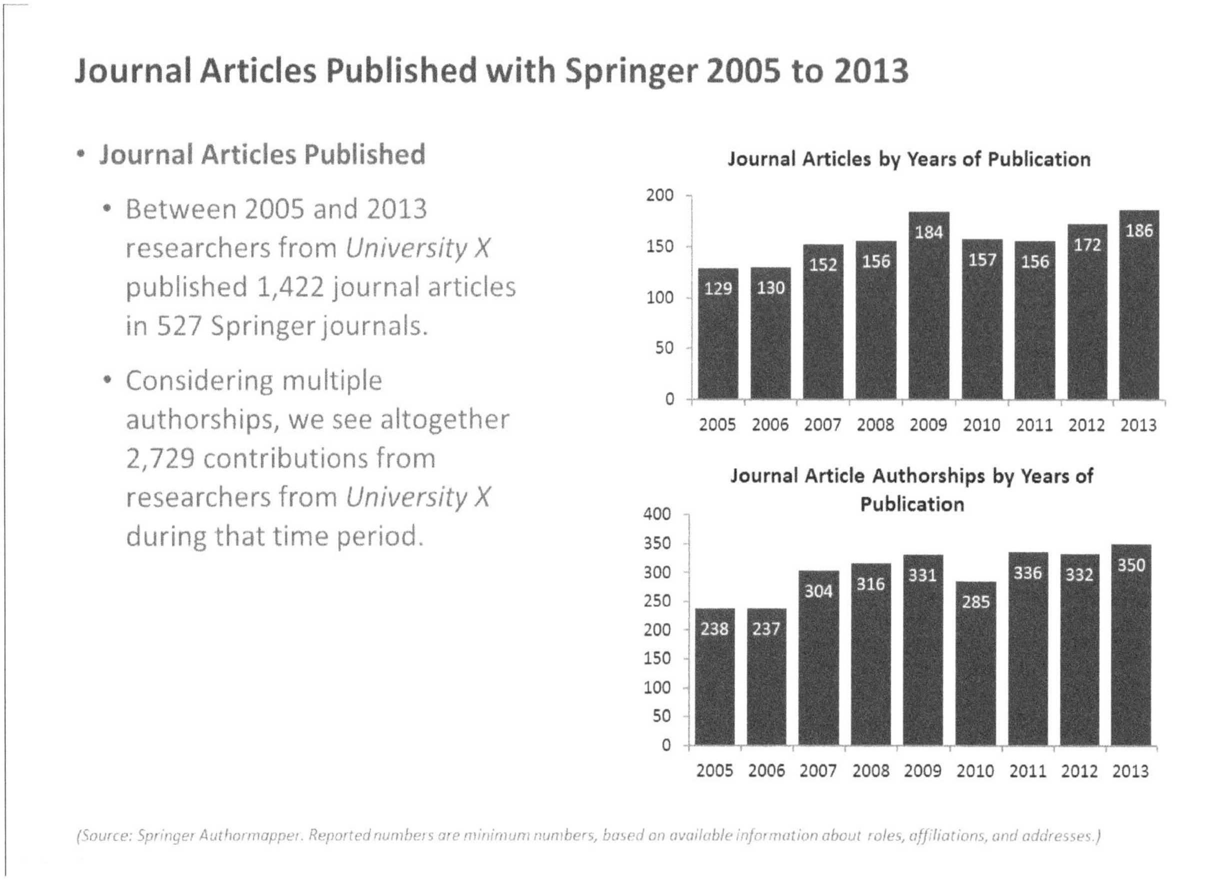

Figure 3. This chart shows the number of journal articles published by authors affiliated with University X from 2005 to 2013.

areas, customers can see which collections might benefit from additional marketing or instruction on campus. Additionally, an account review might reveal problems with the content's accessibility or discoverability which require troubleshooting (either by Springer or the library).

3. **End user behavior analyses:** Usually provided as a complement to the account review, end user behavior analyses look at metrics provided by a licensed service called WebTrekk. This product works in real time and can drill down by individual institution to show how end users arrive at the SpringerLink platform with such metrics as:

    - Entry sources or referrer URLs
    - Search phrases. These may be external (for example, what a user typed into Google while on campus that took them to SpringerLink) or internal (which search terms the end user is entering into SpringerLink's native search box)
    - Number of unique and returning visitors, plus the average amount of time they spend on the site and number of pages looked at
    - Technology used (for example, how many end users were on a PC or laptop versus mobile device? Which operating systems/web browsers were most used?)
    - Most popular visit months, weekdays, or times

There are many more metrics that WebTrekk is capable of analyzing, and they can be examined using multiple time frames. Presenting this information provides additional context to the

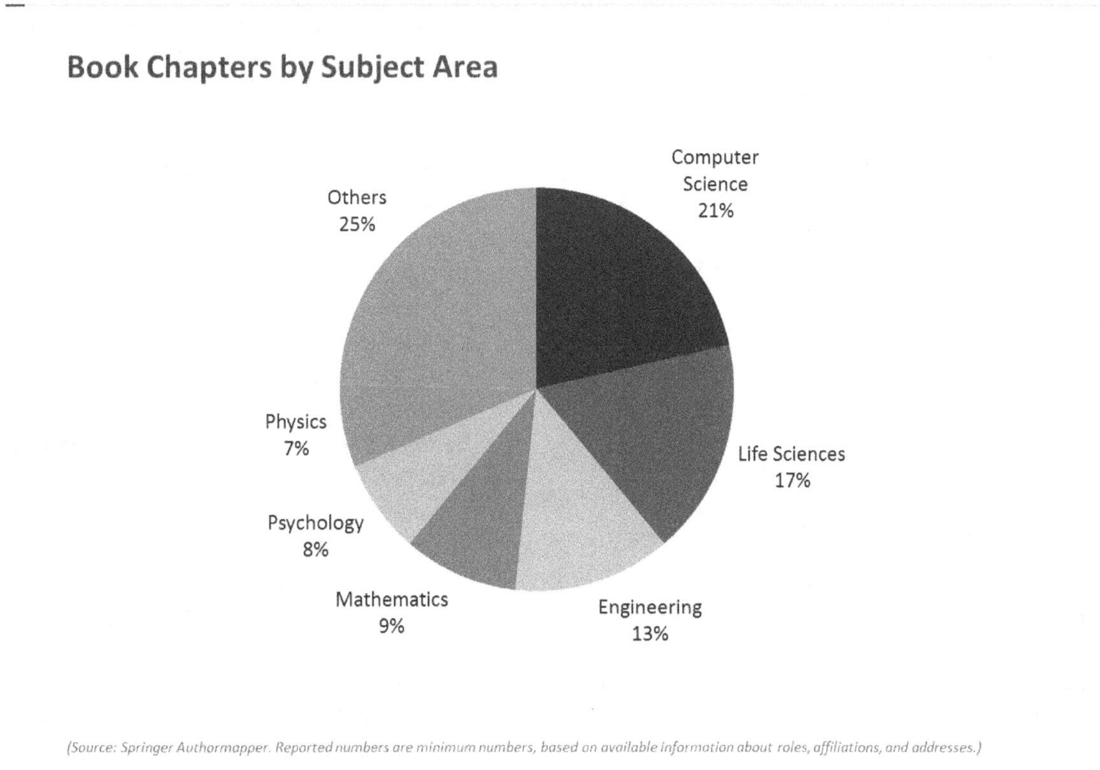

Figure 4. This chart shows volume of book chapter authorships affiliated with University X by subject area.

COUNTER usage reports and account reviews we show to library customers, and can tell a story about the people behind the numbers. Much like with the account reviews, it may also reveal certain access or discovery issues. For example, if a particular library has a full discovery layer but none of the top 20 referrer URLs are from their link resolver, this may warrant further review.

Authorship analyses: Occasionally and upon request, Springer will analyze the volume of authorship affiliated with a particular institution and present it to the library. These analyses examine journal articles, whole books, and book chapters to provide the total numbers (as a whole and also accounting for multiple contributions) along with a breakdown of authorship by subject area. Please see Figures 3 and 4 for specific examples. These reports can help librarians monitor and support local publishing and research trends. They may also help to facilitate relationships between faculty and librarians, or even boost usage of homegrown content. From a marketing standpoint, librarians and publishers might collaborate and use local authorship as a "hook" for usage-based end user campaigns.

4. **Miscellaneous:** Customized usage, cost, or other types of analyses may be provided as needed or upon request. For example, a customer may wish to see the cumulative usage of an e-book package purchased in 2010, or a cost per title versus list price analysis. These miscellaneous reports serve a range of functions both internal (for example, help facilitate a sale or renewal) and external (for example, assist in collection assessment projects).

Next Steps: What Do We Do With This Information?

The next steps Springer takes after providing one or all of these analyses vary depending upon the situation and goals on both sides. For example, during a routine annual "check-in" style of visit, we might just say, "how do you feel about what we just saw? Any concerns or questions?" and leave it there. Where needed, these reports can serve as a springboard to plan usage-boosting initiatives such as trainings, end user marketing campaigns, or reviewing Springer's discoverability within a school's online system. Conversations with librarians are invaluable to learn which information is most useful, which in turn helps Springer to inform future goals and best practices.

Texas A&M System Libraries

Why Review Usage Statistics?

Libraries generally review usage statistics to determine if resources *are* being used and, if so, what is the cost per use. Usage statistics can also be used to determine gaps in the collection and to determine *how* the resource is being used.

Usage is not the same for all resources. For databases, journal packages, e-book collections, and streaming media collections, searches or full-text downloads are normally used, with cost per use being determined based on the cost for the database or package. For individual journal subscriptions and e-book purchases, full-text downloads or title usage/circulation numbers are used, with cost per use being determined based on the cost of the subscription or book. The same applies to individual purchases of streaming media.

Almost all libraries rely on COUNTER reports. These standardized reports provide article/full-text downloads, database/collection usage, and title usage, which are used to determine cost per use. They also provide a variety of other reports, including turnaway reports, which show the number of attempts to access material not available through the libraries current subscription or collection. While COUNTER reports provide an "apples to apples" comparison for electronic resources, not all vendors provide COUNTER reports and not all resources are suitable for COUNTER reports (statistical databases are an example).

What Is Good?

To determine what is "good" usage, libraries generally set a threshold for cost per use, which can vary by resource type. Anything below the threshold is good and anything above the threshold is bad. When setting the threshold, libraries should take into account the average cost of ILL and cost per article from the vendor or other sources (such as the Copyright Clearance Center). The same criteria, either Searches or full-text downloads, should be used for databases and collections. Title usage for these resources may not be as useful because the vendor can add or remove titles at any time. With the advent of Discovery systems, Searches may not be the best criteria to use as Discovery systems can skew those numbers. However, not all resources are included in Discovery systems, so Searches may be a good statistic for those resources.

"Bad" usage statistics can tell us a lot and it's not always that a resource should be dropped. Before eliminating a resource due to poor usage statistics, consider:

- Are users aware of the resource? Do marketing efforts need tuning?
- Does faculty outreach need to be increased?
- Are there searches but no full-text downloads? If so, perhaps:
  - The resource is not being used appropriately, i.e., a Humanities resource is being used for science research.
  - Users may need instruction.
- Consider online tutorials for distance students.
- If journal subscription usage is low on the vendor platform, is the title included in another resource? If so, what is the usage for that platform?

- The user population is small, i.e., the resource supports a small degree program.

If none of these factors contribute to the low usage numbers, then perhaps the resource should be cancelled.

It should be noted that while purchased e-book titles can't be cancelled, specific title usage or non-usage can provide information for future collection development.

An invaluable collection building tool is the Turnaway Report. Turnaway reports can help inform collection development decisions regarding subscriptions to specific journals or purchase of specific e-book or movie titles (for streaming media collections). Turnaway reports can also help inform decisions regarding resource settings, i.e., should unsubscribed content be hidden from default searches.

There's More

While COUNTER reports are good, many libraries are seeking more information about how their resources are being used. Non-COUNTER reports are a good place to start, and many vendors offer these reports in addition to COUNTER reports. Two types of reports that stand out are "Top Search Terms" and "Top Referring Sites." Top Search terms can be valuable in learning not only what terms users are searching for, which can give insight into current course assignments, but also *how* they are searching—is it natural language or are they using Boolean operators? Are they broad searches, such as "C+" or very specific searches, such as "students for a democratic society"?

For individual e-book purchases from the same vendor, title circulation and usage can be enlightening. With purchased e-books, simple title usage or circulation is about that is needed to determine if purchased titles are being used. Hold lists and suggestion lists also provide information regarding collection development.

Other reports that might prove interesting are those that give the time of highest usage, number of user accounts created, and length of visit.

Data That Counts, Charleston Conference 2015

Lorraine Estelle, Director, Project COUNTER

Jo Lambert, JISC Service Manager, JISC

Abstract

Since the first Code of Practice was published in 2003, the COUNTER (Counting Online Usage of Networked Electronic Resources) standard has facilitated the recording and reporting of online usage statistics in a consistent and comparable way. The standard, now in its fourth iteration, has developed over time in response to the changing e-resource environment and to evolving user requirements. Engagement with relevant initiatives and input from vendors is critical to COUNTER's ongoing evolution. Amongst these, COUNTER has worked with NISO on SUSHI (Standardized Usage Harvesting Initiative) to develop a protocol to facilitate the automated harvesting and consolidation of usage statistics from different vendors.

Both COUNTER and SUSHI form the basis of tools to facilitate the gathering and analysis of usage data, and they help support provision of efficient and cost-effective services. One such tool is the Jisc funded JUSP (Journal Usage Statistics Portal), which provides a single point of access to data, enabling libraries to quickly and easily compare usage across a range of publishers and years. Accurate and comparable, usage statistics support analysis and evaluation of e-resources and help to demonstrate their value and impact. JUSP is an important tool that aims to support libraries in this context. This session will outline how COUNTER supports development of tools and services with global reach and impact. It will highlight challenges and opportunities that exist with regard to metrics in terms of developing, gathering, and analyzing data, and will offer some shareable models of good practice.

Introduction

Librarians from across the world use COUNTER usage statistics to inform their decision-making, but as useful as the reports are, their collection can be time-consuming and tedious. However, the combination of the COUNTER Code-of Practice with the National Information Standards Organization (NISO)'s Standardized Usage Statistics Harvesting Initiative (SUSHI) protocol is a game changer. The two standards, if correctly implemented can create an infrastructure on which library consortia and other third parties can build national and regional services. The Journals Usage Statistic Portal (JUSP) and Institutional Repository Usage Statistics (IRUS) in the UK are examples of two such trusted services that are saving librarians and institutional repository managers in the UK much time by removing duplicated manual effort.

The Journals Usage Statistic Portal (JUSP)

Increasing pressure on library budgets means that demonstrating a return on investment for costly e-resources is critical. JUSP is a tool that aims to make this process quicker, easier, and more effective. Jisc, an organization that provides digital solutions for UK education and research, funds JUSP to deliver a service that is free at the point of use for academic libraries. Avoiding the need to visit multiple publisher websites to gather usage statistics, JUSP enables libraries to quickly and easily compare usage across a range of publishers and years through providing a single point of access. Standardised data conforming to the COUNTER standard is gathered on behalf of libraries using the machine-to-machine SUSHI protocol, thereby offering great efficiencies.

The service provides accurate and comparable usage data to support evaluation of e-resources. Apart from viewing and downloading standard usage reports, libraries can access a range of added- value reports to help analyse usage, consider trends over time, and establish value for money to help in purchasing decisions. The service also includes data from gateways and hosts, which help to provide a truer picture of usage when

http://dx.doi.org/10.5703/1288284316296

viewed in conjunction with data direct from publishers.

Currently used by libraries in the UK and Sweden, the service provides access to usage data from around 80 publishers and intermediaries, although this number is constantly growing. COUNTER reports currently gathered are the journal reports JR1, JR1a, JR1 GOA, and from February 2016 the service will include book reports BR1, BR2, and BR3.

Use of JUSP

> Usage statistics are used to inform important decisions and we really want to be sure we can rely on the accuracy of the data; with JUSP we know we can. We will often present this information to academics and it will be scrutinised so it's important for us to be sure that the data is reliable.
>
> —Birkbeck, University of London (speaking of JUSP)

Libraries value JUSP's role in terms of providing accurate, reliable, and standardised content. A series of machine and human validation checks by the JUSP team ensure that errors are significantly reduced. However, the addition of numerous people using the service means that data is constantly scrutinised and problems picked up by just one individual can lead to benefits for everyone. There are instances where a publisher might need to restate data so JUSP can reharvest data on behalf of everyone, potentially avoiding massive duplication of effort.

Quick and convenient access to data via JUSP saves libraries time, enabling them to spend less time on data gathering and more time on data analysis in support of decision-making processes. Reports can be generated at the click of a button, enabling people to respond to requests quickly and easily. Data can be viewed within the JUSP web interface or it can be exported for use within the library's own systems for further analysis of usage, for example by the addition of cost or fund data.

Data can be used for marketing or promotional purposes to consider how usage patterns can be used to promote the library's e-resource collections. As JUSP contains data for more than 90% of UK libraries, this aggregated data enables a comparison of usage with that of others in a similar group, size, or geographical region. These usage profiling reports enable libraries to check whether their own usage is higher or lower than average, to seek reasons for this, and where usage appears higher to use this in library promotion.

IRUS-UK

Institutional repositories (IRs) are key to promoting visibility of research outputs. Given that organisations are keen to demonstrate the value and impact of IRs, IRUS-UK plays an important role.

IRUS-UK is a statistics aggregation service for repositories in the UK, enabling them to share and compare usage statistics using the COUNTER standard. The service collects and then processes usage data from repositories, and consolidates those data into COUNTER-compliant statistics by following the rules of the COUNTER Code of Practice. The service enables repositories to provide consistent, comparable, and trustworthy usage data whilst benchmarking usage of their repository across the UK.

93 UK repositories were using IRUS in December 2015, a number that is constantly growing in support of widespread benchmarking opportunities. The service offers time-saving benefits, supports quality assurance processes, and helps to improve data quality.

By providing a nationwide view of UK institutional repository use, IRUS is helping to demonstrate the importance and value of IRs.

Use of IRUS-UK

> What helps is that it's independent and COUNTER-compliant . . . the fact that it is independent and standards compliant is really important.
>
> —The Open University (speaking of IRUS-UK)

Repository statistics can be inconsistent, and without adherence to an agreed standard it's not possible to compare usage across a range of repositories and software. Reliable, consistent, and comparable measurement is a key feature of IRUS-UK, which is seen as providing an independent and impartial service based on the COUNTER standard.

The service supports institutions in understanding the usage of their IR, enabling a check of total activity, items, and authors attracting significant attention or particular item types with higher numbers of downloads. Key statistics or headline figures can be used in various ways to promote awareness and interest.

Use of IRUS statistics can support advocacy, encouraging researchers to use the repository as they can directly see the impact in terms of usage. It serves as a convenient resource to point researchers toward and can support them with their professional review or by enabling them to track the impact of any dissemination activity in relation to their research.

With data in the portal going back to 2012 for some institutions, IRUS is a really valuable source of data about trends over time. People can check whether repository usage is increasing and how it is changing from one year to the next.

IRUS is being used extensively for benchmarking, both internally and externally. Being able to benchmark the performance of a repository with other institutions of a similar size, for example, provides a wider context and enables useful comparisons to be made. It can highlight trends within an organisation, or the performance of different item types within a repository.

Challenges and Opportunities

Aggregating data at scale means that adherence to standards and use of machine processes is crucial, but there are challenges in terms of delivering shared services in this space.

JUSP is developing an e-books usage statistics service but current activity indicates a mixed picture with regard to COUNTER-compliance, and in some cases vendors are not yet providing machine services to support data harvesting. A concerted effort by all parties is required to make some progress in this area.

Problems arise when vendors or universities make changes to their products or repositories without considering the impact this might have. It's always necessary to consider the wider context. Services such as JUSP and IRUS can highlight the bigger picture and demonstrate how small changes can make a significant difference.

Both JUSP and IRUS use machines to remove many of the onerous, repetitive processes such as downloading and aggregating data. Avoiding this duplication of effort enables greater efficiencies as staff can spend less time on data wrangling and more time analyzing data and making decisions on the basis of that data.

Services such as JUSP offer greater efficiencies for publishers. The Jisc team can interact with publishers over known problems in relation to COUNTER reports for instance and be a single point of contact rather than individual universities contacting a publisher each reporting the same problem.

These services are used by a significant number of UK universities, over 90% in the case of JUSP. This means that the development team can represent the views of the community, and this collective voice can really help to influence change. JUSP insists on COUNTER compliance, but at the same time the team work closely with publishers to help them address any anomalies with the data or their service. The team has regularly helped to test new SUSHI services or reports and particularly during the transition to Release 4 of the COUNTER Code of Practice for e-Resources.

These services provide a means to connect communities of librarians, publishers, ERM vendors, or standards organisations and to share good practices. They offer a practical implementation of a standard, highlighting where there might be issues with the standard or its interpretation or implementation, and it can suggest corrective action.

Conclusion

The information environment has changed considerably since COUNTER implemented Release 4 of the Code of Practice, and work is now underway to develop the next release. The work on Release 5 will be focused on increased utility and efficiency for all of the stakeholders. There will be a move away from a proliferation of different reports and the Excel format. COUNTER will seek to develop fewer reports, designed for SUSHI collection, and in a format that will allow users to filter for the information that they need. Ideally, the new Code of Practice, will enable the development of services such as JUSP and IRUS in many other countries and regions, improving efficiency and enabling librarians, library consortia, and institutional repository managers to concentrate their time on using the data to inform strategy, rather than the manual collection of reports.

Find out more

JUSP: http://jusp.mimas.ac.uk

IRUS UK: http://www.irus.mimas.ac.uk

COUNTER: http://www.projectcounter.org

NISO: http://www.niso.org/about/

SUSHI: http://www.niso.org/workrooms/sushi

Management and Administration

"Flip This House": "Back of the House" Library Staff Engaging the Wider Campus Community

Patrick J. Roth, Head of Systems and Technology, Grand Valley State University

Jeffrey D. Daniels, Head of Knowledge Access and Resource Management Services, Grand Valley State University

Abstract

Procuring and describing content for discoverability are as important now as they ever have been, but we suggest that a successful organization should expect more from faculty and staff members. As technical skill sets become more in demand, "back of the house" staff need to step to the front. In this article we explore how two Grand Valley State University Libraries back of the house departments have partnered with other organizations on campus. Collaboration has reenergized the staff, raised the Libraries's profile, and contributed to the Libraries's overall success.

Traditionally "back of the house" staff work exclusively behind the scenes to grow and support the collections of the library. Even the term itself indicates, "back of the house" staff should remain behind closed doors, working on tasks that, while important, are not easily identifiable to library users. Procuring and describing content for discoverability are as important now as it they ever have been, but a successful organization should expect faculty and staff to do more. As technical skill sets become more in demand campus-wide, the "back of the house" staff are presented with opportunities to step to the front. Two Grand Valley State University (GVSU) Libraries departments typically considered back of the house have partnered with other entities on campus, providing services that are otherwise unavailable. The experiences of these staff members have demonstrated a growing need for back of the house staff to engage with the campus community. Flipping the house by getting these staff members more widely involved has reenergized the staff, raised the Libraries's profile, and contributed to the Libraries's overall success.

Having back of the house staff spend time on outreach isn't a new idea. A 2011 article from Toce and Schofield discusses the value of all library departments providing services that integrate them into the wider campus community and help make the library indispensable. They point out that outreach is traditionally the responsibility of public services departments and instruction librarians, but that technical services departments have unique skills that can lend themselves to other areas on campus. GVSU Libraries firmly believe that Toce and Schofield were correct in their thinking that all library departments can provide service. Through both deliberate partnerships and chance encounters the GVSU Libraries have taken advantage of outreach opportunities. At the GVSU Libraries the Research and Instruction division is primarily responsible for outreach to both faculty and students. They do an excellent job working with the campus community and have done noteworthy work in showcasing the importance of the Libraries. The Knowledge Access and Resource Management Department (KARMS; formerly the Technical Services Department) and the Systems and Technology Department have also begun reaching out and providing services to the campus. This not only has increased the profile of the Libraries, but also has provided additional support around campus for library-provided services.

If Toce and Schofield got it right in 2011, why, in 2015, are so many back of the house departments still solely focused on library-centric tasks? GVSU Libraries found themselves asking these questions in 2012. This thinking led the entire Technology and Information Services (TIS) division to rethink its workflows and approach to providing services. Carlos Rodriquez, Associate Dean of TIS, challenged every staff member in the division to

http://dx.doi.org/10.5703/1288284316297

reexamine their workloads, shifting the focus from task to reason. Why do we catalog material? Why do we have circulation limits. Who is the primary user of our library tools? The resulting changes weren't sweeping, and the division is still responsible for all traditional back of the house functions. The impact was a shift in focus from the task to the patron. Through this focus on the patron it began to become clear that TIS had some services they could offer to other departments at GVSU.

One of the early attempts at tweaking the KARMS team was to add more direct contact with the University community. This was accomplished by a cross-training program with the Operations and User Services team. GVSU Libraries have one service point in the library, handling circulation, reference, and general questions of all kinds. The service point is primarily staffed by student workers, but at all times there is a staff member at the "perching station." This station is within sightline of the service point, and the staff person there is responsible for overseeing the service point and stepping in for more complex requests. The staff member at the perching station also answers chat questions as they come into the library. Six members of the KARMS team began working the service point between two and four hours each week.

There are quite a few benefits to this arrangement. The main benefit has been allowing back of the house staff direct contact with our patrons. When you spend the majority of your time cataloging books, tracking down rush acquisitions, and maintaining and troubleshooting electronic resources, it can be easy to forget the why behind any of those tasks. You can easily begin to focus on the task at hand and lose sight of the reason we do any of that work: supporting the needs of our patrons. Interacting with the patrons just a few hours a week keeps the "why" fresh in their minds. Dealing with patrons face to face and seeing how KARMS work impacts these patrons and keeps the staff motivated to do the best job they can.

Quite a few other benefits also come from this arrangement. While the KARMS team covers between 10 and 20 hours a week of perch station time, the operations team is able to get some work of their own done, further removed from the hustle and bustle, focusing on jobs that require less distraction to do well. The KARMS team members get a change of pace for that little bit of time each day. We have worked really hard for our teams to not be isolated, but still the majority of our work is behind closed doors, focused intently on the computer. Benefits that we didn't anticipate became clear early on. Two of the KARMS team members working the service point are responsible for electronic resource management. While working, they quickly realized as electronic resource questions came to the desk that student employees around would hear them answer questions and frequently say things like "Oh . . . I didn't know that." The same is true for our cataloger, government document specialist, and journal specialist. There are questions that come up where the KARMS team is the most qualified in the organization to answer. We have learned that having them at the service desk creates teachable moments for the student workers.

Other examples of encouraging the KARMS staff to get involved follow similar lines. Two members of the teams are inclusion advocates at GVSU. This roll requires training from Human Resources, and every search committee on campus must have an inclusion advocate. Inclusion advocates are part of a search committee with the added roll of making sure that GVSU creates an environment that values differences across all dimensions of diversity. The KARMS inclusion advocates are therefore on multiple search committees, bringing that expertise to the process, but also exposing them to all types of jobs that the Libraries hire for.

GVSU has received a lot of press in recent years for the Mary Idema Pew Library Learning and Information Commons, which opened in June 2013. This state of the art library is beautiful and unique. Over two years into the new building we still have requests for tours on a regular basis. Several members of the KARMS team have undergone our internal training and serve as tour guides at special events. This is yet another opportunity to get out of the back of the house and interact directly with patrons of the Libraries.

These types of opportunities have benefited the Libraries in a number of ways. The KARMS team is noticeably more comfortable interacting directly with our students, faculty, and staff at GVSU. They bring a very unique set of skills out and about with them, being able to offer their knowledge to better the campus community.

Not all of the services provided by the traditional technical services teams are new ideas, or even new workflows. GVSU, like many academic institutions, has many small departmental libraries. These libraries aren't managed by the Libraries, and these collections are often housed in specific departmental locations across the campus. By simply incorporating this material into standing workflows, the back of the house staff can increase the discoverability of this material exponentially. The KARMS team at GVSU Libraries works with the Office of Undergraduate Research and Scholarship, the Women's Center, the LGBT Resource Center, the Faculty Teaching and Learning Center, the Office of Student life, and the Annis Water Resource Institute. Services offered to these units easily fit into the day-to-day work of the KARMS department. Each departmental library received a location code in the Library Management System (LMS) and then each department collection was cataloged into the LMS. Material included traditional monographs and serials, but also more unique items such as poster tubes and sound recorders have been added to the library catalog. Each location was able to work with the Libraries to determine if they would loan their material and what those loan rules would be. In more than one case the Libraries installed a version of its LMS on a departmental computer, allowing for circulation. With a relatively small outlay of time needed to get the initial collections ingested, the workload has settled into routine. Each department sends over materials as they acquire them, everything from one book at a time to a box of journals at the end of the semester. The KARMS staff processes the material into the collection and returns the material to the specific department. Now these collections can be searched as part of the Libraries collection as well as limited to each location. Furthermore, this material is included in the information sent to the Libraries discovery service. For example, a patron can limit a search using the Libraries's discovery service to just find material owned and located at the LGBT Resource Center.

Possibly the biggest single example of outreach has been the development and hiring of the Metadata and Digital Curation Librarian. GVSU added this new position to the KARMS team about five years ago. Looking at the job description, one sees responsibilities that they would expect from a Cataloging Librarian:

- Tracks developments in metadata schemas and leads the ongoing development and implementation of metadata standards and best practices within the Libraries and across the University.
- Develops best practices for authority control for access points and provides resolution for heading conflicts in the Libraries' catalog (Sierra), institutional repository (Digital Commons), and digital collection management and preservation system (Preservica).

But the intention of this position was to be much more than a standard cataloging position. This position also

- Assists in setting policies, priorities, and practices for the production, management, and preservation of digital content.
- Collaborates with the Scholarly Communications Outreach Coordinator, Digital Initiatives Librarian, Liaison Librarians, and faculty and academic units outside of the library to determine faculty data service needs; and provides advice on the organization and description of research data produced.
- Collaborates with the Scholarly Communications Outreach Coordinator, Digital Initiatives Librarian, Liaison Librarians, and faculty and academic units outside of the library to assist in writing data management plans for grant applications to ensure usability, preservation, and access.

More than five years ago Carlos Rodriguez, associate dean of technology and information services, recognized that researchers on campus were frequently being required to make long-term preservation and access plans for the data collected during research. The University didn't have a department providing the knowledge and support to assist these researchers with data management plans. Today the metadata and digital curation librarian spends a good deal of time consulting with departments and researchers about their data management needs. While still providing the cataloging expertise to the library, this position doesn't have daily cataloging responsibilities, spending more and more time working outside of the Libraries.

Outreach opportunities also exist for Libraries systems departments. Traditionally these departments have focused on supporting Libraries software, managing the content on the Libraries website, and providing technical support to Libraries faculty and staff. While GVSU's systems and technology department's primary responsibilities are internal to the Libraries, we've also begun to work with those outside of the Libraries to provide services and support. This has affected every member of the team and has really impacted how the Libraries are viewed by external departments.

Sometimes opportunities are the result of initiatives started within the systems department. Our digital initiatives librarian was interested in developing a quest based game that could help introduce students to the new library. This started with small discussions within the department and was eventually funded through the Libraries's emerging technology fund, as a pilot. Partnering with a local development company, YETi CGI, a mobile platform was developed that allowed users to complete quests that introduced them to library services, taught them how to find materials, and oriented them to physical spaces in the new library. This was a new role for the systems department as working directly with students is usually left to the public services department and the liaison librarians. After running a successful pilot test, it was decided to work with YETi to further develop LibraryQuest to include more features. More importantly, it was also decided to try and work some information literacy skills into some of the quests. This is very much outside of the scope of our department and required the formation of an internal partnership with the research & instruction division. This group helps inform and develop appropriate information literacy focused tasks for users to complete. This has been very beneficial in helping us better understand the work each department does, which is crucial as we work to support and collaborate with each other.

Another opportunity came about through the building of the new Mary Idema Pew Library. During the planning phase of the library all agreed on the idea that the library should be a place where discovery and creations should both occur. As a result it was determined that the library needed a space where the newest tools and technologies could be available to help students create. Through a partnership with the information technology department, the Atomic Object Technology Showcase was built. Eric Kunnen, the associate director of e-learning and emerging technologies, describes the Technology Showcase as "an immersive and engaging environment for faculty, staff, and students to interact, discover, learn, and share how innovative emerging technologies can enhance teaching and improve student learning" (2015). Though managed and primarily funded by the IT department, the library plays a key role in the Technology Showcase. One of the key technologies in the Technology Showcase is 3D printing, which the library funds, providing free campus-wide access. 3D printing and the other resources available allow us to reach a different group of students than we would through traditional methods. In addition, this has also strengthened our working relationship with the IT department and has allowed us to explore more opportunities to work together.

Another outreach opportunity that arose because of needed expertise is our assistance in website critiques. The GVSU Libraries is always focused on improving our online presence. This is something the Libraries can do but many departments cannot do, as they don't have the staff to do it.

The majority of departments have administrative assistants, support staff, or even student employees manage the content on their websites as part of their jobs; the Libraries are fortunate enough to have a full-time faculty member focus solely on web interfaces. In 2010 the GVSU Libraries hired a new web services librarian who brought a real passion for user experience and usability. Immediately a website usability testing program was implemented and gradual changes that responded to user needs were made. This user-friendly website has caught the attention of other departments on campus. One of the departments that noticed the improvement on the Libraries website was the institutional marketing department. This department oversees all campus websites, built GVSU's content management system, and works with departments to improve their websites. One way they do this is through sessions with departmental website managers, to come and get their websites critiqued. As they noticed the Libraries's website improve, they asked our web services librarian to begin to partner with them at these website critiques. This provided opportunities to showcase the Libraries's expertise, meet and network with other departments, and help students. This also strengthened our relationship with institutional marketing, which in turn has given us more freedom on our website and has also allowed us to influence website policies on campus, such as the move to responsive web design.

Providing services to students no matter their location is something that the Libraries have always done. Whether this means reference services over the phone, e-mail, or online chat, the Libraries are always looking for ways to meet student needs. In the past few years GVSU has seen an influx of nontraditional students and an increase in the number of online courses. The result is that departments that have traditionally served students in a face-to-face capacity are now looking for ways to provide virtual services. In 2013 the Libraries were contacted by the registrar's office about what service we used to provide chat reference. After a brief discussion on who provided our service, the Libraries agreed to contact the vendor and see what it would cost to add another department. If the registrar wanted the full suite of services it would cost them the same as the initial instance has cost the library Libraries. If they were willing to just have a separate chat widget and no additional functionality, it would cost them nothing and the registrar could be added to the Libraries's instance. This was great news to the registrar's office, as they just wanted a trial of the service. The Libraries agreed to help the registrar's office set up the service, train them on some best practices regarding chat services, and provide usage reports at the end of each semester. After the first semester the registrar's office declared the trial a success and expanded the number of staff they had monitoring chat as their virtual questions began to increase and in person visits began to decrease. Shortly after the end of the registrar's trial period the College of Health Professions contacted us about chat services as well. They had spoken with the registrar's office about the service and were wondering if it could be expanded to their office as well. We agreed to provide the same services. The introduction of chat to these departments has been beneficial to all parties involved. The departments get training, reports, and so on without a new system to manage and can reach their students in a new way. The Libraries get to determine which interface is used, giving us control of the look and feel of the interface. In addition, students now have the same user experience with chat service across multiple departments.

Another outreach opportunity to highlight is the Hack Your Campus event that the Libraries hosted and coplanned with various departments on campus. This event was similar to other events held around university campuses where students are asked to submit ideas on how to improve the student experience. The top ideas, selected by judges, were invited to present on their idea and show a plan for how the idea could be implemented. The Libraries's role in this event was coordinating and planning the event, hosting the event, and providing some of the prize money. That's a lot of involvement in something that we really have no expertise in. What we are interested in is innovation and helping students generate, develop, and implement ideas. For this event our digital initiatives librarian worked with the Libraries' liaison to the School of Business, the Center for Entrepreneurship and Innovation, campus dining, university promotions, the provost's office, and others to put on an event that encouraged students to think creatively. This improved the image of the Libraries among the students who participated and helped us create partnerships with other departments. The relationships built during the experience have already resulted in smoother communication when working on other programs and promotions.

Outreach and campus engagement are increasingly important for keeping the Libraries relevant moving forward. The public services arm of the Libraries is already great at doing this, especially as related to library services, instruction, and work with the classroom faculty. The growth opportunity is in back of the house departments finding ways to contribute as well. Our technical skills and ability to manage, describe, and organize large sets of data are not common in most departments on campus, showing the larger campus community and, more importantly, the campus administration our value is vital as budgets continue to get tighter. Many staff are very open to this idea of working with others, but the Libraries need to find a way to allow them to work it into their normal workflows. Supporting the collections and systems of the Libraries will always be the focus of back of the house teams, but outreach and collaboration should also be a priority.

References

Kunnen, E. (2015). Emerging technologies to enhance teaching and enable active learning. *Educause Review, 50*(4). Retrieved from http://er.educause.edu/articles/2015/8/emerging-technologies-to-enhance-teaching-and-enable-active-learning

Toce, J., & Schofield, C. (2011). Technical service outreach strategies for academic libraries. *Technical Services Quarterly, 28*(3): 312–321. Retrieved from http://dx.doi.org/10.1080/07317131.2011.571638

Aligning Collections With Emerging Needs in Research Informatics

Heidi J. Tebbe, Collection Manager for Engineering and Data Science, North Carolina State University Libraries

Darby Orcutt, Assistant Head of Collection Management, North Carolina State University Libraries

Abstract

Some of the North Carolina State University (NCSU) Libraries' largest investments are in collections, digital library development, and technology-rich collaborative spaces. The goal of the NCSU Libraries Fellows Program initiative, "Aligning Collections with Emerging Needs in Research Informatics," is to ensure these areas leverage one another to the benefit of our users in support of emerging research informatics needs through licensing and acquisition of new data sources, as well as leveraging the capabilities of new high-tech library spaces. Over its two years, this initiative seeks to address and mainstream subject specialists' and selectors' consideration of high-tech research informatics needs of users.

Early accomplishments of the initiative include content mining agreements, increased awareness of scholarly APIs, and an ontology to describe research informatics. Ongoing work includes an investigation of relevant collections, licensing terms, and the landscape of the current marketplace; an environmental scan of NCSU research and teaching contexts that would benefit from greater availability of content as data for computational purposes; how-to documentation and training for more technologically sophisticated uses of existing resources; negotiations of select licenses to allow for more flexibility of content use; and revision of our website to promote the research informatics capacities of the Libraries' collections to our users.

Background

Research informatics involves the use of technology to solve complex problems in the humanities, arts, and the social, natural, and applied sciences, through creating, storing, finding, manipulating, and sharing information. Discipline-specific areas of informatics include health informatics, social informatics, and digital humanities.

The NCSU Libraries Fellows Program (http://www.lib.ncsu.edu/fellows) offers new librarians a two-year appointment during which they develop expertise in a functional area and contribute to an initiative of strategic importance. Projects outside of their home department support strategic initiatives while providing concrete and innovative opportunities for fellows to interact with librarians from other departments and achieve at a professional level.

Some of the NCSU Libraries' largest investments are in collections, digital library development, and technology-rich collaborative spaces. The goal of the NCSU Libraries Fellows Program initiative, "aligning collections with emerging needs in research informatics," is to ensure these areas leverage one another to the benefit of our users in support of emerging research informatics needs through licensing and acquisition of new data sources, as well as leveraging the capabilities of new high-tech library spaces.

Over its two years, this initiative seeks to address and mainstream subject specialists' and selectors' consideration of high-tech research informatics needs of users.

Accomplishments

Content Mining Agreements

In June 2014, the NCSU Libraries announced the first of many successful negotiations with content providers for blanket content mining access for North Carolina State researchers, when we became the first institution in the world to offer this model of access to primary historical content from a major for-profit vendor (Gale). These

http://dx.doi.org/10.5703/1288284316298

accomplishments have been documented in several press releases, with more to come soon:

Gale: http://www.infodocket.com/wp-content/uploads/2014/11/final-Gale-data-mining-press-release-1103142.pdf

Unlimited Priorities/Accessible Archives: http://www.accessible-archives.com/2015/03/unlimited-priorities-and-ncsu-libraries-partner-to-create-model-data-mining-agreement/

Adam Matthew: http://news.lib.ncsu.edu/blog/2015/08/14/ncsu-libraries-adam-matthew-digital-strike-groundbreaking-content-mining-agreement/

Let's Eat Lunch and Talk About APIs!

Application programming interfaces, or APIs, are used to build software applications and may be used by scholarly publishers and others to allow users to retrieve data in a greater variety of ways. As such, they are important tools for librarians and researchers to know how to wield.

In April 2015, Heidi Tebbe led a brown bag discussion for subject specialists to increase awareness of APIs. The discussion included topics such as how APIs are used externally (Google Maps, Twitter) and internally (CatalogWS, FacetBrowser 2.0, scholarly publications repository, Suma, GIS Lookup), API vocabulary, potential issues an API user might experience, and things an API user should look for in the documentation (limitations, key, base URL, available resource types, response type).

Web Page for Users Seeking Data Sources

We have also created a list of scholarly resources that offer APIs or other online tools to access or manipulate data. Some of the resources allow large data downloads for research purposes, while others are intended for smaller scale research activities such as experimentation with visualization and development of tools to query journal and citation databases. More information is available at this link: http://go.ncsu.edu/textmining

Herding Research Informatics CATSS

Two essential questions for the initiative are:

1. How does a library evaluate their research informatics offerings?
2. What base knowledge and areas of expertise should library staff acquire?

"Informatics" and "research informatics" are terms that are too broad for effective investigation of these questions, and search results often get overtaken by the more active areas of discipline-specific informatics, such as health informatics. An informatics-specific vocabulary or taxonomy was needed.

A list of "things" related to research informatics was compiled by Tebbe, including visualization, text mining, APIs, and XML. Based on this list, she created a taxonomy with five categories, centered around functionality of the "things":

- Concepts: ideas that are relevant to research informatics
- Activities: things researchers do
- Tools: things researchers use
- Software: formally packaged tools
- Sources: things that provide researchers with data

This hierarchical representation was a good start, but what really was needed was a description of the domain of knowledge related to research informatics. An ontology would provide semantic relationships. A consideration of other ways "things" related to research informatics could be described led Tebbe to TaDiRAH (Taxonomy of Digital Research Activities in the Humanities). While TaDiRAH focuses on tools and methods for digital humanities, the research activities category is broad enough to describe research across disciplines. Research activities is broken down into the following subclasses: capture, creation, enrichment, analysis, interpretation, storage, and dissemination. For the purposes of this ontology, analysis and interpretation are considered to be the same activity.

We also needed a way to make connections with how we present library services. On the Libraries

Research Support portal, we currently have the following "bins": collections, citation management, data and GIS, grants and funding, data management, publishing and copyright, visualization, and measuring research impact.

Combining these ways of describing research informatics, the ontology (https://github.com/NCSU-Libraries/ontology-for-research-informatics) now has the following relationships:

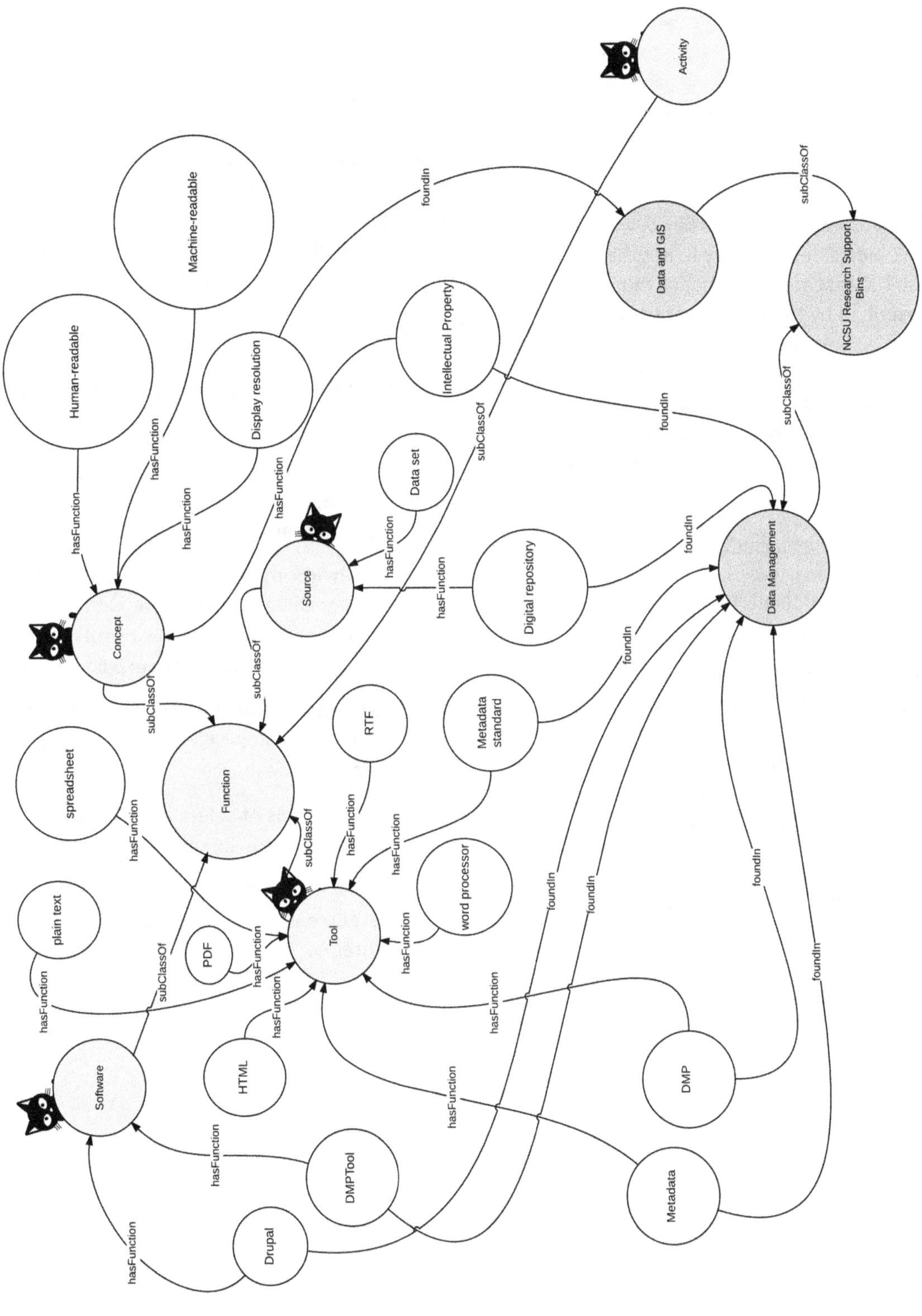

Figure 1. In June 2015, the Libraries' Data Management pages referenced one Concept, three Tools, two types of Software and one Source.

- Thing hasFunction Function
- Thing [is] usedDuring TaDiRAH Research Activity
- Thing [is] foundIn Research Support bin

Additionally, each thing has a definition, a definition source, and Libraries page references, which are Libraries pages or collection items that refer to the thing in question. A thing can only have one function, but can be used during multiple research activities and be found in multiple research support bins.

The value of an ontology like this is directly related to the objects described by it. In other words, almost 150 research informatics things have been described by the ontology, but this is by no means an exhaustive list and that will limit any investigations using the ontology. While the ontology can't provide definitive answers to our questions, it can point to areas that need more investigation and can serve as a starting point for exploration.

Ways to use the ontology include:

- Compare research informatics "things" to website search analytics
- Find the intersection of library departments who mention research informatics things the most with the research activity with the largest number of things to find things with which some library staff need to have some base knowledge
- Find what the Libraries are promoting (or not promoting) on the website

For example, looking at the NCSU Libraries data management "bin," we see one "concept": intellectual property, three "tools": Mmetadata, DMP, and metadata standard, two examples of "software": Drupal and DMPTool, and one "source": digital repository. We could also look at "things" used during the "storage" activity (shown in Figure 1), one of the TaDiRAH research activities closely related to data management, and see what we aren't talking about (namely, PDF, spreadsheet, HTML, word processor, plain text, RTF, dataset, display resolution, machine-readable, and human-readable). Display resolution is mentioned in the data and GIS bin, machine-readable is mentioned on a nonresearch support page, and a few of the things are found in the library collections, but what about the rest? Do they need to be mentioned?

Ongoing Work

Other planned work associated with the initiative include:

- An investigation of relevant collections, licensing terms, and the landscape of the current marketplace
- An environmental scan of NCSU research and teaching contexts that would benefit from greater availability of content as data for computational purposes
- How-to documentation and training for more technologically sophisticated uses of existing resources
- Negotiations of select licenses to allow for more flexibility of content use
- Revision of our web site to promote the research informatics capacities of the Libraries' collections to our users

Learning Mendeley Through Its Certification Program for Librarians

Rajiv Nariani, Science Librarian, York University Libraries

Ithayakuma, Marketing Development Manage, Mendeley

Abstract

York University Libraries (YUL) ended its subscription to their default citation management program in the summer of 2015. The Mendeley Certification Program for Librarians was launched during that time and the science librarian at YUL completed this program. The steps undertaken during the completion of the program led to successful migration to the freely available, and libraries supported, citation management programs. This paper details the various initiatives that were done prior to and during the certification program and how completing the program has benefited our academic community. The certification program has helped solidify relations with faculty and students during the migration process and also provided the librarians opportunities for professional development. The emergence of similar certification programs with added benefits for the academic community may lead to better uptake of new collaborative research management tools.

Introduction

Citation management programs have come to play an important part at York University Libraries (YUL). RefWorks has been the default citation management program at YUL since 2004. Up until 2014 we had over 48,000 RefWorks accounts registered in York's RefWorks system. In 2013, we had over 4,000 accounts created and by 2014 the number had dropped to 2,000 new registered accounts. This was because YUL was coming out of RefWorks. This program had served the faculty, students and staff at York University for the past eleven years. In 2014, YUL started promoting Mendeley and Zotero as the two freely available citation management programs. This paper details the steps involved in migrating to Mendeley and the completion of the Mendeley Certification Program by the science librarian during the summer of 2015.

This paper is divided into three parts:

- Reference management scenario at York University Libraries: prior to starting the certification program
- During the certification program: citation management survey
- Promoting Mendeley: post certification

Prior to the Certification Program

Starting in 2013, York University, like many other Ontario Council of University Libraries (OCUL) institutions, realized that it could not keep up with the ever-increasing costs of subscription-based citation management programs. Besides, our academic community also wanted more features in a program including, easy use of the citation plugin, the ability to capture metadata from web pages and PDFs, the ability to make notes on PDFs and compatibility with Mac. Librarians from OCUL discussed and pursued trials to other citation management programs. As a result, different citation management programs were being taught and promoted at Ontario universities during that period.

In the meanwhile, some of York University science faculty had heard about Mendeley at various science conferences. They were impressed by the unique features in this new citation management program and invited the science librarian (and the author of this paper) to teach this program. Mendeley was integrated in all library workshop sessions for upper undergraduate and graduate students in 2013. In 2014 when YUL decided to come out of subscription-based citation management programs, students and faculty members were provided library support to

http://dx.doi.org/10.5703/1288284316299

transfer their references from RefWorks to Mendeley or Zotero. The messages were posted periodically on the online university newsletter (YFile, 2014). The libraries also offered several bootcamps (Figure 1) for students and faculty to help with the migration process.

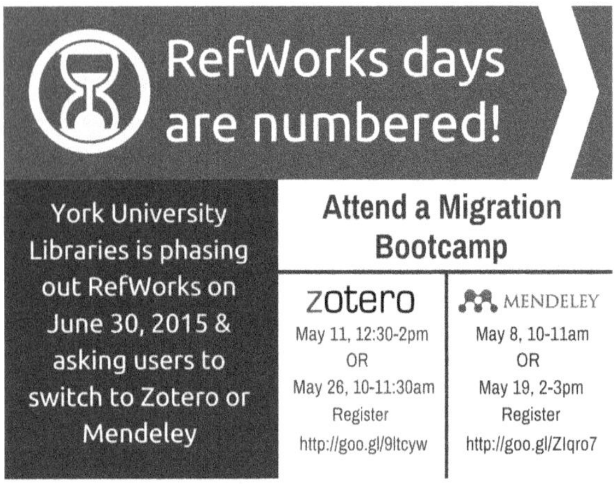

Figure 1. Migration bootcamp.

A citation management team, consisting of the associate university librarian (services), business librarian, science librarian, web librarian, bibliographic services manager, and the acting head of the library computing services, was also formed. Students and faculty could ask related questions about the migration process or request classes for Mendeley and Zotero. A dedicated e-mail account was set up to answer these questions, and members of the citation management team monitored this account.

The Build-Up to the Mendeley Certification Program: Understanding Faculty and Students' Needs

The science librarian was a part of the citation management team, and this provided him an impetus to conduct a survey on citation management tools being used by the science and health science faculty and graduate students. Another objective was to know why a particular program was being used and what features were important to them. It was also another way to inform RefWorks users that the subscription to the program was ending and librarians could help with the migration to a new citation management program.

Method

Two separate online surveys with a similar set of questions were created using Survey Monkey. Each of the surveys had five questions related to the use of citation management software and was sent to faculty members and graduate students in the sciences and health sciences in January 2015. The survey was kept open for three weeks. Initial questions were related to department affiliation and subsequent questions were about the usage of citation management programs and their pertinent features. Survey respondents had the ability to provide open-ended and question-specific comments. The whole survey took fewer than five minutes to complete. The survey link was e-mailed to a total of two hundred faculty members and four hundred graduate students.

Results and Discussions

Who were they?

A total of fifty-nine faculty members and a hundred twenty-five graduate students (Figure 1) completed the survey. We had a higher number of faculty members from psychology (*n* = 19) and kinesiology (*n* = 16), followed by the physics and astronomy faculty (*n* = 6) and chemistry faculty (*n* = 7). A total of ten faculty members from nursing and health science policy and management also participated.

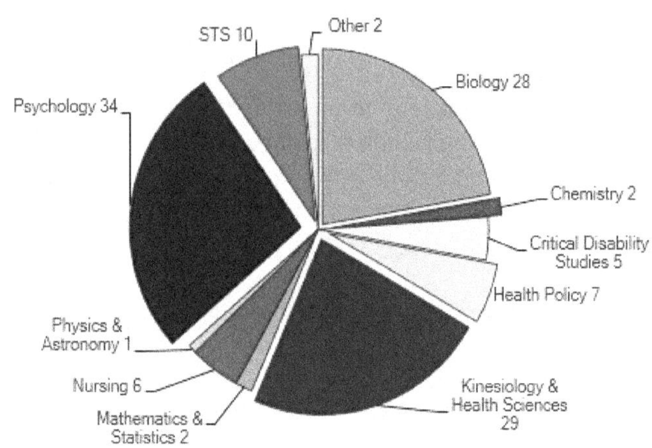

Figure 2. Students from different disciplines.

Similarly, we had a high number of graduate students from psychology (*n* = 34), kinesiology

(n = 29), and biology (n = 28), followed by science and technology studies, and nursing and health policy and management (Figure 2). The higher number in kinesiology and biology students could be because the author is the kinesiology and biology librarian. The psychology department is the largest department in the faculty of health at York University, and this could account for the higher number of psychology graduates completing the survey.

Which citation management programs had faculty and students used, and which one was used most often?

Faculty members and students were asked if they were using any citation management programs. We wanted to know if they had tried more than one program and if there were features in some other programs that were used more often. We also wanted to know the primary citation management program being used by our respondents.

Out of the fifty-nine faculty responses, fourteen had tried two or more citation management programs, and of the hundred twenty-five students, twenty-eight had tried more than one citation management program. Around 13% (n = 8) of the faculty and 17% (n = 20) of the graduate students did not use any citation management programs (Figure 3). Of the twenty students who replied in negative, three had tried at least one citation management program in the past.

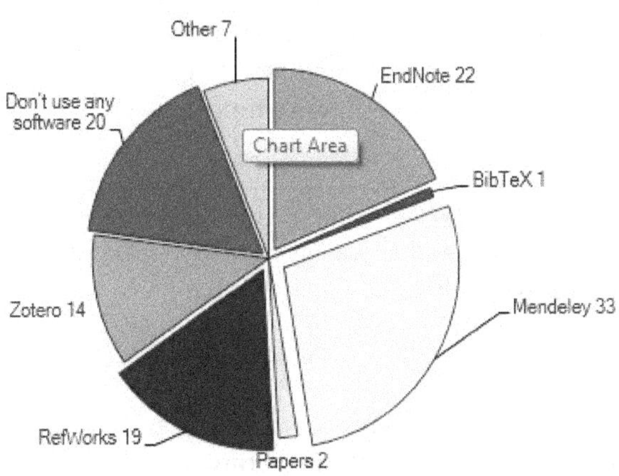

Figure 3. The most often used citation management program (students' responses).

The next question was about the citation management program used most often. Among the fifty-nine faculty members, we had the highest users for EndNote (n = 18), followed by RefWorks (n = 9) and Mendeley (n = 7). Of the one hundred eighteen students who replied to this question, thirty-three were using Mendeley and twenty-two were EndNote users, followed by RefWorks (n = 19) and Zotero (n = 14). Other programs mentioned by students and faculty included WizFolio, JabRef, Papers, Procite, and PERRLA. We had six faculty members and three graduate students who used BibTeX for formatting their references. They were from physics and astronomy, mathematics, and psychology.

> There are tricky issues in BibTex, it would be great if a library resource person was knowledgeable about it for occasional support. For journal submissions it generally works without problems, but textbook chapters sometimes require special formats that it won't do easily. Sometimes free help from the web exists, sometimes not.
>
> Faculty Comment

Our faculty members have been EndNote users for a long time. Many of them have purchased a personal subscription and have created groups and loaded papers in it. They have expressed some apprehension about migrating all the references, documents, and groups from EndNote to a different citation management program.

> I need help to save my massive endnote 7 libraries and be able to move it to newer computer when I get them.
>
> If you do migrate to another system, please choose one where it will be straightforward to transfer our lab's 1000's of references (with subfolders) over to the new system. Thanks!
>
> Faculty comments

Which features were important to them?

One of the objectives of this survey was to know the important features in a citation management program. The top features for our students were

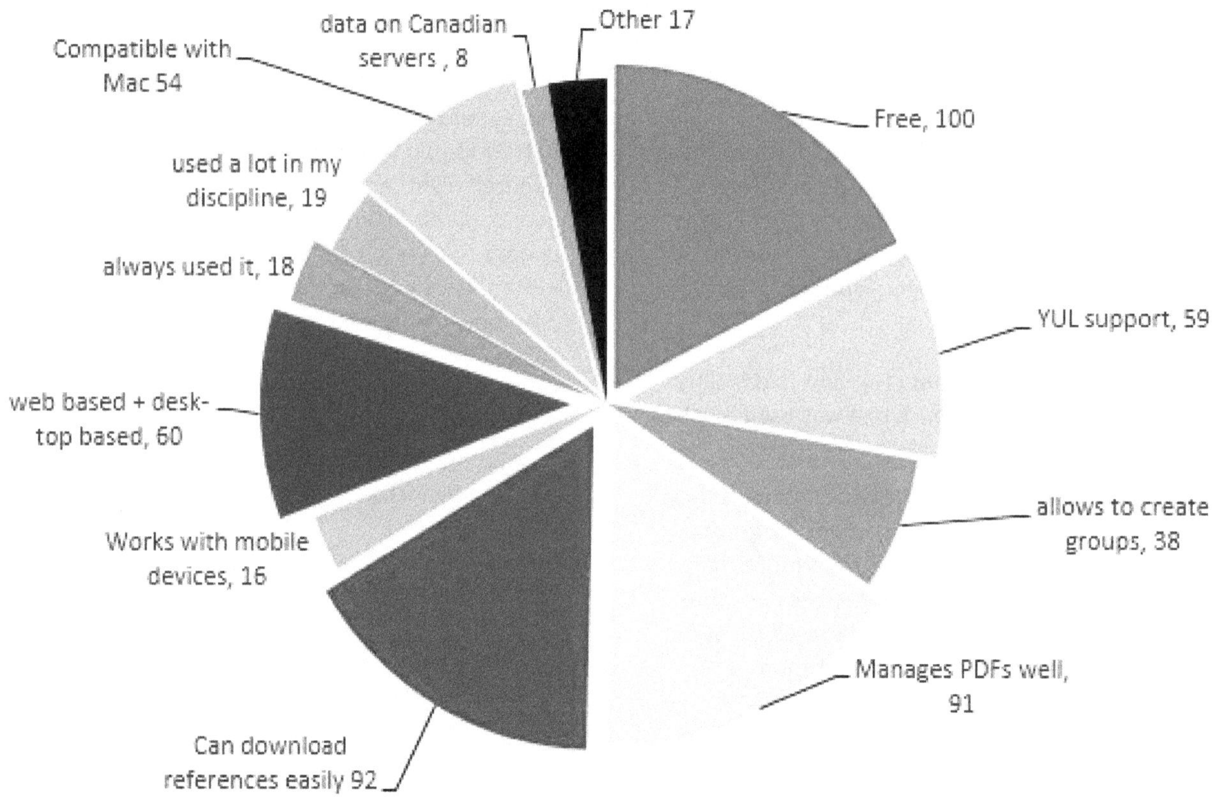

Figure 4. Features important in a citation management program (student responses).

that the citation management program be available free of cost (83%) and should work seamlessly with different databases (76%), handle PDFs well (75%), and be supported by the Libraries (Figure 4). Faculty also valued the ability to easily download references from different databases into the citation management program (80%), and more than half of the respondents wanted the program to extract metadata from the PDFs efficiently and wanted it to be freely available. Other features that scored high with both groups were that the program should have web-based and desktop components and that it was compatible with Macs. Our previous citation management program did not work well with Macintosh. It provided the ability to upload PDFs but could not extract metadata from the PDFs.

Very few survey respondents were concerned if their citation data was not stored on Canadian servers. Also, some faculty members preferred a citation management program because they had always been using one (38%), while some others preferred a particular program because it was used a lot in their areas of study (17%).

The decision to change to a new citation management program was not without challenges for our students, faculty, and librarians. Some of our users had created customized citation styles in Refworks, which needed to be redone in Mendeley. Similarly, the transfer of references, documents and folders, and private groups and PDFs contained in them was a time-consuming process.

> RefWorks was also supported by my old institution and changing over to a new one just seems like too much of a hassle.
>
> Faculty comment

During the migration process a few science faculty members had contacted the librarian to help with the migration of references collected by their lab members. On the positive side, the migration to a new program introduced our faculty and students to new features, which has been appreciated. They found that the newer citation management programs offer a cleaner and a simpler interface. They liked the ability to drag and drop PDFs to their Mendeley library.

> Being able to easily import the reference from online databases is key, and Mendeley has a pretty good feature where it can automatically scrape information from an imported pdf file.
>
> Thanks Rajiv—o far I really like Mendeley.
>
> BIG thanks! I was paying $[X.xx]/month to collaborate with the lab. Much appreciated!
>
> Faculty comments

Upper undergraduate students are also using Mendeley for sharing their research work. They meet up with their liaison librarian and have set up shared groups, and the search strategies and important documents are populated in the shared folder.

> My favourite parts of Mendeley is [*sic*] the ability to add notes, highlights, and folders, as well as create a bibliography automatically on Microsoft Word.
>
> Graduate student comment

During the certification program, the science librarian had the opportunity to invite Mendeley representatives in March and again in May 2015. The science librarian and Mendeley representatives covered some of the new features in the Scopus database and Mendeley. Both events had significant student and faculty attendance, and Mendeley had graciously sponsored refreshments at both occasions. The author also collaborated with Mendeley representatives to present a poster at the Special Libraries Association Annual Conference (Green et al., 2015). The poster showcased Mendeley usage statistics from six North American universities including York University. The various activities done to teach and promote Mendeley formed a part of the documents submitted for the Mendeley Certification Program. Completing all the assessment modules took fewer than five hours, but the time required for promoting and teaching Mendeley was considerably higher. In total, around forty hours were spent on creating and updating the LibGuide, including Mendeley teaching and promotion activities.

The Mendeley Library Guide (Nariani, 2015) has become a ready reference for our users and is used heavily in the library workshops. In 2015 alone it has had over 4,500 hits. The guide has detailed screenshots on installing the Word plugin and creating a bibliography in MS Word. It outlines the steps to transfer documents and citations to Mendeley from different databases. After completing the certification program, the science librarian has fielded a variety of Mendeley-related questions. The common questions asked by our faculty and students were later posted on the Mendeley LibGuide.

Certification and Ahead: Bringing in the New

One of the main benefits of completing the certification program meant that we could distribute one thousand Mendeley Premium accounts to our academic community. The Premium account came with increased storage and the ability to form more private groups. In the third part of the assessment process, the science librarian had detailed how these premium accounts would be distributed. The Mendeley upgrade link was sent to faculty and graduate students through the faculty of health and faculty of science list-servs and as personal e-mails. Incoming students were informed about Mendeley and its features at graduate student orientations in September 2015.

Figure 5. Disturbing freebies and the Mendeley Premium account.

We have organized many classes on Mendeley for undergraduate students and have also distributed the free gifts and premium accounts to upper undergraduate students. The free gifts (except the iPad, which belongs to the author) and the Mendeley Premium account link were also shared at orientation sessions and course workshops (Figure 5).

> I use Mendeley and I find that it is very easy to use. I really appreciate that York offers workshops on how to use it as well. Another great feature is that it uses the document pdfs so I can highlight directly on Mendeley.
>
> Graduate student comment

A *Mendeley: York University* public group has been created, and important Mendeley links and tips are posted on this group. Mendeley (Elsevier) had sent the details about this group to all users registered with the institutional e-mail address. After the certification, the author also delivered a BrightTALK webinar along with two other librarians from Helsinki University in August 2015 (Nariani, 2015). A Mendeley representative provided valuable support in terms of organizing this webinar. The different ways of promoting Mendeley at our institutions and the work involved during the Mendeley Certification program was discussed. The webinar was attended by over 160 participants and was recorded for those who had missed the live session.

Conclusion

The Mendeley Certification Program has allowed York University's science librarians to teach and promote this research tool more effectively. The survey provided excellent know-how about the features in a citation management program valued by our faculty and students. The certification program also provided a springboard to promote a new citation management program during a time of change at York University Libraries. The free premium Mendeley accounts served to assuage faculty and student concerns about the migration process. It also helped the librarian participate in various professional development activities while helping students, faculty, and the wider community engage in scholarly communication.

Academic librarians need to participate in similar vendor-based certification programs, which allow them to grow professionally and provide benefits to their academic community. Publishers at their end need to offer free premium products and upgrades that can be used by our scholars. It is necessary to have regular refresher courses to keep abreast of the new developments. The Mendeley team had recently sent information about the refresher webinars and quizzes which need to be completed in order to maintain the Premium accounts.

At YUL we were anticipating upset patrons with the decision to come out of subscribed citation management programs. Having a citation management team ready much before the actual migration was essential for a smooth transition. The Mendeley certification program along with the premium benefits and innovative features led to an increased uptake of the citation management program at York University Libraries.

References

Green, M., Chang, J., Abaza, Y., Qin, T., Josephine, H., Nariani, R., . . . Berard, L. (2015) *Effect of learning resources on Mendeley user adoption and productivity*. Poster presented at SLA 2015 Annual Conference, Boston, MA, USA. Retrieved from http://scitech.sla.org/wp-content/uploads/2015/06/Effect-of-learning-resources-on-Mendeley-user-adoption_vF-to-share.pdf

Nariani, R. (2015). *Mendeley: Reference Management Program*. Retrieved from http://researchguides.library.yorku.ca/mendeley

Vendorbrarians: Librarians Who Work for Vendors and the Value They Provide to Library Customers

Charlie Remy, Electronic Resources and Serials Librarian, University of Tennessee at Chattanooga

Abstract

A panel of librarians working for different kinds of library vendors discussed their unique and valuable roles inside their organizations. The session was moderated by an Electronic Resources Librarian with an interest in library/vendor relationships. Librarians can add value to their company's relationships with library customers as they share the same basic skill set as their colleagues in libraries and have a better understanding of their needs, industry standards, and the day to day realities of their customers. Topics discussed included the kinds of roles librarians can have at vendors, how these positions compare and contrast with more traditional library work, their identities in the library profession, how library school did and did not prepare them for their jobs, and more.

Background on Panel From the Moderator (Charlie Remy):

I work a great deal with vendors in my role as an electronic resources librarian. Sometimes sales representatives know little about libraries' needs, and this lack of knowledge can even extend to the products they are selling. Libraries have unique requirements compared to businesses or consumers, and time and effort must be spent to familiarize oneself with our organizational cultures and values. Several of my sales representatives or other vendor contacts have library degrees, and I have noticed that I need to explain much less about my library's operations to them. They seem to already "get it." These positive experiences caused me to wonder about the realities of being a vendorbrarian (a librarian working for a vendor).

I am interested in the relationships between libraries and vendors. Traditionally, many librarians have relegated vendors to "the other side"—these interactions perhaps not being the most pleasant part of their job duties. I, however, see vendor relationships as productive partnerships whose end result is providing the user with high quality information that is easily accessible. It does not have to be a negative or adversarial relationship. Librarians could not exist without vendors and vice versa. I believe that librarians working for vendors have the potential to ameliorate what can sometimes be challenging relationships between very different kinds of organizations

Library schools continue to graduate sizable numbers of librarians, yet the professional job market can be rather limited, especially when someone is unable to move far away. This can lead to underemployment (part-time, paraprofessional level work) or unemployment where one might have to choose another profession because of the lack of opportunities. Library school graduates should be made aware that working for a vendor can be a viable and satisfying career option.

Vendors can play a role in combating limited library employment opportunities by creating new positions that harness the knowledge and skill sets of librarians as well as hiring librarians for existing jobs. Discussions like this panel can educate vendors on the value that librarians bring to their organizations and the customers they serve. It is likely that vendors with many librarians on staff can generate goodwill among their customers, which could benefit their bottom lines in the long term.

I deliberately chose a group of panelists working for a variety of companies (for-profit/non-profit, publishers/integrated library systems) so that the audience could see the different kinds of vendors that have librarians on staff. Despite their varying

http://dx.doi.org/10.5703/1288284316300

amounts of traditional library experience, all three panelists share a strong service ethic that is an integral part of librarianship.

Introduction and Explanation of Individual Roles of Each Panelist. Number of Librarians Employed at Each Company.

Bob Boissy: As the manager of account development and strategic alliances at Springer, Bob works with clients post-sale on access, administrative issues, usage, etc. We have four librarians on staff in the US in account development and external policy roles, and others working in metadata jobs in Germany.

Jalyn Kelley: Kelley is the client services manager at IEEE Xplore Digital Library, which is a team of 10 librarians around the world. Our primary goal is to raise awareness and knowledge of the digital library through training and promotional activities. We help our customers get the most out of their existing subscriptions and respond to any librarian-to-librarian questions that arise.

Marliese Thomas: As a solutions architect with Ex Libris Group, I serve as a liaison between account managers, product developers, and clients. I offer technical demonstrations of Alma and Primo products, answer functional questions from librarians, and make recommendations to best suit the institution or consortium's needs.

How Did You Make the Decision to Work for a Vendor and Why? How Did You Get to Where You Are Now?

Bob Boissy: I had two job offers after library school—one in an academic library and one in training/support for a vendor. The vendor position paid $5,000 more in annual salary and the opportunities for advancement were good, so the decision was made to work for the vendor. It was not clear at the time how hard it might be to return to library employment.

Jalyn Kelley: I worked in a virtual corporate library for seven years and while I enjoyed working from home, I wanted more interaction. In this position I have the best of both worlds—travel 60% to 75% of the time and work from home the rest.

Marliese Thomas: I had worked in university libraries for seven years and loved much of my work. However, I wanted something that would give me a wider perspective of how libraries worked, a more diverse skill set. The higher salary doesn't hurt, but I feel I am a more effective librarian and advocate to our profession now, as well.

Specific Examples of Panelists Bringing Value to Customer Experience and Their Vendors in General.

Bob Boissy: I Identify issues with customer implementations early by looking at usage, discovery, catalog, set up, etc.; support local events and survey research; and convene topical meetings to brainstorm solutions to common problems with visibility and use of e-resources.

Jalyn Kelley: Client Services managers are the voices of the customers. We track customer requests for enhancements and help identify issues and trends early. For example, Client Services was able to help internal stakeholders understand the importance of discovery tools and identify issues with linking, which led to the creation of a dedicated Discovery Services Manager position.

Marliese Thomas: I couldn't do my job well if it weren't for all of my previous experiences. Having been a Voyager cataloger and in-the-trenches instruction librarian, I can better empathize with current librarians' pain points and reservations about moving to new systems. I understand why certain things are important and can advocate on their behalf with product managers and account managers.

Challenges of Working for a Vendor

Bob Boissy: I can't respond to controversial issues/topics on listservs or other public venues, and I must adapt to travel demands.

Jalyn Kelley: Differing philosophies, as a librarian I want to provide access to as many people as possible while working to support a sales team.

Marliese Thomas: It goes beyond being self-motivated. Traveling 70% of the time and in a home office the other, I am responsible for my own happiness and work-life balance. Technology is key to keeping me connected with friends, family, and coworkers.

Moving Between the Worlds of Vendors and Libraries For Profit Versus Non-Profit.

Bob Boissy: I went to library school before the arrival of the Internet and never really worked in a library setting. Skills have changed and I feel it is more difficult to move to a library. Academic librarianship seems harder than a vendor job in some technical aspects, and in the variety of prerequisite skills needed.

Jalyn Kelley: There is a segment of the library community that will look down on you for working for a vendor. When I took this position, I was told by one library manager that I would never work in a "real" library again. But I feel more prepared to work in a library environment now that I have vendor experience.

Marliese Thomas: Having previously worked in non-profit corporate, for-profit corporate, and academic venues, it's interesting to be in a mix of them all. You are more direct and responsive, but often have to tailor your speech to the personalities of the clients.

Can Library Schools Prepare Us for This Work? What Do You Wish You Knew From Library School?

Bob Boissy: I am very involved in industry activities and NASIG, and am an ambassador at three library schools. Library school does not require a lot of credits but is useful to introduce students to the scope of library work. I wish I had developed more personal relationships with faculty to get involved in their research, etc.

Jalyn Kelley: I attended library school more than 15 years ago and was in a special libraries track which did not include instructional services courses, presentation skills, etc. If I had known then what I know now, I would have taken marketing and business classes to supplement my library school curriculum.

Marliese Thomas: My library school focused on concepts, so in that sense, it helped prepare me to think of the larger library structure instead of traditional work functions. Also, the people I met through graduate school and interns, mentors, and friends have helped shape and advance my career.

Influence That Librarians Can Have on Vendors Without Actually Working for Them

Bob Boissy: Librarians can influence with many technical recommendations, especially relating to holdings, access, title lists, etc. Librarians need to ask for automated feeds and be more aggressive on data exchange issues. Take part in advisory boards and standards groups and work to apply more market pressure on vendors.

Jalyn Kelley: Take every opportunity to talk to or meet with your vendors and give feedback regularly—the good, the bad, and the ugly.

Marliese Thomas: Make noise. Let us know when something doesn't work, when something makes your life easier. Partner with us, don't fight us.

Questions and Comments From the Audience

Question 1: Do you feel an extra responsibility to advocate for libraries?

Panelists: Yes—concerning: ILL, text/data mining, sharing, and OA; things that don't have commercial value but are important for libraries; goodwill; being engaged with professional organizations; and developing relationships to gather intelligence.

Marliese Thomas: I see now how much impact librarians have on everything my company does. I don't feel the need to advocate for them, as librarians are well-represented in the company, but I want libraries to know how much difference they can make.

Question 2: What are some new skills that you've acquired in this role?

Panelists: Spreadsheets, customer relationship management systems, public speaking, meeting strangers, eating by yourself, self-motivation/accountability, work/life balance with so much travel.

Marliese Thomas: I learned to take care of myself on the road, to be direct without challenging. We develop little routines or rituals for consistency even with all the travel to new places.

Question 3: What things do you miss about working in a library?

Panelists: Helping patrons with research, physically working with people, acquisitions discussions, seeing end results of changes, and the students.

Marliese Thomas: I miss my students. As the outreach librarian, I developed some close relationships with many "kids," and I miss their good natured humor and outlook.

Question 4: (Comment): Some vendorbrarians have regular offices and don't travel much.

Question 5 (Comment): There's a misperception that vendors have a ton of resources.

Panelists: It would be nice to have 3-month paid sabbaticals to work at libraries and vice versa. This would help bridge the gap between libraries and vendors. Speed of decisions can often be much quicker depending on the vendor. Some vendors have to seek approval from a board that changes.

Concluding Thoughts From Moderator

It is clear that these panelists enjoy their vendorbrarian roles despite some challenges such as frequent travel and occasional contrasts in philosophies. Current or aspiring librarians may want to consider working for vendors due to the professional growth opportunities as well as the likelihood for higher salaries in the private sector.

One commonality I noticed among the panelists is a focus on optimizing their products to satisfy a given library's unique set of conditions. They want their customers to get the most out of their content or utilities. This benefits libraries, especially in an era of flat or declining budgets, because it increases the likelihood of a satisfactory return on investment.

In one way or another, the panelists are advocates for library customers within their organizations. They have a solid understanding of library operations and needs as a result of attending library school. Library customers may feel more comfortable providing them with candid feedback that they can in turn articulate with higher-level managers to hopefully improve product offerings, support, and customer service. They can also help to bridge any barriers that may present themselves due to divergent organizational cultures.

My hope is that this panel has demonstrated the value that vendorbrarians provide to both the organizations for which they work and their library customers. Vendors should seriously consider hiring more librarians either for existing roles or creating new positions, particularly in the areas of post-sales support and discovery services. This is a proactive long-term strategy for vendors because it could result in improved library relationships, better returns on investments, and in turn, possibly more sales in the future.

Developing a Weighted Collection Development Allocation Formula

Jeff Bailey, Library Director, Dean B. Ellis Library, Arkansas State University, Jonesboro

Linda Creibaum, Acquisitions and Serials Librarian, Dean B. Ellis Library, Arkansas State University, Jonesboro

Abstract

In this preconference workshop Bailey and Creibaum gave attendees detailed instruction on how to create a spreadsheet-based library collection development allocation formula, one option to manage a library's collection development budget. The presenters demonstrated and led participants through the process of creating customizable Excel-based formulas that can be modified to utilize the criteria relevant to a specific library and institution. The primary element in the success of such a formula is the use of weights applied to each factor contained in the spreadsheet. Potential factors include the number of students majoring in a degree program, total faculty per department, departmental credit hour production, the number of courses offered, and the average costs of books and journals in a discipline. By carefully assigning weights to each factor, the output of the formula results in an equitable allocation of funds to each subject area.

Introduction

Jeff Bailey and Linda Creibaum began by briefly relaying the history, development, and use of a spreadsheet-based allocation formula at the main campus of Arkansas State University. This was followed by a short discussion of how the basic formula may be individualized in a variety of library settings and types.

Attendees were introduced to the skills and resources necessary to enable each to build an allocation formula to help optimize the distribution of their library's financial resources. Discussion included the methods by which the formula can be modified as conditions warrant and as campus circumstances change.

Throughout the workshop the presenters stressed the importance of maintaining comprehensive documentation for every decision and procedure in order to ensure the consistent use of data from one year to the next.

Developing a Library Allocation Formula

Background

In 1997 Arkansas State University's Dean B. Ellis Library used no formula of any kind to provide balanced allocations to the various academic departments for selection of library materials. Collection development budgets had been flat for several years and departmental allocations had grown unbalanced to the point that one department accounted for almost 20% of all library collection expenditures. Funds had not been reallocated or redistributed in many years, and allocations had grown only through inflation. This situation had been allowed to continue for several years and as a result the library had no means to purchase materials in support of new programs, or even to correct the balance or compensate for the inflationary increases in then-current subscription prices.

New library leadership organized a task force that started the process of looking for a more equitable way to allocate funds and manage financial resources. Librarians searched professional literature for methods of making library fund allocations, including the use of a formula, and ultimately decided to develop a formula for the Arkansas State University Library that was based on one used in the 1970s by Colorado State University and described in SPEC Kit #36.

Gathering Data

Before selecting formula factors, it is necessary to gather the relevant data needed to make informed decisions. The presenters led a brainstorming session in which workshop

http://dx.doi.org/10.5703/1288284316301

participants suggested possible factors for inclusion in an allocation formula. Suggestions included:

- Cost of materials
- Circulation of materials by subject area
- Number of students in each major
- Number of majors
- Number of faculty (FTE or head count?)
- Credit hours per discipline
- Prices of books and journals
- Degree levels
- Use of online resources by student majors
- Graduation numbers
- Research income
- Number of campuses
- Preexisting budgeting model
- Longitudinal data over time—change in time periods
- Influential or powerful professors
- Administration's "flavor of the day"
- Publications in disciplines
- Selector behavior—participation
- New programs
- Unique collections
- Consortial purchasing patterns
- Mandate to support nonacademic community
- Faculty assignments/requirements
- Number of BI sessions given
- Remediation—collection needs
- Endowment or donation levels in some disciplines (cash)
- Space concerns
- Electronica
- Gifts (in-kind)
- Ill requests
- Accreditation requirements
- Unbalanced collection
- Freely available resources

Bailey and Creibaum then led an exercise in evaluating and refining the list of suggestions from the brainstorming session to arrive at a list of the most viable factors for an individual campus. It was noted that some factors might be viable at one institution but not at another, and that some brainstorming suggestions might not be appropriate to the formula at all. Duplicates, such as "cost of materials" and "prices of books and journals," were consolidated and suggestions that were not viable for a formula, such as the presence of influential faculty, were eliminated. Workshop participants were reminded that some data may be obtainable at some institutions but not at others. When it is time to begin creating a formula, it is important to gather samples of available data.

Factor Selection

Factor selection for a library's formula should be finalized only after each possibility is carefully considered for completeness of data and relevance to the institution's collection development goals. Presenters emphasized that documentation should be retained for all factors considered for inclusion in the formula, including the specific reason(s) for those not selected. There is a strong possibility that at least some of this information will be needed in the future when considering changes to the formula.

Participants were advised to not get personally attached to the use of any particular factor, as that factor may need to be dropped or modified in the future. To illustrate this point the presenters discussed a modification they made to their library's allocation formula five years ago due to a new area of emphasis on their campus. However, they were forced to remove that factor from the formula in 2015 because they were no longer able to obtain data for that factor, and because it had decreased in relevance in the intervening years.

Weights

Weighting is the assigning of values to indicate the importance or impact of each factor in the formula relative to the other factors. In making an allocation formula there are several considerations to keep in mind when determining the weights. These considerations are particular to each individual institution, and may include input from a library committee, faculty senate, advisory group, or other constituencies.

A library may choose to subdivide factors before assigning weights. An example of this would be subdividing degrees awarded into undergraduate and graduate and assigning a different weighting factor to each. Attendees were advised to do several test runs, as minor changes in weights or factors can sometimes yield unexpected (and unbalanced) results! When developing a formula one should be prepared to make changes throughout the process until planners have agreed upon the final version of the formula and have made the first allocations.

During this time discussion arose regarding the level to which allocations had become outdated or inequitable at some institutions, and how difficult it may be in those libraries to restore balance and equity to their subject allotments, The presenters agreed that drastically changing allocations can be very difficult but they had been successful in doing so on their campus.

Options

Formulas may be utilized to allocate funds separately for print books, e-books, journals, online resources, or any other budgets a library may have, or as a pool for a combination of multiple formulas. Some librarians have indicated they have had difficulty moving funds from one formula to another when more than one is used; for example, moving funds from a print journals fund into an online journals fund managed with a separate formula. Libraries may choose to allocate all of their available funds or keep a percentage or flat amount back for in-house use in accordance with local campus culture and practices. The Arkansas State University Library retains a sizable portion of their funding and uses it to pay for comprehensive resources, backfile purchases, and start-up funds for new degrees. The presenters recommended that other libraries use the same approach.

There are sometimes valid reasons for libraries to make adjustments to individual formula-indicated amounts, including not wanting to reduce any department's existing allocation, choosing to reduce or not increase a funded amount because a department has a history of not spending a satisfactory portion of previous allocations, or adding an amount to help fund the start-up costs of a new program. Additionally, there might be special entities or major campus initiatives that might indicate a department or program should be funded at a level higher than the amount indicated by the formula.

Running the Formula

Attendees were then led through an interactive demonstration of a scaled-down version of the actual allocation formula used at Arkansas State University. During this part of the workshop, Bailey and Creibaum explained various aspects of the formula, demonstrated the relationship of the weights for each factor to the final output, and showed how relatively small changes to weights can make significant changes to departmental funding outcomes. This was accomplished by selectively changing data in the formula and engaging attendees in a discussion of how each change affected the output differently because of the weight assigned to a given factor.

Following this demonstration the attendees were each given online access to the session's PowerPoint presentation and a link to a basic working copy of the formula that was identical to the one that had been used for demonstration purposes during the session.

Closing Comments

Bailey and Creibaum closed by restating that if a library makes the decision to develop and use a collection development allocation formula, it is vitally important to thoroughly document the entire process. This includes documenting why factors were and were not used and how the formula data was gathered. This information will almost certainly be needed for future runs of the formula, whether a library is rerunning an unchanged formula with updated information or has decided to modify the factors or the assigned weights.

While changes to a formula should be kept to a minimum for the sake of consistency, it is important to think of the formula as a living document that will need to be modified from time to time as circumstances change at a library and/or institution.

References

Association of Research Libraries (ARL). (1977). The allocation of materials funds in academic libraries. SPEC Kit 36. Washington, DC: Association of Research Libraries.

Three Heads Are Better Than One: Organizational Changes in Collection Management Leadership

Barbara A. Bishop, Reference Librarian, Auburn University

Adelia B. Grabowsky, Reference Librarian, Auburn University

Liza Weisbrod, Music & Government Documents Librarian, Auburn University

Abstract

Financial pressures, shrinking staff, shifting user expectations, and advances in format access and availability mean that organizational change seems to have become a constant in today's academic library. The area of collection management has not been immune from change; the increasing emphasis on electronic formats, questions about access versus ownership, and the rise of open access have all required adjustment in managing collections. Even with all this change, most academic libraries have retained an organizational structure with a single person serving as a collection management coordinator or decision maker. This presentation details the shift in one academic library from a hierarchical model with a single collection manager overseeing all selectors to a collection management team composed of three peer selectors representing the major areas of humanities, sciences, and social sciences. The team is charged with coordinating the collection and liaison activities of all selectors as well as investigating new collections initiatives, serving as a bridge between reference and technical services, developing a culture of assessment in collection development, and working with the collections budget, the Libraries's development office, and administration. Benefits realized, challenges encountered, and "lessons learned" from this team approach will be discussed and suggestions for implementation in other libraries will be proposed.

Introduction

Collection management is defined by Cogswell as "the systematic management of the planning, composition, funding, evaluation, and use of library collections over extended periods of time, in order to meet specific institutional objectives" (1987, p. 269). Cogswell (1987) discussed six models of collection management which had various reporting structures and varying ties to library divisions but all were similar in being headed by individuals, specifically the library director, a coordinator of collection management, or an associate or assistant dean. More recently, Johnson discussed two models for collection management in academic libraries, a functional model comprised of librarians whose only duties are collection management and a geographic or client-base model with librarians who add collection management to other library duties (2014, p. 61). Libraries may utilize varying components of both models but organizational structure is not as important as "coordination of collection activities and their proper attention within the library's mission and priorities" (Johnson, 2014, p. 62). Johnson (2014) goes on to say that generally coordination is through a single individual who may have various titles. This paper reports on a different approach to the coordination of collection management in an academic library: coordination carried out by a team of three rather than a single individual.

Background

Auburn University is a research institution located in Auburn, Alabama. The University has 22,000 undergraduate students, 4,400 graduate students, 1,200 faculty, 140 undergraduate majors, graduate study in over 110 areas, and professional schools of pharmacy and veterinary medicine. Auburn University Libraries is an ARL library with a serials budget of over $7,000,000.

In 2000, Auburn University Libraries (AUL) underwent a library-wide reorganization and moved to a centralized model for collection management. An assistant dean for collection

http://dx.doi.org/10.5703/1288284316302

development was appointed who handled administrative aspects of collection management and managed between seventeen and twenty subject specialists. He trained new selectors, answered selectors' questions, monitored the approval plan, helped prepare the budget, negotiated with vendors and publishers, worked with library development, and handled gifts and donations. Although subject specialists still selected books and journals, the assistant dean was responsible for major decisions and overall management of the collection.

When the assistant dean retired in 2010, the serials acquisitions librarian took over many of his duties. In addition to her serials obligations, she assumed more collection management responsibilities and had greater involvement with the selectors. As time went on, however, it became clear that the serials acquisitions librarian could not take over every aspect of collection management and a different approach would be needed.

The dean of libraries decided to create a position with a larger collection management component, and the Libraries instituted a search for a collections coordinator. It was intended that the position would be based in the reference department and responsible for working with selectors, developing assessment strategies, exploring and implementing new initiatives, serving as an interface between technical services and the reference departments, and handling the many other aspects of collections management. However, after an extensive search, the Libraries were unable to find the right fit for the job.

In 2013, the dean of libraries decided to try a completely different approach. She would appoint a committee of three people to serve as the collections team for a one-year term. If the team approach turned out to be unworkable, or even a disaster, the committee could be dissolved after a year and another method adopted. The committee is made up of three people, all based in the reference department. One, representing the STEM (science, technology, engineering, and math) sciences, is the health sciences librarian and relatively new to the Libraries and the profession. The communication and journalism librarian, with over two decades of experience, represents the social sciences. The humanities representative also has many years of experience and serves as the music and government documents librarian. All are experienced selectors, although none has any special experience with collection management.

While their subject backgrounds were varied, they also brought differing strengths to the team. The science representative demonstrated a natural affinity for working with numbers and the budget. The social sciences representative enjoyed working with spreadsheets and charts, an invaluable skill in collections. The humanities librarian drew on her twenty years of service in technical services to provide translation and negotiation services between technical services and the reference department.

Duties and Responsibilities

When the Collections Team was formed in late 2013, they were charged with responsibility in six areas: coordinating collections activities, investigating new collection initiatives, acting as a bridge between selectors and technical services, cultivating a culture of assessment, managing the collections budget, and working with development. The collections team began their assignment by establishing suitable methods of communication. On the Libraries's intranet, there was already in place a collection development page that contained usage statistics, journal price histories, and a blog for meeting minutes. The team decided to maintain the intranet page for private or proprietary information but to also create a LibGuide (http://libguides.auburn.edu/collections) to use as a gateway and to host public information. The Collections LibGuide includes information about meetings and deadlines, policies and guidelines, and links to files on the intranet. The team also worked with the Libraries's systems department to establish a team e-mail account and an additional blog for the team's internal use.

A basic responsibility of the team is to coordinate collection activities. An important part of this task is to conduct regular training sessions and provide opportunities for selectors to learn about new resources. The first workshop was conducted by Peggy Johnson (2014), author of *Fundamentals of Collection Development and Management*, on collection development basics. Since then, representatives from YBP have provided training on the approval plan, and the team has conducted in-house training on such topics as interpreting the Voyager acquisitions module, reading the YBP GOBI screens, and working with statistics. Vendor representatives are regularly invited to discuss new products and services. Another aspect of coordinating collection activities involves working with selectors to take advantage of unexpected opportunities. A university hiring initiative provided the opportunity to put together a proposal for electronic backfiles. The collections team polled the selectors for suggestions, worked with the electronic resources librarian to get price quotes, and quickly developed a proposal linked to the initiative.

An important role for the collections team is to act as a bridge between technical services and the selectors. Before the establishment of the team, selectors, especially less-experienced selectors, often did not know who to approach for help and information. Technical services, on the other hand, did not always understand the sort of information selectors needed or the responsibilities of subject liaisons. The team spent (and still spends) time in negotiating, interpreting, and coordinating between the selectors and technical services. Examples include negotiating decision deadlines for journal and database price increases in order to allow selectors time to work with their faculty, coordinating changes in packages, overseeing the approval plan, and managing changes in subject areas. Other areas, such as gifts, also require collaboration between technical services and selectors. The team developed a gift policy so that everyone knows what to accept as well as how to process both the added and discarded material. An upcoming construction project will require weeding the collection, reclassifyng some material, and removing part of the collection to offsite storage. To facilitate this process, the team is acting as the bridge in coordinating the efforts of the technical services, circulation, and reference departments.

The team is also tasked with cultivating a culture of assessment. Working with the assessment librarian and the acquisitions librarian, the team collected data on journal, database, and e-book usage and made them accessible on the Libraries's intranet page along with price histories for databases and journals. The team conducted training on how to calculate cost per use and encouraged the selectors to use this information in collection decisions. The team is currently working on interlibrary loan statistics for selectors' use and to guide the purchase of journal backfiles and packages.

The team is charged with working with library development. One example of working with development is having selectors write thank you letters to donors with stories about how their support provides materials for faculty and students. The team also solicits "wish lists" from selectors and provides that information to the development officer so he is able to inform donors of the cost and value of library material and services. Finally, the team has been called upon to contribute to presentations for donors and faculty representatives.

The last responsibility for the team is to investigate and implement new collection initiatives. Since its creation, the team has implemented patron-driven acquisition programs for e-books and for articles. AUL also joined several open access initiatives for journals, e-books, and digital collections. The Libraries now participate in the SCOAP3 open access physics journals project, Knowledge Unlatched open access social sciences/humanities scholarly books project, and the Reveal Digital underground press crowdsourcing initiative, Independent Voices. The Libraries has introduced a pilot project for one section of the video journal JoVE (*Journal of Video Experience*) and will assess its usage after a year.

Looking forward, there are two areas the collections team plans to concentrate on; the first could be termed macro collection management. AUL selectors do a great job with selecting, evaluating, canceling, and weeding subject-specific resources, but selectors are not able to evaluate large packages or databases which span multiple subject areas. One of the responsibilities of the team is to solicit input from relevant selectors and examine cost and use to determine if other resources or groups of resources supply sufficient access at a better value. The second area of focus is fostering interdisciplinary collecting. Auburn University (AU) has several interdisciplinary programs as well as interdisciplinary research centers. There is also a new initiative at AU which seeks to hire additional faculty with the intent of increasing interdisciplinary research and grant funding. Although some selectors have tried to reach out and form collaborations with one another for interdisciplinary areas, this is an area which needs strengthening, and the collections team will be working on ways to increase communication and collaboration among selectors, faculty, and researchers.

Benefits

One question which should be answered is: why a team? What benefits does a team have over an individual coordinator? The first benefit experienced with a team approach to coordinating collection management is balance. Each member of the team is a liaison to a different subject area, and each also serves as a representative of one of the broader areas of the sciences, social sciences, and humanities. So whether deciding on new pilot projects or allocating gifts or one-time money, each of the three team members holds the others in check so that things don't get too skewed toward one broad area or even one subject area.

Each team member also brings differing strengths to the mix. Coordinating collection management requires many skills. A significant portion of the job involves working with numbers—analyzing use and cost per use and working with the budget. However, just as essential is the ability to communicate information about the collection and collection management needs and activities to audiences which range from selectors to library administration to the provost to potential donors. Deciding what information to present and how to present it effectively is crucial. Finally, coordinating collection management requires facilitating communication between all departments of the library, which requires still another skill set including, but not limited to, an abundance of tact and diplomacy. Each collection team member has different strengths among these various skills, and together the team is more versatile than any individual would be alone.

Another benefit of this team is that members were chosen from the current liaisons/selectors at AUL and thus each possessed an inside view of things that selectors found frustrating with collection management and things they wished were different with the current setup. Additionally, one team member had previously been a cataloger working in technical services, so she had an established relationship with that department and an inside view of their frustrations and desired changes. The collections team is not considered to be a part of public services or a part of technical services; instead the team overlaps both departments and answers ultimately to the dean rather than to either department head.

The final benefit of the team approach is that team members are able to share the load. Before taking on these new duties, each team member had a full-time job that included collection and liaison tasks for assigned subject areas as well as instruction and reference desk responsibilities. Adding in the collection team means sometimes things can get a little crazy. But when one team member is swamped with other duties, the other two can take up the slack for a few days or a week. In the same way, having three team members means that it is very rare that all team members are absent from the library at the same time. Even with conferences and vacations, at least one team member is usually there to answer questions and provide assistance. Sharing the load also means that there is always someone to bounce ideas off of, someone who can argue the other side or point out a differing view; all of which is very helpful in trying to move the library forward.

Challenges

There are challenges as well as benefits to working as a team to coordinate collection management. The first challenge the team faced was how to divide responsibilities. Sometimes, there is a natural division by subject area; for example, the team member responsible for science met with all the science selectors to discuss setting up a pilot project with JoVE. But from the beginning, for most responsibilities, the team has functioned as a team and has not divided up projects along hard lines. Instead, things just seem to get done by the members who have the inclination and the time; everyone pulls their weight and things are completed as a team. What the team did not consider until well into the initial pilot was that each member would need to have individual accomplishments to list on vitae for evaluations, and in the case of one team member, for third year review and then tenure. So although pleased with the way things were working, the team is now more careful to carve out individual responsibilities when possible.

Communication is another challenge faced by the collections team. For communications from others requiring a reply, the team must confer to craft the response which means that sometimes replies are not as quick as they would be when dealing with an individual; however, once this was pointed out, others changed their expectations of response time. The team has also dealt with this challenge by modifying guidelines for decision making and responses. When the pilot began, the team would not make a decision or respond to a question until all three members had time to discuss it. Although that method is still preferred, in the interest of time, as long as two members are able to confer and agree, the decision is made and communicated. There was also initially a problem with communication overlap. When making a decision that needed to be communicated (particularly to selectors), one team member would see the person in the hall and tell them, while another team member might e-mail the decision. Unfortunately, sometimes selectors were being told the same thing two or three times. To solve that problem, delegating which team member will communicate the decision is now part of the decision-making process.

One of the hardest aspects for the team to grasp initially was the collections budget. While each team member had her own collections fund, the collections budget in its entirety was a mystery not only to the team but to all the selectors. There was confusion about where money for various funds came from, what constituted one-time money versus continuing money, and why the former head of acquisitions would start budget discussions with "Well, we have money for books this year . . . but next year looks grim!" One team member compared the collections budget to a bunch of puzzle pieces where the picture was lost and the corners appeared to be missing. Although the team has a better idea of the budget picture and has probably uncovered at least three of the corners, understanding the budget is an ongoing process. The more the team understands, the better able they are to help inform selectors why certain decisions are made regarding spending trends.

By far, the biggest challenge to working as a team is time. Coordinating collection management is a more than a full-time job, and it was taken on by three people who already had full-time jobs. Unlike an individual who would be responsible only for collection management, each team member must decide how to apportion team responsibilities with other individual job duties. Each team member received some reduction in other responsibilities with the expectation that each would be spending about 13 hours a week with collection management; however, that turned out to be overly optimistic. Most weeks, each team member spends more than one-third of their time working on various collection management duties, and how to balance team versus individual responsibilities is a work in progress.

Lessons Learned

Although each team member was an experienced selector and came into the project with an understanding of the basics of collection management, it didn't take long to realize that the bigger picture (especially the budget) was less clear. So the first priority was to learn as much as possible as quickly as possible. All team members found that individual reading followed by discussing what was read was very helpful. Each team member also tries to attend relevant workshops and presentations at conferences whenever possible. The collections team is very fortunate to have a great mentor. AUL Dean Bonnie MacEwan was assistant dean for collections at Penn State before coming to Auburn and she is a wonderful resource. In fact, the team meets with her every other week in order to ask questions and discuss problems.

The second lesson learned is to never assume, especially when dealing with different departments. When the team was formed, it was felt there was a disconnect between public services and technical services. Information was often provided by one department to the other without enough background because those providing the information assumed others understood. Part of the team's job is to insure that communications contain enough background and context for everyone. It is also important to realize that collection management and acquisitions are complicated issues and that mistakes happen. A culture of blame helps no one. A much more helpful approach is to focus on how the mistake can be fixed or prevented from happening again.

Another lesson learned involved transparency. Over the last 20 years, there had been varying levels of transparency regarding the budget at AUL, and each end of the spectrum involves problems. Too little information leaves colleagues wondering why they are being kept in the dark, while too much information can be confusing or off-putting. It is important for the team to decide what level of information is sufficient and also to present information in a consistent and professional manner. Budget information should not be presented in an overly alarmist or overly optimistic manner; instead it is best to just present the facts.

A final lesson learned is the importance of being flexible when coordinating collection management. A selector for political science may need to approach things differently with faculty than the pharmacy selector, so each may need different information or information presented in a different way. It is also important to be flexible about the time selectors are asked to spend on collection duties because they have many other responsibilities.

Conclusion

The use of a team to coordinate collections at Auburn University began as a one year experiment, but before the year was up, the team was asked to make the assignment permanent. Feedback from administration was that they were very happy; feedback from selectors was that they were mostly happy; and feedback from technical services was that progress was being made. Along the way, the team members have learned a great deal. There have been moments of great satisfaction—increasing access for patrons, helping a selector make a more informed decision, putting the Libraries's money to better use, but there are also moments of great frustration. There was an extremely steep learning curve in working with the budget and understanding how it works. There were many times team members left budget meetings asking one another, "Did you understand what that meant?" There were also times when team members felt the bridge being built between reference and technical services was collapsing around them. But overall the team would say that when it comes to collection management, "we are glad we took on this challenge, we think we are making a difference, and most of all we may be tired a lot of the time but we are never, ever bored!"

References

Cogswell, J. A. (1987). The organization of collection management functions in academic research libraries. *The Journal of Academic Librarianship, 13*(5), 268–276.

Johnson, P. (2014). *Fundamentals of collection development and management* (3rd ed.). Chicago: ALA Editions.

Money, Money, Money—Or Not! Budget Realities and Transparency in Collection Development Decision-Making

Mary Gilbert, Assistant University Librarian for Content Management, Towson University

Deborah A. Nolan, Dean of University Libraries, Towson University

Abstract

Each library's budget is unique; however, the importance of providing information about the budget is common across all libraries and is a critical factor in how the library is perceived by its constituents. The cost of e-resources, balancing the collection, and optimizing a flat budget in an era of escalating costs are issues often misinterpreted by the campus community, leading to both misunderstandings and misinformation. Limited budgets, escalating prices, and new acquisitions strategies necessitate clear communication with librarians and faculty about the financial realities and complex decisions surrounding collection development.

One academic library used a two-day workshop format to inform librarians about budget realities in order to provide financial transparency and minimize concerns about budget decisions. Library administrators at a large public university met with librarians to review and clarify funding sources, allocations, expenditures, deficits, high-cost e-resources, collection decision factors, and strategies for acquiring content. With a fuller understanding of the complexities of budget guidelines and limitations, librarians brainstormed solutions to real life collection development scenarios. Both an information-sharing forum and professional development event, the workshop served to update, educate, and generate discussions for both veteran and new librarians.

Strategies described in this paper reflect a comprehensive public university perspective and are scalable and adaptable to other types of institutions.

Introduction

As budgets become more restricted, resources become more expensive, and users' expectations become more demanding, the need for transparency and clear communication about collection budget realities becomes essential. Both librarians and discipline-based faculty need to understand the realities and complexities of collection development in the current environment.

In the interests of transparency and to clear up possible misunderstandings about collection expenditures, the dean of University Libraries and the assistant university librarian for content management developed and presented to the Towson University librarians a two-part forum on the library's collection budget. During the first day of the workshop the library administrators explained and reviewed funding sources, allocations, expenditures, deficits, high-cost e-resources; collection decision factors, and strategies for acquiring content. In part two of the workshop, librarians brainstormed solutions to real-life collection development scenarios and shared suggestions. Participants agreed that the workshops provided an informative foundation for future approaches to collection development. Both an information-sharing forum and professional development event, the workshop served to update, educate, and generate discussions for veteran and new librarians. Subsequently, during the annual fall collection development meeting, librarians presented an abbreviated version of the workshop content to discipline-based faculty, highlighting the realities of a flat budget, clarifying misconceptions, and attempting to alleviate concerns.

Welcome to Reality

Budget questions are always a hot, and often emotional, topic at the university, especially in

http://dx.doi.org/10.5703/1288284316303

today's environment of rising costs, limited funds, flat budgets, and state-imposed financial restrictions. Multiple sources of funds for collections can lead to confusion. Coupled with limitations on income and restriction on expenditures, the allocation/spending process is complex.

Most librarians and faculty are not familiar with the funding model for the library's budget, and they are unclear about how these funds are allocated and spent. The flat university allocation for collections is problematic, and expectations for income from fines, fees, and endowment are unpredictable and low at best.

Expenditures include collections and support for collections; in other words, access and support expenditures. It is usually a shock to see how much the library pays to have the bibliographic records available in the catalog and discovery service, the amount required for copyright permissions, and the fees associated with document delivery. Most users have no idea the library must pay for these access and support services as part of collection management. In fact, nearly 5% of the collections budget goes to support and access.

Most surprising to our constituents is the fact that we routinely run a deficit in our collections budget to simply maintain current resources. This deficit model forces difficult decision-making, reprioritizing, and creative budget management.

Cost Factors

Few users are aware of all the factors contributing to electronic resources costs. For example, the most common pricing model for databases relies on full-time equivalency enrollment (FTE). Calculations based on FTE result in higher licensing costs for a large comprehensive university than for a research-intensive university with fewer students. This discrepancy is particularly visible within library consortia where institutions of varying sizes exist. Although a few vendors do charge by program enrollment instead of university enrollment, this isn't a common pricing model at this time. Additional significant factors affecting costs include inflation (varies from 3%–15%), discipline (science versus humanities), format (electronic versus print), packages (bundling versus single title), and provider (type of publisher). These intricacies may be unfamiliar to librarians not involved in the fiscal side of collection management

Decision-Making

The unanswered question is, "With a limited budget, how do we support the entire curriculum and collection needs of the university community?" The starting point focuses on selection considerations such as current holdings, accreditation requirements, new programs, and program growth or decline.

Each year one of the biggest and most critical issues the library faces revolves around determining what journals and databases to renew, an important and fiscally far-reaching decision, since over 70% of the library's budget goes to support journals and databases.

Cost per use (CPU) of e-resources is one of the principal methods used to determine subscription renewal. In an attempt to save money, however, simply canceling the most expensive databases most likely will not be the most responsible decision. For example, a database costing $40,000 but having over 50,000 searches results in a CPU of only $.08. Another database that costs $8,000 but has only 200 uses would have a $40 cost per use. Relying on CPU as a primary consideration has its limitations and doesn't cover all circumstances, such as low enrollment programs with expensive databases. CPU does, however, give a snapshot of the library's database use and identifies areas of excessive cost per use.

From a practical viewpoint, the library's budget cannot sustain a high CPU, and often will make the decision to cancel the database or journal and instead rely on interlibrary loan to provide requested articles. Additional methods to acquire content and stretch the budget include using demand-driven acquisitions (DDA or PDA) for e-books or to license videos, both of which are methods which focus on use to determine purchase.

Expenditure Guidelines and Alternative Strategies

Each library operates with its own established guidelines for collection development and spending. This institution follows long-established guidelines to assist with decision-making. With over 86% of the collections budget going for electronic resources, reserving some funds for traditional materials such as print books and media is deemed essential. Current guidelines include the following: cancel a journal of like value to add a journal; cancel print journals available electronically or in full-text journal databases; restrict use of departmental allocations to books, DVD's, and music; avoid purchasing duplicate copies; and don't rely on database aggregators for access to full-text journals.

Budget restrictions and pessimistic forecasts lead the library to reconsider current guidelines and explore creative though sometimes unappealing strategies such as canceling journal subscriptions and relying on aggregator databases for full-text journal access; expanding use of interlibrary loan; advocating for shared collection development through the consortium; and dramatically cutting database and journal subscriptions.

Recognizing the library budget limitations, some academic departments have transferred funds from their college accounts to pay for critical resources. In addition some academic departments have requested that the library use their book and media allocations to fund journals and databases. These contributions and minimal endowment income are helpful but practically speaking have marginal effect on buying power.

Scenarios

Collection decisions in a constrained budget climate are difficult and often elicit strong reactions from users. No decision is ideal, and all have pros and cons. To more fully understand the complexities of these decisions, librarians benefit from experiencing the dilemmas firsthand. To do so, librarians worked in small groups to consider actual collection budget scenarios faced by the library. Each scenario group crowd-sourced suggestions and articulated the benefits and pain points of their proposed solutions. The discussion scenarios gave librarians a realistic view of the funding available for collections, the complexities of collection decision-making, and the struggle to stay within the budget.

In scenario one, an academic department requests a new database. The database is heavily used in the trial, has good reviews, and is considered critical to the academic program. The library has already cut low-use databases and spent or encumbered all collection funds. What strategies can be used to acquire this database?

In scenario two, 3 departments offer to contribute funds from their library book/media allocations to subscribe to a database they all want but the library cannot afford. The departments agree to fund 75% if the library will fund 25% of the subscription. Should departmental allocations be used in this manner? How will annual inflation be managed? What if one of the departments drops out of the agreement the following year?

Scenario three is similar to scenario one. Several new journals are requested, and each is deemed critical for the requesting discipline. No library funds are available, and the requesting department strongly resists canceling other journals in its discipline in order to fund the new journals. The library offers to reallocate subscription funds to the new journals by canceling journals in that discipline that are available through aggregators. What are the arguments for and against this solution? Once the issues are considered, what solution is proposed?

Scenario four examines subscriptions to print journals. While the library prioritizes electronic journals over print, some titles are available only in print format. JSTOR provides access to back issues. The library retains print issues until JSTOR catches up and then recycles the print copies. Is this approach a responsible use of resources? Should the library cancel the print subscription, use interlibrary loan for current issues, and rely on aggregators for access to back issues? What factors should be considered in this decision?

Conclusion

While each library's circumstances are different, no library can acquire everything it wants without making hard choices and difficult trade-offs. Limited budgets, escalating prices, and new acquisitions strategies necessitate clear communication about the financial realities and multifaceted decisions surrounding collection development. Academic libraries must deliberately and repeatedly allay unrealistic expectations, misunderstandings, and misinterpretations of their abilities to provide unlimited resources. Conversations and presentations filled with budget numbers tell only part of the story. Librarians immersed in realistic decision-making scenarios gain a more complete view of the dilemmas. Subsequently, librarians are better prepared to explain collection development complexities to their discipline-based faculty.

On the Premises and Beyond: Managing Copyright Policy Through Institutional and Technological Change

Brandy Karl, Copyright Officer, Pennsylvania State University

Abstract

Copyright issues are important to every library, large and small. Libraries, librarians, and library staff are protected by a host of exceptions and copyright rules that are often not followed correctly or at all. This article discusses easy, simple compliance with the laws protecting libraries from infringements made on the traditional library premises.

Further, the library's work is increasingly off-site. From virtual consultations to delivering digitized materials off-site, copyright law can affect the depth and breadth of online services that would otherwise be equivalent to in-person patron services.

The paper describes "virtual library premises" and discusses the legal ramifications of enhancing access to collections for off-site patrons. The paper also explains how offering limited access to digitized in-copyright collections affects library liability under the Copyright Act. It explores whether library premises are restricted to actual physical spaces or whether the concept of the reading room can be extended beyond the four walls of the traditional library.

Introduction and Background

Copyright law is confusing for many libraries and librarians. It is misunderstood and misapplied in a variety of library settings. While the basic exceptions to US copyright law enable the most basic work of lending libraries—that is, the lending of copyrighted materials—many libraries act without knowledge, understanding, or the correct application of library-specific exceptions to copyright law.

These exceptions allow libraries to provide an entire building full of material plus the technology that patrons can use to copy the material in an entirely legal way (for the libraries, at least)—as long as the rules are followed. But these exceptions were drafted at a time before truly complex technologies that come with truly complex licensing agreements were available in the marketplace. Understanding and addressing how old laws apply to new technologies is extremely important in protecting libraries from liability for copyright infringement.

As the place and purpose of libraries shift without the law shifting to accommodate new purposes and methods of service, libraries and librarians must keep careful watch over how their activities do or do not mesh with library exceptions to copyright law.

Copyright Basics for Libraries and Librarians

Librarians are sources of copyright information for their user communities. Consequently, librarians should remain informed about copyright developments, particularly those that can limit or restrict the rights of users or libraries. Librarians should develop a solid understanding of the purpose of the law and knowledge of the details of the law relevant to the activities of the library, the ability to critically analyze circumstances relying on fair use or other limits to the rights of copyright holders, and the confidence to implement the law using good judgment.

—ALA Copyright: An Interpretation of the Code of Ethics (http://www.ala.org/advocacy/proethics/copyright)

The ALA's Interpretation of the Code of Ethics is a tall order to fill for the average librarian, and the list of "librarians should" grows every year.

http://dx.doi.org/10.5703/1288284316304

Copyright law grants to owners of copyrighted works the exclusive rights to reproduce, distribute, display, and publicly perform their works, as well as the right to create derivative works. Duration varies and takes into account a variety of factors, including the date the work was created or published, the death date, where the work was published, and whether registration was renewed, making determining copyright status difficult. The owner of the physical copy is not necessarily the copyright owner, even if there is only one copy. As is most often the case, even with rare copies, your institution may own the copy and none of the rights.

Copyright law developments are fairly rapid, and many areas of the law, especially fair use, have transformed dramatically along with the advent of technologies that allow digital copying, preservation, indexing, and search of copyrighted materials. Although copyright rights are fairly broad, litigation over the scope of owners' copyrights has highlighted the purpose of copyright: to expand public knowledge and understanding. Copyright law achieves this by granting authors exclusive rights, but limits it where the exclusive rights interfere with the purpose of copyright. In flexible areas like fair use the law can relatively rapidly accommodate technological change. Other parts of the copyright statute are not so flexible and were drafted with specific technologies in mind.

Libraries Are Special

Libraries are special under the Copyright Act. While authors and copyright owners enjoy certain rights over their works granted by the law, and users in general enjoy specific use rights that limit authors' rights, the Copyright Act recognizes the special roles that libraries play in collecting, organizing, preserving, and providing access to copyrighted works for the public. In addition to the basic rights provided to everyone under copyright's first sale doctrine—the owner of a physical copy of the work has the right to sell it—the Copyright Act provides multiple exemptions for libraries. Section 108 of the Copyright Act supplies a litany of exceptions granted to libraries from the exclusive copyright rights. All libraries (e.g., public, academic, K–12, government, etc.) are treated the same under the law as long as they are open to the public (or the collections are available to researchers in a specialized field even though they are not affiliated with a private library or archive) and conduct their operations via physical premises—the library exceptions do not apply to libraries that are purely digital.

Many of the special accommodations for libraries come with provisos and additional exceptions and limitations not supplied in a brief overview, but in general are outlined below. It is important to note that these exceptions do not affect in any way the fair use rights of libraries (or anyone else), and do not expand the user's rights—they may still be liable for infringement even though the library is protected from it.

Despite the gigantic exceptions to copyright law that these limitations allow, compliance can be spotty, and many libraries are surprised that they do not take advantage of these easy and cheap ways to limit liability for copyright infringement.

Statutory Exemptions for Library Copying for Library Use

- Libraries may reproduce one copy of a work (but not musical works; pictorial, graphic, or sculptural works; motion pictures; or other audiovisual works other than an audiovisual works dealing with news) so long as the reproduction or distribution is made without any purpose of direct or indirect commercial advantage. The copy must include a notice of copyright or a note that it may be protected if it is lacking a notice.
- Libraries may make three copies of an unpublished work for preservation purposes. Digital copies may be made, but the item cannot already be in a digital format, and those digital copies may not leave the library premises.*

- Libraries may also make three copies of a published work if it is damaged, deteriorating, lost, or stolen; if a replacement cannot be found at a fair price; or if the format is obsolete. The same rules apply regarding digital copies.

It's a bit obvious that these rules can be confusing and hard to manage (and again—they are highlights), even for the largest and most sophisticated libraries. So what do you do when you have a damaged or deteriorating optical disk or want to preserve it? You can make the copy, but it cannot leave the library premises.*

Best Practice Tips: Libraries should implement methods for tracking digital copies of works made under these provisions in their catalogs so that they are not loaned for use outside the premises. Copies made under these provisions should always include a notice of copyright.

Statutory Exemptions for Library Copying for Patron Use

Liability for copyright infringement may arise when libraries copy on behalf of patrons. The Copyright Act allows a library to copy on behalf of a patron or to fulfill an interlibrary loan request under either of the following conditions:

- No more than one article or other contribution to a copyrighted collection or periodical issue, or a copy or phonorecord of a small part of any other copyrighted work
- The entire work, or a substantial part of it, if the library or archives has first determined, on the basis of a reasonable investigation, that a copy of the copyrighted work cannot be obtained at a fair price

If *all* of the following are true:

- The copy becomes the property of the user
- The library has no notice that it would be used for any purpose other than private study, scholarship, or research

The library or archives prominently displays the Register's Notice at the place where orders are accepted, *and* includes the notice on its order form (37 CFR §201.14—find it at http://www.bitlaw.com/source/37cfr/201_14.html).

The notice is very simple and although many libraries do provide adequate notice, many do not. Although parts of the notice seem patently silly—to print it on durable paper in 18-point font, or to place it inside a box on the order form—the requirements are intended to ensure that libraries actually provide notice to the user that they may be liable for copyright infringement if their purposes do not meet the exclusion's requirements. Compliance with the rules is essential to obtain the protections provided to libraries under this exception.

Best Practice Tips: All libraries that make copies on behalf of users should check that their order forms and the place that they are accepted displays the Register's Notice, including any web forms used to accept orders. Many libraries choose to have patrons confirm that the intended use is only for private study, scholarship, or research. There is no need to ask the specific purpose—only confirmation that the purpose is one of those allowed. Develop procedures to handle the "just a quick copy from the photocopier in the back" types of requests—either provide a form or do not allow it at all.

Special Best Practice Tip—A Note About Notice

The Copyright Act does not counsel libraries that they must know the purpose for which a copy has been ordered by a patron—only that they have no notice that it will be used for any purpose besides those outlined above. Unlike in the case of unsupervised copying equipment (see below) where steps may be taken to increase patron privacy and avoid taking notice of patrons' activities, notice may be unavoidable when the library processes patrons' copy requests.

When a library *does* notice that repeated requests from the same or multiple individuals may result in the copying of an entire work where it would otherwise be disallowed, it is incumbent on the library not to fulfill further requests or inquire further as to the purpose of each request, as it now has notice that the requests for copying may not fall within the limited exception.

Statutory Exemptions for Patron Copying for Patron Use

The Copyright Act also allows libraries to supply reproducing equipment for its patrons to copy anything in the library. Although this seems routine to most libraries that have offered photocopiers since they became available, it still represents one of the largest exceptions to copyright law. Libraries can provide the material and the means by which to copy it without being liable for third-party copyright infringement as long as a one simple rule is followed: "That such equipment displays a notice that the making of a copy may be subject to the copyright law." The law does not prescribe the form or content of the notice (and does not except the patron from infringement)—just that the equipment displays the notice.

A shocking number of libraries do not protect themselves by placing the notice on reproducing equipment—which can range from photocopiers, scanners, microfilm reproduction machines, computers, printers, and anything else provided in the library for patron use that may be used to make a copy. A good portion of libraries that have attempted compliance place notices nearby, behind, and next to the reproducing equipment—although it's highly questionable whether that counts as the equipment itself displaying a notice. The statute is clear—the equipment itself should display the notice.

The ALA's suggested notice (since 1977) for unsupervised reproducing equipment is:

> Notice: The copyright law of the United States (Title 17 U.S. Code) governs the making of photocopies or other reproductions of copyrighted material. The person using this equipment is liable for any infringement. (http://www.ala.org/rusa/resources/guidelines/languagesuggested)

Although many libraries choose to have longer or shorter notices, the notice needs to be enough to convey to the user "that the making of a copy may be subject to the copyright law."

Many libraries also forget the "unsupervised" portion of this exception. A common question: What if I notice that a patron is copying an entire book? The proper answer to that may be: Why are you looking? Libraries and librarians need not and should not be supervising in any way patrons' reproductions on the equipment the library provides. It's important as a matter of patron privacy, but also as the key to obtaining the protections of this exception to copyright law. However, if the librarian or library staff has taken notice of the content, amount, or type of a patron's reproductions, the reproducing equipment can no longer be considered unsupervised, and the exception will not apply.

Best Practice Tips: Place the notice *on* the reproducing equipment if at all feasible, and consider screen-based notices wherever possible to reduce administrative burden. Ensure that the notice at least conveys that copying is subject to copyright law. Consider a fair use statement (e.g., "Copying is subject to copyright law. Exercise Fair Use."). Implement a copyright notice audit program to ensure regular checks that notices remain properly placed.

Do not supervise patrons' copying activities. If library staff cannot escape noticing patrons' copying activity and supervising is unavoidable, consider relocating reproducing equipment so that patrons' activities are unsupervised.

Library Exceptions and Technological Change

Section 108 notice compliance is relatively easy and following the instructions laid out in the Copyright Act is not for the most part a difficult task, although it may require complex implementations for very large institutions. To limit liability, many institutions choose not to accept routine copy orders on behalf of a patron and will only reproduce special collections items.

Following the rules for Section 108 library exemptions is absolutely the most inexpensive insurance any library can "purchase" to protect itself from copyright infringement claims.

Fortunately, the rise of personal handheld technologies has further limited library liability for patron copying (both by patrons and for patrons by the libraries) as patrons increasingly turn to self-help solutions and the copyright industries have been unsuccessful in obtaining provisions that would put libraries on the hook for patrons' copyright infringements with their own devices. Patrons now bring their own devices into the library and copy material. Why scan when you can snap with a smartphone and process the pages with a $2 app right into a PDF? Note that in general libraries do not induce, cause, or materially contribute to infringements performed on patrons' own devices; the outcome is always fact-specific—while it may not be able to control patrons' device usage, encouraging them to do so isn't necessarily recommended.

However, the patron copying exemptions were crafted at a time when the only copying technology in the library was a photocopier or a microfilm reader/printer—if a library had them at all. Libraries are full of new technologies that enable patrons to copy anything and everything in the library: photocopiers, printers, computers, flash drives, scanners, and more. Some of these particularly flash drives—make it nearly impossible to display the required notice on the equipment.

Moreover, many libraries maintain extensive technology catalogs that can be checked out and used both in and outside the libraries. Librarians loan just about anything: from charging devices to e-readers to laptops, cameras and video recorders, gaming devices, hard drives, and more. If you can buy it, some library somewhere is lending it to patrons for use both in and outside the library. The rise of lending these types of devices brings serious questions about how the liability of libraries can be limited.

Multiple libraries have begun lending Roku devices—digital video players that stream content onto a connected screen. While Roku streams plenty of free (ad-supported) content, some libraries lending Roku have chosen to add individual Netflix subscriptions to these devices, or redeem "free digital copy" codes that accompany the physical media they have purchased and download the digital copy onto the device. Other libraries simply subscribe to the Netflix DVD service and loan out the DVDs to patrons (or, in academic and school libraries, use them to provide media for the classroom). While the library exceptions and the first sale doctrine always apply, services like these are accompanied by contracts that limit what the library can do with the service—and the first sale doctrine doesn't apply to digital copies at all. The Netflix service is limited to personal, non-commercial use, and there really is no bending the terms of the libraries' agreement with Netflix to sharing with patrons. Although Netflix has not yet enforced the terms of the agreement against any library in a legal forum, it could decide to do so at any time.

Best Practice Tip: Netflix, Kindle Unlimited, and similar services aren't any different than other media services that libraries contract with—the terms of the license must allow the library to provide the service for authorized library users. If the terms of service don't allow loaning or sharing with patrons, consult with your legal department on the relative risks of maintaining a subscription service like Netflix for the benefit of patrons.

*Services for Off-Site Patrons

The library's work is increasingly off-site. From virtual consultations to delivering digitized materials off-site, copyright law can affect the depth and breadth of online services that would otherwise be equivalent to in-person patron services. Just as lending a book from a Kindle account is not the same as lending the physical copy of the book that the library owns, providing services to library patrons outside the confines of the library's physical space isn't the same as providing those same services off-site.

"Virtual Library Premises" can be used to describe the digital off-site services that libraries provide to authorized patrons. The library as an institution has changed from a storehouse of books accompanied by a basic index to a vast array of services, including licensed resources, 24/7 reference assistance, and more. While many libraries provide access to licensed resources for their patrons—whether via journal databases the library is authorized to provide access to for any off-site authorized user, or OverDrive e-book lending—far fewer provide unlicensed resources for library patrons.

Recall the basic library exception outlined above that allows libraries to make limited copies in certain circumstances, including for unpublished (but still copyrighted) works. The statute notes that the work cannot be distributed in digital format, and the copy "is not made available to the public in that format outside the premises of the library or archives." Intentional or not, "to the public" is a clear qualifier on this restriction, and it logically follows that the digital copy can be made available to users that do not constitute "the public" outside the four walls of the library.

Although the definition of premises seems clear in this instance (and has been repeatedly emphasized by Congress), what is the public? There is no real definition of public for this particular provision. Certainly hosting a digitized in-copyright yet unpublished collection on a freely accessible website would constitute making the copies available to the public. However, such collections could be protected in a variety of ways, with more or less risk. On-demand online access to researchers in need via expiring passwords would be the least risky. General access to the entire body of authorized users or patrons of the library itself would carry more risk. For general public libraries, allowing access to all patrons would probably qualify as access "to the public," and libraries experimenting with this type of access would need to critically examine their user base and demand for these types of collections to determine a set of users that would not be considered public.

To be entirely clear, should a court determine that the congressional intent was contrary to the language of the statute and the law prohibit any use of the digital copies outside the library premises, all of these choices would put the library outside the exception, although a fallback fair use position could save a library from liability in certain circumstances. However, the words "to the public" would be completely extraneous if the statute meant that there could be absolutely no access outside the library whatsoever, so according to the rules of statutory construction and interpretation, it seems fairly clear that there can be some although yet undefined non-public virtual access to digitized copies.

Managing Copyright Policy in the Library

Librarians should . . . take a deep breath. While the myriad exceptions can be overwhelming, developing an institutional copyright policy and audit mechanism is manageable, one bite at a time. To be clear, these exceptions aren't new, but many libraries have failed at developing holistic copyright policies that incorporate the provision and lending of new devices, or simply fail to apprehend that innovative lending policies could put them at risk.

Libraries should ensure that they implement policies and procedures that allow them to take greatest advantage of the library exceptions to the Copyright Act, as well as implement ongoing audit procedures to ensure that compliance is maintained. An annual check of reproducing equipment along with a quick checkup of current law and changes can go extremely far in ensuring that libraries maintain the Copyright Act's protections against infringement actions. Further, libraries should consider both copyright and contract law when considering the lending of new devices and services.

Finally, libraries—especially research and academic libraries—should consider whether or not providing not-public digital copies of works to some segment of users would be useful and valuable to their missions and to their patrons, while still remaining within the limits of the Copyright Act. Copyright law is stuffed with careful exceptions that allow libraries to engage in the crucial role of preserving information and copyrighted works and providing access to the public (or non-public, as it were). It's unlikely that the "Next Great Copyright Act" will arrive anytime soon. As much as many libraries would wish for a Copyright Act with broad library exceptions that would allow us to preserve, archive, and digitize, as well as to provide complete public access to unexploited or orphan works, it's unlikely to occur, which may be fortunate for libraries' sake. As we move toward ever more library services and patron interactions off-site, libraries would be wise to take advantage of existing carve-outs and potential exceptions like this one.

Levitating Libraries to the Clouds: A Strategy for Academic Libraries

Mark Dehmlow, Program Director, Information Technology, University of Notre Dame

Abstract

The University of Notre Dame's Office of Information Technology is in the process of implementing a "Cloud First" strategy through which it intends to move 80% of its core technical infrastructure into the cloud by the end of 2017. The strategy advocates a tiered prioritization structure that recommends the hosting (SaaS) model for most services, the AWS (IaaS) model for fewer services, and finally on premises for a handful of the remaining services. As a campus technology partner, the Hesburgh Libraries has begun planning for moving many of our services and infrastructure into the cloud. This initiative represents a radical shift in mindset for technology planning, moving from thinking about technology as assets that need replacement every 5 to 7 years to thinking about IT as a utility, paid monthly based on actual usage. This presentation will cover how the Hesburgh Libraries is devising our plan to move a significant amount of our infrastructure to the cloud, and the phases we have outlined to meet the OIT's 3-year plan. We will cover:

- Our experimentation in Amazon Web Services and how AWS differs from our current infrastructure
- The assessment of library service catalogs, both in terms of function and usage
- Our determination of which hosting models meets the needs of our services (SaaS, PaaS, IaaS, or on premises)
- Planning for the migration and roll out
- Any other considerations libraries may need to evaluate in this process

Introduction

The University of Notre Dame's Office of Information Technology is in the process of implementing a "Cloud First" strategy through which it intends to move 80% of its core technical infrastructure into the cloud by the end of 2017. The strategy advocates a tiered prioritization structure that recommends the hosting (SaaS) model for most services, the AWS (IaaS) model for fewer services, and finally on premises for a handful of the remaining services. As a campus technology partner, the Hesburgh Libraries has begun planning for moving many of our services and infrastructure into the cloud. This initiative represents a radical shift in mindset for technology planning, moving from thinking about technology as assets that need replacement every 5 to 7 years to thinking about IT as a utility, paid monthly based on actual usage.

Cloud First

The central strategy underlying the "Cloud First" program (see Figure 1) is to leverage the efficiencies of hosting applications in the cloud and following a tiered decisioning model that starts with moving most applications to a SaaS hosted model where vendors are not only responsible for infrastructure, but also the entire application stack. This allows organizations to focus on basic configuration, data, and implementation. The "Cloud First" strategy then focuses the next tier of applications being hosted on an infrastructure platform such as Amazon's AWS, so that the underlying infrastructure is provided by the platform and can be implemented quickly, at scale, and without significant redundancy. Whatever doesn't fit the prior models will continue to be hosted on-site, at a data center close to campus (see Figure 2).

http://dx.doi.org/10.5703/1288284316305

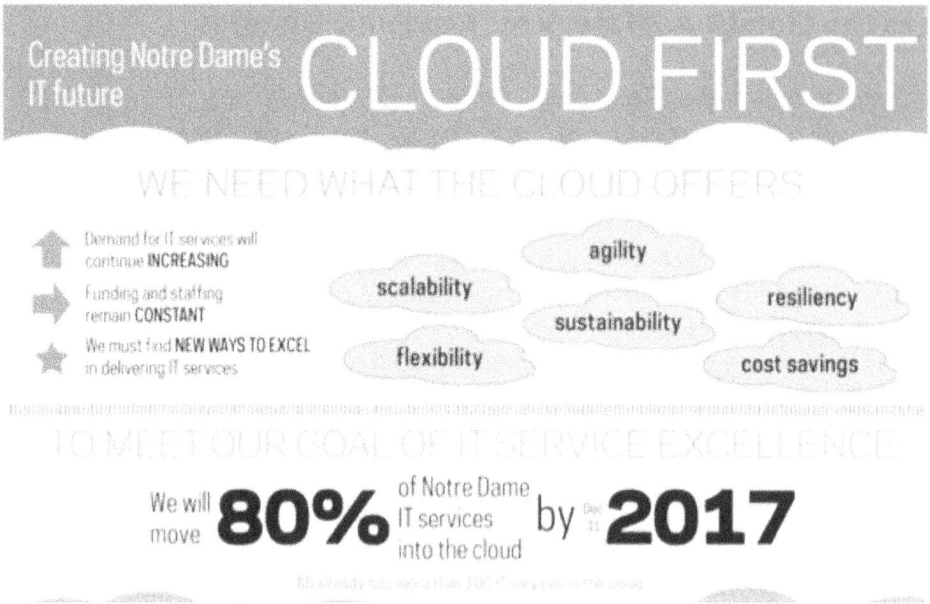

Figure 1. University of Notre Dame Cloud First Marketing Materials (Office of Information Technologies (Cloud First). http://oit.nd.edu/cloud-first/).

Amazon was selected by the University of Notre Dame as its preferred infrastructure provider because they are currently the cloud infrastructure leader in the marketplace, providing some of the most advanced data centers combined with an expansive and extendable set of tools for managing the utilization of their infrastructure.

IT Evolution and Implications of the Cloud

IT infrastructure provisioning has followed a similar arc of abstraction over the years, not unlike that of programming. Early programming focused on writing code to interface with hardware (machine language). Over the years, programmers have abstracted languages—assembly, procedural, and now object oriented, to take advantage of common lower level programming code that often does not need to be rewritten. Increasingly, even within Object Oriented languages, scripting languages, and CSS bundles, coders are writing frameworks and common modules that abstract functionality so that code can be reused and written more quickly. IT Infrastructure is following a similar path, having once relied on mainframe systems which required management by an operator, to racks filled with bare metal servers (one physical server per system), to virtualized systems (one physical server per multiple systems), to now cloud-based infrastructure, an abstracted management environment that allows for all systems to be managed from a web-based dashboard.

SaaS >> IaaS >> On Premise

Figure 2. Tiered decisioning model.

Moving to this model has several potential benefits. The first is cost. When looking at calculating the cost of IT infrastructure, it is important to consider the total cost of ownership for the whole organization, not just the unit provisioning a service. For example, our library does not pay for electricity, the capital costs to provision a data center, networking, data center operations, or many other costs associated with providing IT infrastructure on campus. These costs are absorbed centrally by the University or the Office of Information Technology. As we begin looking at the cost for us to provision our systems in the cloud, we are looking at those costs through a campus-wide stewardship lens. While it is likely to cost the Libraries more to provision systems in the cloud because our IT on campus has always been subsidized centrally, we are still considering the overall impact for the University. Our Office of Information Technology is committed to working with us as we move out into, what is for us, a more expensive IT model.

A more impactful cost consideration is in the repurposing of staff. At our organization, staff are generally more difficult to get funding for because of the long term commitment and added cost of benefits, etc. As new needs continue to emerge, being able to repurpose some of our most skilled, talented, and trainable staff is a huge benefit. Beyond the baseline cost factor, true cloud infrastructure will offer features that are considerably expensive and time-consuming to provide for a single institution—almost infinite scalability, the ability to provision services on-demand, and high availability that is realized by a geographically diverse infrastructure, in some cases implemented on a global scale.

Moving to the cloud, though, requires some shift in thinking about how to acquire and provision infrastructure. Instead of working with fixed budgets that are spent in 5-year cycles for purchasing equipment, the cloud model is a utility model based entirely on usage. It is more efficient in the sense that you use exactly what you pay for and you pay for exactly what you use—with locally implemented servers, there is frequently a lot of idle time where hardware is working at a fraction of capacity. Calculating utility-based estimates and budgeting for unfixed costs is a lot more nuanced and challenging than our historically fixed budgeting model.

Assessment: Preparing for the Cloud

Preparing for a broad infrastructure change required us to undertake a comprehensive service inventory. Like many institutions, this was an activity that we hadn't done for a long time, and it had the benefit of us looking at our environment holistically. We started thinking about what should remain solo, what could be consolidated, and in some cases, what could be decommissioned. In addition to cleaning house and taking inventory, we assessed the service criticality, risk, dependencies, and impact of each service so we could, for the first time, begin to formally assign service-level definitions for each service we run. These definitions include things like who is impacted by an outage and how quickly should we bring services back online. This activity alone is helping to make us a more efficient IT organization.

We then began developing a rubric for how to determine what should go into AWS, what was a candidate for hosting with a vendor, and what we should keep on premise. For AWS, we asked questions like: Is it a web service? (Amazon is optimized for web-based applications.) Does it need extra reliability, scalability, and redundancy? How is it architected? (Applications developed with smaller, separable components are less expensive in the Amazon model.) What is the projected cost to run it in Amazon? For systems we thought could be hosted by a vendor, we asked: What software do they develop and maintain? Can they agree to and meet expected performance such as uptime, data throughput, etc.? How well has their support organization performed?

We looked at several examples and our current thinking about where we felt it was best to host the software.

In addition to evaluating the qualities of our systems that make them a good or bad candidates for the cloud, we have also been monitoring system performance and resource utilization (CPU, memory, network

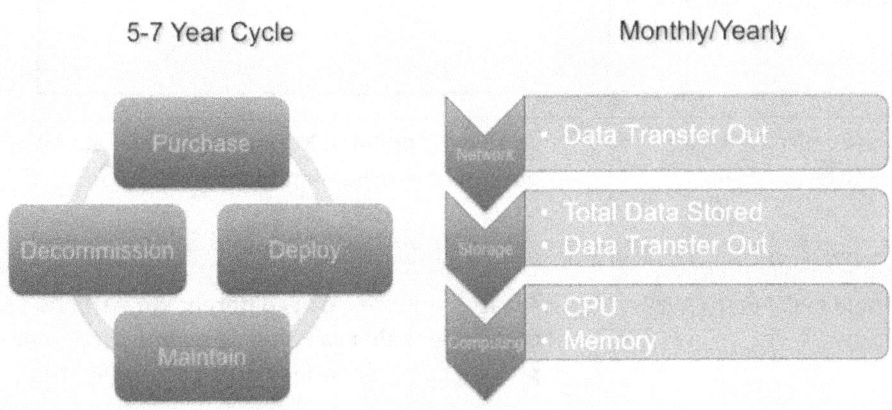

Figure 3. Five–seven year cycle and monthly/yearly.

Table 1. System hosting assessment.

Aleph (Integrated Library System)	
System Characteristics: • client-based • large database • legacy software • vended software	**Candidate for:** *On Premise Hosting*
Primo (Discovery System)	
System Characteristics: • web-based • large indices and database • mature but relatively new software • vended software • vendor has hosting model	**Candidate for:** *Vendor Hosting*
Inventory Management System	
System Characteristics: • web-based • small database • low amount of input/output • newer software and architecture • open source, locally developed	**Candidate for:** *Amazon Web Services*
Hydra/Fedora Based Institutional Repository	
System Characteristics: • web-based • medium database • diverse and complex storage needs • newer software	**Candidate for:** *On Premise, but later Amazon Web Services*

bandwidth, etc.) using software called Ganglia.[1] This is helping us develop predicted costs in Amazon.

The migration plan is then fairly simple. Anything new that we develop, we should look first to AWS as a host. For our existing systems, we will follow our system assessment recommendations.

Amazon Components and Billing Model

Amazon provides many different infrastructure components that can be implemented together to provide comprehensive hosting solutions. The

[1] Ganglia Monitoring System. http://ganglia.sourceforge.net/

following list gives some examples of those components as well as some of the factors that go into calculating the cost of the service.

Amazon Elastic Compute Cloud (EC2)—Server instances

Cost based on:

- Server configuration (OS, Memory, CPU)
- Time in use
- Number of instances

Amazon Simple Storage Service (S3)—Object-based storage

Cost based on:

- Amount of storage
- Data transferred out
- Number of requests against data
- Backups and redundancy

Amazon Relational Database Service (RDS)—Database instances

Cost based on:

- Database size
- Amount of storage
- Number of instances
- Number of requests

Amazon Elastic Load Balancing (ELB)—Load balancing

Cost based on:

- # of load balancers per hour
- Amount of data processed by load balancer

In addition to the technological components for server administration, Amazon also provides a several tools for managing infrastructure including APIs and a tool called Trusted Advisor, which recommends how to optimize service utilization and minimize cost. There are also many third party companies who are developing services like system migration and detailed billing and monitoring services. For a full list of Amazon

Table 2. New IT roles for the cloud.

Title	Role
Systems Architects	Staff who design environments to maximize use of the cloud while ensuring applications work in that environment
DevOps	Hybrid staff who understand both applications development and systems operations and can work as consultants for cloud deployment
Financial Engineers	Staff who can take requirements, estimate usage, and calculate potential costs in the cloud
Business Analyzers	Those who can take requirements and consider the hosting models as well as existing solutions to help answer the questions: Should we build or license, and should we host in the cloud or on premise?

services and a pricing overview, as well as a calculator to help estimate cost, see the following:

- https://aws.amazon.com/products/
- https://media.amazonwebservices.com/AWS_Pricing_Overview.pdf
- http://calculator.s3.amazonaws.com/index.html

Challenges and Organizational Changes

With every solution comes not only benefits but also challenges. For Amazon, these challenges include:

- Vendor lock-in—applications need to be architected appropriately to maximize Amazon's infrastructure and minimize cost
- Knowledge drain—the longer systems administrators are not exercising their traditional skill set, the more they lose knowledge for implementing systems locally
- The complexities of maximizing efficiency of resource utilization in Amazon—what is the right sizing for services, what can be turned off during non-business hours, and can applications be broken into smaller components to reduce large system utilization?

Moving into the cloud will undoubtedly save staff time, but there is a need for new roles to maximize the potential of the cloud. We have begun to identify several new emerging roles.

All of these new roles require a fundamental understanding of technology as well as critical soft skills for working across teams. Increasingly, the necessary roles are interdisciplinary and require flexibility in thinking as well as flexibility in placement within any organization.

Perhaps the most substantial barrier to cloud adoption is organizational culture. The nature of system administrators is to provide for maximal stability, and abstracting infrastructure can obfuscate one's core understanding of that technology and leave staff who work in fairly traditional IT roles feeling uneasy about the future. It is important for organizations to have a strategy for working with staff on such a large logistical and mental transition. First, it requires building a foundation around why. Moving from on-premise to the cloud means sacrificing some flexibility to gain efficiency. It is important to develop a change conversation in the organization and introduce new perspectives. It is also important to challenge assumptions that may be based on old models of thinking. It is good to combat the tendency to ignore sunk cost; people often will talk about how much investment you have made as a means for rejecting change. Helping them understand that cost is cyclical and every significant change has upfront costs that are hopefully offset by the potential benefits is critical. The most important thing is investing in your staff both in terms of assurance and training. For staff, change is scary, especially radical change that appears to be replacing the value they provide for your institution. Building a plan to bring them along with the change and assuring them you are committed to their development and growth so that they can become a core part of the future will help assuage fear, especially as they see you making good on those promises to develop them. Moving into any new way of doing things requires real training and time to experiment with new solutions. Making a goal out of developing competencies in new technologies and investing in their learning will help mitigate demoralization and boost a sense of co-ownership for moving toward new solutions.

Recommendations

After a year of preparatory work and some experience working with Amazon Web Services, we have learned the importance of organizing the transition to the cloud. Ensuring that there is time to conduct the migration in a sane manner is critical for giving staff a chance to get acclimated to a new way of doing things. Giving staff a chance to experiment is also important; complex migrations may not be plug-and-play and how things work in the cloud may feel counterintuitive at times. Budget for experimentation and for making mistakes. With any new technology, it can take some time to fully understand it and the implications of its use. Experimenting at a small scale can mitigate exorbitant costs while providing staff a sandbox to learn in. It is critical to not underestimate the value of change management in the process. Anxieties and demoralization can be tempered considerably through reassuring staff and providing professional growth so that they can clearly see themselves in the future of your organization. It is also important to get application developers involved and provide them with a strong understanding of how a particular cloud environment works. Optimizing applications in the cloud will likely require intentional architecting of applications to work most effectively and efficiently in the cloud. And finally, develop an exit strategy. Who knows exactly what the next major change in infrastructure management will be or when it will come. What is certain is that there will be a new way to provide IT infrastructure more efficiently and effectively in the future at some point, and implementing solutions in a flexible and standardized way can help mitigate problems with future transitions.

Patron-Driven Acquisitions and Interlibrary Loan

Interrogating Demand: Pathways Toward Purchase in Patron-Influenced E-Book Models

Jim Dooley, Head, Collection Services, University of California, Merced

Abstract

E-books are available to academic libraries through a wide variety of acquisition models. The University of California, Merced (UC Merced) Library has used demand-driven acquisitions (DDA) as its principal model for providing access to e-books from its founding in 2005 to the present. This paper will discuss the influence of the situation at UC Merced on the implementation of DDA plans for e-books and the results of the most recent five years of operations of these plans.

E-Books at UC Merced

The University of California, Merced (UC Merced), the tenth campus in the University of California system and the first new American research university in the 21st century, welcomed its first class in 2005. The initial class comprised 875 students, mostly undergraduates. In fall 2015, UC Merced had 6,700 students including almost 400 graduate students. There is a proposal currently under review to construct sufficient academic buildings and student housing to allow the campus to grow to 10,000 students including 1,000 graduate students by 2020.

From the beginning, e-books have been a very important component of collection development at UC Merced. At the present time the library has approximately 1.2 million e-books available and a print collection of approximately 125,000 volumes. Of the 1.2 million available e-books, 800,000 volumes are available through University of California system-wide package licenses with publishers such as Springer, Wiley, and Elsevier. In a majority of cases negotiations for system-wide e-book packages are linked to negotiations for journal packages from the same publishers. This trend has accelerated during the past five years.

The remaining 400,000 e-books are available through a variety of locally licensed models: 128,000 through an ebrary Academic Complete subscription; 216,000 through an EBL demand-driven acquisitions (DDA) plan with purchase on the fourth use after three short-term loans (STLs); and 55,000 through a DDA plan with MyiLibrary with purchase on the second use without STLs.

The Academic Complete subscription provides access to a wide variety of academic titles with unlimited simultaneous users for a very low per title cost. A potential disadvantage is that if the subscription were to be allowed to lapse, all access would be lost. Since UC Merced anticipates being able to maintain the subscription for the foreseeable future, this is not an issue.

One of the main reasons for choosing EBL as the library's principal e-book aggregator, was EBL's use of "non-linear lending." This model is not quite unlimited simultaneous users, but it's close. The model allows a specified number of accesses during a calendar year, usually 300 or 325, before an additional copy needs to be purchased to maintain access to that title. The number of accesses resets each calendar year. This model is extremely useful when faculty assign e-books for class reading. If these books were available with 1-user or even 3-user licenses, the number of turnaways and the resulting frustration could be significant. At UC Merced only one title available under "non-linear lending" has exceeded the number of allowed uses over ten years.

The MyiLibrary DDA plan was originally implemented to provide access to titles not available from EBL. It was also an experiment with a different DDA model that didn't involve the use of STLs. Since the fall of 2014 the MyiLibrary plan has also been used to provide access to titles that

http://dx.doi.org/10.5703/1288284316306

certain publishers were no longer making available through DDA plans with STLs. Content from publishers that no longer support DDA plans of any type is no longer available at UC Merced except for a small number of titles individually purchased.

According to ProQuest the EBL and ebrary catalogues should be combined by the end of 2015. The EBL catalogue has already been deduped against ebrary Academic Complete at UC Merced. The library is currently in the process of examining the new publishers currently with ebrary that will be available when the two catalogues are merged. At this point a number of non-academic publishers have been excluded from the plan. Other publishers may be excluded in the future based on willingness to support short-term loans, the cost of STLs, and the availability of titles under non-linear lending licenses. Now that ProQuest has also acquired MyiLibrary, the expectation is that there will be one unified catalogue of all ProQuest e-books in the not too distant future.

Having almost 275,000 e-books available through DDA is contrary to the collection development practices of most research libraries that carefully circumscribe the size of their DDA pools by subject, publisher, publication year, etc. in order to guard against possible runaway costs. Other than blocking most titles in Library of Congress class R (medicine, nursing, dentistry, etc.), removing certain non-academic publishers and having a $300 per title price limit, there have been no other substantial restrictions on the size of the DDA pool at UC Merced. There is specifically no limit by publication year. The library chose to take this approach primarily due to the rapid, uncoordinated increase in faculty hiring and in the establishment of new programs resulting from the university being in a start-up mode for the first decade of its existence. Both the administration and faculty have tried to expand academic offerings as quickly as possible. Often this has resulted in hiring an individual faculty member in a field that is completely new at UC Merced. In many cases the library did not know that the faculty member had been hired until he or she appeared at the library to request book purchases and journal subscriptions. Since many new faculty, particularly in the humanities, have research agendas that are not shared by other UC Merced faculty, they often request information resources that are not useful to other faculty or programs. These conditions made it practically impossible to manage the DDA plans in the traditional manner. Another reason for taking this approach is that the library did not have and still does not have a sufficient number of librarians to have assigned subject selectors. There simply aren't enough people to do title-by-title selection either for print or electronic monographs.

Because of the emphasis on interdisciplinary work, UC Merced does not have traditional academic departments. Faculty have self-organized into various groups based on disciplinary or cross-disciplinary working relationships. These organizational factors have also made it difficult for the library to initiate and maintain discussions with faculty regarding collection development. Under these circumstances, the best way to support teaching and research has been to cast a wide net with the DDA plans. As academic hiring becomes more stable, it is anticipated that the DDA pool will become more focused.

The experience of UC Merced with the EBL DDA plan for the five-year period from July 1, 2010 through June 30, 2015 is shown in the following statistics:

Total spend: $337, 785

STL spend: $313,047

STLs: $22,

Cost per STL: $13.69

Purchase spend: $24,738

Purchases: $285

Cost per purchase: $86.80

In spite of the large number of available titles, spending remained constant and within budget until the summer of 2014 when a number of publishers significantly raised short-term loan rates without notice. This resulted in the doubling of the monthly cost for the EBL DDA plan. Several steps were taken in September 2014 to once again bring spending under control. Thirteen publishers were completely dropped from the plan. When this action was not sufficient to control spending given the increased STL costs, a $30 cap across the board on individual STLs was instituted. These actions are still in place and have served to bring spending under control. They have also reduced the size of the EBL DDA pool by 50%.

For the comparable period, the experience of UC Merced with the MyiLibrary DDA plan is as follows:

Total spend: $64,362

Purchases: $534

Cost per purchase: $120.53

For UC Merced, DDA, whether employing short-term loans or not, has been and continues to be a cost effective means of providing access to e-books. The results have clearly emphasized access over ownership with 93% of total spending for STLs. Partly this is due to the very large number of available titles and partly due to the comparatively small user base. A very large number of titles that has been accessed once or twice over the decade. At the same time there has been steady usage of the purchased titles after purchase.

Unfortunately, some publishers have taken actions that have raised doubts as to the sustainability of the DDA model going forward. Publishers continue to raise short-term loan rates, often combined with increases in the list price of the book. Since the STL rate is a percentage of the list price, the result has been to make the use of STLs prohibitively expensive for many publishers. Some publishers have instituted embargos on the availability of frontlist titles through DDA. Others have removed all of their titles from DDA plans. The assumption seems to be that if publishers refuse to support DDA or make DDA prohibitively expensive, libraries will have no choice but to purchase e-books up front. Libraries do, however, have a choice; they can choose to not acquire e-books from uncooperative publishers. Hopefully, solutions will be developed that will be sustainable for both libraries and publishers.

Interrogating Demand: Pathways Toward Purchase in Patron-Influenced E-Book Models; University of California-wide Demand-Driven Acquisitions—E-Book Hopes and Dreams Revisited

Kerry P. Scott, University of California–Santa Cruz, Head, Research Support Services, University of California, Santa Cruz

Abstract

From January 2013 to date, the University of California has piloted a system-wide e-book demand driven access (DDA) program comprised of University Press publications in the Arts, Humanities, and Social Sciences. This paper reviews the pilot's progress, specifically focusing on how well it has achieved the hopes and dreams laid out by several of the participating campus librarians prior to the pilot's launch.

In January 2013, nine of the ten University of California campuses initiated a system-wide demand driven (DDA) e-book acquisitions pilot with ebrary as the e-book supplier and YBP as the DDA purchasing management system. The only campus that declined to participate in the pilot program was the University of California San Francisco, our medical campus, due to their specific collection needs. In the areas of the arts, humanities, and social sciences, the pilot focused on making university press titles accessible for short-term loan (STL) and purchase. The attention on the chosen subject areas and the specific presses was by design. The STEM subject areas had been successfully purchasing and demonstrating the need and value of e-books, and the arts, humanities, and social sciences had had fewer opportunities to experiment with e-book acquisition across the UC system. The pilot offered an opportunity for the arts, humanities, and social sciences to test patron interest in e-books. Further, the University of California system-wide collections group wanted to support university presses, and the pilot was a chance to do that by exposing university press content for demand-driven interest across the UCs.

The pilot was overseen by a task force comprised of librarian representatives from the nine participating campuses as well as a licensing expert from the California Digital Library (CDL). The license was negotiated with the CDL representative, and the shared catalog records for the DDA discovery pool were managed by the University of California's Shared Cataloging Program. In total, 63 university presses exposed their DDA-eligible content for the pilot. We included publications from 2010–2015 in the discovery pool and, as of the end of October 2015, 4,620 DDA-eligible records have been uploaded into the UC's shared catalog.

In November 2012, two months prior to the pilot's launch, several UC colleagues put together a presentation for the Charleston Conference that outlined our hopes and dreams for the pilot [see *Collective Collection Building and DDA*, http://dx.doi.org/10.5703/1288284315306]. This paper revisits those hopes and dreams and assesses the pilot against them.

Hopes and Dreams

Prior to the launch of the DDA pilot, the UC system-wide collections group had developed a set of guiding principles for e-book acquisition. The principles became known as the UC E-Book Value Statement. The DDA Pilot afforded an opportunity to test those principles, among which were Digital Rights Management (DRM), full-book ILL lending, and ADA compliance, among others. Given the constraints on collection budgets throughout the system, the pilot was also viewed as an opportunity to expand or redefine the breadth and depth of the UC-wide collections. In theory, if we were collectively purchasing university press titles for the system in e-format, there would be funds left over to redirect to purchases that were unique to the campuses. Finally, we hoped the pilot would provide a

http://dx.doi.org/10.5703/1288284316307

method to improve user access to content as well as help us learn more about how our users interacted with e-books.

A Mixed Bag

In the end, very little of the agreement we reached with ebrary and the 63 publishers included in the pilot matched most of our UC E-Book Value Statement. We did not negotiate publishers out of using DRM or into full-book ILL privileges, and on one campus ADA compliance was an issue—specifically with the ebrary screen reader. While the ebrary screen reader worked, it was not the reader of choice. ADA compliance allows the patron in need of accommodation to identify his or her preferred screen reader, rather than requiring him or her to use the screen reader supplied by the vendor. Expanding the breadth and depth of our system-wide collections was similarly a dream delayed. Print duplication of e-books ordered through the pilot and the inability to effectively and consistently manage deduplication at the campus level was an issue. Instead of repurposing funds for new and unique content, many of the campuses spent funds on the same content in two different formats. Perhaps not surprisingly, print duplication of titles purchased through the e-DDA pilot was highest on the campuses that did not also have a local e-DDA plan in place. Conversely, campuses with a local e-DDA plan that also participated in the system-wide pilot had much lower levels of print duplication for e-book titles included in the pilot. YBP did introduce a method to match local approval profiles against consortial approval profiles and dedupe accordingly, but the campuses did not implement this option. In the future, campuses will likely explore the option as well as develop local methodologies for handling duplication. Given that print and e-book simultaneous publication dates are still not in the majority, in the near term, there will always be some risk of e- and print duplication without intervention.

Where the pilot did realize two of our stated hopes was in improving user access and learning more about patron use of e-books.

As of the end of October 2015:

- 11% of the discovery pool was purchased: 514 titles
- 3,189 short-term loans (STL) were triggered
- 55% of the STLs triggered were for unique titles

The usage data for purchased content was impressive.

- The top used title had 17,601 uses post purchase
- The second top used title had 14,864 uses post purchase
- 26 titles had zero post purchase usage (1% of the purchased titles) but largely represented recently triggered titles (June–October 2015 purchases)

Patrons are using the content and also selecting the publishers we would be most likely to choose on our own.

Our top five triggered publishers did not surprise us:

1. University of California Press
2. University of Chicago Press
3. NYU Press
4. Oxford University Press
5. Stanford University Press

Social science, history, literature, literary criticism, and business and economics were the top five triggered (purchase and STL combined) subject areas, in the order listed.

How Does This All Stack Up?

This has been a productive experiment in consortial e-book purchasing in the arts, humanities and social sciences. [Although we have not been successful in changing the publisher stance about the need for DRM or in influencing a change in ILL practice, we have been able to effectively launch a system-wide e-book program that supports university presses, and that has, based on the usage data gathered to date, served as a useful discovery and access tool for our user population. While we have not quite expanded the breadth and depth of our system-wide collections because of the print duplication issues encountered during the pilot, it is highly likely that duplication issues can be worked out through vendor interventions, local interventions, or both. We have improved access to content and we have learned a lot about usage. Finally, we have determined that much as in STEM, arts, humanities, and social sciences content is desirable in e-format, too.

Balancing Bananas: Collection Assessment of Patron-Driven Acquisitions

Gabrielle Wiersma, Head of Collection Development, University of Colorado–Boulder

Rhonda Glazier, Director of Collections Management, University of Colorado–Colorado Springs

Denise Pan, Associate Director for Technical Services, Auraria Library, University of Colorado–Denver

Stephanie Spratt, Electronic Resources and Serials Librarian, University of Colorado–Colorado Springs

Abstract

The libraries in the University of Colorado (CU) System have been using patron-driven acquisitions (PDA) to build a shared collection of e-books for many years. This paper presents our experiences as both early adopters of PDA and libraries with longstanding PDA e-book programs and describes an analysis of how PDA has impacted collections at each of the libraries in the CU System.

Introduction

The University of Colorado system is comprised of five separately administered libraries, located at four campuses, at three institutions (Boulder, Denver, and Colorado Springs). The materials budget for each separately administered library ranges from $1.3 million to $10.8 million US dollars, and the full-time enrollment (FTE) of students varies from nearly 9,000 to 34,000. The libraries jointly purchase journals, databases, and e-books in order to share costs for core resources and to satisfy an increasing expectation that faculty and students have access to the same content regardless of the campus to which they are primarily affiliated.

In 1999, CU–Boulder participated in one of the first patron-driven acquisition (PDA) pilots on the NetLibrary e-book platform and managed by the Colorado Alliance of Research Libraries (Alliance). The goal of the pilot was to acquire as much e-book content as possible and to make it available to all participating members. The group included the Denver Public Library along with five to seven academic libraries. Outside of price caps on the cost for an individual title, there were few parameters. For one year, MARC records were loaded into member libraries' catalogs and Prospector, the union catalog for the Alliance. Costs were divided among Alliance members using a prorated formula based on library size and materials budgets.

During the pilot, CU–Boulder triggered a substantial number of books about bananas as the result of an undergraduate research assignment. In the spring semester of 2001, an undergraduate geography class at Boulder was assigned to research the production of a crop in a developing country. While the instructor intended to teach students about the economics of crop production and the impact of globalization, all 150 students were given the same instructions to research farm-to-market production of bananas in Central America. Although CU–Boulder held some print books on this topic, students quickly discovered and accessed the NetLibrary e-books. Since the PDA program was established to automatically purchase based on simultaneous use, costs tripled—from $11,000 to more than $37,000—in three months mostly due to multiple, unmediated requests for banana books. The pilot was largely considered a failure because of the rapid rate at which funds were expended and because it resulted in the selection of materials that were deemed inappropriate for the collection. However, it also demonstrated user demand for e-books and illustrated the librarians' roles in the selection of materials in academic libraries.

Ten years later, CU–Boulder was very reluctant to revisit PDA. However, e-books were gaining popularity, while physical space was on the decline. CU–Boulder decided to try again, but with a very different approach. In 2009, CU–Boulder ran a small pilot where fewer than 1,000 e-books

http://dx.doi.org/10.5703/1288284316308

in five subject areas were loaded and available for PDA. Overall, the pilot was very successful and cost was limited. During the pilot, less than $5,000 of the initial deposit was spent. At the end of the pilot 130 or 13% of e-books were used but not purchased. The CU system was able to provide access to e-books valued at approximately $30,000 at no cost. To read more about CU–Boulder's PDA program, see the 2011 Charleston Conference proceedings for "Patron-Driven E-Book Solutions: Moving Beyond the Banana Books Incident" (http://dx.doi.org/10.5703/1288284314973). In addition, CU-system PDA workflows are described in the 2012 Charleston Conference proceedings: "Ebb and Flow: A Selection to Access Workflow for Consortia PDA" (http://dx.doi.org/10.5703/1288284315096).

In 2010, the CU System of five libraries (Boulder, Colorado Springs, Auraria, Health Sciences, and Law) launched a consortial PDA program for MyiLibrary e-books. Unlike previous pilots, the current PDA model utilizes custom, subject-based profiles to identify content within the scope of the libraries' collection development policies. PDA e-books are loaded based on instructions in CU–Boulder's approval plan, but all of the CU libraries load the same discovery (unpurchased) records; significant usage at any campus can trigger a purchase, and all of the purchased content is accessible across all campuses. Since this has become a shared collection, the profiles have been augmented to acquire more e-books in areas that all of the libraries collect, and have been expanded to include subject areas that CU–Boulder does not typically collect (e.g., nursing, sports medicine, criminology, and law).

This mediated version of PDA has increased our libraries' comfort levels; however, it is unclear if PDA is working for all subjects or different types of libraries in the consortia. As such, librarians in the CU system decided to study the impact on the collection at each library as it relates to the MyiLibrary e-book PDA program. The analysis explored several questions including:

- Which subjects have the most PDA e-book records loaded?
- Which subjects are triggering the most purchases?
- Which library is triggering those purchases?
- How does a library analyze the impact of a PDA e-book program on the print book collection?
- As our e-book collection grows, what is the impact on print circulation?
- Are we building collections that support the teaching and research needs of our campuses given existing resources?

Methodology

In order to assess the current PDA program, librarians collected data about the number, subject, cost, and usage of both print and e-books acquired from 2009–2014. This allowed the analysis of data from right before the pilot project began through three years of the PDA program. The cutoff date of 2014 was chosen because a full year of circulation data was preferable for analyzing the print collections. In addition to the aggregate data, books published about chemistry, philosophy, and political science were chosen for additional analysis. These three subjects were chosen because all three campuses had programs in these areas; they represent different disciplines that have different research and resource needs (sciences, social sciences, and humanities); and they have narrowly defined LC call number ranges that facilitate analysis. Usage and circulation statistics for the titles loaded or purchased between 2009 and 2014 were analyzed. While it is evident that online usage stats and circulation are not necessarily equivalent metrics, they do indicate a use and implied need for materials. This data was used in a comparative analysis of print to e-books and also to connect the availability of resources to campus demographic data.

Assessing the Consortial PDA Program

CU's PDA program experienced significant growth both in terms of the number of books available and titles purchased in the first two years of the program. Since then, the libraries have been purchasing e-books at an increasing (but manageable) rate. Although we continue to load and have not weeded records; growth rates for purchased e-books have increased by 20–25% over the past three fiscal years. The CU system libraries currently provide access to more than 20,000 e-books, and have considerable variation in the purchasing patterns and number of records loaded for each subject.

The subject distribution of the e-books that are available varies depending on the format preferences and e-book availability for each subject. The largest number of e-book titles loaded are for political science, followed by business, education, religious studies, engineering, anthropology, law, and sociology. The higher number of science subjects was expected because the profile was designed to be e-preferred for the sciences, but the number of social sciences in the top-ten list was surprising because the profile change to e-preferred for the social sciences happened only recently.

Additional analysis was done to identify the subjects that have triggered the most purchases. Education tops the list, followed by psychology, business, political science, religious studies, anthropology, engineering, biology, criminal justice, and sociology. With the exception of law, this mirrors the list of subjects that also have the most records loaded. This suggests that we are loading e-books in subjects that will get used, but further analysis revealed that purchase rates did vary by subject. On average, the libraries purchased 15% of the titles loaded as PDA e-books. While the top-ten lists of subjects with the most records or that have triggered the most purchases did not include many sciences, subjects like computer science, earth sciences, math, physics, psychology, and sports medicine all had above average purchase rates. In other words, the library may not be loading as many records for these subjects, but we are purchasing a higher percentage of available titles. In contrast, subjects like business, law, political science, and religious studies have below average purchase rates. It could be an indication that many of the titles in these subjects are not needed, or it could be that the research and publication process takes longer in the social sciences and humanities (which tend to be more monograph-based disciplines) and these titles will eventually be used. It could also indicate that researchers in these disciplines do not use e-books (or would prefer print), or that the libraries are simply saving a lot of money by only purchasing the titles that are needed and used instead of buying all of these titles outright. Further analysis is needed to determine why e-books are not being purchased or are purchased at a slower rate in some subjects.

Usage statistics provided further evidence of how e-books are being used in different subject areas. Reports from the MyiLibrary administrative portal contain information about each time a title is accessed including date, time, IP address, broad LC classification, and some subject categories. Comparing the subjects that have the highest use to the subjects with low or zero usage illustrated how e-books are used before and after a purchase. There is significant usage for e-books classed in H (Social Sciences), Q (biology and other life sciences), and B (religious studies and psychology). Again, the subject areas that had significant usage included the subjects with the most records being loaded and titles being purchased. However, further investigation revealed that in some cases there is a lot of concentrated usage on a few titles. This was particularly pronounced in class Q (biology and other life sciences), and L (education) where only five titles generated 20% of the use within that classification. Further analysis is needed to look for patterns or characteristics of the purchased books to better align the approval plan profiles with materials that tend to get used.

Because this is a consortial PDA, it was important to determine which library was triggering a purchase. Each library contributes funds to support the PDA program, and costs are largely based on usage and ability to pay. The libraries analyzed usage statistics to track how usage varied by campus and to determine which library was triggering the most purchases. While trying to do this analysis, it became clear that we cannot tell which library is triggering the purchase, but we can look at usage to see which libraries are generating enough use that could lead to a purchase by analyzing our usage reports, which include unique IP addresses for each campus. The analysis found that CU–Boulder generates 62% of all usage followed by Auraria (Denver) at 25% and UCCS (Colorado Springs) at 11%, which was predictable given the sizes of our institutions and the programs supported at each campus. When looking at the data at the subject level, interesting variations were discovered. For example, in chemistry CU–Boulder generated 88% of the usage with Auraria and UCCS each generating 4%. The Health Sciences Library's usage also generated 4% of the chemistry titles purchased.

Impact on Print Collections

Considerations about consortial PDA e-books naturally led to questions about the print collection at each campus, specifically:

- Are we buying roughly the same number of books in each subject area as we were before PDA?
- If we are buying more e-books, does that mean we are purchasing fewer print books?
- If we are buying fewer print books, are we buying more e-books?
- Or has the overall number of books/rate of growth remained the same despite the introduction of e-books as a format alternative?

Continuing the focused analysis on chemistry, philosophy, and political science, print and consortial PDA e-book purchases were compared. Several interesting trends were noticed. While all three libraries are purchasing fewer print titles each year, the impact of the PDA on the print collection was more subtle than expected. With the number of e-books static across institutions, the percentage of impact on the print collection should have been greatest on the smallest collection (UCCS). However, Auraria's collection was impacted the most by the PDA program with 70% of the chemistry collection in the e-book format; for UCCS, the ratio of print to e-books was closer to 50%, and e-books made up approximately 35% of CU–Boulder's collection.

Just as it was important to analyze usage for e-books, it is important to look at circulation of the print titles. As expected, circulation of titles purchased between 2009 and 2014 in chemistry, philosophy, and political science declined each year. This was expected because titles purchased in later years have fewer chances to circulate than those titles purchased in 2009. This observation led to a secondary analysis for print. In order to compare usage across subjects, the turnover rate for chemistry, philosophy, and political science was calculated. Turnover rate is the number of circulations divided by the number of available titles. For all three libraries, chemistry had the highest turnover rate, followed by philosophy and then political science. Turnover rate for print titles was then compared to a turnover rate of e-books added to the PDA program from 2009 to 2014. The turnover rate for e-book titles was less than the turnover rate for print materials in all three subject areas; however, the turnover rate for e-books followed the same pattern as print with the highest turnover rate in chemistry, followed by philosophy and then political science.

Supporting Teaching and Research

Although each library in the CU System supports programs in chemistry, philosophy, and political science, the number of faculty, students, and degrees offered varies from one campus to another. The analysis needed to include some of this demographic data in order to determine whether or not an individual library's collection was meeting the teaching and research needs for their campuses. Key data included number of faculty and undergraduate and graduate student FTE. To make this data more meaningful, the ratio of titles available to undergraduates, graduates, and faculty at each institution was calculated. This provided an approximate number of print and e-books per FTE for each subject and campus. This data indicates collection size relative to the users it supports and is a metric that can be compared across institutions and subjects.

Conclusion

The findings discussed during the presentation were preliminary. It will be important to delve deeper into the data to answer the more complex questions. For example, can we find a correlation between user demand for monographs by format and discipline? Are our assumptions about how a particular discipline uses information accurate—and can we find the data to verify those assumptions? As the analysis continues, we will be updating and revising the different methodologies used in this study. One of the goals of this project is to develop methodologies that allow for a better comparison between institutions, disciplines, and formats.

CU's consortial PDA program for e-books highlights some of the benefits and challenges of shared collection development. It is clear that when participating in a consortial PDA program, individual institutions give up some control over collection development because individual libraries purchase content based on usage at any participating library. In addition, libraries are not only shifting collection building responsibility to other libraries, but the PDA model empowers patrons affiliated with any of the institutions to make purchases on our behalf. In many cases, students and faculty from multiple institutions are triggering the purchase of materials that are accessible for all CU libraries. Some of the libraries are building collections in areas that are not researched or taught on a particular campus. Overall, the librarians agree that the consortial PDA program supports our goal of building a shared collection of e-books that is accessible to anyone affiliated with the university. This collection provides access to thousands of e-books and serves the overall greater good of the system. Nevertheless, the libraries will continue to assess how well the program meets the needs of each campus and the consortia will adjust accordingly.

Scholarly Communication

CC-BY: Is There Such a Thing as Too Open in Open Access?

LeEtta M. Schmidt, Resource Sharing and Copyright Librarian, University of South Florida Tampa Library

Kyle K. Courtney, Program Manager and Copyright Advisor, Harvard Office of Scholarly Communications

Calvin Manning, LIS Journals Managing Editor, Taylor & Francis

Abstract

Support and demand for researchers to publish in open access (OA) journals has been growing steadily among funding agencies, research organizations, and institutions of higher education. The Wellcome Trust and the Research Councils UK OA policies have begun imposing more finite restrictions, like publishing only under CC-BY licenses, on researchers. CC-BY, or Creative Commons Attribution, is one of several, and the most open, of all creative commons licensing. It most closely embodies the definition of OA, as established by the Berlin Declaration and Bethesda Statement on Open Access, by allowing for the most reuse, including the unrestricted creation of derivatives. Scholars have voiced concern that CC-BY may not be the best license for all disciplines. Libraries, as OA publishers, custodians of institutional repositories, facilitators of scholarly research, and organizers of information, are well-positioned to enhance a discussion on balancing the needs of scholars for minimum control over their work with the goal of OA publishing to most widely disseminate information and scholarship to the public without barriers of country, class, access, or financing.

Background to the Question

Open access has gained momentum as a movement but it is far from mature. Universities, funding agencies, and governments have begun to adopt open access policies for a variety of reasons. This variety of purpose has been criticized by industries research analysts as the reason why open access hasn't grown faster (Aspesi, 2014). For librarians and academic scholars, open access is a new way for researchers to share work that they have traditionally given to publishers for free, while having to pay for access. Open access also allows researchers from all countries and agencies the opportunity to access up to date information and scholarly discourse. For small businesses and economically challenged countries, open access is a way to keep more abreast of scientific discovery than previously possible. For governments and the public, open access is a way to deliver on tax dollars devoted to research funding (Aspesi, 2014). Yet, meaning something different to everyone may actually be a strength in that possible disappointment to some will not stop the greater development of OA.

In addition to the different purposes for OA, there are different methods of achieving OA. Gold open access, where authors publish directly into open access or hybrid journals to make their work immediately available, is often favored by STEM disciplines (Research Councils UK, 2015). gold open access can sometimes require steep author publishing costs (APCs) that many authors and institutions are unprepared to fund (Peterson, Emmett, & Greenberg, 2013). These APCs have also thrown suspicion on hybrid journals that facilitate gold open access publishing within normal subscription journal titles and are receiving money from authors without subsequently altering charges to subscribers for issues with both OA and non-OA articles. On the other hand, Green open access, where authors publish with mainstream subscription publishers and commit to self-archiving their work in a subject or institutional repository, is free of APCs. Access to Green OA publications is not immediate; the research normally becomes available after an embargo period of 12-24 months. This embargo period, and the tendency for authors to lack follow-through on loading their articles into a repository after publishing, lead some to conclude that Green open access does not accomplish the goals of the open access movement (Darley, Reynolds, & Wickham, 2014).

http://dx.doi.org/10.5703/1288284316309

Existing open access policies uphold different ideals on the purpose and execution of OA. Researchers working under these policies, either by institutional affiliation or grant funding, are expected to comply whether or not the specific method or flavor of OA publishing makes sense to them. The RCUK's OA policy requirement that researchers receiving financial support for author publication costs (APCs) must publish under a CC-BY license heightened this discussion on open access publication flavors and how different disciplines function within the OA publishing landscape (Research Councils UK, 2015). Central to this argument is the concern by humanities disciplines that CC-BY publishing, the most open of all creative commons licensing, is not appropriate for scholarly communication in their field (Darley et al., 2014).

Our panel consists of LeEtta Schmidt, Resource Sharing and Copyright Librarian at the University of South Florida, Tampa Library and Editor of the *Journal of Interlibrary Loan, Document Delivery & Electronic Reserve*; Kyle Courtney, Copyright Advisor, Harvard University Office of Scholarly Commons and creator of the Harvard Copyright First Responder Network; and Calvin Manning, Managing Editor for Library and Information Science catalog for US and UK journals at Taylor & Francis.

The panel members were asked to address three questions to further explore the issues that humanities and social sciences have with OA CC-BY and the different ways various disciplines approach open access.

Questions

1. The RCUK's requirement of CC-BY for all researchers receiving article funding costs generated a lot of interest and debate among scholars, particularly in the humanities. Many of these concerns are addressed in the Open Access Journals in Humanities and Social Science Report by the British Academy. What do you perceive are the primary concerns of humanities and social science scholars in regard to OA publishing?
2. In your experience, how do different disciplines react, interact, and respond to OA; what are their differing goals and approaches to OA?
3. In light of these disciplinary differences, what obstacles must OA policy makers consider in order to ensure the future growth and adoption of open access?

Panel Discussion

Kyle

Primary concerns in the humanities and social sciences regarding CC-BY licenses in OA publishing, that I have seen, are the idea of scholarly integrity as well as broader concerns about undesirable activities that could be enabled by what is perceived as lowering the bar of permissions. These concerns break down into three areas, derivatives, commercial uses, and plagiarism. They are elevated by a lack of understanding in this field. In contrast, the sciences have had 20 years of worth of soaking in the open access and CC-BY movement, which has created a greater knowledge and understanding of this particular type of licensing schema. There is no reason why CC-BY should be more harmful or less valuable to the humanities as it is to sciences. I see a lot more misunderstanding on OA itself, CC-BY, and current policies in the humanities than in the sciences. Does this suggest that the humanities people don't read the licenses as carefully as the scientists do? When humanities is derived from reading very carefully? I'm not sure.

Returning to the three areas of concern, a derivative work is something that builds upon an existing work. CC-BY allows others to build upon your work by making a derivative of it. Lawrence Lessig said this is naturally built into the scholarship. The concept is that you build upon what was made before. One of the many benefits of open access publishing in general is that elements such as figures from published research can be reused with attribution as part of teaching material and as part of other published works without having to request permissions. This is the license. This allows article translation, data mining, text mining, image libraries, and data visualization of humanities. These are new to humanities field.

Normal copyright says you need to seek permissions; CC-BY is a license built on copyright. There is protection built into the CC-BY licenses. CC-BY is not just three bullet points. It's actually a page and a half worth of license. It says that it prohibits uses that would distort, mutilate, modify, or take derogatory action to the work that would be prejudicial to the original author's honor or reputation. We shouldn't just boil it down to the three bullet points of what CC-BY allows. We should introduce notions that yes, there are protections for the authors, but that text mining and data visualization are new and novel ways of exploring humanities research that allow you to examine the academic corpus in a way that we haven't considered before. Sciences have been doing this for a while; my notion is that humanities should be able to do this, too. Allowing derivative works would ensure those that are thinking of such future uses would have a chance to try new experimentation with the technology and data collection. Open licenses are necessary to drive the path forward in digital humanities especially, but humanities and social sciences in general.

CC-BY does allow some commercial uses. There two key problems to this. The first is that the definition of what constitutes commercial use now a days is absolutely fuzzy. Not one single court has ruled, nationally or internationally, on what a CC-BY licenses means by commercial or noncommercial use. A German court recently decided that it was just private use that was a commercial activity. We have courts in the US that have, in recent fair use cases, skipped over what is commercial or noncommercial because academics operate in commercial capacities constantly. The sciences do; we have science papers that turn into patents. It doesn't mean the university is suddenly not a nonprofit. There is no clear distinct understanding. In the haze of doubt that overlays this is the idea that if there is a risk of being considered commercial then there is a discouragement to reuse. I would hate to see that. The concept of social sciences and humanities research is the idea of reuse. It is the idea of investment in the past to build upon that scholarship.

The last concern is that CC-BY would somehow encourage plagiarism of the humanities. Plagiarism is a universal issue that everyone is concerned about and a problem that's going to happen regardless of whether you have a license attached. Plagiarism isn't necessarily a law, it's a scholarly no-no. You can't sue someone in court for it. However, CC-BY suddenly gives you this license that says to the authorized user, "if you use this work and don't give attribution you are in violation of the license." It gives you legal recourse.

In my mind, credit to the original author is the coin of the realm. We want to see the impact of our work. This is what drives the motivation for a lot of folks that are writing in this area. Broadly speaking, CC-BY licenses are attribution, indication of modification, and the right to remove attribution if that is what you want. You are in control. It's a very important aspect of this. CC-BY licensing puts the author in the driver's seat in a different way. As you heard in the intro, often you sign away your copyright as an author to the publisher. With CC-BY and open access journals you're giving them a nonexclusive right and you still retain the copyright. With CC-BY licenses on top of that, you say, "I own the copyright and here's how I'll let you use the material and you must, under the law, cite to me." Citation is a major aspect of when we want to measure our academic impact. If we have a law or a license behind it, I think that puts the author in a much better position to decide how and when they want to use their work as opposed to the traditional method where you have to seek, from the publisher, terms for which you can use your work in the future.

Calvin

To return to the first question, another issue is a lack of funding for the humanities as well, especially when looking at the UK's CC-BY requirement. Funding typically goes to the sciences anyway. There's not much for the humanities. It seems like there's a sort of a funding gap. This also applies to the third question we have, which is, what future obstacles are there? I'm not sure how to address that, where the focus is more towards science and less towards humanities for funding, but it seems like one of the obstacles that will have to be overcome. Maybe, in the US, there will have to be a top down approach to OA. It might have to come from a federal level. I'm talking broadly OA and not CC-BY, in this case. Publishers are working on ways to use open access, but APCs are another obstacle for a lot of authors.

It seems like publishers in this instance are kind of like the music industry right now, they've put up a wall and then everyone around them, consumers themselves, realize that they don't need to have that wall. They can go around the industry to get the music they want. They can fund directly the artists they want. I wonder if there could be something similar in OA, a grassroots movement, but I don't know how effective that would be. Also, in looking at the publisher and the development of OA, it's like the concept of the impending singularity, and that is the eventual sentience of robots. As humans, the way the singularity works is that we have to become friends with the first sentient robot, because that robot, once it obtains its own independent thought, is going to be the emissary for humanity to all other sentient robots thereafter. So if you can't become friends with the first sentient robot, you've kind of doomed the human race. I feel like publishers, as humanity in this case, may need to have that kind of sensibility when it comes to OA. OA is coming, when isn't clear, but now is the time to facilitate and show your best side to it.

Kyle

I think you're right in that the movement is coming. We've mentioned the RCUK, Horizon 2020, the Wellcome trust—all notable humanities funders that have mandates for forms of open licensing. The Australian Research Council is another moving in that direction. So it will only be a matter of time before this funder licensing addition comes forward and everyone has to make a choice. Would they cut off their nose to spite their face? Would they say, "well, I really don't like CC-BY so I'm not going to publish with these funding agencies?"

Calvin

I wonder then if it's possible to start a successful Kickstarter campaign? If you had enough people in that community could you say, "I need 10,000 dollars of funding to do this research?" I wonder how you'd go about doing that through something like Kickstarter. I wonder if there is a grassroots campaign to spur more of a top-down approach. When you look at the independent games industry, for games development, and how they're going around the key games publishers to develop the games they want, or the music industry, where people are directly funding tours and albums. There doesn't seem to be a similar movement on OA, where it's really people supporting other people supporting OA, or OA research, or funding, like guerrilla funding.

LeEtta

I think a top-down approach makes the most sense when it comes from funding agencies. Different disciplines will still have issues when the funding agency with a strict OA policy is their only place for funding, but I know that scholars are very sensitive to a top-down approach in institutions and government. Illinois tried it and there were a lot of responses about violated academic freedom (Nelson, 2013). If you're requiring all your faculty to release in OA under a specific license then you are taking away their right to choose where they want to publish.

In some ways I think that a movement in OA needs to be bottom-up to some extent. Most of the issues with the licenses and the movement is just scholar confusion. They don't understand the difference between Green and Gold, they're afraid of predatory journals, they don't know how monograph publishing, especially within the humanities, would fit in the OA environment the way that journal article publishing does. Clearing up this confusion, encouraging faculty to make informed decisions about OA and talk with each other about OA, could begin that bottom up movement.

Calvin

That's something that I've noticed a lot. Working with library and information science most every author I work with understands open access and Green and Gold, but any other discipline I've worked with, sociology, marketing, do not.

Kyle

It's in the DNA of most librarians to understand open access.

Calvin

I was surprised when people didn't understand. I had assumed that all authors did because all authors I work with are librarians. It's interesting that open access seems to have a negative association of an absent peer review system. If you publish open access and are paying an APC you're paying to have your paper published, so people then think there isn't the standard level of peer review scrutinizing for quality control. That's where certain authors aren't aware that it's still the same journal, there's just different funding mechanisms involved.

Kyle

That's because they've had fewer examples. Humanities and social sciences have had fewer examples to prove that the sky does not fall when something goes OA or when the journal gets flipped from subscription to open access. They've had fewer examples to dispel these misunderstandings. It's harder to generate enthusiasm and inspire commitment when you don't have a lot of examples. You get caught in a vicious cycle where slow growth of OA causes slower growth of understanding and good practices. By contrast, to borrow from my colleague Peter Suber, the sciences enjoy not a viscious cycle but a virtuous cycle, where faster growth in OA causes faster growth in understanding. They've had twenty additional years to soak in this, plus the government top-down policy from NIH to test the field. So, to use my gentleman farmer analogy here, this is rocky soil, but we're growing a good crop. There's hope here. There was a time when the growth of OA in the sciences was also slow. It was kept slow by this vicious cycle. But again, twenty years, which is not very long in the history of scholarship, this vicious cycle in the sciences became the virtuous cycle. That means that the reversal is possible. It requires seeding and good fertilizer. I use fish; I put fish in the soil. Pumpkin next to corn; you've got to get it right. So in this regard, how to seed the field of humanities and social sciences to dispel this fear, I think a lot of it is education and understanding of these licenses and that they're not bite size.

The shift in CC-BY's acceptance in sciences was most profoundly noted most recently in January 2015: *Nature* introduced creative commons attribution license for the open access license adoption on its twenty or so open access journals. The percentage of authors choosing CC-BY across all of *Nature*'s open access journals rose from 26% in 2014 to 96% in September 2015. 96% are CC-BY now (Bourke, 2015). That's an amazing stat. But again that's from the sciences that have had the time to steep in this area. I think that there's hope when I look at that, and say "wow that's a tremendous shift in a short period of time." That comes along with the idea that OA helps readers read, retrieve, use, and reuse the research that they need and it helps authors engage with their audience better. The sciences are winning, so let's let the humanities and social sciences take their turn.

Calvin

I wonder, going on your example of *Nature,* it seems like no one similar is stepping up to the plate for the humanities. There is no well-known and well-established leader to wholly accept OA, that I'm aware of, in the humanities section. Societies are another nebulous area. You don't see societies readily accepting OA either, because they still make money on the current schema and depend on that. I think that if we had seen a society taking that approach to OA, there might have been interesting movement, but it's really going to depend on that steeping that you mentioned. Until it becomes the everyday minutia of publishing, opposed to this novel and Wild West where you hear about authors having articles taken and published in books without permission because they were CC-BY. Right now you only hear about extremes because no one is filling the gap.

LeEtta

A lot of scholar's concern is with reputation, so an established person or name, like *Nature,* could make a big difference. Scholars have to publish in a journal with a good reputation in order to get past tenure and promotion and in order to be well-regarded by their peers. If the OA journals available to them don't carry that reputation because they are too new or because the growth of them is very slow, then scholars are continually going to turn away from open access until a journal with a good title and reputation or a society pushes them that way.

Kyle

I like top-down. You know, they're going to give us money to do this, that's great. But I also feel like there should be a grassroots effort among the authors themselves. Like I said, open access CC-BY puts the authors in a driver's seat in a better way. They can control their own works better. I wonder if, instead of handing over your copyrights to a society or to a publisher, you could dispel the myths and say, "Hey CC-BY says you don't have to hand over your full rights, you give them a nonexclusive license, the authors continue to retain control of their work." It's a license that's built atop their copyright. You're saying, "I retain the copyright here and I give you this license to do with as you please." It gives the authors legal recourse to those taking without acknowledging. It gives you control to put your article elsewhere if you want to in the future. Then you get that coin of the realm, mandatory citation, which shows you where and when you are having impact. I'm going to quote Lisa Macklin from dinner last night: she said, "these people are writing to be read first. That's the first and most important thing." The concept there is that they're not necessarily concerned with commercialization, they want exposure. OA, particularly CC-BY, gives them that exposure.

Humanities and social sciences are going to have to become more interdisciplinary, just like every other aspect of other research. You are going to see a new and broader audience open up to your works that you hadn't seen before. Not just the people who belong to that society and get two journals a year. When you make it OA CC-BY, you're going to get scientists that are looking in, politicians, and policy makers. A lot more people have access to your work to give you feedback and will maybe open up your ideas of where your research can go. That's another aspect that's important to the conversation. It could be grassroots. The authors could drive it.

LeEtta

That's where libraries could help too. Obviously, we understand OA and we don't have questions of what's Gold and what's Green and we're already liaising with faculty who don't understand, so it's part of our education efforts. We can spur on that grassroots effort and move the faculty to make their own decisions about how they're licensing their own content instead of signing away their rights.

Kyle

Most humanities work is already based upon scholarship of others and derivative works of reading culture and history. Where do they go for that? The library. They'd want to continue that cycle and work with professional researchers, information professionals, like librarians, that have the ability to do this. We already understand that CC is a well-established legal tool that's being used by another facet of another education community: sciences, and STEM. It seems to be working for them. If all the elements of the infrastructure understand CC licensing then we will be able to use our scholarship more effectively in ways that we can't see right now, like data mining, data visualization, anagrams, word searching, and comparative literature analysis. We will be able to examine that corpus in ways that we hadn't seen before.

LeEtta

I wonder if, as with some of the faculty scholars I've dealt with, the question isn't necessarily about any specific CC licensing. Although, with the RCUK policy it is, but in other policies, there are many other licensing options that are not CC-BY.

You can release your work so that it can be used and copied and disseminated without using a license as open as CC-BY. I think that some of faculty confusion is thinking that all CC licenses are the same. This is also an opportunity to lead faculty to making their own decisions to how they want their work used and what it will mean down the line.

References

Aspesi, C., & Luong, H. (2014). *Reed Elsevier: Goodbye to Berlin—The fading threat of open access.* London: Bernstein Research. Retrieved from http://www.richardpoynder.co.UK/Aspesi.pdf

Bourke, A. (2015). Open access is thriving at nature publishing group. Of schemes and memes: A community blog from *Nature.com*. Retrieved from http://blogs.nature.com/ofschemesandmemes/2015/10/21/open-access-is-thriving-at-nature-publishing-group

Darley, R., Reynolds, D., & Wickham, C. (2014). *Open access journals in humanities and social science.* London: British Academy for the Humanities and Social Sciences. Retrieved from http://www.bisa.ac.UK/files/Research%20Excellence%20Framework/BRIJ1622_British_Academy_Open_Access_Journals_Report_WEB.pdf

Nelson, C. (2013). Open access and academic freedom. *Inside Higher Ed.* Retrieved from https://www.insidehighered.com/views/2013/11/15/essay-impact-open-access-requirements-academic-freedom

Peterson, A. T., Emmett, A., Greenberg, M. L. (2013). Open access and the author-pays problem: Assuring access for readers and authors in a global community of scholars. *Journal of Librarianship and Scholarly Communication, 1*(3). Retrieved from http://dx.doi.org/10.7710/2162-3309.1064

Research Councils UK. (2015). *Review of the implementation of the RCUK policy on open access.* Retrieved from http://www.RCUK.ac.UK/RCUK-prod/assets/documents/documents/Openaccessreport.pdf

Building a Scholarly Communication Boot Camp for East Carolina University Liaisons

Cindy D. Shirkey, Head of Collection Development, East Carolina University

Jeanne Hoover, Scholarly Communication Librarian, East Carolina University

Abstract

A growing demand for scholarly communication expertise led two librarians at East Carolina University to create a series of informative and interactive sessions for liaisons. These boot camp sessions covered topics such as open access, citation management, research impact, data management, authors' rights, copyright, digital humanities, and OER. The goal of the boot camp was to familiarize liaisons with these concepts enough so that they might be able to talk with faculty about them. To achieve this goal, the developers of the sessions used active learning exercises and a flipped classroom model.

East Carolina University (ECU) is a doctoral/research university (DRU) and community engagement institution about 90 minutes east of Raleigh, NC. It serves about 22,000 undergraduates, about 5,000 graduate students, and about 2,000 faculty, 55% of whom are either tenured or on the tenure track. The University has two campuses: a medical campus and the main campus. The medical campus has its own library and the main campus has two: Joyner Library and the Music Library. Between both campuses, the library staff numbers approximately 140, including 18 liaisons.

ECU started out with the head of collection development doing some scholarly communication duties such as overseeing The Scholarship, our institutional repository. Then, in 2013, we hired a temporary staff member to make upgrades to The Scholarship. Shortly after that, the head of collection development was promoted to a new position: assistant director for research and scholarly communication. The temporary position turned into a permanent position: the scholarly communication technician. At this point in 2014 we had two full-time employees working on scholarly communications. In 2015 the assistant director for research and scholarly communication was promoted to assistant director for collections and scholarly communications, and the former STEM librarian was promoted to the scholarly communication librarian and was now put in charge of the scholarly communication technician. The most important takeaway from this is that with each series of promotions, the size of our staff dedicated to scholarly communication grew.

In 2015, the library director recognized and explicitly commented upon the growing need for scholarly communication expertise, so the scholarly communication librarian and the head of collection development collaborated and developed a series of seven workshops that they called a boot camp. The Scholarly Communication Boot Camp was attended by liaisons from both the Joyner and Laupus libraries. Beginning in the fall, each boot camp session was offered twice so as to give liaisons a choice as to when they want to attend.

Being ASERL (Association of Southeastern Research Libraries) members, we were aware that they had been producing and archiving webinars for quite a while. We figured other institutions must be doing the same thing, so we started looking on the web for groups like ASERL. We found a few: ASERL, UKSG, and SPARC being three of the most prolific. But we also found a lot of institutions that have produced just one or two webinars that might fit into a scholarly communication boot camp theme. What helped us when trying to choose materials for a session was to first develop the learning outcomes for that session and then screen webinars, blogs, and articles and see how they might contribute to liaisons' understanding of the topics. Don't be afraid to use snippets of longer webinars if that's

http://dx.doi.org/10.5703/1288284316310

what works best. When evaluating materials you should look at length, speed (if video), clarity, comprehensiveness, and usefulness. Keep in mind that you are never going to find one webinar, video, or article that covers exactly everything you need. Each of our sessions had multiple supporting materials to draw upon.

Internal training for librarians and staff is not a new discussion in the library world. Additionally, it can be extremely costly to bring in external speakers, especially in the era when most libraries are receiving budget cuts every year (Merrill & Lindsay, 2009, p. 85). When planning for our scholarly communication boot camp, we aimed to avoid trainings that required library funds. We looked at similar trainings around campus and at other institutions to help develop our boot camp model.

Due to the ever evolving area of scholarly communication, it is important that training is available to librarians, specifically those in academia. Maria Bonn states that, "Scholarly communication literacy has become a core competency for academic librarians" (2014, p. 132). As topics like open access, data management, and copyright become more important on campus, more librarians need to be familiar with scholarly communication in order to help faculty and students (Bonn, 2014, p. 132). Library personnel training on scholarly communication is also recognized by major associations like the Association of Research Libraries (ARL) and the Association of College and Research Libraries (ACRL). In the ARL/ACRL Institute on Scholarly Communication, training programs for library employees is encouraged (Fowler, Persily, & Stemper, n.d.).

Other libraries have also explored training programs for liaison librarians and other library employees on scholarly communication topics. Julie Rodriguez discussed a training program at Oakland University on open access (p. 397). Her approach to internal training included an elevator pitch presentation for liaisons to develop a short explanation of open access (Rodriguez, 2015, p. 401). Additionally, library employees were invited to open access week events like a brown bag lunch and featured webinars on open access-related topics (Rodriguez, 2015, p. 401). Librarians at the University of Colorado–Boulder (UC–Boulder) explored the scholarly communication needs of their librarians by completing a needs assessment (Bresnahan & Johnson, 2013, p. 414). The UC–Boulder librarians identified the importance of scholarly communication topics and felt these topics would continue to grow in importance over the next five years, especially the topics of copyright and open access (Bresnahan & Johnson, 2013, p. 420). Bresnahan and Johnson also asked their colleagues what type of training they would like to receive on these topics. Most of the librarians felt a workshop, panel, handouts, or even an informal discussion would work well (p. 422). However, most did not want a multi-day training session (p. 422). Merrill and Lindsay used a different model for their internal training program. They started with an overall presentation and followed up with group discussions and shared readings (Merrill & Lindsay, 2009, p. 85). We incorporated a variety of these methods for internal training into our boot camp to fit the needs of the librarians at our institution.

One of the main reasons we created our own was we wanted the flexibility to present the information in the ways we chose. We were able to make it completely relatable to our liaisons' job duties this way. We could have conversations with them about why Altmetrics matters to the humanities or why digital humanities matters on the health science campus. Plus, we wanted to make the boot camp interesting and fun, but at the same time, not juvenile. Another reason was cost. We simply did not have the budget to send people away to other programs, nor was that scalable to the large number of liaisons we wanted to expose to these scholarly communication ideas. Our sessions were also time-effective. Rather than taking a large number of people out for training for a whole day at a time, we spread the time-loss for our participants out over seven months. And finally, it was important that these sessions be portable, since we did have two campuses to reach.

The first session was part of a regular liaisons' meeting and touched briefly upon citation management and open access. We discussed RefWorks, which our library subscribes to, Mendeley, Zotero, and EndNote. For open access we looked at Open Access Explained! by Piled Higher and Deeper (PHD Comics; https://www.youtube.com/watch?v=L5rVH1KGBCY). We talked about Gold and Green Open Access and then also about self-archiving. We kept this session very short because we felt our liaisons were familiar with both of these topics already.

The second session was about research impact. This session, like the ones that followed, was an hour long. In it, we discussed journal, article, and author level measures. We spent the most time on journal level impact factors. We talked about Journal Citation Reports and their inherent problems. We moved on to the Eigenfactor, SJR (SCImago Journal Rank), SNIP (Source Normalized Impact per Paper) through Scopus, and Harzing's Publish or Perish. When we talked about article level factors we started the chat with a discussion about citations, and this segued nicely into our Altmetrics conversation. Finally, we ended the hour with a demonstration of how to calculate the H-index.

Next, in October, we tackled data management. We used a wide variety of sources for this one. First we recommended liaisons become familiar with our Data Management LibGuide: http://libguides.ecu.edu/DataManagement. Next we asked them to view a short video "The DMPTool: A Brief Overview": https://dmptool.org/video. We also asked them to watch the short video "Data Sharing and Management Snafu in 3 Short Acts" (https://www.youtube.com/watch?v=66oNv_DJuPc&feature=youtu.be) to gain an understanding as to why data management is important. And finally, we asked them to view twelve minutes of ASERL's Data Management 101: https://vimeo.com/71525999, by Jen Doty and Wendy Mann.

We moved on to authors' rights for November. The first resource we had liaisons look at for this was Pascal Lupien's PowerPoint entitled "Publishing, authors rights and copyright in the age of open access: common author questions and concerns": pkp.sfu.ca/pkp2013.paper/view/420. We asked them to be familiar with Allyson Mower's presentation on this topic, located at scholarworks.sjsu.edu/oa_digitalrepos/Program/Sessions/3/. We felt that in an ideal world, faculty would know to consult with us before signing away their rights. One way liaisons could help them is by suggesting they use the SPARC Authors Addendum: www.sparc.arl.org/resources/authors/addendum. This resource page talks about why it's important to retain some control over how a work is used, and it links to the Authors Addendum. However, we recognize that it is much more likely that liaisons will deal with faculty who have already signed away their rights. We wanted to let them know that all hope is not lost. Many publishers allow some form of self-archiving. To find out what level of self-archiving a particular publisher allows, liaisons were directed to look up journals on SHERPA/RoMEO: http://www.sherpa.ac.uk/romeo/.

We skipped December so copyright fell in January. We used an ASERL (Association of South Eastern Research Libraries) webinar by Anne Gilliland and Christine Fruin entitled "Helping Students Make Sense of Fair Use," which is #2 in a Copyright & Fair Use 101 Series: www.aserl.org/archive/. We had a lively discussion on the "Four Factors of Fair Use": purpose and character of use, nature of the work being used, amount being used, and effect of the use upon the market.

For the digital humanities chapter we had liaisons look at the Stanford Humanities Center's Digital Humanities page: http://shc.stanford.edu/digital-humanities. We liked this page because it is very well done and it presents a wide array of digital humanities projects. It covers seven different projects. The first is Geography of the Post, which is a geospatial program that maps where post offices were and when they were there. Next is Lacuna Stories, an annotation platform that has been used in certain classes at Stanford University. Writing Rights is about the Declaration of the Rights of Man and of the Citizen. Enchanting the Desert looks at Henry Peabody's slideshow of the Grand Canyon from 1905. Text Technologies covers the long history of the text. And, finally, the Çatalhöyük Living Archive collects data from a long-term dig in Turkey. What we did with this hour session was talk about the depth, breadth, and variety of what's currently falling under the moniker of digital humanities, so this Stanford site was a perfect way to get into that.

The final session featured open educational resources (OER) in the academic classroom. The group was asked to watch a recording of a campus presentation featuring OER projects from faculty members at the College of William and Mary and Old Dominion University. Additionally, we asked liaisons to review the library OER research guide. We also asked liaisons to watch either the ASERL webinar "Your Invitation to Join the Library—OER Community Lessons from the Field" or read blogs and articles related to OER initiatives in higher education and libraries. Since there had been an ongoing discussion about OER in the library this year, we did a short review and update on using OER or alternative textbooks at ECU.

Our philosophy when planning these sessions was simple: flip the class and pay for nothing. We felt that we were working with a group of very bright people who would bring great insights and questions to these sessions, as long as they had quality study materials from which to work. And we felt that other very bright people had done webinars or written articles or blogs on the topics we cared about. It was our work, as the organizers, to pull together the best of the free resources out there and create cohesive classes with them.

We also wanted to make these sessions as painless as possible. One thing we did is run a raffle. For every session a liaison attended, he or she got a ticket. At the end of the series in March we drew one winner for a $50 gift certificate sponsored by the organizers. We also tried to play a game that emphasized active learning with each module. There wasn't really enough time with open access and citation management. We honestly couldn't think of how to turn research impact into a game. But there was a Jeopardy-like game with data management. We played SHERPA/RoMEO red light-green light with author's rights. We did a riff on four square with the four factors of fair use for copyright. We worked out an idea for digital humanities that would allow liaisons to map out their own digital humanities projects based on made-up data we gave them. And then for OER, in March, we played a review game covering all categories.

In the future, we'll have to deal with what happens when a new liaison comes on board. Will we try to recreate the sessions for just one person? Will we simply have the new liaison watch and read the materials assigned previously? Or will we do something else entirely? We think it will depend, at least partially, upon the expertise of the new liaison. We have a good test-case coming up with the arrival of a new STEM librarian. Since the STEM fields are some of the most advanced in terms of scholarly communication, she will need to become familiar with the content of our sessions quickly. At the same time, we do not want to overwhelm her as she is a new librarian and there is much she must learn.

In the course of doing these boot camp sessions we have learned some lessons. First, we learned to always have a back-up plan for complicated subjects. For example, when we tackled impact factor we had a slideshow prepared to help us in going over the main concepts. It turned out to be very helpful for both presentations. This may also reflect that some people are visual learners. Regardless, it aided us in structuring a very difficult topic. We also learned to have a set of discussion questions handy, in case participants didn't have anything they wanted to talk about. Overall, we learned that in order to pull something like this boot camp series off, everyone must be willing to work hard and to prepare sufficiently.

References

Bonn, M. (2014). Tooling up: Scholarly communication education and training. *College & Research Libraries News, 75*(3), 132–135. Retrieved from http://crln.acrl.org/content/75/3/132.full

Bresnahan, M. M., & Johnson, A. M. (2013). Assessing scholarly communication and research data training needs. *Reference Services Review, 41*(3), 413–433. http://dx/doi.org/10.1108/RSR-01-2013-0003

Fowler, K., Persily, G., & Stemper, J. (n.d.). Developing a scholarly communication program in your library. *ARL/ACRL Institute on Scholarly Communication*. Retrieved from http://www.arl.org/focus-areas/scholarly-communication/institute-on-scholarly-communication/2554-developing-a-scholarly-communication-program#.ViUL9n6rSUk

Merrill, A., & Lindsay, E. B. (2009). Growing your own: Building an internal leadership training program. *Library Leadership & Management, 23*(2), 85–87.

Rodriguez, J. E. (2015). Scholarly communications competencies: Open access training for librarians. *New Library World, 116*(7/8), 397–405. http://dx/doi.org/10.1108/NLW-12-2014-0140

E-Book Tune-Up: Maintaining, Sustaining, and Expanding Your Demand-Driven E-Book Program

Jim Davis, President of Docuseek, LLC Caroline C. Mills, Assistant Director for Collection Development, Furman University Libraries

Janet A. Nazar, Content Management Coordinator, Furman University Libraries

Michelle R. Desilets, Reference & Instruction Librarian, Metropolitan State University

Nathan Carlson, Electronic Resources & Discovery Librarian, Metropolitan State University

Abstract

Just like a car, an e-book program needs continuous maintenance in order to run smoothly. What can we do to structure our e-book collections to better meet institutional need? Many factors come into play in building a successful demand-driven acquisition (DDA) program. Student preferences, actual use, collection development, and faculty/staff education and support are all important aspects of maintaining and sustaining a DDA program. This paper describes how the Furman University Library in South Carolina and the Metropolitan State University Library (Metro State) in Minnesota assessed and fine-tuned their respective DDA programs, and the results of these changes.

Introduction

The purpose of this paper is to present a case study of two libraries that take very different approaches to DDA program management and maintenance. It explains what each library has done to make their collection more viable for users, and the results of those changes.

Background of the Demand-Driven Acquisition Program at Furman University

Furman University, a small liberal arts university in Greenville, SC, began an EBL demand-driven acquisition (DDA) program in June 2009 with a deposit of $25,000. Furman's original profile included a few thousand titles published after 2007 in the areas of computer science and information technology, environmental studies, biology and natural history, and botany and zoology. In the first four years of the program there were fewer than 500 short-term loans (STL), only eight books were purchased (see Figure 1 in Appendix) and less than $5,000 was spent.

Assessment of the Program

Motivated by low use of the DDA program, a small task force, including representatives from acquisitions, content management, circulation, and interlibrary loan, was formed in the fall of 2014 to assess the program and propose changes. Based on recent studies ("Ebrary and EBL data study," 2014), the group decided to expand the DDA profile to include titles from the social sciences and arts and humanities in addition to titles from the natural sciences. Fiction and recently published popular titles in the areas of health and fitness, arts and crafts, cooking and wine, and self-help were added based on trends in circulation and book and ILL requests. Languages other than English were included to accommodate changes to the curriculum and in the makeup of the student body. Finally, it was decided to include only items published within the previous three years. Using these criteria, EBL generated a list of titles in their catalog that fit within those parameters. After looking through those titles, the task force chose to exclude several publishers

http://dx.doi.org/10.5703/1288284316311

from the program. Additionally, they asked that titles be excluded based on copyright date, rather than date of publication, in order to avoid electronic reprints of older materials.

Changes to the Program

In November 2014 just over 6,000 DDA titles published prior to 2011 with no recorded STL were withdrawn from the collection, and approximately 65,000 new EBL DDA titles were added.

Six months later the library decided to reduce an existing print approval program and to depend upon the DDA for those titles. Publishers that offer their full catalog through EBL within three months of publication were identified and removed from the print approval plan, resulting in a 30% decrease in received monographs.

In the summer of 2014, because of the continued escalation in costs for short-term loans of e-books from publishers, an extensive cost benefit analysis of our existing demand-driven acquisition autopurchase point was performed. After determining historic institutional use of those publishers, projecting future expenditures based on increased STL pricing, and controlling for multiple use of single titles, it was determined that these increases would cost the institution approximately 10% more while autopurchase would cost approximately 60% more. It was decided at that time to retain our existing purchase point.

Purchase point was examined again in the summer of 2015. After a similar analysis it was determined that it would be most cost effective to autopurchase books from publishers charging 75% of the purchase price for a STL. This change was made in early July 2015.

Challenges

Use of our DDA collection increased immediately, but as use increased, technical problems arose. Users began reporting turnaways. Because we knew our DDA titles were multi-user, we started by looking at our administrative settings. We found that every login from Furman was being authenticated by the same credentials, so EBL saw only one user for our account. Thus, users found that they were blocked from using titles because they "already had the title checked out." Previous low usage of the collection did not make this flaw apparent. Working with EBL Technical Support, Furman was able to establish a system in which individual accounts are generated for each user by identification and authentication through our proxy server (EZproxy). Every account is now recognized as a separate user, eliminating turnaways. An additional problem was the challenge of finding a print book in our Innovative Interfaces, Millennium catalog after loading almost 400,000 e-book titles. The default on our catalog was to display those titles most recently added first, and we found that often you would need to go through two or three pages of results before coming across a print book. This was solved by adding a "print book" limit for those users searching for print.

Results

Increased Use

Short term use of our DDA e-book collection rose after the number of titles available in the catalog was increased in the fall of 2014.

Though use increased dramatically, we found that we were using roughly the same percentage of available titles as we were prior to the expansion (see Figure 2 in Appendix).

Savings

Though our print approval plan reduction took place only three months prior to the end of FY 2014, 5% was saved on approval spending. The following year an additional 30% was saved. Overall, over a two year period we saved twice as much on our modified print approval plan as we spent on our expanded DDA program.

While use of our DDA program has steadily increased, the average costs of these uses has decreased (see Figure 3 in Appendix).

Perception of E-Books

Along with measured increase in use, student perceptions of e-books and their usefulness has shifted.

In both 2012 and 2014 the Furman University Libraries administered the MISO (Measuring Information Service Outcomes) survey to students. Three of the questions on this survey measured perceptions of use of e-books, the value of e-books, and satisfaction with e-books (see Figure 4 in Appendix).

Students were asked "Over the course of a semester, on average how often do you use the following services—library e-book collections?" In 2014 students reported more frequent use of e-books than they did in 2012. An independent-samples t-test identified a statistically significant difference between student-reported frequency of use of e-books in 2012 and 2014.

Additionally, students were asked "How important are these services to you—library e-book collections?" In 2014 students reported that e-books were more important to them than they did in 2012. Again, a statistically significant difference between student-reported importance of e-books in 2012 and 2014 was identified.

Finally, students were asked "How dissatisfied or satisfied are you with the following resources and services—Library e-book collections?" In 2014 students reported a greater satisfaction with e-books than they did in 2012. An independent-samples t-test established that a significant difference existed between student-reported satisfaction with e-books in 2012 and 2014.

Decrease in Circulation

Another trend noticed after the expansion of our DDA program was a substantial decrease in circulation and monograph ILL. Furman, like most academic libraries, has experienced a decrease in circulation of monographs. However, prior to 2014 that decrease had been miniscule. Between FY 2009 and FY 2010 a 2% decrease in circulation and a 15% increase in ILL was observed; between FY 2010 and FY 2011 there was no decrease in circulation and a 10% decrease in ILL. However, between FY 2013 and FY 2014, after expanding our e-book collection, circulation dropped 15% and ILL dropped 10%. Circulation dropped an additional 15% between FY 2014 and FY 2015. Overall, as e-book STLs increased, use of print books decreased (see Figure 5 in Appendix).

Additional Factors

Furman is a member of the Partnership of South Carolina Academic Libraries (PASCAL). Only a few months after Furman's DDA expansion, PASCAL launched an e-book initiative making more than 250,000 e-books available to member libraries through subscriptions to ebrary's Academic Complete, EBSCO's Academic Collection and a small EBL DDA collection. These titles were added to Furman's Catalog, allowing students access to over 300,000 additional e-books (see Figure 6 in Appendix). Rather than causing a decline in DDA use, STLs of Furman's collection remained strong, while use of these additional collections was also substantial.

Continued Maintenance

Several challenges remain part of maintaining and fine-tuning the DDA e-book program. The first is the continuing maintenance of e-book records in our catalog. Updates, deletions, and additions happen continually. It is an ongoing challenge for our cataloging department to continuously maintain e-book records.

Another challenge is preparing for the eventual deselection of e-books when they are no longer relevant to the collection (Levine-Clark, 2011). In the interest of building a permanent library collection the Furman Library has committed to retaining e-book records with one or more STLs or those requested as firm orders by faculty in the catalog for at least ten years. Using the financial report data available on the EBL administrative site, local notes are made in EBL records for STLs, autopurchases, and firm orders or firm order request purchases, and those items will be retained in our DDA collection or purchased if they should become unavailable in DDA format.

As noted above we also changed our autopurchase parameters in late FY 2015. Though only three months of data are available for FY 2016, they show a substantial increase in autopurchases stemming from our decision to autopurchase books from publishers charging 75% of the purchase price for a STL. If this trend remains consistent for the year, a 500% increase in autopurchase and a corresponding decrease in STL may be anticipated (see Figure 7 in Appendix). Depending on budget appropriations it may be necessary to adjust the parameters again at some point in the future.

We will also reassess our print approval plan. In FY 2016 we have found that almost one-third of books that come in through the approval plan are already available in the catalog through our DDA. In January 2016 we will reduce our approval plan further.

Background of the Demand-Driven Acquisition Program at Metropolitan State University

Metropolitan State University (Metro State) is a public state university with a primary, non-residential campus located in Saint Paul, MN. In addition to the main campus, there are three distributed campuses, select courses are offered at area community colleges, and there is a robust online course offering. Initial discussions about DDA began in early 2012 and revolved around how a demand driven approach would benefit our large number of distributed students. A pilot launch of the DDA program began in FY 2013 with a deposit of $20,000. Metro State's original profile included approximately 3,500 titles in the subjects of business, nursing/medicine, law enforcement, and social sciences. In the first seven months, Metro State spent $2,451 on 334 STLs and autopurchased nine titles. The initial autopurchase trigger was the fourth loan of a book. Of the 334 STLS, 57 titles were loaned at least twice and 21 were loaned at least three times. By the end of FY 2013, we had spent just over $17,000 of the initial $20,000 deposit.

Assessment and Changes to the Program

Given the distributed structure of our campuses and the expansion of online-only classes, Metro State librarians recognized the need for more titles that could be accessed from anywhere and linked from our learning management system. After seven months, the librarians began to examine options for expanding the program. First, librarians identified a list of 24 publishers to add to the profile. Publishers included academic and specialty presses such as American Psychiatric Publishing, Brookings Institution, Euromonitor, Kluwer Academic, and McGraw-Hill. The addition of books from these publishers was limited to books within the subject areas identified in the DDA profile. Second, the librarians stopped recommending firm order purchasing unless specifically requested. The modest increase in short-term loans and decrease in purchasing that resulted led the librarians to reconsider how their EBL profile was constituted. Rather than starting with a few basic subjects and relying on the librarians to add what they felt was missing, the library decided to start with every title enabled by default and see what patrons would choose if completely unmediated (see Figure 8 in Appendix).

Challenges

A big challenge for Metropolitan State University was—and continues to be—the unpredictable nature of DDA in terms of budgeting. During the 2014–2015 academic year, funds available for the DDA program were spent down by February 2015. From August 28, 2014, through February 4, 2015, we spent over $21,000 on e-books via the DDA program. We didn't foresee the massive increase in popularity, which resulted in running out of funds before the end of the year. Obviously we needed to adjust our parameters and DDA profile, as this level of spending was not sustainable. In the meantime, we identified alternative funding to keep the DDA program running until the new fiscal year.

Another challenge involved cataloging decisions. Early on we cataloged all available DDA titles in our profile. This step was necessary in order to ensure they were available via our discovery service. This extremely time-consuming endeavor required constant maintenance and upkeep as the titles available changed. When we expanded our DDA profile to offer access to all EBL titles in the fall of 2014, cataloging the 450,000-some titles proved impossible. Fortunately, improved communication between the discovery service and EBL has obviated the need to catalog DDA titles at all.

Results

Use and Expenditures

Metro State's most-used DDA subject areas reinforced the early decision to choose subject areas in support of our distributed programs. Figure 9 (see Appendix) identifies the top two subject areas as business/management and medicine. These subjects support two of our largest areas of study, both of which serve a high number of students from locations other than the main campus.

EBL usage increased each year since Metro State's DDA program launched in FY 2013, as shown in Figure 10 (see Appendix). FY 2015, which included the timeframe when all EBL titles were enabled, experienced the greatest increase.

From FY 2013 to date, Metro State has spent over $74,000 on EBL. Almost half of that amount (i.e., $35,480) was spent in FY 2015 alone (see Figure 11 in Appendix).

Perception of E-Books

Metropolitan State University does not currently administer the MISO survey or a comparable tool to measure perceptions, value, or satisfaction with e-books. However, Metro State librarians have closely monitored the literature on use and perception of e-books. When surveyed, students will express preference for a print-book format (Hoseth & McLure, 2012). When they want to use books for research, however, actual use suggests that students prefer books they can access now versus books they need to drive to campus to check out. The value of e-books to students became very apparent when we spent down our funding for DDA in early 2015. When the student senate became aware of the crisis in DDA funding, they offered to provide the budget to maintain the DDA program through the remainder of the fiscal year. The student senate initiated this offer after they approached the library for background information and statistics. Members of the senate expressed their love of e-books, how they saw e-books as the way of the future, and as a way to remove barriers for students. They also indicated that they hope to see more faculty use e-books as a replacement for cumbersome printed textbooks.

Continued Maintenance

Similar to Furman, Metro State will continue to shift budget from supporting print collections to increasingly supporting electronic collections, including DDA e-books. In fact we modified our collection development policy to stipulate that we purchase e-formats over print formats as a default. Our print collection development is largely based on a demand-driven model as well, and we are also beginning to look at demand-driven options for other resources, such as streaming video.

Conclusion

There is no single solution for e-book DDA program management and maintenance. It is necessary to look at use patterns and user preferences and accommodate them in ways that work with your library budget and institutional priorities. The DDA administrative and acquisitions modules of today enable libraries to quickly and easily modify their e-book program to fit users' unique needs while also meeting the needs of the institution. Don't be afraid to experiment and adjust to see what works for your library. Most of all, don't overlook the management and maintenance of your DDA program, thinking that it will run itself—for optimal performance you must adjust and adapt as conditions and needs change.

References

Ebrary and EBL data study sheds light on ebook use. (2014, February 14). *Health & Medicine Week*, 3354. https://www.highbeam.com/doc/1G1-358920730.html

Hoseth, A., & McLure, M. (2012). Perspectives on e-books from instructors and students in the social sciences. *Reference & User Services Quarterly*, *51*(3), 278–288.

Levine-Clark, M. (2011). Developing a model for long-term management of demand-driven acquisitions. *Against the Grain, 23*(3).

Appendix

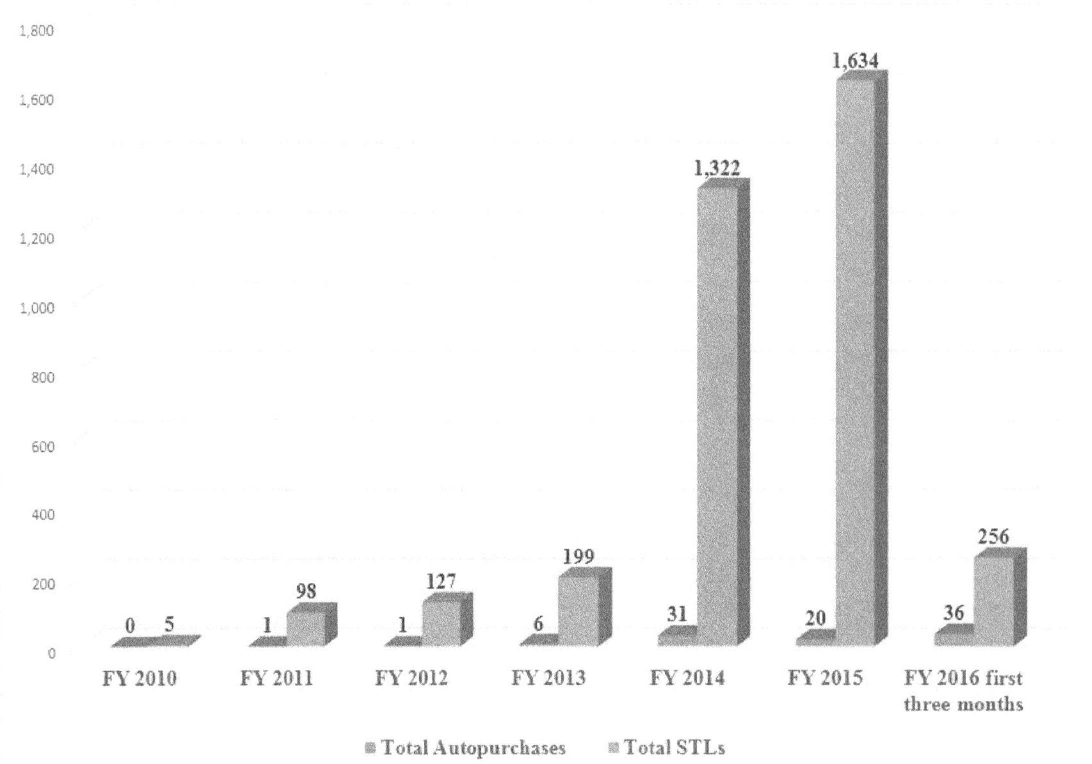

Figure 1. DDA use over the last five fiscal years and for the first three months of FY 2016.

Year	STL	Holdings	% Use of Available Titles
2013	199	11,547	1.72%
2014	1,322	69,547	1.90%
2015	1,634	93,863	1.74%

Figure 2. Percentage use for available holdings over the last three years.

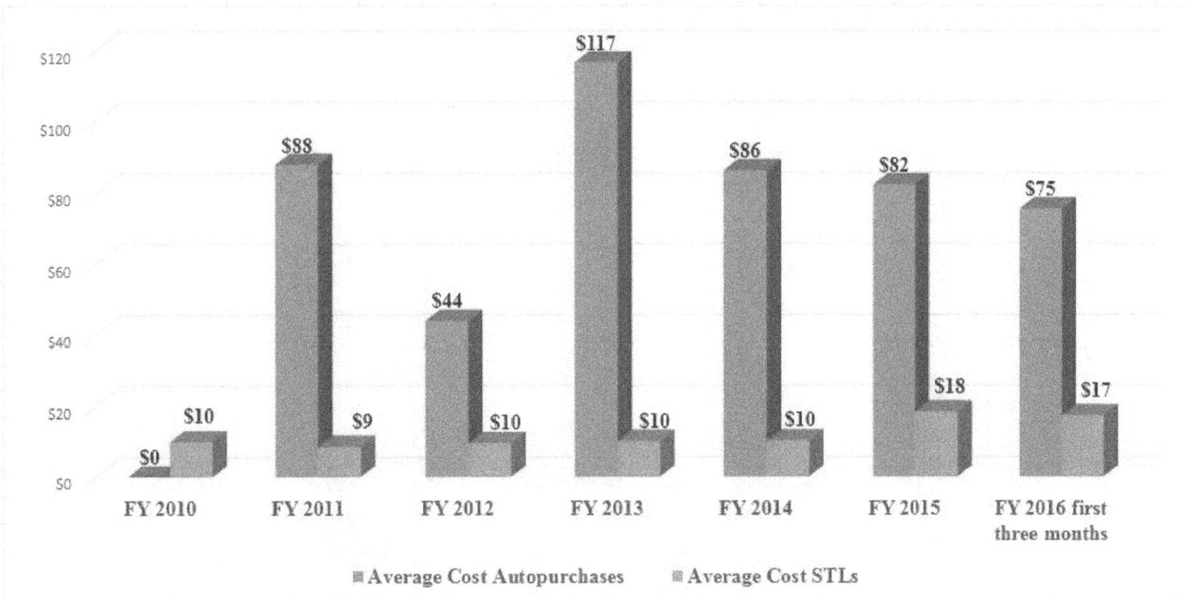

Figure 3. Average costs of both autopurchase and STL per fiscal year, 2010–2016.

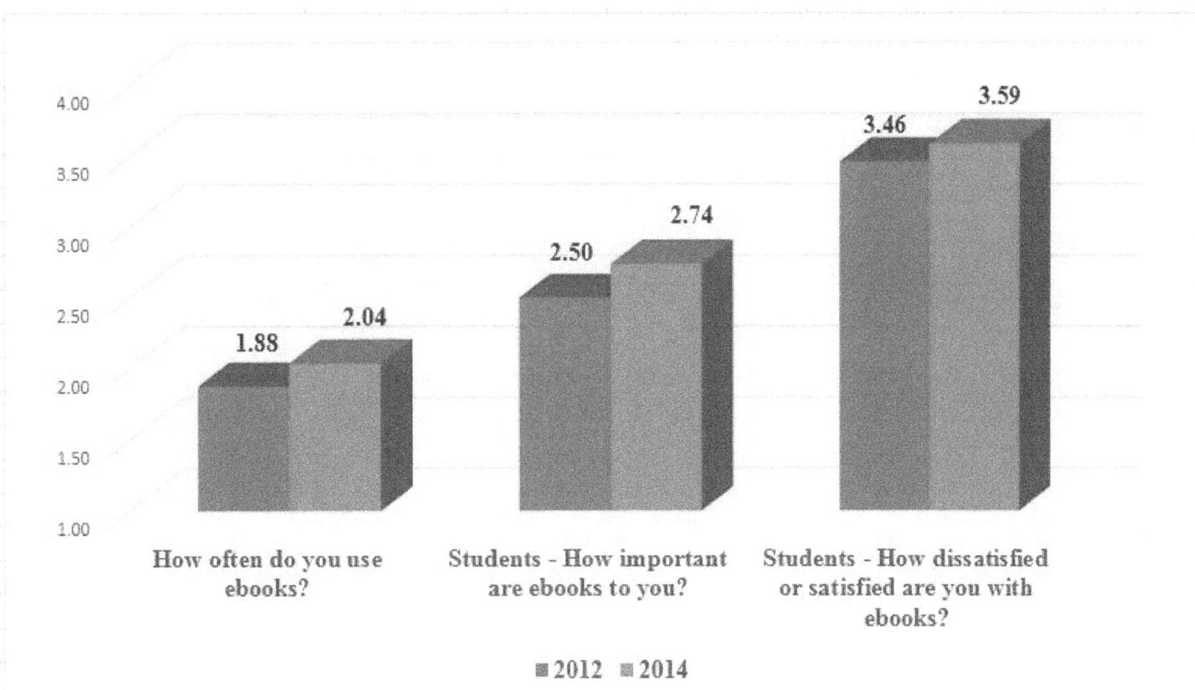

Figure 4. Changes in students' perception of use, importance, and satisfaction with e-books.

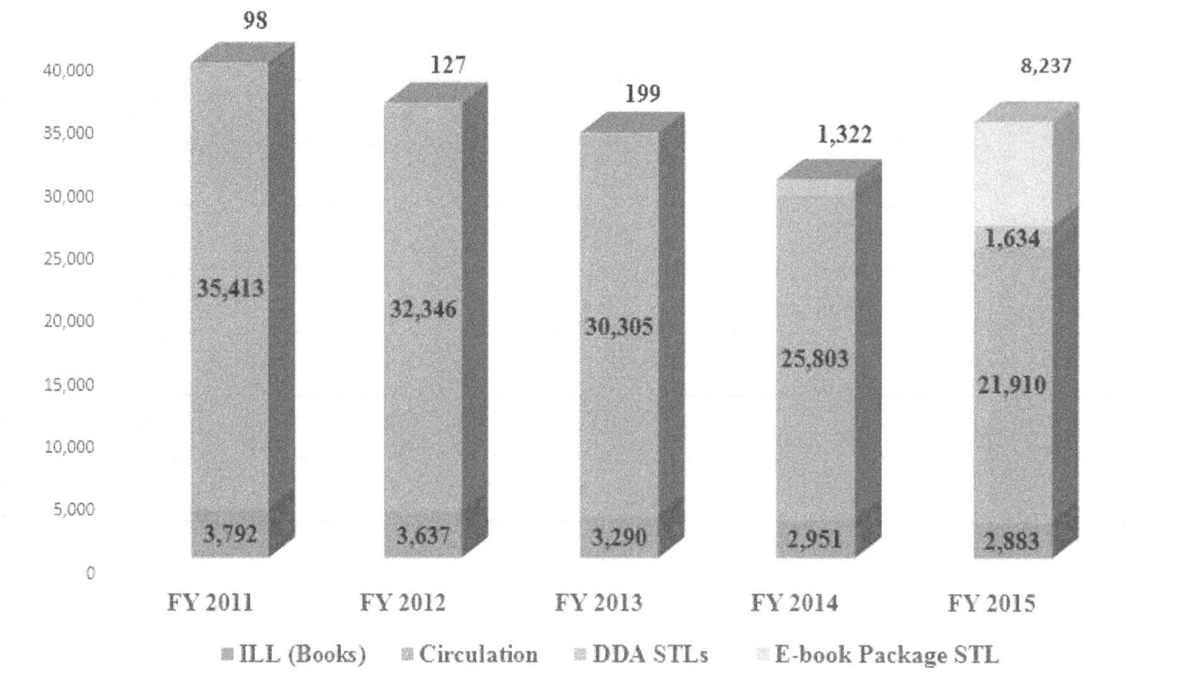

Figure 5. Changes in circulation and ILL transactions between FY 2011 and FY 2015.

Collection	Titles Held	STL
Furman EBL DDA	119,747	2,116
PASCAL ebrary Subscription	149,825	1,710
PASCAL EBSCO Subscription	142,846	1,036
PASCAL EBL DDA	5,534	86

Figure 6. Number of e-book titles available to Furman students in FY 2015 and resulting STLs.

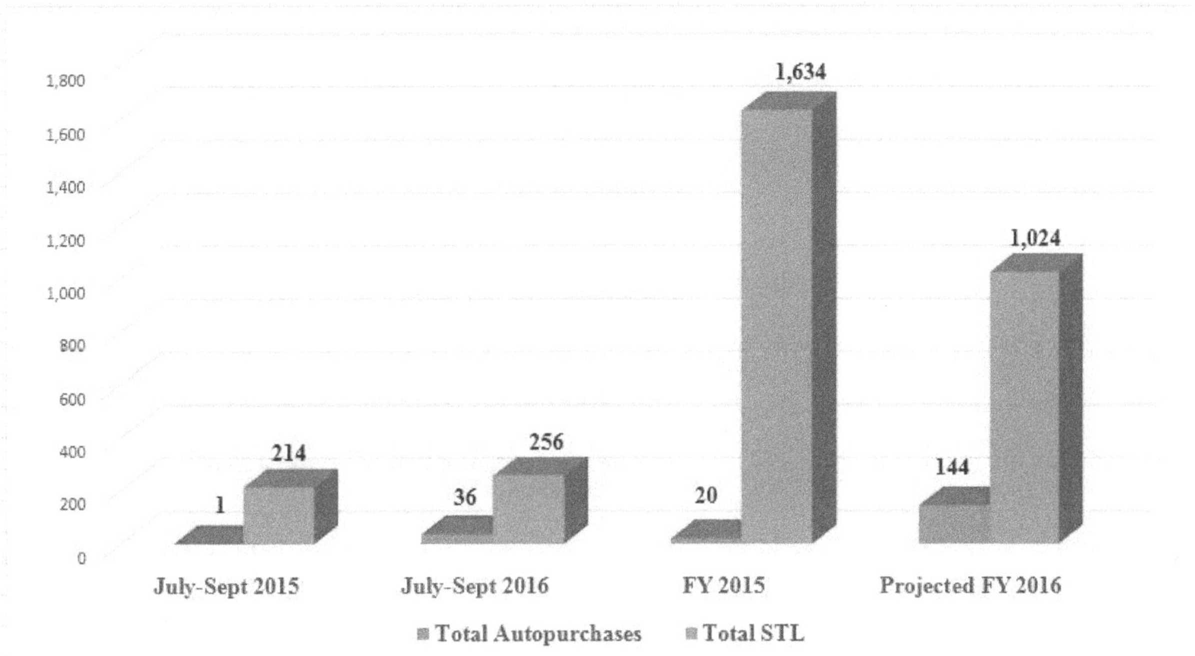

Figure 7. DDA use for the first three months of FY 2015 and FY 2016, total DDA use for FY 2015, and projected use for FY 2016.

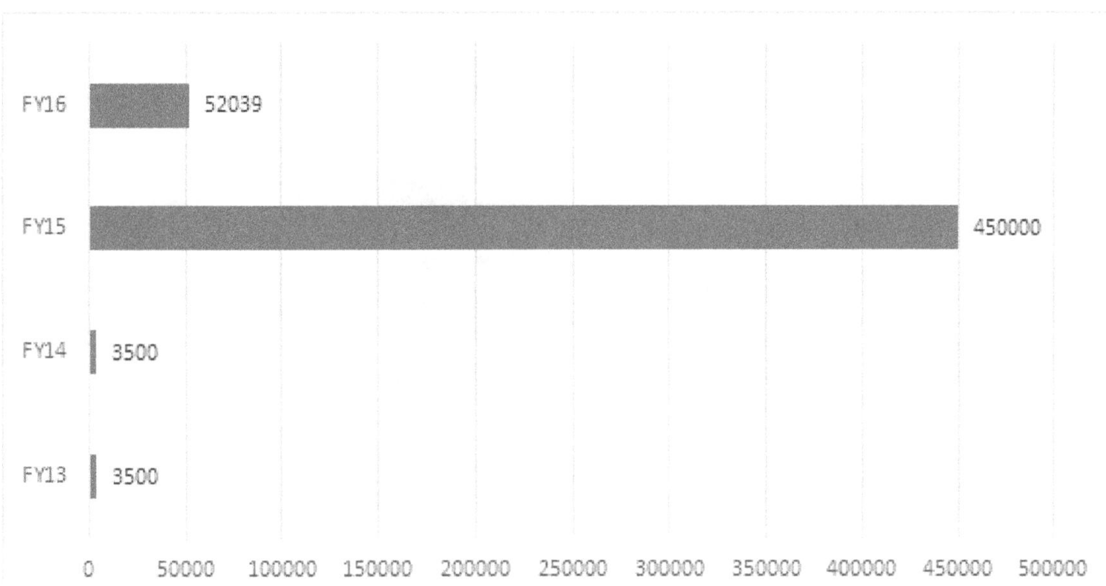

Figure 8. Number of DDA titles available at Metro State, by fiscal year.

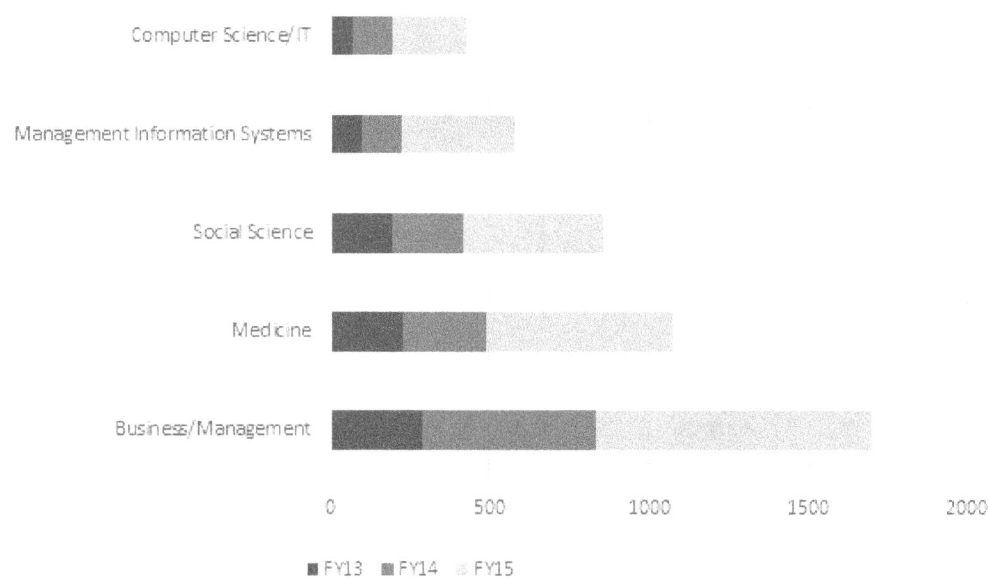

Figure 9. Metro State's most-used DDA subject areas.

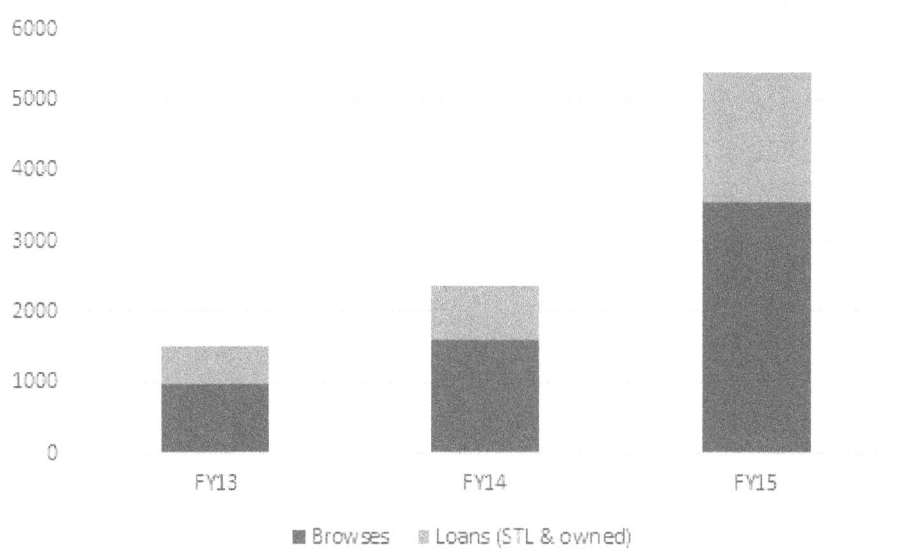

Figure 10. Metro State's EBL usage by fiscal year.

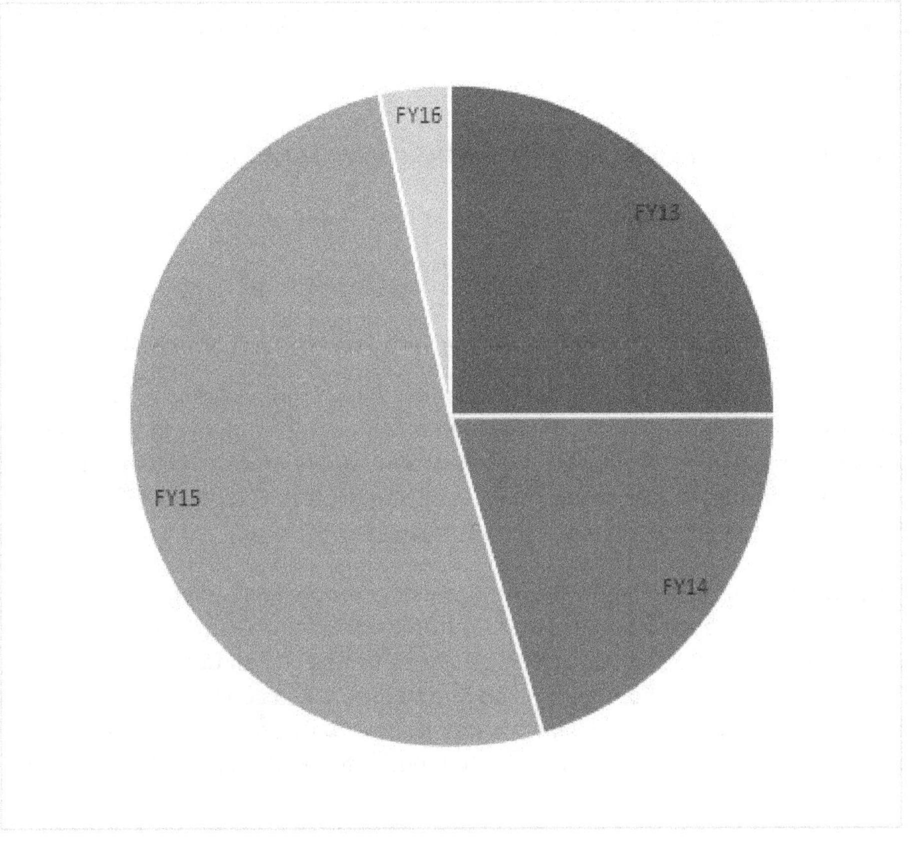

Figure 11. Metro State's EBL expenditures to date, by fiscal year.

Where Do We Go From Here: Choosing a Framework for Assessing Research Data Services and Training

William M. Cross, Director, Copyright and Digital Scholarship, North Carolina State University Libraries

Hilary M. Davis, Interim Head, Collection Management & Director of Research Data Services, North Carolina State University Libraries

Abstract

Research data management has become a critical issue for campus researchers, funding agencies, and libraries, who have made substantial investments of time, energy, and resources into support for managing and sharing data. As data management programs proliferate, however, assessment of research data services has become a notorious challenge for libraries. How can we know—and demonstrate—that our efforts are having an impact, and how can we learn to make them even more effective?

In this session, we will present a survey of several frameworks for assessing research data management services. We will lead a discussion about the application of different frameworks for assessing or auditing existing skill sets, external facing services, and capacity to support an array of research data services. This discussion will be grounded in a demonstration of how we applied one framework to audit the North Carolina State University (NCSU) Libraries's "training ground" model, which serves the dual purpose of developing competencies within our librarians and supporting researchers in their needs to manage, preserve, and share research assets.

Through an active discussion of our efforts, and the efforts of libraries around the world, we can chart a course for effective research data management that can help guide libraries already deep into the process as well as those just getting their feet wet.

Note: This presentation and conference paper is derived in part from the following publication: Davis, H. M., & Cross, W. M. (2015).Using a data management plan review service as a training ground for librarians. *Journal of Librarianship and Scholarly Communication, 3*(2), eP1243.

Introduction

Research data management (RDM) has become a critical issue for campus researchers, funding agencies, and libraries, who have made substantial investments of time, energy, and resources into support for managing and sharing data. As data management programs proliferate, however, assessment of research data services has become a notorious challenge for libraries. Because the practice of data management itself is relatively new and is evolving quickly, nascent library programs that support data management have no established best practices. A program like the Research Data Committee (RDC) in the NCSU Libraries must develop a strategy that helps us understand and demonstrate the impact of our efforts.

These proceedings present an overview on the NCSU Libraries's initial attempts to develop such a strategy. We begin with a survey of several frameworks for assessing research data management services reviewed by the NCSU Libraries. We identify three primary frameworks for assessment of an RDM program and discuss other potential frameworks that were considered. Next, we describe the results of the Libraries's audit process based on one framework, the Joint Task Force on Librarians' Competencies in Support of E-Research and Scholarly Communication (2014). Informed by this audit, we conclude by discussing next steps for the NCSU Libraries RDM program. We anticipate that our experience can be used by other libraries to inform their own programs.

http://dx.doi.org/10.5703/1288284316312

The NCSU Libraries RDM Program and Frameworks for Addressing Program Needs

The NCSU Libraries Research Data Management program has been described in some detail in previous Charleston Conference Proceedings and a recent scholarly article (Davis & Cross, 2015). In brief, the program is more than two years old and uses a committee structure in order to be team-based, light, and nimble. Our "training ground model" (described below) serves to both meet the needs of researchers and prepare librarians in many different departments for greater engagement with research data.

Our audit of the program focused primarily on three related areas: our externally facing services, our existing skillsets, and our capacity to meet the needs of researchers. By focusing on these three areas, we hoped to identify services that are important to our organization as it works to fulfill its role in supporting research data management. Having identified those services, we also hoped that our audit would help to prioritize certain services over others. After a review of the literature, we identified three promising frameworks for assessing a research data management program.

Framework 1: "Joint Task Force Framework"

The first framework we identified was the the Joint Task Force on Librarians' Competencies in Support of E-Research and Scholarly Communication (Joint Task Force, 2014). This framework was developed by a collection of the major players in academic libraries including the Association of Research Libraries (ARL), the Canadian Association of Research Libraries (CARL), the Confederation of Open Access Repositories (COAR), and the Association of European Research Libraries (LIBER). Designed to "outline the competencies needed by librarians in [an] evolving environment," the Joint Task Force framework is a natural fit for evaluation of a library program in RDM.

The Joint Task Force is grounded in three broad areas that are analyzed through specific competencies: providing access to data, advocacy and support for managing data, and managing data collections. As discussed below, this detailed framework which aims "to identify skill gaps in their institution" and "carry out self-assessments" proved to be the cornerstone of our own audit in the NCSU Libraries.

Framework 2: "20 Needed Competencies for Science & Technology Librarians"

While the Joint Task Force framework was the centerpiece of our audit, another framework also provides valuable guidance for assessment of library RDM programs. A group of scholars at the University of Massachusetts Medical School library worked together to identify and describe competencies "needed in order to cultivate [RDM] skills, establish [RDM] roles, and engage successfully in eScience" (Creamer, Morales, Crespo, Kafel, & Martin, 2012).

This framework is grounded in the twenty "needed competencies" identified in the survey. The framework divides these into two distinct areas. The first, "data literacy," includes data sharing, open access, data services, "data interview," data life cycle, IP and copyright, compliance with mandates, data literacy, data management plans, access or locate datasets, and data security. In addition, this framework identifies a number of "technical competencies" such as web 2.0 technologies, data archiving, managing and curating data, metadata standards, digital databases, IR, data mining and visualization, and digital lab notebook applications.

This framework is well organized and provides a rich and detailed set of competencies. It also reflects the health science context that generated it. As such, the framework was useful for establishing context but not a perfect fit for an academic library RDM program.

Framework 3: "Data Management as A Research Tool (DART)"

The third framework we investigated is, in many ways, the most promising. Funded by an IMLS grant, a group of scholars led by Amanda Whitmire has reviewed a large group of data management plans (DMPs) in order to expose the common practices and hurdles faced by scholars in order to provide insight into the detailed individual data management habits of scholars. They have used this review to create a framework branded as "Data Management as a Research Tool" (DART, 2015).

This work builds on research done by Mischo, Schlembach, and O'Donnell (2014) and Parham and Doty (2012) and has generated an analytic rubric "to standardize the review of data management plans as a means to inform targeted expansion or development of research data services at academic libraries" (DART Project, 2015). Early discussion of the framework has been promising and presentations at conferences in the fall of 2015 suggest significant value for academic libraries looking to audit their RDM programs. Unfortunately, no formal documentation was available when we conducted our audit, and only preliminary results were available at the time of our presentation at the Charleston Conference. The DART framework shows great promise and can be expected to be worth watching for future assessment, but simply was not available to inform our audit.

Bringing the Frameworks Together

In addition to these three frameworks, we reviewed several other promising frameworks that informed our efforts. Work done by Raboin, Reznik-Zellen, and Salo (2012) describe shared competencies across three surveyed libraries that include "garnering institutional support, managing the integration of services with new or existing staff structures, and continuing to meet researchers' needs as they evolve." We also incorporated research from peer institutions and model RDM programs such as those documented in Zilinski, Chan-Park, Dasler, and Nicholls' (2013) discussion of commonalities across RDM services at Purdue, Baylor, Maryland, and Michigan.

As discussed above, the Joint Task Force framework ultimately proved to be the most appropriate for our audit. However, we were careful to look to each of the frameworks to add context and nuance to our analysis. Each added something of value to our audit and each provided information that has helped us understand and improve our program. Our discussion below is presented in terms of the Joint Task Force, but subsequent audits are likely to incorporate information from the nascent DART framework as well as more recent scholarship that has been—and will be—produced after our initial audit.

NCSU Libraries's Training Ground Model

Like many libraries, we are in a position of providing support at the point of need, while also training subject liaison librarians in the practical issues and realities of managing research data and research processes. We deployed a Data Management Plan (DMP) Review service to the NC State campus to provide service at the point of need, and to gain access to DMP drafts of our researchers for training purposes. The DMP Review service is managed by a committee of librarians with diverse experience in data management and domain expertise (the Research Data Committee, or RDC). The RDC serves three primary roles: (1) to develop and implement training for librarians and researchers; (2) promote and market those services across campus and to targeted groups; and (3) provide services at the moment of need to support RDM for our university. This group also invites subject liaison librarians to participate in the DMP Review process. Committee membership has strengths in digital scholarship, digital preservation, metadata, geospatial and numeric data, copyright and intellectual property rights, and the grant review process, and includes liaisons with subject expertise. Members rotate annually, allowing new members to get exposure to RDM and inform the future of the committee. To scale out awareness and knowledge within the NCSU Libraries, RDC members have offered workshops and seminars for other library staff on institutional review board protocols, directives for public access to federallyfunded research, strategies for reviewing DMPs, data rights and ownership, and data management for students. Leveraging what we learned through deploying RDM support for campus, these workshops have facilitated rich, engaging training opportunities grounded in actual issues faced by researchers.

The combination of the DMP Review service and the internal training coordinated by our

Table 1. Core competencies for providing access to data and relevant experience gained through the training ground model.

Core Competencies	*Relevant Experience Gained Through Training Ground model*
Identifying datasets, discovery tools	Re3data.org and Data Citation Index to identify datasets and repositories for data deposit
Data centers, repositories, and collections	Mediate with data repositories for eligibility and criteria for data deposit; how data is organized in repositories; emerging standards for data citation
Data organization and structure within these collections	
Data citation/referencing	
Data licensing and intellectual property policies and principles	Licensing language and terms for external datasets; knowledge of licensing options to support sharing and reuse of data
Data manipulation/analysis techniques and tools	Expertise limited to a few librarians with specific geospatial and data analysis skills

committee constitutes our training ground model. This model aims to develop needed competencies for our librarians and provide support to researchers through relevant services and partnerships. The heart of the training ground model is the use of actual DMPs to give librarians hands-on experience and opportunities for peer-to-peer training while reviewing DMPs. We all benefit from seeing how we each find problems and propose solutions, and we each play the role of trainer/trainee on any given DMP. The model presents a reinforcing cycle of support and training: skills gained from the DMP review process provide hands-on training for librarians, sustained marketing lets researchers know that we are a source of help, and, at the point of need, the Committee's shared expertise facilitates immediate support for researchers on a deadline.

Audit of Training Ground Model

In order to identify gaps in our program, we conducted an audit of the DMP Review service in terms of its capacity to develop and enhance competencies as identified by the Joint Task Force on Librarians' Competencies in Support of E-Research and Scholarly Communication. The lack of established benchmarks for what counts as quality service and impact limited our ability to empirically measure the effectiveness or impact of our services; therefore, an audit enabled us to take a first step toward an assessment of our model. The Joint Task Force framework presents competencies in three areas: (1) Providing access to data; (2) advocacy and support for managing data; and (3) managing data collections.

Providing Access to Data

Providing access to data includes competencies for finding datasets, leveraging data centers and how data are organized and structured in those collections, methods for citing data, licensing to support sharing and reuse, and tools and techniques for data manipulation. The DMP Review service builds competencies in finding and identifying datasets, but this is limited since most of the researchers who submit DMPs are using

Table 2. Core competencies for advocacy and support for managing data and relevant experience gained through the training ground model.

Core Competencies	*Relevant Experience Gained Through Training Ground model*
Funders' policies and requirements	Wide range of funding agency requirements for DMPs
Data management plans	Understanding main elements of DMPs; exposure to successful and unsuccessful examples across multiple disciplines
Research practices and workflows	Awareness of researchers' practices and literacy regarding best practices for managing data
Data centers, repositories, and collections for deposit	Identify eligibility for data deposit; investigate how data is organized in repositories; exposure to emerging standards for data citation
Articulate benefits of data sharing and reuse	Ways to help researchers effectively share data and publications while maximizing intellectual property rights
Data sharing options, open access, IPR, licenses	Practices spanning use of commercial grade cloud storage to storage on local media; benefits that established repositories provide (e.g., persistent identifiers, protection of sensitive data, citation tracking, preservation services)
Disciplinary norms and standards for data management	
Data structures, types, and formats	Ways to standardize file-naming, migrate to non-proprietary file formats, document and describe data structure through metadata
Best practices for managing data, standards, metadata, and vocabularies	Variation in metadata standards; in cases where standards do not exist, offer to assist in creating standard practice for research projects
Data publication requirements of specific journals	Data sharing expectations of journals that require data publication; terms in publishers' author agreements that may limit researchers' ability to meet sharing funders' public access mandates
Data audit (i.e., identify range of datasets on campus) and assessment tools (e.g., Data Curation Profiles)	Limited experience in identifying datasets on campus and in employing assessment tools

their own data or have already identified external data sources. The DMP Review service builds competencies in data citation as well as licensing data, for example, when we help researchers find appropriate licenses for data and software. One gap area for our model is that data manipulation and analysis is limited to a few people and is a skill set that needs to be developed more broadly. Table 1 provides an overview of core competencies as outlined by the Joint Task Force and the relevant experience gained through our model.

Advocacy and Support for Managing Data

This category presents competencies in knowledge, expertise, and awareness of funders' policies, DMPs, research practices and workflows, and data repositories to support RDM. By reviewing DMP drafts, we have been exposed to a wide range of practices and are becoming attuned to variable components of DMPs across and within funding agencies (e.g., NSF, USDA, NIH, DOE). The DMP Review service has provided a practical context for us to learn about data repositories across multiple disciplines; in some cases we have contacted data repositories on behalf of researchers to identify eligibility requirements and criteria needed to contribute data.

This category also includes competencies focused on the benefits of sharing data and reuse of data, open access, intellectual property rights, licensing data collections, and disciplinary standards for data management, as well as data types and formats. The DMP Review service supports many of these competencies. For example, we have learned about the drawbacks of commercial-grade cloud storage (e.g., Dropbox and Google Drive) and the benefits of data repositories. Benefits of data repositories

Table 3. Core competencies for managing data collections and relevant experience gained through the training ground model.

Core Competencies	***Relevant Experience Gained Through Training Ground Model***
Metadata standards and schemas, data formats, domain ontologies, data citation, data licensing, and identifiers	Variation in metadata standards; offer to create metadata schema; standards for data citation; licensing options to support sharing and reuse of data; document and author identifiers
Selection and appraisal tech for datasets	Limited experience due to lack of campus data repository
Discovery tools	Some experience in these areas when providing support for researchers in identifying disciplinary or generic data repositories for data deposit; expertise in a few librarians who manage locally curated special collections and university archives
Database design types and structures	
Data linking and data integration techniques	
Data storage infrastructures	
Digital preservation metadata	
Forensic procedures in digital curation	

represent disciplinary norms and standards including persistent identifiers to aid in citation and sharing; support with sensitive data; and tracking citations to databases to monitor the impact of data in the research community.

Finally, this category includes competencies in metadata standards, complying with data publication requirements (and funders' requirements), and a local audit of the range of datasets on campus and use of assessment tools such as the Data Curation Profiles. The audit showed us that we have room for improvement in learning how to develop metadata for research data where standards are lacking. In terms of data publication requirements, as publishers and funders firm up their plans, this will be a constant area for growth for us. When our campus conducts a data inventory, we will be in a position to inform that process. Table 2 provides an overview of core competencies as outlined by the Joint Task Force and the relevant experience ssgained through our model.

Managing Data Collections

Managing data collections competencies include the application of metadata standards and best practices including ontologies and identifiers, selection and appraisal of datasets, discovery tools, database design, data integration and linking, storage infrastructures, preservation metadata, and digital forensics for curation. The biggest gap area for us is the selection and appraisal of data for local storage since we do not currently have a local data repository. Similarly, our model does not fully support competency development in the areas of data integration in the context of data storage infrastructure, digital preservation metadata, and curation forensics. Expertise is concentrated in a few and needs to be broadened to more library staff. Table 3 provides an overview of core competencies as outlined by the Joint Task Force and the relevant experience gained through our model.

Conclusions and Next Steps

The primary objectives of the DMP Review service is to help our researchers be more competitive in the research proposal process and to make research assets more widely available. By equipping librarians with the experience to develop competencies and confidence to support researchers, we can deliver help at the point of need. Conducting our audit has shown us where we have been effective at helping librarians develop skills to support researchers at the grant proposal stage. The DMP Review service has given us the credibility and experience to advocate on behalf of researchers. We have noted the lack of a local data repository as a major liability for research competitiveness and have shared concerns of researchers with IT leaders, leading to the development of a proposal for a local storage solution in the coming months.

The DMP Review service has created opportunities to learn valuable skills while providing time-sensitive service to researchers. However, the gaps identified by the audit point out areas for improvement. To address gaps, we are engaging in the development of a community of practice for data science and data visualization. We are continuing to build out a program of formal, informal training, mentoring, and a support network. We piloted a data science short course for our librarians focusing on topics like data manipulation, data wrangling, first step data analysis, data visualization, and storage infrastructure. We intend to double back and cover the bases to ensure that all of our librarians engaged in research data management support have opportunities to handle raw data, create metadata and discovery-enabled files, get under hood with data repositories, and develop a foundation in digital forensics. We continue to seek partnerships with other units across campus that offer unique skills and support such as data security, options for campus-provided data storage, institutional review board compliance support, technology transfer, and grant proposal development. We are also seeking opportunities to go beyond DMPs to become research partners. In select cases, we are engaged in grant proposals that embed librarians as grant funded senior personnel.

References

Creamer, A., Morales, M. E., Crespo, J., Kafel, D., & Martin, E. R. (2012). An assessment of needed competencies to promote the data curation and management librarianship of health sciences and science and technology librarians in New England. *Journal of eScience Librarianship, 1*(1), Article 4. http://dx.doi.org/10.7191/jeslib.2012.1006

Cross, W., & Davis, H. (2014). Building capacity for research data management support. *Charleston Conference*, November 5–8, 2014. http://dx.doi.org/10.5703/1288284315632

DART Project: Data Management Plans as a Research Tool. (2015). Project overview. Retrieved from http://dmpresearch.library.oregonstate.edu/project-overview

Davis, H. M., & Cross, W. M. (2015).Using a data management plan review service as a training ground for librarians. *Journal of Librarianship and Scholarly Communication, 3*(2), eP1243. http://dx.doi.org/10.7710/2162-3309.1243

Joint Task Force on Librarians' Competencies in Support of E-Research and Scholarly Communication. (2014). Librarians' competencies profile for research data management. Retrieved from https://docs.google.com/document/d/15Kqg6w6AFsdbbaxcRCx7DZ3OERnQk6E0UhQ4UeRu0Cc/

Mischo, W. H., Schlembach, M. C., & O'Donnell, M. N. (2014). An analysis of data management plans in University of Illinois National Science Foundation grant proposals. *Journal of eScience Librarianship, 3*(1): Article 3. http://dx.doi.org/10.7191/jeslib.2014.1060

Parham, S. W., & Doty, C. (2012). NSF DMP content analysis: What are researchers saying? *Bulletin of the American Society for Information Science and Technology, 39(*1), 37–38. http://dx.doi.org/10.1002/bult.2012.1720390113

Raboin, R., Reznik-Zellen, R. C., & Salo, D. (2012). Forging new service paths: Institutional approaches to providing research data management services. *Journal of eScience Librarianship, 1*(3), Article 2. http://dx.doi.org/10.7191/jeslib.2012.1021

Zilinski, L. D., Chan-Park, C., Dasler, R., & Nicholls, N. (2013). Carpe data: Data curation services at four different institutions. Presented at the 2013 DLF Forum, Austin, TX. http://docs.lib.purdue.edu/lib_fspres/39/

In the Highways and Hedges: Library Support for OER Adoption Efforts at Higher Education Institutions Across Virginia

Tara Cassidy, Coordinator of Library Services, Virginia Community College System

Olivia Reinauer, Reference Librarian, Tidewater Community College

Anita R. Walz, Open Education, Copyright & Scholarly Communication, Virginia Tech University

Abstract

A growing number of Virginia higher education libraries are involved in supporting and leading Open Educational Resource (OER) adoption efforts. Statewide, OER initiatives include a unique blend of administrative and grassroots organizations and individuals that work hand in hand to leverage the economic benefits and educational advantages of open educational resources. This article highlights library engagement and leadership, successes and growing pains, on the many levels of OER efforts in Virginia Higher Education.

Introduction: Knowledge Does Not Diminish When It Is Shared

Open educational resources (OER) are:

> Teaching, learning, and research resources that reside in the public domain or have been released under an intellectual property license that permits their free use and repurposing by others. OER include full courses, course materials, modules, textbooks, streaming videos, tests, software, and any other tools, materials, or techniques used to support access to knowledge. (William and Flora Hewlett Foundation, n.d.)

The 2015 NMC Horizon Report designated the proliferation of open educational resources as a midterm trend, "driving EdTech adoption in higher education for three to five years" with real potential for removing cost barriers to education (p. 14, Johnson, Adams Becker, Estrada, & Freeman, 2015).

The OER trend is local, national, and global. It speaks to many audiences, including libraries. Values of the Open Education movement match with nearly all of the ALA's Core Values of Librarianship: access, democracy, education and lifelong learning, intellectual freedom, preservation, the public good, service, and social responsibility (American Library Association, 2004). Perhaps this kinship is part of the reason why so many libraries and librarians find an affinity with open education initiatives as we continue to evolve with learner and faculty needs, and embrace the opportunities afforded by emerging technologies.

Librarians have existing expertise in copyright, licensing, finding, and evaluating information, instruction, faculty development, building relationships, and managing projects. This makes us a natural fit to support and lead our communities in areas of open licensing, evaluating, maintaining and providing access to curated open materials, and open publishing as a number of libraries are moving in this direction. It's up to us to lead as we are able.

Open Education in Virginia, a Rapidly Changing Environment

Virginia open education initiatives in higher education have grown from individual and informal initiatives and gatherings to institutional and multi-institution initiatives, and state-level engagement among individuals, professional association, consortia, and government bodies.

Four notable early initiatives include: Virginia State University's School of Business core curriculum conversion, Tidewater Community College's (TCC) "Z" Degree, Northern Virginia

http://dx.doi.org/10.5703/1288284316313

Community College's (NOVA) Kaleidoscope project, and OpenVA: Virginia's Summit on Open and Digital Learning. In 2010 the School of Business at Virginia State University adopted openly licensed textbooks for nine of its courses (Feldstein et al., 2012). TCC's "Z" degree followed as the first in the country to pilot an entire associate degree (AS in Business Administration) in 2013, resulting in reduced costs and statistically significant improvements in student retention and achievement ("Z-degree," n.d.). OpenVA, a loosely organized group of Virginia Higher Education faculty, educational technologists, and administrators organized statewide meetings in 2013 and 2014 with smaller regional events in 2015 ("OpenVA," n.d.). Also in 2014, NOVA piloted Kaleidoscope, a project supported by EDUCAUSE Next Generation Learning Challenges and Gates Foundation, with the goal of assisting faculty in using open educational resources (Northern Virginia Community College, 2014). In 2015, the Virginia Community College System (VCCS) launched the Zx23 Project to build on Tidewater's success and prior Chancellor-funded projects and replicate the Z-Degree across the 23 Virginia Community Colleges ("Zx23 application," n.d.). Zx23 is packaging OER to establish new degree pathways to existing credentials without traditional textbook cost, and a primary goal of the project is to establish a model for sustaining and supporting the OER infrastructure for degree programs.

The State Council of Higher Education for Virginia (SCHEV) has also played a role in facilitating exploration of open education by co-sponsoring OpenVA, creating and sustaining the Library Advisory Committee (LAC) since the 1970s, and in May 2015 creating the Open Virginia Advisory Committee (OVAC) in support of SCHEV's Statewide Strategic Plan for Higher Education. OVAC representation includes public, private, two- and four-year institution representation as well as representatives from the LAC and was established to:

1. Make recommendations to Council regarding initiatives and policies that may facilitate OER adoption.
2. Organize events to facilitate inter-institutional networking and the sharing of best practices and expertise on issues related to instructional technology and affordable educational resources.

OVAC's current tasks are to conduct an environmental scan to determine the current status of OER/openness at Virginia's higher education institutions, and to develop an outreach plan.

The Virtual Library of Virginia (VIVA) a consortium of 70+ nonprofit academic libraries within the Commonwealth of Virginia, conducted an OER activities survey of member libraries through its Resource Sharing Committee (RSC) in May 2015. Thirty five of 70+ VIVA member libraries responded. Twenty-seven indicated that their institution is currently exploring or using OER. Twenty-one respondents indicated that the library is somewhat or very involved in these efforts. Twenty-seven thought libraries should play a role in OER, and five said maybe—this group was currently not involved. Fifteen respondents thought VIVA should play a role in OER in Virginia, fifteen others said maybe, and two said no. A commissioned task force offered the following recommendations (Virtual Library of Virginia, 2015):

- Educate VIVA members regarding OER and on how some institutions are leveraging OER by promoting current VIVA member OER/affordability efforts. Highlight similar work at other consortia.
- Connect with other state-level groups that are active in this area (SCHEV's OVAC, Virginia 21, and others) to identify potential areas for collaboration
- Leverage VIVA content evaluation expertise to evaluate OER. Highlight only high quality OER in a guide to OER + VIVA-provided resources specifically for teaching and learning.
- Lead by example: Apply open licenses to VIVA web pages and created resources
- Showcase member-created openly licensed learning resources; provide a

platform for faculty to share examples of VIVA resources used in open course materials. This would make it possible to find, adopt, and modify materials rather than each institution creating their own resources.

- Explore ways to help VIVA member institutions working on OER/Affordability initiatives collaborate together better

In spring 2015, VIVA established a listserv to support librarians working with OER/open efforts.

Building a Cross-Institutional Librarian Community

A number of Virginia libraries are corporately and individually engaged in exploring, leading, and supporting open initiatives at and beyond their institutions. These include cross-institutional sharing and networks and OER course-sharing within the VCCS. Institutional, consortia, and public listservs as well as virtual and public in-person events provide valuable cross-institution professional development and networking opportunities. Some of these events include the Virginia Library Association Annual Conference, VCCS's New Horizons Annual Conference, and the new VCCS OER Peer Group. Open networks such as the Virginia Scholarly Communications Forum, and widely advertised institutionally hosted events with live-streaming and event recording are also increasingly offered to internal and public audiences.

The Tidewater Community College (TCC) Z-degree is a high-profile success story from the Virginia two-year system. The college's OER Policy document specifies that librarians will provide support for faculty adopting and developing "Z" courses, and will teach a 6-week online OER training course called Pathways, which is openly licensed and freely available. In 2015, VCCS began the Zx23 Project to scale the Z-degree model beyond Tidewater to all 23 Virginia Community Colleges. A number of community colleges kicked off Zx23 Project teams in September 2015, and each team has a librarian. In response to this, the system library services group began hosting "Zx23 Project Librarian Meetups" in August 2015. The meetups are a recurring web conference call that supports individual librarians participating in the community college Zx23 Project teams. These librarians have welcomed the opportunity for informal cross-college communication to share local project updates, best practices, and ideas on the most effective ways to engage their projects from the library side.

Librarian collaborations extend beyond institutions. Around forty librarians, instructional designers, and administrators from various institution-types attended the Virginia Library Association's (VLA) preconference workshop: "Introduction to OER for Librarians" in October 2015. The workshop was the largest VLA preconference to date. Led by academic librarians, it introduced open licensing, open educational resources, various library OER explorations and initiatives, and a myriad of other topics via direct instruction, storytelling, hands-on activities, and small and large group discussions. The new VIVA OER listserv was promoted along with supplemental resources selected by the presenters. Workshop participant feedback was positive. Broadly summarized, attendees would like to see follow-up on how to start small with OER and get buy-in, where to find/generate funding, how to build faculty relationships, and strategies to move open initiatives forward at the institution level. The VLA conference also featured three other presentations and one poster on OER topics.

Virginia libraries are leading and collaborating to present high profile public events. Several from November 2015 include: Cable Green from Creative Commons who led a discussion on statewide open leadership for librarians and academic technologists at the College of William & Mary; Virginia Tech events featured Andy Mink of the Institute for the Study of Knowledge Management in Education (and OER Commons) who presented on teacher-collaboration and OER as new approaches in education; and Eddie Watson from the University of Georgia presented UGA's OER initiative, which has saved 21,000 students $2 million in textbook costs in 2013–2016. An increasing number of Virginia libraries are highlighting open education and OER during

Open Access Week and Open Education Week, notably Virginia Tech, Virginia Commonwealth University, George Mason University, and others.

Money and Management

Some of the early OER efforts in Virginia developed within the Virginia Community College System. From 2012 to 2015, grants from the VCCS Chancellor's Innovation Fund were awarded to at least seven of the two-year schools. In addition, a separate Chancellor's OER Adoption fund awarded grants of $3,000 toward the development of 15 high-enrollment VCCS OER courses in 2013, and was continued in 2014. The VCCS's Zx23 Project was made possible by a generous grant from The William & Flora Hewlett Foundation; the Zx23 pilot will allow the VCCS to kick-start the process of building out the Z Degree model already in place at Tidewater by providing funding, support, and training to VCCS colleges to begin building pathways to their own Z Degrees.

Coordination among four-year institutions is nascent but growing. At the nineteen four-year institutions responding to the VIVA survey, thirteen indicated knowledge of their institution exploring or using open educational resources. Of these, ten reported that their libraries are somewhat to very involved in their institutions' open initiatives. Most of these libraries reported being in the "exploration" stage, mentioning that they are building collaborative partnerships, offering workshops, actively sharing openly licensed curricular resources, organizing faculty and administration meetings, and creating resource guides and awareness-raising materials. One library works with the Open Textbook Network to host workshops and incentivize reviews of open textbooks. Several libraries reported collaborations with faculty and teaching/learning centers on their campus. Two libraries reported receipt of grant funding for OER adoption grants. Notably, at the College of William and Mary, a collaborative effort between Swem Library and the Department of Academic Technology received funding from the Provost's Creative Adaptation Fund to offer 18 grants of $1,000. These grants, plus training and professional support, will support faculty interested in teaching with OER or those who wish to reduce textbook costs for students (Miller, 2015). The model of an incentive plus workshop and technical assistance model OER initiative has many similarities to the Open Education Initiative funded by the University Libraries and Provost office of the University of Massachusetts Amherst in 2011, and the Alternate Textbook Project at Temple University, which was created by the Temple University Teaching, Learning & Technology Roundtable, also in 2011. Many of these projects use a combination of openlynlicensed and library-subscribed materials available at no additional cost to students.

Platforms and Partners

Because of the decentralized nature of higher education in Virginia (beyond the VCCS), most institutions without a university press utilize a variety of third-party non-profit, university, commercial, or custom-created platforms to find, edit, host, and disseminate openly licensed resources. Faculty from several Virginia institutions share materials with OER Commons, MERLOT II, or on university-hosted platforms. Statewide information regarding use of institutional repositories and systems which allow faculty to share openly licensed materials with the public will (hopefully) be identified by the OVAC survey results in 2016.

The Virginia Community College System (VCCS) partnered with Lumen Learning, first on the Z Degree at Tidewater Community College and currently on the high-profile Zx23 pilot program. As consultants, Lumen aims to guide instructors to adopt existing, quality-assured OER as a starting place. Lumen offers online "office hours" to support the Zx23 pilot teams across the state, as well as assistance with open course creation, maintenance, and hosting on their Candela platform, Lumen's WordPress LMS environment. As part of the Zx23 Project, Candela-hosted OER courses appear in the VCCS LMS environment in a special "OER Courses" menu, enabling VCCS faculty to easily review, copy, and use OER course content in their own course.

What Seems to Be Working So Far?

A commitment to streaming and recording events encourages OER awareness and supports involvement statewide, regardless of institution size or staffing. Furthermore, while the energy and interest of individuals has largely fueled OER efforts in Virginia, "top down" support is also needed from library administrators, deans, provosts, and presidents in order to provide the time, compensation, opportunities, and political support necessary for developing OER policies and programs. We have also found at every level that partnerships among various groups have been key. Open educational resources have many stakeholders, which means that there are many avenues for library outreach and collaboration.

To encourage faculty participation, several Virginia libraries have received grants or institutional funds in order to offer incentive programs. Libraries can also employ strategies such as partnering with faculty who are already advocates for OER, and offering support and training, such as the Pathways course, workshops for professional development credit, or customized one-on-one consultations. We also recommend reaching out to faculty who actually have the power to select their own course materials, or who teach high enrollment courses that can be supported by existing, high quality open textbooks.

To support OER, we also need to train and generate buy-in from librarians. The events and networks discussed in this paper are key factors in building interest and knowledge concerning OER. Librarians new to OER can participate in the same training and professional opportunities offered to faculty, which is also an excellent way to develop relationships with instructors in various departments, and to learn about faculty interests and concerns.

Emerging Challenges

Exploring new ground does not come without its share of growing pains. The first challenge is to develop a shared goal as well as a shared understanding of the term "open." If our goal is only to lower course material costs for students, instructors can select any free resource to use, including library subscriptions. However, if we define open as free to retain, reuse, revise, remix, and redistribute (Wiley, 2014), then open refers only to those materials in the public domain or those licensed for such use. As in nearly every institutional or statewide endeavor, communication can be difficult at times. While admirable efforts are being made, there is always room for improvement, particularly in the early stages of developing a network of support for OER.

In order to support the philosophy of open education, academic libraries and the institutions in which they reside must fully embrace the concept of sharing. One roadblock to sharing is making the philosophical shift to open licensing. While many libraries "practice what they preach" by applying Creative Commons licenses, others have not yet acquired this habit. Technology, while tremendously beneficial to learning, can also present a problem in terms of lack of compatibility among platforms, or the need to host course materials within password-protected learning management systems which limit sharing. In addition, institutions must consider accessibility issues when creating and sharing new open educational resources, as well as access to a sufficient internet speed. Finally, we lack an efficient system for hosting and locating open educational resources. On one hand, this is where librarians can apply their searching expertise. On the other hand, the multiple OER repositories and variety of licenses may intimidate potential adopters.

Faculty encounter other hindrances to OER adoption, including lack of available high-quality material in their discipline and a lack of time or incentives for creating new material. Even when adopting existing resources, courses must be substantially redesigned when shifting away from a textbook, or when replacing a traditional textbook with an open one. Faculty may also need additional technology training in order to successfully incorporate, remix, or revise open educational resources.

Conclusion: The Road Ahead

Although adopting a new approach to course "texts" comes with a learning curve, the authors have encountered a number of pleasant surprises along the way. For one thing, there are many groups and individuals interested in OER for a number of different reasons, including affordability, student success, faculty innovation, pedagogy, and more. This has created opportunities for better partnerships not only among libraries, but also within institutions, and with state-level organizations, policy advisors, and legislators. OER and the open education movement have also allowed librarians to participate in a high-interest, high-visibility area, and to demonstrate our ability to support student learning in what might appear to be a non-traditional area. In Virginia, libraries have leveraged existing networks and developed new channels in order to share our knowledge and experiences in this emerging realm, and have found that stakeholders statewide have welcomed our support and expertise. While we don't know yet where this path will take us, we are enjoying the ride!

References

American Library Association (ALA). (2004, June 29). Core values of librarianship. Retrieved from http://www.ala.org/advocacy/intfreedom/statementspols/corevalues

Feldstein, A., Martin, M., Hudson, A., Warren, K., Hilton, J., & Wiley, D. (2012). Open textbooks and increased student access and outcomes. *European Journal of Open, Distance and E-Learning, 2*. Retrieved from http://files.eric.ed.gov/fulltext/EJ992490.pdf

Johnson, L., Adams Becker, S., Estrada, V., & Freeman, A. (2015). *NMC horizon report: 2015 Higher education edition*. Austin, TX: The New Media Consortium. Retrieved from http://www.nmc.org/publication/nmc-horizon-report-2015-higher-education-edition/

Miller, J. (2015, April 23). Two opportunities for exploring open educational resources at W&M. *Academic technology at the College of William & Mary*. Retrieved from http://at.blogs.wm.edu/two-opportunities-for-exploring-open-educational-resources-at-wm/

Northern Virginia Community College. (2014). NOVA's tenth annual power up your pedagogy conference. Retrieved from http://www.nvcc.edu/cetl/_files/pup.pdf

OpenVA. (n.d.). Retrieved from http://openva.org/

Virtual Library of Virginia (VIVA). (2015). *Findings and recommendation report from the OER/licensed resources task force*. Retrieved from http://vivalib.org/committees/rsc/oer.html

Wiley, D. (2014). The Access Compromise and the 5th R. *iterating toward openness.* Retrieved from http://opencontent.org/blog/archives/3221

William and Flora Hewlett Foundation. (n.d.). *Open educational resources*. Retrieved from http://www.hewlett.org/programs/education/open-educational-resources

Z-degree. (n.d.). *Tidewater Community College*. Retrieved from https://web.tcc.edu/academics/zdegree/index.html

Zx23 application. (n.d.). *EdTech @ VCCS*. Retrieved from http://edtech.vccs.edu/zx23/

Not So Strange Bedfellows: Information Standards for Librarians AND Publishers

Marti Heyman, Open Education, Copyright & Scholarly Communication, Virginia Tech University

Betty Landesman, Open Education, Copyright & Scholarly Communication, Virginia Tech University

Abstract

As our collections become increasingly electronic, standards play an increasingly important role not only for libraries but also for publishers. This session will describe standards and recommended practices that are designed to support the publishing, identification, and retrieval of electronic materials, including KBART (Knowledge Bases and Related Tools), the DOI (Digital Object Identifier), and EPUB. What are they, what do they do, how do they relate to the work of a broad spectrum of attendees, and, particularly, why we should care? The presenters are co-chairs of the NISO (National Information Standards Organization) Content and Collection Management Topic Committee.

As our collections become increasingly electronic, standards play an increasingly important role not only for libraries but also for publishers. This session will describe standards and recommended practices that are designed to support the publishing, identification, and retrieval of electronic materials, including KBART (Knowledge Bases and Related Tools), the DOI (Digital Object Identifier), and EPUB (not an acronym). What are they, what do they do, how do they relate to the work of a broad spectrum of attendees, and, particularly, why we should care? The presenters are co-chairs of the NISO (National Information Standards Organization) Content and Collection Management Topic Committee.

Standards are a collaborative effort by and for members of the information community to facilitate the work of all constituencies by doing things in a specified way to solve a shared problem. Standards and recommended practices may be developed by official standards bodies such as the National Information Standards Organization (NISO) and the International Organization for Standardization (ISO) or emerge from industry groups such as the International Digital Publishing Forum (IDPF) or from member organizations such as the United Kingdom Serials Group (UKSG).

NISO is a membership organization representing all participants in the information community (creators, publishers, aggregators, vendors, libraries, and individual consumers). It identifies, develops, maintains, and publishes technical standards and recommended practices to support information retrieval, repurposing, storage, metadata, and preservation. More information about NISO can be found at http://www.niso.org/.

ISO is an independent, non-governmental organization made up of members from the national standards bodies of 162 countries. It has published nearly 20,000 international standards in the areas of technology and business. More information about ISO can be found at http://www.iso.org.

The IDPF is a global trade and standards organization that promotes the development of electronic publishing applications and products to benefit content creators and consumers as well as makers of reading systems. It develops and maintains the EPUB content publication standard. More information about the IDPF is available at http://idpf.org.

The UKSG is a membership-based organization with members from all parts of the scholarly information community (librarians, publishers, technology vendors, and intermediaries). It works to facilitate an efficient information chain and better understanding among all members of the scholarly and professional information communities. More information about the UKSG is available at http://www.uksg.org.

http://dx.doi.org/10.5703/1288284316314

KBART

KBART is an acronym for Knowledge Bases and Related Tools. It is a National Information Standards Organization (NISO) Recommended Practice, RP-9-2014. A joint project of NISO and the United Kingdom Serials Group (UKSG), it recommends best practices for providing accurate and timely metadata to link resolver knowledge bases by content providers.

KBART was first released in 2010 (Phase I). It provided guidance on the role and importance of accurate and timely metadata supply to link resolvers to support the consistent and correct resolution of OpenURLs. It was revised in 2014 (Phase II) to go beyond basic metadata guidance, focusing on more granular, complex issues causing problems in metadata supply to knowledge bases. It also provides educational and outreach opportunities for all stakeholders and a centralized information portal.

What is the publisher's view of KBART?

- KBART Phase I and Phase II provide guidance on:
  - Routes to providing higher quality data to Discovery Service partners and customers
  - Higher quality data drives effectiveness of discovering and accessing content
- The KBART RP guidelines provide foundation for interoperability of key metadata elements between publishers, content aggregators, and discovery service partners
- Publishers benefit from accurate linking to their content and subsequently the possibility of increased usage of their content
  - Increased revenue and decreased operational costs

What is the library's view of KBART?

- Libraries rely on accurate and consistent information from publishers, aggregators, and link resolver knowledge bases to manage holdings and coverage information for licensed resources
- Inaccurate knowledge base information leads to poor service and user frustration
  - Most users will just go somewhere else (Google, etc.) if our discovery systems say we have an article but access is denied
  - Even if users report a problem, libraries do not have the staff to investigate large numbers of them and to manually update records

More information can be found at the KBART web site at http://www.niso.org/workrooms/kbart.

DOI

DOI is an acronym for Digital Object Identifier, defined as the digital identifier of an object. It is an International Organization for Standardization (ISO) standard, ISO 26324. It allows the registration and use of persistent interoperable identifiers, called DOIs, for use on digital networks. DOI names permanently identify content. If the URLs or services change over time, e.g., the resource moves, this same DOI will continue to resolve to the correct resources or services at their new locations. Publishers collaborate with CrossRef, which maintains a database that keeps track of a current web address associated with each DOI. DOIs are assigned through a federation of worldwide Registration Agencies (RA).

What is the publisher's view of DOI?

- DOIs are coupled with metadata, so they can be modified over time to keep track of the locations and characteristics of the objects they identify, both for publishers and libraries
- Decreased operational costs:
  - Benefit from efficient management and accurate tracking

    - Increased ability to more easily automate processes
- Increased interoperability and collaboration across participants in information community

What is the library's view of DOI?

- Use of the DOI facilitates discovery of the content even If the publisher or platform has changed over time
- Users can find articles quickly and easily without confronting old or broken links

More information can be found at the ISO website at https://www.iso.org/obp/ui/#iso:std:43506:en.

EPUB

EPUB is an International Digital Publishing Forum standard. The current version is EPUB 3.0.1. Previous iterations include:

- Open E-Book Publication Structure (OEB) from 1999
- EPUB 2 (2007 and 2010)

EPUB is a distribution and interchange format standard for digital publications and documents based on web standards. It defines a means of representing, packaging, and encoding structured and semantically enhanced web content for distribution in a single-file format. It allows publishers to produce and send a single digital publication file through distribution and offers consumers interoperability between software/ hardware for unencrypted "reflowable" digital books and other publications to suit the different display dimensions of mobile devices.

What is the publisher's view of EPUB?

- Decreased operational costs:
    - Produce and send *a single digital publication file* through distribution
    - Interoperability between software/hardware
    - Reflowable digital books and other publications for all devices

What is the library's view of EPUB?

- Allows library users to read a book on disparate devices
- Easier viewing on mobile devices
- Display optimized for each device type

More information can be found at the International Digital Publishing Forum website at http://idpf.org/epub.

Summary

Our intention during this poster session was twofold. First, we wanted to highlight three of the standards and recommended practices which have been jointly developed by libraries, publishers, vendors, and other interested parties within the information community. Secondly, we wanted to emphasize that standards and recommended practices benefit all members of the information community, not just publishers and not just libraries. In all cases, the ultimate goal is to provide better, more efficient, and more reliable access to information resources.

"Help, We Started a Journal!": Adventures in Supporting Open Access Publishing Using Open Journal Systems

Anna R. Craft, Metadata Cataloger, University of North Carolina at Greensboro

Abstract

The University Libraries at The University of North Carolina at Greensboro (UNCG) have an active and growing implementation of Open Journal Systems (OJS), a free, open source scholarly publishing platform. But even a free software system is not without its costs, both to the hosting institution and to the creators and staff of individual journals. Institutions that wish to host OJS must be able to install, maintain, and support the product. And while faculty members and other academics are often experts in their content areas, not all of them are prepared to handle other needs associated with creating and publishing an online journal—including decisions that might involve article layout, copyright policies, graphic design, web design, and other technical issues. This article provides an overview of UNCG's support for OJS, as well as challenges, lessons learned, and future directions related to this service.

Introduction

The open access movement continues to grow, change, and offer exciting opportunities for researchers and content creators to share their work. One such opportunity is Open Journal Systems (OJS), a journal management and publishing system that is freely available via the Public Knowledge Project. In 2010, the University Libraries at The University of North Carolina at Greensboro (UNCG) adopted OJS as a platform to support scholarly publishing on campus. The Libraries offer journal hosting to members of the UNCG community—primarily faculty—in an effort to further open access content creation and sharing at UNCG and beyond. This article provides an overview of the OJS service and its support structure within the Libraries, particularly in relation to staffing, as well as questions and issues that have arisen through the development of this service. Challenges, lessons learned, and future directions are also addressed.

Selection and Implementation of OJS at UNCG

The University Libraries at The University of North Carolina at Greensboro (UNCG) have a strong history of supporting and promoting open access initiatives. The Libraries created and continue to develop, host, and maintain an active open access institutional repository (NC DOCKS[1]); they also offer an open access publishing fund to campus faculty, and are active in supporting Open Educational Resources, among other initiatives. In 2010, after requests from campus faculty members for support in the area of open access scholarly publishing, the Libraries adopted OJS as a journal publishing platform. OJS, developed by the Public Knowledge Project (PKP), is a free, open source system designed to aid faculty and researchers in creating and publishing open access journals.[2] The software is available for free download on the PKP website.[3] PKP also offers hosting options for institutions that do not have their own servers, or that are not able or do not wish to maintain local systems.

Five years after adopting OJS, the Libraries' server hosts ten active open access journals, with others in development, and one journal that uses the OJS system only to track and review submissions—not as a public interface. Content areas range across the academic spectrum, including journals focused on archives, mathematics, and service learning.[4] These journals all exist within the same

[1] NC DOCKS, digital online collection of knowledge and scholarship: http://libres.uncg.edu/ir/uncg/
[2] Publish Knowledge Project's (PKP) OJS: https://pkp.sfu.ca/ojs/
[3] To download OJS, visit: https://pkp.sfu.ca/ojs/ojs_download/
[4] A complete list of journals is available on the Libraries's website: http://libjournal.uncg.edu/

http://dx.doi.org/10.5703/1288284316315

OJS implementation. The use of a multi-journal site means that some design and layout options are enforced at the top level, affecting all journals. There are, however, some customizations that can be made at the individual journal level. This issue will be discussed further in the "Roles for journal personnel" section.

Supporting OJS

Roles for Library Personnel

Within the Libraries, three main support roles have developed to facilitate and deliver OJS services on campus. These positions work individually and collaboratively to provide OJS services and to set local policies in the Libraries. They focus efforts in three areas: user support and training, system development and maintenance, and outreach.

The metadata librarian in the technical services department takes the primary role of providing OJS support and training for personnel at the individual journals. Technical and teaching skills are important in this role, which works primarily with managing editors and other journal staff. When new journals are proposed, the Metadata Librarian meets with interested constituencies to discuss journal support services and to demonstrate the use of OJS. At the inception of a new journal, the metadata librarian provides initial in-person training to journal staff. Additional training and other support is provided on an as-needed basis, and might take the form of e-mails, phone calls, or in-person meetings.

The time commitment for support in this area can vary wildly. Most journals are run by faculty members who juggle many commitments during the academic year and who may focus on OJS during the summer or on other breaks from the course calendar. As such, requests for support sometimes spike during summer months. The metadata librarian averages about five hours per week on support and training requests, though there is no way to predict the type and number of support requests in a given time period. But as the number of journals hosted by the University Libraries grows, the number of support requests grows with it.

The second support position, the digital technology consultant, is based in the Libraries's electronic resources and information technology department and serves as the main administrator for the Libraries' OJS implementation. This position spends approximately four hours a week on tasks related to OJS, which might include troubleshooting issues with the software, making changes to top-level site options and stylesheets, and setting up new journals. Strong technology and web development skills are critical in this role.

The third member of the team, the assistant dean for collection management and scholarly communications, is based in the Libraries' administration and provides outreach, publicity, and faculty relations services, particularly to faculty members who may be interested in creating journals. The assistant dean for collection management and scholarly communications also provides general outreach about open access on campus, and as such is well-placed to educate faculty members about the Libraries' offerings, including OJS. On average, this position spends about thirty minutes a week on tasks related to OJS. This role benefits from a strong background in scholarly communications topics and issues, as well as a desire to work with and educate a variety of campus constituencies.

Roles for Journal Personnel

Journal creators come prepared to focus on their content areas and associated tasks, such as identification of article reviewers. But editorial roles are not the only ones that journal managers must be prepared to fill. OJS provides options for use of the following roles within the system:

- Journal managers
- Editors
- Section editors
- Layout editors
- Copyeditors
- Proofreaders
- Reviewers
- Authors

- Readers
- Subscription managers

Journal personnel may have multiple roles assigned to them, such as journal manager and editor. All roles on this list are the responsibility of the individual journals—Libraries' personnel do not handle content, copy editing, layout, or other tasks on this list. While these role assignments are available to all journals, not all of these roles are required. For example, if a journal does not require subscriptions, then there is no need for a subscription manager. And if a journal does not require logins for access to articles, then there is no need for the reader role.

But the roles on the list do not fully describe the skill sets that journal managers may need or want in order to make their journals meet desired standards of consistency and professionalism. Technical and design-related skills are particular areas that potential journal creators should consider.

By selecting OJS as a journal platform, journal creators are committing to working in a powerful but complex online system that has a steep learning curve. Journal managers must be prepared to learn to use this system, or to hire personnel (such as graduate students) to use it for them. Individual journal customization options are limited in a shared OJS system, as many elements of the look-and-feel are controlled at the top; but there are still some options for personalization through graphic and web design. And if a journal wants to explore these types of customization, then they will need staff with skills in these areas, or they will need to outsource this work. If a journal has personnel with skills in the customization of stylesheets, then they will have more options in setting up the look and feel they want for their journal. Similarly, graphic design skills are useful for the creation of banners, logos, and other graphic elements.

One journal at UNCG uses the OJS system only for submission and tracking of manuscripts—not as a public access interface. For a journal with a strong online team in place, this option allows journal personnel to track and assign submissions in the specially designed OJS system, while also allowing them the freedom to personalize the look and feel of the journal to their specifications.

In addition to design and technical aspects of the online system, journals must also consider the layout for their individual articles and other content. Some journals want the traditional two-column layout for their articles, which means they need to have someone on staff who can set up and implement such a template. Further, journal managers must also be prepared to consider policy issues, which could relate to things like open access, copyright, and much more.

Support Requests

Support requests from journal personnel may be directed at any member of the Libraries's OJS support teams. Team members work collaboratively to make sure that requests reach the appropriate person or people on the team. Some support requests are technical in nature, often having to do with the inner workings of the OJS system. These questions might relate to logging in, submitting an article, determining the status of a submission, or ascertaining permissions on a particular user account. Libraries staff can provide guidance and assistance in troubleshooting these topics, and many requests of this type can be solved via e-mail, often with a screen capture included to show a user where to go or what to look for within the OJS interface.

Other technical requests might relate to the look and feel of a journal's public interface within OJS. When requests are made that will affect all journals, the Libraries must consider the time commitment required for the task, along with the potential value for and impact on all hosted journals. While the Libraries's OJS team endeavors to meet the needs of all hosted journals, not all requests can be accommodated.

Despite not providing explicit support in the areas of content, design, layout, and journal policies, the Libraries do still get questions related to many of these topics. Libraries's OJS staff can sometimes provide advice or further information based on previous experiences, perhaps by sharing an example layout template or by providing information about copyright policies at other journals; but ultimately decisions on these topics must be made by managing personnel at the individual journals. Journals have also requested assistance in obtaining International Standard Serial Numbers (ISSNs), an area where the Libraries have been able to provide guidance.

Challenges

The main challenges the Libraries have faced with their OJS services relate to the complexity of the OJS system, turnover of staff, and issues relating to the multi-journal OJS implementation.

OJS was built to support publication of open access journals, and gives journal personnel many options for tracking submissions and sharing them among relevant personnel. The system is very powerful, but it is also very complicated, and for most users it is not an immediately intuitive system. Journal staff need to be comfortable working in a complex online system that enforces processes—for example, a journal editor cannot simply upload a preapproved article and go straight to posting it. Articles must be submitted from users in the author role, and must go through multiple steps before they can be posted. The system allows editors to track and monitor submissions closely and can also send automated e-mails to relevant personnel, if desired. But if a step is missed, it is easy to get stuck or lost in the process, especially for new users and those who are not accustomed to working in online systems.

The learning curve associated with the software, especially combined with journal staff turnover, is one of the biggest challenges the Libraries have faced with this service. Turnover issues exacerbate the learning curve problem. Some journals have made a practice of employing graduate students to do much of the behind-the-scenes legwork of journal creation—working in the OJS system, copy editing, and designing layout for articles. This practice can cause headaches when students graduate—particularly if there is no succession plan in place.

Turnover can affect not only the work of journal creation, but also the continuity of journal existence. In the online environment, it is generally not necessary for journal staff members to be located in the same geographic area. But what happens when a primary journal manager who was based at UNCG leaves the institution? What is the appropriate role of the Libraries in supporting a journal that no longer carries a faculty connection to the institution? Providing support services to distant users is certainly possible, but can be very time-consuming for a support team that has many tasks to handle above and beyond their OJS roles. The Libraries's solution to this issue will be covered in "Lessons learned."

The multi-journal implementation of OJS has also created challenges for the support team. In a single-journal implementation, customizations can be made to fit the exact specifications of the journal. But in a multi-journal site, individualized customizations are not always possible—often a change to the display or design of one journal will affect all other journals. For this reason, the support team has been unable to fill some requests from journal managers.

Lessons Learned

Support for open access publishing through the creation of scholarly journals was a new endeavor for the UNCG University Libraries in 2010. The Libraries have learned several lessons through the implementation and development of the OJS service, particularly related to costs, sustainability, and proactive education models.

This project has reinforced the idea that even though the open source OJS software is free to download and use, it still has costs related to time and expertise. Libraries and other institutions that wish to provide and support OJS services must have staff with skills to handle the technical aspects of the system, both in relation to the server and the user interface. There is no one-size-fits-all support model, and it is difficult to predict the needs of individual journals in advance. A library or other institution that hosts this type of service has the latitude to determine the level of support that they will make available for end users. When planning this type of service, libraries should consider their available staff time and other resources before making commitments to journals.

Sustainability planning for journals is critical, and should particularly be stressed to journal managers. The UNCG University Libraries require that each hosted journal have a primary on-campus contact—this is generally a managing editor or other faculty member with an oversight role in the journal. If this person leaves UNCG and wants the journal to remain active on the Libraries's server, he or she must designate another faculty member at UNCG to be the on-campus contact. Following this policy, the Libraries have facilitated the transfer of one journal that began at UNCG to another institution after changes in the journal's editorial board resulted in no UNCG personnel on staff.

The Libraries's OJS team is also trying to be proactive in educating journal managers—particularly those who are new to OJS—about the tasks that will be part of their work. Discussions with new journal managers touch on the importance of technical, graphic design, and web design skill sets, while noting that the Libraries's OJS team is not able to provide support in these areas unless special arrangements are made.

Through the process of sharing the OJS service with campus, the Libraries have found it strengthens relationships between the Libraries, faculty, and scholarly communities. This service has met the needs of campus faculty who requested support in this area, while facilitating the creation and sharing of new scholarly content on campus and beyond. It also demonstrates and reinforces the Libraries's commitment to open access and new publishing models.

Future Directions

To date, OJS services at the UNCG University Libraries have grown informally, driven by requests from campus faculty. As the number of hosted journals grows, demands for library support grow as well. In a continuing climate of limited resources, project scalability is critical, and the Libraries must consider this when new journals are proposed. To aid in this process, the Libraries would like to create in-house policies to ensure sustainability, as well as local best practices to share with journal managers. The Libraries would also like to continue to raise awareness of the OJS service, for potential new journals as well as for potential readers and scholars who could use the materials. Explorations of impact and readership of the hosted journals are also areas of interest.

Improving the Availability of ISSN—A Joint Project

Gaëlle Béquet, Director, International ISSN Centre/CIEPS

Laurie Kaplan, Content Business Analyst Lead, ProQuest

Abstract

This session described the 2015 pilot project and ongoing cooperation between the International ISSN Centre based in Paris and ProQuest to identify active titles without ISSN. The project is using Ulrich's periodicals database as the initial resource. Under the supervision of the International Centre, national ISSN centers determine whether the ISSN is simply missing or has never been assigned. The outcome of the project will be a benefit to librarians, publishers, and vendors as more titles will have ISSN registered with the national and international ISSN centers and in Ulrich's Periodical Database. This will improve the electronic loading and matching of titles. Gaëlle Béquet, director of the International ISSN Centre, and Laurie Kaplan of ProQuest discussed how the project came to be, the pilot work and refinements to the process, and the ongoing work and schedule for going forward. The audience was encouraged to ask questions and help determine the best way to encourage all interested parties to use the ISSN as an identifier whenever possible.

Librarians, publishers, content vendors, subscription agents, discovery systems, and others need to exchange data on a daily basis. And anything that can make this process more successful by improving the ability to match updates to existing records is of great interest to these parties. Gaëlle Béquet of the International ISSN Centre/CIEPS and Laurie Kaplan of ProQuest developed a joint project between the two organizations to address this very issue.

This project arose out of research that G. Béquet was conducting using Ulrichsweb™, an international database of periodicals produced by ProQuest. She noticed several active titles that did not have ISSN, and contacted L. Kaplan to discuss the possible reasons. After several meetings between the parties, dating back to November 2014 at the Charleston Conference, an agreement was signed to conduct a pilot project, which started in February 2015. The purpose of the project is to improve the assignment rate of ISSN for serial publications worldwide. The impetus for both organizations centered around their reliance on and acknowledgement of the importance of complete and trustworthy bibliographic metadata. The ability to share data to create more complete records was of interest to both parties.

The project has just moved out of the pilot phase, and will involve active serial titles and book series without ISSN in order to have those ISSN assigned by the appropriate ISSN center. Under the supervision of the International Centre, national ISSN centers will determine whether the ISSN is simply missing or has never been assigned.

The starting point is the data behind Ulrich's Periodicals Directory™, an international resource that has been published by ProQuest and its predecessors since 1932. The data in Ulrich's is mostly received directly from the publishers with an emphasis on scholarly publications, which is data the ISSN network is also interested in but may miss during the ISSN registration. The ISSN Centre and ProQuest have had a good working relationship for many years. The US ISSN Center, in fact, has had a ProQuest employee working at the Library of Congress since 2000, improving the ISSN coverage and cataloging of ProQuest resources and contributing to the ISSN assignments for the US Center. Additionally, the ALA ALCTS Outstanding Collaboration Citation was awarded in February 2015 to ProQuest and the US ISSN Center; this project would reinforce the partnership.

In order to determine how to structure the pilot project the ProQuest team conducted research and ran reports from Ulrich's database for active titles, print or online, without ISSN by content type (e.g., academic/scholarly), by serial type (e.g., journal or newsletter), and by country. The pilot project focused on active print and online

http://dx.doi.org/10.5703/1288284316316

titles without ISSN from the Netherlands, initially only academic/scholarly titles, then extended to trade publications and other content types. Working with one local ISSN Center—the Netherlands ISSN Center—facilitated communications by having a consistent team from which to receive feedback. The Netherlands ISSN Center had the ability and the interest to engage in the pilot project, and the ProQuest product managers agreed that improving these records would be a good place to start.

The International ISSN Center and ProQuest agreed to share 16 metadata elements including title and subtitle, language, country, date of publication, related serials, title history, and publisher information. The fields in Ulrich's were mapped to MARC fields to help the ISSN Centers research the titles. The first set of data included 220 titles, many of which were monographic series. The International ISSN Centre team first compared the titles to the ISSN Register. Thirty-eight were found in the register, and this information was returned to the ProQuest team. The remaining 182 titles were sent to ISSN Netherlands for further investigation. During the ensuing months the International ISSN Centre and ProQuest teams met to discuss the progress and clarify any data and terminology issues raised by ISSN Netherlands. An additional 80 records, mostly trade journals, were sent to the Netherlands.

The impact of the pilot project to date is as follows:

- Added over 100 ISSN to Ulrich's and the ISSN Register
- Raised good conversations about monographic series
- Started the conversation regarding how to get publishers to use these new ISSN, and their ISSN in general when posting titles online and when transferring titles among various parties

Based on the success of the pilot the International ISSN Centre and ProQuest agreed to extend the pilot and send over 700 additional titles to the Netherlands, and also to formalize the agreement and extend the work to additional countries, in Europe first and then other parts of the world. At the annual ISSN Directors' meeting that took place October 13–16, 2015 a presentation was made about the partnership with ProQuest to 50 ISSN directors. The directors were informed about the plan to expand geographic coverage of the project. The level of overlapping records with the ISSN Register was low during the pilot. It seemed clear that if the ISSN was missing in the Ulrich's title record it most likely had not been assigned by an ISSN Center, especially since the Ulrich's editors always check the ISSN Portal for ISSN questions. The project should improve the assignment of ISSN to the identified periodicals.

One lesson learned from the pilot project was that it takes a considerable amount of time to research a title using the ISSN Register, the publisher's website, and the open web. It should be noted that legal deposit in the Netherlands was established in 1974. Thus serials published prior to this date may not be part of the national collections. To perform ISSN assignment the team at ISSN Netherlands relies on external large title databases such as GGC_OCLC, the online shared cataloging system within the Netherlands, WorldCat (OCLC), Zeitschriftendatenbank (Germany), SUDOC (France), and the catalogues of the Library of Congress and the British Library. Moreover, the National Library of the Netherlands no longer collects print journals by Elsevier, Kluwer Academic, Brill Academic Publishers, and IOS Press. The Library cannot process and store both print and digital formats of the same journal, and it strives to collect only the digital format. For e-journals, the KB collection is based on separate digital articles. From 2016 onward this policy will be applied to more Dutch publishers. Regarding monographic series, ISSN Netherlands assign ISSN when publishers request it, except for specific publishers like Brill whose book series are automatically assigned ISSN.

In most cases so far we can rely on identical content for both print and digital versions, and this shouldn't be a problem for ISSN assignment since it can be confirmed by the publisher. But sometimes it was already doubtful if the print version was ever published for an existing e-journal (in several cases of Elsevier it appeared no print version was ever published although an ISSN had been requested).

Scarcity of resources at the various ISSN centers may create difficulties regarding projected timeframes. And daily work at the ISSN center suffers when the team is involved in the project work. Starting in January 2016 ProQuest will consider hiring an intern if the local ISSN center requests assistance, to see if this will help reduce the backlog of daily work, enabling the more experienced staff to work on the project.

The outcome of the project will be a benefit to librarians, publishers, and vendors as more titles will have ISSN registered with the national and international ISSN centers and in Ulrich's Periodical Database and Ulrichsweb™. This will improve the electronic loading and matching of titles for any product or system. The value of the project will extend beyond the ISSN network and ProQuest, since publishers, libraries, catalog databases, documentation centers, subscription agencies, academic institutions, retailers, and wholesalers all rely on ISSN as an identification point for serial publications, a way to facilitate distinguishing between serials with identical names, or a record control number. Libraries and others worldwide will benefit from this cooperation as it will result in more complete data being available for active periodicals published around the world.

Both parties acknowledge that assigning ISSN is only the first step in furthering the value of ISSN in the publishing world. Newly assigned ISSN must be incorporated into publisher files and included on publisher websites for the ISSN to become part of the process of transferring and updating titles for librarians. ProQuest and ISSN IC will work together to encourage the use of the newly assigned ISSN by the appropriate publishers and providers of serials content. The NISO PIE-J Recommended Practice also encourages the use of ISSN, and the upcoming revision of ISO-8 will further reinforce the importance of the ISSN for print and online serial publications. Ensuring that more periodicals include ISSN, and that those ISSN are registered with the local center and the International ISSN Centre, can only improve the exchange of data and the citation of data for all parties.

One attendee at the 2015 Charleston Conference presentation suggested two white papers that could be written by the presenters about ISSN for monographic series and the need for publishers and those involved in data exchange to use ISSN. Another attendee remarked that when records have proper ISSN, linking is improved for online journals.

Publishing Our Own Work: Contributing to the Professional Literature Through Systematizing Sharing of Library Reports

Lisa Janicke Hinchliffe, Professor/Coordinator for Information Literacy Services and Instruction, University of Illinois Library at Urbana-Champaign

Sarah E. Crissinger, Information Literacy Librarian, Davidson College

Emily A. Hardesty, Graduate Assistant, University of Illinois Library at Urbana-Champaign

Aaron S. McCollough, Scholarly Communications & Publishing Librarian, University of Illinois Library at Urbana-Champaign

Abstract

Library employees often work on teams, committees, or task forces to do research, and investigation as part of their responsibilities in carrying out the operations of a library; however, much of this work is not published in the professional literature and is only inconsistently recorded in committee documents. As such, this work is hidden both from others in the library who might use it and from the profession at large, meaning that other libraries were not able to benefit from it. To address these challenges, the University of Illinois Library (Urbana-Champaign) established the Library Occasional Reports Series (LibORS) in 2015. This paper presents a case study of the ongoing process of establishing LibORS. Phases of work included exploring what it would mean to commit to publishing and promoting the University Library's work as an organizational practice as well as creating workflows, acquisition criteria, editorial guidelines, a report template, and communication mechanisms.

Why a Library Publication of Library Work?

Faculty and staff of the University of Illinois Library at Urbana–Champaign conduct a wide-ranging program of research and development as part of their responsibilities in carrying out the management and operations of the Library. While some of this work is published in the professional and scholarly literature, much of it is not and is only inconsistently recorded in committee and task force minutes. This work is thus hidden both from others in the Library who might find it useful and also from the profession at large, meaning that other libraries do not benefit as they might from our work, and the University Library does not have as prominent a profile in this area as it should.

Though individual library faculty do publish some of the research that is conducted, it is typically cast as general findings, recommendations, etc., as is appropriate to the scholarly literature. Scholarly articles typically do not present the findings within an organizational context and do not document the specific programs or practices the libraries adopt or the decisions made about how to actually manage a library over time. So, for example, though Mischo, Schlembach, Bishoff, and German (2012) have published a study of transaction log analysis, the Library's reports assessing discovery systems for implementation relative to the Library's operational needs (e.g., WebFeat and Primo) have not been. Likewise, Bowles-Terry, Hensley, and Hinchliffe (2010) coauthored a study on student perceptions of video tutorials; however, there is no easily available Library report of how the User Education Committee examined the Library's instruction strategy as a result. Finding these internal reports as the years pass can also be a challenge since they are not consistently archived or posted online to committee websites.

In addition, librarians are often looking for these sorts of pragmatic evaluations and program development documents from other institutions.

http://dx.doi.org/10.5703/1288284316317

For example, the University Library's Discovery and Delivery Study Team has drawn on reports from the University of Minnesota, North Carolina State University, University of Michigan, Harvard University, and the University of California at Los Angeles in various projects. These research-in-action reports are very helpful in managing a library and understanding decision-making influences and processes.

Finally, the concept of a series of reports—published by the library generated from library operations—fits within the continuum of publications types that the University Library is committed to supporting under the auspices of its recently formalized scholarly communications and publishing unit, which is in the Library's Office of Research. Though monographs and journals are more high-profile publications, supporting publication and dissemination of grey literature is also an important role for library publication programs, evidenced by the profiles in the *Library Publishing Directory* (2016).

Funding and Resources for the Publication

Recognizing that the University of Illinois Library at Urbana-Champaign already had many reports and other documents that would be beneficial to the library community at large but lacked a mechanism for systematically publishing and promoting them, Hinchliffe applied for and received an Innovation Fund grant from the University Library.

The Innovation Fund supports opportunities "to be innovative and make original contributions to the ways in which the Library works" by piloting or advancing new ideas, services, or technologies; investigating new or alternative ideas, technologies, or processes for conducting or organizing Library activities; encouraging users in using and enhancing library-managed content; or initiating or advancing strategic partnerships with other campus units, other libraries, or library consortia or other organizations.

The Library Occasional Report Series (LibORS) proposal was developed around three objectives:

1. To document the research and development work carried out by the University Library
2. To make such reports discoverable by others in the University Library and the profession at large
3. To raise the profile of the University Library as a key contributor to research and development in academic and research libraries.

The Innovation Fund grant funded a graduate assistant for 100 hours. The position was initially filled by Crissinger, who graduated after a few months, and then Hardesty. The graduate assistants are responsible for assisting with reviewing how other libraries publish their reports (starting with the list of libraries that have reported to the Library Publishing Coalition that they publish technical reports series); gathering input from library faculty and staff about how they would suggest LibORS be scoped; developing templates, guidelines, production, and communications processes; and creating reports from existing committee and task force documents.

Hinchliffe serves as the principal investigator of the Innovation Fund grant and manager of the LibORS project. She will also be the inaugural editor of the series, drawing on her previous work as editor of *Research Strategies*, an information literacy scholarly journal, and overseeing newsletters for the ACRL Instruction Section and IFLA Information Literacy Section.

The internal library LibORS Advisory Committee is comprised of Hinchliffe, Crissinger/Hardesty, McCollough and the associate university librarian for research, the chair of the Library Research and Publication Committee appointed by the University Library Executive Committee, and the visiting librarian for library and information science and research support services.

Identifying Technologies and Developing Processes

Operationalizing the LibORS objectives required developing workflows, acquisition criteria,

Subject Content

The Library Occasional Report Series accepts committee and technical reports compiled by the University of Illinois Library faculty, staff, and graduate assistants. These reports can cover a variety of topics, including (but not limited to) instruction, discovery, scholarly communication, user experience, reference, digital humanities, and other important initiatives in the University Library. Reports should be scoped to a specific committee's or initiative's findings.

Criteria

- Report generated from work done within the University of Illinois at Urbana Champaign's Library
- Applicable to the larger library community's conversations and initiatives in specific area(s)
- Requires little to no editing for formatting or grammar
- Follows the Illinois Writing Style Guide at: identitystandards.illinois.edu/writingstyleguide/. The Chicago Manual of Style, 15th edition should be consulted for further questions: chicagomanualofstyle.org/home.html.
- Includes appropriate metadata about the submission and its creators, including date created, authors, committee (and committee charge, if available), original URL/where it was originally published
- Cites any outside information used

How Will My Report Get Published?

1. Reports of any length can be submitted, though reports will usually be 10–20 pages long.
2. Authors are responsible for the accuracy of the report and the statements it includes.
3. The ORS editor will format the report to the ORS template. While the editor will check for basic grammar errors, the report will not go through a rigorous editorial process.
4. All hyperlinks will be checked. All hyperlinks should include an ALT tag for accessibility reasons.
5. There is no uniform citation requirement for reports. However, each report should use a consistent citation style throughout. For example, if the committee uses MLA citation style for the first reference, subsequent references must also follow MLA.
6. The ORS editor will contact all members of the committee that generated the report before it is published and publicized. Further changes will not be made.

Figure 1. Editorial guidelines.

editorial guidelines, a report template, and communication mechanisms. In order to minimize the effort required in order to maximize the output of the series, the design ethos for all of these was intentionally lightweight and built upon existing library technologies and services whenever possible.

Publication Platform

The Library's institutional repository, IDEALS, was selected as the publication platform for LibORS. Also considered were the campus blog platform and the Library's website management system; however, IDEALS offers a number of advantages including permanent handles for the LibORS reports, metadata exposure, and long-term preservation as well as the opportunity to keep the documents for managing the LibORS as a publication in the same repository as the publication itself. The Library Occasional Reports Series community (https://www.ideals.illinois.edu/handle/2142/77875) is a subcommunity of the University Library community (https://www.ideals.illinois.edu/handle/2142/99) and thus also helps to showcase the broader spectrum of the University Library's output as well as promote the IDEALS repository itself. IDEALS also has established account creation and management procedures as well as workflows for file submission that benefit LibORS.

Unfortunately, IDEALS does not create DOIs for submissions, which are needed as part of the assessment of the effectiveness of IDEALS. Though the University Library can create DOIs for text documents through its participation in DataCite, CrossRef DOIs would offer additional advantages and are also needed for other developing publication projects. As such, the University Library is in the process of joining CrossRef. Fortunately, the DOIs can be recorded in the IDEALS record for each report in LibORS once they are created.

Editorial Process and Template Development

Foundational to the creation of LibORS is a set of editorial guidelines for authors to use when submitting a report and for the editor and graduate assistant to use in publishing. Establishing this process raised many questions for the LibORS project team including:

- How do we choose which reports to include in this series?
- What type of reports are valuable?
- How do we decide what is meaningful to the series?

To answer these questions, the team sought advice from faculty and staff in the University Library and the Graduate School of Library and Information Science, reviewed the University's writing style guide, and explored current examples of editorial guidelines for other publications on campus. The guidelines are intended to be easy to follow and lightweight in order to encourage submission to LibORS. See Figure 1 for the guidelines.

After establishing concrete criteria and guidelines for the series, the team then developed a Microsoft Word template into which each submission would be formatted by the designated editor. For each submission that LibORS receives, the editor will arrange the report into the LibORS template, which will later be published as a PDF in IDEALS. The template is complete with official branding from the University of Illinois, a copyright statement, and a sample citation for citing the report. The editorial team hopes that this template will serve as a standard for future committee reports so that little reformatting is needed for submissions.

Marketing and Communications

Also crucial to creating LibORS was establishing a marketing workflow that would effectively promote new reports. Once a report has been formatted into the template and uploaded into IDEALS, the editor will write a blog post on the LibORS WordPress website (http://publish.illinois.edu/libraryreports/), which will include background information about the report, a description of the team or committee that authored the report, and who will benefit from reading the report. The editor will then Tweet a promotional message about the new report with the LibORS Twitter account (@UIUCLibORS). The editorial team chose Twitter as the social media platform to promote the series in light of the many conversations that are held on Twitter among library professionals.

In addition, in order to give LibORS a visual identity, the editorial team sought out the creation of a graphic icon that can be used on social media, the WordPress blog, and the series template. Crystal Sheu, the eLearning Specialist in the Office of Information Literacy in the University Library, worked with the team to develop a visual identity, which LibORS can use in its promotional efforts.

Assessment and Sustainability

LibORS will begin formal publication in 2016, and informal assessment and monitoring will be part of the responsibilities of the graduate assistant and series editor; however, more formal assessment and reporting is planned to determine whether LibORS is achieving its goals and is offering the desired return-on-investment of library resources.

The effectiveness of LibORS will be assessed relative to the project objectives outlined in the Innovation Fund grant proposal.

> Objective 1—*To document the research and development work carried out by the University Library*: This objective is an output objective. Metrics used to assess the benefits will include the number of reports published and the response rate from committees, tasks forces, units, etc. when invited to submit.
>
> Objective 2—*To make such reports discoverable by others in the University Library and the profession at large*: This objective is an output objective. Metrics used to assess the benefits will include an assessment of report adherence to editorial guidelines, degree of full record details in IDEALS, number of subscribers to the publish.illinois.edu WordPress site for the reports series, and number of followers to the UIUCLibORS Twitter account as well as likes and retweets.
>
> Objective 3—*To raise the profile of the University Library as a key contributor to research and development in academic and research libraries*: This objective is an impact objective. An indirect measure of the benefit will be the number of downloads for each report from IDEALS as well as the use of altmetric reports based on the DOIs.

LibORS will only be sustainable with continued allocation of resources to the production of the publications in the series. The work fundedthrough the Innovation Fund proposal provided the up-front investment in establishing templates, practices, and procedures. Much of the production work long-term will be decentralized in that it would be carried out by a committee, task force, team, etc., as a component of doing their work; however, a central editor will be needed to ensure ongoing coordination, publicity, and adjustments of workflow as needed over time.

References

Bowles-Terry, M., Hensley, M., & Hinchliffe, L. (2010). Best practices for online video tutorials: A study of student preferences and understanding. *Communications In Information Literacy, 4*(1), 17–28. Retrieved from http://www.comminfolit.org/index.php/cil/article/view/Vol4-2010AR1

Library Publishing Coalition (LPC). (2016). *Library publishing directory*. Retrieved from http://www.librarypublishing.org/resources/directory/lpd2016

Mischo, W., Schlembach, M., Bishoff, J., & German, E. (2012). User search activities within an academic library gateway: Implications for webscale discovery systems. In M. Popp and D. Dallis (Eds.), *Planning and implementing resource discovery tools in academic libraries* (pp. 153–173). Hershey, PA: Information Science Reference.

Teaching the Library to Students of Higher Education

Steven Weiland, Professor of Higher Education, Michigan State University

Abstract

The academic library and its digital transformation are ignored in graduate programs of higher education administration, which train a significant number of postsecondary professionals. A course in scholarly communications in the digital age recently introduced at one such program includes an invitation to aspiring administrators to study the contributions of the library to the ways that faculty members are coming to understand and capitalize on new technologies in teaching, research, and career development. The library is represented in the course in its traditional and new roles. It is an essential campus location for attention to what technological change means for faculty work.

Introduction: A Gap In Graduate Study of Higher Education

Sociologist Wendy Griswold refers to the academic library as a "sacred space." Its "aura" and the pleasures of reading, she suggests, should be conveyed by the faculty to all students (Cull, 2011). Nevertheless, the campus library can be poorly understood or underestimated even by PhD students in higher education administration. With many of our students dedicated to the academic "success" of undergraduates we might expect that they would be knowledgeable about the need for education in "information literacy" and the library's role in it. But few are. And writing and publishing, with all they can signify across the disciplines, including what libraries do to maintain and advance the communications system, are rarely the subjects of deliberate attention, even by those aspiring to faculty positions.

Of course, that is not unusual among PhD students in many fields. Still, to the degree that higher education administration claims a comprehensive view of academic work, it should make a place in its programs for attention to scholarly communications. In what follows there is first a brief account of higher education administration as a field of graduate study. There is then a report on a course that introduces PhD students at Michigan State University to current developments in scholarly communications. The course is presented in the context of the need to assert the significance of technology's impact on academic communications in relation to the preoccupation among many postsecondary administrators and faculty with online teaching and learning.

The premise was simple: some of our students anticipate faculty careers in higher education programs and thus can benefit from knowledge of what they will encounter as they seek to build publishing records. But the course reflected the belief that whatever postsecondary plans our students have—for most it will be academic middle management—knowledge of scholarly communications and the role of the library is important in understanding faculty work, an essential professional obligation in higher education administration. Examples of such work appear following the description of the course, as does a brief conclusion identifying the unruly and unpredictable nature of scholarly communications today.

Higher Education as a Field of Study

Michigan State University is one of about 100 PhD programs in higher education administration (ranked #4 in the field by *U.S. News and World Report*). Of the 14 members of the Big Ten athletic conference and the Committee on Interinstitutional Collaboration (CIC, which also includes the University of Chicago), 11 offer such programs. And so too do leading private universities like Stanford, USC, Vanderbilt, and NYU. There are over 200 institutions, including most of those offering PhDs, who offer MA programs in higher education, many featuring the

http://dx.doi.org/10.5703/1288284316318

specialized field of student affairs administration (e.g., managing residence halls). Faculty and students associated with both levels of graduate education participate in the activities of the Association for the Study of Higher Education (ASHE) and the American College Personnel Association (ACPA). And the field supports a sizeable group of journals and allied publications, but only rarely do these include an article or report on scholarly communications or libraries (Bray and Major, 2011; Lincoln, 2010).

Why are there so many programs? Because whatever the state of the economy, and the budget difficulties facing many colleges and universities, managerial opportunities on campus continue to grow. While faculty hiring—to full-time tenure track positions—has declined, administrative work continues to expand (Ginsberg, 2011; Marcus, 2014). Campus jobs are available and appealing. Graduate students in higher education administration report that they benefited greatly from undergraduate experience and wish to contribute to the education of succeeding generations. Or, they are dedicated to the reform of the system, particularly in matters of social justice, like access to higher education for underserved minorities.

Many students enrolled in PhD programs are actually working part-time or full-time in institutional positions (where they are enrolled or elsewhere), typically in non-academic units like admissions and financial aid, or in advising and career development roles in academic units. It is not so uncommon to find a college or university president or provost with a PhD in higher education administration. But it is much less so to find a dean or department head with such a degree. In those positions, affiliation with a traditional academic discipline or field matters more.

Moreover, while there are fewer PhD programs in higher education administration than there are in English or economics, or even criminal justice or social work, the field graduates hundreds of students every year. And, as postsecondary management grows, graduates of such programs claim increasing influence on campus. So, from institutional and scholarly perspectives the study of higher education is a sizeable field, worth the attention of academic librarians as a place to make the library's role better known at a time of the digital transformation of teaching and research.

The Other Digital Revolution on Campus

When students of higher education (and faculty and administrators) are invited to think about the impact of digital technologies on higher education it is typically in relation to teaching and learning. And there is national and international attention in the media to MOOCs (Massive Open Online Courses), including what they suggest about leadership roles welcomed by leading American institutions like Stanford, Harvard, and MIT in the founding and management of Coursera and edX. When University of Virginia President Teresa Sullivan ran into conflict with the institution's governing board it was largely because, in their view, she was not responding quickly enough, given what the competition was doing, to apparent opportunities in online education, in credit courses and degree programs as well as MOOCs.

The new course described below addresses another technological transformation. Librarians hardly need to be reminded about the scale and significance of change now underway in scholarly communications (Marcum, Schonfeld, and Thomas, 2015). But their campus colleagues do, faculty and graduate students alike. That is what prompted Middlebury College media studies scholar Jason Mittell (2013) to urge the redirection of academic interest toward the Open Access (OA) movement, an effort that shares the goal of MOOCs in offering direct access to scholarly work. He puts aside the instructional utopian talk of Coursera and edX in favor of a realistic view of what might be accomplished with OA: "Access to the average journal article might do little to change the world. But making the bulk of scholarly research freely available could transform the possibilities of educational uplift, scientific discovery, and public engagement with academic work."

Mittell shares the perspective of the research library that OA has a role in "undercutting the exclusive rights and restrictive access of commercial publishers." As leading publishers themselves devise OA strategies, including what can be gained in fees from authors, change will not come easily. But it is Mittell's goal to convince academic colleagues that MOOCs are over-hyped by high prestige institutions while OA, and allied innovations, are "creating modest but long-lasting change beneath the surface, [altering] traditional practices without proclaiming their own grandeur." Thus, in the spirit of library organization and action, systems of scholarly communication are changing with incremental steps and measured reforms.

Recent efforts in this direction have gained only a fraction of the media attention that has gone to MOOCs. Before Harvard, in collaboration with MIT, put edX in place, the University's esteemed (as a scholar as well as an organizational leader) librarian Robert Darnton had organized Digital Access to Scholarship at Harvard (DASH). Downloads from the pioneering repository have now passed 5.3 million, and Darnton claims it as his primary achievement as a librarian (Ireland, 2015). Indeed, the growth of such repositories, whether aimed at archiving many kinds of digital resources or showcasing faculty work, is one of the most visible features of the OA movement (Marsh, 2015). By now the Directory of Open Access Repositories (OpenDOAR) lists over 2,600 institutional and departmental locations for posting articles and other forms of research. The Coalition of Open Access Policy Institutions (COAPI; housed at SPARC), where OA publishing in some form is mandated, now has almost 70 members. That is in addition to pathmaking disciplinary repositories, particularly, arXiv which has served physicists since 1991 in mathematics, computer science, and other fields in recent years.

Professors and graduate students in these disciplines recognize the opportunities in communications represented by arXiv. Yet, despite a steady increase in the number of institutions mandating OA, and the popularity of unaffiliated and extensive sites like academia.edu and ResearchGate, campus knowledge of the full range of change in scholarly communications—in experiments in peer review, new formats for tracing the impact of publications, and prospects for "enhanced" online texts—is limited. And research libraries themselves vary in ways to incorporate scholarly communications into their operations, including efforts to promote information literacy (ACRL, 2013). A timely information literacy strategy represented in the new course is to recognize relations between the impact of technology on teaching *and* research via interest in "open" as a new framework for thinking about the "political economy" of higher education (Wellen, 2013).

A Course In an e-Book

Open access and repositories are two of many subjects in scholarly communications in the digital age." And the course is organized in a form that reflects its subject, or new publishing formats and their role in teaching and learning. Thus, an e-book I have written is the primary instructional resource. Actually the digital text is titled an *e-Primer* to indicate my intention to introduce the subject to graduate students. It follows from my work as an experienced online teacher, and the course design reflects my pedagogical preferences, representing as they do a heresy according to "best practices" of distance learning (Major, 2015). Thus, my self-paced courses are fully composed online, each with about 60,000 words and hundreds of hyperlinks to allied resources in text, audio, and video, or what is now sometimes called digitally "enhanced" scholarship (Wright, 2014).

A foundational problem for the course is visible in a series of images. A cartoon from *PhD Comics* (phdcomics.com) reduces academic inquiry to "Read . . . Write . . . Rinse [with coffee] . . . Repeat." But in 2009 an OCLC project specified, in more complex fashion, the sequence of steps that shape "Core Scholarly Activities," or searching, collecting, reading, writing, and collaborating (with activities specified for each; Palmer, et al., 2009). Finally, Oxford Internet Institute scholars have plotted the digital work of science and scholarship with a dense graphical display of its intensely networked configuration representing an evolving "e-research ecosystem" (Meyer and Schroeder, 2009). A goal of the course is to maintain the simplicity of the cartoon, or what it can feel like to do the work, while probing the temporal and spatial dimensions of academic inquiry as it is studied and represented in the information sciences and in explorations of the impact of technology on research and communications.

After a brief introduction explaining the origin and goals of the *e-Primer*, including a guide to accessing its linked online resources, the text is organized into six chapters:

1. Our Digital Age
2. Scholars, Scientists, and Information Practices
3. How We Read
4. Writing and Publishing in Electronic Spaces
5. Recognition, Reputation, and Academic Rewards
6. What's Ahead?

A *Glossary* defines essential terms, displaying the subject's vocabulary drawn from several disciplines. In effect, the course design observes the case made by advocates of enhanced digital texts, particularly what they can offer in hypermedia resources. And the course reflects the "long view" of the subject (Mabe, 2010). Such an approach was named too as essential to how we see the scientific and scholarly "threshold" to the future:

> [It] is made up of interlocking components: changes in the nature and status of the document and the book; changes in practices of reading, research, note-taking, and information sharing; changes in the architectural and institutional containers in which such practices are carried out and by means of which they are supported. It was arrived at not suddenly, not with the wave of a digital magic wand, but thanks to a century-long transformation in the culture of communication. (Schnapp and Battles, 2014, pp. 14–15)

Faculty Work In the Digital Age

The *e-Primer* features scientific and scholarly communications, woven as they are into library practices and resources supporting faculty and graduate student research (and, increasingly, support for institutional efforts to promote research by undergraduates). But the course displays too how inventive teaching brings the library's digital resources into the classroom. Thus, Stephen Nichols (2008), an influential medievalist, has explained how he capitalizes on digital versions of French manuscripts to guide his students toward understanding of textual production and literary meaning. Using "digital surrogates" prepared with academic librarians he sees himself as "co-teaching" with the library from easily accessible resources taking the place of modern print versions of work that, in Nichols' view, require the visual experience that only manuscript study can provide. The library supports a novel combination of research and teaching.

Other faculty work shows the differences between disciplines. Thus, chemist Henry Rzepa (2013) reviews his long career in science from the perspective of the steady introduction of new technologies. They reveal to him the distinction between "data" and "discourse." The place of reusable data in scientific communications is crucial and the reason, according to Rzepa, why in one form or another online publications—with their graphical representations—must be as interactive as possible. Still, any progress in data sharing and use will depend on making the most of metadata. In fact, Rzepa displays the scientific origins of the idea of "distant" (or machine) reading that has made the digital humanities appear, to advocates and critics alike, more like science than the conventional activities of literary studies. But Rzepa understands enough about the significance of "discourse" to have made himself an active and widely read blogger in chemistry. It helps to complete what Rzepa calls the "scientific cycle of sharing." Thus, he is a spokesman for "open" science as an indispensable feature of the digital age.

Plainly, Rzepa learned to manage his career in accord with technological innovations in research and publishing. But he worked within the traditional expectation of patient identification of citations for measuring the impact of his work. We can see now, however, signs of how faculty work in the digital age can include very deliberate or even "real-time" attention to the impact of scholarship, often with the aid of the campus library. The University of Toronto urges scholars and scientists—from graduate students to senior faculty—to "get noticed." The UT Library offers this directive: "Success as a scientist is not simply a function of the quality of ideas we hold in our heads . . . . 'Publish or perish' is about surviving, not succeeding. You don't succeed as a scientist by getting papers *published.* You succeed as a scientist by getting them *citeds.*" Media studies scholar Melissa Terras (2012) demonstrates how she utilized the repository at University College, London, and her knowledge of "altmetrics," the new techniques (then at an early stage) for measuring the circulation of scholarly work, to build her reputation and advance her career.

Higher education students in the new course are also invited to see how scholars manage their loyalty to the traditional library even while they capitalize on technology. Historian Anthony Grafton (2009) tells the new story of publishing without paper as anything but a replacement for print: "Sitting at your local coffee shop on your laptop will tell you a lot, especially if you wield your search terms adeptly. But if you want deeper, more local knowledge, you will still have to take the narrower path [at the New York Public Library] that leads between the lions and up the stone stairs. There—as in great libraries around the world—you will use all the new sources, all the time. . . . But these streams of data, rich as they are, will illuminate rather than eliminate the unique books and prints and manuscripts that only the library can put in front of you."

By the end Grafton is happy to recognize what is gained from technology, but he registers too the durability of scholarly habits:

> For now, and for the foreseeable future, if you want to piece together the richest possible mosaic of documents and texts and images, you will have to do it in those crowded public rooms where sunlight gleams on varnished tables, as it has for more than a century, and knowledge is still embodied in millions of dusty, crumbling, smelly, irreplaceable manuscripts and books. (pp. 323–324)

Conclusion: The Wild West?

Like most graduate students in colleges of education, those studying higher education are relentlessly future-minded. They want change and reform. The library can appear to them to be the most conservative of academic locations, and especially so if they believe that printed books are no longer important. Darnton sees the library as the "heart and soul" of the research university, a pervasive force that needs to be understood by anyone with a stake in postsecondary education: "The library still pumps intellectual energy into every corner of campus" (Ireland, 2015).

Teaching the library means representing its vitality in meeting old and new goals, particularly in its contributions to innovation in academic research (e.g., in data curation and the digital humanities) and in scholarly communications, including its own publishing (Okerson and Holzman, 2015). A course must reflect steady change and also how unpredictable or even unruly is the current scene. *Harvard Magazine* recently declared the "Wild West" a suitable metaphor for describing our situation (Lambert, 2015). Accounts abound of the future of the academic library (e.g., CLIR, 2008; *portal:* Jaggars, 2014). They recognize the conditions making necessary a new order of relations in scholarly communications. The Wild West was a place of initiative and anxiety. Students of higher education can be assured that the library is a rich resource for the first, and that it is a place that is not only sacred but serene.

References

Association of College and Research Libraries (ACRL). (2013). Working group on intersections of scholarly communication and information literacy. *Intersections of scholarly communication and information literacy: Creating strategic collaborations for a changing academic environment*. Chicago, IL: ACRL.

Bray, N., & Major, C. (2011). Status of journals in the field of higher education. *Journal of Higher Education, 82*(4), 479–503.

Council on Library and Information Resources (CLIR). (2008). *No brief candle: Reconceiving research libraries for the 21st Century* (pp. 28–34). Washington, DC: CLIR.

Cull, B. (2011, June). Reading revolutions: Online digital text and implications for reading in academe. *First Monday, 16*(6).

Ginsberg, B. (2011). *The fall of the faculty: The rise of the all-administrative university and why it matters*. New York: Oxford University Press.

Grafton, A. (2009). Codex in crisis: The book dematerializes. In Grafton (Ed.), *Worlds made by words: Scholarship and community in the modern West* (pp. 288–324). Cambridge, MA: Harvard University Press.

Ireland, C. (2015, May 11). Robert Darnton closes the book. *Harvard Gazette*. Retrieved from http://news.harvard.edu/gazette/story/2015/05/robert-darnton-closes-the-book/

Lambert, C. (2015). The "wild west" of academic publishing. *Harvard Magazine, January/February, 56–60*, 83.

Lincoln, Y. (2010). Research libraries in the twenty-first century. In J. C. Smart (Ed.), *Higher Education: Handbook of Theory and Research, 25* (pp. 425–448). New York: Springer.

Major, C. (2015). *Teaching online: A guide to theory, research, and practice*. Baltimore, MD: Johns Hopkins University Press.

Marcum, D., Schonfeld, R., & Thomas, S. (2015). *Office of scholarly communication: Scope, organizational placement, and planning in ten research libraries*. New York: Ithaka S+R.

Marcus, J. (2014, February 6). New analysis shows problematic boom in higher ed administrators. *Huffington Post*. Retrieved from http://www.huffingtonpost.com/2014/02/06/higher-ed-administrators-growth_n_4738584.html

Marsh, R. (2015). The role of institutional repositories in developing communication of scholarly research. *OCLC Systems and Services: International Digital Library Perspectives, 31*(4), 163–195.

Mabe, M. A. (2010, October). Scholarly communication: A long view. *New Review of Academic Librarianship*, 132–144.

McCabe, B. (2013). Publish or perish: Academic publishing confronts its digital future. *Johns Hopkins Magazine, 65*(3), 50–57.

Meyer, E., & Schroeder, R. (2009). The world wide web of research and access to knowledge. *Knowledge Management Research & Practice, 7*, 218–233.

Mittel, J. (2013, March 4). The real digital change agent. *Chronicle of Higher Education*. Retrieved from http://chronicle.com/article/The-Real-Digital-Change-Agent/137589/

Nichols, S. (2008). Co-teaching: The library and me. In CLIR (Ed.), *No brief candle: Reconceiving research libraries for the 21st century* (pp. 28–34). Washington, DC: CLIR.

Okerson, A., & Holzman, A. (2015). *The once and future publishing library*. Washington, DC: CLIR.

Palmer, C., Teffau, L., & Pirmann, C. (2009). *Scholarly information practices in the online environment: Themes from the literature and implications for library service development*. Dublin, OH: OCLC.

Jaggars, D. E. (Ed.) (2014). Imagining the future of academic libraries. *portal: Libraries and the Academy, 14*(3).

Rzepa, H. (2013). Changing ways of sharing research in chemistry. In D. Shorley & M. Jubb (Eds.), *The future of scholarly communication* (pp. 3–23). London: Facet.

Schnapp, J., & Battles, M. (2014). *The library beyond the book*. Cambridge, MA: Harvard University Press.

Terras, M. (2012). The impact of social media on the dissemination of research: Results of an experiment. *Journal of Digital Humanities, 1*(3). Retrieved from http://journalofdigitalhumanities.org/1-3/the-impact-of-social-media-on-the-dissemination-of-research-by-melissa-terras/

Wellen, R. (2013). Open access, megajournals, and MOOCs: On the political economy of academic unbundling. *SAGE Open, 3*(4). http://dx.doi.org/10.1177/2158244013507271

Wright, J. (2014, April 21). What enhanced e-books can do for scholarly authors. *Chronicle of Higher Education*. Retrieved from http:// http://chronicle.com/article/What-Enhanced-E-Books-Can-Do/145969/

The Open Movement: What Libraries Can Do

Sheila Corrall, Professor and Chair, Library & Information Science Program, University of Pittsburgh School of Information Sciences

Abstract

Open approaches have moved beyond open access, open source software, and open courseware to developments with open infrastructure and open processes. Open initiatives are gaining momentum as a result of both bottom-up grassroots activism and top-down policy agenda. In a few instances, they have already reached a tipping point; but in many cases they are being pursued separately by specialist groups, suffering from fragmentation, and not always having their expected outcomes or impacts. Our study of open initiatives uses a simple overarching definition of open resources, and introduces a convenient framework enabling shared understanding of three different types of openness—open content, open process, and open infrastructure—illustrated by a dozen examples of open domains relevant to libraries and information services. We explain the common attributes, existing synergies, mutual benefits, and natural limits of open approaches that need to be taken into account when developing and implementing policies and strategies to advance openness in organizations. We argue that librarians and other information specialists can make important contributions in promoting a holistic open culture in education, workplaces, communities, and society; and we identify a continuum of nine potential roles as recommended operational, tactical, and strategic interventions for information professionals, individually and collectively. Practitioners can use the models and tools presented to gain a fuller understanding of the concept of openness and its implications for libraries and their parent institutions; and, more significantly, to review, evaluate, and determine their own current and future roles as advocates, collaborators, and leaders of the open movement.

The Open Movement

Open has been asserted as "the default *modus operandi* for research and higher education" (e-Infranet, 2013), and now extends beyond familiar concepts, such as open access, open source software, and open courseware, to many other examples, including open linked data, open peer review, and open textbooks. Libraries and librarians are getting involved across the whole spectrum of open activities. Notable examples include discussions around support for text and data mining (Orcutt, 2014), and a surge of interest in massive open online courses (MOOCs), evidenced by recent literature, including an environmental scan from ACRL, and a case study of the copyright and permission service at Duke University (Fowler & Smith, 2013; Kazakoff-Lane, 2014; Kaushik, 2015).

Partnership approaches are the dominant model here, with initiatives such as the Global Open Knowledgebase (GOKb) developing open linked data for electronic resource management and scholarly communication using a community-managed approach (Hanson, Song & Wilson, 2015), and the Open Library of Humanities, which is also based on library partner contributions, with libraries funding infrastructure development—rather than purchasing individual journals—in a groundbreaking project enabling humanists to experiment with new models of open access publishing (Eve & Edwards, 2015). Public libraries are also engaging with the open agenda; for example, by hosting open data hackathons and exploring other ways of working with the open data community, while also strengthening links with local government (Carruthers, 2014).

Definitions of Openness

Table 1 (see Appendix) presents sample definitions of open concepts found in the literature and reported in our prior work (Corrall & Pinfield, 2014).

Interpretations of "open" vary for different stakeholder and practitioner groups, especially in the commercial arena (e.g., open standards) and for emergent areas (e.g., open peer review). In

http://dx.doi.org/10.5703/1288284316319

some cases, concepts and terms used for one area of practice have been adopted and adapted for another domain. Thus Suber (2012, pp. 65, 66) uses terminology from open source software to define two "sub-species" of open access:

> Gratis OA is free of charge . . . Users must still seek permission to exceed fair use. Gratis OA removes price barriers but not permission barriers.
>
> Libre OA is free of charge and also free of some copyright and licensing restrictions . . . Libre OA removes price barriers and at least some permission barriers.

In other cases, practitioners have developed their own specific frameworks and meanings for concepts and terms that have more general application, such as the "4 Rs" framework for open educational resources (Wiley, 2010, p. 6):

- Reuse: the right to reuse the content in its unaltered/verbatim form (e.g., make a backup copy of the content)
- Revise: the right to adapt, adjust, modify, or alter the content itself (e.g., translate the content into another language)
- Remix: the right to combine the original or revised content with other content to create something new (e.g., incorporate the content into a mashup)
- Redistribute: the right to share copies of the original content, the revisions, or the remixes with others (e.g., give a copy of the content to a friend)

Open approaches are continuing to evolve in a complex, pluralist knowledge economy, using multiple definitions. The open access movement is among the more mature examples, where research shows OA has reached a tipping point globally, i.e., the stage where a majority of articles are freely available. Studies by Science-Metrix for the European Commission revealed all 34 European countries examined "have tipped towards a majority of papers in OA" and in four countries the aggregate availability for the 2008–2013 period was above 70%; while in North America, the US (67.9%) and Canada (64.4%) have definitely passed the tipping point (Archambault, Caruso & Nicol, 2014, October, p. 20). The complexity of the OA landscape is illustrated by the plethora of interpretations in that field alone. As Archambault et al. (2014, April, p. 4) observe,

> Access—can be open (free), restricted or paid; with unrestricted or restricted usage rights; quality controlled or not; pre-print (pre-refereeing), post-print (post-refereeing), or published version (with final copy editing and page layout); immediate or delayed; permanent or transient.

They provide definitions for 10 categories of access, with subcategories in several instances (not shown here):

- Open Access
- Ideal Open Access
- Restricted Access
- Paid Access
- Restricted Open Access
- Green Open Access
- Gold Open Access
- Robin Hood Open Access or Rogue Open Access
- Delayed Open Access
- Transient Open Access

However, despite the plurality, scholars and practitioners are increasingly identifying theoretical and practical links between open research and open education (Conole & Alevizou, 2010; Esposito, 2013), and also wider connections to open source, open government, open economy, and open society (Peters, 2010; Willinsky, 2005). Others have used Boyer's (1990; 1996) model of scholarship as discovery, integration, application, teaching, and engagement to promote a holistic view of open/social scholarship in the digital world (Greenhow & Gleason, 2014; Scanlon, 2014). The European Network for Co-ordination of Policies and Programmes on e-Infrastructure (e-InfraNet) has made a seminal contribution here in a comprehensive report proclaiming "'Open' as the default *modus operandi* for research and higher education." The project provides a simple overarching definition of Open that can be used to promote a unified interpretation of the concept:

> Open means ensuring that there is little or no barrier to access for anyone who can, or wants to, contribute to a particular development or use its output. (e-InfraNet, 2013, p. 12)

A Typology of Open

We suggest that as an aid to understanding and planning it is useful to think about openness in terms of three basic *types* of open, concerned with *content*, *process*, and *infrastructure*, with the following aims:

- **Open Content**—making content of various sorts freely accessible and available for reuse (e.g., publications, reports, presentations, theses, dissertations, datasets, metadata, learning objects, computer code)
- **Open Process**—carrying out academic or business processes in the public arena (e.g., product and service innovation, software development, scientific work, peer review, pedagogical practices)
- **Open Infrastructure**—creating an interoperable technical environment for education, research, and administration (e.g., standards, systems)

Each open type is represented by distinct open *domains* of activity, though some domains (e.g., open source software) relate to more than one type. Table 2 (see Appendix; taken from Corrall & Pinfield, 2014, p. 298) presents our proposed typology.

As already indicated, although open activities have generally been pursued separately by diverse specialist communities, stakeholders are increasingly seeing connections and identifying important synergies among the different domains:

> As the availability of and access to content and infrastructural resources increases, the need for and use of "open processes" becomes more evident. Where "open content" is used and produced in "open processes" within an open infrastructural setting, a culture of "openness" gradually emerges. (e-Infranet, 2013, p. 13)

The notion of an open *culture* is an important additional dimension of the open landscape that needs to be considered and promoted to advance the open movement. Figure 1 (see Appendix; from Corrall & Pinfield, 2014, p. 299) presents a high-level model of open adding culture to the mix.

In practice, the different open domains overlap and support each other, and in turn stimulate new forms of openness. Thus, open data from research builds on open access to publications, and both often use open source software to make content accessible, such as DSpace from the Massachusetts Institute of Technology (MIT) or EPrints from the University of Southampton (Lynch, 2003). Open educational resources similarly often use open source systems to manage and provide access to course content, and resource sharing is encouraging faculty to share pedagogical practices and promote peer learning; for example, Abelson, Miyagaw and Yue (2012, p. 9) describe an initiative at MIT intended to:

> Share not just the content that MIT uses in teaching—the original OCW model—but also explicit information on how we teach at MIT. This will potentially include pedagogical statements from and interviews with participating faculty, links to exemplary teaching practices, showcases of educational innovations, and other framing information that places the content shared in context of our teaching philosophies.

Such relationships and dependencies are a key feature of the evolving landscape, which mean that policy interventions in one area can have beneficial effects in other domains, as depicted in Figure 2 (see Appendix; Corrall & Pinfield, 2014, p. 301).

The Case for Coordination and Integration

A decade ago, Willinsky (2005) advanced a threefold argument for the "unacknowledged convergence" between open access and open source software. First, the different open domains have a shared "commitment to the unrestricted exchange of information and ideas," evidenced in their shared associations with transparency, public good, and public accountability (resonating with the interests of policy makers). Secondly, they are governed by common "economic principles," based on the efficacy of free knowledge resources, an economy of recognition, and the existence of "free-or-subscribe" models. Thirdly, they have shared characteristics derived from their commitment and principles. We argue that the *de facto* interconnectedness between open domains that continues to develop is a fourth commonality (Corrall & Pinfield, 2014).

In addition, open initiatives share several common attributes: they are generally driven by the impulse of intellectual curiosity; they support an economy of reputation building; and are facilitated by motivation for "competitive sharing." They also offer significant common *benefits* for institutions and individuals, such as visibility and impact, reuse, innovation and agility, cost effectiveness, quality enhancement, and reputation and trust (e-Infranet, 2013; Read, 2011). The potential benefits of openness are important factors to consider when formulating policies or strategies within institutions. It is also important to acknowledge there are "natural" limits to openness, such as the exclusion of royalty-generating literature; restrictions on sharing personal data and commercial information; the existence of a strong mixed economy for software; and selectivity in sharing educational resources arising from concerns about quality, competitiveness, and other issues (Corrall & Pinfield, 2014).

Where Do We Go From Here?

The different open domains are at various stages of evolution and maturity. Open approaches continue to be promoted by diverse communities of practice, but often on parallel tracks, with little or no practical connection between them. Initiatives are being managed at multiple levels—institutional, consortial, national, and international—but with insufficient collaboration and coordination to realize their full potential. The open domains are predicated on shared values; they have common goals and face similar practical issues (e.g., intellectual property rights, business models, sustainability). Librarians and other information specialists are already doing great work in many areas: they have a long history of involvement in open access; they are engaging with the challenges of open data and doing pioneering work on open textbooks (Clobridge, 2015; Corrall, Kennan, & Afzal, 2013; Pinfield, 2015).

Libraries are especially well placed to exploit the synergies and opportunities across the whole open arena, and have the capacity to make operational, tactical, and strategic interventions that will deliver real benefits to their communities and society. Many of the problems identified by others play to our strengths, for example:

> Repository development and implementation presents numerous challenges related to intellectual property rights, data curation, long-term preservation, infrastructure development and interoperability. (Archambault et al., 2014, April, p. 6)

There is also an urgent need for active monitoring of developments globally, which the profession has the expertise, networks, and structures to do. Archambault and colleagues (2014, April, p. 15) have issued an important warning:

> Many mandates being promulgated at the moment run the risk of favouring a shift from BEPA [Back End Paid Access] to FEPA [Front End Paid Access], from inaccessibility to inequality.

Table 3 (see Appendix) shows potential roles for libraries in open domains. The matrix can be used as a tool to assess your current situation and set goals for moving forward by answering the following questions:

- How often are you *now* performing the suggested roles for the defined domains—Frequently? (F) Occasionally? (O) Rarely? (R) Never? (N)

- How often *will* you be performing the suggested roles for the defined domains next year—Frequently? (F) Occasionally? (O) Rarely? (R) Never? (N)

The key area where libraries could—and arguably should—make a substantial contribution is in policy and strategy development for their institutions and communities. Some libraries and information services have prior experience of institutional information strategies from the 1990s, from which lessons can be learned for the open era (Bernbom, 1997; Hughes, 1997; Michalko, 2000). We can also look to management science and other arenas for models and frameworks. Ackoff's (1970) classic concept of *interactive planning*, based on the principles of participation, continuity, and holism, would be a good fit for a concerted effort to develop a unified strategy. The three principles incorporate a stakeholder approach, real-time strategy making, and middle-up-down planning, with the process conceived as:

- *Participative*—everyone who could be affected by the plans should be directly involved or represented in the planning process, to build understanding and help implementation
- *Continuous*—plans should be continuously revised in light of their performance, unexpected developments, and the latest information, to anticipate and respond to changes in the environment
- *Holistic*—every part of a system and every level of it should be planned for simultaneously and interdependently, to coordinate and integrate multiple units and different levels

Another model for consideration is Kipling's (1902F) questions, also known as the 5W1H problem-solving method (or WWWHWaWO), which is used in journalism, engineering, and management, and similarly as an observational framework in social research (Patton, 2002). The six questions can be used to identify issues for consideration in policy development; for example:

- **Why?** (Rationale)—external drivers, institutional missions, individual incentives
- **What?** (Scope)—open types/domains, selection criteria, formats and standards
- **When?** (Timing)—deposit, release, embargoes (publishers, sponsors/funders)
- **Where?** (Venues)—institutional/community repositories, storage locus and access route
- **Who?** (Players)—stakeholder responsibilities, governance arrangements
- **How?** (Practicalities)—openness definitions, license conditions, operational procedures

Libraries are uniquely positioned to collaborate with other stakeholders in coordinating efforts to move beyond atomistic policies and strategies toward the design and delivery of holistic integrated institution-wide endeavors to advance the open agenda. Policy and strategy lag behind thinking and practice, and libraries can take the lead in developing a coherent response.

Acknowledgment

The study presented here forms part of an ongoing program of research conducted with Dr. Stephen Pinfield, University of Sheffield Information School.

References

Abelson, H., Miyagawa, S., & Yue, D. (2012). MIT's ongoing commitment to OpenCourseWare. *MIT Faculty Newsletter, XXIV*(4), 8-9. Retrieved November 5, 2015, from http://web.mit.edu/fnl/volume/244/fnl244.pdf.

Ackoff, R. L. (1970). *A concept of corporate planning.* New York: Wiley.

Archambault, É., Amyot, D., Caruso, J., Campbell, D., Deschamps, P., Nicol, A. . . . Roberge, G. (2014, April 28). *Summary report: Evolution of open access policies and availability, 1996-2013.* Brussels, Belgium: Science-Metrix/European Commission. Retrieved November 5, 2015, from http://science-metrix.com/en/publications/reports/summary-report-evolution-of-open-access-policies-and-availability-1996-2013.

Archambault, É., Caruso, J., & Nicol, A. (2014, October 22). *State-of-art analysis of OA strategies to peer-review publications.* Brussels, Belgium: Science-Metrix/European Commission. Retrieved November 5, 2015, from http://science-metrix.com/en/publications/reports/state-of-art-analysis-of-oa-strategies-to-peer-review-publications.

Bernbom, G. (1997). Institution-wide information strategies. *CAUSE/EFFECT, 20*(1), 8–11. Retrieved November 5, 2015, from http://net.educause.edu/ir/library/pdf/CEM9713.pdf.

Boyer, E. L. (1990). *Scholarship reconsidered: Priorities of the professoriate.* San Francisco, CA: Jossey Bass. Retrieved November 5, 2015, from http://www.umces.edu/sites/default/files/al/pdfs/BoyerScholarshipReconsidered.pdf.

Boyer, E. L. (1996). The scholarship of engagement. *Journal of Public Service & Outreach, 1*(1), 11–20. Retrieved November 5, 2015,from http://openjournals.libs.uga.edu/index.php/jheoe/article/view/253/238.

Carruthers, A. (2014). Open Data Day hackathon 2014 at Edmonton Public Library. *Partnership: The Canadian Journal of Library and Information Practice and Research, 9*(2). Retrieved November 5, 2015, from http://journals2.scholarsportal.info/pdf/19119593/v09i0002/101_oddh2aepl.xml.

Clobridge, A. (2015). Libraries, meet open textbooks. *Online Searcher, 39*(3), 68–70.

Conole, G., & Alevizou, P. (2010). *A literature review of the use of Web 2.0 tools in higher education: A report commissioned by the Higher Education Academy.* Milton Keynes, UK: The Open University. Retrieved November 5, 2015, from https://www.heacademy.ac.uk/sites/default/files/conole_alevizou_2010.pdf.

Corrall, S., & Pinfield, S. (2014, March). Coherence of "open" initiatives in higher education and research: Framing a policy agenda. *Breaking Down Walls: Culture–Context–Computing, iConference 2014 Proceedings* (pp. 293–313). http://dx.doi.org/10.9776/14085. Retrieved November 5, 2015, from https://www.ideals.illinois.edu/handle/2142/47316.

Corrall, S., Kennan, M. A., & Afzal, W. (2013). Bibliometrics and research data management services: Emerging trends in library support for research. *Library Trends, 61*(3), 636–674. http://dx.doi.org/10.1353/lib.2013.0005. Retrieved November 5, 2015, from http://d-scholarship.pitt.edu/18948/.

e-InfraNet (2013). *e-InfraNet: 'Open' as the default modus operandi for research and higher education.* European Network for co-ordination of policies and programmes on e-infrastructures (e-InfraNet Project). Retrieved November 5, 2015, from https://www.surf.nl/binaries/content/assets/surf/en/knowledgebase/2013/e-InfraNet-Open-as-the-Default-Modus-Operandi-for-Research-and-Higher-Education.pdf

Esposito, A. (2013). Neither digital or open, just researchers: Views on digital/open scholarship practices in an Italian university. *First Monday, 18*(1). http://dx.doi.org/10.5210/fm.v18i1.388. Retrieved November 5, 2015, from http://firstmonday.org/ojs/index.php/fm/article/view/3881.

Eve, M. P., & Edwards, C. (2015) Opening the Open Library of Humanities. *Open Library of Humanities, 1*(1), e1. http://dx.doi.org/10.16995/olh.46. Retrieved November 5, 2015, from http://eprints.bbk.ac.uk/13030/1/46-186-4-PB.pdf.

Fowler, L., & Smith, K. (2013). Drawing the blueprint as we build: Setting up a library-based copyright and permissions service for MOOCs. *D-Lib Magazine, 19*(7–8). http://dx.doi.org/10.1045/july2013-fowler. Retrieved November 5, 2015, from http://www.dlib.org/dlib/july13/fowler/07fowler.html.

Greenhow, C., & Gleason, B. (2014). Social scholarship: Reconsidering scholarly practices in the age of social media. *British Journal of Educational Technology, 45*(3), 392–402. http://dx.doi.org/10.1111/bjet.12150.

Hanson, E. M., Song, X., & Wilson, K. (2015). Managing serials data as a community: Partnering with the global open knowledgebase (GOKb). *Serials Review, 41*(3), 146–152. http://dx.doi.org/10.1080/00987913.2015.1064853.

Hughes, A. (1997). Information strategy—Threat or opportunity? *Librarian Career Development, 5*(2), 60–66. http://dx.doi.org/10.1108/09680819710180912.

Kaushik, A. (2015). MOOCs and library and information science domain: A review of selected literature. International Journal of Information Dissemination and Technology, 5(3), 188–195. Retrieved November 5, 2015, from http://www.ijidt.com/index.php/ijidt/article/view/687/268.

Kazakoff-Lane, C. (2014, March 4). *Environmental scan and assessment of OERs, MOOCs and libraries: What effectiveness and sustainability means for libraries' impact on open education.* Chicago, IL: Association of College and Research Libraries. Retrieved November 5, 2015, from http://www.ala.org/acrl/issues/whitepapers.

Kipling, R. (1902). *Just so stories.* London: Macmillan.

Lynch, C. A. (2003). Institutional repositories: Essential infrastructure for scholarship in the digital age. *Portal: Libraries and the Academy, 3*(2), 327–336. http://dx.doi.org/10.1353/pla.2003.0039.

Michalko, J. (2000). Equilibrium and opportunism: Information strategies and the new environment. *New Library World, 101*(1), 6–12. http://dx.doi.org/10.1108/03074800010304352.

Orcutt, D. (2015). Library support for text and data mining. *Online Searcher, 39*(3), 27–30.

Patton, M. Q. (2002). *Qualitative research and evaluation methods* (3rd ed.). Thousand Oaks, CA: SAGE.

Peters, M. A. (2010). Three forms of the knowledge economy: Learning, creativity and openness. *British Journal of Educational Studies, 58*(1), 67–88. http://dx.doi.org/10.1080/00071000903516452.

Pinfield, S. (2015). Making open access work: The "state-of-the-art" in providing open access to scholarly literature. *Online Information Review, 39*(5), 604–636. http://dx.doi.org/10.1108/OIR-05-2015-0167.

Read, M. (2011). Open resources: The need for integration. *EDUCAUSE 2011 Annual Conference, Philadelphia, PA, October 18–21, 2011.* Retrieved November 5, 2015, from http://www.educause.edu/annual-conference/2011/open-resources-need-integration.

Scanlon, E. (2014). Scholarship in the digital age: Open educational resources, publication and public engagement. *British Journal of Educational Technology, 45*(1), 12–23. http://dx.doi.org/10.1111/bjet.12010.

Suber, P. (2012). *Open access*. Cambridge, MA: MIT Press. Retrieved November 5, 2015, from http://mitpress.mit.edu/books/open-access.

Wiley, D. (2010). The open future: Openness as a catalyst for an educational transformation. *EDUCAUSE Review, 45*(4), 14–20. Retrieved November 5, 2015, from http://net.educause.edu/ir/library/pdf/ERM1040.pdf.

Willinsky, J. (2005). The unacknowledged convergence of open source, open access and open science. *First Monday, 10*(8). Retrieved November 5, 2015, from http://firstmonday.org/article/view/1265/1185.

Resources

Anderson, P. (2009). Avoiding abandon-ware: getting to grips with the open development method. Briefing Notes. *OSS Watch*. Retrieved November 5, 2015, from http://oss-watch.ac.uk/resources/odm.

BOAI (2002). Read the Budapest Open Access Initiative. Retrieved November 5, 2015, from http://www.budapestopenaccessinitiative.org/read.

Bradley, J.-C., Owens, K., & Williams, A. (2008, January 9). Chemistry crowdsourcing and open notebook science. *Nature Precedings*. Retrieved November 5, 2015, from http://precedings.nature.com/documents/1505/version/1/files/npre20081505-1.pdf.

Bryant, J. R. (1995). Open systems. *International Journal of Bio-Medical Computing, 39*(1), 31–34.

Chesbrough, H. (2006). Open innovation: A new paradigm for understanding industrial innovation. In H. Chesbrough, W., Vanhaverbeke, & J. West, J. (Eds.), *Open innovation: Researching a new paradigm* (pp. 1–12). Oxford: Oxford University Press.

Dougiamas, M. & Taylor, P. (2003). Moodle: Using learning communities to create an open source course management system. In D. Lassner & C. McNaught (Eds.), *Proceedings of EdMedia: World Conference on Educational Media and Technology 2003* (pp. 171–178). Waynesville, NC: Association for the Advancement of Computing in Education (AACE). Retrieved November 5, 2015, from http://www.editlib.org/p/13739/.

Ehlers, U. D. (2011). Extending the territory: From open educational resources to open educational practices. *Journal of Open, Flexible and Distance Learning, 15*(2), 1–10. Retrieved November 5, 2015, from http://journals.akoaotearoa.ac.nz/index.php/JOFDL/article/viewFile/64/46.

Jones, R., MacGillivray, M., Murray-Rust, P., Pitman, J., Sefton, P., O'Steen, B., & Waites, W. (2011). Open bibliography for science, technology, and medicine. *Journal of Chemoinformatics, 3*(October), 47. http://dx.doi.org/10.1186/1758-2946-3-47. Retrieved November 5, 2015, from http://www.ncbi.nlm.nih.gov/pmc/articles/PMC3206455/.

Keller, P., & Mossink, W. (2008). *Reuse of material in the context of education and research.* Utrecht: SURFDirect. Retrieved November 5, 2015, from http://learn.creativecommons.org/wp-content/uploads/2009/07/090706surfcc_reuse_materiaal_def.pdf.

Lyon, L. (2009). *Open science at web-scale: Optimising participation and predictive potential.* Consultative Report. Bristol: JISC. Retrieved November 5, 2015, from http://opus.bath.ac.uk/30056/.

OCW Consortium (n.d.). What is OpenCourseWare? OpenCourseWareConsortium. Retrieved November 5, 2015, from http://www.oeconsortium.org/faq/what-is-open-courseware/.

Royal Society (2012). *Science as an open enterprise.* London: The Royal Society. Retrieved November 5, 2015, from https://royalsociety.org/topics-policy/projects/science-public-enterprise/Report/.

Undheim, T. A., & Friedrich, J. (2008). The momentum of open standards: A pragmatic approach to software interoperability. *European Journal of ePractice, 5,* 1–13. Retrieved November 5, 2015, from https://joinup.ec.europa.eu/sites/default/files/ePractice-Journal-Volume-5.pdf.

UNESCO (2012). 2012 Paris OER declaration. *World Open Educational Resources (OER) Congress, Paris, June 20–22, 2012.* Paris: UNESCO. Retrieved November 5, 2015, from http://www.unesco.org/new/fileadmin/MULTIMEDIA/HQ/CI/CI/pdf/Events/English_Paris_OER_Declaration.pdf.

Ware, M. (2011). Peer review: Recent experience and future directions. *New Review of Information Networking, 16*(1), 23–53.

Weber S. (2004). *The success of open source*. Cambridge, MA: Harvard University Press.

Appendix

Table 1. Sample definitions of open concepts.

Concept	*Definition*	*Source*
Open access	"...free availability on the public internet, permitting any users to read, download, copy, distribute, print, search, or link to the full texts of these articles, crawl them for indexing, pass them as data to software, or use them for any other lawful purpose, without financial, legal, or technical barriers other than those inseparable from gaining access to the internet itself. The only constraint on reproduction and distribution, and the only role for copyright in this domain, should be to give authors control over the integrity of their work and the right to be properly acknowledged and cited."	BOAI (2002)
Open bibliography	"systematic efforts to create and maintain stores of Openly accessible, machine-readable bibliographic data"	Jones et al. (2011)
Open content	"...a collective name for creative work published under a non-restrictive licence that explicitly permits the work to be copied and – depending on the particular licence chosen – to also be adapted and distributed."	Keller & Mossink (2008, p. 13)
Open courseware (OCW)	"free and open digital publication of high quality college and university-level educational materials. ...organized as courses, and often include course planning materials and evaluation tools as well as thematic content. ...openly licensed, accessible to anyone, anytime via the internet."	OCW Consortium [n.d.]
Open data	"Data that meets the criteria of intelligent openness. Data must be accessible, usable, assessable and intelligible."	Royal Society (2012, p. 12)
Open development	"the community-led development model found within many successful free and open source software projects."	Anderson (2009)
Open educational practices (OEP)	"...collaborative practice in which resources are shared by making them openly available, and pedagogical practices are employed which rely on social interaction, knowledge creation, peer-learning, and shared learning practices."	Ehlers (2011, p. 6)
Open educational resources (OER)	"...teaching, learning and research materials in any medium, digital or otherwise, that reside in the public domain or have been released under an open license that permits no-cost access, use, adaptation and redistribution by others with no or limited restrictions."	UNESCO (2012, p. 1)
Open innovation (OI)	"the use of purposive inflows and outflows of knowledge to accelerate internal innovation, and expand the markets for external use of innovation, respectively. ...assumes that firms can and should use external ideas as well as internal ideas, and internal and external paths to market"	Chesbrough (2006, p. 1)
Open literature review	"...uses a social networking space to aggregate and collectively discuss an evolving body of literature around a set of core research questions."	Conole & Alevizou (2010, p. 6)
Open notebook science	"a form of Open Science where the laboratory notebook is made public in as close to real time as possible"	Bradley, Owens, & Williams (2008)
Open peer review	"the opposite of double blind, in which authors' and reviewers' identities are both known to each other (and sometimes publicly disclosed), but... also used to describe other approaches, such as where the reviewers remain anonymous but their reports are published."	Ware (2011, p. 25)
Open science	"making methodologies, data and results available on the Internet, through transparent working practices"	Lyon (2009, p. 6)
Open source	"...the practice that gives free access in production and development to the source material for an end product; in most cases, one is dealing with software."	Keller & Mossink (2008, p. 9)
Open source software	"The essence of open source is not the software. It is the *process* by which software is created. Think of the software itself as an artifact of the production process. And artifacts are often not the appropriate focus of a broader explanation."	Weber (2004, p. 56)
Open standards	"Open standards are developed in a transparent and collaborative process, are available for free or at a nominal cost and can be implemented royalty free – in particular regarding software interoperability standards – or at reasonable cost."	Undheim & Friedrich, (2008, p. 2)
Open systems	"...conform to internationally agreed standards defining computing environments that allow users to develop, run and interconnect applications and the hardware they run on, from whatever source, without significant conversion costs"	Bryant (1995, p. 32)

Table 2. A typology of open.

Open Type	Open Domain
Open Content	Open access to research publications (OA)
	Open data
	Open educational resources, including open courseware and open textbooks
	Open bibliography/metadata
	Open source software
Open Process	Open development
	Open educational practices
	Open peer review
	Open research, including open literature review and open notebook science
	Open innovation
Open Infrastructure	Open standards
	Open systems

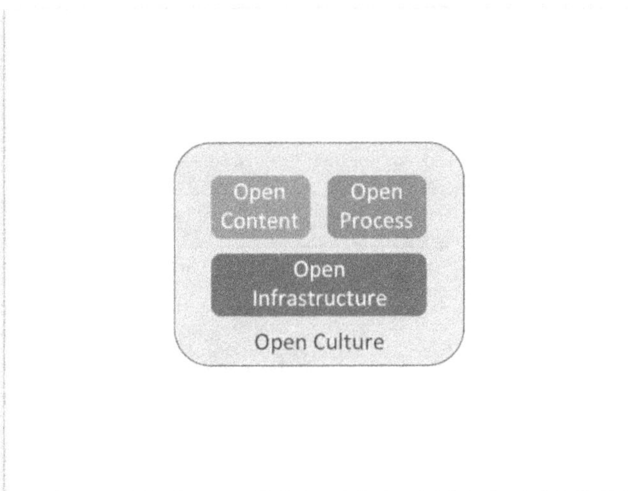

Figure 1. High-level open typology.

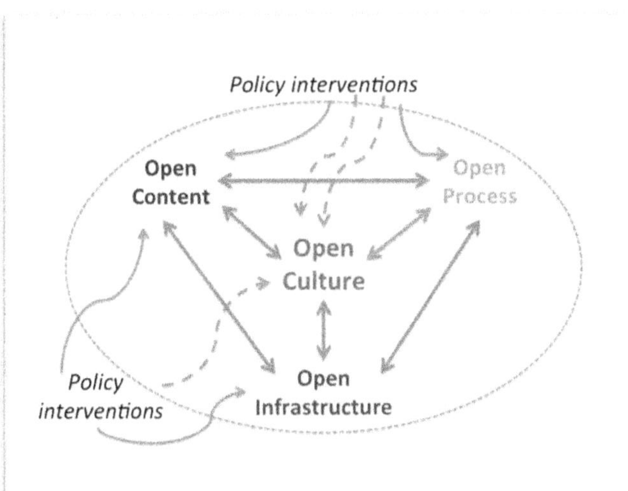

Figure 2. Evolving model of open.

Table 3. Potential roles in open domains.

Types	**Open Content**					**Open Process**				**Open Infrastructure**		
Domains	Open Access	Open Data	Open Educational Resources	Open Bibliography/ Metadata	Open Source Software	Open Development	Open Educational Practices	Open Peer Review	Open Science/ Research	Open Innovation	Open Standards	Open Systems
Roles												
Use												
Educate												
Advocate												
Facilitate												
Mediate												
Collaborate												
Coordinate												
Integrate												
Lead												

Open Access Funds: Getting a Bigger Bang for Our Bucks

Bobby Glushko, Head, Scholarly Communications and Copyright Office, University of Toronto Libraries

Crystal Hampson, Collection Services Librarian, University of Saskatchewan

Patricia Moore, Systems Librarian—Digital Projects and Technologies, Carleton University

Elizabeth Yates, Head Liaison Services (Acting)/Scholarly Communications Librarian, Brock University

Abstract

Many libraries offer open access publishing funds to support authors in paying article processing charges (APC) levied by some OA journals. However, there are few standard practices for managing or assessing these funds. The Open Access Working Group (OAWG) of the Canadian Association of Research Libraries (CARL) was asked to investigate and articulate best practices for successful open access fund management. In spring 2015, the OAWG surveyed Canadian academic libraries with OA funds to review their criteria and collect feedback on current practices. The survey proved timely because many OA funds are under review. Shrinking budgets, ending pilots, and questions around scale and sustainability of funds provide context for some institutions revisiting or reconfiguring these funds. At the same time, Canada's principal funding agencies have issued the new *Tri-Agency Open Access Policy on Publications* (effective May 2015) which mandates open access for funded research and which is increasing the demand from researchers for financial support from their institutions to pay APCs and other OA costs. This paper addresses findings of the survey, some best practices for open access publishing fund management, and counter arguments for OA funds, as well as other strategies developed by international agencies including the Scholarly Publishing and Academic Resources Coalition (SPARC).

Introduction

Worldwide focus on open access to scholarship has grown tremendously over the past decade. Three key contributors to this increased focus on open access (OA) are: shifts in technology to facilitate robust sharing of research, cultural shifts in academe toward more open discourse, and the increasing requirement of funders and funding agencies that research outputs to be made openly available.

A significant number of universities have demonstrated their support for open scholarship by offering funds to support authors who choose to publish in open access journals. These funds are used to pay for article processing charges (APCs) in open access journals or institutional membership fees charged by open access publishers such as PLoS, BioMed Central, or Hindawi.

SPARC, the Scholarly Publishing and Academic Resources Coalition, defines an open access fund as:

> A pool of money set aside by an institution to support publication models that enable free, immediate, online distribution of, and access to, scholarly research. (SPARC, 2014a)

There are 49 institutions in the US (SPARC, 2014c), and 14 institutions in Canada (Yates, 2014) offering campus author funds. These numbers have grown along with the increase in open access funder mandates. While the Canadian government has been slower than other countries in adopting open access mandates, the principal national funding agencies (Natural Sciences and Engineering Research Council of Canada, NSERC; Social Sciences and Humanities Research Council of Canada, SSHRC; and Canadian Institutes of Health research, CIHR) have recently implemented a joint *Tri-Agency Open Access Policy on*

http://dx.doi.org/10.5703/1288284316320

Publications for all research funded after May 2015 (Government of Canada, 2015). The policy may provide impetus for Canadian institutions to increase financial and operational support for open access.

Libraries are often the initiators and managers of open access support initiatives, endeavours which align with the library's overall mission of enabling access to scholarship, and are part of providing concrete support for transformative change within an unsustainable scholarly publishing system (SPARC, 2014b).

The Study: Current Practices for Open Access Funds in Canada

A review of the criteria used by North American libraries and institutions which administer open access funds reveals wide variation in who and what is eligible for these grants (SPARC, 2014a). There is also a lack of common standards for fund management issues such as workflow, budgeting, and accountability.

To assist libraries in maximizing the return on their investment in these funds, the CARL Open Access Working Group established a subcommittee to investigate open access funds in Canada and offer suggestions for best practices for fund management. While this work focused on open access funds at Canadian libraries, the results could also be valuable for institutions in the US and other locations which manage similar funds. To gather evidence for this project, a web-based survey was circulated to the 14 Canadian institutions known to have open access publishing funds, all of whom are CARL members. All 14 institutions answered the survey, which was administered in March and April 2015.

Fund Size & Scope

Most of the 14 open access funds in Canada have been established within the last three years, although some are much older; for example, the University of Calgary has had a fund since 2008. Monetary support ranges from $10,000 for the smallest—at Brock University in St. Catharines, ON—and exceeds $250,000 at larger universities in Ottawa and Calgary. The mode amount is $50,000.

Fund Criteria

Who is eligible for funding?

Best practice: Ensure that eligibility criteria for applicants are transparent and fair, and can be adjusted as needed. Several common themes emerge when examining who and what works are eligible for financial support from these funds. In most universities, faculty members, librarians, staff, graduate students, and postgraduate students were eligible to apply for the OA funds. In some cases, undergraduate students, visiting scholars, part-time and sessional faculty, and researchers affiliated with research institutes could use these funds. In most cases, funding is offered on a first-come, first-served basis. Other common criteria include the following: authors must use any grant funding before applying; first-time applicants only; one application per person per fiscal year; and applicant must be their paper's first author. Adopting broad, inclusive eligibility criteria will increase support for OA across different levels of an institution. Retaining flexibility to adjust eligibility can also be useful, as libraries may not initially realize which populations are interested in OA publishing. Meanwhile, restricting applicants to current members of the institution's community ensures appropriate use of scarce resources.

What is eligible for funding?

Best practice: Develop uniform eligibility criteria. The most common criterion is that funded works must be fully gold OA. It is unusual for author funds to cover hybrid publications. Other common criteria include the following: only OA fees covered, not reprints, colour illustrations, etc.; fee schedule is public; fee waiver for financial hardship; authors must acknowledge OA funding support in their final published paper; and funded article must be deposited in institutional repository. While most OA funds specify that journals must be "fully open access," there is room for confusion about that definition. Many funds use inclusion in the Directory of Open Access Journals (DOAJ) as a criterion for eligibility, which serves as an important measure of quality control and objectivity when adjudicating applications. The Code of Conduct developed by the Open Access Scholarly Publishers' Association

(OASPA) presents another set of useful quality control standards. Key concepts from the Code of Conduct can be utilized as criteria regarding openness and legitimate business practices of eligible publishers. However, given that OASPA membership fees are quite high, the inclusion of actual membership as an eligibility criterion may exclude many smaller OA journals.

Copyright Issues

Best practice: Clarify rights of authors and users. Most institutions surveyed, which require fund recipients to ensure their work carries minimal restrictions on reuse and state that content must be made publicly accessible immediately, had no embargo periods. Two institutions specify that authors must retain rights to their material. Several institutions surveyed require that funded materials be published with Creative Commons licensing, which permits greater reuse of content. A wide range of licenses are used. Libraries can more fully support open scholarship and authors' rights by recommending that funded authors retain full rights to their work and by specifying that funded materials be freely and immediately available to all users. Recommending the least restrictive Creative Commons licensing option—CC-BY—and excluding embargoed materials from funding are two key strategies for promoting the rights of both authors and readers.

Deposit in a Repository

Best practice: Facilitate automatic deposit in a repository. Deposit of funded materials in an institutional repository is mandated by nine institutions. However, compliance may be a challenge. Requiring grant recipients to archive funded work in an institutional repository—if available—further enhances dissemination of their research and strengthens ties their ties to the library, which is usually the entity managing an institutional repository. While a fund's criteria may require deposit, compliance is problematic; developing automatic deposit workflows will enhance compliance and lessen need to "chase" authors.

Workflow and Fund Management

Best practice: Monitor time spent on managing OA funds; provide clear, openly accessible fund documentation. At most Canadian universities, money for OA funds comes from library collections budgets. In some cases, funding also comes from outside the library from entities including research offices and academic faculties. Since the fund was a part of the library budget, fund administration and reporting were under the purview of the libraries. Some libraries shared responsibility for fund management with other campus units including research offices. There are no standard approaches to managing OA funds. Workflows vary widely across institutions and incorporate different units in and outside of the library. Because library staff have expertise in working with publishers and invoices, managing OA funds has seemed like a natural fit. However, tracking the time spent on this work will allow libraries to more clearly evaluate the staffing costs involved. It may also be useful for libraries—particularly those with small staff complements—to "outsource" some fund management responsibilities to university finance departments if possible.

OA funds are complex for both users and staff who manage the processes. Creating clear, easily accessible supporting documentation will make it easier for authors to successfully navigate the application process and reduce time spent by library staff adjudicating applicants. As well, libraries—most of which currently face significant financial pressures—must pursue transparency in reporting how their valuable resources are used to support researchers paying APCs.

Fund Assessment

Best practice: Track quantitative and qualitative measures over time and report statistics among institutions. Fund administrators were seeking recommendations from the project group (the study) on best practices for fund assessment. SPARC's *Open Access Funds in Action* (2014c) provides some basic measures of fund activity. Additional measures were identified by survey respondents or by the project group members (Table 1). These measures allow fund administrators to demonstrate equity of distribution among authors and departments. Distribution per publisher and per journal is also included, to inform management of choice of memberships and to inform future publisher negotiations, particularly if an institution supports articles in hybrid journals.

Table 1. SPARC and additional recommended assessment measures.

SPARC	Additional Useful Measures
$ value of fund	$ amount expended
# articles approved	# applications received # applications rejected and reason for rejection
# payments reimbursed	
# unique submitting authors	# unique successful authors $ per author
# unique departments	$ and # per department
# unique publishers	$ and # per publisher
# unique journals	$ per journal

Tracking quantitative measures over time allows institutions to assess changes in demand, identify trends, and understand the effect of changes to criteria and to funding. Furthermore, the use of common assessment measures, reported to a central body, allows for comparison between institutions, benchmarking, and aggregate reporting; for example, at a national, international, or consortial level.

Qualitative measures gathered from fund recipients will also be necessary to measure the success of the OA fund against its stated purpose. Currently, such measures are generally not being gathered. For funds existing as a service to authors, questions about the quality of the service are needed, such as: timeliness, responsiveness, clarity of criteria, ease of use, and whether the receiving money from the fund made a difference in whether or not the article was published as gold OA. For funds that exist primarily to support OA publishing in general, questions would focus on whether the work would have been published as gold or green OA without the support of the fund and what type of embargo, if any, would have occurred. Tracking qualitative measures over time allows institutions to evaluate the success of service improvement initiatives and impact of the fund.

Fund Changes and Future Implications

Significant changes in the surrounding financial environment occurred in 2015. Institutions' funding in many cases was being reduced. Furthermore, the fall value of the Canadian dollar relative to the US dollar meant an approximately 30% loss in buying power between 2013 and 2015, a particular challenge since the majority of Canadian collections purchases are based on US dollars. Despite the serious financial challenges, nine of fourteen institutions retained their OA fund for the following fiscal year (2015–2016), and four hoped to increase their fund's amount. However, a closer look at the remaining five institutions raises some interesting questions regarding the future of OA funds and potential best practices.

Five OA funds made significant changes. The impetus for change in these cases was financial. Four institutions inactivated their funds, either temporarily or permanently. One of these instead supports a membership with an OA publisher and promotes self-archiving. One institution stopped paying APC micropayments and reduced and refocused their fund on other OA publishing support, including: memberships; other models such as OA e-book publishing initiatives; and models within existing consortial purchases; for example, tokens. One considers their fund temporarily suspended. One fund was closed. We will discuss the final case, the University of Toronto, in more detail.

Who on Campus Should Fund APCs?

Of the 14 funds in total, 10 were funded entirely by the library, nine from the library's collections budget. Two other funds were supported jointly by the library and other campus sources, and two more were funded entirely by other campus sources (the University's research office, either alone or with another source). Four funds that were inactivated were funded entirely by the library. For the jointly supported fund that was reduced in amount and reconfigured, the library's contribution was withdrawn and the fund was subsequently financially supported only by other campus sources.

While the number of funds involved are small, and the majority of institutions retained their funds, these cases raise the question of whether financial support for OA funds is more secure when it is funded by the university's research office or central administration, when such bodies demonstrate willingness to support them, compared to when it is funded just by the library. The answer may center on whether the research office's choice to be involved in the first place was already an indication of strong support from that body. Because this survey did not delve into this question, no conclusion can be drawn based on this study.

Toward Measuring Value for OA Fund Money Within the Collections Budget

A second question relates to how to measure the value for money of OA funds. When funded by the library's collection budget, as is often the case, are OA funds able to demonstrate value for money in a way that can compete with other collections purchases for funding? One or more thousand dollars for one article certainly sounds like a high cost, relatively speaking. What might be a fair way to measure this value?

For other collections content, cost per use is a common measure of comparative value. For gold OA, the cost is one time and the use is not only perpetual but global. Setting aside for a moment the complicating factor of openness on tracking usage, article level use metrics, cumulatively since publication and from the primary locations where the article is stored, could theoretically be factored against the publication's APC to develop a cost per use metric. At the moment, this information is available only on some platforms, and it would be time-consuming to compile it even where it is available. None of the institutions in the survey indicated they were using article-level metrics in this way. While this metric cannot be implemented currently and therefore was not recommended as a best practice at this time, further investigation into it will be valuable.

It is notable that, despite the serious financial context, approximately two-thirds of the institutions with OA funds chose to retain them. Also, three of the five fund-making changes opted for memberships and similar models and other forms of gold OA support. The commitment to gold OA still appears to be high among these institutions, though the choice of models may differ.

A Contrary view—Discontinuing an Open Access Fund—University of Toronto

OA authors' funds are often a popular and important step in advancing open access at Universities. However, after years of administering OA funds, it has become increasingly clear to some observers that authors' funds are often not the most effective use of limited library resources. At the University of Toronto the prime concerns were that OA funds were not scalable, detracted attention from our institutional repository, and were largely being distributed to commercial publishers. Additionally, the author's fund was difficult and cumbersome to maintain and administer, which had the potential to lead to a less than perfect client experience on the part of participating faculty.

History of the University of Toronto OA Fund

The University of Toronto Libraries (UTL) OA Fund Tri-Campus Scholarly Communication Group was designed to raise the profile of open access publishing and to demonstrate UTL support for authors who were early adopters of open access publishing venues.

In the fall and winter of 2011 the University of Toronto Libraries conducted an informal environmental scan to learn more about the policies and procedures of established North American funds with close attention paid to the Canadian exemplars. The Tri-Campus Scholarly Communication Group also considered SPARC's guiding document for "Campus-based Open-access Publishing Funds: A Practical Guide to Design and Implementation" (Tananbaum, 2010) as well as information gathered when UTL hosted international scholarly communication events. Development of policies, procedures, and assessment methods for the fund continued through the spring and summer of 2012, with the initial pilot phase—defined as the first tranche of funding of $55,000 from UT St. George, UT Mississauga, and UT Scarborough—ran from September 2012 to December 2013.

Toward the close of 2013, it became apparent that the remaining funds from the first round of funding would be insufficient to carry the fund through the remainder of the fiscal year. Rather than shutter the fund, which was the course of action originally suggested by the fund administrators, the Chief Librarian contributed an additional $15,000 in funds, which were intended to maintain the fund until the end of the 2013–2014 fiscal year.

Closing the Fund

In May 2015 the Scholarly Communications Committee at University of Toronto agreed to recommend to the UTL Executive that the fund be discontinued in its current form for three main reasons. First, the money spent on the OA fund did not scale at an institution the size of UT; second, the OA fund monies were largely distributed to commercial publishers; and third, the money spent on the author fund could be better spent on other open access efforts, such as support for TSpace, our institutional repository.

The issue of scale was particularly challenging. The University of Toronto employs over 13,000 faculty (Quick Facts, n.d.). The initial tranche of $55,000 in funding enabled us to fund around 35 articles. Funding one article per faculty member a year, at an average cost of $2,000 per article would mean spending 26 million dollars on fees. It's very difficult to advertise a fund that can, at best, serve less than one in 350 of the faculty. Also, because of information management issues, there were frequently cost overruns as applications were submitted after the OA fund had been depleted; UTL chose to fund applications that came in late to avoid a negative reaction from the faculty.

Second, numbers provided by the associate chief librarian for collections and materials management showed that 44% of the fund's fees were paid to commercial publishers, with Springer, Taylor and Francis, and Nature Publishing as the top three recipients. This finding was consistent with other research on open access authors' fees; a recent study for the Research Libraries of the United Kingdom (RLUK) found that four of the top five recipients of authors' fees (APCs) were commercial publishers. Elsevier, Wiley, Nature, and BioMed Central accounted for a vast majority of authors' fees and the money spent on those fees for 2013–2014 (Theo, 2014). This conclusion was strengthened by the following report from *Reed Elsevier: Goodbye to Berlin—The Fading Threat of Open Access (Upgrade to Market-Perform)* (Aspesi & Luong, 2014).

Third, it became clear that in order to assist the faculty in complying with the *Tri-Agency Open Access Policy on Publications* the library needed to focus on the institutional repository. The money spent on APCs could be spent on staffing mediated deposit into the repository, which was scalable at that level of funding and number of faculty. Given substantial faculty anxiety around the open access mandates, it was decided that using those funds on outreach and support for deposit would be a more efficient use of our limited resources.

Moving Forward at the University of Toronto

Moving forward, the University of Toronto Libraries are still committed to supporting open access in a variety of ways. First, the library will continue to provide services supporting use of our institutional repository; transferring funds from the OA authors' fund will enable the library to scale up those services. Second, the library will listen and be receptive to faculty needs around open access; listening to faculty will enable the library to better target limited time and money toward high-return activities. Third, UTL will investigate new methods for supporting open access, whether through publisher/library collaboration, outreach to provincial and federal governments, or engagement with scholars and scholarly societies.

Conclusion

Academic libraries and institutions need to respond to open access. OA author funds remain a common tool in a suite of services for encouraging and supporting open access. However, it is important to review and evaluate these funds and activities. The establishment of benchmarks, assessment, and a solid policy framework is needed to allow deliberation on the value and sustainability of those OA funds. Further, the development of shared and consistent good practices will make the OA funds more effective in meeting their intent. OA funds cannot and should not be the sole initiative on OA, but could be an important part of a larger strategy for addressing open scholarship and open access.

References

Aspesi, C., & Luong, H. (2014, September 24). *Reed Elsevier: Goodbye to Berlin—The fading threat of open access (upgrade to market-perform).* Retrieved from http://www.richardpoynder.co.uk/Aspesi.pdf.

Government of Canada. (2015). *Tri-Agency open access policy on publications.* Retrieved from http://www.science.gc.ca/default.asp?lang=En&n=F6765465-1

Quick facts. (n.d.). *University of Toronto.* Retrieved from https://www.utoronto.ca/about-u -of-t/quick-facts.

SPARC. (2014a). *Campus-based open-access publishing funds.* Retrieved from http://www.sparc.arl.org/resources/funds

SPARC. (2014b). *Funds introduction.* Retrieved from http://www.sparc.arl.org/resources/funds/intro

SPARC. (2014c). *Open access funds in action.* Retrieved from http://www.sparc.arl.org/sites/default/files/OA%20Funds%20in%20Action%20attachment%202014 %20%281%29.pdf

Tananbaum, G. (2010, February 1). Campus-based open-access publishing funds: A practical guide to design and implementation, *SPARC.* Retrieved October 26, 2015 from http://sparcopen.org/wp -content/uploads/2016/01/oafunds-v1.pdf.

Theo. (2014, June 17). Open access in the College of Medicine & Veterinary Medicine. Open scholarship. Retrieved from http://libraryblogs.is.ed.ac.uk/openscholarship/2014/06/

Yates, E. (2014). Library open access publishing funds [PowerPoint slides]. *LinkedIn.* Retrieved from http://www.slideshare.net/ElizabethYates/library-open-access-publishing-funds

The Changing Nature of OA Journals: Helping Scholars Identify the Good, the Bad, and the Political

Matthew C. Torrence, Associate Librarian, University of South Florida

Susan Ariew, University Librarian, University of South Florida

Abstract

When the Open Access (OA) movement began at the beginning of the 21st century, librarians and select scholars saw it as a way to level the playing field by disseminating scholarly work freely, by easing the financial burden placed on rising subscription costs, and by offering alternatives to the traditional publishing model. Predatory and opportunistic OA publishers were quick to arrive on the scene, however, leaving faculty and researchers scrambling for a new and updated vetting process for selecting their publication targets. Jeffrey Beall's blog and Beall's List, along with other important publication directories, have become an important part of the effort to provide oversight and information to scholars about OA publishers. This paper will discuss OA controversies and review sources and opinions on the transformation of academic publishing efforts in the context of OA issues. Recent trends in librarianship demonstrate the need to educate authors on how to comprehensively research journals before submitting manuscripts to them, how to avoid predatory OA publishers, and where scholarly communication is going in terms of oversight and reputability of OA journals. This paper will briefly summarize many of the possible roles of the librarian, as well as discuss and evaluate the impact of Beall's List on both the publishing world and librarianship.

Introduction

The three (3) sections below outline the major topics for this paper, which parallel the discussion held at the Charleston Conference on November 5th, 2015. In order to review and debate the issues related to open access (OA) and Beall's List, the authors divided the issues into following categories: The politics of OA in the lives of faculty and researchers, the politics of Beall's List and its use, and the pragmatic solutions and possible responses to deal with emerging issues in OA publishing.

Typically, the types of OA Journals are defined as follows:

- Hybrid—Subscription journals that are supposed to offer free access to some articles for which extra, usually very high, fees have been paid
- Green—Self-archiving: Option of an author self-archiving the manuscript version after a 12-month embargo period from publication
- Gold—Assigns costs to the authors with no charges for the library or readers
- Platinum—OA journals with no fees

See the (Open access Oxford (OAO) glossary, n.d.)

The last of these types, labeled "Platinum," is a bit more theoretical. While mentioned in the literature by a number of writers, this paper will define these types of OA materials as described by Beall in his work, "Scholarly publishing free for all" (2013b). In this paper, he groups these "Platinum" OA publishers as those that do not require any form of author processing charge (APC), or fees from the institution.

The Politics of Open Access (OA)

Noble causes often have unintended consequences, and the history of OA is rife with these occurrences. The rise of OA and OA politics initially appears to be a response to the ever-increasing and unsustainable pricing of traditional journal publishing models. OA proponents feel that corporations are greedy and that scholars are offering their work for free only to then have the

http://dx.doi.org/10.5703/1288284316321

libraries at their institutions pay outrageous prices for their work. Moreover, there certainly are a number of benefits the OA model offer to authors, including increased exposure and sharing of their work, and the speed of publication. The OA movement is focused on the free exchange of knowledge; one question to answer is "how can such a model be sustainable?" Currently, OA journals of all types are difficult to evaluate in terms of quality, especially without uniform or well-defined criteria. Without consistent criteria and tools, how can we effectively separate the wheat from the chaff?

With the OA movement and increasingly inexpensive methods of online publication and dissemination, there has been a rapid explosion of new OA titles. Many of these, however, often exhibit questionable characteristics. This new environment requires that our profession address in some way the qualities and standards for this increasingly popular form of publishing. A good number of vocal proponents in the OA movement are established and trusted scholars, but some have not addressed the problems and pitfalls of gold OA titles as they relate to promotion/tenure and their impact (Beall, 2013a). Groups and other entities, such as the Open Access Scholarly Publishers Association (OASPA), the Directory of Open Access Journal (DOAJ), and the Scholarly Publishing and Academic Resources Coalition (SPARC), have provided some information about OA and journal quality, but perhaps increased effort and attention by librarians can help to protect and educate our faculty even more about emerging OA journals and publisher misconduct. Academic librarians are well poised to offer more training and consultation. That being said, leadership in the library profession will be required to maximize the benefit of these efforts.

OA proponents have indicated that all outcomes of publically funded research should be free to the public. Is this a valid argument and are all public goods free? Not in all cases, as stated by Beall in his work "The open-access movement isn't really about open-access" (2013a). Jeffrey Beall, a librarian at the Auraria Library, University of Colorado, Denver, is someone that is both concerned with and motivated by the rise of unverified open access publishers. He argues that: "People who are not experts in a given field generally lack both the ability to understand the most complex research in the field and the ability to distinguish between authentic and bogus research in the discipline" (Beall, 2013a). Despite the many benefits of open access, some are questioning the value of technical articles and materials meant for a specialized discourse community being mandated as open to the public. Furthermore, the cost of open access for many authors in the sciences is also skyrocketing.

Academics and researchers are also increasing their scrutiny regarding the value provided by OA in the sciences and the evolution of the current model. In a recent work by Van Noorden, questions regarding costs are debated, along with estimates by the publishing community as to the cost of producing and publishing an article (often \$3,000–\$4,000) and its relationship to the new world of APCs (2013). In another piece, Wolpert portends the "inevitability of open-access." The article provides the telling quote, "The extent to which access to knowledge is constrained and controlled by publishers' business models is at the heart of the discontent researchers have for the current journal-publishing system" (Wolpert, 2013). While some clearly see the rise of OA as a natural or inevitable path, there is plenty of debate about the cost-effectiveness of both traditional and OA models. Cost and politics are, and will be, linked going forward.

Predatory OA Journals and the Politics of Beall's List

Despite the lofty goals of the open-access proponents, the movement itself has given rise to some unsavory practices by open-access publishers only interested in taking an author's money and copyright, and then quickly publishing articles. Many of the worst of these do not have transparency about author fees, preservation, or other practices that ensure an author's work will be shared and maintained by a reputable source. The work of Beall and others that contribute to the identification of these titles and publishers are centered on categorizing what traits and practices define a predatory journal. In 2015, he published his "Criteria for Determining Predatory Open-Access Publishers," which sets forth many of the characteristics of these types of titles and publishers (Beall). In creating his criteria that defines predatory publishers and the candidates for inclusion on Beall's List, his goal is to assist librarians and scholars in recognizing scholarly publishing scams and avoiding them, as well as to expose academic misconduct in scholarly communications (Butler, 2013). While these criteria have started the debate, and figures like Jeffrey Beall are playing a major role, there needs to be more clarity from the various organizations that publish and disseminate these open-access works.

One of Beall's arguments against gold OA has to do with the fact that "junk science" has been published in a few disreputable OA journals (anti-climate change articles, ones that support corporate misconduct, etc.). As more bogus research continues to be published in open-access venues, the public will access it more and many will accept it as valid research. This bogus research will poison discourse in many scientific fields and will create a public that is misinformed on many scientific issues" (Beall, 2013a). At present, OA proponents don't seem to wish to address this issue.

Due to his frequent and vocal opposition of APCs, critics claim that Beall's List is openly hostile to all APC models and virtually all types of OA journals (Berger & Cirasella, 2015).

In many cases, Beall asserts that the APC process is inherently exploitive because it undermines journal quality (2013a). If the publisher's goal is only to garner as many fees from authors as possible, then why not accept everything and publish as many articles as possible, with only bogus peer-review practices? Thus, the rise of the "megajournal" with no focus other than to serve as a pay-for-publish digital repository.

In the ideal model, authors would not be required to pay, which Beall (and others) term the "Platinum" model (2013b). Even if there are no fees charged by the publisher, or publishing body, there ultimately must be some outlay of time or money from the staff required for these efforts. Removing the fee(s), however, does reduce the appearance of a "payola" environment. One question librarians grapple with is whether the APC model is inherently a bad alternative to the traditional model that receives revenue from library and public subscriptions, which rely more on the good will of subscribers and the reputation of the publisher as being a quality source of information. Beall argues that the "author pays" model can appear to work well for certain disciplines and titles, but not in all cases (Beall, 2015b). Beall believes the potential for exploitation of authors and publishing staff is higher with OA, but not that all gold OA is exploitive. He asserts that ethics and quality are often sacrificed with the gold OA model, hence his desire for the "Platinum" model, devoid of APCs (Beall, 2013b). This is a lofty goal, but one that is difficult to meet without strong support of libraries and other institutions and organizations.

Beall's critics assert that OA publishers in developing countries are unfairly targeted (Butler, 2013). According to Shen & Björk's recent work, which relied heavily on Beall's List, most of the more recently identified predatory publishers are in these developing regions (27% from India and 75% from Africa and Asia) (2015). These fraudulent journals are worse than greedy corporations, as they have no commitment to preservation and archiving, stewardship, quality, or long-term reputation. The same study estimates that $74 million went to predatory OA journals in 2014. In addition, "predatory journals have rapidly increased their publication volumes from 53,000 in 2010 to an estimated 420,000 articles in 2014, published by around 8,000 active journals" (Shen & Bjork, 2015). Despite the reliance on Beall's List, what remains to be seen is whether OA advocates are willing to acknowledge Beall's work as legitimate and support it.

The Pragmatic

As stated earlier, the "author pays" (APC) model can appear to work well for certain disciplines and titles, but the costs (if not subsidized by grants or university funding) can be daunting. Solomon and Björk's study of APCs in OA and other journal publishing indicates that "seventy-one percent of journals with an ISI-impact factor charged more than $1,000 USD, whereas the corresponding figure was 15% for journals without an impact factor. The journals charging the highest APCs also have the highest impact factors (*Plos Biology* APC = $2,900, impact factor = 12.9; *NucleidAcids Research* APC = $2,770, impact factor = 7.4)" (2012). In the absence of Beall's List, something would immediately be needed to replace this tool, as librarians increase their efforts in guiding and training faculty in the selection of quality publication targets, based on price, quality, and other important characteristics.

Thus, unless an author has grant funding, he or she cannot afford the high-end APC titles, or publisher hybrid-type fees, for the high impact and established OA titles. One solution to the problem is demonstrated by Texas A&M's OAK Fund, which supports author fees and publishing venues for their faculty (Open Access to Knowledge (OAK) Fund, n.d.). These types of academic and other publishing-support bodies will increasingly rely on Beall's List and other similar sources of information going forward, and libraries continue took for new ways to support their faculty and fund new and hybrid OA models.

Publishing is often a profitable endeavor, however, in both traditional and (some) OA forms. As stated above, the traditional groups have started to adopt hybrid and new funding models. Some universities have found excellent ways of addressing high costs and APC fees by forming teams, or committees, to evaluate the titles and to pay the processing charges for qualified authors and publications. As Beall points out in another of his recent works, "to make up for the low author fees they charge (sometimes as low as $100–$200), [predatory publishers] increase the volume of papers they publish" (2015b). Beall's List provides something not otherwise offered by the library or publishing community and has a great deal of validity (Shen & Bjork, 2015). A vetted whitelist may be a better solution than Beall's blacklist, but whose job is it to create such a list? Additionally, librarians need to distinguish between new and emerging journals and markets from the true predatory titles, and some entity should take up this cause.

The role of librarians as advocates to support their faculty and graduate authors has the potential to be vital to their efforts to achieve publication, promotion, and tenure. If Beall's List disappeared tomorrow, how would the library community perform this duty and protect scholars? As librarians increase their efforts in guiding and training faculty in the selection of quality publication targets, they need to distinguish new and emerging journals and markets from the true predatory titles, and some entity should take up this cause. Librarians have a clear role to offer training, support, and other consultations on publishing options and must position themselves as experts regarding journal quality. As pointed out by Vardi in a recent editorial, it's not just OA journals that can be predatory; it can also be those in the commercial world (2012). As librarians shepherd students and faculty through the various publication processes and choices in both new and emerging OA and traditional publishing firms, there is an increasing need for vigilance.

Conclusions and Future Directions

At the moment, there is mostly silence in the professional library community about predatory journals that are generally destroying the reputation of open access, and there is silence about Beall's List in particular. Many librarians use Beall's List but do not promote it, and when one queries them about that question they say, "Well, I use the list but it shouldn't be just one guy that we rely on for this information." So, the question becomes who should step up to the plate to support Beall's efforts to address the issue of predatory OA journals and begin to solve the problem of publisher misconduct? It is clear that librarians can and should play a role. Digital repositories and academic library supported journal publications offer one solution related to creating OA titles. Another solution might be to increase instruction, consultation, and workshops on desirable publishing practices and options with faculty and graduate students. The University of South Florida Libraries, for example, offers active outreach to faculty (via LibGuides and other sources) to market journal selection and promotion/tenure readiness. This guide is available online at: http://guides.lib.usf.edu/promotion-tenure

Finally, OA advocates need to address the "elephant in the room," regarding predatory OA journals, the emergence of "junk science," and offer potential solutions, or they may risk losing credibility. Continued vigilance in the evaluation of all journal titles is even more important with the growth of OA and OA publishing; librarians, libraries, and research faculty are poised to play a role in defining and redefining standards to evaluate these publications.

References

Beall, J. (2013a). The open-access movement is not really about open access. TripleC: Communication, Capitalism & Critique. *Open Access Journal for a Global Sustainable Information Society, 11*(2), 589–597.

Beall, J. (2013b). Scholarly publishing free for all. *Scholarly Publishing, 16*(2).

Beall, J. (2015b). Predatory journals and the breakdown of research cultures. *Information Development, 31*(5), 473–476.

Berger, M., & Cirasella, J. (2015). Beyond Beall's list. *College & Research Libraries News, 76*(3), 132–135.

Butler, D. (2013). The dark side of publishing. *Nature, 495*(7442), 433–435.

Open Access Oxford (OAO) glossary. (n.d.) Retrieved from http://openaccess.ox.ac.uk/glossary/

Open Access to Knowledge (OAK) Fund. (n.d.) Retrieved from http://scholarlycommunication.library.tamu.edu/oak-fund/

Shen, C., & Bjork, B. C. (2015). "Predatory" open access: A longitudinal study of article volumes and market characteristics. *BMC Medicine, 13*, 230-015-0469-2. http://dx.doi.org/10.1186/s12916-015-0469-2

Solomon, D. J., & Björk, B. (2012). Publication fees in open access publishing: Sources of funding and factors influencing choice of journal. *Journal of the American Society for Information Science and Technology, 63*(1), 98–107.

Van Noorden, R. (2013). Open access: The true cost of science publishing. *Nature, 495*(7442), 426–429. http://dx/doi/org/10.1038/495426a

Vardi, M. Y. (2012). Predatory scholarly publishing. *Communications of the ACM, 55*(7), 5.

Wolpert, A. J. (2013). For the sake of inquiry and knowledge—The inevitability of open access. *New England Journal of Medicine, 368*(9), 785–787.

How Much Do Monographs Cost? And Why Should We Care?

Nancy L. Maron, President, BlueSky to BluePrint, LLC

Charles Watkinson, AUL for Publishing, University of Michigan Library

Meredith Kahn, Women's Studies and Publishing Services Librarian, University of Michigan Library

Shayna Pekala, Scholarly Communication Librarian, Indiana University Libraries

Abstract

What does it cost to make a high quality, digital monograph? What may sound like an obvious question turns out to be a very knotty one, driving to the heart of the essence of scholarly publishing today. It is particularly relevant in an environment where the potential of a sustainable open access (OA) business model for monographs is being explored. Two complementary studies funded by The Andrew W. Mellon Foundation in 2015 have explored this question to understand the costs involved in creating and disseminating scholarly books.

The team at Ithaka S+R studied the full costs of publishing monographs by gathering cost data on a sample of 382 titles across 20 presses. This process involved working with directors, CFOs, and many operational staff to understand the way staff time and effort contribute to the publishing process. In parallel, a separate project at Michigan and Indiana used a top-down model to identify those costs related to monograph publishing at the University of Michigan Press and Indiana University Press. This cost study was part of a larger project in which focus groups and interviews were conducted with faculty and administrators to explore institutional openness to a flipped business model where the costs of producing a monograph would be borne by the author's parent institution.[1]

The data from these two projects will help to understand how an OA monograph model could work. The studies also get at issues critical to the future of scholarly publishing: Which activities are critical to the creation of scholarly books? When does authoring end and publishing begin? How great a role do publishers play in not just producing a book, but in asserting its place in the scholarship and in current debates? A flipped model of funding monographs has major implications for publishers, libraries, and faculty, so a deep understanding of such questions is essential for the long-term health of the scholarly communication ecosystem, especially in the humanities and social sciences.

Once upon a time, in a galaxy far, far away, there was a monograph. A scholar would write a manuscript, identify what she considered to be the best presses publishing works in her field, and submit the work for review to the press. Once the manuscript was accepted, the publishing house would arrange to have the work distributed and sold to libraries, bookstores, and even through direct mail, to people who wanted to read it.

While vestiges remain, that fairy tale world is gone, transformed by new realities:

- **Sales are down**. Publishers routinely report a drop in monograph sales; from the low thousands a decade ago to today's couple of hundred lifetime units. This is unacceptable for many reasons. Publishers are still investing the same sort of effort to create the books that used to

[1] The full study is reported in James Hilton, Carolyn Walters, Paul Courant, Sidonie Smith, Meredith Kahn, Charles Watkinson, . . . Nick Fitzgerald. (2015, Sept 15). A study of direct author subvention for publishing humanities books at two universities: A report to the Andrew W. Mellon Foundation by Indiana University & University of Michigan. Retrieved from http://hdl.handle.net/2027.42/113671

http://dx.doi.org/10.5703/1288284316322

sell 10 times more units. And the raw number of units per title in the marketplace is so low that it suggests an extremely limited potential for impact.

- **Federal mandates are up.** In the past couple of years governments not only in North America but also internationally have asserted the right of taxpayers to have access to the fruits of publicly funded research. The largest funders now make OA a requirement. While this started with the major science and medical funders, even the smaller and humanities focused funders have voiced support for such mandates, and humanities research outputs risk being marginalized if they are not included in this new environment.
- **Some evidence shows OA can work as a business**. While driven by STEM journal publishing (where grants are larger and the need for more and more current content promotes publishing innovation) successful commercial initiatives such as PLoS illustrate how OA models funded by author-side payments can work. This has prompted the question: Could it work for OA monographs as well? Could this be a path both to greater access for the work, and to a more sustainable business model for publishers of monographs?

Some important proposals have been made for funding the production of OA monographs through institutional subventions, most notably the shared proposal of the Association of American Universities and Association of Research Libraries published in spring 2014.[2] Should an OA model for monographs be put into motion on a large scale, it will certainly have wide-ranging impact, not just on publishers, but also on faculty authors, libraries, and university and college administrators.

The Ithaka S+R study that is the central focus of this paper is entitled "Costs of Publishing Monographs: Toward a Transparent Model." The title is meant to underline the notion that (1) there are many elements that comprise monograph costs; and (2) that determining which costs to include in a future business model will be the important and creative next step that lies ahead for funders, publishers, and administrators.

This study started in January 2015 and concluded with publication of the final report in December 2015. It began as a planning grant in 2014, with close support from the Association of American University Presses (AAUP) and several press directors. For the full study, Ithaka S+R worked very closely with an advisory group that included press directors and CFOs of university presses of all sizes, as well as with the AAUP. Kimberly Schmelzinger, previously CFO of Northwestern University Press and now a financial consultant to AAUP, was a key investigator on the project.

While the temptation is to look for a "bottom line" answer to the question "what does a monograph cost" and thus "how much it would cost to subsidize the cost of producing monographs, in a way that alleviates the need for publishers to recoup full costs via sales," some almost philosophical questions need to be addressed first. For example: What should we include in the idea of the "cost?" Do we focus on just the activities needed to produce and distribute the book, or the other costs—the overheads—associated with the people and the press who actually do the work?

The issues are best demonstrated by sharing some data, in this case from University of Michigan Press (see Figure 1). The final report shares data from 20 presses, presented in aggregated form, for each of the 4 AAUP press size categories and Michigan is not necessarily typical. But the data is accessible and shareable and helps demonstrate the issues.

The study gathered costs in several ways. We looked at staff time, by actually asking staffers in five key functional areas of the press—

[2] Raym Crow. (June 2014). AAU/ARL prospectus for an institutionally funded first-book subvention. http://www.arl.org/storage/documents/publications/aau-arl-prospectus-for-institutionally-funded-first-book-subvention-june2014.pdf

acquisitions, manuscript editorial, design, production, and marketing—how they spent their time? How much time on monographs versus other types of publishing? How much time, particularly if you acquire books, on titles that don't actually get published? We then added the direct costs in the same five core areas. Direct costs represent activities the press must pay for "out of pocket" such as using freelancers to copyedit the works, or paying for art for a jacket cover. Finally we added indirect costs, not directly applicable to any one title.

Our final cost model is therefore actually three models: a snapshot of how the cost per book (in this case, we are looking at the average of the 20 titles Michigan used in the study) showing how layers of cost accrete. The **Basic Cost** includes just those costs directly incurred when producing the book. Some have referred to this as the "incremental" cost of a press adding "one more book" to its existing publishing operation. Here, our definition includes staff time and staff overhead, from those who work in the core publishing departments of acquisitions, manuscript editorial, design, production, and marketing. It also includes what we are referring to as direct or "out-of-pocket" expenses which can be captured by title. (For the purposes of this study, this does not include departmental overheads, where publishers were not able to break out costs at the title level.) The Full Cost represents the Basic Cost, plus the press and departmental overheads. Full Cost Plus represents not only the overhead costs included above, but even adds in in-kind contributions, the reported value of resources contributed to the project, but not paid for. These generally included contributed staff time, author-paid fees, and office space.

Among the broad findings from the complete study of 20 presses are that staff costs are the greatest expense overall, and of staff time, acquisitions claims the greatest share. The relative balance of staff versus direct costs is very similar across all sizes of presses in the study. While some factors tend to drive cost (number of illustrations, in particular), there was no significant relationship between cost and, for example, whether the press was at a public or private institution; whether the press pays rent (or enjoys this as a contribution from the university). There may well be some tied to discipline, but those tended to be linked again to the presence of heavily illustrated texts, in art history or archaeology, for example.

Conducted primarily between January and September 2015, "A Study of Direct Author Subvention for Publishing Humanities Books at Two Universities" examined the implications of moving to an institutionally funded model for monographs in the humanities and social sciences for Indiana University and the University of Michigan, two research-intensive public universities. The major focus was on building a picture through interviews with faculty and administrators of the potential implications of a flipped monograph publishing model, funded by the authors' parent institutions, on the scholarly communications environment. While

<table>
<tr><th>Cost type</th><th>Category</th><th>Average cost per title</th><th></th><th>BASIC</th><th>FULL COST</th><th>FULL COST PLUS</th></tr>
<tr><td rowspan="5">Staff time</td><td>Acquisitions Activities</td><td>$5,891</td><td rowspan="5">$15,565</td><td rowspan="11">$23,391</td><td rowspan="12">$26,022</td><td rowspan="14">$28,637</td></tr>
<tr><td>Manuscript Editorial Activities</td><td>$2,250</td></tr>
<tr><td>Production Activities</td><td>$764</td></tr>
<tr><td>Design Activities</td><td>$2,561</td></tr>
<tr><td>Marketing Activities</td><td>$4,098</td></tr>
<tr><td rowspan="5">Direct costs</td><td>Acquisitions</td><td>$400</td><td rowspan="5">$3,132</td></tr>
<tr><td>Manuscript Editorial</td><td>$1,130</td></tr>
<tr><td>Production</td><td>$83</td></tr>
<tr><td>Design</td><td>$1,417</td></tr>
<tr><td>Marketing</td><td>$102</td></tr>
<tr><td>Staff OH</td><td>Staff Time, overhead</td><td>$4,694</td><td>$4,694</td></tr>
<tr><td>G+A</td><td>General and Administrative</td><td>$2,631</td><td>$2,631</td><td></td></tr>
<tr><td rowspan="2">In-kind</td><td>Press & Department level</td><td>$1,523</td><td rowspan="2">$2,614</td><td rowspan="2"></td><td rowspan="2"></td></tr>
<tr><td>Title-level</td><td>$1,091</td></tr>
</table>

Figure 1. University of Michigan Press: Average cost per title.

understanding the cost of monograph production was in this case a subsidiary part of the enterprise and conducted through a less intense study than that conducted by Ithaka S+R, it is encouraging that the average monograph costs reported in Appendix E of the final report was comparable (around $27,000 at both Indiana University Press and University of Michigan Press).

Implications For Stakeholders

As noted in the introduction to this paper, a clear understanding of monograph cost is beneficial for a number of stakeholders, especially in the context of a potential move to a flipped model of funding. In this final section we explore some implications for publishers, libraries, and faculty members.

For Publishers

As university presses move toward new business models (such as "gold" open access), new tools will be needed to assess performance and success beyond sales figures. These new tools could have relevance for "administrators" broadly defined—both within and beyond individual presses—including press directors, campus-level administration charged with overseeing presses, and leadership in the university press community.

The methodology developed by the Ithaka S+R team could be adapted and used by individual presses to create internal tools for tracking and assessing costs, as it provides a straightforward method of describing both direct and indirect costs. With this methodology, presses could take a deep dive into their own lists, and potentially discover new insights about how they expend resources, how those resources translate into published works, and how the performance of those works (via sales, usage metrics, downloads, etc.) compares to their cost of production. The study particularly focuses attention on the large percentages of total expense generated by the acquisitions and marketing functions. This challenges presses to better articulate the undoubted "value add" of those two activities (and make sure that they are optimized).

Presses could also achieve a greater understanding of how the work that goes into titles which are never published (because they do not make it through peer review, are rejected by editorial boards, or are unsuccessful for some other reason) impacts the balance sheet. Perhaps there is also an opportunity for the Association of American University Presses (AAUP) to develop benchmarking tools using this methodology, which could allow presses to compare their performance to that of peer presses beyond just a reliance on sales figures and number of titles produced.

Should proposals for an institutional subvention system progress, publishers will also need to be able to transparently articulate the bases for their monograph cost estimates. These will need to be expressed in a form that institutions find acceptable, and will undoubtedly be subject to some of the same sorts of scrutiny universities already apply to other vendor invoices. As described above, the Ithaka S+R report not only provides a framework for analyzing and expressing costs, but it also provides a sense of the inner and outer bounds of "reasonable" charges.

For Faculty and Administrators

The free-rider problem in university press publishing is commonly understood as the uneven distribution of university presses across the system of higher education. While nearly all faculty in the humanities and humanistic social sciences must publish a monograph to receive tenure, a very small number of universities house presses. The home institution of the university press (not the home institution of the author) bears the cost and risk of publishing those monographs, and university presses don't typically draw their author pool from their home institution. This means that institutions where presses live are shouldering a disproportionate burden in the current system of scholarly communication. As a result, provosts, presidents, regents, and other high-level administrators have begun to ask pointed questions about financial commitments to the university presses who aren't primarily serving the needs of their respective campuses. In the long term, if universities, consortial groups, or others within the academy hope to pursue interventions to address the free-rider problem, understanding and describing the costs associated with university press publishing will be essential.

A stronger understanding of the costs involved in university press publishing for monographs could at first seem to exacerbate these administrators' concerns, as putting a number to these financial commitments might seem to endanger the line item a press represents. However, we believe that greater transparency about the costs of monographs could help administrators on both sides of the free-rider equation understand the value that university presses provide. During interviews at Indiana and Michigan, faculty and administrators consistently identified the editorial (ensuring high-quality work) and certification (reliant on a press's reputation and imprimatur) functions of academic publishing as the most important role that monographs (and the presses who publish them) perform. If administrators begin to understand what it costs to perform these functions, press directors might have stronger footing in conversations around resource allocation.

For Libraries

Under an institutionally funded model, libraries have the opportunity to become more deeply involved in the scholarly monograph publishing enterprise. A major area of library-based support could be in the long-term storage and preservation of the digital objects produced by university presses, likely in the context of an institutional or other digital repository. In addition to providing storage space, libraries could consult with university presses on the creation and management of metadata to maximize access to the resulting digital objects.

Libraries could also contribute to the innovation of scholarly objects. The capacity to support long-form scholarship that goes beyond the PDF and maximizes the unique capabilities of digital technologies will be increasingly desired by faculty authors. Meanwhile, there exists a tradition of technological experimentation within libraries, who have long contributed to the development of tools and platforms that facilitate new forms of scholarship. Libraries could engage in these activities alongside university presses in an effort to expand the definition and capabilities of the scholarly monograph.

If libraries serve as the official digital repository for university press monographs, libraries would need to revise their approaches to collection development. While the overall costs to purchase monographs would decrease (assuming the wide adoption of an institutionally funded model), digital storage and curation costs would increase. This market shift would require libraries to rethink their collection development budgets and strategies.

Finally, the role of libraries in education and outreach related to scholarly communications would become more critical with the adoption of subvention programs. Faculty authors will require a baseline understanding of the scholarly publishing landscape, open access, author's rights, and other relevant topics in order to participate. As experts in these areas, librarians could take an increasingly active role in discussing these issues with faculty and other constituents.

Google Books: It Ain't Over 'Til the Librarian Sings

Bill Hannay, Partner, Schiff Hardin LLP (Chicago); Adjunct Professor, Chicago-Kent College of Law at the Illinois Institute of Technology[1]

Abstract

On October 16, 2015, the US Court of Appeals for the Second Circuit handed down its opinion dismissing the Authors Guild's copyright case against Google Inc.[2] What does it all mean for librarians?

History of the Google Books Case

Let's make a quick trip through the history of this long-running litigation. It all began in 2004 when Google announced the initiation of its Google Print project and its Library Project (now generally called Google Books). A few months later in 2005, the Authors Guild, several individual authors, and various publishers filed a lawsuit in New York City against Google, seeking to enjoin the project from going forward.

As litigation sometimes does, the proceedings began to drag out as the parties filed various motions with the court and engaged in preliminary investigations (known as "discovery"). The parties also began negotiations over a possible settlement in 2006. After extended discussions, the parties filed a proposed settlement agreement on October 28, 2008. Notice of the proposed settlement was widely circulated and produced hundreds of objections. The parties then modified the proposal and, on November 13, 2009, filed a proposed amended settlement agreement with the trial court.

After notice of the amended settlement was circulated in early 2010, another flood of objections was filed, including one from the US Department of Justice which alleged that, if the proposed settlement was adopted, substantial anticompetitive effects would result. On March 22, 2011, US District Judge Chin rejected the amended settlement as not "fair, adequate, and reasonable."

The parties went back to the drawing board but were unable to reach a settlement that was likely to pass muster with the court. So the case resumed its litigation posture, and on May 31, 2012, Judge Chin certified a class of plaintiff-authors and allowed them to proceed to trial.[3] But a little over a year later, the US Court of Appeals for the Second Circuit vacated the class certification and ordered Judge Chin to consider whether or not Google had a legitimate "fair use" defense. He did so, and on November 14, 2013, Judge Chin granted summary judgment to Google on its fair use defense.

The Authors Guild filed an appeal which, almost two years later in October 2015, resulted in affirmance of the District Court's judgment.

Where Are We Now That the Case Is Over?

Is it actually over? Plaintiffs could possibly file a petition for a writ of certiorari with the US Supreme Court, but the likelihood of the Court accepting the case for review—and actually reversing it—seems low.

But the truth of the matter is that, assuming the case is over, the legal result of the case is both extremely sweeping and at the same time

---

[1] Mr. Hannay is is a regular speaker at the Charleston Conference and a contributor to *Against the Grain*.
[2] The Authors Guild et al. v. Google, Inc., 804 F.3d 202 (2d Cir. 2015).
[3] On October 4, 2012, the Association of American Publishers (AAP) and Google announced that they had settled the publishers' part of the Google Books litigation. See http://www.publishers.org/press85/. The settlement provides access to publishers' in-copyright books and journals digitized by Google for its Google Library Project. Other terms—including monetary payments, if any—were not disclosed.

http://dx.doi.org/10.5703/1288284316323

extremely narrow. While millions of individual books have been copied and made part of the Google Books project, all that the Second Circuit has approved are the narrow word search and "snippet" features of the project. The court's opinion is limited to this specific conduct, and there is no court authorization for Google to do anything more than that.

On a book-by-book basis, therefore, very little of the works are actually made available to users of the system.

A Reminder of What Google *Is* doing

Google has made digital copies of millions of books that were submitted to it for that purpose by major libraries. Over 20 million have been scanned since 2004 (at an average cost of $10 per book). In turn, Google has established a publicly available search function for the digital copies.

Specifically, an internet user can use this function to search—without charge or advertising—to determine whether the book contains a specified word or term. The result of the search is that the user can see "snippets" of text containing the searched-for terms.

In addition, participating libraries (i.e., those that have made their books available to Google for scanning) are given a limited right to download and retain digital copies of the books that they submitted.

Google's Search Function Is Quite Limited

The search function in Google Books is quite limited. Only the first usage of the searched-for term on a given page is displayed, for example. Overall, for each book containing the search term, a maximum of three "snippets" containing the term are displayed. (A snippet is a horizontal segment comprising ordinarily an eighth of a page highlighting the term.)

It appears that the Google Books system cannot be fooled into providing more quotations. In particular, a researcher cannot increase the number of snippets revealed on the system simply by repeating the entry of the same search term or by entering searches from different computers. Moreover, one snippet per page and one page out of ten containing the term are randomly "blacklisted" by Google and cannot be displayed. Furthermore, no snippet views of certain books such as dictionaries, cookbooks, and short poems are permitted.

The Second Circuit's Ruling

In analyzing fair use, the Court of Appeals applied the four-part statutory test contained in Section 107 of the Copyright Act of 1976. That Act provides that in determining whether a use is "fair," the factors to be considered must include—

(1) the purpose and character of the use, including whether such use is of a commercial nature or is for nonprofit educational purposes;

(2) the nature of the copyrighted work;

(3) the amount and substantiality of the portion used in relation to the copyrighted work as a whole; and

(4) the effect of the use upon the potential market for or value of the copyrighted work.

Focusing heavily on the first factor (i.e., the purpose and character of the use), the Court of Appeals upheld Google's making of a digital copy to provide a search function as fair use because it is "transformative." It augments public knowledge by making available information *about* authors' books. By contrast, Google does not provide the public with a substantial "substitute" for the substance of the matter protected by the authors' copyrights in the original works. The same is true, at least under present conditions, of Google's provision of the "snippet" function. The search tool permits a researcher to identify those books, out of millions, that do—as well as those that do not—use the terms selected by the researcher.

While Google is a for-profit entity, the court held that profit motivation does not in these circumstances justify denial of fair use. In any event, Google does not charge for the search and snippet functions. (Whether a court might view matters differently if Google were to attempt to monetize these services by charging for them is a question for another day.)

Legal Precedent: Campbell v. Acuff-Rose Music

The Second Circuit devoted considerable attention to interpreting the Supreme Court's 1994 decision on fair use in Campbell v. Acuff-Rose Music.[4] There, a music group called "2 Live Crew" recorded a parody of Roy Orbison's 1964 hit "Pretty Woman" without obtaining a license. The rights holder had sued and lost before the District Court, but won a reversal before the Court of Appeals for the Second Circuit. The appellate court held that the commercial nature of the parody rendered it presumptively unfair under Section 107. The Supreme Court disagreed, however, and reinstated the trial court's dismissal of the claim. The Court held that a commercial parody may be fair use if it is "transformative."

A Caveat Re: "Transformative"

Following the Supreme Court's reasoning in Campbell v. Acuff-Rose Music, the Second Circuit held that Google's use of the copied books was transformative. However, the court issued a strong caveat narrowing the reach of that defense. Speaking for the court, Judge Pierre Leval (who is considered something of an expert on copyright law) stated:

> The word "transformative" cannot be taken too literally as a sufficient key to understanding the elements of fair use. It is rather a suggestive symbol for a complex thought, and does not mean that any and all changes made to an author's original text will necessarily support a finding of fair use.

Derivative Works and "Transformations"

Last year, the Second Circuit had given narrow approval to libraries' pooling of the digital copies of their books provided to them by Google after scanning. Some 80 universities and libraries had submitted over ten million digitized books into the HathiTrust repository, which permits patrons to search for files for particular terms (but does not provide snippets). Patrons with print disabilities (such as blindness) are provided full-text access to the books.

In its 2014 HathiTrust decision,[5] the Second Circuit distinguished between "derivative works" (which are not entitled to a fair use defense) and "transformative works" (which may be). The court said that "[p]aradigmatic examples of derivative works include the translation of a novel into another language, the adaptation of a novel into a movie or play, or the recasting of a novel as an e-book or an audiobook." In Google Books, the court explained that, "[w]hile such changes can be described as transformations, they do not involve the kind of transformative purpose that favors a fair use finding."

The Key to Google Books Is the Limited Nature of Google's Use

The court perceived that the specialized use by Google of the copyrighted work distinguished it from unfair and improper uses. By asking solely whether the work contains a word of interest, Google's search function in effect treats the book as a mere compilation of data rather than exploiting its expressive content. The following quotes from HathiTrust and Google Books illustrate this perspective:

> [T]he result of a word search is different in purpose, character, expression, meaning, and message from the page (and the book) from which it is drawn. —HathiTrust

> [T]he purpose of Google's copying of the original copyrighted books is to make available significant information about those books. —Google Books

This transformation is made greater by the "snippet" function, in the court's view. "Snippet view adds important value to the basic transformative search function."

---

[4] 510 U.S. 569, 114 S. Ct. 1164, 127 L. Ed. 2d 500 (1994).

[5] Authors Guild v. HathiTrust, 755 F.3d 87, 95 (2d Cir. 2014).

> Merely knowing that a term of interest appears in a book does not necessarily tell the searcher whether she needs to obtain the book, because it does not reveal whether the term is discussed in a manner or context falling within the scope of the searcher's interest.

For Transformation, Google Needed to Copy the Whole Book

In order to achieve these transformative search functions, Google needed to copy the whole book. But importantly, though Google in effect makes an unauthorized digital copy of the entire book, it does not reveal that digital copy to the public. The amount and substantiality of what is made accessible to a public is very limited.

Google has constructed the snippet feature in a manner that substantially protects against its serving as a substitute for authors' books. In the court's words:

> Google safeguards from public view the digitized copies it makes and allows access only to the extent of permitting the public to search for the very limited information accessible through the search function and snippet view. The program does not allow access in any substantial way to a book's expressive content.

Recall That Google Tried to Get a Lot More Than This

The actual use made of the copyrighted works is far narrower than Google envisioned a decade ago. Consider the failed 2009 amended settlement: it would have allowed Google to make substantially more extensive use of its scans of copyrighted books than the current arrangement. There, Google sought the right to

(1) sell subscriptions to an electronic books database;

(2) sell online access to individual books; and

(3) sell advertising on pages from books.

The amended settlement (if it had been approved) would have effectively granted Google a monopoly over digital books, and, in particular, orphan books.

But none of these uses exist in the current arrangement.

Libraries' Use of Their Digitized Books Is as Restricted as Google

Reading HathiTrust and Google Books together, it is clear that the participating libraries must use their digital copies to enable only the kinds of searches that the Second Circuit has held to be fair use in connection with Google's offer of such searches to the internet public: i.e., word searches and snippets.

Libraries may not freely disseminate or allow patrons to access the full text of digital copies, and defend by claiming fair use. (Only the narrow category of print-disabled patrons may have access to the full text of the digitized books.)

Can Libraries Be Liable for Copyright Infringement?

With respect to the digital copies that Google has created (and returned to them), if libraries were to misuse them in an infringing manner, those libraries may be liable to authors for copyright infringement.

Also, libraries might incur liability by negligent mishandling of, and failure to protect, their digital copies, leaving them unreasonably vulnerable to hacking.

A Musical Aside

All this suggests to me a Rodgers and Hart song from their 1940 musical *Pal Joey* (which I have "transformed" for fair use purposes):

> If they asked me, I could scan a book,
> That you could read upon a Kindle or Nook.
> You could search the preface inside and out
> So you'd know what data's about.

And the simple secret of the plot
Is just to limit what we disclose a lot.
Then the world discovers as our case ends
On what our fair use law depends.

Now It's Your Turn to Talk . . .

It is important to hear from librarians about Google Books, because in the end, the essential question to be answered is whether the Google Books project has been worth all the effort to create it (and to fight about it). So, I would like to know what you have to say concerning the following questions:

- Is Google Books being used by libraries and library patrons in a productive (and proper) way?
- Is the world (at least the library world) a better place for its creation?

Share your answers with the author at whannay@schiffhardin.com.

You've Licensed It. Now What?

Sylvia K. Miller, Senior Program Manager, Consortium of Humanities Centers and Institutes

David Phillips, Associate Professor of Interdisciplinary Humanities, Innovation, Creativity, and Entrepreneurship (ICE), and Women's, Gender and Sexuality Studies, Wake Forest University

Courtney Berger, Senior Editor and Editorial Department Manager, Duke University Press

Marjorie Fowler, Digital Asset Coordinator, University of North Carolina Press

Rebecca Kennison, Principal, K|N Consultants

John D. Martin III, PhD candidate and teaching fellow, School of Information and Library Science, UNC–Chapel Hill

John McLeod, Director, Office of Scholarly Publishihg Services, Univeresity of North Carolina Press

Chelcie Rowell, Digital Initiatives Librarian, Wake Forest University

Abstract

This article describes the concept of the Publishing Makerspace, which is a publishing environment that is reconfigured as a place where all the components of a scholarly project—books and e-books, virtual and physical exhibits, visualizations, live performance and film—can be integrated using a collaborative process. This place enables the creation of a multimodal publishing environment that fully integrates digital content with manuscripts and "traditional" scholarly content. Starting with an overview of the history of the team that devised this approach and its membership, the article describes the problem that the authors have identified with current approaches to multimodal publishing and outlines a workshop model for engaging in a reconfiguration of the publishing process, including a description of a new publishing and knowledge making ecosystem that includes librarians, publishers, and other collaborators.

What Is a Publishing Makerspace?

This project to redefine publishing is inspired by the experimental spirit of makerspaces in academic libraries. Many academic libraries have carved out physical space where patrons can experiment with designing art installations or objects and use equipment such as 3D printers to prototype their ideas; these workshop spaces and creative laboratories are, in turn, inspired by the makerspaces where engineers and computer scientists come together to take things apart and put them back together in innovative ways. Working in such inventive spaces, whether in open laboratories or prototyping studios, people are finding innovation in using old circuits or tools in new ways. Such makerspaces encourage experimentation, drawing from existing skill sets and encountering a process of discovery that leads to innovation.

In our adaptation of the makerspace concept, the publishing environment is reconfigured as a place where all the components of a scholarly project—books and e-books, virtual and physical exhibits, visualizations, live performance and film—can be integrated using a collaborative process. The goal is to create a multimodal publishing environment that fully integrates digital content with manuscripts and "traditional" scholarly content.

It is important to note that Publishing Makerspace is not solely a digital project or approach. We are interested in crossing the analog-digital divide to

http://dx.doi.org/10.5703/1288284316324

recognize the ongoing interaction and interplay between physical, analog, and digital forms. The result, we hope, will be a more efficient, interoperable process of knowledge creation and production and an enhanced, more meaningful experience for multiple audiences.

What Can the Publishing Makerspace Accomplish?

Our intent is to provide an environment in which scholars work with editors, publishers, librarians, and digital specialists to explore collaborative structures and mechanisms for publication that contribute to public scholarship, that take full advantage of digital platforms, and that provide exciting models for scholarly communication.

From both a publisher's and an author's perspective, the goal of the Publishing Makerspace is to foreground the types of digital content that were hitherto relegated by publishers to appendices, addendums, and supplementary roles, and make them an integral part of the publication. From the point of view of libraries, archives, museums, and other producers of digital content, the goal is to embrace their roles as co-creators of knowledge, enabling new contexts and avenues of discovery for that content. We expect that this new approach will result in more exciting and meaningful multimodal publications and a more efficient process of knowledge production.

In terms of process, our aim is to establish a collaborative relationship among author, editor, librarian, digital specialists, and other relevant experts that makes use of the discrete knowledge and skill sets of each domain to shape the scholarship and be as effective as possible in constructing innovative models of scholarly communication. Our goal is to re-shape and expand the research/authorship process of knowledge production and devise more efficient, interoperable ways to produce multimodal scholarly work.

When successfully applied, the Publishing Makerspace model has the potential to radically alter the publishing landscape and to open up possibilities for collaborative innovation in publishing modes and formats. The end results might include, for example, research publications with various "threads" the reader can follow that replace rigid sequential formats. Another example would be the use of visualizations to enhance illustrations and enable more flexible presentations of data. A physical book could be one artifact of a project, while an online tool could draw from oral history content to allow the reader the opportunity to explore the data and interrelate it in ways previously not possible with analog-only scholarship.

The Team

In a spirit of openness and experimentation, the Publishing Makerspace project brings together people with skills relevant to publishing and opens the possibility of reconfiguring research processes and workflows to encourage new modes of output.

Our team members regard our skills and experience as tools that might be bent to new uses. We also recognized as we began to work together that our cross-functional team might serve as a model for other future Publishing Makerspace teams. Our group currently includes a scholar (David P. Phillips, Wake Forest University); a digital librarian (Chelcie Rowell, Wake Forest University); a technology expert (John D. Martin III, doctoral candidate, School of Information and Library Science, UNC-Chapel Hill); an editor from a university press (Courtney Berger, Duke University Press); a manager of e-books and digital assets, and her colleague who heads their new publishing services operation, from another university press (Marjorie Fowler and John McLeod, University of North Carolina Press); a former publisher and librarian who has started an open access venture (Rebecca Kennison, K|N Consultants); and a former editor and publisher who also has extensive experience with collaborative scholarship (Sylvia Miller, Consortium of Humanities Centers and Institutes).

We also found that our backgrounds melded and overlapped variously; for example, four of us had extensive experience in book production at some point in our careers; three of us had deep experience in libraries; three of us had grappled extensively with business models and sustainability (perhaps needless to say, not at all the same three each time); five of us had been involved in developing digital publications and databases; and so on. A Venn diagram of our collective expertise might look like a mesh net. What might we catch together? Once we had formed our group, we were excited to find out and began to meet and learn from each other right away.

Scholarly Communications Institute

The Publishing Makerspace working group first came together in the Fall of 2014 and had the extraordinary opportunity to refine our goals as one of four groups selected to participate in the prestigious Scholarly Communications Institute (SCI) retreat in Chapel Hill, NC, in November 2014; six members of the group described above participated. At the end of four days of brainstorming and planning, we presented a summary of our ideas and plans to an assembled audience of expert scholarly-communications advisors, including publishers, scholars, librarians, and funders. We received an enthusiastic reaction and several invitations, leading to a talk to UNC-Chapel Hill's Scholarly Communications Working Group, the DH Kitchen at Wake Forest University, a workshop with the PhD Lab in Digital Knowledge at Duke University, and other invitations. Each event has been an opportunity to continue developing and refining the project.

What Does the Design Process Look Like?

At the SCI, we used a design process called a *design charrette*, which David Phillips facilitated based on his experience in design and urban planning.

Charrettes are visioning workshops consisting of multidisciplinary teams of collaborators who explore multiple solutions to complex questions or challenges. This approach is frequently used in urban planning and urban design, with intensive half-day, one-day, or multi-day intense workshops, bringing in a wide range of expertise and knowledge, such as a waterfront neighborhood redesign project that brings in architects, planners, residents, planning officers, and other stakeholders to create teams that draw, sketch, and develop ideas addressing existing design challenges. Borrowing this page from design thinking, we conducted our own design charrette.

In a design charrette, we start with the "faucet," or the idea-generation phase, and end with the "funnel," or process of convergence and refinement. A facilitator walks us through these phases as we narrow in on key objectives and steps toward our goal. Each phase is timed; at SCI we recorded our ideas quickly on post-it notes ("faucet"), which David placed on the wall in constellations that began to form categories ("funnel"), which we then discussed and refined.

Our central question for this visioning exercise was: What would we like the scholarly publishing environment to look like in the Year 2030?

In the backcasting visioning process, we start with the envisioned future and its characteristics and capabilities without the restrictions of considering the limitations of the present that might preclude such a future. Next, as a team, we strategize how to reach back from that future to the present, sketching backward the various steps that would be required to get us from the present to the envisioned future.

We realized that we had modeled a process that could be crucial to authors' visioning of their own Publishing Makerspaces that would lead to important questions such as "How can collaboration with your librarians and digital project specialists help you achieve your envisioned goals?"

The Problem

As our ideas converged on a vision of the future of scholarly publishing during the SCI retreat, our working group stepped back to articulate the central problem that we wanted to address. We agreed that many scholars do not recognize that the fragmented publishing activities that they are pursuing could have dynamic connections and make a more powerful impact if planned in a more coordinated fashion. Other scholars might recognize potential connections but not know

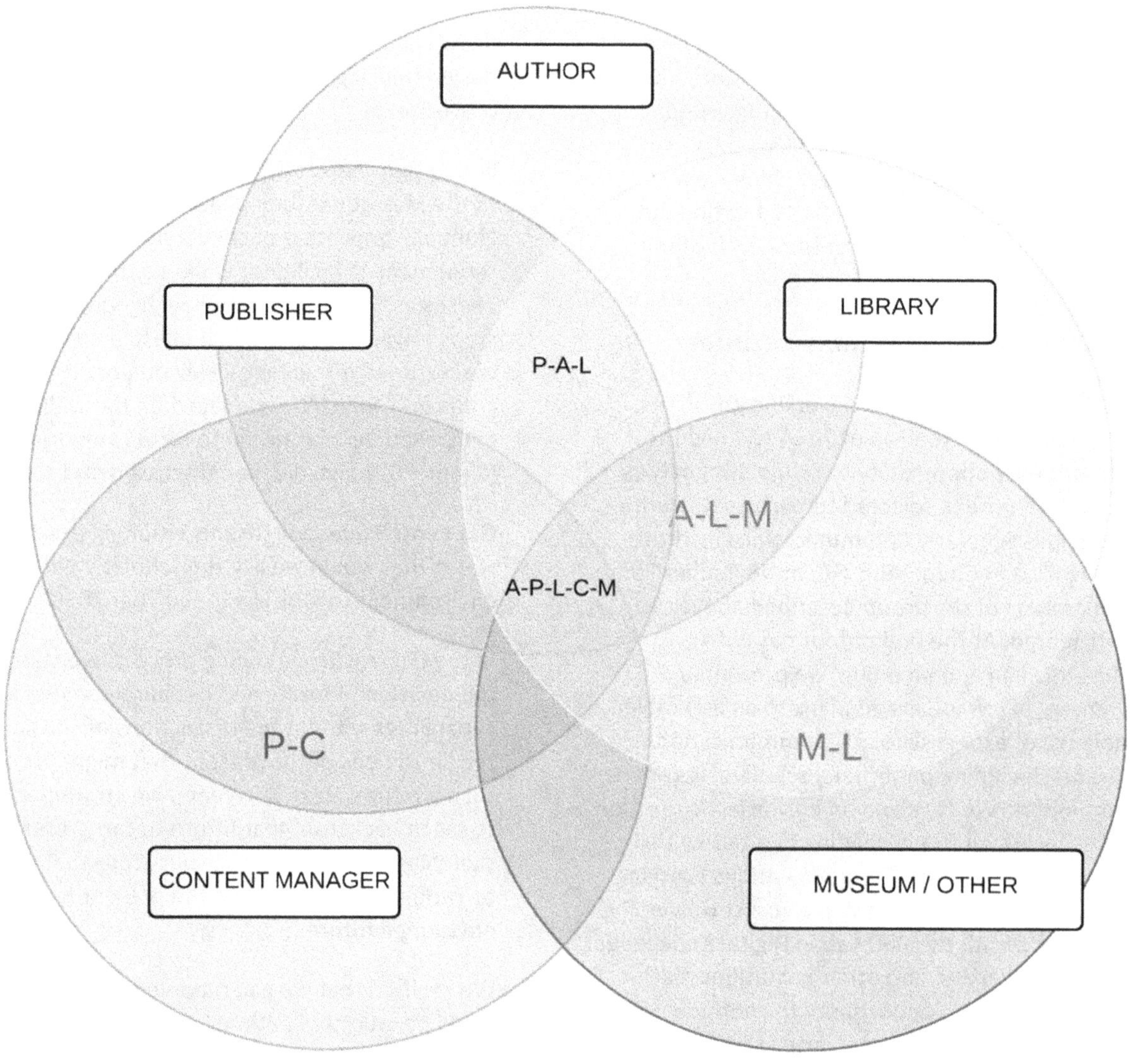

Figure 1. Overlapping collaborative roles: A first sketch of a new publishing ecosystem.

how to realize them. For example, a monograph might have the potential to be more than just a book if linked to an online multimedia archive; exciting possibilities might emerge from the scholar's research that take vision, planning, and practical expertise of multiple types to realize.

More and more, scholars are producing multimodal and multimedia projects that include many content types that do not fit in traditional journal and book publications. But they are operating without the infrastructure and specialized knowledge that will help them to fully realize their goals. Modes of work often include articles, blogs, multimedia interviews, databases, timelines, maps and other visualizations, photographs, collections of historic documents, physical and virtual exhibits, print books, and e-books. Traditional scholarly publishers are seldom able to publish more than a book or article. Libraries and humanities centers and institutes have filled the gap in supporting digital scholarship in experimental forms, often resulting in exciting products, but without much integration with the rest of the scholarly output. A systematic method of making all of the work archivable and discoverable per library and publishing standards has yet to be fully envisioned and deployed.

The Publishing Makerspace Workshop

Having envisioned a future for scholarly publishing in which publishing was redefined to include all forms of scholarship efficiently and elegantly interconnected in useful and enlightening ways, our backcasting exercise encouraged us to identify a practical, feasible first step. Our idea for a first step that would be relatively simple for any author, publisher, library, or other institution to organize was a meeting that we dubbed the Publishing Makerspace Workshop.

The idea for a workshop was inspired partly by the manuscript workshops hosted over the past few years by the John Hope Franklin Humanities Institute, in which a junior scholar has the opportunity to discuss his or her book manuscript with a group of experts in the field; it is a peer-review process done in person. However, the Publishing Makerspace Workshop would happen much earlier in the research process, when the scholarly project is at the proposal stage. While the design-charrette process might enable scholars to overlook current problems in envisioning future realities, participants would likely be acutely conscious of the problems they need to overcome in integrating content. To address this practically, in addition to peer reviewers, the participants in the workshop would be experts in editing, marketing, digital tools for scholarship such as mapping, databases, digital archives, etc., as suggested by the incipient plan for the project.

We are often asked whether Publishing Makerspace is a physical place. We do believe that the initial meeting of a team should happen in person, but subsequent collaboration can be conducted in a virtual space or shared workflow. Publishing Makerspace might be described as a moveable feast that exists wherever and whenever potential collaborators come together to envision and begin to plan a project. While a dedicated space for a team to meet and to work long term is desirable, it need not be a requirement if it sets the bar too high for many collaborations to begin.

Roles in the New Ecosystem

Our first attempt to draw the new ecosystem in which knowledge-makers collaborate from the ground floor is a Venn diagram (Figure 1).

Where the circles overlap, we see librarians, publishers, and others learning from each other and working closely together. Here we focus briefly on the three categories of participants most often represented at the Charleston Conference:

- Librarians have stepped in to fill the gap left by publishers who have been less willing and able to experiment with digital scholarship; libraries continue to provide software development, digitization, hosting, metadata, and archiving services as well as grant-seeking support. They might find that a publisher-like proposal and vetting process will help them to improve control over the allocation of scarce resources.
- Vendors will be increasingly important to the discoverability and accessibility of scholarship as more multimodal scholarship is produced. Digital platforms will need to accommodate multimodal work; file types and metadata will change.
- Publishers offer a useful discipline in identifying and reaching audiences and in budgeting, cost recovery, and sustainability, as well as expertise in visioning, editing, design, and production. Publishers will have to respond creatively to the fact that the forms of scholarship that they produce are often only one piece of a larger whole, and sometimes narrative is not the primary form. Increasingly publishing will become democratized and decentralized. Eventually traditional publishers might have to decide whether to fight this or join it and find their place in the new ecosystem.

An interdisciplinary entity such as a humanities center or institute can be a useful locus of connection for collaborators, as neutral territory.

We have been asked what the business model is for this new kind of publishing. For now, there is not necessarily a new one. Rather, it is a hybrid of existing models. For example, the publisher of the book or article component of a project makes copies available in their usual manner, while archives generally make digital collections freely available for research but might charge permission fees for other uses. The integration of the two (for example, an e-book that includes outbound links to an archive) might produce experimental new business arrangements, and over time, new business models will evolve from new forms of publishing. We are excited to participate in that process, and a couple of our team members are actively involved in developing new business models in other projects, but our focus in Publishing Makerspace is on the scholarship.

We hope that Publishing Makerspace will be a place—whether physical or metaphorical—in which librarians and publishers work together in a collaborative spirit, checking their contentions about business models at the door and appreciating what each collaborator brings to the table.

We also hope that expanding the definition of publishing might influence a change in peer-review practice and the kinds of work that academic promotion committees will consider.

Axioms

As we have developed the idea of the Publishing Makerspace, we have recognized that there are certain principles at the foundation of the project.

1. ***Transparency.*** Publishing has always been collaborative; in a publishing company, acquisitions editors, developmental editors, copy editors, managing editors, designers, typesetters, proofreaders, indexers, publicists, and many others know this in their day-to-day work. If they do their work well, it is invisible. In digital projects, often archivists, programmers, GIS experts, and others are co-creators of knowledge. The Publishing Makerspace advocates surfacing the invisible and admires the Collaborators' Bill of Rights (http://mcpress.media-commons.org/offthetracks/part-one-models-for-collaboration-career-paths-acquiring-institutional-support-and-transformation-in-the-field/a-collaboration/collaborators%E2%80%99-bill-of-rights/).
2. ***Replicability and extensibility.*** We hope that the idea of the Publishing Makerspace Workshop will take off on its own; once we have shared our experiences and published some helpful guidelines online, we do not expect that our team will be needed to help run Publishing Makerspace workshops across the US and around the world.
3. ***Interoperability.*** At this point, the Publishing Makerspace is not a project to build a new publishing technology or platform. However, we are very interested in critiquing and helping to improve existing tools and practices—whether open source or vendor-controlled—to make them interoperable where now they require wasteful and tedious re-keying, re-tagging, re-coding, etc.

Our First Test Run

On November 19, 2015, we had the opportunity to run our first Publishing Makerspace workshop. At the suggestion of our host, Duke University's Franklin Humanities Institute, we began the session with an introduction to the Publishing Makerspace concept and then addressed three scholarly projects in turn, allowing each a half-hour for a lightning-round presentation by the scholar/author, a design-charrette visioning exercise in which the audience and the Publishing Makerspace team participated, followed by a brief discussion.

There was a positive feeling of excitement and creativity in the room, and the scholars were good sports about participating in a visioning exercise in front of an audience; conversations among participants continued long after the event had officially ended. It was helpful to have augmented our team with experts who could address specific aspects of the projects (mapping in two cases and multimedia journal publishing in the third). In retrospect, a half-hour was scarcely enough time for each project; other feedback and assessment will have to be reserved for another article, but it was clear that only actual practice could help us refine the workshop model.

What's Next for the Publishing Makerspace Project?

The project has sparked widespread interest, and we plan to seek funding to support an expansion of our activities. Our wish list includes a website modeled on THATCamp (http://thatcamp.org/help/organize), where people who want to hold a Publishing Makerspace workshop could find guidelines and examples and spin off their own Publishing Makerspace website. Using GitHub for site development, we would incorporate improvements made by individual workshops into the master site. This platform allows for splitting and merging different branches of projects easily and makes the process transparent to all involved. We have started to build an advisory board and listserv, and we continue to seek guinea pigs who would like to try the evolving workshop model to help them develop their ideas both conceptually and technically and find collaborators, while we learn from the experience and refine the workshop model.

As we move toward refining our model and making it available to the public, we are seeking funding to test our prototype, conduct additional research, and implement its principles in several experimental publication projects. Feedback and assessment will be key to the improvement of the model, as will an analysis of the scholarly projects that initially implement the Publishing Makerspace approach. Documentation of the steps involved in the process will enable us to develop tutorials, training modules, and "best practices" literature.

Ultimately, we envision Publishing Makerspace as an approach that any researcher, academic press, or higher educational institution can utilize. We hope to inspire an inclusive view of publishing that will change official tenure-review guidelines at institutions of higher education, in the process expanding the parameters of scholarly publishing to more fully embrace the digital revolution that is transforming the publishing environment. Along the way we look forward to working on some fascinating and exciting scholarly projects.

Techie Issues

The Secret Life of Articles: From Download Metrics to Downstream Impact

Carol Tenopir, Chancellor's Professor, School of Information Sciences, University of Tennessee, Knoxville

Lorraine Estelle, Director, Project COUNTER

Wouter Haak, VP Research Data Management Solutions, Elsevier

Suzie Allard, Professor, School of Information Sciences, Director of Center for Information and Communication Studies, University of Tennessee, Knoxville

Lisa Christian, Research Associate, Center for Information and Communication Studies, University of Tennessee, Knoxville

David Nicholas, Director of CIBER; Adjunct Professor, School of Information Sciences, University of Tennessee, Knoxville

Anthony Watkinson, Principal Consultant, CIBER

Hazel Woodward, Board of Directors, Project COUNTER; Director, Information Power; and retired Librarian, Cranfield University

Peter Shepherd, former Executive Director, Project COUNTER

Robert Anderson, Graduate Research Assistant, University of Tennessee, Knoxville

Suzan Ali Saleh, Graduate Research Assistant, University of Tennessee, Knoxville

Abstract

Traditional citation and download metrics have long been the standard by which we measure the use and value of scholarly articles. However, these methods neglect the usage and real-world impact of newer technologies to access, store, and share downloaded scholarly articles. This session's speakers will share the results of interviews, focus groups, and an international survey with 1,000 scholars to investigate the ways in which they now access, store, share, and use downloaded scholarly articles. By identifying and measuring what traditional metrics fail to examine, the Beyond Downloads project attempts to capture a more complete picture of the use and value of scholarly articles, which is critical for librarians, publishers, and vendors to understand in developing scholarly tools and services. Complete usage can no longer be measured by traditional means alone. The speakers will discuss the findings of their research and the implications for metrics that take into account scholars' changing access, reading, and sharing behaviors.

Introduction

Project COUNTER has long been the standard by which libraries and publishers monitor download counts and usage for articles and journals (Shepherd, 2004). This measurement is then used for a proxy in determining full usage and value. However valuable this estimation is to libraries, it misses an equally important secondary usage—that is, repeat and shared usage information.

Sharing is widespread among the scholarly community, becoming an integral and daily part of the scholarly work life, especially when working in research groups (Zhu & Proctor, 2012; Haustein, Peters, Sugimoto, Thelwall, & Larivière, 2014). Social media and e-mail have become the go-to

http://dx.doi.org/10.5703/1288284316325

methods for sharing (Cheng, Ho, & Lau, 2009; Harley, Acord, Ear-Novell, Lawrence, & King, 2010, Tenopir et al., 2014). The Beyond Downloads project examines the life of a scholarly article beyond the point of download. It examines how and why scholars share scholarly articles, and the format and platform of sharing. This secondary usage is important to consider if we are to estimate or even hope to arrive at a more accurate estimate of the complete value of scholarly articles—for the authors, libraries and, publishers.

Our project research questions included:

1. What are download counts missing?
2. How much do scholars share and what do they share?
3. Are there ways to calculate or measure sharing?
4. What is a more complete use and value of articles?

For regular Charleston attendees, you may remember that we introduced this project last year and reported some of the preliminary results (Tenopir et al., 2014). This year we report the final results. The overall project aimed to define ways to measure non-download usage of digital content and to initiate discussion regarding these issues. This presentation focuses on some of the key takeaways from the research project.

Methodology

We used a multiple-method approach to answering these research questions. The first step was to identify the most frequently and commonly used platforms of sharing scholarly materials. Given the innumerable methods of sharing material in general, we focused on methods scholars are likely to use for sharing research and teaching materials. The second step was to conduct focus groups in the United States and interviews in the United Kingdom. Participants included 29 academics at all levels in the sciences and social sciences—from senior faculty and researchers to doctoral students. Ten participants were in their thirties, while others ranged from their twenties to early sixties. Twenty participants held a PhD, seven held a master's, and two held a bachelor's degree. Twelve participants were professors, four were researchers, five were lecturers, five were PhD students, and three held "other" positions.

This second step helped to inform an international survey of researchers. In late October 2014, an e-mail invitation was sent to a mailing list of 32,956 authors who had previously published in an Elsevier journal. The survey was open until January 16, 2015. We received 1,000 responses for a response rate of 3.03%. Respondents came from 69 countries, with just over a quarter (27.1%) from the United States. Other top respondent nations were: Italy (7.1%), China (7%), Canada (4.0%), United Kingdom (3.8%), and India (3.8%). We also had a range of subject disciplines, mostly coming from the STEM fields. Thirty-four percent were from the sciences, 20.8% from the medical sciences, 21.4% from engineering, 22.4% from the social sciences, and only 1.7% from the humanities. Respondents' ages ranged from 18 to 83, with an average age of 48 years and about a quarter under 39 years old. Eighty-one percent of respondents were in the academic ranks, 3.4% were students, and 11.2% were private or non-academic researchers. Eighty-two percent of respondents held a PhD.

Results

Survey respondents, interviewees, and focus group participants expressed a wide range of behaviors and attitudes. However, this presentation focuses on five main takeaways from the project.

1. Sharing articles is a means to an end. Scholars find sharing useful to further scientific and academic discovery, to facilitate collaboration, and to advance their work.
2. Function drives form. Whether scholars share via a link or PDF depends on the primary channel used for sharing.
3. E-mail is #1. Scholars share primarily via e-mail; however, other forms of scholarly sharing include academic social networks, and social media.

4. The version matters. Scholars want to share the final published version of their articles.
5. The library is key (but not the only source). Scholars' primary source to download scholarly articles is their library subscriptions or databases.

Sharing Articles Is a Means to an End

Researchers and teachers *like* to share. In the survey, we asked, "How did you feel about your work being shared with others?" We received 690 responses to this question. In general, the vast majority of comments were positive. Many respondents say that knowing that their work was being read and shared by others made them feel that their work and their time spent researching was important, that they have a positive impact. They feel validated by this knowledge. Moreover, they expect their work to be shared, as it "is the entire point," according to more than one respondent. Only a few express reservations. Most of these reservations concern using the proper citation.

Why do they share? Sharing is a natural part of scholarship. Scholars say they find sharing useful to further scientific and academic discovery, to facilitate collaboration, and to advance their own work. Sharing is often initiated by others who are interested in an author's work, and the sharing is by the author. But not always. If a scholar has access to an article by someone else that they think is particularly good or useful, or that another person wants, they will likely share it either as a full-text file or a link.

Another common reason for sharing is the lack of access. Articles protected behind a paywall create problems of access for researchers at smaller or private institutions or those from developing countries. Whether someone asks for an article by the respondent or a copy of another researcher's article, respondents report sharing full-text copies to help fulfill these colleagues' information needs—*whether or not the act of sharing is strictly legal*. As one survey respondent states, "It's not like I'm giving away something that they could not get anyhow. But it never dawned on me that, in effect, you know in theory, I am violating copyright." While another reasons, "If I have got it, I will just share it. It is easier than having them go track it down, even if I have got the citation." Convenience and helping others are more important than the letter of the law. Scholars also do not like embargoes. They disagree with statement "Embargo periods that restrict sharing of scholarly articles for (6 months/1 year/2 years) are reasonable" (M = 2.74, 2.07, 1.64, where 1 = strongly disagree; 5 = strongly agree). The longer the embargo period, the more likely they are to disagree or strongly disagree with the idea that embargoes are reasonable.

Scholars who work in a research group are more likely to share their articles and others' articles than those who work alone. Survey respondents mostly agree with the statement that "most of my work is done in a research group" (M = 3.88, where 1 = strongly disagree; 5 = strongly agree). Only 16.3% of participants (128 of 783) disagreed or strongly disagreed with this statement; 12% were neutral (94), and 71.6% agreed or strongly agreed (561). The vast majority of respondents work in research groups most of the time. Furthermore, when working in a group, 66.8% say they share articles more often than otherwise (515 of 771); 30% report their sharing unaffected (231), and only 3.2% report sharing less in groups (25). Moreover, many scholars report that their sharing has increased or will increase. As the number of coauthors on papers and in research teams are increasing, we can expect sharing to increase as well.

Function Drives Form

At first, we assumed that sharing meant the sharing of the full-text article. However, this is not always the case. Early in the project, it became clear that there are two types of saving and sharing downloads—that is, sharing and forwarding a link and sharing the full-text article. Access is key in examining these different sharing behaviors. Sharing a link is most common when the scholar knows the person with whom they are sharing has the same level of access. When access may be an issue, sharing full-text articles comes into play more often. Shared full-texts articles are most often in PDF form.

E-mail is the most popular method for sharing links or full-texts (PDF). In the survey, we asked of respondents, "Thinking back to the last scholarly article that you published, please estimate how many times and/or with how many people you shared references/links/full-text" and provided a list a methods for which to provide their estimates. In all cases, e-mail emerged as the method most used (approximately 10.5 times for both a link or reference and full-text). Learning management software such as Blackboard is the second most used method for sharing a link or reference (13.9 times). Research social networks such as ResearchGate are the second most used method for sharing full-text (10.8 times).

E-mail Is King

As we have stated, e-mail is the most common method of sharing articles. Within the survey, we also asked respondents to rate their preferred method for sharing articles for research and teaching purposes. Again, e-mail came out on top. For research purposes, 73.8% of respondents rank e-mail as their highest preferred method of sharing, followed by cloud services (11.6%) and password-protected internal networks (10.7%).

The picture is similar for teaching, with only learning management systems replacing cloud services. Eighty-three percent of respondents rank e-mail as their most preferred method for sharing articles for teaching, followed by learning management systems (9.6%) and password-protected internal networks (8%). Perhaps the biggest takeaway here is the mundane nature of this behavior. Convenience and ease continue to dominate sharing behaviors.

However, respondents acknowledge that more people are reached by other means than e-mail, cloud services, and learning management systems. Research and general social networks allow them to potentially reach hundreds or even thousands of people. Again, in thinking about the last article they shared of their own work, respondents estimated reaching between 559–4066 through research social networks, 96–614 through general social networks, and 40–189 through internal networks.

Version Matters

Most scholars want to share the final published version—not the author's submitted version or a preprint. Eighty-four percent of respondents report preferring to share the published version of someone else's work, and 77% prefer sharing the published version of their work. This finding differs somewhat by discipline. Medical scientists were the most likely to share the published manuscript of either their own work (84.3%) or another's work (89.7%). Engineers were the least likely (68.5% for their own and 76% for others' work).

Many survey respondents and focus group participants explained their preference for the published version. A focus group participant from the social sciences states, "The main point should be that I share a version that is evidentially the peer-reviewed version (with the publisher and the journal stamp on it)." Another reiterates their intellectual attachment to the final copy, "My feeling is that I've written this, this is my work, they're publishing it. I'm not getting paid for this, they're benefiting from this. I'm a little fish . . . Let them come for me." One survey respondent claims, "Content providers in general have to realize that the relationship between seller and buyer has fundamentally changed in the last 20 years . . . In order to get someone to pay you for something they can get without your permission, you need to (1) make the process of obtaining your product legally at LEAST as effortless as the process of obtaining it illegally. (2) Make it so cheap that it's not worth pirating."

Academics are now utilizing social media in innovative ways to navigate around pay walls in order to disseminate these preferred published versions of scholarly articles. For example, some academics are using the hashtag #icanhazpdf to freely share copyrighted papers (Mohdin, 2015). In the case of sharing other people's work, altruism is a key factor. Many researchers are aware of their position of privilege and are willing to help other less fortunate researchers gain the access they lack.

The Library Is Key

When we asked survey respondents to estimate how many scholarly articles they downloaded for their last research project, the average was 65 articles; for their last teaching term, the average was 36. Still, the most common source for downloads was the library—for research and teaching purposes. This finding follows that of the Tenopir and King scholarly reading studies, which found that the library remained an important and primary resource for scholars (King, Tenopir, Choemprayong, & Wu, 2009; Tenopir, King, Edwards, & Wu, 2009; Tenopir, King, Christian, & Volentine, 2015). Of course, COUNTER allows the library to count these downloads. Over half (54%) of downloads for research and 35% of downloads for teaching come from the library. If we exclude non-responses (or those who selected "0" for each source), we find that 61% of articles for research and 65% of those for teaching come from the library.

But, these numbers may be gross underestimates of use, because when rereading or sharing or returning to that article again, only 9–12% of the time are articles reported as being redownloaded. The rest of the time, readers are returning to a saved copy. If you add the potential 10+ times that an article is shared, you may see why downloads tell only part of the usage story.

Conclusion

Sharing is a natural behavior, which supports research and the dissemination of results. Convenience is a key concern in how researchers choose to share their own work as well as the work of others. Therefore, sharing channels are chosen for their fitness-to-work style. Because sharing is, and has always been, an integral part of the research cycle, new policies and measures must fit preferences and likely behavior patterns. After all, current download counts likely underestimate usage, though the sharing of references and links may balance out discrepancies to a certain extent. Furthermore, these new policies and measurements should not be punitive; rather, they should enable scholars, publishers, and librarians to form a more complete picture of the value of articles—that is, their secret life.

References

Cheng, M.-Y., Ho, S.-Y., & Lau, P. M. (2009). Knowledge sharing in academic institutions: A study of Multimedia University Malaysia. *Electronic Journal of Knowledge Management,* 7(3), 313–324.

Harley, D., Acord, S. K., Earl-Novell, S., Lawrence, S., & King, C. J. (2010). Assessing the future landscape of scholarly communication: An exploration of faculty values and needs in seven disciplines. *Center for Studies in Higher Education.* UC Berkeley: Center for Studies in Higher Education. Retrieved from: https://escholarship.org/uc/item/15x7385g

Haustein, S., Peters, I., Sugimoto, C. R., Thelwall, M., & Larivière, V. (2014). Tweeting biomedicine: An analysis of tweets and citations in the biomedical literature. *Journal of the Association for Information Sciences and Technology, 56*(4). 656–669. http://dx.doi.org/10.1002/asi.23101

King, D. W., Tenopir, C., Choemprayong, S., & Wu, L. (2009). Scholarly journal information seeking and reading patterns of faculty at five U.S. universities. *Learned Publishing,* 22, 126–144. http://dx.doi.org/10.1087/2009208

Mohdin, A. (2015, October 21). Academics have found a way to access insanely expensive research papers—for free, *Quartz*. Retrieved from http://qz.com/528526/academics-have-found-a-way-to-access-insanely-expensive-research-papers-for-free/

Shepherd, P. (2004). COUNTER: Towards reliable vendor usage statistics. *VINE, 4*, 184–189.

Tenopir, C., Hughes, G., Christian, L., Allard, S., Nicholas, D., Watkinson, A., . . . Anderson, R. (2014). *To boldly go beyond downloads: How are journal articles shared and used?* Paper presented at the Charleston Library Conference, Charleston, SC. http://dx.doi.org/10.5703/1288284315614

Tenopir, C., King, D.W., Christian, L., & Volentine, R. (2015). Scholarly article seeking, reading, and use: A continuing evolution from print to electronic in the sciences and social sciences. *Learned Publishing, 28*(2), 93–105. http://dx.doi.org/10.1087/20150203

Tenopir, C., King, D. W., Edwards, S., & Wu, L. (2009). Electronic journals and changes in scholarly article seeking and reading patterns. *Aslib Proceedings: New Information Perspectives, 61*, 5. http://dx.doi.org/10.1108/00012530910932267

Zhu, Y., & Procter, R. (2012). Use of blogs, Twitter, and Facebook by PhD students for scholarly communication: A UK study. *China New Media Communication Annual Conference,* Macao. Retrieved from https://www.escholar.manchester.ac.uk/item/?pid=uk-ac-man-scw:187789

Mitigating Madness: How We Authenticate and Authorize Users to Deliver Databases in a Contractually Complicated Context

Jeremy M. Brown, Associate Director for Technical Services and Systems, Mercer University Libraries

Geoffrey P. Timms, Marine Resources Librarian, College of Charleston

Abstract

During the 2011 overhaul of the Mercer University Libraries website we developed an authentication system to interface with EZProxy and our campus Active Directory system that provides convenient management and delivery of our A–Z database listing. With multiple campuses and seven e-resource privilege groups, we were able to provide persistent URLs for databases to subject librarians, dynamic database lists based upon users' access privileges, convenient integration with our content management system, and a simple backend management interface requiring little expertise to use. We then sought to improve the situation by organizational and license simplification before our 2014 website overhaul: We hired a dedicated licensed content librarian, and systems and technical services personnel worked tirelessly to streamline our seven privilege groups into two by negotiation and policy changes. We then modified our workflows to encourage this simplicity. This paper describes how technical services and systems can design and create an in-house application to ease the dynamic delivery of database information, authentication, and access. Then it describes subsequent improvements upon that system with organizational changes and better business practices.

When the first electronic resources came onto the market, licensing those resources began as an organic process at Mercer University Libraries, as is often the case. Our first licensing model mirrored our print acquisitions model exactly: selecting librarians would choose materials for their clientele, and the resources would be available for the clientele at their locations. The University Libraries subscribed to resources for two main campuses, which began with distinct programs: the Macon campus served a traditional undergraduate population, while the Atlanta campus served graduates and professionals. There are some satellite campuses, that we call the "Centers," which traditionally have served nontraditional students. The University also has a law school and a medical school, the libraries of which are administratively separate from the University Libraries.

Our University culture began with essentially three distinct and independent libraries tailoring electronic resources to serve their distinct programs, without much thought to the collective "University Libraries" institution. However, the greater University ecosystem was evolving beyond the location-bound programs: professional and graduate programs spread to the Centers and Macon campuses, undergraduate disciplines appeared in Atlanta, and nontraditional programs appeared on all campuses. The marketplace was also evolving: new technologies like link resolvers and discovery services appeared on the marketplace, and we had neither the funding nor the personnel to manage three incarnations of each service. Additionally, there was considerable overlap between the pharmacy and nursing programs and the medical school's resources, which led to considerable cooperation across administrative boundaries. That demonstrated the feasibility of intercampus cooperation. By 2010, the time was ripe to figure out how to simplify our electronic resources.

Our library websites existed to serve our clientele, and funnel them to the content we provided. Although we shared an automation system, our websites were built with the electronic resources in mind, and as with those resources, we created three distinct web presences. The first step to simplifying our licenses became an implementation of a single website for three libraries with three distinct sets of electronic resources, and the major problem here was

http://dx.doi.org/10.5703/1288284316326

creating the "database of databases" that would show everyone what they were able to access.

Feature List

We began with two different systems: one system based on a fragile Microsoft Access database, which was hosted on a SharePoint server and accessed via Active Server Pages, and a second based on a MySQL database, which was hosted on a Linux server and accessed via PHP scripts. We authenticated users with EZproxy using lists derived from library patron records in our Innovative Millennium system. These existing systems taught us what we did not like and how to do it better.

Building a system from the ground up gave us an opportunity to take a critical look at the shortcomings and build a list of features to avoid. Those included:

- Maintaining lists of users for our three user populations. We loaded patron records several times a year, and we had to update our lists of users for three different proxies each of those times.
- URL changes wreaked havoc on our websites. Each time a vendor changed URLs, we had to hunt for the database URLs throughout the site. This was tedious.
- EZproxy authentication was tough to explain to library personnel. It was nigh impossible to explain to the public. However, we had to manually create EZproxy URLs for the librarians to use.
- Neither database had a good management interface. Access gave us a tabular interface for data entry, and we managed MySQL with SQL commands. Neither of these was as good as a simple web form.

We identified some new features that would give us solutions to all of those issues, and give us the flexibility to solve our license organization issues until we had time to make our licenses universal across the university:

- Our campus had implemented ActiveDirectory, which was available for us to query. We should use this rather than reloading patron data into the proxy servers.
- We needed a web-accessible administrative interface
- Databases and patrons both needed to be classified by license group
- We needed to support persistent URLs
- Integrating this new system into our new content management system's web editor would promote usage of the system

Authentication

Our remote authentication system was almost where it needed to be. We had already implemented EZproxy's groups feature, so we had a start on classifying databases by license type within the proxy servers. Our old system relied upon users who already had accounts in the campus's ActiveDirectory system. However, we were creating a shadow authentication system that relied upon the university ID number alone. The campus had not implemented a true single sign-on (SSO) system, but at least using ActiveDirectory would allow them to authenticate with the same username and password as they use all over the campus. We determined that the easiest way for us to do this would be with an external web application, and EZproxy's ticketing system.

Since we had disparate licenses, we also needed to authorize our authenticated users. Restated, authorization tells us what privileges the user has. Authentication tells us that the user is who they say they are. Our campus Information Technology unit was rolling out a new student management system in 2010, so we had to create a new student data feed at that time anyway. We load that data into a PostgreSQL (http://www.postgresql.org) database. Because we get different data for employees than we get for students, we load the data separately into separate student and employee tables. We also load this data into our library system. This is visualized in Figure 1 (see Appendix).

At its core, our remote authentication process is a simple process. It collects user authentication information (a username and a password) and queries ActiveDirectory to verify the credentials. After authentication, the system looks at our database to authorize the user. At this point, it constructs a URL with an EZproxy ticket, and sends the user on to the proxy server. The proxy takes over from there. This is visualized in Figure 2 (see Appendix).

We created this application using the CherryPy framework (http://www.cherrypy.org) and a few Python libraries to query the PostgreSQL database and ActiveDirectory. Additionally, we have processes that handle the daily ingest of user data from IT.

The Database of Databases

When looking at the features that we wanted to implement, we are really only looking at a single table of information. This needs to capture the following information:

- Database URL
- Database name
- *Brief* description
- Whether or not to use the proxy. This was to address the desire to add freely accessible databases to this system.
- License groups—initially this included the following groups: Atlanta, Centers, Macon, pharmacy, nursing and any combination of the above. We were later able to reduce that to two possibilities.

We investigated a number of technologies to implement our new database of databases, and we settled upon the Django framework (https://www.djangoproject.com). Django gives us a robust administrative interface for next to no code, once we have implemented our data model. The implementation of the model only required 22 lines of code. We made a number of design decisions that would prevent problems that arose with our previous systems. Chief among those were:

1. Limit description to 512 characters. We could write novels about each resource, but users did not look for that level of detail in this database of databases list. That should be done in a library guide somewhere else.
2. Make the database URL a unique identifier: it is hard to manage URL change when we have dozens of different names for the same resource.

Refer to Figure 3. (see Appendix) for a screen shot of the administrative interface for the data model.

We deployed a series of views that show users' different versions of this data to produce different functionality on the website:

- An A–Z list of the databases that we show on our home page for quick browsing—see Figure 4 (Appendix).
- The actual browse list, with the databases listed alphabetically—see Figure 5 (Appendix). Note the licensing restriction in Figure 6 (Appendix).
- A view that handles persistent URLs. This view shows no content, but rather it looks at authentication, authorization, and the database classification to either redirect directly to the resource, or through a proxy server.

A key function of this system, especially when our licenses were so complicated, was to filter the content so that each authenticated user would only see resources to which he or she was entitled. We also had to build functionality in for manually curated subject lists, which is included in the home page widget. This is not functionality within the application, but it is derived from the same data.

Our persistent links are a key part of this system, and we guaranteed to our users that these will never change but will intelligently use the proxy, and because of that they will work everywhere without making our users understand when to use the EZproxy prefix. For an example, visit: http://libraries.mercer.edu/api/quicklink/2

Website Integration

In 2010 we implemented the Plone (https://plone.org) content management system (CMS), which used the user-friendly TinyMCE web editor so our users no longer needed to know any special markup. However, we anticipated some issues: librarians frequently do not know which URL is the appropriate URL, and it is hard to educate content creators about the Proxy.

Integrating the database of databases into the editor was an important usability feature. A simple "DB" button in the editor invokes the system—see Figure 7 (Appendix). The application window has browse and search tools, and once records are retrieved, the content creator can insert just the link into the database, the link and the description, or everything including the access statement—see Figure 8 (Appendix). The resulting text appears in the editor window.

Relicensing and Workflow Simplification

As we previously pointed out, we knew that our licensing situation was unsustainable. However, setting things right would require time, and thus some interim steps were necessary. The database of databases system bought us time to relicense our resources to address the fact that our programs have spread out across the university's physical locations, and create nearly universal licenses so nearly every student could access nearly every resource.

The primary issue was that too many people had their hands in the licensing task. This created confusion for our vendors, as no one knew which person to talk to, and each person had a slightly different perspective. We created a single position, the Licensed Content Librarian (LCL), to handle all pricing and licensing discussions and be a single voice to all of our vendors. The second task was to charge this new librarian to renegotiate all of our licenses to cover as many students as possible. This was time intensive, and it cost additional money. However, with careful analysis, we were able to shed some redundant resources, and nearly cut the initial estimate in half.

The net result of this position was greatly simplified licensing after nearly two years of work. We ended up with only two license variants, and only three of our 212 databases have any program restrictions placed on them.

A second prong of this reached into the future: we needed to create a stable, forward-thinking workflow for electronic resource licensing. The resulting workflow is beyond the scope of this paper, but it included the following phases: discovery, evaluation, budget, licensing, access, and launching. The LCL was central to every phase of this process, and interacts with all players from selector to end user. The policies also have teeth to ensure that we do not regress to our previous state of affairs: there is the possibility of disciplinary action if personnel attempt to license resources outside of the workflow.

The 2014 Website Update

With our licensing issue solved, we were motivated to evolve the website to a new point. The old site was location centric, and it had four distinct personalities: one for each campus, plus a "University Libraries" personality for off-campus users. The intent when we implemented it was to merge three separate websites into a single website, but we were not able to make many content changes. This compromise caused our home page to be slow—it was buggy and our users frequently got lost in the complexity. The solution was to make the website function-based, rather than location-based. This was mainly a reorganization of content, with a few application twists.

This redesign prompted some updates to our database of databases application: we could now replace the "availability" statement in our database A–Z listing, because virtually everything was available to everyone. It was redundant to say that everything was available, so we removed it, and only disclosed the three resources with access limitations. With the simplified licensing We also had begun the implementation of the EBSCO Discovery Service (EDS), so we needed to classify our resources based upon whether they were indexed by EDS, and we determined that we needed to indicate which organization or individual funded each resource. This added a minor amount of complexity to the data model.

Conclusion

The implementation of this database of databases application taught us quite a bit in a number of areas. The most important lesson learned was the primacy of requirements gathering: when one knows what functionality needs to be implemented, and one knows the problem very well, one can create a robust application. It was very telling when preparing this paper that most of the code that we wrote in 2010 was still there, untouched because it continues to work well half a decade later. We also learned that a complex problem creates complex code, which in turn creates user confusion and bugs. However, this became one of the talking points for our effort to advocate for our licensing simplification project. When that simplification project succeeded, it led to a great simplification in workflows and allowed us to remove hundreds of lines of code from the database of databases web application.

Appendix

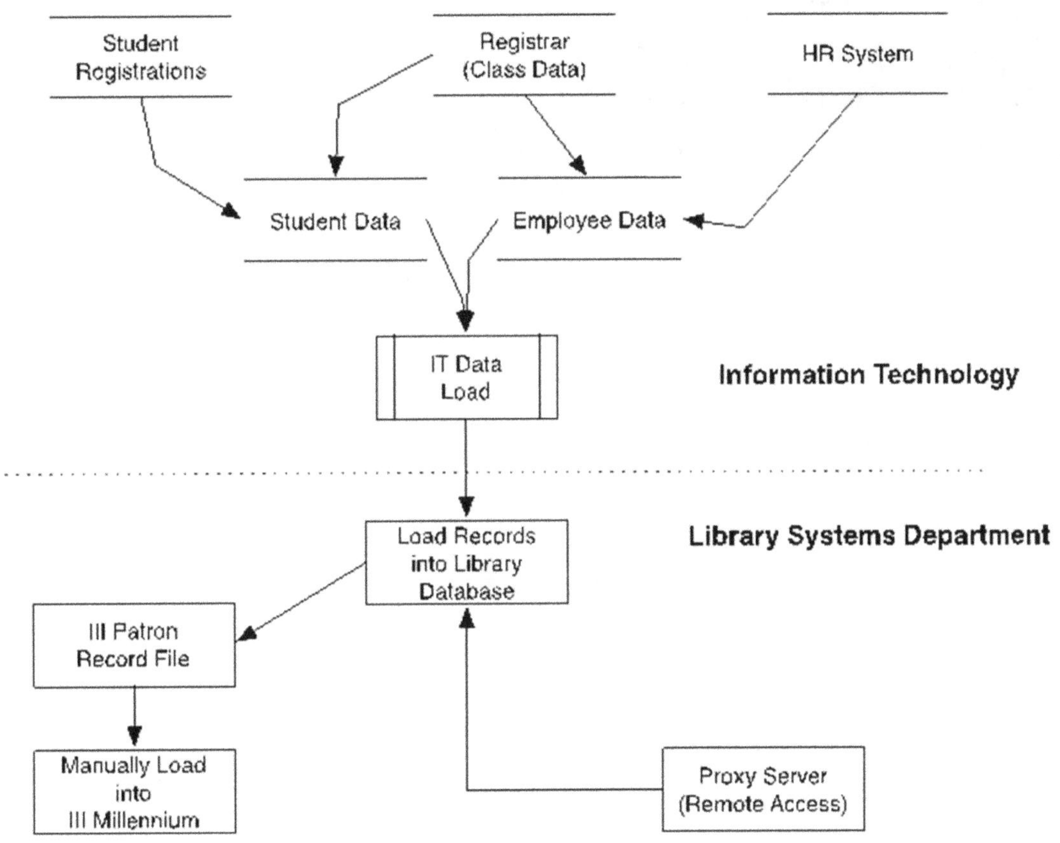

Figure 1. A visualization of the flow of user data from the student system, registration system, and human resources into data files into the library systems. Once the library takes hold of the data, we load it into the database, and then create a patron file for the library system. Our remote authentication process looks directly at the database.

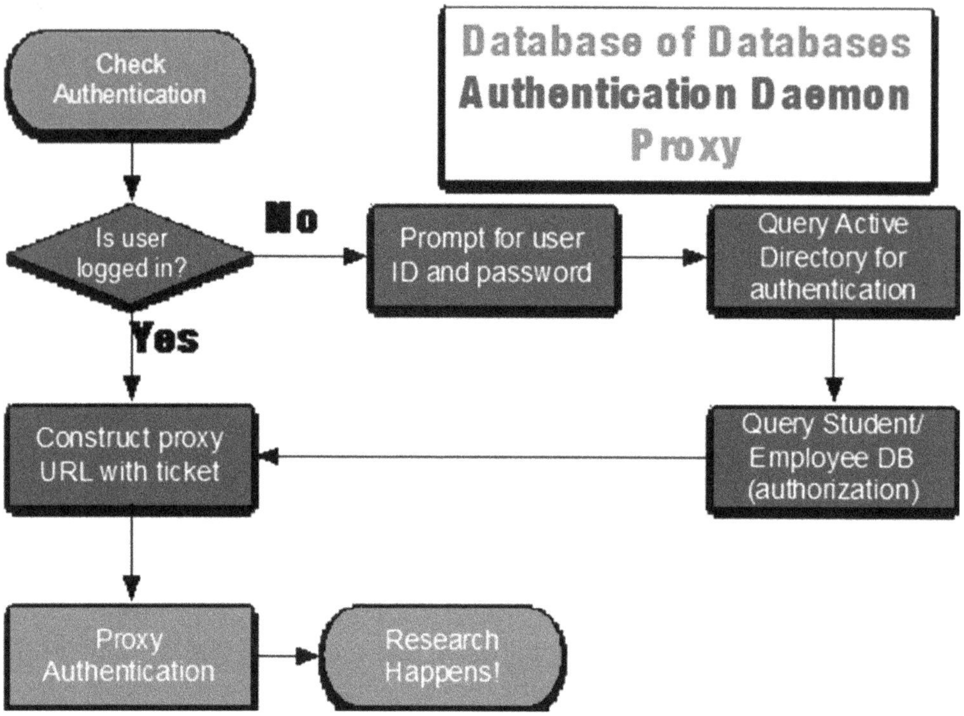

Figure 2. A visualization of the authentication and authorization process.

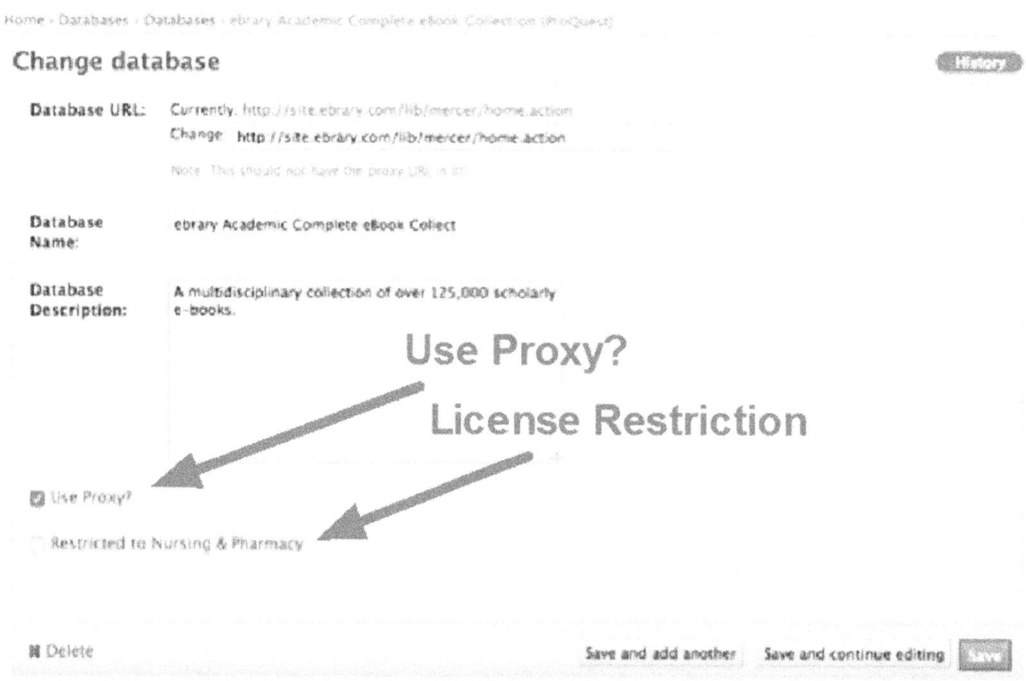

Figure 3. Database of databases data entry, where we capture the URL, name, a short description, whether to use the proxy, and finally which license group. Note: this is an interim stage, where we have already simplified our license choices down to one.

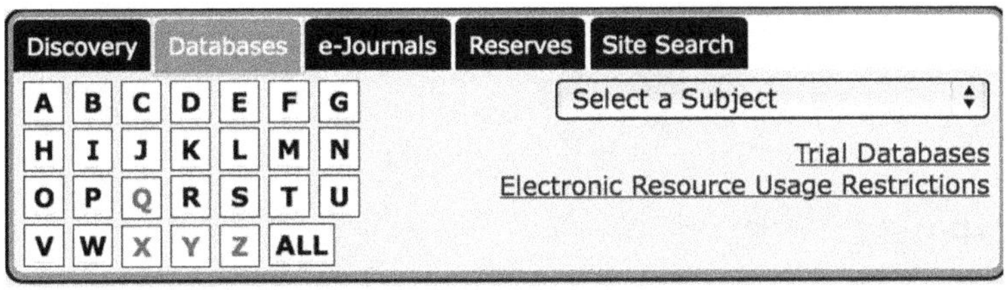

Figure 4. An A–Z browse list for our home page.

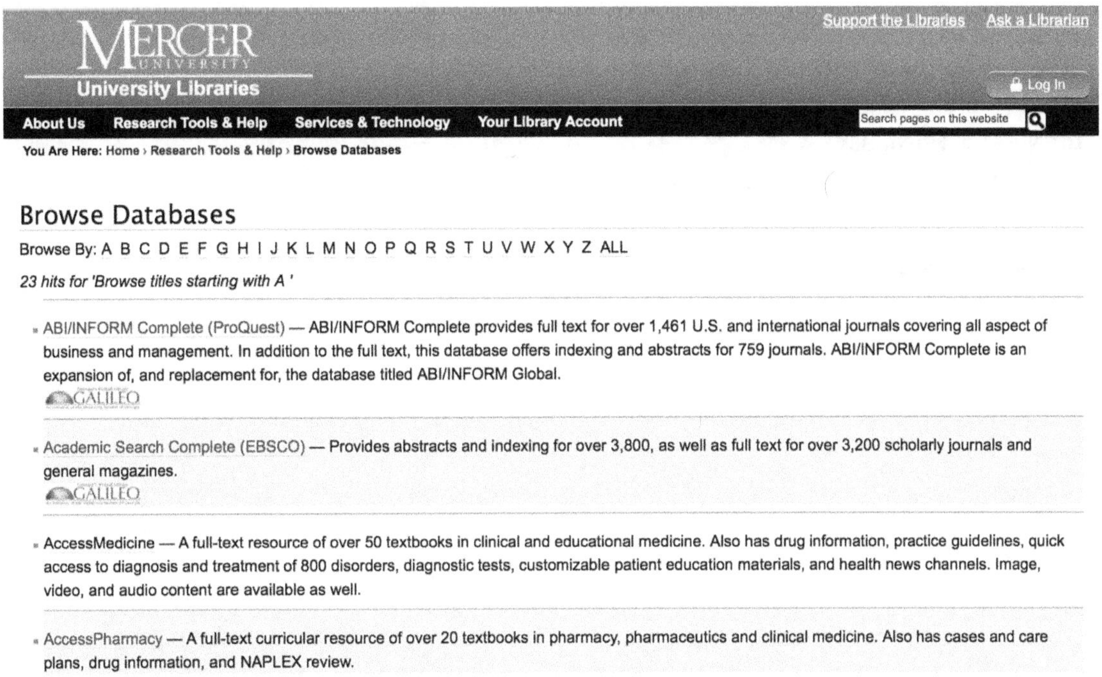

Figure 5. The A–Z listing of each database.

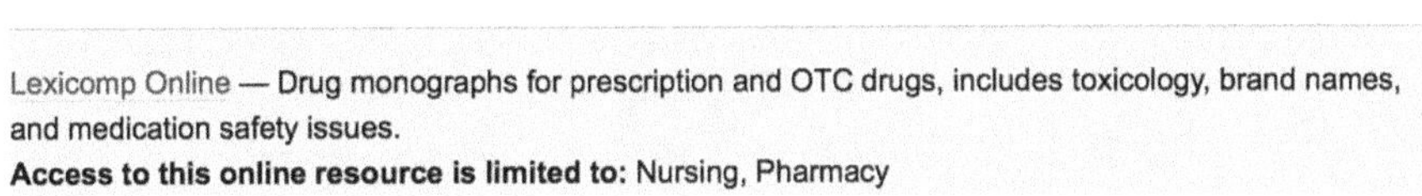

Figure 6. An access-limited resource. Note: in our 2010 implementation, this access statement was on each resource. Now we only show it when a resource is limited.

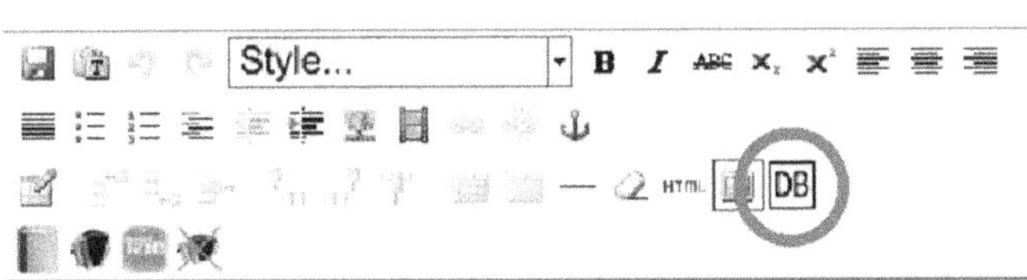

Figure 7. The DB button in the editor toolbar invokes the system.

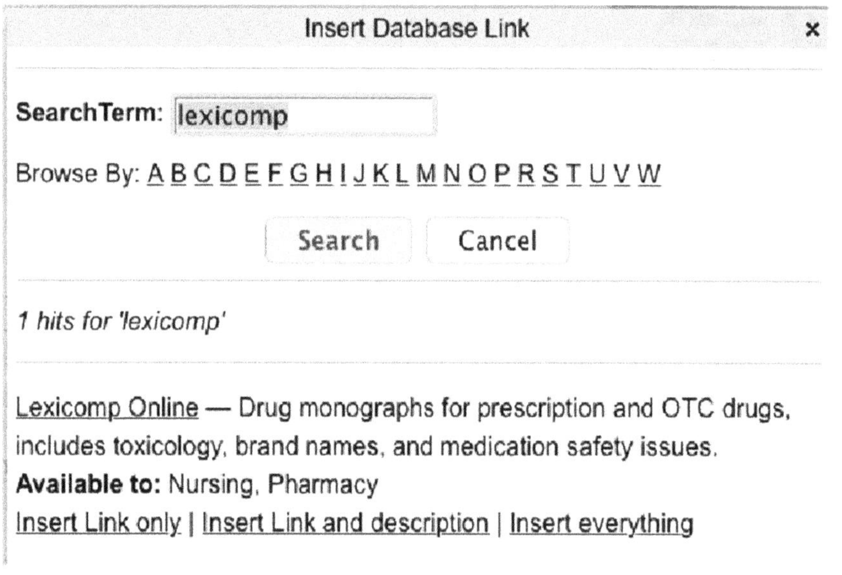

Figure 8. The database integration window.

Don't Share This Item! Developing Digital Collections and Services in a Consumer-Licensed World

William M. Cross, Director, Copyright and Digital Scholarship, North Carolina State University Libraries

Darby Orcutt, Assistant Head of Collection Management, North Carolina State University Libraries

Abstract

Libraries have always faced unique challenges in providing non-academic content for academic use, but the digital age has brought particular problems of "one size fits all" consumer purchase models and vexing methods of digital rights management (DRM), wrapped up with a large bow of legal uncertainty for many institutions. These proceedings describe some practices for sharing consumer-licensed popular materials and confronting legal and technical barriers, as well as what some libraries are considering and encountering in applying the law, fair use, user expectations, and common sense in developing collections and services around digital content that is geared directly to end users.

Digital Collections in a Consumer-Licensed World

Libraries have always faced unique challenges in providing non-academic content for academic use, but the digital age has brought particular problems of "one size fits all" consumer purchase models and vexing methods of DRM, wrapped up with a large bow of legal uncertainty for many institutions. Traditional multimedia content including film and television is increasingly consumed through streaming services (e.g., Netflix, Hulu, and Amazon), and libraries naturally want to enter this space, both because streaming services offer convenience and are often most familiar to patrons. Further, many films and programs are available first or exclusively through proprietary streaming services, including award-winning and culturally significant productions; for example, Netflix's drama *House of Cards* and Amazon's Emmy- and Golden Globe-winning *Transparent*. Collecting new media such as video games raises similar issues, with an increasing number of games available exclusively as digital downloads through Steam or similar services. This trend toward digital and proprietary formats is likely to continue and increase over time, which will leave libraries unable to collect multimedia materials if they cannot engage with these services.

Unfortunately, most of these services are designed for consumer use and present logistical and legal challenges for libraries hoping to share materials with their patrons. The traditional legal protections of first sale and section 108 are, at best, an uncomfortable fit and at times are simply not applicable to consumer-licensed products. These proceedings document the discussion at the 2015 Charleston Conference about these issues.

Current Library Contexts

Few librarian participants in this session indicated that their institutions were currently providing such consumer-oriented media. Several cited extremely risk-adverse legal counsel as a major institutional barrier, some a perceived lack of need or legitimacy of such media, and some concerns about budgeting funds or staff time to such collections.

This latter concern, of staff time, is especially important. These media artifacts are often device-specific, thus requiring that both device and associated media content be circulated or made available within a designated space. Because of the consumer-oriented nature of the content platforms, these media often must be either purchased separately and then "gifted" to an account for user access, or if the vendor does not allow for "gifting," a secure means of hiding library account or credit card information and blocking unauthorized activity must be determined (typically, use of "parental controls"). Thus, consumer-oriented systems must be

http://dx.doi.org/10.5703/1288284316327

carefully reengineered to serve library needs, and the workflows for providing such content are sometimes cumbersome, nearly always unique to the platform and vendor at hand, and may require periodic refreshing as interfaces change (often with little advance notice).

Models for Practice

The North Carolina State University (NCSU) Libraries was an early provider of a circulating Kindle e-books program. Designed as a technology lending program to incubate the use of emerging e-book reader technologies, the Libraries sought to provide user-desired content that could be coupled with these devices in order to encourage their use. This program resulted as well in a quick and easy means of providing popular titles—and even academic titles that were only available in Kindle format. This was and is not a program unique to the NCSU Libraries, and Amazon was consulted and informed along the way in its development, never specifically endorsing yet neither objecting to the Libraries's use of Kindle content.

As consumer-oriented media have grown, the NCSU Libraries has expanded into other media, including video games and streaming video. Increasingly, video games are available in "download only" formats; it is not hard to envision a time when physical media may be altogether unavailable. With robust gaming and game development programs that cross four colleges at the University, we cannot afford to deny our users access to this type of content. Beginning with the Steam platform, and next the PlayStation 4, we are actively building collections of downloaded games for in-house use, and planning to make available circulating consoles to instructors for in-class demonstration purposes. Similarly, an increasing number of films and videos are now only available in streaming formats. To accommodate in-class teaching needs, we are beginning to circulate to instructors Roku devices that can be plugged in in the classroom, with preloaded access to purchased (but not leased) content. While such devices are not now nor envisioned to be the preferred means of accessing such content, the consumer focus means that for much content this is the *only* means by which we can provide access.

Legal Challenges to Including Consumer-Licensed Products

Unfortunately, there are several major conflicts that must be addressed before a library deploys consumer-licensed services including Hulu, Netflix, Amazon Prime, or Steam. Most significantly, consumer-licensed services, especially those that offer streaming content, raise substantive issues about ownership and sharing. Because they do not sell specific items to the library, materials cannot circulate under sec. 109 of the Copyright Act, the "first sale doctrine." Instead, they generally license content for a particular use, and those licenses reflect the assumption that an individual consumer will be making personal, or perhaps familial, use of the content.

The licenses and terms of service for every major consumer-focused service discussed above includes an explicit limitation to "personal" or "private" use which precludes wide-scale sharing of the type done by most libraries. This language is often paired with prohibitions on "sub licensing" or "distribution to third parties." In many contexts this problem is addressed by a distinct institutional license, but we have seen no indication that this model is imminent for these services.

In addition, most of these consumer-focused licenses include terms that are incompatible with many academic institutions' standard license requirements. Licenses for each of the major streaming services require binding arbitration and include provisions requiring choice of law and venue that may conflict with the legal obligations of state institutions. These licenses often also include a limitation on liability and express indemnification language which run afoul of legal and bedrock policy norms of many libraries. Each license also includes some version of a problematic "future license language changes" clause that binds the licensee to terms that may be changed at any time at the discretion of the company. These procedural issues may be seen as "boilerplate" language by corporate offices, but they produce substantial—and at times intractable—challenges for academic libraries.

Conclusions

Despite these legal concerns, some libraries have moved forward with consumer-licensed services in their collection, as well as lending devices that rely on these services for their value. There have also been informal signals reported in blog posts and private conversations that some consumer-licensing companies have no objection to library use, particularly when a one-to-one relationship is maintained between service account and independent use. Certainly we have not seen major litigation around this issue in the way that we have for library practice around digitization and offering electronic reserves, areas viewed as less controversial by many librarians.

These bold actors and quiet conversations suggest that a path forward may exist. Navigating that path will require libraries to think seriously about how they manage risk in a legally uncertain context. It will also require librarians to think about business questions such as the reliability of consumer-licensed products at scale—how will an account designed for a single user function when used by a wide variety of distinct users and user groups—and the reliability of the company over time. A licensed partnership with a scholarly database should assure the library of reliable, sustainable service regardless of corporate mergers and new business plans; an unanticipated use beyond those anticipated by the license may not have such assurances and is not negotiated at arm's length to adapt to the needs of the library and its patrons. The recent lawsuit over accessibility for Netflix content also reminds us that a for-profit company may have values that diverge from the needs and priorities of an academic library. Without a negotiated institutional license, the library has no way to express its priorities, especially when use of the product relies on "flying under the radar" of that company based on fear of a lawsuit.

These challenges may be daunting, but they must be addressed. Streaming content is already becoming the dominant way that media is shared, and libraries must enter that space if their collections are to remain relevant. The Copyright Office has promised to update the law in this area but has no timetable. Libraries also cannot be sure that any changes made by the Copyright Office will reflect the needs of users, rather than of the content industry that has captured so much of the attention of Congress and the Copyright Office.

Partnerships with specific services seem to be the most promising path forward, but they will be complicated by the specific agreements those services have with the content owners from whom they license materials. In the long term, legal changes, institutional licenses, or new business models may solve this problem. Until then, however, libraries will have to find their own path.

How Far Have We Come Since Our "Go Live" Dates, and Where Do We Go from Here?

Ann Kutulas, Cataloger, Tarrant County College

Moon Kim, Acquisitions Librarian, California State University, Fullerton

Susan Flanagan, Collection Development Librarian, Getty Research Institute

Abstract

Next-generation library systems promise new opportunities to expand beyond our existing methodologies, and there has been a surge of institutions migrating to web-based platforms as a result. Extensive research and planning goes into choosing and moving to a new integrated library system (ILS). But what happens after migration and implementation? And how closely does reality align with expectations? Individuals from three libraries who have chosen Ex Libris's Alma as their web-based ILS solution will share their migration experiences and the challenges of working in a constantly changing environment. Strategies on transitioning from an abstract understanding to a live production site will be addressed, as well as the possibilities to collaborate in the future.

Introduction

Migrating to a new ILS will be a different experience for every institution. Some institutions will have a long migration planning period to prepare, while others may have a short turnaround time. The migration and planning stages of the California State University, Fullerton (CSUF), Getty Research Institute (GRI), and Tarrant County College (TCC) to Ex Libris's Alma all vary, but what has been consistent is that the migrations have significantly changed workflows and will continue to change. Even those who have not yet migrated but are in the contemplation stages are re-envisioning workflows that will be constantly changing with every monthly update.

Setting the Stage

The GRI's library is a private art history research institution located in Los Angeles, California with a user base of 1,200 FTE. The library has over a million volumes, and special collections with 75,000 rare volumes, nearly 20,000 feet of archives, 27,000 prints, and 800 collections of rare photographs. Additionally, the library has photo archives of two million study photographs. The library collections, totaling 34 miles of shelving, are located in two buildings: the GRI with 30,000 square feet and an annex, 30 miles away, with 100,000 square feet. Eighty-five percent of the materials are in closed stacks.

Tarrant County College is located in Tarrant County, Texas. It is comprised of five separate campuses: three in Fort Worth, one in Arlington, and one in Hurst, as well as other satellite campuses throughout the county. TCC has about 50,000 enrolled students each semester. There are five main libraries at TCC, with one located on each campus. There is one central technical services department that works with all of the libraries and does acquisitions, cataloging, processing, etc. The collection is comprised of print materials, e-books, periodicals, standing orders, and more.

The California State University (CSU) system is comprised of 23 campuses with a focus on teaching and CSUF is one of the larger CSU campuses, with nearly 32,000 FTE as of fall 2015. CSUF is a Hispanic-serving institution with a heavy emphasis on undergraduate education but offers a number of masters and doctoral degrees. Their collection contains over a million titles in various formats and is an electronic format preferred campus.

http://dx.doi.org/10.5703/1288284316328

Preparing to Migrate and Early Issues

Although every migration will be unique, Ex Libris has a well-defined protocol for facilitating migrations: an assigned implementation team, staff webinars, site visits, and routine conference calls. Some of the protocols have been formalized as a result of the previous migrations and now also includes a migration checklist.

GRI Experience

The GRI had Ex Libris's Voyager for many years, and made the decision to be an early adopter. The GRI moved to Alma and Primo in July 2013, and shortly after that added Rosetta to their suite of Ex Libris products in the fall of 2013.

Moving to Alma was especially challenging for electronic resources, which were handled with a non-Ex Libris product, Serials Solutions. The Voyager to Alma migration was easier as they have a similar information architecture. It was assumed that the Alma Knowledge Base (KB) would have roughly the same number of records as Serials Solutions, but that was not the case. The Alma KB is growing by regularly adding collections and individual records, but its greatest strength remains in the sciences, which does not service a high research art history library.

In acquisitions, there are a number of outstanding issues to be resolved in regards to funds, ledgers, and invoicing. Cases have been submitted to Ex Libris. Post-migration, complexities arose immediately in circulation, or otherwise known as fulfillment in Alma. One of the most prominent problems was the automatic "in transit" feature in Alma. The GRI's turnaround time is fast. Items received in acquisitions are picked up by the circulation staff on the same day. Physically these two departments are fewer than 100 feet apart. The Alma workflow automatically puts the items "in transit," requiring an item to be scanned twice: once upon receipt in acquisitions and once upon arrival in circulation. Shortly after the migration, disabling this functionality was deemed as a high priority.

The GRI did not have Ex Libris migrate the image files to Rosetta, but rather it was done locally because the file structure of the previous system, DigiTool, was an access file, and Rosetta required a master file. The Getty was the first institution of its kind to implement Rosetta.

TCC Experience

TCC as a whole migrated in August 2013, with a short turnaround for migration preparation. Preparation began in March 2013 and the migration took place on August 15, 2013, leaving little time, if any, to prepare data. TCC was set up with an Alma migration team, who established a listserv for questions. Pivotal and then Salesforce were used to document problems and issues.

One of the first items that came up in acquisitions was in regards to the training. Most of the examples and webinars were focused on the individual ordering of items. Most of all TCC's ordering is done by Electronic Data Interchange (EDI) in batches. It was also not something that was easy to duplicate in the sandbox because it is based on incoming imports and then outgoing EDIs. The most challenging part of this was trying to put into place, in Alma, a set of configuration rules that would not stop the Purchase Order Lines (POLs) from packaging and sending out the order right away without waiting. The first time it was set up, the order went into review. After completing the certification class, the migration team was better able to understand the configuration for acquisitions and worked to rectify the situation. Once EDI ordering was up and working, the acquisitions staff was able to do all the ordering in half the time that it took previously.

The concept of work order departments was new to TCC. Since all of the receiving, cataloging, and processing is done in the same area, there is not a significant need for TCC to use this functionality, and it was not adopted. In other words, once an item is received, it remains with the same status until it is taken out of in-process, which puts it "in transit" to one of the five libraries.

A learning curve that was faced right before migration was setting up the Online Computer Library Center (OCLC) gateway to work with Alma. Most of the configuration was straightforward.

The challenging part was understanding how to set up the normalization rules. This was something new. Right before migrating and after some trial and error, the normalization rule was set up for the incoming records for the OCLC gateway, and it is still being used today.

CSUF Experience

CSUF will be migrating from its ILS, Innovative's Millennium, and Ex Libris' SFX and Verde for electronic resources management to Alma. The migration is a critical component in unifying the disparate systems and workflows for managing different types of resources. The CSUF migration is also marked within a larger endeavor at the CSU-wide consortial level to unify all 23 campuses spread across the state of California under a single system. The CSUs as a whole will migrate in the summer of 2017 and similar to other consortial users, the CSUs will have the added layer of the network zone (NZ) in addition to the institution and community zones. There are two CSU campuses, Sacramento and San Marcos, who are already on Alma and will need to be linked to the CSU's NZ as part of the migration. A CSU-wide Alma Sandbox has been established with logins and passwords for various user roles for everyone to explore. As part of the migration, three CSU campuses—Fresno, Northridge, and San Jose—were chosen as the "Vanguard" campuses, and they will undergo a mock Alma migration trial between the end of 2015 and early 2016 to learn system functionalities, assess workflows, and begin work on policies and guidelines for the consortium.

Some of the motivations behind migrating to a new ILS are to take advantage of a cloud-based system that would accommodate growing digital and electronic collections, revitalize workflows, and improve the opportunities to collaborate. A web-based system arrives with functionalities that will allow the CSUs to work directly in the web environment and participate in the development of next-generation library systems.

New implementations will undoubtedly learn from the experience of early adopters, and the CSU migration is no exception. The CSUs are reviewing the migration of the sister consortium in the Pacific Northwest, the Orbis Cascade Alliance, and closely monitoring other consortial Ex Libris migrations in addition to the development of consortial features in areas such as vendor records management, consortial licensing, and consortial collections building.

Current Workflows

GRI

After the first year, the Getty's electronic resources and acquisitions are largely in order and operational. In acquisitions, the GRI has implemented some Alma-suggested workflows, but have found it easier to stay with previous workflows for serials check-in and print plus online orders. With a small staff, most tasks are assigned to one person. For example, one staff member handles all aspects of standing orders. Therefore, the task list workflow feature is not heavily used except for claiming.

As a library with 85% of the collection in two storage facilities, paging is a huge task for the Getty's circulation staff. The main storage building of 100,000 square feet is 30 miles away. Fifteen percent of the collection is in open stacks in two different physical sites: the Getty Center and the Getty Villa, which are 15 miles apart. For open stack materials, patrons are to get the volumes and check them out to themselves on OPAC self-checkout stations in the building in which they are located. Set up for patron records was complex. Circulation needed to identify where staff were located (Center or Villa) and set up their records to allow them to page from buildings they were not physically in. This took one year to resolve. From 2013– 2014, patrons needed to send an e-mail to circulation to request the open stacks materials for the building in which they were not physically located. Retrieving requested books and charging them to patrons takes more time in Alma than it did in Voyager. One cannot charge a requested book out to a patron by scanning the barcode of the book and have Alma match the book to the patron's record. The circulation staff must first search for the patron's name on the printed call slip, and then scan the book to be charged out.

Introducing the Primo discovery system was a challenge. For staff who use the GRI's Ex Libris products daily, there was a short but steep learning curve. With many meetings and documenting procedures on an internal wiki, the Primo team was able to move forward and resolve issues in a systematic way. After about six months, everyone was trained and familiar with the features and limitation of the system.

As for the public, that was another story. The Getty is a specialized research library with a unique international client base who may visit for only a week or stay for years. Explaining "discovery" to the public with varying degrees of familiarity with the system was not easy. However, one of the strengths of a discovery system is to use a central index to find journal articles, including ones that the library does not own. As a developing central index, Primo does not have all the resources the Getty subscribes to. Therefore, users are only getting partial content. The nearly impossible task for the reference librarians is to explain what is in Primo and what is not. And as Primo Central Index grows, what was not there a month ago, may be available a month later. Although adding resources is a good thing, it has been difficult to predict when collections will be added, and therefore challenging to keep users up-to-date. The good news is that as Primo's index expands, the ability to reveal our rich collections will be even more helpful to researchers.

TCC

At TCC, one of the biggest changes in acquisitions was that the ISBN was used for EDI ordering. Brief machine-readable cataloging (MARC) order records are imported; then the order information is sent out through EDI to the vendor. In the past, the order would use the ISBN that was in the first 020 field on the MARC record. This meant having to sometimes manipulate the records to have the ISBN for the item being ordered in that first 020 field. It would then go into the purchase order line (POL) and be sent out on the order. At the beginning in Alma, this still happened with the option of being able to choose the ISBN in the POL to use the correct ordering, but a couple of months after TCC went to Alma, and a Salesforce case later, this changed. The Alma developers were able to have a way for TCC to directly map the ISBN from the incoming order record to the POL. This meant that TCC did not need to re-lay on the 020 fields. The ISBN of the ordered item went to a different field on the MARC record, and was then mapped in Alma directly to the POL identifier. This meant that the ordered item's ISBN, from the vendor, sent out within the EDI, without any additional work from acquisitions. Thus saving the acquisitions department a lot of time. There have now been more fields that are able to be mapped, saving even more processing time of items.

In cataloging, there have also been some time savers. TCC sometimes has to relink items. If the items are in process, then Alma does not allow relinking of the holdings. But on the item record itself it is now possible to change the process type on the items to make them available and able to be relinked. Also more recently Alma now added a way to merge records in the metadata editor.

Moving Forward

Cultural Shift or at Least Acceptance

As evidenced in the examples above, migrating to a new system will present new and exciting challenges, but there needs to be staff buy-in, or at least acceptance of the changes that will occur. A new and unfamiliar system will require training, willingness to reassess workflows, and troubleshooting abilities. Empowering everyone to ask questions and become involved is an expensive undertaking from an operations point of view, but a necessary process to create a smooth transition. A new system might result in a whole new set of duties or a change to a colleague's portfolio of responsibilities. Having everyone on the same page through open and clear channels of communication minimizes the confusion and stress during and after migration.

One of the harsh realities of working in a system that is in development is that not every desired feature will be available, but Alma users can submit enhancement requests for nonexistent functionalities. There may be other instances when a button's functionality or potential is not obvious; for example, in the electronic collection records, the "current" or "perpetual" access type radio buttons showed up unexpectedly early in 2015. Although it is obvious what the purpose of these buttons is within the context of electronic collection records, there were local discussions as to why this functionality surfaced as a new button and how it relates to the type of information contained in license records.

Monthly Updates

The most noticeable change with Alma is that there are monthly updates. Although the systematic updates reduce the work of systems staff who have traditionally maintained the local ILS, the work now is decentralized to staff working in the functional areas to check the monthly Alma release notes for anything that would affect existing processes. Sometimes there is nothing but other times the changes can be significant. It is important to stay up-to-date with the changes and enhancements to keep surprises to a minimum. Occasionally, staff might encounter unexpected changes rolled out into the production site prematurely. In the spring of 2015, there were a number major changes with electronic collection records and the handling of license records that surfaced in production before their scheduled monthly release. Although this was a nice preview of what was in store for the upcoming release, it was a timely reminder that the system is constantly changing.

Reviewing Existing Workflows and Configurations

Sometimes it is not enough to simply keep up with the updates but routinely review existing workflows and local configurations. It is hard to see the bigger picture of Ex Libris' direction when the changes happen incrementally over time. Or in larger institutions with compartmentalized units responsible for a fraction of the entire workflow, changes in the system might go unnoticed, perpetuating outdated workflows that are not optimizing the system or the institution for efficiency. Alma changes and is dynamic. Maintaining the status quo would not take advantage of all Alma has to offer. Staying abreast of developments in the system, understanding the changes in relation to existing functionalities, and vigilance with regard to workflows will offer a more holistic view in identifying local strategies for institutional needs.

Problem With Documentation

It is challenging to document workflows in a system that is changing regularly. Ex Libris's documentation is naturally changing as well because the system is changing. Alma's flexibility in allowing many different ways of performing the same task or function makes it even more difficult to document workflows. For instance, a patron hold can be placed on an item through the purchase order line, or through the inventory; depending on how the hold request was initiated, a hold request can be created in more than one functional area. One method of overcoming the constant need to update documentation is to rely on Ex Libris's step-by-step documentation, if available, and locally document the reasons as to why a particular decision was made. Providing the framework to guide the work at the macro level might sometimes be necessary over detailed instructions.

Working Collaboratively and the Benefits

As consumers, there is a vested interest in the development of the product. User engagement benefits not only the vendor but also the users in the long run, and as such, Alma users become involved with the development process. There are many ways to participate through groups such as the International Group of Ex Libris Users (IGeLU) or Ex Libris Users of North America (ELUNA) that coordinate the product enhancement cycles and meet annually.

Working at a small institution where one person might carry out all technical services functions, learning from one's counterparts in other organizations becomes necessary to carry out tasks. Connecting with other institutions regarding Alma is often facilitated through the listservs. In addition to user groups, conferences, and listservs, one may partake in topical, local, consortial or regional meetings to network with others utilizing the same vendor's ILS. It might even be desirable to learn about other ILS developments and see what benefits those systems possess and offer. There is no shortage of venues and opportunities to work with colleagues, but the important thread is to continue working together to innovate and improve the systems to ultimately better serve our users.

Future

Once a library is up and running for about six months, most staff are up to speed, migration issues are addressed, and life becomes more manageable. Issues that do arise are submitted using the case reporting function, or the library identifies internal solutions. System upgrades are monthly with documentation available well in advance. Alma and Primo Central Index updates are posted regularly. Daily issues are discussed on the listservs, and the Ex Libris client phone conferences decrease over time.

As the number of libraries that are now on Alma increases, it is possible to learn of different institutional practices and processes. This has meant a lot more sharing of resources and hearing about different experiments or outcomes without having to test out the entire monthly release by oneself. Alma is a different Alma from the time of the early adopters' migrations to now, having gone through numerous updates. Although there are still areas that are being developed and enhanced, there have been noted improvements over its initial release. Many users have cited cases where Alma has improved efficiency in some areas and as Alma continues to mature, more improvements will be documented. The overall good news is that there have been a lot of changes with Alma since its inception, and it is constantly getting better with every new monthly release. The future road map also looks very bright and promising because of the dedication of the users deeply invested in improving this system.

Index

Z

www.ingramcontent.com/pod-product-compliance
Lightning Source LLC
LaVergne TN
LVHW082010200926
848481LV00010B/2826